The Path of Transformation

The Path of Transformation

How Healing Ourselves Can Change the World

SHAKTI GAWAIN

NATARAJ PUBLISHING
A Division of

NEW WORLD LIBRARY
NOVATO, CALIFORNIA

Nataraj Publishing
A Division of

New World Library
14 Pamaron Way
Novato, California 94949

Revised edition © 2000 by Shakti Gawain
Original edition © 1993 by Shakti Gawain

Front cover design by Alexandra Honig
Text design by Tona Pearce Myers

Library of Congress Cataloging-in-Publication Data
Gawain, Shakti 1948–
The path of transformation : how healing ourselves can change the
world / by Shakti Gawain.
p. cm.
Originally published: 1993.
Includes bibliographical references.
ISBN 1-57731-154-X
1. Conduct of life. I. Title.
BJ1581.G35 2000
158.1—dc21   00-020076

First printing of revised edition, March 2000.
ISBN 1-57731-154-X
Printed in Canada on acid-free paper
Distributed to the trade by Publishers Group West

10 9 8 7 6 5

*To all the teachers and friends
who have helped me along my own
transformational path.*

CONTENTS

Acknowledgments   viii

Publisher's Preface   ix

Introduction   xiii

PART I — HOW WE CAN CHANGE THE WORLD

Chapter   1: What Is Your Vision of the Future?   3

Chapter   2: Facing the Future   5

Chapter   3: Healing Crises in Our Personal Lives   9

Chapter   4: The World in a Healing Crisis   15

Chapter   5: Creating Real Change   21

Chapter   6: Blame and Responsibility   27

Chapter   7: Taking Action   33

Chapter   8: The Consciousness Journey   43

Chapter   9: A Cosmic Perspective on Life   51

Chapter   10: The Path of the Material World   55

Chapter   11: The Path of Transcendence   57

Chapter   12: The Path of Transformation   67

PART II — ON THE PATH OF TRANSFORMATION

Chapter   13: Finding Your Inner Teacher   73

Chapter   14: Developing Inner Guidance   81

Chapter 15: The Four Levels of Existence   91

Chapter 16: Healing the Spiritual Level   97

Chapter 17: Healing the Mental Level   105

Chapter 18: Healing the Emotional Level   115

Chapter 19: Healing the Physical Level   125

Chapter 20: Integration   143

Chapter 21: Discovering Our Many Selves   147

Chapter 22: Our Relationships As Mirrors   163

Chapter 23: The World As Our Mirror   177

Chapter 24: Consciousness and Spirituality   191

Chapter 25: Making a Difference in the World   201

Chapter 26: Seven Steps on the Path of Transformation   217

Chapter 27: Fulfilling Our Higher Purpose   227

Chapter 28: Envisioning the Future Together   233

Appendix: Relaxation Exercise   237
Recommended Resources   241
About the Author   245

ACKNOWLEDGMENTS

$\mathcal{M}$y heartfelt thanks go to my editor, Hal Bennett. Your creativity and expertise have added greatly to the book, and to my enjoyment in writing it.

I'd like to express my appreciation to Jane Hogan for your vision and hard work in the creation of Nataraj Publishing, Kathy Altman for the ideas you contributed to the book and your overall support, and all the other people associated with Nataraj Publishing who have helped, directly or indirectly, to bring this book into form.

For the revised edition, I'd like to thank Lora O'Connor for your suggestions, as well as Georgia Hughes, Marc Allen, and everyone at New World Library.

Last, but certainly not least, a special thanks to my husband and partner, Jim Burns, for your loving support on all levels.

PUBLISHER'S PREFACE

S hakti Gawain walks her talk. It has been an honor, even a saving grace, to have known her through most of her adult life.

She was a fervent student and seeker when I met her. She was twenty-six, and had just returned from a two-year journey around the world. She had spent the last year in India, and the experience had ignited her passion for a different way of life. India awakened her to the world of the spirit.

She spent years integrating her India experience, and continued to explore all kinds of other paths, and to learn and grow. When I met her, we were both what were fondly called "workshop junkies" in the San Francisco Bay area.

When she turned thirty, she wrote *Creative Visualization*, a book that pulled together and expressed what she had learned through her searching and questioning. It turned out she had a wonderful gift as a writer. Her words touched people in a gentle, caring way and led them into new worlds and new lives of greater possibilities.

She kept learning new things, finding new teachers and guides — always fully and sometimes painfully honest about herself and her ongoing struggles and the process of growth as she worked with the people attending her seminars and talks. Seven years after *Creative Visualization* was published, she wrote *Living in the Light*.

Both of her books were very successful, and Shakti was faced with the problem that a lot of people wanted to put her up on a pedestal and make her their guru. She absolutely refused to play that game, however, and instead taught and encouraged her students to find and follow their own inner wisdom.

Shortly after *Living in the Light* was published, she met Drs. Hal and Sidra Stone, the creators of the Psychology of Selves and the powerful technique of Voice Dialoque. They are the authors of several great books, including *Embracing Our Selves* and their recent *Partnering: A New Kind of Relationship*. Working deeply with the Stones over several years helped Shakti tremendously, and she incorporated some of their most important and powerful principles into her own work with people and in her writing. She has been able to bring the Stones' understanding of the intricate workings of our psyches, with all our different "subpersonalities," to a much broader audience.

Seven years after *Living in the Light* was published, she wrote her third major book, *The Path of Transformation*. During those years, her insight deepened tremendously, and she continued to work very closely with the Stones. She also relaxed a great deal more, and enjoyed life more. She had an almost electric intensity in her early years — one reason why the name Shakti fit her so well (it means "life energy" in the Sanskrit language). Her growth and maturity brought her a calmness and a clarity and even a sense of peace that is contagious.

It takes a special kind of insight to do what Shakti does: She has an analytical, scientific mind that she rigorously applies to everything she has learned. Yet she is also able to see the broad picture in a way few others can.

In this book, she writes of the three different kinds of paths that we choose to walk — either the path of the material world, the path of transcendence, or the path of transformation. I don't know if anyone else today has seen it in quite the same way. Her insight is fresh and unique, and helps me to see my own path and the paths of others with more understanding and clarity. Many other writers and teachers talk about our physical, emotional, mental, and spiritual bodies, but Shakti brings a great depth to it that allows us to use her words as tools that can affect the quality of our lives.

In a way, *The Path of Transformation* was ahead of its time. Now, seven years after its initial publication, Shakti has revised it for the twenty-first century. It contains much that will be necessary and helpful to us in this new millennium. During and after reading *The Path of Transformation*, we're moved to do a lot of reflection about ourselves, and to do some deep inner work that inevitably leads to growth and healthy change. By the time we finish, we realize we are on a wonderful and important path: fulfilling our higher purpose and creating the future together.

What is more important than that?

— Marc Allen
Publisher
Author of *Visionary Business*

INTRODUCTION

*I*f you have just picked up this book and are wondering whether or not you want to read it, perhaps the following will help you out. If one or more of the following statements applies to you, then the chances are very good that you will find this book worthwhile reading:

- You are searching for a deeper meaning and purpose in your life.
- You are facing one or more major challenges in your personal life regarding your health and well-being, your relationships, your life work, your finances, creativity, or anything else.
- You are deeply concerned about world problems such as famine, disease, poverty, war, racism, sexism, drug addiction, the disintegration of the family, the destruction of the environment, and you are:
   a) Doing everything in your power to find solutions to these problems on social, political, and/or spiritual levels; or,
   b) Feeling helpless, not knowing what to do about these seemingly overwhelming

problems, wondering what, if anything, you can do to really make a difference.

- You have done a lot of spiritual practice, perhaps devoted to one or more specific paths or teachers, yet are feeling stuck in certain areas of your life. You are wondering why you aren't progressing faster, or why you can't apply your spiritual knowledge more successfully in your daily life.

- You have done a lot of psychological work on yourself and are yearning for a more expanded vision of life's possibilities.

- You have done a lot of work in recovery (healing an addiction or dependency) and are wondering what's next.

- You are a "New Age" person who holds an optimistic view of life, but wonder why you keep encountering painful experiences or angry, needy, or otherwise "unenlightened" people.

- You are drawn toward doing personal growth work but you can't stand the "flakier" aspects of the New Age movement.

- You have never done any personal growth work that you know of, and you aren't even sure what it is, but you sense the need for something deeper and more meaningful in your life.

- You are going through a major transition in your life, letting go of something old and opening to the new.

- You've been experiencing upset or upheaval in your life, and you are wondering why.

If anything on the list applies to you, read on...

Why I Wrote This Book

As we begin a new millennium, life on our planet seems to be intensifying. Most of us are faced with challenging personal problems — in our jobs, our relationships and families, our finances, our health. We're not sure how to best meet these challenges. Our traditional ways of living, working, and relating to each other and our environment don't seem to be functioning very well anymore, yet we have few role models for effective new ways.

Even more overwhelming are the problems confronting humanity as a whole. On a planetary level, things seem to be getting worse and worse. We wonder why there is so much pain, suffering, and struggle all over the world. Most of us have no idea of what we can do to help, so we do little or nothing.

I wrote this book to address these issues and to share the ideas and perspectives that are helping me the most in facing my own problems and the global situation. I want to clarify the challenges I see facing us in the new millennium and how we can best meet them. My intentions are to provide understanding and tools for dealing more effectively with personal issues, and to explain from my own viewpoint why the world is in such turmoil and what I believe we can do about it.

I also wish to address some of the confusion I see in the consciousness movement, otherwise known as the New Age movement, or human potential movement. As I have traveled around for many years, giving workshops all over the world, I have grown concerned about certain issues that many sincere seekers seem to be struggling with. I believe that a number of these struggles arise from the fact that many New Age philosophies and leaders are drawing from wisdom of ancient spiritual traditions without fully adapting them to the modern world and our present stage of human evolution. Too many people are striving to follow a path which, as I see it, ultimately will not meet their needs or the needs of the world.

Another issue I have tried to address here is that many traditional forms of psychotherapy, while providing a certain amount of help and guidance, exclude the spiritual or transpersonal dimension of human life, and so leave out a significant part of the healing paradigm. Since a majority of people in the modern world are suffering from a lack of any connection with their spiritual essence, this leaves a major hole in the healing process. All too often, the deeper levels of emotional healing are not dealt with, either. Few people know where to turn for profound healing on all levels.

I am concerned, as well, by the growing chasm I see between many people who are conscientiously working to effect political, social, and environmental reform, and those who are equally committed to their inner growth process. Both groups have visions of a healthier, more harmonious world and a commitment to work hard for positive change. There is little agreement, however, about how real change can be accomplished. We need to work together, to understand and respect each other's contributions.

Changing our lives and changing the world cannot be

accomplished either by focusing exclusively on external solutions or by following a traditional transcendent, spiritual path in which the reality and importance of the physical world are minimized or denied. Rather, we need to choose an alternative — which I call the path of transformation — in which we commit ourselves to the integration of our spiritual and human aspects and learn to live as whole beings, in balance and fulfillment on the earth.

Today's challenges can only be met powerfully and effectively through a shift in consciousness, which in fact is already well under way worldwide. We need to recognize, to the depths of our souls, that we are all part of one whole, that what each of us does individually has a powerful impact on us all. Our global crises relate to and mirror our individual processes. Only through healing ourselves on all levels — physical, emotional, mental, and spiritual — can we heal our families, our communities, and our planet.

I hope this book can provide guidance for readers at all stages of the consciousness journey — those who are just beginning as well as those who are already on the path and wish to move deeper. It is my wish that what I've written here will help all my readers grasp the importance of healing, developing, and integrating all aspects of our own being.

I hope, also, that what I've tried to communicate in these pages will be helpful to those who have already done considerable inner work and integration on all levels and now want to bring their knowledge forth into the world in more meaningful and powerful ways.

The message of this book is really quite simple: Each one of us makes a real and substantial difference on this planet. And by making a commitment to your own consciousness journey, you are indeed taking a significant role in the transformation of the world.

PART ONE

How We Can Change the World

Never doubt that a small group of thoughtful,
committed citizens can change the world.
Indeed it is the only thing that ever has.

— Margaret Mead

CHAPTER ONE

What Is Your Vision of the Future?

*I*n this book we will be exploring our thoughts, feelings, fears, and visions about our own personal futures, and the future of our world. To begin our exploration, I'd like to invite you to do the brief exercise that follows. The purpose of this exercise is to help you get in touch with some of your own thoughts and feelings before reading what I have to say.

So before you read further, I'd like to ask you to take a few moments, read through the following exercise once, then close your eyes and try it. (If you prefer not to do this, that's fine — just go on to the next chapter.)

Sit comfortably in a quiet place. If you wish, have a pen and paper or your journal within easy reach. Close your eyes and take a few slow, deep breaths. Take a moment to relax. Then ask yourself, "What is my vision of the future? How do I feel about it?"

First, focus your attention on how you see, think, and

feel about your own personal future. How do you imagine your future prospects in your career, your finances, your relationships, your family, friends, your physical health and fitness (including how you feel about your aging process), and your overall personal well-being?

Just sit quietly and note whatever thoughts, feelings, and images come up for you. Try to be very honest with yourself and acknowledge all the thoughts and feelings you have about these things, both positive and negative. Some of your inner responses to these questions might seem contradictory or confusing. For example, you might simultaneously have both positive and negative feelings about the same thing. That's perfectly natural and quite okay. Just acknowledge the full range of your feelings.

Now, expand your focus to imagine the future of your community, your country, humanity, the natural environment, the planet. Just notice the images, thoughts, and feelings that come to you when you ask yourself to imagine the future of the world. Again, try to be as honest as you can, and don't worry if your inner responses seem somewhat contradictory or confusing. For example, you might find yourself thinking, "There's so much potential for positive changes...but I wonder if we will destroy ourselves before we get a chance to make those changes!"

When you feel complete with the exercise, open your eyes. If you wish, take your pen and paper or your journal and write down as much as you can about what came to you as you imagined your personal future and the future of our planet. If you prefer, use colored pens or crayons and draw your images and feelings.

CHAPTER TWO

Facing
the Future

*Humanity is in an ongoing process of
conscious evolution. At this time, we are taking
a giant step in consciousness — a great leap
in our evolutionary process.*

*H*ow do you feel about the future? If you are like
most of us, you may find yourself having very
mixed feelings when you consider that question.

If you are an especially optimistic person, or happen
to be having a particularly good day, you might imagine a
bright, glowing future for yourself and for all of us. If
you're a more cynical or pessimistic person, or if you are
having a difficult day, you may foresee a dim or dark
future for yourself and others.

I've found, however, that most people who are asked
this question, myself included, experience at least some
conflicting feelings. On one hand we feel hope, excitement, a certain fascination with what the future may
bring. On the other hand, we feel some doubt, fear,

perhaps even dread or despair. Oftentimes we feel a deep confusion and helplessness about what to do. We barely know how to effectively address our own personal problems, much less the gigantic problems we see out there in the world.

It is entirely appropriate that so many of us are experiencing this mixture of feelings. Nobody would deny that this is a very scary time, perhaps the most frightening time that has ever existed on this planet. Most people are struggling with painful personal problems. Our relationships don't seem to be working the way we think they should. Marriages are falling apart. Children are being abused. Many people are depressed and anxiety ridden, or frustrated, or even violent. A friend or family member (or we ourselves) may be suffering from a disease for which we have no cure. Some of us have no jobs; others are dissatisfied with the jobs we have. Many of us are workaholics who are burning ourselves out. Perhaps we are dealing with our own or a loved one's addictions to alcohol, drugs, food, or other substances or activities.

As if all this weren't enough, when we look beyond our personal lives, we see even worse problems. We have wars all over the planet. Many countries are suffering from cruel, repressive governments. The Third World countries are being exploited by the industrialized nations. Economic chaos and disasters are threatening. There is a worldwide threat of terrorism. We have increasing violence in our cities, and homelessness has become a terrible problem. We have a drug epidemic that's out of control. Most frightening of all, we are in the process of destroying the natural environment upon which our lives depend.

It's unpleasant and uncomfortable to face these realities and our feelings about them, so most of us try to focus on other things. Yet, in order to have the courage to confront our personal and planetary problems, and try to solve them, we must first be honest enough to acknowledge the confusing, frightening feelings we may have and how overwhelming it all seems. The first step we must take in dealing with any challenge is to acknowledge what it is and how we feel about it. It is only through facing our fears and difficulties that we can find creative and effective solutions.

If our personal lives are so difficult, and the world is in such a mess (reconfirmed every evening on the news), why should we feel anything except despair? Why feel hopeful at all? The reason is that although this is a frightening time, it is simultaneously the most powerful time that has ever existed on this planet.

Humanity is in an ongoing process of conscious evolution. At this time, we are taking a giant step in consciousness — a great leap in our evolutionary process. It's probably the most exciting event that has ever taken place on this plane of reality. And I believe that on a soul level we have all chosen to be here at this time in order to take part in it. So we've committed ourselves to being here and doing this, we've put our hearts and souls into it, and now we're looking rather anxiously and breathlessly to see whether or not it's going to work! Somewhere, deep inside us, we know what is possible, and we're wondering if we're going to be able to manifest that. It's a big question.

I believe that the answer to that question lies in the

hands of every one of us. Through our personal commitment to the process of growth and change, each one of us has the power not only to transform our own life, but to contribute tremendously to the transformation of life on our planet.

CHAPTER THREE

Healing Crises
in Our Personal Lives

A healing crisis occurs at the point when we have
outgrown an old pattern or way of being, but are
still unconsciously holding onto that old way
because it feels safe and familiar.

*A*s you may have noticed, it often takes a personal crisis of some kind to catalyze real change and growth
in our lives. Upon reflection, you can probably remember
how a period of great upheaval, filled with confusion and
pain — perhaps triggered by an event such as the death of
a loved one, the ending of a relationship, a financial set-
back or loss of a job, or an accident or illness — has ultimately led to greater understanding, awareness, and new
opportunities in your life. If you look at the lives of people
you know, you may very well see the same pattern. Times
of chaos and uncertainty can lead to new doors opening,
especially when we are willing and able to look for the
growth opportunities in a situation rather than simply
being overwhelmed by outside circumstances.

It is the nature of the human soul to constantly move forward into greater challenge, expansion, and awareness. The primary job of the human personality, however, is to try to survive in physical form and get our physical and emotional needs met as best we can. There are certain parts of our personalities that want to change and grow, recognizing that growing is necessary and beneficial. Other parts of us prefer to cling to whatever has worked for us in the past. These conservative inner voices argue, "We've survived so far, haven't we? Why change something that's working okay?" These are the aspects of our psyches that urge us to stay with old patterns that feel safe and comfortable, rather than risking new things that we're not sure will work.

It is important to acknowledge these seemingly conflicting drives within us in order to understand how they affect the choices we make in our lives, and how, contrary to what might be our first impressions, they can actually work together. The tension between the parts of us that want to grow and change and the parts that want to remain safe in familiar territory is responsible for triggering what we call a "healing crisis."

A healing crisis occurs at the point when we have outgrown an old pattern or way of being, but are still unconsciously holding onto that old way because it feels safe and familiar. Our response to a healing crisis can vary greatly, both according to who we are and in reaction to other influences that may be affecting us at the time. We may be feeling relatively comfortable and content in a pattern that is no longer vital, unaware that our soul — which always welcomes forward motion — is ready to guide us to a new level. Or we may be feeling stuck and frustrated, wanting to make a change but not quite willing or able to. So we unconsciously create some kind of physical, emotional, mental, or spiritual crisis that shakes us out of the old and propels us into the new.

Healing crises are always uncomfortable and can often be painful and sometimes even terrifying. It can feel as if our world is in danger of coming to an end. It can seem as if our lives are falling apart. We may see disaster and doom everywhere. Oftentimes we blame ourselves and feel that we've done something horribly wrong or that we are, in some way, terribly lacking.

In fact, we have simply outgrown an old form, an old way of relating to the world. An old way of being is dissolving, making way for a new, more expanded, and more conscious way. The outer forms in our lives mirror this internal process. So we may lose a job or a relationship because it is too limiting; it would not allow us to expand in the direction we need to go. We may lose a loved one through death because both our souls are moving onto new levels — one of us continuing within the physical body, the other passing into a nonphysical reality. We may contract a serious illness in order to confront ourselves with the necessity for change, or confront a choice between continuing our own journey in physical form or moving forward into non-physical reality.

If you have ever gone through crises such as these, and have taken the opportunity to grow from them, you can probably recognize, in retrospect, how vitally important the experience was. From your present vantage point you may even realize that you would never want to return to your previous way of life or level of consciousness.

I know, in my own life, that there have been times, such as during the ending of a relationship, when I experienced a great deal of pain, convinced that my whole world was falling apart. Yet, as I look back at those times and see them in the context of a continuing journey, I can see how necessary they were — more like the opening of doors than the closing of them.

Fortunately, as we progress in the evolution of our consciousness, and gain more understanding of the growth process, most often we don't have to learn through severe crises. We learn to respond more quickly to the subtler clues that life gives us that it's time for a change! Because we've been through difficult times before and felt the positive results, we have a little more trust. It's easier each time to surrender to change, to let go of the old and open to the new. Still, it's always frightening and difficult to some degree, and we need to have great compassion for ourselves and others who are going through a healing crisis.

A friend of mine had an experience that perfectly illustrates this. She had enjoyed a successful business partnership with a man for many years. Then one day he announced that he wanted to dissolve their partnership and go out on his own. My friend was devastated, feeling that she would never be able to make it without his expertise and support. In the process, she confronted many of her fears and doubts and became aware of certain self-defeating patterns of her behavior. She used the entire process as a learning experience. Today she has a successful business of her own and is very much enjoying her newfound strength and independence. At the time it happened, the change had seemed like a disaster to her, yet it led to healing, growth, and expansion.

I believe that in the Eastern philosophical and spiritual tradition, there is a greater understanding of the process of change and growth than we have in the West. In the Hindu religion, there is a trinity of three main gods — Brahma, the creator; Vishnu, the preserver; and Shiva, the destroyer. In the West, we may find it rather horrifying to worship "The Destroyer" right along with "The Creator." Yet this concept represents a profound understanding of the natural polarities of life — that life includes death and rebirth, and that old forms are constantly being destroyed, making way for the new. In fact, Shiva, is called the cosmic dancer — the god of music, dance, and the arts — and it is said his dance keeps the universe in motion.*

---

* When I was in India, many years ago, I was so profoundly moved by the image and energy of Shiva that I took the name Shakti, which is the feminine form of Shiva. The name of our publishing company, Nataraj, refers to Shiva as the cosmic dancer.

CHAPTER FOUR

The World in a Healing Crisis

Everything that we have been sweeping under the rug and denying for centuries is coming out in the open, demanding the birth of a new awareness. Now is the time to confront the fact that we are still clinging to patterns of thinking and behaving that no longer work.

*J*ust as we may experience a healing crisis on the individual level when we are ready to go through major change and transformation, the same is true on a collective or global level. That is exactly what is happening now. As we begin this new millennium, humanity is making an evolutionary leap in consciousness. And this forward movement of the collective soul is now being experienced throughout the world as a healing crisis on the planetary level.

To fully grasp this, we have to understand how the process of conscious evolution works. As we grow, evolve, and expand our consciousness, individually and collectively, the old forms we have created no longer fit. It's as if our awareness is getting bigger, and so it can no longer fit into the forms that used to work. These forms were once quite appropriate; they supported us and allowed us to express ourselves. But now they are no longer working for us. As we grow, it's as if we literally push beyond these old forms that have been containing us. As we step out of them they begin to crumble. They must fall apart to create space for expansion. From that more expanded awareness, we create new, more flexible forms that support us in our new level of consciousness.

On a personal level, we can see this process in action when we lose a job that used to be satisfying but no longer is, or a relationship falls apart that used to feel safe and comfortable but now feels increasingly restrictive. On a collective level we see this process as we watch economic and political systems crumble and institutions fall apart or change drastically. The fall of the Berlin Wall, the dissolution of the Soviet Union, and the shift away from our "cold war" mentality are dramatic examples of this transformational process that took place in the latter years of the twentieth century. While these might seem like positive changes, it is sometimes more difficult to see our economic crises, violence in our cities, and our drug epidemics as an evolution in consciousness. But remember that the old institutions have to crumble to make way for the new. What we are witnessing is the "falling apart" aspect of the process. We are now ready to recognize and acknowledge what didn't work about our old way of doing things, so that we can recreate things in a new and more conscious way.

Both individually and collectively, when we gain new awareness of what's possible, we look at how we've been doing things and have a new perspective on our behavior. What seemed perfectly normal up to now may suddenly seem very limited, ineffective, or even a bit crazy. It's as if we've found a bit of consciousness to stand on, and this allows us to look back and see our former lack of consciousness.

For example, in your personal life, you may begin to recognize a pattern that you have in a relationship as dysfunctional and self-defeating. You may even find yourself continuing to act out this pattern for a while because part of you is still holding on to the familiar behavior, even though you recognize its limitations and notice how it doesn't really work for you. You can become aware of this only because another part of you has already recognized that there are other possible ways of behaving. Eventually, you will find yourself shifting into a new, more satisfying way of doing things.

A woman I know had always been driven by the need to make a lot of money. She was quite successful at this, but she pushed herself relentlessly in order to achieve her goals, working endless hours and sacrificing her personal life and other emotional needs in the process. She entered therapy and began to realize how out of balance her life had become. For about a year, however, she was unable to extricate herself from her driven lifestyle. She had become aware of the pain it caused her, but couldn't bring herself to make any significant changes. Finally, an illness forced her to reduce the hours she was working, and she began to use her evenings and weekends to rest and nurture herself. Eventually, she took a few months, devoting her time to herself and getting in touch with what she really wanted and needed to be happy. During that time, she made some important decisions and discoveries about herself. Today she has a job she loves. She works normal hours, makes less money than before, and enjoys her life much more.

While we are unconsciously living out our old forms of behavior we may actually numb ourselves to our pain. Then, when we finally shift into the new form of behavior we find ourselves feeling much happier and more satisfied. The truly uncomfortable time is that in-between stage where we are becoming conscious of what doesn't work but are still caught in the middle of it. It is at this time that whatever we have been doing to numb ourselves to the pain ceases to work as well as it once did — and then we discover how much pain we are really in. As difficult as this might be, it is a necessary and powerful stage we must go through. We must have patience and compassion for ourselves, knowing that real change takes time.

Today we are in this challenging middle stage on a worldwide level. Many of us are waking up and realizing that a lot of things in our world aren't working. It's time to make changes, but we aren't sure yet how to make them. We're bumbling around, acutely aware of how painful and destructive our old habits are but not quite knowing what else to do.

Let's look at the example of war. Down through most of recorded human history, in most cultures, war has been seen as inevitable, natural, an appropriate and effective way to deal with conflict. But in recent times, increasing numbers of people are recognizing war as unnecessarily destructive, a barbaric and foolish way for human beings to try to solve problems. In fact, to many of us it's starting to look completely insane. Men and women everywhere are simply refusing to take part in it or to consider it a viable way to handle any conflict whatsoever. Yet there continue to be plenty of wars going on. This is because a large portion of the collective whole is still operating according to the old pattern; it doesn't yet know what else to do.

The good news, in my view, is that our collective consciousness is expanding and growing in this and many other areas. More and more people are becoming aware that we have fundamental challenges to overcome — in our families, our educational systems, our cities, our governments, our economic systems, our international relations, our planetary environment — and that we must find new ways to confront these problems.

In this new millennium, everything that we have been sweeping under the rug and denying for centuries is coming out in the open, demanding the birth of a new awareness. Now is the time to confront the fact that we are still clinging to patterns of thinking and behaving that no longer work. We are beginning to open up, both individually and collectively, to the realization that it is time to create our lives and our world differently. Now is the time for change and transformation.

CHAPTER FIVE

Creating
Real Change

*Like the proverbial pebble dropped into a still
pond, the shifts of consciousness we make in
our personal lives send out small but important
waves that ripple through the whole world.*

Most people reading this book will agree that the
time has come for profound transformation in
our lives and in the world. Indeed, this transformation is
already under way. But the question arises, "How can we
support and contribute to that process? How can we do
our part, as individuals, to make sure it's going in a positive direction? How *do* we create real change in our personal lives and in the world?"

The simple answer to that question is this: We change
the world most effectively by becoming more conscious.
There is a quote attributed to Mohandas Ghandi that says
this well: "You must be the change you wish to see in the
world." As each of us becomes more aware on an individual level, we see change reflected in our personal lives.

Old problems and patterns gradually melt away and we meet new difficulties and new challenges with a widening perspective and increasing wisdom. Our lives become more balanced, more fulfilling, and more in alignment with our soul's purpose. Since each one of us is an integral part of the collective consciousness, we each have a subtle but powerful effect on that mass consciousness (and vice versa). Like the proverbial pebble dropped into a still pond, the shifts of consciousness we make in our personal lives send out small but important waves that ripple through the whole world.

When we, as individuals, grow in awareness, the mass consciousness shifts accordingly. As the mass consciousness changes, it pulls along other individuals who may be clinging to old patterns, or who are simply unaware of how to proceed. So as a few wake up, everyone begins to awaken. And as the collective consciousness expands, the social, economic, and political forms of the world change and respond to those new levels of awareness.

I'm sure that many of you reading this book are already familiar with the concept of creating our own reality — the idea that we each take a very active part in creating the kind of world we experience. This metaphysical principle is based on the awareness that everything in the universe is made of one vital element, which we can call "energy" or "life force." This being so, everything in life is interconnected. Our thoughts and feelings are a form of energy, as are our physical bodies and seemingly solid material like stone and metal. Many modern physicists, observing this same phenomenon in science, agree that our thoughts, feelings, physical bodies, and the material world around us are all mutually interrelated and constantly affecting one another.

This helps us to understand how we are each constantly creating our own subjective experiences of reality. Our own deepest beliefs and expectations about ourselves, about others, and about life determine how we perceive external reality, what kinds of people, events, and situations we draw to us, and are drawn to, and how we interpret everything that happens to us.

In a very real way, what we experience in our lives is a mirrored image of the values, beliefs, and images we hold within us, consciously or unconsciously. What we experience shifts considerably as we become more aware. One obvious example of this can be seen if we go into therapy or join twelve-step programs to change a harmful or addictive pattern of behavior. As we change, our whole circle of friends may change, reflecting new interests and new needs. We become aware of a whole new range of possibilities we couldn't have seen before. We find relationships that are emotionally and spiritually much more fulfilling than anything we were capable of enjoying before. And along with this, our feelings toward ourselves change, becoming more positive and self-affirming, raising self-esteem. With greater self-esteem and awareness a whole new world of possibility opens up to us, one that was invisible to us until we changed.

Because our experiences accurately mirror our inner consciousness, we can actually learn to use our impressions of the external world as reflections of our inner selves. Just as looking into the bathroom mirror in the morning allows us to see our faces and physical bodies, so the mirrors provided by our experiences of the external world can allow us to become more aware of our own deepest beliefs, thoughts, and emotional patterns. Using our experiences in the world as our reflection, we can learn what attitudes and beliefs we have that need to be healed or expanded.

Not long ago, for example, a client of mine became aware that in every one of his jobs he had a difficult time with a domineering, unreasonable co-worker or supervisor. It seemed that these people were always looking over his shoulder, telling him every move to make and being both hypercritical and argumentative. Through first accepting the idea that the repetitive experience was a mirror of some kind, and then asking what this reflection was revealing about himself, he became aware of a pattern established in his early childhood. He had been raised by a domineering stepfather, a relationship that had been confusing and difficult for him. Through that relationship he had established a deep unconscious emotional pattern that continued to draw him into similar relationships in his adulthood. Once he was able to recognize this, however, and become more aware of his beliefs, feelings, and needs around this pattern, the pattern shifted.

Along with his new awareness, he began to create a new, more harmonious work environment, one in which he no longer became enmeshed with domineering people. Instead of projecting his power onto authority figures, he began to claim his own natural sense of strength. As he owned his own power and authority in a healthy way, others began to treat him with more respect.

It is an extremely empowering step on our journey of consciousness to understand that we do in fact create our own reality, and that we can take responsibility for our own life experience. Instead of feeling like a victim of circumstances, or blaming other people for our problems, we can make fuller use of the fact that we each have the creative power of the universe within us.

As we begin working with this mirror concept in our daily lives, it becomes a powerful and trustworthy guide, shining a clear and brilliant light on a path that might otherwise be quite confusing to us. We begin to see the problems that are reflected to us in our lives as graphic illustrations showing us where we are currently unconscious. With this gift of awareness, we can heal and expand our consciousness further. Once we recognize that the difficulties and imbalances in our lives are reflections of our own unconscious patterns, we have a powerful tool to become aware of and change those patterns. After a relatively short period of employing this tool in our lives, we become aware of how much power we actually have to create the lives we truly want.

CHAPTER SIX

Blame and Responsibility

Choosing to be responsible instead of blaming ourselves is saying, "Yes, I am a powerful, creative being, learning every day, from every experience, and learning how to create. Now that I see and appreciate what I've created, how can I learn from my reality, refine and improve it?"

*I*n recent years, the concept that we create our own reality has gained a great deal of popularity, especially in the personal growth movement. Like most principles, the idea that our external reality reflects our internal one can be easily misunderstood. Unfortunately, it is frequently misused and can cause a great deal of unnecessary harm. One woman I heard about refused to go to her doctor when she became seriously ill because she felt so guilty about having somehow "created" this illness. Obviously, this is a terrible, and potentially tragic, misuse of this principle. In this book, I hope to clarify how to use this concept in a healing and empowering way.

It is extremely important to grasp that we are creating our experience of reality in this life not just on the personality level, but from the soul level. In other words, on a deep spiritual level we may be choosing certain circumstances and experiences that contribute to our consciousness growth and development. These may not always feel comfortable or be understandable on the personality level. For example, we might unconsciously choose an illness or other seeming misfortune as the most effective or fastest way to learn, grow, and evolve.

In order to use the mirror of consciousness principle constructively, we need to recognize the difference between responsibility and blame. Many of us have spent our entire lives seeing other people or external circumstances as the cause of our difficulties — we've blamed the outside world for our troubles. Unfortunately, when we finally grasp the concept that we are responsible for our own lives, too many of us begin to *blame ourselves* for the problems that exist in our reality. For example, if I have an illness and I learn that on some level I am creating that reality, I might think, "What's the matter with me that I am creating this illness? If I were a more conscious person I'd be well — or I'd be able to heal myself instantly!" Or, if I am having financial difficulties I might say to myself, "The universe is abundant, so I ought to be able to create prosperity in my own life. There must be something really bad or lacking in me since I am living in poverty."

This kind of self-recrimination is anything but taking responsibility for our lives. Rather, it is self-blame. The peculiar thing about blame is that it discourages us from moving forward. And in this respect, the effect is the same whether we are blaming other people or blaming ourselves.

Unfortunately, I see all too many people on the personal growth journey who struggle with this idea of the mirror of consciousness and beat themselves up with blame, not grasping the true meaning of taking responsibility for their realities. When we are blaming ourselves or others, this is fundamentally a disempowering act. It comes from a sense of helplessness and makes us feel worse, actually magnifying that helplessness. Taking responsibility, meanwhile, involves claiming our power to create and to change.

Blame is based on the negative assumption that something wrong or bad is happening and therefore someone is in error. Taking an attitude of responsibility, on the other hand, requires us to look at every situation as a potentially valuable learning experience. We need to cultivate the ability to appreciate the reality we've already created, and see the problems in it as gifts that can help us grow and evolve.

We are not to blame for the way our lives are unfolding. Blaming ourselves for our present reality is like blaming a child for being ten years old instead of twenty or thirty. We are evolving in a natural way. We've done the best we have known how up until now. One of the ironic things about life is that from moment to moment we have only a limited knowledge about our lives, and we can only make choices and decisions on the basis of what we know. To ask more than that of any human being is as futile and unreasonable as asking a six-month-old child to explain what she wants instead of crying. Blaming is a static state, one of standing in place and not moving on, while responsibility — the ability to respond — is dynamic, the very essence of forward movement.

By looking at the reality we have manifested in a "response-able" way, rather than a blaming way, we can learn much more. We can become more conscious and aware of our own patterns. Choosing to be responsible instead of blaming ourselves is saying, "Yes, I am a powerful, creative being, learning every day, from every experience, and learning how to create. Now that I see and appreciate what I've created, how can I learn from my reality, refine and improve it?"

As we do our consciousness work, spiritually and psychologically, we become more and more aware of our own deeply held assumptions and belief systems about life, and our habitual emotional patterns and reactions. We can begin to see how these factors of our "inner reality" shape and influence our experience of what we commonly think of as "external reality." We find that as we heal our emotional wounds and change our beliefs, the experiences of our lives change, sometimes almost miraculously. We begin to have a genuine experience of how we are creating our own personal reality.

Many times, in workshops, with my clients, and in my own private life, I have seen this kind of transformation occur. I am thinking now of a young woman who attended a workshop I gave in Los Angeles. She had not spoken to her sister for years, owing to a conflict they'd had in their early twenties. During the workshop, she realized she had been clinging to her old pattern of blaming and feeling like a victim, and the only thing it ever got her was a feeling of sadness over not having her sister's friendship anymore. She was able to express and release the feelings that were keeping her separated from her sister, and in the process felt greatly relieved.

During the lunch break, she called her office to check for phone messages. One of the messages was from her sister. She called her back and discovered that her sister, also, had gone through a similar healing process of her own. When she returned to the workshop, she shared this story with us, saying how grateful she was to be able to be close to her sister again. Seemingly, their relationship had been healed across the miles in the instant that she saw the old pattern of blame and was able to let go of it.

Once we are able to embrace this concept of creating our own reality, it becomes quite easy to embrace the concept that we also participate in creating the world reality. Just as we are each creating our individual reality, the mass consciousness is creating the collective reality. Whatever attitudes and beliefs are held most deeply and powerfully in the mass consciousness will, for better or worse, be manifested in the collective reality of the world. Unresolved conflict and pain, held in the consciousness of millions of people the world over, can — and I believe does — get reflected back to us in war, in violence in our cities, and in our collective disregard for the rights of other human beings and the well-being of the Earth.

As the mass consciousness evolves, the collective experience of reality gradually changes. We see evolution taking place in physical form in our world through new ideas, changing religious beliefs, the emergence of new social and political systems, and the development of new technologies. Our world as it is today is a clear and accurate reflection of our present collective consciousness.

It is, I believe, absolutely critical that we understand and learn to more fully appreciate how our evolution as individuals automatically changes the collective consciousness of our world. While we might feel that we are mere drops in a vast ocean of consciousness, the interesting thing is that the evolution of each "mere drop" is a tremendously powerful force. It takes a relatively small number of souls moving into alignment with universal forces to have a great impact on our global reality.

We must never underestimate the potent impact we each have on the collective consciousness, whether we are taking responsibility for it or not. As we cultivate our own consciousness growth process, we affect others profoundly and we spur forward the mass consciousness in its evolution. Through our individual efforts we truly can change the world. This is happening even now as you sit reading this book.

Interestingly, since we're integrally connected in consciousness, no one individual can evolve far ahead of everyone else. We are all contained within a certain force field of consciousness. Though we may take a role close to the leading edge, we cannot leave our fellow beings far behind since in essence we are all one. So we have no choice but to evolve together, bringing all our brothers and sisters along with us.

CHAPTER SEVEN

Taking
Action

We begin to see that for our personal or social/political actions to be most effective, we need to start with a deep understanding and commitment to our own consciousness processes.

*A*s we discuss how we can make real change through our consciousness, the question naturally arises, "Are we supposed to just sit around and try to get conscious, and assume somehow that's going to improve our lives and the world? Don't we have to take action in order to make our lives work, and don't we need to get involved in social and political activities in order to deal with the very real problems and challenges that exist in the world?"

Of course, taking action is a vital part of bringing our consciousness into form and making real change. Direct, powerful, and committed action is vitally important on both a personal and social/political level. Whether or not we commit ourselves to such actions is not so much the issue as where the motivation for that action comes from within us.

The pitfall is this: If we put our *primary* attention and commitment into external action, we repeat an old pattern, one that is at the root of much of the trouble we're in today — and that is believing that the cause of the problem, as well as the power to correct it, exists primarily in the external world.

If we try to solve our problems only externally, which we often do by trying to fix or change other people or institutions, we give away our power. We project it out there, into the external world, instead of owning where it really exists, and where we can actually do something about it — inside us.

For example, many people who were active in the women's movement, and who worked very hard to change the old patriarchal values in our society came to the point of a personal impasse in their forties or fifties. Clearly they had helped to change our society for the better, but they found they could move ahead in their personal lives only after confronting in themselves some of the same gender biases they had been fighting in the external world. This phenomenon was well documented in Gloria Steinem's book *Revolution from Within: A Book of Self-Esteem,** and is further explained in Sidra Stone's fascinating book *The Shadow King: The Invisible Force That Holds Women Back.***

When our primary focus is to go out and try to change things in the external world, we may accomplish some of our goals, but ultimately our effectiveness may be limited. Lasting change comes only when we get completely away

---

* Published by Little, Brown and Company, New York, 1992.
** Published by Nataraj/New World Library, Novato, California, 1997.

from thinking that the core problem is *out there* some-where, that our peace of mind can be won only by chang-ing others. The kind of thinking that we must change in ourselves is the belief that it's somebody else's fault, it's those other people, it's that situation, it's that other coun-try, that other race, that government, those politicians, or those unconscious people who are responsible for the way things are. We need to let go of this way of thinking not just because it's a *nice* or *spiritually aware* thing to do, but because it is the only way we can discover and take respon-sibility for our own power.

Where do we begin? We begin by first understanding and fully embracing the awareness that all those people and institutions reflect aspects of ourselves. They are man-ifestations of our own consciousness and the process that is going on inside us at this very moment. When we take on this kind of responsibility — and believe me, it is one of the biggest responsibilities we will ever assume — we say with conviction, "Yes, I can understand how this situation reflects a part of my own inner conflict. I can see how these people mirror aspects of me. I can see how these things that are going on in the world may reflect things that are going on in my own life. I take responsibility (but not blame) for what I see."

Once we accept this responsibility to hold our power within ourselves and we see the world as mirroring aspects of ourselves, then we can take a particular kind of external action that will be extremely effective. This kind of action begins with owning our center of power and responsibility within ourselves.

It is only from that place of power and responsibility that we can put our energy into action, supporting our awareness. We need to walk our talk. We need to say what we honestly feel, and act on what we know. We need to talk about, act upon, give our time, energy, and money to causes we believe in. We need to live our truth as fully as possible, every moment of our lives.

Deena Metzger, author of *Writing for Your Life,* works with people to help them achieve what she calls "personal disarmament." She sees the inner life of the individual as being much like a nation-state, one that contains multiple selves, governed as countries are governed. Problems and issues that afflict nations also affect our own "inner countries." Sometimes the citizens of this nation-state of the psyche live in harmony and peace; at other times they may be in rebellion, fighting one another. We need to be able to recognize the different interests and needs of these various selves, to sometimes negotiate agreements with them, and to not keep one group or the other buried, or hidden away. Perhaps even more importantly, we need to recognize what kind of government we have: Dictatorial and repressive? Laissez-faire to the point of laxness? Openly democratic, allowing each self to have its say?

The nation-state of the self doesn't just keep to itself, isolated from others. Rather, that inner state interacts with the outer world in ways that affect the world just as much as real nations do. We project our inner conflicts, our rebellions, repressions, and fears to the outside world all the time. I have found it helpful to look at our inner worlds in this way — to identify what kind of inner governments we have, what inner selves we allow to openly express and enjoy themselves, and what inner selves we repress and try to hold down.

As a political liberal I used to feel irritated and judgmental toward people with a conservative viewpoint. Now I recognize that they represent a conservative side of my own inner nation-state that I am less in touch with than my liberal side. Recently, while visiting a friend's family, her brother began to express opinions that I strongly disagreed with, having to do with a local environmental issue. Rather than jumping immediately into a highly polarized argument, I paused to acknowledge my annoyance inwardly and to remind myself that this person was mirroring a part of me — a citizen of my own inner nation — that I have trouble accepting. After that I was able to make a few clear points from my own perspective, which at least gave him something to think about without needlessly antagonizing him.

If I'm able to see someone in my life as a reflection of myself, and then have the courage to speak my truth to that person when appropriate, while simultaneously recognizing that part of myself they are mirroring to me, I'm taking responsibility for the whole process. I'm speaking and living my truth. And there is no way that I can be more effective either in the external world or in my inner life.

We begin to see that for our personal or social/political actions to be most effective, we need to start with a deep understanding and commitment to our own consciousness process. This begins by recognizing that we truly do have a strong influence on creating the realities we experience, that we tend to draw to us those people and experiences that reflect our own consciousness in some way.

Working from that base, we can learn what it is to take action from our own deepest inner sense of truth. We can discover the power of doing what we genuinely feel moved to do, what our hearts tell us is the right thing to do. Too often we base our actions on external standards or rules of behavior we've blindly adopted. Or we take a particular path of action because it seems like a rational idea or a theoretically good course to pursue.

Some years ago, I met a psychiatrist in his mid-forties who had come to a major turning point in his life over this very issue. His life was literally falling apart, and he no longer wanted to see patients. He said he was tired of hearing about people's problems, largely because he was convinced that he wasn't helping them in any way.

As he began questioning his own motives, he quickly saw that he had never really felt any great urge to become a doctor. In fact, the decision to go to medical school was one he'd made when he was still a teenager. It was a decision based on neither his knowledge of what psychiatrists do, nor on anything that came from his own heart. It was a decision based primarily on the fact that his best friend had chosen to study psychiatry and his own parents had been enthusiastic and supportive of the idea.

This man had been wise enough to recognize that he had little to offer his patients except what he had learned in his medical training; nothing was coming from his heart. His feelings of impotence, reflected by his belief that he was not helping his patients, was coming from something he felt within him — that he was not operating from his own inner truth.

A couple of years later, I learned that this man had sold his practice and was working part-time in an emergency room, putting most of his time and energy into developing his creative talents. He had written two articles for magazines on controversial topics and had gotten lots of lively reactions. He was feeling very excited about the possibility of using his writing skills to make a difference in the world.

When we look at our own lives, or the lives of friends and acquaintances, it is easy to see that this man is by no means alone in his search. His is just one example among perhaps millions showing that we need to follow not just what our heads tell us are appropriate actions, but what we feel in our guts. We need to be asking what it is that enlivens, empowers, excites us, turns us on, makes us genuinely feel satisfied and fulfilled. That's what actually heals us, and heals the world.

In the political world there are examples of whole societies or even nations that have followed their hearts in the way I'm describing. During the Second World War, for example, the people of Norway, as well as the citizens of a small settlement called Mondragon in the Basque area of Spain, refused to cooperate with the Fascist takeovers of their regions. Following the truths of their own hearts, they were guided to find ways not only to resist the violent military machine that was sweeping Europe, but did so with little bloodshed as well. They ended up strengthening their own resolve to create societies that even today are some of the most productive, wealthy, and humane in the whole world.

We have the greatest healing effect on the world when we allow the life force to move through our own bodies. Our power comes not simply by what we say or do. Rather, our words and actions are vehicles for our life energy. What really transforms is the life force moving through us.

When you are in touch with your inner truth and you walk into a room, you may have an impact on the lives of everyone there simply because you have so much life force moving through you. You need not even say or do anything, other than simply be there. On some level, conscious or unconscious, people feel this and are affected by it. It stimulates their own life energy and begins to trigger change and growth for them. It may catalyze some type of healing crisis in their lives. And so they experience growth as a result, and you have contributed to the healing of this planet, probably without even knowing it.

A friend of mine told me an interesting story. A few years ago, she committed herself to a process of emotional healing and recovery from addiction. As a result of her example, her brother also got deeply involved in his healing process. He recently told her that he had gone back to their hometown in New England and found that at least twenty of their friends were involved in similar processes of recovery, healing, and growth, all as a direct or indirect result of the influence of my friend and her brother.

Having seen examples of these phenomena many, many times over the years, I am convinced that our commitment to our own growth and healing processes serves as a catalyst for countless others — our family, our friends, and even people whose names we may never know. The power of being committed to the truths of our own hearts releases energy into our bodies and into the world that can heal some of the most grievous and long-standing troubles of the world.

How exactly does all this work? How does commitment to the truths of their heart in one person ripple through entire communities like this? We don't really know how it happens, but it is clear that it does — and much more often than we might think. The fact that it happens at all suggests that the concept of oneness, that we are all one, is indeed a fact of life, not just an obscure spiritual abstraction. Our own thoughts, feelings, and actions are not isolated occurrences taking place within the confines of our own bodies, but are in fact manifestations of the one spiritual and energetic source that moves through every one of us. It is no more possible for one of us to change without changing the rest as it is for a single wave to crest in the ocean without affecting the whole.

CHAPTER EIGHT

The Consciousness Journey

*Consciousness is not a destination at
which we finally arrive. It is an ongoing,
ever-deepening, infinitely expanding process,
a journey that perhaps has no end.*

*A*t this point you might ask, "If the way to create real
change in my life and in the world is primarily
through my own consciousness growth, what exactly does
that mean? What is consciousness growth?"

Let us begin with a statement that may at first seem
quite obvious — that consciousness is awareness and understanding, while unconsciousness is a lack of the same.
Consciousness growth, then, is the process of becoming
aware of things we were formerly unaware of. It is really as
simple as that.

Consciousness growth happens naturally as a part of
every being's evolution. For example, a baby's consciousness grows as she becomes aware of her fingers and toes
and learns how to move them and play with them. A man

grows in consciousness when, as a result of a serious illness and a decision to regain his health, he learns that certain foods and behavior patterns are detrimental, while others promote his health and well-being.

In our society, consciousness is generally associated with the mind, that is, "improving your mind," or gaining mental skills that allow you to perform a particular task better or "know more" in order to pass a test, get a higher degree in college, or become an expert in a certain field. In the sense that we are discussing it here, however, our consciousness growth involves our four levels of existence — the spiritual, the mental, the emotional, and the physical.

We might attend college, for example, in order to become more aware and knowledgeable about a particular subject. But we might not realize that in the process of attending school we may be developing on many other levels as well, raising our self-esteem, perhaps, and discovering more about our soul's purpose.

Life is fundamentally a journey of consciousness, a journey of growing awareness. However, most of us aren't fully aware of this evolutionary process of our lives, nor do we understand in depth how it works. Therefore, most people are as yet *unconsciously* involved in a process of consciousness growth!

We make a great leap forward when we recognize the evolutionary nature of our lives and begin to understand how it works. As this awareness increases, we can choose to embrace our lives as a consciousness process, and make a commitment to that process, to keep it in focus and do whatever we can to move through it much more rapidly.

By doing so, most people enjoy their lives more, finding deeper fulfillment and satisfaction than ever before.

Making a commitment to your consciousness growth means making a decision to become aware of and understand as much as you can about yourself, others, life, and the universe. It involves looking at life as a learning experience in which every single thing that happens to us can be seen as a potential gift to help us develop our full potential.

One ironic thing about the consciousness journey is that with every new step we take, we become aware of things we were unaware of before. Facing our previous unconsciousness can be very difficult and unpleasant. Until we become comfortable with the journey itself, seeing that over time our lives become more fulfilled by following such a path, the discovery of what we don't know can cause us to feel quite fearful. As humans, we like to believe that we know where we stand at any given moment. We like to feel that our beliefs are complete or "right" or unquestionable. Most people on a consciousness journey, however, learn that our awareness is constantly changing and that as consciousness evolves there is peace of mind and security that come with letting go of the need to be right. So one of the first things we learn as we embark on this journey is the willingness to face our unconsciousness.

Like a light in the darkness, our awareness automatically illuminates areas where we have not been aware. Until we are able to stop criticizing or castigating ourselves for our ignorance, our journey cannot move along freely. It is a process that flourishes in a spirit of acceptance, compassion, and adventure. We need to see ourselves much as we see young children who are growing and learning. In a sense, we are all children in an evolutionary process, moving as quickly as it is appropriate for us to go. And we must always bear in mind that there is much more to learn than any of us can learn in a single lifetime.

It is important to understand that *the consciousness journey is lifelong.* In fact, it is most likely many lives long. But certainly it will continue throughout our present lifetime. Consciousness is not a destination at which we finally arrive. It is an ongoing, ever-deepening, infinitely expanding process, a journey that perhaps has no end.

Because we live in a quick-fix, meal-in-a-minute, results-oriented society, I feel it is very important to emphasize the lifelong, ever-evolving nature of the consciousness journey. It is important to understand that it is a process rather than a product. All too many teachers and healers espouse the idea that there is a specific destination or defined goal that we're seeking. Too many promise that "enlightenment" can be had, once and for all, simply by following their prescription, that if you read this book, attend this workshop, practice this meditation, follow this diet or this program, your life will be healed, your problems cured, miracles will happen, and you'll never again have any difficulties in your life.

The product-oriented approach to consciousness is very appealing to the part of us that yearns for an instant remedy, a magic recipe. We don't want to go through any pain or discomfort. We quickly grow impatient with self-examination. We don't want to take the time to find our own path. We want an all-knowing, all-powerful authority figure to give us answers and tell us exactly what to do. We want a spiritual white knight to sweep us up and carry us away from the trials and tribulations of being human. We want to pack our bags and fly away into a never-never land of enlightenment, the quicker the better.

Unfortunately, it simply doesn't happen this way. The journey of a human being is much more complex than this, and involves an intense willingness to embrace all aspects of life. We don't find our way by avoiding, skipping over, or running away from anything.

I warn against these promised shortcuts and miracle cures not because I think the consciousness journey should be difficult but because there are actual hazards in pursuing instant enlightenment. At the top of the list of such hazards is that when we are offered such promises and they don't work, we usually blame ourselves. Over the years I have encountered far too many people in the personal growth movement who keep beating themselves up because they think something is wrong with them. They have been on a consciousness journey for many years, and they feel they should be far more evolved than they seem to be. They still have relationship problems, health problems, work problems. They've attended prosperity workshops, have said their prosperity affirmations faithfully, but they're still having financial difficulties. They know they create their own reality, yet they haven't managed to heal themselves. They've followed a spiritual teacher for years, yet they're not feeling anywhere near enlightened. They are filled with doubt, many are quite disillusioned, and most end up asking themselves, "What's wrong with me?"

The answer is that there is nothing wrong with them. Like the rest of us, they are human beings on an ongoing, lifelong journey. Consciousness growth is a challenging process, one that involves us both individually and collectively. Our own evolution affects the larger whole, the consciousness of the planet, and the evolution of that whole affects us. Every time we move to a new level of awareness — individually or collectively — we are confronted with new areas of denial, ignorance, pain, and, ultimately, healing. The process moves in cycles, so at times we feel clear and powerful, and at other times we feel lost in confusion. At times we feel stuck, being challenged to move ever more deeply into a specific area of healing. We struggle and resist for a time but when we can finally embrace those aspects of ourselves that we're resisting, we move quickly through them, finally at peace again for a time.

I'm not denying that miracles happen. They do! Sometimes a specific workshop, or therapy session, or meditation provides a breakthrough; something shifts and our lives are never again the same. Sometimes, a shift occurs for no apparent reason at all — it's just time. We can enjoy and appreciate such wonderful moments of change and growth. But we need to understand them for what they are — powerful steps on an infinite and fascinating journey.

It's important to know, also, that the journey consists of many different kinds of steps. Tools or techniques that are helpful and appropriate at one place in the journey may not be effective in the next. We may need to find a different approach than we've ever tried before. Once we've mastered a certain principle or teaching, we don't usually get to rest on our laurels for very long! Life keeps pushing us to the next area of growth, which may require a very different understanding.

For example, you may have learned to meditate deeply, and know how to find your center in the midst of emotional upheaval and external chaos. This ability may serve you well at a certain time in your life. And you may come to a different time in your life, when this approach alone no longer feels right or is simply no longer effective. It may be time to explore feelings and express your emotions, or to risk taking more direct action in the world. Whatever our next step is, life has a way of pushing, pulling, and prodding us toward it, by any means necessary!

I think of periods in my own life when the most important lesson of the time was to learn how to let go, to let go of an old belief and make room for something new, or to let go of a close friendship or lover. At another time, the lesson seemed to be just the opposite — to learn how to hold my ground, to stand up for the beliefs that were true for me, or to do everything I could to work through difficulties I was having with another person in my life.

The journey of consciousness is a spiral. We move in cycles, but each cycle takes us to a deeper level. When we find a familiar lesson coming around again, we should never jump to the conclusion that it's coming up because we didn't learn it the first time around. Instead, we need to remind ourselves that we are always moving into deeper levels of awareness that cause us to take a new and different look what may seem, at first glance, to be the same old issue.

It's helpful to see our consciousness growth process as an adventure, perhaps the ultimate one. We don't know where the process is going to take us, but on some deep level we know that it's going to be worthwhile. Sometimes the going gets rough or turns into just plain drudgery. At other times it's easy and fun. There are moments of clarity and inspiration. And there are moments that are dark and scary. The important thing is not to focus on the destination, being at peace with the fact that there isn't any final end point. *We need to become fascinated with the journey itself,* so that every moment in the process of learning, growth, and expansion becomes its own rich reward.

CHAPTER NINE

A Cosmic Perspective on Life

The time has come for the reunion and integration of male and female principles into a balanced and harmonious form. This is what is happening now, and this is why it's very exciting to be alive on this planet right now!

In order to clarify the consciousness process as I see it, I'd like to take a step back and give you a cosmic perspective of the universe, life on earth, why we are here, what we are doing, and what it's all about!

There are many different levels of reality in the universe, many different realms of existence. The physical plane is only one of those realms. On the purely spiritual plane, we are all part of one infinite intelligent life force. In other realms we may exist as individual entities, yet we can still be very aware of and connected to our oneness. We exist in all these realms simultaneously. Those of us who are currently focused in physical reality touch into the other realms through our nightly dreams, through prayer and meditation, and sometimes through psychic or "paranormal" experiences.

The physical plane is the most dense realm of existence. It's solid and slow compared with other levels where impulse and creation are often one and the same. On the dense physical plane, time becomes an important factor, taking hours, days, months, years, or even decades to bring things into physical form. I believe that the physical plane was created in order to fully explore and develop our creative power. It is a plane of duality where all things exist as polarities.

One way to think of it is this: The oneness wanted to explore "two-ness," or "otherness." It wanted to develop its opposite. Or to phrase it more poetically, the universe wanted to make love to itself, so it created the physical world in order to develop separation and reunion.

So physical reality can be viewed as a place of exploration and discovery, a place that's in a constant creative, evolutionary process. We are all divine, eternal beings, aspects of the essential oneness of life. As such, we have chosen to focus our attention and awareness here in physical reality for a time, in order to learn, grow, and develop, in order to give something to and receive something from the experience.

Since the material plane is so dense, it is a difficult and challenging place for a spiritual entity to hang out. We might well think of ourselves as the gambler/adventurers of the universe — the cosmic risk-takers. I can almost hear a conversation between two entities contemplating coming into physical form:

"Hey, want to do Earth? I hear it's a major challenge. Let's see if we can handle it!"

"Okay, I'm up for an adventure. How about if we meet there in about thirty Earth years?"

Then they get in here on the physical plane, feel the density, and they start thinking: "Oh, my God, what have I done? Get me out of here!"

I'm joking about this, of course, but in fact a large number of people I meet have a strong basic yearning to leave their physical bodies and return to another less dense realm. I believe this is because the journey of physical existence is inherently quite difficult. Yet there is great learning to be had here, and the possibility of incredible rewards and satisfactions, or we wouldn't be here doing this.

The first major experience to be explored on the physical plane is that of individuality, limitation, and separation — the opposite of the essential spiritual experience of oneness and limitlessness. Because the experience of oneness is already so powerful, we've needed to develop its opposite principle — individuality — equally strongly. Another way to think of this is that the feminine principle (spirit) was already fully developed; we needed to birth and develop the male principle (form) to match her power so that we could ultimately experience their union.*

It's taken us a few million years of earthly existence to develop and strengthen this male principle of separation, individuality, and self-expression. We've developed it to the point that it now balances the feminine. If we continue to go in the direction we've been traveling, however, we will have gone too far, destroying our physical existence

---

* I describe this concept in greater detail in my book *Return to the Garden.*

altogether. The time has come for the reunion and integration of male and female principles into a balanced and harmonious form. This is what is happening now, and this is why it's very exciting to be alive on this planet right now!

CHAPTER TEN

The Path of the Material World

Down through history, a majority of human beings have been focusing on what I call the path of the material world — the process of learning to survive and succeed in the physical realm.

$\mathcal{F}$or most of us in the Western world, being born into a physical body has resulted in our forgetting about our spiritual origins. Our primary task has been to explore this dense realm of the physical world and develop a sense of ourselves as unique individuals. If we had remained strongly conscious of the spiritual level of our existence, the pull of the oneness experience might have been too powerful and compelling, and we might not have wanted to remain focused here. So we developed a mechanism of denial to shut out our connection to our essential being.

Unfortunately, the mechanisms we've developed to shut out our sense of oneness have left us each feeling fundamentally alone in the universe, lost and empty. However, it clearly has allowed us to concentrate on the work we set out to do here — to survive and develop as individuals on the physical plane. To do this we each had to develop a unique physical body and personality. And the lost, empty, lonely feelings we experienced have provided a perfect driving force to move us out into life — discovering, developing, creating — in an effort to find satisfaction and fulfillment.

Down through history, a majority of human beings have been focusing on what I call the path of the material world — the process of learning to survive and succeed in the physical realm. In order to do this, we have had to mostly disconnect from awareness of any other level of our being and lose ourselves in the world of physical form, believing in its reality more than any other. This has been a painful, but necessary, evolutionary step. In a sense we have all sacrificed our deeper happiness in order to fulfill this mission.

I want to emphasize that there is nothing wrong with being materially oriented. It is a necessary and very important stage in our individual growth process and our human evolution. We have needed to discover, experience, and develop the many aspects of our lives as human beings fully participating on the physical plane. A vast majority of humanity today is primarily focused on this fascinating process.

Many of us who are now on consciousness journeys began this lifetime by following the path of the material world, but at some point we have sensed that other alternatives exist, and we have begun our spiritual reawakening.

CHAPTER ELEVEN

The Path of Transcendence

While it may help to remind us that our physical existence is not all there is, the transcendent path does tend to create a growing chasm between spirit and form, between who we are as spiritual beings and who we are as human personalities in physical bodies.

*I*n recent history, it seems that the majority of people have been mainly focused on the path of the material world, developing skills necessary for physical existence. Meanwhile, there has always been a small number of individuals who have taken a very different path. Whether guided by religious practices of the East or the West, this latter group — including monks, nuns, priests, yogis, rabbis, and other types of spiritual leaders, as well as solitary ascetics or simply faithful devotees — has focused primarily on remembering and developing their awareness of the spiritual level of being. In doing so, they have played an important role in the evolution of our planet, maintaining our connection with spirit. From the perspective of the mass consciousness, we have all been working together —

the majority focusing on mastering the physical world, while the few held our link to the spiritual realm.

For each individual, however, there has been a kind of split, a choice to be made between form and spirit. We could either be worldly or we could be spiritual, but we couldn't be both — or so it was believed!

In both the Eastern and Western traditions, there has been the belief and the implication that to focus on the spiritual path you must renounce the world. To be truly committed to a spiritual life, you had to stay as far as you could from the "worldly" aspects of life, such as relationships (especially sexual or emotionally intimate ones), business, money, and material possessions. All these things were seen as temptations or attachments that hook us into worldly involvement and draw us away from the spiritual focus. From the traditional spiritual perspective, the only solution to the apparent conflict between these two realities was to commit to spirit and minimize our involvement with the material world. The ultimate goal was to leave the limited world of form by leaving our physical bodies, thus returning fully to the realm of spirit.

I call this traditional spiritual approach the "path of transcendence." It focuses on a very important step in the evolution of consciousness — remembering that we are not simply physical forms, lost in and limited by the material world, but are in essence unlimited, eternal spiritual beings, a part of the oneness of all life. This is a vitally important and beautiful step that all of us must make at some time. Remembering the essence of who we are, that we exist beyond our physical form, gives us a much clearer perspective on our lives and on our human problems. It allows us to transcend the apparent limitations of human form and reclaim our true place in the universe. I believe it is primarily a search for this perspective that led so many in our culture to experiment with psychedelic drugs, and has motivated so many Westerners to study traditional Eastern philosophies and practices such as meditation. This yearning for spiritual transcendence has also given rise to many of the New Age philosophies and groups that have developed.

However, like any stage in the development of consciousness, the path of transcendence can have its own problems and limitations if you don't move on to the next step. To a great degree, the transcendent spiritual philosophies and practices have been a reaction to the pain and limitation of feeling stuck and imprisoned in the world of the material plane. While it may help to remind us that our physical existence is not all there is, the transcendent path does tend to create a growing chasm between spirit and form, between who we are as spiritual beings and who we are as human personalities in physical bodies.

The transcendent spiritual view is that the physical world is fundamentally unreal, an illusion in which we have become imprisoned. Our human bodies and personalities are traps from which we must escape to find true liberation in the higher realms. We must strive therefore to transcend our human experience, our physical and emotional needs, and our feelings and passions. Ultimately we want to leave our physical bodies and the physical world so that we can merge in oneness with pure spirit.

This philosophy seems to imply that the physical plane is just a big mistake, or perhaps a type of hell or purgatory through which we must pass, learning the error of our ways before we are allowed to get back where we really belong. There's the implication — and sometimes overt claim — that life here on earth is inherently inferior to what our existence can be in the higher realms. The experience of individuality we have here is seen as negative; we simply need to get back as fast as possible to the experience of pure oneness. There's often a feeling that there's something wrong with us for being here on the physical plane, that we are lesser beings than those inhabiting other realms.

It is my belief that this system of thought ignores the obvious fact that this physical realm has been created for a reason, and that on some level we've chosen to be here rather than remain solely on the spiritual plane. Regardless of how it may look and feel sometimes, there's something very powerful and exciting happening here. The physical world is not just some big mistake on the part of Creative Intelligence — God's goof! I'm quite convinced that we didn't just come here in order to see how quickly we could escape. There's a unique experience of infinite value and richness to be had here if we're willing to see and embrace it.

For many people currently following a transcendent philosophy, the term "ego" has become almost a dirty word. One hears a great deal of talk in the New Age movement, for example, about "getting rid of," or "letting go of" the ego. The ego is designated as our enemy, the part that tries to keep us from embracing our spiritual awareness — and any effort to even suggest that the ego has any value is seen as nothing more than the ego fighting to justify itself. Unfortunately, this belief simply deepens the confusion and fear. It's a bit like attributing anything we don't like to the "work of the devil."

By treating the ego as our enemy, we unwittingly create an adversarial thought system, a belief that there are "good parts" and "bad parts" within us, and we have to weed out the latter. Ironically, this is a form of blaming that keeps us searching for someone or something to blame and sets up false conflicts.

The idea that we have something to gain by getting rid of the ego is based on misunderstandings of the ego's actual function. Our egos are simply our awareness of ourselves as individuals. The term "ego" can be roughly equated with the term "personality." It is that aspect of our consciousness that is concerned with our survival and well-being on the physical plane.

There is nothing inherently good or bad about the ego; it is simply a fact of life, like the physical body. And without an ego, we could not survive for a moment in the physical realm. So if we get rid of the ego, we have to leave our body. The attempt to suppress our ego simply deepens the split and intensifies our inner conflict. Any time we try to get rid of or deny a part of ourselves or a part of life, we get into terrible conflicts in which the denied aspect starts fighting for its very existence! So, of course, we experience the ego as "resisting" our attempt to get rid of it.

A far less contradictory or frustrating approach, and

one that is much more productive, is to understand that the function of ego is to ensure our survival as an individual with a physical form. Rather than fruitlessly attempting to annihilate our egos, we need to appreciate them for what they are and foster cooperation between ego and spirit. We can then educate our egos to the fact that opening to our spiritual essence can actually enhance our lives on Earth. We can develop an aware ego or conscious personality that embraces our spiritual energy and views our human existence within the larger universal perspective.

Very few people on the path of transcendence ever fully achieve their avowed goal — a kind of "enlightenment" that involves becoming totally identified with one's spiritual self and mostly disowning one's human feelings and needs — i.e. "ego." Those who have done so, such as many Christian saints and martyrs, often have died at an early age, frequently with much physical suffering, stemming, I believe, from the denial of the physical body.

So-called enlightened masters who have achieved some level of transcendence can be fascinating teachers, especially when we are just embarking on a consciousness journey and are needing inspiration and a powerful source of guidance and authority. However, most transcendent masters or saints, having denied the world, can only live in relative seclusion, surrounded by devotees who care for their earthly needs and protect them, at least to some extent, from having to deal with everyday practicalities. And unfortunately, they all too often prove to have feet of clay — at least some human tendencies that keep stubbornly reappearing (although usually in secret). Most often these involve the very energies that they and their followers have been trying hard to transcend — sexuality, aggression, pleasure, and the desire for money and worldly possessions.

Throughout history there have been scandals and tragedies surrounding the emergence of the repressed "shadow" side of transcendent spiritual leaders. So we have the "celibate" priests, nuns, and yogis, or the married fundamentalist ministers, who are discovered to have secret lovers; most often these illicit sexual encounters are with their own followers, who are overly trusting and dependent. Other examples of the problem range from church leaders who are corrupted by financial greed to tragic incidents such as the Jonestown disaster at Guyana, or the fiery deaths of the Branch Davidians near Waco, Texas.

The vast majority of seekers on the path of transcendence never make it anywhere close to so-called "enlightenment," and relatively few find self-acceptance or peace. I'm afraid that most people who choose the transcendent path eventually find themselves mired down in the apparent split between the physical and the spiritual — torn between the needs of the soul and the desires of the ego. Try as they might to subdue their humanness and rise above it, they often find themselves battling with conflicting parts of themselves. Sometimes, even after years of meditation and other spiritual practices, they find themselves filled with self-criticism, feeling like failures. Instead of achieving the enlightened state they seek, they end up chastising themselves for not being further along in their spiritual development.

The transcendent path does very little to address the problems of the physical world. Indeed, it regards the material plane as an illusion or dream from which we need to awaken — or escape! More often than not, those on a transcendent path literally abandon the physical world. They treat everything that happens in that realm as an illusion, not to be taken seriously in any way. After all, if our commitment is to try to transcend the world, how could we find any value in trying to transform it?

We can see the results of narrowly limiting ourselves to either the material path or the transcendent path by looking at the Western industrialized countries, where the material path is fiercely pursued, and of the Eastern countries where the transcendent path has been pursued just as strongly. Devoted almost exclusively to material development, the Western cultures have developed a technology so advanced that we now have the power to destroy our world — if not through atomic weaponry, then through pollution. In some Eastern or Third World countries where there are very strong spiritual traditions, there has been a tendency to focus on the transcendent energies to the point where physical existence falls into neglect, chaos, and extreme poverty.

It is important to understand that the path of the material world and the path of transcendence each has its place in our individual development and in the evolution of human consciousness. However, neither of them alone offers us what we need to meet the many challenges we face today in our personal and planetary lives. For this reason it concerns me to see so many people today who are involved in the human potential or New Age movements still attempting to follow an essentially transcendental philosophy. In order to truly heal our lives and change the world we need to take another step — onto the path of transformation.

CHAPTER TWELVE

The Path of Transformation

*Through lovingly embracing the full range of
our experience — human and divine — we can
heal the split that has existed between spirit and
form, in ourselves individually and in the
whole world. We can bring the full power and
awareness of our spiritual being into our
human lives and all our worldly endeavors.*

*A*t this time in our evolution we have an exciting new
way to focus our consciousness journey. I call it the
path of transformation. Rather than being limited by physical reality, as on the path of the material world, or seeking
to escape the physical form so we can return to the realm
of spirit, as on the transcendent path, the path of transformation challenges us to create an entirely new reality. This
new reality is created not by denying either the physical or
the spiritual but, on the contrary, by integrating the two. It
is a path that can lead us to the discovery and development
of a whole new way of life.

In the process of human evolution, we have had to travel
the first two paths. We needed to forget our spiritual origins long enough to develop our consciousness of physical

reality. Then we needed to wake up from the limitation of that reality and remember the spiritual realm. Now the time has come and we are ready to dissolve the split between the two and bring those two realities into one integrated experience.

In order to do this we must strengthen our awareness of our essential roots as spiritual beings. And from that deeply rooted awareness, we must learn to fully embrace our human experience, the reality of our bodies and personalities. Through lovingly embracing the full range of our experience — human and divine — we can heal the split that has existed between spirit and form, in ourselves individually and in the whole world. We can bring the full power and awareness of our spiritual being into our human lives and all our worldly endeavors. Only then do we begin to discover the power and fulfillment that is possible in the physical form. We begin to experience what life on earth is really all about!

This process is already well under way. If you are reading this book, you are most likely already on a transformational path, knowingly or not. If you feel like your life has recently been shaken up and turned upside down, then you know for sure that you are!

Following the path of transformation is not necessarily easy. In fact, it can be extremely challenging. Many people at this time are clinging to their material focus, or to their transcendent philosophy, unconsciously hoping they will never have to face the transformational journey. However, if you want to remain in the physical world and continue to evolve, there really is no other choice. In fact, the process is not nearly as arduous as many people fear it will be. While difficult and painful at times, it is also utterly rewarding, exciting, and beautiful.

Rather than rejecting or trying to get beyond all the challenging experiences of our humanness, we can find the beauty and passion in them. We can learn to consciously create our physical reality as an expression of our spiritual being. We can learn to live in the physical world as it was intended to be.

By making a personal commitment to our own individual transformational process, we automatically begin to transform the world around us. As we discover and express more and more of the spiritual potential within us here and now in our human lives, our personal reality changes to reflect our shifts in consciousness. The world around us changes as we change. And since we are all linked through the mass consciousness, as we grow we affect everyone else in the world. In choosing to follow the path of transformation, we are not only changing our own lives, we are changing the world.

In Part II, we will discuss more specifically the practical steps involved in following the path of transformation.

PART TWO

On the Path of Transformation

If you really want to help this world, what you will have to teach is how to live in it. And that no one can do who has not himself learned how to live in it in the joyful sorrow and sorrowful joy of the knowledge of life as it is.

— Joseph Campbell

CHAPTER THIRTEEN

Finding Your Inner Teacher

*Once we've developed a relationship with our
own inner teacher and guide, we have access to
an unerring source of clarity, wisdom, and
direction, right inside us at all times!*

*H*ow do we follow the path of transformation? One
of the first steps is to establish a personal connection with the universal intelligence, or higher power. This
higher power exists within everything and everyone. It's
the infinitely wise aspect of our being that simply "knows"
everything that we need to be aware of at any given time,
providing us with guidance from moment to moment, step
by step throughout our lives.

There is nothing complicated or mysterious about this
higher power. It's a very natural part of our existence. It
comes to us through our intuitive sense, our gut feelings.
We are all born into this world with this intuitive guidance
system. And if we had all been raised in a more enlightened
way, we would have learned to follow this inner guidance
throughout our lives. Instead, most of us did not receive

much support or encouragement in trusting our own deepest feelings. In fact, many of us were actively taught not to trust ourselves but instead to follow an external authority. Or we were encouraged to be rational — to the exclusion of our intuitive faculties.

As adults we can take responsibility for rediscovering and reconnecting with our natural intuitive sense. As we learn to listen to and follow our intuition, we develop an increasingly trusting and powerful relationship with our own inner guidance.

On the path of transformation, it is essential to develop this relationship with our inner guidance because on this path there are no final outside authorities. There are no holy texts or priests, or ministers, or gurus who represent the absolute word of God. There is no dogma to follow. Instead, our primary guidance must come from our inner source.

In the Eastern transcendent traditions, and in many of the New Age groups that are modeled after them, there is a belief that one must surrender to an enlightened teacher in order to progress on one's spiritual journey. However, from the perspective of the transformational path, there are no fully enlightened teachers. The traditional masters and gurus are only enlightened in the transcendent sense. They may be able to teach us a great deal about our spiritual development, but they can't show us how to integrate that fully into our human lives on earth, since they have not yet learned to do that themselves.

We are not alone on this new path. There are teachers who can help us with certain aspects of the journey.

However, there is no one who has already absolutely "made it" on this journey, because we are all still learning. We are all moving along the path, more or less together. In a very real way we are each other's teachers and mirrors, reflecting the other's process. Some people are more developed in certain ways and can teach the rest of us what they have learned. Each person's journey is unique, however, so ultimately no one but you knows what you need to do.

Do we, then, *need* teachers on the path of transformation? And if so, what is their appropriate role in our lives? How can we relate to them in a way that is healthy and most supportive to our growth?

Yes, I believe that most of us absolutely need teachers on this path. Of course teachers come in many forms, not all of them human. For example, nature is one of our greatest teachers.

Most of us also have human teachers, healers, and guides who come in many different forms and often play crucial roles at certain times in our journey. Someone in our lives, for instance, may be the initial catalyst or inspiration that helps us get on a consciousness path. In the earlier states of our process, almost all of us need information, feedback, support, and guidance of some sort. In a sense, we are all in the childhood stage of the consciousness journey and may need a wise parental figure to show us the way. As we gain more knowledge and experience, we gradually develop more trust in ourselves, but we still may need wiser and more experienced people as resources, much as we do when we are adolescents and young adults learning to take our place in the community.

Eventually, once we are mature in our consciousness process, we primarily follow our own inner direction. Yet the nature of life is constant growth, so at times of stress or crisis, or whenever we are going through a major change, or a deepening or expansion of consciousness, we may once again need some outer guidance.

The pitfall in relating to teachers or healers of any kind is the tendency we have to give too much of our power away to them. When we haven't yet fully recognized and owned our inner wisdom, goodness, creativity, and power, we tend to project these qualities onto our mentors and teachers. This is perfectly natural. As we grow, we become aware that these qualities reside in us, and we begin to claim them more and more as our own. A clear and wise teacher helps and supports us in the process of owning our own power. Such a teacher encourages us to take independent steps as soon as we feel we are ready.

Unfortunately, there are many teachers, therapists, and healers who are unclear in this regard. They are overly attached to being in a power position with their students or clients, or to having them remain dependent for too long. This takes care of certain emotional — and often financial — needs on the part of the leader, but it inhibits or severely impairs the growth and empowerment process of the client or student.

I know many people who have suffered greatly from this type of overattachment to a leader or teacher. In fact, one close friend of mine spent years healing herself — both emotionally and physically — after finally breaking away from a teacher who had many fine qualities but unconsciously entrapped her students in dependent relationships with her.

So I must warn readers to beware of teachers, workshop leaders, therapists, healers, or any others who claim to have all the answers (or more than anyone else), who regard themselves as more enlightened or farther along the path than anyone else, or who generally seem to have an inflated sense of themselves. They may be very developed in certain areas, and have much to share, but we need to be cautious and maintain healthy skepticism in our relationships with them. Proceed with caution, especially if you notice that there seems to be a circle of very dependent devotees who seldom become more empowered in their own lives or move on to other involvements, and who never move into a relationship of more equality and balance with the leader. It may also be a danger signal if you feel consistently one-down or inferior to a teacher and he or she seems to cultivate that kind of relationship.

The key to relating to a teacher or healer in a healthy, empowering way is to recognize that person as a mirror of your own inner qualities. If you admire someone for his or her wisdom, love, power, or whatever, recognize that you have those exact qualities within you and that you are drawn to this person as a reflection of the parts of yourself that you need and want to develop. Allow your teacher or therapist to inspire you and show you the way to develop yourself. Afford your teacher respect, admiration, and appreciation, but remind yourself that you are with him or her to learn to love, respect, and honor yourself as much! Our teachers are in our lives essentially to help us develop, strengthen, and deepen our relationship to our own inner teacher.

I have had many wonderful teachers, therapists, and guides over the years, and each one has helped me in a special way. Like most people, I put them on pedestals at first and gave my power away to them. Once or twice I became involved in a very dependent role for a while. However, each of these experiences was extremely valuable ultimately in helping me to develop my trust in my own inner teacher. Now I have certain people in my life who are teachers and mentors for me. I can turn to them when I need help, support, and guidance, and we have a relationship of mutual trust, honor, and love.

Because so many of us have been thoroughly conditioned against trusting our inner sources, we simply may not know where to begin the process of developing our relationship with our inner teacher. There are teachers and therapists available in most communities who can help us get on a path of trusting our own inner processes more fully. We recognize these teachers not because they claim to know all the answers but because they are offering skills to help us find those answers ourselves. Even with the best of teachers, however, there comes a time when we may need to let them go, having developed in ourselves the skills we need to trust our own inner guidance. In the next chapter, I will discuss more specifically how we can learn and cultivate this trust in ourselves.

Once we've developed a relationship with our own inner teacher and guide, we have access to an unerring source of clarity, wisdom, and direction, right inside us at all times! Needless to say, this can be quite comforting, especially in moments of fear and confusion. It gives us the basic sense of trust that we need to have the courage to make this journey. From it we gain the confidence that we are not alone, that there is a higher power guiding our way and helping us along.

CHAPTER FOURTEEN

Developing Inner Guidance

Most of us have been trained to automatically deny, ignore, or discount our intuitive feelings to the point where we don't even know we have them. So we need to retrain ourselves to recognize and pay attention to our inner promptings.

How do we go about establishing and developing a relationship with our inner guide? I've been teaching a process for doing this for many years, and I'm happy to say that most people find it easy to do once they understand the principles and have the opportunity to practice a few simple steps.

One principle to remember is that when we are following our intuitive sense we are following our natural way of living. If doing this seems difficult at first, it is because we have been trained not to do what comes naturally to us. When we pursue these abilities, we are not trying to cultivate supernormal capacities. On the contrary, the process is really one of *unlearning* habits that have prevented us from being able to sense what's true and right for us in our lives.

Most of us have been trained to automatically deny, ignore, or discount our intuitive feelings to the point where we don't even know we have them. So we need to retrain ourselves to recognize and pay attention to our inner promptings.

As you go through the following exercise, remind yourself that we all have intuitive inner guidance. Just because we may not feel it or trust it right now doesn't mean it isn't there. It's always there. What you are doing now is learning to reconnect with it.

Here are some simple steps that can help you contact and cultivate your inner guidance:

1. Relax. If you know a particular relaxation or meditation technique that works for you, such as counting your breaths, saying a mantra, progressive relaxation (often taught in natural childbirth classes), or anything else that allows you to relax your body and quiet your mind, use it. I have included a relaxation exercise in the Appendix of this book for those who would like a program to follow.

In the modern world, we are so accustomed to living in a more or less constant state of stress that we are hardly able to recognize the difference between how it feels to be in a state of tension and how it feels to be relaxed. If you have difficulty with the relaxation exercise I include, you may want to consider taking a class in stress reduction or meditation or using an appropriate audio or videotape.

If you consistently have real difficulty learning

to relax, try doing something enjoyable that requires physical exertion, such as walking or running outdoors, or playing lively music and dancing until you feel tired. Then lie down and relax deeply.

Choose a time and place where you will not be disturbed by other people, or the phone, and where you will not be reminded of things you need to be doing. Try putting on some soft, soothing music. Sit or lie down comfortably with your spine straight and supported, and take a few minutes to quiet your mind.

2. Once you feel relaxed, allow your awareness to move into a deep place in the core of your body, near your heart or your solar plexus (wherever feels right to you). Affirm that in this place deep inside, you have access to your inner guidance. You can do this with a simple affirmation, such as, "I am moving into the place, deep within me, where I can sense and trust my inner guidance."

3. Ask a question, such as, "What do I need to know (or remember) in my life right now?" or, "What direction do I need to take in my life right now?" Or you can ask something more specific, such as, "What is my next step in relation to my career?" or, "Show me how to take better care of myself."

4. Once you have posed the question, just let it go, and relax quietly, being receptive and open. Notice what thoughts, feelings, or images come to

you in response to the question(s) you have asked. If you feel that nothing relevant comes to you, or you feel as confused or uncertain as ever, that's okay, just let it go for now. Guidance doesn't necessarily come immediately in the form of definite ideas or feelings — although it may, especially as you practice and gain more confidence. It often comes later, through a gradually dawning awareness or feeling about the issue. Or it may come through some seemingly external means — you walk into a bookstore and "just happen" to pick up a book and read a relevant paragraph, or a friend makes a chance remark that strikes a strong chord for you.

5. Once you feel complete with this exercise, just get up and go about your life.

Practice this simple meditation once a day — or at the very least twice a week. Most people find that the best times of the day to do this are in the morning upon awakening or before they go to sleep at night. But find what works best for you.

6. Throughout the day, pause and notice your gut feelings about things. Over the next few days, try to notice and be especially aware of your thoughts, feelings, and experiences related to the issue you've asked about. Practice following any intuitive impulses or gut feelings you have, and notice how things work out. You will probably discover that there is a particular quality to following your intuitive sense. For example, many people describe it as a sense of "being in

the flow," or "being centered," or a feeling of "quiet excitement."

When you are faced with even a simple choice or decision, such as where to eat lunch, whether or not to call a friend, or which movie to see, briefly quiet your mind and go inside. Instead of making your choice on the basis of logical reasoning, or what you think is "correct," or what others might wish, go by what your intuitive guidance tells you.

Pay attention to whatever feedback you get from the way things unfold in your external experience. See how things work out when you follow your inner guidance. If things don't seem to be working out, it may be because you are not yet fully attuned with your inner guidance. You may be following other feelings instead. The best indication that you are in tune with your inner truth is that you feel more alive as a result. Also, things generally work more easily. Doors open. There's a sense of following a certain flow of energy.

Start with small steps first. Don't make radical moves such as quitting your job, leaving a relationship, or spending a large sum of money because you think you have gotten an "intuitive hit" to do that. Start with simple feelings in the moment — this feels right to me or this doesn't. For example, if you are invited to a social event, check in with yourself to see if it feels right before accepting or declining. Live by your inner truth in small, simple ways before you tackle major issues. Seemingly, small steps in this regard may be very significant. As you practice these small steps, you build power and confidence in your connection to your inner guidance.

If you try the six steps I have suggested for a while and don't feel that you are getting any stronger sense of connection with your inner guidance, here are some further suggestions that may help you:

- You are probably trying too hard to make something happen instead of simply allowing it to happen. You may be making the process into a bigger deal than it really is. Relax and let go. Stop trying to make anything amazing happen. Just listen a little more deeply than usual for your own sense of truth.

- If you feel a lot of confusion and inner conflict, and can't distinguish your intuitive sense from all your other thoughts and feelings, try to identify some of the different voices inside you. Take different color pens and write out what each of them has to say.

  For example, if you are trying to figure out whether to change a particular course you have been following in your life — in your career, a hobby, a relationship — you might discover that there is a very fearful voice. Try using a black pen to thoroughly write out what this voice is saying: i.e., "Don't try anything new, it might be a disaster!" You might discover that you have a conservative voice that tells you, "Maybe you'd better stay with what's familiar." You could use a blue pen to write what this voice is saying. You might get in touch with a creative voice that tells you, "I have a wonderful idea for starting a new business!" You might like to record these thoughts with a green pen. Then again, you may find that you have a risk-taking voice that says, "Go ahead, do something new and exciting!" Record what it has to say with a red pen.

You may, of course, have other voices that I have not mentioned here — a self-critical voice, a rebellious one, a vulnerable or playful child. You may become aware of a voice that sounds like one of your parents, your spouse, your boss, or someone else you know or have known. Whatever comes up for you, take the time to write down everything it says, using whatever colored pen or pencil best fits. After you've done this, just let it go for a while.

- Try not to get caught up in needing to have an immediate answer. Life is an ongoing, unfolding process, and you may not be ready yet for a decision or a definite direction. You may be "in process." Inner guidance seldom gives us long-term information; it usually just lets us know what we need in the moment. Sometimes, inner guidance may be saying, "Just wait, don't do anything, allow yourself to be in confusion." When clarity is meant to come, it will. That is the nature of inner guidance.

- If you feel really blocked for a long period of time, you probably need to do some emotional healing work. When we are holding our emotions inside us, it can be difficult or even impossible to contact our intuitive feelings. If you feel you may be having difficulties of this kind, find a good therapist or support group and begin the process of learning to experience and express your emotions. Once you've done a certain amount of deep emotional healing, you will automatically be more in touch with your intuition.

- If you are following what you think are your intuitive feelings, but you aren't feeling more enlivened and aware, and your life doesn't seem to be in motion, then you probably are confusing your intuitive feelings with other emotions or impulses. You may need some help clarifying what's what.

  Also, it's very important to learn to distinguish intuitive feelings and impulses from addictive ones. If I have a drinking problem or an eating disorder, and I have a sudden strong impulse to have a drink or eat an ice cream sundae, that is not my intuitive guidance. If I'm a workaholic and I have a deep feeling that I need to go into the office on Sunday despite my family's objections, I probably need to question where that impulse is coming from. Our intuitive guidance is always trying to help us in the

direction of bringing balance and real fulfillment into our lives. In order to hear it clearly,
we have to be able to recognize our addictive
tendencies and learn not to be controlled by
them. If you sense that you may have an active
addiction, seek help from a twelve-step program
or therapist specializing in addiction.

• And finally, remember that developing inner
guidance is a lifelong, ever-deepening process.
I've been working on it for years, and I'm still
learning and developing my ability to sense and
trust my inner truth. Like all things in life, the
process goes in cycles. Sometimes, my inner
guidance is coming through clear and strong,
and I feel completely in the flow of life. At other
times I feel confused and lost, uncertain why
things are happening the way they are and not
knowing what to do about them. I've learned to
trust those times, too, and know that eventually
I come out the other side with greater awareness. A friend of mine calls this "the lull," which
is as natural a part of our lives as the normal
pause between heartbeats or between the exhalation and inhalation of breath.*

Inner guidance is always there inside us, and
it is always correct, wise, and loving. We may

---

* My book, *Living in the Light,* as well as my new book and tape on this
topic, *Developing Intuition,* have many exercises to help you develop
your ability to follow your intuitive guidance.

lose touch with it, or misinterpret it at times. We may try to push too hard and get ahead of ourselves. But our inner teacher never abandons us. We are never alone.

CHAPTER FIFTEEN

The Four Levels of Existence

All four levels of being are closely related to and affected by one another. As we heal one level, we support the healing process of all the other levels as well.

*H*uman life consists of four levels or aspects of being — spiritual, mental, emotional, and physical. The path of transformation involves clearing, healing, developing, and integrating all four of these levels.

All of these aspects are equally important. There isn't one that we can skip or neglect if we want to experience wholeness. We need to focus time and attention on healing and developing each one. As we do this, all four levels naturally begin to balance and become more fully integrated with one another.

We may begin our consciousness journey at any of these levels. It's different for each person. For example, many people get involved in a consciousness process because they have a physical crisis — a disease, an accident, a weight issue, or an addiction problem. Or they simply develop an interest in living a healthier lifestyle; they start learning more about nutrition and exercise, one thing leads to another, and eventually they are discovering all kinds of new ideas and ways of living that take them beyond just the physical level.

For example, I started practicing hatha yoga as a physical discipline. It eventually led me to an interest in meditation and a greater connection to my spirituality.

For other people it may be an emotional crisis or need that brings them into the journey. Perhaps someone seeks counseling for grief over the loss of a loved one, and begins to discover much more about themselves that they want to explore even further. Or because of an addiction problem (which is emotional as well as physical) they join a twelve-step program (Alcoholics Anonymous, Narcotics Anonymous, etc.), which brings them to a commitment to their personal growth process.

Still others may enter the process on the mental level. Motivated initially by intellectual curiosity they begin by reading philosophy, psychology, or consciousness books. I have heard many stories about people who by chance picked up a particular book, and their lives were never quite the same again.

Others begin by studying religion or spiritual teachings of some kind, or of a spiritual leader or guru. After progressing on a spiritual path for a while, they discover there is healing work that needs to be done emotionally, or physically.

So there are many different ways the process may get started. Once we have begun, we usually move from one level to another at different times, or we may work on two, three, or all four levels simultaneously. Each person's path is unique.

Generally, however, no matter where we start our consciousness journey, or how we proceed with it, there's a certain underlying evolutionary process that unfolds from the spiritual to the physical.

Somewhere along the line, we have a profound spiritual experience. Such an event may appear to happen by chance, before we even know there is a conscious path to follow. In fact, that event may be the catalyst precipitating a crisis which, in turn, leads to the beginning of our journey into a greater level of consciousness. Or it may happen later, after we are already conscious seekers. In any case, whenever it happens, it changes our life forever. It gives us a glimpse of a higher perspective on life, and a taste of the feelings of love, power, and bliss that are possible to experience.

I remember meeting a woman in her mid-forties who had been faced with cancer twelve years before. During an operation, she had a near-death experience, in which she saw herself bathed in white light that was helping in her healing. When the operation was over, she kept having recurring visions of the light. At the same time that she was bathed in this light she was filled with feelings of complete and total peace and oneness.

Prior to this time she had never considered herself to be a spiritual or religious person. But after the experience she began to pursue that path, one she has been on ever since. She said that what happened to her in surgery opened her eyes to a very different level of reality than she had ever before recognized.

This is a fairly dramatic example of a life-changing spiritual experience. For many of us it may take a more subtle or gradual form. But the eventual result is the same.

Having had these experiences, we can no longer be content with a limited way of living; we are compelled to seek greater awareness. We try to understand what happened to us so that we can repeat and/or expand the experience. This leads to experimentation with spiritual practices, and exploration on the mental level as we let go of old ideas and open up to new ones. Eventually, usually after a few years of work on the spiritual and mental levels, we find ourselves increasingly bumping into the emotional level of our being. For many of us, the emotional level can feel like a wall that seems to prevent us from fully living our spiritual beliefs in our daily lives.

Our old emotional patterns seem to be keeping us from living our new philosophies. For example, we may have had moments of spiritual clarity or breakthrough in which we really felt that there is a higher power taking care of us. We may understand that idea intellectually and be committed to living our lives accordingly, trusting our inner guidance to show us what we need to know. Yet we may repeatedly find ourselves wrestling with feelings of fear, even terror, unable to let go of our old ways of controlling our lives.

This is a perfectly natural part of the process. Just because we've experienced something at the spiritual level, and we now understand it mentally, we haven't necessarily integrated it at the emotional level. To heal ourselves at the emotional level of our being demands a whole different focus, requiring time, patience, and compassion for ourselves. And it usually requires a lot of help from other people as well.

Once we have done a substantial amount of work on the spiritual, mental, and emotional levels, we have the great challenge of bringing it all into the physical level. Here we have the opportunity to actually bring everything we have been learning and discovering into our daily lives, living fully and freely, moment by moment. This often requires some healing of the body itself.

In the next four chapters, I will explain a little more about these levels and how the healing and transformational process takes place on each one of them.

All four levels of being are closely related to and affected by one another. As we heal one level, we support the healing process of all the other levels as well. Strengthening our spiritual connection gives us the inspiration and strength to face deep emotional healing, for example. As we do our emotional healing work, we release blocked energies on the mental and physical levels as well. And the more in tune we are with our physical bodies, the more energy we feel on every level. We may begin the process on any level and explore the others at different times in our lives. The ultimate goal is the integration of them all.

CHAPTER SIXTEEN

Healing the Spiritual Level

Spiritual healing occurs as we begin to consciously reconnect with our essential being — the wise, loving, powerful, creative entity that we are at our core. Through this connection with our spiritual essence…we experience a sense of safety, trust, and fulfillment, a feeling of belonging in the universe.

*M*ost of us who have grown up in the modern world have experienced a profound disconnection from our spiritual selves and from the universal source. This causes an underlying feeling of emptiness, insecurity, and meaninglessness in our lives. Unconsciously we seek to fill this inner void in many fruitless ways. We may strive for money, power, and success as a way of feeling secure, or we may devote ourselves to our families or careers as a way of finding meaning and purpose. We may succumb to various addictive behaviors, using food, drugs, work, or sex to try to fill the empty feeling. Unfortunately, none of these efforts affects the underlying problem.

The lack of spiritual connection in our culture is at the root of many of our social as well as personal ills. The epidemic use of drugs, the proliferation of gangs, and violence have their roots in the deepest levels of spiritual alienation and need. The development of bizarre religious cults is also symptomatic of the search for meaning and authentic spiritual experience. When we live in or visit areas that have been particularly hard hit by the breakdown of our socioeconomic systems, we encounter much depression and rage that come about when people have no spiritual or psychological base for dealing with the pressures they are facing.

Spiritual healing occurs as we begin to consciously reconnect with our essential being — the wise, loving, powerful, creative entity that we are at our core. Through this connection with our spiritual essence, we begin to reexperience our oneness with all other beings and with all of nature. The more we connect with this essential oneness, the more we experience a sense of safety, trust, and fulfillment, a feeling of belonging in the universe. We experience our inner emptiness being filled by the spirit within.

This contact with our spiritual self gives us an expanded perspective of our lives, both as individuals and as part of humanity. Rather than just being caught up in the daily frustrations and struggles of our personality, we are able to see things from the perspective of the soul. We're able to look at the bigger picture of life on earth, which helps us to understand a lot more about why we're here and what we're doing. It helps to make our daily problems seem not quite so huge, and makes our lives feel more meaningful.

For example, the island of Kauai, where I live part of the time, was struck by a powerful hurricane a few years ago. The island was devastated. No one died, but thousands of buildings were destroyed or, like my home, severely damaged. There were shortages of water, food, power, and shelter. Many lost not only their homes but all their possessions, their businesses, and their jobs. It was a frightening and stressful time.

Yet, for those with a spiritual perspective, it was clearly a transformational event. Almost everyone going through it reconnected with their deepest values and priorities — the sense that life, family, and community are so much more important than physical possessions. Many people were forced to get clear about changes they needed to make, or new steps they needed to take in their lives. While the experience brought pain and suffering to many, it also brought tremendous healing for those who are able to see it that way.

The spiritual level gives us a foundation from which we can more easily move into other levels of healing. Without at least starting our spiritual healing it can be difficult, or even impossible, to find the hope, understanding, and strength we need to confront the difficulties and challenges of healing the other levels.

Spiritual healing begins when we find a way to make regular contact with the spiritual aspect of ourselves. This means developing a spiritual practice that works for us, and then making a commitment to doing it on a regular basis, daily or at least weekly. For some people this might be silent meditation, alone or in a group; it might be attending church services or some other type of group inspirational activity. For others it might take place through regular contact with nature — walks in the woods, hikes in the mountains, sitting quietly near a river or the ocean.

A spiritual practice need not be religious in the usual sense. Many people find their spiritual connection primarily through physical activity — walking, running, dancing, bicycling. Others find it through a creative activity such as painting or making music. Some find it in serving others, and some find it in quiet moments with family and loved ones. A friend of mine takes a day of silence each week. All his close friends know this is his day of rest — to rest his voice, his mind, and his body and listen keenly to his internal guidance. If a full day is not possible for you, start with an hour or two in the morning or late afternoon or evening, when you will simply be alone, with a quiet mind and no outside distractions — no phone, no television, no visitors.

For many people, Sunday is a good day to honor our spiritual needs since this is a day our society has traditionally set aside for spiritual or religious nurturing. One of my friends doesn't have any organized religious affiliations but keeps her time open on Sunday mornings to listen to what she alone needs, freeing herself from obligations and plans. In this way she renews her inner self, and makes ready for a busy schedule during the coming week.

Find whatever works for you; just make certain that you have some form of spiritual inspiration and renewal as a regular part of your life.

The steps described in chapter 14, "Developing Inner Guidance," provide one form of spiritual practice. Our inner guidance comes from the spiritual center within us, so as we learn to trust and follow our intuition, we are building a strong relationship with our spiritual being.

Meditation
Tuning in to Your Spiritual Being

Meditation is a way of taking time to become aware of our thoughts, feelings, and bodily sensations, and then to allow ourselves to drop into a deeper level of being. Here is a simple exercise that can help you begin your spiritual practice.

Find a spot to designate as your place of spiritual retreat, somewhere close to home or work so that you have regular, easy access to it. It's wonderful if this place can be outdoors, with some natural beauty around it. Most importantly, though, it should be quiet, peaceful, and comfortable. It could be a spot in your backyard, a special room in your house, or a corner of a room.

Make it special by designating a certain chair, pillow, and/or blanket that you only use while meditating. Make sure you will be uninterrupted for at least fifteen minutes, or longer if possible.

Find a comfortable position either sitting or lying down. Make sure it's a position where your body can completely relax.

Take a deep breath, slowly, filling your lungs. Then exhale, slowly and easily, and let your body relax. Take another deep breath, and as you exhale, relax your body a little more. With every breath, as you exhale, relax your body a little more deeply.

Notice the thoughts that are going through your mind. Watch them for a while as they parade across your consciousness, like one of those electronic billboards: "Well, here I am trying to watch my thoughts. Let's see, what am I thinking? This reminds me of the time I went to that meditation retreat....There was that weird guy there. He reminded me of...whoops, I'm supposed to be watching my thoughts." Imagine your mind slowing down and going slightly out of focus. Thoughts will continue to arise, but don't hold onto them. As soon as you notice you are having a thought, let it go.

As you continue to breathe deeply and slowly, notice how you are feeling emotionally. Don't try to analyze why you are feeling that way, and don't try to change how you are feeling. Simply acknowledge and accept how you are feeling. For example, "I notice that I'm feeling a little depressed right now," or, "I'm aware that I'm feeling anxious, remembering all the work I have to do," or, "I'm feeling calm and peaceful at the moment." Allow the feeling(s) to just be there. You need do nothing about them except to accept them.

Continue to breathe deeply and slowly as you relax your body, accept your feelings, and allow your mind to slow down a little.

Now, imagine moving your awareness deeper inside, deeper and deeper into the core of your being, deeper than your body, your mind, or your emotions. Allow yourself to sit quietly and just be with yourself in a deep place inside. Know that this is the place where you can contact your spiritual being.

Sit quietly. Continue to notice any thoughts, feelings, or images that come to you. Notice and accept anything that happens within you. If you wish, ask for guidance or inspiration, or whatever you feel you need. Accept whatever comes, or doesn't come, without analyzing it.

After you've been there quietly for fifteen minutes (or as long as you wish), give thanks to your spiritual being. Then get up slowly and gently, and go about your life.

Sometimes when you do this, you may feel that nothing happens. Or you may find at times that you obsess about certain thoughts or feelings and can't really relax. This is normal and natural. As you practice this meditation regularly for a while, you will probably find it gets easier to drop into a relaxed, quiet state of mind. If not, then take a class in meditation or relaxation techniques, or try a different method of spiritual practice.

Here are some of the many practices that people find helpful for learning to relax and meditate: progressive relaxation; counting your breaths; dancing to your favorite music until you sweat; sitting quietly while focusing on an object such as a flower, the flame of a candle, a sound; chanting, drumming, or listening to music that is calming and repetitive.*

---

* Many simple and powerful meditations and spiritual practices can be found in the book *Coming Home: The Return to True Self* by Martia Nelson. Please see the Recommended Resources section in the back of this book.

CHAPTER SEVENTEEN

Healing the Mental Level

*To experience balance, integration, and
well-being, we need belief systems and thought
processes that support and are in harmony
with the other three levels of our existence —
the physical, emotional, and spiritual.*

The mental level of our being is our intellect, that is,
the rational mind. In order to clear and heal the
mental level, we need to become conscious of our
thoughts and underlying belief systems. We need to educate ourselves about other ideas and beliefs, and eventually be able to consciously choose the ideas that make
most sense to us and make our lives work the best.

We've all learned certain viewpoints and attitudes
about the world through the early influences of our families, religions, schools, and our culture as a whole. Around
the time of Columbus, for example, most people believed
the world was flat, and if you sailed far enough out at sea
you'd fall off the edge of the Earth. People held that picture of the Earth in their minds and saw it as the truth

because that was what their parents, teachers, and society believed and taught. When explorers like Christopher Columbus successfully challenged these beliefs, however, it created a whole new belief about the world in our minds.

There's a wonderful story told by Deepak Chopra that teaches us something important about this point. When training baby elephants in India, trainers start by chaining one hind leg of the animal to a large tree. In a short time the elephant becomes so accustomed to the chain that he no longer tries to free himself. The trainers then reduce the size of the chain. In time, the elephant is so conditioned to the restraint that even a tiny cord around that foot will stop him. Yet it is certainly not the cord that holds him; rather, it is his belief that he is restrained.

Like the elephant, our belief systems color our experience of the world, and we tend to keep interpreting our experiences and recreating our world based on our core beliefs about ourselves, other people, life. As we mature and have new and different experiences of life, however, new ideas and perspectives may challenge our beliefs. Every moment of our lives we are all involved in an ongoing process of sorting out and evolving our philosophy of life.

To experience balance, integration, and well-being, we need belief systems and thought processes that support and are in harmony with the other three levels of our existence — the physical, emotional, and spiritual. We need to have a spiritual understanding, or life philosophy, that helps us find meaning in our lives. We need to have an understanding and acceptance of our emotions that help us to accept ourselves. And we need to know how to care for our physical bodies in a healthy way.

If you have a belief that your physical body is inferior to your spiritual self, for example, and that it is unworthy of your care or attention, you are holding onto a mental attitude that will cause conflict and lack of well-being in your system. But if you were to reeducate yourself to understand how important and worthy your physical body is, and you learned to take good care of it, you would find more balance and harmony in your entire system.

In the process of becoming more conscious, we are constantly learning new ideas, viewpoints, and philosophies, and weighing them against the ones we already hold. Gradually, we begin letting go of the old ideas that are too limiting for us, while retaining the ones that still serve us and incorporating new ones that are more expansive, deepening, and empowering.

For example, I used to believe that there wasn't much I could do about the circumstances of my life, that I didn't have much power to change them. Then I learned the idea that I create my own reality. I found that idea much more empowering, so I eventually chose to adopt that belief system. As I did this, I began to experience the world in a very different way and began to see that I really could have a great deal of power over the circumstances of my life.

I had grown up believing that I would choose a life career and go to college for many years in order to achieve my goals. But after four years of college I still didn't know exactly what I wanted to do! I discovered a new philosophy, that by trusting and following my intuitive guidance and creative impulses, my life would develop in interesting and fulfilling ways. A fascinating and successful career has unfolded from following this belief system — and I never went back to college!

Many people are confused about the process of healing the mental level. They think they must always practice "positive thinking," using that technique to block out their negative thoughts. They're afraid their negative thoughts will hurt them. Perhaps they have been stuck in negative thoughts and feelings at one time in their lives. Now that they are feeling more positive, they don't want to acknowledge *any* negatives for fear of "slipping back" into a negative perspective. So they deny or repress all their negative thoughts and concentrate only on the positive ones. For some people this works fairly well for a while, but eventually all those denied or repressed thoughts and feelings have to come to the surface, one way or another. That is why many people who attempt to practice positive thinking are quite surprised to discover that efforts to get rid of their negative thinking actually make matters worse. Rather than diminishing their negative thoughts and feelings, they find themselves caught up in them even more.

Remember that the first step in any healing process is always acknowledgment and acceptance of what is true right now. We don't heal anything by trying to block it out, get rid of, or pretend it doesn't exist. We heal it by accepting that it's there, and then becoming aware that there are other choices possible. So we need to acknowledge and accept our "negative" thoughts as part of who we are, and at the same time recognize and develop other perspectives and ideas that give us more expansive possibilities.

Here's a common example: Someone recognizes that there's a part of her that says she's not worthy or deserving of happiness. She notices herself sometimes getting stuck in these self-critical thoughts. Whenever she makes a mistake, her inner critic says, "You see, this is just further proof that you can't do anything right."

She can't change this by simply censoring herself every time her inner critic speaks up. Rather, she needs to acknowledge those thoughts, and perhaps delve a little more deeply into them. One question she might ask herself is: "Where did these thoughts come from, anyway?" Upon reflection, she realizes that the voice in her head is very similar to her mother's voice, who used to criticize her just as she now criticizes herself.

With this awareness, she can begin seeking out tools for learning to heal and transform her inner critic.* If she had simply tried to block out her negative thoughts, she would have lost the opportunity to learn from them, and she might have spent the rest of her life struggling to repress her negative thoughts instead of finding a way to truly heal them.

Some people have had the childhood experience of being told they were stupid, or they had their abilities compared unfavorably with a sibling or classmate. Many girls were given the message, directly or indirectly, that females are less intelligent, or that they are less important than

---

* There is an excellent and most helpful book on this topic by Drs. Hal and Sidra Stone, *Embracing Your Inner Critic*. See the Recommended Resources section.

males. And many people with more intuitive, holistic, right-brain learning styles were never supported by our left-brain, logically oriented society and school system; as a result, many have drawn the mistaken conclusion that they are less intelligent than others.

People who have suffered these types of traumas in early life may have learned to doubt, discount, or deny their own intellect. In this case, the mental healing process must involve reclaiming one's own natural intelligence and learning to trust it. Our society tends to reward only one kind of intelligence. But there are actually many different kinds of intelligence. In his book, *Raising a Magical Child,* Joseph Chilton Pearce talks about the seven intelligences:*

Physical intelligence
Emotional intelligence
Intellectual intelligence
Social intelligence
Conceptual intelligence
Intuitive intelligence
Imaginative intelligence

To this list we could add many others, such as:

Spiritual intelligence
Musical intelligence
"Tracking" (wilderness) intelligence
"Street smarts"

---

* Published by Dutton, New York, 1992.

Similarly, some people are more oriented to what has come to be called "right-brain" abilities — the more artistic, nonlinear, less structured activities. Others are more oriented to "left-brain" abilities — structured, linear processes such as mathematics, verbal, and technical skills.

Certainly, each type of intelligence has its own niche. For example, if you were lost in a jungle you'd obviously be much better off with a guide who had "tracking" intelligence than you would with a person who was a great academic! And if your car broke down fifty miles from the nearest town, the person with physical intelligence (which includes the mechanical) is probably going to be a lot more helpful than the one with intellectual intelligence.

In each kind of intelligence is a clue to the gift we have come here to give. Every one of us has our own gift, from the agile rock climber to the "fix-it genius," to the single mother who raises three healthy kids and maintains a full-time job. It is ironic but very true that we are often the last ones in the world to be able to see and acknowledge our own gifts or areas of intelligence. Most of us are pretty blind to the things we do best. While low self-esteem can contribute to this blindness, a bigger factor is that we live with our genius every day and it just seems "normal" to us.

When I was a kid, I read and wrote constantly. The library was my favorite place and I used to imagine a whole shelf full of books that I had written! This was, and is, one of my areas of intelligence and it is a course I have recognized and been able to follow through most of my life. However, it is not always easy to immediately recognize our gifts.

For example, my editor, Hal Bennett, tells how in his childhood he loved reading and writing but was discouraged by his inability to diagram sentences and remember rules of grammar, which were required in school. Eventually he became convinced that he was, in his words, "just plain stupid where school was concerned," and he virtually gave up trying. He graduated from high school only by taking special summer classes, and his family never expected him to go any further with his schooling.

When he was twenty-one, he enrolled in a night school class in creative writing that completely changed the course of his life. He wrote a short story that the class loved and that later was published in a literary magazine. That was the encouragement he needed to pursue his gift and his unique intelligence. Since the days of that creative writing class he has gone on to get university degrees in writing and holistic health, and a doctorate in psychology. He has published twelve books of his own, and another twenty as a coauthor. But what he best loves is working with other writers to help them develop and refine their work.

The path he followed in his life was to pursue his early interests even though he felt discouraged and had many mixed messages about what he could and couldn't do. A similar path can be helpful for anyone who has somehow been discouraged from pursuing their own gifts and early interests.

Exercise

Rediscovering Your Native Intelligence

Think about the various kinds of intelligences I listed in the paragraphs above — or any other kinds of intelligence you may have observed on your own. What kinds of intelligence do you have? It may be a unique combination of several of the intelligences noted above, plus one or more others you may have thought of.

To help you open your eyes to your type of intelligence, remember back to the activities you gravitated toward as a kid. Exploring nature? Reading? Making up stories? Playing with animals? Putting on plays? Taking things apart to see how they work? Sports? Music? What else?

Take a moment to write down a list of things that you do well or that you really like to do. Is there a common thread that runs through them? Follow the thread. It will lead you to your own unique intelligence.

As you get in touch with your own intelligence, you may also recognize that you were rewarded, discouraged, belittled, or encouraged in the area of your greatest interest. If you had negative experiences where your intelligence is concerned, start reaffirming your abilities right now by recognizing that your natural gifts and unique intelligence are found in those activities and interests toward which you were drawn in your early life. There is a reason you gravitated in that direction, and the inner compass that pointed in that particular direction is rarely, if ever, wrong.

If you need to do some healing around your gift, look for ways that you might start today to develop those early interests. Pursue skills and knowledge in that area by taking classes, by getting to know other people who have successful careers in your field of interest, by reading more about it, and — perhaps most important of all — by doing it for yourself, starting right now.

Begin doing it with the faith that your early interests are trustworthy indicators that reveal your true gift. Start giving yourself time to focus more of your attention on those early interests. Find some way to get hands-on experience: If your early interest is writing, start a writing journal or take a writing class. If you are interested in mechanical things, get a broken-down machine that intrigues you and take it apart. If working with people is your passion, sign up for volunteer work at an agency that helps people. These firsthand involvements not only revive and reaffirm your interests and your natural intelligence, they also get you on your way to actualizing those most important parts of yourself that may have been lost.

CHAPTER EIGHTEEN

Healing the
Emotional Level

*Our feelings are an important part of the life
force that is constantly moving through us.
If we don't allow ourselves to fully experience
our emotions, we stop the natural flow
of that life force.*

For most of us, exploring the spiritual realm is primarily a pleasant, expansive experience. And because we are such a mental culture we are fairly comfortable with the mental aspect of our journey. However, a great many people are stuck at the level where emotional healing needs to take place. Most people are frightened at the prospect of doing deep emotional healing work.

We live in a society that's generally terrified of emotions. Our patriarchal mentality is highly suspicious of the feminine aspect of our being — the feeling, intuitive part of us. The rational side of us is trying to ensure our safety in the physical world, and fears the loss of control that deep emotion brings. Since our culture admires the more rational approach to life, and disrespects the more feeling side of us, we have all learned, to one degree or another, to hide and deny our feelings — even from ourselves. We've learned to bury most of our feelings deep inside, and show the world only what seems safe, which usually isn't very much.

Most of us are particularly uncomfortable with what are commonly considered "negative" feelings, such as fear, hurt, sadness, grief, and anger. In reality, there is no such thing as a negative feeling. We call things negative because we don't understand them and therefore we fear them. All of these feelings are natural and important. They each serve a meaningful function in the human experience. Rather than rejecting and avoiding them, we need to explore and discover the gift each one offers us. And we need to understand that to fully feel anything, we have to be comfortable feeling the fullness of its opposite. In order to feel real joy, for example, we must be able to embrace our sadness. In order to open to love, we need to accept our fear as part of our experience. Interestingly enough, we are often just as afraid of too much of a "positive" feeling as we are of the so-called "negative" ones. We don't want to feel too much love, joy, or passion. We prefer the cool middle ground where we can feel in control.

While most of us have learned to repress our feelings, some people have the opposite problem: they are too easily overwhelmed by their emotions and have difficulty maintaining any emotional equilibrium. They are often carrying the repressed emotions of other people around them, feeling and expressing everyone else's feelings as well as their own. Still others are stuck in one particular emotion and are constantly reacting from that place — anger perhaps, or fear. These are all symptoms of emotional imbalances that need healing.

Due at least in part to our fear of feeling, there is a great deal of ignorance and misinformation about healing the emotional level. Many people, in fact, don't even acknowledge that emotions exist! How many times have you read or heard reference to the *three* levels of existence — body, mind, and spirit? The emotional level is not even acknowledged, but is simply lumped into the mind category. This comes from the traditional transcendent approach, where the importance of the human experience is minimized, and emotions, so much a part of that human experience, are underemphasized, or even dismissed as fabrications of the mind.

Many teachers and healers confuse the mental and emotional levels, or treat them as one. You may have heard or read discussions, for example, of how our thoughts affect our physical health, with no reference whatsoever of how our feelings affect our physical health. Yet blocked emotions are certainly one of the main causes of most physical ailments.

Of course, our mental and emotional energies are intertwined, as are all levels of our being. It's not possible to completely separate any of them from the others. But thoughts and feelings, while certainly connected and strongly influencing each other, are very different. Part of healing the emotional level is learning to distinguish between thinking and feeling. In beginning workshops, for example, when a person is asked how they *feel* about, let's say, their boss firing them unexpectedly, the reply may be, "Well, he had no grounds for doing that. I always did my work and then some!" That is a thinking response. A feeling response would be, "I'm angry! And I'm scared."

Our thoughts are much more connected to our conscious mind and our will, whereas our feelings come from a deeper, less rational place. To some degree we can consciously choose our thoughts, but the only choice we have about our feelings is how we handle them. The person who got fired, for instance, might choose to indulge himself in critical or vengeful thoughts about his boss, or he might choose to focus on thoughts about how to get another job, or better yet, what his true vocation is. However, the underlying emotions of anger and fear are there, regardless. He can choose how he handles those feelings by sitting at home feeling depressed, or going to the office and yelling at the boss, or talking his feelings out with a friend or a therapist, then going job-hunting. In other words, he can repress his feelings, or act them out in a destructive way, or he can choose to explore, express, accept them, and then find appropriate actions to take care of himself.

It's rather shocking to discover how few people seem to understand the process of emotional healing — even many therapists and healers who are supposedly helping people with that process. Many professionals who are able to help people up to a certain point don't know how to guide them through the deeper levels of emotional healing. This is partly because in order to guide others successfully we need to have done our own deep healing work, and many therapists have done little if any of this. Fortunately all this is slowly changing; more is being learned every day about emotional healing, and more people are having the courage to go through it. I certainly don't consider myself an expert by any means, but I have learned a good deal from several excellent teachers I've worked with, from going through my own deep emotional healing process and from guiding many others through theirs.

When we were infants and children, we had many strong feelings. What we needed was to have people acknowledge and respond to these feelings in appropriate ways. For example, we needed to hear things like this: "I understand that you're really upset that your brother got to go and you didn't." Or, "I can see that you're feeling really sad about grandpa being sick."

In essence, as children we need reflection and validation of our feelings from our parents, families, teachers, and the surrounding world. We need to be assured that we have a right to our feelings, that our feelings aren't wrong or bad. We need to feel that others can understand and empathize with us when we are experiencing strong feelings. In short, we need to be allowed to have our own feeling experience.

Having our feelings validated is, of course, quite different from being allowed to do whatever we want. Children need to be given clear limits and boundaries about their behavior just as much as they need to be assured that having feelings is okay. Thus, at the same time that a parent might be telling the child, "You can't go out and play now," she could acknowledge that child's feelings, "I know you are disappointed about that. I understand that you're upset because you want to ride your bike right now!"

Because our parents and families were not supported in their own emotional experience as children, most of them did not know how to do that for us. More often than not, they gave us messages that told us that our feelings were wrong, bad, inappropriate, or intolerable, such as, "There's no reason to feel that way." Or, "Cheer up! Things aren't so bad!" Or, the classic, "Big boys (or girls) don't cry." As a result, most of us learned to bury our feelings and present what was considered appropriate.

Even as parents, we may find ourselves treating our own children in ways that we were treated. We tend to pass on the same attitudes and patterns that our parents taught us. If we never healed the belief our parents taught us, for example, that anger or fear is an "unacceptable" feeling, we will tend to pass that lesson on to our own children. And they, in turn, will have the same confusion about their feelings that we have about our own.

No matter how hard parents try, and they all do the best they are capable of, children inevitably experience some degree of emotional hurt, neglect, and abandonment. Because we are so vulnerable as children, we are deeply wounded by these experiences, and we carry our wounds inside us for the rest of our lives — or until we do our conscious emotional healing work.

In emotional healing work we learn to give ourselves, and allow ourselves to receive from others, whatever we didn't receive as young children. We learn to accept and experience all our feelings and, when appropriate, to communicate these feelings in a way that allows others to understand us. We open the way to our emotional healing through the experience of having at least one other person hear, understand, and empathize with what we are feeling, without denying or rejecting those feelings in any way.

If we have denied or stuffed down a lot of our feelings, we need to have a safe place and experienced guide to help us begin to get in touch with, experience, and release them. Then we need to develop tools for staying current with our feelings by allowing ourselves to acknowledge and experience them as they arise. It is important to get in touch with the needs underneath our feelings and learn how to communicate those needs effectively. Underneath most of our emotions are our basic needs for love, acceptance, security, and self-esteem. We need to know the vulnerable child who still lives deep inside each of us, and learn to become the loving parent our inner child requires.

If we want to experience the full range of our being in this lifetime, we need to commit ourselves to heal the emotional wounds from our childhood and early life. This deep level of emotional healing takes time. It cannot be rushed or forced. It needs to unfold in its own time, sometimes taking a number of years to move through the deeper levels. Fortunately, as each layer is healed, life becomes more and more fulfilling and rewarding.

Our feelings are an important part of the life force that is constantly moving through us. If we don't allow ourselves to fully experience our emotions, we stop the natural flow of that life force. Energy gets blocked in our physical bodies and may remain that way for years or even a lifetime, unless it is released. This leads to emotional and physical pain and disease. Repressed feelings = blocked energy = emotional and physical ailments.

Accepting our emotions, allowing ourselves to feel them, and learning to communicate them constructively and appropriately allows them to move through us easily and naturally. This enables the full free flow of the life force through our physical bodies, which brings emotional and physical healing. Experiencing feelings = free-flowing energy = emotional and physical health and well-being.

Our emotions are like the weather, constantly changing — sometimes dark, sometimes light, at times wild and intense, at other times calm and quiet. Trying to resist or control your feeling experience is like trying to control the weather — an exercise in futility and frustration! Besides, if all we ever experienced were sunny days of exactly 75-degree temperature, life might become quite boring. When we can appreciate the beauty of the rain, the wind, and the snow as well as the sun, we are free to enjoy the fullness of life.

Exercise
Healing the Emotional Level

If you become aware of having lost your feeling of well-being during the day, try this simple exercise:

Lie or sit down in a comfortable position and focus your attention, for a moment, on the area of your discomfort, remembering that emotions are held in the body as tension, pain, or other expressions of uneasiness. Usually, you will experience this discomfort somewhere in your torso. Let your attention rest near this discomfort in a caring and soothing way. Let yourself feel the quality of the sensations in that area.

When you find your attention drifting, refocus and bring your awareness back to the sensations in your torso.

Give permission to your intuitive guidance to bring forth any issues concerning these feelings. You can do this simply by asking, "Is there something you want me to know?" Then be careful that you don't abandon the area of feeling.

Let yourself receive a sense of what is going on there. Allow yourself to feel as fully as possible any emotions that come up. Just attending to the area in this way, allowing yourself to feel it, will encourage any blocked energy to move more easily through it.

CHAPTER NINETEEN

Healing the Physical Level

The overall process of physical healing takes place in our lives as we learn to feel, listen to, and trust our bodies again. Our bodies... communicate to us clearly and specifically, if we are willing to listen to them.

Since the spiritual, mental, and emotional aspects of our being are all housed in our physical body, every bit of healing work that we do on the other three levels is reflected in our physical health and well-being. Our body is where we integrate and express all four levels of our existence. All the consciousness we gain on the other levels shows up in how alive we feel in our daily life. As the other levels are healed, our consciousness is freed to be more present in the moment. We naturally feel more in touch with our body and we are able to live in it more fully.

Of course, the physical body has its own specific healing process as well. As with the other levels, there are certain basic principles, common to everyone, yet each person's needs are unique as well.

In modern civilization, we are not generally encouraged to respect or be sensitive to our physical bodies. In fact, many of us are quite disconnected from our true physical needs. We can see clear evidence of this in the sedentary, nonphysical lives of many modern urban dwellers. We see it in the concrete jungles we humans seem prone to create everywhere we go. Millions of people are living and working every day in buildings that completely cut them off from anything natural. Many of these buildings don't even have natural light or air. And worst of all, we are polluting our air and water and dumping toxic chemicals that saturate the soil in which we grow our food.

Just as our own physical bodies are physical manifestations and vehicles for our individual consciousness, so the earth is the physical manifestation and home for our collective consciousness. Thus, our awareness of, and relationship to the physical plane is reflected to us both in how we treat our own bodies and how we treat our Earth body.

One reason we are experiencing disconnectedness from our physical being has to do with the increasing emphasis on the intellect over the past few hundred years, and most particularly over the past century. Our eagerness to explore the mental level, and the resulting development of the technological age, has tended to cut us off from awareness of our natural physical selves.

Another contribution to the problem of disconnecting from the physical has been the attitude toward the body fostered by the traditional, transcendent spiritual approach, embraced by most world religions. The body is seen as the enemy of spirit, the seat of human needs, emotions, attachments, and passions. And it is the goal of these religions to subdue and rise above these human aspects. Therefore, the body is seen as lowly — inferior to mind and spirit, or even downright evil. Thus, our bodies are ignored or denigrated.

We are all born with a natural awareness of our bodies' needs and feelings, but we have learned to literally tune out the body. We may ignore it completely except when it's in extreme distress, so the body quickly learns that it has to get sick or have an accident in order to get attention. And even then, the attention we give may be in the form of trying to mask or get rid of the symptoms as quickly as possible so that we can resume our unconscious life patterns again. We learn to avoid looking deeper to discover the root of the problem — what the body is really trying to communicate to us.

Still, there are many of us who think we're paying a lot of positive attention to our physical health because we are interested in nutrition and exercise. All too often, however, we are pushing our bodies to do the things we have mentally decided should be good for us — following a rigid diet or driving ourselves to perform a strenuous exercise program — rather than listening to the real messages our bodies are trying to give us.

One of the major things that makes it possible to shut out our bodies' signals effectively is the use of drugs. Most of us are becoming aware of the epidemic of drug, alcohol, tobacco, and other addictions we are currently suffering, as people frantically try to cope with their spiritual and emotional pain by shutting it out. Fortunately, as we realize the futility and destructiveness of this method of dealing with our problems, more and more people are reaching out and finding healing. In fact, this may be the way a majority are getting involved with transformational processes — through twelve-step programs such as Alcoholics Anonymous and other treatment modalities.

Still, we remain a drug-oriented society, prone to cutting off our bodies' communications to us by popping a pill or ingesting a substance. For example, a great number of people use coffee to wake themselves up and keep themselves going throughout the day. It is available everywhere. Unfortunately, it revs up the nervous system so that we can't feel or follow our natural energy.

Because we've abdicated responsibility for our own bodies' well-being, we have become overly dependent on outside authorities when it comes to physical health. Of course, we must seek help from doctors and other professional health practitioners when we are in need of expert assistance, but we need to balance our reliance on others with self-awareness and self-trust as well. We need to see our helping professionals not as ultimate authorities but as "resource people" assisting us on our healing paths.

A friend of mine went to a doctor who had been highly recommended concerning a growth on her foot. The doctor advised surgery. My friend had the operation, which proved unsuccessful. She was in considerable pain for some time. Another doctor she consulted said he would not have advised the surgery. My friend realized that she had not even paused to consider her own feelings or decide whether to get a second opinion before following the first doctor's advice. I'm not implying that a second opinion is always indicated; rather, I'm suggesting that it is just as important to check into our own sense of things as it is to check what the experts say.

The overall process of physical healing takes place in our lives as we learn to feel, listen to, and trust our bodies again. Our bodies usually know what they need. They communicate to us clearly and specifically, if we are willing to listen to them. We must cultivate the art of understanding and interpreting their signals accurately.

Our bodies communicate their physical needs — what and when they desire to eat, how and when they desire rest or movement or physical contact from other people. Once we move through artificial, addictive cravings that we may have developed — using alcohol, drugs, caffeine, sugar, overeating, overexercising, etc. — and get down to the body's true desires and responses, we have a very reliable guide for our physical needs. When we learn to listen to our bodies and heed their messages, we are well on the way to healing.

Keep in mind that your body is also an important bellwether of your spiritual, mental, and emotional needs. If you have ignored a need on another level — say, you have not paid attention to a yearning you have been feeling for spiritual nurturing — your body will eventually manifest that need in a physical form: headaches, perhaps, or an upper respiratory infection. This seems especially true of the feeling level, perhaps because this is the most blocked or neglected area for most of us. If we have not taken care of our emotional needs and feelings, they eventually try to get through to us through physical discomfort and disease. I believe that most, if not all, of our physical ailments are related to spiritual, mental, and emotional causes.

Generally, an illness or accident is an indication that we may need to look a little deeper at our own needs and feelings, or pay more attention to following our inner guidance. It may be the symptom of an inner conflict that we need to deal with more directly. For example, my friend and associate Kathy Altman is a wonderfully nurturing and responsible person. She is great at taking care of my needs and everyone else's but not so good at allowing herself to receive help from others. Once when we were organizing a large retreat in Hawaii she injured her ankle and was unable to handle all the logistics herself. She was forced to ask for help and support from others. This was difficult but, of course, healing for her. And everyone else was delighted to have the opportunity to care for her a bit.

The fact that physical ailments may be linked to emotional or other causes *does not mean that because we have an ailment we have failed to become a conscious person!* Too often, people who embrace the idea that physical diseases have roots in spiritual, mental, and emotional causes use this idea to beat themselves up. They feel that if only they had properly done their inner work, they could have prevented the problem.

Unfortunately, all too many teachers and healers unintentionally support these feelings of shame or guilt by implying that thinking the right thoughts, saying the right affirmations, eating the right diet, or whatever ought to keep you perfectly healthy. Needless to say, it's not so simple. We can eat a pure diet, meditate every day, exercise regularly, express our feelings often, use affirmations and visualization, and still get sick! The consciousness process is complex and often mysterious. We can't always know exactly why something is happening. Remember that our soul uses every avenue available to educate and enlighten us.

A physical ailment is not necessarily a negative occurrence. In fact, it is always an opportunity for learning, growth, and healing on all levels — not only for the person with the ailment, but also for the loved ones who are affected by it. This is true for minor or major illnesses or accidents, although of course the more serious the problem, the greater the intensity of the learning. As difficult as it can be to accept, any ailment can be viewed as a gift, an opportunity to look at ourselves and our lives and learn something. It presents a possibility for real change and movement.

The most constructive and effective way to deal with an ailment is to acknowledge that you have it, that you are not "guilty" for having it, but that you wish to use the experience to deepen and expand your consciousness.

Naturally, it doesn't usually feel like an opportunity for change and growth at the time. Most likely, it feels painful, frightening, confusing, discouraging. Part of the healing process is to allow ourselves to experience those feelings. It can be helpful to put a kind of framework around the experience, one that goes something like this: "Even though this feels terrible and I don't understand it, I know that there is a gift of learning and healing for me here. I'm open to receiving that and understanding it at the appropriate time." This empowers our inner guidance to show us what we need to learn from the experience.

For example, I was recently ill with a virulent flu — the virus from Hell! For months I'd been under a lot of pressure. I had more than my usual number of commitments to attend to, including writing this book. When I got the flu, I was still under as much pressure as ever, but I felt too sick to do anything but lie in bed. It was stressful to feel myself falling behind in my responsibilities. I had no energy to cope with anything — a strange feeling, for I am generally healthy and energetic.

The symptoms lingered for almost two weeks, and I found myself falling into a deep depression, in which some very dark feelings of hopelessness and meaninglessness came to the surface. Finally, with the help of a therapist friend, I was able to get in touch with the underlying emotions. I had been driving myself so hard for two or three months, trying to do so much (which tends to be my pattern), that my inner child had become hopeless and discouraged, convinced that she would never again have any rest, nurturing, or fun! Once I expressed these feelings, I felt much lighter emotionally, and the next day I was finally physically well.

Since then I have been more able to balance my hard work with rest and pleasure. This is an issue I have been working on for many years, and the illness seems to have taken me to a new level of healing. In addition, I gained tremendous understanding and empathy for those who suffer from depression. I had rarely experienced this feeling of not being able to cope with life, and now I know how frightening and debilitating it can be. This can only help me be a more compassionate and skilled facilitator for others suffering from similar symptoms.

The illness I had was clearly a combination of physical (there was a terrible virus going around) and emotional factors (I was stressed out and needed a break). I don't know which came first, the virus or the overwork, but clearly they worked together. The result is that I received a gift. And now I feel great! So this was not an experience I could or should have avoided. It was a perfect step on my journey.

Obviously, with a life-threatening illness or accident, the stakes are higher, the feelings much more intense. The opportunities for growth are also that much more powerful. Many people discover that a critical illness causes them to confront major issues and through this confrontation gain life-changing awareness.

Again, we need to be careful about judging ourselves or others for having a serious illness or for any of the results that follow. We need to understand that death can be a legitimate and positive choice, not a failure to heal. Who are we to judge the journey of our own or another's soul? A life-threatening illness may cause one person to choose life and make any necessary changes to heal themselves. Another person may consciously or unconsciously choose death. Perhaps they have accomplished what they needed in this life, or they feel that they'll be able to accomplish the next step more effectively on a different plane of existence, or in another lifetime.

A friend of mine recently related the story of his mother's death to me. He told of sitting with her through the last few weeks of her life, beginning when she was in severe denial about her terminal illness all the way through to her very peaceful and conscious death. Being in her mid-eighties, she felt that she had accomplished everything she had ever dreamed of doing and she was quite content with her life. She had a very large tumor growing in her pancreas, and one day when her doctor touched it and asked her if she was feeling any pain, she replied with a smile, "Oh, no. I am grateful for it. It is letting me leave this life and go on."

If you are suffering from a critical illness, one of the most important things you can do is try to get in touch with, and acknowledge, that part of you that wants to die and is choosing death. Find out why it is making this choice. Allow the feeling its full expression. You may also need to feel and acknowledge that part of you that wants to live. Find out why it is making that choice. Allow yourself to consciously feel the conflict between the two; then, sit with the unresolved conflict for as long as you need to until it begins to resolve itself in some way. You may need support and facilitation from a therapist or counselor experienced in this field to do this.

It may be shocking to think that you have a part of you that *wants* to die. You may not be consciously in touch with this part at all. Few of us are. However, in my experience, anyone dealing with a life-threatening illness has a part of their psyche choosing death, consciously or unconsciously. Often, it has its roots in the vulnerable child within, who is somehow not getting his or her needs met. Sometimes it has to do with a very heavy inner critic or inner tyrant who is generating a feeling of self-hate.

In some cases the body itself can be feeling unappreciated and unsupported, perhaps because the person has a transcendent spiritual philosophy and considers the body unimportant, unreal, or even corrupt. Or there may be a spiritual aspect that simply feels ready to move on, as with my friend's mother in the story above. By getting in touch with the parts that want to die and the parts that don't, it's possible to make the choice a more conscious one.

One of the best techniques for doing this work is the Voice Dialogue process, described in the chapter "Discovering Our Many Selves."* Of course, use these techniques in conjunction with whatever medical and/or healing care you need.

How do we go about healing the physical level of our being? The first step, especially if we have an acute or serious ailment, is to get the most immediate and effective treatment we can find. The second step is to learn more about ongoing ways to maintain and strengthen our physical health. This might include treatment and support from the appropriate medical and/or alternative practitioners. The third step, which can be done simultaneously with the first and second, is to look into the emotional, mental, and spiritual factors that may contribute to the physical problem, then get whatever help you might need to heal those areas.

---

* Please see the books by Hal and Sidra Stone listed in the Recommended Resources section.

Choosing a treatment method for a physical problem can be confusing. In this day and age, we have many choices available — including Western medicine and surgery, classic Chinese medicine, Ayurvedic medicine, homeopathy, herbology, naturopathy, acupuncture, chiropractic, massage and bodywork, exercise therapies, as well as diet and nutrition.

My personal feeling is that all these modalities, and others I may have failed to mention, have value and are appropriate in particular situations. I have benefited from nearly all of them at certain times in my life. Many of them, such as hatha yoga, exercise, massage, chiropractic care, acupuncture, and good nutrition are part of my regular health-maintenance regime.

Increasingly, we are finding that there are medical doctors and clinics throughout the country who work with both mainstream medicine and alternative methods. Such people can be invaluable resources when faced with a serious illness. They can be tremendously helpful in providing you with the information you will want when making choices that have to do with your treatment.*

It's important to find out what works for you, whether it's for maintaining good health, treating problems when they arise, or restoring strength and health following radical treatment such as surgery. In my experience, the more acute the problem, the more likely it is that Western

---

* One good source of information is the monthly newsletter, *Self Healing*, published by Dr. Andrew Weil. Write *Self Healing*, 42 Pleasant Street, Waterton, MA 02172 or call (800) 523-3296 for information.

medicine will be called for, since it generally employs the strongest and fastest methods for dealing with immediate symptoms or the disturbance of a normal physical function. For subtler problems, some of the so-called alternative methods may actually be more effective. For example, Western medicine may not be able to help when it comes to many back problems, but by working with a chiropractor, massage therapist, and/or body worker, we can slowly heal and retrain the physical body so that the problem doesn't recur. In many cases, the skill, wisdom, and sensitivity of the practitioner may be a more important factor than the method they use.

Explore, discover, and learn as much as you can about the alternatives available to you, then trust your inner guidance about what's best for you. Seek the advice of appropriate professionals. Really listen to what they have to say. Take in feedback from friends and loved ones. Then listen deeply to your own sense of truth and make your own decisions about the best course of action.

Having done what you need to do to make sure your body is getting the care it needs, turn your attention to the other levels of your being. Find out what you need emotionally, mentally, and spiritually. Then take steps to care for those needs.

Remember that our bodies are wonderful communicators. They let us know what they need. Cultivate the art and practice of feeling, sensing, and listening to what your body is saying. As we learn to respond to our bodies' needs, we gradually become attuned to our own natural rhythms and to those of the Earth.

Mother Earth is our greatest teacher. If we pay attention we can learn from her everything we need to know about living on the physical plane. Every day, in every way, she demonstrates to us her natural rhythms and cycles, all the natural laws of life.

Most of the indigenous cultures of the world had a deep understanding and reverence for humanity's connection with the Earth. Their belief systems were built around the essential connections between our Mother Earth and our physical, emotional, mental, and spiritual well-being, both collectively and individually. The resurgence of interest in the wisdom of indigenous peoples reflects a recognition that we have a great deal to learn from them about creating healthy relationships with ourselves, each other, and the Earth.

The pressures of modern life tend to move us further and further from the natural cycles and rhythms of the Earth. We get up when the alarm clock rings; we go to bed after the eleven o'clock news. Life is structured according to what we *think* needs to be done, not according to our sensitivity to a natural rhythm. Yet, separated though we may be, we are still part of the Earth. We need to acknowledge that, and to respect the Earth's rhythms and live in accordance with them.

We are not machines that can produce the same output each and every day, endlessly. Our mental and emotional states are different on sunny summer days than they are on cloudy winter days. And there are a myriad of other subtle changes throughout the day that affect us. If we can acknowledge and accept these differences each day, we can move more within the flow of life.

In order to get more in touch with our Earth connections, it is essential to be outside a little every day, even if it is just for a few moments. It is only by having that direct contact with the natural world that we can become conscious of the subtle changes occurring throughout the year. If you live in the city, it's a little more difficult to stay in touch with nature, but almost anyone can get outside, observe the sky, and feel the sun and the air.

Daily physical movement is an important part of maintaining a healthy, happy body and soul. As we move our bodies, the life force can flow freely through, healing and replenishing our physical form and bringing us pleasure and joy.

I am convinced that life in a physical body is meant to be an ecstatic experience. Through commitment to our healing and to our transformational process we can open to more and more of life's many gifts.

Exercise
Moving Meditation

Find a time when you can have some privacy in your home. (That may be a challenging enough exercise right there, for most people!) Move the furniture aside, if necessary, to make some space for yourself in a room where you have a tape player. Then try this moving meditation.

Pretend that your body is a musical instrument tuning up in preparation for playing in an orchestra. Select some of your favorite music and start to move to it gently.

You may want to pay attention to your body's natural order, starting with moving your head for a minute or two, following the rhythm of the music.

Next, switch to your shoulders and move them any way you choose, staying with them for a few minutes.

Follow each part of your body for a few minutes until you feel it has been given enough time to warm up and express itself — your arms, hands, chest, hips, thighs, knees, and feet.

When you reach your feet, you might want to work back up in the reverse order — knees, thighs, hips, etc. — for further warm-up. When you feel you have "tuned up your instrument," begin to let your whole body move spontaneously to the music. Imagine that the music is actually moving throughout you, that your body is being "played" like an instrument by the sound.

Try this exercise for at least twenty minutes a day for one week and see how different you feel. Note which parts of your body are expressive. Which ones feel tight? Give each part time for expression and you will notice them begin to change.*

---

* Adapted from the work of Gabrielle Roth, author of *Maps to Ecstasy: A Healing Journey for the Untamed Spirit*. She has also produced some excellent music tapes that are great for doing this exercise. See the Recommended Resources section.

Exercise

Communicating with Your Body

If you have an ache or pain in, let's say, your lower back, sit quietly and then imagine that this part of yourself is able to talk to you. Ask it what it wants or needs. Ask it what it would like you to know. Sit and listen for answers that will come to you as an idea, an imagined voice, or perhaps in a dream or daydream. You might also try journal writing, with your nondominant hand representing the voice of your body, or any part of your body.

This exercise is one of the best ways I know to begin developing good communications with your body. As you learn more and more about feeling, sensing, and listening to what it is telling you, you will begin to discover not only what your body needs but how to get to the real source of your discomfort or illness, which is the first step toward lasting health and balance.*

---

* If you would like more help in discovering what your body is communicating to you, there are many therapists and body workers who work with the body-mind-emotion connection. There are two Voice Dialogue facilitators who specialize in helping you understand your body's communications — Judith Hendin and Judith Stone. They each work differently, and both are excellent. You can find out more about them on the Voice Dialogue Web site: delos-inc.com or call Judith Hendin at (610) 330-9778 or Judith Stone at (310) 459-0429.

CHAPTER TWENTY

Integration

There is a simple universal principle:
Everything in the universe wants to be accepted.
All aspects of creation want to be loved
and appreciated and included.

A key word on the path of transformation is "integration." Simply stated, this means "joining together
into one functional whole." Within our present context,
it means becoming more fully realized beings, developing, expressing, and embodying all aspects of who we are
as fully as possible in our daily lives. Living on earth successfully means embracing and integrating our animal
(physical), human (emotional and mental), and divine
(spiritual) selves.

The physical world is a plane of duality. It contains
infinite polarities, meaning that for every truth there is an
equal and opposite truth. For minds like ours, influenced
by rational, linear thought systems, the existence of duali-
ties — wherein every truth has its polar opposite — seems

paradoxical and difficult to comprehend. To understand the whole and not be confused by the dualistic world we have made, we need to draw from our more intuitive, right-brained, holistic selves, which aren't troubled by the fact that truth can seem paradoxical and are quite comfortable with exploring polarities.

For every essential energy within us, there is potentially an equal, opposite energy to balance it — for example, doing and being, giving and receiving, power and vulnerability. The more we can develop and embrace these opposites of life within ourselves, the more conscious, integrated, and balanced we become. Life is always guiding us in the direction that will help us develop the qualities that we most need.

In order to fully express one energy, it is necessary to integrate its opposite. It can even be said that the way to one quality is through its opposite. For example, you truly have strength only to the degree that you've accepted and embraced its opposite — your weakness or vulnerability. Just as being a good teacher requires us to be willing to learn, so to be truly wise we must learn to accept our own foolishness.

Most of us are very good at accepting and expressing one side of any given polarity, and not so good at accepting and expressing the other side. One person might be comfortable in a leadership role but be unable to accept a subordinate position; another person might be comfortable as a follower but not as a leader. Or one might stay in the safe middle ground, afraid to explore either extreme — unable to lead or follow. If we're identified with one polarity, life frequently pushes us toward its opposite. If we're only comfortable in the middle, it may guide us first in one direction and then the other.

If we wish to integrate our inner polarities we can't reject any parts of ourselves, not even the ones we're not yet comfortable with. Integration means expanding to include them. We judge some of our feelings, thoughts, and energies as negative, and we classify other aspects of ourselves and life in general as positive. We attempt to get rid of the negative things and experience only the positive ones. But the things we call negative are just the things we're afraid of or don't really understand. We don't want to experience them and so we try to get rid of them. But they can never go away because they are a part of us and a part of life.

Blocking what we have defined as "negative" aspects of ourselves requires a huge amount of energy, and this means that we are robbing ourselves of our potential power. By spending more and more of our energy trying to keep the door shut on our "negative" selves, trying not to experience aspects that we think are negative and frightening, we drain our life force. We can actually die from using our energy to close off our energy!

Life is trying to teach us how to open the door and begin to look at those parts of ourselves that we've been frightened of, that we've hated, that we think are bad and ugly and awful and scary. Life is helping us to discover the hidden aspects of ourselves that we need, that we want, that we can't really live without.

There is a simple universal principle: Everything in the

universe wants to be accepted. All aspects of creation want to be loved and appreciated and included. So, any quality or energy you are not allowing yourself to experience or express will keep coming up inside you, or around you, until you recognize it as a part of you, and accept it and integrate it into your personality and your life.

If, for instance, you were taught that it is wrong and bad to express anger, and you never allowed yourself to do that, you may have a lot of anger building up inside you. Eventually, it might come out in an explosion, or it may cause you to feel depressed, or it might contribute to the development of a physical illness. Also, you may find that you are attracting angry people into your life, or your mate or one of your children might be very angry. Once you learn to express your anger in appropriate and constructive ways, however, it can empower and enrich your life. You will likely find the people in your life less angry as well.

Whatever we don't like, whatever we reject, whatever we try to get away from or get rid of will haunt us. It will bug us. It will follow us around and fly right in our face. It will pursue us in our dreams. It will cause problems in our lives through our relationships, our health, our finances, until we are willing and able to confront it, recognize it, and embrace it as a part of ourselves. Once we do that, it's no longer a problem. It's no longer a big deal. It no longer runs our life. We begin to have an increasingly large range of choices and possibilities.

How, exactly, do we go about the integration process I describe here? That's what the next few chapters are about.

CHAPTER TWENTY-ONE

Discovering Our Many Selves

*The fact is that within each personality are
many different subpersonalities, or selves.
To better understand our own inner conflicts
and inconsistencies we need to become
aware of these selves.*

As modern, civilized adults, we expect ourselves to
feel and behave in a rational, consistent manner
most of the time. But the fact is that our feelings and
behavior are often quite inconsistent from one hour or
day to the next. For example, we may feel quite clear and
confident at one point in time, and at another moment
feel completely the opposite — insecure, confused, uncertain. Furthermore, we often experience inner conflict,
whether consciously or unconsciously. Maybe one part of
us wants to make a radical change in our life, like leaving
a job or a relationship, while another part wants to keep
the status quo. Or there may be a part that wants to work
hard and succeed, while a conflicting part wants to relax
and take it easy.

The fact is that within each personality are many different subpersonalities, or selves. To better understand our own inner conflicts and inconsistencies we need to become aware of these selves. The process of consciousness growth involves getting to know our many inner selves and bringing them into balance and integration in our personalities.

The universe consists of an infinite number of essential qualities, energies, and archetypes. As spiritual beings, each of us is a microcosm of the macrocosm — containing bits of all that exists in the universe. When we are born into physical bodies, we have the potential for developing and expressing all of these energies in our human personality.

The formation of personality can be imagined as being somewhat like the different layers of an onion. At the core is our essential spiritual being, with additional layers growing around that core as we experience the world and begin to develop ways of functioning within it. The first layer of personality to develop around that essential core is the infant. The infant continues to be very closely connected to the spiritual self, so it is intensely aware and sensitive, with a tremendously powerful and magnetic presence.

On the physical level, the tiny infant is completely helpless, vulnerable, and dependent. In order to survive, it must attract the love and care of the mother, family, and/or other people around it. So it begins to experiment with expressing itself in different ways, soon discovering which expressions produce the best results. It may discover that smiling and cooing bring love and warmth, and crying when it's uncomfortable also brings the needed attention.

Or it may find that when it cries it gets ignored or even punished.

As the child grows, it continues to experiment with a variety of energies and behaviors. It watches parents and others in the environment, and imitates them. The behaviors that bring approval and reward, or that allow it to escape punishment or the pain of abandonment, are incorporated into the personality, becoming another layer of the onion. Energies and expressions that produce disapproval, or that go unrewarded by the outside world, or that bring unwelcome attention such as criticism, ridicule, or punishment, are eventually scrapped or repressed and do not become an obvious part of the outward personality. Though they may be eliminated from the everyday personality, these expressions don't necessarily go away. Instead, they may very well go underground and remain undeveloped, or they can pop out at unguarded moments.

This process of developing and expressing certain aspects of ourselves while repressing or disowning others continues throughout our childhood, adolescence, and adulthood. The energies that we feel most comfortable expressing become our primary selves — the dominant parts of the personality. We become closely identified with our primary selves, and think that's who we are. In fact, until we become conscious of this process of personality development, our primary selves really run our lives.

In my family, for example, intellectual pursuits were highly valued and rewarded with positive attention, so I developed primary selves that are rational and articulate. My mother was a strong role model, a powerful, adventurous, and successful career woman. So I developed primary selves that were similar to hers — strong, competent, hardworking, and willing to take risks. Since my parents were divorced when I was three, and my mother needed to work, I developed a sense of responsibility and independence very early. As a sensitive child, I could feel my parents' (and others') emotional pain, and I tried to give them support. So even when I was a young girl, the "caretaking mother" energy in me became a strong primary self.

How we describe ourselves, or how someone who knows us well describes us, is usually a pretty good description of our primary selves. If I were asked to describe myself as a young adult, I would probably have said that I was intelligent, responsible, serious, outgoing, and caring.

Our primary selves are very strong, real energies. They are like people that live inside us and make almost all our decisions. Their underlying purpose is to protect and defend the vulnerable child energy that still lives deep within us — the first layer of the onion. Usually we are quite unaware that we have a vulnerable child inside of us, and that much of our behavior is rooted in our unconscious attempt to meet this child's needs and protect it from harm. We are also largely unaware of our primary selves as distinct energies. We are so totally identified with them we think that's who we really are.

Our primary selves may occupy 90 percent (or even more) of our personality and our time; even so, these selves are only a part of who we actually are. The primary selves developed as the best way we could find to survive and succeed in our family and cultural environment. They are the energies that were the most successful at getting our early needs met.

We have many other energies, often very different or seemingly the opposite of our primary selves, that were neglected or repressed in the past because they failed to get us the attention and approval we wanted, or because they resulted in disapproval or punishment from our family, teachers, or community. Since these energies are nevertheless a natural part of us, they don't go away just because we don't express them. They remain inside us, dormant, or perhaps pushing their way out at moments when our primary selves are off guard. These repressed or undeveloped energies are our disowned selves.

In my case, since my primary selves are serious, responsible, and hardworking, some of my disowned energies are carefree, lighthearted, and playful. Since I'm such a "doer," a less developed energy in me is the ability to relax and just "be."

Our disowned selves are just as important to us as our primary selves. They represent our potential for expanding, developing, and expressing ourselves in new ways. They are not negative, though they may seem that way to us at first. They may have become distorted through being repressed for so long. So when we become aware of a disowned self within us, it may seem very negative or frightening at first. But as we get more in touch with it, allow it to express itself, and come to understand it, we see that at its root, it is a positive, natural quality that is necessary to our well-being and wholeness.

For example, if you are very identified with a primary self that is kind, considerate, and loving, you might very well discover that one of your disowned selves is just the opposite — selfish and seemingly uncaring of others. These qualities no doubt sound very negative to you, and you wonder, "Why would I want to develop and embrace that part of myself? I don't want to be selfish and thoughtless of others. In fact, I'd like to get rid of that part of me completely."

However, you can't get rid of any part of you. You can deny it and repress it, in which case it will eventually cause problems in your life. Or you can acknowledge and accept it as a natural, human part of you, in which case it is no longer such a big deal. And consider this: if your primary self is caring, considerate, and giving to others 90 percent of the time, you are probably giving far too much. This will eventually drain you so there is nothing left to give.

Giving too much is not really good for you or anyone else, because you are out of balance. Getting in touch with and owning the opposite quality of selfishness — i.e., being aware of your *own* needs and taking care of them — provides you with the balance that you need. By learning to take care of yourself better, you will actually have more to give to others.

Embracing your disowned selves does not mean becoming totally identified with them or displacing your primary selves. It means finding an appropriate balance between the two so that your life works better and you feel more integrated, more whole.

Another word for our disowned selves is our "shadow." A shadow self is simply any part of us that we have not recognized and accepted. Since that self is a part of us, it can't go away just because it has been rejected. So it follows us through life like our shadow, until we notice and acknowledge it.

For many of us, the aspects of ourselves that we are most likely to disown are the instinctual energies — those associated with our sexuality and the aggressive drives. One reason for this is that most of us learn very early that these drives are feared and distrusted by civilized society and often condemned by traditional religion. Since these energies are powerful expressions of the life force itself, when we disown them we end up repressing a great deal of our natural vitality. The repression of these forces — a key source of chronic stress — can eventually lead to emotional depression and physical illness. Embracing these energies does not mean we turn them loose to run rampant in our lives. It means finding a balance where we can acknowledge, appreciate, and enjoy our instinctual selves while maintaining our awareness of consideration for others, the need for boundaries, appropriateness of our behavior, and so on.

Our culture places such a high value on strength and self-sufficiency that many of us disown or deny any feelings of need we may have. It's hard for us to admit that we need or want help or support from anyone. Any feelings of need or dependency seem very shameful. Yet, without the ability to accept and acknowledge our feelings of need and vulnerability, and we can't reach out for help when appropriate, we can't receive love, we can't embrace our humanity. Instead, we develop primary selves that are supercompetent, independent, and distrustful of others. This predicament has been most typical of men in the traditional male role, but it has increasingly become a woman's problem as well.

At the opposite pole, some people become closely identified with need and vulnerability. If these qualities become a person's primary self, they lose all sense of strength and independence. This personality structure develops because the person discovers early in life that expressing power is dangerous or incurs criticism. It's safer or more comfortable to be vulnerable, dependent, passive. Without access to their power to assert themselves and take care of themselves, these highly dependent people can become victimized by others. Traditionally, this has been more common for women, but in these changing times many men find themselves with this problem, too.

How do we find balance and integration between our primary and our disowned selves? The first and most important step is to become aware of and identify our primary selves. The very act of noticing them as parts of us means that we have taken a step away from being so completely identified with them that we are literally swallowed up by them. While perhaps seeming subtle, this step is, in fact, extremely powerful. Remember that the major part of change comes from awareness — simply becoming conscious of the way things are.

As we become more aware of our primary selves we

begin to develop an "aware ego" — a conscious part of our personality — which knows all the various selves and helps to orchestrate balance and harmony. As our recognition of our primary selves increases, so also do the choices we have in our lives. For example, when I was able to see my hardworking, intellectual energies as primary selves, I also began to see that there were other possibilities. Life didn't have to be all hard work. The fact is that as long as I clung only to these qualities, acting as if they absolutely had to be followed at all times, other aspects of myself were neglected.

As we develop an aware ego that is able to observe the primary selves with more objectivity and detachment, we find ourselves becoming much more open to a wider and wider range of choices. As we separate from complete identification with our primary selves, our disowned energies begin to filter into the space that is created. They will do this gradually and naturally, so that we simply begin to feel more and more balanced. Once the aware ego has developed, our lives tend to be much more relaxed and open, and we become quite comfortable with those selves we previously denied or repressed.

This doesn't mean that we try to get rid of our primary selves. On the contrary, they are vital parts of us that we still need! They've helped us grow and survive and get this far in life. We want to keep them with us. The increased consciousness provided by our aware ego simply gives us a greater range of conscious choices about our lives. Instead of having my hardworking responsible self running 95 percent of my life, and making almost all my decisions for me, I prefer to have it as a trusted advisor. Then I may gradually begin choosing to work a little less hard and be a little less responsible, and allow my disowned energies of relaxation, carefreeness, and play come into my life, enriching it immensely.

In this process it is quite important to appreciate and acknowledge our primary selves for all that they have done to take care of us, and let them know we still want them. This may sound strange, but the subpersonalities are like real people who have the need to be loved, understood, appreciated, and included. They have a job to do and they don't want to be disregarded. If they feel that we are trying to get rid of them or undermine them, they will fight back hard, often in very devious ways, and sabotage our efforts to grow and change. Every part of us is important and needs to know it will have its rightful place in our psyche and our lives.*

Underneath the complex structure of our personality, with all its primary and disowned subpersonalities, there lies the energy of the original vulnerable child we once

---

* Readers may wonder how the concept of many selves relates to multiple personality disorder. To simplify, we all have many different selves or subpersonalities within us; if a person suffers severe abuse or trauma in early life, however, these energies may fragment into many different parts, with very little holding them together and little or no awareness of one another. Rather than having the various selves working together as a more or less integrated whole, as they do in most healthy personalities, the person with multiple personality disorder shifts from one self to another, as if that was his or her only self. Fortunately, many who suffer from multiple personality disorder are finding healing through therapy.

were. Although we may have lost conscious touch with the child, it never grows up or goes away. It remains a deep part of us throughout our lives. Essentially, our entire personality has developed in order to take care of the child, try to get its needs met, and protect it from harm. Paradoxically, the child usually gets buried beneath the multiple layers of our personality, forgotten at a conscious level. Unconsciously, however, most of the other selves are constantly attempting to take care of the child in various (often conflicting) ways.

As we gain awareness, we usually discover that many of the ways we've been trying to meet our inner child's needs are outdated, limited, or even self-destructive. For example, if we grew up in a dysfunctional family situation we may have developed a defensive posture to protect the child in us from getting hurt. We don't let anyone close to us emotionally. Later, we may become aware that this behavior is preventing us — and particularly our inner child — from getting the nurturing and love it wants or needs. As adults with aware egos, we can choose to change this pattern and allow certain people close to our inner child once again.

At this point, we have begun to take conscious charge of the process. But to do this we need to get acquainted with our inner child, find out how it feels and what it needs, and learn to consciously care for it in an effective way. In a sense we need to become aware, caring parents to our own child self.

Healing our relationship with our inner child is one of the most important and profound steps on our consciousness journey. Because the child is the deepest part of our personality, it is the key to our emotional well-being. Until we have conscious access to our sensitive, vulnerable child self, and are able to express its needs and feelings, we can't create and sustain true intimacy in our relationships. In addition to feeling deeply, the child is the part of us that knows how to play, have fun, and enjoy life. Without our playful child energy, life becomes too serious and drab.

Because the child is the first layer of personality, it is closely linked to our spiritual essence. Discovering and embracing our inner child opens the doorway to our soul. So our relationship with our inner child is the source of our creativity, natural wisdom, and our spiritual well-being.

Much of my understanding about the many selves within us, and the importance of developing the aware ego, has come from studying and working with Drs. Hal and Sidra Stone. Their understanding of the psychology of selves is quite profound, and the method they have created for getting to know and understand our many subpersonalities — Voice Dialogue — is one of the most powerful tools for consciousness that I have ever experienced. Their work relates to and draws from many other disciplines — Jungian analysis, Gestalt therapy, psychosynthesis, to name just a few. But it takes a few steps beyond anything else. I have found it extraordinarily helpful, both in my own personal healing process and in my work with others.

Hal and Sidra are wise and wonderful teachers who lead workshops and trainings all over the world. They are the authors of several excellent books and numerous tapes. (In the Recommended Resources section of this book, you'll find more information about their written and recorded material, as well as their workshops.)

Voice Dialogue is one very effective way of discovering and healing your inner child, and there are many other ways as well. There are numerous support groups and therapists specializing in helping people do their inner child work. Al-Anon has special groups for Adult Children of Alcoholics or other dysfunctional family situations, with special focus on learning to love and care for your inner child. The books, seminars, and television programs of John Bradshaw have helped millions of people understand the importance of doing their inner child work. There is an excellent book by Lucia Cappachione, Ph.D., *Recovery of Your Inner Child,* which shows you how to get in touch with and heal your inner child through writing with your non-dominant hand. Also my tape, *Meditations,* has a meditation called "Discovering Your Inner Child" that you may find helpful. All these items are listed more fully in the Recommended Resources section of this book.

Exercise
Getting Acquainted with Your Primary Selves

To get a sense of your primary selves, make a list of six to twelve of your strongest, and most obvious, personality characteristics. If you have difficulty identifying what these might be, think of how you present yourself to the world most of the time. Then jot down a list of those descriptive words. Try not to be judgmental or to evaluate your qualities in either a positive or negative way. Be as objective as possible.

Once you have made this list, take a look at it and see if it seems to describe your primary ways of operating in the world. These are some of your primary selves. As you become more aware of these, you might also become aware that your innermost feelings are not necessarily represented by these selves. For example, your primary selves might include ones that are aggressive, outgoing, and funny while deep inside you feel shy, sad, and very "guarded" or "private." These inner feelings are likely to be disowned selves.

How do your primary selves operate in your life? For instance, you might see that one of your primary selves is a "good mother" or "good father," and the way it operates in your life is that it is very aware and caring of the needs of others, but may not be in touch with the needs of your own inner child.

Now go through your list and, for every primary quality listed, see if you can think of an opposite quality. Make two columns on a piece of paper, listing your primary quality in the first column, the opposite of that quality in the second. If you think of more than one opposite quality for a single primary quality, write them both down. If you can't think of an opposite word, just leave it blank. Here's an example of one person's list:

Primary Qualities	Opposites
Introverted	Outgoing
Intellectual	Emotional; Physical
Shy	Bold
Kind	Selfish

Organized	Spontaneous
Humorous	Serious
Hardworking	Lazy; Relaxed
Creative	?

If you find you have many negative or judgmental words in your second column, see if you can think of a positive way of describing that same quality. For example, in the list above the person wrote two words opposite "hardworking;" the first was "lazy," which has negative connotations, the second was "relaxed," which has positive associations. If you can't think of a positive synonym for the second column, let it go for now.

Look at the second column of words and see if some of them might describe disowned or less-developed selves. Then, ask yourself how you might benefit by developing those opposite qualities.

You may find you already have sets of opposite words in your *primary qualities* column. This may mean that you have developed some opposite primary selves, who may be in conflict within you.

Most people find they are most balanced and most effective in their lives when they are able to draw from both sides of any pair of opposites. How can you learn to accept and find balance between both sides of you?

The most effective way that I know of is to do some work with a trained Voice Dialogue facilitator. There are many of them all over the world, and you can find out if there is one in your area by contacting Hal and Sidra Stone's office. Some Voice Dialogue facilitators even do sessions over the phone, so that is a possibility if there is no one in your area.

One simple technique that can help you begin to accept your inner contradictions and find balance is to come up with an *oxymoron* to describe two polarities within you. An oxymoron is a name that describes one person or thing that incorporates what may seem to be contradictory qualities, such as "the hermit-extrovert;" "the selfish saint;" and "the spontaneous organizer." Play around with this idea until you find the label that describes these contradictory qualities and it will help you to both understand your gifts and choose situations where those gifts are best applied.

For example, one person described himself as a "hermit-extrovert" because he was most effective when he could work alone but in a way that involved him with a large group of people. In his profession, he was a creative engineer who was part of a team developing new products. While the team came together to compare notes once a week, most of his actual work was done at his home office more than a hundred miles from the company's main offices.

As you become more aware of your inner contradictions and polarities, don't feel that you need to resolve them, fix them, or immediately find perfect balance and integration. Uncomfortable though it may be, the important thing is to become *conscious* of what's going on inside you without trying to *control* it. The important thing is to start becoming more aware of your different selves and see how they work in your life. More balance and integration will happen over time.

CHAPTER TWENTY-TWO

Our Relationships As Mirrors

If we learn to see our relationships as the wonderfully accurate mirrors they are, revealing to us where we need to go with our own inner process, we can see much about ourselves that we would otherwise have a great deal of difficulty learning.

One of the biggest differences between the path of the material world, the path of transcendence, and the path of transformation is in how we view our relationships.

On the material path we see relationships as an end in themselves. We form relationships of various kinds in order to satisfy our needs for love, companionship, security, stimulation, sexual fulfillment, financial stability, and so on. Our focus tends to be on the external form of the relationship and on what is being exchanged, be it friendship, work, affection, respect, money, or security. Because we view relationships primarily in the light of getting needs met, we tend to try to control them, to try to make them the way we want them. Consciously or unconsciously, we try to manipulate other people in order to get what we want from them. The control we assert limits how we experience our relationships.

On the path of transcendence, relationships are often viewed as impediments that keep us from evolving beyond the physical form. Because our relationships bring out all of our human feelings, needs, and emotional attachments, they are seen as distractions and thus detrimental to our spiritual journey. People who are seriously committed to the transcendent path try to stay as unattached as possible. Since sexuality is such a strong force physically and emotionally, involving our animal instincts and human feelings, it is often looked upon as the opposite of spirituality. Therefore, many devotees of the transcendent path either take a vow of celibacy and try to avoid sex altogether, or they try to transmute it into a "higher" energy, following sacred disciplines that keep the experience focused on its spiritual aspects.

On the path of transformation we embrace both our humanness and our spirituality. Instead of attempting to escape or ignore them, we honor our human needs for relationship, and we learn to be more conscious of how to communicate those needs and how to take good care of ourselves and each other in the process. We also recognize that we are spiritual beings, not limited to our human form and emotions, but connected to the unlimited oneness of the universe. Rather than denying our sexuality, we embrace it as one of the most important expressions of our life force.

On the path of transformation there is a further vital step we must take, one that allows us to have a different perspective on relationships than we would if we followed a material or spiritual path. On the transformational path we need to recognize that our relationships can be powerful mirrors, reflecting back to us what we need to learn. When we learn how to use these reflections, our relationships can become one of the most powerful avenues we have for becoming conscious.

Our primary relationship is really with ourselves. Each of us is involved in developing all aspects of our being and bringing them into relationship with one another — becoming whole. Our relationships with other people continually reflect exactly where we are in that process. For example, for many years I yearned to find the right man to be my life partner. I created many relationships with men who were unavailable or inappropriate in certain ways. Eventually, I realized they were reflecting my own inner ambivalence about committed relationship and the ways that I didn't truly love myself. It was only after I did some deep emotional healing work, learning to truly love and be committed to myself, that I met a wonderful man who is now my husband.

If we learn to see our relationships as the wonderfully accurate mirrors they are, revealing to us where we need to go with our own inner process, we can see much about ourselves that we would otherwise have a great deal of difficulty learning. Any and every relationship in our lives — with our friends, co-workers, neighbors, our children and other family members as well as our primary partners — can be a reflection to us in this way. Even an encounter with a stranger can sometimes be an important learning experience.

It's very difficult to look inside ourselves and see what's going on in there — particularly to see what we're unaware of. That's why it's important to look at our relationships as mirrors of our inner processes. Used in this way, relationships become one of the most valuable sources of healing and teaching in our lives. To understand how this works, we need to remind ourselves that we each, through our individual consciousness, create and shape how we experience external reality. This is as true in our relationships as in every other area of our lives — the relationships we create and shape reflect back to us what we are holding within our consciousnesses. We draw to us and are drawn to people who match and reflect some aspect of ourselves.

Generally, we find that the easiest people to get along with are those who reflect aspects of ourselves that we feel comfortable with and accept — reflections of our primary selves, or complementary energies that we appreciate. These are usually people who we consciously seek out or are drawn to in everyday friendship. If you are primarily a physically active person who loves sports, you may feel most comfortable with people who are similarly athletic. On the other hand, you may also enjoy a relationship with a friend who is somewhat more intellectual and less physical than you because it stretches your mind in a way that you accept and enjoy — it stimulates a less-developed aspect of you in a way that is comfortable and nonconfrontational. Your friend is reflecting your intellectual self, and you may be reflecting his or her physical or athletic self. In this case, you are both comfortable with the reflections you are receiving, so the relationship is a harmonious one.

The people in our lives who make us uncomfortable, who annoy us, who we feel judgmental or even combative toward, reflect parts of ourselves that we reject — usually aspects of our disowned selves, the shadow side of our personality. If you are a gentle, soft-spoken person, you may be very irritated by a person who seems loud and pushy. Or if you are a direct, outspoken person you may feel uncomfortable with those who hold back and seem overly timid. The fact is that in both cases you are mirroring each other's disowned energies. The quiet person is being shown their undeveloped assertive side, and the aggressive person is being shown their undeveloped reflective side.

Oftentimes we find ourselves attracted to our opposites — people who have developed opposite qualities from the ones we most identify with. In these relationships, we are unconsciously seeking to become whole, and drawn to people who express those energies that are undeveloped in our own personalities. On some level, we recognize that they have the potential to help us become more balanced.

People who express our opposite aspects can be our most powerful teachers if we allow them to be. But first we must acknowledge that they express what we need to develop in ourselves. Early in a relationship, we often sense that the other person is bringing us exactly what we need. It is, in fact, their differentness that is so attractive to us. However, unless we are able to acknowledge that this person is offering us a reflection of something we need to see in ourselves, the differentness that drew us to them can become a major source of conflict. After a while, we may begin to resent them for the ways they are different and begin trying to change them to be more like us!

Of course, it's important in any relationship to learn constructive ways to communicate honestly about our needs, our likes and dislikes, and so forth. However, along with letting the other person know our feelings, including ways we might wish they would change, we need to remind ourselves that we brought them into our lives to teach and inspire us to develop new aspects of ourselves. Our challenge, then, is to be open to discovering the parts of ourselves that they mirror for us, and to learn how we can express those parts of ourselves more in our own lives. For example, Joanne really loved the fact that her friend Tina was a free spirit who loved to "go with the flow." However, it began to annoy her that Tina was often late for appointments. She needed to communicate to Tina her desire not to be kept waiting. At the same time, she needed to keep in mind that Tina was in her life to help her get more in touch with her own spontaneity, and to remind her to enjoy the present moment more often.

One very common relationship problem is the conflict between order and spontaneity. Some years ago, this dynamic was the central dramatic premise for the very popular play, movie, and television series *The Odd Couple*. Almost any two people who live together get into this polarization — one of them is neat and one of them is messy. Their arguments focus on trying to get the other person to change. But seen from a transformational point of view, the real conflict is between the very structured, organized, linear side of ourselves and our more spontaneous, intuitive, and creative aspects. One person is playing out one side, while the other is playing out the other side.

You can have endless conflicts between you and this other person until you recognize that the person is mirroring your own inner conflict and is showing you what you want or need to develop in yourself. On the transformational path, you seek the balance between those two extremes by developing those "opposite" aspects in yourself so that you both become more whole. Interestingly enough, when you find more balance in yourself the other person will often shift into a more balanced place as well, even though he or she knows nothing about the process! This is because we are energetically linked and strongly affected by one another.

It is very common in a relationship for one person to want greater commitment, depth, and intimacy while the other wants more freedom, more time alone, more space. This outer conflict mirrors essential polarities within each of us. We all want closeness, intimacy, and commitment; at the same time, we fear loss of freedom and individuality. If you have this kind of conflict in a relationship, take a look at what it might represent about these polarities in yourself.

Another conflict that often comes up in close relationships is that one of the people takes a more rational approach to life and seems relatively detached or aloof emotionally; the other may be highly emotional.

So, for example, if a very rational man finds himself with a very emotional woman, the message being mirrored to him is that he can become more whole by developing his emotional side, by getting more in touch with his feelings.

And the message being mirrored to the woman is that she can become more whole by cultivating a more impersonal, detached, and rational energy that will give her life greater balance. If the two people don't begin to integrate their opposite energies — instead of trying to change each other — they will eventually polarize even further, the man becoming even more rational and the woman even more emotional.

Interestingly, as this occurs the "symptoms" of their need to develop the opposite side of themselves become more exaggerated and uncomfortable. In utter frustration, they may withdraw completely from each other and from others in their lives who reflect their opposite aspects. They can begin to heal their relationships and their lives when they see their conflicts as mirrors. Either person can begin to break the impasse by taking steps to recognize their primary selves and develop their opposite side.

Not long ago, I worked with a woman whose relationship with her husband clearly illustrated this point. He was trained as a computer engineer and spent most of his hours at work focused on very rational, linear, mental activities. She was a nursery school teacher, where she worked with the emotions of very young children all day. She described the early years of her marriage to him as "blissful." She had never felt more complete or whole. His cool, detached way of approaching problems gave her a sense of calmness and security that her life alone had lacked.

In time, however, she began to feel frustrated with the relationship. He retreated into his computer whenever she got emotional. She became nearly hysterical every time he tried to "explain away" what she was feeling. The chasm between them grew until she could barely stand to be in the same room with him. She accused him of being totally unable to deal with anything emotional; he accused her of being totally irrational, lacking any ability to "work things out."

Eventually, she began to learn to see his behavior as a mirror, reflecting back to her what she needed to develop in herself. Rather than seeing her husband as her enemy — which she acknowledged that she had begun to do — she began to view him as a teacher for her. In time, the tension between them eased, and the very same qualities that they had begun to hate in each other became valuable guides, pointing the way not only to a more harmonious relationship but to a greater sense of balance within themselves.

It can be difficult for us to recognize or accept that people we have problems with are actually mirroring for us the disowned parts of ourselves. One simple way to tell if you are doing this is to check in with your feelings; if you are feeling very judgmental toward that person, the chances are very good that they are mirroring your shadow side. Underneath, you may be jealous. Perhaps this person is expressing a kind of energy that you hold back or don't allow yourself to express.

It's important to remember that mirroring in the way I'm describing is very different than making the other person a "role model." A role model is a person we admire and want to emulate. But in mirroring, our own self-discovery and self-development are the goals; we're not trying to be like another person. The goal is to become more ourselves. The fact is that the person mirroring our own needs may be even more out of balance than we are. They certainly don't have to be people we look up to, as we might do with a role model. We don't have to become like they are, or go to an extreme opposite from the way we've been. However, we may need to allow ourselves to develop a little more of that energy that we are seeing reflected back to us.

If you are a quiet, reserved, perhaps overly modest and self-effacing person, for example, you might feel judgmental toward someone who always seems to seize the center of attention. They may be mirroring that part of you that would like to receive more attention but is afraid to. It's not necessary to emulate this person, for they may very well be out of balance in the opposite direction from you. Instead, allow that person to be a catalyst for your growth process. Try to see the *essence* of the quality that this person reflects to you — in this case, the desire for love and attention — and begin to investigate how you can nurture and express that part of yourself *in your own way.*

We avoid the things that we're afraid of because we think there will be dire consequences if we confront them. But the truly dire consequences in our lives come from avoiding things that we need to learn about or discover. We must instead learn to be more open and accepting of the things we're afraid of, whether it's exploring our emotions, or learning to balance our checkbook! Acceptance is simply a willingness to look at, confront, and understand something instead of pushing it away.

Acceptance doesn't mean that we have to allow things into our lives that aren't good for us. Obviously, we wouldn't go out and commit a crime because we believed there was something to be gained by learning to confront fears we have about such behavior. We don't become whole unless we recognize the need to set boundaries and be able to discriminate between what's right and not right for us.

Being willing to learn from our relationships does not mean that we should stay in situations that are not good for us. If a relationship is physically or emotionally abusive, what we have to learn from it is how to set boundaries and protect ourselves. This could mean going into couples counseling to seek real and lasting resolutions. Or it could mean leaving the relationship if that is the only way we can effectively take care of ourselves.

People can criticize or abuse us only to the degree that we accept or allow it. First we must take steps externally to take care of ourselves. Then we must look inside to heal the way that we criticize or abuse ourselves; out of the knowledge we gain in this way we can learn to love and support ourselves instead.

A woman I know was raised by an emotionally and physically abusive father. She developed an internal "abusive father" energy that told her constantly how worthless and undeserving she was. She married a man who mirrored her pattern of internal self-abuse, constantly criticizing and belittling her and occasionally hitting her. She tolerated the situation for years because to her it all seemed normal;

she believed, at least on some level, she deserved the abuse. Once she began therapy, she was able to recognize that her husband was reflecting her deepest beliefs about herself. She gradually developed an ability to stand up for herself and eventually she left the relationship. After going through a deep emotional healing process, she eventually remarried, this time to a man who was kind and supportive, reflecting the way she had learned to treat herself.

For many of us, our relationships have been such a painful struggle that it's difficult to believe we could get to a place in our lives when our relationships are primarily supportive and satisfying. Yet, if we are willing to do our deep emotional work, our relationships can mirror every step of progress that we make in our relationships with ourselves. As we become more integrated our relationships become more supportive and loving — a reflection of our aliveness, self-love, and self-expression.

The art and science of using our relationships as reflections of our consciousness process is fascinating and complex. In this chapter I have merely touched upon some of the basic ideas. In fact, I am planning to write a book on this topic. Meanwhile, I highly recommend the books *Partnering: A New Kind of Relationship* and *Embracing Each Other: Relationship as Teacher, Healer, and Guide* by Drs. Hal and Sidra Stone, as well as their tapes, *The Dance of Selves in Relationship* and *Understanding Your Relationships*. I also found the book *Getting the Love You Want* by Dr. Harville Hendrix interesting and helpful. These books and tapes are listed in the Recommended Resources section.

Exercise
Using the Mirror of Relationship

Difficulties we are having in our relationships often mirror parts of ourselves that we need to heal. Such difficulties may involve a family member, a close friend, a co-worker, or even people with whom we have only a brief encounter, such as a clerk in a store.

If you are having difficulty with a present relationship, or if you frequently encounter certain kinds of difficult people — for example, a needy person or a person who doesn't respect your boundaries — take a moment to look closely at what they are reflecting.

Begin by closing your eyes and relaxing for a few moments. Then bring to mind a difficult relationship. Think about what, exactly, bothers you about this person. What quality or trait does this person have that makes you uncomfortable or that you judge?

Once you have identified the quality or qualities that bother you, ask yourself what the positive aspect or essence of that quality might be. For example, if you see them as lazy, what could be the positive aspect of laziness? It could be the ability to relax.

Ask yourself how it might benefit you to develop a bit more of that quality in yourself. Could it help you find more balance in your life? If you are judging someone as lazy, for example, chances are you are a very active, driven type of person who could benefit from developing a greater ability to relax. This person is a mirror, reflecting the disowned quality of relaxation to you, so that you can become more aware of what you need to develop.

Here are some other examples: If you find someone too needy, they may be reflecting the disowned part of you that has emotional needs. You may be too identified with strength and self-sufficiency and need to get more in touch with your vulnerability. If you find someone too domineering, perhaps you are overly timid and need to develop more assertiveness. If you judge someone as selfish, it's possible that you are too giving.

Remember that you don't need to become like this person. They may be too far to the extreme or expressing themselves in a distorted way. However, you can use the discomfort of this relationship to help you discover the essential qualities you need to develop in order to feel more whole and fulfilled.

Once you have identified what quality this person is reflecting to you, imagine yourself having integrated more of that quality in yourself. Imagine yourself more able to relax, for example, or more able to show your vulnerability in close relationships, or more assertive, or more able to receive.

CHAPTER TWENTY-THREE

The World As Our Mirror

*If we have the courage to look at the social and
political forces in the world as reflections
of the forces at work within each of us,
we can more effectively take responsibility
not only for our own personal healing,
but for the healing of our planet.*

On the path of transformation we are concerned with not only our own personal process of healing and integration, but with the healing process going on in our world. We recognize the interrelationship between our individual consciousness journey and the evolution of the consciousness of humanity.

Just as the imbalances in our individual consciousness are reflected in our personal relationships and in the daily events of our lives, so the imbalances in the collective consciousness are reflected in our communities, our nation, our relationships with other countries, and our relationships to the Earth. Since we are each a participant in the mass consciousness, influencing it and being influenced by it, the world itself becomes a mirror that helps us see ourselves more clearly and understand ourselves more deeply. If we have the courage to look at the social and political forces in the world as reflections of the forces at work within each of us, we can more effectively take responsibility not only for our own personal healing, but for the healing of our planet.

Again, I want to remind you that taking responsibility for our part in the creation of our world does not mean taking or assigning blame. Obviously, no single one of us, as an individual, is to blame for the problems that exist in the world. Nor are we to blame for our own personal circumstances or difficulties. Rather, as spiritual beings, we have each chosen to play an important part in the fascinating, unfolding process of evolution that is taking place on this planet. We are doing this for our own learning and empowerment, and we each have special gifts that are needed in this world.

As we discussed in the last few chapters, we have many different aspects within us, and we are all in the process of bringing those energies into balance and integration in our bodies, our personalities, and our lives. As we have seen, our inner conflicts are frequently reflected in the conflicts we experience in our personal relationships. We literally project our unconscious inner conflicts into our external environment. When they are mirrored back to us in difficulties with other people, or difficulties accomplishing some of the things we want in our lives, we thereby create the possibility for becoming more aware of these inner conflicts and healing them. The people we are in conflict with are usually mirroring some parts of ourselves that we are uncomfortable with, or have not yet resolved.

A client of mine, for example, had a long history of negative encounters with authority figures, including the police and the legal system. Through our work together, he recognized that he had rejected and disowned the structured, authoritarian part of himself because of a negative, conflicted relationship he had with his father, who strongly identified with these energies. And so he continued to attract to himself people and situations that forced him to confront the aspects of himself that he had avoided or tried to get rid of — his authoritarian shadow side. It's interesting to note, of course, that his father had also created, in his son, an excellent mirror for him to see his own reflection, for his son was literally a reflection of his own shadow, those energies of the older man that wanted to rebel against all rules and structure! Once the son was able to recognize the value in having a certain amount of "law and order" in life, and could embrace the structured, authoritarian aspects of himself, he began to feel more understanding toward his father and developed better communication and more closeness with him before the older man died.

Just as the dramas of our personal relationships have their roots in our individual psyches, so the social and political events in our world are rooted in the spiritual and psychological workings of the mass consciousness in which each of us is a participant. Community, national, and international conflict is a mass projection of individual internal conflicts, and of the internal conflicts within the societies involved. These inner conflicts are projected onto other people, other races, other cultures, other religions, and then externalized in the form of disputes, wars, revolutions, riots, and other efforts to weaken or annihilate whoever or whatever mirrors our disowned energies.

Just as we each have an individual shadow, groups have a collective shadow consisting of those qualities and energies they have collectively denied or repressed. We can see that collective shadow in operation whenever a group or nation projects its disowned energies onto another race, ethnic group, or country, transforming it into a feared and dreaded enemy. If you don't have an enemy, you don't have anyone on which to project your shadow, and thus are forced to face yourself. It can be painful and difficult to look at ourselves. It always seems much easier to create a racial conflict or a war — at least, world events would suggest that this way of dealing with our shadows seems to be a more automatic response for most of us.

If we look at the opposing sides of social and political conflicts, we can often see what each group is trying to disown in itself. We see how those disowned parts are reflected by the other parties involved. In a traditional patriarchal society, for example, the masculine principle of rationality and order is celebrated while the intuitive, feeling, feminine principle is suppressed. This is reflected in the fact that men play a more dominant role, at least appearing to hold the power, while women are more subservient, oppressed, or disempowered. This is an external reflection of what's happening internally in each person — the masculine aspect within men is controlling and suppressing the feminine within them, often because it is a "mystery" that they fear and distrust.

Meanwhile, the women have an internalized, patriarchal, masculine energy within them that suppresses their feminine power and devalues them because they are women.* In a strongly patriarchal society, most participants, both men and women, are consciously or unconsciously supporting that process.

As we — both men and women — have begun to bring our masculine and feminine energies into balance, integrating them internally, the external roles of men and women have been changing accordingly. As the external roles become more balanced, they support further internal balance. The internal and external processes reflect and support each other. However, as we move out of the old patriarchal mentality and women begin to reclaim their own power, there is an initial tendency for many women to project their suppressed or denied, internal, dominating, patriarchal energy onto men in general and blame them for the women's oppression. And many men deal with their fear of their own feminine energy by attempting to control women and keep them in subservient roles. As the process is evolving, however, more members of both sexes are gaining the ability to take responsibility for their own part in the process.

Some years ago, Sam Keen published a fascinating book that he called *Faces of the Enemy*. It was a collection of

---

* Dr. Sidra Stone has written a fascinating book on this topic, *The Shadow King: The Invisible Force that Holds Women Back*. See Recommended Resources.

war posters and political cartoons, depicting the *faces of the enemy* in highly stylized, distorted forms. Keen showed how during a war or revolution the enemy is portrayed as a stereotype that shows very little variation and has very little to do with the actual characteristics of the society involved. In the cartoons and posters, every member of a whole society was depicted as being alike. Usually, the impression given was that the entire race or culture was subhuman and capable of the most inhuman acts.*

This is not to say that the qualities we dislike in ourselves don't also actually exist in people who are acting out those qualities in the external world. Most often they do. However, the point is that until we learn to take responsibility for our own shadows, we will continue to project our denied aspects outside us — a process that actually empowers those people and forces that mirror them.

Sometimes an internal human conflict is played out in a particularly dramatic, intense, and often tragic way on the world stage. While such events can be extraordinarily painful, destructive, and horrifying, they can also be transformational, created on some level by the mass consciousness in order to wake ourselves up. The most extreme example of this in recent history — so gruesome that one hesitates to even try to discuss it in these terms — was the Holocaust. Hitler and the Nazis demonstrated the incredible extreme of the human tendency to blame, scapegoat, and victimize other people. In allowing this to

---

* From the book by Sam Keen, *Faces of the Enemy*, published by Harper and Row, New York, 1986.

take place, the German people, as well as those of us across the ocean who put off even denouncing Hitler's actions, acted out the tendency we all have to deny unpleasant realities and follow along with authority figures rather than risk a confrontation by speaking out or acting upon our own inner truth. And those who were persecuted revealed to all of us the ultimate horror that can be experienced through identifying with the victim aspect of our consciousness.

Of course, there is much more to it than we have the space to develop here, but it is also important to begin taking a look at all such human carnage as something that arises out of unhealed aspects of our collective consciousness. From a human perspective, all such events are numbingly horrifying and make absolutely no sense at all. From a larger perspective, however, it's perhaps possible to see them as a way that the collective consciousness dramatically acts out unconscious forces so that we can recognize, claim, and heal them. The impact of these experiences is so intense that the mass consciousness has to make a leap forward in its evolution. Of course, it takes time for these lessons to penetrate the consciousness of all cultures and individuals; hence we are still seeing plenty of terrible conflicts, many of them all too similar to the Holocaust, such as the so-called "ethnic cleansing" going on in many countries.

A very interesting example of internal polarities being played out on the world stage was the confrontation in the early 1990s between the United States, headed by George Bush, and Iraq, headed by Saddam Hussein. The United

States has become identified, at least in the minds of most Americans and our allies, with being the "good guys" — the ones who use our tremendous power in the world for good, justice, and peace. George Bush, very much identified with the good guy stance, represented "might for right" leadership.

The shadow side of the U.S., as mirrored in Saddam Hussein, has as its source the many political and economic forces and individuals within this country that are motivated by *anything but* goodness, justice, and truth, but rather by fear, greed, and lust for power. Saddam Hussein is the perfect representative of this shadow side of ourselves. He unabashedly represented pure, self-serving aggression and the philosophy of "might makes right." Given the energies involved, perhaps we had to go to war with him. But in doing so, did we fail to recognize and own the reflection of our shadow?

One of the clearest and most obvious examples of how we project our disowned energies onto another group of people, and then attempt to suppress those energies by oppressing the people who represent them to us, is in racial conflicts. It's interesting that throughout the world, people with lighter skin color tend to oppress darker-skinned people — those who literally represent their shadow side. Darker-skinned people, at least on some level, have apparently, down through history, bought into the belief system that they are somehow inferior; thus, their light-skinned external oppressors eventually come to represent, within their unconscious minds, "proof" that supports their own internalized oppressive belief structure. When they begin to rebel and fight back against the external power structure, they simultaneously (consciously or unconsciously) confront and fight their internal self-doubt and self-hatred, reclaiming their own power and self-respect. One example of this was reflected in the slogan "Black is beautiful," which grew out of the victories of the Civil Rights movement of the 1960s and 1970s, and in its own way reflected a healing within the oppressed.

As I mentioned earlier in this book (see page 36), Deena Metzger gives a fascinating example of how she recognized the "political process" within her own psyche. This is excerpted from her excellent article, "Personal Disarmament: Negotiation with the Inner Government":*

In a small, segregated country, called Zebra, the Sun minority has relegated the Shade majority to reservations far from the cities and the centers of power. Some Shades work for the Suns or are exhibited in the lavish national parks developed for the enjoyment of foreigners. The government is a theocracy, with a dictator who has allegiance to the oligarchy and priests.

The dictator, as well as the rest of the Sun minority, knows nothing of the culture, mores, values, or spiritual inclinations of the Shades; nevertheless, fear and control of the Shades is behind every governmental decision. It is fully believed that if the Shades came near prominence or power, the entire way of being of the country would be altered. The minority does not fear for its lives; it

---

* Published in *Revision*, vol. 12, no. 4.

fears for its way of life. To change this would be worse than death.

One day there is a serious power outage. The power lines have been cut. Up to this point, energy has been the major export of this country. The country is paralyzed. The Shades do not deny they cut the lines but assert that the power has always belonged to them....

Deena goes on to explain:

This scenario could describe conditions in any one of numerous countries. In fact, it is a description of my own inner state of being, a political description of the nation-state of my own psyche. I have come to understand that an individual is also a country, that one contains multiple selves who are governed as nations are governed, and that the problems and issues that afflict nations also afflict individuals. For most of my life, I have been completely unconscious of the real mode of government and the status of the beings within my territory....

Therefore, albeit unwillingly, slowly, and painstakingly, I began to dismantle the minority supremacist government. I did this although the Suns insisted this meant the end of progress and growth, that it meant disaster.... I came to understand that the system of government that controlled me internally was similar to the systems of government in the world.... It was heartbreaking to realize that all the work I'd done in the world was undermined by the constant seepage of contrary values from my inner being. I could not be a democrat in the world or promote democracy while I was a tyrant within.... I couldn't hope to accomplish change in the outside world until I changed the inner one....

When I lectured on Personal Disarmament at the Peace Tent at the Non-Governmental Organizations, United Nations Conference on Women in Nairobi in July 1985, I asked an audience of African, American, and European women who it was that ruled their inner countries.

The majority painfully acknowledged that they were ruled by tyrants. They agreed that nothing could change in the world until they also altered their inner conditions.... It wasn't that we thought we needed to stop efforts in the public world, but that there was other urgent work, on the inner plane, which had to be pursued simultaneously.

Important strides can be made through social, political, legal, and other types of external action toward dealing with the problems of racism, sexism, religious bigotry, poverty, violence, and all the other ills that plague humanity. However, I don't believe that for any of these problems we can find broad, lasting solutions, reaching the deepest levels of our being, until we as individuals are able to confront, acknowledge, and heal these ills at their source — within our own psyches. It is here that we will find the roots of our own racism, sexism, homophobia, prejudice, blame, fear, greed, inner poverty, and hunger for satisfaction. If we truly want to stop tyrannizing others, or being victims of others, we must learn how to confront and heal the inner forces that cause us to tyrannize and victimize ourselves. We must learn to love, respect, and honor all aspects of ourselves. By building a foundation of self-love and self-respect, and by integrating all aspects of ourselves, we can at last honestly respect, forgive, and have compassion for all our fellow beings. It is here that we find the key to transform the quality of life on our planet.

One of the most serious reflections that we all need to take in and deal with is the way we human beings are exploiting and polluting our natural environment and the Earth we live on. To me, this seems to mirror our deep disconnection from our spiritual essence and the resulting loss of awareness of our relationship to the whole of existence. Our insensitivity and mistreatment of the natural world all around us reflects our denial of our inner nature. Our amazing disregard for the long-term results of our actions mirrors how out of touch we are with the rhythms and cycles of life.

As we do our inner healing work and reclaim our natural feelings and energies, we automatically become more aware and sensitive to the energies of the world around us. Through reconnecting with and honoring our spiritual being, we recognize the spirit in everyone and everything. We learn to live in attunement with that spirit, in harmony and in balance with the Earth.

Exercise

Reading the Reflections in Your Mirror

Think of a problem or an issue in your community (or country or world) that particularly concerns you. Ask yourself if there is any way it might reflect or relate to an issue or process within you. Imagine that all the players in the drama represent parts of yourself. What would need to happen for the issue to be resolved or healed?

Here are some examples:

One man was concerned about crowded and inhuman conditions in prisons and the fact that prisoners are locked up and punished rather than being rehabilitated. He asked what part of himself was feeling imprisoned, what parts of him were jailers, and what part represented the society that condemned the imprisoned part. And then he asked himself how he might go about rehabilitating his own "inner prisoner."

One woman was especially worried about poverty and homelessness. She asked if there was a part of herself that felt homeless and impoverished. And she then asked how she could provide that part of herself with what she needed.

Another man was upset by the fact that the industrialized nations are using most of the world's resources, while the underdeveloped nations live in poverty. He asked what were the developed aspects of himself that were using most of his available resources, while other aspects languished? And he then asked how he could bring them into balance.

A woman found that she was angry at the fact that criminals often go unpunished while their victims suffered. She asked who, within herself, was "getting away with murder" while another part felt like a victim? And what would she need to do to stop the inner murdering and release herself from being a victim?

Most of us feel concerned about almost all of these problems. Whatever we feel *most* "emotionally charged" about in the external world, however, is usually most closely related to our personal issues.

In doing this exercise, please keep in mind that finding a correlation or synchronicity between your personal issues and world issues is *not* to imply that we are to blame for those issues. However, as we heal our personal conflicts we do contribute to healing world problems.

If you do not find any relationships between world problems and your own, or you feel confused about this exercise, simply let it go. Keep open to the possibility of an insight about it arising some time in the future.

CHAPTER TWENTY-FOUR

Consciousness and Spirituality

*Unconditional love is something that arises
naturally when we can accept all our feelings
and love all parts of us, including the parts
that aren't unconditionally loving.*

*I*t has been tremendously helpful for me to understand the difference between consciousness and spirituality. Spirituality is one type of energy — the energy that
links us to our deepest essential nature and to the universal source. Consciousness is the awareness of all of the
energies within us. Thus, it is quite possible to follow a
spiritual path that is not necessarily a consciousness path.
That is, we can work on developing the spiritual dimension of our being, without necessarily developing the other
aspects. We can become spiritually developed and totally
identified with our "spiritual self." In this case, we usually
disown many other energies, especially the physical and
emotional ones. That's why we see so many people who are
highly attuned spiritually, but may be completely out of
balance in their physical and emotional lives.

Consciousness, on the other hand, involves developing and integrating all the many aspects of our being, including but not limited to the spiritual. The path of transcendence is a spiritual path, while the path of transformation is a consciousness path. Contacting and developing our spiritual nature is an important part of the consciousness journey, but there are many other important parts as well. The path of transformation involves a powerful commitment to every level of growth.

One of my concerns about the New Age movement is its focus on transcendence rather than transformation. Many are hoping that by developing spiritually they can rise above their problems and not have to face the challenge of integrating their spiritual and human natures. They feel comfortable and safe exploring the spiritual and mental realms, but hope to avoid the more painful or difficult emotional healing work. Of course, it is a perfectly legitimate option to choose a transcendent path, but it will not bring about profound healing and wholeness for the individual or for the world. And ironically, the peace of mind that so many people seek on the transcendent path cannot be fully achieved by focusing exclusively on that reality.

Fortunately, in recent decades, the human potential movement has been integrating a variety of therapies, physical systems, and spiritual practices. At human potential centers such as Esalen Institute in California and The Open Center in New York City, for example, it is not unusual to find classes being offered that include bodywork, meditation, yoga, intuition training, movement

classes, recovery groups, and psychotherapeutic techniques. And the recovery movement, spearheaded by
Alcoholics Anonymous, is having a powerful impact on the
consciousness of the world today, applying the twelve-step
processes for profound healing in a variety of life issues
that range from early abandonment to drug addiction.

What stops people from embarking on the transformational path? For many, it is simply a lack of knowledge.
They aren't aware that such an opportunity exists, or perhaps they aren't sure how to go about finding it. Hopefully
this book can provide a kind of trail map for this journey.

But lack of knowledge is not the only roadblock on the
consciousness path. Another one is fear. We all fear the
unknown, of course, and this particular journey certainly is
unpredictable in many ways. That's why it is so important
to cultivate a personal relationship with our inner guidance. Unless we feel some sense of a higher force working
with us, it is simply too frightening to leave our familiar territory.

Many people are afraid of emotional healing work.
There are so many misunderstandings and stereotypes
about psychotherapy — and, unfortunately, there are also
many less than adequate and even harmful therapists and
healers, and many people who have had negative, disap-
pointing, or downright traumatic experiences with them.
So it is extremely important to choose your helpers wisely
and carefully.

I have found that most people are afraid that if they
begin exploring deep feelings, they will get stuck there and
never emerge. When feelings have been repressed and

disowned, they feel very intense and powerful, and it is easy to feel that they might overwhelm us forever if we ever gave them the opportunity.

The facts are quite different, however. If we move into our healing process at our own pace, without pushing ourselves, and with the right support, it is not nearly as difficult as we might fear. Each of us has an internal mechanism that guides the pace of our journey. Once we allow ourselves to experience an emotion freely, we discover that rather than washing us away, the wave of feeling gradually subsides and leaves us with a deep sense of wonderful peace.

In my own healing process, as well as with thousands of others I have participated in and guided over the last twenty years, I can say wholeheartedly that deep healing is possible and is within the reach of anyone willing to make the commitment and follow through on it.

In New Age circles there is much talk about unconditional love. Many teachers urge their followers to practice forgiveness, be nonjudgmental, and love fully without conditions, and many sincere seekers are earnestly trying to follow these teachings. There is a problem with the way these ideas are often presented, however. Of course, judgments are unpleasant, separating, and uncomfortable for all concerned. Forgiveness is a powerful and healing force for both the giver and the recipient. And there's nothing more blissful than giving and/or receiving unconditional love. There is a lot of confusion and misunderstanding about these processes, however, and much of what is being taught is coming from the transcendent rather than the transformative approach.

Again, we must recognize the difference between our spiritual essence and our human personality. As spiritual beings, we are always at one with universal love, which is always unconditional and nonjudgmental. The personality, however, has the goal of learning to live in the physical world and getting our emotional needs met. On the personality level, we are fundamentally concerned with protecting and caring for the vulnerable child within us; our feelings of love are entwined with our needs for safety, trust, and intimacy. We have powerful defense mechanisms in our personalities that can close off our feelings of love when we don't feel safe.

Rather than denying or trying to suppress these feelings and reactions, we need to respect and appreciate the function of our human personality. It is not by nature unconditionally loving. Much healing can take place when we recognize this as a given and are able to honor both our spiritual and our human nature.

When we feel judgmental, rather than denying those feelings, we need to look deeply into them to discover what is triggering them. Usually, we feel judgmental when we are frustrated because we have not followed our own truth in some way, or because we are having to confront another person who is reflecting one of our disowned selves back to us. So, instead of simply blocking ourselves from experiencing our judgmental feelings, we need to realize that our judgments can provide us with clues for the things we need to look at in ourselves. Ultimately, our judgments are healing gifts. If we try to suppress or ignore the feelings, we miss the opportunity for learning and consciousness. Condemning ourselves for being judgmental is simply judging ourselves for being judgmental!

As for forgiveness, many people try to forgive too soon, in order to avoid feeling emotions they are afraid of. When we have been emotionally wounded, we may have many feelings, including hurt, fear, grief, withdrawal, anger, rage, and even the desire for revenge. If we can allow ourselves to acknowledge and freely experience all these emotions as they arise, without trying to "fix" or change anything, we will eventually arrive naturally at a feeling of forgiveness.

Forgiveness occurs when we have completed the learning process of a particular experience and are ready to release it and move on. If we rush to forgive before we are actually ready, we may short-circuit our own learning process, repress our other feelings, and miss an opportunity for greater healing. There is definitely an important place and time for rituals of forgiveness, but only when we know we aren't using forgiveness as a way to avoid other parts of the process.

The key to unconditional love is found in the love our spirit has for our personality. When we can tap into spirit, we can unconditionally love ourselves — including the parts of us that are angry, judgmental, needy, and selfish. Then we naturally feel compassion and acceptance toward others as well. We recognize in them the same human attributes that we have learned to accept in ourselves. By loving and honoring our own personality in this way, we gain clear vision about other people's development on the personality level. We can maintain appropriate boundaries, making wise choices about whom it's appropriate to get close to. At the same time, through our connection with our divine essence, we naturally recognize and acknowledge the spiritual being in everyone else, even those with whom we know we must maintain some distance.

In recent years, with the recovery movement, many people have learned how to be loving even as they are setting boundaries and distancing themselves from loved ones who are having problems with addictive behavior. For example, they often have to learn that the most loving and compassionate act can be to confront the addictive person with the raw truth about how they are hurting other people. People who actually get through the recovery process often attribute the beginning of their healing to having a loved one confront them in this way and insist that they get into a treatment program or support group.

Hal Bennett recently shared a story with me that perhaps helps to illustrate this point further. When he first graduated from college he got a job teaching a group of children with serious behavioral problems. After the first week of working with them, he was about to resign. He told his supervisor that the children were too violent with him and with each other. Indeed, each week there were runs to the emergency room to repair everything from bloody noses to broken arms. Hal's head teacher asked him to give it two more weeks, and to keep two things in mind: First, that he could not succeed with these children until he learned how to love them, and second, that he would never learn to love them until he had accepted the fact that virtually any one of them was capable of stabbing him in the back if he didn't watch himself.

In the beginning this seemed like an impossible contradiction. But after two weeks he had begun to see the wisdom in what his supervisor had said. Prior to their conversation, his judgments had rightly identified the children's behavior as violent and potentially dangerous to him and others. But there was a part of this labeling process that also created a substantial wall between himself and the kids. In his mind, he had rejected them because of their behavior, telling himself that they were unworthy of his or anyone else's attention.

When he began to understand what his supervisor had told him, he accepted the fact that the children were violent in their behavior, but he stopped seeing that behavior as a reason for rejecting them. He began to see beyond their outward actions, to see that within each of them was still a very tender, loving spirit. In order to get to that spirit, he had to find ways to deal with their violence — not to deny it, but to help them learn how to relate to each other in more appropriate ways.

Learning to transform the violent behavior, which came from a very deep place of hurt and deprivation, required him to look at his own angry and violent feelings and begin healing them, too. He and the four other teachers assigned to these children worked together both to confront their own feelings and to seek more effective ways of creating a healing environment. Hal ended up staying at

this school for another three years, and as part of a very dedicated teaching team, helped to transform the lives of nearly thirty children.

Remember that it doesn't really work to *try* to feel love, or any other feeling. Our feelings are not controlled by our will, and most attempts to assert this kind of power over them leads to denial, repression, and disowning parts of ourselves, or to an expression of feeling that is not authentic. By acknowledging and honoring any feeling — no matter how "unacceptable" we might have previously judged it to be — we create space for its opposite. So *trying* to love unconditionally is a contradiction. Unconditional love is something that arises naturally when we can accept all our feelings and love all parts of us, including the parts that aren't unconditionally loving.

Meditation
Accepting Ourselves and Others

Get in a comfortable position, lying down or sitting up with your back straight and supported. Take a few slow, deep breaths and let your body and mind relax into a quiet state of being.

Ask to be in touch with the part of you that is judgmental. Ask it who or what it feels judgmental about and why. Ask how this judgment reflects on any parts of yourself that you don't accept.

Now ask to be in touch with the spiritual aspect of your being that is unconditionally loving. Ask that loving part of

you if it can teach you how to accept all aspects of yourself, including your judgmental self and the parts of you that it rejects. Imagine a beautiful pink light of love and acceptance all around you. Now imagine looking at others with the compassion that you are gaining through accepting yourself.

CHAPTER TWENTY-FIVE

Making a Difference
in the World

As we clear out our spiritual, mental, emotional, and physical blocks and limitations, the creative life force can move through us more fully and freely. This life energy naturally moves us to take action that is in harmony with our being, in alignment with our higher purpose, and necessary and effective in the world.

*I*n my early youth, I was intensely involved in political and social causes. I was raised in a politically active, liberal family, and I was encouraged to express my views and take action supporting the principles I believed in. I wrote letters to the editor of the newspaper; I wrote to my elected representatives (although I was too young to vote); I volunteered in the local Head Start program, and took part in many demonstrations. My first month in college I was jailed overnight for protesting the Vietnam War. I believed that I could make a difference, and I was determined to do everything I could to make this world a better place.

Gradually a certain disillusionment crept in and took over my experience. Politically, events were not encouraging.

The Kennedy and King assassinations, the defeat of candidates and causes I believed in, the Vietnam War dragging on...all these were very disheartening to me. When Nixon was elected President, I gave up. Ironically, by the time I was old enough to vote, I didn't bother.

Much more profound than my political discouragement was the fact that I was going through a deep existential crisis, questioning the very meaning and purpose of my life. I felt vaguely empty, alone, dissatisfied; I wondered who I was and why I existed. My search for meaning and fulfillment opened me to the beginning of my consciousness journey.

For many years my focus was primarily inward, seeking to know and understand myself and the essential nature of life. Intuitively, I sensed that real changes and true satisfaction in life could only be found by addressing these core issues. I worked hard to know and develop myself on all levels — spiritual, mental, emotional, and physical. I went through a profound healing process that was sometimes painful and difficult, as well as fascinating and exciting. From the beginning, as I discovered helpful ideas and tools, and gradually gained wisdom, I found myself sharing what I was learning with others through counseling, leading workshops, and writing books.*

During all this time, I had very little interest in the external reality of the world. I seldom read newspapers or watched television, so I knew little about current events. I wasn't trying to avoid these things. I just didn't feel much

---

* If you are interested in knowing more specifically about my life, I have shared my personal story in *Return to the Garden*.

connection with them. Although I knew I was part of the mass consciousness that created this world, I was more strongly focused on a different reality. It felt like I, and others who were on a consciousness path, were in the process of building a whole new world *inside ourselves.* I was completely absorbed in the task of transforming my own awareness and creating a new reality, so I had very little energy for the old world around me.

My process, I believe, is quite typical of a great many people of my generation. It is a process that has been greatly misunderstood and misinterpreted, especially by the media. I have read many newspaper and magazine articles lamenting the passing of the idealism and activism of the 1960s and early '70s. If one were to believe these articles, that idealism and activism have all evaporated into nothingness. No doubt some people did abandon their beliefs, but for many of us, the process of radical change deepened. It did not fade at all but became more internal, more quiet and personal.

It has also been very fashionable in the popular media, and even in the politically oriented alternative media, to criticize any type of personal growth activities as "narcissistic and self-indulgent." While such criticism may be valid for certain individuals, it completely misses the mark in terms of what most of us on a consciousness journey have been doing. Rather than avoiding the external world, we have been laying the inner groundwork for outer change.

Here is my general view of the evolution of consciousness in the twentieth century:

In the first half of the century, most of the world was

consumed by intense cataclysmic events — two world wars, a major economic depression, and mass genocide. These catalyzed tremendous growth for humanity, forcing us to face our darkest shadows and deepest fears, and compelling us to begin to see the world and humanity as one whole, interrelated system.

The '50s was an era of restabilization along with an effort to attempt to find order, balance, and some semblance of "normalcy." The late '50s and '60s brought a tremendous opening up to the nonrational forces of life — the instinctual, emotional, intuitive, and spiritual — first through rhythm-and-blues and then rock-and-roll music, and later through psychedelic drugs. There was huge rebellion against the limits of the overly linear, logical, and controlled Western mind, and the corresponding social, political, and military power structure.

In the '70s, for the first time in Western history, a significant number of people were actually experiencing nonlinear, transpersonal, and even mystical states of consciousness. This opened the way for many to seek spiritual understanding, healing practices, and alternative life-styles. Many Westerners became fascinated with the wisdom of the East, and/or of the Earth-centered spirituality of indigenous peoples, such as Native Americans.

In the '80s and '90s, many of us continued to deepen and expand our consciousness journeys. Much of our learning and growth came as we brought that process more into the world of form, through creating and nurturing careers and families. This was often painful and difficult. In the past, the vast majority of human beings lived in one geographical location, had one job, and stayed in one marriage for their entire lives. Finding that we could no longer do these things in the old ways, we've tried to discover new ways to live in the world, with few role models to guide us. Often feeling confused, and frequently feeling like failures in our attempts, we have nevertheless had the courage to keep risking.

Now, as we begin the new millennium, the evolutionary process is gaining speed and intensity. The new world that we have been creating internally is being born, and the birth is not an easy one. We are undergoing a difficult labor! However, we are beginning to see it take shape in the form of an increasing number of people seeking social and political reform, and in an increasing number seeking consciousness, not in order to escape the troubles of today's world but in order to take part in healing them.

Because this new world is emerging, the old one is dying and falling apart all around us. Old forms, institutions, and systems simply aren't working anymore. To the degree that we are attached to that world — and it is difficult not to be — we feel frightened and confused. To the degree that we are already involved in the creation of the new, we feel elated and excited.

Most of us have a foot in both worlds and feel somewhat caught between realities, not quite knowing which to trust or believe in. We are frightened by the pain and chaos we see in the world. We're not sure how to handle our own personal life challenges. The problems of the world seem completely overwhelming. We'd like to do something to help, but we're not sure what to do.

Many of us who have been intensely focused primarily on an inner journey and/or the healing and development of our personal lives are feeling our energy begin to move outward again. All things move in cycles. Having gone deeply within, it is now time for many of us to begin to participate more openly and actively in the larger world. Synchronistically, this internal shift is being reflected by many things happening on our planet at this time. For one thing, our earthly environment seems to be deteriorating rapidly and we are growing increasingly concerned that we must tend to the problems immediately and effectively or it is going to be too late. Another factor is the changing political climate in the world and in our country.

When I first began getting ideas and writing notes for this book, the world was still visibly dominated by the old patriarchal, cold war mentality. It was still the Reagan/Bush era in this country, and the Soviet Union was still intact. There was a pervasive feeling of deadness and denial. I felt, however, that great change was happening, just under the surface, and I wanted to write a book that could help awaken people to that change and support those who were already at the forefront.

In the years since, the atmosphere of the world has shifted considerably. The Soviet Union has dissolved, and the cold war is officially over. Many nations are undergoing massive change and "shake-ups" in their political and social structures.

The inner consciousness work we have been doing is finally becoming manifest in a more visible way in this new worldwide atmosphere of change and transformation.

These are exciting times; we are beginning to see the results of much hard work. It is only a beginning; there is tremendous chaos, struggle, and frustration around the process of change. But it is difficult to deny that it is happening.

For many of us on a consciousness journey, this atmosphere of change is reigniting our hope and our vision, inspiring us to get involved in the world in some more active way. Yet, these feelings may generate some new inner conflicts. Especially for those who have been following a transcendent spiritual path, there may be tremendous contradictions to be faced between separating ourselves from worldly involvement and plunging into the middle of things. How do we become involved in the external world without losing the internal connection we've worked so hard to achieve?

Just as the world is at a great turning point, so is the consciousness movement. Rather than following a transcendent path and withdrawing from the world, we must commit ourselves to the transformational path and take responsibility for changing the world.

We must remember that trying to solve the world's problems through a primarily external focus is not very effective, either. The world is full of people attempting to find solutions to community and planetary problems with little success and much struggle, because they are not fully confronting deeper levels of the issues. As well-meaning as we may be, if we try to "fix" things outside ourselves without healing the underlying causes of the problem in our own consciousness, we simply perpetuate the problem.

For example, in recent years there have been many gatherings to visualize world peace. I am, as many know, a great believer in the power of visualization, having written the book, *Creative Visualization,* many years ago. So I encourage people to continue to use this powerful tool for achieving personal and collective goals. However, visualizing world peace or anything else will only be effective if we are willing to do the personal consciousness work that will support it. If we are identified with love, light, and peaceful energies, and we project our disowned aggression onto others, then our attempts to create world peace, or even peaceful lives of our own, will most likely fail. If we are able to own our natural aggression in a healthy way, claiming our inner warrior as the important part of us that he is, and making him a part of our lives, then aggression will not be a shadow that we project onto others. The masters of Eastern martial arts understand this principle — if you are at peace with your inner warrior and know how to skillfully channel that energy, that power will radiate from you and you will most likely never need to be overtly aggressive.

Ultimately, if we want to live peaceful lives and create a peaceful world, we must start by building the foundation for that peace within ourselves. This process includes accepting and integrating the parts of ourselves that are aggressive and capable of making war.

How can we fulfill our desire to actively make a difference in the world? We must discover how to take action that is a natural extension of our consciousness process. These actions can only be effective if they are firmly rooted in the soil of our inner healing work — everything that I have been describing in this book.

First, we must understand that we are all truly part of one whole, that all of creation is, at the deepest level, one consciousness, one intelligence. Therefore, we must remind ourselves that *everything* we do has meaning and significance; to some degree, *all* our actions affect everyone. We must do our inner work with the knowledge that in healing ourselves we contribute to healing everyone and everything.

It's fairly easy to see that we affect the people we personally encounter, and to understand that they in turn affect the people they interact with, so that our influence spreads out into the world through every personal contact. We may need to make a leap of faith to grasp that through the collective consciousness — in which we are all active participants — we also affect people on the other side of the world. We affect each other even though we may never have any personal contact.

Everyone on the planet who is involved in a personal growth process is part of an important stage in our evolution, one that could be called the "healing generation." It is our destiny to do a tremendous amount of inner work so that the generations that follow us will not have so much healing to do, and can get on with whatever work they come here to accomplish! For many of us, it may very well be that the inner work we do will be our greatest contribution to humanity.

Certainly, if we want our external actions to be as powerful and effective as possible, we need to be deeply committed to our ongoing, ever-deepening consciousness journey. We need to remember to use every important relationship, every significant experience we have, as a mirror, providing us with reflections that help us continue to learn how we can express more of our potential and live more consciously.

Everything we think, feel, say, and do has some effect on other people and the world around us. Therefore, the most powerful and important thing we can do to change the world is simply to do our best to live a conscious life on a daily basis. Remember, this does not mean living up to some lofty spiritual ideal — always being unconditionally loving, accepting, and forgiving. Trying too hard to conform to *any* model of perfection, no matter how appealing it might be, will always lead to disappointment and feelings of failure. We don't have to be saints before we can start making a difference!

To me, living consciously means accepting our human weaknesses and imperfections without judging ourselves harshly, and being willing to learn from our unconscious patterns of behavior once we become aware of them. It means looking at our experiences as gifts that can help us grow, recognizing everyone and everything we encounter as a potential teacher. It means taking responsibility (not blame) for our thoughts, feelings, and actions, recognizing that they do have an effect on others. It means listening and reaching deeply inside ourselves to find our inner sense of truth, then doing our best to speak and live that truth moment to moment and day by day. And it means generously sharing the gift of our being, as well as our special talents and abilities, with others.

To live consciously we need to reclaim and develop our awareness of how we live on the earth. Most of us need to learn to live more simply, without using up so many resources and creating so much waste. This does not mean that we need to live in poverty or suffer feelings of deprivation and scarcity. Quite the contrary! As we become aware of our *real* needs — spiritually, mentally, emotionally, and physically — and as we learn to truly fulfill these needs, we will find we have less need for much of the external stuff that we're using to try to fill our emptiness. As true needs are filled, false needs dissolve, along with the fears that have driven us. As we are filled from within with our own spirit, and as our life force moves more freely through our bodies, as we move into alignment with our souls and our higher purpose, we feel a part of the natural flow and abundance of the universe. We come to appreciate the wealth in life's simpler things.

This doesn't mean we can't enjoy our material possessions and the products of our remarkable technology. I believe that when we are in balance with ourselves, we will find a harmonious way to balance the needs of our environment along with enjoying the fruits of our material creativity. Meanwhile, most of us need to develop more awareness and better habits in the use of our resources. The little things matter — such things as buying healthier and more natural foods, with less packaging, fewer chemical additives, and less processing, avoiding products that are toxic or that come in nonrecyclable containers, carrying along your own canvas bag when shopping, recycling at home and at the office. All of these can seem like small things but each one can make a big difference, especially as we teach our children these practices.

Another important part of living consciously, of course, is how we treat our fellow humans — and our animal friends as well — on a daily basis. Of course, we all say and do things that we later regret and feel bad about. That is an unavoidable part of being human, *especially* when we are actively engaged in learning new ways of living and relating, rather than following the safe path we may have found in the past. So we need to allow ourselves plenty of room to express ourselves in ways that may not always turn out to be harmonious or successful. However, we can also make an extra effort, when we are able, to share our love and caring with others, with our families, friends, and co-workers, and even in small ways, such as making eye contact and saying a real thank you to the toll taker on the bridge, or having a little extra patience with a store clerk who's obviously having a difficult day.

Living consciously means living creatively, looking at each new day not only as an opportunity to learn but also as an opportunity to enjoy sharing our special gifts, talents, and inspirations, in small and large ways.

As we do our inner healing work, we automatically tap into more and more of our own natural creative energy. As we clear out our spiritual, mental, emotional, and physical blocks and limitations, the creative life force can move through us more fully and freely. This life energy naturally moves us to take action that is in harmony with our being, in alignment with our higher purpose, and necessary and effective in the world.

By following your creative ideas and impulses, you may find yourself doing unusual and unexpected things, some of which may develop in interesting ways. For example, a friend of mine who is a composer had created the music for a film on ecology. When the film played in the local community, he had the impulse to buy tickets for all his friends to go and see it, in order to help raise their consciousness about the topic. The event truly did help them to become more aware and caring of the environment. Everyone who went was so inspired that they got together to brainstorm some ways to get the film better exposure. They purchased copies of the film on video and took it around to different school districts for the children to see.

While no single person felt that it had taken a huge amount of time, energy, or money to do what they did, their efforts made a tremendous difference in the world, spreading a message that was important and healing.

This is a good example of "right action." Here are some guidelines that may help you discover how to take your own right action:

- Make a commitment to yourself to discover meaningful and effective action that you can take to contribute to and support healing and transformation in the world. Look around you to see some of the problems and issues in your immediate environment or out in your community.

- When you find yourself attracted to an issue you would like to help heal in the external world, ask yourself if there is anything you need to do first on an *inner* level. How might this problem reflect an issue within your own psyche, and what do you need to do to resolve that issue within yourself? If you don't get an answer or see any clear correlation, don't worry. Let it go, but keep the question open as you proceed. At some point you may have a further insight about this.

- Then ask your inner guidance for clarity and direction for any kind of action you are thinking about taking in relation to the issue. If no inner guidance comes, let it go for a while. Something may come up later. If nothing does, this may not be an area where you are meant to take action. Instead, notice where you *do* have energy to do something.

- When you feel an impulse in a certain direction, follow it. Continue to ask for guidance and follow it as best you can. When you don't feel clear about your direction, rest.

- Don't bite off more than you can chew or be too ambitious in your plans. Take small steps and remember that the little things can count as much as the big ones.

- Do what you genuinely have energy to do. Try not to act out of guilt or fear. As much as possible, follow your inspiration. Do what is exciting, enlivening, and/or personally satisfying to you.

For example, a woman I know read an article in the newspaper telling how the local school district, for financial reasons, had to cut its after-school program of arts classes for young people. She felt distressed by this because when she was a child a similar after-school class had led her to her lifelong love of dance and theater. She asked her inner guidance to let her know if there was something she could do to help. A few days later she had a strong feeling to call the school district and volunteer her help. She ended up teaching after-school theater classes for several years and absolutely loved her experience with the children.

Many of the things we are guided to do in our lives may not seem to have a direct connection with helping anyone or healing the world. Remember that the greatest contribution that you can make is in the aliveness that comes from simply being yourself, living your truth, and doing what you love. The passionate expression of who we are will heal the world.

CHAPTER TWENTY-SIX

Seven Steps on the Path of Transformation

*Remember that healing doesn't happen overnight
— it's an ongoing process. Often it may be
uncomfortable, at times painful, but there are
few ventures in life that are more fascinating
and rewarding. Trust your own process and give
it time and space to unfold on its own way.*

Some of you may be just beginning your consciousness process. Others may have been doing this work for years, yet reading this book has perhaps given you a new insight or a different perspective.

For those who are wishing to consciously begin or to deepen and renew your transformational journey, here are seven fundamental steps:

Step 1. Making a Commitment

Make a conscious commitment to yourself to follow your truth as best you can, and to do whatever it takes to learn, grow, heal, and gain awareness. You may want to do this privately, or with your partner, family, friends, or a group. If you wish, make a statement of commitment and create a ritual to formalize the event for yourself: write it in your journal, do a meditation in a special place, walk on the beach and shout it to the ocean, find a power object that symbolizes the step you are taking and keep it with you or create a personal altar of special objects, wear a special ring or other piece of jewelry, create a work of art that expresses your feelings about this step, or anything else that feels right for you.

Step 2. Following Inner Guidance

Develop a relationship with your own inner teacher by practicing the art of listening to and following your inner intuitive guidance. I have described this in chapters on "Finding Your Inner Teacher" and "Developing Inner Guidance."

Step 3. Finding Support

Reach out for the support you need for your journey. Many of us have the idea that we must be completely self-sufficient, making changes in our lives without assistance from anyone. We may feel that it is somehow shameful or embarrassing to admit we need help. The fear of acknowledging our vulnerability in this way is one of the old limiting patterns that we need to heal. As human beings we do need each other. We are a socially oriented species, and we need to have a feeling of belonging within a family, group, or community. And the consciousness process is far too complex and difficult to manage alone. Of course there are times when we need to face being alone, turning inward for answers and trusting our own sense of self rather than looking to others. Learning to discern when we need support and when we need to be independent is all part of the process.

For you, support may be in the form of a good friend or group of friends, your partner and/or family, a mentor or a trusted adviser, a doctor or healing practitioner, a counselor or therapist, a teacher, a class, a professional organization, a church or spiritual group, a workshop, a therapy group, a recovery group or twelve-step program.

Be careful and selective when choosing your support systems. Make certain they really address and satisfy your own specific needs. A good rule of thumb is that generally you should come away from the experience feeling better about yourself, feeling empowered, enlivened, or more at peace. Of course there may be times when you feel differently — shaken or disturbed because an old pattern is being challenged, perhaps. But overall, the feeling should be a positive one for you. Beware of any situation where you frequently feel belittled, criticized, confused, frustrated, or disempowered. This may indicate that someone is on a power trip. Be particularly cautious if they tell you it's for your own good, or if they say that you are being resistant if you question their techniques.

We all need at least one person or group with whom we can be fully ourselves, where we can feel safe to share our innermost thoughts and deepest feelings, where we feel accepted for who we are, including the qualities we might consider our flaws or weaknesses. Aside from this basic support, we may also require more specific kinds: the need for inspiration, the need for help in learning skills, or the need for help from a health practitioner. A support person can be any friend or specialist who assists you on the transformational path, either directly or indirectly.

The type of support you need will probably vary from time to time. Sometimes we outgrow our support people, or we find ourselves moving in different directions, choosing very different paths. When we do, it can be difficult to let go of our old support people, even when we recognize that it is time to do so. Sometimes it is vital to let go and move on. Again, knowing when to stay and when to go is a wisdom that is only gained by meeting the challenge when it comes up in your life.

Keep in mind, too, that as wonderful as our friends and family may be, there are times when we need support from a more objective source. Our loved ones have their own attachments and investments in our lives and can't always offer us the perspective we need. Also, they may not have the skills or expertise we need in a given area. And expecting all our needs for emotional support to be met by our spouse, partner, family, or closest friends may simply be too great a burden on them, especially when we're going through an emotional crisis or deep healing. Getting outside or professional guidance at these times can be crucial to our own well-being and to the well-being of our loved ones.

When seeking support, get as clear as you can about what you need. This doesn't mean that you have to know exactly what you need; just get in touch with whatever you are aware of and go from there. Ask for inner guidance to direct you toward appropriate support. For example, you may realize that you need to learn to communicate better in relationships, but not be sure exactly what that would look like, or what skills you need. Ask friends and acquaintances for recommendations and referrals to good therapists, support groups, or workshops. Consult any other sources you can think of. When you find something that sounds interesting or feels appropriate, check it out. Don't be afraid to interview a potential adviser, healer, or therapist to see how you feel about them and how you work together. It is a good idea to start out on a trial basis. Above all, trust your gut feelings about what's right for you, and keep following your inner guidance.

Step 4. Using Tools

Find tools that can help you with your process on all four levels — spiritual, mental, emotional, and physical. Allow yourself to explore, investigate, and discover different ideas, techniques, and practices that attract your interest to find out what works best for you at any given time. When you are in an exploratory phase, you may read books, listen to tapes, or watch videos on various topics, take classes, consult with experts or advisers until you find a skill or method that works for you. Then you may find yourself concentrating on a particular practice or two for awhile. Again, remember that your needs change as you grow; tools that you once used regularly may be placed on the shelf for a while or discarded altogether as you find new ones. You may also find that there is a time for letting go of all tools for growth, and just allow yourself to be for a while!

Some of the tools that have been most important in my

process over the years are (more or less in the order they came into my life): dance, hatha yoga, meditation, the idea that we create our own reality, the techniques of creative visualization and affirmation, contacting and clearing core beliefs, many different kinds of emotional release work and therapeutic modalities, massage and body work, the practice of trusting and following inner guidance, balancing male and female energies, twelve-step work with codependency issues, the psychology of selves and Voice Dialogue, learning from nature, and the wisdom of indigenous peoples. There have been many others as well. I mention these not to endorse them specifically, but to give you an idea of the range of different tools that have helped me at various times — and still are helping me.

Step 5. Allowing Healing

Make consciousness growth a high priority in your life. Create time and space to allow your healing process to occur on all levels. Regardless of the type of support you've created or the tools you have chosen, the basic healing process involves gaining insight and awareness about yourself, learning to accept and be comfortable with all aspects of yourself, learning to trust, care for, and love yourself.

Because of the unconsciousness and denial that exists on the planet today, we have all been wounded to some degree. Some, of course, have suffered more than others, and therefore may need to spend more of their time and energy healing. Try not to compare your process with anyone else's. We all have our own journey to make and each one is different, depending on the lessons we came into this life to learn and the gifts we came to give. Wherever the deepest pain exists, there will be the greatest learning — and there also will you find much that you will have to share with others.

Remember that healing doesn't happen overnight — it's an ongoing process. Often it may be uncomfortable, at times painful, but there are few ventures in life that are more fascinating and rewarding. Trust your own process and give it time and space to unfold in its own way.

Step 6. Expressing Creativity

Discover ways to express your creativity. Everyone is naturally creative, and expressing our creativity is an important part of finding wholeness and fulfillment. In fact, the inability to express our natural creative energy is a root cause of many addictions, as well as much of our spiritual, mental, emotional, and physical pain. The more healing we experience on all levels, the more our creativity begins to emerge.

If you feel your creativity has been blocked, you may need to do some emotional healing, specifically in this area. Get some support to help you discover how and why it got stopped or suppressed, and what is standing in the way of letting it flow.

Getting in touch with and healing your inner child may be a key for unlocking your creativity. Young children are endlessly creative because they have not yet become inhibited. Our creativity often gets dampened or smothered once we begin to develop the inner *perfectionist* and *critic*. Our perfectionist tells us how things should be done and sets very high standards for us. Our inner critic points out every time we fall short of perfection. (Being human, this is most of the time!) This can make us unwilling to try new things or express ourselves for fear that we won't do it well enough. We may need to do some conscious healing work with our inner critic and perfectionist, who are actually just trying to protect us from external criticism by trying to shape us up to be as perfect as possible. Keeping their best intentions in mind, it can be a good idea to get them to relax a bit. Then it becomes much easier to contact the naturally spontaneous child within us and encourage him/her to start expressing more in our lives.

To encourage our own creativity we need to lighten up a bit, have some fun, be adventurous. We need to take some risks to express ourselves in new and different ways. Take small steps first. Try some things that seem fun and creative to you — draw a picture, build something, take a cooking class, an art, dance, or martial arts class, take up a musical instrument, join an amateur theater group, take up a sport, write a poem or short story, plant a garden. Do it strictly for your own enjoyment, not for anyone else's approval. The purpose of our creativity is our own fulfillment; the goal is not to please other people or win their approval.

Remember that creativity expresses itself in many ways and each person has his or her own unique way. You may express your creativity primarily through your work, through raising your children, through a favorite hobby, through remodeling or decorating your home, through how you manage your money, through the way you dress, or through gardening, or cooking, or healing.

Step 7. Sharing with Others

Passing on to others what we have received and learned is an important part of completing that process at each level of our healing and growth. We have not fully integrated anything until we have manifested it in our experience in a way that impacts others in some transformational way.

This is not something we have to try to do, however. It simply happens automatically as we follow the other six steps. Primarily it happens on an energetic level. The more inner healing we accomplish, the more life force can move through our bodies. This life energy has an impact on everyone we encounter, regardless of our words or actions. The universe literally flows through us to "knock people alive," to awaken or speed up their transformational process. As we become more conscious, we influence the mass consciousness to shift, and this affects everyone's reality.

In a more obvious and specific way, as we express our creativity more fully and freely in our work and through our other interests, we make a contribution to others. Many of us may be drawn toward some form of consciousness or healing work, wishing to pass on to others the support and tools that have been so valuable to us. This is extremely rewarding and fulfilling, and the reflection we receive from the people we work with definitely helps us integrate our own consciousness process even more deeply. Also, as many have discovered, serving others can be one of the greatest highs available on the planet!

It doesn't really matter what our specific activities are, however. If our talent and our joy lies in repairing automobiles, studying an obscure insect species in a remote forest, selling computers, or baby-sitting children, and we do it with love and integrity, we will have a healing effect on everyone we encounter, and on the Earth itself.

Seven Steps on the Path of Transformation

1. Making a Commitment

2. Following Inner Guidance

3. Finding Support

4. Using Tools

5. Allowing Healing

6. Expressing Creativity

7. Sharing with Others

CHAPTER TWENTY-SEVEN

Fulfilling Our Higher Purpose

Our higher purpose is what we came here
to do on a soul level. We are born with the
specific interests, talents, and abilities
to fulfill that purpose.

*E*very one of us comes into this life with lessons to
learn and gifts to give. The more we learn and grow,
the more we become capable of developing and sharing
these natural gifts.

As we follow the seven steps on the path of transformation, we find ourselves guided toward discovering and
fulfilling our higher purpose in life. That higher purpose
is, quite literally, the sharing of our gifts.

Our higher purpose is what we came here on a soul
level to do. We are born with the specific interests, talents,
and abilities to fulfill that purpose. As we come into life we
most likely choose — in some mysterious, forgotten way —
the family and environment that will give us the exact
combination of support and challenges to overcome that

we most need to effectively accomplish our goals. Some of us choose more support in our early life, others choose environments of physical, emotional, mental, and/or spiritual challenge! Regardless of the environments we've come from, if we can successfully reap the knowledge that is available in them, we are well on our way to recognizing and expressing our higher purpose.

Chances are that our higher purpose is already showing itself in our lives. It is usually there from the very beginning, expressing itself through who we are as children. Whatever things we do naturally and easily, whatever our innate talents and interests, whatever knowledge and skills we've been led to develop, and whatever people and activities we are drawn to provide us with clues about our higher purpose. We may already be expressing that purpose so naturally and easily that it's just no big deal. If so, we will have a feeling of fulfillment and contentment where that aspect of our lives is concerned.

Many of us have yet to discover our higher purpose, in which case there will probably be a sense of dissatisfaction and restlessness until we do. It has often been said that we ourselves are most blind to our greatest gifts. Many times, it is our friends and loved ones who see them most clearly. Often, these gifts, which others value so highly in us, are things that come very easily and perhaps even automatically to us. Part of what makes them so difficult for us to recognize is that they are associated with things that we find easy, enjoyable, and effortless for us to do.

It is through these gifts that we can get in touch with our higher purpose. To do this, first think about a close friend. Since we are mirrors to each other, bring them into your mind and ask them first what they value in you. What do you bring to their life that they feel improves it? You might even ask, what is it in me that reflects the very best in you?

The answers you get may seem very modest or commonplace at first, but try not to underestimate their importance. In fact, after you've begun to get in touch with your gifts, start looking for ways that you might use them in a more conscious way. For example, a woman I know found that what her closest friends valued most in her was her ability to listen to others in a way that they found both calming and empowering. She herself had never thought of this as being a special gift since it was something that came to her so naturally. Once she became aware of it, however, she began to see many of the ways that her listening did, in fact, seem to give people encouragement, giving them the courage they needed to solve problems they were having or to go forward with plans when they were procrastinating.

The more conscious she became of this gift, the more she saw it as an expression of a higher purpose. The last I spoke with her, she was exploring all the ways that she might express her talents professionally. Her choices at that time included taking a job with a company that teaches communication skills or going back to school to earn the necessary degrees to become a psychotherapist. Both these paths promised to make good use of her natural abilities.

I recently saw a delightful news story on television. They were doing a special "human interest" feature about a man who drives a street-sweeping machine. It seems that from earliest childhood, he had a great fascination with street sweepers! His mother showed pictures he had drawn and models he had made of them when he was a boy. Now he owns his own machine, and simply loves driving it for a living. He was very warmhearted, friendly, and obviously enjoying his life tremendously. He seemed to be radiating wonderful energy everywhere he went. One would not normally think of driving a street sweeper as fulfilling one's higher purpose, but clearly this man was doing so!

As I mentioned earlier, when I was a child I used to read and write stories all the time. I used to imagine that some day I would walk into a library and there would be a whole shelf full of books written by me! At the time, I was reading books about horses and other animals, so I thought that's what I probably would be writing.

Years went by, and I forgot all about this vision, and never wrote a thing. It wasn't until I had written and published my first book, *Creative Visualization,* that I remembered my childhood dream of being a writer. I've now learned, of course, that writing and teaching about consciousness is a major part of my higher purpose. This is not something I ever planned or decided to do. It evolved naturally out of my process, and out of who I am as a being. I teach and write because I am compelled to, for my own learning, as well as to share my gifts with others. It's something I can't *not* do!

If you don't feel that you are in touch with your higher purpose and you would like to be, ask your inner guidance to begin to bring you information, awareness, and clarity about it. Ask yourself what things you most enjoy doing, or just seem to find yourself doing frequently. How do you express yourself most easily and naturally? What fantasies did you have as a child? What are your fantasies and visions for yourself now? Spend some time exploring them.

Don't expect immediate answers to these questions. Be patient with yourself. The process of discovering and fulfilling your higher purpose may take years. It cannot be forced or rushed, since it is all part of your unfolding journey. Allow yourself to be with the questions without demanding answers. When answers do come, they may come in surprising ways and unexpected moments. Keep in mind that doing your consciousness work will automatically bring your higher purpose into focus and clarity over time.

Remember that your higher purpose is not just what you do. It is also who you are — your unique combination of energy, personality, and physical form brings something special into the world. Keep in mind that you have never seen anyone with the same higher purpose as yours, since yours is unique! Your higher purpose has not been invented until you manifest it.

Martha Graham, the great dancer and choreographer, expressed it beautifully:

> There is vitality, a life force, an energy, a quickening that is translated through you into action. And because there is only one you in all time, this expression is unique. And if you block it, it will never exist through any other medium...the world will not have it. It is not your business to determine

how good it is, nor how valuable, nor how it compares with other expressions. It is your business to
keep it yours clearly and directly, to keep the channel open.*

* Agnes De Mille, *Dance to the Piper,* Atlantic Monthly Press, New
York, 1952.

CHAPTER TWENTY-EIGHT

Envisioning the
Future Together

*F*or a long time, I felt deeply troubled both by the difficulties I was experiencing in my own personal life and by the pain and suffering I saw in the world. Through many years of consciousness work, I had developed a strong connection with my spiritual self. From that perspective I could see the perfection of the whole process; I had a strong faith that there was meaning and purpose in it all, and that it would all work out well eventually. The human part of me felt more unsure; on the emotional level I had fears and doubts about my own future and the future of the planet. I wondered if my own personal needs would ever get fulfilled, much less the needs of all the beings on this Earth.

As my healing process has deepened and continued,

I've found a great deal more integration within myself. This is being reflected as my life is gradually becoming more balanced and satisfying. Some of my most difficult patterns are slowly dissolving and I'm finding new ways to live my life that work better. Many of my deepest heart's desires are being fulfilled. Do I get stuck and feel frustrated? Yes, frequently! But not as profoundly or as lengthily as before. Watching my life, and the lives of many others near and dear to me, unfold in amazing ways has deepened my confidence that the principles I have been living and teaching really do work.

Along with my own healing has come a stronger sense of trust in the healing process going on in our world. Before, I wasn't quite sure whether we would actually be able to effect change quickly enough, or whether we would simply have to move onto another level of existence to continue our journeys.

I still feel pangs of fear and doubt sometimes when I am forced to confront some of the more upsetting aspects of our current reality. I expect that many external circumstances may get worse as the old order crumbles. Yet deep inside, I feel more strongly than ever before that we are participants in an amazing evolutionary and transformational process that is taking place here on Earth. I believe that we will succeed at our task, and that many of us will see results manifested in form within our lifetimes.

I'd like to invite you to join me and all the other readers of this book in envisioning the future. Just as at the beginning of the book, I'm going to ask you to close your eyes and imagine the future. This time I'd like you to pay special attention to your most creative fantasies. If doubts and fears come, acknowledge them and allow them to be there, too. Then turn your attention to developing your vision. Don't limit it in any way. Allow it to be as expansive as you would like.

Get in a comfortable position with your pen and paper, journal, crayons, or whatever tools you'd like within easy reach. Close your eyes, and take a few slow, deep breaths. Let your awareness move into a quiet place deep inside of you. Ask yourself, "What is my vision of the future?"

First, focus your attention on imagining your own personal future as you would most like it to be. If you're not quite sure how you want it to be, just allow yourself to go with one fantasy about it, knowing that you can change it whenever you want to. Imagine your relationship with yourself as fulfilling as possible on all levels — spiritual, mental, emotional, and physical. Imagine everything in your life reflecting the balance and harmony within your own being — your relationship, your work, your finances, your living situation, your creative pursuits. Allow them all to be wonderfully successful and satisfying.

Now expand your focus to imagine the future of the world around you — your community, your country, humanity, the natural environment, our planet. Allow them all to reflect the integration and wholeness you have found within yourself. Imagine the new world emerging and developing in a healthy, balanced, expansive way. Really let your imagination soar. Envision the world as you would love it to be, a paradise on Earth.

When you feel complete with this process, open your eyes. If you wish, write or draw your vision.

Thank you for joining me. Bless you.

Relaxation
Exercise

This exercise is designed for very deep relaxation. Just as with learning any kind of new activity, such as riding a bicycle or running, it takes a while to train your body and mind to respond in a new way. The instructions given here will help you achieve a balanced and effective relaxation response in a minimum of time. Once you have done this longer version a few times, you'll discover that you can enter a deeply relaxed state within just a few seconds by closing your eyes and taking a few deep breaths.

Some people find that conscious relaxation of this kind is enhanced by playing very soft, relaxing music in the background. Make sure it remains very peaceful throughout.

First give yourself permission to take five to ten minutes to relax deeply, without having to think about other things you should be doing. Choose a quiet place and time of day when this will be possible.

Loosen any tight clothing.

Sit in an alert, upright position, hands gently resting in your lap with your palms open.

Take a deep breath and exhale slowly, allowing your shoulders to be loose and relaxed.

Open your mouth wide. Yawn, or pretend you are yawning.

Let the areas around your eyes and forehead be relaxed and loose. Let the areas around your nose, mouth, and jaw be relaxed.

Breathe slowly and easily.

If ideas or feelings come into your mind at this time, pretend they are a telephone ringing in the distance, perhaps in a neighbor's house. Acknowledge that "someone is calling," but you do not have to answer.

Take a deep breath, inhaling gently and slowly, imagining the breath entering your right nostril. Hold the breath for a moment, then exhale slowly and comfortably, imagining that you are exhaling through your left nostril.

Take another deep breath, this time imagining your breath entering your left nostril and exiting your right.

Focus your attention on how your breath feels: cooling, as it enters your nostrils, perhaps gently expanding your chest as it fills your lungs, then slightly warming your nostrils as you exhale. You may wish to visualize the air as having a beautiful, vibrant color as it enters and exits your body.

Repeat this breathing pattern until you have done at least four full cycles. A full cycle is one inhalation and one exhalation.

Now with each cycle, focus your attention on one area of your body:

Be aware of your scalp relaxing.

Be aware of your eyes, ears, and jaw relaxing.

Be aware of your neck relaxing.

Be aware of your shoulders relaxing.

Be aware of your chest relaxing.

Be aware of your upper back relaxing.

Be aware of your arms and hands relaxing.

Be aware of your abdomen relaxing.

Be aware of your buttocks relaxing.

Be aware of your legs relaxing.

Be aware of your feet relaxing.

Now let your breathing pattern return to normal as you enjoy the relaxed state you have created.

For several weeks, practice this relaxation exercise whenever the opportunity arises or whenever you feel a need to unwind and rest at work, at home, or in your recreational life.

RECOMMENDED RESOURCES

Books

Allen, Marc. *A Visionary Life: Conversations on Personal and Planetary Evolution.* New World Library, 1998.

Arrien, Angeles. *The Fourfold Way: Walking the Paths of the Warrior, Teacher, Healer, and Visionary.* HarperSanFrancisco, 1993.

Capacchione, Lucia. *The Power of Your Other Hand: A Course in Channeling the Inner Wisdom of the Right Brain.* Newcastle Publishing Co., Inc., 1988.

Capacchione, Lucia. *Recovery of Your Inner Child.* Simon & Schuster, 1991.

Gawain, Shakti. *Creating True Prosperity.* Nataraj Publishing/New World Library, 1997.

Gawain, Shakti. *Awakening: A Daily Guide to Conscious Living.* Nataraj Publishing/New World Library, 1991.

Gawain, Shakti. *Creative Visualization.* Nataraj Publishing/New World Library, 1978. Revised Edition 1995.

Gawain, Shakti. *Four Levels of Healing: A Guide to Balancing the Spiritual, Mental, Emotional, and Physical Aspects of Life.* Nataraj Publishing/New World Library, 1997.

Gawain, Shakti (with Laurel King). *Living in the Light: A Guide to Personal and Planetary Transformation.* Nataraj Publishing/New World Library, 1986. Revised Edition 1998.

Gawain, Shakti. *Developing Intuition.* Nataraj Publishing/New World Library, 2000.

Hendrix, Harville. *Getting the Love You Want.* Henry Holt & Co., 1988.

Luvaas, Tanha. *Notes from My Inner Child.* Nataraj Publishing/New World Library, 1993.

Macy, Joanna and Molly Young Brown. *Coming Back to Life: Practices to Reconnect Our Lives, Our World.* New Society Publishers, 1998.

Metzger, Deena. *Writing for Your life: A Guide and Companion to the Inner Worlds.* HarperSanFrancisco, 1992.

Nelson, Martia. *Coming Home: The Return to True Self.* Nataraj Publishing/New World Library, 1993.

Stone, Hal and Sidra. *Embracing Our Selves: The Voice Dialogue Manual.* Nataraj Publishing/New World Library, 1989.

Stone, Hal and Sidra. *Embracing Each Other: Relationship as Teacher, Healer, and Guide.* Nataraj Publishing/New World Library, 1989.

Stone, Hal and Sidra. *Embracing Your Inner Critic: Turning Self-Criticism into a Creative Asset.* HarperSanFrancisco, 1993.

Stone, Hal and Sidra. *Partnering: A New Kind of Relationship.* Nataraj Publishing/New World Library, 2000.

Stone, Sidra. *The Shadow King: The Invisible Force that Holds Women Back.* Delos Inc., 1997.

Audiotapes:

Gawain, Shakti

Creating True Prosperity: Book on Tape. Nataraj Publishing/
New World Library, 1997.
Creative Visualization: Book on Tape. Nataraj Publishing/
New World Library, 1995.
Creative Visualization Meditations. Nataraj Publishing/New
World Library, 1996.
*The Four Levels of Healing: A Guide to Balancing the
Spiritual, Mental, Emotional, and Physical Aspects of Life.*
Nataraj Publishing/New World Library, 1997.
Living in the Light: Book on Tape. Abridged version. Nataraj
Publishing/New World Library, 1998.
Meditations. Nataraj Publishing/New World Library, 1997.
The Path of Transformation: Book on Tape. Abridged version.
Nataraj Publishing/New World Library, 1993.

Stone, Hal and Sidra

The Child Within. Delos, 1990.
The Dance of Selves in Relationships. Delos. 1990.
Decoding Your Dreams. Delos, 1990.
Meet the Pusher. Delos, 1990.
Meet Your Inner Critic. Delos, 1990.
Meeting Your Selves. Delos, 1990.
Understanding Your Relationships. Delos, 1990.

These tapes are all available through Drs. Hal and
Sidra Stone, P.O. Box 604, Albion, CA 95410-0604.
Telephone: (707) 937-2424; E-Mail: delos@mcn.org.

Videotapes

Gawain, Shakti. *The Path of Transformation*. Video of live talk. Hay House, Inc., 1992.

Gawain, Shakti. *Creative Visualization Workshop Video*. Nataraj Publishing/New World Library, 1995.

Gawain, Shakti. *Living in the Light*. Video. Zolar Entertainment, 1995.

Workshop Information

Shakti Gawain gives talks and leads workshops all over the United States and in many other countries. She also conducts retreats, intensives, and training programs. If you would like to be on her mailing list and receive workshop information contact:

Shakti Gawain, Inc.

P.O. Box 377, Mill Valley, CA 94942

Telephone: (415) 388-7140

Fax: (415) 388-7196

E-mail: staff@shaktigawain.com

www.shaktigawain.com

For information about workshops and training given by Drs. Hal and Sidra Stone contact:

Delos, Inc.

P.O. Box 604, Albion CA 95410

Telephone: (707) 937-2424

E-mail: delos@mcn.org

www.delos-inc.com

ABOUT THE AUTHOR

A pioneer in the field of personal growth and consciousness, Shakti Gawain is the author of many
bestselling books including *Creative Visualization, Living in
the Light, The Four Levels of Healing,* and *Creating True
Prosperity.* She leads workshops internationally and has
facilitated thousands of individuals in developing greater
balance and wholeness in their lives. She and her husband
live in Mill Valley, California, and on the island of Kauai.

An Introduction to Programming Using Visual Basic 5.0

Third Edition

An Introduction to Programming Using Visual Basic 5.0

Third Edition

David I. Schneider
University of Maryland

 Prentice Hall, Upper Saddle River, New Jersey 07458

Library of Congress Cataloging-in-Publication Data

Schneider, David I.
        An Introduction to programming using Visual Basic 5.0 / David
    I. Schneider.—3rd ed.
            p.   cm.
        Includes index.
        ISBN 0-13-875857-3 (pbk.)
        1. Microsoft Visual BASIC. 2. BASIC (Computer program language)
    I. Title.
    QA76.73.B3S333   1998
    005.26'8—dc21   97-28306
                                                               CIP

Publisher: *ALAN APT*
Acquisitions editor: *LAURA STEELE*
Editor-in-chief: *MARCIA HORTON*
Managing editor: *BAYANI MENDOZA DE LEON*
Director of production and manufacturing: *DAVID W. RICCARDI*
Production editor: *KATHARITA LAMOZA*
Interior design and composition: *REBECCA EVANS & ASSOCIATES*
Art director: *HEATHER SCOTT*
Cover designer: *TAMARA NEWNAM-CAVALLO*
Cover contributor: *GABRIEL SCHNEIDER*
Manufacturing buyer: *DONNA SULLIVAN*
Editorial assistant: *TONI D. HOLM*

©1998 by Prentice-Hall, Inc.
Simon & Schuster / A Viacom Company
Upper Saddle River, New Jersey 07458

The author and publisher of this book have used their best efforts in preparing this book. These efforts include the development, research, and testing of the theories and programs to determine their effectiveness. The author and publisher make no warranty of any kind, expressed or implied, with regard to these programs or the documentation contained in this book. The author and publisher shall not be liable in any event for incidental or consequential damages in connection with, or arising out of, the furnishing, performance, or use of these programs.

TRADEMARK INFORMATION

IBM is a registered trademark of International Business Machines Corporation.
Hercules is a trademark of Hercules Computer Technology.
Microsoft is a registered trademark of Microsoft Corporation.

Printed in the United States of America

10 9 8 7 6 5

ISBN   0-13-875857-3

PRENTICE-HALL INTERNATIONAL (UK) LIMITED, *London*
PRENTICE-HALL OF AUSTRALIA PTY. LIMITED, *Sydney*
PRENTICE-HALL CANADA INC., *Toronto*
PRENTICE-HALL HISPANOAMERICANA, S.A., *Mexico*
PRENTICE-HALL OF INDIA PRIVATE LIMITED, *New Delhi*
PRENTICE-HALL OF JAPAN, INC., *Tokyo*
SIMON & SCHUSTER ASIA PTE. LTD., *Singapore*
EDITORA PRENTICE-HALL DO BRASIL, LTDA., *Rio de Janeiro*

Preface

This text provides an introduction to programming using Microsoft® Visual Basic™ 5.0 on IBM PC and IBM PC compatible computers running Windows. Due to its extraordinary combination of power and ease of use, Visual Basic has become the tool of choice for developing user-friendly Windows applications in the business world. In addition, Microsoft has made Visual Basic the language used to take full control of its best selling Windows applications such as Microsoft Word, Access, and Excel. Not only is Visual Basic the state of the art in Basic programming, but Visual Basic is fun! Learning Visual Basic was very exciting to me, and most students have similar reactions when they see how easy it is to build powerful visual interfaces using it.

My objectives when writing this text were as follows:

1. To develop focused chapters. Rather than covering many topics superficially, I concentrate on important subjects and cover them thoroughly.

2. To use examples and exercises with which students can relate, appreciate, and feel comfortable. I frequently use real data. Examples do not have so many embellishments that students are distracted from the programming techniques illustrated.

3. To produce compactly written text that students will find both readable and informative. The main points of each topic are discussed first and then the peripheral details are presented as comments.

4. To teach good programming practices that are in step with modern programming methodology. Problem-solving techniques and structured programming are discussed early and used throughout the book.

5. To provide insights into the major applications of computers.

Unique and Distinguishing Features

Exercises for Most Sections. Each section that teaches programming has an exercise set. The exercises both reinforce the understanding of the key ideas of the section and challenge the student to explore applications. Most of the exercise sets require the student to trace programs, find errors, and write programs. The answers to all the odd-numbered exercises in Chapters 2 through 6 and selected odd-numbered exercises from Chapters 7 through 14 are given at the end of the text.

Practice Problems. Practice problems are carefully selected exercises located at the end of a section, just before the exercise set. Complete solutions are given following the exercise set. The practice problems often focus on points that are potentially confusing or are best appreciated after the student has worked on them. The reader should seriously attempt the practice problems and study their solutions before moving on to the exercises.

Programming Projects. Beginning with Chapter 3, nearly every chapter contains programming projects. The programming projects not only reflect the variety of ways that computers are used in the business and engineering communities, but also present some games and general-interest topics. The large number and range of difficulty of the programming projects provide the flexibility to adapt the course to the interests and abilities of the students. Some programming projects in later chapters can be assigned as end-of-the-semester projects.

Comments. Extensions and fine points of new topics are reserved for the "Comments" portion at the end of each section so that they will not interfere with the flow of the presentation.

Case Studies. Each of the four case studies focuses on an important programming application. The problems are analyzed and the programs are developed with hierarchy charts and pseudocode. The programs are available to students on an accompanying CD.

Chapter Summaries. In Chapters 3 through 14, the key results are stated and the important terms are summarized at the end of the chapter.

Procedures. The early introduction of general procedures in Chapter 4 allows structured programming to be used in simple situations before being applied to complex problems. However, the text is written so that the presentation of procedures easily can be postponed until decision and repetition structures have been presented. In Chapters 5 and 6 (and Sections 7.1 and 7.2), all programs using procedures appear at the ends of sections and can be deferred or omitted.

Arrays. Arrays are introduced gently in two sections. The first section presents the basic definitions and avoids procedures. The second section presents the techniques for manipulating arrays and shows how to pass arrays to procedures.

Appendix on Debugging. The placement of the discussion of Visual Basic's sophisticated debugger in Appendix D allows the instructor flexibility in deciding when to cover this topic.

Reference Appendices. Appendices serve as a compact reference manual for Visual Basic's environments and statements.

Visual Basic CD. A CD containing the Control Creation Edition version of VB 5.0 is packaged with each book. This version has most of the features of the other versions of VB 5.0. The main differences are that the Control Creation Edition does not allow compilation to an EXE file and is not able to create and access databases.

Examples and Case Studies Files. The programs from all examples and case studies from the text have been copied onto the accompanying CD. The CD also contains all databases and text files used in the examples, and many of the text files used in exercises.

Instructors Diskette. A diskette containing every program in the text, the solution to every exercise and programming project, and a test item file for each chapter is available to the instructor.

What's New in the Third Edition

1. An entire chapter on object-oriented programming has been added. After presenting the fundamentals of classes and objects, the chapter shows how to declare and raise events in objects, and gives substantial examples of the ways objects interact with other objects.

2. One of the most publicized innovations of VB 5.0 is it's ability to create ActiveX controls easily and quickly. Section 13.4 shows how to build ActiveX controls.

3. The Web Browser control is used to gain direct access to the Internet.

4. Section 14.3 shows how to use VBScript to make Web pages interactive.

5. The help features (QuickInfo and List Properties/Methods) added in Visual Basic 5.0 are discussed.

6. Standard naming conventions for controls are used throughout the book.

7. The discussion of debugging and error-trapping has been expanded.

Acknowledgments

Many talented instructors, students, and programmers provided helpful comments and thoughtful suggestions at each stage in the preparation of this text. I extend my gratitude for their contributions to the quality of the book to A. Abonomah, University of Akron; Timothy Babbitt, Rochester Institute of Technology; William Barnett, Northwestern State University; Sherry Barriclow, Grand Valley State University; Nancy Beals, Microsoft; Robert Berman, Wayne State University; William Burrows, University of Washington; David Chao, San Francisco State University; Christopher Chisolm, University of Nebraska, Omaha; Robert Coil, Cincinnati State Technical and Community College; Gary Cornell, University of Connecticut; Ward Deutschman, Briarcliff; Ralph Duffy, North Seattle Community College; Pat Fenton, West Valley College; David Fichbohm, Golden Gate University; Mickie Goodro, Casper College; Wade T. Graves, Grayson Community College; Gary Haw, MIPS Software Dev. Inc.; Shelly Hawkins, Microsoft; Tom Janicki, Kent State University; Dana Johnson, North Dakota State University; Dan Joseph, Rochester Institute of Technology; Del Kimber, Clemson University; Paul Lecoq, San Francisco Community College; David Leitch, Devry Institute; David Letcher, The College of New Jersey; Kieran Mathieson, Oakland University; Charlie Miri, Delaware Tech; George Nezlek, DePaul University; Ron Notes, Hebrew Academy of Greater Washington; Mike Paul, Berry University; T. S. Pennington, Maple Woods Community College; Arland Richmond, Computer Learning Center; David Rosser, Essex County College; Arturo Salazar, San Francisco State; Janie Schwark, Microsoft; Mike Talber, Portland Community College; Steve Turek, Devry Institute of Technology, Kansas City; Jac Van Deventer, Washington State University; Randy Weinberg, St. Cloud State University; Laurie Werner, Miami University; Melinda White, Santa Fe Community College; Ronald Williams, Central Piedmont Community College.

Rebecca Evans & Associates used state-of-the-art technology to compose the text. Donna Sullivan of Prentice Hall did a fantastic job to keep the book on schedule.

David Lakein, Boris Kozintsev, and Heather Muise provided valuable assistance and advice throughout the preparation of the book. Their clear thinking and insights into programming contributed considerably to the success of the book.

My editor, Laura Steele, not only capably handled the many details needed to bring the book to production, but her ideas and enthusiasm nurtured me during the preparation of this revision.

Last, but not least, I am grateful to the Microsoft Corporation for its commitment to producing outstanding programming languages and for its permission to include a copy of the Control Creation Edition of Visual Basic 5.0 with each book.

Contents

Chapter 1 **An Introduction to Computers and Visual Basic** **1**

    1.1   An Introduction to Computers 2
    1.2   Using Windows 95 4
    1.3   Disks and Folders 16
    1.4   An Introduction to Visual Basic 22
    1.5   Biographical History of Computing 25

Chapter 2 **Problem Solving** **31**

    2.1   Program Development Cycle 32
    2.2   Programming Tools 34

Chapter 3 **Fundamentals of Programming in Visual Basic** **43**

    3.1   Visual Basic Objects 44
    3.2   Visual Basic Events 58
    3.3   Numbers 71
    3.4   Strings 84
    3.5   Input and Output 98
    3.6   Built-In Functions 118
    Summary 136
    Programming Projects 138

Chapter 4 **Procedures** **141**

    4.1   Subprograms, Part I 142
    4.2   Subprograms, Part II 163
    4.3   Functions 176
    4.4   Modular Design 189
    Summary 194
    Programming Projects 194

Chapter 5 **Decisions** **197**

    5.1   Relational and Logical Operators 198
    5.2   IF Blocks 203
    5.3   Select Case Blocks 219
    5.4   A Case Study: Weekly Payroll 235
    Summary 243
    Programming Projects 243

Chapter 6	Repetition	247

6.1 Do Loops 248
6.2 Processing Lists of Data with Do Loops 260
6.3 For...Next Loops 274
6.4 A Case Study: Analyze a Loan 287
Summary 295
Programming Projects 295

Chapter 7	Arrays	301

7.1 Creating and Accessing Arrays 302
7.2 Using Arrays 320
7.3 Control Arrays 335
7.4 Sorting and Searching 348
7.5 Two-Dimensional Arrays 367
7.6 A Case Study: Calculating with a Spreadsheet 381
Summary 390
Programming Projects 391

Chapter 8	Sequential Files	397

8.1 Sequential Files 398
8.2 Using Sequential Files 411
8.3 A Case Study: Recording Checks and Deposits 419
Summary 429
Programming Projects 429

Chapter 9	Random-Access Files	435

9.1 User Defined Data Types 436
9.2 Random-Access Files 446
Summary 453
Programming Projects 454

Chapter 10	The Graphical Display of Data	455

10.1 Introduction to Graphics 456
10.2 Line Charts 468
10.3 Bar Charts 476
10.4 Pie Charts 483
Summary 493
Programming Projects 493

Chapter 11	Additional Controls and Objects	495

11.1 List Boxes and Combo Boxes 496
11.2 Nine Elementary Controls 508
11.3 Five Additional Objects 523
Summary 541
Programming Projects 542

Chapter 12   Database Management   **545**

    12.1 An Introduction to Databases   **546**
    12.2 Relational Databases and SQL   **557**
    12.3 Data-Bound Grid Control; Creating and Designing Databases   **569**
    Summary   **584**
    Programming Projects   **585**

Chapter 13   Object-Oriented Programming   **587**

    13.1 Classes and Objects   **588**
    13.2 Collections and Events   **604**
    13.3 Class Relationships   **614**
    13.4 Building ActiveX Controls   **623**
    Summary   **633**
    Programming Projects   **633**

Chapter 14   Communicating with Other Applications   **637**

    14.1 OLE   **638**
    14.2 Accessing the Internet with Visual Basic   **648**
    14.3 Web Page Programming with VBScript   **654**
    Summary   **663**

Appendixes   **665**

    Appendix A   ANSI Values   **665**
    Appendix B   How To   **667**
    Appendix C   Visual Basic Statements, Functions, Methods,
                  Properties, Events, Data Types, and Operators   **681**
    Appendix D   Visual Basic Debugging Tools   **721**

Answers to Selected Odd-Numbered Exercises   **731**

Index   **803**

1

An Introduction to Computers and Visual Basic

1.1 **An Introduction to Computers** / 2

1.2 **Using Windows 95** / 4
- Mouse Pointers • Mouse Actions • Starting Windows 95
- Windows and Its Little Windows • Using the Notepad
- Ending Windows 95

1.3 **Disks and Folders** / 16
Using My Computer

1.4 **An Introduction to Visual Basic** / 22
- Why Windows and Why Visual Basic?
- How You Develop a Visual Basic Application

1.5 **Biographical History Of Computing** / 25
- 1800s • 1930s • 1940s • 1950s • 1960s • 1970s
- 1980s • 1990s

1.1 AN INTRODUCTION TO COMPUTERS

An Introduction to Programming Using Visual Basic 5.0 is a book about problem solving with computers. The programming language used is Visual Basic, but the principles taught apply to many modern programming languages. The examples and exercises present a sampling of the ways that computers are used in society.

Computers are so common today that you certainly have seen them in use and heard some of the terminology applied to them. Here are some of the questions that you might have about computers and programming.

Question: What is meant by a personal computer?

Answer: The word personal does not mean that the computer is intended for personal, as opposed to business, purposes. Rather, it indicates that the machine is operated by one person at a time instead of by many people.

Question: What are the main components of a personal computer?

Answer: The visible components are shown in Figure 1.1. Instructions are entered into the computer by typing them on the keyboard or by reading them from a diskette in a diskette drive or from a hard disk. Characters normally appear on the monitor as they are typed. Information processed by the computer can be displayed on the monitor, printed on the printer, or recorded on a diskette or hard drive. Hidden from view inside the system unit are the microprocessor and the memory of the computer. The microprocessor, which can be thought of as the brain of the computer, carries out all computations. The memory stores the instructions and data that are processed by the computer.

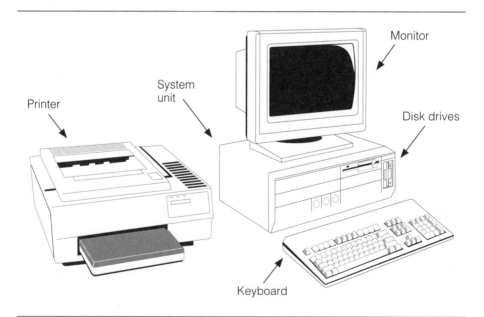

Figure 1.1 Components of a personal computer.

Question: What are some uses of computers in our society?

Answer: Whenever we make a phone call, a computer determines how to route the call and calculates the cost of the call. Banks store all customer transactions on computers and process these data to revise the balance for each customer. Airlines record all reservations into computers. This information, which is said to form a database, can be accessed to determine the status of any flight. NASA uses computers to calculate the trajectories of satellites. Business analysts use computers to create pie and bar charts that give visual impact to data.

Question: What are some topics covered in this text that students can use immediately?

Answer: Computer files can be created to hold lists of names, addresses, and phone numbers, which can be alphabetized and printed in entirety or selectively. Line graphs or attractive tables can be created to enhance the data in a term paper. Mathematical computations can be carried out for science, business, and engineering courses. Personal financial transactions, such as bank deposits and loans, can be recorded, organized, and analyzed.

Question: How do we communicate with the computer?

Answer: There are many languages that are used to communicate with the computer. At the lowest level, there is machine language, which is understood directly by the microprocessor, but is awkward for humans. Visual Basic is an example of a higher-level language. It consists of instructions to which people can relate, such as Print, Let, and Do. The Visual Basic software translates Visual Basic programs into machine language programs.

Question: How do we get computers to perform complicated tasks?

Answer: Tasks are broken down into a sequence of instructions that can be expressed in a computer language. (This text uses the language Visual Basic.) The sequence of instructions is called a program. Programs range in size from two or three instructions to tens of thousands of instructions. Instructions are typed on the keyboard and stored in the computer's memory. (They also can be stored permanently on a diskette or hard disk.) The process of executing the instructions is called running the program.

Question: Are there certain features that all programs have in common?

Answer: Most programs do three things: take in data, manipulate them, and give desired information. These operations are referred to as input, processing, and output. The input data might be held in a portion of the program, reside on a diskette or hard drive, or be provided by the computer operator in response to requests made by the computer while the program is running. The processing of the input data takes place inside the computer and can take from a fraction of a second to many hours. The output data are either displayed on the screen, printed on the printer, or recorded onto a disk. As a simple example, consider a program that computes sales tax. An item of input data is the cost of the thing purchased. The processing consists of multiplying the cost by a certain percentage. An item of output data is the resulting product, the amount of sales tax to be paid.

Question: What are the meanings of the terms hardware and software?

Answer: The term **hardware** refers to the physical components of the computer, including all peripherals, central processing unit, disk drives, and all mechanical and electrical devices. Programs are referred to as **software**.

Question: What are the meanings of the terms programmer and user?

Answer: A **programmer** is a person who solves problems by writing programs on a computer. After analyzing the problem and developing a plan for solving it, he or she writes and tests the program that instructs the computer how to carry out the plan. The program might be run many times, either by the programmer or by others. A **user** is any person who uses a program. While working through this text, you will function both as a programmer and a user.

Question: What is meant by problem solving?

Answer: Problems are solved by carefully reading them to determine what data are given and what outputs are requested. Then a step-by-step procedure is devised to process the given data and produce the requested output. This procedure is called an **algorithm**. Finally, a computer program is written to carry out the algorithm. Algorithms are discussed in Section 2.2.

Question: What types of problems are solved in this text?

Answer: Carrying out business computations, creating and maintaining records, alphabetizing lists, and drawing line graphs are some of the types of problems we will solve.

Question: What is the difference between standard BASIC and Visual Basic?

Answer: In the early 1960s, two mathematics professors at Dartmouth College developed BASIC to provide their students with an easily learned language that could tackle complicated programming projects. As the popularity of BASIC grew, refinements were introduced that permitted structured programming, which increases the reliability of programs. Visual Basic is a version of BASIC that was written by the Microsoft Corporation to incorporate object-oriented programming into BASIC and to allow easy development of Windows applications.

1.2 USING WINDOWS 95

Programs such as Visual Basic, which are designed for Microsoft Windows, are supposed to be easy to use—and they are once you learn a little jargon and a few basic techniques. This section explains the jargon, giving you enough of an understanding of Windows to get you started in Visual Basic. Although

Windows may seem intimidating if you've never used it before, you only need to learn a few basic techniques, which are covered right here.

Mouse Pointers

When you use Windows, think of yourself as the conductor and Windows as the orchestra. The conductor in an orchestra points to various members, does something with his or her baton, and then the orchestra members respond in certain ways. For a Windows user, the baton is called the **pointing device**; most often it is a **mouse**. The idea is that as you move the mouse across your desk, a pointer moves along the screen in sync with your movements. Two basic types of mouse pointers you will see in Windows are an arrow and an hourglass.

The **arrow** is the ordinary mouse pointer you use to point at various Windows objects before activating them. You will usually be instructed to "Move the pointer to . . . ." This really means "Move the mouse around your desk until the mouse pointer is at . . . ."

The **hourglass** mouse pointer pops up whenever Windows is saying: "Wait a minute; I'm thinking." This pointer still moves around when you move the mouse, but you can't tell Windows to do anything until it finishes what it's doing and the mouse pointer no longer resembles an hourglass. (Sometimes you can press the Esc key to tell Windows to stop what it is doing.)

Note: The mouse pointer can take on many other shapes, depending on which document you are using and what task you are performing. For instance, when entering text in a word processor or Visual Basic, the mouse pointer appears as a thin, large, uppercase I (referred to as an I-Beam).

Mouse Actions

After you move the (arrow) pointer to a place where you want something to happen, you need to do something with the mouse. There are four basic things you can do with a mouse—point, click, double-click, and drag.

Tip: You can pick the mouse up off your desk and replace it without moving the mouse pointer. This is useful, for example, when the mouse pointer is in the center of the screen but the mouse is about to fall off your desk!

Pointing means moving your mouse across your desk until the mouse pointer is over the desired object on the screen.

Clicking (sometimes people say single-clicking) means pressing and releasing the left mouse button once. Whenever a sentence begins "Click on . . . ," you need to

1. Move the mouse pointer until it is at the object you are supposed to click on.

2. Press and release the left mouse button.

An example of a sentence using this jargon might be "Click on the button marked Yes." You also will see sentences that begin "Click inside the. . . ." This means to move the mouse pointer until it is inside the boundaries of the object, and then click.

Double-clicking means clicking the left mouse button twice in quick succession (that is, pressing it, releasing it, pressing it, and releasing it again *quickly* so that

Windows doesn't think you single-clicked twice). Whenever a sentence begins "Double-click on . . . ", you need to

1. Move the mouse pointer until it is at the object you are supposed to double-click on.

2. Press and release the left mouse button twice in quick succession.

For example, you might be instructed to "Double-click on the little box at the far left side of your screen."

Note: An important Windows convention is that clicking selects an object so you can give Windows or the document further directions about it, but double-clicking tells Windows (or the document) to do something.

Dragging usually moves a Windows object. If you see a sentence that begins "Drag the . . . ", you need to

1. Move the mouse pointer until it is at the object.

2. Press the left mouse button and hold it down.

3. Now move the mouse pointer until the object moves to where you want it to be.

4. Finally, release the mouse button.

Sometimes this whole activity is called *drag and drop*.

The general rule in Windows is that double-clicking on the icon that represents a program starts the program. Here are two important icons.

Starting Windows 95

Windows 95 starts automatically when you turn on your computer. After a little delay, you will first see the Windows logo and finally a screen looking something like Figure 1.2. The four little pictures (with labels) are called **icons**. You double-click on the My Computer icon to see your computer's contents and manage your files. The Network Neighborhood icon is used to see available resources on the network and the Recycle Bin is a temporary storage place for deleted files. You click on the **Start button** (at the bottom left corner of the screen) to run programs such as Visual Basic, end Windows, and carry out several other tasks. (The Start menu also can be accessed with Ctrl+Esc.)

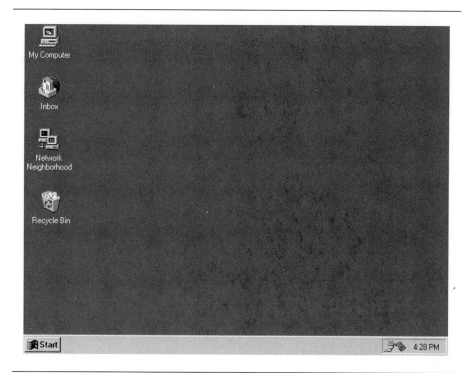

Figure 1.2 Windows 95 desktop.

Windows and Its Little Windows

Windows gets its name from the way it organizes your screen into rectangular regions. When you run a program, the program runs inside a bordered rectangular box. Unfortunately Windows jargon calls all of these windows, so there's only a lowercase "w" to distinguish them from the program called Windows.

When Windows' attentions are focused on a specific window, the bar at the top of the window is highlighted and the window is said to be **active**. The active window is the only one that can be affected by your actions. An example of a sentence you might see is "Make the window active." This means that if the title bar of the window is not already highlighted, click inside the window. At this point, the (new) window will be responsive to your actions.

Using the Notepad

We will explore the Windows application Notepad in detail to illustrate the Windows environment. The Notepad is used extensively in this text to create data files for documents. Most of the concepts learned here carry over to Visual Basic and other Windows applications.

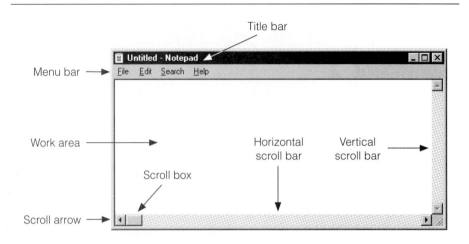

Figure 1.3 The Notepad window.

To invoke Notepad from Windows 95, click the Start button, point to Programs, point to Accessories, and click Notepad. As its name suggests, Notepad is an elementary word processor. You can type text into the Notepad window, edit the text, print the text on the printer, and save the text for later recall.

The blinking vertical line is called the **cursor**. Each letter you type will appear at the cursor. The Notepad window is divided into four parts. The part containing the cursor is called the **Work area**. It is the largest and most important part of the window because documents are typed into this window.

The **Title bar** at the top of the screen holds the name of the document currently being written. Until the document is given a name, the document is called "Untitled."

You can change the window to exactly suit your needs. To adjust the size:

1. Move the mouse pointer until it is at the place on the boundary you want to adjust. The mouse pointer changes to a double-headed arrow.

2. Drag the border to the left or right or up or down to make it smaller or larger.

3. When you are satisfied with the new size of the window, release the left mouse button.

If the Work area contains more information than can fit on the screen, you need a way to move through this information so you can see it all. For example, you will certainly be writing instructions in Visual Basic that are longer than one screen. You can use the mouse to march through your instructions with small steps or giant steps. A **Vertical scroll bar** lets you move from the top to the bottom of the window; a **Horizontal scroll bar** lets you move within the left and right margins of the window. Use this Scroll bar when the contents of the window are too wide to fit on the screen. Figure 1.3 shows both Vertical and Horizontal scroll bars.

A scroll bar has two arrows at the end of a channel and sometimes contains a box (usually called the **Scroll box**). The Scroll box is the key to moving rapidly; the arrows are the key to moving in smaller increments. Dragging the Scroll box enables you to quickly move long distances to an approximate location in your document. For example, if you drag the Scroll box to the middle of the channel, you'll scroll to approximately the middle of your document.

The **Menu bar** just below the Title bar is used to call up menus, or lists of tasks. Several of these tasks are described in this section.

Documents are created from the keyboard in much the same way they would be written with a typewriter. In computerese, writing a document is referred to as editing the document; therefore, the Notepad is called a **text editor**. Before discussing editing, we must first examine the workings of the keyboard.

There are several different styles of keyboards. Figure 1.4 contains a typical keyboard. The keyboard is divided into several parts. The largest portion looks and functions like an ordinary typewriter keyboard. The row of keys above this portion consists of 12 keys labeled F1 through F12, called the **function keys**. (On many keyboards, the function keys are located on the left side.) Function keys are used to perform certain tasks with a single keystroke. For instance, pressing the function key F5 displays the time and date. The right portion of the keyboard, called the **numeric keypad**, is used either to move the cursor or to enter numbers. Press the **Num Lock** key a few times and notice the tiny light labeled NUM LOCK blink on and off. When the light is on, the numeric keypad produces numbers; otherwise, it moves the cursor. The Num Lock key is called a toggle key because it "toggles" between two states. When the numeric keypad is in the cursor-moving state, the four arrow keys each move the cursor around the existing document.

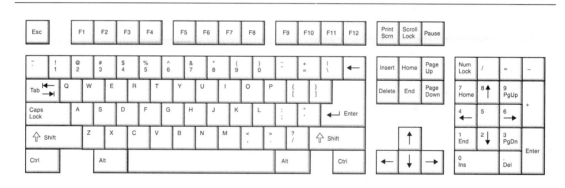

Figure 1.4 IBM PC keyboard.

Two very important keys may not have names printed on them. The **Enter** key is the key with the hooked arrow (and/or the word Enter). It is used to start a new line of a document. The Enter key corresponds to the carriage return on a typewriter. The **Backspace** key is the gray key with the left-pointing arrow located above the Enter key. It moves the cursor one space to the left and erases any character in that location.

After the Notepad has been invoked, the following routine will introduce you to the keyboard.

1. Click on the Work area of the Notepad.

2. Type a few words into the Notepad.

3. Use the right and left cursor-moving keys on the numeric keypad to move the cursor.

4. Press the **Home** key to move the cursor back to the beginning of the line. In general, the Home key moves the cursor to the beginning of the line on which it currently is located.

5. Now press the **End** key (on the numeric keypad). The cursor will move to the end of the line.

6. Type some letters using the central typewriter portion of the keyboard. The two **Shift** keys are used to obtain uppercase letters or the upper character of keys showing two characters.

7. Press the **Caps Lock** key and then type some letters. The letters will appear in uppercase. We say the keyboard is in uppercase mode. To toggle back to lowercase mode, press the Caps Lock key again. Only alphabetic keys are affected by Caps Lock. *Note:* When the keyboard is in the uppercase state, the tiny light labeled CAPS LOCK on the keyboard is lit.

8. Type some letters and then press the Backspace key a few times. It will erase letters one at a time. Another method of deleting a letter is to move the cursor to that letter and press the **Del** key. (Del stands for "Delete.") The backspace key erases the character to the left of the cursor, and the Del key erases the character at the cursor.

9. Hold down the **Ctrl** key (Ctrl stands for "Control") and press the **Del** key. This combination erases the portion of the line to the right of the cursor. We describe this combination as **Ctrl + Del**. (The plus sign indicates that the Ctrl key is to be held down while pressing the Del key.) There are many useful key combinations like this.

10. Type a few letters and use the appropriate cursor-moving key to move the cursor under one of the letters. Now type any letter and notice that it is inserted at the cursor position and that the letters following it move to the right. This is because the Notepad uses **insert mode**. Visual Basic has an additional mode, called **overwrite mode**, in which a typed letter overwrites the letter located at the cursor position. In Visual Basic, overwrite mode is invoked by pressing the **Ins** key. (Ins stands for "Insert.") Pressing this toggle key again reinstates insert mode. The cursor size indicates the active mode; a large cursor means overwrite mode.

11. The key to the left of the Q key is called the **Tab** key. It is marked with a pair of arrows, the upper one pointing to the left and the lower one pointing to the right. At the beginning of the line, pressing the Tab key indents the cursor several spaces.

12. Type more characters than can fit on one line of the screen. Notice that the leftmost characters scroll off the screen to make room for the new characters.

13. The Enter key is used to begin a new line on the screen in much the same way that the carriage return lever is used on a manual typewriter.

14. The **Alt** key activates the Menu bar. Then, pressing one of the underlined letters, such as F, E, S, or H, selects a menu. (From the Menu bar, a menu can also be selected by pressing the right-arrow key to highlight the name and then pressing the Enter key.) As shown in Figure 1.5, after a menu is opened, each option has one letter underlined. You can press an underlined letter to select an option. (Underlined letters are called **Access** keys.) For instance, pressing A from the file menu selects the option "Save As". Selections also can be made with the cursor-moving keys and the Enter key. **Note 1:** You can select menus and options without the use of keys by clicking on them with the mouse. **Note 2:** You can close a menu, without making a selection, by clicking anywhere outside the menu, or pressing the Esc key twice.

Figure 1.5 A menu and its options.

15. The **Esc** key (Esc stands for "Escape") is used to return to the Work area.

16. Press and release Alt, then press and release F, and then press N. (This key combination is abbreviated Alt/File/New or Alt/F/N.) The dialog box in Figure 1.6 will appear and ask you if you want to save the current document. Decline by pressing N or clicking on the No button.

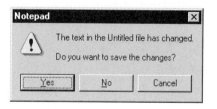

Figure 1.6 A "Do you want to save the changes?" dialog box.

17. Type the following information into the Notepad. (It gives the names of employees, their hourly wages, and the number of hours worked in the past week.) This document is used in Section 3.5. **Note:** We follow the convention of surrounding words with quotation marks to distinguish words from numbers, which are written without quotation marks.

"Mike Jones", 7.35, 35
"John Smith", 6.75, 33

18. Let's store the document as a file on a disk. To save the document, press Alt/File/Save As. A dialog box appears to request a file name for the document. The cursor is in a narrow rectangular box labeled "File Name:".

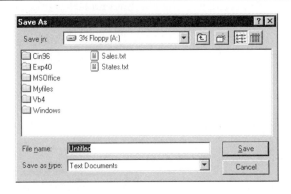

Figure 1.7 Save As dialog box.

Type a drive letter, a colon, and a name, and then press the Enter key or click on Save. For instance, you might type A:PERSONEL. The document will then be stored on drive A. This process is called **saving** the document. Notepad automatically adds a period and the extension txt to the name. Therefore, the complete file name is PERSONEL.TXT on the disk. ***Note:*** If you want to save the document in a specific folder (directory) of the disk, also type the folder (directory). For instance, you might type A:\MYFILES\ PERSONEL. See Section 1.3 for a discussion of folders. (***Note:*** You can move around in any dialog box by repeatedly pressing the Tab key.)

19. Press the key combination Alt/File/New to clear PERSONEL.TXT from Notepad.

20. Restore PERSONEL.TXT as the document in the Notepad by pressing Alt/File/Open, typing PERSONEL (possibly preceded by a drive letter and a colon, such as A:, and a folder) at the cursor position, and then pressing the Enter key.

21. Press Alt/File/Exit to exit Notepad.

Ending Windows 95

To close Windows, click the Start button and then click Shut Down. You are presented with a message box that looks like the right window in Figure 1.8. Click Yes. (If you forgot to save changes to documents, Windows will prompt you to save changes.) A screen message will appear to let you know when you can safely turn off your computer.

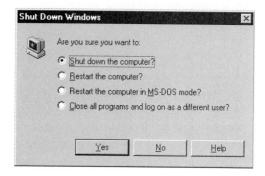

Figure 1.8 Dialog box for ending Windows.

Comments

1. The key sequences discussed in this section follow the format key1+key2 or key1/key2. The plus sign (+) instructs you to hold down key1 and then press key2. The slash symbol (/) tells you to release key1 before pressing key2. Some useful key combinations that we have not discussed yet are the following:

(a) Ctrl+Home: moves the cursor to the beginning of the document
(b) Ctrl+End: moves the cursor to the end of the document
(c) Alt/F/P/Enter: prints a copy of the current document on the printer

2. When the work area is completely filled with lines of text, the document scrolls upward to accommodate additional lines. The lines that have scrolled off the top can be viewed again by pressing the **PgUp** key. The **PgDn** key moves farther down the document.

3. There are two methods to clear the work area. You can either erase the lines one at a time with Ctrl+Del or erase all lines simultaneously and begin a new document with Alt/F/N. With the second method, a dialog box may query you about saving the current document. In this case, use Tab to select the desired option and press the Enter key. The document name in the Title bar might change to Untitled.

4. Notepad can perform many of the tasks of word processors, such as search and block operations. However, these features needn't concern us presently. A discussion of them can be found in Appendix B, under "HOW TO: Use the Editor."

5. TXT is the default extension for files created with Notepad.

6. The title bar of the Notepad window, or of any window, contains buttons that can be used to maximize, minimize, or close the window. See Figure 1.9.

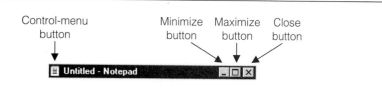

Figure 1.9 Title bar of the Notepad window.

You can click on the Maximize button to make the Notepad window fill the entire screen, click on the Minimize button to change the Notepad window into a button on the taskbar, or click on the Close button to exit Notepad. As long as a window isn't maximized, you can usually move it around the screen by dragging its title bar. (Recall that this means to move the mouse pointer until it is in the title bar, hold down the left mouse button, move the mouse until the window is where you want it to be, and then release the mouse button.) **Note 1:** If you have maximized a window, the Maximize button changes to a pair of rectangles called the **Restore button.** Click on this button to return the window to its previous size. **Note 2:** If the Notepad window has been minimized, it can be restored to its previous size by double-clicking on the icon or clicking on the button that was created when the Minimize button was clicked.

7. You should end Windows by the procedures discussed in this section whenever possible. It is a bad idea to end Windows by just shutting off your machine.

PRACTICE PROBLEMS 1.2

(Solutions to practice problems always follow the exercises.)
Assume you are using Windows' Notepad.

1. Give two ways to open the Edit menu.

2. Assume the Edit menu has been opened. Give three ways to pick a menu item.

EXERCISES 1.2

1. What does an hourglass icon mean?

2. Describe "clicking" in your own words.

3. Describe "double-clicking" in your own words.

4. Describe "dragging" in your own words.

5. What is the blinking vertical line in Notepad called, and what is its purpose?

6. How can you tell when a window is active?

7. What is the difference between "Windows" and "windows"?

8. What is the purpose of the vertical scroll bar in Notepad?

9. How do you open Notepad when the Notepad icon is visible?

10. By what name is a Notepad document known before it is named as part of being saved on disk?

11. What is a toggle key?

Figure 1.10 shows many of the special keys on the keyboard. In Exercises 12 through 36, select the key (or key combination) that performs the task in Windows' Notepad.

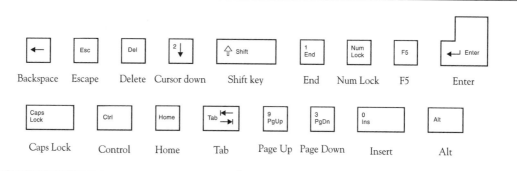

Figure 1.10 Some special keys.

12. Scroll the document to view a higher part.

13. Scroll the document to view a lower part.

14. Erase the line containing the cursor.

15. Erase the character to the left of the cursor.

16. Access the Start menu.

17. Toggle the numeric keypad between states.

18. Erase the character to the right of the cursor.

19. Toggle the case for alphabetic characters.

20. Move the cursor to the beginning of the line containing the cursor.

21. Move the cursor to the end of the line containing the cursor.

22. Display the time and date.

23. Cause the upper character of a double-character key to be displayed.

24. Move the cursor down to the next row of the screen.

25. Print a copy of the current document on the printer.

26. Exit Notepad.

27. Move the cursor to the beginning of the document.

28. Move the cursor to the end of the document.

29. Move the cursor from the Work area to the Menu bar.

30. Cancel a dialog box.

31. Move from the Menu bar to the Work area.

32. Move from one option rectangle of a dialog box to another rectangle.

33. Save the current document on a diskette.

34. Clear the current document from the Work area and start a new document.

35. Create a blank line in the middle of a document.

36. Remove a pull-down menu from the screen.

SOLUTIONS TO PRACTICE PROBLEMS 1.2

1. Press Alt/Edit or click on the word Edit in the toolbar to display the Edit menu. The jargon says the menu is "dropped down" or "pulled down."

2. Press the Down arrow key to highlight the item and then press the Enter key, press the underlined letter in the name of the item, or click on the item.

1.3 DISKS AND FOLDERS

Modern computers have a hard disk, a diskette drive, and usually a CD drive. The hard disk is permanently housed inside the computer. You can read information from all three drives, but can only write information to the hard disk and to diskettes. Most diskette drives accommodate the type of diskette shown in Figure 1.11. This diskette has a plastic jacket and measures $3\frac{1}{2}''$ on each side.

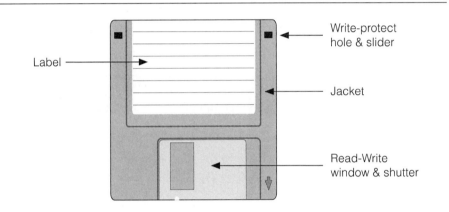

Figure 1.11 $3\frac{1}{2}''$ diskette.

When the diskette is inserted into a drive, the shutter slides to the right and exposes the read-write window. The diskette drive records and reads data through the read-write window. The write-protect hole is normally covered. When the write-protect hole is uncovered by sliding the slider on the back of the diskette, nothing can be erased from or recorded on the diskette. To insert a diskette, hold the diskette with the label facing up and the read/write window pointing toward the diskette drive. You insert the diskette by just pushing it into the drive until you hear a click. You remove it by pressing the button on the drive.

When handling a diskette, be careful not to touch the exposed surface in the read-write window. Also, do not remove a diskette from a diskette drive while the little light on the diskette drive is lit.

We use the word **disk** to refer to either the hard disk, a diskette, or a CD. Each drive is identified by a letter. Normally, the hard drive is identified by C, the diskette by A, and the CD drive by D.

Disk management is handled by the computer's operating system. VB 5.0 requires that your computer use a Windows 95 operating system.

Disks hold not only programs but also collections of data stored in **data files**. The term file refers to either a data file or a program file. We created a data file in Section 1.2. Each file has a name consisting of a base name followed by an optional extension consisting of a period and one or more characters. Letters, digits, spaces, periods and a few other assorted characters (see Comment 1) can be used in filenames. Extensions are normally used to identify the type of file. For example, spreadsheets created with Excel have the extension xls, documents created with Word have the extension doc, and files created with Notepad have the extension txt. Some examples of file names are "Annual Sales.xls," "Letter to Mom.doc," and Phone.txt.

Because a disk is capable of holding thousands of files, locating a specific file can be quite time-consuming. Therefore, related files are grouped into collections that are stored in separate areas of the disk. For instance, one area might hold all your Visual Basic programs, and another the documents created with your word processor.

Think of a disk as a large folder, called the **root folder**, that contains several smaller folders, each with its own name. (The naming of folders follows the same rule as the naming of files.) Each of these smaller folders can contain yet other named folders. Each folder is identified by listing its name preceded by the names of the successively larger folders that contain it, with each folder name preceded by a backslash. Such a sequence is called a **path**. For instance, the path \SALES\NY.90\JULY identifies the folder JULY, contained in the folder NY.90, which in turn is contained in the folder SALES. Think of a file, along with its name, as written on a slip of paper that can be placed into either the root folder or one of the smaller folders. The combination of a drive letter followed by a colon, a path, and a file name is called a **filespec**, an abbreviation of "file specification." Some examples of filespecs are C:\VB5\VB.EXE and A:\PERSONAL\INCOME96.TXT.

In DOS and earlier versions of Windows, folders were called directories. Many Visual Basic objects and commands still refer to folders as directories. Windows 95 contains two programs (My Computer and Windows Explorer) that help you view, organize, and manage the folders and files on your disks. We will carry out these tasks with My Computer. We will learn how to create, rename, copy, move, and delete folders and files.

Using My Computer

To invoke My Computer, double-click on the My Computer icon. Your initial window will show an icon for each drive (and a few other icons). If you click on one of the drive icons a second window containing the folders and files for that drive will appear. Figure 1.12 shows a possible pair of windows. A folder is identified by a folder icon, a file created with Notepad is identified by a small spiral notepad, and an executable file is identified by a rectangle (with a thin bar across top) icon.

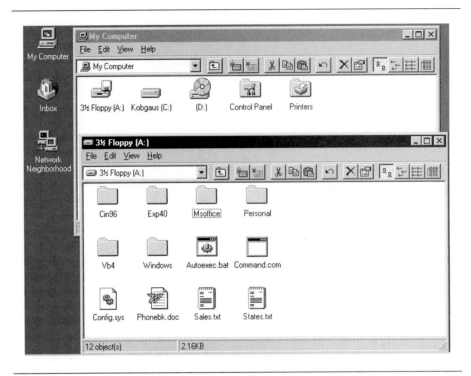

Figure 1.12 Windows created with My Computer.

To open a folder, double-click on that folder. A window with the folder's name in its title bar will appear. This window will contain an icon for each subfolder and file of the original folder. Figure 1.13 shows such a window.

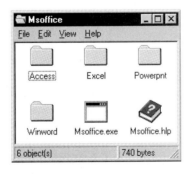

Figure 1.13 A window produced by opening a folder.

To create a new folder:

1. Open the folder that is to contain the new folder as a subfolder.

   Note: Initially, the root folder is open.

2. On the File menu, point to New, and then click Folder. (Or press Alt/File/New/Folder.)

   The new folder appears with a temporary name.

3. Type a name for the folder and then press the Enter key.

To rename a folder or file:

1. Click on the folder or file.

2. On the File menu, click Rename. (Or press Alt/File/Rename.)

The current name will appear highlighted inside a rectangle.

3. Type the new name and then press the Enter key.

To delete a folder or file:

1. Click on the folder or file.

2. On the File menu, click Delete. (Or Press Alt/File/Delete.)

A "Confirm File Delete" input box containing the name of the folder or file will appear.

3. Click on the Yes button.

To copy a folder or file:

1. Click on the folder or file to be copied.

2. On the Edit menu, click Copy. (Or press Alt/Edit/Copy.)

3. Open the folder or disk where the copy is to be placed.

4. On the Edit menu, click Paste. (Or press Alt/Edit/Paste.)

To move a folder or file:

1. Click on the folder or file to be moved.

2. On the Edit menu, click on Cut. (Or press Alt/Edit/Cut.)

3. Open the folder where the folder or file is to be placed.

4. On the Edit menu, click Paste. (Or press Alt/Edit/Paste.)

You also can carry out some of the preceding operations by "drag and drop." For details, see the Help Topics accessed through the My Computer Help menu. For instance, you can delete a folder or file by dragging it to the Recycle Bin and releasing the left mouse button.

Comments

1. File names can consist of digits, letters of the alphabet, spaces, and the characters & ! _ @ ' ' ~ ( ) { } – # % . + , ; = [ ] $.

2. File names can consist of up to 255 characters including spaces. However, a name cannot contain the following characters: \ / : ? * " > < |

3. Names of folders do not usually have an extension.

4. Neither Windows nor Visual Basic distinguishes between uppercase and lowercase letters in folders and file names. For instance, the names COSTS95.TXT, Costs95.Txt, and costs95.txt are equivalent. From now on, we will use uppercase letter in this book.

5. Because you cannot write to a CD drive, you cannot rename or delete files or folders residing on a CD drive.

6. When you delete a folder directory containing other subfolders or files, you will be queried about the removal of these subfolders and files.

7. Most diskettes purchased these days are "preformatted." Formatting prepares the disk for use with your computer and deletes any previous information stored on it. If you have a diskette that has not been formatted, you must format it yourself before you can use it.

   To format a diskette:

   (a) Insert the diskette in a drive and select the drive in My Computer.
   (b) From the File menu, choose Format.
   (c) In the Format Disk dialog box, specify the various options. (Most likely, the default values will be appropriate.)
   (d) Click the Start button.

8. You can obtain further information about My Computer by selecting "Search for Help on" from its Help menu and then specifying a topic.

9. Refer to Step 18 in the Notepad walkthrough of Section 1.2, and suppose you typed A:\MYFILES\PERSONEL into the "File Name:" box. The disk drive and directory could have been specified with other parts of the dialog box.

   (a) Click on the arrow to the right of the "Save in:" box and click on "3 1/2 Floppy (A:)" to select the A: drive.
   The large box in the center of the "Save As" window shows the subfolder of the selected drive.
   (b) Open the desired folder by double-clicking on it.
   The folder will replace the drive in the "Save in:" box and its subfolders will appear in the large box. This process can be repeated as many times as required to locate the desired folder.
   (c) Return to the "File name:" box and type in PERSONEL.
   (d) Press the Enter key or click on the Save button.

10. There are many uses of dialog boxes such as the one discussed in comment 9. For instance, they pop up to report errors in a Visual Basic document. In general, the Tab key is used to move around inside a dialog box and the Enter key makes a selection. Although dialog boxes often have a cancel button, the Esc key also can be used to remove the dialog box from the screen.

11. In DOS and earlier versions of Windows, file names were limited to no more than eight characters followed by an optional extension of at most 3 characters. This is referred to as the 8.3 format. In this text we use the 8.3 format so that folders also can be explored in DOS, and the programs we write also can be run in earlier versions of Visual Basic using Windows 3.1.

12. Some books use the word "path" to mean what we call "filespec."

PRACTICE PROBLEMS 1.3

1. Give two ways to remove all information from a diskette.

2. Suppose the path for a file is C:\GAMES\BOARD\CHESS.EXE. How many folders must you open in My Computer to reach the file?

EXERCISES 1.3

1. Explain why "Who is there?" is not a valid file name.

2. Explain why "FOUR STAR HOTEL ***" is not a valid name.

3. What is wrong with the filespec "C:/SPORTS/TENNIS.DOC"?

4. What is wrong with the filespec "A$:\GREAT\FILMS\CITIZEN KANE"?

5. Suppose "C:\U.S.A\MARYLAND\MONTGOMERY COUNTY\SILVER SPRING.DOC" is the filespec for a file. How many folders (counting the root folder) must you open in My Computer to reach the file?

6. Suppose the filespec for a file is A:\ANIMAL\BIRDS\ROBIN.DOC. How many folders must you open in My Computer to reach the file?

7. The folder Windows (or WIN95) contains a folder named System. How many folders does System contain?

8. The file VB5.EXE (or VB5CCE.EXE) is created when Visual Basic is installed on a computer. Determine the filespec for this file.

The folder Windows (or WIN95) contains a folder named System. Open System and then press Alt/V/D to select the Details option from the View menu. In Exercises 9-12, give the effect of clicking on the specified button in the bar just below the toolbar.

9. Size

10. Type

11. Modified

12. Name

13. Suppose your computer has just one diskette drive. How could you use the procedures discussed in this section to copy a file in the root directory of a diskette onto another diskette?

14. Open the folder on your hard disk containing Visual Basic. How many subfolders does the folder contain directly? How many files does the folder contain directly?

In Exercises 15 and 16, carry out the stated tasks.

15. (a) Take a blank diskette and create two folders (directories) named Laurel and Hardy.
    (b) Create a subdirectory of Laurel called Stan.
    (c) Use Notepad to create a file containing the sentence "Here's another nice mess you've gotten me into." and save the file with the name QUOTE.TXT in the directory Laurel.
    (d) Copy the file QUOTE.TXT into the folder (directory) Hardy.
    (e) Rename the new copy of the file QUOTE.TXT as Line.txt.
    (f) Delete the original copy of the file QUOTE.TXT.

16. (a) Take a blank diskette, create a folder (directory) named Slogans, and create two subdirectories of Slogans named Coke and CocaCola.
    (b) Use Notepad to create a file containing the sentence "It's the real thing." and save the file with the name COKE1970.TXT in the folder (directory) Coke.

(c) Use Notepad to create a file containing the phrase "The ideal brain tonic." and save the file with the name COKE1892.TXT in the folder (directory) Coke.

(d) Copy the two files in Coke into the folder (directory) CocaCola.

(e) Delete the folder (directory) Coke.

(f) Rename the folder (directory) CocaCola as Coke.

SOLUTIONS TO PRACTICE PROBLEMS 1.3

1. First way: Use the Delete command from the File menu of My Computer. Second way: Format the diskette.

2. Three, counting the root folder. You can think of clicking on the C: icon as opening the root folder. After that, you must open folder Games and then folder Board. Chess.exe will be in the folder Board.

1.4 AN INTRODUCTION TO VISUAL BASIC

Visual Basic is the most exciting development in programming in many years. Visual Basic is the next generation of BASIC and is designed to make user-friendly programs easier to develop.

Prior to the creation of Visual Basic, developing a friendly user interface usually required teams of programmers using arcane languages like "C" that came in 10-pound boxes with thousands of pages of documentation. Now they can be done by a few people using a language that is a direct descendent of BASIC—the language most accessible to beginning programmers.

Visual Basic 5.0 requires the Microsoft Windows 95 operating system. Although you don't need to be an expert user of Microsoft Windows, you do need to know the basics before you can master Visual Basic—that is, you need to be comfortable with manipulating a mouse, you need to know how to manipulate a window, and you need to know how to use Notepad and My Computer. However, there is no better way to master Microsoft Windows than to write applications for it—and that is what Visual Basic is all about.

Why Windows and Why Visual Basic?

What people call **graphical user interfaces**, or GUIs (pronounced "gooies"), have revolutionized the microcomputer industry. Instead of the cryptic C:\> prompt that DOS users have long seen (and that some have long feared), users are presented with a desktop filled with little pictures called icons. Icons provide a visual guide to what the program can do.

Similarly, along with the revolution in how programs look was a revolution in how they feel. Consider a program that requests information for a database. Figure 1.14 shows how such a DOS-based BASIC program gets its information. The program requests the six pieces of data one at a time, with no opportunity to go back and alter previously entered information. After the program requests the six pieces of data, the screen clears and the six inputs are again requested one at a time. Figure 1.15 shows how an equivalent Visual Basic program gets its information. The boxes may be filled in any order. When the user clicks on a box with the mouse, the cursor moves to that box. The user can either type in new information or edit the existing information. When the user is satisfied that all the information is correct, he or she just clicks on the Write to Database button. The boxes will clear and the data for another person can be entered. After all names have been entered, the user clicks on the Exit button. In Figure 1.14, the program is in control; in Figure 1.15, the user is in control!

```
Enter Name (Enter EOD to terminate): Bill Clinton
Enter Address: 1600 Pennsylvania Avenue
Enter City: Washington
Enter State: DC
Enter Zipcode: 20500
Enter Phone Number: 202-395-3000
```

Figure 1.14 Input screen of a DOS-based BASIC program to create a database.

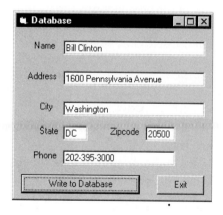

Figure 1.15 Input screen of a Visual Basic program to fill a database.

How You Develop a Visual Basic Application

One of the key elements of planning a Visual Basic application is deciding what the user sees—in other words, designing the screen. What data will he or she be entering? How large a window should the application use? Where will you place the command buttons, the "buttons" the user clicks on to activate the applications? Will the applications have places to enter text (text boxes) and places to display output? What kind of warning boxes (message boxes) should the application use? In Visual Basic, the responsive objects a program designer places on windows are called **controls**.

Two features make Visual Basic different from almost any other programming tool:

1. You literally draw the user interface, much like using a paint program. Next, and perhaps more importantly,

2. When you're done drawing the interface, the command buttons, text boxes, and other objects that you have placed in a blank window will automatically recognize user actions such as mouse movements and button clicks. That is,

the sequence of procedures executed in your program is controlled by "events" that the user initiates, rather than by a predetermined sequence of procedures in your program.

In any case, only after you design the interface does anything like traditional programming occur. Objects in Visual Basic recognize events like mouse clicks; how the objects respond to them depends on the instructions you write. You always need to write instructions in order to make controls respond to events. This makes Visual Basic programming fundamentally different from conventional programming.

Programs in conventional programming languages run from the top down. For older programming languages, execution starts from the first line and moves with the flow of the program to different parts as needed. A Visual Basic program works completely differently. The core of a Visual Basic program is a set of independent groups of instructions that are activated by the events they have been told to recognize. This is a fundamental shift. Instead of designing a program to do what the programmer thinks should happen, the user is in control.

Most of the programming instructions in Visual Basic that tell your program how to respond to events like mouse clicks occur in what Visual Basic calls *event procedures*. Essentially, anything executable in a Visual Basic program is either in an event procedure or is used by an event procedure to help the procedure carry out its job. In fact, to stress that Visual Basic is fundamentally different from ordinary programming languages, Microsoft uses the term *project*, rather than *program*, to refer to the combination of programming instructions and user interface that makes a Visual Basic application possible.

Here is a summary of the steps you take to design a Visual Basic application:

1. Decide how the windows that the user sees will look.

2. Determine which events the objects on the window should recognize.

3. Write the event procedures for those events.

Now here is what happens when the program is running:

1. Visual Basic monitors the window and the objects in the window to detect any event that an object can recognize (mouse movements, clicks, keystrokes, and so on).

2. When Visual Basic detects an event, it examines the program to see if you've written an event procedure for that event.

3. If you have written an event procedure, Visual Basic executes the instructions that make up that event procedure and goes back to Step 1.

4. If you have not written an event procedure, Visual Basic waits for the next event and goes back to Step 1.

These steps cycle continuously until the application ends. Usually, an event must happen before Visual Basic will do anything. Event-driven programs are reactive more than active—and that makes them more user-friendly.

The Different Versions of Visual Basic

Visual Basic 1.0 first appeared in 1991. It was followed by version 2.0 in 1992, version 3.0 in 1993, version 4.0 in 1995, and version 5.0 in 1997. Because Microsoft has publicly announced that Visual Basic is a key product for the company, Microsoft will continue to add further enhancements to the language. For example, Microsoft is using versions of Visual Basic to control all its applications, such as Microsoft Office. Master Visual Basic and you will be well-prepared for almost any office computer environment.

Visual Basic 5.0 comes in four editions—Learning, Professional, Enterprise, and Control Creation Edition. All editions require either Windows 95 or Windows NT. You can use any edition of Visual Basic 5.0 with this textbook.

1.5 BIOGRAPHICAL HISTORY OF COMPUTING

The following people made important contributions to the evolution of the computer and the principles of programming.

1800s

George Boole: a self-taught British mathematician; devised an algebra of logic that later became a key tool in computer design. The logical operators presented in Section 5.1 are also known as Boolean operators.

Charles Babbage: a British mathematician and engineer; regarded as the father of the computer. Although the mechanical "analytical engine" that he conceived was never built, it influenced the design of modern computers. It had units for input, output, memory, arithmetic, logic, and control. Algorithms were intended to be communicated to the computer via punched cards, and numbers were to be stored on toothed wheels.

Augusta Ada Byron: a mathematician and colleague of Charles Babbage; regarded as the first computer programmer. She encouraged Babbage to modify the design based on programming considerations. Together they developed the concepts of decision structures, loops, and a library of procedures. Decision structures, loops, and procedures are presented in Chapters 5, 6, and 4 of this text, respectively.

Herman Hollerith: the founder of a company that was later to become IBM; at the age of 20, he devised a computer that made it possible to process the data for the U.S. Census of 1890 in one-third the time required for the 1880 census. His electromagnetic "tabulating machine" passed metal pins through holes in punched cards and into mercury-filled cups to complete an electric circuit. Each location of a hole corresponded to a characteristic of the population.

1930s

Alan Turing: a gifted and far-sighted British mathematician; made fundamental contributions to the theory of computer science, assisted in the construction of some of the early large computers, and proposed a test for detecting intelligence within a machine. His theoretical "Turing machine" laid the foundation for the development of general-purpose programmable computers. He changed the course of the Second World War by breaking the German "Enigma" code, thereby making secret German messages comprehensible to the Allies.

John V. Atanasoff: a mathematician and physicist at Iowa State University; declared by a federal court in Minnesota to be the inventor of the first electronic digital special-purpose computer. Designed with the assistance of his graduate assistant, Clifford Berry, this computer used vacuum tubes (instead of the less efficient relays) for storage and arithmetic functions.

1940s

Howard Aiken: a professor at Harvard University; built the Mark I, a large-scale digital computer functionally similar to the "analytical engine" proposed by Babbage. This computer, which took 5 years to build and used relays for storage and computations, was technologically obsolete before it was completed.

Grace M. Hopper: retired in 1986 at the age of 79 as a rear admiral in the United States Navy; wrote the first major subroutine (a procedure used to calculate sin x on the Mark I computer) and one of the first assembly languages. In 1945, she found that a moth fused onto a wire of the Mark I was causing the computer to malfunction, thus the origin of the term "debugging" for finding errors. As an administrator at Remington Rand in the 1950s, Dr. Hopper pioneered the development and use of COBOL, a programming language for the business community written in English-like notation.

John Mauchley and J. Presper Eckert: electrical engineers working at the University of Pennsylvania; built the first large-scale electronic digital general-purpose computer to be put into full operation. The ENIAC used 18,000 vacuum tubes for storage and arithmetic computations, weighed 30 tons, and occupied 1500 square feet. It could perform 300 multiplications of two 10-digit numbers per second, whereas the Mark I required 3 seconds to perform a single multiplication. Later they designed and developed the UNIVAC I, the first commercial electronic computer.

John von Neumann: a mathematical genius and member of the Institute of Advanced Studies in Princeton, New Jersey; developed the stored program concept used in all modern computers. Prior to this development, instructions were programmed into computers by manually rewiring connections. Along with Hermann H. Goldstein, he wrote the first paper on the use of flowcharts.

Stanislaw Ulam: American research mathematician and educator; pioneered the application of random numbers and computers to the solution of problems in mathematics and physics. His techniques, known as Monte Carlo methods or computer simulation, are used to determine the likelihoods of various outcomes of games of chance and to analyze business operations.

Maurice V. Wilkes: an electrical engineer at Cambridge University in England and student of von Neumann; built the EDSAC, the first computer to use the stored program concept. Along with D. J. Wheeler and S. Gill, he wrote the first computer programming text, *The Preparation of Programs for an Electronic Digital Computer* (Addison-Wesley, 1951), which dealt in depth with the use and construction of a versatile subroutine library.

John Bardeen, Walter Brattain, and William Shockley: physicists at Bell Labs; developed the transistor, a miniature device that replaced the vacuum tube and revolutionized computer design. It was smaller, lighter, more reliable, and cooler than the vacuum tube.

1950s

John Backus: a programmer for IBM; in 1953, headed a small group of programmers who wrote the most extensively used early interpretive computer system, the IBM 701 Speedcoding System. An interpreter translates a high-level language program into machine language one statement at a time as the program is executed. In 1957, Backus and his team produced the compiled language Fortran, which soon became the primary academic and scientific language. A compiler translates an entire program into efficient machine language before the program is executed. Visual Basic combines the best of both worlds. It has the power and speed of a compiled language and the ease of use of an interpreted language.

Donald L. Shell: in 1959, the year that he received his Ph.D. in mathematics from the University of Cincinnati, published an efficient algorithm for ordering (or sorting) lists of data. Sorting has been estimated to consume nearly one-quarter of the running time of computers. The Shell sort is presented in Chapter 7 of this text.

1960s

John G. Kemeny and Thomas E. Kurtz: professors of mathematics at Dartmouth College and the inventors of BASIC; led Dartmouth to national leadership in the educational uses of computing. Kemeny's distinguished career included serving as an assistant to both John von Neumann and Albert Einstein, serving as president of Dartmouth College, and chairing the commission to investigate the Three Mile Island nuclear power plant accident. In recent years, Kemeny and Kurtz have devoted considerable energy to the promotion of structured BASIC.

Corrado Bohm and Guiseppe Jacopini: European mathematicians; proved that any program can be written with the three structures discussed in Section 2.2: sequences, decisions, and loops. This result led to the systematic methods of modern program design known as structured programming.

Edsger W. Dijkstra: professor of computer science at the Technological University at Eindhoven, The Netherlands; stimulated the move to structured programming with the publication of a widely read article, "Go To Statement Considered Harmful." In that article, he proposes that GOTO statements be abolished from all high-level languages such as BASIC. The modern programming structures available in Visual Basic do away with the need for GOTO statements.

Harlan B. Mills: IBM Fellow and professor of computer science at the University of Maryland; has long advocated the use of structured programming. In 1969, Mills was asked to write a program creating an information database for the *New York Times*, a project that was estimated to require 30 person-years with traditional programming techniques. Using structured programming techniques, Mills single-handedly completed the project in 6 months. The methods of structured programming are used throughout this text.

Donald E. Knuth: professor of computer science at Stanford University; is generally regarded as the preeminent scholar of computer science in the world. He is best known for his monumental series of books, *The Art of Computer Programming*, the definitive work on algorithms.

Ted Hoff, Stan Mazer, Robert Noyce, and Federico Faggin: engineers at the Intel Corporation; developed the first microprocessor chip. Such chips, which serve as the central processing units for microcomputers, are responsible for the extraordinary reduction in the size of computers. A computer with greater power than the ENIAC now can be held in the palm of the hand.

1970s

Ted Codd: laid the groundwork for relational databases in his seminal paper, "A Relational Model of Data for Large Shared Data Banks," that appeared in the June 1970 issue of the *Communications of the ACM*. Relational databases are studied in Chapter 12 of this text.

Paul Allen and Bill Gates: cofounders of Microsoft Corporation; developed languages and the operating system for the IBM PC. The operating system, known as MS-DOS, is a collection of programs that manage the operation of the computer. In 1974, Gates dropped out of Harvard after 1 year, and Allen left a programming job with Honeywell to write software together. Their initial project was a version of BASIC for the Altair, the first microcomputer. Microsoft is one of the most highly respected software companies in the United States and a leader in the development of programming languages.

Stephen Wozniak and Stephen Jobs: cofounders of Apple Computer Inc.; started the microcomputer revolution. The two had met as teenagers while working summers at Hewlett-Packard. Another summer, Jobs worked in an orchard, a job that inspired the names of their computers. Wozniak designed the Apple computer in Jobs' parents' garage, and Jobs promoted it so successfully that the company was worth hundreds of millions of dollars when it went public. Both men resigned from the company in 1985.

Dan Bricklin and Dan Fylstra: cofounders of Software Arts; wrote VisiCalc, the first electronic spreadsheet program. An electronic spreadsheet is a worksheet divided into rows and columns, which analysts use to construct budgets and estimate costs. A change made in one number results in the updating of all numbers derived from it. For instance, changing a person's housing expenses will immediately produce a change in total expenses. Bricklin got the idea for an electronic spreadsheet after watching one of his professors at Harvard Business School struggle while updating a spreadsheet at the blackboard. VisiCalc became so popular that many people bought personal computers just so they could run the program. A simplified spreadsheet is developed as a case study in Section 7.6 of this text. Chapter 13 shows how to use Visual Basic as a front end to access a spreadsheet.

Robert Barnaby: a dedicated programmer; best known for writing WordStar, one of the most popular word processors. Word processing programs account for 30 percent of all software sold in the United States. The Visual Basic editor uses WordStar-like commands.

1980s

William L. Sydnes: manager of the IBM Entry Systems Boca engineering group; headed the design team for the IBM Personal Computer. Shortly after its introduction in 1981, the IBM PC dominated the microcomputer field. Visual Basic runs on IBM Personal Computers and compatibles.

Mitchell D. Kapor: cofounder of Lotus Corporation; wrote the business software program 1-2-3, the most successful piece of software for personal computers. Lotus 1-2-3 is an integrated program consisting of a spreadsheet, a database manager, and a graphics package. Databases are studied in Chapters 8 and 9 of this text and graphics in Chapter 10.

Tom Button: group product manager for applications programmability at Microsoft; headed the team that developed QuickBasic, QBasic, and Visual Basic. These modern, yet easy-to-use languages, have greatly increased the productivity of programmers.

Alan Cooper: director of applications software for Coactive Computing Corporation; is considered the father of Visual Basic. In 1987, he wrote a program called Ruby that delivered visual programming to the average user. A few years later, Ruby was combined with QuickBasic to produce Visual Basic, the remarkably successful language that allows Windows programs to be written from within Windows easily and efficiently.

Tim Berners-Lee: British computer scientist, proposed the World Wide Web project in 1989 while working in Switzerland. His brainchild has grown into a global phenomenon. Chapter 13 shows how to use Visual Basic to browse the Web.

1990s

Marc Andreessen: while a graduate student at the University of Illinois, led a small band of fellow students to develop Mosaic, a program that allowed the user to move around the World Wide Web by clicking on words and symbols. Andreesssen went on to cofound Netscape Communications Corporation; today Netscape is the world's leading Web browser. Chapter 13 shows how to use Visual Basic to build a simplified Web browser.

2

Problem Solving

2.1 Program Development Cycle / 32
• Performing a Task on the Computer • Program Planning

2.2 Programming Tools / 34
• Flowcharts • Pseudocode • Hierarchy Chart • Direction of Numbered New York Streets Algorithm • Class Average Algorithm

2.1 PROGRAM DEVELOPMENT CYCLE

We learned in the first chapter that hardware refers to the machinery in a computer system (such as the monitor, keyboard, and CPU) and software refers to a collection of instructions, called a **program** (or **project**), that directs the hardware. Programs are written to solve problems or perform tasks on a computer. Programmers translate the solutions or tasks into a language the computer can understand. As we write programs, we must keep in mind that the computer will only do what we instruct it to do. Because of this, we must be very careful and thorough with our instructions.

Performing a Task on the Computer

The first step in writing instructions to carry out a task is to determine what the **output** should be, that is, exactly what the task should produce. The second step is to identify the data, or **input**, necessary to obtain the output. The last step is to determine how to **process** the input to obtain the desired output, that is, to determine what formulas or ways of doing things can be used to obtain the output.

This problem-solving approach is the same as that used to solve word problems in an algebra class. For example, consider the following algebra problem:

How fast is a car traveling if it goes 50 miles in 2 hours?

The first step is to determine the type of answer requested. The answer should be a number giving the rate of speed in miles per hour (the output). The information needed to obtain the answer is the distance and time the car has traveled (the input). The formula

$$rate = distance / time$$

is used to process the distance traveled and the time elapsed in order to determine the rate of speed. That is,

$$rate = 50 \text{ miles} / 2$$
$$= 25 \text{ miles} / \text{hour}$$

A pictorial representation of this problem-solving process is

We determine what we want as output, get the needed input, and process the input to produce the desired output.

In the following chapters, we discuss how to write programs to carry out the preceding operations. But first, we look at the general process of writing programs.

Program Planning

A recipe provides a good example of a plan. The ingredients and the amounts are determined by what is to be baked. That is, the *output* determines the *input* and the *processing*. The recipe, or plan, reduces the number of mistakes you might make if you tried to bake with no plan at all. Although it's difficult to imagine an architect building a bridge or a factory without a detailed plan, many programmers (particularly students in their first programming course) frequently try to write programs without first making a careful plan. The more complicated the problem, the more complex the plan must be. You will spend much less time working on a program if you devise a carefully thought out step-by-step plan and test it before actually writing the program.

Many programmers plan their programs using a sequence of steps, referred to as the **program development cycle**. The following step-by-step process will enable you to use your time efficiently and help you design error-free programs that produce the desired output.

1. ***Analyze:*** Define the problem.

   Be sure you understand what the program should do, that is, what the output should be. Have a clear idea of what data (or input) are given and the relationship between the input and the desired output.

2. ***Design:*** Plan the solution to the problem.

   Find a logical sequence of precise steps that solve the problem. Such a sequence of steps is called an **algorithm**. Every detail, including obvious steps, should appear in the algorithm. In the next section, we discuss three popular methods used to develop the logic plan: flowcharts, pseudocode, and top-down charts. These tools help the programmer break a problem into a sequence of small tasks the computer can perform to solve the problem.

   Planning also involves using representative data to test the logic of the algorithm by hand to ensure that it is correct.

3. ***Choose the interface:*** Select the objects (text boxes, command buttons, etc.).

   Determine how the input will be obtained and how the output will be displayed. Then create objects to receive the input and display the output. Also, create appropriate command buttons to allow the user to control the program.

4. ***Code:*** Translate the algorithm into a programming language.

   Coding is the technical word for writing the program. During this stage, the program is written in Visual Basic and entered into the computer. The programmer uses the algorithm devised in Step 2 along with a knowledge of Visual Basic.

5. ***Test and debug:*** Locate and remove any errors in the program.

   Testing is the process of finding errors in a program, and **debugging** is the process of correcting errors found during the testing process. (An error in a program is called a **bug.**) As the program is typed, Visual Basic points out certain types of program errors. Other types of errors will be detected by Visual Basic when the program is executed; however, many errors due to typing mistakes, flaws in the algorithm, or incorrect usages of the Visual Basic language rules only can be uncovered and corrected by careful detective work. An example of such an error would be using addition when multiplication was the proper operation.

6. **Complete the documentation:** Organize all the material that describes the program.

Documentation is intended to allow another person, or the programmer at a later date, to understand the program. Internal documentation consists of statements in the program that are not executed, but point out the purposes of various parts of the program. Documentation might also consist of a detailed description of what the program does and how to use the program (for instance, what type of input is expected). For commercial programs, documentation includes an instruction manual. Other types of documentation are the flowchart, pseudocode, and top-down chart that were used to construct the program. Although documentation is listed as the last step in the program development cycle, it should take place as the program is being coded.

2.2 PROGRAMMING TOOLS

This section discusses some specific algorithms and develops three tools used to convert algorithms into computer programs: flowcharts, pseudocode, and hierarchy charts.

You use algorithms every day to make decisions and perform tasks. For instance, whenever you mail a letter, you must decide how much postage to put on the envelope. One rule of thumb is to use one stamp for every five sheets of paper or fraction thereof. Suppose a friend asks you to determine the number of stamps to place on an envelope. The following algorithm will accomplish the task.

1. Request the number of sheets of paper; call it Sheets.   *(input)*

2. Divide Sheets by 5.   *(processing)*

3. Round the quotient up to the next highest whole number; call it Stamps.   *(processing)*

4. Reply with the number Stamps.   *(output)*

The preceding algorithm takes the number of sheets (Sheets) as input, processes the data, and produces the number of stamps needed (Stamps) as output. We can test the algorithm for a letter with 16 sheets of paper.

1. Request the number of sheets of paper; Sheets = 16.

2. Dividing 5 into 16 gives 3.2.

3. Rounding 3.2 up to 4 gives Stamps = 4.

4. Reply with the answer, 4 stamps.

This problem-solving example can be pictured by

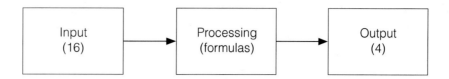

Of the program design tools available, the three most popular are the following:

Flowcharts: graphically depict the logical steps to carry out a task and show how the steps relate to each other.

Pseudocode: uses English-like phrases with some Visual Basic terms to outline the task.

Hierarchy charts: show how the different parts of a program relate to each other.

Flowcharts

A flowchart consists of special geometric symbols connected by arrows. Within each symbol is a phrase presenting the activity at that step. The shape of the symbol indicates the type of operation that is to take place. For instance, the parallelogram denotes input or output. The arrows connecting the symbols, called **flowlines**, show the progression in which the steps take place. Flowcharts should "flow" from the top of the page to the bottom. Although the symbols used in flowcharts are standardized, no standards exist for the amount of detail required within each symbol.

A table of the flowchart symbols adopted by the American National Standards Institute (ANSI) follows. Figure 2.1 contains the flowchart for the postage stamp problem.

Symbol	Name	Meaning
⟶	*Flowline*	Used to connect symbols and indicate the flow of logic.
▭	*Terminal*	Used to represent the beginning (Start) or the end (End) of a task.
▱	*Input/Output*	Used for input and output operations, such as reading and printing. The data to be read or printed are described inside.
▭	*Processing*	Used for arithmetic and data-manipulation operations. The instructions are listed inside the symbol.
◇	*Decision*	Used for any logic or comparison operations. Unlike the input/output and processing symbols, which have one entry and one exit flowline, the decision symbol has one entry and two exit paths. The path chosen depends on whether the answer to a question is "yes" or "no."

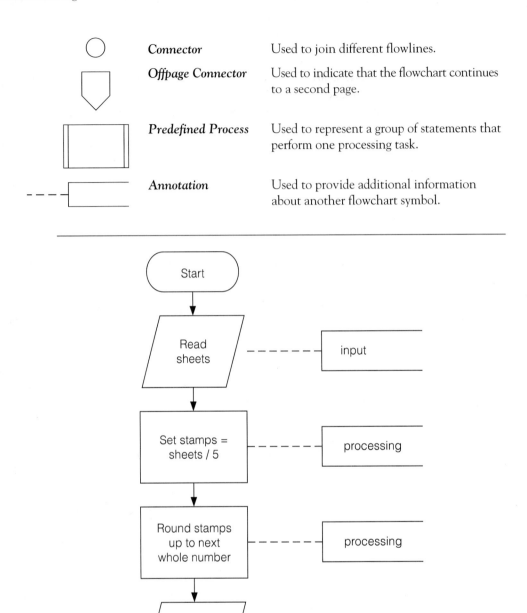

Symbol	Name	Description
○	**Connector**	Used to join different flowlines.
▽	**Offpage Connector**	Used to indicate that the flowchart continues to a second page.
▯	**Predefined Process**	Used to represent a group of statements that perform one processing task.
▭	**Annotation**	Used to provide additional information about another flowchart symbol.

Figure 2.1 Flowchart for the postage stamp problem.

The main advantage of using a flowchart to plan a task is that it provides a pictorial representation of the task, which makes the logic easier to follow. We can clearly see every step and how each step is connected to the next. The major disadvantage with flowcharts is that when a program is very large, the flowcharts may continue for many pages, making them hard to follow and modify.

Pseudocode

Pseudocode is an abbreviated version of actual computer code (hence, *pseudo-code*). The geometric symbols used in flowcharts are replaced by English-like statements that outline the process. As a result, pseudocode looks more like computer code than does a flowchart. Pseudocode allows the programmer to focus on the steps required to solve a problem rather than on how to use the computer language. The programmer can describe the algorithm in Visual Basic-like form without being restricted by the rules of Visual Basic. When the pseudocode is completed, it can be easily translated into the Visual Basic language.

The following is pseudocode for the postage stamp problem:

Program: Determine the proper number of stamps for a letter
Read Sheets *(input)*
Set the number of stamps to sheets / 5 *(processing)*
Round the number of stamps up to the next whole number *(processing)*
Display the number of stamps *(output)*

Pseudocode has several advantages. It is compact and probably will not extend for many pages as flowcharts commonly do. Also, the plan looks like the code to be written and so is preferred by many programmers.

Hierarchy Chart

The last programming tool we'll discuss is the **hierarchy chart**, which shows the overall program structure. Hierarchy charts are also called structure charts, HIPO (Hierarchy plus Input-Process-Output) charts, top-down charts, or VTOC (Visual Table of Contents) charts. All these names refer to planning diagrams that are similar to a company's organization chart.

Hierarchy charts depict the organization of a program but omit the specific processing logic. They describe what each part, or **module**, of the program does and they show how the modules relate to each other. The details on how the modules work, however, are omitted. The chart is read from top to bottom and from left to right. Each module may be subdivided into a succession of sub-modules that branch out under it. Typically, after the activities in the succession of submodules are carried out, the module to the right of the original module is considered. A quick glance at the hierarchy chart reveals each task performed in the program and where it is performed. Figure 2.2 contains a hierarchy chart for the postage stamp problem.

The main benefit of hierarchy charts is in the initial planning of a program. We break down the major parts of a program so we can see what must be done in general. From this point, we can then refine each module into more detailed plans using flowcharts or pseudocode. This process is called the **divide-and-conquer** method.

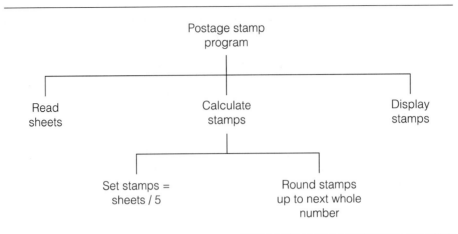

Figure 2.2 Hierarchy chart for the postage stamp problem.

The postage stamp problem was solved by a series of instructions to read data, perform calculations, and display results. Each step was in a sequence; that is, we moved from one line to the next without skipping over any lines. This kind of structure is called a **sequence structure**. Many problems, however, require a decision to determine whether a series of instructions should be executed. If the answer to a question is "Yes," then one group of instructions is executed. If the answer is "No," then another is executed. This structure is called a **decision structure**. Figure 2.3 contains the pseudocode and flowchart for a decision structure.

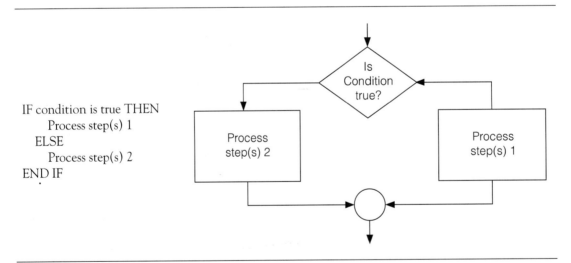

IF condition is true THEN
    Process step(s) 1
  ELSE
    Process step(s) 2
END IF

Figure 2.3 Pseudocode and flowchart for a decision structure.

The sequence and decision structures are both used to solve the following problem.

Direction of Numbered New York Streets Algorithm

Problem: Given a street number of a one-way street in New York, decide the direction of the street, either eastbound or westbound.

Discussion: There is a simple rule to tell the direction of a one-way street in New York: Even numbered streets run eastbound.

Input: Street number

Processing: Decide if the street number is divisible by 2.

Output: "Eastbound" or "Westbound"

Figures 2.4 through 2.6 contain the flowchart, pseudocode, and hierarchy chart for the New York numbered streets problem.

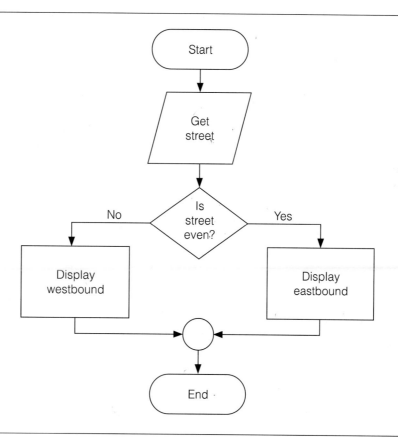

Figure 2.4 Flowchart for the New York numbered streets problem.

Program: Determine the direction of a numbered NYC street.

Get Street
IF Street is even THEN
    Display Eastbound
  ELSE
    Display Westbound
END IF

Figure 2.5 Pseudocode for the New York numbered streets problem.

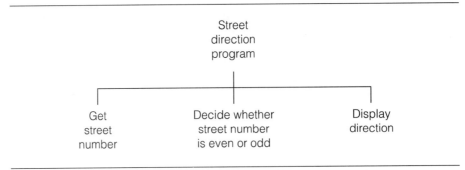

Figure 2.6 Hierarchy chart for the New York numbered streets problem.

The solution to the next problem requires the repetition of a series of instructions. A programming structure that executes instructions many times is called a **loop structure**.

We need a test (or decision) to tell when the loop should end. Without an exit condition, the loop would repeat endlessly (an infinite loop). One way to control the number of times a loop repeats (often referred to as the number of passes or iterations) is to check a condition before each pass through the loop and continue executing the loop as long as the condition is true.

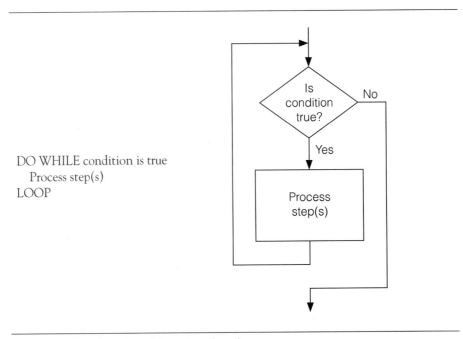

DO WHILE condition is true
    Process step(s)
LOOP

Figure 2.7 Pseudocode and flowchart for a loop.

Class Average Algorithm

Problem: Calculate and report the grade-point average for a class.

Discussion: The average grade equals the sum of all grades divided by the number of students. We need a loop to read and then add (accumulate) the grades for each student in the class. Inside the loop, we also need to total (count) the number of students in the class. See Figures 2.8 through 2.10.

Input: Student grades

Processing: Find the sum of the grades; count the number of students; calculate average grade = sum of grades / number of students.

Output: Average grade

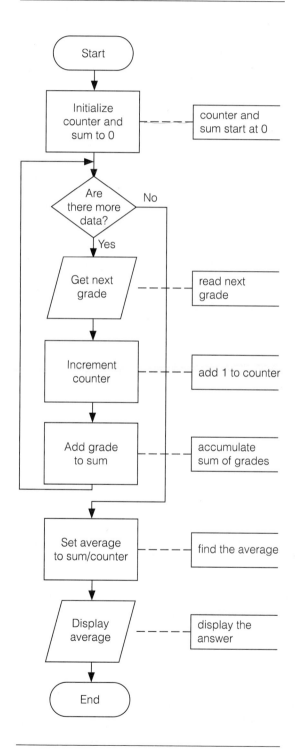

Figure 2.8 Flowchart for the class average problem.

Program: Determine the average grade of a class
Initialize Counter and Sum to 0
DO WHILE there are more data
    Get the next Grade
    Add the Grade to the Sum
    Increment the Counter
LOOP
Compute Average = Sum / Counter
Display Average

Figure 2.9 Pseudocode for the class average problem.

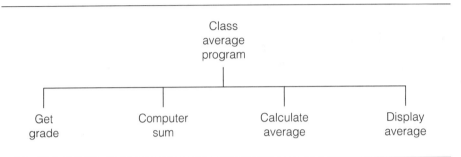

Figure 2.10 Hierarchy chart for the class average problem.

Comments

1. Tracing a flowchart is like playing a board game. We begin at the Start symbol and proceed from symbol to symbol until we reach the End symbol. At any time, we will be at just one symbol. In a board game, the path taken depends on the result of spinning a spinner or rolling a pair of dice. The path taken through a flowchart depends on the input.

2. The algorithm should be tested at the flowchart stage before being coded into a program. Different data should be used as input and the output checked. This process is known as **desk-checking**. The test data should include nonstandard data as well as typical data.

3. Flowcharts, pseudocode, and hierarchy charts are universal problem-solving tools. They can be used to construct programs in any computer language, not just Visual Basic.

4. Flowcharts are used throughout this text to provide a visualization of the flow of certain programming tasks and Visual Basic control structures. Major examples of pseudocode and hierarchy charts appear in the case studies.

5. There are four primary logical programming constructs: sequence, decision, loop, and unconditional branch. Unconditional branch, which appears in some languages as Goto statements, involves jumping from one place in a program to another. Structured programming uses the first three constructs, but forbids the fourth. One advantage of pseudocode over flowcharts is that pseudocode has no provision for unconditional branching and thus forces the programmer to write structured programs.

6. Flowcharts are time-consuming to write and update. For this reason, professional programmers are more likely to favor pseudocode and hierarchy charts. Because flowcharts so clearly illustrate the logical flow of programming techniques, however, they are a valuable tool in the education of programmers.

7. There are many styles of pseudocode. Some programmers use an outline form, whereas others use a form that looks almost like a programming language. The pseudocode appearing in the case studies of this text focuses on the primary tasks to be performed by the program and leaves many of the routine details to be completed during the coding process. Several Visual Basic keywords, such as, Print, If, Do, and While, are used extensively in the pseudocode appearing in this text.

8. Many people draw rectangles around each item in a hierarchy chart. In this text, rectangles are omitted to encourage the use of hierarchy charts by making them easier to draw.

3

Fundamentals of Programming in Visual Basic

3.1 Visual Basic Objects / 44
• A Text Box Walkthrough • A Command Button Walkthrough • A Label Walkthrough • A Picture Box Walkthrough

3.2 Visual Basic Events / 58
• An Event Procedure Walkthrough

3.3 Numbers / 71
• Arithmetic Operations • Scientific Notation • Variables • Print Method

3.4 Strings / 84
• Variables and Strings • Concatenation • Declaring Variable Types • Using Text Boxes for Input and Output • ANSI Character Set • The KeyPress Event Procedure

3.5 Input and Output / 98
• Reading Data from Files • Input from an Input Box • Formatting Output with Print Zones • Tab Function • Spc Function • Using a Message Box for Output • The Line Continuation Character • Output to the Printer • Rem Statement

3.6 Built-In Functions / 118
• Numeric Functions: Sqr, Int • String Functions: Left, Mid, Right, UCase, Trim • String-Related Numeric Functions: Len, InStr • Format Function • Generating Random Numbers: Rnd

Summary / 136

Programming Projects / 138

3.1 VISUAL BASIC OBJECTS

Visual Basic programs display a Windows style screen (called a **form**) with boxes into which users type (and edit) information and buttons that they click to initiate actions. The boxes and buttons are referred to as **controls**. Forms and controls are called **objects**. In this section, we examine forms and four of the most useful Visual Basic controls.

Note: If Visual Basic has not been installed on your computer, you can install it by following the steps outlined on the first page of Appendix B.

Invoking the Control Creation Edition of Visual Basic 5.0: Appendix B explains how to install the Control Creation Edition and add an icon labeled VB5CCE to the Windows desktop. To invoke VB5.0, double-click the VB5CCE icon.

Invoking the Learning, Professional, or Enterprise Editions of Visual Basic 5.0: To invoke Visual Basic, click the Start button, point to Programs, point to Microsoft Visual Basic 5.0, and click on Visual Basic 5.0.

With all versions of Visual Basic 5.0, the center of the screen will contain the New Project window of Figure 3.1. The main part of the window is a tabbed dialog box with three tabs—New, Existing, and Recent. (If the New tab is not in the foreground, click on it to bring it to the front.) The number of project icons showing are either three (with the Control Creation and Learning Editions) or nine (with the Professional and Enterprise Editions).

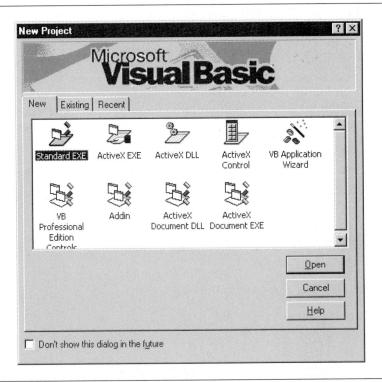

Figure 3.1 New Project window from Professional Edition of VB 5.0.

Double-click the Standard EXE icon to bring up the initial Visual Basic screen in Figure 3.2. The appearance of this screen varies slightly with the different versions of Visual Basic.

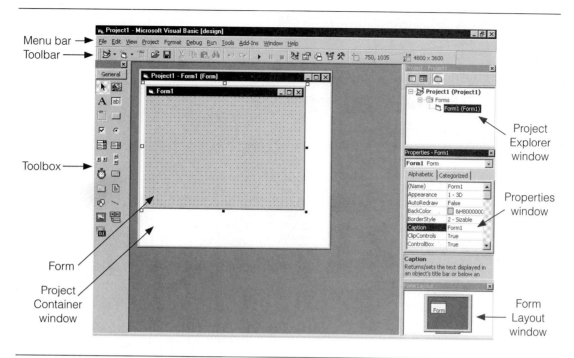

Figure 3.2 The initial Visual Basic screen.

The menu bar displays the commands you use to work with Visual Basic. Some of the menus, like File, Edit, View, and Window, are common to most Windows applications. Others, such as Project, Format, and Debug, provide commands specific to programming in Visual Basic.

The Toolbar is a collection of icons that carry out standard operations when clicked. For example, the fifth icon, which looks like a diskette, can be used to save the current program to a disk. To display the function of a Toolbar icon, position the mouse pointer over the icon for a few moments.

The large stippled Form window, or *form* for short, becomes a Windows window when a program is executed. All information displayed by the program appears on the form. The information is displayed either directly on the form or in controls that have been placed on the form. The **Form Layout** window allows you to position the location of the form at run time relative to the entire screen using a small graphical representation of the screen.

The **Project Explorer window** is seldom needed for our purposes until Chapter 13. The **Properties window** is used to change how objects look and react.

The icons in the **Toolbox** represent objects that can be placed on the form. The four objects discussed in this chapter are text boxes, labels, command buttons, and picture boxes.

Text boxes: You use a text box primarily to get information, referred to as **input**, from the user.

Labels: A label is placed next to a text box to tell the user what type of information to enter into the text box.

Command buttons: The user clicks a command button to initiate an action.

Picture boxes: You use a picture box to display text or graphics.

A Text Box Walkthrough

1. Double-click on the text box icon. (The text box icon consists of the bold letters ab and a vertical bar cursor inside a rectangle and is the fourth icon in the Toolbox.) A rectangle with eight small squares, called sizing handles, appears at the center of the screen. See Figure 3.3.

Figure 3.3 A text box with sizing handles.

2. Click anywhere on the form outside the rectangle to remove the handles.

3. Click on the rectangle to restore the handles. An object showing its handles is (said to be) **selected**. An object can have its size altered, location changed, and other properties modified.

4. Move the mouse arrow to the handle in the center of the right side of the text box. The arrow should change to a double arrow (◄►). Hold down the left mouse button and move the mouse to the right. The text box is stretched to the right. Similarly, grabbing the text box by one of the other handles and moving the mouse stretches the text box in another direction. For instance, you use the handle in the upper-left corner to stretch the text box up and to the left. Handles also can be used to make the text box smaller.

5. Move the mouse arrow to any point of the text box other than a handle, hold down the left mouse button, and move the mouse. You can now drag the text box to a new location. Using Steps 4 and 5, you can place a text box of any size anywhere on the form.

   Note: The text box should now be selected; that is, its sizing handles should be showing. If not, click anywhere inside the text box to select it.

6. Press the delete key, Del, to remove the text box from the form. Step 7 gives an alternative way to place a text box of any size at any location on the form.

7. Click on the text box icon in the Toolbox. Then move the mouse pointer to any place on the form. (When over the form, the mouse pointer becomes a pair of crossed thin lines.) Hold down the left mouse button and move the mouse on a diagonal to generate a rectangle. Release the mouse button to obtain a selected text box. You can now alter the size and location as before.

   Note: The text box should now be selected; that is, its sizing handles should be showing. If not, click anywhere inside the text box to select it.

8. Press F4 to activate the Properties window. (You can also activate the properties window by clicking on it or clicking on the Properties window icon.) See Figure 3.4. The first line of the Properties window (called the **object box**) reads "Text1 TextBox". Text1 is the current name of the text box. The two tabs permit you to view the list of properties either alphabetically or grouped into categories. Text boxes have 40 properties which can be grouped into 7 categories. Use the up- and down-arrow keys (or the up- and down-scroll arrows) to glance through the list. The left column gives the property

and the right column gives the current setting of the property. We discuss four properties in this walkthrough.

Object
box →

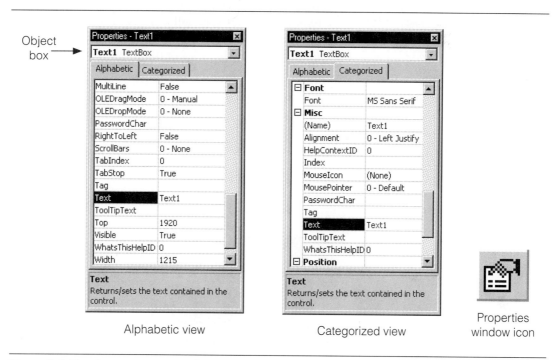

Alphabetic view   Categorized view   Properties
window icon

Figure 3.4 Text box properties window.

9. Move to the Text property with the up- and down-arrow keys. (Alternatively, scroll until the property is visible and click on the property.) The Text property is now highlighted. The Text property determines the words in the text box. Currently, the words are set to "Text1" in the **Settings box** on the right.

10. Type your first name. As you type, your name replaces "Text1" in both the settings box and the text box. See Figure 3.5. (Alternatively, you could have clicked on the settings box and edited its contents.)

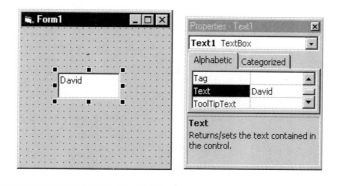

Figure 3.5 Setting the text property to David.

11. Click at the beginning of your name in the settings box and add your title, such as Mr., Ms., or The Honorable. (If you mistyped your name, you can easily correct it now.)

12. Press Shift+Ctrl+F to move to the first property that begins with the letter F. Now use the down-arrow key or the mouse to highlight the property ForeColor. The foreground color is the color of the text.

13. Click on the down arrow in the right part of the Settings box and then click on the Palette tab to display a selection of colors. See Figure 3.6. Click on one of the solid colors, such as blue or red. Notice the change in the color of your name.

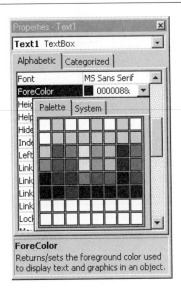

Figure 3.6 Setting the ForeColor property.

14. Highlight the Font property with a single click of the mouse. The current font is named MS Sans Serif.

15. Click on the ellipsis (...) box in the right part of the settings box to display a dialog box. See Figure 3.7. The three lists give the current name (MS Sans Serif), current style (Regular), and current size (8) of the font. You can change any of these attributes by clicking. Click on Italics in the style list and click on 12 in the size list. Now click on the OK button to see your name displayed in a larger italics font.

16. Click on the text box and resize it to be about 3 inches wide and 1 inch high.

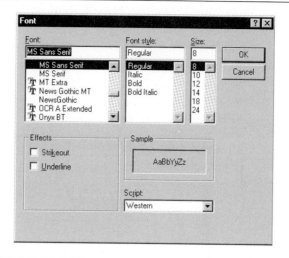

Figure 3.7 The Font Dialog box.

Visual Basic programs consist of three parts—interface, values of properties, and code. Our interface consists of a form with a single object, a text box. We have set a few properties for the text box—the text (namely, your name), the foreground color, the font style, and the font size. In Section 3.2, we see how to place code into a program. Visual Basic endows certain capabilities to programs that are independent of any code. We will now run the existing codeless program and experience these capabilities.

17. Press F5 to run the program. (Alternatively, a program can be run from the menu by pressing Alt/R/S or by clicking on the Start icon ▶, the twelfth icon on the Toolbar.) Notice that the dots have disappeared from the form.

18. The cursor is at the beginning of your name. Press the End key to move the cursor to the end of your name. Now type in your last name, and then keep typing. Eventually, the words will scroll to the left.

19. Press Home to return to the beginning of the text. You have a full-fledged word processor at your disposal. You can place the cursor anywhere you like to add or delete text. You can drag the cursor across text to create a block, place a copy of the block in the clipboard with Ctrl+C, and then duplicate it anywhere with Ctrl+V.

20. To terminate the program, press Alt+F4. Alternatively, you can end a program by clicking on the End icon ■, the fourteenth icon on the Toolbar, or clicking on the form's close button ☒.

21. Select the text box, activate the Properties window, select the MultiLine property, click on the down-arrow button, and finally click on True. The MultiLine property has been changed from False to True.

22. Run the program and type in the text box. Notice that now words wrap around when the end of a line is reached. Also, text will scroll up when it reaches the bottom of the text box.

23. End the program.

24. Press Alt/F/V or click on the Save Project icon ▣ to save the work done so far. A Save File As dialog box appears. See Figure 3.8. Visual Basic creates two disk files to store a program. The first, with the extension .frm, is entered into the Save File As dialog box and the second, with the extension .vbp, into a Save Project As dialog box. As noted earlier, Visual Basic refers to programs as **projects**.

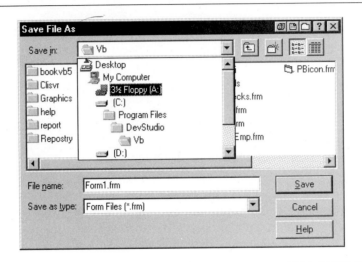

Figure 3.8 The Save File As dialog box.

25. Type a file name, such as *testprog* into the "File name" box. The extension .frm automatically will be appended to the name. Do not press the Enter key yet. (Pressing the Enter key has the same effect as clicking Save.) The selection in the large window tells where your program will be saved. Alter these as desired. (**Suggestion:** If you are using a computer in a campus computer lab, you probably should use a diskette to save your work. If so, place the diskette in a drive, say, the A drive, and select 3½ Floppy (A:) in the Drives or "Save in" box.)

26. Click the Save button when you are ready to go on. (Alternatively, press Tab several times until the Save button is highlighted and then press Enter.) The Save Project As dialog box appears.

27. Type a file name into the File Name box. You can use the same name, such as *testprog*, as before. Then proceed as in Steps 25 and 26. (The extension .vbp will be added.)

28. Press Alt/F/N to begin a new program. (As before, select Standard EXE.)

29. Place three text boxes on the form. (Move each text box out of the center of the form before creating the next.) Notice that they have the names Text1, Text2, and Text3.

30. Run the program. Notice that the cursor is in Text1. We say that Text1 has the **focus**. (*Focus* is the ability to receive user input through the mouse or keyboard.) Any text typed will display in that text box.

31. Press Tab once. Now, Text2 has the focus. When you type, the characters appear in Text2.

32. Press Tab several times and then press Shift+Tab a few times. With Tab, the focus cycles through the objects on the form in the order the objects were created. With Shift+Tab, the focus cycles in the reverse order.

33. End the program.

34. Press Alt/F/O or click on the Open Project icon to reload your first program. When a dialog box asks if you want to save your changes, click the No button or press N. An Open Project dialog box appears on the screen. Click on the Recent tab to see a list of the programs most recently opened or saved. Your first program and its location should appear at the top of the list. (**Note:** You can also find any program by clicking on the Existing tab and using the dialog box to search for the program.)

35. Click on the name of your first program and then click on the Open button. Alternatively, double-click on the name. (You also have the option of typing the name into the File Name box and then clicking the Open button.)

A Command Button Walkthrough

1. Press Alt/F/N and double-click on Standard EXE to start anew. There is no need to save anything.

2. Double-click on the command button icon to place a command button in the center of the form. (The rectangular-shaped command button icon is the sixth icon in the Toolbox.)

3. Activate the Properties window, highlight the Caption property, and type "Please Push Me". See Figure 3.9. Notice that the letters appear on the command button as they are typed. The button is too small.

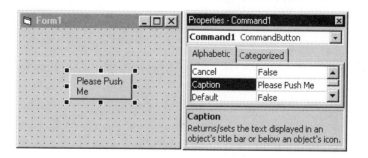

Figure 3.9 Setting the caption property.

4. Click on the command button to select it and then enlarge it to accommodate the phrase "Please Push Me" on one line.

5. Run the program and click on the command button. The command button appears to move in and then out. In Section 3.2, we write code that is activated when a command button is pushed.

6. End the program and select the command button.

7. From the Properties window, edit the Caption setting by inserting an ampersand (&) before the first letter, P. Notice that the ampersand does not show on the button. However, the letter following the ampersand is now underlined. See Figure 3.10. Pressing Alt+P while the program is running triggers the same event as clicking the command button. Here, the letter P is referred to as the **access key** for the command button. (The access key is always the key following the ampersand.)

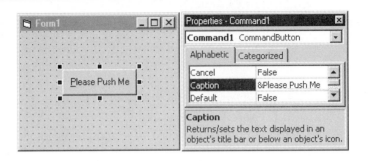

Figure 3.10 Designating P as an access key.

8. End the program.

A Label Walkthrough

1. Press Alt/F/N and double-click on Standard EXE to start anew. There is no need to save anything.

2. Double-click on the label icon to place a label in the center of the form. (The label icon, a large letter A, is the third icon in the Toolbox.)

3. Activate the Properties window, highlight the Caption property, and type "Enter Your Phone Number". Such a label would be placed next to a text box into which the user will enter a phone number.

4. Click on the label to select it and then widen it until all words are on the same line.

5. Make the label narrower until the words occupy two lines.

6. Activate the Properties window and double-click on the Alignment property. Double-click two more times. The combination of sizing and alignment permits you to design a label easily.

7. Run the program. Nothing happens, even if you click on the label. Labels just sit there. The user cannot change what a label displays unless you write code to allow the change.

8. End the program.

A Picture Box Walkthrough

1. Press Alt/F/N and double-click on Standard EXE to start anew. There is no need to save anything.

2. Double-click on the picture box icon to place a picture box in the center of the form. (The picture box icon is the second icon in the Toolbox. It contains a picture of the sun shining over a desert.)

3. Enlarge the picture box.

4. Run the program. Nothing happens and nothing will, no matter what you do. Although picture boxes look like text boxes, you can't type in them.

However, you can display text in them with statements discussed later in this chapter, you can draw lines and circles in them with statements discussed in Chapter 10, and you can insert pictures into them.

5. End the program and click the picture box to select it.

6. Activate the Properties window and double-click on the Picture property. A Load Picture dialog box appears. See Figure 3.11.

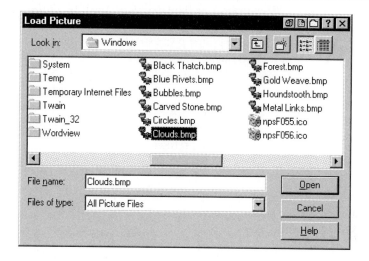

Figure 3.11 The Load Picture dialog box.

7. Select the Windows folder and then double-click on one of the picture files. A good candidate is Clouds.bmp, shown in Figure 3.12. See comment 17 at the end of this section.

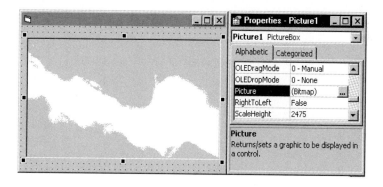

Figure 3.12 A picture box filled with the clouds.bmp picture.

8. Click on the picture box and press Del to remove the picture box.

Comments

1. When selecting from a list, double-clicking has the same effect as clicking once and pressing Enter.

2. On a form, the Tab key cycles through the objects that can get the focus, and in a dialog box, it cycles through the items.

3. The form itself is also an object and has properties. For instance, you can change the text in the title bar with the Caption property. You can move the form by dragging the title bar of its project container window. Although the project container window does not have sizing handles, you can size it by grabbing it by one of its corners, bottom edge, or sides and dragging the mouse.

4. The name of an object is used in code to refer to the object. By default, objects are given names like Text1 and Text2. You can use the Properties window to change the Name property of an object to a more suggestive name. (The Name property is always the first property in the list of properties. An object's Name must start with a letter and can be a maximum of 40 characters. It can include numbers and underline (_) characters, but can't include punctuation or spaces.) Also, Microsoft recommends that each name begin with a three letter prefix that identifies the type of the control. See the table below. Beginning with Section 3.2, we will use suggestive names and these prefixes whenever possible.

Object	Prefix	Example
command button	cmd	cmdComputeTotal
form	frm	frmPayroll
label	lbl	lblInstructions
picture box	pic	picClouds
text box	txt	txtAddress

5. The Name and Caption properties of a command button are both initially set to something like Command1. However, changing one of these properties does not affect the setting of the other property. Similarly for the Name and Caption properties of forms and labels, and for the Name and Text properties of text boxes.

6. The color settings appear as strings of digits and letters preceded by &H and trailed with &. Don't concern yourself with the notation at this time.

7. Here are some fine points on the use of the Properties window.
   (a) Press Shift+Ctrl+*letterkey* to highlight the first property that begins with that letter. Successive pressings highlight successive properties that begin with that letter.
   (b) To change the selected object from the Properties window, click on the down-arrow icon at the right of the Object box of the Properties window. Then select the new object from the pull-down list.

8. Some useful properties that have not been discussed are the following:
   (a) BorderStyle: Setting the BorderStyle to "0 – None" removes the border from an object.
   (b) Visible: Setting the Visible property to False hides an object when the program is run. The object can be made to reappear with code.
   (c) BackColor: Specifies the background color for a text box, label, picture box, or form. Also specifies the background color for a command button having Style set to "1 – Graphical." (Such a command button can display a picture.)
   (d) BackStyle: The BackStyle property of a label is opaque by default. The rectangular region associated with the label is filled with the label's background color and caption. Setting the background style of a label

to transparent causes whatever is behind the label to remain visible; the background color of the label essentially becomes "see through."

(e) Font: Can be set to any of Windows' fonts, such as Courier and Times Roman. Two unusual fonts are Symbols and Wingdings. For instance, with the Wingdings font, pressing the keys for %, &, ', and J yield a bell, a book, a candle, and a smiling face, respectively. To view the character sets for the different Windows' fonts, click on the Start button, and successively select Programs, Accessories, and Character Map. Then click on Character Map or press the Enter key. After selecting a font, hold down the left mouse button on any character to enlarge the character and obtain the keystroke that produces that character.

9. When you click on a property in the Properties window, a description of the property appears just below the window. Additional information about many of the properties can be found in Appendix C. You can obtain very detailed (and somewhat advanced) information about a property by clicking on the property and pressing F1.

10. Most properties can be set or altered with code as the program is running instead of being preset from the Properties window. For instance, a command button can be made to disappear with a line such as Let Command1.Visible = False. See Section 3.2 for details.

11. The BorderStyle and MultiLine properties of a text box can be set only from the Properties window. You cannot alter them during run time.

12. Of the objects discussed in this section, only command buttons have true access keys.

13. If you inadvertently double-click an object in a form, a window containing two lines of text will appear. (The first line begins Private Sub.) This is a code window and is discussed in the next section. To remove this window, click on its Close button.

14. Objects can be grouped together by attaching them to a picture box. (To attach an object to a picture box, click on the icon in the Toolbox, move the mouse to a point inside the picture box, and drag the mouse until the object has the shape you want. Do not use the double-click method to create the object.)

15. To enlarge (or decrease) the Project Container window, position the mouse cursor anywhere on the right or bottom edge and drag the mouse. To enlarge (or decrease) the form, select the form and drag one of its sizing handles. Alternatively, you can enlarge either the Project Container window or the form by clicking on its Maximize button.

16. We will nearly always be selecting the Standard EXE icon from the New Project window. (Only in Section 13.4 do we select another icon—the ActiveX Control.)

17. If the file Clouds.bmp is not in the Windows directory of your computer, you may be able to find it in the directory C:\Program Files\DevStudio\VB\samples\Pguide\PalMode. If not, you can use any picture file in place of Clouds.bmp. The CD accompanying this textbook contains several picture files in the folder Pictures.

PRACTICE PROBLEMS 3.1

1. What is the difference between the Caption and the Name of a command button?

2. Suppose in an earlier session you created an object that looks like an empty rectangle. It might be a picture box, a text box with Text property set to nothing (blanked out by deleting all characters), or a label with a blank caption and BorderStyle property set to Fixed Single. How might you determine which it is?

EXERCISES 3.1

1. Why are command buttons sometimes called "push buttons"?

2. How can you tell if a program is running by looking at the screen?

3. Create a form with two command buttons, run the program, and click on each button. Do you notice anything different about a button after it has been clicked?

4. Design an experiment to convince yourself that picture boxes can get the focus, but labels cannot.

5. Place three command buttons vertically on a form with Command3 above Command2, and Command2 above Command1. Then run the program and successively press Tab. Notice that the command buttons receive the focus from bottom to top. Experiment with various configurations of command buttons and text boxes to convince yourself that objects get the focus in the order in which they were created.

6. While a program is running, an object is said to **lose focus** when the focus moves from that object to another object. In what three ways can the user cause an object to lose focus?

In Exercises 7 through 28, carry out the task. Use a new form for each exercise.

7. Place CHECKING ACCOUNT in the title bar of a form.

8. Create a text box containing the words PLAY IT, SAM in blue letters.

9. Create an empty text box with a yellow background.

10. Create a text box containing the word HELLO in large italic letters.

11. Create a text box containing the sentence "After all is said and done, more is said than done." The sentence should occupy three lines and each line should be centered in the text box.

12. Create a borderless text box containing the words VISUAL BASIC in bold white letters on a red background.

13. Create a text box containing the words VISUAL BASIC in Courier font.

14. Create a command button containing the word PUSH.

15. Create a command button containing the word PUSH in large italic letters.

16. Create a command button containing the word PUSH in nonbold letters with the letter P underlined.

17. Create a command button containing the word PUSH with the letter H as access key.

18. Create a command button containing the caption HALF MOON, a white background, and the picture file MOON7.BMP from the Pictures folder of the CD accompanying this book.

19. Create a label containing the word ALIAS.

20. Create a label containing the word ALIAS in white on a blue background.

21. Create a label with a border containing the centered italicized word ALIAS.

22. Create a label containing VISUAL on the first line and BASIC on the second line. Each word should be right justified.

23. Create a label containing a picture of a diskette. (**Hint:** Use the Wingdings character <.) Make the diskette as large as possible.

24. Create a label with a border containing the bold word ALIAS in the Terminal font.

25. Create a picture box with a yellow background.

26. Create a picture box with no border and a red background.

27. Create a picture box containing two command buttons.

28. Create a picture box with a blue background containing a picture box with a white background.

In Exercises 29 through 36, create the interface shown in the figure. (These exercises give you practice creating objects and assigning properties. The interfaces do not necessarily correspond to actual programs.)

29.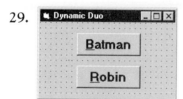

30.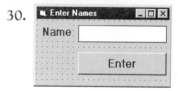

31.

32.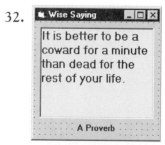

33.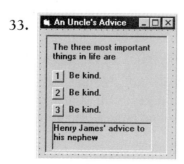

34.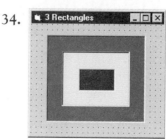

35.

This picture is contained in the file picbox.bmp in the Pictures folder of the CD accompanying this book.

36.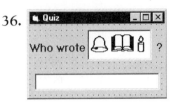

37. Create a replica of your bank check on a form. Words common to all checks, such as PAY TO THE ORDER OF, should be contained in labels. Items specific to your checks, such as your name at the top left, should be contained in text boxes. Make the check on the screen resemble your check as much as possible.

38. Create a replica of your campus ID on a form. Words that are on all student IDs, such as the name of the college, should be contained in labels. Information specific to your ID, such as your name and social security number, should be contained in text boxes. Simulate your picture with a text box containing a smiling face—a size 24 Wingdings J.

39. If you are familiar with Paintbrush (one of Windows' Accessories), use Paintbrush to make a drawing and then save it as a .bmp file. In Visual Basic, create a picture box containing the picture.

SOLUTIONS TO PRACTICE PROBLEMS 3.1

1. The Caption is the text appearing on the command button, whereas the Name is the designation used to refer to the command button. Initially, they have the same value, such as Command1. However, they can each be changed independently of the other.

2. Click on the object to select it and then press F4 to activate its Properties window. The Object box gives the Name of the object (in bold letters) and its type, such as Label, TextBox, or PictureBox.

   We have examined only four of the objects from the Toolbox. To determine the type of one of the other objects, hold the mouse pointer over it for a few seconds.

3.2 VISUAL BASIC EVENTS

When a Visual Basic program is run, a form and its controls appear on the screen. Normally, nothing happens until the user takes an action, such as clicking a control or pressing the Tab key. Such an action is called an **event**.

The three steps to creating a Visual Basic program are as follows:

1. Create the interface; that is, generate, position, and size the objects.

2. Set properties; that is, set relevant properties for the objects.

3. Write the code that executes when the events occur.

This section is devoted to Step 3.

Code consists of statements that carry out tasks. Visual Basic has a repertoire of over 200 statements and we will use many of them in this text. In this section, we limit ourselves to statements that change properties of objects while a program is running.

Properties of an object are changed in code with statements of the form

```
Let objectName.property = setting
```

where *objectName* is the name of the form or a control, *property* is one of the properties of the object, and *setting* is a valid setting for that object. Here are three such statements.

The statement

```
Let txtBox.Font.Size = 12
```

sets the size of the characters in the text box named txtBox to 12.

The statement

```
Let txtBox.Font.Bold = True
```

converts the characters in the text box to boldface.

The statement

```
Let txtBox.Text = ""
```

clears the contents of the text box; that is, it invokes the blank setting.

Most events are associated with objects. The event *clicking cmdButton* is different from the event *clicking picBox*. These two events are specified cmdButton_Click and picBox_Click. The statements to be executed when an event occurs are written in a block of code called an **event procedure**. The structure of an event procedure is

```
Private Sub objectName_event()
  statements
End Sub
```

The word Sub in the first line signals the beginning of the event procedure, and the first line identifies the object and the event occurring to that object. The last line signals the termination of the event procedure. The statements to be executed appear between these two lines. (**Note:** The word Private indicates that the event procedure cannot be invoked by an event from another form. This will not concern us until much later in the text. The word *Sub* is an abbreviation of *Subprogram*.) For instance, the event procedure

```
Private Sub cmdButton_Click()
  Let txtBox.Text = ""
End Sub
```

clears the contents of the text box when the command button is clicked.

An Event Procedure Walkthrough

The form in Figure 3.13, which contains a text box and a command button, will be used to demonstrate what event procedures are and how they are created. Three event procedures will be used to alter the appearance of a phrase that is typed into the text box. The event procedures are txtPhrase_LostFocus, txtPhrase_GotFocus, and cmdBold_Click.

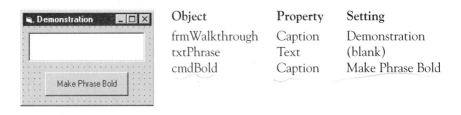

Object	Property	Setting
frmWalkthrough	Caption	Demonstration
txtPhrase	Text	(blank)
cmdBold	Caption	Make Phrase Bold

Figure 3.13 The interface for the event procedure walkthrough.

1. Create the interface in Figure 3.13. The Name properties of the form, text box, and command button should be set as shown in the Object column. The caption property of the form should be set to Demonstration, the Text property of the text box should be made blank, and the Caption property of the command button should be set to Make Phrase Bold.

2. Double-click on the text box. A window, called a **code window**, appears. See Figure 3.14. Just below the title bar are two drop-down list boxes. The left box is called the Object box and the right box is called the Procedure box. (When you position the mouse pointer over one of these list boxes, its type appears.)

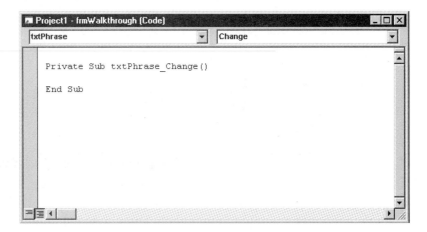

Figure 3.14 A code window.

3. Click on the down-arrow button to the right of the Procedure box. The pull-down menu that appears contains a list of all possible event procedures associated with text boxes. See Figure 3.15.

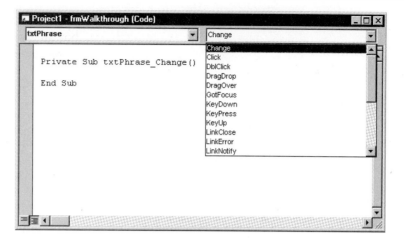

Figure 3.15 Pull-down menu of event procedures.

4. Scroll down the list of event procedures and click on LostFocus. (LostFocus is the last event procedure.) The lines

```
Private Sub txtPhrase_LostFocus()

End Sub
```

appear in the code window with a blinking cursor poised at the beginning of the blank line.

5. Type the line

```
Let txtPhrase.Font.Size = 12
```

between the existing two lines. (We usually indent lines inside procedures.) (After you type each period, the editor displays a list containing possible choices of items to follow the period. See Figure 3.16. This new feature, which was added in Visual Basic 5.0, is called "List Properties/Methods." In Figure 3.16, instead of typing the word "Size," you can double-click on "Size" in the displayed list or highlight the word "Size" and press Tab.) The screen appears as in Figure 3.17. We have now created an event procedure that is activated whenever the text box loses the focus.

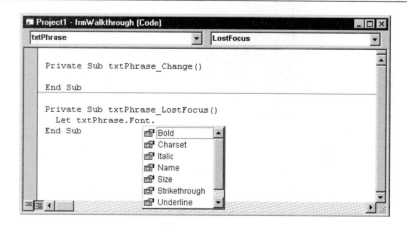

Figure 3.16 A LostFocus event procedure.

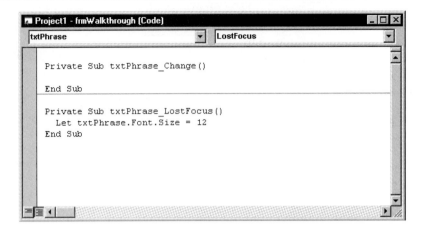

Figure 3.17 A LostFocus event procedure.

6. Let's create another event procedure for the text box. Click on the down-arrow button to the right of the Procedure box, scroll up the list of event procedures, and click on GotFocus. Then type the lines

```
Let txtPhrase.Font.Size = 8
Let txtPhrase.Font.Bold = False
```

between the existing two lines. See Figure 3.18.

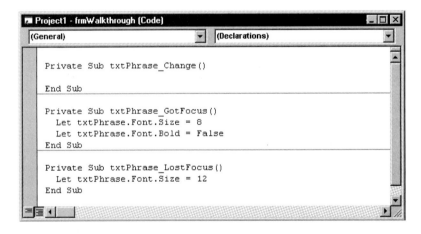

Figure 3.18 A GotFocus event procedure.

7. The txtPhrase_Change event procedure in Figure 3.18 was not used and can be deleted. To delete the procedure, highlight it by dragging the mouse across the two lines of code, and then press the Del key.

8. Let's now create an event procedure for the command button. Click on the down-arrow button to the right of the Object box. The pull-down menu contains a list of the objects, along with a mysterious object called (General). See Figure 3.19. (We'll discuss (General) later in this chapter.)

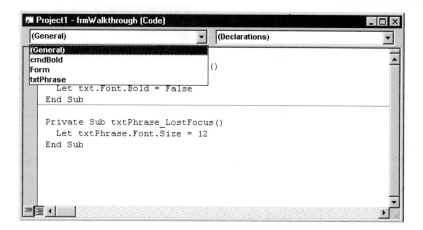

Figure 3.19 List of objects.

9. Click on cmdBold. The event procedure cmdBold_Click is displayed. Type in the line

```
Let txtPhrase.Font.Bold = True
```

The screen appears as in Figure 3.20 and the program is complete.

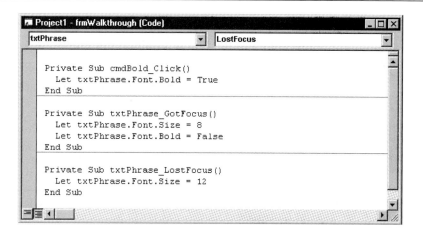

Figure 3.20 The three event procedures.

10. Now run the program by pressing F5.

7. Each color can be identified by a sequence of digits and letters beginning with &H. The common colors and their identifying sequences are red (&HFF&), green (&HFF00&), blue (&HFF0000&), yellow (&HFFFF&), black (&H0&), and white (&HFFFFFF&). Whereas these sequences are not required when assigning colors from the Properties window, they are necessary when assigning colors at run time. For instance, the statement

```
Let picBox.BackColor = &HFFFF&
```

gives picBox a yellow background.

8. For statements of the form Let *object.property* = *setting*, with properties Caption, Text, or Font.Name, the setting must be surrounded by quotes. (For instance, Let lblTwo.Caption = "Name", Let txtBox.Text = "45", and Let picBox.Font.Name = "Courier".)

9. Code windows have many features of word processors. For instance, the operations cut, copy, paste, find, undo, and redo can be carried out with the sixth through eleventh icons of the toolbar. These operations, and several others, also can be initiated from the Edit menu.

10. Names of existing event procedures associated with a control are *not* automatically changed when you rename the control. You must change them yourself and also must change any references to the control. Therefore, you should finalize the names of your controls before you put any code into their event procedures.

11. If you find the automatic List Properties/Method feature distracting, you can turn it off by pressing Tools/Options, selecting the Editor page, and clicking on Auto List Members. If you do so, you can still display a list manually at the appropriate time time by pressing Ctrl+J.

12. Earlier versions of Visual Basic used the property FontSize instead of Font.Size. Although Font.Size is preferred, FontSize is allowed for compatibility. Similarly, properties such as FontBold, FontItalic, and FontName have been included for compatibility with earlier versions of Visual Basic.

PRACTICE PROBLEM 3.2

1. You can always locate an existing event procedure by searching through the code window with the Pg Up and Pg Dn keys. Give another way.

Comments

1. To hide the code window, press the right mouse button and click on Hide. You can also hide it by clicking on the icon at the left side of the title bar and clicking on Close. To view a hidden code window, press Alt/View/Code. To hide a form, close its container. To view a hidden form, press Alt/View/ Object.

2. The form is the default object in Visual Basic code. That is, code such as

```
Let Form1.property = setting
```

can be written as

```
Let property = setting
```

Also, event procedures associated with Form1 appear as

```
Form_event()
```

rather than

```
Form1_event()
```

3. Another useful command is SetFocus. The statement

```
object.SetFocus
```

moves the focus to the object.

4. We have ended our programs by clicking the End icon or pressing Alt+F4. A more elegant technique is to create a command button, call it cmdQuit, with caption Quit and the event procedure:

```
Private Sub cmdQuit_Click()
   End
End Sub
```

5. Certain words, such as Sub, End, and Let, have special meanings in Visual Basic and are referred to as **reserved words** or **keywords**. The Visual Basic editor automatically capitalizes the first letter of a reserved word and displays the word in blue.

6. Visual Basic can detect certain types of errors. For instance, consider the line

```
Let txtBox.Font.Size = 12
```

from the walkthrough. Suppose you neglected to type the number 12 to the right of the equal sign before pressing the Enter key. Visual Basic would tell you something was missing by displaying the left message box at the top of page 66. On the other hand, suppose you misspell the keyword Let. You might notice something is wrong when Let doesn't turn blue. If not, you will certainly know about the problem when the program is run because Visual Basic will display the right message box on the right at the top of page 66 when you click on the command button. After you click on OK, the offending word will be highlighted.

7. Each color can be identified by a sequence of digits and letters beginning with &H. The common colors and their identifying sequences are red (&HFF&), green (&HFF00&), blue (&HFF0000&), yellow (&HFFFF&), black (&H0&), and white (&HFFFFFF&). Whereas these sequences are not required when assigning colors from the Properties window, they are necessary when assigning colors at run time. For instance, the statement

```
Let picBox.BackColor = &HFFFF&
```

gives picBox a yellow background.

8. For statements of the form Let *object.property* = *setting*, with properties Caption, Text, or Font.Name, the setting must be surrounded by quotes. (For instance, Let lblTwo.Caption = "Name", Let txtBox.Text = "45", and Let picBox.Font.Name = "Courier".)

9. Code windows have many features of word processors. For instance, the operations cut, copy, paste, find, undo, and redo can be carried out with the sixth through eleventh icons of the toolbar. These operations, and several others, also can be initiated from the Edit menu.

10. Names of existing event procedures associated with a control are *not* automatically changed when you rename the control. You must change them yourself and also must change any references to the control. Therefore, you should finalize the names of your controls before you put any code into their event procedures.

11. If you find the automatic List Properties/Method feature distracting, you can turn it off by pressing Tools/Options, selecting the Editor page, and clicking on Auto List Members. If you do so, you can still display a list manually at the appropriate time time by pressing Ctrl+J.

12. Earlier versions of Visual Basic used the property FontSize instead of Font.Size. Although Font.Size is preferred, FontSize is allowed for compatibility. Similarly, properties such as FontBold, FontItalic, and FontName have been included for compatibility with earlier versions of Visual Basic.

PRACTICE PROBLEM 3.2

1. You can always locate an existing event procedure by searching through the code window with the Pg Up and Pg Dn keys. Give another way.

EXERCISES 3.2

In Exercises 1 through 6, describe the string displayed in the text box when the command button is clicked.

1.
```
Private Sub cmdButton_Click()
    Let txtBox.Text = "Hello"
End Sub
```

2.
```
Private Sub cmdButton_Click()
    Let txtBox.ForeColor = &HFF&
    Let txtBox.Text = "Hello"
End Sub
```

3.
```
Private Sub cmdButton_Click()
    Let txtBox.Font.Italic = True
    Let txtBox.Text = "Hello"
End Sub
```

4.
```
Private Sub cmdButton_Click()
    Let txtBox.Font.Size = 24
    Let txtBox.Text = "Hello"
End Sub
```

5.
```
Private Sub cmdButton_Click()
    Let txtBox.Text = "Hello"
    Let txtBox.Visible = False
End Sub
```

6.
```
Private Sub cmdButton_Click()
    Let txtBox.Font.Bold = True
    Let txtBox.Text = "Hello"
End Sub
```

In Exercises 7 through 10, assume the three objects on the form were created in the order txtOne, txtTwo, and lblOne. Also assume that txtOne has the focus. Determine the output displayed in lblOne when Tab is pressed.

7.
```
Private Sub txtOne_LostFocus()
    Let lblOne.ForeColor = &HFF00&
    Let lblOne.Caption = "Hello"
End Sub
```

8.
```
Private Sub txtOne_LostFocus()
    Let lblOne.Caption = "Hello"
End Sub
```

9.
```
Private Sub txtTwo_GotFocus()
    Let lblOne.Font.Name = "Courier"
    Let lblOne.Font.Size = 24
    Let lblOne.Caption = "Hello"
End Sub
```

10.
```
Private Sub txtTwo_GotFocus()
    Let lblOne.Font.Italic = True
    Let lblOne.Caption = "Hello"
End Sub
```

In Exercises 11 through 16, determine the errors.

11.
```
Private Sub cmdButton_Click()
    Let frmHi. = "Hello"
End Sub
```

12.
```
Private Sub cmdButton_Click()
    Let txtOne.ForeColor = "red"
End Sub
```

13.
```
Private Sub cmdButton_Click()
    Let txtBox.Caption = "Hello"
End Sub
```

14.
```
Private Sub cmdButton_Click()
    Let lblTwo.Text = "Hello"
End Sub
```

15.
```
Private Sub cmdButton_Click()
    Let lblTwo.BorderStyle = 2
End Sub
```

16.
```
Private Sub cmdButton_Click()
    Let txtOne.MultiLine = True
End Sub
```

In Exercises 17 through 32, write a line (or lines) of code to carry out the task.

17. Display "E.T. phone home." in lblTwo.

18. Display "Play it, Sam." in lblTwo.

19. Display "The stuff that dreams are made of." in red letters in txtBox.

20. Display "Life is like a box of chocolates." in Courier font in txtBox.

21. Delete the contents of txtBox.

22. Delete the contents of lblTwo.

23. Make lblTwo disappear.

24. Remove the border from lblTwo.

25. Give picBox a blue background.

26. Place a bold red "Hello" in lblTwo.

27. Place a bold italics "Hello" in txtBox.

28. Make picBox disappear.

29. Give the focus to cmdButton.

30. Remove the border from picBox.

31. Place a border around lblTwo and center its contents.

32. Give the focus to txtBoxTwo.

33. Describe the GotFocus event in your own words.

34. Describe the LostFocus event in your own words.

35. Labels and picture boxes have an event called DblClick that responds to a double-clicking of the left mouse button. Write a simple program to test this event. Determine whether or not you can trigger the DblClick event without also triggering the Click event.

36. Why do you think that text boxes do not support the Click event?

In Exercises 37 through 42, the interface and initial properties are specified. Write the code to carry out the stated task.

37. When one of the three command buttons is pressed, the words on the command button are displayed in the label with the stated alignment.

Object	Property	Setting
frmEx37	Caption	Alignment
lblShow	Caption	(blank)
cmdLeft	Caption	Left Justify
cmdCenter	Caption	Center
cmdRight	Caption	Right Justify

38. When one of the command buttons is pressed, the face changes to a smiling face (Wingdings character "J") or a frowning face (Wingdings character "L").

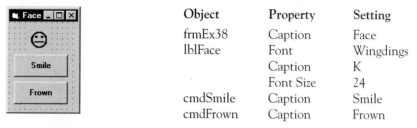

Object	Property	Setting
frmEx38	Caption	Face
lblFace	Font	Wingdings
	Caption	K
	Font Size	24
cmdSmile	Caption	Smile
cmdFrown	Caption	Frown

39. Pressing the command buttons alters the background and foreground colors in the text box.

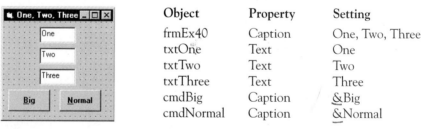

Object	Property	Setting
frmEx39	Caption	Colorful Text
lblBack	Caption	Background
cmdRed	Caption	&Red
cmdBlue	Caption	&Blue
txtShow	Text	Beautiful Day
	MultiLine	True
	Alignment	2 – Center
lblFore	Caption	Foreground
cmdWhite	Caption	&White
cmdYellow	Caption	&Yellow

40. While one of the three text boxes has the focus, its text is bold. When it loses the focus, it ceases to be bold. The command buttons enlarge text (Font.Size = 12) or return text to normal size (Font.Size = 8.25).

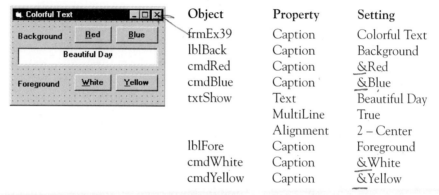

Object	Property	Setting
frmEx40	Caption	One, Two, Three
txtOne	Text	One
txtTwo	Text	Two
txtThree	Text	Three
cmdBig	Caption	&Big
cmdNormal	Caption	&Normal

41. When you click on one of the three small text boxes at the bottom of the form, an appropriate saying is displayed in the large text box. Use the sayings "I like life, it's something to do."; "The future isn't what it used to be."; and "Tell the truth and run."

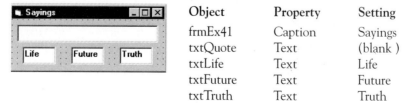

Object	Property	Setting
frmEx41	Caption	Sayings
txtQuote	Text	(blank)
txtLife	Text	Life
txtFuture	Text	Future
txtTruth	Text	Truth

42. After the user types something into the text box, the user can change the font by clicking on one of the command buttons.

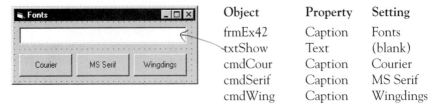

Object	Property	Setting
frmEx42	Caption	Fonts
txtShow	Text	(blank)
cmdCour	Caption	Courier
cmdSerif	Caption	MS Serif
cmdWing	Caption	Wingdings

In Exercises 43 through 48, write a program with a Windows-style interface to carry out the task.

43. Allow the user to click on command buttons to change the size of the text in a text box and alter its appearance between bold and italics.

44. A form contains two text boxes and one large label between them with no caption. When the focus is on the first text box, the label reads "Enter your full name." When the focus is on the second text box, the label reads "Enter your phone number, including area code."

45. Use the same form and properties as in Exercise 38, with the captions for the command buttons replaced with Vanish and Reappear. Clicking a button should produce the stated result.

46. Simulate a traffic light with three small square picture boxes placed vertically on a form. Initially, the bottom picture box is solid green and the other picture boxes are white. When the Tab key is pressed, the middle picture box turns yellow and the bottom picture box turns white. The next time Tab is pressed, the top picture box turns red and the middle picture box turns white. Subsequent pressing of the Tab key cycles through the three colors. *Hint:* First, place the bottom picture box on the form, then the middle picture box, and finally the top picture box.

47. The form contains four square buttons arranged in a rectangular array. Each button has the caption "Push Me." When you click on a button, the button disappears and the other three become or remain visible.

48. The form contains two text boxes into which the user types information. When the user clicks on one of the text boxes, it becomes blank and its contents are displayed in the other text box.

SOLUTION TO PRACTICE PROBLEM 3.2

1. With the code window showing, click on the arrow to the right of the Object box and then select the desired object. Then click on the arrow to the right of the Procedure box and select the desired event procedure.

3.3 NUMBERS

Much of the data processed by computers consists of numbers. In "computer-ese," numbers are often called **numeric constants**. This section discusses the operations that are performed with numbers and the ways numbers are displayed.

Arithmetic Operations

The five arithmetic operations are addition, subtraction, multiplication, division, and exponentiation. (Because exponentiation is not as familiar as the others, it is reviewed in detail in Comment 11.) Addition, subtraction, and division are denoted in Visual Basic by the standard symbols +, −, and /, respectively. However, the notations for multiplication and exponentiation differ from the customary mathematical notations.

Mathematical Notation	Visual Basic Notation
$a \cdot b$ or $a \times b$	$a * b$
a^r	$a \wedge r$

(The asterisk [*] is the upper character of the 8 key on the top row of the keyboard. The caret [^] is the upper character of the 6 key at the top of the keyboard.) **Note:** In this book, the proportional font used for text differs from the monospaced font used for programs. In the program font, the asterisk appears as a five-pointed star (*).

One way to show a number on the screen is to display it in a picture box. If n is a number, then the instruction

```
Picture1.Print n
```

Method

displays the number n in the picture box. If the Picture1.Print instruction is followed by a combination of numbers and arithmetic operations, it carries out the operations and displays the result. Print is a reserved word and the Print operation is called a **method**. Another important method is Cls. The statement

```
Picture1.Cls
```

Method

erases all text and graphics from the picture box Picture1.

EXAMPLE 1   The following program applies each of the five arithmetic operations to the numbers 3 and 2. Notice that 3 / 2 is displayed in decimal form. Visual Basic never displays numbers as common fractions. **Note 1:** The star in the fifth and eighth lines is the computer font version of the asterisk. **Note 2:** The word Run in the phrasing [Run ...] indicates that F5 should be pressed to execute the program. **Note 3:** All programs appearing in examples and case studies are available to readers of this book. See the discussion on the next to last page of the book for details.

Below is the form design and a table showing the names of the objects on the form and the settings, if any, for properties of these objects. This form design is also used in the discussion and examples in the remainder of this section.

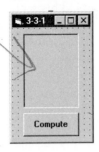

Object	Property	Setting
frm3_3_1	Caption	3-3-1
picResults		
cmdCompute		

```
Private Sub cmdCompute_Click()
  picResults.Cls
  picResults.Print 3 + 2
  picResults.Print 3 - 2
  picResults.Print 3 * 2
  picResults.Print 3 / 2
  picResults.Print 3 ^ 2
  picResults.Print 2 * (3 + 4)
End Sub
```

[Run and then click the command button.]

Scientific Notation

Let us review powers of 10 and scientific notation. Our method of decimal notation is based on a systematic use of exponents.

$$10^1 = 10 \qquad\qquad 10^{-1} = 1/10 = .1$$
$$10^2 = 100 \qquad\qquad 10^{-2} = .01$$
$$10^3 = 1000 \qquad\qquad 10^{-3} = .001$$
$$\vdots \qquad\qquad\qquad\qquad \vdots$$
$$10^n = \underbrace{1000...0}_{n \text{ zeros}} \qquad\qquad 10^{-n} = \underbrace{.000...01}_{n \text{ digits}}$$

Scientific notation provides a convenient way of writing numbers by using powers of 10 to stand for zeros. Numbers are written in the form $b \cdot 10^r$, where b is a number from 1 up to (but not including) 10, and r is an integer. For example, it is much more convenient to write the diameter of the sun (1,400,000,000 meters) in scientific notation: $1.4 \cdot 10^9$ meters. Similarly, rather than write .0000003 meters for the diameter of a bacterium, it is simpler to write $3 \cdot 10^{-7}$ meters.

Any acceptable number can be entered into the computer in either standard or scientific notation. The form in which Visual Basic displays a number depends on many factors, with size being an important consideration. In Visual Basic, $b \cdot 10^r$ is usually written as bEr. (The letter E is an abbreviation for *exponent*.) The following forms of the numbers just mentioned are equivalent.

1.4 * 10^9	1.4E+09	1.4E+9	1.4E9	1400000000
3 * 10^–7	3E–07	3E–7	.0000003	

The computer displays r as a two-digit number, preceded by a plus sign if r is positive and a minus sign if r is negative.

EXAMPLE 2   The following program illustrates scientific notation. The computer's choice of whether to display a number in scientific or standard form depends on the magnitude of the number.

```
Private Sub cmdCompute_Click()
  picResults.Cls
  picResults.Print 1.2 * 10 ^ 34
  picResults.Print 1.2 * 10 ^ 8
  picResults.Print 1.2 * 10 ^ 3
  picResults.Print 10 ^ -20
  picResults.Print 10 ^ -2
End Sub
```

[Run and then click the command button.]

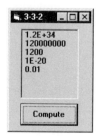

Variables

In applied mathematics problems, quantities are referred to by names. For instance, consider the following high school algebra problem. "If a car travels at 50 miles per hour, how far will it travel in 14 hours? Also, how many hours are required to travel 410 miles?" The solution to this problem uses the well-known formula

$$\text{distance} = \text{speed} \times \text{time elapsed}$$

Here's how this problem would be solved with a computer program.

```
Private Sub cmdCompute_Click()
  picResults.Cls
  Let speed = 50
  Let timeElapsed = 14
  Let distance = speed * timeElapsed
  picResults.Print distance
  Let distance = 410
  Let timeElapsed = distance / speed
  picResults.Print timeElapsed
End Sub
```

[Run and then click the command button. The following is displayed in the picture box.]

```
700
8.2
```

The third line of the event procedure sets the speed to 50 and the fourth line sets the time elapsed to 14. The fifth line multiplies the value for the speed by the value for the time elapsed and sets the distance to this product. The next line displays the answer to the first question. The last three lines before the End Sub statement answer the second question in a similar manner.

The names *speed*, *timeElapsed*, and *distance*, which hold numbers, are referred to as **variables**. Consider the variable *timeElapsed*. In the fourth line, its value was set to 14. In the eighth line, its value was changed as the result of a computation. On the other hand, the variable *speed* had the same value, 50, throughout the program.

In general, a variable is a name that is used to refer to an item of data. The value assigned to the variable may change during the execution of the program. In Visual Basic, variable names can be up to 255 characters long, must begin with a letter, and can consist only of letters, digits, and underscores. (The shortest variable names consist of a single letter.) Visual Basic does not distinguish between uppercase and lowercase letters used in variable names. Some examples of variable names are *total*, *numberOfCars*, *taxRate_1994*, and *n*. As a convention, we write variable names in lowercase letters except for the first letters of additional words (as in *numberOfCars*). "Let" statements assign values to variables and "Print" methods display the values of variables.

If *var* is a variable and *num* is a constant, then the statement

```
Let var = num
```

assigns the number *num* to the variable *var*. Actually, the computer sets aside a location in memory with the name *var*, and places the number *num* in it. The statement

```
picBox.Print var
```

looks into this memory location for the value of the variable and displays the value in the picture box.

A combination of constants, variables, and arithmetic operations that can be evaluated to yield a number is called a **numeric expression**. Expressions are evaluated by replacing each variable by its value and carrying out the arithmetic. Some examples of expressions are 2 * distance + 7, n + 1, and (a + b) / 3.

EXAMPLE 3   The following program displays the value of an expression.

```
Private Sub cmdCompute_Click()
  picResults.Cls
  Let a = 5
  Let b = 4
  picResults.Print a * (2 + b)
End Sub
```

[Run and then click the command button. The following is displayed in the picture box.]

30

If *var* is a variable, then the statement

```
Let var = expression
```

first evaluates the expression on the right and *then* assigns its value to the variable. For instance, the event procedure in Example 3 can be written as

```
Private Sub cmdCompute_Click()
  picResults.Cls
  Let a = 5
  Let b = 4
  Let c = a * (2 + b)
  picResults.Print c
End Sub
```

The expression a * (2 + b) is evaluated to 30 and then this value is assigned to the variable *c*.

Because the expression in a Let statement is evaluated *before* an assignment is made, a statement such as

```
Let n = n + 1
```

is meaningful. It first evaluates the expression on the right (that is, it adds 1 to the original value of the variable *n*), and then assigns this sum to the variable *n*. The effect is to increase the value of the variable *n* by 1. In terms of memory locations, the statement retrieves the value of *n* from *n*'s memory location, uses it to compute *n* + 1, and then places the sum back into *n*'s memory location.

Print Method

Consider the following event procedure.

```
Private Sub cmdDisplay_Click()
  picResults.Cls
  picResults.Print 3
  picResults.Print -3
End Sub
```

[Run and then click the command button.]

Notice that the negative number –3 begins directly at the left margin, whereas the positive number 3 begins one space to the right. The Print method always displays nonnegative numbers with a leading space. The Print method also displays a trailing space after every number. Although the trailing spaces are not apparent here, we will soon see evidence of their presence.

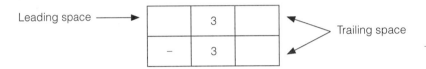

The Print methods used so far only display one number per line. After displaying a number, the cursor moves to the leftmost position and down a line for the next display. Borrowing from typewriter terminology, we say that the computer performs a carriage return and a line feed after each number is displayed. The carriage return and line feed, however, can be suppressed by placing a semicolon at the end of the Print method.

EXAMPLE 4   The following program illustrates the use of semicolons in Print methods. The output reveals the presence of the space trailing each number. For instance, the space trailing –3 combines with the leading space of 99 to produce two spaces between the numbers.

```
Private Sub cmdDisplay_Click()
    picResults.Cls
    picResults.Print 3;      ← Same line
    picResults.Print -3;
    picResults.Print 99;
    picResults.Print 100
End Sub
```

[Run and then click the command button.]

Semicolons can be used to display several numbers with one Print method. If *m*, *n*, and *r* are numbers, a line of the form

```
picBox.Print m; n; r;
```

or

```
picBox.Print m; n; r
```

displays the three numbers, one after another, separated only by their leading and trailing spaces. For instance, the Print methods in preceding Example 4 can be replaced by the single line

```
picBox.Print 3; -3; 99; 100
```

Comments

1. Numbers must not contain commas, dollar signs, or percent signs. Also, mixed numbers, such as 8 1/2, are not allowed.

2. In this text, we use lowercase letters for variable names. For names such as *interestRate*, however, we capitalize the first letter of the second word to improve readability. Visual Basic allows any type of capitalization you like and helps you to be consistent with the use of uppercase letters in a variable name. For instance, if you use the variable name *interestRate* in a program and later enter a line using *InterestRate*, the appearance of the first variable name will automatically be changed to *InterestRate* by Visual Basic.

3. Some people think of the equal sign (=) in a Let statement as an arrow pointing to the left. This stresses the fact that the value on the right is assigned to the variable on the left.

4. Parentheses should be used when necessary to clarify the meaning of an expression. When there are no parentheses, the arithmetic operations are performed in the following order: (1) exponentiations; (2) multiplications and divisions; (3) additions and subtractions. In the event of ties, the leftmost operation is carried out first. Table 3.1 summarizes these rules.

( )	Inner to outer, left to right
^	Left to right in expression
* /	Left to right in expression
+ −	Left to right in expression

Table 3.1 Level of precedence for arithmetic operations.

5. Visual Basic statements and certain other words that have a specific meaning in the Visual Basic language cannot be used as names of variables. For instance, the statements Let print = 99 and Let end = 99 are not valid. Words such as Print and End are called **restricted keywords**. Some other common restricted keywords are Call, If, Select, and Sub. If a restricted keyword is used as a variable name, you will soon be warned that something is wrong. As soon as the cursor is moved from the line, an error message will appear and the line will turn red. The use of some other keywords (such as Error, Height, Name, Rate, Time, Val, Width, and Year) as variable names

does not trigger an immediate warning, but generates an error message when the program is run. Although there is a way to get Visual Basic to accept this last group of keywords as variable names, we will never use keywords as variable names. Most of the items in Appendix C, other than properties, are reserved words. You can tell immediately when you inadvertently use a reserved word as a variable in a Let statement because Visual Basic automatically capitalizes the first letter of keywords. For instance, if you type "let rate = 50" and press the Enter key, the line will change to "Let Rate = 50".

6. Grammatical errors, such as misspellings or incorrect punctuations, are called **syntax errors**. Certain types of syntax errors are spotted by the smart editor when they are entered, whereas others are not detected until the program is executed. When Visual Basic spots an error, it displays a dialog box. Some incorrect statements and their errors are given below.

Statement	Reason for Error
picBox.Primt 3	Misspelling of keyword
picBox.Print 2 +	No number follows the plus sign
Let 9W = 5	9W is not a valid variable name

7. Errors detected while a program is running are called **run-time errors**. Although some run-time errors are due to improper syntax, others result from the inability of the computer to carry out the intended task. For instance, if the value of *numVar* is 0, then the statement

```
Let numVarInv = 1/numVar
```

interrupts the program with the run-time error "Division by zero." If the file DATA.TXT is not in the root folder of the C drive, then a statement that refers to the file by the filespec "C:\DATA.TXT" produces the run-time error "File not found."

The dialog box generated by a run-time error states the type of error and has a row of four command buttons captioned Continue, End, Debug, and Help. If you click on the Debug command button, Visual Basic will highlight in yellow the line of code that caused the error. (**Note:** After a run-time error occurs, the program is said to be in break mode. See the first page of Appendix D for a discussion of the three program modes.)

8. A third type of error is the so-called **logical error**. Such an error occurs when a program does not perform the way it was intended. For instance, the lines

```
Let ave = firstNum + secondNum / 2
picBox.print "The average of the two numbers is"; ave
```

are syntactically correct. However, the missing parentheses in the first line are responsible for an incorrect value being generated. Appendix D discusses debugging tools that can be used to detect and correct logical errors.

9. The omission of the asterisk to denote multiplication is a common error. For instance, the expression a(b + c) is not valid. It should read a * (b + c).

10. The largest number that most of the numeric variables considered in this text can represent is 3.402823E+38. Attempting to generate larger values produces the message "Overflow." The numbers generated by the programs in this text usually have a maximum of seven digits.

11. *A Review of Exponents.* The expression 2^3 means $2 \cdot 2 \cdot 2$, the product of three 2's. The number 3 is called the **exponent**, and the number 2 is called the **base**. In general, if r is a positive integer and a is a number, then a^r is defined as follows:

$$a^r = \underbrace{a \cdot a \ldots a}_{r \text{ factors}}$$

The process of calculating a^r is called *raising a to the rth power*. Some other types of exponents are the following:

$a^{1/2} = \sqrt{a}$		$9^{1/2} = 3$
$a^{1/n} = \sqrt[n]{a}$	n positive integer	$16^{1/4} = 2$
$a^{m/n} = (\sqrt[n]{a})^m$	m, n positive integers	$8^{2/3} = (\sqrt[3]{8})^2 = 4$
$a^{-r} = 1/a^r$	$a \neq 0$	$10^{-2} = .01$

12. More than one statement can be placed on a single line of a program provided the statements are separated by colons. For instance, the code inside the event procedure in Example 3 can be written as

```
picResults.Cls: Let a = 5: Let b = 4: picResults.Print a * (2 + b)
```

In general, though, programs are much easier to follow if just one statement appears on each line. In this text, we almost always use single-statement lines.

PRACTICE PROBLEMS 3.3

1. Evaluate $2 + 3 * 4$.

2. Complete the table by filling in the value of each variable after each line is executed.

	a	b	c
`Private Sub cmdCompute_Click()`			
`Let a = 3`	3	—	—
`Let b = 4`	3	4	—
`Let c = a + b`	3	4	7
`Let a = c * a`	21	3	7
`picResults.Print  a - b`		—	0
`Let b = b * b`	16	4	0
`End Sub`			

EXERCISES 3.3

In Exercises 1 through 6, evaluate the numeric expression.

1. 3 * 4

2. 7 ^ 2

3. 1 / (2 ^ 5)

4. 3 + (4 * 5)

5. (5 − 3) * 4

6. 3 * ((−2) ^ 5)

In Exercises 7 through 10, write the number in scientific notation as it might be displayed by the computer.

7. 3 billion

8. 12,300,000

9. 4 / (10 ^ 8)

10. 32 * (10 ^ 20)

In Exercises 11 through 16, determine whether or not the name is a valid variable name.

11. balance

12. room&Board

13. fOrM_1040

14. 1040B

15. expenses?

16. INCOME 1987

In Exercises 17 through 22, evaluate the numeric expression where a = 2, b = 3, and c = 4.

17. (a * b) + c

18. a * (b + c)

19. (1 + b) * c

20. a ^ c

21. b ^ (c − a)

22. (c − a) ^ b

In Exercises 23 through 28, write an event procedure to calculate and display the value of the expression.

23. $7 \cdot 8 + 5$

24. $(1 + 2 \cdot 9)^3$

25. 5.5% of 20

26. $15 − 3(2 + 3^4)$

27. 17 (3 + 162)

28. 4 1/2 − 3 5/8

In Exercises 29 and 30, complete the table by filling in the value of each variable after each line is executed.

29.

	x	y
`Private Sub cmdCompute_Click()`		
`Let x = 2`	2	
`Let y = 3 * x`	2	6
`Let x = y + 5`	11	6
`picResults.Cls`	---	---
`picResults.Print x + 4`		
`Let y = y + 1`	7	
`End Sub`		

30.

	bal	inter	withDr
`Private Sub cmdCompute_Click()`			
`Let bal = 100`	100		
`Let inter = .05`	100	.05	
`Let withDr = 25`	100	.05	25
`Let bal = bal + inter * bal`			
`Let bal = bal - withDr`			
`End Sub`			

100.05

In Exercises 31 through 38, determine the output displayed in the picture box by the lines of code.

31.
```
Let amount = 10
picOutput.Print amount - 4
```

32.
```
Let a = 4
Let b = 5 * a
picOutput.Print a + b; b - a
```

33.
```
picOutput.Print 1; 2;
picOutput.Print 3; 4
picOutput.Print 5 + 6
```

34.
```
Let number = 5
Let number = 2 * number
picOutput.Print number
```

35.
```
picOutput.Print a + 1
Let a = 4
Let b = a ^ 2
picOutput.Print a * b
```

36.
```
Let tax = 200
Let tax = 25 + tax
picOutput.Print tax
```

37. Let x = 3
```
picOutput.Print x ^ x; x + 3 * x
```
3
27, 24

38. Let n = 2
```
picOutput.Print 3 * n
Let n = n + n
picOutput.Print n + n
```

In Exercises 39 through 42, identify the errors.

39. Let a = 2
```
Let b = 3
Let a + b = c
picOutput.Print c
```

40. Let a = 2
```
Let b = 3
Let c = d = 4
picOutput.Print 5((a + b) / (c + d)
```

41. Let balance = 1,234
```
Let deposit = $100
picOutput.Print balance + deposit
```

42. Let .05 = interest
```
Let balance = 800
picOutput.Print interest * balance
```

In Exercises 43 and 44, rewrite the code with fewer lines.

43.
```
picOutput.Print 1;
picOutput.Print 2;
picOutput.Print 1 + 2
```

44. Let a = 1
```
Let b = a + 2
picOutput.Print b
```

In Exercises 45 through 52, write code starting with Private Sub cmdCompute_ Click() and picOutput.Cls statements, ending with an End Sub statement, and having one line for each step. Lines that display data should use the given variable names.

45. The following steps calculate a company's profit.

(a) Assign the value 98456 to the variable *revenue*.
(b) Assign the value 45000 to the variable *costs*.
(c) Assign the difference between the variables *revenue* and *costs* to the variable *profit*.
(d) Display the value of the variable *profit* in a picture box.

46. The following steps calculate the amount of a stock purchase.

(a) Assign the value 25.625 to the variable *costPerShare*.
(b) Assign the value 400 to the variable *numberOfShares*.
(c) Assign the product of *costPerShare* and *numberOfShares* to the variable *amount*.
(d) Display the value of the variable *amount* in a picture box.

47. The following steps calculate the price of an item after a 30% reduction.

(a) Assign the value 19.95 to the variable *price*.
(b) Assign the value 30 to the variable *discountPercent*.
(c) Assign the value of (*discountPercent* divided by 100) times *price* to the variable *markDown*.
(d) Decrease price by *markDown*.
(e) Display the value of *price* in a picture box.

48. The following steps calculate a company's break-even point, the number of units of goods the company must manufacture and sell in order to break even.

(a) Assign the value 5000 to the variable *fixedCosts*.
(b) Assign the value 8 to the variable *pricePerUnit*.
(c) Assign the value 6 to the variable *costPerUnit*.
(d) Assign the value *fixedCosts* divided by (the difference of *pricePerUnit* and *costPerUnit*) to the variable *breakEvenPoint*.
(e) Display the value of the variable *breakEvenPoint* in a picture box.

49. The following steps calculate the balance after 3 years when $100 is deposited in a savings account at 5% interest compounded annually.

(a) Assign the value 100 to the variable *balance*.
(b) Increase the variable *balance* by 5% of its value.
(c) Increase the variable *balance* by 5% of its value.
(d) Increase the variable *balance* by 5% of its value.
(e) Display the value of the variable *balance* in a picture box.

50. The following steps calculate the balance after 3 years when $100 is deposited at the beginning of each year in a savings account at 5% interest compounded annually.

(a) Assign the value 100 to the variable *balance*.
(b) Increase the variable *balance* by 5% of its value and add 100.
(c) Increase the variable *balance* by 5% of its value and add 100.
(d) Increase the variable *balance* by 5% of its value and add 100.
(e) Display the value of the variable *balance* in a picture box.

51. The following steps calculate the balance after 10 years when $100 is deposited in a savings account at 5% interest compounded annually.

(a) Assign the value 100 to the variable *balance*.
(b) Multiply the variable *balance* by 1.05 raised to the 10th power.
(c) Display the value of the variable *balance* in a picture box.

52. The following steps calculate the percentage profit from the sale of a stock.

(a) Assign the value 10 to the variable *purchasePrice*.
(b) Assign the value 15 to the variable *sellingPrice*.
(c) Assign to the variable *percentProfit*, 100 times the value of the difference between *sellingPrice* and *purchasePrice* divided by *purchasePrice*.
(d) Display the value of the variable *percentProfit* in a picture box.

In Exercises 53 through 58, write an event procedure to solve the problem and display the answer in a picture box. The program should use variables for each of the quantities.

53. Suppose each acre of farmland produces 18 tons of corn. How many tons of corn can be produced on a 30-acre farm?

54. Suppose a ball is thrown straight up in the air with an initial velocity of 50 feet per second and an initial height of 5 feet. How high will the ball be after 3 seconds? **Note:** The height after t seconds is given by the expression $-16t^2 + v_o t + h_o$, where v_o is the initial velocity and h_o is the initial height.

55. If a car left Washington, D.C., at two o'clock and arrived in New York at seven o'clock, what was its average speed? **Note:** New York is 233 miles from Washington.

56. A motorist wants to determine her gas mileage. At 23,340 miles (on the odometer), the tank is filled. At 23,695 miles, the tank is filled again with 14.1 gallons. How many miles per gallon did the car average between the two fillings?

57. A U.S. geological survey showed that Americans use an average of 1600 gallons of water per person per day, including industrial use. How many gallons of water are used each year in the United States? **Note:** The current population of the United States is about 260 million people.

58. According to FHA specifications, each room in a house should have a window area equal to at least 10 percent of the floor area of the room. What is the minimum window area for a 14-ft by 16-ft room?

SOLUTIONS TO PRACTICE PROBLEMS 3.3

1. 14. Multiplications are performed before additions. If the intent is for the addition to be performed first, the expression should be written (2 + 3) * 4.

2.

	a	b	c
`Private Sub cmdCompute_Click()`			
`Let a = 3`	3	–	–
`Let b = 4`	3	4	–
`Let c = a + b`	3	4	7
`Let a = c * a`	21	4	7
`picResults.Print a - b`	21	4	7
`Let b = b * b`	21	16	7
`End Sub`			

Each time a Let statement is executed, only one variable has its value changed (the variable to the left of the equal sign).

3.4 STRINGS

There are two primary types of data that can be processed by Visual Basic: numbers and strings. Sentences, phrases, words, letters of the alphabet, names, phone numbers, addresses, and social security numbers are all examples of strings. Formally, a **string constant** is a sequence of characters that is treated as a single item. Strings can be assigned names with Let statements, can be displayed with Print methods, and there is an operation called concatenation (denoted by &) for combining strings.

Variables and Strings

A **string variable** is a name used to refer to a string. The allowable names of string variables are identical to those of numeric variables. The value of a string variable is assigned or altered with Let statements and displayed with Print methods just like the value of a numeric variable.

EXAMPLE 1 The following code shows how Let and Print are used with strings. The string variable *today* is assigned a value by the fourth line and this value is displayed by the fifth line. The quotation marks surrounding each string constant are not part of the constant and are not displayed by the Print method. (The form design for Examples 1 through 6 consists of a command button and picture box, as shown in Example 1 of the previous section.)

```
Private Sub cmdButton_Click()
  picBox.Cls
  picBox.Print "hello"
  Let today = "9/17/95"
  picBox.Print today
End Sub
```

[Run and then click the command button. The following is displayed in the picture box.]

```
hello
9/17/97
```

If $x, y, \ldots, z$ are characters and *strVar1* is a string variable, then the statement

```
Let strVar1 = "xy...z"
```

assigns the string constant $xy\ldots z$ to the variable, and the statement

```
picBox.Print "xy...z"
```

or

```
picBox.Print strVar1
```

displays the string $xy\ldots z$ in a picture box. If *strVar2* is another string variable, then the statement

```
Let strVar2 = strVar1
```

assigns the value of the variable *strVar1* to the variable *strVar2*. (The value of *strVar1* will remain the same.) String constants used in Let or picBox.Print statements must be surrounded by quotation marks, but string variables are never surrounded by quotation marks.

As with numbers, semicolons can be used with strings in picBox.Print statements to suppress carriage returns and line feeds. However, picBox.Print statements do not display leading or trailing spaces along with strings.

EXAMPLE 2   The following program illustrates the use of the Let statement and Print method.

```
Private Sub cmdShow_Click()
  picOutput.Cls
  Let phrase = "win or lose that counts."
  picOutput.Print "It's not whether you "; phrase
  picOutput.Print "It's whether I "; phrase
End Sub
```

[Run and then click the command button. The following is displayed in the picture box.]

```
It's not whether you win or lose that counts.
It's whether I win or lose that counts.
```

EXAMPLE 3   The following program has strings and numbers occurring together in a picBalance.Print instruction.

```
Private Sub cmdCompute_Click()
  picBalance.Cls
  Let interestRate = 0.0655
  Let principal = 100
  Let phrase = "The balance after a year is"
  picBalance.Print phrase; (1 + interestRate) * principal
End Sub
```

[Run and then click the command button. The following is displayed in the picture box.]

```
The balance after a year is 106.55
```

Concatenation

Two strings can be combined to form a new string consisting of the strings joined together. The joining operation is called **concatenation** and is represented by an ampersand (&). For instance, "good" & "bye" is "goodbye". A combination of strings and ampersands that can be evaluated to form a string is called a **string expression**. The Let statement and Print method evaluate expressions before assigning them to variables or displaying them.

EXAMPLE 4   The following program illustrates concatenation.

```
Private Sub cmdDisplay_Click()
  picQuote.Cls
  Let quote1 = "The ballgame isn't over, "
  Let quote2 = "until it's over."
  Let quote = quote1 & quote2
  picQuote.Print quote & "   Yogi Berra"
End Sub
```

[Run and then click the command button. The following is displayed in the picture box.]

```
The ballgame isn't over, until it's over.   Yogi Berra
```

Declaring Variable Types

So far, we have not distinguished between variables that hold strings and variables that hold numbers. There are several advantages to specifying the type of values, string or numeric, that can be assigned to a variable. A statement of the form

```
Dim variableName As String
```

specifies that only strings can be assigned to the named variable. A statement of the form

```
Dim variableName As Single
```

specifies that only numbers can be assigned to the named variable. The term Single derives from *single-precision real number*. After you type the space after the word "As," the editor displays a list of all the possible next words. In this text we use only a few of the items from this list.

A Dim statement is said to **declare** a variable. From now on we will declare all variables. However, all the programs will run correctly even if the Dim statements are omitted. Declaring variables is regarded as good programming practice because it makes programs easier to read and helps prevent certain types of errors.

EXAMPLE 5   The following rewrite of Example 3 declares all variables.

```
Private Sub cmdCompute_Click()
  Dim interestRate As Single
  Dim principal As Single
  Dim phrase As String
  picBalance.Cls
  Let interestRate = 0.0655
  Let principal = 100
  Let phrase = "The balance after a year is"
  picBalance.Print phrase; (1 + interestRate) * principal
End Sub
```

Several Dim statements can be combined into one. For instance, the first three Dim statements of Example 5 can be replaced by

```
Dim interestRate As Single, principal As Single, phrase As String
```

The dollar sign provides an alternative way to identify a variable as being a string variable. A statement of the form

```
Dim var As String
```

can be replaced by

```
Dim var$
```

In the event you do not declare a variable with a Dim statement, you can still designate a type for it by appending a special character, called a **type declaration tag** to the end of the variable name. Use an exclamation mark for a numeric variable (that is, a single-precision variable) and a dollar sign for a string variable. For instance, a program can contain lines such as the following:

```
Let price! = 65.99
Let nom$ = "John"
```

Visual Basic actually has several different types of numeric variables. So far, we have used only single-precision numeric variables. Single-precision numeric variables can hold numbers of magnitude from as small as 1.4×10^{-45} to as large as 3.4×10^{38}. Another type of numeric variable, called **Integer**, can only hold whole numbers from −32768 to 32767. Integer type variables are declared with a statement of the form

```
Dim intVar As Integer
```

The type declaration tag for Integer variables is the percent symbol. The Integer data type uses less memory than the Single data type and statements using the Integer type execute faster. (This is only useful in programs with many calculations, such as the programs in later chapters that use For...Next loops.) Of course, Integer variables are limited because they cannot hold decimals or large numbers. We will use Integer variables extensively with For...Next loops in Chapter 6 and occasionally when the data clearly consist of small whole numbers.

Other types of numeric variables are Long, Double, and Currency. We do not use them in this text. If you want to learn about them, consult Appendix C. In this text, whenever we refer to a numeric variable without mentioning a type, we mean type Single or Integer.

Using Text Boxes for Input and Output

The contents of a text box is always a string. Therefore, statements such as

```
Let strVar = txtBox.Text
```

and

```
Let txtBox.Text = strVar
```

can be used to assign the contents of the text box to the string variable *strVar* and vice versa.

Numbers are stored in text boxes as strings. Therefore, they should be converted to numbers before being assigned to numeric variables. If *str* is a string representation of a number, then

```
Val(str)
```

is that number. Conversely, if *num* is a number, then

```
Str(num)
```

is a string representation of the number. Therefore, statements such as

```
Let numVar = Val(txtBox.Text)
```

and

```
Let txtBox.Text = Str(numVar)
```

can be used to assign the contents of the text box to the numeric variable *numVar* and vice versa. **Note:** When a nonnegative number is converted to a string with Str, its first character (but not its last character) is a blank space.

EXAMPLE 6 The following program converts miles to furlongs and vice versa. **Note:** A furlong is 1/8th of a mile.

Object	Property	Setting
frm3_4_6	Caption	Convertor
lblMile	Alignment	1 – Right Justify
	Caption	Miles
txtMile	Text	0
lblFurlong	Alignment	1 – Right Justify
	Caption	Furlongs
txtFurlong	Text	0

The two text boxes have been named txtMile and txtFurlong. With the Event procedures shown, typing a number into a text box and pressing Tab results in the converted number being displayed in the other text box.

```
Private Sub txtMile_LostFocus()
  Let txtFurlong.Text = Str(8 * Val(txtMile.Text))
End Sub

Private Sub txtFurlong_LostFocus()
  Let txtMile.Text = Str(Val(txtFurlong.Text) / 8)
End Sub
```

ANSI Character Set

Each of the 47 different keys in the center typewriter portion of the keyboard can produce two characters, for a total of 94 characters. Adding 1 for the space character produced by the space bar makes 95 characters. These characters have numbers ranging from 32 to 126 associated with them. These values, called the ANSI (or ASCII) values of the characters, are given in Appendix A. Table 3.2 shows a few of the values.

32 (space)	48 0	66 B	122 z
33 !	49 1	90 Z	123 {
34 "	57 9	97 a	125 }
35 #	65 A	98 b	126 ~

Table 3.2 A few ANSI values.

Most of the best-known fonts, such as Ariel, Courier, Helvetica, and Times Roman, are essentially governed by the ANSI standard, which assigns characters to the numbers from 32 to 255. Table 3.3 shows a few of the higher ANSI values.

162 ¢	177 ±	181 μ	190 ¾
169 ©	178 ²	188 ¼	247 ÷
176 °	179 ³	189 ½	248 φ

Table 3.3 A few higher ANSI values.

If *n* is a number between 32 and 255, then

    Chr(n)

is the string consisting of the character with ANSI value *n*. If *str* is any string, then

Returns only first characters value ASCII

    Asc(str)

is the ANSI value of the first character of *str*. For instance, the statement

    Let txtBox.Text = Chr(65)

displays the letter A in the text box and the statement

    picBox.Print Asc("Apple")

displays the number 65 in the picture box.

Concatenation can be used with Chr to obtain strings using the higher ANSI characters. For instance, with one of the fonts that conforms to the ANSI standard, the statement

    Let txtBox.Text = "32" & Chr(176) & " Fahrenheit"

displays 32° Fahrenheit in the text box.

The KeyPress Event Procedure

When a text box has the focus and the user presses a key, the KeyPress event procedure identifies the key pressed. When a key is pressed, the event procedure assigns the ANSI value of the key to an Integer variable called *KeyAscii*. The general form of the procedure is

    Private Sub ControlName_KeyPress(KeyAscii As Integer)
        statements
    End Sub

The statements usually involve the variable *KeyAscii*. Also, a character does not appear in the text box until End Sub is reached. At that time, the character with ANSI value *KeyAscii* is displayed.

EXAMPLE 7 The following program allows the user to determine the ANSI values of the standard (typewriter) keys of the keyboard. The statement Let txtCharacter. Text = "" removes any previously typed character from the text box.

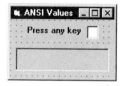

Object	Property	Setting
frm3_4_7	Caption	ANSI Values
lblPress	Caption	Press any key
txtCharacter	Text	(blank)
picOutput		

```
Private Sub txtCharacter_KeyPress(KeyAscii As Integer)
  Let txtCharacter.Text = ""
  picOutput.Cls
  picOutput.Print Chr(KeyAscii); " has ANSI value"; KeyAscii
End Sub
```

[Run and then press a key. For instance, if A is pressed, the following is displayed in the picture box.]

```
A has ANSI value 65
```

The KeyPress procedure can alter the character typed into the text box. For instance, if the statement

```
Let KeyAscii = 65
```

is placed in a KeyPress event procedure, the letter A is displayed when any standard key is pressed. In Chapter 5, we use a decision structure to prevent the user from typing unwanted keys. For instance, if we want the user to enter a number into a text box, we can intercept and discard any key presses that are not digits. The statement

```
Let KeyAscii = 0
```

placed in a KeyPress event procedure discards the key pressed. Finally, a program can be made more friendly by letting the Enter key (ANSI value 13) move the focus in the same way that the Tab key moves the focus. This requires having a KeyPress event procedure for each object that is to respond to the Enter key and then setting the focus to the next object when the value of *KeyAscii* is 13.

Comments

1. The string "", which contains no characters, is called the **null string** or the **empty string**. It is different from " ", the string consisting of a single space. String variables that have not been assigned values by Let statements initially have "" as their default values. (Numeric variables have default value 0.)

2. The statement picBox.Print, with no string or number, simply skips a line in the picture box.

3. Assigning string values to numeric variables or numeric values to string variables results in the error message "Type mismatch."

4. In Visual Basic 5.0, the maximum allowable number of characters in a string is approximately 2 billion.

5. The quotation mark character (") can be placed into a string constant by using Chr(34). For example, after the statement

```
Let txtBox.Text = "George " & Chr(34) & "Babe" & Chr(34) & " Ruth"
```

is executed, the text box contains

```
George "Babe" Ruth
```

6. Most major programming languages require that all variables be declared before they can be used. Although declaring variables with Dim statements is optional in Visual Basic, you can tell Visual Basic to make declaration mandatory. The steps are as follows:

   (a) From any code window, click on the down-arrow to the right of the object box and click on (General).
   (b) Type

   ```
   Option Explicit
   ```

   and press Enter.

   Then, if you use a variable without first declaring it in a Dim statement, the message "Variable not defined" will appear as soon as you attempt to run the program. One big advantage of using Option Explicit is that mistypings of variable names will be detected. Otherwise, malfunctions due to typing errors are often difficult to detect.

7. You can have Visual Basic automatically place Option Explicit in every program you write. The steps are as follows:

   (a) Press Alt/T/O and click on the Editor tab to invoke the editor options.
   (b) If the square to the left of "Require Variable Declaration" does not contain a check mark, click on the square.

8. Variables that are not (explicitly) declared with Dim statements are said to be **implicitly declared**. Such variables, which have a data type called Variant, can hold strings, numbers, and several other kinds of information.

9. You can display the type of a variable with the following steps—position the cursor over the word, press the right mouse button, and click on Quick Info.

10. Val can be applied to strings containing nonnumeric characters. If the beginning of the string *str* represents a number, then Val(*str*) is that number; otherwise, it is 0. For instance, Val("123Blastoff") is 123, and Val("ab3") is 0.

11. The KeyPress event also applies to command buttons and picture boxes.

12. Concatenation of strings also can be represented by a plus sign (+). However, restricting the plus sign to operations on numbers eliminates ambiguity and provides self-documenting code.

13. If Val is omitted from the statement

```
Let numVar = Val(txtBox.Text)
```

or Str is omitted from the statement

```
Let txtBox.Text = Str(numVar)
```

Visual Basic does not complain, but simply makes the conversion for you. However, errors can arise from omitting Val and Str. For instance, if the contents of txtBox1.Text is 34 and the contents of txtBox2.Text is 56, then the statement

```
Let numVar = txtBox1.Text + txtBox2.Text
```

assigns the number 3456 rather than 90 to *numVar*. (This is because Visual Basic does not perform the conversion until just before the assignment.) If txtBox1 is empty, then the statement

```
Let numVar = 3 * txtBox1.Text
```

will crash the program and produce the error message "Type mismatch." We follow the standards of good programming practice by always using Val and Str to convert values between text boxes and numeric variables. Similar considerations apply to conversions involving label captions.

14. Variable names should describe the role of the variable. Also, some programmers use a prefix such as sng or str to identify the type of a variable. For example, they would use names like sngInterestRate and strFirstName.

PRACTICE PROBLEMS 3.4

1. Compare the following two statements, where *phrase* is a string variable and *balance* is a numeric variable.

```
picBox.Print "It's whether I "; phrase
picBox.Print "The balance is"; balance
```

Why is the space preceding the second quotation mark necessary for the first picBox.Print statement, but not necessary for the second picBox.Print statement?

2. A label's caption is a string and can be assigned a value with a statement of the form

```
Let lblOne.Caption = strVar
```

What is one advantage to using a label for output as opposed to a text box?

3. Write code to add the numbers in txtBox1 and txtBox2 and place the sum in lblThree.

EXERCISES 3.4

In Exercises 1 through 14, determine the output displayed in the picture box by the lines of code.

1. ```
picOutput.Print "Hello"
picOutput.Print "12" & "34"
```

2. ```
picOutput.Print "Welcome; my friend."
picOutput.Print "Welcome"; "my friend."
```

3. ```
picOutput.Print "12"; 12; "TWELVE"
```
```

4. `picOutput.Print Chr(104) & Chr(105)`

5.
```
Dim r As String, b As String
   Let r = "A ROSE"
   Let b = " IS "
   picOutput.Print r; b; r; b; r
```

6.
```
Dim n As Single, x As String
   Let n = 5
   Let x = "5"
   picOutput.Print n
   picOutput.Print x
```

7.
```
Dim houseNumber As Single
   Dim street As String
   Let houseNumber = 1234
   Let street = "Main Street"
   picOutput.Print houseNumber; street
```

8.
```
Dim p As String, word As String
   Let p = "f"
   Let word = "lute"
   picOutput.Print p & word
```

9.
```
Dim quote As String, person As String, qMark As String
   Let quote = "We're all in this alone."
   Let person = "Lily Tomlin"
   Let qMark = Chr(34)
   picOutput.Print qMark & quote & qMark & "  " & person
```

10.
```
Dim letter As String
   Let letter = "D"
   picOutput.Print letter; " is the"; Asc(letter) - Asc("A") + 1;
   picOutput.Print "th letter of the alphabet."
```

11.
```
picOutput.Print Str(17); Val("2B")
   picOutput.Print Str(-20); Val("16.00")
```

12.
```
Dim a As Single, b As Single
   Let a = 1
   Let b = 2
   picOutput.Print Val(Str(a)); Str(a + b)
   picOutput.Print Str(4 - a)
```

13.
```
Dim num1 As Single, num2 As String
   Let num1 = 3567
   Let num2 = Str(num1)
   picOutput.Print "The number of digits in"; num2; " is"; 4
```

14.
```
Dim address As String
   Let address = "1600 Pennsylvania Avenue"
   picOutput.Print "Bill, your house number is"; Val(address)
```

In Exercises 15 through 20, identify any errors.

15.
```
Dim phone As Single
   Let phone = "234-5678"
   picOutput.Print "My phone number is "; phone
```

16.
```
Dim x As String, y As Single
   Let x = "2"
   Let y = 3
   picOutput.Print x + y
```

17.
```
Dim quote As String
   Let quote = I came to Casablanca for the waters.
   picOutput.Print quote; "  "; "Bogart"
```

18.
```
Dim strVar As String
Let strVar = Str(23Skidoo)
picOutput.Print strVar
```

19.
```
Dim end As String
Let end = "happily ever after."
picOutput.Print "They lived "; end
```

20.
```
Dim hi-Yo As String
Let hi-Yo = Silver
picOutput.Print "Hi-Yo "; hi-Yo
```

21. Write an event procedure that allows the user to press a command button by pressing any key while the focus is on the command button.

22. Describe the KeyPress event in your own words.

In Exercises 23 through 26, write code starting with Private Sub cmdDisplay_ Click() and picOutput.Cls statements, ending with an End Sub statement, and having one line for each step. Lines that display data should use the given variable names.

23. The following steps give the name and birth year of a famous inventor.

    (a) Declare all variables used in the steps below.
    (b) Assign "Thomas" to the variable *firstName*.
    (c) Assign "Alva" to the variable *middleName*.
    (d) Assign "Edison" to the variable *lastName*.
    (e) Assign 1847 to the variable *yearOfBirth*.
    (f) Display the inventor's full name followed by a comma and his year of birth.

24. The following steps compute the price of ketchup.

    (a) Declare all variables used in the steps below.
    (b) Assign "ketchup" to the variable *item*.
    (c) Assign 1.80 to the variable *regularPrice*.
    (d) Assign .27 to the variable *discount*.
    (e) Display the phrase "1.53 is the sale price of ketchup."

25. The following steps display a copyright statement.

    (a) Declare all variables used in the steps below.
    (b) Assign "Prentice Hall, Inc." to the variable *publisher*.
    (c) Display the phrase "© Prentice Hall, Inc."

26. The following steps give advice.

    (a) Declare all variables used in the steps below.
    (b) Assign "Fore" to the variable *prefix*.
    (c) Display the phrase "Forewarned is Forearmed."

In Exercises 27 through 32, the interface and initial properties are specified. Write the code to carry out the stated task.

27. After values are placed in the x and y text boxes, pressing Compute Sum places x + y in the sum picture box.

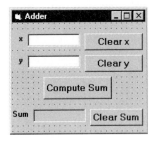

Object	Property	Setting
frmEx27	Caption	Adder
lblX	Caption	x
txtNum1	Text	(blank)
cmdClearX	Caption	Clear x
lblY	Caption	y
txtNum2	Text	(blank)
cmdClearY	Caption	Clear y
cmdCompute	Caption	Compute Sum
lblSum	Caption	Sum
picSum		
cmdClearSum	Caption	Clear Sum

28. When cmdCelsius is pressed, the temperature is converted from Fahrenheit to Celsius, the title bar changes to Celsius, cmdCelsius is hidden, and cmdFahr becomes visible. If cmdFahr is now pressed, the temperature is converted from Celsius to Fahrenheit, the title bar reverts to Fahrenheit, cmdFahr is hidden, and cmdCelsius becomes visible. Of course, the user can change the temperature in the text box at any time. (**Note:** The conversion formulas are $C = (5/9) * (F - 32)$ and $F = (9/5) * C + 32$.)

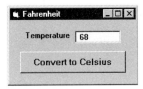

Object	Property	Setting
frmEx28	Caption	Fahrenheit
lblTemp	Caption	Temperature
txtTemp	Text	0
cmdCelsius	Caption	Convert to Celsius
cmdFahr	Caption	Convert to Fahrenheit
	Visible	False

29. If n is the number of seconds between lightning and thunder, the storm is $n/5$ miles away. Write a program that requests the number of seconds between lightning and thunder and reports the distance of the storm.

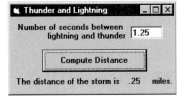

Object	Property	Setting
frmStorm	Caption	Thunder and Lightning
lblNumSec	Caption	Number of seconds between lightning and thunder
txtNumSec	Text	(blank)
cmdCompute	Caption	Compute Distance
lblDistance	Caption	The distance of the storm is
lblNumMiles	Caption	(blank)
lblMiles	Caption	miles.

30. Write a program to request the name of a baseball team, the number of games won, and the number of games lost as input, and then display the percentage of games won.

Object	Property	Setting
frmBaseball	Caption	Baseball
lblTeam	Caption	Team
txtTeam	Text	(blank)
lblWon	Caption	Games Won
txtWon	Text	(blank)
lblLost	Caption	Games Lost
txtLost	Text	(blank)
cmdCompute	Caption	Compute Percentage
picPercent		

31. The number of calories burned per hour by bicycling, jogging, and swimming are 200, 475, and 275, respectively. A person loses 1 pound of weight for each 3500 calories burned. Write a program that allows the user to input the number of hours spent at each activity, and then calculates the number of pounds worked off.

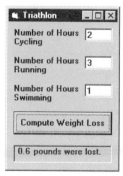

Object	Property	Setting
frmTriathlon	Caption	Triathlon
lblCycle	Caption	Number of Hours Cycling
txtCycle	Text	(blank)
lblRun	Caption	Number of Hours Running
txtRun	Text	(blank)
lblSwim	Caption	Number of Hours Swimming
txtSwim	Text	(blank)
cmdCompute	Caption	Compute Weight Loss
picWtLoss		

32. The American College of Sports Medicine recommends that you maintain your *training heart rate* during an aerobic workout. Your training heart rate is computed as $.7 * (220 - a) + .3 * r$, where a is your age and r is your resting heart rate (your pulse when you first awaken). Write a program to request a person's age and resting heart rate and then calculate the training heart rate. (Determine *your* training heart rate.)

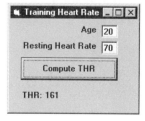

Object	Property	Setting
frmWorkout	Caption	Training Heart Rate
lblAge	Caption	Age
txtAge	Text	(blank)
lblRestHR	Caption	Resting Heart Rate
txtRestHR	Text	(blank)
cmdCompute	Caption	Compute THR
lblTHR	Caption	THR:
lblTrainHR	Caption	(blank)

In Exercises 33 through 37, write a program with a Windows-style interface to carry out the task. The program should use variables for each of the quantities and display the outcome with a complete explanation, as in Example 5.

33. If a company's annual revenue is $550,000 and its expenses are $410,000, what is its net income (revenue minus expenses)?

34. If the price of a 17-ounce can of corn is 68 cents, what is the price per ounce?

35. If a company earns $5.25 per share for the year and the price of one share of stock is $68.25, what is the company's price-to-earnings ratio (that is, price/earnings)?

36. If the radius of the earth is 6170 kilometers, what is the volume of the earth? **Note:** The volume of a sphere of radius r is $(4/3) * (3.14159) * r^3$.

37. How many pounds of grass seed are needed to seed a lawn 40 feet by 75 feet if 40 ounces are recommended for 2000 square feet? **Note:** There are 16 ounces in a pound.

38. A store manager needs three shelf signs. Write a program to produce the output that follows. The words "SALE! Everything on this shelf" and "% off!" should appear only once in the program.

SALE! Everything on this shelf 10% off!
SALE! Everything on this shelf 30% off!
SALE! Everything on this shelf 50% off!

39. Write a program that displays a command button and a label on the screen, with the label initially containing 0. Each time the command button is pressed, the number in the label should increase by 1.

40. Allow the user to enter any quantity of positive numbers. As each number is entered, display the sum of the numbers and the quantity of numbers entered. The user should be able to start anew at any time.

41. Calculate the amount of a waiter's tip, given the amount of the bill and the percentage tip. (Test the program with $20 and 15 percent.)

SOLUTIONS TO PRACTICE PROBLEMS 3.4

1. In the second picBox.Print statement, the item following the second quotation mark is a positive number, which is displayed with a leading space. Because the corresponding item in the first picBox.Print statement is a string, which is *not* displayed with a leading space, a space had to be inserted before ˙he quotation mark.

2. The user cannot enter data into a label from the keyboard. Therefore, if a control is to be used for output only, a label is preferred. **Note:** When using a label for output, you might want to set its BorderStyle property to "1-Fixed Single".

3. `lblThree.Caption = Str(Val(txtBox1.Text) + Val(txtBox2.Text))`

3.5 INPUT AND OUTPUT

So far we have relied on the Let statement to assign values to variables. Data also can be stored in files and accessed through Input# statements, or data can be supplied by the user in a text box or input box. The Print method, with a little help from commas and the Tab and Spc functions, can spread out and align the display of data in a picture box or on a printer. Message boxes grab the user's attention and display temporary messages. Rem statements allow the programmer to document all aspects of a program, including a description of the input used and the output to be produced.

Reading Data from Files

In Chapter 1, we saw how to create data files with Windows' Notepad. (As a rule of thumb, and simply as a matter of style, we enclose each string in quotation marks.) A file can have either one item per line or many items (separated by commas) can be listed on the same line. Usually, related items are grouped together on a line. For instance, if a file consisted of payroll information, each line would contain the name of a person, that person's hourly wage, and the number of hours that person worked during the week, as shown in Figure 3.24.

```
"Mike Jones", 7.35, 35
"John Smith", 6.75, 33
```

Figure 3.24 Contents of PERSONEL.TXT.

The items of data will be assigned to variables one at a time in the order they appear in the file. That is, "Mike Jones" will be the first value assigned to a variable. After all the items from the first line have been assigned to variables, subsequent requests for values will be read from the next line.

Data stored in a file can be read in order (that is, sequentially) and assigned to variables with the following steps.

1. Choose a number from 1 to 255 to be the **reference number** for the file.

2. Execute the statement

   ```
   Open "filespec" For Input As #n
   ```

   where n is the reference number. This procedure is referred to as **Opening a file for input**. It establishes a communications link between the computer and the disk drive for reading data *from* the disk. Data then can be input from the specified file and assigned to variables in the program.

3. Read items of data in order, one at a time, from the file with Input# statements. The statement

   ```
   Input #n, var
   ```

   reads to this variable

   causes the program to look in the file for the next available item of data and assign it to the variable *var*. In the file, individual items are separated by commas or line breaks. The variable in the Input# statement should be the same type (that is, string versus numeric) as the data to be assigned to it from the file.

4. After the desired items have been read from the file, close the file with the statement

   ```
   Close #n
   ```

EXAMPLE 1 Write a program that uses a file for input and produces the same output as the following code. (The form design for all examples in this section consists of a command button and a picture box.)

```
Private Sub cmdDisplay_Click()
  Dim houseNumber As Single, street As String
  picAddress.Cls
  Let houseNumber = 1600
  Let street = "Pennsylvania Ave."
  picAddress.Print "The White House is located at"; houseNumber; street
End Sub
```

[Run and then click the command button. The following is displayed in the picture box.]

```
The White House is located at 1600 Pennsylvania Ave.
```

SOLUTION   Use Windows' Notepad to create the file DATA.TXT containing the following two lines:

1600
"Pennsylvania Ave."

In the following code, the fifth line looks for the first item of data, 1600, and assigns it to the numeric variable *houseNumber*. (Visual Basic records that this piece of data has been used.) The sixth line looks for the next available item of data, "Pennsylvania Ave.", and assigns it to the string variable *street*. **Note:** You will have to alter the Open statement in the fourth line to tell it where the file DATA.TXT is located. For instance, if the file is in the root directory (that is, folder) of a diskette in drive A, then the line should read Open "A:\DATA.TXT" For Input As #1. If the file is located in the subdirectory (that is, folder) VB5 of the C drive, then the statement should be changed to "Open "C:\VB5\DATA.TXT" For Input As #1".

```
Private Sub cmdReadFile_Click()
  Dim houseNumber As Single, street As String
  picAddress.Cls
  Open "DATA.TXT" For Input As #1
  Input #1, houseNumber
  Input #1, street
  picAddress.Print "The White House is located at"; houseNumber; street
  Close #1
End Sub
```

A single Input# statement can assign values to several different variables. For instance, the two Input# statements in the solution of Example 1 can be replaced by the single statement

```
  Input #1, houseNumber, street
```

In general, a statement of the form

```
  Input #n, var1, var2, ..., varj
```

has the same effect as the sequence of statements

```
Input #n, var1
Input #n, var2
    .
    .
    .
Input #n, varj
```

EXAMPLE 2   The following program uses the file PERSONEL.TXT in Figure 3.24 to compute weekly pay. Notice that the variables in the Input# statement are the same types (string, numeric, numeric) as the constants in each line of the file.

```
Private Sub cmdCompute_Click()
  Dim nom As String, wage As Single, hrs As Single
  picPay.Cls
  Open "PERSONEL.TXT" For Input As #1
  Input #1, nom, wage, hrs
  picPay.Print nom; hrs * wage
  Input #1, nom, wage, hrs
  picPay.Print nom; hrs * wage
  Close #1
End Sub
```

[Run and then click the command button. The following will be displayed in the picture box.]

```
Mike Jones 257.25
John Smith 222.75
```

In certain situations, we must read the data in a file more than once. This is accomplished by closing the file and reopening it. After a file is closed and then reopened, subsequent Input# statements begin reading from the first entry of the file.

EXAMPLE 3   The following program takes the average annual amounts of money spent by college graduates for several categories and converts these amounts to percentages. The data are read once to compute the total amount of money spent and then read again to calculate the percentage for each category. The purpose of the fifth line is to initialize the numeric variable *total*, which keeps a running total of the amounts. **Note:** These figures were compiled for the year 1990 by the Bureau of Labor Statistics.

COSTS.TXT consists of the following four lines:

```
"Transportation", 7232
"Housing", 14079
"Food", 5649
"Other", 15833
```

```
Private Sub cmdCompute_Click()
  Dim total As Single, category As String, amount As Single
  Open "COSTS.TXT" For Input As #1
  picPercent.Cls
  Let total = 0
```

```
    Input #1, category, amount
    Let total = total + amount
    Input #1, category, amount
    Let total = total + amount
    Input #1, category, amount
    Let total = total + amount
    Input #1, category, amount
    Let total = total + amount
    Close #1
    Open "COSTS.TXT" For Input As #1
    Input #1, category, amount
    picPercent.Print category; amount / total
    Input #1, category, amount
    picPercent.Print category; amount / total
    Input #1, category, amount
    picPercent.Print category; amount / total
    Input #1, category, amount
    picPercent.Print category; amount / total
    Close #1
End Sub
```

[Run and then click the command button. The following is displayed in the picture box.]

```
Transportation 0.1689996
Housing 0.3290024
Food 0.1320076
Other 0.3699904
```

Input from an Input Box

Normally, a text box is used to obtain input described by a label. Sometimes, we want just one piece of input and would rather not have a text box and label stay on the screen forever. The problem can be solved with an **input box**. When a statement of the form

```
    Let stringVar = InputBox(prompt,title)
```

is executed, an input box similar to the one shown in Figure 3.25 pops up on the screen. After the user types a response into the rectangle at the bottom of the screen and presses Enter (or clicks OK), the response is assigned to the string variable. The message to be displayed can consist of any string, and the title parameter can be omitted.

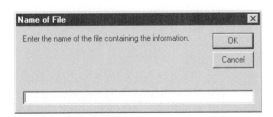

Figure 3.25 Sample input box.

When you type the parenthesis following the word InputBox, the editor displays a line containing the general form of the InputBox statement. See Figure 3.26. This feature, which was added in Visual Basic 5.0, is called **Quick Info**. The parameters *prompt* and *title* are strings that specify the message to be displayed and the caption in the title bar. Optional parameters are surrounded by brackets. All the parameters in the general form of the InputBox statement are optional except for *prompt*.

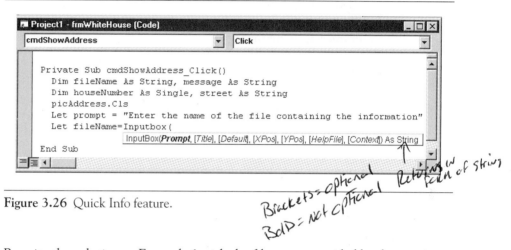

Figure 3.26 Quick Info feature.

EXAMPLE 4 Rewrite the solution to Example 1 with the file name provided by the user in an input box.

```
Private Sub cmdDisplay_Click()
    Dim fileName As String, prompt As String, title As String
    Dim houseNumber As Single, street As String
    picAddress.Cls
    Let prompt = "Enter the name of the file containing the information."
    Let title = "Name of File"
    Let fileName = InputBox(prompt, title)
    Open fileName For Input As #1
    Input #1, houseNumber
    Input #1, street
    picAddress.Print "The White House is located at"; houseNumber; street
    Close #1
End Sub
```

[Run and then click the command button. The input box of Figure 3.25 appears on the screen. Type DATA.TXT (possibly preceded with a path) into the input box and click on OK. The input box disappears and the following appears in the picture box.]

```
The White House is located at 1600 Pennsylvania Ave.
```

The response typed into an input box is treated as a single string value, no matter what is typed. (Quotation marks are not needed, and if included, are considered as part of the string.) Numeric data typed into an input box should be converted to a number with Val before it is assigned to a numeric variable or used in a calculation.

Formatting Output with Print Zones

Each line in a picture box can be thought of as being subdivided into zones, as shown in Figure 3.27. Each zone contains 14 positions, where the width of a position is the average width of the characters in the font.

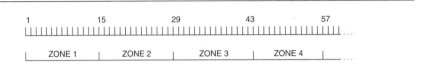

Figure 3.27 Print zones.

We have seen that when the Print method is followed by several items separated by semicolons, the items are displayed one after another. When commas are used instead of semicolons, the items are displayed in consecutive zones. For instance, if the Font property of picBox is set to Courier, when the motto of the state of Alaska is displayed with the statements

```
picBox.Print "North", "to", "the", "future."
picBox.Print "123456789012345678901234567890123456789012345678901234567890"
```

the resulting picture box is

```
North           to              the             future.
123456789012345678901234567890123456789012345678901234567890
```

where each word is in a separate print zone. This same output can be achieved with the code

```
Dim a As String, b As String, c As String, d As String
Let a = "North"
Let b = "to"
Let c = "the"
Let d = "future."
picBox.Print a, b, c, d
picBox.Print "123456789012345678901234567890123456789012345678901234567890"
```

EXAMPLE 5 The following program uses Print zones to organize expenses for public and private schools into columns of a table. The data represent the average expenses for 1993–94. (The Font setting for picTable is the default font MS Sans Serif.)

```
Private Sub cmdDisplay_Click()
  picTable.Cls
  picTable.Print " ", "Pb 2-yr", "Pr 2-yr", "Pb 4-yr", "Pr 4-yr"
  picTable.Print
  picTable.Print "Tuit & Fees", 1229, 6175, 2527, 11025
  picTable.Print "Bks & Suppl", 533, 566, 552, 556
  picTable.Print "Board", 1643, 1589, 1601, 1722
  picTable.Print "Trans", 923, 890, 870, 824
  picTable.Print "Other Exp", 1044, 970, 1259, 1073
  picTable.Print " ", "_____", "_____", "_____", "_____"
  picTable.Print "Total", 5372, 10190, 6809, 15200
End Sub
```

[Run and then click the command button. The resulting picture box is shown.]

	Pb 2-yr	Pr 2-yr	Pb 4-yr	Pr 4-yr
Tuit & Fees	1229	6175	2527	11025
Bks & Suppl	533	566	552	556
Board	1643	1589	1601	1722
Trans	923	890	870	824
Other Exp	1044	970	1259	1073
	-----------	----------	----------	----------
Total	5372	10190	6809	15200

Tab Function

If an item appearing in a Print statement is preceded by

Tab(*n*);

where *n* is a positive integer, that item will be displayed (if possible) beginning at the *n*th position of the line. (Exceptions are discussed in Comment 8.)

EXAMPLE 6 The following program uses the Tab function to organize data into columns of a table. The data represent the number of bachelor's degrees conferred (in units of 1000). (*Source:* National Center of Educational Statistics.)

```
Private Sub cmdDisplay_Click()
  picTable.Cls
  picTable.Print Tab(10); "1970-71"; Tab(20); "1980-81"; Tab(30); "1990-91"
  picTable.Print
  picTable.Print "Male"; Tab(10); 476; Tab(20); 470; Tab(30); 490
  picTable.Print "Female"; Tab(10); 364; Tab(20); 465; Tab(30); 560
  picTable.Print "Total"; Tab(10); 840; Tab(20); 935; Tab(30); 1050
End Sub
```

[Run and then click the command button. The resulting picture box is shown.]

	1970-71	1980-81	1990-91
Male	476	470	490
Female	364	465	560
Total	840	935	1050

Spc Function

A statement of the form

picBox.Print *item1*; Spc(*n*); *item2*

inserts *n* spaces between the two items. The width of each space is the average width of the characters in the font. For example, the statement

picBox.Print "North"; Spc(5); "to"; Spc(10); "the"; Spc(5); "future."

results in the output

North	to	the	future.

Using a Message Box for Output

Sometimes you want to grab the user's attention with a brief message such as "Correct" or "Nice try, but no cigar." You want this message only to appear on the screen until the user has read it. This mission is easily accomplished with a **message box** such as the one shown in Figure 3.28. When a statement of the form

```
MsgBox prompt, , title
```

is executed, where *prompt* and *title* are strings, a message box with *prompt* displayed and the title bar caption *title* appears, and stays on the screen until the user presses Enter or clicks OK. For instance, the statement MsgBox "Nice try, but no cigar.", , "Consolation" produces Figure 3.28. If you use double quotation marks ("") for *title*, the title bar will be blank.

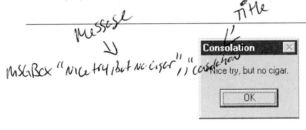

Figure 3.28 Sample message box.

The Line Continuation Character

Up to 1023 characters can be typed in a line of code. If you use a line with more characters than can fit in the window, Visual Basic scrolls the window toward the right as needed. However, most programmers prefer having lines that are no longer than the width of the code window. This can be achieved with the underscore character (_) preceded by a space. Make sure the underscore doesn't appear inside quotation marks though. For instance, the line

```
Let msg = "640K ought to be enough for anybody. (Bill Gates, 1981)"
```

can be written as

```
Let msg = "640K ought to be enough for " & _
          "anybody. (Bill Gates, 1981)"
```

Output to the Printer

You print text on a sheet of paper in the printer in much the same way you display text in a picture box. Visual Basic treats the printer as an object named Printer. If *expr* is a string or numeric expression, then the statement

```
Printer.Print expr
```

sends *expr* to the printer in exactly the same way picBox.Print sends output to a picture box. You can use semicolons or commas for print zones, Tab, and Spc.

Font properties can be set with statements like

```
Let Printer.Font.Name = "Script"
Let Printer.Font.Bold = True
Let Printer.Font.Size = 12
```

Another useful printer command is

```
Printer.NewPage
```

which starts a new page.

Windows' print manager usually waits until an entire page has been completed before starting to print. To avoid losing information, execute the statement

```
Printer.EndDoc
```

when you are finished printing.

The statement

```
PrintForm
```

prints the content of the form.

Rem Statement

Now that we have the capability to write more complicated programs, we must concern ourselves with program documentation. **Program documentation** is the inclusion of comments that specify the intent of the program, the purpose of the variables, the nature of the data in the files, and the tasks performed by individual portions of the program. If *text* is any information whatsoever, then the statement

```
Rem text
```

is completely ignored when the program is executed. Program documentation appears whenever the program is displayed or printed. Also, a line can be documented by adding

```
'text
```

to the end of the line. Rem statements and text following an apostrophe appear green on the screen.

EXAMPLE 7   Document the program in Example 2.

SOLUTION   In the following program, the first Rem statement describes the entire program, the three apostrophes precede the meanings of the variables, and the second Rem statement tells the nature of the items in each line of the file.

```
Private Sub cmdComputePay_Click()
  Rem Compute weekly pay
  Dim nom As String      'Employee name
  Dim wage As Single     'Hourly pay
  Dim hrs As Single      'Number of hours worked during week
  picPay.Cls
  Open "PERSONEL.TXT" For Input As #1
  Rem person's name, person's wage, person's hours worked
  Input #1, nom, wage, hrs
  picPay.Print nom; hrs * wage
  Input #1, nom, wage, hrs
  picPay.Print nom; hrs * wage
  Close #1
End Sub
```

Some of the benefits of documentation are as follows:

1. Other people can easily comprehend the program.

2. The program can be understood when read later.

3. Long programs are easier to read because the purposes of individual pieces can be determined at a glance.

Comments

1. The text box and input box provide a whole new dimension to the capabilities of a program. The user, rather than the programmer, can provide the data to be processed.

2. A string used in a file does not have to be enclosed by quotation marks. The only exceptions are strings containing commas or leading and trailing spaces.

3. If an Input# statement looks for a string and finds a number, it will treat the number as a string. Suppose the first two entries in the file DATA.TXT are the numbers 2 and 3.

```
Private Sub cmdButton_Click()
  Dim a As String, b As String
  picBox.Cls
  Open "DATA.TXT" For Input As #1
  Input #1, a, b
  picBox.Print a + b
  Close #1
End Sub
```

[Run and then click the command button. The following is displayed in the picture box.]

23

4. If an Input# statement looks for a number and finds a string, the Input# statement will assign the value 0 to the numeric variable. For instance, suppose the first two entries in the file DATA.TXT are "ten" and 10. Then after the statement

```
Input #1, num1, num2
```

is executed, where *num1* and *num2* are numeric variables, the values of these variables will be 0 and 10.

5. If all the data in a file have been read by Input# statements and another item is requested by an Input# statement, a box will appear displaying the message "Input past end of file."

6. Numeric data in a text box, input box, or file must be a constant. It *cannot* be a variable or an expression. For instance, num, 1 / 2, and 2 + 3 are not acceptable.

7. To skip a Print zone, just include two consecutive commas.

8. The Tab function cannot be used to move the cursor to the left. If the position specified in a Tab function is to the left of the current cursor position, the cursor will move to that position on the next line. For instance, the line

```
picBox.Print "hello"; Tab(3); "good-bye"
```

results in the output

```
hello
  good-bye
```

9. The statement Close, without any reference number, closes all open files.

10. Windows allows you to alternate between Visual Basic and Notepad without exiting either application. To invoke Notepad with Windows 95, click on the Start button; successively select Programs, Accessories, and Notepad; and then click on Notepad or press the Enter key. Now that both Visual Basic and Notepad have been invoked, you can go from one application to the other by holding down the Alt key and repeatedly pressing the Tab key until the name of the other application appears. When the Alt key is released, the named application becomes active.

PRACTICE PROBLEMS 3.5

1. What is the difference in the outcomes of the following sets of lines of code?

```
Input #1, num1, num2
picOutput.Print num1 + num2


Input #1, num1
Input #1, num2
picOutput.Print num1 + num2
```

2. What is the difference in the outcomes of the following sets of lines of code?

```
Let strVar = InputBox("How old are you?", "Age")
Let numVar = Val(strVar)
picOutput.Print numVar


Let numVar = Val(InputBox("How old are you?", "Age"))
picOutput.Print numVar
```

EXERCISES 3.5

In Exercises 1 through 14, assume that the file DATA.TXT (shown to the right of the code) has been opened for input with reference number 1. Determine the output displayed in the picture box by the lines of code.

1.
```
Dim num As Single
Input #1, num
picOutput.Print num * num
```
DATA.TXT
4

2.
```
Dim word As String
Input #1, word
picOutput.Print "un" & word
```
DATA.TXT
"speakable"

3.
```
Dim str1 As String, str2 As String
Input #1, str1, str2
picOutput.Print str1; str2
```
DATA.TXT
"base"
"ball"

4.
```
Dim num1 As Single, num2 As Single
Dim num3 As Single
Input #1, num1, num2, num3
picOutput.Print (num1 + num2) * num3
```
DATA.TXT
3
4
5

5.
```
Dim yrOfBirth As Single, curYr As Single
Input #1, yrOfBirth
Input #1, curYr        'Current year
picOutput.Print "Age:"; curYr - yrOfBirth
```
DATA.TXT
1976
1996

6.
```
Dim str1 As String, str2 As String
Input #1, str1
Input #1, str2
picOutput.Print str1 & str2
```
DATA.TXT
"A, my name is "
"Alice"

7.
```
Dim word1 As String, word2 As String
Input #1, word1
Input #1, word2
picOutput.Print word1 & word2
```
DATA.TXT
"set", "up"

8.
```
Dim num As Single, sum As Single
Let sum = 0
Input #1, num
Let sum = sum + num
Input #1, num
Let sum = sum + num
picOutput.Print "Sum:"; sum
```
DATA.TXT
123, 321

9.
```
Dim building As String
Dim numRooms As Single
Input #1, building, numRooms
picOutput.Print "The "; building;
picOutput.Print " has" numRooms; "rooms."
```
DATA.TXT
"White House", 132

10.
```
Dim nom As String        'Name of student
Dim grade1 As Single     'Grade on 1st exam
Dim grade2 As Single     'Grade on 2nd exam
Dim average As Single    'Ave of grades
Input #1, nom, grade1, grade2
Let average = (grade1 + grade2) / 2
picOutput.Print nom; " ======> "; average
Input #1, nom, grade1, grade2
Let average = (grade1 + grade2) / 2
picOutput.Print nom; " ======> "; average
```

DATA.TXT
"Al Adams", 72, 88
"Betty Brown", 76, 82

11.
```
Dim num1 As Single, num2 As Single
Dim str1 As String, str2 As String
Input #1, num1, str1
Input #1, str2, num2
picOutput.Print num1; str1; str2; num2
Close #1
Open "DATA.TXT" For Input As #1
picOutput.Print num2
Input #1, num2
picOutput.Print num2
```

DATA.TXT
1, "One", "Two", 2

12.
```
Dim num As Integer, str As String
Input #1, num, str
picOutput.Print num; str
Close #1
Open "DATA.TXT" For Input As #1
Input #1, num, str
picOutput.Print num, str
```

DATA.TXT
4, "calling birds"
3, "French hens"

13.
```
Dim college As String
Dim yrFounded As Single
Dim yrStr As String, yr As Single
Input #1, college, yrFounded
Let yrStr = InputBox("What is the current year?")
Let yr = Val(yrStr)
picOutput.Print college; " is";
picOutput.Print yr - yrFounded; "years old."
```

DATA.TXT
"Harvard University", 1636

(Assume that the response is *1996*.)

14.
```
Dim hourlyWage As Single, nom As String
Dim hoursWorked As Single, message As String
Input #1, hourlyWage, nom
Let message = "Hours worked by " & nom & ":"
Let hoursWorked = Val(InputBox(message))
picOutput.Print "Pay for "; nom; " is";
picOutput.Print hoursWorked * hourlyWage
```

DATA.TXT
7.50, "Joe Smith"

(Assume that the response is *10*.)

In Exercises 15 through 28, determine the output displayed in the picture box by the following lines of code.

15.
```
Dim bet As Single     'Amount bet at roulette
Let bet = Val(InputBox("How much do you want to bet?", "Wager"))
picOutput.Print "You might win"; 36 * bet; "dollars."
```

(Assume that the response is 5.)

16.
```
Dim word As String
Let word = InputBox("Word to negate:")
picOutput.Print "un"; word
```

(Assume that the response is *tied*.)

17.
```
Dim lastName As String, message As String, firstName As String
Let lastName = "Jones"
Let message = "What is your first name Mr. " & lastName
Let firstName = InputBox(message)
picOutput.Print "Hello "; firstName; " "; lastName
```

(Assume that the response is *John*.)

18.
```
Dim intRate As Single  'Current interest rate
Let intRate = Val(InputBox("Current interest rate?"))
picOutput.Print "At the current interest rate, ";
picOutput.Print "your money will double in";
picOutput.Print 72 / intRate; "years."
```

(Assume that the response is 6.)

19.
```
picOutput.Print 1; "one", "won"
```

20.
```
picOutput.Print 1, 2; 3
```

21.
```
picOutput.Print "one",
picOutput.Print "two"
```

22.
```
picOutput.Print "one", , "two"
```

23.
```
Let picOutput.Font.Name = "Courier"     'Fixed-width font
picOutput.Print "1234567890"
picOutput.Print Tab(4); 5
```

24.
```
Let picOutput.Font.Name = "Courier""    'Fixed-width font
picOutput.Print "1234567890"
picOutput.Print "Hello"; Tab(3); "Good-bye"
```

25.
```
Let picOutput.Font.Name = "Courier"
picOutput.Print "1234567890"
picOutput.Print "one", Tab(12); "two"
```

26.
```
Let picOutput.Font.Name = "Courier"
picOutput.Print "1234567890"
picOutput.Print Tab(3); "one"
picOutput.Print Spc(3); "two"
```

27.
```
Let picOutput.Font.Name = "Courier"
picOutput.Print "1234567890"
picOutput.Print Spc(2); "one"; Tab(8); "two"
```

28.
```
Let picOutput.Font.Name = "Courier New"
   picOutput.Print "1234567890"
   picOutput.Print Spc(1); "1"; Spc(2); "2"
   picOutput.Print 1; 2
```

In Exercises 29 through 40, assume that the file DATA.TXT (shown to the right of the code) has been opened for input with reference number 1. Identify any errors.

29.
```
Dim str1 As String, str2 As String
   Input #1, str1, str2
   picOutput.Print "Hello "; str1
```
DATA.TXT
"John Smith"

30.
```
Dim num As Single
   Input #1, num
   picOutput.Print 3 * num
```
DATA.TXT
1 + 2

31.
```
Rem  Each line of DATA.TXT contains
   Rem  building, height, # of stories
   Dim building As String
   Dim ht As Single
   Input #1, building, ht
   picOutput.Print building, ht
   Input #1, building, ht
   picOutput.Print building, ht
```
DATA.TXT
"World Trade Center", 1350, 110
"Sears Tower", 1454, 110

32.
```
Dim num As Single
   Let num = InputBox("Pick a number from 1 to 10.")
   picOutput.Print "Your number is"; num
```

33.
```
Dim statePop As Single
   Let statePop = Val(InputBox("State Population?"))
   picOutput.Print "The population should grow to";
   picOutput.Print 1.01 * statePop; "by next year."
```

(Assume that the response is 8,900,000)

34. `Let info = InputBox()`

35. `Let Printer.Name = Courier`

36. `Let txtBox.Text = "one", "two"`

37. `Let lblTwo.Caption = 1, 2`

38. `Printer.Print "Hello"; Tab(200); "Good-bye"`

39. `Let Form.Caption = "one"; Spc(5); "two"`

40.
```
Dim rem As Single   'Number to remember
   Input #1, rem
   picOutput.Print "Don't forget to ";
   picOutput.Print "remember the number"; rem
```
DATA.TXT
4

41. Fill in the table with the value of each variable after each line is executed. Assume the file DATA.TXT consists of the two lines

"phone", 35.25
"postage", 14.75

Event Procedure	category	amount	total
`Private Sub cmdDetermineTotal_Click()`			
`Dim category As String`			
`Dim amount As Single`			
`Dim total As Single`			
`Open "DATA.TXT" For Input As #1`			
`Input #1, category, amount`			
`Let total = total + amount`			
`Input #1, category, amount`			
`Let total = total + amount`			
`picOutput.Print total`			
`Close #1`			
`End Sub`			

42. Fill in the table with the value of each variable after each line is executed. Assume the file DATA.TXT consists of the single line

2, 3, 5

Event Procedure	num1	num2	num3
`Private Sub cmdButton_Click()`			
`Dim num1 As Single, num2 As Single`			
`Dim num3 As Single`			
`Open "DATA.TXT" For Input As #1`			
`Input #1, num1, num2, num3`			
`Let num1 = num2 + num3`			
`Close #1`			
`Open "DATA.TXT" For Input As #2`			
`Input #2, num1, num3`			
`Let num3 = num3 + 1`			
`Close #2`			
`End Sub`			

In Exercises 43 through 46, write code starting with Private Sub cmdDisplay_
Click() and picOutput.Cls statements, ending with an End Sub statement,
and having one line for each step. Lines that display data should use the given
variable names.

43. The following steps display the increase in the enrollment in selected courses
taken by high school graduates. Assume the file DATA.TXT consists of the
two lines

"Algebra I", 65.1, 77.2
"Geometry", 45.7, 61.0

(a) Declare all variables used in the steps below.
(b) Use an Input# statement to assign values to the variables *course, percent1982*, and *percent1987*.
(c) Display a sentence giving the percentage change in enrollment from 1982 to 1987.
(d) Repeat steps (b) and (c).

44. The following steps display information about Americans' eating habits.
Assume the file DATA.TXT consists of the single line

"soft drinks", "million gallons", 23

(a) Declare all variables used in the steps below.
(b) Open the file DATA.TXT for input.
(c) Use an Input# statement to assign values to the variables *food, units*, and *quantityPerDay*.
(d) Display a sentence giving the quantity of a food item consumed by Americans in 1 day.

45. The following steps calculate the percent increase in a typical grocery basket of goods.

(a) Declare all variables used in the steps below.
(b) Assign 200 to the variable *begOfYearPrice*.
(c) Request the price at the end of the year with an input box and assign it to the variable *endOfYearPrice*.
(d) Assign 100 * (*endOfYearPrice* – *begOfYearPrice*) / *begOfYearPrice* to the variable *percentIncrease*.
(e) Display a sentence giving the percent increase for the year.

(Test the program with a $215 end-of-year price.)

46. The following steps calculate the amount of money earned in a walk-a-thon.

(a) Declare all variables used in the steps below.
(b) Request the amount pledged per mile from an input box and assign it to the variable *pledge*.
(c) Request the number of miles walked from an input box and assign it to the variable *miles*.
(d) Display a sentence giving the amount to be paid.

(Test the program with a pledge of $2.00 and a 15-mile walk.)

In Exercises 47 and 48, write a line of code to carry out the task.

47. Pop up a message box stating "The future isn't what it used to be."

48. Pop up a message box with "Taking Risks Proverb" in the title bar and the message "You can't steal second base and keep one foot on first."

49. Table 3.4 summarizes the month's activity of three checking accounts. Write a program that displays the account number and the end-of-month balance for each account, and then displays the total amount of money in the three accounts. Assume the data are stored in a data file.

Account Number	Beginning-of-Month Balance	Deposits	Withdrawals
AB4057	1234.56	345.67	100.00
XY4321	789.00	120.00	350.00
GH2222	321.45	143.65	0.00

Table 3.4 Checking account activity.

50. Table 3.5 contains a list of colleges with their student enrollments and faculty sizes. Write a program to display the names of the colleges and their student/faculty ratios, and the ratio for the total collection of students and faculty. Assume the data for the colleges are stored in a data file.

	Enrollment	Faculty
Ohio State	48676	3724
Univ. of MD, College Park	30646	1638
Princeton	6419	886

Table 3.5 Colleges.
Source: The World Almanac, 1997.

51. Write a program to compute semester averages. Each line in a data file should contain a student's social security number and the grades for three hourly exams and the final exam. (The final exam counts as two hourly exams.) The program should display each student's social security number and semester average, and then the class average. Use the data in Table 3.6.

Soc. Sec. No.	Exam 1	Exam 2	Exam 3	Final Exam
123-45-6789	67	85	90	88
111-11-1111	93	76	82	80
123-32-1234	85	82	89	84

Table 3.6 Student grades.

52. Table 3.7 gives the 1995 populations of three New England states. Write a program that calculates the average population and then displays the name of each state and the difference between its population and the average population. The states and their populations should be stored in a data file.

Maine	1241
Massachusetts	6074
Connecticut	3275

Table 3.7 1995 Population (in thousands) of three New England states.

53. Write a program to produce Table 3.8. (The amounts are given in millions of dollars.) For each person, the name, sport, salary or winnings, and endorsements should be contained in a data file. The totals should be computed by the program.

Athlete	Sport	Salary or Winnings	Endorsements	Total
M. Jordan	basketball	29.3	193.2	222.5
E. Holyfield	boxing	110.3	7.5	117.8
A. Agassi	tennis	11.3	63.5	74.8
W. Gretsky	hockey	36.8	31.5	68.3

Table 3.8 1990–96 earnings (in millions) of athletes.

54. Write a program to calculate the amount of a waiter's tip given the amount of the bill and the percentage tip. The output should be a complete sentence that reiterates the inputs and gives the resulting tip. For example, if $20 and 15% are the inputs, then the output might read "A 15% tip on $20 dollars is $3 dollars."

55. Design a form with two text boxes labeled "Name" and "Phone number". Then write an event procedure that shows a message box stating "Be sure to include the area code!" when the second text box receives the focus.

In Exercises 56 and 57, write lines of code corresponding to the given flowchart. Assume that the data needed are contained in a file.

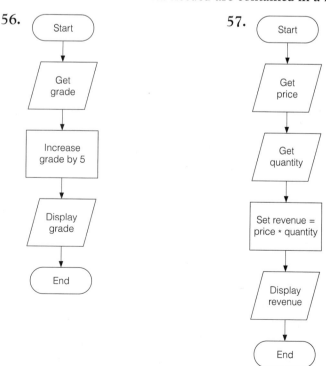

56. Start → Get grade → Increase grade by 5 → Display grade → End

57. Start → Get price → Get quantity → Set revenue = price * quantity → Display revenue → End

---

3.6 BUILT-IN FUNCTIONS

Visual Basic has a number of built-in functions that greatly extend its capability. These functions perform such varied tasks as taking the square root of a number, counting the number of characters in a string, and capitalizing letters. Functions associate with one or more values, called the *input*, a single value, called the *output*. The function is said to **return** the output value. The two functions considered in what follows have numeric input and output.

Numeric Functions: Sqr, Int

The function Sqr calculates the square root of a number. The function Int finds the greatest integer less than or equal to a number. Therefore, Int discards the decimal part of positive numbers. Some examples follow:

```
Sqr(9) is 3.          Int(2.7) is 2.
Sqr(0) is 0.          Int(3) is 3.
Sqr(2) is 1.414214.   Int(-2.7) is -3.
```

The terms inside the parentheses can be either numbers (as shown), numeric variables, or numeric expressions. Expressions are first evaluated to produce the input.

EXAMPLE 1   The following program evaluates each of the functions for a specific input given by the value of the variable *n*.

```
Private Sub cmdEvaluate_Click()
  Dim n As Single
  Rem Evaluate functions at a variable
  picResults.Cls
  Let n = 6.25
  picResults.Print Sqr(n); Int(n)
End Sub
```

[Run and then click the command button. The following is displayed in the picture box.]

```
2.5  6
```

EXAMPLE 2   The following program evaluates each of the preceding functions at an expression.

```
Private Sub cmdEvaluate_Click()
  Dim a As Single, b As Single
  Rem Evaluate functions at expressions
  picResults.Cls
  Let a = 2
  Let b = 3
  picResults.Print Sqr(5 * b + 1); Int(a ^ b)
End Sub
```

[Run and then click the command button. The following is displayed in the picture box.]

4   8

EXAMPLE 3   The following program shows an application of the Sqr function.

```
Private Sub cmdFindHyp_Click()
  Dim leg1 As Single, leg2 As Single, hyp As Single
  Rem  Find the length of the hypotenuse of a right triangle
  picHyp.Cls
  Let leg1 = Val(txtFirst.Text)
  Let leg2 = Val(txtSecond.Text)
  Let hyp = Sqr(leg1 ^ 2 + leg2 ^ 2)
  picHyp.Print "The length of the hypotenuse is"; hyp
End Sub
```

[Run, type 3 and 4 into the text boxes, and then click the command button.]

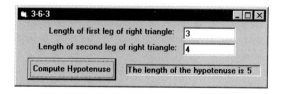

EXAMPLE 4   The following program rounds a positive number to the nearest integer.

```
Private Sub cmdRound_Click()
  Dim n As Single, r As Single
  Rem Round positive number to nearest integer
  picValue.Cls
  Let n = Val(txtNumber.Text)
  Let r = Int(n + 0.5)
  picValue.Print "The rounded value of"; n; "is"; r
End Sub
```

[Run, type 3.6 into the text box, and then click the command button.]

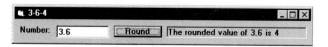

[Run, type 2.4 into the text box, and then click the command button.]

The idea in Example 4 can be extended to round a number to two decimal places, an essential task for financial applications. Just replace the sixth line by

```
Let r = Int(100 * n + 0.5) / 100
```

Then, substitute some different values for *n* and carry out the computation to check that the formula works.

EXAMPLE 5   The following program shows how Int is used to carry out long division. When the integer *m* is divided into the integer *n* with long division, the result is a quotient and a remainder. See Figure 3.29.

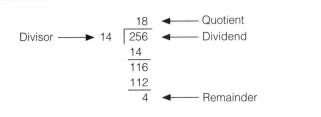

Figure 3.29 Long division.

```
Private Sub cmdDivide_Click()
  Dim divisor As Single, dividend As Single
  Dim quotient As Single, remainder As Single
  Rem Long division
  picResult.Cls
  Let divisor = Val(txtDivisor.Text)
  Let dividend = Val(txtDividend.Text)
  Let quotient = Int(dividend / divisor)
  Let remainder = dividend - quotient * divisor
  picResult.Print "The quotient is"; quotient
  picResult.Print "The remainder is"; remainder
End Sub
```

[Run, type 14 and 256 into the text boxes, and then click the command button.]

String Functions: Left, Mid, Right, UCase, Trim

The functions Left, Mid, and Right are used to extract characters from the left end, middle, and right end of a string. Suppose *str* is a string and *m* and *n* are positive integers. Then Left(*str*, *n*) is the string consisting of the first *n* characters of *str* and Right(*str*, *n*) is the string consisting of the last *n* characters of *str*. Mid(*str*, *m*, *n*) is the string consisting of *n* characters of *str*, beginning with the *m*th character. UCase(*str*) is the string *str* with all of its lowercase letters capitalized. Trim(*str*) is the string *str* with all leading and trailing spaces removed. Some examples are as follows:

```
Left("fanatic", 3) is "fan".        Right("fanatic", 3) is "tic".
Left("12/15/93", 2) is "12".        Right("12/15/93", 2) is "93".
Mid("fanatic", 5, 1) is "t".        Mid("12/15/93", 4, 2) is "15".
UCase("Disk") is "DISK".            UCase("12three") is "12THREE".
Trim(" 1  2 ") is "1  2".           Trim("-12 ") is "-12".
```

The strings produced by Left, Mid, and Right are referred to as **substrings** of the strings from which they were formed. For instance, "fan" and "t" are substrings of "fanatic". The substring "fan" is said to begin at position 1 of "fanatic" and the substring "t" is said to begin at position 5.

Like the numeric functions discussed before, Left, Mid, Right, UCase, and Trim also can be evaluated for variables and expressions.

EXAMPLE 6 The following program evaluates the functions above for variables and expressions. Note that spaces are counted as characters.

```
Private Sub cmdEvaluate_Click()
    Dim str1 As String, str2 As String
    Rem Evaluate functions at variables and expressions.
    picResults.Cls
    Let str1 = "Quick as"
    Let str2 = "a wink"
    picResults.Print Left(str1, 7)
    picResults.Print Mid(str1 & str2, 7, 6)
    picResults.Print UCase(str1 & str2)
    picResults.Print "The average "; Right(str2, 4); " lasts .1 second."
    picResults.Print Trim(str1); str2
End Sub
```

[Run and then click the command button. The following is displayed in the picture box.]

```
Quick a
as a w
QUICK AS A WINK
The average wink lasts .1 second.
Quick asa wink
```

String-Related Numeric Functions: Len, InStr

The functions Len and InStr operate on strings, but produce numbers. The function Len gives the number of characters in a string. The function InStr searches for the first occurrence of one string in another and gives the position at which the string is found. Suppose *str1* and *str2* are strings. The value of Len(*str1*) is the number of characters in *str1*. The value of InStr(*str1*, *str2*) is 0 if *str2* is not a substring of *str1*. Otherwise, its value is the first position of *str2* in *str1*. Some examples of Len and InStr follow:

```
Len("Shenandoah") is 10.          InStr("Shenandoah", "nand") is 4.
Len("Just a moment") is 13.       InStr("Just a moment", " ") is 5.
Len(" ") is 1.                    InStr("Croissant", "ist") is 0.
```

EXAMPLE 7   The following program evaluates functions at variables and expressions. The ninth line locates the position of the space separating the two names. The first name will end one position to the left of this position and the last name will consist of all but the first *n* characters of the full name.

```
Private Sub cmdAnalyze_Click()
    Dim nom As String     'Name
    Dim n As Integer      'Location of space
    Dim first As String   'First name
    Dim last As String    'Last name
    Rem Evaluate functions at variables and expressions.
    picResults.Cls
    Let nom = txtFullName.Text
    Let n = InStr(nom, " ")
    Let first = Left(nom, n - 1)
    Let last = Right(nom, Len(nom) - n)
    picResults.Print "Your first name is "; first
    picResults.Print "Your last name has"; Len(last); "letters."
End Sub
```

[Run, type John Doe into the text box, and then click the command button.]

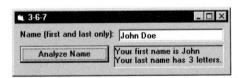

Format Function

The Visual Basic function Format is used to display numbers and dates in familiar forms and to right-justify numbers. We will look at a few variations of this versatile function. (See the discussion of Format in Appendix C for more nuances.)

Here are some examples of how numbers are converted to convenient strings with Format.

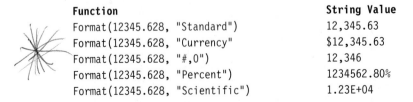

Function	String Value
Format(12345.628, "Standard")	12,345.63
Format(12345.628, "Currency")	$12,345.63
Format(12345.628, "#,0")	12,346
Format(12345.628, "Percent")	1234562.80%
Format(12345.628, "Scientific")	1.23E+04

The strings "Currency", "Standard", "#,0", "Percent", and "Scientific" are referred to as format strings. If *num* is a number, a numeric expression, or the string representation of a number, and *fmt* is a format string, then

Format(*num*, *fmt*)

is a string consisting of a formatted version of the number.

The format strings "Standard" and "Currency" convert numbers to string representations having two decimal places and commas every three digits to the left of the decimal point. Numbers less than 1 in magnitude have a zero to the left of the decimal point. "Currency" attaches a leading dollar sign and encloses negative numbers in parentheses. Accountants normally use parentheses to denote negative numbers.

Function	String Value
Format(1 / 4, "Standard")	0.25
Format(2 + 3.759, "Currency")	$5.76
Format(-1234, "Standard")	-1,234.00
Format(-1234, "Currency")	($1,234.00)
Format(".2", "Currency")	$0.20

The format string "#,0" rounds numbers to whole numbers and places commas every three digits to the left of the decimal point. The format strings "Percent" and "Scientific" convert numbers to string representations consisting of percentages and scientific notation, respectively. Both forms include two decimal places. The scientific notations consist of a number between 1 and 9.99 followed by an exponent and possibly preceded by a minus sign.

Function	String Value
Format(-3.6, "#,0")	-4
Format(.06265, "Percent")	6.27%
Format(1 / 8, "Percent")	12.50%
Format(-600.228, "Scientific")	-6.00E+02
Format(1 / 8, "Scientific")	1.25E-01

If *dateString* represents a date in a form such as 7/4/96 and *fmt* is a format string, then

Format(*dateString*, *fmt*)

is a string consisting of a formatted version of the date. Two useful format strings are "Long Date" and "Medium Date", which produce the results implied by their names.

Function	String Value
Format("7/4/96", "Long Date")	Thursday, July 04, 1996
Format("7/4/96", "Medium Date")	04-Jul-96

Format can be used with fixed-width fonts, such as Courier or Terminal, to display columns of numbers so that the decimal points are lined up. If *num* is a number, a numeric expression, or a string representation of a number, and *fmt* is a string of *n* "at" symbols, then

Format(*num*, *fmt*)

is a string of *n* characters with the number right-justified in a field of *n* spaces. Actually, if *num* is any string, such as a string produced by a Format function, then the value of Format(num, fmt) contains the string right-justified in a field of *n* spaces. In the following table, each string value has length 10. For instance, in the second example, the string value consists of seven spaces followed by the string "123".

Function	String Value
Format(1234567890, "@@@@@@@@@@")	1234567890
Format(123, "@@@@@@@@@@")	123
Format("1234.56", "@@@@@@@@@@")	1234.56
Format("$1,234.56", "@@@@@@@@@@")	$1,234.56

EXAMPLE 8 The following program produces essentially the first two columns of the table in Example 5 of the previous section. However, Format is used to right-justify the expense categories and to align the numbers.

Object	Property	Setting
frmExpenses	Caption	Public 2-year College Expenses
cmdDisplay	Caption	Display Expenses
picTable	Font.Name	Courier

```
Private Sub cmdDisplay_Click()
  Dim fmt1 As String, fmt2 As String, fmt3 As String
  Dim col1 As String, col2 As String
  Rem Average expenses of commuter students (1993-94)
  picTable.Cls
  picTable.Print Tab(19); "Pb 2-yr"
  picTable.Print
  Let fmt1 = "@@@@@@@@@@@@@@@@@"
  Let fmt2 = "#,0"
  Let fmt3 = "@@@@@@"
  Let col1 = Format("Tuition & Fees", fmt1)
  Let col2 = Format(1229, fmt2)
  Let col2 = Format(col2, fmt3)
  picTable.Print col1; Tab(19); col2
  Let col1 = Format("Books & Supplies", fmt1)
  Let col2 = Format(533, fmt2)
  Let col2 = Format(col2, fmt3)
  picTable.Print col1; Tab(19); col2
  Let col1 = Format("Board", fmt1)
  Let col2 = Format(1643, fmt2)
  Let col2 = Format(col2, fmt3)
  picTable.Print col1; Tab(19); col2
  Let col1 = Format("Transportation", fmt1)
  Let col2 = Format(923, fmt2)
  Let col2 = Format(col2, fmt3)
  picTable.Print col1; Tab(19); col2
  Let col1 = Format("Other Expenses", fmt1)
  Let col2 = Format(1044, fmt2)
  Let col2 = Format(col2, fmt3)
  picTable.Print col1; Tab(19); col2
  picTable.Print Tab(19); "——"
```

```
    Let col1 = Format("Total", fmt1)
    Let col2 = Format(5372, fmt2)
    Let col2 = Format(col2, fmt3)
    picTable.Print col1; Tab(19); col2
End Sub
```

[Run and then click the command button.]

```
                      Pb 2-yr
    Tuition & Fees    1,229
  Books & Supplies      533
            Board    1,643
    Transportation      923
    Other Expenses    1,044
                     _____
             Total    5,372
```

Generating Random Numbers: Rnd

Consider a specific collection of numbers. We say that a process selects a number at **random** from this collection if any number in the collection is just as likely to be selected as any other and the number cannot be predicted in advance. Some examples follow:

Collection	Process
1, 2, 3, 4, 5, 6	toss a die
0 or 1	toss a coin: 0 = tails, 1 = heads
–1, 0, 1, . . . , 36	spin a roulette wheel (interpret –1 as 00)
1, 2, . . . , n	write numbers on slips of paper, pull one from hat
numbers from 0 to 1	flip the spinner in Figure 3.30

Handwritten margin note: LND = Selects # between 0±1 Randomize = Chooses the seed

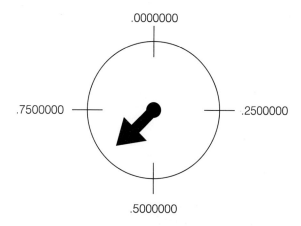

Figure 3.30 Spinner to randomly select a number between 0 and 1.

The function Rnd, which acts like the spinner in Figure 3.30, returns a random number. The statement

```
picBox.Print Rnd
```

randomly displays a number from 0 up to (but not including) 1. The statement

```
Let numVar = Rnd
```

randomly assigns a number between 0 and 1 to the variable *numVar*. A different number will be assigned each time Rnd is called in the program, and any number greater than or equal to 0 and less than 1 is just as likely to be generated as any other. Therefore, although Rnd looks like a numeric variable, it does not act at all like a variable.

With appropriate scaling, the Rnd function can generate random numbers from other collections. The statement

```
picBox.Print Int(6 * Rnd) + 1;
```

displays a number from the set 1, 2, 3, 4, 5, 6. Because Rnd always has a value from 0 to 1, excluding 1, 6 * Rnd has a value from 0 to 6 (excluding 6), and Int(6 * Rnd) has one of the values 0, 1, 2, 3, 4, 5. Adding 1 shifts the resulting number into the desired range.

Suppose the preceding statement is repeated many times. The integers generated should exhibit no apparent pattern. They should look very much like a sequence of integers obtained from successively rolling a die. For instance, each of the six integers should appear about one-sixth of the time and be reasonably spread out in the sequence. The longer the sequence, the more likely this is to occur.

Rnd normally generates the same sequence of numbers each time a program is run. However, Visual Basic has another function, Randomize, that changes the sequence of numbers generated by Rnd. This statement will be used in all programs in this text.

EXAMPLE 9   The DC Lottery number is obtained by selecting a Ping-Pong ball from each of three separate bowls. Each ball is numbered with an integer from 0 through 9. Write a computer program to produce a lottery number. (Such a program is said to **simulate** the selection of Ping-Pong balls.)

SOLUTION   The value of Int(10 * Rnd) will be an integer from 0 through 9, and each of these integers has the same likelihood of occurring. Repeating the process three times produces the requested digits.

```
Private Sub cmdDisplayANumber_Click()
  Rem Display a lottery number
  picNumber.Cls
  Randomize
  picNumber.Print Int(10 * Rnd);
  picNumber.Print Int(10 * Rnd);
  picNumber.Print Int(10 * Rnd)
End Sub
```

[Run and then click the command button. One possible output to be displayed in the picture box is as follows.]

8   3   9

Comments

1. Requesting the square root of a negative number terminates the execution of the program and gives the error message "Invalid procedure call or argument."

2. If *n* is greater than the length of *str*, then the value of Left(*str*, *n*) will be the entire string *str*. A similar result holds for Mid and Right.

3. Visual Basic has a function called LCase that is analogous to UCase. LCase converts all uppercase letters in a string to lowercase letters.

4. Because the values of the functions Left, Mid, Right, UCase, and Format are strings, they are referred to as **string-valued functions**.

5. Mid is an important function. It will be used several times in this book to examine each letter of a string.

6. Trim is useful when reading data from a text box. Sometimes users type spaces at the end of input. Unless the spaces are removed, they can cause havoc elsewhere in the program. Also, Trim is useful in trimming the leading spaces from numbers that have been converted to strings with Str.

7. The InStr function has a useful extension. The value of InStr(*n*, *str1*, *str2*) is the position of the first occurrence of *str2* in *str1* in position *n* or greater. For instance, InStr(5, "Mississippi", "ss") is 6.

8. In Example 5, we found that 4 is the remainder when 256 is divided by 14. Mathematicians say "4 = 256 modulo 14." Visual Basic has an operation, Mod, that performs this calculation directly. If *m* and *n* are positive integers, then *n* Mod *m* is the remainder when *n* is divided by *m*. Visual Basic also has an operation called **integer division**, denoted by \, which gives the quotient portion of a long division problem.

9. Recall that the function Mid has the form Mid(*str*, *m*, *n*) and returns the substring of *str* starting with position *m* and having length *n*. Visual Basic does its best to please for unexpected values of *m* and *n*. If *m* is greater than the length of the string or *n* is 0, then the empty string is returned. If *m* + *n* is greater than the length of the string, then Mid(*str*, *m*, *n*) is the right part of the string beginning with the *m*th character. For instance, the value of Mid("abcdef", 3, 9) is "cdef".

10. When Format is used with the "Currency" format string, negative numbers are indicated by parentheses instead of minus signs. If you prefer minus signs, use the format string "$#,0.00" instead. For instance, the value of Format("–1234", "$#,0.00") is "–$1,234.00".

11. When Format is used with the "#,0" format string, commas are placed every three positions to the left of the decimal point. If you prefer to omit the commas, use the format string "0" instead. For instance, the value of Format(1234.6, "0") is 1235.

12. Each time the function Rnd appears in a program, it will be reassigned a value. For instance, the task attempted (but not accomplished) by the first set of lines that follows is achieved by the second set of lines. Because each of the Rnd's in the first set of lines will assume a different value, it is highly unlikely that the square of the first one will equal the product of the last two.

```
Rem Generate the square of a randomly chosen number
Randomize
picBox.Print "The square of"; Rnd; "is"; Rnd * Rnd

Rem Generate the square of a randomly chosen number
Randomize
Let numVar = Rnd
picBox.Print "The square of"; numVar; "is"; numVar * numVar
```

13. Additional information about the keywords, function, methods, and properties discussed in this chapter appear in Appendix C. You can obtain a detailed (and somewhat advanced) discussion about an item appearing in code by clicking on the item and pressing F1. Other ways of obtaining help are presented in Appendix B.

PRACTICE PROBLEMS 3.6

1. What is the value of InStr("Computer", "E")?

2. What is the value of Sqr(12 * Len("WIN"))?

3. Write an expression that will randomly select an uppercase letter from the alphabet.

4. When will Int(n / 2) be the same as n / 2?

EXERCISES 3.6

In Exercises 1 through 18, find the value of the given function.

1. `UCase("McD's")`   2. `Sqr(64)`

3. `Int(10.75)`   4. `Left("harp", 2)`

5. `Sqr(3 * 12)`   6. `Int(9 - 2)`

7. `Left("ABCD", 2)`   8. `Mid("ABCDE", 2, 3)`

9. `Mid("shoe", 4, 1)`   10. `UCase("$2 bill")`

11. `Len("shoe")`   12. `InStr("shoe", "h")`

13. `InStr("shoe", "f")`   14. `Len("s" & Left("help", 2))`

15. `Right("snow", 3)`   16. `Right("123", 1)`

17. `Len(Trim(Str(32)))`   18. `Len(Trim(Str(-32)))`

In Exercises 19 through 35, find the value of the given function where *a* and *b* are numeric variables, *c* and *d* are string variables; *a* = 5, *b* = 3, *c* = "Lullaby", and *d* = "lab".

19. `Len(d)`   20. `Sqr(4 + a)`

21. `Int(-a / 2)`   22. `UCase(d)`

23. Sqr(a - 5)

24. Int(b * .5)

25. Left(c, Len(d))

26. Mid(c, a, 3)

27. Mid(c, a - b, 2 * a)

28. Left(d, b - 2)

29. UCase(c)

30. InStr(c, d)

31. InStr(c, "r")

32. Len(c & Left(d, 2))

33. Right(c, 2)

34. Right("Sky" & d, 5)

35. Trim(Str(a + b)) & d

In Exercises 36 through 43, determine the output produced by the lines of code.

36. Let numVar = 3.67
```
picOutput.Print Int(10 * numVar + .5) / 10;
Let numVar = 7.345
picOutput.Print Int(10 * numVar + .5) / 10
```

37. Let week = "SunMonTueWedThuFriSat"
```
Let strVar = InputBox("Day of week (1 to 7)")
picOutput.Print "Today is "; Mid(week, 3 * Val(strVar) - 2, 3)
```

(Assume that the response is 5.)

38. Let today = InputBox("Date (mm/dd/yy)")
```
picOutput.Print "The year is 19" & Mid(today, 7, 2)
```

(Assume that the response is *10/23/96.*)

39. Let word = "Hello"
```
picOutput.Print Mid(word, Len(word), 1)
```

40. Let nom = txtName.Text
```
picOutput.Print Left(nom, 1) & Mid(nom, InStr(nom, " ") + 1, 1)
```

(Assume that txtName.Text is *Bill Clinton.*)

41. Let response = InputBox("Do you like jazz (yes or no)")
```
Let num = Int(InStr("YyNn", Left(response, 1)) / 2 + .5)
Let response = Mid("yesno ", 3 * num - 2, 3)
picOutput.Print "I guess your answer is "; response
```

(Assume that the response is *yup* or *Yeah.*)

42. Let num = 123
```
Let strVar = Str(num)
picOutput.Print "xxx"; Right(strVar, Len(strVar) - 1)
```

43. Let numStr = Trim(Str(37))
```
Let strVar = " Yankees"
picOutput.Print "19"; numStr; UCase(strVar)
```

In Exercises 44 through 77, determine the output displayed in the text box by the following lines of code.

44. Let txtBox.Text = Format(7654.321, "Standard")

45. Let txtBox.Text = Format(3.2E+05, "Standard")

```
46. Let txtBox.Text = Format(-.0005, "Standard")

47. Let txtBox.Text = Format(32, "Standard")

48. Let txtBox.Text = Format(58 + 2, "Standard")

49. Let txtBox.Text = Format(3E-2, "Standard")

50. Let txtBox.Text = Format(7654.3, "Currency")

51. Let txtBox.Text = Format(-23, "Currency")

52. Let txtBox.Text = Format(".25", "Currency")

53. Let txtBox.Text = Format(3 / 4, "Currency")

54. Let txtBox.Text = Format(-5555555.555, "Currency")

55. Let txtBox.Text = Format((1 + .05) * 10, "Currency")

56. Let txtBox.Text = Format(12345.8, "#,0")

57. Let txtBox.Text = Format(.43, "#,0")

58. Let txtBox.Text = Format(-.249, "#,0")

59. Let txtBox.Text = Format(-2345.256, "0")

60. Let txtBox.Text = Format(1000 * Sqr(9), "0")

61. Let txtBox.Text = Format(-Sqr(2), "#,0")

62. Let txtBox.Text = Format(.05, "Percent")

63. Let txtBox.Text = Format(.06253, "Percent")

64. Let txtBox.Text = Format(1 / 4, "Percent")

65. Let txtBox.Text = Format(1, "Percent")

66. Let txtBox.Text = Format(-Sqr(2), "Percent")

67. Let txtBox.Text = Format(.005 + .02002, "Percent")

68. Let txtBox.Text = Format(5.5 * 10 ^ 5, "Scientific")

69. Let txtBox.Text = Format(.0002, "Scientific")

70. Let txtBox.Text = Format(-23E+04, "Scientific")

71. Let txtBox.Text = Format(34 + 66, "Scientific")

72. Let txtBox.Text = Format(12.345, "Scientific")

73. Let txtBox.Text = Format(-Sqr(2), "Scientific")

74. Let txtBox.Text = Format("12/31/99", "Long Date")
```

(**Note:** The year 1999 ends on a Friday.)

```
75. Let txtBox.Text = Format("1/1/2000", "Long Date")

76. Let txtBox.Text = Format("12/13/99", "Medium Date")

77. Let txtBox.Text = Format("1/2/2000", "Medium Date")
```

In Exercises 78 through 81, what will be displayed in the picture box by the following statements?

78. `picOutput.Print "Pay to France "; Format(27267622, "Currency")`

79. `picOutput.Print "Manhattan", Format(24, "Currency")`

80. `picOutput.Print "Name"; Tab(10); "Salary"`
    `picOutput.Print "Bill"; Tab(10); Format(123000, "Currency")`

81. `picOutput.Print "Name"; Tab(10); Format("Salary", "@@@@@@@@@@")`
    `Let strVar = Format(123000, "Currency")`
    `picOutput.Print "Bill"; Tab(10); Format(strVar, "@@@@@@@@@@")`

(Assume that the setting for Font is "Courier".)

In Exercises 82 through 89, determine the format string, *fmt,* for which the lines of code on the left produce the output shown on the right. Assume that the setting for Font is "Courier".

82. `picOutput.Print "1234567890"`   Output: 1234567890
    `picOutput.Print Format(98765.123, fmt)`   98,765.12

83. `picOutput.Print "1234567890"`   Output: 1234567890
    `picOutput.Print Format("2.5", fmt)` $2.50

84. `picOutput.Print "1234567890"`   Output: 1234567890
    `picOutput.Print Format(.0125, fmt)`   1.25%

85. `picOutput.Print "1234567890"`   Output: 1234567890
    `picOutput.Print Format(123, fmt)`   123

86. `picOutput.Print "1234567890"`   Output: 1234567890
    `picOutput.Print Format(-123.459, fmt)`   ($123.46)

87. `picOutput.Print "1234567890"`   Output: 1234567890
    `picOutput.Print Format(201.3, fmt)`   2.01E+02

88. `picOutput.Print "1234567890"`   Output: 1234567890
    `picOutput.Print Tab(3); Format(.3, fmt)`   0

89. `picOutput.Print "1234567890"`   Output: 1234567890
    `picOutput.Print Spc(3); Format(23, fmt)`   23.00

In Exercises 90 through 95, determine the output displayed on the printer by the following lines of code.

90. `Let Printer.Font.Name = "Courier"   'Fixed-width font`
    `Printer.Print "1234567890"`
    `Printer.Print Format(123, "@@@@@@@@@@")`

91. `Let Printer.Font.Name = "Courier"   'Fixed-width font`
    `Printer.Print "1234567890"`
    `Printer.Print Format("abcd", "@@@@@@@@@@")`

92. `Let Printer.Font.Name = "Courier"   'Fixed-width font`
    `Printer.Print "1234567890"`
    `Printer.Print Format("$1,234.56", "@@@@@@@@@@")`

93.
```
Let Printer.Font.Name = "Courier"    'Fixed-width font
Printer.Print "1234567890"
Let strVar = Str(1234.559)
Printer.Print Format(strVar, "@@@@@@@@@@")
```

94.
```
Let Printer.Font.Name = "Courier"    'Fixed-width font
Printer.Print "1234567890"
Printer.Print Format(1 / 4, "@@@@@@@@@@")
```

95.
```
Let Printer.Font.Name = "Courier"    'Fixed-width font
Printer.Print "1234567890"
Let numVar = 25
Let strVar = Format(numVar, "Currency")
Printer.Print Format(strVar, "@@@@@@@@@@")
```

In Exercises 96 through 103, determine any errors.

96.
```
Let strVar = "Thank you"
picOutput.Print InStr(strVar, k)
```

97. `picOutput.Print Left(3, "goodbye")`

98.
```
Let firstName = InputBox("Enter your first name.")
picOutput.Print "Your first name is "; firstName
```

(Assume that the response is Left("John Doe", 4).)

99.
```
Let num1 = 7
Let num2 = 5
picOutput.Print Sqr(num1 - 2 * num2)
```

100.
```
Dim numString As String
  Let numString = 123
  picOutput.Print 2 * Val(numString)
```

101. `picOutput.Print Format(123.45, Standard)`

102. `Let txtBox.Text = Format($7654.3, "Currency")`

103. `Let txtBox.Text = (1234.568, "Standard")`

104. `Is Str(Val("32")) the same string as "32"?`

105. `Is Trim(Str(Val("32"))) the same string as "32"?`

In Exercises 106 through 111, determine the range of values that can be generated by the given expression.

106. `Int(38 * Rnd) - 1`

107. `Int(10 * Rnd) + 10`

108. `2 * Rnd`

109. `Int(52 * Rnd) + 1`

110. `Chr(Int(3 * Rnd) + 65)`

111. `Chr(Int(26 * Rnd) + 97)`

In Exercises 112 through 117, write an expression that will randomly select a value from the given range.

112. An integer from 1 through 100

113. A number from 2 through 4 (excluding 4)

114. An even integer from 2 through 100

115. Either 0 or 1

116. The answer to a multiple-choice question, where the answers range from *a* to *d*

117. A white piano key from an octave; that is, one of the letters A through G

118. Suppose txtBox.Text contains a positive number. Write code to replace this number with its units digit.

119. Suppose a text box contains a (complete) phone number. Write code to display the area code.

120. The formula $s = \sqrt{24d}$ gives an estimate of the speed of a car in miles per hour that skidded *d* feet on dry concrete when the brakes were applied. Write a program that requests the distance skidded and then displays the estimated speed of the car. (Try the program for a car that skids 54 feet.)

121. A college graduation is to be held in an auditorium with 2000 seats available for the friends and relatives of the graduates. Write a program that requests the number of graduates as input and then displays the number of tickets to be distributed to each graduate. Assume each graduate receives the same number of tickets. (Try the program for 325 graduates.)

122. Suppose you decide to give three pieces of Halloween candy to each trick-or-treater. Write a program that requests the number of pieces of candy you have and displays the number of children you can treat. (Try the program for 101 pieces of candy.)

123. The optimal inventory size for a specific item is given by the formula $s = \sqrt{2qh/c}$, where *q* is the quantity to be sold each year, *h* is the cost of placing an order, and *c* is the annual cost of stocking one unit of the item. Write a program that requests the quantity, ordering cost, and storage cost as input and displays the optimum inventory size. (Use the program to compute the optimal inventory size for an item selling 3025 units during the year, where placing an order costs $50, and stocking a unit for 1 year costs $25.)

124. Write a program that requests a whole number of inches and converts it to feet and inches. (Try the program with 72, 53, and 8 inches.)

125. Write a program that requests a number and the number of decimal places to which the number should be rounded, and then displays the rounded number.

126. Write a program that requests a letter, converts it to uppercase, and gives its first position in the sentence "THE QUICK BROWN FOX JUMPS OVER A LAZY DOG." For example, if the user responds by typing *b* into the text box, then the message *B first occurs in position 11* is displayed.

127. Write a program that requests an amount of money between 1 and 99 cents and gives the number of quarters to be used when making that amount of change. (Try each of the amounts 85, 43, and 15 as input.)

128. Write a program that requests a day of the week (Sunday, Monday, . . . , Saturday) and gives the numerical position of that day in the week. For example, if the user responds by typing *Wednesday* into the text box, then the message *Wednesday is day number 4* is displayed.

129. On the nautical clock, hours of the day are numbered from 0 to 23, beginning at midnight. Write a program to convert nautical hours to standard hours. For example, if the user responds by typing *17* into the text box, then the message *The standard hour is 5* is displayed. **Note:** Let 12 o'clock in standard hours appear as 0.

130. Write a program that requests a sentence, a word in the sentence, and another word, and then displays the sentence with the first word replaced by the second. For example, if the user responds by typing "What you don't know won't hurt you" into the first text box and *know* and *owe* into the second and third text boxes, then the message "What you don't owe won't hurt you" is displayed.

131. Write a program that requests a positive number containing a decimal point as input, and then displays the number of digits to the left of the decimal point and the number of digits to the right of the decimal point.

132. When *P* dollars are deposited in a savings account at interest rate *r* compounded annually, the balance after *n* years is $P(1 + r)^n$. Write a program to request the principal *P* and the interest rate *r* as input, and compute the balance after 10 years, as shown in the sample output on the left below.

133. Redo Exercise 132 to achieve the output shown on the right above. The principal and interest should be entered as 1000 and .05, but should be converted to nice forms when the button is pressed. (The balance is displayed in a label.) Also, the two text boxes should become empty when they receive the focus to allow for additional computations.

134. Write a program to generate a rent receipt. The program should request the person's name, amount received, and the current date in text boxes and print a receipt of the type shown on the right below.

Received from Jane Smith the sum of $645.50

Signed _____
Wednesday, April 02, 1997

135. Write a program to produce Table 3.9 on the printer. (The population is for 1995, the area is given in square miles, and the density is in people per square mile.) For each state, the name, capital, population, and area should be contained in a file. The densities should be computed by the program.

State	Capital	Population	Area	Density
Alaska	Juneau	603,617	570,374	1.06
New York	Albany	18,136,000	47,224	304.04
Texas	Austin	18,723,990	261,914	71.49

Table 3.9 State Data.

Source: The World Almanac of the U.S.A., 1996.

136. Table 3.10 provides approximate information about certain occupations and projects the percent change in job openings from 1990 to 2005. Write a program to produce this table on the printer. Place the data in a file. Notice that the names of the occupations and the numbers are right-justified.

Occupation	Current Number of Jobs	% Change	Weekly Median Earning
Computer programmer	565,000	63	$653
Teacher, Secondary School	1,280,000	45	$648
Physician	580,000	41	$2,996

Table 3.10 Job openings to 2005 and 1990 earnings.

Source: Bureau of Labor Statistics.

137. Write a program to randomly select a month and year during the 1990s. A typical outcome is 6 / 1997.

138. Write a program to randomly select one of the 64 squares on a chess board. **Note:** Each square is represented by a letter (from *a* to *h*, giving the column starting from white's left) and a number (from 1 to 8, giving the row starting from white's side). A typical outcome is d5.

139. Write an event procedure to drive the user crazy. Assume that the focus is on a text box. Each time the user presses a key, have a randomly selected letter from A to Z appear in the text box.

SOLUTIONS TO PRACTICE PROBLEMS 3.6

1. 0. There is no uppercase letter E in the string "Computer". InStr distinguishes between upper- and lowercase.

2. 6. Len("WIN") is 3, 12 * 3 is 36, and Sqr(36) is 6. This expression is an example of function composition. The inner function will be evaluated first.

3. Chr(Int(26 * Rnd) + 65). Uppercase letters have the 26 ANSI values ranging from 65 to 90. The value of 26 * Rnd is a number from 0 through 26 (excluding 26). The value of Int(26 * Rnd) is a whole number from 0 to 25, and therefore the value of Int(26 * Rnd) + 65 is a whole number from 65 to 90.

4. When n / 2 is an integer, that is, when *n* is an even number. (This idea will be used later in the text to determine whether an integer is even.)

Chapter 3
Summary

1. The Visual Basic screen consists of a collection of objects for which various properties can be set. Some examples of *objects* are text boxes, labels, command buttons, picture boxes, and the form itself. Objects placed on the form are called *controls*. Some useful properties are Text (set the text displayed by a text box), Caption (set the title of a form, the contents of a label, or the words on a command button), Font.Size (set the size of the characters displayed), Alignment (set the placement of the contents of a label), MultiLine (text box to display text on several lines), Picture (display drawing in picture box), ForeColor (set foreground color), BackColor (set background color), Visible (show or hide object), BorderStyle (alter and possibly remove border), Font.Bold (display boldface text), and Font.Italic (display italic text).

2. An event procedure is called when a specific event occurs to a specified object. Some event procedures are *object*_Click (*object* is clicked), *object*_Lost-Focus (*object* loses the focus), *object*_GotFocus (*object* receives the focus), and *object*_KeyPress (a key is pressed while *object* has the focus).

3. Visual Basic methods such as Print and Cls are applied to objects and are coded as *object*.Print and *object*.Cls.

4. Two types of *constants* can be stored and processed by computers, *numbers* and *strings*.

5. The arithmetic *operations* are +, –, *, /, and ^. The only string operation is &, concatenation. An *expression* is a combination of constants, variables, functions, and operations that can be evaluated.

6. A *variable* is a name used to refer to data. Variable names can be up to 255 characters long, must begin with a letter, and may contain letters, digits, and underscores. Dim statements explicitly declare variables and specify the types of the variables. In this book, variables have types Single, Integer, and String.

7. Values are assigned to variables by Let and Input# statements. The values assigned by Let statements can be constants, variables, or expressions. Input# statements look to data files for constants. String constants used in Let statements must be surrounded by quotation marks, whereas quotation marks are optional for string constants input with Input#. InputBox can be used to request that the user type in a constant.

8. The Print method displays information in a picture box or on the printer. *Semicolons*, *commas*, and *Tab* and *Spc* control the placement of the items on a particular line. A temporary message can be displayed on the screen using the MsgBox statement.

9. You control the printer with the Printer object and write to it with statements of the form Printer.Print *expression*. You set properties with statements of the form Let Printer.*property* = *setting*. Printer.NewPage starts a new page and PrintForm does a screen dump. A series of commands to the Printer object must end with EndDoc, which actually produces the final printed page.

10. Rem statements are used to explain formulas, state the purposes of variables, and articulate the purposes of various parts of a program.

11. The Format function provides detailed control of how numbers, dates, and strings are displayed. Numbers can be made to line up uniformly and be displayed with dollar signs, commas, and a specified number of decimal places. Dates can be converted to a long or medium form. Strings can be right-justified.

12. *Functions* can be thought of as accepting numbers or strings as input and returning numbers or strings as output.

Function	Input	Output
Asc	string	number
Chr	number	string
InStr	string, string	number
Int	number	number
LCase	string	string
Left	string, number	string
Len	string	number
Mid	string, number, number	string
Right	string, number	string
Rnd		number
Sqr	number	number
Str	number	string
Trim	string	string
UCase	string	string
Val	string	number

Chapter 3
Programming Projects

1. Write a program that allows the user to specify two numbers and then adds, subtracts, or multiplies them when the user clicks on the appropriate command button. The output should give the type of arithmetic performed and the result.

2. Suppose automobile repair customers are billed at the rate of $35 per hour for labor. Also, costs for parts and supplies are subject to a 5 percent sales tax. Write a program to print out a simplified bill. The customer's name, the number of hours of labor, and the cost of parts and supplies should be entered into the program via text boxes. When a command button is clicked, the customer's name (indented) and the three costs should be displayed in a picture box, as shown in the sample run in Figure 3.31.

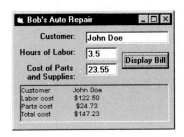

Figure 3.31 Sample run for Programming Project 2.

3. Write a program to generate the following personalized form letter. The person's name and address should be read from text boxes.

```
Mr. John Jones
123 Main Street
Juneau, Alaska  99803

Dear Mr. Jones,

    The Jones family has been selected as the
first family on Main Street to have the opportunity
to purchase an Apex solar-powered flashlight. Due to limited
supply, only 1000 of these amazing inventions will be available
in the entire state of Alaska. Don't delay. Order today.

                        Sincerely,
                        Cuthbert J. Twillie
```

4. At the end of each month, a credit card company constructs the table in Figure 3.32 to summarize the status of the accounts. Write a program to produce this table. The first four pieces of information for each account should be read from a data file. The program should compute the finance charges (1.5 percent of the unpaid past due amount) and the current amount due. Format the last column to be aligned right.

```
Account   Past Due   Payments   Purchases   Finance    Current
Number    Amount                            Charges    Amt Due

123-AB    123.45     10.00      934.00      1.70       $1,049.15
456-CD    134.56     134.56     300.00      0.00         $300.00
```

Figure 3.32 Status of credit card accounts.

5. Table 3.11 gives the distribution of the U.S. population (in thousands) by age group and sex. Write a program to produce the table shown in Figure 3.33. For each age group, the column labeled %Males gives the percentage of the people in that age group that are male, similarly for the column labeled %Females. The last column gives the percentage of the total population in each age group. (**Note:** Store the information in Table 3.11 in a data file. For instance, the first line in the file should be "Under 20", 36743, 34993. Read and add up the data once to obtain the total population, and then read the data again to produce the table.)

Age Group	Males	Females
Under 20	36,743	34,993
20–64	72,003	73,893
Over 64	12,854	15,818

Table 3.11 U.S. resident population (1990).

```
              U.S. Population (in thousands)

Age group   Males    Females   %Males   %Females   %Total

Under 20    36,743   34,993    51.22%   48.78%     29.12%
20-64       72,003   73,893    49.35%   50.65%     59.23%
Over 64     12,854   15,818    44.83%   55.17%     11.64%
```

Figure 3.33 Output of Programming Project 5.

6. Write a program to convert a U.S. Customary System length in miles, yards, feet, and inches to a Metric System length in kilometers, meters, and centimeters. A sample run is shown in Figure 3.34. After the number of miles, yards, feet, and inches are read from the text boxes, the length should be converted entirely to inches and then divided by 39.37 to obtain the value in meters. The Int function should be used to break the total number of meters into a whole number of kilometers and meters. The number of centimeters should be displayed to one decimal place. Some of the needed formulas are as follows:

total inches = 63360 * miles + 36 * yards + 12 * feet + inches
total meters = total inches / 39.37
kilometers = Int(meters / 1000)

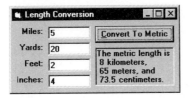

Figure 3.34 Sample run for Programming Project 6.

4

Procedures

4.1 **Subprograms, Part I / 142**
  • Variables and Expressions as Arguments

4.2 **Subprograms, Part II / 163**
  • Passing Values Back from Subprograms
  • Local Variables • Form-level Variables

4.3 **Functions / 176**

4.4 **Modular Design / 189**
  • Top-Down Design • Structured Programming
  • Advantages of Structured Programming

Summary / 194

Programming Projects / 194

4.1 SUBPROGRAMS, PART I

Structured program design requires that problems be broken into small problems to be solved one at a time. Visual Basic has two devices, subprograms and functions, that are used to break problems into manageable chunks. Subprograms and functions are known as **procedures**. To distinguish them from event procedures, subprograms and functions are referred to as *general procedures*. Procedures also eliminate repetitive code, can be reused in other programs, and allow a team of programmers to work on a single program.

In this section, we show how subprograms are defined and used. The programs in this section are designed to demonstrate the use of subprograms rather than to accomplish sophisticated programming tasks. Later chapters of the book use procedures for more substantial programming efforts.

A **subprogram** is a part of a program that performs one or more related tasks, has its own name, is written as a separate part of the program, and is accessed via a Call statement. The simplest type of subprogram has the form

```
Private Sub SubprogramName()
    statement(s)
End Sub
```

Consider the following program that calculates the sum of two numbers. This program will be revised to incorporate subprograms.

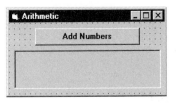

Object	Property	Setting
frmArithmetic	Caption	Arithmetic
cmdAdd	Caption	Add Numbers
picResult		

```
Private Sub cmdAdd_Click()
    Dim num1 As Single, num2 As Single
    Rem Display the sum of two numbers
    picResult.Cls
    picResult.Print "This program displays a sentence "
    picResult.Print "identifying two numbers and their sum."
    picResult.Print
    Let num1 = 2
    Let num2 = 3
    picResult.Print "The sum of"; num1; "and"; num2; "is"; num1 + num2
End Sub
```

[Run and then click the command button. The following is displayed in the picture box.]

```
This program displays a sentence
identifying two numbers and their sum.

The sum of 2 and 3 is 5
```

The tasks performed by this program can be summarized as follows:

Explain purpose of program.

Display numbers and their sum.

Subprograms allow us to write and read the program in such a way that we first focus on the tasks and later on how to accomplish each task.

EXAMPLE 1   The following program uses a subprogram to accomplish the first task of the preceding program. When the statement Call ExplainPurpose is reached, execution jumps to the Sub ExplainPurpose statement. The lines between Sub ExplainPurpose and End Sub are executed, and then execution continues with the line following the Call statement. **Note:** Do not type this program into the computer until you have read the two paragraphs following the example.

```
Private Sub cmdAdd_Click()
  Dim num1 As Single, num2 As Single
  Rem Display the sum of two numbers
  picResult.Cls
  Call ExplainPurpose
  picResult.Print
  Let num1 = 2
  Let num2 = 3
  picResult.Print "The sum of"; num1; "and"; num2; "is"; num1 + num2
End Sub

Private Sub ExplainPurpose()
  Rem Explain the task performed by the program
  picResult.Print "This program displays a sentence"
  picResult.Print "identifying two numbers and their sum."
End Sub
```

Subprograms are not typed into event procedure windows. Instead, they are in the portion of the code window called (General). The steps for creating a subprogram are as follows.

1. Activate a code window if one is not already active.

2. Select Add Procedure from the Tools menu with the mouse or the key combination Alt/T/P.

3. Type in the name of the subprogram. (Omit parentheses.)

4. The word Sub should appear selected in the Type box. If not, click on the circle to the left of the word Sub.

5. The word Public should appear selected in the Scope box. Switch the selection to Private. **Note:** Actually either one is OK. A Public procedure is available to all forms, whereas a Private procedure is only available to the form in which it was defined.

6. Press the Enter key or click the OK button.

7. A separator line and two lines of code have been added at the bottom of the code window. The first line says Private Sub *SubName*( ), and the cursor appears on a blank line just above the words End Sub.

8. Type the statements of the subprogram into this window.

9. To return to the form, just click on it or press Shift+F7.

The following steps are used to edit a general procedure.

1. Make the code window active if it is not already active. (For instance, you can just press F7 or click on the View Code icon in the Project window.)

2. Click on the down-arrow at the right side of the Object box (on the top left part of the code window) and select (General).

3. Click on the down-arrow at the right side of the Procedure box and click on the desired procedure. **Note:** Clicking on the item denoted "(Declarations)" moves to the top of the code window where you can declare special types of variables that will be discussed later.

The second task performed by the addition program also can be handled by a subprogram. The values of the two numbers, however, must be transmitted to the subprogram. This transmission is called **passing**.

EXAMPLE 2 The following revision of the program in Example 1 uses a subprogram to accomplish the second task. The statement Call Add(2, 3) causes execution to jump to the Private Sub Add(num1 As Single, num2 As Single) statement, which assigns the number 2 to *num1* and the number 3 to *num2*.

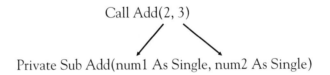

Call Add(2, 3)

Private Sub Add(num1 As Single, num2 As Single)

After the lines between Private Sub Add (num1 As Single, num2 As Single) and End Sub are executed, execution continues with the line following Call Add(2, 3), namely, the End Sub statement in the event procedure. **Note 1:** When you create the subprogram Add, you must type in "(num1 As Single, num2 As Single)" after leaving the Add Procedure dialog box.

```
Private Sub cmdAdd_Click()
  Rem Display the sum of two numbers
  picResult.Cls
  Call ExplainPurpose
  picResult.Print
  Call Add(2, 3)
End Sub

Private Sub Add(num1 As Single, num2 As Single)
  Rem Display numbers and their sum
  picResult.Print "The sum of"; num1; "and"; num2; "is"; num1 + num2
End Sub
```

```
Private Sub ExplainPurpose()
  Rem Explain the task performed by the program
  picResult.Print "This program displays a sentence"
  picResult.Print "identifying two numbers and their sum."
End Sub
```

Subprograms make a program easy to read, modify, and debug. The event · procedure gives an unencumbered description of what the program does and the subprograms fill in the details. Another benefit of subprograms is that they can be called several times during the execution of the program. This feature is especially useful when there are many statements in the subprogram.

EXAMPLE 3 The following extension of the program in Example 2 displays several sums.

```
Private Sub cmdAdd_Click()
  Rem Display the sums of several pairs of numbers
  picResult.Cls
  Call ExplainPurpose
  picResult.Print
  Call Add(2, 3)
  Call Add(4, 6)
  Call Add(7, 8)
End Sub

Private Sub Add(num1 As Single, num2 As Single)
  Rem Display numbers and their sum
  picResult.Print "The sum of"; num1; "and"; num2; "is"; num1 + num2
End Sub

Private Sub ExplainPurpose()
  Rem Explain the task performed by the program
  picResult.Print "This program displays sentences"
  picResult.Print "identifying pairs of numbers and their sums."
End Sub
```

[Run and then click the command button. The following is displayed in the picture box.]

```
This program displays sentences
identifying pairs of numbers and their sums.

The sum of 2 and 3 is 5
The sum of 4 and 6 is 10
The sum of 7 and 8 is 15
```

The variables *num1* and *num2* appearing in the subprogram Add are called **parameters**. They are merely temporary place holders for the numbers passed to the subprogram; their names are not important. The only essentials are their type, quantity, and order. In the Add subprogram, the parameters must be numeric variables and there must be two of them. For instance, the subprogram could have been written

```
Private Sub Add(this As Single, that As Single)
  Rem Display numbers and their sum
  picResult.Print "The sum of"; this; "and"; that; "is"; this + that
End Sub
```

A string also can be passed to a subprogram. In this case, the receiving parameter in the subprogram must be followed by the declaration As String.

EXAMPLE 4   The following program passes a string and two numbers to a subprogram. When the subprogram is first called, the string parameter *state* is assigned the string constant "Hawaii", and the numeric parameters *pop* and *area* are assigned the numeric constants 1134750 and 6471, respectively. The subprogram then uses these parameters to carry out the task of calculating the population density of Hawaii. The second Call statement assigns different values to the parameters.

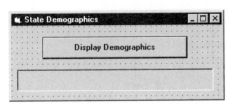

Object	Property	Setting
frmStates	Caption	State Demographics
cmdDisplay	Caption	Display Demographics
picDensity		

```
Private Sub cmdDisplay_Click()
  Rem Calculate the population densities of states
  picDensity.Cls
  Call CalculateDensity("Hawaii", 1134750, 6471)
  Call CalculateDensity("Alaska", 570345, 591000)
End Sub

Private Sub CalculateDensity(state As String, pop As Single, area As Single)
  Dim rawDensity As Single, density As Single
  Rem  The density (number of people per square mile)
  Rem  will be displayed rounded to a whole number
  Let rawDensity = pop / area
  Let density = Int(rawDensity + .5)   'round to whole number
  picDensity.Print "The density of "; state; " is"; density;
  picDensity.Print "people per square mile."
End Sub
```

[Run and then click the command button. The following is displayed in the picture box.]

```
The density of Hawaii is 175 people per square mile.
The density of Alaska is 1 people per square mile.
```

The parameters in the density program can have any names, as with the parameters in the addition program of Example 3. The only restriction is that the first parameter be a string variable and that the last two parameters be numeric variables. For instance, the subprogram could have been written

```
Private Sub CalculateDensity(x As String, y As Single, z As Single)
  Dim rawDensity As Single, density As Single
  Rem The density (number of people per square mile)
```

```
      Rem will be rounded to a whole number
      Let rawDensity = y / z
      Let density = Int(rawDensity + .5)
      picDensity.Print "The density of "; x; " is"; density;
      picDensity.Print "people per square mile."
    End Sub
```

When nondescriptive names are used for parameters, the subprogram should contain Rem statements giving the meanings of the variables. Possible Rem statements for the preceding program are

```
Rem x    name of the state
Rem y    population of the state
Rem z    area of the state
```

Variables and Expressions as Arguments

The items appearing in the parentheses of a Call statement are called **arguments**. These should not be confused with parameters, which appear in the heading of a subprogram. In Example 3, the arguments of the Call Add statements were constants. These arguments also could have been variables or expressions. For instance, the event procedure could have been written as follows. See Figure 4.1.

```
Private Sub cmdAdd_Click()
    Dim x As Single, y As Single, z As Single
    Rem Display the sum of two numbers
    picResult.Cls
    Call ExplainPurpose
    picResult.Print
    Let x = 2
    Let y = 3
    Call Add(x, y)
    Call Add(x + 2, 2 * y)
    Let z = 7
    Call Add(z, z + 1)
End Sub
```

Figure 4.1 Passing arguments to parameters.

This feature allows values obtained as input from the user to be passed to a subprogram.

EXAMPLE 5 The following variation of the addition program requests the two numbers as input from the user. Notice that the names of the arguments, *x* and *y*, are different than the names of the parameters. The names of the arguments and parameters may be the same or different; what matters is that the order, number, and types of the arguments and parameters match.

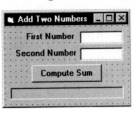

Object	Property	Setting
frmAdd	Caption	Add Two Numbers
lblFirstNum	Caption	First Number
txtFirstNum	Text	(blank)
lblSecondNum	Caption	Second Number
txtSecondNum	Text	(blank)
cmdCompute	Caption	Compute Sum
picResult		

[handwritten: Anything entered into a text box is a string]

```
Private Sub cmdCompute_Click()
  Dim x As Single, y As Single
  Rem This program requests two numbers and
  Rem displays the two numbers and their sum.
  Let x = Val(txtFirstNum.Text)
  Let y = Val(txtSecondNum.Text)
  Call Add(x, y)
End Sub

Private Sub Add(num1 As Single, num2 As Single)
  Rem Display numbers and their sum
  picResult.Cls
  picResult.Print "The sum of"; num1; "and"; num2; "is"; num1 + num2
End Sub
```

[Run, type 23 and 67 into the text boxes, and then click the command button.]

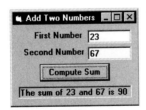

EXAMPLE 6 The following variation of Example 4 obtains its input from the file DEMO-GRAP.TXT. The second Call statement uses different variable names for the arguments to show that using the same argument names is not necessary. See Figure 4.2.

DEMOGRAP.TXT contains the following two lines:

"Hawaii", 1134750, 6471
"Alaska", 570345, 591000

```
Private Sub cmdDisplay_Click()
  Dim state As String, pop As Single, area As Single
  Dim s As String, p As Single, a As Single
  Rem Calculate the population densities of states
  picDensity.Cls
  Open "DEMOGRAP.TXT" For Input As #1
```

```
    Input #1, state, pop, area
    Call CalculateDensity(state, pop, area)
    Input #1, s, p, a
    Call CalculateDensity(s, p, a)
    Close #1
End Sub

Private Sub CalculateDensity(state As String, pop As Single, area As Single)
  Dim rawDensity As Single, density As Single
  Rem The density (number of people per square mile)
  Rem will be rounded to a whole number
  Let rawDensity = pop / area
  Let density = Int(rawDensity + .5)
  picDensity.Print "The density of "; state; " is "; density;
  picDensity.Print " people per square mile."
End Sub
```

[Run and then click the command button. The following is displayed in the picture box.]

```
The density of Hawaii is 175 people per square mile.
The density of Alaska is 1 people per square mile.
```

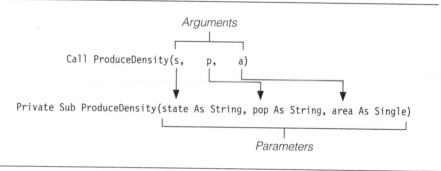

Figure 4.2 Passing arguments to parameters in Example 6.

Arguments and parameters also can be used to pass values from subprograms back to event procedures or other subprograms. This important property of subprograms is explored in detail in the next section.

Comments

1. In this text, subprogram names begin with uppercase letters in order to distinguish them from variable names. Like variable names, however, they can be written with any combination of uppercase and lowercase letters. To improve readability, the Visual Basic editor will automatically ensure that the capitalization of a subprogram name is consistent throughout a program. For instance, if you type Private Sub SubPROGRAMNAME and also type Call SubprogramName, the second name will be changed to match the first. **Note:** Parameters appearing in a Sub statement are not part of the subprogram name.

2. The rules for naming subprograms are identical to the rules for naming numeric variables. The name chosen for a subprogram should describe the task it performs.

3. Subprograms allow programmers to focus on the main flow of the program and defer the details of implementation. Modern programs use subprograms liberally. An event procedure acts as a supervisor, delegating tasks to the subprograms. This method of program construction is known as **modular** or **top-down** design.

4. As a rule, a subprogram should perform only one task, or several closely related tasks, and should be kept relatively small.

5. After a subprogram has been defined, Visual Basic automatically reminds you of the subprogram's parameters when you type in Call statements. As soon as you type in the left parenthesis of a Call statement, a banner appears giving the names and types of the parameters. The help feature is called **Parameter Info**. See Figure 4.3.

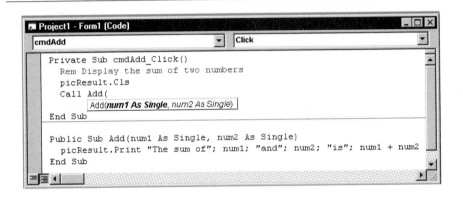

Figure 4.3 The Parameter Info help feature.

6. To delete a subprogram, erase every line of the subprogram.

7. In this text, the first line inside a subprogram is often a Rem statement describing the task performed by the subprogram. If necessary, several Rem statements are devoted to this purpose. Conventional programming practice also recommends that all variables used by the subprogram be listed in Rem statements with their meanings. In this text, we give several examples of this practice, but only adhere to it when the variables are especially numerous or lack descriptive names.

8. Although both constants and expressions can be used as arguments in Call statements, only variables can be used as parameters in Sub statements.

9. A subprogram can call another subprogram. If so, after the End Sub of the called subprogram is reached, execution continues with the line in the calling subprogram that follows the Call statement.

10. An alternative method of creating a subprogram is to move the cursor to a blank line outside of any procedure, type Private Sub *SubName*, and press the Enter key.

11. When you write a subprogram without parameters, Visual Basic automatically adds a pair of empty parentheses at the end of the subprogram name. However, Call statements should not use the empty parentheses.

12. The first lines of event procedures and subprograms end with a pair of parentheses. With the event procedures we have discussed, the parentheses are usually empty, whereas with subprograms, the parentheses often contain parameters.

PRACTICE PROBLEMS 4.1

1. What is displayed in the picture box by the following code when the command button is clicked?

```
Private Sub cmdButton_Click()
   Rem Demonstrate subprograms calling other subprograms
   Call FirstPart
   picOutput.Print 4;
End Sub

Private Sub FirstPart()
   picOutput.Print 1;
   Call SecondPart
   picOutput.Print 3;
End Sub

Private Sub SecondPart
   picOutput.Print 2;
End Sub
```

2. What is wrong with the following code?

```
Private Sub cmdDisplay_Click()
   Dim phone As String
   Let phone = txtPhoneNumx.Text
   Call AreaCode(phone)
End Sub

Private Sub AreaCode()
   picOutput.Print "Your area code is "; Left(phone, 3)
End Sub
```

EXERCISES 4.1

In Exercises 1 through 34, determine the output displayed in the picture box when the command button is clicked.

```
1. Private Sub cmdDisplay_Click()
     Rem Quote from Kermit
     Call Quotation
     picOutput.Print "          Kermit the frog"
   End Sub

   Private Sub Quotation()
     Rem Display a quotation
     picOutput.Print "It isn't easy being green."
   End Sub

2. Private Sub cmdDisplay_Click()
     picOutput.Print "Today ";
     Call WhatDay
     picOutput.Print "of the rest of your life."
   End Sub

   Private Sub WhatDay()
     picOutput.Print "is the first day ";
   End Sub
```

3. ```
Private Sub cmdDisplay_Click()
    Call Question
    Call Answer
End Sub

Private Sub Answer()
  picOutput.Print "Because they were invented in the northern"
  picOutput.Print "hemisphere where sundials move clockwise."
End Sub

Private Sub Question()
  picOutput.Print "Why do clocks run clockwise?"
End Sub
```

4. ```
Private Sub cmdDisplay_Click()
    Call FirstName
    picOutput.Print "How are you today?"
End Sub

Private Sub FirstName()
  Dim nom As String
  Let nom = InputBox("What is your first name?", "Name")
  picOutput.Print "Hello " + UCase(nom)
End Sub
```

   (Assume that the response is *Bill*.)

5. ```
Private Sub cmdDisplay_Click()
    Rem The fates of Henry the Eighth's six wives
    Call CommonFates
    picOutput.Print "died;"
    Call CommonFates
    picOutput.Print "survived."
End Sub

Private Sub CommonFates()
  Rem The most common fates
  picOutput.Print "Divorced, beheaded, ";
End Sub
```

6. ```
Private Sub cmdDisplay_Click()
    picOutput.Print "A rose";
    Call Rose
    Call Rose
    picOutput.Print "."
End Sub

Private Sub Rose()
  picOutput.Print ", is a rose";
End Sub
```

7. ```
Private Sub cmdDisplay_Click()
    Rem Good advice to follow
    Call Advice
End Sub

Private Sub Advice()
  picOutput.Print "Keep cool, but don't freeze."
  Call Source
End Sub
```
```

```
   Private Sub Source()
     picOutput.Print "Source: A jar of mayonnaise."
   End Sub
```

8.
```
Private Sub cmdDisplay_Click()
    Call Answer
    Call Question
End Sub

   Private Sub Answer()
     picOutput.Print "The answer is 9W."
     picOutput.Print "What is the question?"
   End Sub

   Private Sub Question()
     Rem Note: "Wagner" is pronounced "Vagner"
     picOutput.Print
     picOutput.Print "Do you spell your name with a V, Mr. Wagner?"
   End Sub
```

9.
```
Private Sub cmdDisplay_Click()
    Call Piano(88)
End Sub

   Private Sub Piano(num As Integer)
     picOutput.Print num; "keys on a piano"
   End Sub
```

10.
```
Private Sub cmdDisplay_Click()
    Rem Opening line of Moby Dick
    Call FirstLine("Ishmael")
End Sub

   Private Sub FirstLine(nom As String)
     Rem Display first line
     picOutput.Print "Call me "; nom
   End Sub
```

11.
```
Private Sub cmdDisplay_Click()
    Rem Opening line of Tale of Two Cities
    Call Times("best")
    Call Times("worst")
End Sub

   Private Sub Times(word As String)
     Rem Display first line
     picOutput.Print "It was the "; word; " of times."
   End Sub
```

12.
```
Private Sub cmdDisplay_Click()
    Call Potato(1)
    Call Potato(2)
    Call Potato(3)
    picOutput.Print 4
End Sub

   Private Sub Potato(quantity As Integer)
     picOutput.Print quantity; "potato,";
   End Sub
```

13.
```
cmdDisplay_Click()
    Dim nom As String
    Rem Analyze a name
    Let nom = "Gabriel"
    Call AnalyzeName(nom)
End Sub

Private Sub AnalyzeName(nom As String)
    Rem Display length and first letter
    picOutput.Print "Your name has"; Len(nom); "letters."
    picOutput.Print "The first letter is "; Left(nom, 1)
End Sub
```

14.
```
Private Sub cmdDisplay_Click()
    Dim color As String
    Let color = InputBox("What is your favorite color?")
    Call Flattery(color)
End Sub

Private Sub Flattery(color As String)
    picOutput.Print "You look dashing in "; color
End Sub
```

(Assume that the response is *blue*.)

15.
```
Private Sub cmdDisplay_Click()
    Dim num As Integer
    Let num = Val(InputBox("Give a number from 1 to 26."))
    Call Alphabet(num)
End Sub

Private Sub Alphabet(num As Integer)
    picOutput.Print Left("abcdefghijklmnopqrstuvwxyz", num)
End Sub
```

(Assume that the response is *5*.)

16.
```
Private Sub cmdDisplay_Click()
    Dim size As Single
    Let size = 435
    Call House(size)
    picOutput.Print "of Representatives"
End Sub

Private Sub House(size As Single)
    picOutput.Print size; "members in the House ";
End Sub
```

17.
```
Private Sub cmdDisplay_Click()
    Dim num As Single
    Let num = 144
    Call Gross(num)
End Sub

Private Sub Gross(amount As Single)
    picOutput.Print amount; "items in a gross"
End Sub
```

18.
```
Private Sub cmdDisplay_Click()
    Dim a As String
    Let a = "mile"
    Call Acres(a)
End Sub

Private Sub Acres(length As String)
    picOutput.Print "640 acres in a square "; length
End Sub
```

19.
```
Private Sub cmdDisplay_Click()
    Dim candy As String
    Let candy = "M&M's Plain Chocolate Candies"
    Call Brown(candy)
End Sub

Private Sub Brown(item As String)
    picOutput.Print "30% of "; item; " are brown."
End Sub
```

20.
```
Private Sub cmdDisplay_Click()
    Dim annualRate As Single
    Let annualRate = .08
    Call Balance(annualRate)
End Sub

Private Sub Balance(r As Single)
    Dim p As Single
    p = Val(InputBox("What is the principal?"))
    picOutput.Print "The balance after 1 year is"; (1 + r) * p
End Sub
```

(Assume that the response is *100*.)

21.
```
Private Sub cmdDisplay_Click()
    Dim hours As Single
    Let hours = 24
    Call Minutes(60 * hours)
End Sub

Private Sub Minutes(num As Single)
    picOutput.Print num; "minutes in a day"
End Sub
```

22.
```
Private Sub cmdDisplay_Click()
    Dim a As String, b As String
    Let a = "United States"
    Let b = "acorn"
    Call Display(Left(a, 3) + Mid(b, 2, 4))
End Sub

Private Sub Display(word As String)
    picOutput.Print word
End Sub
```

23. ```
Private Sub cmdDisplay_Click()
    Dim word As String
    Let word = InputBox("Enter a word.")
    Call T(InStr(word, "t"))
End Sub

Private Sub T(num As Integer)
    picOutput.Print "t is the"; num; "th letter of the word."
End Sub
```

(Assume that the response is *computer*.)

**24.** ```
Private Sub cmdDisplay_Click()
    Dim states As Single, senators As Single
    Let states = 50
    Let senators = 2
    Call Senate(states * senators)
End Sub

Private Sub Senate(num As Single)
    picOutput.Print "The number of members of the U.S. Senate is"; num
End Sub
```

25. ```
Private Sub cmdDisplay_Click()
    Call DisplaySource
    Call Language("BASIC", 22)
    Call Language("Assembler", 16)
    Call Language("C", 15)
    Call Language("Pascal", 13)
End Sub

Private Sub DisplaySource()
    picOutput.Print "According to a poll in the May 31, 1988"
    picOutput.Print "issue of PC Magazine, 75% of the people polled"
    picOutput.Print " write programs for their companies."
    picOutput.Print "The four most popular languages used are as follows."
End Sub

Private Sub Language(nom As String, users As Single)
    picOutput.Print users; "percent of the respondents use "; nom
End Sub
```

**26.** ```
Private Sub cmdDisplay_Click()
    Rem Sentence using number, thing, and place
    Call Sentence(168, "hour", "a week")
    Call Sentence(76, "trombone", "the big parade")
End Sub

Private Sub Sentence(num As Single, thing As String, where As String)
    picOutput.Print num; thing; "s in "; where
End Sub
```

27.
```
Private Sub cmdDisplay_Click()
    Dim pres As String, college As String
    Open "CHIEF.TXT" For Input As #1
    Input #1, pres, college
    Call PresAlmaMater(pres, college)
    Input #1, pres, college
    Call PresAlmaMater(pres, college)
    Close #1
End Sub

Private Sub PresAlmaMater(pres As String, college As String)
    picOutput.Print "President "; pres; " is a graduate of "; college
End Sub
```

(Assume that the file CHIEF.TXT contains the following two lines)

"Bush", "Yale University"
"Clinton", "Georgetown University"

28.
```
Private Sub cmdDisplay_Click()
    Dim nom As String, yob As Integer
    Let nom = InputBox("Name?")
    Let yob = Val(InputBox( "Year of birth?"))
    Call AgeIn2000(nom, yob)
End Sub

Private Sub AgeIn2000(nom As String, yob As Integer)
    picOutput.Print nom; ", in the year 2000 your age will be"; 2000 - yob
End Sub
```

(Assume that the responses are *Gabriel* and *1980*.)

29.
```
Private Sub cmdDisplay_Click()
    Dim word As String, num As Integer
    Let word = "Visual Basic"
    Let num = 6
    Call FirstPart(word, num)
End Sub

Private Sub FirstPart(term As String, digit As Integer)
    picOutput.Print "The first"; digit; "letters are ";
    picOutput.Print Left(term, digit)
End Sub
```

30.
```
Private Sub cmdDisplay_Click()
    Dim object As String, tons As Single
    Let object = "The Statue of Liberty"
    Let tons = 250
    Call HowHeavy(object, tons)
End Sub

Private Sub HowHeavy(what As String, weight As Single)
    picOutput.Print what; " weighs"; weight; "tons"
End Sub
```

31.
```
Private Sub cmdDisplay_Click()
    Dim word As String
    Let word = "worldly"
    Call Negative("un" & word, word)
End Sub

Private Sub Negative(neg As String, word As String)
    picOutput.Print "The negative of "; word; " is "; neg
End Sub
```

32.
```
Private Sub cmdDisplay_Click()
    Dim age As Integer, yrs As Integer, major As String
    Let age = Val(InputBox("How old are you?"))
    Let yrs = Val(InputBox("In how many years will you graduate?"))
    Let major = InputBox("What sort of major do you have (Arts or Sciences)?")
    Call Graduation(age + yrs, Left(major, 1))
End Sub

Private Sub Graduation(num As Integer, letter As String)
    picOutput.Print "You will receive a B"; UCase(letter);
    picOutput.Print " degree at age"; num
End Sub
```

(Assume that the responses are *19, 3,* and *arts.*)

33.
```
Private Sub cmdDisplay_Click()
    Call HowMany(24)
    picOutput.Print "a pie."
End Sub

Private Sub HowMany(num As Integer)
    Call What(num)
    picOutput.Print " baked in ";
End Sub

Private Sub What(num As Integer)
    picOutput.Print num; "blackbirds";
End Sub
```

34.
```
Private Sub cmdDisplay_Click()
    picOutput.Print "All's";
    Call PrintWell
    Call PrintWords(" that ends")
    picOutput.Print "."
End Sub

Private Sub PrintWell()
    picOutput.Print " well";
End Sub

Private Sub PrintWords(words As String)
    picOutput.Print words;
    Call PrintWell
End Sub
```

In Exercises 35 through 38, find the errors.

35.
```
Private Sub cmdDisplay_Click()
    Dim n As Integer
    Let n = 5
    Call Alphabet
End Sub

Private Sub Alphabet(n As Integer)
    picOutput.Print Left("abcdefghijklmnopqrstuvwxyz", n)
End Sub
```

36.
```
Private Sub cmdDisplay_Click()
    Dim word As String, number As Single
    Let word = "seven"
    Let number = 7
    Call Display(word, number)
End Sub

Private Sub Display(num As Single, term As String)
    picOutput.Print num; term
End Sub
```

37.
```
Private Sub cmdDisplay_Click()
    Dim nom As String
    Let nom = InputBox("Name")
    Call Print(nom)
End Sub

Private Sub Print(handle As String)
    picOutput.Print "Your name is "; handle
End Sub
```

38.
```
Private Sub cmdDisplay_Click()
    Dim num As Integer
    Let num = 2
    Call Tea(num)
End Sub

Private Sub Tea()
    picOutput.Print "Tea for"; num
End Sub
```

In Exercises 39 through 42, rewrite the program so the output is performed by calls to a subprogram.

39.
```
Private Sub cmdDisplay_Click()
    Dim num As Integer
    Rem Display a lucky number
    picOutput.Cls
    Let num = 7
    picOutput.Print num; "is a lucky number."
End Sub
```

40.
```
Private Sub cmdDisplay_Click()
    Dim nom As String
    Rem Greet a friend
    picOutput.Cls
    Let nom = "Jack"
    picOutput.Print "Hi, "; nom
End Sub
```

41.
```
Private Sub cmdDisplay_Click()
    Dim tree As String, ht As Single
    Rem Information about trees
    picOutput.Cls
    Open "TREES.TXT" For Input As #1
    Input #1, tree, ht
    picOutput.Print "The tallest "; tree; " in the U.S. is"; ht; "feet."
    Input #1, tree, ht
    picOutput.Print "The tallest "; tree; " in the U.S. is"; ht; "feet."
    Close #1
End Sub
```

(Assume that the file TREES.TXT contains the following two lines.)

"redwood", 362
"pine", 223

42.
```
Private Sub cmdDisplay_Click()
    Dim major As String, enrolled As Single
    Rem Undergraduate majors at U of MD, College Park
    picOutput.Cls
    Open "MAJORS.TXT" For Input As #1
    Input #1, major, enrolled
    picOutput.Print "In 1992, the University of Maryland had";
    picOutput.Print enrolled; major; " majors."
    Input #1, major, enrolled
    picOutput.Print "In 1992, the University of Maryland had";
    picOutput.Print enrolled; major; " majors."
    Close #1
End Sub
```

(Assume that the file MAJORS.TXT contains the following two lines.)

"computer science", 914
"economics", 556

43. Write a program that requests a number as input and displays three times the number. The output should be produced by a call to a subprogram named Triple.

44. Write a program that requests a word as input and displays the word followed by the number of letters in the word. The output should be produced by a call to a subprogram named Length.

45. Write a program that requests a word and a column number from 1 through 10 as input and displays the word tabbed over to the column number. The output should be produced by a call to a subprogram named PlaceNShow.

46. Write a program that requests three numbers as input and displays the average of the three numbers. The output should be produced by a call to a subprogram named Average.

In Exercises 47 through 50, write a program that, when cmdDisplay is clicked, will display in picOutput the output shown. The last two lines of the output should be displayed by one or more subprograms using data passed by variables from an event procedure.

47. (Assume that the following is displayed.)

```
According to a 1991 survey of college freshmen
taken by the Higher Educational Research Institute:

 18 percent said they intend to major in business
  2 percent said they intend to major in computer science
```

48. (Assume that the current date is 12/31/1995, the label for txtBox reads "What is your year of birth?", and the user types 1976 into txtBox before cmdDisplay is clicked.)

```
You are now 19 years old.
You have lived for more than 6935 days.
```

49. (Assume that the label for txtBox reads "What is your favorite number?" and the user types 7 into txtBox before cmdDisplay is clicked.)

```
The sum of your favorite number with itself is 14
The product of your favorite number with itself is 49
```

50. (Assume that the following is displayed.)

```
In the year 1990,
533,600 college students took a course in Spanish
272,600 college students took a course in French
```

51. Write a program to display four verses of *Old McDonald Had a Farm*. The primary verse, with variables substituted for the animals and sounds, should be contained in a subprogram. The program should use the file FARM.TXT.

FARM.TXT contains the following four lines:

```
"lamb", "baa"
"firefly", "blink"
"chainsaw", "brraap"
"computer", "beep"
```

The first verse of the output should be

```
Old McDonald had a farm. Eyi eyi oh.
And on his farm he had a lamb. Eyi eyi oh.
With a baa baa here and a baa baa there.
Here a baa, there a baa, everywhere a baa baa.
Old McDonald had a farm. Eyi eyi oh.
```

52. Write a program that displays the word WOW vertically in large letters. Each letter should be drawn in a subprogram. For instance, the subprogram for the letter W follows.

```
Private Sub DrawW()
  Rem Draw the letter W
  picWow.Print "**            **"
  picWow.Print " **          **"
  picWow.Print "  **  **  **"
  picWow.Print "   **    **"
  picWow.Print
End Sub
```

53. Write a program to display the data from Table 4.1. The occupations and numbers of people for 1982 and 1991 should be contained in a file. A subprogram, to be called three times, should read the three pieces of data for an occupation, calculate the percent change from 1982 to 1991, and display the four items. **Note:** The percent change is calculated as 100 * (1991 value – 1982 value) / (1982 value).

Occupation	1982	1991	Change
Computer analysts, programmers	719	1321	84%
Data processing equipment repairers	98	152	55%
Social workers	407	603	48%

Table 4.1 Occupations experiencing the greatest growth from 1982 to 1991 (numbers in thousands).

Source: Bureau of Labor Statistics

54. Write a program to compute tips for services rendered. The program should request the person's occupation, the amount of the bill, and the percentage tip as input and pass this information to a subprogram to display the person and the tip. A sample run is shown.

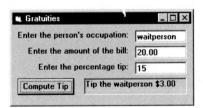

SOLUTIONS TO PRACTICE PROBLEMS 4.1

1. 1 2 3 4

After the subprogram Second is called, execution continues with the remaining statements in the subroutine First before returning to the event procedure.

2. The statement Private Sub AreaCode( ) must be replaced by Private Sub AreaCode(phone As String). Whenever a value is passed to a subprogram, the Sub statement must provide a parameter to receive the value.

4.2 SUBPROGRAMS, PART II

The previous section introduced the concept of a subprogram, but left some questions unanswered. Why can't the value of a variable be passed from an event procedure to a subprogram by just using the variable in the subprogram? How do subprograms pass values back to an event procedure? The answers to these questions provide a deeper understanding of the workings of subprograms and reveal their full capabilities.

Passing Values Back from Subprograms

Suppose a variable, call it *arg*, appears as an argument in a Call statement, and its corresponding parameter in the Sub statement is *par*. After the subprogram is executed, *arg* will have whatever value *par* had in the subprogram. Hence, not only is the value of *arg* passed to *par*, but the value of *par* is passed back to *arg*.

EXAMPLE 1   The following program illustrates the transfer of the value of a parameter to its calling argument.

```
Private Sub cmdDisplay_Click()
  Dim amt As Single
  Rem Illustrate effect of value of parameter on value of argument
  picResults.Cls
  Let amt = 2
  picResults.Print amt;
  Call Triple(amt)
  picResults.Print amt
End Sub

Private Sub Triple(num As Single)
  Rem Triple a number
  picResults.Print num;
  Let num = 3 * num
  picResults.Print num;
End Sub
```

[Run and then click the command button. The following is displayed in the picture box.]

```
 2  2  6  6
```

Although this feature may be surprising at first glance, it provides a vehicle for passing values from a subprogram back to the place from which the subprogram was called. Different names may be used for an argument and its corresponding parameter, but only one memory location is involved. Initially, the cmdButton_Click( ) event procedure allocates a memory location to hold the value of *amt* (Figure 4.4(a)). When the subprogram is called, the parameter *num* becomes the subprograms's name for this memory location (Figure 4.4(b)). When the value of *num* is tripled, the value in the memory location becomes 6 (Figure 4.4(c)). After the completion of the procedure, the parameter name *num* is forgotten; however, its value lives on in *amt* (Figure 4.4(d)). The variable *amt* is said to be **passed by reference**.

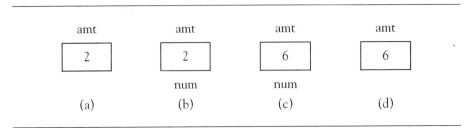

Figure 4.4 Passing a variable by reference to a subprogram.

Passing by reference has a wide variety of uses. In the next example, it is used as a vehicle to transport a value from a subprogram back to an event procedure.

EXAMPLE 2   The following variation of the addition program from the previous section uses a subprogram to acquire the input. The variables *x* and *y* are not assigned values prior to the execution of the first Call statement. Therefore, before the Call statement is executed, they have the value 0. After the Call statement is executed, however, they have the values 2 and 3. These values then are passed by the second Call statement to the subprogram Add.

Object	Property	Setting
frmAdd	Caption	Add Two Numbers
lblFirstNum	Caption	First Number
txtFirstNum	Text	(blank)
lblSecondNum	Caption	Second Number
txtSecondNum	Text	(blank)
cmdCompute	Caption	Compute Sum
picResult		

```
Private Sub cmdCompute_Click()
  Dim x As Single, y As Single
  Rem Display the sum of the two numbers
  Call GetNumbers(x, y)
  Call Add(x, y)
End Sub

Private Sub Add(num1 As Single, num2 As Single)
  Dim sum As Single
  Rem Display numbers and their sum
  picResult.Cls
  Let sum = num1 + num2
  picResult.Print "The sum of"; num1; "and"; num2; "is"; sum
End Sub

Private Sub GetNumbers(num1 As Single, num2 As Single)
  Rem Record the two numbers in the text boxes
  Let num1 = Val(txtFirstNum.Text)
  Let num2 = Val(txtSecondNum.Text)
End Sub
```

[Run, type 2 and 3 into the text boxes, and then click the command button.]

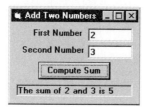

 In most situations, a variable with no preassigned value is used as an argument of a Call statement for the sole purpose of carrying back a value from the subprogram.

EXAMPLE 3   The following variation of Example 2 allows the cmdCompute_Click event procedure to be written in the input-process-output style.

```
Private Sub cmdCompute_Click()
  Dim x As Single, y As Single, s As Single
  Rem Display the sum of two numbers
  Call GetNumbers(x, y)
  Call CalculateSum(x, y, s)
  Call DisplayResult(x, y, s)
End Sub

Private Sub CalculateSum(num1 As Single, num2 As Single, sum As Single)
  Rem Add the values of num1 and num2
  Rem and assign the value to sum
  Let sum = num1 + num2
End Sub

Private Sub DisplayResult(num1 As Single, num2 As Single, sum As Single)
  Rem Display a sentence giving the two numbers and their sum
  picResult.Cls
  picResult.Print "The sum of"; num1; "and"; num2; "is"; sum
End Sub

Private Sub GetNumbers(num1 As Single, num2 As Single)
  Rem Record the two numbers in the text boxes
  Let num1 = Val(txtFirstNum.Text)
  Let num2 = Val(txtSecondNum.Text)
End Sub
```

Local Variables

When the same variable name appears in two different subprograms or in a subprogram and an event procedure, Visual Basic gives the variables separate identities and treats them as two different variables. A value assigned to a variable in one part of the program will not affect the value of the like-named variable in the other part of the program, unless, of course, the values are passed by a Call statement. Also, each time a subprogram is called, all declared variables that are not parameters assume their default values. (Numeric variables have default value 0, and string variables default to the empty string.) The variables in a subprogram are said to be local to the subprogram in which they reside.

EXAMPLE 4   The following program illustrates the fact that each time a subprogram is called, its variables are set to their default values; that is, numerical variables are set to 0 and string variables are set to the empty string.

```
Private Sub cmdDisplay_Click()
  Rem  Demonstrate that variables in a subprogram do
  Rem  not retain their values in subsequent calls
  picResults.Cls
  Call Three
  Call Three
End Sub

Private Sub Three()
  Dim num As Single
  Rem Display the value of num and assign it the value 3
  picResults.Print num;
  Let num = 3
End Sub
```

[Run and then click the command button. The following is displayed in the picture box.]

```
0  0
```

EXAMPLE 5   The following program illustrates the fact that variables are local to the part of the program in which they reside. The variable x in the event procedure and the variable x in the subprogram are treated as different variables. Visual Basic handles them as if their names were separate, such as *xcmdDisplay_Click* and *xTrivial*. Also, each time the subprogram is called, the value of variable x inside the subprogram is reset to 0.

```
Private Sub cmdDisplay_Click()
  Dim x As Single
  Rem Demonstrate the local nature of variables
  picResults.Cls
  Let x = 2
  picResults.Print x;
  Call Trivial
  picResults.Print x;
  Call Trivial
  picResults.Print x;
End Sub

Private Sub Trivial()
  Dim x As Single
  Rem Do something trivial
  picResults.Print x;
  Let x = 3
  picResults.Print x;
End Sub
```

[Run and then click the command button. The following is displayed in the picture box.]

```
2  0  3  2  0  3  2
```

Form-level Variables

Visual Basic provides a way to make a variable visible to *every* procedure in a form's code without being passed. Such a variable is called a **form-level variable**. Form-level variables appear at the top of the code window and are separated from the rest of the code by a horizontal separator line. Inside the code window, you can move to them either by pressing Ctrl+Home or clicking on General in the Object list box. Form-level variables are said to reside in the (Declarations) section of (General) and are declared with the following steps.

1. Invoke a code window if one is not already active.

2. Click on the down-arrow to the right of the Object list box.

3. Click on (General).

4. Click on (Declarations) in the Procedure list box.

5. Type in a declaration statement, such as Dim strVar As String, and press the Enter key.

When a form-level variable is assigned a value by a procedure, it retains that value when the procedure is exited. In this text, we rarely use form-level variables until Chapter 7.

EXAMPLE 6 The following program contains the form-level variables *num1* and *num2*. Their Dim statement does not appear inside a procedure.

```
Dim num1 As Single, num2 As Single    'In (Declarations) section of (General)

Private Sub cmdDisplay_Click()
  Rem Display the sum of two numbers
  Let num1 = 2
  Let num2 = 3
  picResults.Cls
  Call AddAndIncrement
  picResults.Print
  picResults.Print "num1 = "; num1
  picResults.Print "num2 = "; num2
End Sub

Private Sub AddAndIncrement()
  Rem Display numbers and their sum
  picResults.Print "The sum of"; num1; "and"; num2; "is"; num1 + num2
  Let num1 = num1 + 1
  Let num2 = num2 + 1
End Sub
```

[Run and click the command button. The following is displayed in the picture box.]

```
The sum of 2 and 3 is 5

num1 = 3
num2 = 4
```

In the preceding example, we had to click a command button to assign values to the form-level variables. In some situations, we want to assign a value immediately to a form-level variable, without requiring the user to perform some specific action. Visual Basic has a special event procedure called Form_Load that is automatically activated as soon as the program is run, even before the form is created. The Form_Load template is invoked by double-clicking on the form itself.

EXAMPLE 7 The following program demonstrates the use of Form_Load.

```
Dim pi As Single    'In (Declarations) section of (General)

Private Sub Form_Load()
  Rem  Assign a value to pi
  Let pi = 3.14159
End Sub

Private Sub cmdCompute_Click()
  Rem Display the area of a circle of radius 5
  picArea.Cls
  picArea.Print "The area of a circle of radius 5 is"; pi * 5 * 5
End Sub
```

[Run and then click the command button. The following is displayed in the picture box.]

```
The area of a circle of radius 5 is 78.53975
```

Comments

1. In addition to the reasons presented earlier, some other reasons for using subprograms follow:

   (a) Programs with subprograms are easier to debug. Each subprogram can be checked individually before being placed into the program.

   (b) The task performed by a subprogram might be needed in another program. The subprogram can be reused with no changes. Programmers refer to the collection of their most universal subprograms as a **library** of subprograms. (The fact that variables appearing in subprograms are local to the subprograms is quite helpful when reusing subprograms in other programs. There is no need to worry if a variable name in the subprogram is used for a different purpose in another part of the program.)

   (c) Often, programs are written by a team of programmers. After a problem has been broken into distinct and manageable tasks, each programmer is assigned a single subprogram to write.

   (d) Subprograms make large programs easier to understand. Some programming standards insist that each subprogram be at most two pages long.

(e) Subprograms permit the following program design, which provides a built-in outline of an event procedure. A reader can focus on the main flow first, and then go into the specifics of accomplishing the secondary tasks.

```
Private Sub Object_Event()
  Rem An event procedure written entirely as subprograms
    Call FirstSubprogram      'Perform first task
    Call SecondSubprogram     'Perform second task
    Call ThirdSubprogram      'Perform third task
End Sub
```

2. Subprograms can call other subprograms. In such cases, the calling subprogram plays the role of the event procedure with respect to the called subprogram. Complex problems are thereby broken into simpler tasks, which are then broken into still more elementary tasks. This approach to problem solving is called **top-down design**.

3. In Appendix D, the section "Stepping Through a Program Containing a Procedure: Chapter 4" uses the Visual Basic debugger to trace the flow through a program and observe the interplay between arguments and parameters.

4. The Form_Load event procedure is activated just before the form and its controls appears on the screen. Therefore, it cannot contain statements such as

```
picBox.Print "Hello".
```

PRACTICE PROBLEMS 4.2

1. What does the following code display in the picture box when the command button is clicked?

```
Private Sub cmdDisplay_Click()
  Dim b As Integer, c As Integer
  Let b = 1
  Let c = 2
  Call Rhyme
  picOutput.Print b; c
End Sub
```

```
Private Sub Rhyme()
  Dim b As Integer, c As Integer
  picOutput.Print b; c; "buckle my shoe."
  Let b = 3
End Sub
```

2. When a variable appears as a parameter in the top line of a subprogram (without ByVal), how do we know if its role is to receive a value from an event procedure or to pass a value back to an event procedure, or both?

EXERCISES 4.2

In Exercises 1 through 18, determine the output displayed in the picture box when the command button is clicked.

1.
```
Private Sub cmdDisplay_Click()
    Dim num As Single
    Let num = 7
    Call AddTwo(num)
    picOutput.Print num
End Sub

Private Sub AddTwo(num As Single)
    Let num = num + 2
End Sub
```

2.
```
Private Sub cmdDisplay_Click()
    Dim term As String
    Let term = "Fall"
    Call Plural(term)
    picOutput.Print term
End Sub

Private Sub Plural(term As String)
    Let term = term & "s"
End Sub
```

3.
```
Private Sub cmdDisplay_Click()
    Dim dance As String
    Let dance = "Can "
    Call Twice(dance)
    picOutput.Print dance
End Sub

Private Sub Twice(dance As String)
    Let dance = dance & dance
End Sub
```

4.
```
Private Sub cmdDisplay_Click()
    Dim num As Single, fmt As String
    Let num = 1234.967
    Call GetFormatString(fmt)
    picOutput.Print "The number is "; Format(num, fmt)
End Sub

Private Sub GetFormatString(formatString As String)
    Let formatString = "Currency"
End Sub
```

5.
```
Private Sub cmdDisplay_Click()
    Dim a As Single
    Let a = 5
    Call Square(a)
    picOutput.Print a
End Sub

Private Sub Square(num As Single)
    Let num = num * num
End Sub
```

6.
```
Private Sub cmdDisplay_Click()
    Dim state As String
    Let state = "NEBRASKA"
    Call Abbreviate(state)
    picOutput.Print state
End Sub

Private Sub Abbreviate(a As String)
    Let a = Left(a, 2)
End Sub
```

7.
```
Private Sub cmdDisplay_Click()
    Dim word As String
    Call GetWord(word)
    picOutput.Print "Less is "; word
End Sub

Private Sub GetWord(w As String)
  Let w = "more"
End Sub
```

8.
```
Private Sub cmdDisplay_Click()
    Dim hourlyWage As Single, annualWage As Single
    Let hourlyWage = 10
    Call CalculateAnnualWage(hourlyWage, annualWage)
    picOutput.Print "Approximate Annual Wage:"; annualWage
End Sub

Private Sub CalculateAnnualWage(hWage As Single, aWage As Single)
  Let aWage = 2000 * hWage
End Sub
```

9.
```
Private Sub cmdDisplay_Click()
    Dim nom As String, yob As Integer
    Call GetVita(nom, yob)
    picOutput.Print nom; " was born in the year"; yob
End Sub

Private Sub GetVita(nom As String, yob As Integer)
  Let nom = "Gabriel"          'name
  Let yob = 1980               'year of birth
End Sub
```

10.
```
Private Sub cmdDisplay_Click()
    Dim word1 As String, word2 As String
    Let word1 = "fail"
    Let word2 = "plan"
    picOutput.Print "If you ";
    Call Sentence(word1, word2)
    Call Exchange(word1, word2)
    picOutput.Print " then you ";
    Call Sentence(word1, word2)
End Sub

Private Sub Exchange(word1 As String, word2 As String)
  Dim temp As String
  Let temp = word1
  Let word1 = word2
  Let word2 = temp
End Sub

Private Sub Sentence(word1 As String, word2 As String)
  picOutput.Print word1; " to "; word2;
End Sub
```

11.
```
Private Sub cmdDisplay_Click()
  Dim state As String
  Let state = "Ohio "
  Call Team
End Sub

Private Sub Team()
  Dim state As String
  picOutput.Print state;
  picOutput.Print "Buckeyes"
End Sub
```

12.
```
Private Sub cmdDisplay_Click )
  Dim a As Single
  Let a = 5
  Call Multiply(7)
  picOutput.Print a * 7
End Sub

Private Sub Multiply(num As Single)
  Dim a As Single
  Let a = 11
  picOutput.Print a * num
End Sub
```

13.
```
Private Sub cmdDisplay_Click()
  Dim a As Single
  Let a = 5
  Call Multiply(7)
End Sub

Private Sub Multiply(num As Single)
  Dim a As Single
  picOutput.Print a * num
End Sub
```

14.
```
Private Sub cmdDisplay_Click()
  Dim nom As String, n As String
  Let nom = "Ray"
  Call Hello(nom)
  picOutput.Print n; " and "; nom
End Sub

Private Sub Hello(nom As String)
  Dim n As String
  Let n = nom
  Let nom = "Bob"
  picOutput.Print "Hello "; n; " and "; nom
End Sub
```

15.
```
Private Sub cmdDisplay_Click()
  Dim num As Single
  Let num = 1
  Call Amount(num)
  Call Amount(num)
End Sub

Private Sub Amount(num As Single)
  Dim total As Single
  Let total = total + num
  picOutput.Print total;
End Sub
```

16.
```
Private Sub cmdDisplay_Click()
  Dim river As String
  Let river = "Wabash"
  Call Another
  picOutput.Print river
  Call Another
End Sub

Private Sub Another()
  Dim river As String
  picOutput.Print river;
  Let river = "Yukon"
End Sub
```

17.
```
Private Sub cmdDisplay_Click()
    Dim explorer As String
    Let explorer = "de Leon"
    Call Place(explorer)
End Sub

Private Sub Place(nom As String)
    picOutput.Print explorer; " discovered Florida"
End Sub
```

18.
```
Private Sub cmdDCompute_Click()
    Dim tax As Single, price As Single, total As Single
    Let tax = .05
    Call GetPrice("bicycle", price)
    Call ProcessItem(price, tax, total)
    Call DisplayResult(total)
End Sub

Private Sub DisplayResult(total As Single)
    picOutput.Print "With tax, the price is "; Format(total, "currency")
End Sub

Private Sub GetPrice(item As String, price As Single)
    Dim strVar As String
    Let strVar = InputBox("What is the price of a " & item & "?")
    Let price = Val(strVar)
End Sub

Private Sub ProcessItem(price As Single, tax As Single, total As Single)
    Let total = (1 + tax) * price
End Sub
```

(Assume that the cost of the bicycle is $200.)

In Exercises 19 and 20, find the errors.

19.
```
Private Sub cmdCompute_Click()
    Dim a As Single, b As Single, c As Single
    Let a = 1
    Let b = 2
    Call Sum(a, b, c)
    picOutput.Print "The sum is"; c
End Sub

Private Sub Sum(x As Single, y As Single)
    Dim c As Single
    Let c = x + y
End Sub
```

20.
```
Private Sub cmdDisplay_Click()
    Dim ano As String
    Call GetYear(ano)
    picOutput.Print ano
End Sub

Private Sub GetYear(yr As Single)
    Let yr = 1995
End Sub
```

In Exercises 21 through 24, rewrite the program so input, processing, and output are each performed by Calls to subprograms.

21.
```
Private Sub cmdCompute_Click()
    Dim price As Single, tax As Single, cost As Single
    Rem Calculate sales tax
    picOutput.Cls
    Let price = InputBox("Enter the price of the item:")
    Let tax = .05 * price
    Let cost = price + tax
    picOutput.Print "Price: "; price
    picOutput.Print "Tax: "; tax
    picOutput.Print "————-"
    pjcOutput.Print "Cost: "; cost
End Sub
```

22.
```
Private Sub cmdDisplay_Click()
    Dim nom As String, n As Integer, firstName As String
    Rem Letter of acceptance
    picOutput.Cls
    Let nom = InputBox("What is your full name?")
    Let n = InStr(nom, " ")
    Let firstName = Left(nom, n - 1)
    picOutput.Print "Dear "; firstName; ","
    picOutput.Print "We are proud to accept you to Gotham College."
End Sub
```

23.
```
Private Sub cmdDisplay_Click()
    Dim length As Single, wdth As Single, area As Single
    Rem Determine the area of a rectangle
    picOutput.Cls
    Let length = Val(txtLength.Text)
    Let wdth = Val(txtWidth.Text)
    Let area = length * wdth
    picOutput.Print "The area of the rectangle is"; area
End Sub
```

24.
```
Private Sub cmdCompute_Click()
    Dim a As String, feet As Single, inches As Single
    Dim totalInches As Single, centimeters As Single
    Rem Convert feet and inches to centimeters
    picOutput.Cls
    Let a = "Give the length in feet and inches.  "
    Let feet = Val(InputBox(a & "Enter the number of feet."))
    Let inches = Val(InputBox(a & "Enter the number of inches. "))
    Let totalInches = 12 * feet + inches
    Let centimeters = 2.54 * totalInches
    picOutput.Print "The length in centimeters is"; centimeters
End Sub
```

In Exercises 25 and 26, write a line of code to carry out the task. Specify where in the program the line of code would occur.

25. Declare the variable *nom* as a string variable visible to all parts of the program.

26. Declare the variable *nom* as a string variable visible only to the Form_Click event.

In Exercises 27 through 32, write a program to perform the stated task. The input, processing, and output should be performed by calls to subprograms.

27. Request a person's first name and last name as input and display the corresponding initials.

28. Request the amount of a restaurant bill as input and display the amount, the tip (15 percent), and the total amount.

29. Request the cost and selling price of an item of merchandise as input and display the percentage markup. Test the program with a cost of $4 and a selling price of $6. **Note:** The percentage markup is 100 * ((selling price – cost) / cost).

30. Read the number of students in public colleges (10.8 million) and private colleges (3.1 million) from a file, and display the percentage of college students attending public colleges.

31. Read a baseball player's name (Sheffield), times at bat (557), and hits (184) from a file and display his name and batting average. **Note:** Batting average is calculated as (hits)/(times at bat).

32. Request three numbers as input and then calculate and display the average of the three numbers.

33. The Hat Rack is considering locating its new branch store in one of three malls. The following file gives the monthly rent per square foot and the total square feet available at each of the three locations. Write a program to display a table exhibiting this information along with the total monthly rent for each mall.

MALLS.TXT contains the following three lines:

"Green Mall", 6.50, 583
"Red Mall", 7.25, 426
"Blue Mall", 5.00, 823

34. Write a program that uses the data in the following file CHARGES.TXT to display the end-of-month credit card balances of three people. (Each line gives a person's name, beginning balance, purchases during month, and payment for the month.) The end-of-month balance is calculated as [finance charges] + [beginning-of-month balance] + [purchases] – [payment], where the finance charge is 1.5 percent of the beginning-of-month balance.

CHARGES.TXT contains the following three lines:

"John Adams", 125.00, 60.00, 110.00
"Sue Jones", 0, 117.25, 117.25
"John Smith", 350.00, 200.50, 300.00

35. Write a program to produce a sales receipt. Each time the user clicks on a command button, an item and its price should be read from a pair of text boxes and displayed in a picture box. Use a form-level variable to track the sum of the prices. When the user clicks on a second command button (after all the entries have been made), the program should display the sum of the prices, the sales tax (5 percent of total), and the total amount to be paid. Figure 4.5 shows a sample output of the program.

```
Light bulbs    2.65
Soda           3.45
Soap           1.15
             --------
Sum            7.25
Tax            0.36
Total          7.61
```

Figure 4.5 Sales receipt for Exercise 35.

SOLUTIONS TO PRACTICE PROBLEMS 4.2

1. 0 0 buckle my shoe.
   1 2

This program illustrates the local nature of the variables in a subprogram. Notice that the variables *b* and *c* appearing in the subprogram have no relationship whatsoever to the variables of the same name in the event procedure. In a certain sense, the variables inside the subprogram can be thought of as having alternate names, such as *bRhyme* and *cRhyme*.

2. You cannot determine this by simply looking at the parameters. The code of the subprogram must be examined.

4.3 FUNCTIONS

Visual Basic has many built-in functions. In one respect, functions are like miniature programs. They use input, they process the input, and they have output. Some functions we encountered earlier are listed in Table 4.2.

Function	Example	Input	Output
Int	Int(2.6) is 2	number	number
Chr	Chr(65) is "A"	number	string
Len	Len("perhaps") is 7	string	number
Mid	Mid("perhaps",4,2) is "ha"	string,number,number	string
InStr	InStr("to be"," ") is 3	string,string	number

Table 4.2 Some Visual Basic built-in functions.

Although the input can involve several values, the output always consists of a single value. The items inside the parentheses can be constants (as in Table 4.2), variables, or expressions.

In addition to using built-in functions, we can define functions of our own. These new functions, called **user-defined functions**, are defined in much the same way as subprograms and are used in the same way as built-in functions. Like built-in functions, user-defined functions have a single output that can be string or numeric. User-defined functions can be used in expressions in exactly the same way as built-in functions. Programs refer to them as if they were constants, variables, or expressions. Functions are defined by function blocks of the form

```
Private Function FunctionName(var1 As Type1, var2 As Type2, ...) As dataType
   statement(s)
   FunctionName = expression
End Function
```

The variables in the top line are called **parameters** and variables inside the function block that are not parameters are local. Function names should be suggestive of the role performed and must conform to the rules for naming variables. The type *dataType*, which specifies the type of the output, will be one of String, Integer, Single, and so on. In the preceding general code, the next-to-last line assigns the output, which must be of type *dataType*, to the function name. Two examples of functions are as follows:

```
Private Function FtoC(t As Single) As Single      ← output
   Rem Convert Fahrenheit temperature to Celsius
   FtoC = (5 / 9) * (t - 32)
End Function
```

```
Private Function FirstName(nom As String) As String
   Dim firstSpace As Integer
   Rem Extract the first name from the full name nom
   Let firstSpace = InStr(nom, " ")
   FirstName = Left(nom, firstSpace - 1)
End Function
```

In each of the preceding functions, the value of the function is assigned by a statement of the form *FunctionName = expression*. (Such a statement also can be written as Let *FunctionName = expression*.) The variables *t* and *nom* appearing in the preceding functions are parameters. They can be replaced with any variable of the same type without affecting the function definition. For instance, the function FtoC could have been defined as

```
Private Function FtoC(temp As Single) As Single
   Rem Convert Fahrenheit temperature to Celsius
   FtoC = (5 / 9) * (temp - 32)
End Function
```

Like subprograms, functions can be created from a code window with Alt/T/P. The only difference is that the circle next to the word Function should be selected. After the name is typed and the OK button is clicked, the lines Private Function *FunctionName( )* and End Function will be placed automatically (separated by a blank line) in the code window.

EXAMPLE 1   The following program uses the function FtoC.

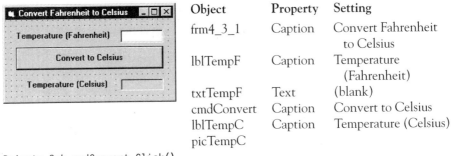

Object	Property	Setting
frm4_3_1	Caption	Convert Fahrenheit to Celsius
lblTempF	Caption	Temperature (Fahrenheit)
txtTempF	Text	(blank)
cmdConvert	Caption	Convert to Celsius
lblTempC	Caption	Temperature (Celsius)
picTempC		

```
Private Sub cmdConvert_Click()
  picTempC.Cls
  picTempC.Print FtoC(Val(txtTempF.Text))
End Sub

Private Function FtoC(t As Single) As Single
  Rem Convert Fahrenheit temperature to Celsius
  FtoC = (5 / 9) * (t - 32)
End Function
```

[Run, type 212 into the text box, and then click the command button.]

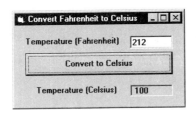

EXAMPLE 2   The following program uses the function FirstName.

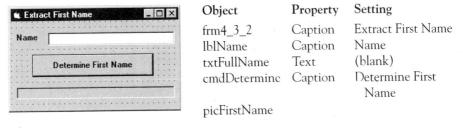

Object	Property	Setting
frm4_3_2	Caption	Extract First Name
lblName	Caption	Name
txtFullName	Text	(blank)
cmdDetermine	Caption	Determine First Name
picFirstName		

```
Private Sub cmdDetermine_Click()
  Dim nom As String
  Rem Determine a person's first name
  Let nom = txtFullName.Text
  picFirstName.Cls
  picFirstName.Print "The first name is "; FirstName(nom)
End Sub

Private Function FirstName(nom As String) As String
  Dim firstSpace As Integer
  Rem Extract the first name from a full name
  Let firstSpace = InStr(nom, " ")
  FirstName = Left(nom, firstSpace - 1)
End Function
```

[Run, type Thomas Woodrow Wilson into the text box, and then click the command button.]

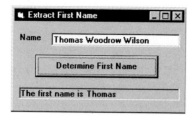

The input to a user-defined function can consist of one or more values. Two examples of functions with several parameters follow. One-letter variable names have been used so the mathematical formulas will look familiar and be readable. Because the names are not descriptive, the meanings of these variables are carefully stated in Rem statements.

accept → *Return*

```
Private Function Hypotenuse(a As Single, b As Single) As Single
   Rem  Calculate the hypotenuse of a right triangle
   Rem  having sides of lengths a and b
   Hypotenuse = Sqr(a ^ 2 + b ^ 2)
End Function
```

```
Private Function FV(p As Single,r As Single,c As Single,n As Single) As Single
   Dim i As Single, m As Single
   Rem Find the future value of a bank savings account
   Rem p  principal, the amount deposited
   Rem r  annual rate of interest
   Rem c  number of times interest is compounded per year
   Rem n  number of years
   Rem i  interest per period
   Rem m  total number of times interest is compounded
   Let i = r / c
   Let m = c * n
   FV = p * ((1 + i) ^ m)
End Function
```

EXAMPLE 3   The following program uses the Hypotenuse function.

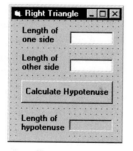

Object	Property	Setting
frm4_3_3	Caption	Right Triangle
lblSideOne	Caption	Length of one side
txtSideOne	Text	(blank)
lblSideTwo	Caption	Length of other side
txtSideTwo	Text	(blank)
cmdCalculate	Caption	Calculate Hypotenuse
lblHyp	Caption	Length of hypotenuse
picHyp		

```
Private Sub cmdCalculate_Click()
  Dim a As Single, b As Single
  Rem Calculate length of the hypotenuse of a right triangle
  Let a = Val(txtSideOne.Text)
  Let b = Val(txtSideTwo.Text)
  picHyp.Cls
  picHyp.Print Hypotenuse(a, b)
End Sub

Private Function Hypotenuse(a As Single, b As Single) As Single
  Rem Calculate the hypotenuse of a right triangle
  Rem having sides of lengths a and b
  Hypotenuse = Sqr(a ^ 2 + b ^ 2)
End Function
```

[Run, type 3 and 4 into the text boxes, and then click the command button.]

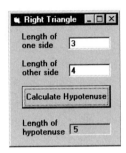

EXAMPLE 4　The following program uses the future value function. With the responses shown, the program computes the balance in a savings account when $100 is deposited for 5 years at 4 percent interest compounded quarterly. Interest is earned 4 times per year at the rate of 1 percent per interest period. There will be 4 * 5 or 20 interest periods.

Object	Property	Setting
frm4_3_4	Caption	Bank Deposit
lblAmount	Caption	Amount of bank deposit
txtAmount	Text	(blank)
lblRate	Caption	Annual rate of interest
txtRate	Text	(blank)
lblNumComp	Caption	Number of times interest is compounded per year
txtNumComp	Text	(blank)
lblNumYrs	Caption	Number of years
txtNumYrs	Text	(blank)
cmdCompute	Caption	Compute Balance
lblBalance	Caption	Balance
picBalance		

```
Private Sub cmdCompute_Click()
  Dim p As Single, r As Single, c As Single, n As Single
  Rem Find the future value of a bank deposit
  Call InputData(p, r, c, n)
  Call DisplayBalance(p, r, c, n)
End Sub


Private Sub DisplayBalance(p As Single,r As Single,c As Single,n As Single)
  Dim balance As Single
  Rem Display the balance in the picture box
  picBalance.Cls
  Let balance = FV(p, r, c, n)
  picBalance.Print Format(balance, "Currency")
End Sub


Private Function FV(p As Single,r As Single,c As Single,n As Single) As Single
  Dim i As Single, m As Single
  Rem Find the future value of a bank savings account
  Rem p  principal, the amount deposited
  Rem r  annual rate of interest
  Rem c  number of times interest is compounded per year
  Rem n  number of years
  Rem i  interest per period
  Rem m  total number of times interest is compounded
  Let i = r / c
  Let m = c * n
  FV = p * ((1 + i) ^ m)
End Function


Private Sub InputData(p As Single, r As Single, c As Single, n As Single)
  Rem Get the four values from the text boxes
  Let p = Val(txtAmount.Text)
  Let r = Val(txtRate.Text)
  Let c = Val(txtNumComp.Text)
  Let n = Val(txtNumYrs.Text)
End Sub
```

[Run, type 100, .04, 4, and 5 into the text boxes, then click the command button.]

EXAMPLE 5 Some computer languages have a useful built-in function called Ceil that is similar to the function Int, except that it rounds noninteger numbers up to the next integer. For instance, Ceil(3.2) is 4 and Ceil(–1.6) is –1. The following program creates Ceil in Visual Basic as a user-defined function.

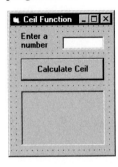

Object	Property	Setting
frm4_3_5	Caption	Ceil Function
lblNumber	Caption	Enter a number
txtNumber	Text	(blank)
cmdCalculate	Caption	Calculate Ceil
picResults		

```
Private Function Ceil(x As Single) As Single
  Rem Round nonintegers up
  Ceil = -Int(-x)
End Function

Private Sub cmdCalculate_Click()
  Rem Demonstrate the Ceil function
  picResults.Print "Ceil("; txtNumber.Text; ") ="; Ceil(Val(txtNumber.Text))
End Sub
```

[Run, type 4.3 into the text box, click the command button, type 4 into the text box, and then click the command button again.]

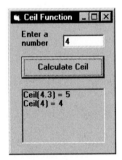

There are many reasons for employing user-defined functions.

1. User-defined functions are consistent with the modular approach to program design. Once we realize a particular function is needed, we can give it a name but save the task of figuring out the computational details until later.

2. Sometimes a single formula must be used several times in a program. Specifying the formula as a function saves repeated typing of the same formula, improves readability, and simplifies debugging.

3. Functions written for one program can be used in other programs. Programmers maintain a collection, or library, of functions that might be needed.

Comments

1. The word **procedure** refers to either a function or a subprogram.

2. Functions can perform the same tasks as subprograms. For instance, they can request input and display text; however, they are primarily used to calculate a single value. Normally, subprograms are used to carry out other tasks.

3. Functions differ from subprograms in the way they are accessed. Subprograms are invoked with Call statements, whereas functions are invoked by placing them where you would otherwise expect to find a constant, variable, or expression.

4. Functions can invoke other functions or subprograms.

5. Functions, like subprograms, need not have any parameters. Unlike subprograms, when a parameterless function is used, the function name may be followed by an empty set of parentheses. The following program uses a "parameterless" function.

```
Private Sub cmdButton_Click()
  Rem Request and display a saying
  picBox.Cls
  picBox.Print Saying()        '() is optional
End Sub


Private Function Saying() As String
  Rem Retrieve a saying from the user
  Saying = InputBox("What is your favorite saying?")
End Function
```

[Run, click the command button, and then type *Less is more.* into the message box.]

The saying *Less is more.* is displayed in the picture box.

6. An alternative method of creating a function is to move the cursor to a blank line outside of any procedure, type Private Function *FunctionName*, and press the Enter key.

7. When a variable argument is passed by reference to a subprogram or function, any changes to the corresponding parameter inside the procedure will change the value of the original argument when the procedure finishes. This change can be prevented by surrounding the argument by an extra pair of parentheses or by preceding the parameter in the top line of the procedure definition with ByVal. In this case, the argument is said to be **passed by value**.

PRACTICE PROBLEMS 4.3

1. Suppose a program contains the lines

```
Dim n As Single, x As String
picOutput.Print arc(n, x)
```

What types of inputs and output (numeric or string) does the function arc have?

2. What is displayed in the picture box when cmdCompute is clicked?

```
Private Sub cmdCompute_Click()
  Dim gallonsPerBushel As Single, apples As Single
  Rem How many gallons of apple cider can we make?
  Call GetData(gallonsPerBushel, apples)
  Call DisplayNumOfGallons(gallonsPerBushel, apples)
End Sub

Private Function Cider(g As Single, x As Single) As Single
  Cider = g * x
End Function

Private Sub DisplayNumOfGallons(galPerBu As Single, apples As Single)
  picOutput.Cls
  picOutput.Print "You can make"; Cider(galPerBu, apples);
  picOutput.Print "gallons of cider."
End Sub

Private Sub GetData(gallonsPerBushel As Single, apples As Single)
  Rem  gallonsPerBushel    Number of gallons of cider one bushel
  Rem                      of apples makes
  Rem  apples              Number of bushels of apples available
  Let gallonsPerBushel = 3
  Let apples = 9
End Sub
```

EXERCISES 4.3

In Exercises 1 through 10, determine the output displayed in the picture box when the command button is clicked.

```
1. Private Sub cmdConvert_Click()
     Dim temp As Single
     Rem Convert Celsius to Fahrenheit
     Let temp = 95
     picOutput.Print CtoF(temp)
   End Sub

   Private Function CtoF(t As Single) As Single
     CtoF = (9 / 5) * t + 32
   End Function

2. Private Sub cmdDisplay_Click()
     Dim acres As Single
     Rem acres     Number of acres in a parking lot
     Let acres = 5
     picOutput.Print "You can park about"; Cars(acres); "cars."
   End Sub

   Private Function Cars(x As Single) As Single
     Rem Parking cars
     Cars = 100 * x
   End Function
```

3.
```
Private Sub cmdDisplay_Click()
    Dim p As Single
    Rem Rule of 72
    Let p = Val(txtPopGr.Text)        'Population growth as a percent
    picOutput.Print "The population will double in";
    picOutput.Print DoublingTime(p); "years."
End Sub


Private Function DoublingTime(x As Single) As Single
    Rem Estimate time required for a population to double
    Rem at a growth rate of x percent
    DoublingTime = 72 / x
End Function
```

(Assume that the text box contains the number 3.)

4.
```
Private Sub cmdDisplay_Click()
    Dim initVel As Single, initHt As Single
    Rem Calculate max. ht. of a ball thrown straight up in the air
    Let initVel = Val(txtVel.Text)    'Initial velocity of ball
    Let initHt = Val(txtHt.Text)      'Initial height of ball
    picOutput.Print MaximumHeight(initVel, initHt)
End Sub


Private Function MaximumHeight(v As Single, h As Single) As Single
    MaximumHeight = h + v ^ 2 / 64
End Function
```

(Assume that the text boxes contain the values 96 and 256.)

5.
```
Private Sub cmdDisplay_Click()
    Dim r As Single, h As Single
    Rem Compute volume of a cylinder
    Let r = 1
    Let h = 2
    Call DisplayVolume(r, h)
    Let r = 3
    Let h = 4
    Call DisplayVolume(r, h)
End Sub


Private Function Area(r As Single) As Single
    Rem Compute area of a circle of radius r
    Area = 3.14159 * r ^ 2
End Function


Private Sub DisplayVolume(r As Single, h As Single)
    picOutput.Print "Volume of cylinder having base area"; Area(r)
    picOutput.Print "and height"; h; "is"; h * Area(r)
End Sub
```

6.
```
Private Sub cmdDisplay_Click()
    Dim days As String, num As Integer
    Rem Determine the day of the week from its number
    Let days = "SunMonTueWedThuFriSat"
    Let num = Val(InputBox("Enter the number of the day"))
    picOutput.Print "The day is "; DayOfWeek(days, num)
End Sub

Private Function DayOfWeek(x As String, n As Integer) As String
    Dim position As Integer
    Rem x    string containing 3-letter abbreviations of days of the week
    Rem n    the number of the day
    Let position = 3 * n - 2
    DayOfWeek = Mid(x, position, 3)
End Function
```

(Assume that the response is 4.)

7.
```
Private Sub cmdDisplay_Click()
    Dim a As String
    Rem Demonstrate local variables
    Let a = "Choo "
    picOutput.Print TypeOfTrain()
End Sub

Private Function TypeOfTrain() As String
    Dim a As String
    Let a = a & a
    TypeOfTrain = a & "train"
End Function
```

8.
```
Private Sub cmdDisplay_Click()
    Dim num As Single
    Rem Triple a number
    Let num = 5
    picOutput.Print Triple(num);
    picOutput.Print num
End Sub

Private Function Triple(x As Single) As Single
    Dim num As Single
    Let num = 3
    Triple = num * x
End Function
```

9.
```
Private Sub cmdDisplay_Click()
    Dim word As String
    Let word = "moral"
    Call Negative(word)
    Let word = "political"
    Call Negative(word)
End Sub

Private Function AddA(word As String) As String
    AddA = "a" & word
End Function
```

```
   Private Sub Negative(word As String)
     picOutput.Print word; " has the negative "; AddA(word)
   End Sub
```

10.
```
Private Sub cmdDisplay_Click()
    Dim city As String, pop As Single, shrinks As Single
    Open "DOCS.TXT" For Input as #1
    Input #1, city, pop, shrinks
    Call DisplayData(city, pop, shrinks)
    Input #1, city, pop, shrinks
    Call DisplayData(city, pop, shrinks)
    Close #1
End Sub

Private Sub DisplayData(city As String, pop As Single, shrinks As Single)
  picOutput.Print city; " has"; ShrinkDensity(pop, shrinks);
  picOutput.Print "psychiatrists per 100,000 people."
End Sub

Private Function ShrinkDensity(pop As Single, shrinks As Single) As Integer
  ShrinkDensity = Int(100000 * (shrinks / pop))
End Function
```

(Assume that the file DOCS.TXT contains the following two lines.)

"Boston", 2824000, 8602
"Denver", 1633000, 3217

In Exercises 11 and 12, identify the errors.

11.
```
Private Sub cmdDisplay_Click()
    Dim answer As Single
    Rem Select a greeting
    Let answer = Val(InputBox("Enter 1 or 2."))
    picOutput.Print Greeting(answer)
End Sub

Private Function Greeting(x As Single) As Single
  Greeting = Mid("hellohi ya", 5 * x - 4, 5)
End Function
```

12.
```
Private Sub cmdDisplay_Click()
    Dim word As String
    Let word = InputBox("What is your favorite word?")
    picOutput.Print "When the word is written twice,";
    picOutput.Print Twice (word); "letters are used."
End Sub

Private Function Twice(w As String) As Single
  Rem Compute twice the length of a string
  Twice(w) = 2 * Len(w)
End Function
```

In Exercises 13 through 21, construct user-defined functions to carry out the primary task(s) of the program.

13. To determine the number of square centimeters of tin needed to make a tin can, add the square of the radius of the can to the product of the radius and height of the can, and then multiply this sum by 6.283. Write a program that requests the radius and height of a tin can in centimeters as input and displays the number of square centimeters required to make the can.

14. According to Plato, a man should marry a woman whose age is half his age plus seven years. Write a program that requests a man's age as input and gives the ideal age of his wife.

15. Write a program that accepts a number (m) and a small positive integer (n) as input and rounds m to n decimal places.

16. In order for exercise to be beneficial to the cardiovascular system, the heart rate (number of heart beats per minute) must exceed a value called the training heart rate, THR. A person's THR can be calculated from his age and resting heart rate (pulse when first awakening) as follows:

    (a) Calculate the maximum heart rate as 220 – age.
    (b) Subtract the resting heart rate from the maximum heart rate.
    (c) Multiply the result in step (b) by 60 percent and then add the resting heart rate.

    Write a program to request a person's age and resting heart rate as input and display her THR. (Test the program with an age of 20 and a resting heart rate of 70, and then determine *your* training heart rate.)

17. The three ingredients for a serving of popcorn at a movie theater are popcorn, butter substitute, and a bucket. Write a program that requests the cost of these three items and the price of the serving as input and then displays the profit. (Test the program where popcorn costs 5 cents, butter substitute costs 2 cents, the bucket costs 25 cents, and the selling price is $2.)

18. Rewrite the population density program from Example 4 of Section 4.1 using a function to calculate the population density.

19. The original cost of airmail letters was 5 cents for the first ounce and 10 cents for each additional ounce. Write a program to compute the cost of a letter whose weight is given by the user in a text box. **Hint:** Use the function Ceil discussed in Example 5. (Test the program with the weights 4, 1, 2.5, and .5 ounce.)

20. Suppose a fixed amount of money is deposited at the beginning of each month into a savings account paying 6% interest compounded monthly. After each deposit is made, [new balance] = 1.005 * [previous balance one month ago] + [fixed amount]. Write a program that requests the fixed amount of the deposits as input and displays the balance after each of the first four deposits. A sample outcome when 800 is typed into the text box for the amount deposited each month follows.

```
Month 1    800.00
Month 2   1604.00
Month 3   2412.02
Month 4   3224.08
```

21. Write a program to request the name of a United States senator as input and display the address and greeting for a letter to the senator. Assume the name has two parts and use a function to determine the senator's last name. A sample outcome when Robert Smith is typed into the text box holding the senator's name follows.

```
The Honorable Robert Smith
United States Senate
Washington, DC 20001

Dear Senator Smith,
```

SOLUTIONS TO PRACTICE PROBLEMS 4.3

1. The first argument, *n*, takes numeric values and the second argument, *x*, takes string values; therefore, the input consists of a number and a string. From the two lines shown here, there is no way to determine the type of the output. This can be determined only by looking at the definition of the function.

2. You can make 27 gallons of cider. In this program, the function was used by a subprogram rather than by an event procedure.

4.4 MODULAR DESIGN

Top-Down Design

Large problems usually require large programs. One method programmers use to make a large problem more understandable is to divide it into smaller, less complex subproblems. Repeatedly using a "divide-and-conquer" approach to break up a large problem into smaller subproblems is called **stepwise refinement**. Stepwise refinement is part of a larger methodology of writing programs known as **top-down design**. The term top-down refers to the fact that the more general tasks occur near the top of the design and tasks representing their refinement occur below. Top-down design and structured programming emerged as techniques to enhance programming productivity. Their use leads to programs that are easier to read and maintain. They also produce programs containing fewer initial errors, with these errors being easier to find and correct. When such programs are later modified, there is a much smaller likelihood of introducing new errors.

The goal of top-down design is to break a problem into individual tasks, or modules, that can easily be transcribed into pseudocode, flowcharts, or a program. First, a problem is restated as several simpler problems depicted as modules. Any modules that remain too complex are broken down further. The process of refining modules continues until the smallest modules can be coded directly. Each stage of refinement adds a more complete specification of what tasks must be performed. The main idea in top-down design is to go from the general to the specific. This process of dividing and organizing a problem into tasks can be pictured using a hierarchy chart. When using top-down design, certain criteria should be met:

1. The design should be easily readable and emphasize small module size.

2. Modules proceed from general to specific as you read down the chart.

3. The modules, as much as possible, should be single-minded. That is, they should only perform a single well-defined task.

4. Modules should be as independent of each other as possible, and any relationships among modules should be specified.

This process is illustrated with the following example.

EXAMPLE 1   Write a hierarchy chart for a program that gives certain information about a car loan. The amount of the loan, the duration (in years), and the interest rate should be input. The output should consist of the monthly payment and the amount of interest paid during the first month.

SOLUTION   In the broadest sense, the program calls for obtaining the input, making calculations, and displaying the output. Figure 4.6 shows these tasks as the first row of a hierarchy chart.

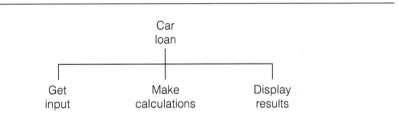

Figure 4.6 Beginning of a hierarchy chart for the car loan program.

Each of these tasks can be refined into more specific subtasks. (See Figure 4.7 for the final hierarchy chart.) Most of the subtasks in the second row are straightforward and so do not require further refinement. For instance, the first month's interest is computed by multiplying the amount of the loan by one-twelfth of the annual rate of interest. The most complicated subtask, the computation of the monthly payment, has been broken down further. This task is carried out by applying a standard formula found in finance books; however, the formula requires the number of payments.

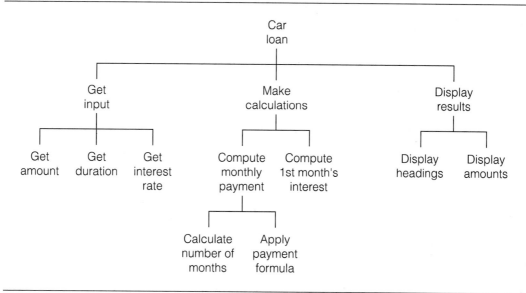

Figure 4.7 Hierarchy chart for the car loan program.

It is clear from the hierarchy chart that the top modules manipulate the modules beneath them. While the higher-level modules control the flow of the program, the lower-level modules do the actual work. By designing the top modules first, specific processing decisions can be delayed.

Structured Programming

A program is said to be **structured** if it meets modern standards of program design. Although there is no formal definition of the term **structured program**, computer scientists are in uniform agreement that such programs should have modular design and use only the three types of logical structures discussed in Chapter 2: sequences, decisions, and loops.

Sequences: Statements are executed one after another.

Decisions: One of two blocks of program code is executed based on a test for some condition.

Loops (iteration): One or more statements are executed repeatedly as long as a specified condition is true.

Chapters 5 and 6 are devoted to decisions and loops, respectively.

One major shortcoming of the earliest programming languages was their reliance on the GoTo statement. This statement was used to branch (that is, jump) from one line of a program to another. It was common for a program to be composed of a convoluted tangle of branchings that produced confusing code referred to as *spaghetti code*. At the heart of structured programming is the assertion of E. W. Dijkstra that GoTo statements should be eliminated entirely because they lead to complex and confusing programs. Two Italians, C. Bohm and G. Jacopini, were able to prove that GoTo statements are not needed and that any program can be written using only the three types of logic structures discussed before.

Structured programming requires that all programs be written using sequences, decisions, and loops. Nesting of such statements is allowed. All other logical constructs, such as GoTos, are not allowed. The logic of a structured program can be pictured using a flowchart that flows smoothly from top to bottom without unstructured branching (GoTos). The portion of a flowchart shown in Figure 4.8(a) contains the equivalent of a GoTo statement and, therefore, is not structured. A correctly structured version of the flowchart in which the logic flows from the top to the bottom appears in Figure 4.8(b).

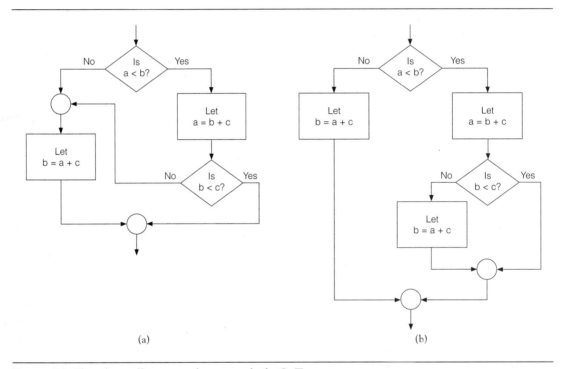

(a)   (b)

Figure 4.8 Flowcharts illustrating the removal of a GoTo statement.

Advantages of Structured Programming

The goal of structured programming is to create correct programs that are easy to write, understand, and change. Let us now take a closer look at the way modular design, along with a limited number of logical structures, contributes to attaining these goals.

1. *Easy to write.*

Modular design increases the programmer's productivity by allowing him or her to look at the big picture first and focus on the details later. During the actual coding, the programmer works with a manageable chunk of the program and does not have to think about an entire complex program.

Several programmers can work on a single large program, each taking responsibility for a specific module.

Studies have shown structured programs require significantly less time to write than standard programs.

Often, procedures written for one program can be reused in other programs requiring the same task. Not only is time saved in writing a program, but reliability is enhanced because reused procedures will already be tested and debugged. A procedure that can be used in many programs is said to be **reusable**.

2. *Easy to debug.*

Because each procedure is specialized to perform just one task, a procedure can be checked individually to determine its reliability. A dummy program, called a **driver**, is set up to test the procedure. The driver contains the minimum definitions needed to call the procedure to be tested. For instance, if the procedure to be tested is a function, the driver program assigns diverse values to the arguments and then examines the corresponding function value. The arguments should contain both typical and special-case values.

The program can be tested and debugged as it is being designed with a technique known as **stub programming**. In this technique, the key event procedures and perhaps some of the smaller procedures are coded first. Dummy procedures, or stubs, are written for the remaining procedures. Initially, a stub procedure might consist of a Print method to indicate that the procedure has been called, and thereby confirm that the procedure was called at the right time. Later, a stub might simply display values passed to it in order to confirm not only that the procedure was called, but also that it received the correct values from the calling procedure. A stub also can assign new values to one or more of its parameters to simulate either input or computation. This provides greater control of the conditions being tested. The stub procedure is always simpler than the actual procedure it represents. Although the stub program is only a skeleton of the final program, the program's structure can still be debugged and tested. (The stub program consists of some coded procedures and the stub procedures.)

Old-fashioned unstructured programs consist of a sequence of instructions that are not grouped for specific tasks. The logic of such a program is cluttered with details and therefore difficult to follow. Needed tasks are easily left out and crucial details easily neglected. Tricky parts of the program cannot be isolated and examined. Bugs are difficult to locate because they might be present in any part of the program.

3. *Easy to understand.*

The interconnections of the procedures reveal the modular design of the program.

The meaningful procedure names, along with relevant comments, identify the tasks performed by the modules.

The meaningful variable names help the programmer to recall the purpose of each variable.

4. *Easy to change.*

Because a structured program is self-documenting, it can easily be deciphered by another programmer.

Modifying a structured program often amounts to inserting or altering a few procedures rather than revising an entire complex program. The programmer does not even have to look at most of the program. This is in sharp contrast to the situation with unstructured programs that require an understanding of the entire logic of the program before any changes can be made with confidence.

Chapter 4
Summary

1. A *general procedure* is a portion of a program that is accessed by event procedures or other general procedures. The two types of general procedures are *subprograms* and *user-defined functions*.

2. Subprograms are defined in blocks beginning with Sub statements and ending with End Sub statements. They are accessed by Call statements.

3. User-defined functions are defined in blocks beginning with Function statements and ending with End Function statements. A function is activated by a reference in an expression and returns a value.

4. In any procedure, the arguments appearing in the calling statement must match the parameters of the Sub or Function statement in number, type, and order. They need not match in name.

5. A variable declared in the (Declarations) section of (General) is *form-level*. Such a variable is available to every procedure in the form's code and retains its value from one procedure invocation to the next. Form-level variables are often initialized in the Form_Load event procedure.

6. A variable appearing inside a procedure is *local* to the procedure if it is declared in a Dim statement within the procedure or if it is not a form-level variable and does not appear in the parameter list. The values of these variables are reinitialized each time the procedure is called. A variable with the same name appearing in another part of the program is treated as a different variable.

7. Structured programming uses modular design to refine large problems into smaller subproblems. Programs are coded using the three logical structures of sequences, decisions, and loops.

Chapter 4
Programming Projects

1. The numbers of calories per gram of carbohydrate, fat, and protein are 4, 9, and 4, respectively. Write a program that requests the nutritional content of a 1-ounce serving of food and displays the number of calories in the

serving. The input and output should be handled by subprograms and the calories computed by a function. A sample run for a typical breakfast cereal is shown in Figure 4.9

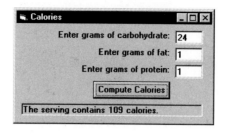

Figure 4.9 Sample run for Programming Project 1.

2. About 18 million PCs were sold during 1994. Table 4.3 gives the market share for the four largest vendors. Write a program that displays the number of computers sold by each of the Big Four. The input and output should be handled by subprograms and the number of computers calculated by a function.

Company	Market Share
Compaq	12.8%
Apple	12.2%
Packard Bell	10.8%
IBM	10.2%

Table 4.3 Market shares of leading PC companies.

3. Table 4.4 gives the revenues (in millions of dollars) of several major beverage companies. Write a program that displays the percentage growth for each company. Subprograms should be used for input and output and the percentage growth should be computed with a function. **Note:** The percentage growth is 100 ∗ ([1992 revenues] − [1991 revenues]) / [1991 revenues].

Company	1991 Revenues	1992 Revenues
PepsiCo	19,292	21,970
Coca-Cola Company	11,572	13,074
A&W Brands	123	130
Snapple Beverage Corp.	95	232

Table 4.4 Growth of beverage companies.
Source: Nordby International (*Beverage World*, July 1993)

4. A fast-food vendor sells pizza slices ($1.25), fries ($1.00), and soft drinks ($.75). Write a program to compute a customer's bill. The program should request the quantity of each item ordered in a subprogram, calculate the total cost with a function, and use a subprogram to display an itemized bill. A sample output is shown in Figure 4.10.

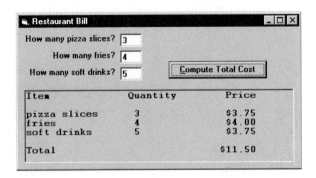

Figure 4.10 Sample run for Programming Project 4.

5. Write a program to generate a Business Travel Expense attachment for an income tax return. The program should request as input the name of the organization visited, the date and location of the visit, and the expenses for meals and entertainment, airplane fare, lodging, and taxi fares. (Only 50% of the expenses for meals and entertainment are deductible.) A possible form layout and run are shown in Figures 4.11 and 4.12, respectively. Subprograms should be used for the input and output.

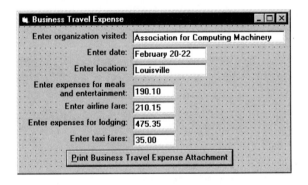

Figure 4.11 Form with sample data for Programming Project 5.

```
Business Travel Expense

Trip to attend meeting of
Association for Computing Machinery
February 20–22 in Louisville

Meals and entertainment     $190.10
Airplane fare               $210.15
Lodging                     $475.35
Taxi fares                   $35.00

Total other than Meals and Entertainment: $720.50

50% of Meals and Entertainment: $95.05
```

Figure 4.12 Output on printer for sample run of Programming Project 5.

5

Decisions

5.1 Relational and Logical Operators / 198
• Logical Operators

5.2 IF Blocks / 203

5.3 Select Case Blocks / 219

5.4 A Case Study: Weekly Payroll / 235
• Designing the Weekly Payroll Program • Pseudocode for
the Display Payroll Event • Writing the Weekly Payroll
Program • The User Interface

Summary / 243

Programming Projects / 243

5.1 RELATIONAL AND LOGICAL OPERATORS

A **condition** is an expression involving relational operators (such as < and =) that is either true or false when evaluated. Conditions also may incorporate logical operators (such as And, Or, and Not).

The relational operator *less than* (<) can be applied to both numbers and strings. The number a is said to be less than the number b if a lies to the left of b on the number line. For instance, $2 < 5$, $-5 < -2$, and $0 < 3.5$.

The string a is said to be less than the string b if a precedes b alphabetically when using the ANSI (or ASCII) table to alphabetize their values. For instance, "cat" < "dog", "cart" < "cat", and "cat" < "catalog". Digits precede uppercase letters, which precede lowercase letters. Two strings are compared working from left to right, character by character, to determine which one should precede the other. Therefore, "9W" < "bat", "Dog" < "cat", and "Sales-89" < "Sales-retail".

Table 5.1 shows the different mathematical relational operators, their representations in Visual Basic, and their meanings.

Mathematical Notation	Visual Basic Notation	Numeric Meaning	String Meaning
=	=	equal to	identical to
≠	<>	unequal to	different from
<	<	less than	precedes alphabetically
>	>	greater than	follows alphabetically
≤	<=	less than or equal to	precedes alphabetically or is identical to
≥	>=	greater than or equal to	follows alphabetically or is identical to

Table 5.1 Relational operators.

EXAMPLE 1   Determine whether each of the following conditions is true or false.

(a) 1 <= 1
(b) 1 < 1
(c) "car" < "cat"
(d) "Dog" < "dog"

SOLUTION   (a) True. The notation <= means "less than *or* equal to." That is, the condition is true provided either of the two circumstances holds. The second one (equal to) holds.

(b) False. The notation < means "strictly less than" and no number can be strictly less than itself.

(c) True. The characters of the strings are compared one at a time working from left to right. Because the first two match, the third character decides the order.

(d) True. Because uppercase letters precede lowercase letters in the ANSI table, the first character of "Dog" precedes the first character of "dog."

Conditions also can involve variables, numeric operators, and functions. To determine whether a condition is true or false, first compute the numeric or string values and then decide if the resulting assertion is true or false.

EXAMPLE 2 Suppose the numeric variables *a* and *b* have values 4 and 3, and the string variables *c* and *d* have values "hello" and "bye". Are the following conditions true or false?

(a) $(a + b) < 2 * a$
(b) $(Len(c) - b) = (a / 2)$
(c) $c < ("good" \& d)$

SOLUTION (a) The value of a + b is 7 and the value of 2 * a is 8. Because 7 < 8, the condition is true.
(b) True, because the value of Len(c) – b is 2, the same as (a / 2).
(c) The condition "hello" < "goodbye" is false because "h" follows "g" in the ANSI table.

Logical Operators

Programming situations often require more complex conditions than those considered so far. For instance, suppose we would like to state that the value of a numeric variable, *n*, is strictly between 2 and 5. The proper Visual Basic condition is

$$(2 < n) \text{ And } (n < 5)$$

The condition (2 < n) And (n < 5) is a combination of the two conditions 2 < n and n < 5 with the logical operator And.
    The three main logical operators are And, Or, and Not. If *cond1* and *cond2* are conditions, then the condition

    cond1 And *cond2*

is true if both *cond1* and *cond2* are true. Otherwise, it is false. The condition

    cond1 Or *cond2*

is true if either *cond1* or *cond2* (or both) is true. Otherwise, it is false. The condition

    Not *cond1*

is true if *cond1* is false, and is false if *cond1* is true.

EXAMPLE 3 Suppose the numeric variable *n* has value 4 and the string variable *answ* has value "Y". Determine whether each of the following conditions is true or false.

(a) $(2 < n)$ And $(n < 6)$
(b) $(2 < n)$ Or $(n = 6)$
(c) Not $(n < 6)$
(d) $(answ = "Y")$ Or $(answ = "y")$
(e) $(answ = "Y")$ And $(answ = "y")$
(f) Not $(answ = "y")$
(g) $((2 < n)$ And $(n = 5 + 1))$ Or $(answ = "No")$
(h) $((n = 2)$ And $(n = 7))$ Or $(answ = "Y")$
(i) $(n = 2)$ And $((n = 7)$ Or $(answ = "Y"))$

SOLUTION   (a) True, because the conditions (2 < 4) and (4 < 6) are both true.

(b) True, because the condition (2 < 4) is true. The fact that the condition (4 = 6) is false does not affect the conclusion. The only requirement is that at least one of the two conditions be true.

(c) False, because (4 < 6) is true.

(d) True, because the first condition becomes ("Y" = "Y") when the value of *answ* is substituted for *answ*.

(e) False, because the second condition is false. Actually, this compound condition is false for every value of *answ*.

(f) True, because ("Y" = "y") is false.

(g) False. In this logical expression, the compound condition ((2 < n) And (n = 5 + 1)) and the simple condition (answ = "No") are joined by the logical operator Or. Because both of these conditions are false, the total condition is false.

(h) True, because the second Or clause is true.

(i) False. Comparing (h) and (i) shows the necessity of using parentheses to specify the intended grouping.

The use of parentheses with logical operators improves readability; however, they can be omitted sometimes. Visual Basic has an operator hierarchy for deciding how to evaluate logical expressions without parentheses. First, all arithmetic operations are carried out, and then all expressions involving >, <, and = are evaluated to true or false. The logical operators are next applied, in the order Not, then And, and finally Or. For instance, the logical expression in part (g) of Example 3 could have been written 2 < n And n = 5 + 1 Or answ = "No". In the event of a tie, the leftmost operator is applied first.

EXAMPLE 4   Place parentheses in the following condition to show how it would be evaluated by Visual Basic.

a < b + c Or d < e And Not f = g

SOLUTION   ((a <(b + c)) Or ((d < e) And (Not (f = g))))

The step-by-step analysis of the order of operations is

a < (b + c)	Or	d < e	And	Not f = g	arithmetic operation
(a < (b + c))	Or	(d < e)	And	Not (f = g)	relational expressions
(a < (b + c))	Or	(d < e)	And	(Not (f = g))	Not
(a < (b + c))	Or	((d < e)	And	(Not (f = g)))	And
((a < (b + c))	Or	((d < e)	And	(Not (f = g))))	Or

Comments

1. A condition involving numeric variables is different from an algebraic truth. The assertion (a + b) < 2 * a, considered in Example 2, is not a valid algebraic truth because it isn't true for all values of *a* and *b*. When encountered in a Visual Basic program, however, it will be considered true if it is correct for the current values of the variables.

2. Conditions evaluate to either true or false. These two values often are called the possible **truth values** of the condition.

3. A condition such as 2 < n < 5 should never be used, because Visual Basic will not evaluate it as intended. The correct condition is (2 < n) And (n < 5).

4. A common error is to replace the condition Not (2 < 3) by condition (3 > 2). The correct condition is (3 >= 2).

PRACTICE PROBLEMS 5.1

1. Is the condition "Hello " = "Hello" true or false?

2. Complete Table 5.2.

cond1	cond2	cond1 And cond2	cond1 Or cond2	Not cond2
true	true	true		
true	false		true	
false	true			false
false	false			

Table 5.2 Truth values of logical operators.

EXERCISES 5.1

In Exercises 1 through 12, determine whether the condition is true or false. Assume a = 2 and b = 3.

1. $3 * a = 2 * b$

2. $(5 - a) * b < 7$

3. $b <= 3$

4. $a \wedge b = b \wedge a$

5. $a \wedge (5 - 2) > 7$

6. $3E{-}02 < .01 * a$

7. $(a < b)$ Or $(b < a)$

8. $(a * a < b)$ Or Not $(a * a < a)$

9. Not $((a < b)$ And $(a < (b + a)))$

10. Not $(a < b)$ Or Not $(a < (b + a))$

11. $((a = b)$ And $(a * a < b * b))$ Or $((b < a)$ And $(2 * a < b))$

12. $((a = b)$ Or Not $(b < a))$ And $((a < b)$ Or $(b = a + 1))$

In Exercises 13 through 24, determine whether the condition is true or false.

13. "9W" <> "9w"

14. "Inspector" < "gadget"

15. "Car" < "Train"

16. "J" >= "J"

17. "99" > "ninety-nine"

18. "B" > "?"

19. ("Duck" < "pig") And ("pig" < "big")

20. "Duck" < "Duck" + "Duck"

21. Not (("B" = "b") Or ("Big" < "big"))

22. Not ("B" = "b") And Not ("Big" < "big")

23. (("Ant" < "hill") And ("mole" > "hill")) Or Not
(Not ("Ant" < "hill") Or Not ("Mole" > "hill"))

24. (7 < 34) And ("7" > "34")

In Exercises 25 through 34, determine whether or not the two conditions are equivalent, that is, whether they will be true or false for exactly the same values of the variables appearing in them.

25. a <= b; (a < b) Or (a = b)

26. Not (a < b); a > b

27. (a = b) And (a < b); a <> b

28. Not ((a = b) Or (a = c)); (a <> b) And (a <> c)

29. (a < b) And ((a > d) Or (a > e));
((a < b) And (a > d)) Or ((a < b) And (a > e))

30. Not ((a = b + c) Or (a = b)); (a <> b) Or (a <> b + c)

31. (a < b + c) Or (a = b + c); Not ((a > b) Or (a > c))

32. Not (a >= b); (a <= b) Or Not (a = b)

33. Not (a >= b); (a <= b) And Not (a = b)

34. (a = b) And ((b = c) Or (a = c));
(a = b) Or ((b = c) And (a = c))

In Exercises 35 through 39, write a condition equivalent to the negation of the given condition. (For example, a <> b is equivalent to the negation of a = b.)

35. a > b   **36.** (a = b) Or (a = d)

37. (a < b) And (c <> d)   **38.** Not ((a = b) Or (a > b))

39. (a <> "") And (a < b) And (Len(a) < 5)

SOLUTIONS TO PRACTICE PROBLEMS 5.1

1. False. The first string has six characters, whereas the second has five. Two strings must be 100 percent identical to be called equal.

2.

cond1	cond2	cond1 And cond2	cond1 Or cond2	Not cond2
true	true	true	true	false
true	false	false	true	true
false	true	false	true	false
false	false	false	false	true

5.2 IF BLOCKS

An If block allows a program to decide on a course of action based on whether a certain condition is true or false. A block of the form

```
If condition Then
    action1
  Else
    action2
End If
```

causes the program to take *action1* if *condition* is true and *action2* if *condition* is false. Each action consists of one or more Visual Basic statements. After an action is taken, execution continues with the line after the If block. Figure 5.1 contains the pseudocode and flowchart for an If block.

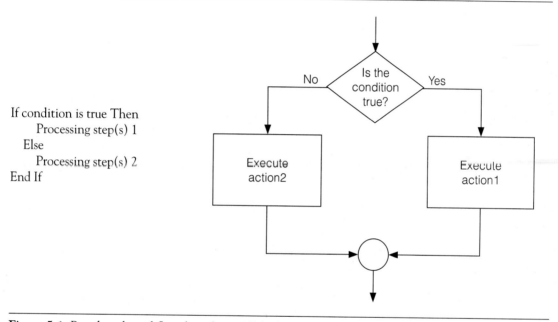

If condition is true Then
    Processing step(s) 1
Else
    Processing step(s) 2
End If

Figure 5.1 Pseudocode and flowchart for an If block.

EXAMPLE 1   Write a program to find the larger of two numbers input by the user.

SOLUTION   In the following program, the condition is Val(txtFirstNum.Text) > Val(txtSecondNum.Text), and each action consists of a single Let statement. With the input 3 and 7, the condition is false and so the second action is taken.

Object	Property	Setting
frmMaximum	Caption	Maximum
lblFirstNum	Caption	First Number
	Alignment	Right Justify
txtFirstNum	Text	(blank)
lblSecondNum	Caption	Second Number
	Alignment	Right Justify
txtSecondNum	Text	(blank)
cmdFindLarger	Caption	Find Larger Number
picResult		

```
Private Sub cmdFindLarger_Click()
  Dim largerNum As Single
  picResult.Cls
  If Val(txtFirstNum.Text) > Val(txtSecondNum.Text) Then
      Let largerNum = Val(txtFirstNum.Text)
    Else
      Let largerNum = Val(txtSecondNum.Text)
  End If
  picResult.Print "The larger number is"; largerNum
End Sub
```

[Run, type 3 and 7 into the text boxes, and press the command button.]

EXAMPLE 2   Write a program that requests the costs and revenue for a company and displays the message "Break even" if the costs and revenue are equal or otherwise displays the profit or loss.

SOLUTION   In the following program, action2 is another If block.

Object	Property	Setting
frm5_2_2	Caption	Profit/Loss
lblCosts	Caption	Costs
	Alignment	Right justify
txtCosts	Text	(blank)
lblRev	Caption	Revenue
	Alignment	Right justify
txtRev	Text	(blank)
cmdShow	Caption	Show financial status
picResult		

```
Private Sub cmdShow_Click()
    Dim costs As Single, revenue As Single, profit As Single, loss As Single
    Let costs = Val(txtCosts.Text)
    Let revenue = Val(txtRev.Text)
    picResult.Cls
    If costs = revenue Then
        picResult.Print "Break even"
      Else
        If costs < revenue Then
            Let profit = revenue - costs
            picResult.Print "Profit is "; Format(profit, "Currency")
          Else
            Let loss = costs - revenue
            picResult.Print "Loss is "; Format(loss, "Currency")
        End If
    End If
End Sub
```

[Run, type 9500 and 8000 into the text boxes, and press the command button.]

EXAMPLE 3 The If block in the following program has a logical operator in its condition.

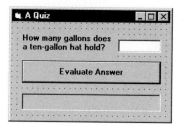

Object	Property	Setting
frmQuiz	Caption	A Quiz
lblQuestion	Caption	How many gallons does a ten-gallon hat hold?
txtAnswer	Text	(blank)
cmdEvaluate	Caption	Evaluate Answer
picSolution		

```
Private Sub cmdEvaluate_Click()
  Dim answer As Single
  Rem Evaluate answer
  picSolution.Cls
  Let answer = Val(txtAnswer.Text)
  If (.5 <= answer) And (answer <= 1) Then
      picSolution.Print "Good, ";
    Else
      picSolution.Print "No, ";
  End If
  picSolution.Print "it holds about 3/4 of a gallon."
End Sub
```

[Run, type 10 into the text box, and press the command button.]

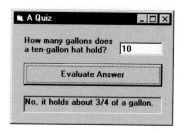

The Else part of an If block can be omitted. In its absence, a false condition causes execution to continue with the statement after the If block. This important type of If block appears in the next example.

EXAMPLE 4   The following program offers assistance to the user before presenting a quotation.

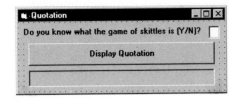

Object	Property	Setting
frm5_2_4	Caption	Quotation
lblQuestion	Caption	Do you know what the game of skittles is (Y/N)?
txtAnswer	Text	(blank)
cmdDisplay	Caption	Display Quotation
picQuotation		

```
Private Sub cmdDisplay_Click()
  Dim message As String
  Let message = "Skittles is an old form of bowling " & _
                "in which a wooden disk is used to " & _
                "knock down nine pins arranged in a square."
  If UCase(txtAnswer.Text) = "N" Then
      MsgBox message, , ""
  End If
  picQuotation.Print "Life ain't all beer and skittles.";
  picQuotation.Print " - Du Maurier (1894)"
End Sub
```

[Run, type N into the text box, and press the command button.]

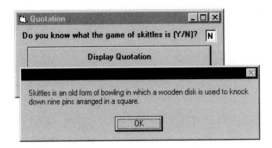

[Press OK.]

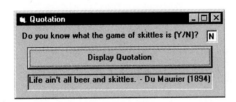

An extension of the If block allows for more than two possible alternatives with the inclusion of ElseIf clauses. A typical block of this type is

```
If condition1 Then
    action1
  ElseIf condition2 Then
    action2
  ElseIf condition3 Then
    action3
  Else
    action4
End If
```

This block searches for the first true condition, carries out its action, and then skips to the statement following End If. If none of the conditions is true, then Else's action is carried out. Execution then continues with the statement following the block. In general, an If block can contain any number of ElseIf clauses. As before, the Else clause is optional.

EXAMPLE 5 Redo Example 1 so that if the two numbers are equal, the program so reports.

SOLUTION
```
Private Sub cmdFindLarger_Click()
    picResult.Cls
    If Val(txtFirstNum.Text) > Val(txtSecondNum.Text) Then
        picResult.Print "The larger number is "; txtFirstNum.Text
      ElseIf Val(txtSecondNum.Text) > Val(txtFirstNum.Text) Then
        picResult.Print "The larger number is "; txtSecondNum.Text
      Else
        picResult.Print "The two numbers are equal."
    End If
End Sub
```

[Run, type 7 into both text boxes, and press the command button.]

If blocks allow us to define functions whose values are not determined by a simple formula. The function in Example 6 uses an If block.

EXAMPLE 6 The Social Security or FICA tax has two components—the Social Security benefits tax, which in 1997 is 6.2 percent on the first $65,400 of earnings for the year, and the Medicare tax, which is 1.45 percent of earnings. Write a program to calculate an employee's FICA tax for a specific paycheck.

SOLUTION

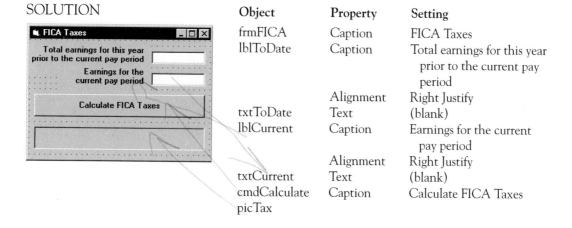

Object	Property	Setting
frmFICA	Caption	FICA Taxes
lblToDate	Caption	Total earnings for this year prior to the current pay period
	Alignment	Right Justify
txtToDate	Text	(blank)
lblCurrent	Caption	Earnings for the current pay period
	Alignment	Right Justify
txtCurrent	Text	(blank)
cmdCalculate	Caption	Calculate FICA Taxes
picTax		

```
Private Sub cmdCalculate_Click()
  Dim FicaTaxes As Single
  Let FicaTaxes = FICA(Val(txtToDate.Text), Val(txtCurrent.Text))
  picTax.Cls
  picTax.Print "Your FICA taxes for the current"
  picTax.Print "pay period are "; Format(FicaTaxes, "Currency")
End Sub

Private Function FICA(ytdEarnings As Single, curEarnings As Single) As Single
  Dim socialSecurityBenTax As Single, medicare As Single
  Rem  Calculate Social Security benefits tax and Medicare tax
  Rem  for a single pay period
  Let socialSecurityBenTax = 0
  If (ytdEarnings + curEarnings) <= 65400 Then
      Let socialSecurityBenTax = .062 * curEarnings
    ElseIf ytdEarnings < 65400 Then
      Let socialSecurityBenTax = .062 * (65400 - ytdEarnings)
  End If
  Let medicare = .0145 * curEarnings
  FICA = socialSecurityBenTax + medicare
End Function
```

[Run, type 12345.67 and 543.21 into the text boxes, and press the command button.]

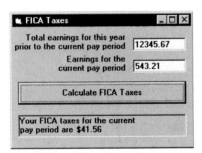

Comments

1. The actions of an If block and the words Else and ElseIf do not have to be indented. For instance, the If block of Example 1 can be written

```
If Val(txtFirstNum.Text) > Val(txtSecondNum.Text) Then
Let largerNum = Val(txtFirstNum.Text)
Else
Let largerNum = Val(txtSecondNum.Text)
End If
```

However, because indenting improves the readability of the block, it is regarded as good programming style. As soon as you see the word If, your eyes can easily scan down the program to find the matching End If and the enclosed Else and ElseIf clauses. You then immediately have a good idea of the size and complexity of the block.

2. Constructs in which an If block is contained inside another If block are referred to as **nested** If blocks.

3. Care should be taken to make If blocks easy to understand. For instance, in Figure 5.2, the block on the left is difficult to follow and should be replaced by the clearer block on the right.

```
If cond1 Then                        If cond1 And cond2 Then
    If cond2 Then                        action
        action                       End If
    End If
End If
```

Figure 5.2 A confusing If block and an improvement.

4. Some programs call for selecting among many possibilities. Although such tasks can be accomplished with complicated nested If blocks, the Select Case block (discussed in the next section) is often a better alternative.

5. In Appendix D, the section "Stepping Through Programs Containing Decision Structures: Chapter 5" uses the Visual Basic debugging tools to trace the flow through an If block.

6. Visual Basic also has a single-line If statement of the form

```
If condition Then action1 Else action2
```

which is a holdover from earlier, unstructured versions of BASIC; it is seldom used in this text.

PRACTICE PROBLEMS 5.2

1. Suppose the user is asked to input a number into txtNumber for which the square root is to be taken. Fill in the If block so that the lines of code below either will display the message "Number can't be negative" or will display the square root of the number.

```
Private Sub cmdTakeSquareRoot_Click()
  Dim num As Single
  Rem Check reasonableness of data
  Let num = Val(txtNumber.Text)
  If

  End If
End Sub
```

2. Improve the block

```
If a < b Then
    If c < 5 Then
        picBox.Print "hello"
    End If
End If
```

EXERCISES 5.2

In Exercises 1 through 12, determine the output displayed in the picture box when the command button is clicked.

1.
```
Private Sub cmdDisplay_Click()
    Dim num As Single
    Let num = 4
    If num <= 9 Then
        picOutput.Print "Less than ten"
      Else
        If num = 4 Then
            picOutput.Print "Equal to four"
        End If
    End If
End Sub
```

2.
```
Private Sub cmdDisplay_Click()
    Dim gpa As Single
    Let gpa = 3.49
    If gpa >= 3.5 Then
        picOutput.Print "Honors ";
    End If
    picOutput.Print "Student"
End Sub
```

3.
```
Private Sub cmdDisplay_Click()
    Dim a As Single
    Let a = 5
    If 3 * a - 4 < 9 Then
        picOutput.Print "Remember, "
    End If
    picOutput.Print "Tomorrow is another day."
End Sub
```

4.
```
Private Sub cmdDisplay_Click()
    Dim change As Single
    Let change = 356          'Amount of change in cents
    If change >= 100 Then
        picOutput.Print "Your change contains";
        picOutput.Print Int(change / 100); "dollars."
      Else
        picOutput.Print "Your change contains no dollars."
    End If
End Sub
```

5.
```
Private Sub cmdDisplay_Click()
    Dim a As Single, b As Single, c As Single
    Let a = 2
    Let b = 3
    Let c = 5
    If a * b < c Then
        Let b = 7
```

```
      Else
         Let b = c * a
      End If
      picOutput.Print b
   End Sub
```

6.
```
Private Sub cmdDisplay_Click()
   Dim a As Single, b As Single
   Let a = Val(InputBox("Enter a number."))
   Let b = Val(InputBox("Enter another number."))
   If a > b Then
      Let a = a + 1
    Else
      Let b = b + 1
   End If
   picOutput.Print a; b
End Sub
```

(Assume that the responses are *7, 11*.)

7.
```
Private Sub cmdDisplay_Click()
   Dim length As Single
   Rem Cost of phone call from NY to LA
   Call InputLength(length)
   Call DisplayCost(length)
End Sub

Private Function Cost(length As Single) As Single
  If length < 1 Then
     Cost = .46
    Else
     Cost = .46 + (length - 1) * .36
  End If
End Function

Private Sub DisplayCost(length As Single)
  Rem Display the cost of a call
  picOutput.Print "Cost of call: "; Format(Cost(length), "Currency")
End Sub

Private Sub InputLength(length As Single)
  Rem Request the length of a phone call
  Let length = Val(InputBox("Duration of the call in minutes?"))
End Sub
```

(Assume that the response is *31*.)

8.
```
Private Sub cmdDisplay_Click()
    Dim letter As String
    Let letter = InputBox("Enter A, B, or C.")
    If letter = "A" Then
        Call DisplayAmessage
      ElseIf letter = "B" Then
        Call DisplayBmessage
      ElseIf letter = "C" Then
        Call DisplayCmessage
      Else
        picOutput.Print "Not a valid letter"
    End If
End Sub

Private Sub DisplayAmessage()
  picOutput.Print "A, my name is Alice."
End Sub

Private Sub DisplayBmessage()
  picOutput.Print "To be or not to be."
End Sub

Private Sub DisplayCmessage()
  picOutput.Print "Oh, say can you see."
End Sub
```

(Assume that the response is B.)

9.
```
Private Sub cmdDisplay_Click()
    Dim vowels As Integer
    Let vowels = 0      'Number of vowels
    Call ExamineLetter(vowels)
    Call ExamineLetter(vowels)
    Call ExamineLetter(vowels)
    picOutput.Print "The number of vowels is"; vowels
End Sub

Private Sub ExamineLetter(vowels As Integer)
  Dim ltr As String
  Let ltr = InputBox("Enter a letter.")
  Let ltr = UCase(ltr)
  If ltr = "A" Or ltr = "E" Or ltr = "I" Or ltr = "O" Or ltr = "U" Then
      Let vowels = vowels + 1
  End If
End Sub
```

(Assume that the three responses are U, b, and a.)

10.
```
Private Sub cmdDisplay_Click()
    Dim a As Single
    Let a = 5
    If (a > 2) And (a = 3 Or a < 7) Then
        picOutput.Print "Hi"
    End If
End Sub
```

11.
```
Private Sub cmdDisplay_Click()
    Dim num As Single
    Let num = 5
    If num < 0 Then
        picOutput.Print "neg"
      Else
        If num = 0 Then
            picOutput.Print "zero"
          Else
            picOutput.Print "positive"
        End If
    End If
End Sub
```

12.
```
Private Sub cmdDisplay_Click()
    Dim msg As String, age As Integer
    Let msg = "You are eligible to vote"
    Let age = Val(InputBox("Enter your age."))
    If age >= 18 Then
        picOutput.Print msg
      Else
        picOutput.Print msg & " in"; 18 - age; "years"
    End If
End Sub
```

(Assume that the response is *16*.)

In Exercises 13 through 20, identify the errors.

13.
```
Private Sub cmdDisplay_Click()
    Dim num As Single
    Let num = .5
    If 1 < num < 3 Then
        picOutput.Print "Number is between 1 and 3."
    End If
End Sub
```

14.
```
Private Sub cmdDisplay_Click()
    Dim num As Single
    Let num = 6
    If num > 5 And < 9 Then
        picOutput.Print "Yes"
      Else
        picOutput.Print "No"
    End If
End Sub
```

15.
```
Private Sub cmdDisplay_Click()
    If 2 <> 3
        picOutput.Print "Numbers are not equal"
    End If
End Sub
```

16.
```
Private Sub cmdDisplay_Click()
    Dim major As String
    If major = "Business" Or "Computer Science" Then
        picOutput.Print "Yes"
    End If
End Sub
```

17.
```
Private Sub cmdDisplay_Click()
    Dim numName As String, num As Single
    Let numName = "Seven"
    Let num = Val(InputBox("Enter a number."))
    If num < numName Then
        picOutput.Print "Less than"
      Else
        picOutput.Print "Greater than"
    End If
End Sub
```

18.
```
Private Sub cmdDisplay_Click()
    Dim switch As String
    Rem Change switch from "on" to "off", or from "off" to "on"
    Let switch = InputBox("Enter on or off.")
    If switch = "off" Then
        Let switch = "on"
    End If
    If switch = "on" Then
        Let switch = "off"
    End If
End Sub
```

19.
```
Private Sub cmdDisplay_Click()
    Dim j As Single, k As Single
    Rem Display "OK" if either j or k equals 4
    Let j = 2
    Let k = 3
    If j Or k = 4 Then
        picOutput.Print "OK"
    End If
End Sub
```

20.
```
Private Sub cmdDisplay_Click()
    Dim query As String, answer1 As String, answer2 As String
    Rem Is your program correct?
    Let query = "Are you certain everything in your program is correct?"
    Let answer1 = InputBox(query)
    Let answer1 = UCase(Left(answer1, 1))
    If answer1 = "N" Then
        picOutput.Print "Don't patch bad code, rewrite it."
      Else
        Let query = "Does your program run correctly"
        Let answer2 = InputBox(query)
        Let answer2 = UCase(Left(answer2, 1))
```

```
        If answer2 = "Y" Then
            picOutput.Print "Congratulations"
          Else
            picOutput.Print "One of the things you are certain"
            picOutput.Print "about is wrong."
        End If
    End Sub
```

In Exercises 21 through 26, simplify the code.

21.
```
If a = 2 Then
    Let a = 3 + a
  Else
    Let a = 5
End If
```

22.
```
If Not (answer <> "y") Then
    picOutput.Print "YES"
  Else
    If (answer = "y") Or (answer = "Y") Then
        picOutput.Print "YES"
    End If
End If
```

23.
```
If j = 7 Then
    Let b = 1
  Else
    If j <> 7 Then
        Let b = 2
    End If
End If
```

24.
```
If a < b Then
    If b < c Then
        picOutput.Print b; "is between"; a; "and"; c
    End If
End If
```

25.
```
Let message = "Is Alaska bigger than Texas and California combined?"
Let answer = InputBox(message)
If Left(answer, 1) = "Y" Then
    Let answer = "YES"
End If
If Left(answer, 1) = "y" Then
    Let answer = "YES"
End If
If answer = "YES" Then
    picOutput.Print "Correct"
  Else
    picOutput.Print "Wrong"
End If
```

26.
```
Let message = "How tall (in feet) is the Statue of Liberty?"
Let feet = Val(InputBox(message))
If feet <= 141 Then
    picOutput.Print "Nope"
End If
If feet > 141 Then
    If feet < 161 Then
        picOutput.Print "Close"
      Else
        picOutput.Print "Nope"
    End If
End If
picOutput.Print "The Statue of Liberty is 151.08 feet"
picOutput.Print "from base to torch."
```

27. Write a program to determine how much to tip the waiter in a fine restaurant. The tip should be 15 percent of the check, with a minimum of $1.

28. Write a quiz program to ask "Who was the first Ronald McDonald?" The program should display "Correct" if the answer is Willard Scott and otherwise should display "Nice try."

29. A computer store sells diskettes at $1 each for small orders or at 70 cents apiece for orders of 25 diskettes or more. Write a program that requests the number of diskettes ordered and displays the total cost. (Test the program for purchases of 5, 25, and 35 diskettes.)

30. A copying center charges 5 cents per copy for the first 100 copies and 3 cents per copy for each additional copy. Write a program that requests the number of copies as input and displays the total cost. (Test the program with the quantities 25 and 125.)

31. Write a txtBox_KeyPress event procedure that allows the user to type only digits into the text box.

32. Suppose a program has a command button with the caption "Quit." Suppose also that the Name property of this command button is cmdQuit. Write a cmdQuit_Click event procedure that gives the user a second chance before ending the program. The procedure should use an input box to request that the user confirm that the program should be terminated, and then only end the program if the user responds in the affirmative.

33. Write a program to handle a savings account withdrawal. The program should request the current balance and the amount of the withdrawal as input and then display the new balance. If the withdrawal is greater than the original balance, the program should display "Withdrawal denied." If the new balance is less than $150, the message "Balance below $150" should be displayed.

34. Write a program that requests three scores as input and displays the average of the two highest scores. The input and output should be handled by subprograms and the average should be determined by a function.

35. A lottery drawing produces three digits. Write a program that uses Rnd to generate three digits and then displays "Lucky seven" if two or more of the digits are 7.

36. Federal law requires hourly employees be paid "time-and-a-half" for work in excess of 40 hours in a week. For example, if a person's hourly wage is $8 and he works 60 hours in a week, his gross pay should be

$$(40 \times 8) + (1.5 \times 8 \times (60 - 40)) = \$560.$$

Write a program that requests as input the number of hours a person works in a given week and his hourly wage, and then displays his gross pay.

37. Write a program that requests a word (with lowercase letters) as input and translates the word into pig latin. The rules for translating a word into pig latin are as follows:

(a) If the word begins with a consonant, move the first letter to the end of the word and add *ay*. For instance, *chip* becomes *hipcay*.

(b) If the word begins with a vowel, add *way* to the end of the word. For instance, *else* becomes *elseway*.

38. The current calendar, called the Gregorian calendar, was introduced in 1582. Every year divisible by 4 was declared to be a leap year with the exception of the years ending in 00 (that is, those divisible by 100) and not divisible by 400. For instance, the years 1600 and 2000 are leap years, but 1700, 1800, and 1900 are not. Write a program that requests a year as input and states whether or not it is a leap year. (Test the program on the years 1994, 1995, 1900, and 2000.)

39. Create a form with a picture box and two command buttons captioned Bogart and Raines. When Bogart is first pressed, the sentence "I came to Casablanca for the waters." is displayed in the picture box. The next time Bogart is pressed, the sentence "I was misinformed." is displayed. When Raines is pressed, the sentence "But we're in the middle of the desert." is displayed. Run the program and then press Bogart, Raines, Bogart to obtain a dialogue.

40. Write a program that allows the user to use one command button to toggle the appearance of the text in a text box between bold and italics and use another pair of command buttons to increase or decrease the size of the text to the next available point size. (Point sizes available in the default MS Sans Serif font are 8, 10, 12, 14, 18, and 24.)

41. Write a program that allows the user 10 tries to answer the question "Which U.S. President was born on July 4?" After three incorrect guesses, the program should pop-up the hint, "He once said, 'If you don't say anything, you won't be called upon to repeat it.' " in a message box. After seven incorrect guesses, the program should give the hint, "His nickname was 'Silent Cal.' " The number of guesses should be displayed in a label. **Note:** Calvin Coolidge was born on July 4, 1872.

42. Write a program that reads a test score from a text box each time a command button is clicked and then displays the two highest scores whenever a second command button is clicked. Use two form-level variables to track the two highest scores.

43. The flowchart in Figure 5.3 calculates New Jersey state income tax. Write a program corresponding to the flowchart. (Test the program with taxable incomes of $15,000, $30,000, and $60,000.)

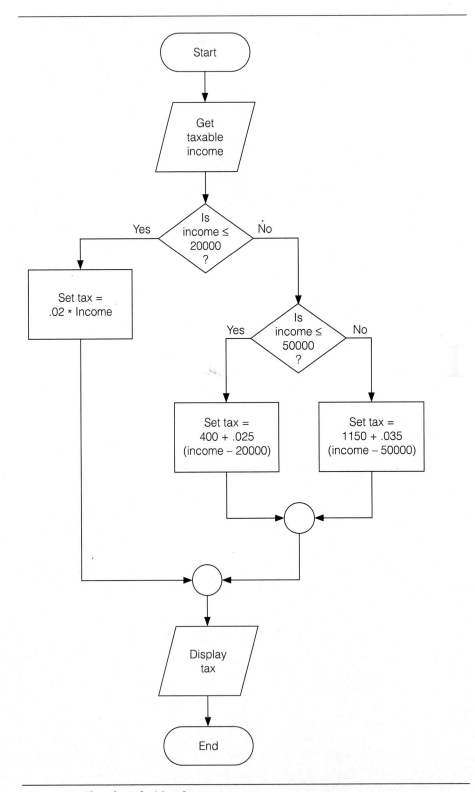

Figure 5.3 Flowchart for New Jersey state income tax program.

44. Write a program to play "Hide and Seek" with this picture of the treetops (in the file Trees.bmp in the Pictures folder of the CD accompanying this book) or with any other picture of your choosing. When the command button is pressed, the picture should disappear and the caption on the button should change to Show Picture. The next time the button is pressed, the picture should reappear and the caption revert to Hide Picture, and so on. (**Note:** This picture shows the autumn view from the author's office.)

Object	Property	Setting
frmHide	Caption	Hide and Seek
picTrees	Picture	Trees.bmp
cmdButton	Caption	Hide Picture

SOLUTIONS TO PRACTICE PROBLEMS 5.2

1.
```
If num < 0 Then
    MsgBox "Number can't be negative.", , "Input Error"
    txtNumber.Text = ""
    txtNumber.SetFocus
  Else
    picSquareRoot.Print Sqr(num)
End If
```

2. The Print method will be executed when a < b is true and c < 5 is also true. That is, it will be executed when both of these two conditions are true. The clearest way to write the block is

```
If (a < b) And (c < 5) Then
    picBox.Print "hello"
End If
```

5.3 SELECT CASE BLOCKS

A Select Case block is an efficient decision-making structure that simplifies choosing among several actions. It avoids complex nested If constructs. If blocks make decisions based on the truth value of a condition; Select Case choices are determined by the value of an expression called a **selector**. Each of the possible actions is preceded by a statement of the form

```
Case valueList
```

where *valueList* itemizes the values of the selector for which the action should be taken.

EXAMPLE 1   The following program converts the finishing position in a horse race into a descriptive phrase. After the variable *position* is assigned a value from txtPosition, the computer searches for the first Case statement whose value list contains that value and executes the succeeding statement. If the value of *position* is greater than 5, then the statement following Case Else is executed.

Object	Property	Setting
frmRace	Caption	Horse Race
lblPosition	Caption	Finishing position (1, 2, 3, . . .)
txtPosition	Text	(blank)
cmdDescribe	Caption	Describe Position
picOutcome		

```
Private Sub cmdDescribe_Click()
  Dim position As Integer
  Let position = Val(txtPosition.Text)
  picOutcome.Cls
  Select Case position
    Case 1
      picOutcome.Print "Win"
    Case 2
      picOutcome.Print "Place"
    Case 3
      picOutcome.Print "Show"
    Case 4, 5
      picOutcome.Print "You almost placed"
      picOutcome.Print "in the money."
    Case Else
      picOutcome.Print "Out of the money."
    End Select
End Sub
```

[Run, type 2 into the text box, and press the command button.]

EXAMPLE 2   In the following variation of Example 1, the value lists specify ranges of values. The first value list provides another way to specify the numbers 1, 2, and 3. The second value list covers all numbers from 4 on.

```
Private Sub cmdDescribe_Click()
  Dim position As Integer
  Rem Describe finishing positions in a horse race
  picOutcome.Cls
  Let position = Val(txtPosition.Text)
```

```
    Select Case position
      Case 1 To 3
        picOutcome.Print "In the money."
        picOutcome.Print "Congratulations"
      Case Is > 3
        picOutcome.Print "Not in the money."
    End Select
End Sub
```

[Run, type 2 into the text box, and press the command button.]

The general form of the Select Case block is

```
Select Case selector
  Case valueList1
    action1
  Case valueList2
    action2
      .
      .
  Case Else
    action of last resort
End Select
```

where Case Else (and its action) is optional, and each value list contains one or more of the following types of items separated by commas:

1. a constant

2. a variable

3. an expression

4. an inequality sign preceded by Is and followed by a constant, variable, or expression

5. a range expressed in the form *a* To *b*, where *a* and *b* are constants, variables, or expressions.

Different items appearing in the same list must be separated by commas. Each action consists of one or more statements. After the selector is evaluated, the computer looks for the first value list item containing the value of the selector and carries out its associated action. Figure 5.4 contains the flowchart for a Select Case block. The pseudocode for a Select Case block is the same as for the equivalent If block.

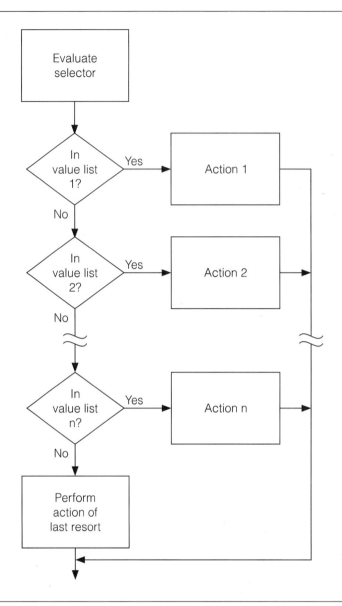

Figure 5.4 Flowchart for a Select Case block.

EXAMPLE 3 The following program illustrates several different types of value lists. With the response shown, the first action was selected because the value of y − x is 1.

Object	Property	Setting
frm5_3_3	Caption	One, Two, Buckle My Shoe
lblEnterNum	Caption	Enter a number from 1 to 10
txtNumber	Text	(blank)
cmdInterpret	Caption	Interpret Number
picPhrase		

```
Private Sub cmdInterpret_Click()
  Dim x As Integer, y As Integer, num As Integer
  Rem One, Two, Buckle My Shoe
  picPhrase.Cls
  Let x = 2
  Let y = 3
  Let num = Val(txtNumber.Text)
  Select Case num
    Case y - x, x
      picPhrase.Print "Buckle my shoe."
    Case Is <= 4
      picPhrase.Print "Shut the door."
    Case x + y To x * y
      picPhrase.Print "Pick up sticks."
    Case 7, 8
      picPhrase.Print "Lay them straight."
    Case Else
      picPhrase.Print "Start all over again."
  End Select
End Sub
```

[Run, type 4 into the text box, and press the command button.]

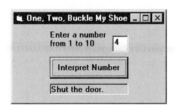

In each of the three preceding examples, the selector was a numeric variable; however, the selector also can be a string variable or an expression.

EXAMPLE 4   The following program has the string variable *firstName* as a selector.

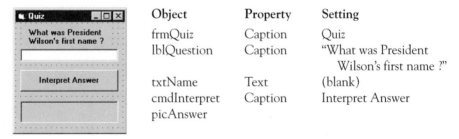

Object	Property	Setting
frmQuiz	Caption	Quiz
lblQuestion	Caption	"What was President Wilson's first name ?"
txtName	Text	(blank)
cmdInterpret	Caption	Interpret Answer
picAnswer		

```
Private Sub cmdInterpret_Click()
  Dim firstName As String
  Rem Quiz
  picAnswer.Cls
  Let firstName = txtName.Text
  Select Case firstName
    Case "Thomas"
      picAnswer.Print "Correct."
```

```
      Case "Woodrow"
        picAnswer.Print "Sorry, his full name was"
        picAnswer.Print "Thomas Woodrow Wilson."
      Case "President"
        picAnswer.Print "Are you for real?"
      Case Else
        picAnswer.Print "Nice try, but no cigar."
    End Select
End Sub
```

[Run, type Woodrow into the text box, and press the command button.]

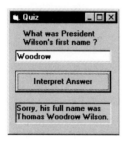

EXAMPLE 5 The following program has the selector Left(anyString, 1), a string expression. In the sample run, only the first action was carried out even though the value of the selector was in both of the first two value lists. The computer stops looking as soon as it finds the value of the selector.

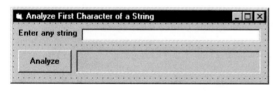

Object	Property	Setting
frm5_3_5	Caption	Analyze First Character of a String
lblEnter	Caption	Enter any string
txtString	Text	(blank)
cmdAnalyze	Caption	Analyze
picResult		

```
Private Sub cmdAnalyze_Click()
  Dim anyString As String
  Rem Analyze the first character of a string
  picResult.Cls
  Let anyString = UCase(txtString.Text)
  Select Case Left(anyString, 1)
    Case "S", "Z"
      picResult.Print "The string begins with a sibilant."
    Case "A" To "Z"
      picResult.Print "The string begins with a nonsibilant."
    Case "0" To "9"
      picResult.Print "The string begins with a digit."
    Case Is < "0"
      picResult.Print "The string begins with a character of ANSI"
      picResult.Print " value less than 48 (e.g. +, &, #, or %)."
    Case Else
      picResult.Print "The string begins with one of the following:"
      picResult.Print "      : ; < = > ? @ [ \ ] ^ _ `"
  End Select
End Sub
```

[Run, type Sunday into the text box, and press the command button.]

EXAMPLE 6 The color of the beacon light atop Boston's John Hancock Building forecasts the weather according to the following rhyme. Write a program that requests a color (blue or red) and a mode (steady or flashing) as input and displays the weather forecast. The program should contain a Select Case block with a string variable as selector.

Steady blue, clear view.
Flashing blue, clouds due.
Steady red, rain ahead.
Flashing red, snow instead.

SOLUTION

Object	Property	Setting
frmWeather	Caption	Weather Beacon
lblColor	Caption	Color of the light
txtColor	Text	(blank)
lblMode	Caption	Mode (S or F)
txtMode	Text	(blank)
cmdInterpret	Caption	Interpret Beacon
picForecast		

```
Private Sub cmdInterpret_Click()
  Dim color As String, mode As String
  Rem Interpret a weather beacon
  picForecast.Cls
  Let color = txtColor.Text
  Let mode = txtMode.Text
  Select Case UCase(mode) & UCase(color)
    Case "SBLUE"
      picForecast.Print "CLEAR VIEW"
    Case "FBLUE"
      picForecast.Print "CLOUDS DUE"
    Case "SRED"
      picForecast.Print "RAIN AHEAD"
    Case "FRED"
      picForecast.Print "SNOW AHEAD"
  End Select
End Sub
```

[Run, type red and S into the text boxes, and press the command button.]

EXAMPLE 7   Select Case is useful in defining functions that are not determined by a formula. The following program assumes the current year is not a leap year.

Object	Property	Setting
frm5_3_7	Caption	Seasons
lblSeason	Caption	Season
txtSeason	Text	(blank)
cmdNumber	Caption	Number of Days
picNumDays		

```
Private Sub cmdNumber_Click()
  Dim season As String
  Rem Determine the number of days in a season
  picNumDays.Cls
  Let season = txtSeason.Text
  picNumDays.Print season; " has"; NumDays(season); "days."
End Sub

Private Function NumDays(season As String) As Integer
  Rem Look up the number of days in a given season
  Select Case UCase(season)
    Case "WINTER"
      NumDays = 87
    Case "SPRING"
      NumDays = 92
    Case "SUMMER", "AUTUMN", "FALL"
      NumDays = 93
  End Select
End Function
```

[Run, type Summer into the text box, and press the command button.]

Comments

1. Some programming languages do not allow a value to appear in two different value lists; Visual Basic does. If a value appears in two different value lists, the action after the first value list will be carried out.

2. In Visual Basic, if the value of the selector does not appear in any of the value lists and there is no Case Else clause, execution of the program will continue with the statement following the Select Case block.

3. The Case statements and their actions do not have to be indented; however, because indenting improves the readability of the block, it is regarded as good programming style. As soon as you see the words Select Case, your eyes

can easily scan down the block to find the matching End Select statement. You immediately know the number of different cases under consideration.

4. The items in the value list must evaluate to a constant of the same type, string or numeric, as the selector. For instance, if the selector evaluates to a string value, as in

```
Dim firstName As String
Let firstName = txtBox.Text
Select Case firstName
```

then the clause

```
Case Len(firstName)
```

would be meaningless.

5. If the word Is, which should precede an inequality sign in a value list, is accidentally omitted, the smart editor will automatically insert it when checking the line.

6. A Case clause of the form Case b To c selects values from *b* to *c* inclusive. However, the extreme values can be excluded by placing the action inside an If block beginning with If (*selector* <> b) And (*selector* <> c) Then.

7. The value of *b* must be less than or equal to the value of *c* in a Case clause of the form Case b To c.

8. Every Select Case block can be replaced by an If block. Select Case is preferable to an If block when the possible choices have more or less the same importance.

9. In Appendix D, the section "Stepping Through Programs Containing Selection Structures: Chapter 5" uses the Visual Basic debugging tools to trace the flow through a Select Case block.

PRACTICE PROBLEMS 5.3

1. Suppose the selector of a Select Case block is the numeric variable *num*. Determine whether each of the following Case clauses is valid.

(a) `Case 1, 4, Is < 10`

(b) `Case Is < 5, Is >= 5`

(c) `Case "2"`

2. Do the following two programs always produce the same output for a whole number grade from 0 to 100?

```
Let grade = Val(txtBox.Text)
Select Case grade
  Case Is >= 90
    picOutput.Print "A"
  Case Is >= 60
    picOutput.Print "Pass"
  Case Else
    picOutput.Print "Fail"
End Select
```

```
Let grade = Val(txtBox.Text)
Select Case grade
  Case Is >= 90
    picOutput.Print "A"
  Case 60 To 89
    picOutput.Print "Pass"
  Case 0 To 59
    picOutput.Print "Fail"
End Select
```

EXERCISES 5.3

In Exercises 1 through 8, for each of the responses shown in the parentheses, determine the output displayed in the picture box when the command button is clicked.

1.
```
Private Sub cmdDisplay_Click()
  Dim age As Single
  Let age = Val(InputBox("What is your age?"))
  Select Case age
    Case Is < 6
      Let price = 0
    Case 6 To 17
      Let price = 3.75
    Case Is >= 17
      Let price = 5
  End Select
  picOutput.Print "The price is "; Format(price, "Currency")
End Sub
```

(8.5, 17)

2.
```
Private Sub cmdDisplay_Click()
  Dim n As Single
  Let n = Val(InputBox("Enter a number from 5 to 12"))
  Select Case n
    Case 5
      picOutput.Print "case 1"
    Case 5 To 7
      picOutput.Print "case 2"
    Case 7 To 12
      picOutput.Print "case 3"
  End Select
End Sub
```

(7, 5, 11.2)

3.
```
Private Sub cmdDisplay_Click()
  Dim age As Integer
  Let age = Val(InputBox("Enter age (in millions of years)"))
  Select Case age
    Case Is < 70
      picOutput.Print "Cenozoic Era"
    Case Is < 225
      picOutput.Print "Mesozoic Era"
    Case Is <= 600
      picOutput.Print "Paleozoic Era"
    Case Else
      picOutput.Print "?"
  End Select
End Sub
```

(100, 600, 700)

4.
```
Private Sub cmdDisplay_Click()
    Dim yearENIAC As Integer
    Call AskQuestion(yearENIAC)
    Call ProcessAnswer(yearENIAC)
End Sub

Private Sub AskQuestion(yearENIAC As Integer)
    Dim message As String
    Rem Ask question and obtain answer
    Let message = "In what year was the ENIAC computer completed?"
    Let yearENIAC = Val(InputBox(message))
End Sub

Private Sub ProcessAnswer(yearENIAC As Integer)
    Rem Respond to answer
    Select Case yearENIAC
        Case 1945
            picOutput.Print "Correct"
        Case 1943 To 1947
            picOutput.Print "Close, 1945."
        Case Is < 1943
            picOutput.Print "Sorry, 1945. Work on the ENIAC began ";
            picOutput.Print "in June 1943."
        Case Is > 1947
            picOutput.Print "No, 1945. By then IBM had built a stored-program ";
            picOutput.Print "computer."
    End Select
End Sub
```

(1940, 1945, 1950)

5.
```
Private Sub cmdDisplay_Click()
    Dim nom As String
    Let nom = InputBox("Who developed the stored program concept")
    Select Case UCase(nom)
        Case "JOHN VON NEUMANN", "VON NEUMANN"
            picOutput.Print "Correct"
        Case "JOHN MAUCHLY", "MAUCHLY", "J. PRESPER ECKERT", "ECKERT"
            picOutput.Print "He worked with the developer, von Neumann, on the ENIAC."
        Case Else
            picOutput.Print "Nope"
    End Select
End Sub
```

(Grace Hopper, Eckert, John von Neumann)

6.
```
Private Sub cmdDisplay_Click()
    Dim message As String, a As Single, b As Single, c As Single
    Let message = "Analyzing solutions to the quadratic equation "
    Let message = message & "A*X^2 + B*X + C = 0.  Enter the value for "
    Let a = Val(InputBox(message & "A"))
    Let b = Val(InputBox(message & "B"))
    Let c = Val(InputBox(message & "C"))
```

```
      Select Case b * b - 4 * a * c
        Case Is < 0
          picOutput.Print "The equation has no real solutions."
        Case Is 0
          picOutput.Print "The equation has exactly one solution."
        Case Is > 0
          picOutput.Print "The equation has two solutions."
      End Select
    End Sub
```

$(1,2,3; 1,5,1; 1,2,1)$

7.
```
Private Sub cmdDisplay_Click()
    Dim num1 As Single, word As String, num2 As Single
    Rem State a quotation
    Let num1 = 3
    Let word = "hello"
    Let num2 = Val(InputBox("Enter a number"))
    Select Case 2 * num2 - 1
      Case num1 * num1
        picOutput.Print "Less is more."
      Case Is > Len(word)
        picOutput.Print "Time keeps everything from happening at once."
      Case Else
        picOutput.Print "The less things change, the more they remain the same."
    End Select
End Sub
```

$(2, 5, 6)$

8.
```
Private Sub cmdDisplay_Click()
    Dim whatever As Single
    Let whatever = Val(InputBox("Enter a number"))
    Select Case whatever
      Case Else
        picOutput.Print "Hi"
    End Select
End Sub
```

$(7, -1)$

In Exercises 9 through 16, identify the errors.

9.
```
Private Sub cmdDisplay_Click()
    Dim num As Single
    Let num = 2
    Select Case num
      picOutput.Print "Two"
    End Select
End Sub
```

10.
```
Private Sub cmdDisplay_Click()
    Dim num1 As Single, num2 As Single
    Let num1 = 5
    Let num2 = 7
    Select Case num1
      Case 3 <= num1 <= 10
        picOutput.Print "Between 3 and 10"
      Case num2 To 5; 4
        picOutput.Print "Near 5"
    End Select
End Sub
```

11.
```
Private Sub cmdDisplay_Click()
    Dim a As String
    Let a = "12BMS"
    Select Case a
      Case 0 To 9
        picOutput.Print "Begins with a digit"
      Case Else
    End Select
End Sub
```

12.
```
Private Sub cmdDisplay_Click()
    Dim word As String
    Let word = "hello"
    Select Case Left(word, 1)
      Case h
        picOutput.Print "Begins with h"
    End Select
End Sub
```

13.
```
Private Sub cmdDisplay_Click()
    Dim word As String
    Let word = InputBox("Enter a word from the United States motto")
    Select Case UCase(word)
      Case "E"
        picOutput.Print "This is the first word of the motto."
      Case Left(word, 1) = "P"
        picOutput.Print "The second word is PLURIBUS."
      Case Else
        picOutput.Print "The third word is UNUM."
    End Select
End Sub
```

14.
```
Private Sub cmdDisplay_Click()
    Dim num As Single
    Let num = 5
    Select Case num
      Case 5, Is <> 5
        picOutput.Print "Five"
      Case Is > 5
        picOutput.Print "Greater than 5"
End Sub
```

15.
```
Private Sub cmdDisplay_Click()
    Dim a As Single
    Let a = 3
    Select Case a
      Case a < 5
        Print "Less than five"
      Case a >= 5
        Print "Not less than five"
    End Select
End Sub
```

16.
```
Private Sub cmdDisplay_Click()
    Dim purchase As Single
    Let purchase = Val(InputBox("Quantity purchased?"))
    Select Case purchase
      Case Is < 10000
        picOutput.Print "Five dollars per item."
      Case Is 10000 To 30000
        picOutput.Print "Four dollars per item."
      Case Is > 30000
        picOutput.Print "Three dollars per item."
    End Select
End Sub
```

In Exercises 17 through 22, suppose the selector of a Select Case block, *word,*
evaluates to a string value. Determine whether the Case clause is valid.

17. `Case "un" & "til"`

18. `Case "hello", Is < "goodbye"`

19. `Case 0 To 9`

20. `Case word <> "No"`

21. `Case Left("abc", 1)`

22. `Case word Then`

In Exercises 23 through 26, rewrite the code using a Select Case block.

23.
```
If a = 1 Then
    picOutput.Print "one"
Else
    If a > 5 Then
        picOutput.Print "two"
    End If
End If
```

24.
```
If a = 1 Then
    picOutput.Print "lambs"
End If
If a <= 3 And a < 4 Then
    picOutput.Print "eat"
End If
If a = 5 Or a > 7 Then
    picOutput.Print "ivy"
End If
```

25.
```
If a < 5 Then
    If a = 2 Then
        picOutput.Print "yes"
    Else
        picOutput.Print "no"
    End If
Else
    If a = 2 Then
        picOutput.Print "maybe"
    End If
End If
```

26.
```
If a = 3 Then
    Let a = 1
End If
If a = 2 Then
    Let a = 3
End If
If a = 1 Then
    Let a = 2
End If
```

27. Table 5.3 gives the terms used by the National Weather Service to describe
the degree of cloudiness. Write a program that requests the percentage of
cloud cover as input and then displays the appropriate descriptor.

Percentage of Cloud Cover	Descriptor
0–30	clear
31–70	partly cloudy
71–99	cloudy
100	overcast

Table 5.3 Cloudiness descriptors.

28. Table 5.4 shows the location of books in the library stacks according to their call numbers. Write a program that requests the call number of a book as input and displays the location of the book.

Call Numbers	Location
100 to 199	basement
200 to 500 and over 900	main floor
501 to 900 except 700 to 750	upper floor
700 to 750	archives

Table 5.4 Location of library books.

29. Write an interactive program that requests a month of the year and then gives the number of days in the month. If the response is February, the user should be asked whether or not the current year is a leap year. The first request should be made in a subprogram and the computation should be carried out in a function.

30. Figure 5.5 shows some geometric shapes and formulas for their areas. Write a program that requests the user to select one of the shapes, requests the appropriate lengths, and then gives the area of the figure. Input and output should be handled by subprograms, and the areas should be computed by functions.

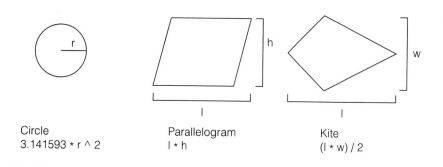

Circle
3.141593 * r ^ 2

Parallelogram
l * h

Kite
(l * w) / 2

Figure 5.5 Areas of geometric shapes.

31. Write an interactive program that requests an exam score and assigns a letter grade with the scale 90–100 (A), 80–89 (B), 70–79 (C), 60–69 (D), 0–59 (F). The input should be accomplished by a subprogram and the computation carried out in a function. (Test the program with the grades 84, 100, and 57.)

32. (Computerized quiz show.) Write a program that asks the contestant to select one of the numbers 1, 2, or 3 and then calls a subprogram that asks the question and requests the answer. The program should then tell the contestant if the answer is correct. Use the following three questions:

1. Who was the only living artist to have his work displayed in the Grand Gallery of the Louvre?
2. Who said "Computers are useless. They can only give you answers."?
3. By what name is Pablo Blasio better known?

Note: These questions have the same answer, Pablo Picasso.

33. IRS informants are paid cash awards based on the value of the money recovered. If the information was specific enough to lead to a recovery, the informant receives 10 percent of the first $75,000, 5 percent of the next $25,000, and 1 percent of the remainder, up to a maximum award of $50,000. Write a program that requests the amount of the recovery as input and displays the award. (Test the program on the amounts $10,000, $125,000, and $10,000,000.) (**Note:** The source of this formula is *The Book of Inside Information*, Boardroom Books, 1993.)

34. Table 5.5 contains information on several states. Write a program that requests a state and category (flower, motto, and nickname) as input and displays the requested information. If the state or category requested is not in the table, the program should so inform the user.

State	Flower	Nickname	Motto
California	Golden poppy	Golden State	Eureka
Indiana	Peony	Hoosier State	Crossroads of America
Mississippi	Magnolia	Magnolia State	By valor and arms
New York	Rose	Empire State	Ever upward

Table 5.5 State flowers, nicknames, and mottos.

35. Write a program that, given the last name of one of the four most recent Presidents, displays his state and a colorful fact about him.

Note: Carter: Georgia, The only soft drink served in the Carter White House was Coca-Cola.; Reagan: California, His secret service code name was Rawhide.; Bush: Texas, He was the third left-handed president.; Clinton: Arkansas, In college he did a good imitation of Elvis Presley.

36. Table 5.6 contains the meanings of some abbreviations doctors often use for prescriptions. Write a program that requests an abbreviation and gives its meaning. The user should be informed if the meaning is not in the table.

Abbreviation	Meaning
ac	before meals
ad lib	freely as needed
bid	twice daily
gtt	a drop
hs	at bedtime
qid	four times a day

Table 5.6 Physicians' abbreviations.

37. The user enters a number into a text box and then clicks on the appropriate command button to have either one of three pieces of humor or one of three insults displayed in the large label below the buttons. Place the humor and insults in general procedures, with Select Case statements in each to display the appropriate phrase. Also, if the number entered is not between 1 and 3, the text box should be cleared.

Note: Some possible bits of humor are "I can resist everything except temptation.", "I just heard from Bill Bailey. He's not coming home.", and "I have enough money to last the rest of my life, unless I buy something." Some possible insults are "How much would you charge to haunt a house?", "I bet you have no more friends than an alarm clock.", and "When your IQ rises to 30, sell."

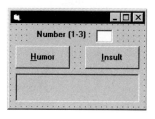

Object	Property	Setting
frmEx37	Caption	(blank)
lblNumber	Alignment	1 – Right Justify
	Caption	Number (1–3):
txtNumber	Text	(blank)
cmdHumor	Caption	&Humor
cmdInsult	Caption	&Insult
lblSentence	BorderStyle	Fixed Single
	Caption	(blank)

Form for Exercise 37   Objects and Properties for Exercise 37

SOLUTIONS TO PRACTICE PROBLEMS 5.3

1. (a) Valid. These items are redundant because 1 and 4 are just special cases of Is < 10. However, this makes no difference in Visual Basic.

   (b) Valid. These items are contradictory. However, Visual Basic looks at them one at a time until it finds an item containing the value of the selector. The action following this Case clause will always be carried out.

   (c) Valid. However, since the selector has numeric type, would be better as `Case 2`.

2. Yes. However, the program on the right is clearer and therefore preferable.

5.4 A CASE STUDY: WEEKLY PAYROLL

This case study processes a weekly payroll using the 1996 Employer's Tax Guide. Table 5.7 shows typical data used by a company's payroll office. These data are processed to produce the information in Table 5.8 that is supplied to each employee along with his or her paycheck. The program should request the data from Table 5.7 for an individual as input and produce output similar to that in Table 5.8.

The items in Table 5.8 should be calculated as follows:

Current Earnings: Hourly wage times hours worked (with time-and-a-half after 40 hours)

Year-to-Date Earnings: Previous year-to-date earnings plus current earnings

FICA Tax: Sum of 6.2 percent of first $62,700 of earnings (Social Security benefits tax) and 1.45 percent of total wages (Medicare tax)

Federal Income Tax Withheld: Subtract $49.04 from the current earnings for each withholding exemption and use Table 5.9 or Table 5.10, depending on marital status

Check Amount: [Current earnings] – [FICA taxes] – [Income tax withheld]

Name	Hourly Wage	Hours Worked	Withholding Exemptions	Marital Status	Previous Year-to-Date Earnings
Al Johnson	26.25	38	4	Married	$61,865.00
Ann Jones	14.00	35	3	Married	$21,840.50
John Smith	7.95	50	1	Single	$12,900.15
Sue Williams	27.50	43	2	Single	$41,890.50

Table 5.7 Employee data.

Name	Current Earnings	Yr. to Date Earnings	FICA Taxes	Income Tax Wh.	Check Amount
Al Johnson	997.50	62,862.50	66.23	101.60	829.67

Table 5.8 Payroll information.

Adjusted Weekly Income	Income Tax Withheld
$0 to $50	0
Over $50 to $489	15% of amount over $50
Over $489 to $1033	$65.85 + 28% of amount over $489
Over $1033 to $2,361	$218.17 + 31% of amount over $1,033
Over $2,361 to $5,100	$629.85 + 36% of amount over $2,361
Over $5,100	$1,615.89 + 39.6% of amount over $5,100

Table 5.9 1996 federal income tax withheld for a single person.

Adjusted Weekly Income	Income Tax Withheld
$0 to $124	0
Over $124 to $851	15% of amount over $124
Over $851 to $1,725	$109.05 + 28% of amount over $851
Over $1,725 to $2,920	$353.77 + 31% of amount over $1,725
Over $2,920 to $5,152	$724.22 + 36% of amount over $2,920
Over $5,152	$1,527.74 + 39.6% of amount over $5,152

Table 5.10 1996 federal income tax withheld for a married person.

Designing the Weekly Payroll Program

After the data for an employee have been gathered from the text boxes, the program must compute the five items appearing in Table 5.8 and then display the payroll information. The five computations form the basic tasks of the program.

1. Compute current earnings.

2. Compute year-to-date earnings.

3. Compute FICA tax.

4. Compute federal income tax withheld.

5. Compute paycheck amount (that is, take-home pay).

Tasks 1, 2, 3, and 5 are fairly simple. Each involves applying a formula to given data. (For instance, if hours worked is at most 40, then Current Earnings = Hourly Wage times Hours Worked.) Thus, we won't break down these tasks any further. Task 4 is more complicated, so we continue to divide it into smaller subtasks.

4. *Compute Federal Income Tax Withheld.* First, the employee's pay is adjusted for exemptions, and then the amount of income tax to be withheld is computed. The computation of the income tax withheld differs for married and single individuals. Task 4 is, therefore, divided into the following subtasks:

4.1 Compute pay adjusted by exemptions.
4.2 Compute income tax withheld for single employee.
4.3 Compute income tax withheld for married employee.

The hierarchy chart in Figure 5.6 shows the stepwise refinement of the problem.

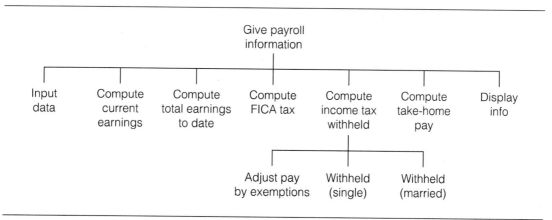

Figure 5.6 Hierarchy chart for the weekly payroll program.

Pseudocode for the Display Payroll Event

INPUT employee data (Subprogram InputData)
COMPUTE CURRENT GROSS PAY (Function Gross_Pay)
COMPUTE TOTAL EARNINGS TO DATE (Function Total_Pay)
COMPUTE FICA TAX (Function FICA_Tax)
COMPUTE FEDERAL TAX (Function Fed_Tax)
   Adjust pay for exemptions
   IF employee is single THEN
       COMPUTE INCOME TAX WITHHELD from adjusted pay using tax
       brackets for single taxpayers (Function TaxSingle)
     ELSE
       COMPUTE INCOME TAX WITHHELD from adjusted pay using tax
       brackets for married taxpayers (Function TaxMarried)
   END IF
COMPUTE CHECK (Function Net_Check)
Display payroll information (Subprogram ShowPayroll)

Writing the Weekly Payroll Program

The cmdDisplay event procedure calls a sequence of seven subprograms. Table 5.11 shows the tasks and the procedures that perform the tasks.

Task	Procedure
0. Input employee data.	InputData
1. Compute current earnings.	Gross_Pay
2. Compute year-to-date earnings.	Total_Pay
3. Compute FICA tax.	FICA_Tax
4. Compute federal income tax withheld.	Fed_Tax
4.1 Compute adjusted pay.	Fed_Tax
4.2 Compute amount withheld for single employee.	TaxSingle
4.3 Compute amount withheld for married employee.	TaxMarried
5. Compute paycheck amounts.	Net_Check
6. Display payroll information.	ShowPayroll

Table 5.11 Tasks and their procedures.

The User Interface

Figure 5.7 Template for entering payroll data.

Object	Property	Setting
frmPayroll	Caption	Weekly Payroll
lblName	Alignment	1 – Right Justify
	Caption	Employee Name
txtName	Text	(blank)
lblWage	Alignment	1 – Right Justify
	Caption	Hourly Wage
txtWage	Text	(blank)
lblHours	Alignment	1 – Right Justify
	Caption	Number of Hours Worked
txtHours	Text	(blank)
lblExempts	Alignment	1 – Right Justify
	Caption	Number of Exemptions
txtExempts	Text	(blank)
lblMarital	Alignment	1 – Right Justify
	Caption	Marital Status (M or S)
txtMarital	Text	(blank)
lblPriorPay	Alignment	1– Right Justify
	Caption	Total Pay Prior to this Week
txtPriorPay	Text	(blank)
cmdDisplay	Caption	Display Payroll
cmdNext	Caption	Next Employee
cmdQuit	Caption	Quit
picResults		

Table 5.12 Objects and initial properties for the weekly payroll program.

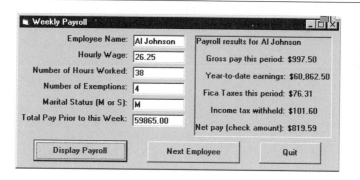

Figure 5.8 Sample run of weekly payroll.

```
Rem Program to compute employees' weekly payroll
Rem
Rem ******************************************************************
Rem *           Variable Table                                      *
Rem *                                                               *
Rem *   exempts          Number of exemptions for employee          *
Rem *   fedTax           Federal income tax withheld this week      *
Rem *   ficaTax          FICA taxes for this week                   *
Rem *   hrsWorked        Hours worked this week                     *
Rem *   hrWage           Hourly wage                                *
Rem *   medicare         Medicare tax for this week                 *
Rem *   mStatus          Marital status: S for Single; M for Married *
Rem *   empName          Name of employee                           *
```

```
Rem *  grossPay          This week's pay before taxes              *
Rem *  check             Paycheck this week (take-home pay)        *
Rem *  prevPay           Total pay for year excluding this week    *
Rem *  socialSecurity  Social Security tax for this week           *
Rem *  totalPay          Total pay for year including this week    *
Rem *************************************************************

Private Sub cmdDisplay_Click()
  Dim empName As String, hrWage As Single, hrsWorked As Single
  Dim exempts As Single, mStatus As String, prevPay As Single
  Dim grossPay As Single, totalPay As Single, ficaTax As Single
  Dim fedTax As Single, check As Single
  Rem Obtain data, compute payroll, display results
  Call InputData(empName, hrWage, hrsWorked, exempts, mStatus, prevPay)
  Let grossPay = Gross_Pay(hrWage, hrsWorked)
  Let totalPay = Total_Pay(prevPay, grossPay)
  Let ficaTax = FICA_Tax(grossPay, prevPay, totalPay)
  Let fedTax = Fed_Tax(grossPay, exempts, mStatus)
  Let check = Net_Check(grossPay, ficaTax, fedTax)
  Call ShowPayroll(empName, grossPay, totalPay, ficaTax, fedTax, check)
End Sub

Private Sub cmdNext_Click()
  Rem Clear all text boxes for next employee's data
  Let txtName.Text = ""
  Let txtWageEarn.Text = ""
  Let txtHrsYtd.Text = ""
  Let txtExempFica.Text = ""
  Let txtMarTax.Text = ""
  Let txtPayChk.Text = ""
  picResults.Cls
End Sub

Private Sub cmdQuit_Click()
  End
End Sub

Private Function Net_Check(pay As Single, ficaTax As Single, fedTax As Single) As Single
  Rem Compute amount of money given to employee
  Net_Check = pay - ficaTax - fedTax
End Function

Private Function Fed_Tax(pay As Single, exempts As Single, mStatus As String) As Single
  Dim adjPay As Single
  Rem Compute federal income tax
  Let adjPay = pay - (49.04 * exempts)
  If adjPay < 0 Then
      Let adjPay = 0
  End If
  If mStatus = "S" Then
      Fed_Tax = TaxSingle(adjPay)
    Else
      Fed_Tax = TaxMarried(adjPay)
  End If
End Function
```

```
Private Function FICA_Tax(pay As Single, prevPay As Single, totalPay As Single) As Single
   Dim socialSecurity As Single, medicare As Single
   Rem Compute social security and medicare tax
   Let socialSecurity = 0
   If totalPay <= 62700 Then
       Let socialSecurity = .062 * pay
     ElseIf prevPay < 62700 Then
       Let socialSecurity = .062 * (62700 - prevPay)
   End If
   Let medicare = .0145 * pay
   FICA_Tax = socialSecurity + medicare
End Function


Private Function Gross_Pay(hrWage As Single, hrsWorked As Single) As Single
   Rem Compute weekly pay before taxes
   If hrsWorked <= 40 Then
       Gross_Pay = hrsWorked * hrWage
     Else
       Gross_Pay = 40 * hrWage + (hrsWorked - 40) * 1.5 * hrWage
   End If
End Function


Private Function Total_Pay(prevPay As Single, pay As Single) As Single
   Rem Compute total pay before taxes
   Total_Pay = prevPay + pay
End Function


Private Sub InputData(empName As String, hrWage As Single, hrsWorked As Single,
                      exempts As Single, mStatus As String, prevPay As Single)
   Rem Enter above two lines as one
   Rem Get payroll data for employee
   Let empName = txtName.Text
   Let hrWage = Val(txtWageEarn.Text)
   Let hrsWorked = Val(txtHrsYtd.Text)
   Let exempts = Val(txtExempFica.Text)
   Let mStatus = Left(UCase(txtMarTax.Text), 1) 'M or S
   Let prevPay = Val(txtPayChk.Text)
End Sub


Private Sub ShowPayroll(empName As String, pay As Single, totalPay As Single,
                        ficaTax As Single, fedTax As Single, check As Single)
   Rem Enter above two lines as one
   Rem Display results of payroll computations
   picResults.Cls
   picResults.Print "Payroll results for "; empName
   picResults.Print
   picResults.Print "   Gross pay this period: "; Format(pay, "Currency")
   picResults.Print
   picResults.Print "   Year-to-date earnings: "; Format(totalPay, "Currency")
   picResults.Print
   picResults.Print "   Fica Taxes this period: "; Format(ficaTax, "Currency")
   picResults.Print
   picResults.Print "     Income tax withheld: "; Format(fedTax, "Currency")
   picResults.Print
   picResults.Print "Net pay (check amount): "; Format(check, "Currency")
End Sub
```

```
Private Function TaxMarried(adjPay As Single) As Single
  Rem Compute federal tax for married person based on adjusted pay
  Select Case adjPay
    Case 0 To 124
      TaxMarried = 0
    Case 124 To 851
      TaxMarried = .15 * (adjPay - 124)
    Case 851 To 1725
      TaxMarried = 109.5 + .28 * (adjPay - 851)
    Case 1725 To 2920
      TaxMarried = 353.77 + .31 * (adjPay - 1725)
    Case 2920 To 5152
      TaxMarried = 724.22 + .36 * (adjPay - 2920)
    Case Is > 5152
      TaxMarried = 1527.74 + .396 * (adjPay - 5152)
  End Select
End Function

Private Function TaxSingle(adjPay As Single) As Single
  Rem Compute federal tax for single person based on adjusted pay
  Select Case adjPay
    Case 0 To 50
      TaxSingle = 0
    Case 50 To 489
      TaxSingle = .15 * (adjPay - 50)
    Case 489 To 1033
      TaxSingle = 65.85 + .28 * (adjPay - 489)
    Case 1033 To 2361
      TaxSingle = 218.17 + .31 * (adjPay - 1033)
    Case 2361 To 5100
      TaxSingle = 629.85 + .36 * (adjPay - 2361)
    Case Is > 5100
      TaxSingle = 1615.89 + .396 * (adjPay - 5100)
  End Select
End Function
```

Comments

1. In ComputeFICATax, care has been taken to avoid computing social security benefits tax on income in excess of $62,700 per year. The logic of the program makes sure an employee whose income crosses the $62,700 threshold during a given week is only taxed on the difference between $62,700 and his previous year-to-date income.

2. The two functions TaxMarried and TaxSingle use Select Case to incorporate the tax brackets given in Tables 5.9 and 5.10 for the amount of federal income tax withheld. The upper limit of each Case clause is the same as the lower limit of the next Case clause. This ensures fractional values for adjPay, such as 50.50 in the TaxSingle function, will be properly treated as part of the higher salary range.

Chapter 5
Summary

1. The *relational operators* are <, >, =, <>, <=, and >=.

2. The principal *logical operators* are And, Or, and Not.

3. A *condition* is an expression involving constants, variables, functions, and operators (arithmetic, relational, and/or logical) that can be evaluated as either True or False.

4. An If block decides what action to take depending on the truth values of one or more conditions. To allow several courses of action, the If and Else parts of an If statement can contain other If statements.

5. A Select Case block selects one of several actions depending on the value of an expression, called the *selector*. The entries in the *value* lists must have the same type (string or numeric) as the selector.

Chapter 5
Programming Projects

1. Table 5.13 gives the price schedule for Eddie's Equipment Rental. Full-day rentals cost one-and-a-half times half-day rentals. Write a program that displays Table 5.13 in a picture box when an appropriate command button is clicked and displays a bill in another picture box based on the item number and time period chosen by a customer. The bill should include a $30.00 deposit.

Piece of Equipment	Half-Day	Full-Day
1. Rug cleaner	$16.00	$24.00
2. Lawn mower	$12.00	$18.00
3. Paint sprayer	$20.00	$30.00

Table 5.13 Price schedule for Eddie's Equipment Rental.

A possible form layout and sample run is shown in Figure 5.9.

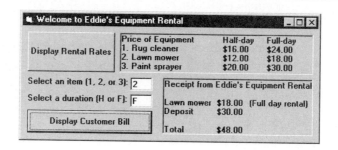

Figure 5.9 Form layout and sample run for Programming Project 1.

2. The American Heart Association suggests that at most 30 percent of the calories in our diet come from fat. Whereas food labels give the number of calories and amount of fat per serving, they often do not give the percentage of calories from fat. This percentage can be calculated by multiplying the number of grams of fat in one serving by 9, dividing that number by the total number of calories per serving, and multiplying the result by 100. Write a program that requests the name, number of calories per serving, and the grams of fat per serving as input, and tells us whether the food meets the American Heart Association recommendation. A sample run is as follows:

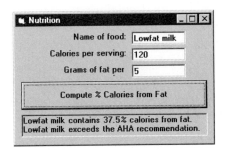

3. Table 5.14 gives the 1995 federal income tax rate schedule for single tax-payers. Write a program that requests the taxable income and calculates the federal income tax. Use a subprogram for the input and a function to calculate the tax.

Taxable Income Over	But Not Over	Your Tax Is	Of Amount Over
$0	$23,350	15%	$0
$23,350	$56,550	$3,502.50 + 28%	$23,350
$56,550	$117,950	$12,798.50 + 31%	$56,550
$117,950	$256,500	$31,832.50 + 36%	$117,950
$256,500		$81,710.50 + 39.6%	$256,500

Table 5.14 1995 federal income tax rates for single taxpayers.

4. Write a program to determine the real roots of the quadratic equation $ax^2 + bx + c = 0$ (where $a \neq 0$) after requesting the values of a, b, and c. Use a subprogram to ensure that a is nonzero. **Note:** The equation has 2, 1, or 0 solutions depending on whether the value of $b{\wedge}2 - 4 * a * c$ is positive, zero, or negative. In the first two cases, the solutions are given by the quadratic formula $(-b \pm \mathrm{Sqr}(b{\wedge}2 - 4 * a * c)) / (2 * a)$.

5. Table 5.15 contains seven proverbs and their truth values. Write a program that presents these proverbs one at a time and asks the user to evaluate them as true or false. The program should then tell the user how many questions were answered correctly and display one of the following evaluations: Perfect (all correct), Excellent (5 or 6 correct), You might consider taking Psychology 101 (less than 5 correct).

Proverb	Truth Value
The squeaky wheel gets the grease.	True
Cry and you cry alone.	True
Opposites attract.	False
Spare the rod and spoil the child.	False
Actions speak louder than words.	True
Familiarity breeds contempt.	False
Marry in haste, repent at leisure.	True

Table 5.15 Seven proverbs.

Source: "You Know What They Say . . .," by Alfie Kohn, *Psychology Today*, April 1988.

6. Write a program to find the day of the week for any date after 1582, the year our current calendar was introduced. The program should

(a) Request the year and the number of the month as input.

(b) Determine the number of days in the month. **Note:** All years divisible by 4 are leap years, with the exception of those years divisible by 100 and not by 400. For instance, 1600 and 2000 are leap years, but 1700, 1800, and 1900 are not.

(c) Request the number of the day as input. The prompt should list the possible range for the number.

(d) Determine the day of the week with the following algorithm.

(1) Treat January as the 13th month and February as the 14th month of the previous year. For example 1/23/1986 should be converted to 13/23/1985 and 2/6/1987 should be converted to 14/6/1986.

(2) Denote the number of the day, month, and year by d, m, and y, respectively. Compute

$$w = d + 2*m + \mathrm{Int}(.6 * (m+1)) + y + \mathrm{Int}(y/4) - \mathrm{Int}(y/100) + \mathrm{Int}(y/400) + 2$$

(3) The remainder when w is divided by 7 is the day of the week of the given date, with Saturday as the zeroth day of the week, Sunday the first day of the week, Monday the second, and so on.

A sample run of the program for a famous date in U.S. history follows.

Test the program with the following memorable dates in the history of the U.S. space program.

On Tuesday, February 20, 1962, John Glenn became the first American to orbit the earth.

On Sunday, July 20, 1969, Neil Armstrong became the first person to set foot on the moon.

On Saturday, June 18, 1983, Sally Ride became the first American woman to travel in space.

7. Write a program to analyze a mortgage. The user should enter the amount of the loan, the annual rate of interest, and the duration of the loan in months. When the user clicks on the command button, the information that was entered should be checked to make sure it is reasonable. If bad data have been supplied, the user should be so advised. Otherwise, the monthly payment and the total amount of interest paid should be displayed. The formula for the monthly payment is

```
payment = p * r / (1 - (1 + r) ^ (-n))
```

where p is the amount of the loan, r is the monthly interest rate (annual rate divided by 12) given as a number between 0 (for 0 percent) and 1 (for 100 percent), and n is the duration of the loan. The formula for the total interest paid is

```
total interest = n * payment - p
```

8. Write a program using the form in Figure 5.10. Each time the command button is pressed, Rnd is used to simulate a coin toss and the values are updated. The figure shows the status after 27 coin tosses. **Note:** You can produce tosses quickly by just holding down the Enter key. Although the percentage of heads initially will fluctuate considerably, it should stay close to 50% after many (say, 1000) tosses.

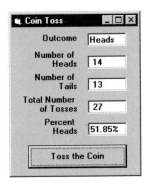

Figure 5.10 Form for Programming Project 8.

6

Repetition

6.1 Do Loops / 248

6.2 Processing Lists of Data With Do Loops / 260
• EOF Function • Counters and Accumulators
• Flags • Nested Loops

6.3 For...Next Loops / 274

6.4 A Case Study: Analyze A Loan / 287
• Designing the Analyze a Loan Program • The User
Interface • Writing the Analyze a Loan Program
• Pseudocode for the Analyze a Loan Program

Chapter Summary / 295

Programming Projects / 295

6.1 DO LOOPS

A **loop**, one of the most important structures in Visual Basic, is used to repeat a sequence of statements a number of times. At each repetition, or **pass**, the statements act upon variables whose values are changing.

The **Do loop** repeats a sequence of statements either as long as or until a certain condition is true. A Do statement precedes the sequence of statements and a Loop statement follows the sequence of statements. The condition, along with either the word While or Until, follows the word Do or the word Loop. When Visual Basic executes a Do loop of the form

```
Do While condition
  statement(s)
Loop
```

it first checks the truth value of *condition*. If *condition* is false, then the statements inside the loop are not executed and the program continues with the line after the Loop statement. If *condition* is true, then the statements inside the loop are executed. When the statement Loop is encountered, the entire process is repeated beginning with the testing of *condition* in the Do While statement. In other words, the statements inside the loop are repeatedly executed only as long as (that is, while) the condition is true. Figure 6.1 contains the pseudocode and flowchart for this loop.

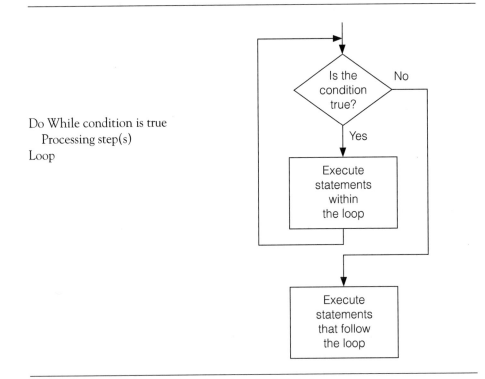

```
Do While condition is true
  Processing step(s)
Loop
```

Figure 6.1 Pseudocode and flowchart for a Do While Loop.

EXAMPLE 1   Write a program that displays the numbers from 1 through 10.

SOLUTION   The condition in the Do loop is "num <= 10".

```
Private Sub cmdDisplay_Click()
  Dim num As Integer
  Rem Display the numbers from 1 to 10
  Let num = 1
  Do While num <= 10
    picNumbers.Print num;
    Let num = num + 1
  Loop
End Sub
```

[Run and click the command button. The following is displayed in the picture box.]

```
1  2  3  4  5  6  7  8  9  10
```

Do loops are commonly used to ensure that a proper response is received from the InputBox function.

EXAMPLE 2   The following program requires the user to give a password before a secret file can be accessed.

Object	Property	Setting
frm6_1_2	Caption	Read File
lblFiles	Caption	The available files are: HUMOR.TXT, INSULTS.TXT, and SECRET.TXT.
lblName	Caption	Name of file to open
txtName	Text	(blank)
cmdDisplay	Caption	Display First Item of File
picItem		

```
Private Sub cmdDisplay_Click()
  Dim passWord As String, info As String
  If UCase(txtName.Text) = "SECRET.TXT" Then
      Let passWord = ""
      Do While passWord <> "SHAZAM"
        Let passWord = InputBox("What is the password?")
        Let passWord = UCase(passWord)
      Loop
  End If
  Open txtName.Text For Input As #1
  Input #1, info
  picItem.Cls
  picItem.Print info
  Close #1
End Sub
```

[Run, type SECRET.TXT into the text box, and click the command button.]

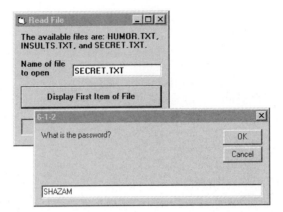

Note: If a file other than SECRET.TXT is requested, the statements inside the loop are not executed.

In Examples 1 and 2, the condition was checked at the top of the loop, that is, before the statements were executed. Alternatively, the condition can be checked at the bottom of the loop when the statement Loop is reached. When Visual Basic encounters a Do loop of the form

```
Do
    statement(s)
Loop Until condition
```

it executes the statements inside the loop and then checks the truth value of *condition*. If *condition* is true, then the program continues with the line after the Loop statement. If *condition* is false, then the entire process is repeated beginning with the Do statement. In other words, the statements inside the loop are executed at least once and then are repeatedly executed **until** the condition is true. Figure 6.2 shows the pseudocode and flowchart for this type of Do loop.

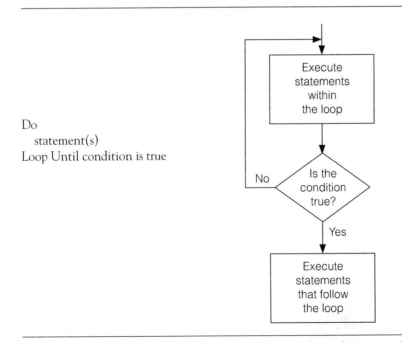

Do
    statement(s)
Loop Until condition is true

Figure 6.2 Pseudocode and flowchart for a Do loop with condition tested at the bottom.

EXAMPLE 3 The following program is equivalent to Example 2, except that the condition is tested at the bottom of the loop.

```
Private Sub cmdDisplay_Click()
    Dim passWord As String, info As String
    If UCase(txtName.Text) = "SECRET.TXT" Then
        Do
            Let passWord = InputBox("What is the password?")
            Let passWord = UCase(passWord)
        Loop Until passWord = "SHAZAM"
    End If
    Open txtName.Text For Input As #1
    Input #1, info
    picItem.cls
    picItem.Print info
    Close #1
End Sub
```

Do loops allow us to calculate useful quantities for which we might not know a simple formula.

EXAMPLE 4 Suppose you deposit $100 into a savings account and let it accumulate at 7 percent interest compounded annually. The following program determines when you will be a millionaire.

Object	Property	Setting
frmInterest	Caption	7% Interest
lblAmount	Caption	Amount Deposited
txtAmount	Text	(blank)
cmdYears	Caption	Years to become a millionaire
picWhen		

```
Private Sub cmdYears_Click()
    Dim balance As Single, numYears As Integer
    Rem Compute years required to become a millionaire
    picWhen.Cls
    Let balance = Val(txtAmount.Text)
    Let numYears = 0
    Do While balance < 1000000
        Let balance = balance + .07 * balance
        Let numYears = numYears + 1
    Loop
    picWhen.Print "In"; numYears; "years you will have a million dollars."
End Sub
```

[Run, type 100 into the text box, and press the command button.]

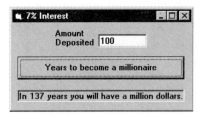

Comments

1. Be careful to avoid infinite loops, that is, loops that are never exited. The following loop is infinite because the condition "num < > 0" will always be true. **Note:** The loop can be terminated by pressing Ctrl+Break.

```
Private Sub cmdButton_Click()
  Dim num As Single
  Rem An infinite loop
  Let num = 7
  Do While num <> 0
    Let num = num - 2
  Loop
End Sub
```

Notice that this slipup can be avoided by changing the condition to "num >= 0".

2. The statements between Do and Loop do not have to be indented. However, because indenting improves the readability of the program, it is regarded as good programming style. As soon as you see the word Do, your eyes can easily scan down the program to find the matching Loop statement. You know immediately the size of the loop.

3. Visual Basic allows the use of the words While and Until either at the top or bottom of a Do loop. In this text, the usage of these words is restricted for the following reasons.

   (a) Because any While statement can be easily converted to an Until statement and vice versa, the restriction produces no loss of capabilities and the programmer has one less matter to think about.
   (b) Restricting the use simplifies reading the program. The word While proclaims testing at the top and the word Until proclaims testing at the bottom.
   (c) Certain other major structured languages, such as Pascal, only allow While at the top and Until at the bottom of a loop. Therefore, following this convention will make life easier for people already familiar with Pascal or planning to learn it.
   (d) Standard pseudocode uses the word While to denote testing a loop at the top and the word Until to denote testing at the bottom.

4. Good programming practice requires that all variables appearing in a Do loop be assigned values before the loop is entered, rather than relying on default values. For instance, the code at the left in what follows should be replaced with the code at the right.

```
Rem Add 1 through 10              Rem Add 1 through 10
Do While num < 10                Let num = 0
  Let num = num + 1              Let sum = 0
  Let sum = sum + num            Do While num < 10
Loop                               Let num = num + 1
                                   Let sum = sum + num
                                 Loop
```

PRACTICE PROBLEMS 6.1

1. How do you decide whether a condition should be checked at the top of a loop or at the bottom?

2. Change the following loop so it will be executed at least once.

```
Do While continue = "Yes"
  Let answer = InputBox("Do you want to continue (Y or N)")
  If UCase(answer) = "Y" Then
      Let continue = "Yes"
    Else
      Let continue = "No"
  End If
Loop
```

EXERCISES 6.1

In Exercises 1 through 6, determine the output displayed in the picture box when the command button is clicked.

1.
```
Private Sub cmdDisplay_Click()
  Dim q As Single
  Let q = 3
  Do While q < 15
    Let q = 2 * q - 1
  Loop
  picOutput.Print q
End Sub
```

2.
```
Private Sub cmdDisplay_Click()
  Dim balance As Single, interest As Single, n As Integer
  Let balance = 1000
  Let interest = .1
  Let n = 0                'Number of years
  Do
    picOutput.Print n; balance
    Let balance = (1 + interest) * balance
    Let n = n + 1
  Loop Until balance > 1200
  picOutput.Print n
End Sub
```

3. ```
Private Sub cmdDisplay_Click()
    Dim num As Single, message As String
    Rem Display a message
    Let num = 4
    Do
      Select Case num
        Case 1
          Let message = "grammer!"
          Let num = -1
        Case 2
          Let message = "re a su"
          Let num = (5 - num) * (3 - num)
        Case 3
          Let message = "per pro"
          Let num = 4 - num
        Case 4
          Let message = "You a"
          Let num = 2 * num - 6
      End Select
      picOutput.Print message;
    Loop Until num = -1
End Sub
```

4. ```
Private Sub cmdQuiz_Click()
    Dim prompt As String, firstYear As Integer
    Rem Computer-assisted instruction
    Let prompt = "In what year was the IBM PC first produced?"
    Do
      Let firstYear = Val(InputBox(prompt))
      Select Case firstYear
        Case 1981
          picQuiz.Print "Correct. The computer was an instant"
          picQuiz.Print "success. By the end of 1981, there was"
          picQuiz.Print "such a backlog of orders that customers"
          picQuiz.Print "had a three-month waiting period."
        Case Is < 1981
          picQuiz.Print "Later. The Apple II computer, which"
          picQuiz.Print "preceded the IBM PC, appeared in 1977."
        Case Is > 1981
          picQuiz.Print "Earlier. The first successful IBM PC clone,"
          picQuiz.Print "the Compaq Portable, appeared in 1983."
      End Select
      picQuiz.Print
    Loop Until firstYear = 1981
End Sub
```

(Assume that the first response is *1980* and the second response is *1981*.)

5. ```
Private Sub cmdDisplay_Click()
    Rem Calculate the remainder in long division
    picOutput.Print Remainder(3, 17)
End Sub
```
```

```
Private Function Remainder(divisor As Single, dividend As Single) As Single
   Dim sum As Single
   Let sum = 0
   Do While sum <= dividend
      Let sum = sum + divisor
   Loop
   Remainder = dividend - sum + divisor
End Function
```

6.
```
Private Sub cmdDisplay_Click()
   Dim info As String, counter As Integer, letter As String
   Rem Simulate InStr; search for the letter t
   Let info = "Potato"
   Let counter = 0
   Let letter = ""
   Do While (letter <> "t") And (counter < Len(info))
      Let counter = counter + 1
      Let letter = Mid(info, counter, 1)
      If letter = "t" Then
          picOutput.Print counter
      End If
   Loop
   If letter <> "t" Then
       picOutput.Print 0
   End If
End Sub
```

In Exercises 7 through 10, identify the errors.

7.
```
Private Sub cmdDisplay_Click()
   Dim q As Single
   Let q = 1
   Do While q > 0
      Let q = 3 * q - 1
      picOutput.Print q;
   Loop
End Sub
```

8.
```
Private Sub cmdDisplay_Click()
   Dim num As Integer
   Rem Display the numbers from 1 to 5
   Do While num <> 5
      Let num = 1
      picOutput.Print num;
      Let num = num + 1
   Loop
End Sub
```

9.
```
Private Sub cmdDisplay_Click()
   Dim answer As String
   Rem Repeat until a yes response is given
   Loop
      Let answer = InputBox("Did you chop down the cherry tree (Y/N)?")
   Do Until UCase(answer) = "Y"
End Sub
```

10.
```
Private Sub cmdDisplay_Click()
    Dim n As Integer, answer As String
    Rem Repeat as long as desired
    Do
      Let n = n + 1
      picOutput.Print n
      Let answer = InputBox("Do you want to continue (Y/N)?")
    Until UCase(answer) = "Y"
End Sub
```

In Exercises 11 through 20, replace each phrase containing Until with an equivalent phrase containing While, and vice versa. For instance, the phrase Until sum = 100 would be replaced by While sum < > 100.

11. `Until num < 7`

12. `Until nom = "Bob"`

13. `While response = "Y"`

14. `While total = 10`

15. `While nom <> ""`

16. `Until balance >= 100`

17. `While (a > 1) And (a < 3)`

18. `Until (ans = "") Or (n = 0)`

19. `Until Not (n = 0)`

20. `While (ans = "Y") And (n < 7)`

In Exercises 21 and 22, write simpler and clearer code that performs the same task as the given code.

21.
```
Private Sub cmdDisplay_Click()
    Dim nom As String
    Let nom = InputBox("Enter a name:")
    picOutput.Print nom
    Let nom = InputBox("Enter a name:")
    picOutput.Print nom
    Let nom = InputBox("Enter a name:")
    picOutput.Print nom
End Sub
```

22.
```
Private Sub cmdDisplay_Click()
    Dim loopNum As Integer, answer As String
    Let loopNum = 0
    Do
      If loopNum >= 1 Then
         Let answer = InputBox("Do you want to continue (Y/N)?")
         Let answer = UCase(answer)
        Else
         Let answer = "Y"
      End If
      If (answer = "Y") Or (loopNum = 0) Then
         Let loopNum = loopNum + 1
         picOutput.Print loopNum
      End If
    Loop Until answer <> "Y"
End Sub
```

23. Write a program that displays a Celsius-to-Fahrenheit conversion table. Entries in the table should range from –40 to 40 degrees Celsius in units of 5 degrees. **Note:** The formula f = (9 / 5) * c + 32 converts Celsius to Fahrenheit.

24. World population doubled from 2.7 billion in 1951 to 5.4 billion in 1991. If we assume that the world population has been doubling every 40 years, write a program to determine in what year the world population would have been less than 5.4 million.

25. Recall that the function Rnd has a random value between 0 and 1 (excluding 1), and so the expression Int(6*Rnd)+1 has a random whole number value between 1 and 6. Write a program that repeatedly "throws" a pair of dice and tallies the number of tosses and the number of those tosses that total (lucky) seven. The program should stop when 100 lucky sevens have been tossed. The program should then report the approximate odds of tossing a lucky seven. (The odds will be "1 in" followed by the result of dividing the number of tosses by the number of tosses that came up lucky sevens.)

26. Write a program to display all the numbers between 1 and 100 that are perfect squares. (A perfect square is an integer that is the square of another integer; 1, 4, and 16 are examples of perfect squares.)

27. Write a program to display all the numbers between 1 and 100 that are part of the Fibonacci sequence. The Fibonacci sequence begins 1, 1, 2, 3, 5, 8, . . . , where each new number in the sequence is found by adding the previous two numbers in the sequence.

28. The population of Mexico City in 1995 was 15.6 million people and was growing at the rate of 3 percent each year. Write a program to determine when the population will reach 30 million.

29. An old grandfather clock reads 6:00 p.m. Somewhere not too long after 6:30 p.m., the minute hand will pass directly over the hour hand. Write a program using a loop to make better and better guesses as to what time it is when the hands exactly overlap. Keep track of the positions of both hands using the minutes at which they are pointing. (At 6:00 p.m., the minute hand points at 0 while the hour hand points at 30.) You will need to use the fact that when the minute hand advances m minutes, the hour hand advances $m/12$ minutes. (For example, when the minute hand advances 60 minutes, the hour hand advances 5 minutes from one hour mark to the next.) To make an approximation, record how far the minute hand is behind the hour hand, then advance the minute hand by this much and the hour hand by 1/12 this much. The loop should terminate when the resulting positions of the minute and hour hands differ by less than .0001 minute. (The exact answer is 32 and 8/11 minutes after 6.)

30. Write a program that requests a word containing the two letters r and n as input and determines which of the two letters appears first. If the word does not contain both of the letters, the program should so advise the user. (Test the program with the words *colonel* and *merriment*.)

31. The coefficient of restitution of a ball, a number between 0 and 1, specifies how much energy is conserved when a ball hits a rigid surface. A coefficient of .9, for instance, means a bouncing ball will rise to 90 percent of its initial height after each bounce. Write a program to input a coefficient of restitution and a height in meters and report how many times a ball bounces before it rises to a height of less than 10 centimeters. Also report the total distance traveled by the ball before this point. The coefficients of restitution of a tennis ball, basketball, super ball, and softball are .7, .75, .9, and .3, respectively.

In Exercises 32 through 35, write a program to solve the stated problem.

32. *Savings Account.* $15,000 is deposited into a savings account paying 5 percent interest and $1000 is withdrawn from the account at the end of each year. Approximately how many years are required for the savings account to be depleted?

33. Rework Exercise 32 so that the amount of money deposited initially is input by the user and the program computes the number of years required to deplete the account. **Note:** Be careful to avoid infinite loops.

34. $1000 is deposited into a savings account, and an additional $1000 is deposited at the end of each year. If the money earns interest at the rate of 5 percent, how long will it take before the account contains at least $1 million?

35. A person born in 1980 can claim, "I will be x years old in the year x squared." Write a program to determine the value of x.

36. Illustrate the growth of money in a savings account. When the user presses the command button, values for Amount and Interest Rate are obtained from text boxes and used to calculate the number of years until the money doubles and the number of years until the money reaches a million dollars. Use the following form design. **Note:** The balance at the end of each year is $(1 + r)$ times the previous balance, where r is the annual rate of interest in decimal form. Use Do loops to determine the number of years.

Object	Property	Setting
frmInterest	Caption	Compound Interest
lblAmount	Alignment	1 – Right Justify
	Caption	Amount
txtAmount	Text	(blank)
lblRate	Alignment	1 – Right Justify
	Caption	Interest Rate (Annual)
txtRate	Text	(blank)
cmdDetermine	Caption	Determine Years
lblDouble	Alignment	1 – Right Justify
	Caption	Doubling Time (Years)
picDouble		
lblMillion	Alignment	1 – Right Justify
	Caption	Reach a Million (Years)
picMillion		

Form for Exercise 36   Objects and Properties for Exercise 36

37. Allow the user to enter a sentence. Then, depending on which command button the user clicks, display the sentence entirely in capital letters or with just the first letter of each word capitalized.

In Exercises 38 and 39, write a program corresponding to the flowchart.

38. The flowchart in Figure 6.3 requests an integer greater than 1 as input, and factors it into a product of prime numbers. (**Note:** A number is prime if its only factors are 1 and itself. Test the program with the numbers 660 and 139.)

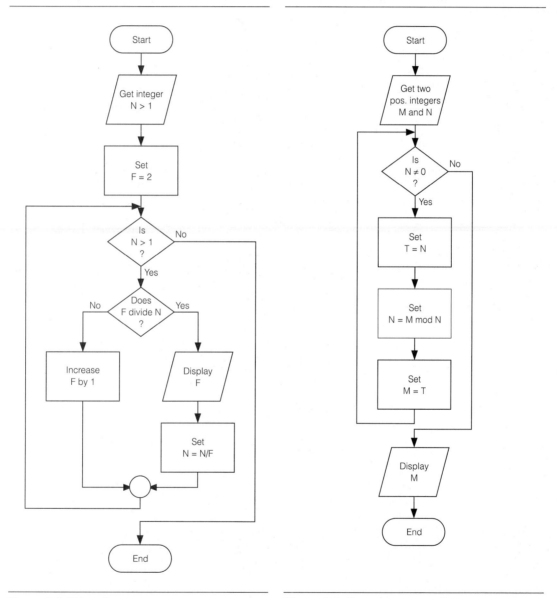

Figure 6.3 Prime factors.

Figure 6.4 Greatest common divisor.

39. The flowchart in Figure 6.4 finds the greatest common divisor of two positive integers input by the user. (The greatest common divisor of two positive integers is the largest integer that divides both numbers.) Write a program that corresponds to the flowchart.

6.2 PROCESSING LISTS OF DATA WITH DO LOOPS

One of the main applications of programming is the processing of lists of data. Do loops are used to display all or selected items from lists, search lists for specific items, and perform calculations on the numerical entries of a list. This section introduces several devices that facilitate working with lists. **Counters** calculate the number of elements in lists, **accumulators** sum numerical values in lists, **flags** record whether certain events have occurred, and the **EOF function** indicates the end of a file. **Nested loops** add yet another dimension to repetition.

EOF Function

Data to be processed are often retrieved from a file by a Do loop. Visual Basic has a useful function, EOF, that tells us if we have reached the end of the file from which we are reading. Suppose a file has been opened with reference number n. At any time, the condition

```
EOF(n)
```

will be true if the end of the file has been reached, and false otherwise.

One of the first programs I wrote when I got my computer stored a list of names and phone numbers and printed a phone directory. I first had the program display the directory on the screen and later changed the Picture1.Print statements to Printer.Print statements to produce a printed copy. I stored the names in a file so I could easily add, change, or delete entries.

EXAMPLE 1   The following program displays the contents of a telephone directory. The names and phone numbers are contained in the file PHONE.TXT. The loop will repeat as long as the end of the file is not reached.

PHONE.TXT contains the following four lines:

"Bert", "123-4567"
"Ernie", "987-6543"
"Grover", "246-8321"
"Oscar", "135-7900"

Object	Property	Setting
frmPhone	Caption	Directory
cmdDisplay	Caption	Display Phone Numbers
picNumbers		

```
Private Sub cmdDisplay_Click()
  Dim nom As String, phoneNum As String
  picNumbers.Cls
  Open "PHONE.TXT" For Input As #1
  Do While Not EOF(1)
    Input #1, nom, phoneNum
    picNumbers.Print nom, phoneNum
  Loop
  Close #1
End Sub
```

[Run and press the command button.]

The program in Example 1 illustrates the proper way to process a list of data contained in a file. The Do loop should be tested at the top with an end-of-file condition. (If the file is empty, no attempt is made to input data from the file.) The first set of data should be input *after* the Do statement and then the data should be processed. Figure 6.5 contains the pseudocode and flowchart for this technique.

Do While there are still data in the file
  Get an item of data
  Process the item
Loop

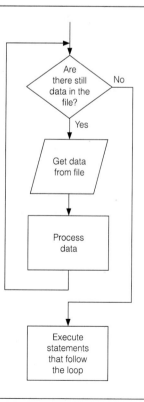

Figure 6.5 Pseudocode and flowchart for processing data from a file.

Sequential files can be quite large. Rather than list the entire contents, we typically search the file for a specific piece of information.

EXAMPLE 2   Modify the program in Example 1 to search the telephone directory for a name specified by the user. If the name does not appear in the directory, so notify the user.

SOLUTION   We want to keep searching as long as there is no match *and* we have not reached the end of the list. Therefore, the condition for the Do While statement is a compound logical expression with the operator And. After the last pass through the loop, we will know whether the name was found and be able to display the requested information.

Object	Property	Setting
frmPhone	Caption	Phone Number
lblName	Caption	Name to look up
txtName	Text	(blank)
cmdDisplay	Caption	Display Phone Number
picNumber		

```
Private Sub cmdDisplay_Click()
  Dim nom As String, phoneNum As String
  Open "PHONE.TXT" For Input As #1
  Do While (nom <> txtName.Text) And (Not EOF(1))
    Input #1, nom, phoneNum
  Loop
  Close #1
  picNumber.Cls
  If nom = txtName.Text Then
      picNumber.Print nom, phoneNum
    Else
      picNumber.Print "Name not found."
  End If
End Sub
```

[Run, type Grover into the text box, and press the command button.]

Counters and Accumulators

A **counter** is a numeric variable that keeps track of the number of items that have been processed. An **accumulator** is a numeric variable that totals numbers.

EXAMPLE 3 The following program counts and finds the value of coins listed in a file.

COINS.TXT contains the following entries: 1, 1, 5, 10, 10, 25

Object	Property	Setting
frmCoins	Caption	Coins
cmdAnalyze	Caption	Analyze Change
picValue		

```
Private Sub cmdAnalyze_Click()
  Dim numCoins As Integer, sum As Single, value As Single
  Open "COINS.TXT" For Input As #1
  Let numCoins = 0
  Let sum = 0
  Do While Not EOF(1)
    Input #1, value
    Let numCoins = numCoins + 1
    Let sum = sum + value
  Loop
  picValue.Cls
  picValue.Print "The value of the"; numCoins; "coins is"; sum; "cents."
  Close #1
End Sub
```

[Run and press the command button.]

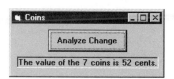

The value of the counter, *numCoins*, was initially 0 and changed on each execution of the loop to 1, 2, 3, 4, 5, and finally 6. The accumulator, *sum*, initially had the value 0 and increased with each execution of the loop to 1, 2, 7, 17, 27, and finally 52.

Flags

A **flag** is a variable that keeps track of whether a certain event has occurred. Typically, it is initialized with the value 0 and then assigned a nonzero value when the event occurs. It is used within a loop to provide information that will be taken into consideration after the loop has terminated. The flag also provides an alternative method of terminating a loop.

EXAMPLE 4 The following program counts the number of words in the file WORDS.TXT and then reports whether the words are in alphabetical order. In each execution of the loop, a word is compared to the next word in the list. The flag variable, called *orderFlag*, is initially assigned the value 0 and is set to 1 if a pair of adjacent words is out of order. The technique used in this program will be used in Chapter 7 when we study sorting. **Note:** The statement in line 7, Let word1 = "", is a device to get things started. Each word must first be read into the variable *word2*.

WORDS.TXT contains the following winning words from the U.S. National Spelling Bee:

"cambist", "croissant", "deification"
"hydrophyte", "incisor", "maculature"
"macerate", "narcolepsy", "shallon"

Object	Property	Setting
frmWords	Caption	Word Analysis
cmdAnalyze	Caption	Analyze Words
picReport		

```
Private Sub cmdAnalyze_Click()
  Dim orderFlag As Integer, wordCounter As Integer
  Dim word1 As String, word2 As String
  Rem Count words.  Are they in alphabetical order?
  Let orderFlag = 0
  Let wordCounter = 0
  Let word1 = ""
  Open "WORDS.TXT" For Input As #1
  Do While Not EOF(1)
    Input #1, word2
    Let wordCounter = wordCounter + 1
    If word1 > word2 Then
        Let orderFlag = 1
    End If
    Let word1 = word2
  Loop
  Close #1
  picReport.Print "The number of words is"; wordCounter
  If orderFlag = 0 Then
      picReport.Print "The words are in alphabetical order."
    Else
      picReport.Print "The words are not in alphabetical order."
  End If
End Sub
```

[Run and press the command button.]

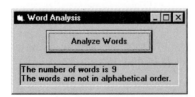

Nested Loops

The statements inside of a Do loop can consist of another Do loop. Such a configuration is referred to as **nested loops** and is useful in repeating a single data-processing routine several times.

EXAMPLE 5 Modify the program in Example 2 to allow the user to look through several lists of names. Suppose we have several different phone directories, the names of which are listed in the file LISTS.TXT. (For instance, the file LISTS.TXT might contain the entries CLIENTS.TXT, FRIENDS.TXT, and KINFOLK.TXT.) A sought-after name might be in any one of the files.

SOLUTION The statements in the inner Do loop will be used to look up names as before. At least one pass through the outer Do loop is guaranteed and passes will continue as long as the name is not found and phone lists remain to be examined.

```
Private Sub cmdDisplay_Click()
   Dim foundFlag As String, fileName As String
   Dim nom As String, phoneNum As String
   Open "LISTS.TXT" For Input As #1
   Let foundFlag = "no"
   Let nom = ""
   Do While (foundFlag = "no") And (Not EOF(1))
      Input #1, fileName
      Open fileName For Input As #2
      Do While (nom <> txtName.Text) And (Not EOF(2))
         Input #2, nom, phoneNum
      Loop
      Close #2
      picNumber.Cls
      If nom = txtName.Text Then
          picNumber.Print nom, phoneNum
          Let foundFlag = "yes"
      End If
   Loop
   Close #1
   If foundFlag = "no" Then
       picNumber.Print "Name not found."
   End If
End Sub
```

Comment

1. In Appendix D, the section "Stepping Through a Program Containing a Do Loop: Chapter 6" uses the Visual Basic debugging tools to trace the flow through a Do loop.

PRACTICE PROBLEMS 6.2

1. Determine the output of the following program, where the file SCORES.TXT contains the three scores 150, 200, and 300.

```
Private Sub cmdComputeTotal_Click()
  Dim sum As Single, score As Single
  Rem Find the sum of a collection of bowling scores
  Let sum = 0
  Open "SCORES.TXT" For Input As #1
  Input #1, score
  Do While Not EOF(1)
    Let sum = sum + score
    Input #1, score
  Loop
  Close #1
  picTotal.Print sum
End Sub
```

2. Why didn't the preceding program produce the intended output?

3. Correct the preceding program so it has the intended output.

EXERCISES 6.2

In Exercises 1 through 10, determine the output displayed in the picture box when the command button is clicked.

1.
```
Private Sub cmdDisplay_Click()
  Dim total As Single, num As Single
  Let total = 0
  Open "DATA.TXT" For Input As #1
  Do While Not EOF(1)
    Input #1, num
    Let total = total + num
  Loop
  Close #1
  picOutput.Print total
End Sub
```

(Assume that the file DATA.TXT contains the following entries.)

5, 2, 6

2.
```
Private Sub cmdDisplay_Click()
  Dim nom As String
  Open "DATA.TXT" For Input As #1
  Do While Not EOF(1)
    Input #1, nom
    picOutput.Print nom
  Loop
  Close #1
End Sub
```

(Assume that the file DATA.TXT contains the following entries.)

"Brooke", "Andre"

3.
```
Private Sub cmdDisplay_Click()
   Dim dessert As String
   Rem Display list of desserts
   Open "DESSERTS.TXT" For Input As #1
   Do While Not EOF(1)
     Input #1, dessert
     picOutput.Print dessert
   Loop
   Close #1
End Sub
```

(Assume that the file DESSERTS.TXT contains the following entries.)

"pie", "cake", "melon"

4.
```
Private Sub cmdDisplay_Click()
   Dim city As String, pop As Single
   Open "CITYPOPS.TXT" For Input As #1
   Do While Not EOF(1)
     Input #1, city, pop
     If pop >= 7 Then
         picOutput.Print city, pop
     End If
   Loop
   Close #1
End Sub
```

(Assume that the file CITYPOPS.TXT contains the following four lines that give a city and its population in millions.)

"San Francisco", 5.6
"Boston", 4
"Chicago", 8
"New York", 17.7

5.
```
Private Sub cmdDisplay_Click()
   Dim firstLetter As String, fruit As String
   Let firstLetter = ""
   Open "FRUITS.TXT" For Input As #1
   Do While Not EOF(1)
     Input #1, fruit
     If Left(fruit, 1) <> firstLetter Then
         If firstLetter <> "" Then
             picOutput.Print
         End If
         Let firstLetter = Left(fruit, 1)
         picOutput.Print Tab(3); firstLetter
     End If
     picOutput.Print fruit
   Loop
   Close #1
End Sub
```

(Assume that the file FRUITS.TXT contains the following entries.)

"Apple", "Apricot", "Avocado", "Banana", "Blueberry", "Grape", "Lemon", "Lime"

6.
```
Private Sub cmdDisplay_Click()
    Dim num As Single
    Rem Display list of numbers
    Open "DATA.TXT" For Input As #1
    Input #1, num
    Do While Not EOF(1)
      picOutput.Print num;
      Input #1, num
    Loop
    Close #1
End Sub
```

(Assume that the file DATA.TXT contains the following entries.)

2, 3, 8, 5

7.
```
Private Sub cmdDisplay_Click()
    Dim animal As String, groupName As String
    Call InputAnimal(animal)
    If animal <> "" Then
        Call SearchList(animal, groupName)
        Call DisplayResult(animal, groupName)
    End If
End Sub


Private Sub DisplayResult(anml As String, gName As String)
  If gName = "" Then
      picOutput.Print "Animal not found."
    Else
      picOutput.Print "A group of "; anml; "s is called a "; gName
  End If
End Sub


Private Sub InputAnimal(anml As String)
  Rem Request the name of an animal as input
  Let anml = InputBox("Please enter the name of an animal")
End Sub


Private Sub SearchList(anml As String, gName As String)
  Dim creature As String, groupName As String
  Let creature = ""
  Open "ANIMALS.TXT" For Input As #1
  Do While (creature <> anml) And Not EOF(1)
    Input #1, creature, groupName
  Loop
  If EOF(1) Then
      Let gName = ""
    Else
      Let gName = groupName
  End If
  Close #1
End Sub
```

(Assume that the file ANIMALS.TXT contains the following three lines that give an animal and the name of a group of those animals. Assume the response is *duck*.)

"lion", "pride"
"duck", "brace"
"bee", "swarm"

8.
```
Private Sub cmdDisplay_Click()
    Dim excerpt As String
    Let excerpt = "I think I can. "
    Call Duplicate30(s)
    Let excerpt = "We're off to see the wizard, " & _
            "the wonderful wizard of OZ."
    Call Duplicate30(excerpt)
End Sub

Private Sub Duplicate30(sentence As String)
    Dim flag As Integer
    Let flag = 0      'flag tells whether loop has been executed
    Do While Len(sentence) < 30
      Let flag = 1
      Let sentence = sentence & sentence
    Loop
    If flag = 1 Then
        picOutput.Print sentence
      Else
        picOutput.Print "Loop not executed."
    End If
End Sub
```

9.
```
Private Sub cmdDisplay_Click()
    Dim word As String, cWord As String
    Open "WORDS.TXT" For Input As #1
    Do While Not EOF(1)
      Input #1, word
      If Left(word, 1) = "c" Then
          Let cWord = word
      End If
    Loop
    Close #1
    picOutput.Print cWord
End Sub
```

(Assume that the file WORDS.TXT contains the following saying data.)

"time", "is", "a", "child", "idly", "moving", "counters", "in", "a", "game", "Heraclitus"

10.
```
Private Sub cmdDisplay_Click()
    Dim max As Single, value As Single, rowMax As Single
    Let max = 0
    Open "DATA.TXT" For Input As #1
    Do While Not EOF(1)
      Input #1, value
      Let rowMax = 0
```

```
        Do While value <> -2
          If value > rowMax Then
              Let rowMax = value
          End If
          Input #1, value
        Loop
        picOutput.Print rowMax
        If rowMax > max Then
            Let max = rowMax
        End If
      Loop
      Close #1
      picOutput.Print max
    End Sub
```

(Assume that the file DATA.TXT contains the following entries.)

5, 7, 3, –2, 10, 12, 6, 4, –2, 1, 9, –2

In Exercises 11 through 14, identify the errors.

11.
```
Private Sub cmdDisplay_Click()
    Dim num As Single
    Open "DATA.TXT" For Input As #1
    Do While (Not EOF(1)) And (num > 0)
      Input #1, num
      picOutput.Print num
    Close #1
End Sub
```

(Assume that the file DATA.TXT contains the following entries.)

7, 6, 0, –1, 2

12.
```
Private Sub cmdDisplay_Click()
    Dim flag As Integer, num As Single
    Let flag = 0
    Do While flag <> 1
      Let num = Val(InputBox("Enter a number"))
      If num * num < 0 Then
          Let flag = 1
      End If
    Loop
End Sub
```

13.
```
Private Sub cmdDisplay_Click()
    Dim president As String
    Rem Display names of some U.S. Presidents
    Open "PRES.TXT" For Input As #1
    Input #1, president
    Do
      picOutput.Print president
      Input #1, president
    Loop Until EOF(1)
    Close #1
End Sub
```

(Assume that the file PRES.TXT contains the following entries.)

"Lincoln", "Washington", "Kennedy", "Clinton"

14.
```
Private Sub cmdDisplay_Click()
    Dim num As Single
    Open "DATA.TXT" For Input As #1
    If EOF(1) Then
        Let num = 0
      Else
        Input #1, num
    End If
    Do While 1 < num < 5
      picOutput.Print num
      If EOF(1) Then
          Let num = 0
        Else
          Input #1, num
      End If
    Loop
    Close #1
End Sub
```

(Assume that the file DATA.TXT contains the following entries)

3, 2, 4, 7, 2

15. Write a program to find and display the largest of a collection of positive numbers contained in a data file. (Test the program with the collection of numbers 89, 77, 95, and 86.)

16. Write a program to find and display those names that are repeated in a data file. Assume the file has already been sorted into alphabetical order. When a name is found to be repeated, only display it once.

17. Suppose the file GRADES.TXT contains student grades on a final exam. Write a program that displays the average grade on the exam and the percentage of grades that are above average.

18. Suppose the file BIDS.TXT contains a list of bids on a construction project. Write a program to analyze the list and report the two highest bids.

19. Suppose the file USPRES.TXT contains the names of the United States Presidents in order from Washington to Clinton. Write a program that asks the user to type a number from 1 to 42 into a text box, and then, when a command button is clicked, displays the name of the President corresponding to that number.

20. Table 6.1 shows the different grades of eggs and the minimum weight required for each classification. Write a program that processes a data file that lists the weights of a sample of eggs. The program should report the number of eggs in each grade and the weight of the lightest and heaviest egg in the sample. (**Note:** Eggs weighing less than 1.5 ounces cannot be sold in supermarkets.) Figure 6.6 shows a sample output of the program.

Grade	Weight (in ounces)
Jumbo	2.5
Extra Large	2.25
Large	2
Medium	1.75
Small	1.5

25 Jumbo eggs
132 Extra Large eggs
180 Large eggs
150 Medium eggs
95 Small eggs
Lightest egg: 1.52 ounces
Heaviest egg: 2.72 ounces

Table 6.1 Grades of eggs.

Figure 6.6 Output for Exercise 20.

21. Write a program to request a positive integer as input and carry out the following algorithm. If the number is even, divide it by 2. Otherwise, multiply the number by 3 and add 1. Repeat this process with the resulting number and continue repeating the process until the number 1 is reached. After the number 1 is reached, the program should display how many iterations were required. **Note:** A number is even if Int(num / 2) = num / 2. (Test the program with the numbers 9, 21, and 27.)

22. Suppose the file USPRES.TXT contains the names of all United States Presidents, and the file USSENATE.TXT contains the names of all former and present U.S. Senators. Write a program with nested loops that uses these files to display the names of all Presidents who served in the Senate.

23. Suppose the file SONNET.TXT contains Shakespeare's Sonnet #18. Each entry in the file consists of a line of the sonnet enclosed in quotes. Write a program using nested loops to analyze this file line by line and report the average number of words in a line and the average length of a word in the sonnet.

24. Suppose the file SALES.TXT contains information on the sales during the past week at a new car dealership. Assume the file begins as shown in Figure 6.7. The file contains the following for each salesperson at the dealership: the name of the salesperson, pairs of numbers giving the final sales price and the dealer cost for each sale made by that salesperson, a pair of zeros to indicate the end of data for that salesperson. Write a program to display the name of each salesperson and the commission earned for the week. Assume the commission is 15% of the profit on each sale.

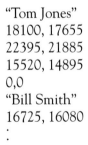

"Tom Jones"
18100, 17655
22395, 21885
15520, 14895
0,0
"Bill Smith"
16725, 16080
.
.
.

Figure 6.7 Sales data file for Exercise 24.

25. Write a program to do the following. (The program should use a flag.)

    (a) Ask the user to input a sentence that possibly contains one pair of parentheses.

    (b) Display the sentence with the parentheses and their contents removed.

    Test the program with the following sentence as input: BASIC (Beginners All-purpose Symbolic Instruction Code) is the world's most widely known computer language.

26. The salespeople at a health club keep track of the members who have joined in the last month. Their names and types of membership, Bronze, Silver, or Gold, are stored in the data file NEWMEMBS.TXT. Write a program that displays all the Bronze members, then the Silver members, and finally the Gold members.

27. Table 6.2 gives the prices of various liquids. Write a program that requests an amount of money as input and displays the names of all liquids for which a gallon could be purchased with that amount of money. The information from the table should be recovered from a data file. As an example, if the user has $2.35, then the following should be displayed in the picture box:

    You can purchase one gallon of any of the following liquids.

    Bleach
    Gasoline
    Milk

Liquid	Price	Liquid	Price
Apple Cider	2.60	Milk	2.30
Beer	6.00	Gatorade	4.20
Bleach	1.40	Perrier	6.85
Coca-Cola	2.55	Pancake Syrup	15.50
Gasoline	1.30	Spring Water	4.10

Table 6.2 Some comparative prices per gallon of various liquids.

SOLUTIONS TO PRACTICE PROBLEMS 6.2

1. 350

2. When the third score was read from the file, EOF(1) became true. With EOF(1) true, the loop terminated and the third score was never added to *sum*. In addition, if the data file had been empty or contained only one piece of data, then the error message "Input past end of file" would have been displayed.

3.
```
Private Sub cmdComputeTotal_Click()
    Dim sum As Single, score As Single
    Rem Find the sum of a collection of bowling scores
    Let sum = 0
    Open "SCORES.TXT" For Input As #1
    Do While Not EOF(1)
        Input #1, score
        Let sum = sum + score
    Loop
    Close #1
    picTotal.Print sum
End Sub
```

6.3 FOR...NEXT LOOPS

When we know exactly how many times a loop should be executed, a special type of loop, called a For...Next loop, can be used. For...Next loops are easy to read and write, and have features that make them ideal for certain common tasks. The following code uses a For...Next loop to display a table.

```
Private Sub cmdDisplayTable_Click()
  Dim i As Integer
  Rem Display a table of the first 5 numbers and their squares
  picTable.Cls
  For i = 1 To 5
    picTable.Print i; i ^ 2
  Next i
End Sub
```

[Run and click on cmdDisplayTable. The following is displayed in the picture box.]

```
1   1
2   4
3   9
4   16
5   25
```

The equivalent program written with a Do loop is as follows.

```
Private Sub cmdDisplayTable_Click()
  Dim i As Integer
  Rem Display a table of the first 5 numbers and their squares
  picTable.Cls
  Let i = 1
  Do While i <= 5
    picTable.Print i; i ^ 2
    Let i = i + 1
  Loop
End Sub
```

In general, a portion of a program of the form

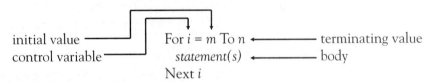

initial value ———— For $i = m$ To n ←———— terminating value
control variable ———— statement(s) ←———— body
                      Next i

constitutes a For...Next loop. The pair of statements For and Next cause the statements between them to be repeated a specified number of times. The For statement designates a numeric variable, called the **control variable**, that is initialized and then automatically changes after each execution of the loop. Also, the For statement gives the range of values this variable will assume. The Next statement increments the control variable. If $m \leq n$, then i is assigned the values m, $m + 1, \ldots, n$ in order, and the body is executed once for each of these values. If $m > n$, then execution continues with the statement after the For...Next loop.

When program execution reaches a For...Next loop such as the one shown previously, the For statement assigns to the control variable i the initial value m and checks to see whether i is greater than the terminating value n. If so, then execution jumps to the line following the Next statement. If $i <= n$, the statements inside the loop are executed. Then, the Next statement increases the value of i by 1 and checks this new value to see if it exceeds n. If not, the entire process is repeated until the value of i exceeds n. When this happens, the program moves to the line following the loop. Figure 6.8 contains the pseudocode and flowchart of a For...Next loop.

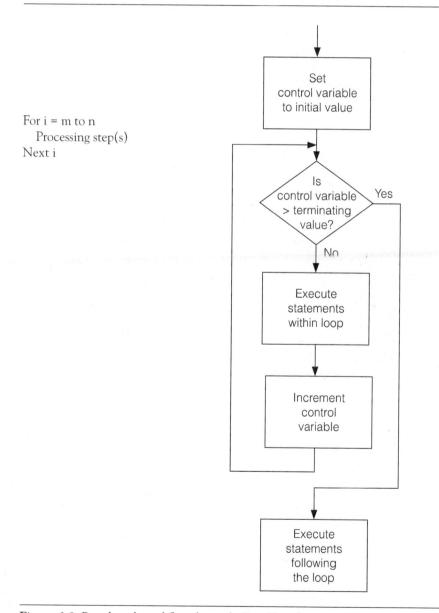

For i = m to n
    Processing step(s)
Next i

Figure 6.8 Pseudocode and flowchart of a For...Next loop.

The control variable can be *any* numeric variable. The most common single letter names are i, j, and k; however, if appropriate, the name should suggest the purpose of the control variable.

EXAMPLE 1   Suppose the population of a city is 300,000 in the year 1990 and is growing at the rate of 3 percent per year. The following program displays a table showing the population each year until 1995.

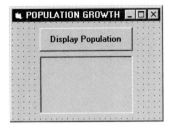

Object	Property	Setting
frm6_3_1	Caption	POPULATION GROWTH
cmdDisplay	Caption	Display Population
picTable		

```
Private Sub cmdDisplay_Click()
  Dim pop As Single, yr As Integer
  Rem Display population from 1990 to 1995
  picTable.Cls
  Let pop = 300000
  For yr = 1990 To 1995
    picTable.Print yr, Format(pop, "#,#")
    Let pop = pop + .03 * pop
  Next yr
End Sub
```

[Run and click the command button.]

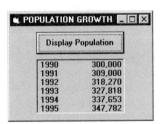

The initial and terminating values can be constants, variables, or expressions. For instance, the For statement in the preceding program can be replaced by

```
Let firstYr = 1990
Let lastYr = 1995
For yr = firstYr To lastYr
```

In Example 1, the control variable was increased by 1 after each pass through the loop. A variation of the For statement allows any number to be used as the increment. The statement

```
For i = m To n Step s
```

instructs the Next statement to add *s* to the control variable instead of 1. The numbers *m*, *n*, and *s* do not have to be whole numbers. The number *s* is called the **step value** of the loop.

EXAMPLE 2 The following program displays the values of the index of a For...Next loop for terminating and step values input by the user.

Object	Property	Setting
frm6_3_2	Caption	For index = 0 To n Step s
lblN	Caption	n:
txtEnd	Text	(blank)
lblS	Caption	s:
txtStep	Text	(blank)
cmdDisplay	Caption	Display Values of index
picValues		

```
Private Sub cmdDisplay_Click()
  Dim n As Single, s As Single, index As Single
  Rem Display values of index ranging from 0 to n Step s
  picValues.Cls
  Let n = Val(txtEnd.Text)
  Let s = Val(txtStep.Text)
  For index = 0 To n Step s
    picValues.Print index;
  Next index
End Sub
```

[Run, type 3.2 and .5 into the text boxes, and click the command button.]

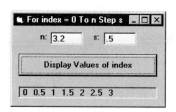

In the examples considered so far, the control variable was successively increased until it reached the terminating value. However, if a negative step value is used and the initial value is greater than the terminating value, then the control value is decreased until reaching the terminating value. In other words, the loop counts backward or downward.

EXAMPLE 3 The following program accepts a word as input and displays it backwards.

Object	Property	Setting
frm6_3_3	Caption	Write Backwards
lblWord	Caption	Enter Word
txtWord	Text	(blank)
cmdReverse	Caption	Reverse Letters
picTranspose		

```
Private Sub cmdReverse_Click()
  picTranspose.Cls
  picTranspose.Print Reverse(txtWord.Text)
End Sub
```

```
Private Function Reverse(info As String) As String
  Dim m As Integer, j As Integer, temp As String
  Let m = Len(info)
  Let temp = ""
  For j = m To 1 Step -1
    Let temp = temp + Mid(info, j, 1)
  Next j
  Reverse = temp
End Function
```

[Run, type SUEZ into the text box, and click the command button.]

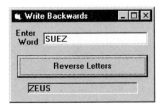

Note: The initial and terminating values of a For...Next loop can be expressions. For instance, the third and fifth lines of the function in Example 3 can be consolidated to

```
For j = Len(info) To 1 Step -1
```

The body of a For...Next loop can contain *any* sequence of Visual Basic statements. In particular, it can contain another For...Next loop. However, the second loop must be completely contained inside the first loop and must have a different control variable. Such a configuration is called **nested loops**. Figure 6.9 shows several examples of valid nested loops.

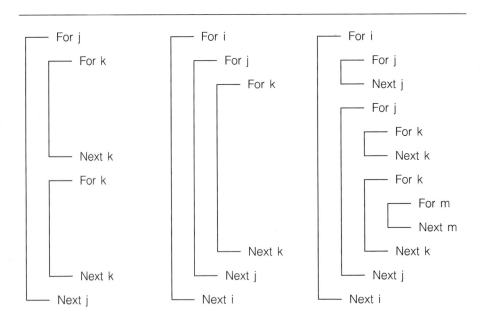

Figure 6.9 Nested loops.

EXAMPLE 4 Write a program to display the products of the integers from 1 to 4.

SOLUTION In the following program, *j* denotes the left factors of the products and *k* denotes the right factors. Each factor takes on a value from 1 to 4. The values are assigned to *j* in the outer loop and to *k* in the inner loop. Initially, *j* is assigned the value 1 and then the inner loop is traversed four times to produce the first row of products. At the end of these four passes, the value of *j* will still be 1 and the value of *k* will have been incremented to 5. The picTable.Print statement just before Next j guarantees that no more products will be displayed in that row. The first execution of the outer loop is then complete. Following this, the statement Next j increments the value of *j* to 2. The statement beginning For k is then executed. It resets the value of *k* to 1. The second row of products is displayed during the next four executions of the inner loop, and so on.

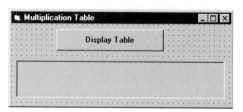

Object	Property	Setting
frmMultiply	Caption	Multiplication Table
cmdDisplay	Caption	Display Table
picTable		

```
Private Sub cmdDisplay_Click()
  Dim j As Integer, k As Integer
  picTable.Cls
  For j = 1 To 4
    For k = 1 To 4
      picTable.Print j; "x"; k; "="; j * k,
    Next k
    picTable.Print
  Next j
End Sub
```

[Run and press the command button.]

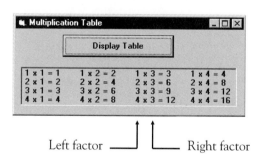

Left factor —————┘ └————— Right factor

Comments

1. The body of a For...Next loop need not be indented. However, because indenting improves the readability of the program, it is good programming style. As soon as you see the word For, your eyes can easily scan down the program to find the matching Next statement. You then know two facts immediately: the number of statements in the body of the loop and the number of passes that will be made through the loop.

2. For and Next statements must be paired. If one is missing, the program will generate the error message "For without Next" or "Next without For."

3. Consider a loop beginning with For i = m To n Step s. The loop will be executed exactly once if m equals n no matter what value s has. The loop will not be executed at all if m is greater than n and s is positive, or if m is less than n and s is negative.

4. The value of the control variable should not be altered within the body of the loop; doing so might cause the loop to repeat indefinitely or have an unpredictable number of repetitions.

5. Noninteger step values can lead to roundoff errors with the result that the loop is not executed the intended number of times. For instance, a loop beginning with For i = 1 To 2 Step .1 will be executed only 10 times instead of the intended 11 times. It should be replaced with For i = 1 To 2.01 Step .1.

PRACTICE PROBLEMS 6.3

1. Why won't the following lines of code work as intended?

```
For i = 15 To 1
  picBox.Print i;
Next i
```

2. When is a For...Next loop more appropriate than a Do loop?

EXERCISES 6.3

In Exercises 1 through 12, determine the output displayed in the picture box when the command button is clicked.

1.
```
Private Sub cmdDisplay_Click()
    Dim i As Integer
    For i = 1 To 4
      picOutput.Print "Pass #"; i
    Next i
End Sub
```

2.
```
Private Sub cmdDisplay_Click()
    Dim i As Integer
    For i = 3 To 6
      picOutput.Print 2 * i;
    Next i
End Sub
```

3.
```
Private Sub cmdDisplay_Click()
    Dim j As Integer
    For j = 2 To 8 Step 2
      picOutput.Print j;
    Next j
    picOutput.Print "Who do we appreciate?"
End Sub
```

4.
```
Private Sub cmdDisplay_Click()
    Dim countdown As Integer
    For countdown = 10 To 1 Step -1
      picOutput.Print countdown;
    Next countdown
    picOutput.Print "blastoff"
End Sub
```

5.
```
Private Sub cmdDisplay_Click()
    Dim num As Integer, i As Integer
    Let num = 5
    For i = num To 2 * num + 3
      picOutput.Print i;
    Next i
End Sub
```

6.
```
Private Sub cmdDisplay_Click()
    Dim i As Single
    For i = 3 To 5 Step .25
      picOutput.Print i;
    Next i
    picOutput.Print i
End Sub
```

7.
```
Private Sub cmdDisplay_Click()
    Dim recCount As Integer, miler As Integer
    Dim nom As String, mileTime As String
    Rem First entry in data file is number of records in file
    Open "MILER.TXT" For Input As #1
    Input #1, recCount
    For miler = 1 To recCount
      Input #1,  nom, mileTime
      picOutput.Print nom, mileTime
    Next miler
    Close #1
End Sub
```

(Assume that the file MILER.TXT contains the following four lines.)

3
"Steve Cram", "3:46.31"
"Steve Scott", "3:51.6"
"Mary Slaney", "4:20.5"

8.
```
Private Sub cmdDisplay_Click()
    Dim recCount As Integer, total As Integer
    Dim i As Integer, score As Integer
    Rem First entry in data file is number of records in file
    Open "SCORES.TXT" For Input As #1
    Input #1, recCount
    Let total = 0
    For i = 1 To recCount
      Input #1, score
      Let total = total + score
    Next i
    Close #1
    picOutput.Print "Average ="; total / recCount
End Sub
```

(Assume that the file SCORES.TXT contains the following entries.)

4, 89, 85, 88, 98

9.
```
Private Sub cmdDisplay_Click()
    Dim i As Integer, j As Integer
    For i = 0 To 2
      For j = 0 To 3
        picOutput.Print i + 3 * j + 1; "  ";
      Next j
      picOutput.Print
    Next i
End Sub
```

10.
```
Private Sub cmdDisplay_Click()
    Dim i As Integer, j As Integer
    For i = 1 To 5
      For j = 1 To i
        picOutput.Print "*";
      Next j
      picOutput.Print
    Next i
End Sub
```

11.
```
Private Sub cmdDisplay_Click()
    Dim word As String, num1 As Integer, num2 As Integer
    Let word = InputBox("Please enter a word")
    Let num1 = Int((20 - Len(word)) / 2)
    Let num2 = 20 - num1 - Len(word)
    Call Asterisks(num1)
    picOutput.Print word;
    Call Asterisks(num2)
End Sub

Private Sub Asterisks(num As Integer)
  Dim i As Integer
  Rem Display num asterisks
  For i = 1 To num
    picOutput.Print "*";
  Next i
End Sub
```

(Assume that the response is *Hooray*.)

12.
```
Private Sub cmdDisplay_Click()
    Dim info As String, i As Integer, letter As String
    Rem Display an array of letters
    Let info = "DATA"
    For i = 1 To Len(info)
      Let letter = Mid(info, i, 1)
      Call DisplayFive(letter)
      picOutput.Print        'Move to next line
    Next i
  End Sub

Private Sub DisplayFive(letter As String)
  Dim i As Integer
  Rem Display letter five times
  For i = 1 To 5
    picOutput.Print letter;
  Next i
End Sub
```

In Exercises 13 through 16, identify the errors.

13.
```
Private Sub cmdDisplay_Click()
    Dim j As Single
    For j = 1 To 25.5 Step -1
      picOutput.Print j
    Next j
End Sub
```

14.
```
Private Sub cmdDisplay_Click()
    Dim i As Integer
    For i = 1 To 3
      picOutput.Print i; 2 ^ i
End Sub
```

15.
```
Private Sub cmdDisplay_Click()
    Dim i As Integer
    For i = 1 To 99
      If i Mod 2 = 0 Then
          Next i
        Else
          picOutput.Print i
      End If
    Next i
End Sub
```

16.
```
Private Sub cmdDisplay_Click()
    Dim i As Integer, j As Integer
    For i = 1 To 6
      For j = 1 To 3
          picOutput.Print i / j;
      Next i
    Next j
End Sub
```

In Exercises 17 and 18, rewrite the program using a For...Next loop.

17.
```
Private Sub cmdDisplay_Click()
    Dim num As Integer
    Let num = 1
    Do While num <= 10
      picOutput.Print num
      Let num = num + 2
    Loop
End Sub
```

18.
```
Private Sub cmdDisplay_Click()
    picOutput.Print "hello"
    picOutput.Print "hello"
    picOutput.Print "hello"
    picOutput.Print "hello"
End Sub
```

In Exercises 19 through 37, write a program to complete the stated task.

19. Display a row of 10 stars (asterisks).

20. Request a number from 1 to 20 and display a row of that many stars (asterisks).

21. Display a 10-by-10 square of stars.

22. Request a number and call a subprogram to display a square having that number of stars on each side.

23. Find the sum $1 + 1/2 + 1/3 + 1/4 + \ldots + 1/100$.

24. Find the sum of the odd numbers from 1 through 99.

25. You are offered two salary options for ten days of work. Option 1: $100 per day. Option 2: $1 the first day, $2 the second day, $4 the third day, and so on, with the amount doubling each day. Write a program to determine which option pays better.

26. When $1000 is deposited at 5 percent simple interest, the amount grows by $50 each year. When money is invested at 5 percent compound interest, then the amount at the end of each year is 1.05 times the amount at the beginning of that year. Write a program to display the amounts for 10 years for a $1000 deposit at 5 percent simple and compound interest. The first few lines displayed in the picture box should appear as in Figure 6.10.

Years	Amount Simple Interest	Amount Compound Interest
1	$1,050.00	$1,050.00
2	$1,100.00	$1,102.50
3	$1,150.00	$1,157.63

Figure 6.10 Growth of $1000 at simple and compound interest.

27. According to researchers at Stanford Medical School (as cited in *Medical Self Care*), the ideal weight for a woman is found by multiplying her height in inches by 3.5 and subtracting 108. The ideal weight for a man is found by multiplying his height in inches by 4 and subtracting 128. Request a lower and upper bound for heights and then produce a table giving the ideal weights for women and men in that height range. For example, when a lower bound of 62 and an upper bound of 65 are specified, Figure 6.11 shows the output displayed in the picture box:

Height	Wt - Women	Wt - Men
62	109	120
63	112.5	124
64	116	128
65	119.5	132

Figure 6.11 Output for Exercise 27.

28. Table 6.3 contains statistics on professional quarterbacks. Read this information from a data file and generate an extended table with two additional columns, Pct Comp (Percent Completions) and Avg Gain (Average Gain per Completed Pass).

Name	Att	Comp	Yards
Young	279	180	2517
Rypien	421	249	3564
Bono	237	141	1617
Aikman	363	237	2754

Table 6.3 1991 Passing statistics (attempts, completions, yards gained).

29. Request a sentence and display the number of sibilants (that is, letters S or Z) in the sentence. The counting should be carried out by a function.

30. Request a number, *n*, from 1 to 30 and one of the letters *S* or *P*. Then calculate the sum or product of the numbers from 1 to *n* depending upon whether *S* or *P* was selected. The calculations should be carried out with functions.

31. Suppose $800 is deposited into a savings account earning 4 percent interest compounded annually, and $100 is added to the account at the end of each year. Calculate the amount of money in the account at the end of 10 years. (Determine a formula for computing the balance at the end of 1 year based on the balance at the beginning of the year. Then write a program that starts with a balance of $800 and makes 10 passes through a loop containing the formula to produce the final answer.)

32. A TV set is purchased with a loan of $563 to be paid off with five monthly payments of $116. The interest rate is 1 percent per month. Display a table giving the balance on the loan at the end of each month.

33. *Radioactive Decay.* Cobalt 60, a radioactive form of cobalt used in cancer therapy, decays or dissipates over a period of time. Each year, 12 percent of the amount present at the beginning of the year will have decayed. If a container of cobalt 60 initially contains 10 grams, determine the amount remaining after 5 years.

34. *Supply and Demand.* This year's level of production and price for most agricultural products greatly affects the level of production and price next year. Suppose the current crop of soybeans in a certain country is 80 million bushels and experience has shown that for each year,

[price this year] = 20 – .1 * [quantity this year]

[quantity next year] = 5 * [price this year] –10

where quantity is measured in units of millions of bushels. Generate a table to show the quantity and price for each of the next 12 years.

35. Request a number greater than 3 and display a hollow rectangle of stars (asterisks) with each outer row and column having that many stars. Use a fixed-width font such as Courier or Terminal so that the space and asterisk will have the same width. (See Figure 6.12(a).)

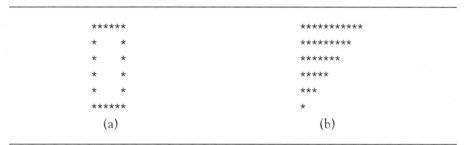

Figure 6.12 Outputs for Exercises 35 and 36.

36. Request an odd number and display a triangle similar to the one in Figure 6.12(b) with the input number of stars in the top row.

37. Allow any two integers, *m* and *n*, between 2 and 12 to be specified and then generate an *m*-by-*n* multiplication table. Figure 6.13 shows the output when *m* is 5 and *n* is 7. To obtain a nicely lined up table, use a fixed-space font such as Courier or Terminal together with the following function, which right-justifies a value in a field six spaces wide.

```
Private Function RightJustify6(what As Integer) As String
  Dim strVar As String
  Let strVar = Format(what, "#")
  RightJustify6 = Format(s, "@@@@@@")
End Function
```

1	2	3	4	5	6	7
2	4	6	8	10	12	14
3	6	9	12	15	18	21
4	8	12	16	20	24	28
5	10	15	20	25	30	35

Figure 6.13 Output for Exercise 37.

38. Write a program to create the histogram in Figure 6.14. A data file should hold the years and values. The first entry in the data file could be used to hold the title for the histogram.

```
1980 ** 2
1985 *** 3
1990 ******** 8
1995 ********** 10
```

People Employed in Computing Services (in 100,000s)

Figure 6.14 Histogram for Exercise 38.
Source: Bureau of Labor Statistics

39. A man pays $1 to get into a gambling casino. He loses half of his money there and then has to pay $1 to leave. He goes to a second casino, pays another $1 to get in, loses half his money again and then pays another $1 to leave. Then, he goes to a third casino, pays another $1 to get in, loses half of his money again, and then pays another $1 to get out. After this, he's broke. Write a program to determine the amount of money he began with by testing $5, then $6, and so on.

40. Write a program to estimate how much a young worker will make before retiring at age 65. Request the worker's name, age, and starting salary as input. Assume the worker receives a 5 percent raise each year. For example, if the user enters Helen, 25, and 20000, then the picture box should display the following:

Helen will earn about $2,415,995.25

Exercises 41 through 44 require the Rnd function presented in Section 3.6.

41. Write a program that selects a word at random from among 20 words in a file.

42. Write a program to simulate the tossing of a coin 100 times and display the numbers of "heads" and "tails" that occur.

43. A company has a sequential file containing the names of people who have qualified for a drawing to win an IBM Personal Computer. Write a program to select a name at random from the file. Assume the file contains at most 1000 names. Test your program on a file consisting of five names.

44. A club has 20 members. Write a program to select two different people at random to serve as president and treasurer. (The names of the members should be contained in a file.)

SOLUTIONS TO PRACTICE PROBLEMS 6.3

1. The loop will never be entered because 15 is greater than 1. The intended first line might have been

```
For i = 15 To 1 Step -1
```

or

```
For i = 1 To 15
```

2. If the exact number of times the loop will be executed is known before entering the loop, then a For...Next loop should be used. Otherwise, a Do loop is more appropriate.

6.4 A CASE STUDY: ANALYZE A LOAN

This case study develops a program to analyze a loan. Assume the loan is repaid in equal monthly payments and interest is compounded monthly. The program should request the amount (principal) of the loan, the annual rate of interest, and the number of years over which the loan is to be repaid. The four options to be provided by command buttons are as follows.

1. Calculate the monthly payment. The formula for the monthly payment is

$$\text{payment} = p * r / (1 - (1 + r) \char`\^ (-n))$$

where p is the principal of the loan, r is the monthly interest rate (annual rate divided by 12) given as a number between 0 (for 0 percent) and 1 (for 100 percent), and n is the number of months over which the loan is to be repaid. Because a payment computed in this manner can be expected to include fractions of a cent, the value should be rounded up to the next nearest cent. This corrected payment can be achieved using the formula

$$\text{correct payment} = -\text{Int}(-100 * \text{payment}) / 100$$

2. Display an amortization schedule, that is, a table showing the balance on the loan at the end of each month for any year over the duration of the loan.

Also show how much of each monthly payment goes toward interest and how much is used to repay the principal. Finally, display the total interest paid over the duration of the loan. The balances for successive months are calculated with the formula

$$\text{balance} = (1 + r) * b - m$$

where r is the monthly interest rate (annual rate / 12, a fraction between 0 and 1), b is the balance for the preceding month (amount of loan left to be paid), and m is the monthly payment.

3. Show the effect of changes in the interest rate. Display a table giving the monthly payment for each interest rate from 1 percent below to 1 percent above the specified annual rate in steps of one-eighth of a percent.

4. Quit

Designing the Analyze-a-Loan Program

For each of the tasks described in preceding options 1 to 4, the program must first look at the text boxes to obtain the particulars of the loan to be analyzed. Thus, the first division of the problem is into the following tasks:

1. Input the principal, interest, and duration.

2. Calculate the monthly payment.

3. Calculate the amortization schedule.

4. Display the effects of interest rate changes.

5. Quit.

Task 1 is a basic input operation and Task 2 involves applying the formula given in Step 1; therefore, these tasks need not be broken down any further. The demanding work of the program is done in Tasks 3 and 4, which can be divided into smaller subtasks.

3. *Calculate amortization schedule.* This task involves simulating the loan month by month. First, the monthly payment must be computed. Then, for each month, the new balance must be computed together with a decomposition of the monthly payment into the amount paid for interest and the amount going toward repaying the principal. That is, Task 3 is divided into the following subtasks:

3.1 Calculate monthly payment.
3.2 Calculate new balance.
3.3 Calculate amount of monthly payment for interest.
3.4 Calculate amount of monthly payment for principal.

4. *Display the effects of interest rate changes.* A table is needed to show the effects of changes in the interest rate on the size of the monthly payment. First, the interest rate is reduced by one percentage point and the new monthly payment is computed. Then the interest rate is increased by regular increments until it reaches one percentage point above the original rate, with new monthly payment amounts computed for each intermediate interest rate. The subtasks for this task are then:

4.1 Reduce the interest rate by 1 percent.
4.2 Calculate the monthly payment.
4.3 Increase the interest rate by 1/8 percent.

The hierarchy chart in Figure 6.15 shows the stepwise refinement of the problem.

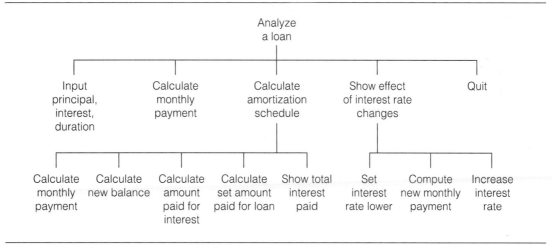

Figure 6.15 Hierarchy chart for the Analyze a Loan Program.

The User Interface

Figure 6.16 shows a possible form design. Figures 6.17 and 6.18 show possible runs of the program for each task available through the command buttons. The width and height of the picture box were adjusted by trial and error to handle the extensive output generated.

Figure 6.16 Template for loan analysis.

Object	Property	Setting
frmLoan	Caption	Analysis of a Loan
lblAmt	Alignment	1 – Right Justify
	Caption	Amount of Loan:
txtAmt	Text	(blank)
lblApr	Alignment	1 – Right Justify
	Caption	Interest APR:
txtApr	Text	(blank)
lblYrs	Alignment	1 – Right Justify
	Caption	Number of Loan Years
txtYrs	Text	(blank)
cmdPayment	Caption	Calculate Monthly Payment
cmdRateTable	Caption	Display Interest Rate Change Table
cmdAmort	Caption	Display Amortization Schedule
cmdQuit	Caption	Quit
picDisp		

Table 6.4 Objects and initial properties for the loan analysis program.

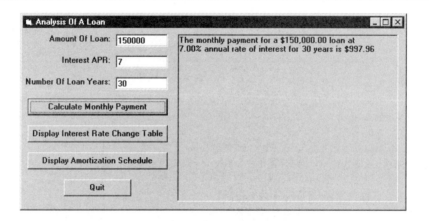

Figure 6.17 Monthly payment on a 30-year loan.

Figure 6.18 Interest rate change table for a 30-year loan.

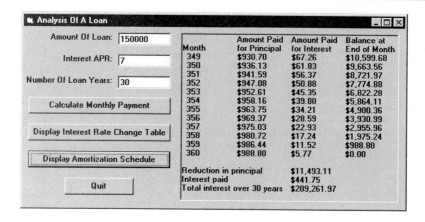

Figure 6.19 Amortization of year 30 of a loan.

Writing the Analyze a Loan Program

Table 6.5 shows each task discussed before and the procedure that carries out the task.

Pseudocode for the Analyze a Loan Program

Calculate Monthly Payment command button:
    INPUT LOAN DATA (Subprogram InputData)
    COMPUTE MONTHLY PAYMENT (Function Payment)
    DISPLAY MONTHLY PAYMENT (Subprogram ShowPayment)

Display Interest Rate Change Table command button:
    INPUT LOAN DATA (Subprogram InputData)
    Decrease annual rate by .01
    DO
        Compute monthly interest rate
        COMPUTE MONTHLY PAYMENT (Function Payment)
        Increase annual rate by .00125
    LOOP UNTIL annual rate > original annual rate + .01

Display Amortization Schedule command button:
    INPUT LOAN DATA (Subprogram InputData)
    DISPLAY AMORTIZATION SCHEDULE (Subprogram ShowAmortSched)
    Compute monthly interest rate
    COMPUTE MONTHLY PAYMENT (Function Payment)
    Display amortization table
    Display total interest paid

Task	Procedure
1. Input principal, interest, duration.	InputData
2. Calculate monthly payment.	ShowPayment
3. Calculate amortization schedule.	ShowAmortSched
3.1 Calculate monthly payment.	Payment
3.2 Calculate new balance.	Balance
3.3 Calculate amount paid for loan.	ShowAmortSched
3.4 Calculate amount paid for interest.	ShowAmortSched
4. Show effect of interest rate changes.	ShowInterestChanges
4.1 Reduce interest rate.	ShowInterestChanges
4.2 Compute new monthly payment.	Payment
4.3 Increase interest rate.	ShowInterestChanges

Table 6.5 Tasks and their procedures.

```
Rem Analyze a loan
Rem
Rem ****************************************************
Rem *                                                *
Rem *          Variable Table                        *
Rem *                                                *
Rem *                                                *
Rem * numMonths       Number of months to pay loan   *
Rem * principal       Amount of loan                 *
Rem * yearlyRate      Yearly interest rate           *
Rem *                                                *
Rem ****************************************************
Rem

Private Function Balance(mPayment As Single, prin As Single, mRate As Single) As Single
  Dim newBal As Single
  Rem Compute balance at end of month
  Let newBal = (1 + mRate) * prin
  If newBal <= mPayment Then
      Let mPayment = newBal
      Balance = 0
    Else
      Balance = newBal - mPayment
  End If
End Function

Private Sub cmdAmort_Click()
  Dim principal As Single, yearlyRate As Single
  Dim numMonths As Integer
  Call InputData(principal, yearlyRate, numMonths)
  Call ShowAmortSched(principal, yearlyRate, numMonths)
End Sub

Private Sub cmdPayment_Click()
  Dim principal As Single, yearlyRate As Single
  Dim numMonths As Integer
  Call InputData(principal, yearlyRate, numMonths)
  Call ShowPayment(principal, yearlyRate, numMonths)
End Sub
```

```
Private Sub cmdQuit_Click()
  End
End Sub


Private Sub cmdRateTable_Click()
  Dim principal As Single, yearlyRate As Single
  Dim numMonths As Integer
  Call InputData(principal, yearlyRate, numMonths)
  Call ShowInterestChanges(principal, yearlyRate, numMonths)
End Sub


Private Sub InputData(prin As Single, yearlyRate As Single, numMs As Integer)
  Dim percentageRate As Single, numYears As Integer
  Rem Input the loan amount, yearly rate of interest, and duration
  Let prin = Val(txtAmt.Text)
  Let percentageRate = Val(txtApr.Text)
  Let numYears = Val(txtYrs.Text)
  Let yearlyRate = percentageRate / 100
  Let numMs = numYears * 12
End Sub


Private Function Payment(prin As Single, mRate As Single, numMs As Integer) As Single
  Dim payEst As Single
  If numMs = 0 Then
      Let payEst = prin
    ElseIf mRate = 0 Then
      Let payEst = prin / numMs
    Else
      Let payEst = prin * mRate / (1 - (1 + mRate) ^ (-numMs))
  End If
  Payment = -Int(-payEst * 100) / 100   'round up to nearest cent
End Function


Private Sub ShowAmortSched(prin As Single, yearlyRate As Single, numMs As Integer)
  Dim msg As String, startMonth As Integer, mRate As Single
  Dim monthlyPayment As Single, totalInterest As Single
  Dim yearInterest As Single, oldBalance As Single
  Dim monthNum As Integer, newBalance As Single
  Dim principalPaid As Single, interestPaid As Single
  Dim reducPrin As Single, loanYears As String
  Rem Display amortization schedule
  Let msg = "Please enter year (1-" & Str(numMs / 12)
  Let msg = msg & ") for which amorization is to be shown:"
  Let startMonth = 12 * Val(InputBox(msg)) - 11
  picDisp.Cls
  picDisp.Print "", "Amount Paid ",
  picDisp.Print "Amount Paid", "Balance at"
  picDisp.Print "Month", "for Principal",
  picDisp.Print "for Interest", "End of Month"
  Let mRate = yearlyRate / 12   'monthly rate
  Let monthlyPayment = Payment(prin, mRate, numMs)
  Let totalInterest = 0
  Let yearInterest = 0
  Let oldBalance = prin
  For monthNum = 1 To numMs
```

```
      Let newBalance = Balance(monthlyPayment, oldBalance, mRate)
      Let principalPaid = oldBalance - newBalance
      Let interestPaid = monthlyPayment - principalPaid
      Let totalInterest = totalInterest + interestPaid
      If monthNum >= startMonth And monthNum <= startMonth + 11 Then
          picDisp.Print Tab(2); Format(monthNum, "#"),
            picDisp.Print Format(principalPaid, "Currency"),
            picDisp.Print Format(interestPaid, "Currency"),
            picDisp.Print Format(newBalance, "Currency")
          Let yearInterest = yearInterest + interestPaid
      End If
      Let oldBalance = newBalance
    Next monthNum
    Let reducPrin = 12 * monthlyPayment - yearInterest
    Let loanYears = Str(numMs / 12)
    picDisp.Print
    picDisp.Print "Reduction in principal",
    picDisp.Print Format(reducPrin, "Currency")
    picDisp.Print "Interest paid", ,
    picDisp.Print Format(yearInterest, "Currency")
    picDisp.Print "Total interest over" & loanYears & " years",
    picDisp.Print Format(totalInterest, "Currency")
End Sub


Private Sub ShowInterestChanges(prin As Single, yearlyRate As Single, numMs As Integer)
  Dim newRate As Single, mRate As Single, py As Single
  Dim pymnt As String
  Rem Display affect of interest changes
  picDisp.Cls
  picDisp.Print , "Annual"
  picDisp.Print , "Interest rate", "Monthly Payment"
  Let newRate = yearlyRate - .01
  Do
    Let mRate = newRate / 12   'monthly rate
    Let py = Payment(prin, mRate, numMs)
    Let pymnt = Format(py, "currency")
    picDisp.Print , Format(newRate * 100, "#.000") + "%", pymnt
    Let newRate = newRate + .00125
  Loop Until newRate > yearlyRate + .01
End Sub


Private Sub ShowPayment(prin As Single, yearlyRate As Single, numMs As Integer)
  Dim mRate As Single, prn As String, apr As String
  Dim yrs As String, pay As Single, pymnt As String
  Rem Display monthly payment amount
  Let mRate = yearlyRate / 12   'monthly rate
  Let prn = Format(prin, "Currency")
  Let apr = Format(yearlyRate * 100, "#.00")
  Let yrs = Format(numMs / 12, "#")
  Let pay = Payment(prin, mRate, numMs)
  Let pymnt = Format(pay, "Currency")
  picDisp.Cls
  picDisp.Print "The monthly payment for a " & prn & " loan at "
  picDisp.Print apr & "% annual rate of interest for ";
  picDisp.Print yrs & " years is " & pymnt
End Sub
```

Comments

1. Tasks 3.1 and 3.2 are performed by functions. Using functions to compute these quantities simplifies the computations in ShowAmortSched.

2. Because the payment was rounded up to the nearest cent, it is highly likely that the payment needed in the final month to pay off the loan will be less than the normal payment. For this reason, ShowAmortSched checks if the balance of the loan (including interest due) is less than the regular payment, and if so, makes appropriate adjustments.

3. The standard formula for computing the monthly payment cannot be used if either the interest rate is zero percent or the loan duration is zero months. Although both of these situations do not represent reasonable loan parameters, provisions are made in the function Payment so that the program can handle these esoteric situations.

Chapter 6
Summary

1. A Do loop repeatedly executes a block of statements either as long as or until a certain condition is true. The condition can be checked either at the top of the loop or at the bottom.

2. The EOF function tells us if we have read to the end of a file.

3. As various items of data are processed by a loop, a *counter* can be used to keep track of the number of items and an *accumulator* can be used to sum numerical values.

4. A *flag* is a variable used to indicate whether or not a certain event has occurred.

5. A For...Next loop repeats a block of statements a fixed number of times. The *control variable* assumes an initial value and increments by one after each pass through the loop until it reaches the terminating value. Alternative increment values can be specified with the Step keyword.

Chapter 6
Programming Projects

1. Write a program to display a company's payroll report in a picture box. The program should read each employee's name, hourly rate, and hours worked from a file and produce a report in the form of the sample run shown in Figure 6.20. Employees should be paid time-and-a-half for hours in excess of 40.

```
Payroll Report for Week ending 8/15/97

Employee      Hourly Rate   Hours Worked   Gross Pay

Al Adams      $6.50         38             $247.00
Bob Brown     $5.70         50             $313.50
Carol Coe     $7.00         40             $280.00

Final Total   $840.50
```

Figure 6.20 Sample output from Programming Project 1.

2. Table 6.6 shows the standard prices for items in a department store. Suppose prices will be reduced for the annual George Washington's Birthday Sale. The new price will be computed by reducing the old price by 10 percent, rounding up to the nearest dollar, and subtracting 1 cent. If the new price is greater than the old price, the old price is used as the sale price. Write a program to display in a picture box the output shown in Figure 6.21.

Item	**Original Price**
GumShoes	39.00
SnugFoot Sandals	21.00
T-Shirt	7.75
Maine Handbag	33.00
Maple Syrup	6.75
Flaked Vest	24.00
Nightshirt	26.00

Table 6.6 Washington's Birthday Sale.

```
                        Sale
Item                    Price
GumShoes                35.99
SnugFoot Sandals        18.99
T-Shirt                  6.99
Maine Handbag           29.99
Maple Syrup              6.75
Flaked Vest             21.99
Nightshirt              23.99
```

Figure 6.21 Output of Project 2.

3. The Rule of 72 is used to make a quick estimate of the time required for prices to double due to inflation. If the inflation rate is r percent, then the Rule of 72 estimates that prices will double in $72/r$ years. For instance, at an inflation rate of 6 percent, prices double in about $72/6$ or 12 years. Write a program to test the accuracy of this rule. The program should display a table showing, for each value of r from 1 to 20, the rounded value of $72/r$ and the actual number of years required for prices to double at an r percent inflation rate. (Assume prices increase at the end of each year.) Figure 6.22 shows the first few rows of the output.

```
Interest    Rule
Rate (%)    of 72     Actual
    1         72         70
    2         36         36
    3         24         24
```

Figure 6.22 Rule of 72.

4. Table 6.7 shows the number of bachelor degrees conferred in 1980 and 1989 in certain fields of study. Tables 6.8 and 6.9 show the percentage change and a histogram of 1989 levels, respectively. Write a program that allows the user to display any one of these tables as an option and quit as a fourth option.

Field of Study	1980	1989
Business and management	185,361	246,659
Computer and info. science	11,154	30,637
Education	118,169	96,988
Engineering	68,893	85,273
Social sciences	103,519	107,714

Table 6.7 Bachelor degrees conferred in certain fields.

Source: U.S. National Center of Educational Statistics

Field of Study	% Change (1980–1989)
Business and management	33.1
Computer and info. science	174.7
Education	−17.9
Engineering	23.8
Social sciences	4.1

Table 6.8 Percentage change in bachelor degrees conferred.

Business and management	************************	246,659
Computer and info. science	***	30,637
Education	**********	96,988
Engineering	*********	85,273
Social sciences	**********	107,714

Table 6.9 Bachelor degrees conferred in 1989 in certain fields.

5. *Least Squares Approximation.* Table 6.10 shows the 1988 price of a gallon of fuel and the consumption of motor fuel for several countries. Figure 6.23 displays the data as points in the xy plane. For instance, the point with coordinates $(1, 1400)$ corresponds to the USA. Figure 6.23 also shows the straight line that best fits these data in the least squares sense. (The sum of the squares of the distances of the 11 points from this line is as small as possible.) In general, if $(x_1, y_1), (x_2, y_2), \ldots, (x_n, y_n)$ are n points in the xy coordinate system, then the least squares approximation to these points is the line $y = mx + b$, where

$$m = \frac{n * (\text{sum of } x_i * y_i) - (\text{sum of } x_i) * (\text{sum of } y_i)}{n * (\text{sum of } x_i * x_i) - (\text{sum of } x_i)^2}$$

and

$$b = ((\text{sum of } y_i) - m * (\text{sum of } x_i))/n$$

Write a program that calculates and displays the equation of the least squares line, and then allows the user to enter a fuel price and uses the equation of the line to predict the corresponding consumption of motor fuel. (Place the numeric data from the table in a data file.) A sample run is shown in Figure 6.24.

Country	Price per gallon in U.S. Dollars	Tons of Oil per 1000 Persons	Country	Price per gallon in U.S. Dollars	Tons of Oil per 1000 Persons
USA	$1.00	1400	France	$3.10	580
W.Ger.	$2.20	620	Norway	$3.15	600
England	$2.60	550	Japan	$3.60	410
Austria	$2.75	580	Denmark	$3.70	570
Sweden	$2.80	700	Italy	$3.85	430
Holland	$3.00	490			

Table 6.10 A comparison of 1988 fuel prices and per capita motor fuel use.

Source: World Resources Institute

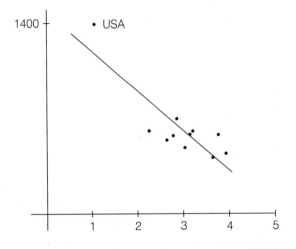

Figure 6.23 Least-squares fit to data from Table 6.10.

Least Squares Fuel Consumption

The equation of the least squares line is y = (-291.4) x & 1471.1

Price per gallon: 4.00   Estimate Consumption

The corresponding use is 305.5 tons of oil per 1000 people

Figure 6.24 Sample run of Programming Project 5.

6. Write a program to provide information on the height of a ball thrown straight up into the air. The program should request the initial height, *h* feet, and the initial velocity, *v* feet per second, as input. The four options to be provided by command buttons are as follows:

(a) Determine the maximum height of the ball. **Note:** The ball will reach its maximum height after $v/32$ seconds.

(b) Determine approximately when the ball will hit the ground. **Hint:** Calculate the height after every .1 second and observe when the height is no longer a positive number.

(c) Display a table showing the height of the ball every quarter second for 5 seconds or until it hits the ground.

(d) Quit.

The formula for the height of the ball after *t* seconds, $h + v * t - 16 * t * t$, should be specified in a user-defined function. (Test the program with *v* = 148 and *h* = 0. This velocity is approximately the top speed clocked for a ball thrown by a professional baseball pitcher.)

7. *Depreciation to a Salvage Value of 0.* For tax purposes an item may be depreciated over a period of several years, *n*. With the *straight-line* method of depreciation, each year the item depreciates by $1/nth$ of its original value. With the *double-declining* balance method of depreciation, each year the item depreciates by $2/nths$ of its value at the *beginning* of that year. (In the last year it is depreciated by its value at the beginning of the year.) Write a program that

(a) Requests a description of the item, the year of purchase, the cost of the item, the number of years to be depreciated (estimated life), and the method of depreciation. The method of depreciation should be chosen by clicking one of two command buttons.

(b) Displays a depreciation schedule for the item similar to the schedule shown in Figure 6.25.

```
Description: Computer
Year of purchase: 1994
Cost: $2000.00
Estimated life: 5
Method of depreciation: double-declining balance
```

Year	Value at Beg of Yr	Amount Deprec During Year	Total Depreciation to End of Year
1994	2,000.00	800.00	800.00
1995	1,200.00	480.00	1,280.00
1996	720.00	288.00	1,568.00
1997	432.00	172.80	1,740.80
1998	259.20	259.20	2,000.00

Figure 6.25 Depreciation schedule.

8. *The Twelve Days of Christmas.* Each year, Provident National Bank of Philadelphia publishes a Christmas price list. See Table 6.11. Write a program that requests an integer from 1 through 12 and then lists the gifts for that day along with that day's cost. On the nth day, the n gifts are 1 partridge in a pear tree, 2 turtle doves, . . . n of the nth item. The program also should give the total cost of all twelve days. As an example, Figure 6.26 shows the output in the picture box when the user enters 3.

Item	Cost	Item	Cost
partridge in a pear tree	27.50	swan-a-swimming	1000.00
turtle dove	25.00	maid-a-milking	4.25
French hen	5.00	lady dancing	289.50
calling bird	70.00	lord-a-leaping	292.50
gold ring	60.00	piper piping	95.75
geese-a-laying	25.00	drummer drumming	95.00

Table 6.11 Christmas price index.

```
The gifts for day 3 are
 1 partridge in a pear tree
 2 turtle doves
 3 French hens
Cost:     $92.50


Total cost for the twelve days: $71,613.50
```

Figure 6.26 Sample output for Programming Project 8.

7

Arrays

7.1 **Creating And Accessing Arrays** / 302

7.2 **Using Arrays** / 320
• Ordered Arrays • Using Part of an Array • Passing Arrays between Procedures

7.3 **Control Arrays** / 335
• Control Array Event Procedures • Creating Control Arrays at Run Time

7.4 **Sorting and Searching** / 348
• Bubble Sort • Shell Sort • Searching

7.5 **Two-dimensional Arrays** / 367

7.6 **A Case Study: Calculating With a Spreadsheet** / 381
• The Design of the Program • The User Interface
• Coding the Program

Summary / 390

Programming Projects / 391

7.1 CREATING AND ACCESSING ARRAYS

A **variable** (or simple variable) is a name to which the computer can assign a single value. An **array variable** is a collection of simple variables of the same type to which the computer can efficiently assign a list of values.

Consider the following situation. Suppose you want to evaluate the exam grades for 30 students. Not only do you want to compute the average score, but you also want to display the names of the students whose scores are above average. You might place the 30 pairs of student names and scores in a data file and run the program outlined.

```
Private Sub cmdButton_Click()
   Dim student1 As String, score1 As Single
   Dim student2 As String, score2 As Single
   Dim student3 As String, score3 As Single
        .
        .
        .
   Dim student30 As String, score30 As Single
   Rem Analyze exam grades
   Open "SCORES.TXT" For Input As #1
   Input #1, student1, score1
   Input #1, student2, score2
   Input #1, student3, score3
        .
        .
        .
   Input #1, student30, score30
   Rem Compute the average grade
        .
        .
        .
   Rem Display names of above average students
        .
        .
        .
End Sub
```

This program is going to be uncomfortably long. What's most frustrating is that the 30 Dim statements and 30 Input# statements are very similar and look as if they should be condensed into a short loop. A shorthand notation for the many related variables would be welcome. It would be nice if we could just write

```
For i = 1 To 30
   Input #1, studenti, scorei
Next i
```

Of course, this will not work. The computer will treat *studenti* and *scorei* as two variables and keep reassigning new values to them. At the end of the loop they will have the values of the thirtieth student.

Visual Basic provides a data structure called an **array** that lets us do what we tried to accomplish in the loop. The variable names will be similar to those in the Input statement. They will be

```
student(1), student(2), student(3), ..., student(30)
```

and

```
score(1), score(2), score(3), ..., score(30).
```

We refer to these collections of variables as the array variables *student*( ) and *score*( ). The numbers inside the parentheses of the individual variables are called **subscripts**, and each individual variable is called a **subscripted variable** or **element**. For instance, *student*(3) is the third subscripted variable of the array *student*( ), and *score*(20) is the 20th subscripted variable of the array *score*( ). The elements of an array are assigned successive memory locations. Figure 7.1 shows the memory locations for the array *score*( ).

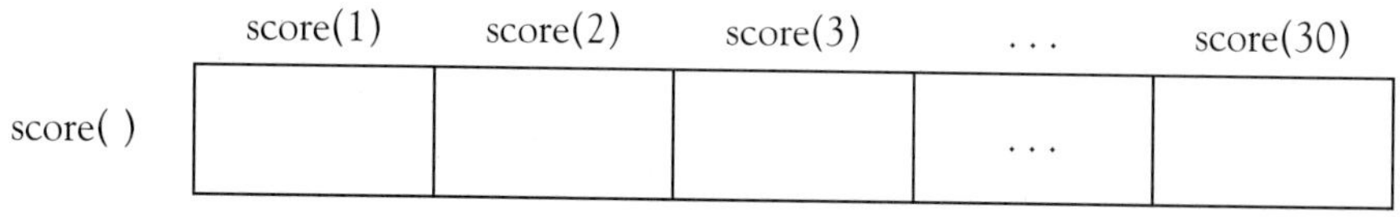

	score(1)	score(2)	score(3)	. . .	score(30)
score( )				. . .	

Figure 7.1 The array *score*( ).

Array variables have the same kinds of names as simple variables. If *array-Name* is the name of an array variable and *n* is a whole number, then the statement

```
Dim arrayName(1 To n) As varType
```

placed in the (Declarations) section of (General) reserves space in memory to hold the values of the subscripted variables *arrayName*(1), *arrayName*(2), *array-Name*(3), . . . , *arrayName*(n). (Recall from Section 4.1 that the (Declarations) section of (General) is accessed from any code window by selecting these values in the Object and Procedure boxes.) The spread of the subscripts specified by the Dim statement is called the **range** of the array, and the Dim statement is said to **dimension** the array. In particular, the statements

```
Dim student(1 To 30) As String
Dim score(1 To 30) As Integer
```

dimension the arrays needed for the preceding program. An array holds either all string values or all numeric values, depending on whether *varType* is String or one of the numeric type names.

As with any variable created in the (Declarations) section of (General), these array variables are form-level as discussed in Chapter 4. Recall that form-level variables can be accessed from any procedure in the program and continue to exist and retain their values as long as the program is running.

Values can be assigned to subscripted variables with Let statements and displayed with Print methods. The statement

```
Dim score(1 To 30) As Integer
```

sets aside a portion of memory for the numeric array *score*( ) and places the default value 0 in each element.

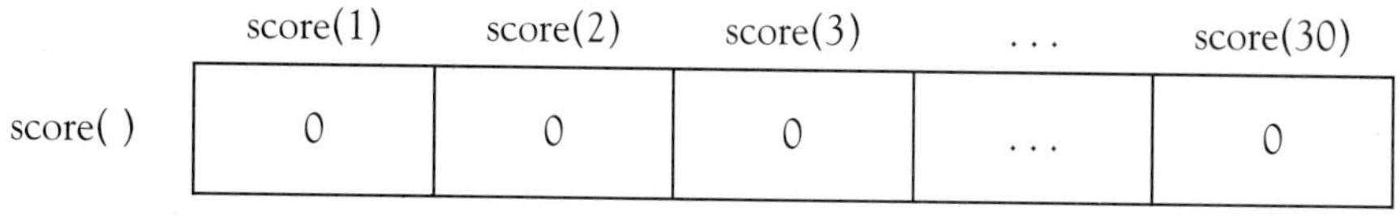

	score(1)	score(2)	score(3)	. . .	score(30)
score( )	0	0	0	. . .	0

The statements

```
Let score(1) = 87
Let score(3) = 92
```

assign values to the first and third elements.

	score(1)	score(2)	score(3)	. . .	score(30)
score( )	87	0	92	. . .	0

The statements

```
For i = 1 To 4
  picBox.Print score(i);
Next i
```

then produce the output 87 0 92 0   in picBox.

EXAMPLE 1   The following program creates a string array consisting of the names of the first five World Series winners. Figure 7.2 shows the array created by the program.

```
Rem Create array for five strings
Dim teamName(1 To 5) As String    'in (Declarations) section of (General)

Private Sub cmdWhoWon_Click()
  Dim n As Integer
  Rem Fill array with World Series Winners
  Let teamName(1) = "Red Sox"
  Let teamName(2) = "Giants"
  Let teamName(3) = "White Sox"
  Let teamName(4) = "Cubs"
  Let teamName(5) = "Cubs"
  Rem Access array of five strings
  Let n = Val(txtNumber.Text)
  picWinner.Cls
  picWinner.Print "The "; teamName(n); " won World Series number"; n
End Sub
```

[Run, type 2 into the text box, and click the command button.]

	teamName(1)	teamName(2)	teamName(3)	teamName(4)	teamName(5)
teamName( )	Red Sox	Giants	White Sox	Cubs	Cubs

Figure 7.2 The array *teamName*( ) of Example 1.

In Example 1, the array *teamName* was assigned values within the cmdWhoWon_Click event procedure. Every time the command button is clicked, the values are reassigned to the array. This manner of assigning values to an array can be very inefficient, especially in programs with large arrays where the task of the program (in Example 1, looking up a fact) may be repeated numerous times for different user input. When, as in Example 1, the data to be placed in an array are known at the time the program first begins to run, a more efficient location for the statements that fill the array is in Visual Basic's Form_Load event procedure. The Form_Load event procedure is executed by Visual Basic only once, and this execution is guaranteed to occur before the execution of any other event or general procedure in the program. Example 2 uses the Form_Load procedure to improve on Example 1.

EXAMPLE 2 Modify Example 1 to request the name of a baseball team as input and search the array to determine whether or not the team name appears in the array. Load the array values only once.

```
Rem Create array for five strings
Dim teamName(1 To 5) As String  'in (Declarations) section of (General)

Private Sub cmdDidTheyWin_Click()
  Dim team As String, foundFlag As Integer, n As Integer
  Rem Search for an entry in a list of strings
  Let team = txtName.Text
  Let foundFlag = 0
  Let n = 0
  Do
    Let n = n + 1
    If UCase(teamName(n)) = UCase(team) Then
        Let foundFlag = 1
    End If
  Loop Until (foundFlag = 1) Or (n = 5)
  picWinner.Cls
  If foundFlag = 0 Then
      picWinner.Print "The "; team; " did not win any";
      picWinner.Print " of the first five World Series."
    Else
      picWinner.Print "The "; teamName(n); " won World Series number"; n
  End If
End Sub

Private Sub Form_Load()
  Rem Fill array with World Series winners
  Let teamName(1) = "Red Sox"
  Let teamName(2) = "Giants"
  Let teamName(3) = "White Sox"
  Let teamName(4) = "Cubs"
  Let teamName(5) = "Cubs"
End Sub
```

[Run, type White Sox into the text box, and click the command button.]

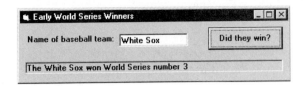

We could have written the program in Example 2 with a For...Next loop beginning For n = 1 To 5. However, such a loop would unnecessarily search the entire list when the sought-after item is found early. The wasted time could be significant for a large array.

In some applications, arrays are only needed temporarily to help a procedure complete a task. Visual Basic also allows us to create array variables that are local to a specific procedure and that exist temporarily while the procedure is executing. If the statement

```
Dim arrayName(1 To n) As varType
```

is placed inside an event procedure or general procedure, then space for n subscripted variables is set aside in memory each time the procedure is invoked and released when the procedure is exited.

In Example 1, values were assigned to the elements of the array with Let statements. However, data for large arrays are more often stored in a data file and read with Input# statements. Example 3 uses this technique. Also, because the task of the program is likely to be performed only once during a run of the program, a local array is utilized.

EXAMPLE 3 Table 7.1 gives names and test scores from a mathematics contest given in 1953. Write a program to display the names of the students scoring above the average for these eight students.

Richard Dolen	135	Paul H. Monsky	150
Geraldine Ferraro	114	Max A. Plager	114
James B. Fraser	92	Robert A. Schade	91
John H. Maltby	91	Barbara M. White	124

Table 7.1 The top scores on the Fourth Annual Mathematics Contest Sponsored by the Metropolitan NY section of the MAA.

Source: The Mathematics Teacher, February 1953

SOLUTION The following program creates a string array to hold the names of the contestants and a numeric array to hold the scores. The first element of each array holds data for the first contestant, the second element of each array holds data for the second contestant, and so on. See Figure 7.3. Note that the two arrays can be dimensioned in a single Dim statement by placing a comma between the array declarations.

```
Private Sub cmdShow_Click()
  Dim total As Integer, student As Integer, average As Single
  Rem Create arrays for names and scores
  Dim nom(1 To 8) As String, score(1 To 8) As Integer
  Rem Assume the data has been placed in the file "SCORES.TXT"
  Rem (The first line of the file is "Richard Dolen", 135)
  Open "SCORES.TXT" For Input As #1
  For student = 1 To 8
    Input #1, nom(student), score(student)
  Next student
  Close #1
  Rem Analyze exam scores
  Let total = 0
  For student = 1 To 8
    Let total = total + score(student)
  Next student
  Let average = total / 8
  Rem Display all names with above average grades
  picTopStudents.Cls
  For student = 1 To 8
    If score(student) > average Then
        picTopStudents.Print nom(student)
    End If
  Next student
End Sub
```

[Run and click the command button.]

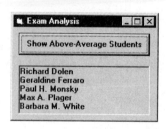

---

	nom(1)	nom(2)	. . .	nom(8)
nom( )	Richard Dolen	Geraldine Ferraro	. . .	Barbara M. White

	score(1)	score(2)	. . .	score(8)
score( )	135	114	. . .	124

Figure 7.3 Arrays created by Example 3.

In Example 3, the number of students to be processed had to be known at the time the program was written. In actual practice, the amount of data that a program will be processing is not known in advance. Programs should be flexible and incorporate a method for handling varying amounts of data. Visual Basic makes this possible with the statement

```
ReDim arrayName (1 to n) As varType
```

which can use variables or expressions when indicating the subscript range. However, ReDim statements can only be used inside procedures.

EXAMPLE 4   The following program reworks Example 3 for the case when the amount of data is not known in advance.

```
Private Sub cmdShow_Click()
  Dim numStudents As Integer, nTemp As String, sTemp As Integer
  Dim student As Integer, Total As Integer, average As Single
  Rem Determine amount of data to be processed
  Let numStudents = 0
  Open "SCORES.TXT" For Input As #1
  Do While Not EOF(1)
    Input #1, nTemp, sTemp
    Let numStudents = numStudents + 1
  Loop
  Close #1
  Rem Create arrays for names and scores
  ReDim nom(1 To numStudents) As String, score(1 To numStudents) As Integer
  Open "SCORES.TXT" For Input As #1
  For student = 1 To numStudents
    Input #1, nom(student), score(student)
  Next student
  Close #1
  Rem Analyze exam scores
  Let Total = 0
  For student = 1 To numStudents
    Let Total = Total + score(student)
  Next student
  Let average = Total / numStudents
  Rem Display all names with above average grades
  picTopStudents.Cls
  For student = 1 To numStudents
    If score(student) > average Then
        picTopStudents.Print nom(student)
    End If
  Next student
End Sub
```

An alternative approach to program flexibility that does not require reading the data file twice is to require that the data file begin with a line that holds the number of records to be processed. If SCORES.TXT is modified by adding a new first line that gives the number of students, then the fourth through eighteenth lines of Example 4 can be replaced with

```
Rem Create arrays for names and scores
Open "SCORES.TXT" For Input As #1
Input #1, numStudents
ReDim nom(1 To numStudents) As String, score(1 To numStudents) As Integer
For student = 1 To numStudents
  Input #1, nom(student), score(student)
Next student
Close #1
```

In Example 4, the ReDim statement allowed us to create arrays whose size was not known before the program was run. On the other hand, the arrays that were created were local to the event procedure cmdShow_Click. Many applications require form-level arrays whose size is not known in advance. Unfortunately, Dim statements cannot use variables or expressions to specify the subscript range. The solution offered by Visual Basic is to allow the (Declarations) section of (General) to contain Dim statements of the form

```
Dim arrayName() As varType
```

where no range for the subscripts of the array is specified. An array created in this manner will be form-level, but cannot be used until a ReDim statement is executed in a procedure to establish the range of subscripts. It is important to note that both the Dim statement and the ReDim statement must include identical "As *varType*" clauses.

EXAMPLE 5   Suppose the data file WINNERS.TXT contains the names of the teams who have won each of the World Series, with the first line of the file giving the number of World Series that have been played. Write a program that displays the numbers, if any, of the World Series that were won by the team specified by the user.

```
Rem Create form-level array
Dim teamName() As String
Dim seriesCount As Integer

Private Sub cmdDidTheyWin_Click()
  Dim teamToFind As String, numWon As Integer, series As Integer
  Rem Search for World Series won by user's team
  Let teamToFind = txtName.Text
  Let numWon = 0
  picSeriesWon.Cls
  For series = 1 To seriesCount
    If UCase(teamName(series)) = UCase(teamToFind) Then
        Let numWon = numWon + 1
        If numWon = 1 Then
           picSeriesWon.Print "The "; teamName(series);
           picSeriesWon.Print " won the following World Series: ";
         Else
           Rem Separate from previous
           picSeriesWon.Print ",";
```

```
                    If (numWon = 5) Or (numWon = 16) Then
                        Rem Start a new line at 5th and 16th win
                        picSeriesWon.Print
                    End If
                End If
                Rem First world series played in 1903
                picSeriesWon.Print Str(series + 1902);
            End If
        Next series
        If numWon = 0 Then
            picSeriesWon.Print "The "; teamToFind; " did not win any World Series."
        End If
    End Sub

    Private Sub Form_Load()
      Dim series As Integer
      Rem Fill array with World Series winners
      Open "WINNERS.TXT" For Input As #1
      Input #1, seriesCount
      ReDim teamName(1 To seriesCount) As String
      For series = 1 To seriesCount
        Input #1, teamName(series)
      Next series
      Close #1
    End Sub
```

[Run, type Yankees into the text box, and click the command button.]

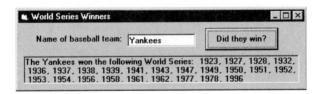

The range of an array need not just begin with 1. A statement of the form

```
Dim arrayName(m To n) As varType
```

where *m* is less than or equal to *n*, creates an array with elements *arrayName*(*m*), *arrayName*(*m* + 1), *arrayName*(*m* + 2), . . . , *arrayName*(*n*). Similarly for ReDim.

EXAMPLE 6   The following program segment stores the names of the 40th, 41st, and 42nd presidents in the array pictured in Figure 7.4.

```
Rem Place names of last three presidents in an array
Dim pres(40 To 42) As String

Private Sub Form_Load()
  Let pres(40) = "Ronald Reagan"
  Let pres(41) = "George Bush"
  Let pres(42) = "Bill Clinton"
End Sub
```

	pres(40)	pres(41)	pres(42)
pres( )	Ronald Reagan	George Bush	Bill Clinton

Figure 7.4 The array created by Example 6.

An array can be used as either a checklist or frequency table, as in the next example. The function Asc associates each character with its position in the ANSI table.

EXAMPLE 7 The following program requests a sentence as input and records the number of occurrences of each letter of the alphabet. The array *count*( ) has range Asc("A") To Asc("Z"), that is, 65 To 90. The number of occurrences of each letter is stored in the element whose subscript is the ANSI value of the uppercase letter.

```
Private Sub cmdAnalyze_Click()
  Dim index As Integer, letterNum As Integer, sentence As String
  Dim letter As String, column As Integer
  Rem Count occurrences of different letters in a sentence
  ReDim charCount(Asc("A") To Asc("Z")) As Integer
  For index = Asc("A") To Asc("Z")
    Let charCount(index) = 0
  Next index
  Rem Consider and tally each letter of sentence
  Let sentence = UCase(txtSentence.Text)
  For letterNum = 1 To Len(sentence)
    Let letter = Mid(sentence, letterNum, 1)
    If (letter >= "A") And (letter <= "Z") Then
        Let index = Asc(letter)
        Let charCount(index) = charCount(index) + 1
    End If
  Next letterNum
  Rem List the tally for each letter of alphabet
  Let picLetterCount.Font = "Courier"
  picLetterCount.Cls
  Let column = 1    'Next column at which to display letter & count
  For letterNum = Asc("A") To Asc("Z")
    Let letter = Chr(letterNum)
    picLetterCount.Print Tab(column); letter;
    picLetterCount.Print Tab(column + 1); charCount(letterNum);
    Let column = column + 6
    If column > 42 Then    'only room for 7 sets of data in a line
        picLetterCount.Print
        Let column = 1
    End If
  Next letterNum
End Sub
```

[Run, type in the given sentence, and click the command button.]

Comments

1. Arrays must be dimensioned in a Dim or ReDim statement before they are used. If a statement such as Let $a(6) = 3$ appears without a previous Dim or ReDim of the array $a(\ )$, then the error message "Sub or Function not defined" will be displayed when an attempt is made to run the program.

2. Subscripts in ReDim statements can be numeric expressions. Subscripts whose values are not whole numbers are rounded to the nearest whole number. Subscripts outside the range of the array produce an error message as shown in what follows when t has the value 6 in the For...Next loop.

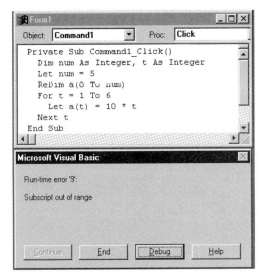

3. The two arrays in Example 3 are referred to as **parallel arrays** because subscripted variables having the same subscript are related.

4. The integers m and n in the statement Dim *arrayName*(m To n) As *varType* can be positive, negative, or zero. The only restriction is that m cannot be greater than n. The same holds true for ReDim statements.

5. Until a value is assigned to an element of an array, the element has its default value. Numeric variables have a default value of 0, and string variables have the default value "", the empty string.

6. The statement Dim *arrayName*(0 To n) As *varType* can be replaced by the statement Dim *arrayName*(n) As *varType*. The same holds for the ReDim statement.

PRACTICE PROBLEMS 7.1

1. When should arrays be used to hold data?

2. (a) Give an appropriate Dim statement to declare a string array to hold the names of the *Time* magazine "Man of the Year" awards for the years 1980 through 1989.

   (b) Write a statement to assign to the array element for 1982 the name of that year's winner, "The Computer".

EXERCISES 7.1

In Exercises 1 through 6, determine the output displayed in the picture box when the command button is clicked. All Dim statements for arrays are in the (Declarations) section of (General).

1.
```
Dim a(1 To 20) As Integer

Private Sub cmdDisplay_Click()
  Let a(5) = 1
  Let a(10) = 2
  Let a(15) = 7
  picOutput.Print a(5) + a(10);
  picOutput.Print a(5 + 10);
  picOutput.Print a(20)
End Sub
```

2.
```
Dim sq(1 To 5) As Integer

Private Sub cmdDisplay_Click()
  Dim i As Integer, t As Integer
  For i = 1 To 5
    Let sq(i) = i * i
  Next i
  picOutput.Print sq(3)
  Let t - 3
  picOutput.Print sq(5 - t)
End Sub
```

3.
```
Dim fh(1 To 4) As String

Private Sub cmdDisplay_Click()
  Dim i As Integer, n As Integer
  Open "HORSEMEN.TXT" For Input As #1
  For i = 1 To 4
    Input #1, fh(i)
  Next i
  picOutput.Print fh(4)
  Let n = 1
  picOutput.Print fh(2 * n + 1)
  Close #1
End Sub
```

   (Assume that the file HORSEMEN.TXT contains the following entries.)

   "Miller", "Layden", "Crowley", "Stuhldreher"

4.
```
Dim s(1 To 4) As Integer

Private Sub cmdDisplay_Click()
  Dim t As Integer, k As Integer
  Open "DATA.TXT" For Input As #1
  Let t = 0
  For k = 1 To 4
    Input #1, s(k)
    Let t = t + s(k)
  Next k
```

```
    picOutput.Print t
    Close #1
  End Sub
```

(Assume that the file DATA.TXT contains the following entries.)

3, 5, 2, 1

5. `Dim p(1 To 6) As Integer`

```
Private Sub cmdDisplay_Click()
  Dim k As Integer
  Open "DATA.TXT" For Input As #1
  For k = 1 To 6
    Input #1, p(k)
  Next k
  For k = 6 To 1 Step -1
    picOutput.Print p(k);
  Next k
End Sub
```

(Assume that the file DATA.TXT contains the following entries.)

4, 3, 11, 9, 2, 6

6. `Dim a(1 To 4) As Integer`
`Dim b(1 To 4) As Integer`
`Dim c(1 To 4) As Integer`

```
Private Sub cmdDisplay_Click()
  Dim i As Integer
  Open "DATA.TXT" For Input As #1
  For i = 1 To 4
    Input #1, a(i), b(i)
  Next i
  For i = 1 To 4
    Let c(i) = a(i) * b(i)
    picOutput.Print c(i);
  Next i
End Sub
```

(Assume that the file DATA.TXT contains the following entries.)

2, 5, 3, 4, 1, 3, 7, 2

In Exercises 7 through 12, identify the errors.

7. `Dim companies(1 To 100) As String`

```
Private Sub Form_Load()
  Dim recCount As Integer, i As Integer
  Open "COMPLIST.TXT" For Input As #1
  Input #1, recCount
  ReDim companies(1 To recCount) As String
  For i = 1 To recCount
    Input #1, companies(i)
  Next i
  Close #1
End Sub
```

8.
```
Dim p(1 To 100) As Single

Private Sub cmdDisplay_Click()
  Dim i As Integer
  For i = 1 To 200
    Let p(i) = i / 2
  Next i
End Sub
```

9.
```
Dim a(1 To 10) As Integer

Private Sub cmdDisplay_Click()
  Dim i As Integer, k As Integer
  Open "DATA.TXT" For Input As #1
  For i = 1 To 9
    Input #1, a(i)
  Next i
  Close #1
  For k = 1 To 9
    Let a(k) = a(5 - k)
  Next k
End Sub
```

(Assume that the file DATA.TXT contains the following entries.)

1, 2, 3, 4, 5, 6, 7, 8, 9

10.
```
Let maxRecords = 100
Dim patients(1 To maxRecords) As String

Private Sub cmdDisplay_Click()
  Dim recCount As Integer, i As Integer
  Open "PATIENTS.TXT" For Input As #1
  Let recCount = 0
  Do While (Not EOF(1)) And (recCount < maxRecords)
    Let recCount = recCount + 1
    Input #1, patients(recCount)
  Loop
  Close #1
  picOutput.Cls
  picOutput.Print recCount; "records were read"
End Sub
```

11.
```
Dim b(2 To 8 Step 2) As Integer

Private Sub cmdDisplay_Click()
  Dim t As Integer
  Open "DATA.TXT" For Input As #1
  For t = 2 To 8 STEP 2
    Input #1, b(t)
  Next t
  Close #1
End Sub
```

(Assume that the file DATA.TXT contains the following entries.)

1, 4, 8, 19

12. ```Dim names()```

```
Private Sub Form_Load
  Dim i As Integer, recCount As Integer
  Open "DATA.TXT" For Input As #1
  Input #1, recCount
  ReDim names(1 to recCount) As String
  For i = 1 to recCount
    Input #1, names(i)
  Next i
  Close #1
End Sub
```

(Assume that the file DATA.TXT contains the following entries.)

3, "Tom", "Dick", "Harry"

13. Assuming the array *river*( ) is as shown below, fill in the empty rectangles to show the progressing status of *river*( ) after the execution of each program segment.

	river(1)	river(2)	river(3)	river(4)	river(5)
river( )	Nile	Ohio	Amazon	Volga	Thames

```
Let temp = river(1)
Let river(1) = river(5)
Let river(5) = temp
```

	river(1)	river(2)	river(3)	river(4)	river(5)
river( )					

```
Let temp = river(1)
For i = 1 To 4
  Let river(i) = river(i + 1)
Next i
Let river(5) = temp
```

	river(1)	river(2)	river(3)	river(4)	river(5)
river( )					

14. Assuming the array *cat*( ) is as shown below, fill in the empty rectangles to show the final status of *cat*( ) after executing the nested loops.

	cat(1)	cat(2)	cat(3)	cat(4)
cat( )	Morris	Garfield	Socks	Felix

```
For i = 1 To 3
  For j = 1 To 4 - i
    If cat(j) > cat(j + 1) Then
        Let temp = cat(j)
        Let cat(j) = cat(j + 1)
        Let cat(j + 1) = temp
    End If
  Next j
Next I
```

	cat(1)	cat(2)	cat(3)	cat(4)
cat( )				

15. The subscripted variables of the array $a(\ )$ have the following values: $a(1) = 6$, $a(2) = 3$, $a(3) = 1$, $a(4) = 2$, $a(5) = 5$, $a(6) = 8$, $a(7) = 7$. Suppose $i = 2$, $j = 4$, and $k = 5$. What values are assigned to n when the following Let statements are executed?

   (a) `Let n = a(k) - a(i)`   (c) `Let n = a(k) * a(i + 2)`
   (b) `Let n = a(k - i) + a(k - j)`   (d) `Let n = a(j - i) * a(i)`

16. The array *monthName*( ) holds the following three-character strings.

   `monthName(1)="Jan", monthName(2)="Feb", ..., monthName(12)="Dec"`

   (a) What is displayed by the following statement?

   `picMonth.Print monthName(4), monthName(9)`

   (b) What value is assigned to *winter* by the following statement?

   `Let winter = monthName(12) & "," & monthName(1) & "," & monthName(2)`

17. Modify the program in Example 3 to display each student's name and the number of points his or her score differs from the average.

18. Modify the program in Example 3 to display only the name(s) of the student(s) with the highest score.

In Exercises 19 through 30, write a line of code or program segment to complete the stated task.

19. Inside a procedure, dimension the string array *bestPicture*( ) to have subscripts ranging from 1975 to 1995.

20. In the (Declarations) section of (General), dimension the string array *info*( ) to have subscripts ranging from 10 to 100.

21. Dimension the string array *marx*( ) with subscripts ranging from 1 to 4 so that the array is visible to all parts of the program. Assign the four values Chico, Harpo, Groucho, and Zeppo to the array as soon as the program is run.

22. Dimension the string array *stooges*( ) with subscripts ranging from 1 to 3 so that the array is visible only to the event procedure cmdStooges_Click. Assign the three values Moe, Larry, Curly to the array as soon as the command button is clicked.

23. The arrays $a(\ )$ and $b(\ )$ have been dimensioned to have range 1 to 4, and values have been assigned to $a(1)$ through $a(4)$. Reverse the order of these values and store them in $b(\ )$.

24. Given two arrays, $p(\ )$ and $q(\ )$, each with range 1 to 20, compute the sum of the products of the corresponding array elements, that is

    ```
    p(1)*q(1) + p(2)*q(2) + ... + p(20)*q(20)
    ```

25. Display the values of the array $a(\ )$ of range 1 to 30 in five columns as shown below.

    ```
    a(1)    a(2)     a(3)     a(4)     a(5)
     .       .        .        .        .
     .       .        .        .        .
     .       .        .        .        .
    a(26)   a(27)    a(28)    a(29)    a(30)
    ```

26. A list of 20 integers, all between 1 and 10, is contained in a data file. Determine how many times each integer appears and have the program display the frequency of each integer.

27. Compare two arrays $a(\ )$ and $b(\ )$ of range 1 to 10 to see if they hold identical values, that is, if $a(i) = b(i)$ for all i.

28. Calculate the sum of the entries with odd subscripts in an array $a(\ )$ of range 1 to 9.

29. Twelve exam grades are stored in the array *grades*$(\ )$. Curve the grades by adding 7 points to each grade.

30. Read 10 numbers contained in a data file into an array and then display three columns as follows: Column 1 should contain the original 10 numbers, column 2 should contain these numbers in reverse order, and column 3 should contain the averages of the corresponding numbers in columns 1 and 2.

31. Thirty scores, each lying between 0 and 49, are given in a data file. These scores are used to create an array *frequency*$(\ )$ as follows:

    frequency(1) = # of scores < 10
    frequency(2) = # of scores such that 10 <= score < 20
    frequency(3) = # of scores such that 20 <= score < 30
    frequency(4) = # of scores such that 30 <= score < 40
    frequency(5) = # of scores such that 40 <= score < 50.

    Write a program to display the results in tabular form as follows:

Interval	Frequency
0 to 10	frequency(1)
10 to 20	frequency(2)
20 to 30	frequency(3)
30 to 40	frequency(4)
40 to 50	frequency(5)

32. Given the following flight schedule,

Flight #	Origin	Destination	Departure Time
117	Tucson	Dallas	8:45 a.m.
239	LA	Boston	10:15 a.m.
298	Albany	Reno	1:35 p.m.
326	Houston	New York	2:40 p.m.
445	New York	Tampa	4:20 p.m.

write a program to load this information into four arrays of range 1 to 5, *flightNum( )*, *orig( )*, *dest( )*, and *deptTime( )*, and ask the user to request a flight number. Have the computer find the flight number and display the information corresponding to that flight. Account for the case where the user requests a nonexistent flight.

33. Table 7.2 contains the names and number of units of the top 10 pizza chains in 1995. Write a program to place these data into a pair of parallel arrays, compute the total number of units for these 10 chains, and display a table giving the name and percentage of total units for each of the companies.

Name	Units	Name	Units
1. Pizza Hut	12,140	6. Chuck E. Cheese	319
2. Domino's	5,257	7. Godfather's	520
3. Little Caesar's	4,720	8. Shakey's	310
4. Papa John's	878	9. Pizza Inn	477
5. Round Table	558	10. California Pizza Kitchen	77

Table 7.2 Top 10 pizza chains for 1995 (and numbers of units).
Source: Restaurants & Institutions, July 1996

34. A retail store has five bins, numbered 1 to 5, each containing a different commodity. At the beginning of a particular day, each bin contains 45 items. Table 7.3 shows the cost per item for each of the bins and the quantity sold during that day.

Bin	Cost per Item	Quantity Sold
1	3.00	10
2	12.25	30
3	37.45	9
4	7.49	42
5	24.95	17

Table 7.3 Costs of items and quantities sold for Exercise 34.

Write a program to

(a) place the cost per item and the quantity sold from each bin into parallel arrays.
(b) display a table giving the inventory at the end of the day and the amount of revenue obtained from each bin.
(c) compute the total revenue for the day.
(d) list the number of each bin that contains fewer than 20 items at the end of the day.

35. Write a program that asks the user for a month by number and then displays the name of that month. For instance, if the user inputs 2, the program should display February. **Hint:** Create an array of 12 strings, one for each month of the year.

Exercises 36 and 37 require the Rnd function presented in Section 3.6.

36. Write a program to select the winning lottery numbers. The selection should consist of six randomly chosen whole numbers from 1 through 40 (with no repeats).

37. Write a program to simulate 1000 rolls of a die and report the number of times each integer occurs.

SOLUTIONS TO PRACTICE PROBLEMS 7.1

1. Arrays should be used when

   (a) several pieces of data of the same type will be entered by the user
   (b) computations must be made on the items in a data file *after* all of the items have been read
   (c) lists of corresponding data are being analyzed.

2. (a) `Dim manOfTheYear(1980 To 1989)`

   (b) `Let manOfTheYear(1982) = "The Computer"`

7.2 USING ARRAYS

This section considers three aspects of the use of arrays: processing ordered arrays, reading part of an array, and passing arrays to procedures.

Ordered Arrays

An array is said to be ordered if its values are in either ascending or descending order. The following arrays illustrate the different types of ordered and unordered arrays. In an ascending ordered array, the value of each element is less than or equal to the value of the next element. That is,

$$[\text{each element}] \le [\text{next element}].$$

For string arrays, the ANSI table is used to evaluate the "less than or equal to" condition.

Ordered Ascending Numeric Array

dates( )	1492	1776	1812	1929	1969

Ordered Descending Numeric Array

discov( )	1610	1541	1513	1513	1492

Ordered Ascending String Array

king( )	Edward	Henry	James	John	Kong

Ordered Descending String Array

lake( )	Superior	Ontario	Michigan	Huron	Erie

Unordered Numeric Array

rates( )	8.25	5.00	7.85	8.00	6.50

Unordered String Array

char( )	G	R	E	A	T

Ordered arrays can be searched more efficiently than unordered arrays. In this section we use their order to shorten the search. The technique used here is applied to searching sequential files in Chapter 8.

EXAMPLE 1 The following program places an ordered list of names into an array, requests a name as input, and informs the user if the name is in the list. Because the list is ordered, the search of the array ends when an element is reached whose value is greater than or equal to the input name. On average, only half the ordered array will be searched. Figure 7.5 shows the flowchart for this search.

```
Rem Create array to hold 10 strings
Dim nom(1 To 10) As String

Private Sub cmdSearch_Click()
  Dim n As Integer, name2Find As String
  Rem Search for a name in an ordered list
  Let name2Find = UCase(Trim(txtName.Text))
  Let n = 0     'n is the subscript of the array
  Do
    Let n = n + 1
  Loop Until (nom(n) >= name2Find) Or (n = 10)
  Rem Interpret result of search
  picResult.Cls
  If nom(n) = name2Find Then
      picResult.Print "Found."
    Else
      picResult.Print "Not found."
  End If
End Sub

Private Sub Form_Load()
  Rem Place the names into the array
  Rem All names must be in uppercase
  Let nom(1) = "AL"
  Let nom(2) = "BOB"
  Let nom(3) = "CARL"
  Let nom(4) = "DON"
  Let nom(5) = "ERIC"
```

```
   Let nom(6) = "FRED"
   Let nom(7) = "GREG"
   Let nom(8) = "HERB"
   Let nom(9) = "IRA"
   Let nom(10) = "JUDY"
End Sub
```

[Run, type Don into the text box, and click the command button.]

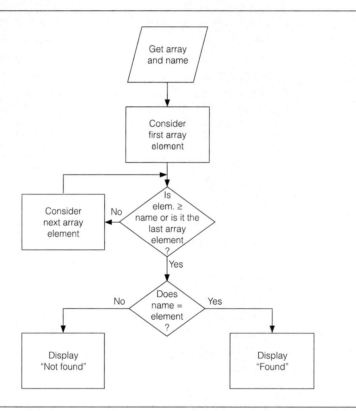

Figure 7.5 Flowchart for a search of an ordered array.

Using Part of an Array

In some programs, we must dimension an array before knowing how many pieces of data are to be placed into the array. In these cases, we dimension the array large enough to handle all reasonable contingencies. For instance, if the array is to hold exam grades and class sizes vary from 5 to 100 students, we would use a statement such as Dim grades(1 To 100) As Integer. In such situations, we must employ a **counter variable** to keep track of the number of values actually stored in the array. We create this counter variable using a Dim statement in the (Declarations) section of (General) so that all procedures will have access to it.

EXAMPLE 2   The following program requests a list of companies and then displays them along with a count.

```
Rem Demonstrate using only part of an array
Dim stock(1 To 100) As String
Dim counter As Integer

Private Sub cmdResult_Click()
  If (counter < 100) Then
      Let counter = counter + 1
      Let stock(counter) = txtCompany.Text
      Let txtCompany.Text = ""
      txtCompany.SetFocus
    Else
      MsgBox "No space to record additional companies.", , ""
      Let txtCompany.Text = ""
      cmdSummarize.SetFocus
  End If
End Sub

Private Sub cmdSummarize_Click()
  Dim i As Integer
  Rem List stock companies that have been recorded
  picStocks.Cls
  picStocks.Print "You own the following"; counter; "stocks."
  For i = 1 To counter
    picStocks.Print stock(i) & "  ";
    Rem Move to new line after every 5 stocks
    If Int(i / 5) = i / 5 Then
        picStocks.Print
    End If
  Next i
End Sub

Private Sub Form_Load()
  Rem Initialize count of companies
  Let counter = 0
End Sub
```

[Run, type in eleven companies (press Record Name after each company) and press Summarize.]

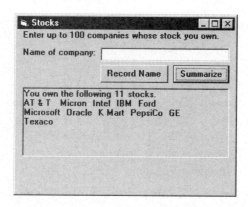

Suppose you have two ordered lists of customers (possibly with some customers on both lists) and you want to consolidate them into a single ordered list. The technique for creating the third list, called the **merge algorithm**, is as follows.

1. Compare the two names at the top of the first and second lists.
    (a) If one name alphabetically precedes the other, copy it onto the third list and cross it off its original list.
    (b) If the names are the same, copy the name onto the third list and cross out the name from the first and second lists.
2. Repeat Step 1 with the current top names until you reach the end of either list.
3. Copy the names from the remaining list onto the third list.

EXAMPLE 3   The following program stores two lists of names in arrays and merges them into a third list. Although at most 10 names will be placed into the third array, duplications will reduce this number. Because the variable r identifies the next position to insert a name in the third array, $r - 1$ is the number of names in the array.

```
Rem Create arrays to hold list of names
Dim list1(1 To 5) As String, list2(1 To 5) As String
Dim newList(1 To 10) As String

Private Sub cmdMerge_Click()
  Dim m As Integer, n As Integer, r As Integer
  Dim numNames As Integer, i As Integer
  Rem Merge two lists of names
  Let m = 1    'Subscript for first array
  Let n = 1    'Subscript for second array
  Let r = 1    'Subscript and counter for third array
  Do While (m <= 5) And (n <= 5)
    Select Case list1(m)
      Case Is < list2(n)
        Let newList(r) = list1(m)
        Let m = m + 1
      Case Is > list2(n)
        Let newList(r) = list2(n)
        Let n = n + 1
      Case list2(n)
        Let newList(r) = list1(m)
        Let m = m + 1
        Let n = n + 1
    End Select
    Let r = r + 1
  Loop
  Rem If one of the lists has items left over copy them into the third list
  Rem At most one of the following two loops will be executed
  Do While m <= 5        'Copy rest of first array into third
    Let newList(r) = list1(m)
    Let r = r + 1
    Let m = m + 1
  Loop
```

```
    Do While n <= 5        'Copy rest of second array into third
      Let newList(r) = list2(n)
      Let r = r + 1
      Let n = n + 1
    Loop
    Let numNames = r - 1
    Rem Show result of merging lists
    picMergedList.Cls
    For i = 1 To numNames
      picMergedList.Print newList(i) & "  ";
    Next i
End Sub

Private Sub Form_Load()
  Rem Fill list1 with names
  Let list1(1) = "Al"
  Let list1(2) = "Carl"
  Let list1(3) = "Don"
  Let list1(4) = "Greg"
  Let list1(5) = "Judy"
  Rem Fill list2 with names
  Let list2(1) = "Bob"
  Let list2(2) = "Carl"
  Let list2(3) = "Eric"
  Let list2(4) = "Greg"
  Let list2(5) = "Herb"
End Sub
```

[Run and click the command button.]

Passing Arrays between Procedures

An array that is not dimensioned in the (Declarations) section of (General) but rather is declared in a procedure is local to that procedure and unknown in all other procedures. However, an entire local array can be passed to another procedure. The name of the array, followed by an empty set of parentheses, must appear as an argument in the calling statement, and an array variable name of the same type must appear as a corresponding parameter in the procedure definition of the procedure that is to receive the array.

EXAMPLE 4   The following program illustrates passing an array to both a subprogram and a function.

```
Private Sub cmdDisplayAverage_Click()
  Rem Pass array to subprogram and function
  Dim score(1 To 10) As Integer
  Call FillArray(score())
  picAverage.Cls
  picAverage.Print "The average score is"; Sum(score()) / 10
End Sub

Private Sub FillArray(s() As Integer)
  Rem Fill array with scores
  Let s(1) = 85
  Let s(2) = 92
  Let s(3) = 75
  Let s(4) = 68
  Let s(5) = 84
  Let s(6) = 86
  Let s(7) = 94
  Let s(8) = 74
  Let s(9) = 79
  Let s(10) = 88
End Sub

Private Function Sum(s() As Integer) As Integer
  Dim total As Integer, index As Integer
  Rem Add up scores
  Let total = 0
  For index = 1 To 10
    Let total = total + s(index)
  Next index
  Sum = total
End Function
```

[Run and click the command button.]

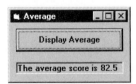

Sometimes it is also necessary to pass a form-level array from one procedure to another. For example, you might have a sorting procedure (discussed in Section 7.3) and three form-level arrays to be sorted. The sorting procedure would be called three times, each time passing a different form-level array. The method for passing a form-level array to another procedure is the same as the method for passing a local array.

EXAMPLE 5   The following program incorporates all three topics discussed in this section. It reads ordered lists of computer languages and spoken languages into form-level arrays, requests a new language as input, and inserts the language into its proper array position (avoiding duplication). The language arrays are dimensioned to hold up to 20 names; the variables *numCompLangs* and *numSpokLangs* record the actual number of languages in each of the ordered arrays. The original contents of the data files are

COMPLANG.TXT: ADA, C, Cobol, Fortran, Pascal, Visual Basic
SPOKLANG.TXT: Cantonese, English, French, Mandarin, Russian, Spanish

Object	Property	Setting
frmAdding	Caption	Adding to an Ordered Array
lblNew	Caption	New language:
txtLang	Text	(blank)
cmdAddComp	Caption	Add to Computer List
cmdAddSpok	Caption	Add to Spoken List
picAllLang		

```
Dim compLang(1 To 20) As String
Dim spokLang(1 To 20) As String
Dim numCompLangs As Integer
Dim numSpokLangs As Integer


Private Sub AddALang(lang() As String, langCount As Integer)
  Dim language As String, n As Integer, i As Integer
  Rem Insert a language into an ordered array of languages
  Let language = Trim(txtLang.Text)
  Let n = 0
  Do
    Let n = n + 1
  Loop Until (UCase(lang(n)) >= UCase(language)) Or (n = langCount)
  If UCase(lang(n)) < UCase(language) Then      'Insert new language at end
      Let lang(langCount + 1) = language
      Let langCount = langCount + 1
    ElseIf UCase(lang(n)) > UCase(language) Then      'Insert before item n
      For i = langCount To n Step -1
        Let lang(i + 1) = lang(i)
      Next i
      Let lang(n) = language
      Let langCount = langCount + 1
  End If
End Sub


Private Sub cmdAddComp_Click()
  Rem Insert language into ordered array of computer languages
  Call AddALang(compLang(), numCompLangs)
  Call DisplayArray(compLang(), numCompLangs)
End Sub


Private Sub cmdAddSpok_Click()
  Rem Insert language into ordered array of spoken languages
  Call AddALang(spokLang(), numSpokLangs)
```

```
      Call DisplayArray(spokLang(), numSpokLangs)
End Sub

Private Sub DisplayArray(lang() As String, howMany As Integer)
  Dim i As Integer
  Rem Display the languages in the array
  picAllLang.Cls
  For i = 1 To howMany
    picAllLang.Print lang(i) & "  ";
  Next i
End Sub

Private Sub Form_Load()
  Rem Fill computer language array from COMPLANG.TXT
  Let numCompLangs = 0
  Open "COMPLANG.TXT" For Input As #1
  Do While (Not EOF(1)) And (numCompLangs < 20)
    Let numCompLangs = numCompLangs + 1
    Input #1, compLang(numCompLangs)
  Loop
  Close #1
  Rem Fill spoken language array from SPOKLANG.TXT
  Let numSpokLangs = 0
  Open "SPOKLANG.TXT" For Input As #1
  Do While (Not EOF(1)) And (numSpokLangs < 20)
    Let numSpokLangs = numSpokLangs + 1
    Input #1, spokLang(numSpokLangs)
  Loop
  Close #1
End Sub
```

[Run, type in German, and click Add to Spoken List.]

[Type in FORTRAN and click Add to Computer List.]

Comments

1. In Examples 1 and 5 we searched successive elements of an ordered list beginning with the first element. This is called a **sequential search**. An efficient alternative to the sequential search is the **binary search**, which is considered in the next section.

2. A single element of an array can be passed to a procedure just like any ordinary numeric or string variable.

```
Private Sub cmdButton_Click()
  Dim num(1 To 20) As Integer
  Let num(5) = 10
  picOutput.Print Triple(num(5))
End Sub

Private Function Triple(x As Integer) As Integer
  Triple = 3 * x
End Function
```

When the program is run and the command button clicked, 30 will be displayed.

3. Visual Basic provides two functions that simplify working with arrays that have been passed to a procedure. If an array has been dimensioned with the range *m* To *n*, then the values of the functions LBound(*arrayName*) and UBound(*arrayName*) are *m* and *n*.

```
Private Sub cmdButton_Click()
  Dim pres(40 To 42) As String
  Let pres(40) = "Reagan"
  Let pres(41) = "Bush"
  Let pres(42) = "Clinton"
  Call Display(pres())
End Sub

Private Sub Display(a() As String)
  Dim i As Integer
  For i = LBound(a) To UBound(a)
    picOutput.Print a(i) & "  ";
  Next i
End Sub
```

When the program is run and the command button clicked, "Reagan Bush   Clinton" will be displayed.

PRACTICE PROBLEMS 7.2

1. Can an array be in both ascending and descending order at the same time?

2. How can the Select Case block in Example 3 be changed so all entries of both arrays (including duplicates) are merged into the third array?

EXERCISES 7.2

In Exercises 1 and 2, decide if the array is ordered.

1. month()

January	February	March	April	May

2. pres()

Adams	Adams	Bush	Johnson	Johnson

In Exercises 3 through 8, determine the output displayed in the picture box when the command button is clicked.

3.
```
Private Sub cmdDisplay_Click()
    Dim lake(1 To 5) As String
    Let lake(3) = "Michigan"
    Call DisplayThird(lake())
End Sub

Private Sub DisplayThird(lake() As String)
  Rem Display the third element of an array
  picOutput.Print lake(3)
End Sub
```

4.
```
Private Sub cmdDisplay_Click()
    Dim i As Integer, num As Integer
    Dim square(1 To 20) As Integer
    Let num = Val(InputBox("Enter a number from 1 to 20:"))
    For i = 1 To num
      Let square(i) = i ^ 2
    Next i
    Call Total(square(), num)
End Sub

Private Sub Total(array() As Integer, n As Integer)
  Dim sum As Integer
  Let sum = 0
  For i = 1 To n
    Let sum = sum + array(i)
  Next i
  picOutput.Print "The sum of the first"; n; "elements is"; sum
End Sub
```

(Assume that the response is 4.)

5.
```
Private Sub cmdDisplay_Click()
    Dim i As Integer
    Dim value(1 To 5) As Integer
    Call FillArray(value())
    For i = 1 To 4
      Select Case value(i)
        Case Is < value(i + 1)
          picOutput.Print "less than"
        Case Is > value(i + 1)
          picOutput.Print "greater than"
        Case Else
          picOutput.Print "equals"
      End Select
    Next i
End Sub
```

```
Private Sub FillArray(array() As Integer)
  Rem Place values into an array of five elements
  Open "DATA.TXT" For Input As #1
  For i = 1 To 5
    Input #1, array(i)
  Next i
  Close #1
End Sub
```

(Assume that the file DATA.TXT contains the following entries.)

3, 7, 1, 1, 17

6.
```
Private Sub cmdDisplay_Click()
  Dim ocean(1 To 5) As String
  Let ocean(1) = "Pacific"
  Call Musical(ocean(1))
End Sub
```

```
Private Sub Musical(sea As String)
  picOutput.Print "South "; sea
End Sub
```

7.
```
Private Sub cmdDisplay_Click()
  Dim rainfall(1 To 12) As Single
  Let rainfall(1) = 2.4
  Let rainfall(2) = 3.6
  Let rainfall(3) = 4.0
  picOutput.Print "The total rainfall for the first quarter is";
  picOutput.Print Total(rainfall(),3)
End Sub
```

```
Private Function Total(rainfall() As Single, n As Integer) As Single
  Dim sum As Single, i As Integer
  Let sum = 0
  For i = 1 To n
    Let sum = sum + rainfall(i)
  Next i
  Total = sum
End Function
```

8.
```
Private Sub cmdDisplay_Click()
  Dim i As Integer
  Dim num(1 To 8) As Integer
  Open "DATA.TXT" For Input As #1
  For i = 1 To 8
    Input #1, num(i)
  Next i
  Close #1
  picOutput.Print "The array has"; Nonzero(num()); "nonzero entries."
End Sub
```

```
Private Function Nonzero(digit() As Integer) As Integer
  Dim count As Integer, i As Integer
  Let count = 0
  For i = 1 To 8
    If digit(i) <> 0 Then
        Let count = count + 1
    End If
  Next i
  Nonzero = count
End Function
```

(Assume that the file DATA.TXT contains the following entries.)

5, 0, 2, 1, 0, 0, 7, 7

In Exercises 9 through 12, identify the error.

9.
```
Private Sub cmdDisplay_Click()
    Dim city(1 To 3) As String
    Call Assign(city())
    picOutput.Print city
End Sub

Private Sub Assign(town() As String)
  Let town(1) = "Chicago"
End Sub
```

10.
```
Private Sub cmdDisplay_Click()
    Dim planet(1 To 9) As String
    Call Assign(planet)
    picOutput.Print planet(1)
End Sub

Private Sub Assign(planet As String)
  Let planet(1) = "Venus"
End Sub
```

11.
```
Private Sub cmdDisplay_Click()
    Dim prompt As String, n As Integer
    Dim number As Single, product As Single, i As Integer
    Rem Multiply several numbers together
    Dim num(1 To 5) As Single
    Let prompt = "Enter a positive number to multiply by, or, to see the "
    Let prompt = prompt & "product, press Enter without giving a number. "
    Let prompt = prompt & "(Five numbers maximum can be specified.)"
    Let n = 0
    Do
      Let n = n + 1
      Let number = Val(InputBox(prompt))
      If number > 0 Then
          Let num(n) = number
      End If
```

```
     Loop Until (number <= 0) Or (n = 5)
     Let product = 1
     For i = 1 To n
       Let product = product * num(i)
     Next i
     picOutput.Print "The product of the numbers entered is "; product
   End Sub
```

12.
```
Private Sub cmdDisplay_Click()
    Dim hue(0 To 15) As String
    Let hue(1) = "Blue"
    Call Favorite(hue())
End Sub

Private Sub Favorite(tone() As String)
    Let tone(1) = hue(1)
    picOutput.Print tone
End Sub
```

In Exercises 13 and 14, find the error in the program and rewrite the program to correctly perform the intended task.

13.
```
Private Sub cmdDisplay_Click()
    Dim i As Integer
    Dim a(1 To 10) As Integer
    Dim b(1 To 10) As Integer
    For i = 1 To 10
      Let a(i) = i ^ 2
    Next i
    Call CopyArray(a(), b())
    picOutput.Print b(10)
End Sub

Private Sub CopyArray(a() As Integer, b() As Integer)
    Rem Place a's values in b
    Let b() = a()
End Sub
```

14.
```
Private Sub cmdDisplay_Click()
    Dim a(1 To 3) As Integer
    Let a(1) = 42
    Let a(2) = 7
    Let a(3) = 11
    Call FlipFirstTwo(a())
    picOutput.Print a(1); a(2); a(3)
End Sub

Private Sub FlipFirstTwo(a() As Integer)
    Rem Swap first two elements
    Let a(2) = a(1)
    Let a(1) = a(2)
End Sub
```

Suppose an array has been dimensioned in the (Declarations) section of (General) with the statement Dim scores(1 To 50) As Single and numbers assigned to each element by the Form_Load event procedure. In Exercises 15 through 18, write a procedure to perform the stated task.

15. Determine if the array is in ascending order.

16. Determine if the array is in descending order.

17. With a single loop, determine if the array is in ascending order, descending order, both, or neither.

18. Assuming the array is in ascending order, count the numbers that appear more than once in the array.

In Exercises 19 and 20, suppose arrays *a*( ), *b*( ), and *c*( ) are form-level and that arrays *a*( ) and *b*( ) have each been assigned 20 numbers in ascending order (duplications may occur) by a Form_Load event procedure. For instance, array *a*( ) might hold the numbers 1, 3, 3, 3, 9, 9, ...

19. Write a procedure to place all the 40 numbers from arrays *a*( ) and *b*( ) into *c*( ) so that *c*( ) is also ordered. The array *c*( ) could contain duplications.

20. Write a procedure to place the numbers from *a*( ) and *b*( ) into *c*( ) so that *c*( ) is ordered but contains no duplications.

21. Write a program to dimension an array with the statement Dim state(1 To 50) As String and maintain a list of certain states. The list of states should always be in alphabetical order and occupy consecutive elements of the array. The command buttons in the program should give the user the following options:

    (a) Take the state specified by the user in a text box and insert it into its proper position in the array. (If the state is already in the array, so report.)
    (b) Take the state specified by the user in a text box and delete it from the array. (If the state is not in the array, so report.)
    (c) Display the states in the array.
    (d) Quit.

22. Write a program that requests a sentence one word at a time from the user and then checks whether the sentence is a *word palindrome*. A word palindrome sentence reads the same, word by word, backward and forward (ignoring punctuation and capitalization). An example is "You can cage a swallow, can't you, but you can't swallow a cage, can you?" The program should hold the words of the sentence in an array and use procedures to obtain the input, analyze the sentence, and declare whether the sentence is a word palindrome. (Test the program with the sentences, "Monkey see, monkey do." and "I am; therefore, am I?")

23. Write a program to display the average score and the number of above average scores on an exam. Each time the user clicks a "record score" command button, a grade should be read from a text box. The average score and the number of above average scores should be displayed in a picture box whenever the user clicks on a "show average" command button. (Assume the class contains at most 100 students.) Use a function to calculate the average and another

function to determine the number of scores above average. **Note:** Pass the functions an array parameter for the grades and a numeric parameter for the number of elements of the array that have been assigned values.

24. Suppose an array of 1000 names is in ascending order. Write a procedure to search for a name input by the user. If the first letter of the name is found in N through Z, then the search should begin with the 1000th element of the array and proceed backwards.

Exercises 25 and 26 require the Rnd function presented in Section 3.6.

25. Write a program to randomly select 50 different people from a group of 100 people whose names are contained in a data file. **Hint:** Use an array of 100 elements to keep track of whether or not a person has been selected.

26. *The Birthday Problem.* Given a random group of 23 people, how likely is it that two people have the same birthday? To answer this question, write a program that creates an array of range 1 To 23, randomly assigns to each subscripted variable one of the integers from 1 through 365, and checks to see if any of the subscripted variables have the same value. (Make the simplifying assumption that no birthdays occur on February 29.) Now expand the program to repeat the process 100 times and determine the percentage of the time that there is a match. **Note:** This program may take a few minutes to run.

SOLUTIONS TO PRACTICE PROBLEMS 7.2

1. Yes, provided each element of the array has the same value.

2. The third Case tests for duplicates and only assigns one array element to the third array if duplicates are found in the two arrays. Thus, we remove the third Case and change the first Case so it will process any duplicates. A situation where you would want to merge two lists while retaining duplications is the task of merging two ordered arrays of test scores.

```
Select Case first(m)
  Case Is <= second(n)
    Let third(r) = first(m)
    Let m = m + 1
  Case Is > second(n)
    Let third(r) = second(n)
    Let n = n + 1
End Select
```

7.3 CONTROL ARRAYS

We have seen many examples of the usefulness of subscripted variables. They are essential for writing concise solutions to many programming problems. Because of the great utility that subscripts provide, Visual Basic also provides a means of constructing arrays of text boxes, labels, command buttons, and so on. Because text boxes, labels, and command buttons are referred to generically in Visual Basic as controls, arrays of these objects are called **control arrays**.

Unlike variable arrays, which can only be created by Dim statements once a program is running, at least one element of a control array must be created when the form is designed. The remaining elements can be created either during form design, or, perhaps more typically, with the Load statement when the program is running.

To create the first element of an array of text boxes, create an ordinary text box, then access the Properties window, and select the property called Index. By default this property is blank. Change the Index property to 0 (zero). Your text box is now the first element in a subscripted control array. If the name of a text box is *txtBox* and its Index property is 0, then assigning a value to the text box during run time requires a statement of the form

```
Let txtBox(0).Text = value
```

Arrays are not of much use if they contain only a single element. To create additional elements of the *txtBox*( ) control array during form design, make sure that the element you just created is active by clicking on it. Next, press Ctrl+C (or open the Edit menu and select Copy). Visual Basic has now recorded all the properties associated with *txtBox*(0) and is ready to reproduce as many copies as you desire. To create a copy, press Ctrl+V (or open the Edit menu and select Paste). The copy of *txtBox*(0) appears in the upper-left corner of the form. The value of the Index property for this new text box is 1; thus the text box is referred to as *txtBox*(1). Move this text box to the desired position. Press Ctrl+V again and another copy of *txtBox*(0) appears in the upper left corner of the form. Its Index property is 2. Move *txtBox*(2) to an appropriate position. Continue copying *txtBox*(0) in this manner until all desired controls have been created.

It is important to note that all properties of *txtBox*(0) are being passed to the other elements of the *txtBox*( ) control array, with the exception of the Index, Top, and Left properties. Thus, as a matter of efficiency, before you begin copying *txtBox*(0), set all properties that you want carried over to all elements of *txtBox*( ). For example, if you desire to have the Text property blank for all *txtBox*( ) elements, set the Text property of *txtBox*(0) to (blank) before starting the copying process.

The preceding discussion gave a process for creating an array of text boxes. This same process applies to creating arrays of labels or any other control. In summary, the following steps create an array of controls while designing a form:

1. Add one instance of the desired control to the form.

2. Set the Index property of this control to 0.

3. Set any other properites of the control that will be common to all elements of the array.

4. Click on the control and then press Ctrl+C to prepare to make a copy of the control.

5. Press Ctrl+V to create a copy of the control. Position this control as desired.

6. Repeat Step 5 until all desired elements of the control array have been created.

EXAMPLE 1 A department store has five departments. Write a program to request the amount of sales for each department and display the total sales.

SOLUTION We use a control array of five labels and a control array of five text boxes to handle the input. For the label captions we use "Department 1", "Department 2", and so on. Because these labels are the same except for the number, we wait until run time and use a For...Next loop inside the Form_Load ( ) event procedure to assign the captions to each element of the *lblDepart*( ) control array. At design time, before making copies of *lblDepart*(0), we set the Alignment property to "1 – Right Justify" so that all elements of the array inherit this property. Similarly, the Text property of *txtSales*(0) is set to (blank) before copying.

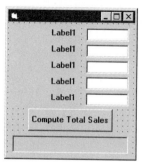

Object	Property	Setting
lblDepart()	Index	0 to 4
	Alignment	1 – Right Justify
txtSales( )	Index	0 to 4
	Text	(blank)
cmdCompute	Caption	Compute Total Sales
picTotal		

```
Private Sub Form_Load()
  Dim depNum As Integer
  For depNum = 0 To 4
    Let lblDepart(depNum).Caption = "Department" & Str(depNum + 1)
  Next depNum
End Sub


Private Sub cmdCompute_Click()
  Dim depNum As Integer, sales As Single
  Let sales = 0
  For depNum = 0 To 4
    Let sales = sales + Val(txtSales(depNum).Text)
  Next depNum
  picTotal.Cls
  picTotal.Print "Total sales were " & Format(sales, "Currency")
End Sub
```

[Run, type the following data into the text boxes, and click the command button.]

Control Array Event Procedures

In Chapter 3 we discussed several events related to text boxes. One example was the GotFocus event procedure. If *txtBox* is an ordinary text box, then the GotFocus event procedure begins with the statement

```
Private Sub txtBox_GotFocus()
```

If, on the other hand, we make *txtBox* a control array, the GotFocus event procedure begins with the statement

```
Private Sub txtBox_GotFocus(Index As Integer)
```

(handwritten annotation: Is the Element of Control array)

Two points should be noted. First, even though we may have a dozen or more elements in the *txtBox( )* control array, we will have just one txtBox_GotFocus event procedure to deal with. Second, Visual Basic passes to this one event procedure the value of the Index property for the element of the control array that has the focus. We may wish to respond in the same manner whenever any element of *txtBox( )* has the focus, in which case we simply ignore the value of *Index*. If, on the other hand, we wish to respond in different ways, depending on which element has the focus, then we write the GotFocus event procedure in the form

```
Private Sub txtBox_GotFocus(Index As Integer)
  Select Case Index
    Case 0
      action when txtBox(0) gets the focus
    Case 1
      action when txtBox(1) gets the focus
      .
      .
  End Select
End Sub
```

In general, all event procedures for a control array have the additional parameter Index As Integer. This additional parameter can be used, if desired, to base the action taken by the event procedure on which element of the control array underwent the event.

EXAMPLE 2 Create an electronic dialing pad.

SOLUTION The following form contains a control array of 10 command buttons. Each time a command button is clicked, the Index parameter conveys the digit to be added onto the phone number. This program illustrates using the Index parameter without employing a Select Case statement.

Object	Property	Setting
cmdDigit( )	Index	0 to 9
	Caption	(same as Index)
lblPhoneNum	BorderStyle	1 – Fixed Single
	Caption	(blank)

```
Private Sub cmdDigit_Click(Index As Integer)
  Let lblPhoneNum.Caption = lblPhoneNum.Caption & Format(Index, "0")
  If Len(lblPhoneNum.Caption) = 3 Then
      Let lblPhoneNum.Caption = lblPhoneNum.Caption & "-"
    ElseIf Len(lblPhoneNum.Caption) = 8 Then
      MsgBox "Dialing ...", , ""
      Let lblPhoneNum.Caption = ""
  End If
End Sub
```

Creating Control Arrays at Run Time

We have discussed the process for creating an entire control array while designing a form, that is, at design time. However, copying and positioning control array elements can become tedious if the number of elements is large. Also, the actual number of elements needed in a control array may not be known until a response from the user is processed at run time. In light of these concerns, Visual Basic provides a solution via the Load statement that only requires us to create the first element of a control array during design time. The remaining elements are then created as needed at run time. Before we discuss creating arrays at run time, we must consider a preliminary topic—the Left, Top, Width, and Height properties of controls. These properties specify the location and size of controls.

The standard unit of measurement in Visual Basic is called a **twip**. There are 1440 twips to the inch. When a control is active, the two panels on the right side of the toolbar give the location and size of the control, respectively. Figure 7.6(a) shows an active text box, named Text1. The first panel says that the left side of the text box is 960 twips from the left side of the form, and the top of the text box is 720 twips down from the title bar of the form. In terms of properties, Text1.Left is 960, and Text1.Top is 720. Similarly, the numbers 1935 and 975 in the second panel give the width and height of the text box in twips. In terms of properties, Text1.Width is 1935 and Text1.Height is 975. Figure 7.6(b) shows the meanings of these four properties.

The location and size properties of a control can be altered at run time with statements such as

```
Let Text1.Left = 480
```

which moves the text box to the left or

```
Let Text2.Top = Text1.Top + 1.5 * Text1.Height
```

which places Text2 a comfortable distance below Text1. As a result of the second statement, the distance between the two text boxes will be half the height of Text1.

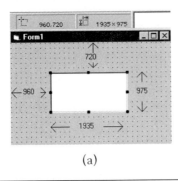
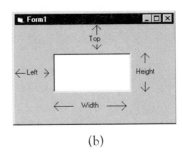

(a)   (b)

Figure 7.6 The location and size of a control.

If *controlName* is the name of a control whose Index property was assigned a value during form design (thus creating the beginnings of a control array) and *num* is a whole number that has not yet been used as an index for the *control-Name*( ) array, then the statement

        Load *controlName(num)*

copies all the properties of *controlName*(0), including the Top and Left properties, and creates the element *controlName(num)* of the *controlName*( ) array. The only property of *controlName(num)* that may differ from that of *controlName*(0) is the Visible property. The Load statement always sets the Visible property of the created element to False. After creating a new element of a control array, you will want to adjust the Top and Left properties so that the new element has its own unique location on the form, and then set the Visible property of the new element to True.

EXAMPLE 3   Write a program to create a control array of 12 labels and a control array of 12 text boxes. Position the labels and text boxes so that they form two columns, with the labels to the left of the text boxes and the text boxes one immediately below the other. Use text boxes whose height is as small as possible. Use labels whose height is just large enough to display a single line. Assign the captions Jan, Feb, and so on, to the labels.

SOLUTION   When designing the form, we place the first label to the left of the first text box and set the Index property of both controls to 0. The height of the shortest text box is 285 units and the height of a label just tall enough for a single line is 255 units. We use the text box's Height property as the unit of vertical spacing for both the new text box elements and the new label elements. The following is the form at design time and at run time.

Object	Property	Setting
frm 7_3_3	Caption	Year
lblMonth	Index	0
	Caption	Jan
txtInfo	Index	0
	Text	(blank)

```
Private Sub Form_Load()
  Dim i As Integer, monthNames As String
  Let monthNames = "FebMarAprMayJunJulAugSepOctNovDec"
  For i = 1 To 11
    Load lblMonth(i)
    Load txtInfo(i)
    Let lblMonth(i).Top = lblMonth(i - 1).Top + txtInfo(0).Height
    Let txtInfo(i).Top = txtInfo(i - 1).Top + txtinfo(0).Height
    Let lblMonth(i).Caption = Mid(monthNames, 3 * i - 2, 3)
    Let lblMonth(i).Visible = True
    Let txtInfo(i).Visible = True
  Next i
End Sub
```

Comments

1. In the discussion and examples of control arrays, the initial index was always 0. For a particular application it may be more natural to have the lowest index of a control array be 1 or even 1995. To achieve this when creating just the first element at design time and the remaining controls at run time, set the Index property of the first element to the desired lowest index value at design time, then Load the other elements using the desired indexes at run time. (The Load statement copies the properties of the element with the lowest index, whatever that lowest index may be.) For example, at design time you might create *txtSales*(1995) and then at run time execute the statements

```
For yearNum = 1996 to 2005
  Load txtSales(yearNum)
Next yearNum
```

To create an entire control array at design time with indexes starting at a value other than 0, first create the control array using an initial index of 0. Once all elements have been created, use the Properties window to adjust the index of each element of the control array, starting with the element having the highest index.

PRACTICE PROBLEMS 7.3

1. Suppose an event procedure has the first line

```
Private Sub txtBox_GotFocus()
```

How do you know whether txtBox is the name of an ordinary control or a control array?

2. Assume element 0 of the txtBox control array was created during design time. What is the shortcoming of the following event procedure?

```
Private Sub Form_Load()
  Load txtBox(1)
  Let txtBox(1).Visible = True
End Sub
```

3. What is the effect of adding the following line to the event procedure in Problem 2?

```
Let txtBox(1).Top = txtBox(0).Top + 2 * txtBox(0).Height
```

EXERCISES 7.3

In Exercises 1 to 4, design the given form using the indicated number and type of controls.

1. A control array of four text boxes, a command button, and a picture box.

2. A control array of three command buttons and a picture box.

3. A contol array of six labels, a control array of six text boxes, and a command button.

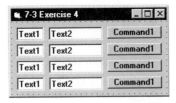

4. Two control arrays of four text boxes each and a control array of four command buttons.

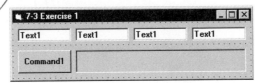

In Exercises 5 to 10, give the effect of the statement.

5. `Let txtBox.Width = .5 * txtBox.Width`

6. `Let txtBox.Top = .5 * txtBox.Height`

7. `Let txtBox.Left = txtBox.Top`

8. `Let txtBox.Width = txtBox.Height`

9. `Let txtBox.Width = Form1.Width`

10. `Let txtBox.Width = .5 * Form1.Width`

In Exercises 11 through 18, suppose the control array cmdButton( ) consists of the two command buttons cmdButton(0) and cmdButton(1) placed vertically, and write an event procedure to carry out the indicated task.

11. When a button is clicked on, it disappears.

12. When a button is clicked on, it moves 100 twips to the right.

13. When the button is clicked, its caption turns italic and the caption of the other button turns nonitalic.

14. When a button is clicked, the other button assumes the caption of the clicked on button, but with the letters reversed.

15. When a button is clicked, it moves 100 twips to the right of the other button.

16. When a button is clicked, it moves 100 twips below the other button.

17. When a button is clicked, it doubles in width.

18. When a button is clicked, it becomes twice the width of the other button.

In Exercises 19 and 20, write lines of code to carry out the given tasks.

19. Suppose the text box txtBox with index 0 was created at design time. Create a new text box at run time and place it 100 twips below the original text box.

20. Suppose the text box txtBox with index 0 was created at design time. Create two additional text boxes at run time and place them below the original text box. Then italicize the contents of a text box when the text box gets the focus.

In Exercises 21 through 24, identify the error.

IS TWIP
35

21.
```
Private Sub cmdButton(1)_Click
    Let cmdButton(1).ForeColor = &HFFFF&
End Sub
```

22. `Load cmdButton(Index As Integer)`

23.
```
Private Sub Form_Load()
    Dim i As Integer
    For i = 0 To 5
      Load lblID(i)
      Let lblID(i).Caption = Str(1995 + i)
      Let lblID(i).Top = lblID(i - 1).Top + lblID(i - 1).Height
      Let lblID(i).Visible = True
    Next i
End Sub
```

24.
```
Private Sub Form_Load()
    Dim i As Integer
    For i = 1 To 12
      Load txtBox(i)
      Let txtBox.Text(i) = ""
      Let txtBox.Left(i) = txtBox.Left(i - 1) + txtBox.TextWidth(i - 1)
    Next i
    Let txtBox.Visible(i - 1) = True
End Sub
```

In Exercises 25 through 28, use the following form (already filled in by the user) to determine the output displayed in the picture box when the command button is clicked. The text boxes on the form consist of four control arrays— *txtWinter*( ), *txtSpring*( ), *txtSummer*( ), and *txtFall*( )—with each control array having indexes ranging from 1 to 4.

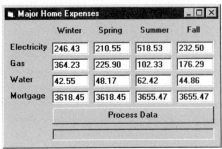

25.
```
Private Sub cmdProcessData_Click()
    Dim itemNum As Integer, total As Single
    Let total = 0
    For itemNum = 1 to 4
      Let total = total + Val(txtWinter(itemNum).Text)
    Next itemNum
    picBox.Print "Home expenses for winter were ";
    picBox.Print Format(total, "Currency")
End Sub
```

26.
```
Private Sub cmdProcessData_Click()
    Dim total As Single
    Let total = 0
    Let total = total + Val(txtWinter(3).Text)
    Let total = total + Val(txtSpring(3).Text)
    Let total = total + Val(txtSummer(3).Text)
    Let total = total + Val(txtFall(3).Text)
    picBox.Print "Annual water bill was ";
    picBox.Print Format(total, "Currency")
End Sub
```

27.
```
Private Sub cmdProcessData_Click()
    Dim itemNum As Integer, diff As Single, total As Single
    Let total = 0
    For itemNum = 1 To 4
      Let diff = Val(txtSummer(itemNum).Text) - Val(txtWinter(itemNum).Text)
      Let total = total + diff
    Next itemNum
    picBox.Print "Summer bills exceeded winter by ";
    picBox.Print Format(total, "Currency")
End Sub
```

28.
```
Private Sub cmdProcessData_Click()
    Dim itemNum As Integer, total As Single
    Let total = 0
    For itemNum = 1 To 4
      Let total = total + TotalCateg(itemNum)
    Next itemNum
    picBox.Print "Total major expenses were ";
    picBox.Print Format(total, "Currency")
End Sub
```

```
Private Function TotalCateg(itemNum As Integer) As Single
  Dim total As Single
  Let total = 0
  Let total = total + Val(txtWinter(itemNum).Text)
  Let total = total + Val(txtSpring(itemNum).Text)
  Let total = total + Val(txtSummer(itemNum).Text)
  Let total = total + Val(txtFall(itemNum).Text)
  TotalCateg = total
End Function
```

For Exercises 29 through 32, the design-time appearance of a form follows along with the properties assigned to the controls. Determine the appearance of the form after the given program segment is executed.

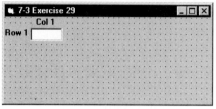

Object	Property	Setting
frmExer	Caption	7-3 Exercise 29
lblSide	Index	1
	Caption	Row 1
lblTop	Index	1
	Caption	Col 1
txtInfo	Index	1
	Text	(blank)

29.
```
Dim itemNum As Integer
For itemNum = 2 To 4
  Load lblSide(itemNum)
  Load txtInfo(itemNum)
  Let lblSide(itemNum).Top=lblSide(itemNum-1).Top + 1.5*txtInfo(1).Height
  Let txtInfo(itemNum).Top=txtInfo(itemNum-1).Top + 1.5*txtInfo(1).Height
  Let lblSide(itemNum).Caption = "Row" & Str(itemNum)
  Let lblSide(itemNum).Visible = True
  Let txtInfo(itemNum).Visible = True
Next itemNum
```

30.
```
Dim itemNum As Integer
For itemNum = 2 To 4
  Load lblTop(itemNum)
  Load txtInfo(itemNum)
  Let lblTop(itemNum).Left=lblTop(itemNum-1).Left + 1.5*txtInfo(1).Width
  Let txtInfo(itemNum).Left=txtInfo(itemNum-1).Left + 1.5*txtInfo(1).Width
  Let lblTop(itemNum).Caption = "Col" & Str(itemNum)
  Let lblTop(itemNum).Visible = True
  Let txtInfo(itemNum).Visible = True
Next itemNum
```

31.
```
Dim itemNum As Integer
For itemNum = 2 To 4
  Load lblTop(itemNum)
  Load txtInfo(itemNum)
  Let lblTop(itemNum).Left = lblTop(itemNum - 1).Left + txtInfo(1).Width
  Let txtInfo(itemNum).Left = txtInfo(itemNum - 1).Left + txtInfo(1).Width
  Let lblTop(itemNum).Caption = "Col" & Str(itemNum)
  Let lblTop(itemNum).Visible = True
  Let txtInfo(itemNum).Visible = True
Next itemNum
```

32.
```
Dim itemNum As Integer
For itemNum = 2 To 4
   Load lblTop(itemNum)
   Load lblSide(itemNum)
   Load txtInfo(itemNum)
   Let lblTop(itemNum).Left = lblTop(itemNum - 1).Left + txtInfo(1).Width
   Let lblSide(itemNum).Top = lblSide(itemNum - 1).Top + txtInfo(1).Height
   Let txtInfo(itemNum).Left = txtInfo(itemNum - 1).Left + txtInfo(1).Width
   Let txtInfo(itemNum).Top = txtInfo(itemNum - 1).Top + txtInfo(1).Height
   Let lblTop(itemNum).Caption = "Col" & Str(itemNum)
   Let lblSide(itemNum).Caption = "Row" & Str(itemNum)
   Let lblTop(itemNum).Visible = True
   Let lblSide(itemNum).Visible = True
   Let txtInfo(itemNum).Visible = True
Next itemNum
```

33. Modify the form given for Exercises 25 through 28 by deleting the command button and picture box and adding a row of labels below the row of Mortgage text boxes (use a control array named *lblQuarterTot*) and a column of labels to the right of the Fall text boxes (use a control array named *lblCategTot*). The purpose of these new labels is to hold the totals of each column and each row. Write an event procedure that updates the totals displayed on these new labels whenever the cursor is moved from one text box to another.

34. Write a program to compute a student's grade-point average. The program should use InputBox in the Form_Load event procedure to request the number of courses to be averaged and then create elements in two text box control arrays to hold the grade and semester hours credit for each course. After the student fills in these text boxes and clicks on a command button, the program should use a function to compute the grade-point average. Another subprogram should display the GPA and then display one of two messages. A student with a GPA of 3 or more should be informed that he has made the honor roll. Otherwise, the student should be congratulated on having completed the semester. In either case, the student should be wished a merry vacation.

35. Simulate a traffic light with a control array consisting of three small square picture boxes placed vertically on a form. Initially, the bottom picture box is solid green and the other picture boxes are white. When the Tab key is pressed, the middle picture box turns yellow and the bottom picture box turns white. The next time Tab is pressed, the top picture box turns red and the middle picture box turns white. Subsequent pressing of the Tab key cycles through the three colors. **Hint:** First, place the bottom picture box on the form, then the middle picture box, and finally the top picture box.

36. (A primitive typewriter.) Create a form containing a picture box and a control array of 26 small command buttons, each having one of the letters of the alphabet as its caption. When a command button is pressed, its letter should be added to the text in the picture box.

37. *Multiple-choice Quiz.* Write a program to ask multiple-choice questions with four possible answers. Figure 7.7 shows a typical question. The user selects an answer by clicking on a command button and is informed as to the correctness of the answer by a message box. When the user gives a correct answer, a new question is presented. The program ends when all questions have been presented or when the user clicks on the quit command button. Questions and correct answers should be read from a data file. The numbered command buttons should be elements of a command button control array. The question and answers should be displayed using a five-element control array of labels.

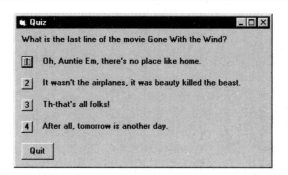

Figure 7.7 A typical question for Exercise 37.

38. Table 7.4 gives the U.S. Census Bureau projections for the populations (in millions) of the states predicted to be the most populous in the year 2010. Write a program that stores the 2010 data in an array and provides a control array of text boxes for the input of the current population of each of these states. When a command button is clicked, the percentage population growth for each state should be displayed in a control array of labels. In a picture box below these five values, the program should display the average percentage population growth for the five states. (Figure 7.8 shows a possible form design and run with sample data for 1990.) The growth is calculated using the formula

growth = (projected pop. − current pop.) / current pop.

Percentage growth can be obtained using Format(growth, "Percentage"). Test the program with the current populations shown in Figure 7.8.

State	Population in 2010
California	36.9
Texas	21.4
New York	20.3
Illinois	13.5
Florida	13.0

Table 7.4 State popuations in the Year 2010.

Figure 7.8 Sample run for Exercise 38.

SOLUTIONS TO PRACTICE PROBLEMS 7.3

1. It is an ordinary control. If it were a control array, the parentheses at the end of the line would contain the words "Index As Integer."

2. The new text box will be placed in the exact same location as the original text box. An additional line, like the one in Practice Problem 3, is needed.

3. The new text box will be placed below the original text box, with space between them equal to the height of the text boxes.

7.4 SORTING AND SEARCHING

A **sort** is an algorithm for ordering an array. Of the many different techniques for sorting an array, we discuss two, the **bubble sort** and the **Shell sort**. Both sorts require the interchange of values stored in a pair of variables. If *var1*, *var2*, and *temp* are all variables of the same type (that is, all numeric or all string), then the statements

```
Let temp = var1
Let var1 = var2
Let var2 = temp
```

assign *var1*'s value to *var2*, and *var2*'s value to *var1*.

EXAMPLE 1   Write a program to alphabetize two words supplied in text boxes.

SOLUTION
```
Private Sub cmdAlphabetize_Click()
    Dim firstWord As String, secondWord As String, temp As String
    Rem Alphabetize two words
    Let firstWord = txtFirstWord.Text
    Let secondWord = txtSecondWord.Text
    If firstWord > secondWord Then
        Let temp = firstWord
        Let firstWord = secondWord
        Let secondWord = temp
    End If
    picResult.Cls
    picResult.Print firstWord; " before "; secondWord
End Sub
```

[Run, type the following text shown into the text boxes, and click the command button.]

Bubble Sort

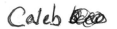

Caleb Reed

The bubble sort is an algorithm that compares adjacent items and swaps those that are out of order. If this process is repeated enough times, the list will be ordered. Let's carry out this process on the list Pebbles, Barney, Wilma, Fred, Dino. The steps for each pass through the list are as follows:

1. Compare the first and second items. If they are out of order, swap them.

2. Compare the second and third items. If they are out of order, swap them.

3. Repeat this pattern for all remaining pairs. The final comparison and possible swap are between the second-to-last and last elements.

The first time through the list, this process is repeated to the end of the list. This is called the first pass. After the first pass, the last item (Wilma) will be in its proper position. Therefore, the second pass does not have to consider it and so requires one less comparison. At the end of the second pass, the last two items will be in their proper position. (The items that must have reached their proper position have been underlined.) Each successive pass requires one less comparison. After four passes, the last four items will be in their proper positions and, hence, the first will be also.

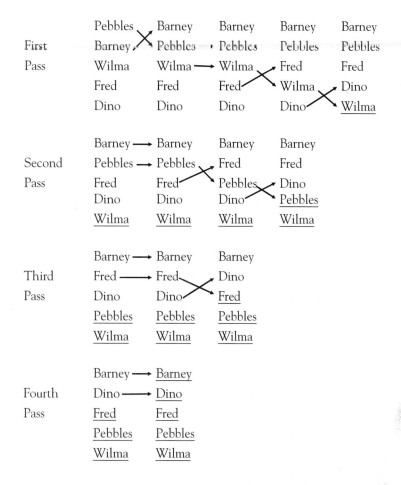

EXAMPLE 2   Write a program to alphabetize the names Pebbles, Barney, Wilma, Fred, Dino.

SOLUTION✱ Sorting the list requires a pair of nested loops. The inner loop performs a single pass and the outer loop controls the number of passes.

```
Dim nom(1 To 5) As String

Private Sub cmdSort_Click()
  Dim passNum As Integer, i As Integer, temp As String
  Rem Bubble sort names
  For passNum = 1 To 4     'Number of passes is 1 less than number of items
    For i = 1 To 5 - passNum           'Each pass needs 1 less comparison
      If nom(i) > nom(i + 1) Then
          Let temp = nom(i)
          Let nom(i) = nom(i + 1)
          Let nom(i + 1) = temp
      End If
    Next i
  Next passNum
  Rem Display alphabetized list
  picNames.Cls
  For i = 1 To 5
    picNames.Print nom(i),
  Next i
End Sub

Private Sub Form_Load()
  Rem Fill array with names
  Let nom(1) = "Pebbles"
  Let nom(2) = "Barney"
  Let nom(3) = "Wilma"
  Let nom(4) = "Fred"
  Let nom(5) = "Dino"
End Sub
```

[Run and click the command button.]

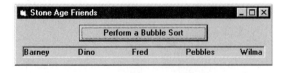

EXAMPLE 3   Table 7.5 contains facts about the 10 most populous metropolitan areas with listings in ascending order by city name. Sort the table in descending order by population.

Metro Area	Population in Millions	Median Income per Household	% Native to State	% Advanced Degree
Boston	4.2	$40,666	73	12
Chicago	8.1	$35,918	73	8
Dallas	3.9	$32,825	64	8
Detroit	4.7	$34,729	76	7
Houston	3.7	$31,488	67	8
Los Angeles	14.5	$36,711	59	8
New York	18.1	$38,445	73	11
Philadelphia	5.9	$35,797	70	8
San Francisco	6.3	$41,459	60	11
Washington	3.9	$47,254	32	17

Note: Column 4 gives the percentage of residents who were born in their current state of residence. Column 5 gives the percentage of residents age 25 or older with a graduate or professional degree.

Table 7.5 The 10 most populous metropolitan areas.

Source: The 1990 Census

SOLUTION
Data are read from a file into parallel arrays by the Form_Load event procedure. When cmdDisplayStats is clicked, the collection of parallel arrays is sorted based on the array *pop*( ). Each time two items are interchanged in the array *pop*( ), the corresponding items are interchanged in each of the other arrays. This way, for each city, the items of information remain linked by a common subscript.

```
Dim city(1 To 10) As String, pop(1 To 10) As Single, income(1 To 10) As Single
Dim natives(1 To 10) As Single, advDeg(1 To 10) As Single

Private Sub cmdDisplayStats_Click()
  Call SortData
  Call ShowData
End Sub

Private Sub Form_Load()
  Dim i As Integer
  Rem Assume the data for city name, population, medium income, % native,
  Rem and % advanced degree have been placed in the file "CITYSTAT.TXT"
  Rem (First line of file is "Boston", 4.2, 4066, 73, 12)
  Open "CITYSTAT.TXT" For Input As #1
  For i = 1 To 10
    Input #1, city(i), pop(i), income(i), natives(i), advDeg(i)
  Next i
  Close #1
End Sub

Private Sub ShowData()
  Dim i As Integer
  Rem Display ordered table
  picTable.Cls
  picTable.Print , "Pop. in", "Med. income", "% Native", "% Advanced"
  picTable.Print "Metro Area", "millions", "per hsd", "to State", "Degree"
  picTable.Print
```

```
     For i = 1 To 10
       picTable.Print city(i); Tab(16); pop(i), income(i), natives(i), advDeg(i)
     Next i
   End Sub

   Private Sub SortData()
     Dim passNum As Integer, index As Integer
     Rem Bubble sort table in descending order by population
     For passNum = 1 To 9
       For index = 1 To 10 - passNum
         If pop(index) < pop(index + 1) Then
             Call SwapData(index)
         End If
       Next index
     Next passNum
   End Sub

   Private Sub SwapData(index As Integer)
     Rem Swap entries
     Call SwapStr(city(index), city(index + 1))
     Call SwapNum(pop(index), pop(index + 1))
     Call SwapNum(income(index), income(index + 1))
     Call SwapNum(natives(index), natives(index + 1))
     Call SwapNum(advDeg(index), advDeg(index + 1))
   End Sub

   Private Sub SwapNum(a As Single, b As Single)
     Dim temp As Single
     Rem Interchange values of a and b
     Let temp = a
     Let a = b
     Let b = temp
   End Sub

   Private Sub SwapStr(a As String, b As String)
     Dim temp As String
     Rem Interchange values of a and b
     Let temp = a
     Let a = b
     Let b = temp
   End Sub
```

[Run and click the command button.]

Metropolitan Statistics

Display Statistics on 10 Most Populous Metropolitan Areas

Metro Area	Pop. in millions	Med. income per hsd	% Native to State	% Advanced Degree
New York	18.1	38445	73	11
Los Angeles	14.5	36711	59	8
Chicago	8.1	35918	73	8
San Francisco	6.3	41459	60	11
Philadelphia	5.9	35797	70	8
Detroit	4.7	34729	76	7
Boston	4.2	40666	73	12
Dallas	3.9	32825	64	8
Washington	3.9	47254	32	17
Houston	3.7	31488	67	8

Shell Sort

The bubble sort is easy to understand and program. However, it is too slow for really long lists. The Shell sort, named for its inventor, Donald L. Shell, is much more efficient in such cases. It compares distant items first and works its way down to nearby items. The interval separating the compared items is called the **gap**. The gap begins at one-half the length of the list and is successively halved until eventually each item is compared with its neighbor as in the bubble sort. The algorithm for a list of n items is as follows.

1. Begin with a gap of $g = \text{Int}(n / 2)$.

2. Compare items 1 and $1 + g$, 2 and $2 + g$, . . . , $n - g$ and n. Swap any pairs that are out of order.

3. Repeat Step 2 until no swaps are made for gap g.

4. Halve the value of g.

5. Repeat Steps 2, 3, and 4 until the value of g is 0.

The Shell sort is illustrated in what follows. Crossing arrows indicate that a swap occurred.

Initial Gap = Int([Number of Items] / 2) = Int(5 / 2) = 2

	Pebbles → Pebbles	Pebbles	Pebbles
First	Barney	Barney → Barney	Barney
Pass	Wilma → Wilma	Wilma	Dino
	Fred	Fred —— Fred	Fred
	Dino	Dino	Dino	Wilma

Because there was a swap, use the same gap for the second pass.

	Pebbles	Dino	Dino	Dino
Second	Barney	Barney → Barney	Barney
Pass	Dino	Pebbles	Pebbles → Pebbles
	Fred	Fred —— Fred	Fred
	Wilma	Wilma	Wilma → Wilma

Again, there was a swap, so keep the current gap.

	Dino —— Dino	Dino	Dino
Third	Barney	Barney → Barney	Barney
Pass	Pebbles → Pebbles	Pebbles → Pebbles
	Fred	Fred —— Fred	Fred
	Wilma	Wilma	Wilma → Wilma

There were no swaps for the current gap of 2, so

Next Gap = Int([Previous Gap] / 2) = Int(2 / 2) = 1

Fourth
Pass

Dino	Barney	Barney	Barney	Barney
Barney	Dino	Dino	Dino	Dino
Pebbles	Pebbles	Pebbles	Fred	Fred
Fred	Fred	Fred	Pebbles	Pebbles
Wilma	Wilma	Wilma	Wilma	Wilma

Because there was a swap (actually two swaps), keep the same gap.

Fifth
Pass

Barney	Barney	Barney	Barney	Barney
Dino	Dino	Dino	Dino	Dino
Fred	Fred	Fred	Fred	Fred
Pebbles	Pebbles	Pebbles	Pebbles	Pebbles
Wilma	Wilma	Wilma	Wilma	Wilma

Because there were no swaps for the current gap, then

Next Gap = Int([Previous Gap] / 2) = Int(1 / 2) = 0

and the Shell sort is complete.

Notice that the Shell sort required 14 comparisons to sort the list whereas the bubble sort required only 10 comparisons for the same list. This illustrates the fact that for very short lists, the bubble sort is preferable; however, for lists of 30 items or more, the Shell sort will consistently outperform the bubble sort. Table 7.6 shows the average number of comparisons required to sort arrays of varying sizes.

Array Elements	Bubble Sort Comparisons	Shell Sort Comparisons
5	10	15
10	45	57
15	105	115
20	190	192
25	300	302
30	435	364
50	1225	926
100	4950	2638
500	124,750	22,517
1000	499,500	58,460

Table 7.6 Efficiency of bubble and Shell sorts.

EXAMPLE 4 Use the Shell sort to alphabetize the parts of a running shoe (see Figure 7.9).

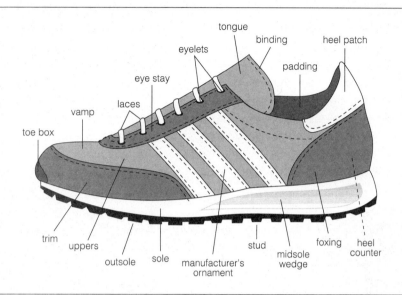

Figure 7.9 Running shoe.

SOLUTION   In the following program, the data are read into an array that has been dimensioned so as to guarantee more than enough space. In the event procedure Form_Load, the variable *numParts* provides the subscripts for the array and serves as a counter. The final value of *numParts* is available to all subprograms because the variable was created in the (Declarations) section of (General). The subprogram Sort-Data uses a flag to indicate if a swap has been made during a pass.

```
Dim part(1 To 50) As String
Dim numParts As Integer

Private Sub cmdDisplayParts_Click()
  Rem Sort and display parts of running shoe
  Call SortData
  Call ShowData
End Sub

Private Sub Form_Load()
  Rem Read part names
  Let numParts = 0     'Number of parts
  Open "SHOEPART.TXT" For Input As #1
  Do While (Not EOF(1)) And (numParts < UBound(part))
    Let numParts = numParts + 1
    Input #1, part(numParts)
  Loop
  Close #1
End Sub

Private Sub ShowData()
  Dim i As Integer
  Rem Display sorted list of parts
  picParts.Cls
```

```
   For i = 1 To numParts
     picParts.Print part(i),
     If i Mod 5 = 0 Then    'only put 5 items per line
         picParts.Print
     End If
   Next i
End Sub

Private Sub SortData()
  Dim gap As Integer, doneFlag As Integer
  Dim index  As Integer, temp As String
  Rem Shell sort shoe parts
  Let gap = Int(numParts / 2)
  Do While gap >= 1
    Do
      Let doneFlag = 1
      For index = 1 To numParts - gap
        If part(index) > part(index + gap) Then
            Let temp = part(index)
            Let part(index) = part(index + gap)
            Let part(index + gap) = temp
            Let doneFlag = 0
        End If
      Next index
    Loop Until doneFlag = 1
    Let gap = Int(gap / 2)         'Halve the length of the gap
  Loop
End Sub
```

[Run and click the command button.]

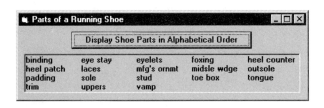

Searching

Suppose we had an array of 1000 names in alphabetical order and wanted to locate a specific person in the list. One approach would be to start with the first name and consider each name until a match was found. This process is called a **sequential search**. We would find a person whose name begins with "A" rather quickly, but 1000 comparisons might be necessary to find a person whose name begins with "Z." For much longer lists, searching could be a time-consuming matter. However, when the list has already been sorted into either ascending or descending order, there is a method, called a **binary search**, that shortens the task considerably.

Let us refer to the sought item as *quarry*. The binary search looks for *quarry* by determining in which half of the list it lies. The other half is then discarded and the retained half is temporarily regarded as the entire list. The process is repeated until the item is found. A flag can indicate if *quarry* has been found.

The algorithm for a binary search of an ascending list is as follows (Figure 7.10 contains the flowchart for a binary search):

1. At each stage, denote the subscript of the first item in the retained list by *first* and the subscript of the last item by *last*. Initially, the value of *first* is 1, the value of *last* is the number of items in the list, and the value of *flag* is 0.

2. Look at the middle item of the current list, the item having the subscript $middle = \text{Int}((first + last) / 2)$.

3. If the middle item is *quarry*, then *flag* is set to 1 and the search is over.

4. If the middle item is greater than *quarry*, then *quarry* should be in the first half of the list. So the subscript of *quarry* must lie between *first* and *middle* – 1. That is, the new value of *last* is *middle* – 1.

5. If the middle item is less than *quarry*, then *quarry* should be in the second half of the list of possible items. So the subscript of *quarry* must lie between *middle* + 1 and *last*. That is, the new value of *first* is *middle* + 1.

6. Repeat Steps 2 through 5 until *quarry* is found or until the halving process uses up the entire list. (When the entire list has been used up, *first* > *last*.) In the second case, *quarry* was not in the original list.

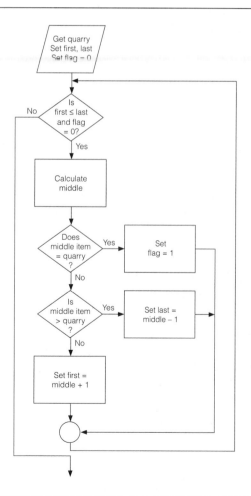

Figure 7.10 Flowchart for a binary search.

EXAMPLE 5   Assume the array *firm*( ) contains the alphabetized names of 100 corporations. Write a program that requests the name of a corporation as input and uses a binary search to determine whether or not the corporation is in the array.

SOLUTION

```
Dim firm(1 TO 100) As String
Dim numFirms As Integer

Private Sub BinarySearch(corp As String, result As String)
  Dim foundFlag As Integer
  Dim first As Integer, middle As Integer, last As Integer
  Rem Array firm() assumed already ordered alphabetically
  Rem Binary search of firm() for corp
  Let foundFlag = 0                      '1 indicates corp found
  Let first = 1
  Let last = numFirms
  Do While (first <= last) And (foundFlag = 0)
    Let middle = Int((first + last) / 2)
    Select Case UCase(firm(middle))
      Case corp
        Let foundFlag = 1
      Case Is > corp
        Let last = middle - 1
      Case Is < corp
        Let first = middle + 1
    End Select
  Loop
  If foundFlag = 1 Then
      Let result = "found"
    Else
      Let result = "not found"
  End If
End Sub

Private Sub cmdSearch_Click()
  Dim corp As String, result As String
  Let corp = UCase(Trim(txtCorporation.Text))
  Call BinarySearch(corp, result)
  Rem Display results of search
  picResult.Cls
  picResult.Print corp; " "; result
End Sub

Private Sub Form_Load()
  Rem Fill array with data from FIRMS.TXT
  Open "FIRMS.TXT" For Input As #1
  Let numFirms = 0
  Do While (Not EOF(1)) And (numFirms < UBound(firm))
    Let numFirms = numFirms + 1
    Input #1, firm(numFirms)
  Loop
End Sub
```

[Run, type IBM into the text box, and click the command button.]

Suppose the corporation input in Example 5 is in the second half of the array. On the first pass, *middle* would be assigned $Int((1 + 100)/2) = Int(50.5) = 50$ and then *first* would be altered to $50 + 1 = 51$. On the second pass, *middle* would be assigned $Int((51 + 100))/2 = Int(75.5) = 75$. If the corporation is not the array element with subscript 75, then either *last* would be assigned 74 or *first* would be assigned 76 depending upon whether the corporation appears before or after the 75th element. Each pass through the loop halves the range of subscripts containing the corporation until the corporation is located.

In Example 5, the binary search merely reported whether or not an array contained a certain item. After finding the item, its array subscript was not needed. However, if related data are stored in parallel arrays (as in Table 7.5), the subscript of the found item can be used to retrieve the related information in the other arrays. This process, called a **table lookup**, is used in the following example.

EXAMPLE 6 Use a binary search procedure to locate the data for a city from Example 3 requested by the user.

SOLUTION The following program does not include a sort of the data file CITYSTAT.TXT because the file is already ordered alphabetically.

```
Dim city(1 To 10) As String, pop(1 To 10) As Single, income(1 To 10) As Single
Dim natives(1 To 10) As Single, advDeg(1 To 10) As Single

Private Sub cmdDisplayStats_Click()
  Dim searchCity As String, result As Integer
  Rem Search for city in the metropolitan areas table
  Call GetCityName(searchCity)
  Call FindCity(searchCity, result)
  picResult.Cls
  If result > 0 Then
      Call ShowData(result)
    Else
      picResult.Print searchCity & " not in file"
  End If
End Sub

Private Sub FindCity(searchCity As String, result As Integer)
  Dim first As Integer, middle As Integer, last As Integer
  Dim foundFlag As Integer
  Rem Binary search table for city name
  Let first = 1
  Let last = 10
```

```
    Do While (first <= last) And (foundFlag = 0)
      Let middle = Int((first + last) / 2)
      Select Case UCase(city(middle))
        Case searchCity
          Let foundFlag = 1
        Case Is > searchCity
          Let last = middle - 1
        Case Is < searchCity
          Let first = middle + 1
      End Select
    Loop
    If foundFlag = 1 Then
        Let result = middle
      Else
        Let result = 0
    End If
End Sub

Private Sub Form_Load()
  Dim i As Integer
  Rem Assume that the data for city name, population, medium income, % native,
  Rem and % advanced degree have been placed in the file "CITYSTAT.TXT"
  Rem (First line of file is "Boston", 4.2, 4066, 73, 12)
  Open "CITYSTAT.TXT" For Input As #1
  For i = 1 To 10
    Input #1, city(i), pop(i), income(i), natives(i), advDeg(i)
  Next i
  Close #1
End Sub

Private Sub GetCityName(searchCity As String)
  Rem Request name of city as input
  Let searchCity = UCase(Trim(txtCity.Text))
End Sub

Private Sub ShowData(index As Integer)
  Rem Display city and associated information
  picResult.Print , "Pop. in", "Med. income", "% Native", "% Advanced"
  picResult.Print "Metro Area", "millions", "per hsd", "to State", "Degree"
  picResult.Print
  picResult.Print city(index), pop(index), income(index),
  picResult.Print natives(index), advDeg(index)
End Sub
```

[Run, type San Francisco into the text box, and click the command button.]

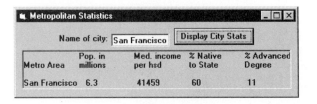

Comments

1. Suppose our bubble sort algorithm is applied to an ordered list. The algorithm will still make $n-1$ passes through the list. The process could be shortened for some lists by flagging the presence of out-of-order items as in the Shell sort. It may be preferable not to use a flag, because for greatly disordered lists, the flag would slow down an already sluggish algorithm.

2. In Example 3, parallel arrays already ordered by one field were sorted by another field. Usually, parallel arrays are sorted by the field to be searched when accessing the file. This field is called the **key field**.

3. Suppose an array of 2000 items is searched sequentially, that is, one item after another, in order to locate a specific item. The number of comparisons would vary from 1 to 2000, with an average of 1000. With a binary search, the number of comparisons would be at most 11, because $2^{11} > 2000$.

4. The built-in function UCase converts all the characters in a string to uppercase. UCase is useful in sorting and searching arrays of strings when the alphabetic case (upper or lower) is unimportant. For instance, Examples 5 includes UCase in the Select Case comparisons, and so the binary search will locate "Mobil" in the array even if the user entered "MOBIL".

5. The Visual Basic function Timer can be used to determine the speed of a sort. Precede the sort with the statement Let t = Timer. After the sort has executed, the statement Picture1.Print Timer – t will display the duration of the sort in seconds.

PRACTICE PROBLEMS 7.4

1. The pseudocode for a bubble sort of an array of n items follows. Why is the terminating value of the outer loop $n-1$ and the terminating value of the inner loop $n-j$?

```
For j = 1 To n - 1
  For k = 1 To n - j
    If [kth and (k+1)st items are out of order] Then [interchange them]
  Next k
Next j
```

2. Complete the table by filling in the values of each variable after successive passes of a binary search of a list of 20 items, where the sought item is in the 13th position.

First	Last	Middle
1	20	10
11	20	

EXERCISES 7.4

In Exercises 1 through 4, determine the output displayed in the picture box when the command button is clicked.

1.
```
Private Sub cmdDisplay_Click()
    Dim p As Integer, q As Integer, temp As Integer
    Let p = 100
    Let q = 200
    Let temp = p
    Let p = q
    Let q = temp
    picOutput.Print p; q
End Sub
```

2.
```
Dim gag(1 To 2) As String

Private Sub cmdDisplay_Click()
  If gag(2) < gag(1) Then
      Dim temp As String
      Let temp = gag(2)
      Let gag(2) = gag(1)
      Let gag(1) = temp
  End If
  picOutput.Print gag(1), gag(2)
End Sub

Private Sub Form_Load()
  Open "DATA.TXT" For Input As #1
  Input #1, gag(1), gag(2)
  Close #1
End Sub
```

(Assume that the file DATA.TXT contains the following entries.)

"Stan", "Oliver"

3.
```
Private Sub cmdDisplay_Click()
    Dim x As Single, y As Single, temp As Single
    Dim swappedFlag As Integer
    Open "DATA.TXT" For Input As #1
    Input #1, x, y
    Close #1
    Let swappedFlag = 0
    If y > x Then
        Let temp = x
        Let x = y
        Let y = temp
        Let swappedFlag = 1
    End If
    picOutput.Print x; y;
    If swappedFlag = 1 Then
        picOutput.Print "Numbers interchanged."
    End If
End Sub
```

(Assume that the file DATA.TXT contains the following entries.)

7, 11

4.
```
Dim a(1 To 3) As Integer

Private Sub cmdDisplay_Click()
  Dim j As Integer, k As Integer, temp As Integer
  For j = 1 To 2
    For k = 1 To 3 - j
      If a(k) > a(k + 1) Then
          Let temp = a(k)
          Let a(k) = a(k + 1)
          Let a(k + 1) = temp
      End If
    Next k
  Next j
  For j = 1 To 3
    picOutput.Print a(j);
  Next j
End Sub

Private Sub Form_Load()
  Dim j As Integer
  Open "DATA.TXT" For Input As #1
  For j = 1 To 3
    Input #1, a(j)
  Next j
  Close #1
End Sub
```

(Assume that the file DATA.TXT contains the following entries.)

7, 4, 3

In Exercises 5 and 6, identify the errors.

5.
```
Dim c(1 To 4) As Integer, d(1 To 4) As Integer

Private Sub cmdDisplay_Click()
  Rem swap two items
  Let c(4) = d(4)
  Let d(4) = c(4)
  picOutput.Print c(4), d(4)
End Sub

Private Sub Form_Load()
  Dim i As Integer
  Open "DATA.TXT" For Input As #1
  For i = 1 To 4
    Input #1, c(i), d(i)
  Next i
  Close #1
End Sub
```

(Assume that the file DATA.TXT contains the following entries.)

1, 2, 3, 4, 5, 6, 7, 8

6.
```
Dim a(1 To 3) As Integer, b(1 To 3) As Integer

Private Sub cmdDisplay_Click()
  Dim temp(1 To 3) As Integer
  Let temp() = a()
  Let a() = b()
  Let b() = temp()
End Sub

Private Sub Form_Load()
  Dim i As Integer
  Open "DATA.TXT" For Input As #1
  For i = 1 To 3
    Input #1, a(i), b(i)
  Next i
  Close #1
End Sub
```

(Assume that the file DATA.TXT contains the following entries.)

1, 3, 5, 7, 9, 11

7. Which type of search would be best for the following array?

1	2	3	4	5
Paul	Ringo	John	George	Pete

8. Which type of search would be best for the following array?

1	2	3	4	5
Beloit	Green Bay	Madison	Milwaukee	Oshkosh

9. Consider the items Tin Man, Dorothy, Scarecrow, and Lion in that order. After how many swaps in a bubble sort will the list be in alphabetical order?

10. How many comparisons will be made in a bubble sort of six items?

11. How many comparisons will be made in a bubble sort of n items?

12. Modify the program in Example 2 so that it will keep track of the number of swaps and comparisons and display these numbers before ending.

13. Rework Exercise 9 using the Shell sort.

14. How many comparisons would be made in a Shell sort of six items if the items were originally in descending order and were sorted in ascending order?

15. If a list of six items is already in the proper order, how many comparisons will be made by a Shell sort?

16. The following subprogram fills an array of 200 integers with values between 0 and 63 that are in need of sorting. Write a program that uses the subprogram and sorts the array *nums( )* with a bubble sort. Run the program and time the execution. Do the same for the Shell sort.

```
Private Sub FillArray(nums() As Integer)
  Rem Generate numbers from 0 to 63 and place in array
  Let nums(1) = 5
  For i = 2 To 200
    Let nums(i) = (9 * nums(i - 1) + 7) Mod 64
  Next i
End Sub
```

17. Suppose a list of 5000 numbers is to be sorted, but the numbers consist of only 1, 2, 3, and 4. Describe a method of sorting the list that would be much faster than either the bubble or Shell sort.

18. The bubble sort gets its name because in an ascending sort successive passes cause "lighter" items to rise to the top like bubbles in water. How did the Shell sort get its name?

19. What is the maximum number of comparisons required to find an item in a sequential search of 16 items? What is the average number of comparisons? What is the maximum number of comparisons required to find an item in a binary search of 16 items?

20. Redo Exercise 19 with 2^n items, where n is any positive integer.

In Exercises 21 through 32, write a short program (or procedure) to complete the stated task.

21. Exchange the values of the variables x, y, and z so that x has y's value, y has z's value, and z has x's value.

22. Display the names of the seven dwarfs in alphabetical order. For the contents of a data file use

    Doc, Grumpy, Sleepy, Happy, Bashful, Sneezy, Dopey

23. Table 7.7 lists 10 of the most attended exhibits in the history of the National Gallery of Art. Read the data into a pair of parallel arrays and display a similar table with the exhibit names in alphabetical order.

Exhibit	Attendance (in thousands)
Rodin Rediscovered	1053
Treasure Houses of Britain	999
Treasures of Tutankhamen	836
Chinese Archaeology	684
Ansel Adams	652
Splendor of Dresden	617
Wyeth's Helga Pictures	558
Post-Impressionism	558
Matisse in Nice	537
John Hay Whitney Collection	513

Table 7.7 National Gallery of Art's hits.

24. Table 7.8 presents statistics on the five leading athletic footwear brands. Read the data into three parallel arrays and display a similar table with sales in descending order.

Brand	Sales ($ millions)	Ad Spending ($ millions)
Converse	400	22
Keds	690	11
L.A. Gear	984	24
Nike	3386	120
Reebok	2672	78

Table 7.8 Leading athletic footwear brands.

Source: The 1994 Information Please Business Almanac

25. Accept 10 words to be input in alphabetical order and store them in an array. Then accept an 11th word as input and store it in the array in its correct alphabetical position.

26. An airline has a list of 200 flight numbers in an ascending ordered array. Accept a number as input and do a binary search of the list to determine if the flight number is valid.

27. Modify the program in Exercise 16 to compute and display the number of times each of the numbers from 0 through 63 appears.

28. Allow a number n to be input by the user. Then accept as input a list of n numbers. Place the numbers into an array and apply a bubble sort.

29. Write a program that accepts a word as input and converts it into Morse code. The dots and dashes corresponding to each letter of the alphabet are as follows:

A ·−	H ····	O −−−	V ···−
B −···	I ··	P ·−−·	W ·−−
C −·−·	J ·−−−	Q −−·−	X −··−
D −··	K −·−	R ·−·	Y −·−−
E ·	L ·−··	S ···	Z −−··
F ··−·	M −−	T −	
G −−·	N −·	U ··−	

30. Write a program that accepts an American word as input and performs a binary search to translate it into its British equivalent. Use the following list of words for data and account for the case when the word requested is not in the list.

American	British	American	British
attic	loft	ice cream	ice
business suit	lounge suit	megaphone	loud hailer
elevator	lift	radio	wireless
flashlight	torch	sneakers	plimsolls
french fries	chips	truck	lorry
gasoline	petrol	zero	nought

31. Write a program that accepts a student's name and seven test scores as input and calculates the average score after dropping the two lowest grades.

32. Suppose letter grades are assigned as follows:

97 and above	A+	74–76	C
94–96	A	70–73	C–
90–93	A–	67–69	D+
87–89	B+	64–66	D
84–86	B	60–63	D–
80–83	B–	0–59	F
77–79	C+		

Write a program that accepts a grade as input and displays the corresponding letter. **Hint:** This problem shows that when you search an array, you don't always look for equality. Set up an array *range*( ) containing the values 97, 94, 90, 87, 84, . . . , 59 and the parallel array *letter*( ) containing A+, A, A–, B+, . . . , F. Next, perform a sequential search to find the first i such that *range*(i) is less than or equal to the input grade.

33. The *median* of a set of n measurements is a number such that half the n measurements fall below the median and half fall above. If the number of measurements n is odd, the median is the middle number when the measurements are arranged in ascending or descending order. If the number of measurements n is even, the median is the average of the two middle measurements when the measurements are arranged in ascending or descending order. Write a program that requests a number n and a set of n measurements as input and then displays the median.

34. Write a program with two command buttons labeled Ascending Order and Descending Order that displays the eight vegetables in V8 in either ascending or descending alphabetic order. The vegetables (tomato, carrot, celery, beet, parsley, lettuce, watercress, and spinach) should be stored in a form-level array.

SOLUTIONS TO PRACTICE PROBLEMS 7.4

1. The outer loop controls the number of passes, one less than the number of items in the list. The inner loop performs a single pass, and the jth pass consists of $n - j$ comparisons.

2.

First	Last	Middle
1	20	10
11	20	15
11	14	12
13	14	13

7.5 TWO-DIMENSIONAL ARRAYS

Each array discussed so far held a single list of items. Such array variables are called **single-subscripted variables**. An array can also hold the contents of a table with several rows and columns. Such arrays are called **two-dimensional arrays** or **double-subscripted variables**. Two tables follow. Table 7.9 gives the road mileage between certain cities. It has four rows and four columns. Table 7.10 shows the leading universities in three disciplines. It has three rows and five columns.

	Chicago	Los Angeles	New York	Philadelphia
Chicago	0	2054	802	738
Los Angeles	2054	0	2786	2706
New York	802	2786	0	100
Philadelphia	738	2706	100	0

Table 7.9 Road mileage between selected U.S. cities.

	1	2	3	4	5
Business	U of PA	U of IN	U of MI	UC Berk	U of VA
Comp Sci.	MIT	Cng-Mellon	UC Berk	Cornell	U of IL
Engr/Gen.	U of IL	U of OK	U of MD	Cng-Mellon	CO Sch. of Mines

Table 7.10 University rankings.

Source: A Rating of Undergraduate Programs in American and International Universities, Dr. Jack Gourman, 1996

Two-dimensional array variables store the contents of tables. They have the same types of names as other array variables. The only difference is that they have two subscripts, each with its own range. The range of the first subscript is determined by the number of rows in the table, and the range of the second subscript is determined by the number of columns. The statement

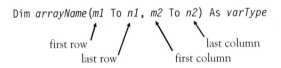

```
Dim arrayName(m1 To n1, m2 To n2) As varType
```

placed in the (Declarations) section of (General), dimensions an array of type *varType* corresponding to a table with rows labeled from *m1* To *n1* and columns labeled from *m2* To *n2*. The entry in the *j*th row, *k*th column is *arrayName(j,k)*. For instance, the data in Table 7.9 can be stored in an array named rm( ). The statement

```
Dim rm(1 To 4, 1 To 4) As Single
```

will dimension the array. Each element of the array has the form *rm(row, column)*. The entries of the array are

rm(1,1)=0	rm(1,2)=2054	rm(1,3)=802	rm(1,4)=738
rm(2,1)=2054	rm(2,2)=0	rm(2,3)=2786	rm(2,4)=2706
rm(3,1)=802	rm(3,2)=2786	rm(3,3)=0	rm(3,4)=100
rm(4,1)=738	rm(4,2)=2706	rm(4,3)=100	rm(4,4)=0

As with one-dimensional arrays, when a two-dimensional array is created using Dim in the (Declarations) section of (General), the array becomes a form-level subscripted variable, and is therefore accessible in all event procedures and general procedures and retains whatever values are assigned until the program is terminated. Two-dimensional arrays also can be created with Dim that are local to a procedure and cease to exist once the procedure is exited. When the range of the subscripts is given by one or more variables, the proper statement to use is

```
ReDim arrayName(m1 To n1, m2 To n2) As varType
```

The data in Table 7.10 can be stored in a two-dimensional string array named *univ*( ). The statement

```
Dim univ(1 To 3, 1 To 5) As String
```

will dimension the array as form-level. Some of the entries of the array are

univ(1,1) = "U of PA"
univ(2,3) = "UC Berk"
univ(3,5) = "CO Sch. of Mines"

EXAMPLE 1 Write a program to store and access the data from Table 7.9.

SOLUTION Data are read from the data file DISTANCE.TXT into a two-dimensional form-level array using a pair of nested loops. The outer loop controls the rows and the inner loop controls the columns.

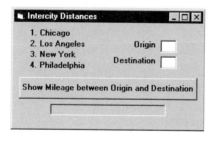

Object	Property	Setting
frmDist	Caption	Intercity Distances
lblCh	Caption	1. Chicago
lblLA	Caption	2. Los Angeles
lblNY	Caption	3. New York
lblPh	Caption	4. Philadelphia
lblOrig	Caption	Origin
txtOrig	Text	(blank)
lblDest	Caption	Destination
txtDest	Text	(blank)
cmdShow	Caption	Show Mileage between Origin and Destination
picMiles		

```
Dim rm(1 To 4, 1 To 4) As Single  'In (Declarations) section of (General)

Private Sub cmdShow_Click()
  Dim row As Integer, col As Integer
  Rem Determine road mileage between cities
  Let row = Val(txtOrig.Text)
  Let col = Val(txtDest.Text)
```

```
      If (row >= 1 And row <= 4) And (col >= 1 And col <= 4) Then
          Call ShowMileage(rm(), row, col)
        Else
          MsgBox "Origin and Destination must be numbers from 1 to 4", , "Error"
      End If
      txtOrig.SetFocus
  End Sub

  Private Sub Form_Load()
    Dim row As Integer, col As Integer
    Rem Fill two-dimensional array with intercity mileages
    Rem Assume the data have been placed in the file "DISTANCE.TXT"
    Rem (First line of the file is 0,2054,802,738)
    Open "DISTANCE.TXT" For Input As #1
    For row = 1 To 4
      For col = 1 To 4
        Input #1, rm(row, col)
      Next col
    Next row
    Close #1
  End Sub

  Private Sub ShowMileage(rm() As Single, row As Integer, col As Integer)
    Rem Display mileage between cities
    picMiles.Cls
    picMiles.Print "The road mileage is"; rm(row, col)
  End Sub
```

[Run, type 3 into the Origin box, type 1 into the Destination box, and click the command button.]

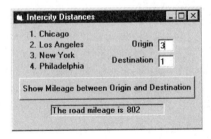

So far, two-dimensional arrays have been used only to store data for convenient lookup. In the next example, an array is used to make a valuable computation.

EXAMPLE 2   The Center for Science in the Public Interest publishes *The Nutrition Scorebook*, a highly respected rating of foods. The top two foods in each of five categories are shown in Table 7.11 along with some information on their composition. Write a program to compute the nutritional content of a meal. The table should be read into an array and then the program should request the quantities of each food item that is part of the meal. The program should then compute the amounts of each nutritional component consumed by summing each column with each entry weighted by the quantity of the food item.

	Calories	Protein (grams)	Fat (grams)	Vit A (IU)	Calcium (mg)
spinach (1 cup)	23	3	0.3	8100	93
sweet potato (1 med.)	160	2	1	9230	46
yogurt (8 oz.)	230	10	3	120	343
skim milk (1 cup)	85	8	0	500	302
whole wheat bread (1 slice)	65	3	1	0	24
brown rice (1 cup)	178	3.8	0.9	0	18
watermelon (1 wedge)	110	2	1	2510	30
papaya (1 lg.)	156	2.4	0.4	7000	80
tuna in water (1 lb)	575	126.8	3.6	0	73
lobster (1 med.)	405	28.8	26.6	984	190

Table 7.11 Composition of 10 top-rated foods.

SOLUTION Coding is simplified by using a control array of labels to hold the food names and a control array of text boxes to hold the amount input by the user. In the following template, the label captions have been assigned an initial value of "(food name)" so that the labels can be seen. The five nutrients of interest and the actual names and nutrient values of the foods to be used in building a meal are read from the data file NUTTABLE.TXT.

Object	Property	Setting
frmMeal	Caption	Nutrition in a Meal
lblFood	Caption	(food name)
	Index	0 – 9
lblQnty	Caption	Quantity in Meal
txtQnty	Text	(blank)
	Index	0 – 9
cmdAnalyze	Caption	Analyze Meal Nutrition
picAnalysis		

```
Dim nutName(1 To 5) As String          'nutrient names
Dim nutTable(1 To 10, 1 To 5) As Single 'nutrient values for each food

Private Sub cmdAnalyze_Click()
  Rem Determine the nutritional content of a meal
  Dim quantity(1 To 10) As Single 'amount of food in meal
  Call GetAmounts(quantity())
  Call ShowData(quantity())
End Sub

Private Sub Form_Load()
  Dim i As Integer, j As Integer, foodName As String
  Rem Fill arrays; assign label captions
  Open "NUTTABLE.TXT" For Input As #1
  For i = 1 To 5
    Input #1, nutName(i)
  Next i
```

```
   For i = 1 To 10
     Input #1, foodName
     Let lblFood(i - 1).Caption = foodName
     For j = 1 To 5
       Input #1, nutTable(i, j)
     Next j
   Next i
   Close #1
End Sub

Private Sub GetAmounts(quantity() As Single)
  Dim i As Integer
  Rem Obtain quantities of foods consumed
  For i = 1 To 10
    Let quantity(i) = Val(txtQnty(i - 1).Text)
  Next i
End Sub

Private Sub ShowData(quantity() As Single)
  Dim col As Integer, row As Integer
  Dim amount As Single, nutWid As Single
  Rem Display amount of each component
  picAnalysis.Cls
  picAnalysis.Print "This meal contains the"
  picAnalysis.Print "following quantities"
  picAnalysis.Print "of these nutritional"
  picAnalysis.Print "components:"
  picAnalysis.Print
  For col = 1 To 5
    Let amount = 0
    For row = 1 To 10
      Let amount = amount + quantity(row) * nutTable(row, col)
    Next row
    picAnalysis.Print nutName(col) & ":"; Tab(16); amount
  Next col
End Sub
```

[Run, type the following quantities into each text box, and click the command button.]

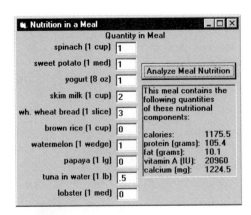

Comment

1. Three- (or higher-) dimensional arrays can be defined by statements similar to those used for two-dimensional arrays. A three-dimensional array uses three subscripts, and the assignment of values requires a triple-nested loop. As an example, a meteorologist might use a three-dimensional array to record temperatures for various dates, times, and elevations. The array might be created by the statement

```
Dim temps(1 To 31, 1 To 24, 0 To 14) As Single
```

PRACTICE PROBLEMS 7.5

1. Consider the road mileage program in Example 1. How can the program be modified so the actual names of the cities can be supplied by the user?

2. In what types of problems are two-dimensional arrays superior to parallel arrays?

EXERCISES 7.5

In Exercises 1 through 8, determine the output displayed in the picture box when the command button is clicked. All Dim statements for arrays are in the (Declarations) section of (General).

1. ```
Dim a(1 To 20, 1 To 30) As Single

Private Sub cmdDisplay_Click()
  Let a(3, 5) = 6
  Let a(5, 3) = 2 * a(3, 5)
  picOutput.Print a(5, 3)
End Sub
```

2. ```
Dim years(1 To 100, 1 To 50) As Single

Private Sub cmdDisplay_Click()
  Dim x As Single, y As Single
  Let x = 7
  Let y = 8
  Let years(x, y) = 1937
  picOutput.Print years(7, 8) + 50
End Sub
```

3. ```
Dim w(1 To 10, 1 To 15) As String

Private Sub cmdDisplay_Click()
  Dim d As String, n As Integer
  Let d = "Dorothy"
  Let w(1, 1) = d
  Let n = 1
  picOutput.Print w(n, n)
End Sub
```
```

4. `Dim actor(1 To 5, 1 To 5) As String`

```
Private Sub cmdDisplay_Click()
  Dim a As Integer, b As Integer, temp As Integer
  Let a = 2
  Let b = 3
  Let actor(a, b) = "Bogart"
  Let temp = a
  Let a = b
  Let b = temp
  picOutput.Print "1. "; actor(a, b)
  picOutput.Print "2. "; actor(b, a)
End Sub
```

5. `Dim a() As Single`

```
Private Sub cmdDisplay_Click()
  Dim p As Integer, q As Integer
  Dim j As Integer, k As Integer
  Open "DATA.TXT" For Input As #1
  Input #1, p, q
  ReDim a(1 To p, 1 To q) As Single
  For j = 1 To p
    For k = 1 To q
      Input #1, a(j, k)
      picOutput.Print a(j, k);
    Next k
    picOutput.Print
  Next j
  Close #1
End Sub
```

(Assume that the file DATA.TXT contains the following entries.)

2, 3, 4, 1, 6, 5, 8, 2

6. `Dim a(1 To 4, 1 To 5) As Integer`

```
Private Sub cmdDisplay_Click()
  Dim j As Integer, k As Integer
  For j = 1 To 4
    For k = 1 To 5
      Let a(j, k) = (j - k) * j
      picOutput.Print a(j, k);
    Next k
    picOutput.Print
  Next j
End Sub
```

7. `Dim s(1 To 3, 1 To 3) As Single`

```
Private Sub cmdDisplay_Click()
  Dim j As Integer, k As Integer
  Open "DATA.TXT" For Input As #1
```

```
      For j = 1 To 3
        For k = 1 To 3
          Input #1, s(j, k)
        Next k
      Next j
      Close #1
      For j = 1 To 3
        picOutput.Print s(j, j);
      Next j
    End Sub
```

(Assume that the file DATA.TXT contains the following entries.)

1, 2, 3, 4, 3, 2, 3, 4, 5

8.
```
Dim m() As Integer

Private Sub cmdDisplay_Click()
  Dim x As Integer, y As Integer
  Dim j As Integer, k As Integer
  Open "DATA.TXT" For Input As #1
  Input #1, x, y
  ReDim m(1 To x, 1 To y) As Integer
  For j = 1 To x
    For k = 1 To y - j
      Input #1, m(j, k)
      picOutput.Print m(j, k) - k;
    Next k
    picOutput.Print
  Next j
  Close #1
End Sub
```

(Assume that the file DATA.TXT contains the following entries.)

2, 3, 6, 3, 2, 1, 3, 4, 9, 8

In Exercises 9 and 10, identify the errors.

9.
```
Dim a(1 To 3, 1 To 4) As Integer

Private Sub cmdDisplay_Click()
  Dim j As Integer, k As Integer
  Rem Fill an array
  Open "DATA.TXT" For Input As #1
  For j = 1 To 4
    For k = 1 To 3
      Input #1, a(j, k)
    Next k
  Next j
  Close #1
End Sub
```

(Assume that the file DATA.TXT contains the following entries.)

1, 2, 3, 4, 5, 6, 7, 8, 9, 0, 1, 2

10.
```
Dim score(1 To 3, 1 To 3) As Integer

Private Sub Form_Load()
  Dim j As Integer, k As Integer, student As Integer
  Rem Fill array from data file
  Open "SCORES.TXT" For Input As #1
  For j = 1 To 3
    Input #1, student
    For k = 1 To 3
      Input #1, score(k, j)
    Next k
  Next j
End Sub

Private Sub cmdDisplay_Click()
  Dim student As Integer, exam As Integer
  Rem Report individual scores
  Let student = Val(txtStudent.Text)
  Let exam = Val(txtExam.Text)
  If (student >= 1 And student <= 3) And (exam >= 1 And exam <= 3) Then
    picOutput.Print score(student, exam)
  End If
End Sub
```

(Assume that the file SCORES.TXT contains the following three lines.)

1, 80, 85, 90
2, 72, 80, 88
3, 87, 93, 90

In Exercises 11 through 14, write a procedure to perform the stated task.

11. Given an array dimensioned with the statement Dim a(1 To 10, 1 To 10) As Single, set the entries in the jth column to j (for $j = 1, \ldots, 10$).

12. Given an array dimensioned with the statement Dim a(1 To 10, 1 To 10) As Single, and values assigned to each entry, compute the sum of the values in the 10th row.

13. Given an array dimensioned with the statement Dim a(1 To 10, 1 To 10) As Single, and values assigned to each entry, interchange the values in the second and third rows.

14. Given an array dimensioned with the statement Dim a(1 To 3, 1 To 45) As Single, and values assigned to each entry, find the greatest value and the locations (possibly more than one) at which it occurs.

In Exercises 15 through 24, write a program to perform the stated task.

15. A company has two stores (1 and 2), and each store sells three items (1, 2, and 3). The following tables give the inventory at the beginning of the day and the amount of each item sold during that day.

	Item		
	1	2	3
Store 1	25	64	23
2	12	82	19

Beginning Inventory

	Item		
	1	2	3
Store 1	7	45	11
2	4	24	8

Sales for Day

(a) Record the values of each table in an array.

(b) Adjust the values in the first array to hold the inventories at the end of the day and display these new inventories.

(c) Calculate and display the total number of items in the store at the end of the day.

16. Table 7.12 gives the results of a survey on the uses of computers in the workplace. Each entry shows the percentage of respondents from the educational attainment category that use the computer for the indicated purpose.

(a) Place the data from the table in an array.

(b) Determine the average of the percentages in the Databases column.

Educational Attainment	Word Processing	Spread-sheets	Databases	Communi-cations	Desktop Publishing
Not a high school graduate	54.4	22.2	9.9	20.4	20.6
High school graduate	52.5	25.8	13.3	29.4	17.6
Some college	49.5	33.9	20.6	38.5	18.0
Four years of college	40.0	41.5	28.8	45.1	17.0
More than 4 yr of college	29.3	41.9	35.3	48.5	10.4

Table 7.12 Computer use on the job by educational attainment.
Source: U.S. Center of Educational Statistics, *Digest of Educational Statistics,* 1994

17. A university offers 10 courses at each of three campuses. The number of students enrolled in each is presented in Table 7.13.

		Course									
		1	2	3	4	5	6	7	8	9	10
	1	5	15	22	21	12	25	16	11	17	23
Campus	2	11	23	51	25	32	35	32	52	25	21
	3	2	12	32	32	25	26	29	12	15	11

Table 7.13 Number of students enrolled in courses.

(a) Find the total number of course enrollments on each campus.

(b) Find the total number of students taking each course.

18. Table 7.14 gives the 1994 and 1995 sales for the five leading quick-service restaurants.

   (a) Place the data into an array.
   (b) Calculate the total change in sales for these five restaurants.

	1994 sales $MM	1995 sales $MM
1. McDonald's	26.0	29.9
2. Burger King	7.5	8.4
3. KFC	7.1	7.3
4. Taco Bell	4.5	4.9
5. Wendy's	4.2	4.5

Table 7.14 Top quick-service restaurants.

Source: Restaurants & Institutions, July 1996

19. The scores for the top three golfers at the 1997 Masters tournament are shown in Table 7.15.

   (a) Place the data into an array.
   (b) Compute the total score for each player.
   (c) Compute the average score for each round.

	Round			
	1	2	3	4
Tiger Woods	70	66	65	69
Tom Kite	77	69	66	70
Tommy Tolles	72	72	72	67

Table 7.15 1997 Masters leaders.

20. Table 7.16 contains part of the pay schedule for federal employees. Table 7.17 gives the number of employees of each classification in a certain division. Place the data from each table into an array and compute the amount of money this division pays for salaries during the year.

	Step			
	1	2	3	4
GS–1	13,132	13,570	14,006	14,442
GS–2	14,764	15,116	15,606	16,019
GS–3	16,111	16,647	17,184	17,720
GS–4	18,085	18,688	19,292	19,895
GS–5	20,233	20,908	21,582	22,257
GS–6	22,554	23,305	24,057	24,809
GS–7	25,061	25,897	26,737	27,568

Table 7.16 1996 pay schedule for federal white-collar workers.

	1	2	3	4
GS–1	0	0	2	1
GS–2	2	3	0	1
GS–3	4	2	5	7
GS–4	12	13	8	3
GS–5	4	5	0	1
GS–6	6	2	4	3
GS–7	8	1	9	2

Table 7.17 Number of employees in each category.

21. Consider Table 7.10, the rankings of three university departments. Write a program that places the data into an array, allows the name of a college to be input, and gives the categories in which it appears. Of course, a college might appear more than once or not at all.

22. Table 7.18 gives the monthly precipitation for a typical Nebraska city during a 5-year period.

	Jan.	Feb.	Mar.	Apr.	May	June	July	Aug.	Sept.	Oct.	Nov.	Dec.
1986	0.88	1.11	2.01	3.64	6.44	5.58	4.23	4.34	4.00	2.05	1.48	0.77
1987	0.76	0.94	2.09	3.29	4.68	3.52	3.52	4.82	3.72	2.21	1.24	0.80
1988	0.67	0.80	1.75	2.70	4.01	3.88	3.72	3.78	3.55	1.88	1.21	0.61
1989	0.82	0.80	1.99	3.05	4.19	4.44	3.98	4.57	3.43	2.32	1.61	0.75
1990	0.72	0.90	1.71	2.02	2.33	2.98	2.65	2.99	2.55	1.99	1.05	0.92

Table 7.18 Monthly precipitation (in inches) for a typical Nebraska city.

Write a program that reads the table from a data file into an array and then displays in a picture box the following output.

```
Total precipitation for each year
1986  36.53
1987  31.59
1988  28.56
1989  31.96
1990  22.81

Average precipitation for each month
Jan   Feb   Mar   Apr   May   Jun   Jul   Aug   Sep   Oct   Nov   Dec
0.77  0.91  1.91  2.94  4.33  4.08  3.62  4.10  3.50  2.09  1.32  0.77
```

23. Suppose a course has 15 students enrolled and five exams were given during the semester. Write a program that accepts each student's name and grades as input and places the names in a one-dimensional array and the grades in a two-dimensional array. The program should then display each student's name and semester average. Also, the program should display the median for each exam. (For an odd number of grades, the median is the middle grade. For an even number of grades, it is the average of the two middle grades.)

24. An *n*-by-*n* array is called a magic square if the sums of each row, each column, and each diagonal are equal. Write a program to determine if an array is a magic square and use it to determine if either of the following arrays is a magic square. **Hint**: If at any time one of the sums is not equal to the others, the search is complete.

(a)	1	15	15	4	(b)	11	10	4	23	17
	12	6	7	9		18	12	6	5	24
	8	10	11	5		25	19	13	7	1
	13	3	2	16		2	21	20	14	8
						9	3	22	16	15

25. A company has three stores (1, 2, and 3), and each store sells five items (1, 2, 3, 4, and 5). The following tables give the number of items sold by each store and category on a particular day, and the cost of each item.

(a) Place the data from the left-hand table in a two-dimensional array and the data from the right-hand table in a one-dimensional array.

(b) Compute and display the total dollar amount of sales for each store and for the entire company.

		Item				
		1	2	3	4	5
	1	25	64	23	45	14
Store	2	12	82	19	34	63
	3	54	22	17	43	35

Number of Items Sold During Day

Item	Cost
1	$12.00
2	$17.95
3	$95.00
4	$86.50
5	$78.00

Cost per Item

SOLUTIONS TO PRACTICE PROBLEMS 7.5

1. The function FindCityNum can be used to determine the subscript associated with each city. This function and the modified event procedure cmdShow_Click are as follows.

```
Private Function FindCityNum(city As String) As Integer
  Select Case UCase(city)
    Case "CHICAGO"
      FindCityNum = 1
    Case "LOS ANGELES"
      FindCityNum = 2
    Case "NEW YORK"
      FindCityNum = 3
    Case "PHILADELPHIA"
      FindCityNum = 4
    Case Else
      FindCityNum = 0
  End Select
End Function

Private Sub cmdShow_Click()
  Dim orig As String, dest As String
  Dim row As Integer, col As Integer
  Rem Determine road mileage between cities
  Let orig = txtOrig.Text
  Let dest = txtDest.Text
  Let row = FindCityNum(orig)
  Let col = FindCityNum(dest)
  If (row < 1 Or row > 4) Then
      MsgBox "City of origin not available", , "Error"
    ElseIf (col < 1 Or col > 4) Then
      MsgBox "Destination city not available", , "Error"
    Else
      Call ShowMileage(rm(), row, col)
  End If
  txtOrig.SetFocus
End Sub
```

2. Both parallel arrays and two-dimensional arrays are used to hold related data. If some of the data are numeric and some are string, then parallel arrays must be used because all entries of an array must be of the same type. Parallel arrays should also be used if the data will be sorted. Two-dimensional arrays are best suited to tabular data.

7.6 A CASE STUDY: CALCULATING WITH A SPREADSHEET

Spreadsheets are one of the most popular types of software used on personal computers. A spreadsheet is a financial planning tool in which data are analyzed in a table of rows and columns. Some of the items are entered by the user and other items, often totals and balances, are calculated using the entered data. The outstanding feature of electronic spreadsheets is their ability to recalculate an entire table after changes are made in some of the entered data, thereby allowing the user to determine the financial implications of various alternatives. This is called "What if?" analysis.

The Design of the Program

Figure 7.11 contains an example of a spreadsheet used to analyze a student's financial projections for the four quarters of a year. Column F holds the sum of the entries in columns B through E, rows 6 and 14 hold sums of the entries in rows 3 through 5 and 9 through 13, respectively, and row 16 holds the differences of the entries in rows 6 and 14. Because the total balance is negative, some of the amounts in the spreadsheet must be changed and the totals and balances recalculated.

	A	B	C	D	E	F
1		Fall	Winter	Spring	Summer	Total
2	**Income**					
3	Job	1000	1300	1000	2000	5300
4	Parents	200	200	200	0	600
5	Scholarship	150	150	150	0	450
6	**Total**	1350	1650	1350	2000	6350
7						
8	**Expenses**					
9	Tuition	400	0	400	0	800
10	Food	650	650	650	650	2600
11	Rent	600	600	600	400	2200
12	Books	110	0	120	0	230
13	Misc	230	210	300	120	860
14	**Total**	1990	1460	2070	1170	6690
15						
16	**Balance**	–640	190	–720	830	–340

Figure 7.11 Spreadsheet for student's financial projections.

The 96 locations in the spreadsheet that hold information are called **cells**. Each cell is identified by its row number and column letter. For instance, cell 14, C contains the amount 1460. For programming purposes, each column is identified by a number, starting with 1 for the leftmost column. Thus cell 14, C will be cell 14, 3 in our program.

This case study develops a program to produce a spreadsheet with the five columns of numbers shown in Figure 7.11, three user-specified categories of income, and five user-specified categories of expenses. The following tasks are to be selected by command buttons:

1. Start a new spreadsheet. All current category names and values are erased and the cursor is placed in the text box of the first income category.

2. Quit.

Three additional tasks need to be performed as the result of other events:

1. Create the spreadsheet when the form is loaded.

2. Limit the user to editing category names and quarterly values.

3. Display totals after a change is made in the spreadsheet.

The User Interface

Each cell in the spreadsheet will be an element of a text box control array. A control array of labels is needed for the numeric labels to the left of each row and another control array of labels for the alphabetic labels at the top of each column. Finally, two command buttons are required. The task of controlling which cells the user can edit will be handled by a GotFocus event. The task of updating the totals will be handled by a LostFocus event. Figure 7.12 shows one possible form design with all control elements loaded. For this application of a spreadsheet, the headings that have been assigned to cells in rows 1, 2, 6, 8, 14, and 16 are fixed; the user will not be allowed to edit them. The other entries in column A, the category names, may be edited by the user, but we have provided the set from Figure 7.11 as the default.

	A	B	C	D	E	F
1		Fall	Winter	Spring	Summer	Total
2	Income					
3	Job					
4	Parents					
5	Scholarship					
6	Total					
7						
8	Expenses					
9	Tuition					
10	Food					
11	Rent					
12	Books					
13	Misc					
14	Total					
15						
16	Balance					

Figure 7.12 Template for spreadsheet.

Because processing the totals for the spreadsheet involves adding columns and rows of cells, coding is simplified by using a control array of text boxes so that an index in a For...Next loop can step through a set of cells. A two-dimensional array of text boxes seems natural for the spreadsheet. Unfortunately, only a single index is available for control arrays in Visual Basic. However, a single dimensional array of text boxes can be used without much difficulty if we define a function Indx that connects a pair of row (1 to 16) and column (1 to 6) values to a unique index (1 to 96) value. An example of such a rule would be Indx(row,column)=(row–1)*6+column. Successive values of this function are generated by going from left to right across row 1, then left to right across row 2, and so on.

A solution to the spreadsheet problem that uses one control array of text boxes and two control arrays of labels follows. The text box control array *txtCell*( ) provides the 96 text boxes needed for the spreadsheet cells. Because the proposed Indx function advances by one as we move from left to right across a row of cells, the cells must be positioned in this order as they are loaded. The label control array *lblRowLab*( ) provides a label for each of the rows of cells, while label control array *lblColLab*( ) provides a label for each column of cells. Figure 7.13 shows the layout of the form at design time. The properties for the controls are given in Table 7.19. The Height and Width properties given for the text box will assure enough room on the screen for all 96 cells. These dimensions can be obtained by creating a normal size text box, then reducing its width by one set of grid marks and its height by two sets of grid marks.

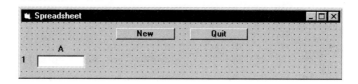

Figure 7.13 Controls at design time.

Object	Property	Setting
frmSpreadsheet	Caption	Spreadsheet
cmdNew	Caption	New
cmdQuit	Caption	Quit
lblRowLab	Caption	1
	Index	1
lblColLab	Caption	A
	Index	1
txtCell	Text	(blank)
	Index	1
	Height	1095
	Width	285

Table 7.19 Objects and their properties.

Coding the Program

The top row of Figure 7.14 shows the different events to which the program must respond. Table 7.20 identifies the corresponding event procedures and the general procedures they call. Let's examine each event procedure.

1. **Form_Load** assigns the number of rows (16) and columns (6) in our spreadsheet to the form-level variables *maxRow* and *maxCol*. Form_Load then calls three general procedures to create and initialize the spreadsheet.

   The procedure CreateSpreadsheet loads each element of the *txtCell( )* control array in order from left to right, top to bottom. Cell 1, which is to be the first cell in the first row, is not loaded because it was created at design time. The Top property of a new cell is set so that the top edge of the new cell overlaps the bottom edge of the previous cell in the column. The Top property of the first cell in a column is not modified, and so the value of the Top property is the same as cell 1. Similarly, the Left property of a new cell is set so that the left edge of the new cell overlaps the right edge of the previous cell in the row. The Left property of the first cell in a row is not modified, and so the value of the Left property is the same as cell 1. CreateSpreadsheet also loads the additional row and column label elements and assigns an appropriate caption. CreateSpreadsheet's final task is to set the Height and Width properties of Form1 to accommodate all the objects that have been loaded. The numbers 500 and 200, which appear in these statements, were obtained by trial and error and are necessary to account for the space used by the form caption and borders.

   The procedure SetStructure assigns heading values to various cells of the spreadsheet in accordance with the specific application we were asked to program. The user will not be able to alter the value in these cells, because the rules for which cells are to be totaled, and where these totals are to be placed are "hard wired" into the program and cannot be changed by the user. SetStructure also assigns values to a set of form-level variables so that other procedures in the program can be coded using meaningful names rather than possibly obscure numbers. Besides Form_Load, SetStructure is also called by the cmdNew_Click event procedure.

   The procedure SetDefaults assigns the income and expense category headings shown in Figure 7.11 to the appropriate cells. The user may change these headings at any time, and must supply them if the "New" command is issued.

2. **txtCell_GotFocus** checks to see if the cell that has received the focus may, according to the rules of this application, be edited by the user. The row and column numbers for the cell are computed from the cell's index. If the cell that has received the focus is in a column after *stopCol*, the last editable column, then the column to be edited is changed to *startCol*, the first editable column, and the row to be edited is advanced by one. If the row to be edited does not contain any editable cells, then the row to be edited is advanced to the next row containing editable cells. (When the focus goes past the last row of editable cells, the next editable row is the first editable row, that is, *incStartRow*.) Finally, focus is set to the adjusted row and column, but only if an adjustment has been made. If the test Indx(row,col)<>Index were not made and focus were reset to a cell that already had the focus, then the GotFocus event procedure would be invoked again as a result of the SetFocus, and then again as a result of the SetFocus performed by this invocation of GotFocus, and so on, resulting in an infinite loop.

3. **txtCell_LostFocus** invokes the general procedure DisplayTotals when the cursor leaves one of the spreadsheet cells. DisplayTotals in turn invokes five general procedures that each compute one set of needed totals and display the results by assigning values to appropriate text boxes. TotalIncome adds up the income for each quarter and saves the results in the array *iTot*( ). Similarly, TotalExpenses adds up the expenses for each quarter and saves the results in the array *eTot*( ). ComputeBalances takes the results stored in *iTot*( ) and *eTot*( ) and subtracts them to determine the balance for each quarter. TotalRows adds the four quarters for each category and assigns the results to the text boxes at the right end of each row. Finally, Determine-GrandTotals adds the values in *iTot*( ) and *eTot*( ) to determine the values for the right end of the "balance" row and each "total" row.

4. **cmdNew_Click** prepares for the entry of a new spreadsheet by setting the Text property of each element of the control array *txtCell*( ) to the null string and then setting focus to the first cell in the spreadsheet.

5. **cmdQuit_Click** ends the program.

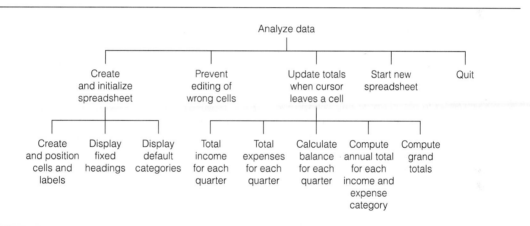

Figure 7.14 Hierarchy chart for spreadsheet program.

1. Create & Initialize spreadsheet	Form_Load
1.1 Create & position cells & labels	CreateSpreadsheet
1.2 Display fixed headings	SetStructure
1.3 Display default categories	SetDefaults
2. Prevent editing of wrong cells	txtCell_GotFocus
3. Update totals when cursor leaves a cell txtCell_LostFocus (DisplayTotals)	
3.1 Total income each quarter	TotalIncome
3.2 Total expenses each quarter	TotalExpenses
3.3 Compute balances each quarter	ShowBalances
3.4 Total each income & expense category	TotalRows
3.5 Determine grand totals	ShowGrandTotals
4. Start a new spreadsheet	cmdNew_Click
5. End program	cmdQuit_Click

Table 7.20 Tasks and their procedures.

```
Rem Spreadsheet Program
Rem ********************************************************************
Rem *                                                                  *
Rem *              Variable Table                                      *
Rem *                                                                  *
Rem *    txtCell()            Control array for data cells             *
Rem *    lblRowLab()          Control array for numeric row labels     *
Rem *    lblColLab()          Control array for alphabetic column labels *
Rem *    maxCol               Number of columns in spreadsheet         *
Rem *    maxRow               Number of rows in spreadsheet            *
Rem *    incStartRow          Row where income categories begin        *
Rem *    incStopRow           Row where income categories end          *
Rem *    incTotRow            Row where income total is displayed      *
Rem *    expStartRow          Row where expense categories begin       *
Rem *    expStopRow           Row where expense categories end         *
Rem *    expTotRow            Row where expense total is displayed     *
Rem *    balRow               Row where balance is displayed           *
Rem *    startCol             Column where numeric data begins         *
Rem *    stopCol              Column where numeric data ends           *
Rem *    totCol               Column where total for each row is displayed *
Rem *                                                                  *
Rem ********************************************************************
Dim maxCol As Integer
Dim maxRow As Integer
Dim incStartRow As Integer
Dim incStopRow As Integer
Dim incTotRow As Integer
Dim expStartRow As Integer
Dim expStopRow As Integer
Dim expTotRow As Integer
Dim balRow As Integer
Dim startCol As Integer
Dim stopCol As Integer
Dim totCol As Integer

Private Sub cmdNew_Click()
  Dim row As Integer, col As Integer
  Rem Clear all data and total text boxes
  For col = 1 To maxCol
    For row = 1 To maxRow
      Let txtCell(Indx(row, col)).Text = ""
    Next row
  Next col
  Call SetStructure
  Rem Place cursor in first data txtCell
  txtCell(Indx(1, 1)).SetFocus
End Sub

Private Sub cmdQuit_Click()
  End
End Sub

Private Sub CreateSpreadsheet()
  Dim row As Integer, col As Integer, i As Integer
  Dim cellHeight As Single, cellWidth As Single
```

```
      Dim cellTop As Single, cellLeft As Single
      Let cellHeight = txtCell(1).Height
      Let cellWidth = txtCell(1).Width
      Rem Create cells
      For row = 1 To maxRow
        For col = 1 To maxCol
          Let i = Indx(row, col)
          If Not (col = 1 And row = 1) Then
             Load txtCell(i)
          End If
          If row > 1 Then
             Let cellTop = txtCell(Indx(row - 1, col)).Top
             Let txtCell(i).Top = cellTop + cellHeight
          End If
          If col > 1 Then
             Let cellLeft = txtCell(Indx(row, col - 1)).Left
             Let txtCell(i).Left = cellLeft + cellWidth
          End If
          Let txtCell(i).Visible = True
        Next col
      Next row
      Rem Create Row Labels
      For row = 2 To maxRow
        Load lblRowLab(row)
        Let lblRowLab(row).Top = lblRowLab(row - 1).Top + cellHeight
        Let lblRowLab(row).Caption = Format(row, "0")
        Let lblRowLab(row).Visible = True
      Next row
      Rem Create Column Labels
      For col = 2 To maxCol
        Load lblColLab(col)
        Let lblColLab(col).Left = lblColLab(col - 1).Left + cellWidth
        Let lblColLab(col).Caption = Chr(col + 64)
        Let lblColLab(col).Visible = True
      Next col
      Rem Set form height and width to accommodate all objects
      Let i = Indx(maxRow, maxCol)
      Let frmSpreadsheet.Height = txtCell(i).Top + cellHeight + 500
      Let frmSpreadsheet.Width = txtCell(i).Left + cellWidth + 200
   End Sub

   Private Sub DisplayTotals()
      ReDim itot(startCol To stopCal) As Single
      ReDim etot(startCol To stopCal)  As Single
      Rem Calculate and show totals for Income each quarter
      Call TotalIncome(itot())
      Rem Calculate and show totals for Expenses each quarter
      Call TotalExpenses(etot())
      Rem Calculate and show Balances for each quarter
      Call ShowBalances(itot(), etot())
      Rem Calculate and show the Total of each Income & Expense category
      Call TotalRows
      Rem Calculate and show grand totals of quarter totals and balances
      Call ShowGrandTotals(itot(), etot())
   End Sub
```

```
Private Sub Form_Load()
  Rem Establish number of rows and columns. Trial and error show
  Rem that a maximum of 20 rows and 8 columns will fit the screen.
  Rem For this particular application, 16 rows and 6 columns are adequate.
  Let maxRow = 16
  Let maxCol = 6
  Call CreateSpreadsheet
  Call SetStructure
  Call SetDefaults
End Sub

Private Function Indx(row As Integer, col As Integer) As Integer
  Indx = (row - 1) * maxCol + col
End Function

Private Sub SetDefaults()
  Rem Set default values specific to this application
  Let txtCell(Indx(3, 1)).Text = "Job"
  Let txtCell(Indx(4, 1)).Text = "Parents"
  Let txtCell(Indx(5, 1)).Text = "Scholarship"
  Let txtCell(Indx(9, 1)).Text = "Tuition"
  Let txtCell(Indx(10, 1)).Text = "Food"
  Let txtCell(Indx(11, 1)).Text = "Rent"
  Let txtCell(Indx(12, 1)).Text = "Books"
  Let txtCell(Indx(13, 1)).Text = "Misc"
End Sub

Private Sub SetStructure()
  Let txtCell(Indx(1, 2)).Text = "Fall"
  Let txtCell(Indx(1, 3)).Text = "Winter"
  Let txtCell(Indx(1, 4)).Text = "Spring"
  Let txtCell(Indx(1, 5)).Text = "Summer"
  Let txtCell(Indx(1, 6)).Text = "Total"
  Let txtCell(Indx(1, 6)).ForeColor = QBColor(2)
  Let txtCell(Indx(2, 1)).Text = "Income"
  Let txtCell(Indx(2, 1)).ForeColor = QBColor(5)
  Let txtCell(Indx(6, 1)).Text = "Total"
  Let txtCell(Indx(6, 1)).ForeColor = QBColor(2)
  Let txtCell(Indx(8, 1)).Text = "Expenses"
  Let txtCell(Indx(8, 1)).ForeColor = QBColor(5)
  Let txtCell(Indx(14, 1)).Text = "Total"
  Let txtCell(Indx(14, 1)).ForeColor = QBColor(2)
  Let txtCell(Indx(16, 1)).Text = "Balance"
  Let txtCell(Indx(16, 1)).ForeColor = QBColor(2)
  Let incStartRow = 3
  Let incStopRow = 5
  Let incTotRow = 6
  Let expStartRow = 9
  Let expStopRow = 13
  Let expTotRow = 14
  Let balRow = 16
  Let startCol = 2
  Let stopCol = 5
  Let totCol = 6
End Sub
```

```
Private Sub ShowBalances(itot() As Single, etot() As Single)
  Dim col As Integer
  For col = startCol To stopCol
    Let txtCell(Indx(balRow, col)).Text = Format(itot(col) - etot(col), "0")
  Next col
End Sub


Private Sub ShowGrandTotals(itot() As Single, etot() As Single)
  Dim col As Integer, iTotal As Single, eTotal As Single
  Rem Compute and display grand totals for income, expenses, and balance
  Let iTotal = 0
  Let eTotal = 0
  For col = startCol To stopCol
    Let iTotal = iTotal + itot(col)
    Let eTotal = eTotal + etot(col)
  Next col
  Let txtCell(Indx(incTotRow, totCol)) = Format(iTotal, "0")
  Let txtCell(Indx(expTotRow, totCol)) = Format(eTotal, "0")
  Let txtCell(Indx(balRow, totCol)) = Format(iTotal - eTotal, "0")
End Sub


Private Sub TotalExpenses(etot() As Single)
  Dim row As Integer, col As Integer
  Rem Total expenses for each of four quarters
  For col = startCol To stopCol
    Let etot(col) = 0
    For row = expStartRow To expStopRow
      Let etot(col) = etot(col) + Val(txtCell(Indx(row, col)).Text)
    Next row
    Let txtCell(Indx(expTotRow, col)).Text = Format(etot(col), "0")
  Next col
End Sub


Private Sub TotalIncome(itot() As Single)
  Dim row As Integer, col As Integer
  Rem Total income for each of four quarters
  For col = startCol To stopCol
    Let itot(col) = 0
    For row = incStartRow To incStopRow
      Let itot(col) = itot(col) + Val(txtCell(Indx(row, col)).Text)
    Next row
    Let txtCell(Indx(incTotRow, col)).Text = Format(itot(col), "0")
  Next col
End Sub


Private Sub TotalRows()
  Dim row As Integer, col As Integer, rowTot As Single
  Rem Total each income category
  For row = incStartRow To incStopRow
    Let rowTot = 0
    For col = startCol To stopCol
      Let rowTot = rowTot + Val(txtCell(Indx(row, col)).Text)
    Next col
    Let txtCell(Indx(row, totCol)).Text = Format(rowTot, "0")
  Next row
```

```
    Rem Total each expense category
    For row = expStartRow To expStopRow
      Let rowTot = 0
      For col = startCol To stopCal
        Let rowTot = rowTot + Val(txtCell(Indx(row, col)).Text)
      Next col
      Let txtCell(Indx(row, totCol)).Text = Format(rowTot, "0")
    Next row
End Sub

Private Sub txtCell_GotFocus(Index As Integer)
  Dim row As Integer, col As Integer
  Rem Force focus into a data txtCell for this application
  Let row = Int((Index - 1) / maxCol) + 1
  Let col = ((Index - 1) Mod maxCol) + 1
  If col > stopCol Then
      Let row = row + 1
      Let col = startCol
  End If
  If row < incStartRow Then
      Let row = incStartRow
    ElseIf (row > incStopRow) And (row < expStartRow) Then
     .Let row = expStartRow
    ElseIf row > expStopRow Then
      Let row = incStartRow
  End If
  If Indx(row, col) <> Index Then
      txtCell(Indx(row, col)).SetFocus
  End If
End Sub

Private Sub txtCell_LostFocus(Indx As Integer)
  Call DisplayTotals
End Sub
```

Chapter 7
Summary

1. For programming purposes, tabular data are most efficiently processed if stored in an *array*. The *ranges* of variable arrays are specified by Dim or ReDim statements.

2. An array of labels, text boxes, or command buttons, referred to in general as a *control array*, can be created by assigning a value (usually zero) to the *Index* property of the control at design time. Additional elements of the control array are created either at design time by using Ctrl+C and Ctrl+V to copy the first element in the array or at run time by using the Load statement. New elements created in either way inherit all the properties of the first element except the Index, Visible (if created with Load), Top (when copied at design time), and Left (when copied at design time) properties.

3. Two of the best known methods for ordering (or *sorting*) arrays are the *bubble sort* and the *Shell sort*.

4. Any array can be searched *sequentially* to find the subscript associated with a sought-after value. Ordered arrays can be searched most efficiently by a *binary search*.

5. A table can be effectively stored in a *two-dimensional array*.

Chapter 7
Programming Projects

1. Table 7.21 contains some lengths in terms of feet. Write a program that displays the nine different units of measure, requests the unit to convert from, the unit to convert to, and the quantity to be converted, and then displays the converted quantity. A typical outcome is shown in Figure 7.15.

1 inch = .0833 foot	1 rod = 16.5 feet
1 yard = 3 feet	1 furlong = 660 feet
1 meter = 3.2815 feet	1 kilometer = 3281.5 feet
1 fathom = 6 feet	1 mile = 5280 feet

Table 7.21 Equivalent lengths.

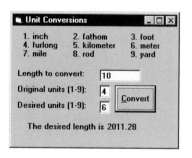

Figure 7.15 Possible outcome of Project 1.

2. Statisticians use the concepts of **mean** and **standard deviation** to describe a collection of data. The mean is the average value of the items, and the standard deviation measures the spread or dispersal of the numbers about the mean. Formally, if $x_1, x_2, x_3, \ldots, x_n$ is a collection of data, then

$$\text{mean} = m = \frac{x_1 + x_2 + x_3 + \ldots + x_n}{n}$$

$$\text{standard deviation} = s = \sqrt{\frac{(x_1 - m)^2 + (x_2 - m)^2 + (x_3 - m)^2 + \ldots + (x_n - m)^2}{n - 1}}$$

Write a computer program to

(a) Place the exam scores 59, 60, 65, 75, 56, 56, 66, 62, 98, 72, 95, 71, 63, 77, 65, 77, 65, 59, 85, and 62 into an array.

(b) Calculate the mean and standard deviation of the exam scores.

(c) Assign letter grades to each exam score, ES, as follows:

$$ES \geq m + 1.5s \qquad A$$
$$m + .5s \leq ES < m + 1.5s \qquad B$$
$$m - .5s \leq ES < m + .5s \qquad C$$
$$m - 1.5s \leq ES < m - .5s \qquad D$$
$$ES < m - 1.5s \qquad F$$

For instance, if m were 70 and s were 12, then grades of 88 or above would receive A's, grades between 76 and 87 would receive B's, and so on. A process of this type is referred to as *curving grades*.

(d) Display a list of the exam scores along with their corresponding grades.

3. *Rudimentary Translator.* Table 7.22 gives English words and their French and German equivalents. Store these words in a data file and read them into three parallel arrays, one for each language. Write a program that sorts all three arrays according to the array of English words. The program should then request an English sentence as input from the keyboard and translate it into French and German. For example, if the English sentence given is MY PENCIL IS ON THE TABLE, then the French translation will be MON CRAYON EST SUR LA TABLE, and the German translation will be MEIN BLEISTIFT IST AUF DEM TISCH.

YES	OUI	JA	LARGE	GROS	GROSS
TABLE	TABLE	TISCH	NO	NON	NEIN
THE	LA	DEM	HAT	CHAPEAU	HUT
IS	EST	IST	PENCIL	CRAYON	BLEISTIFT
YELLOW	JAUNE	GELB	RED	ROUGE	ROT
FRIEND	AMI	FREUND	ON	SUR	AUF
SICK	MALADE	KRANK	AUTO	AUTO	AUTO
MY	MON	MEIN	OFTEN	SOUVENT	OFT

Table 7.22 English words and their French and German equivalents.

4. Write a program that allows a list of no more than 50 personal computer vendors and their percent changes in market share for a particular year to be input and displays the information in two lists titled *gainers* and *losers*. Each list should be sorted by the *magnitude* of the percent change. Try your program on the 1991 data for the top 10 U.S. vendors in Table 7.23. **Note:** You will need to store the data initially in an array to determine the number of gainers and losers.

Company	% Change	Company	% Change
Apple	2.8	Gateway 2000	1.4
AST	0.7	IBM	–1.5
Bull/ZDS	0.0	Packard Bell	0.3
Compaq	–0.5	Tandy	1.1
Everex	0.2	Toshiba	–0.02

Table 7.23 Changes in market share of personal computer and single-user workstation market.

Source: International Data Corp. (*Industry Surveys*, Dec. 31, 1992)

5. Each team in a six-team soccer league played each other team once. Table 7.24 shows the winners. Write a program to

(a) Place the team names in a one-dimensional array.
(b) Place the data from Table 7.24 in a two-dimensional array.
(c) Place the number of games won by each team in a one-dimensional array.
(d) Display a listing of the teams giving each team's name and number of games won. The list should be in decreasing order by the number of wins.

	Jazz	Jets	Owls	Rams	Cubs	Zips
Jazz	—	Jazz	Jazz	Rams	Cubs	Jazz
Jets	Jazz	—	Jets	Jets	Cubs	Zips
Owls	Jazz	Jets	—	Rams	Owls	Owls
Rams	Rams	Jets	Rams	—	Rams	Rams
Cubs	Cubs	Cubs	Owls	Rams	—	Cubs
Zips	Jazz	Zips	Owls	Rams	Cubs	—

Table 7.24 Soccer league winners.

6. A poker hand can be stored in a two-dimensional array. The statement

```
Dim hand(1 TO 4, 1 TO 13) As Integer
```

declares a 52-element array, where the first dimension ranges over the four suits and the second dimension ranges over the thirteen denominations. A poker hand is specified by placing ones in the elements corresponding to the cards in the hand. See Figure 7.16.

Write a program that requests the five cards as input from the user, creates the related array, and passes the array to subprograms to determine the type of the hand: flush (all cards have the same suit), straight (cards have consecutive denominations—ace can come either before 2 or after King), straight flush, four-of-a-kind, full house (3 cards of one denomination, 2 cards of another denomination), three-of-a-kind, two pairs, one pair, or none of the above.

	A	2	3	4	5	6	7	8	9	10	J	Q	K
Club	0	0	0	0	0	0	0	0	1	0	0	0	0
Diamond	1	0	0	0	0	0	0	0	0	0	0	0	0
Heart	1	0	0	0	0	0	0	0	0	0	0	1	0
Spade	0	0	0	0	1	0	0	0	0	0	0	0	0

Figure 7.16 Array for the poker hand A♥ A♦ 5♠ 9♣ Q♥.

7. *Airline Reservations.* Write a reservation system for an airline flight. Assume the airplane has 10 rows with 4 seats in each row. Use a two-dimensional array of strings to maintain a seating chart. In addition, create an array to be used as a waiting list in case the plane is full. The waiting list should be "first come, first served," that is, people who are added early to the list get priority over those added later. Allow the user the following three options:

(1) Add a passenger to the flight or waiting list.
    (a) Request the passenger's name.
    (b) Display a chart of the seats in the airplane in tabular form.
    (c) If seats are available, let the passenger choose a seat. Add the passenger to the seating chart.
    (d) If no seats are available, place the passenger on the waiting list.
(2) Remove a passenger from the flight.
    (a) Request the passenger's name.
    (b) Search the seating chart for the passenger's name and delete it.
    (c) If the waiting list is empty, update the array so the seat is available.
    (d) If the waiting list is not empty, remove the first person from the list, and give him or her the newly vacated seat.
(3) Quit.

8. The Game of Life was invented by John H. Conway to model some genetic laws for birth, death, and survival. Consider a checkerboard consisting of an *n*-by-*n* array of squares. Each square can contain one individual (denoted by 1) or be empty (denoted by –). Figure 7.17(a) shows a 6-by-6 board with four of the squares occupied. The future of each individual depends on the number of his neighbors. After each period of time, called a *generation*, certain individuals will survive, others will die due to either loneliness or overcrowding, and new individuals will be born. Each nonborder square has eight neighboring squares. After each generation, the status of the squares change as follows:

(a) An individual *survives* if there are two or three individuals in neighboring squares.
(b) An individual *dies* if he has more than three individuals or less than two in neighboring squares.
(c) A new individual is *born* into each empty square with exactly three individuals as neighbors.

Figure 7.17(b) shows the status after one generation. Write a program to do the following:

(a) Dimension an *n*-by-*n* array, where *n* is input by the user, to hold the status of each square in the current generation. To specify the initial configuration, have the user input each row as a string of length *n*, and break the row into 1's or dashes with Mid.

(b) Dimension an *n*-by-*n* array to hold the status of each square in the next generation. Compute the status for each square and produce the display in Figure 7.17(b). **Note:** The generation changes all at once. Only current cells are used to determine which cells will contain individuals in the next generation.

(c) Assign the next generation values to the current generation and repeat as often as desired.

(d) Display the number of individuals in each generation.

Hint: The hardest part of the program is determining the number of neighbors a cell has. In general, you must check a 3-by-3 square around the cell in question. Exceptions must be made when the cell is on the edge of the array. Don't forget that a cell is not a neighbor of itself.

(Test the program with the initial configuration shown in Figure 7.18. It is known as the figure-eight configuration and repeats after eight generations.)

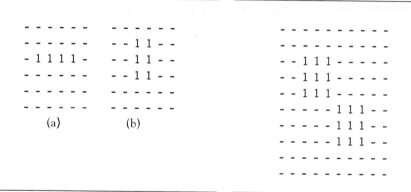

```
- - - - - -        - - - - - -
- - - - - -        - - 1 1 - -
- 1 1 1 1 -        - - 1 1 - -
- - - - - -        - - 1 1 - -
- - - - - -        - - - - - -
- - - - - -        - - - - - -
    (a)                (b)
```

```
- - - - - - - - - -
- - - - - - - - - -
- - 1 1 1 - - - - -
- - 1 1 1 - - - - -
- - 1 1 1 - - - - -
- - - - - 1 1 1 - -
- - - - - 1 1 1 - -
- - - - - 1 1 1 - -
- - - - - - - - - -
- - - - - - - - - -
```

Figure 7.17 Two generations.   **Figure 7.18** The figure eight.

9. Simulate the game Concentration. The Form_Load routine should create an array of 20 command buttons placed vertically on a form. A list of 10 words should be randomly assigned as potential captions for the buttons, with each word assigned to two command buttons. Initially, none of the buttons should show their words. However, when a button is clicked on, its word is revealed as its caption. After two words have been revealed, either both of the command buttons should become invisible (if their words match) or their captions should again become blank (if the two words do not match). When all matches have been found, a message box should display the number of tries (pairs of words exposed) and an appropriate remark about the user's concentration ability. Possible remarks might be, "You must have ESP" (less than 14 tries), "Amazing concentration" (14 to 20 tries), "Can't hide anything from you" (21 to 28 tries), "Perhaps a nap would recharge your concentration" (29 to 37 tries), and "Better find a designated driver" (more than 37 tries).

8

Sequential Files

8.1 Sequential Files / 398
• Creating a Sequential File • Adding Items to a
Sequential File • Error Trapping

8.2 Using Sequential Files / 411
• Sorting Sequential Files • Merging Sequential Files
• Control Break Processing

8.3 A Case Study: Recording Checks and Deposits / 419
• The Design of the Program • The User Interface
• Coding the Program

Summary / 429

Programming Projects / 429

8.1 SEQUENTIAL FILES

Throughout this text we have processed data from files created with Windows' Notepad and saved on a disk. Such files are stored on disk as a sequence of characters. (Two special characters, called the "carriage return" and "line feed" characters, are inserted at the end of each line to indicate where new lines should be started.) Such files are called **sequential files**. In this section, we create sequential files from Visual Basic programs and develop techniques for using sequential files.

Creating a Sequential File

There are many ways to organize data in a sequential file. The technique presented here is easy to implement. Other techniques are discussed in the comments. The following steps create a new sequential file and write data to it.

1. Choose a **file name**. With Windows 3.1, a file name is a string consisting of a base name of at most eight characters followed by an optional extension consisting of a period and at most three characters. Letters, digits, and a few other assorted characters (see Comment 1) can be used in either the name or the extension. Blank spaces are not allowed. Some examples of file names are INCOME.86, CUSTOMER.TXT, and FORT500. Windows 95 allows the base name to contain as many as 255 characters. Because we want our files to be available with both operating systems, we will follow the Windows 3.1 naming rules.

 2. Choose a number from 1 through 511 to be the **reference number** of the file. While the file is in use, it will be identified by this number.

3. Execute the statement

   ```
   Open "filespec" For Output As #n
   ```

   where *n* is the reference number. This process is referred to as **opening a file for output**. It establishes a communications link between the computer and the disk drive for storing data *onto* the disk. It allows data to be output from the computer and recorded in the specified file.

4. Place data into the file with the Write# statement. If *a* is a string, then the statement

   ```
   Write #n, a
   ```

   writes the string *a* surrounded by quotation marks into the file. If *c* is a number, then the statement

   ```
   Write #n, c
   ```

   writes the number *c*, without any leading or trailing spaces, into file number *n*. The statement

   ```
   Write #n, a, c
   ```

   writes *a* and *c* as before, but with a comma separating them. Similarly, if the statement Write #n is followed by a list of several strings and/or numbers separated by commas, then all the strings and numbers appear as before, separated by commas. After each Write# statement is executed, the "carriage return" and "line feed" characters are placed into the file.

5. After all the data have been recorded in the file, execute

```
Close #n
```

where *n* is the reference number. This statement breaks the communications link with the file and dissociates the number *n* from the file.

EXAMPLE 1 The following program illustrates the different aspects of the Write# statement. Notice the absence of leading and trailing spaces for numbers and the presence of quotation marks surrounding strings.

```
Private Sub cmdCreateFile_Click()
  Dim name1 As String, name2 As String
  Rem Demonstrate use of Write # statement
  Open "PIONEER.TXT" For Output As #1
  Write #1, "ENIAC"
  Write #1, 1946
  Write #1, "ENIAC", 1946
  Let name1 = "Eckert"
  Let name2 = "Mauchly"
  Write #1, 14 * 139, "J.P. " & name1, name2, "John"
  Close #1
End Sub
```

[Run, click the command button, and then load the file PIONEER.TXT into Windows' Notepad. The following will appear on the screen.]

"ENIAC"
1946
"ENIAC",1946
1946,"J.P. Eckert","Mauchly","John"

Caution: If an existing sequential file is opened for output, the computer will erase the existing data and create a new empty file.

Write# allows us to create files just like the Notepad files that appear throughout this text. We already know how to read such files with Input#. The remaining major task is adding data to the end of sequential files.

Adding Items to a Sequential File

Data can be added to the end of an existing sequential file with the following steps.

1. Choose a number from 1 through 511 to be the reference number for the file. This number need not be the same number that was used when the file was created.

2. Execute the statement

```
Open "filespec" For Append As #n
```

where *n* is the reference number. This procedure is called **opening a file for append**. It allows data to be output from the computer and recorded at the end of the specified file.

3. Place data into the file with the Write# statement.

4. After all the data have been recorded into the file, close the file with the statement Close #*n*.

The Append option for opening a file is intended to add data to an existing file. However, it also can be used to create a new file. If the file does not exist, then the Append option acts just like the Output option and creates the file.

The three options, Output, Input, and Append, are referred to as **modes**. A file should not be open in two modes at the same time. For instance, after a file has been opened for output and data have been written to the file, the file should be closed before being opened for input.

An attempt to open a nonexistent file for input terminates the program with the "File not found" error message. There is a function that tells us whether a certain file has already been created. If the value of

```
Dir("filespec")
```

is the empty string "", then the specified file does not exist. Therefore, prudence often dictates that files be opened for input with code such as

```
If Dir("filespec") <> "" Then
    Open "filespec" For Input As #1
  Else
    Let message = "Either no file has yet been created or "
    Let message = message & "the file is not where expected."
    MsgBox message, , "File Not Found"
End If
```

There is one file-management operation that we have yet to discuss—deleting an item of information from a file. An individual item of the file cannot be changed or deleted directly. A new file must be created by reading each item from the original file and recording it, with the single item changed or deleted, into the new file. The old file is then erased and the new file renamed with the name of the original file. Regarding these last two tasks, the Visual Basic statement

```
Kill "filespec"
```

removes the specified file from the disk and the statement

```
Name "filespec1" As "filespec2"
```

changes the name of the file identified by *filespec1* to the new name *filespec2*. (**Note:** The Kill and Name statements cannot be used with open files. So doing generates a "File already open" message.)

EXAMPLE 2 The following program creates and manages a file of names and years of birth.

Object	Property	Setting
frm8_1_2	Caption	Access YOB.TXT
lblName	Caption	Name
txtName	Text	(blank)
lblYOB	Caption	Year of Birth
txtYOB	Text	(blank)
cmdAdd	Caption	Add Above Person to File
cmdLookUp	Caption	Look up Year of Birth
cmdDelete	Caption	Delete Above Person from File

```
Private Sub cmdAdd_Click()
  Dim message As String
  Rem Add a person's name and year of birth to file
  If (txtName.Text <> "") And (txtYOB.Text <> "") Then
      Open "YOB.TXT" For Append As #1
      Write #1, txtName.Text, Val(txtYOB.Text)
      Close #1
      Let txtName.Text = ""
      Let txtYOB.Text = ""
      txtName.SetFocus
    Else
      Let message = "You must enter a name and year of birth."
      MsgBox message, , "Information Incomplete"
  End If
End Sub


Private Sub cmdLookUp_Click()
  Dim message As String
  Rem Determine a person's year of birth
  If txtName.Text <> "" Then
      If Dir("YOB.TXT") <> "" Then
          Call DisplayYearOfBirth
        Else
          Let message = "Either no file has yet been created or "
          Let message = message & "the file is not where expected."
          MsgBox message, , "File Not Found"
      End If
    Else
      MsgBox "You must enter a name.", , "Information Incomplete"
  End If
  txtName.SetFocus
End Sub


Private Sub cmdDelete_Click()
  Dim message As String
  Rem Remove a person from the file
  If txtName.Text <> "" Then
      If Dir("YOB.TXT") <> "" Then
          Call DeletePerson
```

```
            Else
                Let message = "Either no file has yet been created or "
                Let message = message & "the file is not where expected."
                MsgBox message, , "File Not Found."
            End If
        Else
            MsgBox "You must enter a name.", , "Information Incomplete"
        End If
        txtName.SetFocus
End Sub

Private Sub DeletePerson()
    Dim nom As String, yob As Integer, flag As String
    Let flag = "Not found"
    Open "YOB.TXT" For Input As #1
    Open "TEMP" For Output As #2
    Do While Not EOF(1)
        Input #1, nom, yob
        If nom <> txtName.Text Then
            Write #2, nom, yob
        Else
            Let flag = "Found"
        End If
    Loop
    Close #1
    Close #2
    Kill "YOB.TXT"
    Name "TEMP" As "YOB.TXT"
    If flag = "Not found" Then
        MsgBox "The name was not found.", , ""
    Else
        Let txtName.Text = ""
        Let txtYOB.Text = ""
    End If
End Sub

Private Sub DisplayYearOfBirth()
    Dim nom As String, yob As Integer
    Rem Find the year of birth for the name in txtName
    Let txtYOB.Text = ""
    Open "YOB.TXT" For Input As #1
    Let nom = ""
    Do While (nom <> txtName.Text) And (Not EOF(1))
        Input #1, nom, yob
    Loop
    If nom = txtName.Text Then
        Let txtYOB.Text = Str(yob)
    Else
        MsgBox "Person is not in file.", , ""
        Let txtName.Text = ""
    End If
    Close #1
End Sub
```

[Run. After several names have been added, the file might look as shown in Figure 8.1.]

```
"Barbra",1942
"Ringo",1940
"Sylvester",1946
```

Figure 8.1 Sample contents of YOB.TXT.

Error Trapping

If you try to Open a file on a diskette in drive A and there is no diskette in drive A, the program will crash with the error message "Disk not ready." Visual Basic has a device, called **error-trapping**, for preventing this and many other types of errors. If an error occurs while error-trapping is active, two things happen. An identifying number is assigned to an object called Err, and the program jumps to some lines of code called an **error-handling routine**, which takes corrective measures based on the value of Err. Some errors and the values they generate are as follows:

Type of error	Value of Err
Subscript out of range	9
Division by zero	11
File not found	53
File already open	55
Disk full	61
File already exists	68
Disk not ready	71

To set up error-trapping inside a procedure, do the following:

1. Make the first line of the procedure

```
On Error GoTo ErrorHandler
```

2. Type in the lines to carry out the purpose of the procedure.

3. Make the last lines of the procedure

```
Exit Sub
ErrorHandler:
error-handling routine
Resume
```

The statement "On Error GoTo ErrorHandler" activates error-trapping. If an error occurs during the execution of a line of the procedure, the program will jump to the error-handling routine. The statement "Resume" causes the program to jump back to the line causing the error. The statement "Exit Sub", which causes an early exit from the procedure, prevents the error-handling routine from being entered when no error occurs. For instance, the following procedure has an error-handling routine that is called when a file cannot be found.

```
Private Sub OpenFile()
  On Error GoTo ErrorHandler
  Dim fileName As String
```

```
        Let fileName = InputBox("Enter the name of the file to be opened.")
        Open fileName For Input As #1
        Exit Sub
    ErrorHandler:
      Select Case Err
        Case Err = 53
          MsgBox "File not found. Try Again."
          Let fileName = InputBox("Enter the name of the file to be opened.")
        Case Err = 71
          MsgBox "The drive door might be open - please check."
      End Select
      Resume
    End Sub
```

The word "ErrorHandler", which is called a **line label**, can be replaced by any word of at most 40 letters. The line, which is placed just before the error-handling routine, must start at the left margin and must end with a colon. If "Resume" is replaced by "Resume Next", then the program will jump to the line following the line causing the error.

The line label must be in the same procedure as the On Error statement. However, the error-handling routine can call another procedure.

There are two variations of the On Error statement. The statement "On Error GoTo 0" turns off error-trapping. The statement "On Error Resume Next" specifies that when a run-time error occurs, execution continues with the statement following the statement where the error occurred.

Comments

1. Sequential files make efficient use of disk space and are easy to create and use. Their disadvantages are as follows:

   (a) Often a large portion of the file must be read in order to find one specific item.
   (b) An individual item of the file cannot be changed or deleted easily.

   Another type of file, known as a **random-access file**, has neither of the disadvantages of sequential files; however, random-access files typically use more disk space, require greater effort to program, and are not flexible in the variety and format of the stored data. Random-access files are discussed in Chapter 9.

2. Consider the sequential file shown in Figure 8.1 at the end of Example 2. This file is said to consist of three records of two fields each. A **record** holds all the data about a single individual. Each item of data is called a **field**. The three records are

   "Barbra", 1942
   "Ringo", 1940
   "Sylvester", 1946

   and the two fields are

   name field, year of birth field

3. To obtain a complete list of error messages and the associated values of Err, click on "Microsoft Visual Basic Help Topics" in the Help menu, click the Contents tab, double-click "Trappable Errors," and double-click "Core Visual Basic Language Errors." You can obtain detailed information about a specific error message by double-clicking on it.

PRACTICE PROBLEMS 8.1

1. Compose a subprogram RemoveDups that could be used in Example 2 to delete from YOB.TXT all repeated records except the first instance of a name matching the name in txtName. (Assume that the existence of YOB.TXT is checked prior to the execution of this subprogram.)

2. Compose a subprogram AddNoDuplicate to add a name and year of birth to the end of the file YOB.TXT only if the name to be added is not already present in the file. (Assume that the existence of YOB.TXT is checked prior to the execution of this subprogram.)

EXERCISES 8.1

In Exercises 1 through 4, determine the output displayed in the picture box when the command button is clicked.

1.
```
Private Sub cmdDisplay_Click()
    Dim salutation As String
    Open "GREETING.TXT" For Output As #1
    Write #1, "Hello"
    Write #1, "Aloha"
    Close #1
    Open "GREETING.TXT" For Input As #1
    Input #1, salutation
    picOutput.Print salutation
    Close #1
End Sub
```

2.
```
Private Sub cmdDisplay_Click()
    Dim salutation As String, welcome As String
    Open "GREETING.TXT" For Output As #2
    Write #2, "Hello", "Aloha"
    Close #2
    Open "GREETING.TXT" For Input As #1
    Input #1, salutation, welcome
    picOutput.Print welcome
    Close #1
End Sub
```

3.
```
Private Sub cmdDisplay_Click()
    Dim salutation As String
    Open "GREETING.TXT" For Output As #2
    Write #2, "Hello"
    Write #2, "Aloha"
    Write #2, "Bon Jour"
    Close #2
    Open "GREETING.TXT" For Input As #1
    Do While Not EOF(1)
      Input #1, salutation
      picOutput.Print salutation
    Loop
    Close #1
End Sub
```

4. Assume the contents of the file GREETING.TXT are as shown in Figure 8.2.

```
Private Sub cmdDisplay_Click()
  Dim file As String, salutation As Integer, g As String
  Let file = "GREETING.TXT"
  Open file For Append As #3
  Write #3, "Buenos Dias"
  Close #3
  Open file For Input As #3
  For salutation = 1 To 4
    Input #3, g
    picOutput.Print g
  Next salutation
  Close #3
End Sub
```

"Hello"
"Aloha"
"Bon Jour"

Figure 8.2 Contents of the file GREETING.TXT.

5. Assume that the contents of the file GREETING.TXT are as shown in Figure 8.2. What is the effect of the following program?

```
Private Sub cmdDisplay_Click()
  Dim g As String
  Open "GREETING.TXT" For Input As #1
  Open "WELCOME" For Output As #2
  Do While Not EOF(1)
    Input #1, g
    If g <> "Aloha" Then
        Write #2, g
    End If
  Loop
  Close
End Sub
```

6. Assume that the contents of the file YOB.TXT is as shown in Figure 8.1. What is the effect of the following program?

```
Private Sub cmdDisplay_Click()
  Dim flag As Integer, nom As String, year As Integer
  Open "YOB.TXT" For Input As #1
  Open "YOB2.TXT" For Output As #2
  Let flag = 0
  Let nom = ""
  Do While (nom < "Clint") And (Not EOF(1))
    Input #1, nom, year
    If nom >= "Clint" Then
        Write #2, "Clint", 1930
        Let flag = 1
    End If
    Write #2, nom, year
  Loop
```

```
      Do While Not EOF(1)
        Input #1, nom, year
        Write #2, nom, year
      Loop
      If flag = 0 Then
          Write #2, "Clint", 1930
      End If
      Close
   End Sub
```

In Exercises 7 through 12, identify any errors. Assume that the contents of the files YOB.TXT and GREETING.TXT are as shown in Figures 8.1 and 8.2.

7.
```
Private Sub cmdDisplay_Click()
    Open YOB.TXT For Append As #1
    Write #1, "Michael"
    Close #1
End Sub
```

8.
```
Private Sub cmdDisplay_Click()
    Dim nom As String, yr As Integer
    Open "YOB.TXT" For Output As #2
    Input #2, nom, yr
    picOutput.Print yr
    Close #2
End Sub
```

9.
```
Private Sub cmdDisplay_Click()
    Dim i As Integer, g As String
    Open "GREETING.TXT" For Input As #1
    For i = 1 To EOF(1)
      Input #1, g
      picOutput.Print g
    Next i
    Close #1
End Sub
```

10.
```
Private Sub cmdDisplay_Click()
    Dim g As String
    Open "GREETING.TXT" For Input As #1
    Do While Not EOF
      Input #1, g
      picOutput.Print g
    Loop
    Close #1
End Sub
```

11.
```
Private Sub cmdDisplay_Click()
    Dim nom As String, g As String
    Open "GREETING.TXT" For Input As #1
    Let nom = "NEW.GREET.TXT"
    Open "nom" For Output As #2
    Do While Not EOF(1)
      Input #1, g
      Write #2, g
    Loop
    Close
End Sub
```

12.
```
Private Sub cmdDisplay_Click()
    Open "GREETING.TXT" For Input As #1
    Close "GREETING.TXT"
End Sub
```

Exercises 13 through 20 are related and use the data in Table 8.1. The file created in Exercise 13 should be used in Exercises 14 through 20.

13. Write a program to create the sequential file COWBOY.TXT containing the information in Table 8.1.

Colt Peacemaker	12.20
Holster	2.00
Levi Strauss Jeans	1.35
Saddle	40.00
Stetson	10.00

Table 8.1 Prices paid by cowboys for certain items in mid-1800s.

14. Write a program to display all items in the file COWBOY.TXT that cost more than $10.

15. Write a program to add the data *Winchester rifle, 20.50* to the end of the file COWBOY.TXT.

16. Suppose an order is placed for 3 Colt Peacemakers, 2 Holsters, 10 pairs of Levi Strauss Jeans, 1 saddle, and 4 Stetsons. Write a program to

    (a) Create the sequential file ORDER.TXT to hold the numbers 3, 2, 10, 1, 4.

    (b) Use the files COWBOY.TXT and ORDER.TXT to display a sales receipt with three columns giving the name of each item, the quantity ordered, and the cost for that quantity.

    (c) Compute the total cost of the items and display it at the end of the sales receipt.

17. Write a program to request an additional item and price from the user. Then create a sequential file called COWBOY2.TXT containing all the information in the file COWBOY.TXT with the additional item (and price) inserted in its proper alphabetical sequence. Run the program for both of the following data items: *Boots, 20* and *Horse, 35.*

18. Suppose the price of saddles is reduced by 20 percent. Use the file COWBOY. TXT to create a sequential file, COWBOY3.TXT, containing the new price list.

19. Write a program to create a sequential file called COWBOY4.TXT containing all the information in the file COWBOY.TXT except for the data *Holster, 2.*

20. Write a program to allow additional items and prices to be input by the user and added to the end of the file COWBOY.TXT. Include a method to terminate the process.

21. Suppose the file YOB.TXT contains many names and years, and that the names are in alphabetical order. Write a program that requests a name as input and either gives the person's age or reports that the person is not in the file. *Note:* Because the names are in alphabetical order, usually there is no need to search to the end of the file.

22. Suppose the file YOB.TXT contains many names and years. Write a program that creates two files, called SENIORS.TXT and JUNIORS.TXT, and copies all the data on people born before 1940 into the file SENIORS and the data on the others into the file JUNIORS.TXT.

23. A publisher maintains two sequential files, HARDBACK.TXT and PAPERBCK.TXT. Each record consists of the name of a book and the quantity in stock. Write a program to access these files. (The program should allow for the case when the book is not in the file.) A run of the program might look as follows:

24. Fill in the missing code for the error-handling routine to handle a "division by zero" error.

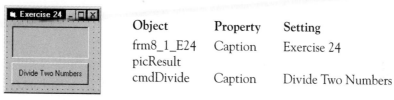

Object	Property	Setting
frm8_1_E24	Caption	Exercise 24
picResult		
cmdDivide	Caption	Divide Two Numbers

```
Private Sub cmdDivide_Click()
  On Error GoTo ErrorHandler
  Dim a As Single, b As Single, c As Single
  picResult.Cls
  Let a = Val(InputBox("Enter the numerator."))
  Let b = Val(InputBox("Enter the denominator."))
  Let c = a / b
  picResult.Print "The quotient of"
  picResult.Print a; "and"; b
  picResult.Print "is"; c
  Exit Sub
ErrorHandler:
  missing code
End Sub
```

25. Visual Basic cannot Kill a file that is open. Attempting to do so generates a "File already open" error. Write a short program that uses error-trapping to prevent such an error.

SOLUTIONS TO PRACTICE PROBLEMS 8.1

1. A record in YOB.TXT is kept if the name in the record does not match the search name, or if the name in the record matches the search name and a flag indicates that the search name has not been found previously.

```
Private Sub RemoveDups()
  Dim nom As String, yob As Integer, flag As String
  Let flag = "Not found"
  Open "YOB.TXT" For Input As #1
  Open "TEMP" For Output As #2
  Do While Not EOF(1)
    Input #1, nom, yob
    If nom <> txtName.Text Then
        Write #2, nom, yob
      Else
        If flag = "Not Found" Then
            Write #2, nom, yob
        End If
        Let flag = "Found"
    End If
  Loop
  Close #1
  Close #2
  Kill "YOB.TXT"
  Name "TEMP" As "YOB.TXT"
  If flag = "Not found" Then
      MsgBox "The name was not found.", , ""
    Else
      Let txtName.Text = ""
      Let txtYOB.Text = ""
  End If
End Sub
```

2. The file YOB.TXT is first opened for Input and scanned for the new name. If the name is not found, YOB.TXT is reopened for Append and the name and year of birth are added to the end of the file.

```
Private Sub AddNoDuplicate()
  Dim nom As String, yob As Integer, found As Integer
  Open "YOB.TXT" For Input As #1
  Let found = 0
  Do While (Not(EOF(1))) And (found = 0)
    Input #1, nom, yob
    If nom = txtName.Text Then
        Let found = 1
    End If
  Loop
  Close #1
  If found = 0 Then
      Open "YOB.TXT" For Append As #1
      Write #1, txtName.Text, Val(txtYOB.Text)
      Close #1
  End If
End Sub
```

8.2 USING SEQUENTIAL FILES

In addition to being accessed for information, sequential files are regularly updated by modifying certain pieces of data, removing some records, and adding new records. These tasks can be performed most efficiently if the files are first sorted.

Sorting Sequential Files

The records of a sequential file can be sorted on any field by first reading the data into parallel arrays and then sorting on a specific array.

EXAMPLE 1 Compose a program to sort the sequential file YOB.TXT of the previous section by year of birth.

SOLUTION

```
Private Sub cmdSort_Click()
    Dim numPeople As Integer
    Rem Sort data from YOB.TXT file by year of birth
    Let numPeople = 3             'Number of people in file
    ReDim nom(1 To numPeople) As String
    ReDim yearBorn(1 To numPeople) As Integer
    Call ReadData(nom(), yearBorn(), numPeople)
    Call SortData(nom(), yearBorn(), numPeople)
    Call ShowData(nom(), yearBorn(), numPeople)
    Call WriteData(nom(), yearBorn(), numPeople)
End Sub

Private Sub ReadData(nom() As String, yearBorn() As Integer, numPeople As
        Integer)
    Dim index As Integer
    Rem Read data from file into arrays
    Open "YOB.TXT" For Input As #1
    For index = 1 To numPeople
      Input #1, nom(index), yearBorn(index)
    Next index
    Close #1
End Sub

Private Sub ShowData(nom() As String, yearBorn() As Integer, numPeople As
        Integer)
    Dim index As Integer
    Rem Display the sorted list
    picShowData.Cls
    For index = 1 To numPeople
      picShowData.Print nom(index), yearBorn(index)
    Next index
End Sub
```

```
Private Sub SortData(nom() As String, yearBorn() As Integer, numPeople As Integer)
  Dim passNum As Integer, index As Integer
  Rem Bubble sort arrays by year of birth
  For passNum = 1 To numPeople - 1
    For index = 1 To numPeople - passNum
      If yearBorn(index) > yearBorn(index + 1) Then
          Call SwapData(nom(), yearBorn(), index)
      End If
    Next index
  Next passNum
End Sub

Private Sub SwapData(nom() As String, yearBorn() As Integer, index As Integer)
  Dim stemp As String, ntemp As Integer
  Rem Swap names and years
  Let stemp = nom(index)
  Let nom(index) = nom(index + 1)
  Let nom(index + 1) = stemp
  Let ntemp = yearBorn(index)
  Let yearBorn(index) = yearBorn(index + 1)
  Let yearBorn(index + 1) = ntemp
End Sub

Private Sub WriteData(nom() As String, yearBorn() As Integer, numPeople As Integer)
  Dim index As Integer
  Rem Write data back into file
  Open "YOB.TXT" For Output As #1
  For index = 1 To numPeople
    Write #1, nom(index), yearBorn(index)
  Next index
  Close #1
End Sub
```

If the program is run, the command button pressed, and then YOB.TXT is examined using Windows' Notepad, the following will be seen:

"Ringo",1940
"Barbra",1942
"Sylvester",1946

Merging Sequential Files

In Section 7.2, we considered an algorithm for merging two arrays. This same algorithm can be applied to merging two ordered files.

Suppose you have two ordered files (possibly with certain items appearing in both files), and you want to merge them into a third ordered file (without duplications). The technique for creating the third file is as follows.

1. Open the two ordered files For Input and open a third file For Output.

2. Try to get an item of data from each file.

3. Repeat steps (a) and (b) below until an item of data is not available in one of the files.

   (a) If one item precedes the other, write it into the third file and try to get another item of data from its file.
   (b) If the two items are identical, write one into the third file and try to get another item of data from each of the two ordered files.

4. At this point, an item of data has most likely been retrieved from one of the files and not yet written to the third file. In this case, write that item and all remaining items in that file to the third file.

5. Close the three files.

EXAMPLE 2 The following program merges two ordered files of numbers into a third file.

Object	Property	Setting
frmMerge	Caption	Merge Two Files
lblNameFirst	Caption	Name of first file:
txtNameFirst	Text	(blank)
lblNameSecond	Caption	Name of second file:
txtNameSecond	Text	(blank)
lblNameMerged	Caption	Name for merged file:
txtNameMerged	Text	(blank)
cmdProceed	Caption	Proceed to Merge
picProgress		

```
Private Sub cmdProceed_Click()
  Dim file1 As String, file2 As String, file3 As String
  Dim have1data As String, have2data As String
  Dim num1 As Single, num2 As Single
  Dim recCount As Integer
  Rem Merge two ordered files
  picProgress.Cls
  Let file1 = txtNameFirst.Text
  Let file2 = txtNameSecond.Text
  Let file3 = txtNameMerged.Text
  Open file1 For Input As #1
  Open file2 For Input As #2
  Open file3 For Output As #3
  Let have1data = Get1data(num1)
  Let have2data = Get2data(num2)
  Let recCount = 0
  Do While (have1data = "T") And (have2data = "T")
    Select Case num1
      Case Is < num2
        Write #3, num1
        Let have1data = Get1data(num1)
      Case Is > num2
        Write #3, num2
```

```
        Let have2data = Get2data(num2)
      Case num2
        Write #3, num1
        Let have1data = Get1data(num1)
        Let have2data = Get2data(num2)
    End Select
    Let recCount = recCount + 1
  Loop
  Do While (have1data = "T")
    Write #3, num1
    Let recCount = recCount + 1
    Let have1data = Get1data(num1)
  Loop
  Do While (have2data = "T")
    Write #3, num2
    Let recCount = recCount + 1
    Let have2data = Get2data(num2)
  Loop
  Close #1, #2, #3
  picProgress.Print recCount; "records written to "; file3
End Sub

Private Function Get1data(num1 As Single) As String
  Rem If possible, read next value from file 1
  Rem Return a value of "T" when new data are read; "F" if data not available
  If Not EOF(1) Then
      Input #1, num1
      Get1data = "T"
    Else
      Get1data = "F"
  End If
End Function

Private Function Get2data(num2 As Single) As String
  Rem If possible, read next value from file 2
  Rem Return a value of "T" when new data are read; "F" if data not available
  If Not EOF(2) Then
      Input #2, num2
      Get2data = "T"
    Else
      Get2data = "F"
  End If
End Function
```

Control Break Processing

Suppose a small real estate company stores its sales data for a year in a sequential file in which each record contains four fields: month of sale (1 through 12), day of sale (1 through 31), address, and price. Typical data for the sales of the first quarter of a year are shown in Figure 8.3. The records are ordered by date of sale.

```
Month          Day    Address              Price
January        9      102 Elm Street       $203,000
January        20     1 Main Street        $315,200
January        25     5 Maple Street       $123,450
February       15     1 Center Street      $100,000
February       23     2 Vista Drive        $145,320
March          15     205 Rodeo Circle     $389,100
```

Figure 8.3 Real estate sales for first quarter of year.

Figure 8.4 shows the output of a program that displays the total sales for the quarter year, with a subtotal for each month.

```
January    9      102 Elm Street          $203,000.00
January    20     1 Main Street           $315,200.00
January    25     5 Maple Street          $123,450.00

           Subtotal for January:          $641,650.00

February   15     1 Center Street         $100,000.00
February   23     2 Vista Drive           $145,320.00

           Subtotal for February:         $245,320.00

March      15     205 Rodeo Circle        $389,100.00

           Subtotal for March:            $389,100.00

Total for First Quarter: $1,276,070.00
```

Figure 8.4 Output of Example 3.

A program to produce the output of Figure 8.4 must calculate a subtotal at the end of each month. The variable holding the month triggers a subtotal whenever its value changes. Such a variable is called a **control variable** and each change of its value is called a **break**.

EXAMPLE 3 Write a program to produce the output of Figure 8.4. Assume the data of Figure 8.3 are stored in the sequential file HOMESALE.TXT.

SOLUTION The following program allows for months with no sales. Because monthly subtotals will be printed, the month-of-sale field is an appropriate control variable.

```
Private Sub cmdCreateReport_Click()
  Dim currentMonth As String, newMonth As String
  Dim dayNum As Integer, address As String
  Dim price As Currency, monthTotal As Currency
  Dim yearTotal As Currency, done As Integer
  Rem Display home sales by month
  picReport.Cls
  Open "HOMESALE.TXT" For Input As #1
```

```
        Let currentMonth = ""           'Name of month being subtotaled
        Let monthTotal = 0
        Let yearTotal = 0
        Let done = 0                     'Flag to indicate end of list
        Do While done = 0
          If Not EOF(1) Then
              Input #1, newMonth, dayNum, address, price
            Else
              Let done = 1               'End of list
          End If
          If (newMonth <> currentMonth) Or (done = 1) Then 'Control break processing
              If currentMonth <> "" Then      'Don't print subtotal before 1st month
                  picReport.Print
                  picReport.Print Tab(15); "Subtotal for " & currentMonth & ":";
                  picReport.Print Tab(38); Format(monthTotal, "Currency")
                  picReport.Print
              End If
              Let currentMonth = newMonth
              Let monthTotal = 0
          End If
          If done = 0 Then
              picReport.Print newMonth;
              picReport.Print Tab(11); Format(dayNum, "0");
              picReport.Print Tab(18); address;
              picReport.Print Tab(38); Format(price, "Currency")
              Let yearTotal = yearTotal + price
          End If
          Let monthTotal = monthTotal + price
        Loop
        Close #1
        picReport.Print "Total for First Quarter: "; Format(yearTotal, "Currency")
      End Sub
```

Comments

1. In the examples of this and the previous section, the files to be processed have been opened and closed within a single event procedure or subprogram. However, the solution to some programming problems requires that a file be opened just once the instant the program is run and stay open until the program is terminated. This is easily accomplished by placing the Open statement in the Form_Load event procedure and the Close and End statements in the click event procedure for a command button labeled "Quit."

PRACTICE PROBLEMS 8.2

1. The program in Example 2 contains three Do loops. Explain why at most one of the last two loops will be executed. Under what circumstances will neither of the last two loops be executed?

2. Modify the program in Example 2 so that duplicate items will be repeated in the merged file.

EXERCISES 8.2

Exercises 1 through 4 are related. They create and maintain the sequential file AVERAGE.TXT to hold batting averages of baseball players.

1. Suppose the season is about to begin. Compose a program to create the sequential file containing the name of each player, his times at bat, and his number of hits. The program should allow the user to type a name into a text box and then click a command button to add a record to the file. The times at bat and number of hits initially should be set to 0. (**Hint:** Open the file for Output in the Form_Load event procedure and Close the file when a "Quit" command button is clicked.)

2. Each day, the statistics from the previous day's games should be used to update the file. Write a program to read the records one at a time and allow the user to enter the number of times at bat and the number of hits in yesterday's game for each player in appropriate text boxes on a form. When a command button is clicked, the program should update the file by adding these numbers to the previous figures. (**Hint:** Open files in the Form_Load event procedure. Close the files and end the program when all data have been processed.)

3. Several players are added to the league. Compose a program to update the file.

4. Compose a program to sort the file AVERAGE.TXT with respect to batting averages and display the players with the top 10 batting averages. **Hint:** The file must be read once to determine the number of players and again to load the players into an array.

Exercises 5 and 6 refer to the ordered file BLOCK.TXT containing the names of people on your block and the ordered file TIMES.TXT containing the names of all people who subscribe to the *New York Times*.

5. Write a program that creates a file consisting of the names of all people on your block who subscribe to the *New York Times*.

6. Write a program that creates a file consisting of the names of all *New York Times* subscribers who do not live on your block.

7. Suppose a file of positive integers is in ascending order. Write a program to determine the maximum number of times any integer is repeated in the file. (For instance, if the entries in the file are 5, 5, 6, 6, 6, and 10, then the output is 3.)

8. Suppose each record of the file SALES.TXT contains a salesperson's name and the dollar amount of a sale, and the records are ordered by the names. Write a program to display the name, number of sales, and average sale amount for each salesperson. For instance, if the first four records of the file are

"Adams", 123.45
"Adams", 432.15
"Brown", 89.95
"Cook", 500.00

then the first two entries of the output would be

Salesperson	Number of Sales	Average Sale Amount
Adams	2	$277.80
Brown	1	$89.95

9. An elementary school holds a raffle to raise funds. Suppose each record of the file RAFFLE.TXT contains a student's grade (1 through 6), name, and the number of raffle tickets sold, and that the records are ordered by grade. Write a program using a control break to display the number of tickets sold by each grade and the total number of tickets sold.

10. *Multiple Control Breaks.* Suppose the sorted sequential file CENSUS.TXT contains names of all residents of a state, where each record has the form "lastName","firstName". Write a program to determine, in one pass through the file, the most common last name and most common full name. (**Note:** In the unlikely event of a tie, the program should display the first occurring name.) For instance, the output in the picture box might be as follows.

```
The most common last name is Brown
The most common full name is John Smith
```

In Exercises 11 and 12, suppose the file MASTER.TXT contains the names and phone numbers of all members of an organization, where the records are ordered by name.

11. Suppose the ordered file MOVED.TXT contains the names and new phone numbers of all members who have changed their phone numbers. Write a program to update the file MASTER.TXT.

12. Suppose the ordered file QUIT.TXT contains the names of all members who have left the organization. Write a program to update the file MASTER.TXT.

13. Suppose a file must be sorted by Visual Basic, but is too large to fit into an array. How can this be accomplished?

14. What are some advantages of files over arrays?

SOLUTIONS TO PRACTICE PROBLEMS 8.2

1. Execution proceeds beyond the first Do loop only when EOF becomes True for one of the input files. Because each of the last two Do loops executes only if EOF is not True, at most one loop can execute.

   Neither of the last two loops will be executed if each input file is empty or if the last entries of the files are the same.

2. Change the SELECT CASE block to the following:

```
Select Case num1
  Case Is <= num2
    Write #3, num1
    Input #1, num1
  Case Is > num2
    Write #3, num2
    Input #2, num2
End Select
```

8.3 A CASE STUDY: RECORDING CHECKS AND DEPOSITS

The purpose of this section is to take you through the design and implementation of a quality program for personal checkbook management. Nothing in this chapter shows off the power of Visual Basic better than the program in this section. That a user-friendly checkbook management program can be written in only four pages of code clearly shows Visual Basic's ability to improve the productivity of programmers. It is easy to imagine an entire finance program, similar to programs that have generated millions of dollars of sales, being written in only a few weeks by using Visual Basic!

The Design of the Program

Though there are many commercial programs available for personal financial management, they include so many bells and whistles that their original purposes—keeping track of transactions and reporting balances—have become obscured. The program in this section was designed specifically as a checkbook program. It keeps track of expenditures and deposits and produces a printed report. Adding a reconciliation feature would be easy enough, although we did not include one.

The program is supposed to be user-friendly. Therefore, it showcases many of the techniques and tools available in Visual Basic.

The general design goals for the program included the abilities to

- Automatically enter the user's name on each check and deposit slip.
- Automatically provide the next consecutive check or deposit slip number. (The user can override this feature if necessary.)
- Automatically provide the date. (Again, this feature can be overridden.)
- For each check, record the payee, the amount, and optionally a memo.
- For each deposit slip, record the source, the amount, and optionally a memo.
- Display the current balance at all times.
- Produce a printout detailing all transactions.

The User Interface

With Visual Basic we can place a replica of a check or deposit slip on the screen and let the user supply the information as if actually filling out a check or deposit slip. Figure 8.5 shows the form in its check mode. A picture box forms the boundary of the check. Below the picture box are two labels for the current balance and four command buttons.

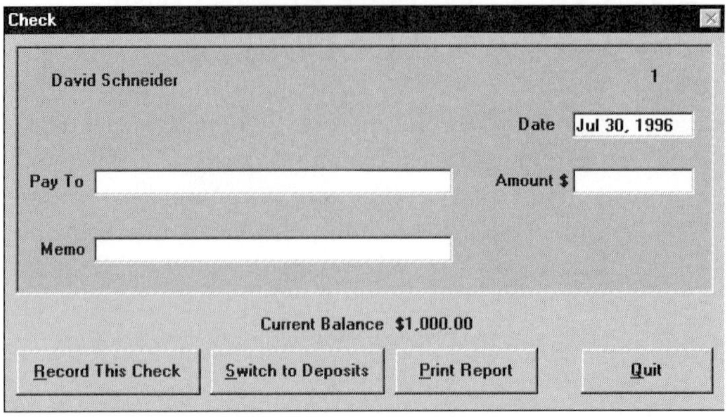

Figure 8.5 Template for entering a check.

The first time the program is run, the user is asked for his or her name, the starting balance, and the numbers of the first check and deposit slip. Suppose the user's name is David Schneider, the first check has number 1, the starting balance is $1000, and the first deposit slip is also number 1. Figure 8.5 shows the form after the three pieces of input. The upper part of the form looks like a check. The check has a color of light turquoise blue (or cyan). The Date box is automatically set to today's date, but can be altered by the user. The user fills in the payee, amount, and optionally a memo. When the user pushes the Record This Check button, the information is written to a file, the balance is updated, and check number 2 appears.

To record a deposit, the user pushes the Switch to Deposits button. The form then appears as in Figure 8.6. The form's title bar now reads Deposit Slip, the words Pay To changes to Source, and the color of the slip changes to yellow. Also, in the buttons at the bottom of the form, the words Check and Deposit are interchanged. A deposit is recorded in much the same way as a check. When the Print Report button is pushed, a printout similar to the one in Figure 8.7 is printed on the printer.

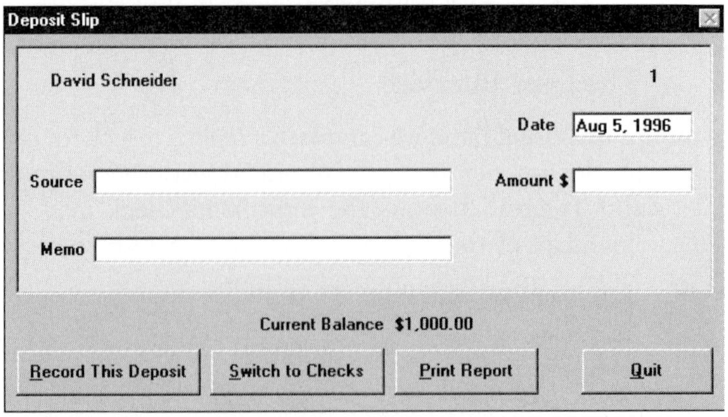

Figure 8.6 Template for entering a deposit slip.

Feb 5, 1995

Name: David Schneider   Starting balance: $1,000.00

Date	Transaction	Amount	Balance
Jan 21, 1996	Check #: 1 Paid to: Land's End Memo: shirts	$75.95	$924.05
Jan 29, 1996	Check #: 2 Paid to: Bethesda Coop Memo: groceries	$125.00	$799.05
Feb 5, 1996	Deposit #: 1 Source: Prentice Hall Memo: typing expenses	$245.00	$1,044.05

Ending Balance: $1,044.05

Figure 8.7 Sample printout of transactions.

The common design for the check and deposit slip allows one set of controls to be used for both items. Figure 8.8 shows the controls and their suggestive names. The caption of the label lblToFrom will change back and forth between Pay To and Source.

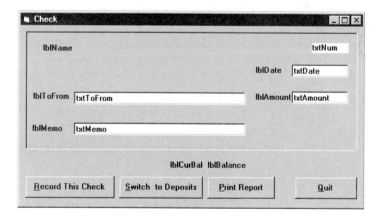

Figure 8.8 Control names for checkbook management program.

Table 8.2 lists the objects and their initial properties. Because the program will always begin by displaying the next check, the various captions and the Background property of the picture box could have been set at design time. We chose instead to leave these assignments to the SetupCheck subprogram, which is normally used to switch from deposit entry to check entry, but also can be called by the Form_Load event procedure to prepare the initial mode (check or deposit) for the form. However, in order to write the setup subprograms, we do note the values that Visual Basic displays for the Background property if we select the light blue or yellow colors from the third row of the color palette. These values are &H00FFFF00& and &H0000FFFF&, respectively.

Object	Property	Setting
frmCheckbook		
picBox		
lblName	BackStyle	0 – Transparent
txtNum	BorderStyle	0 – None
lblDate	BackStyle	0 – Transparent
	Caption	Date
txtDate		
lblToFrom	BackStyle	0 – Transparent
txtToFrom		
lblAmount	BackStyle	0 – Transparent
	Caption	Amount $
txtAmount		
lblMemo	BackStyle	0 – Transparent
	Caption	Memo
txtMemo		
lblCurBal	Caption	Current Balance
lblBalance		
cmdRecord		
cmdMode		
cmdPrint	Caption	&Print Report
cmdQuit	Caption	&Quit

Table 8.2 Objects and initial properties for the checkbook management program.

The transactions are stored in a data file named CHKBOOK.TXT. The first four entries of the file are the name to appear on the check or deposit slip, the starting balance, the number of the first check, and the number of the first deposit slip. After that, each transaction is recorded as a sequence of eight items—the type of transaction, the contents of txtToFrom, the current balance, the number of the last check, the number of the last deposit slip, the amount of money, the memo, and the date.

Coding the Program

The top row of Figure 8.9 shows the different events to which the program must respond. Table 8.3 identifies the corresponding event procedures and the general procedures they call.

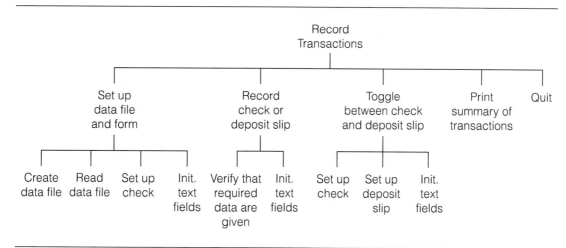

Figure 8.9 Hierarchy chart for checkbook management program.

Task	Procedure
1. Set up data file and form	Form_Load
1.1 Create data file	CreateDataFile
1.2 Read data file	ReadDataFile
1.3 Set up check	SetupCheck
1.4 Initialize text fields	InitializeFields
2. Record check or deposit slip	cmdRecord_Click
2.1 Verify that required data are given	AllDataGiven
2.2 Initialize text fields	InitializeFields
3. Toggle between check & deposit slip	cmdMode_Click
3.1 Set up check	SetupCheck
3.2 Set up deposit slip	SetupDeposit
3.3 Initialize text fields	InitializeFields
4. Print summary of transaction	cmdPrint_Click
5. Quit	cmdQuit_Click

Table 8.3 Tasks and their procedures.

Let's examine each event procedure.

1. Form_Load first looks to see if the file CHKBOOK.TXT has been created. The function Dir returns "CHKBOOK.TXT" if the file exists and otherwise returns the empty string. If CHKBOOK.TXT does not exist, the routine CreateDataFile is called. CreateDataFile prompts the user for the name to appear on the checks and deposit slips, the starting balance, and the numbers of the first check and deposit slip, and then writes these items to the data file. If CHKBOOK.TXT does exist, the routine ReadDataFile is called to read through the entire file to determine all information needed to proceed. The event procedure calls SetupCheck to set the transaction type to Check and set the appropriate captions and background colors for a check. The event procedure then calls InitializeFields, which initializes all the text boxes.

In the first Let statement of the procedure, the drive is specified as the A drive. Therefore, the data file will be written to and read from a diskette on the A drive. Feel free to change the letter A to whatever drive you prefer. You may even want to specify an entire path.

2. **cmdRecord_Click** first confirms that the required fields contain entries. This is accomplished by calling the function AllDataGiven. If the value returned is "YES", then cmdRecord_Click opens the data file for output as Append, sends eight pieces of data to the file, and then closes the file. When AllDataGiven returns "NO", the function itself pops up a message box to tell the user where information is needed. The user must type in the information and then press the Record button again.

3. **cmdMode_Click** toggles back and forth from a check to a deposit slip. It calls SetupCheck, or its analog SetupDeposit, and then calls InitializeFields.

4. **cmdPrint_Click** prints out a complete history of all transactions, as shown in Figure 8.7.

5. **cmdQuit_Click** ends the program.

```
Rem Record Checks and Deposits
Rem
Rem *************************************************************************
Rem *                                                                      *
Rem *   fileName      Name of the file containing previous data, if any    *
Rem *   nameOnChk     Name to appear on checks                             *
Rem *   lastCkNum     Number of last check written                        *
Rem *   lastDpNum     Number of last deposit slip processed               *
Rem *   curBal        Current balance in account                          *
Rem *   transType     Type of transaction, check or deposit               *
Rem *                                                                      *
Rem *************************************************************************

Dim fileName As String, nameOnChk As String
Dim lastCkNum As Integer, lastDpNum As Integer
Dim curBal As Single, transType As String

Private Function AllDataGiven() As String
  Dim message As String
  Rem If one of the four required pieces of information
  Rem is missing, assign its name to message
  Let message = ""
  If txtDate.Text = "" Then
      Let message = "Date"
      txtDate.SetFocus
    ElseIf txtToFrom.Text = "" Then
      If transType = "Check" Then
          Let message = "Pay To"
        Else
          Let message = "Source"
      End If
      txtToFrom.SetFocus
```

```
     ElseIf txtAmount.Text = "" Then
        Let message = "Amount"
        txtAmount.SetFocus
      ElseIf txtNum.Text = "" Then
        If transType = "Check" Then
           Let message = "Check Number"
          Else
           Let message = "Deposit Number"
        End If
        txtNum.SetFocus
    End If
    If message = "" Then
        Rem All required data fields have been filled; recording can proceed
        AllDataGiven = "YES"
      Else
        Rem Advise user of required data that are missing
        MsgBox "The '" & message & "' field must be filled", , "Error"
        AllDataGiven = "NO"
    End If
End Function


Private Sub cmdMode_Click()
  Rem Toggle from Check to/from Deposit Slip
  If transType = "Check" Then
      Call SetupDeposit
    Else    'transType = "Deposit"
      Call SetupCheck
  End If
  Call InitializeFields
  txtToFrom.SetFocus
End Sub


Private Sub cmdPrint_Click()
  Dim temp As String, lineNo As Integer
  Dim nameOnChk As String, balance As Single, ck As Integer, dp As Integer
  Dim toFrom As String, amount As String, memo As String, theDate As String
  Rem Print out a detailed list of all transactions.
  Let temp = frmCheckbook.Caption              'Save the current form caption
  Let frmCheckbook.Caption = "Printing..."     'Set form caption to indicate printing
  Let lineNo = 1                               'Line number being printed
  Open fileName For Input As #1                'Open the file
  Input #1, nameOnChk, balance, ck, dp         'Read in the file header
  Rem Print the details of the individual transactions.
  Do Until EOF(1)
    If lineNo >= 57 Then
        Rem 57 or more lines have been printed; start a new page
        Printer.NewPage
        Let lineNo = 1
    End If
    If lineNo = 1 Then
        Rem Print the report header
        Printer.Print
        Printer.Print "Name: ";nameOnChk;Tab(65);Format(Date, "mmm d, yyyy")
        Printer.Print
```

```
            Printer.Print , "Starting balance: "; Format(balance, "Currency")
            Printer.Print
            Printer.Print "Date", "Transaction"; Tab(50); "Amount";
            Printer.Print Tab(65); "Balance"
            Printer.Print "____", "_____"; Tab(50); "_____";
            Printer.Print Tab(65); "_____"
            Printer.Print
            Printer.Print
            Let lineNo = 10
        End If
        Input #1, transType, toFrom, balance, ck, dp, amount, memo, theDate
        If transType = "Check" Then
            Printer.Print theDate, "Check #: "; ck; Tab(50); amount;
            Printer.Print Tab(65); Format(balance, "Currency")
            Printer.Print , "Paid to: "; toFrom
          Else              'Transaction was a deposit
            Printer.Print theDate, "Deposit #: "; dp; Tab(50); amount;
            Printer.Print Tab(65); Format(balance, "Currency")
            Printer.Print , "Source: "; toFrom
        End If
        Let lineNo = lineNo + 2
        Rem If there was a memo, then print it.
        If memo <> "" Then
            Printer.Print , "Memo: "; memo
            Let lineNo = lineNo + 1
        End If
        Printer.Print
        Let lineNo = lineNo + 1
    Loop
    Close #1                        'Close the file
    Rem Print the ending balance
    Printer.Print
    Printer.Print , "Ending Balance: "; Format(balance, "Currency")
    Printer.EndDoc                      'Send the output to the Printer
    Let frmCheckbook.Caption = temp     'Restore the form caption
    txtToFrom.SetFocus                  'Set focus for the next entry
End Sub

Private Sub cmdQuit_Click()
  Rem  Exit the program
  End
End Sub

Private Sub cmdRecord_Click()
  Dim amt As String, amount As Single, itemNum As Integer
  Rem Check to ensure all required fields are filled
  If AllDataGiven() = "YES" Then
      Let amt = txtAmount.Text 'Amount of transaction as string
      Let amount = Val(amt)     'Amount of transaction as number
      Let amt = Format(amt, "Currency")
      Let itemNum = Val(txtNum.Text)
      If transType = "Check" Then
          Let curBal = curBal - amount
          Let lastCkNum = itemNum
```

```
        Else              'transType = "Deposit"
           Let curBal = curBal + amount
           Let lastDpNum = itemNum
        End If
        Let lblBalance.Caption = Format(curBal, "Currency")
        Open fileName For Append As #1
        Write #1, transType, txtToFrom.Text, curBal, lastCkNum, lastDpNum, amt, _
                txtMemo.Text, txtDate.Text
        Close #1
        Call InitializeFields
        txtToFrom.SetFocus
    End If
End Sub


Private Sub CreateDataFile()
   Dim startBal As Single, ckNum As integer
   Rem The first time the program is run, create a data file
   Open fileName For Output As #1
   Let nameOnChk = InputBox("Name to appear on checks:")
   Let startBal = Val(InputBox("Starting balance:"))
   Let ckNum = Val(InputBox("Number of the first check:"))
   Let lastCkNum = ckNum - 1    'Number of "last" check written
   Let ckNum = Val(InputBox("Number of the first deposit slip:"))
   Let lastDpNum = ckNum - 1    'Number of "last" deposit slip processed
   Let curBal = startBal        'Set current balance
   Rem First record in data file records name to appear on checks
   Rem plus initial data for account
   Write #1, nameOnChk, startBal, lastCkNum, lastDpNum
   Close #1
End Sub


Private Sub Form_Load()
   Dim drive As String
   Rem If no data file exists, create one. Otherwise, open the
   Rem data file and get the user's name, last used check and
   Rem deposit slip numbers, and current balance.
   Rem In next line adjust drive as necessary
   Let drive = "A:"                   'Drive (or path) for data file
   Let fileName = drive & "CHKBOOK.TXT"  'Program uses one data file
   If Dir(fileName) = "" Then
       Rem Data file does not exist, so create it and obtain initial data
       Call CreateDataFile
     Else
       Call ReadDataFile
   End If
   Rem Set name and balance labels
   Let lblName.Caption = nameOnChk
   Let lblBalance.Caption = Format(curBal, "Currency")
   Rem Set the date field to the current date
   Let txtDate.Text = Format(Date, "mmm d, yyyy")
   Call SetupCheck                   'Always start session with checks
   Call InitializeFields
End Sub
```

```
Private Sub InitializeFields()
  Rem Initialize all text entry fields except date
  Let txtToFrom.Text = ""
  Let txtAmount.Text = ""
  Let txtMemo.Text = ""
  If transType = "Check" Then
      Rem Make txtNum text box reflect next check number
      Let txtNum.Text = Format(lastCkNum + 1, "#")
    Else              'transType = "Deposit"
      Rem Make txtNum text box reflect next deposit slip number
      Let txtNum.Text = Format(lastDpNum + 1, "#")
  End If
End Sub


Private Sub ReadDataFile()
  Dim t As String, s As String, n As String, m As String, d As String
  Rem Recover name to appear on checks, current balance,
  Rem number of last check written, and number of last deposit slip processed
  Open fileName For Input As #1
  Input #1, nameOnChk, curBal, lastCkNum, lastDpNum
  Do Until EOF(1)
    Rem Read to the end of the file to recover the current balance and the
    Rem last values recorded for ckNum and dpNum.
    Rem t, s, n, m and d are dummy variables and are not used at this point
    Input #1, t, s, curBal, lastCkNum, lastDpNum, n, m, d
  Loop
  Close #1
End Sub


Private Sub SetupCheck()
  Rem Prepare form for the entry of a check
  Let transType = "Check"
  Let frmCheckbook.Caption = "Check"
  Let lblToFrom.Caption = "Pay To"
  Let cmdRecord.Caption = "&Record This Check"
  Let cmdMode.Caption = "&Switch to Deposits"
  Let picBox.BackColor = &H00FFFF00&" ' color of check is light blue
  Let txtNum.BackColor = &H00FFFF00&
End Sub


Private Sub SetupDeposit()
  Rem Prepare form for the entry of a deposit
  Let transType = "Deposit"
  Let frmCheckbook.Caption = "Deposit Slip"
  Let lblToFrom.Caption = "Source"
  Let cmdRecord.Caption = "&Record This Deposit"
  Let cmdMode.Caption = "&Switch to Checks"
  Let picBox.BackColor = &H0000FFFF& ' color of deposit slip is yellow
  Let txtNum.BackColor = &H0000FFFF&
End Sub
```

Chapter 8
Summary

1. When sequential files are *opened*, we must specify whether they will be created and written to, added to, or read from by use of the terms Output, Append, or Input. The file must be *closed* before the operation is changed. Data are written to the file with Write# statements and retrieved with Input# statements. The EOF function tells if we have read to the end of the file.

2. A sequential file can be ordered by placing its data in arrays, sorting the arrays, and then writing the ordered data into a file. This process should precede adding, deleting, or altering items in a master file.

Chapter 8
Programming Projects

1. Table 8.3 gives the leading eight soft drinks and their percentage share of the market. Write and execute a program to place these data into a sequential file. Then write a second program to use the file to

   (a) display the eight brands and their gross sales in billions. (The entire soft drink industry grosses about $40 billion.)
   (b) calculate the total percentage market share of the leading eight soft drinks.

Coke Classic	20.2	Diet Pepsi	5.7
Pepsi	15.5	Mountain Dew	5.6
Diet Coke	8.8	Sprite	4.9
Dr. Pepper	6.1	7 Up	2.8

Table 8.3 Leading soft drinks and percentages of market share.
Source: Beverage Digest, 1996

2. Suppose the sequential file ALE.TXT contains the information shown in Table 8.4. Write a program to use the file to produce Table 8.5 in which the baseball teams are in descending order by the percentage of games won.

Team	Won	Lost
Baltimore	88	74
Boston	85	77
Detroit	53	109
New York	92	70
Toronto	74	88

Table 8.4 American League East games won and lost in 1996.

American League East			
	W	L	Pct
New York	92	70	.568
Baltimore	88	74	.543
Boston	85	77	.525
Toronto	74	88	.457
Detroit	53	109	.327

Table 8.5 Final 1996 American League East standings.

3. Write a rudimentary word processing program. The program should do the following:

   (a) Use InputBox to request the name of the sequential file to hold the document being created.
   (b) Set the label for a text box to "Enter Line 1" and allow the user to enter the first line of the document into a text box.
   (c) When the Enter key is pressed or a "Record Line" command button is clicked, determine if the line is acceptable. Blank lines are acceptable input, but lines exceeding 60 characters in length should not be accepted. Advise the user of the problem with a message box, and then set the focus back to the text box so that the user can edit the line to an acceptable length.
   (c) When an acceptable line is entered, write this line to the file and display it in a picture box.
   (d) Change the prompt to "Enter Line 2", clear the text box, allow the user to enter the second line of the document into the text box, and carry out (c) for this line using the same picture box. (Determine in advance how many lines the picture box can display and only clear the picture box when the lines already displayed do not leave room for a new line.)
   (e) Continue as in (d) with appropriate labels for subsequent lines until the user clicks on a "Finished" command button.
   (f) Clear the picture box and display the number of lines written and the name of the data file created.

4. Write a program that counts the number of times a word occurs in the sequential file created in Programming Project 3. The file name and word should be read from text boxes. The search should not be sensitive to the case of the letters. For instance, opening a file that contained the first three sentences of the directions to this problem and searching for "the" would produce the output: "the" occurs six times.

5. *Create and Maintain Telephone Directories.* Write a program to create and maintain telephone directories. Each directory will be a separate sequential file. The following command buttons should be available:

   (a) Select a directory to access. A list of directories that have been created should be stored in a separate sequential file. When a request is made to open a directory, the list of available directories should be displayed as part of an InputBox prompt requesting the name of the directory to be accessed. If the user responds with a directory name not listed, the desire to create a new directory should be confirmed, and then the new directory created and added to the list of existing directories.

(b) Add name and phone number (as given in the text boxes) to the end of the current directory.

(c) Delete name (as given in the text box) from the current directory.

(d) Sort the current directory into name order.

(e) Print out the names and phone numbers contained in the current directory.

(f) Terminate the program.

6. Table 8.6 contains the statistics for a stock portfolio.

Stock	Number of Shares	Date Purchased	Purchase Price/Share	Current Price/Share
AT&T	200	12/4/84	18 3/4	51 1/4
GM	600	4/16/85	61 5/8	47 1/2
IBM	300	8/8/85	129 1/4	103 5/8
Xerox	400	11/16/85	56 5/8	50 1/8
Exxon	100	3/1/86	52 1/4	83 7/8

Table 8.6 Stock portfolio.

(a) Compose a program to create the sequential file STOCKS.TXT containing the information in Table 8.6.

(b) Compose a program to perform the following tasks. A possible form design is shown in Figure 8.10.

(1) Display the information in the file STOCKS.TXT as in Table 8.6 when the user clicks on a "Display Stocks" command button.

(2) Add an additional stock onto the end of the file STOCKS.TXT when the user clicks on an "Add Stock" command button. The data for the new stock should be read from appropriately labeled text boxes.

(3) Update the Current Price/Share of a stock in the file STOCKS.TXT when the user clicks on an "Update Price" command button. The name of the stock to be updated and the new price should be read from the appropriate text boxes. The file STOCKS.TXT should then be copied to a temp file until the specified stock is found. The update record for this stock should then be written to the temp file, followed by all remaining records in STOCKS.TXT. Finally, the original STOCKS.TXT file should be erased and the temp file renamed to STOCKS.TXT.

(4) Process the data in the file STOCKS.TXT and produce the display shown in Figure 8.11 when a "Show Profit/Loss" command button is clicked.

(5) Quit.

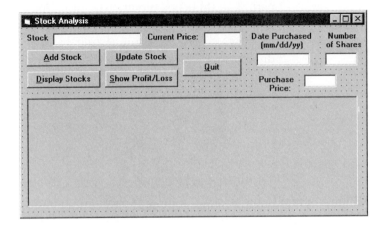

Figure 8.10 Possible form design for Programming Project 6.

Stock	Cost	Current Value	Profit (or Loss)
AT&T	$3,750.00	$10,250.00	$6,500.00
GM	$36,975.00	$28,500.00	($8,475.00)
IBM	$38,775.00	$31,087.50	($7,687.50)
Xerox	$22,650.00	$20,050.00	($2,600.00)
Exxon	$5,225.00	$8,387.50	$3,162.50

Figure 8.11 Output of Project 6.

7. A department store has a file containing all sales transacted for a year. Each record contains a customer's name, zip code, and amount of the sale. The file is ordered first by zip code and then by name. Write a program to display the total sales for each customer, the total sales for each zip code, and the total sales for the store. For instance, if the first six records of the file are

```
"Adams, John", 10023, 34.50
"Adams, John", 10023, 60.00
"Jones, Bob", 10023, 62.45
"Green, Mary", 12345, 54.00
"Howard, Sue", 12345, 79.25
"Smith, George", 20001, 25.10
```

then the output in the picture box will begin as shown in Figure 8.12.

```
Customer      Total Sales
Adams, John   $94.50
Jones, Bob    $62.45
      Total sales of zip code 10023: $156.95
Green, Mary   $54.00
```

Figure 8.12 Sample output for Programming Project 7.

8. *Savings Account.* FILE1.TXT is a sequential file containing the name, account number, and beginning-of-month balance for each depositor. FILE2.TXT is a sequential file containing all the transactions (deposits and withdrawals) for the month. Use FILE2.TXT to upgrade FILE1.TXT. For each customer, print a statement similar to the one received from banks that shows all trans-actions and the end-of-month balance. Also, record all overdrawn accounts in a file. (As an optional embellishment, deduct a penalty if the balance fell below a certain level any time during the month. The penalty could include a fixed fee of $10 plus a charge of $1 for each check and deposit.) **Hint:** Assume no more than 500 transactions have occurred.

9. A fuel economy study was carried out for five models of cars. Each car was driven for 100 miles of city driving, and then the model of the car and the number of gallons used were placed in the sequential file MILEAGE.TXT with the statement

```
Write #1, modelName, gallons
```

Table 8.7 shows the first entries of the file. Write a program to display the models and their average miles per gallon in decreasing order with respect to mileage. The program should utilize three parallel arrays of range 1 to 5. The first array should record the name of each model of car. This array is initially empty; each car model name is added when first encountered in reading the file. The second array should record the number of test vehicles for each model. The third array should record the total number of gallons used by that model. **Note:** The first array must be searched each time a record is read to determine the appropriate index to use with the other two arrays.

Model	Gal	Model	Gal	Model	Gal
LeBaron	4.9	Cutlass	4.5	Cutlass	4.6
Escort	4.1	Escort	3.8	LeBaron	5.1
Beretta	4.3	Escort	3.9	Escort	3.8
Skylark	4.5	Skylark	4.6	Cutlass	4.4

Table 8.7 Gallons of gasoline used in 100 miles of city driving.

9

Random-Access Files

9.1 User Defined Data Types / 436
   • Fixed-Length Strings • Records

9.2 Random-Access Files / 446

   Summary / 453

   Programming Projects / 454

9.1 USER DEFINED DATA TYPES

Records provide a convenient way of packaging as a single unit several related variables of different types. Before we can explore this powerful variable type, we must first explore a new category of variable, the fixed-length string.

Fixed-Length Strings

Fixed-length string variables are named following the same rules as other variable types. They are declared by statements of the form

```
Dim var As String * n
```

where n is a positive integer. After such a declaration, the value of *var* will always be a string of length n. Suppose *info* is an ordinary string and a statement of the form

```
Let var = info
```

is executed. If *info* has more than n characters, then only the first n characters will be assigned to *var*. If *info* has less than n characters, then spaces will be added to the end of the string to guarantee that *var* has length n.

EXAMPLE 1 The following program uses fixed-length strings. In the output, San Francisco is truncated to a string of length 9 and Detroit is padded on the right with two blank spaces.

```
Private Sub cmdGo_Click()
   Dim city As String * 9
   Rem Illustrate fixed-length strings
   picOutput.Cls
   picOutput.Print "123456789"
   Let city = "San Francisco"
   picOutput.Print city
   Let city = "Detroit"
   picOutput.Print city; "MI"
   picOutput.Print Len(city)
End Sub
```

[Set picOutput's Font property to Courier. Run and click the command button.]

Care must be taken when comparing an ordinary (variable-length) string with a fixed-length string or comparing two fixed-length strings of different lengths.

EXAMPLE 2 In the following program, the strings assigned to the variables *town*, *city*, and *municipality* have lengths 7, 9, and 12, respectively, and therefore are all different.

```
Private Sub cmdGo_Click()
  Dim town As String * 7
  Dim city As String * 9
  Dim municipality As String * 12
  Rem Illustrate fixed-length strings
  Let town = "Chicago"
  Let city = "Chicago"
  Let municipality = "Chicago"
  picOutput.Cls
  If (city = town) Or (city = municipality) Then
      picOutput.Print "same"
    Else
      picOutput.Print "different"
  End If
  picOutput.Print "123456789012345"
  picOutput.Print city & "***"
  picOutput.Print town & "***"
  picOutput.Print municipality & "***"
End Sub
```

[Set picOutput's Font property to Courier. Run and click the command button.]

There are times when we want to consider the values assigned to variables of different types as being the same, such as *city* and *town* in Example 2. In this situation, the function RTrim comes to the rescue. If *info* is an ordinary string or a fixed-length string, then the value of

```
RTrim(info)
```

is the (variable-length) string consisting of *info* with all right-hand spaces removed. For instance, the value of RTrim("hello   ") is the string "hello". In Example 2, if the If block is changed to

```
If (RTrim(city) = town) And (RTrim(city) = RTrim(municipality)) Then
    picOutput.Print "same"
  Else
    picOutput.Print "different"
End If
```

then the first line of the output will be "same".

Records

In this text, we have worked with numbers, strings, arrays, and now fixed-length strings. Strings and numbers are built-in data types that can be used without being declared, although we have always elected to declare numeric and string variables using Dim statements. On the other hand, arrays and fixed-length strings are user-defined data types that must be declared with a Dim statement before being used. A record is a user-defined data type that groups related variables of different types.

Figure 9.1 shows an index card that can be used to hold data about colleges. The three pieces of data—name, state, and year founded—are called **fields**. Each field functions like a variable in which information can be stored and retrieved. The **length** of a field is the number of spaces allocated to it. In the case of the index card, we see that there are three fields having lengths 30, 2, and 4, respectively. The layout of the index card can be identified by a name, such as collegeData, called a record type.

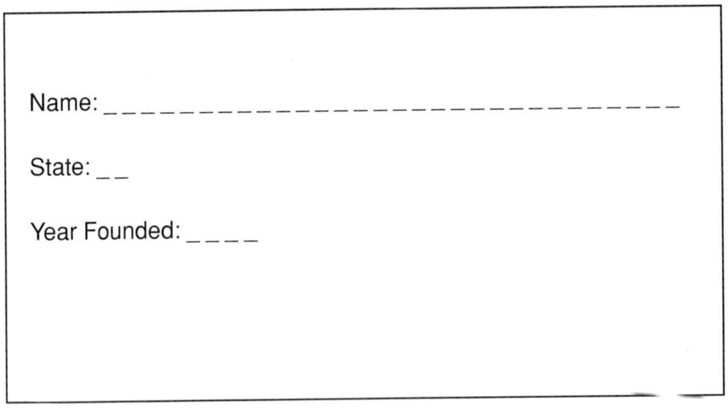

```
Name: _ _ _ _ _ _ _ _ _ _ _ _ _ _ _ _ _ _ _ _ _ _ _ _ _ _ _ _ _

State: _ _

Year Founded: _ _ _ _
```

Figure 9.1 An index card having three fields.

For programming purposes, the layout of the record is declared by a block of statements similar to

```
Type collegeData
  nom As String * 30
  state As String * 2
  yearFounded As Integer
End Type
```

Each character of a string is stored in a piece of memory known as a byte. Therefore, a field of type String * *n* requires *n* bytes of memory. However, numbers (that is, the integer or single-precision numbers we use in this text) are stored in a different manner than strings. Integer numbers *always* use two bytes of memory, whereas single-precision numbers *always* use four bytes of memory.

Visual Basic requires that Type declarations, such as the preceding record structure *collegeData*, be placed in either (General) or in a special file, referred to as a BAS Module. When placed in the (General) portion of a form, the word "Type" must be preceded by "Private" and the record type is only valid for that form. When placed in a BAS module, the word "Type" may be preceded by either "Private" (valid for the current BAS module) or "Public" (valid throughout the entire program). In this text, we will primarily place our declarations inside BAS Modules and make them Public.

To create a BAS Module for the program currently being designed, press Alt/P/M and double-click on Module. A window like the one in Figure 9.2 will appear. This window is where our Type declarations will be entered. To switch between this BAS Module window and the form(s), press Ctrl+R to activate the Project Explorer and double-click on a form or module. (When the program is saved, the information in the BAS Module will be saved in a separate file with the extension bas.) You can also switch between the BAS Module and form windows by clicking on any portion of the desired window that is sticking out from behind the currently active window.

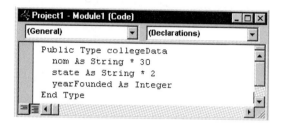

Figure 9.2 BAS Module window for type declarations.

A record variable capable of holding the data for a specific college is declared in the form code by a statement such as

```
Dim college As collegeData
```

Each field is accessed by giving the name of the record variable and the field, separated by a period. For instance, the three fields of the record variable college are accessed as *college.nom*, *college.state*, and *college.yearFounded*. Figure 9.3 shows a representation of the way the record variable is organized.

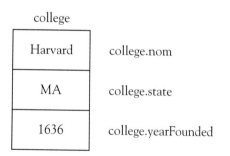

Figure 9.3 Record variable with values assigned to the fields.

In general, a record type is created in a BAS Module by a Type block of the form

```
Public Type recordType
  fieldName1 As fieldType1
  fieldname2 As fieldType2
    .
    .
    .
End Type
```

where *recordType* is the name of the user-defined data type; *fieldName1*, *fieldName2*, . . . are the names of the fields of the record variable; and *fieldType1*, *fieldType2*, . . . are the corresponding field types, either String * *n*, (for some *n*), Integer, or Single in this text. In the form code, a record variable *recordVar* is declared to be of the user-defined type by a statement of the form

```
Dim recordVar As recordType
```

EXAMPLE 3   The following program processes records.

```
Rem In BAS Module        user.
Public Type collegeData  defined
  nom As String * 30      data
  state As String * 2
  yearFounded As Integer
End Type

Rem In Form Module
Private Sub cmdProcess_Click()
  Dim century As Integer, when As String
  Rem Demonstrate use of records
  picResult.Cls
  Dim college As collegeData
  Let college.nom = txtCollege.Text
  Let college.state = txtState.Text
  Let college.yearFounded = Val(txtYear.Text)
  Let century = 1 + Int(college.yearFounded / 100)
  picResult.Print RTrim(college.nom); " was founded in the" & Str(century);
  picResult.Print "th century in "; college.state
  Dim university As collegeData
  Let university.nom = "M.I.T."
  Let university.state = "MA"
  Let university.yearFounded = 1878
  If college.yearFounded < university.yearFounded Then
      Let when = "before "
    Else
      Let when = "after "
  End If
  picResult.Print RTrim(college.nom); " was founded ";
  picResult.Print when; RTrim(university.nom)
End Sub
```

[Run, type the following data into text boxes, and press the command button.]

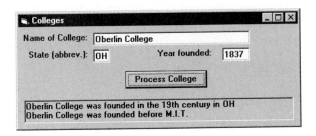

Dim statements can be used in procedures to declare a local record variable. When records are passed to and from procedures, the parameter in the Private Sub or Function statement must have the form

parameter As *recordType*

EXAMPLE 4   The following program uses procedures to perform the same tasks as the program in Example 3.

```
Rem In BAS Module
Public Type collegeData
  nom As String * 30
  state As String * 2
  yearFounded As Integer
End Type

Rem In Form Module
Private Sub cmdProcess_Click()
  Rem Demonstrate use of records
  picBox.Cls
  Dim college As collegeData
  Call GetDat(college)
  Call DisplayStatement(college)
End Sub

Private Sub DisplayStatement(school As collegeData)
  Dim century As Integer, when As String
  Let century = 1 + Int(school.yearFounded / 100)
  picBox.Print RTrim(school.nom); " was founded in the" & Str(century);
  picBox.Print "th century in "; school.state
  Dim university As collegeData
  Let university.nom = "M.I.T."
  Let university.state = "MA"
  Let university.yearFounded = 1878
  If school.yearFounded < university.yearFounded Then
      Let when = "before "
    Else
      Let when = "after "
  End If
  picBox.Print RTrim(school.nom); " was founded ";
  picBox.Print when; RTrim(university.nom)
End Sub

Private Sub GetDat(school As collegeData)
  Let school.nom = txtCollege.Text
  Let school.state = txtState.Text
  Let school.yearFounded = Val(txtYear.Text)
End Sub
```

Comments

1. Record variables are similar to arrays in that they both store and access data items using a common name. However, the elements in an array must be of the same data type, whereas the fields in a record variable can be a mixture of different data types. Also, the different elements of an array are identified by their indices, whereas the fields of a record are identified by a name following a period.

2. If the record variables *recVar1* and *recVar2* have the same type, then all the field values of *recVar2* can be assigned simultaneously to *recVar1* by the statement

   ```
   Let recVar1 = recVar2
   ```

3. Statements of the form

   ```
   picBox.Print recVar
   ```

   are invalid, where *recVar* is a record variable. Each field of a record must appear separately in a picBox.Print statement. Also, comparisons involving records using the relational operators <, >, =, <>, <=, and >= are valid only with the record fields, and not with the records themselves.

4. In addition to being declared as numeric or fixed-length string data types, the elements of a user-defined variable type can also be declared as other types of records. However, we do not use such structures in this text.

5. An array of fixed-length strings is declared by a statement of the form

   ```
   Dim arrayName (a To b) As String * n
   ```

6. An array of records would be declared with a statement such as

   ```
   Dim colleges(1 To 8) As collegeData
   ```

   and information would be accessed with statements such as

   ```
   picBox.Print colleges(1).nom
   ```

7. When fixed-length strings are passed to and from procedures, the corresponding parameter in the Sub or Function statement must be an ordinary (variable-length) string.

8. Most data types can be used as field types appearing in a Type block, including (variable-length) strings. However, the String data type is not allowed in Type blocks that will be used with random-access files.

PRACTICE PROBLEMS 9.1

1. Find the errors in the following event procedure. Assume that the record variable *squad* will be used to place information into a random-access file.

   ```
   Private Sub cmdDisplay_Click()
     Public Type Team
       school As String
       mascot As String
     End Type
   ```

```
    Dim squad As Team
    Let squad.school = "Rice"
    Let squad.mascot = "Owls"
    picOutput.Print squad.school & " " & squad.mascot
End Sub
```

2. Correct the code in Problem 1.

EXERCISES 9.1

In Exercises 1 through 4, determine the output displayed in the picture box when the command button is clicked.

1.
```
Private Sub cmdDisplay_Click()
    Dim ocean As String * 10
    Dim river As String * 10
    Let ocean = "Pacific"
    Let river = "Mississippi"
    picOutput.Print ocean; river
End Sub
```

2.
```
Private Sub cmdDisplay_Click()
    Dim color As String
    Dim colour as String * 6
    Let colour = "Blue"
    Let color = "Red"
    picOutput.Print colour; color; colour
End Sub
```

3.
```
Rem In BAS Module
Public Type appearance
  height As Single
  weight As Single
  eyeColor As String * 5
End Type

Rem In Form code
Private Sub cmdDisplay_Click()
  Dim person1 As appearance
  Dim person2 As appearance
  Let person1.height = 72
  Let person1.weight = 170
  Let person1.eyeColor = "brown"
  Let person2.height = 12 * 6
  Let person2.weight = person1.weight
  Let person2.eyeColor = "brownish green"
  If person1.height = person2.height Then
      picOutput.Print "heights are same"
  End If
  picOutput.Print person2.weight
  If person1.eyeColor = person2.eyeColor Then
      picOutput.Print "eye colors are same"
  End If
End Sub
```

4.
```
Rem In BAS Module
Public Type testData
  nom As String * 5
  score As Single
End Type

Rem In Form Module
Private Sub cmdDisplay_Click()
  Dim i As Integer
  Dim student As testData
  Open "SCORES.TXT" For Input As #1
  picOutput.Cls
  For i = 1 to 3
    Call GetScore(student)
    Call PrintScore(student)
  Next i
  Close #1
End Sub

Private Sub GetScore(student As testData)
  Input #1, student.nom, student.score
End Sub

Private Sub PrintScore(student As testData)
  picOutput.Print student.nom; student.score
End Sub
```

(Assume that the file SCORES.TXT contains the following three lines.)

"Joe", 18
"Moe", 20
"Albert", 25

In Exercises 5 through 10, determine the errors.

5.
```
Rem In BAS Module
Public Type zodiac
  nom As String * 15
  sign As String * 11
End Type

Rem In Form code
Private Sub cmdDisplay_Click()
  Dim astrology As zodiac
  Let nom = "Michael"
  Let sign = "Sagittarius"
End Sub
```

6.
```
Private Sub cmdDisplay_Click()
  Public Type address
    street As String * 30
    city As String * 20
    state As String * 2
    zip As String * 10
  End Type
```

```
Dim whiteHouse As address
Let whiteHouse.street = "1600 Pennsylvania Avenue"
Let whiteHouse.city = "Washington"
Let whiteHouse.state = "DC"
Let whiteHouse.zip = "20500"
End Sub
```

7.
```
Rem In BAS Module
Public Type employee
  name As String * 15
  socSecNum As String * 11
  payRate As Single
  exemptions As Integer
  maritalStat As String * 1

Rem In Form code
Private Sub cmdDisplay_Click()
  Let employee.name = "Bob"
End Sub
```

8.
```
Public Type print
  firstWord As String * 5
  secondWord As String * 5
End Type
```

9.
```
Public Type values
  label As String * 5
  var2 As Number
End Type
```

10.
```
Rem In BAS Module
Public Type vitamins
  a As Single
  b As Single
End Type

Rem In Form code
Private Sub cmdDisplay_Click()
  Dim minimum As vitamins
  Let minimum.b = 200
  Let minimum.a = 500
  picOutput.Print minimum
End Sub
```

In Exercises 11 through 14, write a Type block to declare a user-defined data type of the given name and types of elements.

11. Name: planet; Elements: planetName, distanceFromSun

12. Name: taxData; Elements: SSN, grossIncome, taxableIncome

13. Name: car; Elements: make, model, year, mileage

14. Name: party; Elements: numberOfGuests, address

15. Write a program that reads words from three text boxes and then displays them in a picture box in the first three zones without using any commas in the picOutput.Print statement. Do this by declaring the variables used to hold the words as fixed-length strings of the appropriate length, and setting the Font property of the picture box to Courier.

16. Write a program to look up data on notable tall buildings. The program should declare a user-defined data type named "building" with the elements "nom", "city", "height", and "stories". This interactive program should allow the user to type the name of a building into a text box and then search through a data file to determine the city, height, and number of stories of the building when a command button is pressed. If the building is not in the data file, then the program should so report. Use the information in Table 9.1 for the data file.

Building	City	Height (ft)	Stories
Empire State	New York	1250	102
Sears Tower	Chicago	1454	110
Texas Commerce Tower	Houston	1002	75
Transamerica Pyramid	San Francisco	853	48

Table 9.1 Tallest buildings.

SOLUTIONS TO PRACTICE PROBLEMS 9.1

1. The event procedure contains two errors, both related to the Type declaration. First, the Type declaration cannot be inside a procedure. Instead, we enter the Type declaration in a BAS Module. Second, strings in a Type declaration to be used with a random-access file must be of fixed length; an asterisk and a whole number must follow String in defining the elements *school* and *mascot*.

2. In addition to correcting the errors that Visual Basic notices, we also need to keep the output looking as intended, thus the addition of the RTrim functions that follow.

```
Rem In BAS Module
Public Type Team
  school As String * 20
  mascot As String * 20
End Type

Rem In Form code
Private Sub cmdDisplay_Click()
  Dim squad As Team
  Let squad.school = "Rice"
  Let squad.mascot = "Owls"
  picOutput.Print RTrim(squad.school) & " " & RTrim(squad.mascot)
End Sub
```

9.2 RANDOM-ACCESS FILES

A random-access file is like an array of records stored on a disk. The records are numbered 1, 2, 3, and so on, and can be referred to by their numbers. Therefore, a random-access file resembles a box of index cards, each having a numbered tab. Any card can be selected from the box without first reading every index card preceding it; similarly, any record of a random-access file can be read without having to read every record preceding it.

One statement suffices to open a random-access file for all purposes: creating, appending, writing, and reading. Suppose a record type has been defined with a Type block and a record variable, called *recVar*, has been declared with a Dim statement. Then after the statement

```
Open "filespec" For Random As #n Len = Len(recVar)
```

is executed, records may be written, read, added, and changed. The file is referred to by the number n. Each record will have as many characters as allotted to each value of recVar.

Suppose appropriate Type, Dim, and Open statements have been executed. The two-step procedure for entering a record into the file is as follows.

1. Assign a value to each field of a record variable.

2. Place the data into record r of file #n with the statement

```
Put #n, r, recVar
```

where recVar is the record variable from Step 1.

[handwritten annotations: File #, Counter, Variable Name]

EXAMPLE 1   The following program creates and writes records to the random-access file COLLEGES.TXT.

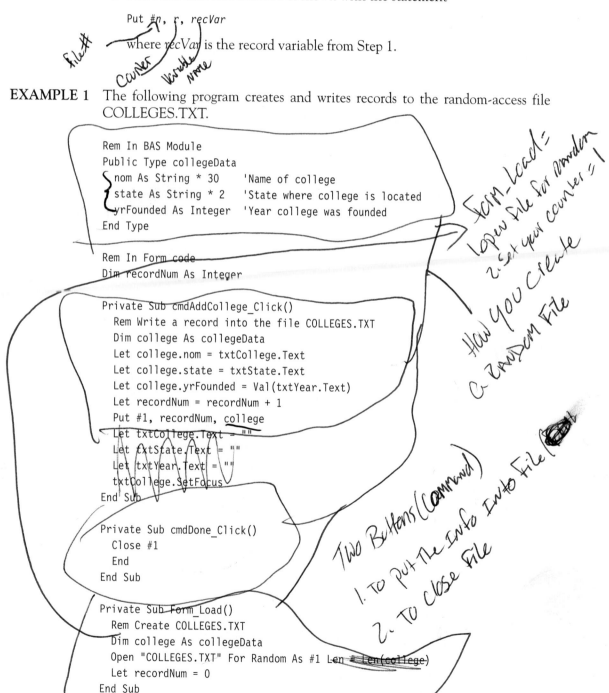

```
Rem In BAS Module
Public Type collegeData
    nom As String * 30        'Name of college
    state As String * 2       'State where college is located
    yrFounded As Integer      'Year college was founded
End Type

Rem In Form code
Dim recordNum As Integer

Private Sub cmdAddCollege_Click()
    Rem Write a record into the file COLLEGES.TXT
    Dim college As collegeData
    Let college.nom = txtCollege.Text
    Let college.state = txtState.Text
    Let college.yrFounded = Val(txtYear.Text)
    Let recordNum = recordNum + 1
    Put #1, recordNum, college
    Let txtCollege.Text = ""
    Let txtState.Text = ""
    Let txtYear.Text = ""
    txtCollege.SetFocus
End Sub

Private Sub cmdDone_Click()
    Close #1
    End
End Sub

Private Sub Form_Load()
    Rem Create COLLEGES.TXT
    Dim college As collegeData
    Open "COLLEGES.TXT" For Random As #1 Len = Len(college)
    Let recordNum = 0
End Sub
```

[handwritten annotations: Form_Load = 1 open file for random, 2 set your counter = 1 / How you create a random file / Two Buttons (command) 1. To put the info into file (add) 2. To close file]

[Run and type into the text boxes the data shown in the following first window. Click the "Add College to File" command button. Record number 1 is added to COLLEGES.TXT and the text boxes are cleared. Proceed to record the data shown for the other two colleges and then click the "Done" command button.]

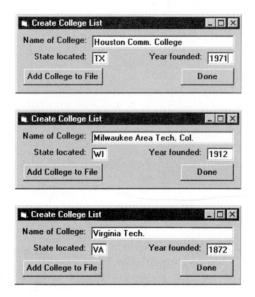

The two-step procedure for reading data from a record is as follows:

1. Execute the statement

   ```
   Get #n, r, recVar
   ```

   to assign record *r* of file #*n* to the record variable *recVar*.

2. Use the field variables of the record variable to either display values with picBox.Print or to transfer values to other variables with Let.

EXAMPLE 2   Write a program to display the entire contents of the random-access file COLLEGES.TXT.

SOLUTION
```
Rem In BAS Module
Public Type collegeData
  nom As String * 30      'Name of college
  state As String * 2     'State where college is located
  yrFounded As Integer    'Year college was founded
End Type

Rem In Form code
Private Sub cmdDisplay_Click()
  Call DisplayFile
End Sub

Private Sub DisplayFile()
  Dim recordNum As Integer
```

```
   Rem Access the random-access file COLLEGES.TXT
   Dim college As collegeData
   Open "COLLEGES.TXT" For Random As #1 Len = Len(college)
   picOutput.Cls
   picOutput.Print "College", , "State", "Year founded"
   For recordNum = 1 To 3
     Get #1, recordNum, college
     picOutput.Print college.nom, college.state, college.yrFounded
   Next recordNum
   Close #1
End Sub
```

[Run and click the command button.]

```
┌─────────────────────────────────────────────┐
│ ▪ Three Colleges                    _ □ ✕    │
├─────────────────────────────────────────────┤
│           ┌───────────────────┐             │
│           │  Display Colleges  │             │
│           └───────────────────┘             │
│ College                State    Year founded │
│ Houston Comm. College   TX         1971      │
│ Milwaukee Area Tech. Col.  WI      1912      │
│ Virginia Tech.          VA         1872      │
└─────────────────────────────────────────────┘
```

The total number of characters in the file with reference number *n* is given by the value of the function

```
   LOF(n)
```

The number of the last record in the file can be calculated by dividing this value by the record length. The LOF function, rather than the EOF function, should be used to determine when the end of the file has been reached. For instance, in Example 2, the For statement in the subprogram DisplayFile can be written as

```
   For recordNum = 1 To LOF(1) / Len(college)
```

Also, the pair of statements

```
   Let lastRecord = LOF(1) / Len(college)
   Put #1, lastRecord + 1, college
```

can be used to add a record to the end of the file.

Comments

1. Random-access files are also known as **direct-access** or **relative** files. Because each record has the same number of characters, the computer can calculate where to find a specified record and, therefore, does not have to search for it sequentially.

2. Unlike sequential files, random-access files needn't be closed between placing information into them and reading from them.

3. Random-access files do not have to be filled in order. For instance, a file can be opened and the first Put statement can be Put #*n*, 9, *recVar*. In this case, space is allocated for the preceding eight records.

4. If the record number *r* is omitted from a Put or Get statement, then the record number used will be the one following the number most recently used in a Put or Get statement. For instance, if the line

```
Put #1, , college
```

is added to the program in Example 1 after the existing Put statement, then the information on Houston Comm. College will occupy records 1 and 2, Milwaukee Area Tech. Col. records 3 and 4, and Virginia Tech. records 5 and 6 of the file COLLEGES.TXT.

5. Users often enter records into a random-access file without keeping track of the record numbers. If file *#n* is open, then the value of the function

```
Loc(n)
```

is the number of the record most recently written to or read from file *n* with a Put or Get statement.

6. Each record in a random-access file has the same length. This length can be any number from 1 to 32767.

7. When the statement Open "COLLEGES.TXT" For Random As #1 Len = Len(college) is typed, the words "For Random" can be omitted. The smart editor will insert them automatically.

8. The decision of whether to store data in a sequential file or in a random-access file depends on how the data are to be processed. If processing requires a pass though all the data in the file, then sequential files are probably desirable. If processing involves seeking out one item of data, however, random-access files are the better choice.

PRACTICE PROBLEM 9.2

1. In Example 2, the first picOutput.Print statement clearly displays "State" in the third print zone. Why will the second picOutput.Print statement also display the value of college.state in the third print zone?

EXERCISES 9.2

In Exercises 1 through 8, determine the output displayed in the picture box when the command button is clicked. For each problem, assume that the file COLLEGES.TXT was just created by Example 1 and that the given code replaces the ????? in the following program.

```
Rem In BAS Module
Public Type collegeData
  nom As String * 30      'Name of college
  state As String * 2     'State where college is located
  yrFounded As Integer    'Year college was founded
End Type
```

```
Rem In Form code
Private Sub cmdDisplay_Click()
  Dim i As Integer
  Dim college As collegeData
  picOutput.Cls
  Open "COLLEGES.TXT" For Random As #1 Len = Len(college)
  ?????
  Close #1
End Sub
```

1. ```
Get #1, 3, college
picOutput.Print college.state
```

2. ```
Get #1, 3, college
picOutput.Print LOF(1); Loc(1)
```
=

3. ```
For i = 1 To LOF(1) / Len(college)
   Get #1, i, college
    picOutput.Print college.state
Next i
picOutput.Print Loc(1)
```

2ʳᵈ record

4. ```
Let college.yrFounded = 1876
Put #1, 2, college
Get #1, 2, college
picOutput.Print college.nom; college.yrFounded
```

5. ```
Let college.nom = "Harvard"
Let college.state = "MA"
Let college.yrFounded = 1636
Put #1, 4, college
For i = 3 To 4
  Get #1, i, college
   picOutput.Print college.nom, college.state, college.yrFounded
Next i
```

3rd & 4th Records

6. ```
Let college.nom = "Michigan State"
Let college.state = "MI"
Let college.yrFounded = 1855
Put #1, 1, college
For i = 1 To 3
  Get #1, i, college
   picOutput.Print college.nom
Next i
```

7. ```
Get #1, 1, college
Get #1, , college
picOutput.Print college.nom, college.state, college.yrFounded
```

8. ```
Let lastRec = LOF(1) / Len(college)
Get #1, lastRec, college
picOutput.Print college.nom, college.state, college.yrFounded
```

— last Rec ?

In Exercises 9 through 12, identify the errors. Assume the given code replaces the ????? in the following program.

```
Rem In BAS Module
Public Type filmCredits
   nom As String * 25      'Name of actor or actress
   film As String * 35     'Name of film
End Type

Rem In Form code
Private Sub cmdDisplay_Click()
   Dim lastRec As Integer
   Dim actor As filmCredits
   ?????
End Sub
```

9. ```
   Open "ACTORS.TXT" For Random As #2 Len = Len(filmCredits)
   Let actor.nom = "Bogart"
   Let actor.film = "Casablanca"
   Put #2, 3, actor
   Close #2
   ```

10. ```
    Open "ACTRESS.TXT For Random As #3 Len = Len(actor)
    Let actor.nom = "Garland"
    Let actor.film = "Wizard of Oz"
    Let lastRec = LOF(3) / Len(actor)
    Put #3, lastRec + 1, actor
    Close #3
    ```

11. ```
    Open "ACTORS.TXT" For Random As #1 Len = Len(actor)
    Let actor.nom = "Stallone"
    Let actor.film = "Rocky"
    Put #1, 1, actor
    Get #1, 1, actor
    Close #1
    picBox.Print actor
    ```

12. ```
    Open "ACTRESS.TXT" For Random As #3 Len = Len(actor)
    Put #1, 1, actor
    Close #1
    ```

13. Give an Open statement and Type block for a random-access file named NUMBERS.TXT in which each record consists of three numbers.

14. Give an Open statement and Type block for a random-access file named ACCOUNTS.TXT in which each record consists of a person's name (up to 25 characters) and the balance in their savings account.

15. Consider the sequential file YOB.TXT discussed in Section 8.1 and assume the file contains many names. Write a program to place all the information into a random-access file.

16. Write a program that uses the random-access file created in Exercise 15 and displays the names of all people born before 1970.

17. Write a program that uses the random-access file created in Exercise 15 to determine a person's year of birth. The program should request that the name be typed into a text box, then search for the proper record when the command button is pressed, and either give the year of birth or report that the person is not in the file.

18. Write a program that uses the random-access file created in Exercise 15 and adds the data *Joan, 1934* to the end of the file.

Exercises 19 through 22 refer to the file COLLEGES.TXT. Assume many colleges have been added to the file in no particular order.

19. Write a program to allow additional colleges to be added to the end of the file using the same user interface as shown in Example 1.

20. Modify the program in Exercise 19 to issue an error message rather than record the data if the name of the college input has more than 25 characters.

21. Write a program to find the two oldest colleges.

22. Write a program to display the data on any college whose name is typed into a text box by the user. The college should be identified by name and located by a sequential search of the records. **Note:** Remember to take into account that each college name retrieved from the file will contain 25 characters.

23. Extend the program in Exercise 22 in the following way: After the information on a college is displayed, exchange its record with the previous record, unless, of course, the displayed record is the first record. (A familiar rule of thumb for office filing is, 80 percent of the action involves 20 percent of the records. After the program has been used many times, the most frequently requested records will tend to be near the top of the file and the average time required for searches should decrease.)

SOLUTION TO PRACTICE PROBLEM 9.2

1. The value of college.nom will have length 25 for each college. Therefore, it will extend into the second print zone and force the value of college.state into the third print zone.

Chapter 9
Summary

1. A *fixed-length string* is a variable declared with a statement of the form Dim *var* As String * n. The value of *var* is always a string of n characters.

2. A *record* is a composite user-defined data type with a fixed number of fields that can be of most data types. Type statements (in this text appearing in the (Declarations) section of a BAS Module) define record types and Dim statements are used to declare a variable to be of that type.

3. After a record type has been specified, the associated *random-access file* is an ordered collection of record values numbered 1, 2, 3, and so on. Record values are placed into the file with Put statements and read from the file with Get statements. At any time, the value of LOF(*n*) / Len(*recordVar*) is the number of the highest record value in the file and the value of Loc is the number of the record value most recently accessed by a Put or Get statement.

Chapter 9
Programming Projects

1. *Balance a Checkbook.* Write an interactive program to request information (payee, check number, amount, and whether or not the check has cleared) for each check written during a month and store this information in a random file. The program should then request the balance at the beginning of the month and display the current balance and the payee and amount for every check still outstanding.

2. A teacher maintains a random-access file containing the following information for each student: name, social security number, grades on each of two hourly exams, and the final exam grade. Assume the random-access file GRADES.TXT has been created with string fields of lengths 25 and 11 and three numeric fields, and all the names and social security numbers have been entered. The numeric fields have been initialized with zeros. Write a program with the five command buttons "Display First Student," "Record Grade(s) & Display Next Student," "Locate Student," "Print Grade List," and "Done" to allow the teacher to do the following.

   (a) Enter all the grades for a specific exam.
   (b) Locate and display the record for a specific student so that one or more grades may be changed.
   (c) Print a list of final grades that can be posted. The list should show the last four digits of the social security number, the grade on the final exam, and the semester average of each student. The semester average is determined by the formula (exam1 + exam2 + 2 * finalExam) / 4.

10

The Graphical
Display of Data

10.1 Introduction to Graphics / 456
• Specifying a Coordinate System • Graphics Methods
for Drawing Lines, Points, and Circles • Positioning Text

10.2 Line Charts / 468
• Line Styling

10.3 Bar Charts / 476

10.4 Pie Charts / 483

Summary / 493

Programming Projects / 493

10.1 INTRODUCTION TO GRAPHICS

Visual Basic has impressive graphics capabilities. Figure 10.1 shows four types of charts that can be displayed in a picture box and printed by the printer.

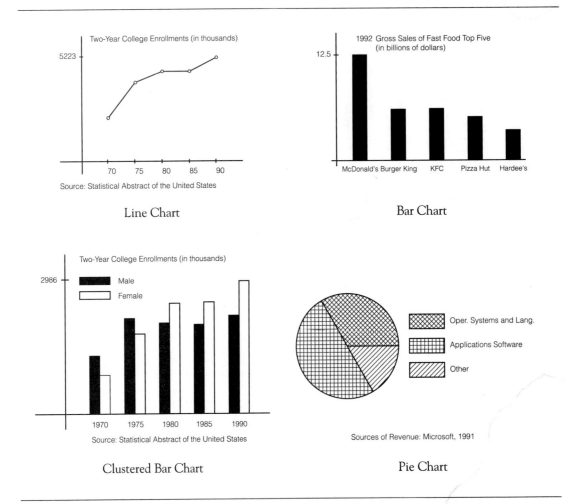

Figure 10.1 Four types of charts.

The construction of each of these charts involves three basic steps: (1) define a coordinate system; (2) use graphics methods to draw the appropriate lines, rectangles, and circles; and (3) place text at appropriate points on the chart. The basic tools for accomplishing each of these steps follow.

Specifying a Coordinate System

Suppose we have a piece of paper, a pencil, and a ruler and we want to graph a line extending from (2, 40) to (5, 60). We would most likely use the following three-step procedure:

1. Use the ruler to draw an x axis and a y axis. Focus on the first quadrant because both points are in that quadrant.

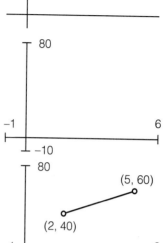

2. Select scales for the two axes. For instance, we might decide that the numbers on the x axis range from −1 to 6 and that the numbers on the y axis range from −10 to 80.

3. Plot the two points and use the ruler to draw the straight-line segment joining them.

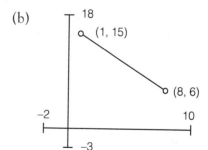

EXAMPLE 1 (a) Draw a coordinate system with the numbers on the x axis ranging from −2 to 10, and the numbers on the y axis ranging from −3 to 18.
(b) Draw the straight line from (1, 15) to (8, 6).
(c) Draw the straight line from (−2, 0) to (10, 0).

SOLUTION (a) 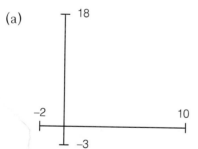 (b)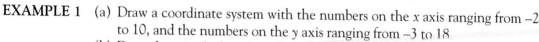

(c) The point (−2, 0) is the left-hand end point of the x axis and the point (10, 0) is the right-hand end point; therefore, the line joining them is just the portion of the x axis we have pictured.

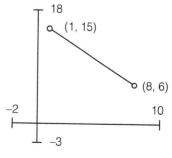

We draw these graphs on the screen with the same three steps we use with paper, pencil, and ruler. The only difference is that we first do Step 2 and then Steps 1 and 3. The Visual Basic method Scale is used to specify the range of values for the axes and the method Line serves as the ruler.

The statement

```
picBox.Scale (a, d)-(b, c)
```

specifies that numbers on the *x* axis range from *a* to *b* and that numbers on the *y* axis range from *c* to *d*. See Figure 10.2. The ordered pair (*a, d*) gives the coordinates of the top left corner of the picture box, and the ordered pair (*b, c*) gives the coordinates of the bottom right corner of the picture box.

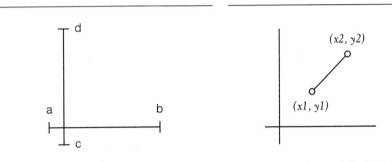

Figure 10.2 Result of Scale method.   **Figure 10.3** Result of the Line method.

Graphics Methods for Drawing Lines, Points, and Circles

After an appropriate coordinate system has been specified by a picBox.Scale statement, graphics can be drawn in the picture box using the Line and Circle methods. The statement

```
picBox.Line (x1, y1)-(x2, y2)
```

draws the line segment from the point with coordinates (*x1, y1*) to the point with coordinates (*x2, y2*) in the picture box (see Figure 10.3). In particular, the statement picOutput.Line (*a*, 0)–(*b*, 0) draws the *x* axis and the statement Picture1.Line (0, *c*)–(0, *d*) draws the *y* axis.

The following event procedure produces the graph of Example 1, part (b):

```
Private Sub cmdDraw_Click()
  picOutput.Cls
  picOutput.Scale (-2, 18)-(10, -3)   'Specify coordinate system
  picOutput.Line (-2, 0)-(10, 0)    'Draw x-axis
  picOutput.Line (0, -3)-(0, 18)    'Draw y-axis
  picOutput.Line (1, 15)-(8, 6)    'Draw the straight line
End Sub
```

EXAMPLE 2   Consider Figure 10.4.

(a) Give the statement that specifies the range for the numbers on the axes.
(b) Give the statements that will draw the axes.
(c) Give the statement that will draw the line.

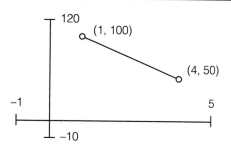

Figure 10.4 Graph for Example 2.

SOLUTION   (a) `picOutput.Scale (-1, 120)-(5, -10)`

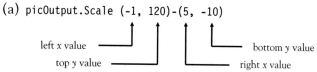

    left *x* value   bottom *y* value
      top *y* value   right *x* value

(b) *x* axis: `picOutput.Line (-1, 0)-(5, 0)`

                      a   b

    y axis: `picOutput.Line (0, -10)-(0, 120)`

                      c   d

(c) `picOutput.Line (1, 100)-(4, 50)`

There are two other graphics methods that are just as useful as the Line method. The statement

    `picOutput.PSet (x, y)`

plots the point with coordinates (*x*, *y*). The statement

    `picOutput.Circle (x, y), r`

draws the circle with center (*x*, *y*) and radius *r*.

EXAMPLE 3   Write an event procedure to plot the point (7, 6) in a picture box and draw a circle of radius 3 about the point.

SOLUTION   The rightmost point to be drawn will have *x* coordinate 10; therefore the numbers on the *x* axis must range beyond 10. In the following event procedure, we allow the numbers to range from –2 to 12. See Figure 10.5.

```
Private Sub cmdDraw_Click()
  Rem Draw circle with center (7, 6) and radius 3
  picOutput.Cls                       'Clear picture box
  picOutput.Scale (-2, 12)-(12, -2)'Specify coordinate system
  picOutput.Line (-2, 0)-(12, 0)    'Draw x-axis
  picOutput.Line (0, -2)-(0, 12)    'Draw y-axis
  picOutput.PSet (7, 6)             'Draw center of circle
  picOutput.Circle (7, 6), 3        'Draw the circle
End Sub
```

[Run and then click the command button. The resulting picture box is shown in Figure 10.5.]

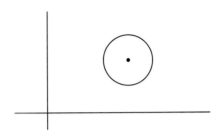

Figure 10.5 Graph for Example 3.

The numbers appearing in the Scale, Line, PSet, and Circle methods can be replaced by variables or expressions. The following example demonstrates this feature.

EXAMPLE 4   Write an event procedure to draw a graph of the square root function.

SOLUTION   We will graph the function for values of *x* from 0 to 100. See Figure 10.6.

```
Private Sub cmdDraw_Click()
  Dim r As Single, h As Single, x As Single
  Rem Graph the Square Root Function
  Let r = 100                         'Largest x-value used
  Let h = 10                          'Largest y-value used
  picOutput.Cls
  picOutput.Scale (-20, 12)-(120, -2)  'Specify coordinate system
  picOutput.Line (-5, 0)-(r, 0)        'Draw x-axis
  picOutput.Line (0, -1)-(0, h)        'Draw y-axis
  For x = 0 To r Step 0.2              'Plot about 500 points
    picOutput.PSet (x, Sqr(x))         'Plot point on graph
  Next x
End Sub
```

[Run and then click the command button. The resulting picture box is shown in Figure 10.6.]

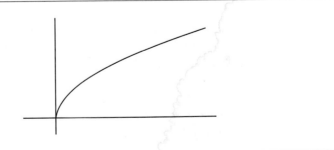

Figure 10.6 Graph of the square root function.

Positioning Text

There are times when text is placed on the screen in conjunction with graphics. This would be the case if a graph were to be titled or a tick mark needed a label. The ability to position such text appropriately in the picture box is essential to good-looking graphs. A picture box has two properties, CurrentX and CurrentY, and two methods, TextHeight and TextWidth, that allow us to precisely position text alongside graphics.

The properties CurrentX and CurrentY record the precise horizontal and vertical location at which the next character of text will be printed. By assigning appropriate values to these properties prior to executing a Print method, text can be positioned very precisely in the picture box. In the following event procedure, the coordinates of the right end of the tick mark are $(x, y) = (.1, 3)$. As a first attempt at labeling a tick mark on the y axis, the CurrentX and CurrentY properties are set to these coordinates. The results are shown in Figure 10.7(a).

```
Private Sub cmdDraw_Click()
  picOutput.Cls
  picOutput.Scale (-4, 4) - (4, -4)
  picOutput.Line (-4, 0) - (4, 0)    'Draw x-axis
  picOutput.Line (0, -4) - (0, 4)    'Draw y-axis
  picOutput.Line (-.1, 3) - (.1, 3) 'Draw tick mark
  Let picOutput.CurrentX = .1        'Right end of tick mark
  Let picOutput.CurrentY = 3         'Same vertical position as tick mark
  picOutput.Print "y=3"             'Label for tick mark
End Sub
```

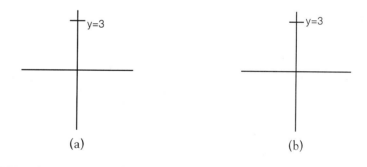

(a)   (b)

Figure 10.7 Placing labels: (a) first attempt and (b) second attempt.

Note that the top of the text is even with the tick mark. This reflects the fact that the value of the CurrentY property used by Visual Basic is the location for the **top** of the character cursor. Ideally, the text should be moved up so that the tick mark aligns with the middle of the text. To do this, the value of the CurrentY property needs to be increased by one-half the height of the text. The following statement assigns a corrected value to the CurrentY property by using the TextHeight method to obtain the height of the text being used as the tick mark label.

```
Let picOutput.CurrentY = 3 - picOutput.TextHeight("y=3") / 2
```

The result of using this corrected value for CurrentY is shown in Figure 10.7(b).

When the TextHeight method is used, all characters have the same height. Thus the height of a string can be obtained by asking for the height of any single character. The following procedure uses the TextHeight method with a space character to center the text cursor at the requested graphic point.

```
Private Sub PositionText(x As Single, y As Single)
  Rem Center text cursor at the point (x, y)
  Let picOutput.CurrentX = x
  Let picOutput.CurrentY = y + picOutput.TextHeight(" ") / 2
End Sub
```

Another useful picture box method is TextWidth. Whereas the Len function returns the number of characters in a string, the TextWidth method takes into account the varying widths of characters and returns the physical width of the entire string in the units of the current scale for the picture box. The TextWidth method is essential when centering text, as illustrated in the following example.

EXAMPLE 5   Write an event procedure to display the phrase "Th-that's all folks!" centered and double underlined in a picture box with x values ranging from 0 to 6 and y values ranging from 0 to 4.

SOLUTION   Centering text requires knowing the coordinates of the center of the picture box, which for the given ranges will be the point (3, 2). Next, we need the width and height of the text being centered. These values are available using the TextWidth and TextHeight methods. The text cursor needs to start with a CurrentX that is half the text's width to the left of center and a CurrentY that is half the text's height above center. The first underline can be placed at half the text's height below center. The additional distance down to the second underline should be in proportion to the height of the text. We decided after some experimenting to use a proportion of 1/6th.

```
Private Sub cmdDraw_Click()
  Rem Center and double underline a phrase
  Dim xCenter As Single, yCenter As Single, phrase as String
  Dim w As Single, h As Single, leftEdge As Single, rightEdge As Single
  Dim ul1Pos As Single, ul2Pos As Single
  picOutput.Scale (0, 4)-(6, 0)
  picOutput.Cls
  Let xCenter = 3
  Let yCenter = 2
  Let phrase = "Th-that's all Folks!"
  Let w = picOutput.TextWidth(phrase)
  Let h = picOutput.TextHeight(" ")
  Let picOutput.CurrentX = xCenter - w / 2
  Let picOutput.CurrentY = yCenter - h / 2
  picOutput.Print phrase
  Let leftEdge = xCenter - w / 2
  Let rightEdge = xCenter + w / 2
  Let ul1Pos = yCenter + h / 2
  Let ul2Pos = ul1Pos + h / 6
  picOutput.Line (leftEdge, ul1Pos)-(rightEdge, ul1Pos)
  picOutput.Line (leftEdge, ul2Pos)-(rightEdge, ul2Pos)
End Sub
```

[Run and then click the command button. The resulting picture box follows.]

```
Th-that's all Folks!
```

Comments

1. In Examples 1 through 4, examples that produce graphs, the range of numbers on the axes extended from a negative number to a positive number. Actually, any value of *a*, *b*, *c*, and *d* can be used in a Scale method. In certain cases, however, you will not be able to display one or both of the axes on the screen. (For instance, after picOutput.Scale (1, 10)–(10, –1) has been executed, the *y* axis cannot be displayed.)

2. The following technique can be used to determine a good range of values for a Scale method when graphs with only positive values are to be drawn.

   (a) Let *r* be the *x* coordinate of the rightmost point that will be drawn by any Line, PSet, or Circle method.
   (b) Let *h* be the *y* coordinate of the highest point that will be drawn by any Line, PSet, or Circle method.
   (c) Let the numbers on the *x* axis range from about –[20% of *r*] to about *r* + [20% of *r*]. Let the numbers on the *y* axis range from about –[20% of *h*] to about *h* + [20% of *h*]. That is, use

   ```
   picOutput.Scale (-.2 * r, 1.2 * h)-(1.2 * r, -.2 * h)
   ```

3. The radius of a circle uses the scale specified for the *x* axis.

4. If one or both of the points used in the Line method fall outside the picture box, the computer only draws the portion of the line that lies in the picture box. This behavior is referred to as **line clipping** and is used for the Circle method also.

5. A program can execute a picOutput.Scale statement more than once. Executing a new picOutput.Scale statement has no effect on the text and graphics already drawn; however, future graphics statements will use the new coordinate system. This technique can be used to produce the same graphics figure in different sizes and/or locations within the picture box. The output from the following event procedure in shown in Figure 10.8.

```
Private Sub cmdDraw_Click()
  Dim i As Integer
  picOutput.Cls
  For i = 0 To 3
    picOutput.Scale (0, 2 ^ i)-(2 ^ i, 0)
    picOutput.Line (0, 0)-(.5, 1)
    picOutput.Line (.5, 1)-(.8, 0)
    picOutput.Line (.8, 0)-(0, .8)
    picOutput.Line (0, .8)-(1, .5)
    picOutput.Line (1, .5)-(0, 0)
  Next i
End Sub
```

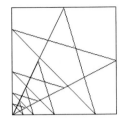

Figure 10.8 Output from Comment 5.

6. The programs in this section can be modified to produce colorful displays. The numbers 0 through 15 identify colors as shown in Table 10.1.

0 Black	4 Red	8 Gray	12 Light red
1 Blue	5 Magenta	9 Light blue	13 Light magenta
2 Green	6 Yellow	10 Light green	14 Light Yellow
3 Cyan	7 White	11 Light cyan	15 High-intensity white

Table 10.1 Values for colors from the QBColor function.

Lines, points, and circles can be drawn in these colors through use of the QBColor function. To use color c, place ", QBColor(c)" at the end of the corresponding graphics statement. For instance, the statement

```
picBox.Line (x1, y1)-(x2, y2), QBColor(4)
```

draws a red line.

PRACTICE PROBLEMS 10.1

Suppose you want to write a program to draw a line from (3, 45) to (5, 80).

1. Use the technique of Comment 2 to select appropriate values for the Scale method.

2. Write an event procedure to draw the axes, the line, and a small circle around each end point of the line.

3. Write the statements that draw a tick mark on the y axis at height 80 and label it with the number 80.

EXERCISES 10.1

1. Determine the Scale method corresponding to the coordinate system of Figure 10.9.

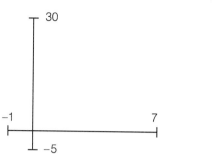

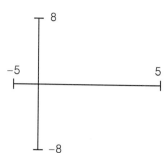

Figure 10.9 Coordinate system for Exercise 1.

Figure 10.10 Coordinate system for Exercise 2.

2. Determine the Scale method corresponding to the coordinate system of Figure 10.10.

3. Suppose the statement picBox.Scale (–1, 40)–(4, –8) has been executed. Write down the statements that draw the *x* axis and the *y* axis.

4. Suppose the statement picBox.Scale (–3, 1)–(18, –.2) has been executed. Write down the statements that draw the *x* axis and the *y* axis.

In Exercises 5 through 8, write an event procedure to draw a line between the given points. Select an appropriate Scale method, draw the axes, and draw a small circle around each end point of the line.

5. (3, 200), (10, 150)

6. (4, 4), (9, 9)

7. (2, .5), (4, .3)

8. (5, 30), (6, 30)

In Exercises 9 through 20, write an event procedure to draw the given figures in a picture box. Draw the axes only when necessary.

9. Draw a circle whose center is located at the center of the picture box.

10. Draw a tick mark on the *x* axis at a distance of 5 from the origin.

11. Draw a tick mark on the *y* axis at a distance of 70 from the origin.

12. Draw a circle whose leftmost point is at the center of the picture box.

13. Draw four small quarter-circles, one in each corner of the picture box.

14. Draw a triangle with two sides of the same length.

15. Draw a rectangle.

16. Draw a square.

17. Draw five concentric circles, that is, five circles with the same center.

18. Draw a point in the center of the picture box.

19. Draw a circle and a line that is tangent to the circle.

20. Draw two circles that touch at a single point.

In Exercises 21 through 24, consider the following event procedure. What would be the effect on the circle if the picOutput.Scale statement were replaced by the given picOutput.Scale statement?

```
Private Sub cmdDraw_Click()
  picOutput.Cls
  picOutput.Scale (-5, 5)-(5, -5)     'Specify coordinate system
  picOutput.Circle (0, 0), 3          'Draw circle centered at origin
End Sub
```

21. `picOutput.Scale (-8, 8)-(8,-8)`   **22.** `picOutput.Scale (-5, 8)-(5, -8)`

23. `picOutput.Scale (-8, 5)-(8, -5)`   **24.** `picOutput.Scale (-4, 4)-(4, -4)`

In Exercises 25 through 27, write an event procedure to perform the given task.

25. Draw a graph of the function $y = x^2$ for x between 0 and 10.

26. Draw a graph of the function $200 / (x + 5)^2$ for x between 0 and 20.

27. Draw displays such as the one in Figure 10.11. Let the user specify the maximum number (in this display, 8).

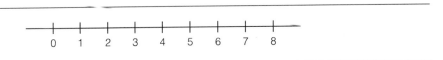

Figure 10.11 Display for Exercise 27.

In Exercises 28 through 30, use the statement picOutput.Scale (0, 50)– (100, 0).

28. Write a program to produce Figure 10.12. Let the maximum line number (in this display, 3) be specified by the user.

———————————— LINE 1

———————————— LINE 2

———————————— LINE 3

Figure 10.12 Display for Exercise 28.

29. Write a program to produce a sheet of graph paper.

30. Write a program to produce a form for a course schedule. See Figure 10.13.

COURSE SCHEDULE						
Time	Mon.	Tues.	Wed.	Thurs.	Fri.	Sat./Sun.

Figure 10.13 Course schedule.

SOLUTIONS TO PRACTICE PROBLEMS 10.1

1. The largest value of any x coordinate is 5. Because 20% of 5 is 1, the numbers on the x axis should range from -1 to 6 ($= 5 + 1$). Similarly, the numbers on the y axis should range from -16 to 96 ($= 80 + 16$). Therefore, an appropriate scaling statement is

```
picOutput.Scale (-1, 96)-(6, -16)
```

2.
```
Private Sub cmdDraw_Click()
   picOutput.Scale (-1, 96)-(6, -16)  'Specify coordinate system
   picOutput.Line (-1, 0)-(6, 0)      'Draw x-axis
   picOutput.Line (0, -16)-(0, 96)    'Draw y-axis
   picOutput.Line (3, 45)-(5, 80)     'Draw the line
   picOutput.Circle (3, 45), .1       'Draw small circle about left end point
   picOutput.Circle (5, 80), .1       'Draw small circle about right end point
End Sub
```

The radius for the small circles about the end points was determined by trial and error. As a rule of thumb, it should be about 2 percent of the length of the x axis.

3. Add the following lines before the End Sub statement of the preceding event procedure. The length of the tick mark was taken to be the diameter of the circle. See Figure 10.14 for the output of the entire program.

```
picOutput.Line (-.1, 80)-(.1, 80)   'Draw tick mark
Let picOutput.CurrentX = .1         'Prepare cursor position for label
Let picOutput.CurrentY = 80 + picOutput.TextHeight(" ") / 2
picOutput.Print "80"                'Display label
```

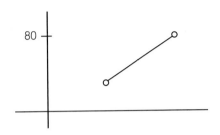

Figure 10.14 Final output from practice problems.

10.2 LINE CHARTS

A line chart displays the change in a certain quantity in relation to another quantity (often time). The following steps produce a line chart.

1. Look over the data to be displayed. A typical line chart displays between 5 and 20 items of data corresponding to evenly spaced units of time: years, months, or days. The positions on the x axis will contain labels such as "Jan Feb Mar Apr ..." or "91 92 93 94 ...". These labels can be placed at the locations 1, 2, 3, ... on the x axis.

2. Choose a coordinate system based on the number of data items and the size of the quantities. A convenient scale for the x axis is from –1 to one more than the number of data items. The scale for the y axis is determined by the largest quantity to be displayed.

3. Draw the line segments. It is a good idea to draw a small circle around the end points of the line segments.

4. Draw and label tick marks on the coordinate axes. The x axis should have a tick mark for each time period. The y axis should have at least one tick mark to indicate the magnitude of the quantities displayed.

5. Title the chart and give the source of the data.

EXAMPLE 1　Table 10.2 gives enrollment data for 2-year colleges taken from the *Statistical Abstract of the United States*. Write a program to display the total enrollments for the given years in a line chart.

Year	1970	1975	1980	1985	1990
Male	1317	2165	2047	2002	2237
Female	906	1805	2479	2529	2986
Total	2223	3970	4526	4531	5223

Table 10.2 Two-year college enrollments (in thousands).

SOLUTION　Figure 10.15 shows the graph that results from executing the following program. The data in ENROLL.TXT are taken from the first and last lines of Table 10.2.

For example, the first line in the file is "1970", 2223. (Explanatory remarks follow the program.)

```
Rem In (Declarations) section of (General)
Dim numYears As Integer, maxEnroll As Single

Private Sub cmdDraw_Click()
  Rem Line Chart of Total Two-Year College Enrollments
  Let numYears = 5
  ReDim label(1 To numYears) As String
  ReDim total(1 To numYears) As Single
  Call ReadData(label(), total())
  Call DrawAxes
  Call DrawData(total())
  Call ShowTitle
  Call ShowLabels(label())
End Sub

Private Sub DrawAxes()
  Rem Draw axes
  picEnroll.Scale (-1, 1.2 * maxEnroll) - (numYears + 1, -.2 * maxEnroll)
  picEnroll.Line (-1, 0)-(numYears + 1, 0)
  picEnroll.Line (0, -.1 * maxEnroll)-(0, 1.2 * maxEnroll)
End Sub

Private Sub DrawData(total() As Single)
  Dim i As Integer
  Rem Draw lines connecting data and circle data points
  For i = 1 To numYears
    If i < numYears Then
        picEnroll.Line (i, total(i))-(i + 1, total(i + 1))
    End If
    picEnroll.Circle (i, total(i)), .01 * numYears
  Next i
End Sub

Private Sub Locate(x As Single, y As Single)
  Let picEnroll.CurrentX = x
  Let picEnroll.CurrentY = y
End Sub

Private Sub ReadData(label() As String, total() As Single)
  Dim i As Integer
  Rem Assume the data have been placed in the file "ENROLL.TXT"
  Rem (First line of the file is "1970",2223)
  Rem Read data into arrays, find highest enrollment
  Let maxEnroll = 0
  Open "ENROLL.TXT" For Input As #1
  For i = 1 To numYears
    Input #1, label(i), total(i)
    If total(i) > maxEnroll Then
        Let maxEnroll = total(i)
    End If
  Next i
  Close #1
End Sub
```

```
Private Sub ShowLabels(label() As String)
  Dim i As Integer, lbl As String, lblWid As Single
  Dim lblHght As Single, tickFactor As Single
  Rem Draw tick marks and label them
  For i = 1 To numYears
    Let lbl = Right(label(i), 2)
    Let lblWid = picEnroll.TextWidth(lbl)
    Let tickFactor = .02 * maxEnroll
    picEnroll.Line (i, -tickFactor)-(i, tickFactor)
    Call Locate(i - lblWid / 2, -tickFactor)
    picEnroll.Print lbl
  Next i
  Let lbl = Str(maxEnroll)
  Let lblWid = picEnroll.TextWidth(lbl)
  Let lblHght = picEnroll.TextHeight(lbl)
  Let tickFactor = .02 * numYears
  picEnroll.Line (-tickFactor, maxEnroll)-(tickFactor, maxEnroll)
  Call Locate(-tickFactor - lblWid, maxEnroll - lblHght / 2)
  picEnroll.Print lbl
End Sub

Private Sub ShowTitle()
  Rem Display source and title
  Call Locate(-.5, -.1 * maxEnroll)
  picEnroll.Print "Source: Statistical Abstract of the United States"
  Call Locate(.5, 1.2 * maxEnroll)
  picEnroll.Print "Two-Year College Enrollments (in thousands)"
End Sub
```

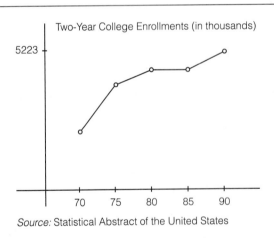

Figure 10.15 Chart for Example 1.

Remarks on the program in Example 1

1. The value of *tickFactor* in the subprogram ShowLabels was set to 2 percent of the scale determiners (*numYears* and *maxEnroll*) for the *x* and *y* axes. This percentage is appropriate for picture boxes that occupy 1/4th to 1/3rd of the screen. Smaller picture boxes might require a factor of 3 percent or 4 percent for good-looking tick marks. Picture boxes that almost fill the screen might have good results with a factor as small as 1 percent.

2. In the subprogram ShowLabels, the TextWidth and TextHeight methods were used to obtain the width and height of each label. These values were used together with the coordinates of the appropriate end of the tick mark to assign values to CurrentX and CurrentY for proper placement of the label relative to the graphics.

3. In the event procedure cmdDraw_Click, the number of data points (5) was assigned to the variable *numYears*, and then *numYears* was used as a parameter to all other subprograms. This feature makes it easy to add additional data to the line chart. For instance, if we decide to include the data for one additional year, we will only have to change the value of *numYears* and add one more line to the data file.

Line Styling

Patterned, or "styled," lines can be drawn between two points. Some available line styles are shown in Figure 10.16. Each line has an associated number identifying its style. If *s* is one of the numbers in the figure, then the statements

```
Let picBox.DrawStyle = s
picBox.Line (a, b)-(c, d)
```

draw the line from (a, b) to (c, d) in the style corresponding to the number *s*.

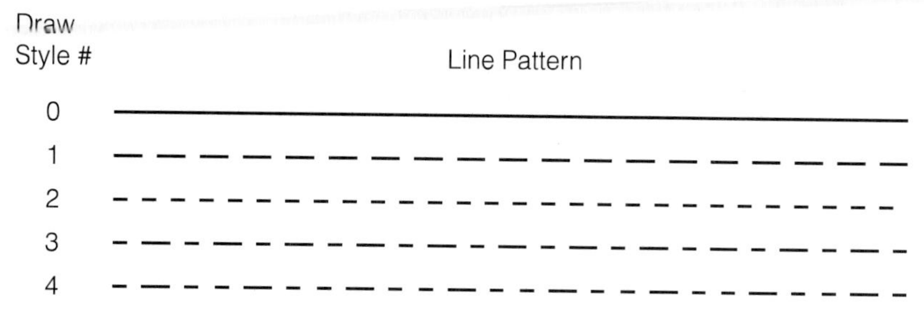

Figure 10.16 Line patterns.

Styling is useful when displaying several line charts on the same coordinate system.

EXAMPLE 2   Alter the program in Example 1 so that it will draw line charts displaying the male, female, and total enrollments of 2-year colleges.

SOLUTION   The data file must be changed to contain the enrollment figures for males and females, and arrays must be created to hold this information. The totals can be computed from the other numbers. The styled lines for male and female enrollments must be drawn. Finally, legends must be given to identify the different line charts. Figure 10.17 shows the picture box that results from the modified program.

```
Rem In (Declarations) section of (General)
Dim numYears As Integer, maxEnroll As Single

Private Sub cmdDraw_Click()
  Rem Line Chart of Total Two-Year College Enrollments
  Let numYears = 5
  ReDim label(1 To numYears) As String
  ReDim male(1 To numYears) As Single
  ReDim female(1 To numYears) As Single
  ReDim total(1 To numYears) As Single
  Call ReadData(label(),male(),female(),total())
  Call DrawAxes
  Call DrawData(male(), female(), total())
  Call ShowTitle
  Call ShowLabels(label())
  Call ShowLegend
End Sub

Private Sub DrawAxes()
  Rem Draw axes
  picEnroll.Scale (-1, 1.2 * maxEnroll) - (numYears + 1, -.2 * maxEnroll)
  picEnroll.Line (-1, 0)-(numYears + 1, 0)
  picEnroll.Line (0, -.1 * maxEnroll)-(0, 1.2 * maxEnroll)
End Sub

Private Sub DrawData(male() As Single, female() As Single, total() As Single)
  Dim i As Integer
  For i = 1 To numYears
    If i < numYears Then
        Rem Draw lines connecting data points
        Let picEnroll.DrawStyle = 2
        picEnroll.Line (i, male(i))-(i + 1, male(i + 1))
        Let picEnroll.DrawStyle = 1
        picEnroll.Line (i, female(i))-(i + 1, female(i + 1))
        Let picEnroll.DrawStyle = 0
        picEnroll.Line (i, total(i))-(i + 1, total(i + 1))
    End If
    Rem Draw small circles around data points
    picEnroll.Circle (i, male(i)), .01 * numYears
    picEnroll.Circle (i, female(i)), .01 * numYears
    picEnroll.Circle (i, total(i)), .01 * numYears
  Next i
End Sub

Private Sub Locate(x As Single, y As Single)
  Let picEnroll.CurrentX = x
  Let picEnroll.CurrentY = y
End Sub

Private Sub ReadData(label() As String, male() As Single, _
                     female() As Single, total() As Single)
  Rem The two lines above should be enter as one line
  Dim i As Integer
  Rem Assume the data has been placed in the file "ENROLLMF.TXT"
  Rem (First line of file is "1970",1317,906)
  Rem Read data into arrays, find highest enrollment
```

```
      Open "ENROLLMF.TXT" For Input As #1
    Let maxEnroll = 0
    For i = 1 To numYears
      Input #1, label(i), male(i), female(i)
      Let total(i) = male(i) + female(i)
      If maxEnroll < total(i) Then
          Let maxEnroll = total(i)
      End If
    Next i
    Close #1
  End Sub

  Private Sub ShowLabels(label() As String)
    Dim i As Integer, lbl As String, lblWid As Single
    Dim lblHght As Single, tickFactor As Single
    Rem Draw tick marks and label them
    For i = 1 To numYears
      Let lbl = Right(label(i), 2)
      Let lblWid = picEnroll.TextWidth(lbl)
      Let tickFactor = .02 * maxEnroll
      picEnroll.Line (i, -tickFactor)-(i, tickFactor)
      Call Locate(i - lblWid / 2, -tickFactor)
      picEnroll.Print lbl
    Next i
    Let lbl = Str(maxEnroll)
    Let lblWid = picEnroll.TextWidth(lbl)
    Let lblHght = picEnroll.TextHeight(lbl)
    Let tickFactor = .02 * numYears
    picEnroll.Line (-tickFactor, maxEnroll)-(tickFactor, maxEnroll)
    Call Locate(-tickFactor - lblWid, maxEnroll - lblHght / 2)
    picEnroll.Print lbl
  End Sub

  Private Sub ShowLegend()
    Rem Show legend
    Let picEnroll.DrawStyle = 2
    picEnroll.Line (.1, 1.05 * maxEnroll)-(.9, 1.05 * maxEnroll)
    Call Locate(1, 1.1 * maxEnroll)
    picEnroll.Print "Male"
    Let picEnroll.DrawStyle = 1
    picEnroll.Line (.1, .95 * maxEnroll)-(.9, .95 * maxEnroll)
    Call Locate(1, maxEnroll)
    picEnroll.Print "Female"
    Let picEnroll.DrawStyle = 0
    picEnroll.Line (.1, .85 * maxEnroll)-(.9, .85 * maxEnroll)
    Call Locate(1, .9 * maxEnroll)
    picEnroll.Print "Total"
  End Sub

  Private Sub ShowTitle()
    Rem Display source and title
    Call Locate(.5, -.1 * maxEnroll)
    picEnroll.Print "Source: Statistical Abstract of the United States"
    Call Locate(.5, 1.2 * maxEnroll)
    picEnroll.Print "Two-Year College Enrollments (in thousands)"
  End Sub
```

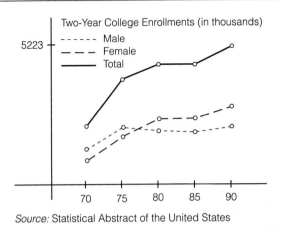

Source: Statistical Abstract of the United States

Figure 10.17 Chart for Example 2.

PRACTICE PROBLEMS 10.2

Consider the programs of Examples 1 and 2 that draw the three-line chart of two-year college enrollments.

1. The enrollments for 1965 were Males—734, Females—439, Total—1173. Change the program to include these data.

2. Suppose the enrollment data were given in units of millions instead of thousands. How would this affect the appearance of the three-line chart?

3. Why wasn't 1990 (or 90) used in the picEnroll.Scale statement to determine the scale for the x axis? It is the largest value of x.

EXERCISES 10.2

In Exercises 1 and 2, determine a picOutput.Scale statement that could have been used to obtain the chart.

1.

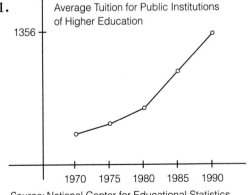

Source: National Center for Educational Statistics

2.

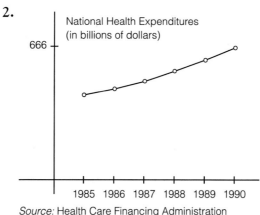

Source: Health Care Financing Administration

In Exercises 3 through 7, write a program to display the given information in a line chart.

3. The Consumer Price Index is a measure of living costs based on changes in retail prices, with 1967 taken as the base year.

Year	1967	1971	1975	1979	1983	1987	1991
CPI	100.0	121.3	161.2	217.7	297.4	335.0	399.9

Source: Bureau of Labor Statistics

4. Workers with Personal Computers (in millions)

Year	1981	1984	1987	1990
Workers	2	6	14	24

Source: Future Computing Incorporated

5. Freshman Life Goals (% of students committed to goal)

	1968	1976	1984	1992
Be very well off financially	45	57	70	73
Develop a meaningful philosophy of life	80	57	45	46

Source: Higher Education Research Institute

6. Normal Monthly Precipitation (in inches)

	Jan	Apr	July	Oct
Mobile, AL	4.6	5.35	7.7	2.6
Phoenix, AZ	.7	.3	.7	.6
Portland, OR	6.2	2.3	.5	3.0
Washington, DC	2.8	2.9	3.9	2.9

Source: Statistical Abstract of the United States

7. Age Distribution (%) of the Labor Force

	16–24	25–34	35–54	Over 54
1975	24	24	36	15
1990	17	29	42	12
2005	16	21	48	15

Source: The 1994 Information Please Business Almanac

SOLUTIONS TO PRACTICE PROBLEMS 10.2

1. Change *numYears* to 6 in the cmdDraw_Click event procedure and add the following line to the beginning of the data file.

   "1965", 734, 439

2. Not at all. The value of *maxEnroll*, 5940 would change to 5.94 but the picEnroll.Scale statement would scale the y axis with respect to this new value of *maxEnroll* and the line charts would look exactly the same as before.

3. If 1990 (or 90) had been used, the line charts would have been unreadable. Line charts are used to illustrate from about 3 to 15 pieces of data. These are best placed at the numbers 1, 2, 3, ... on the x axis. In many cases the classifications given below the tick marks are words (such as Jan, Feb, ...) instead of numbers.

10.3 BAR CHARTS

Drawing bar charts requires a variation of the line statement. If $(x1, y1)$ and $(x2, y2)$ are two points on the screen, then the statement

    picBox.Line (x1, y1) - (x2, y2), , B

draws a rectangle with the two points as opposite corners. If B is replaced by BF, a solid rectangle will be drawn (see Figure 10.18).

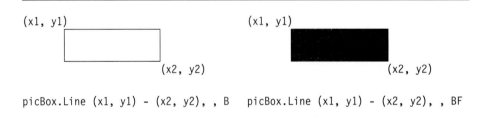

Figure 10.18 Line method with B and BF options.

EXAMPLE 1 The populations of California and New York are 30 and 18 million, respectively. Draw a bar chart to compare the populations.

SOLUTION The following program produces the chart shown in Figure 10.19. The first five lines are the same as those of a line chart with two pieces of data. The base of the rectangle for California is centered above the point $(1, 0)$ on the x axis and extends .3 unit to the left and right. (The number .3 was chosen arbitrarily; it had to be less than .5 so that the rectangles would not touch.) Therefore, the upper left corner of the rectangle has coordinates $(.7, 30)$ and the lower right corner has coordinates $(1.3, 0)$. Figure 10.20 shows the coordinates of the principal points of the rectangles.

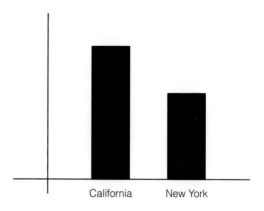

Figure 10.19 Bar chart for Example 1.

```
Private Sub cmdDisplayPop_Click()
  Rem Populations of California and New York
  picPop.Scale (-1, 40)-(3, -5)        'Specify coordinates
  picPop.Line (-1, 0)-(3, 0)           'Draw x-axis
  picPop.Line (0, -5)-(0, 40)          'Draw y-axis
  picPop.Line (.7, 30)-(1.3, 0),,BF    'Draw solid rectangle for CA
  picPop.Line (1.7, 18)-(2.3, 0),,BF   'Draw solid rectangle for NY
  Let picPop.CurrentY = -1
  Let picPop.CurrentX = .7
  picPop.Print "California";
  Let picPop.CurrentX = 1.7
  picPop.Print "New York";
End Sub
```

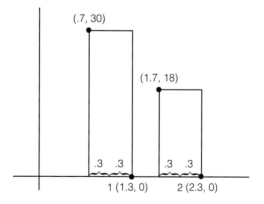

Figure 10.20 Coordinates of principal points of Example 1.

Any program that draws a line chart can be easily modified to produce a bar chart. Multiple line charts are converted into so-called **clustered bar charts**.

EXAMPLE 2 Display the 2-year college enrollments for males and females in a clustered bar chart. Use the data in Table 10.2 of Section 10.2.

SOLUTION The output of the following program appears in Figure 10.21. This program is very similar to the program that produced Figure 10.17 of Section 10.2.

```
Private Sub cmdDraw_Click()
  Dim numYears As Integer, maxEnroll As Single
  Rem Bar Chart of Total Two-Year College Enrollments
  Let numYears = 5
  ReDim label(1 To numYears) As String
  ReDim male(1 To numYears) As Single
  ReDim female(1 To numYears) As Single
  Call ReadData(label(), male(), female(), numYears, maxEnroll)
  Call DrawAxes(numYears, maxEnroll)
  Call DrawData(male(), female(), numYears)
  Call ShowTitle(maxEnroll)
  Call ShowLabels(label(), numYears, maxEnroll)
  Call ShowLegend(maxEnroll)
End Sub


Private Sub DrawAxes(numYears As Integer, maxEnroll As Single)
  Rem Draw axes
  picEnroll.Scale (-1, 1.2 * maxEnroll) - (numYears + 1, -.2 * maxEnroll)
  picEnroll.Line (-1, 0)-(numYears + 1, 0)
  picEnroll.Line (0, -.1 * maxFnroll)-(0, 1.2 * maxEnroll)
End Sub


Private Sub DrawData(male() As Single, female() As Single, _
                     numYears As Integer)
  Dim i As Integer
  Rem Draw rectangles
  For i = 1 To numYears
    picEnroll.Line (i - .3, male(i))-(i, 0), , BF
    picEnroll.Line (i, female(i))-(i + .3, 0), , B
  Next i
End Sub


Private Sub Locate(x As Single, y As Single)
  Let picEnroll.CurrentX = x
  Let picEnroll.CurrentY = y
End Sub


Private Sub ReadData(label() As String, male() As Single,
                     female() As Single, numYears As Integer,
                     maxEnroll As Single)
  Rem The three lines above should be entered as one line
  Dim i As Integer
  Rem Assume the data have been placed in the file ENROLLMF.TXT
  Rem (First line is file is "1970",1317,906)
  Rem Read data into arrays, find highest enrollment
  Open "ENROLLMF.TXT" For Input As #1
  Let maxEnroll = 0
```

```
      For i = 1 To numYears
        Input #1, label(i), male(i), female(i)
        If male(i) > maxEnroll Then
            Let maxEnroll = male(i)
        End If
        If female(i) > maxEnroll Then
            Let maxEnroll = female(i)
        End If
      Next i
      Close #1
    End Sub

    Private Sub ShowLabels(label() As String, numYears As Integer, _
                          maxEnroll As Single)
      Dim i As Integer, lbl As String, lblWid As Single
      Dim lblHght As Single, tickFactor As Single
      Rem Draw tick marks and label them
      For i = 1 To numYears
        Let lbl = label(i)
        Let lblWid = picEnroll.TextWidth(lbl)
        Let tickFactor = .02 * maxEnroll
        picEnroll.Line (i, -tickFactor)-(i, tickFactor)
        Call Locate(i - lblWid / 2, -tickFactor)
        picEnroll.Print lbl
      Next i
      Let lbl = Str(maxEnroll)
      Let lblWid = picEnroll.TextWidth(lbl)
      Let lblHght = picEnroll.TextHeight(lbl)
      Let tickFactor = .01 * numYears
      picEnroll.Line (-tickFactor, maxEnroll)-(tickFactor, maxEnroll)
      Call Locate(-tickFactor - lblWid, maxEnroll - lblHght / 2)
      picEnroll.Print lbl
    End Sub

    Private Sub ShowLegend(maxEnroll As Single)
      Rem Show legend
      picEnroll.Line (.1, 1.05 * maxEnroll)-(.9, .95 * maxEnroll), , BF
      Call Locate(1, 1.05 * maxEnroll)
      picEnroll.Print "Male"
      picEnroll.Line (.1, .9 * maxEnroll)-(.9, .8 * maxEnroll), , B
      Call Locate(1, .9 * maxEnroll)
      picEnroll.Print "Female"
    End Sub

    Private Sub ShowTitle(maxEnroll As Single)
      Rem Display source and title
      Call Locate(-.5, -.1 * maxEnroll)
      picEnroll.Print "Source: Statistical Abstract of the United States"
      Call Locate(.5, 1.2 * maxEnroll)
      picEnroll.Print "Two-Year College Enrollments (in thousands)"
    End Sub
```

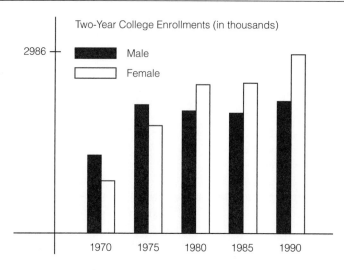

Figure 10.21 Chart for Example 2.

Comments

1. Any line chart can be converted to a bar chart and vice versa. Line charts are best suited for displaying quantities that vary with time. The slopes of the individual line segments clearly portray the rates at which the quantity is changing. Bar charts excel in contrasting the magnitudes of different entities.

2. The Line method can produce colored rectangles. The statement picBox.Line $(x1, y1)$–$(x2, y2)$, QBColor(c), B draws a rectangle in color c of Table 10.1 in Section 10.1. A solid rectangle of color c will be produced if B is replaced by BF. The use of color permits clustered bar charts with three bars per cluster.

3. In Section 10.4, we discuss a method to fill in rectangles using various patterns, such as horizontal lines and crosshatches. Using this technique, we can create black-and-white clustered bar charts having three or more bars per cluster.

PRACTICE PROBLEMS 10.3

Consider the bar chart in Figure 10.22.

1. How does this bar chart differ from the other charts considered so far?

2. Outline methods to achieve the effects referred to in the solution to Practice Problem 1.

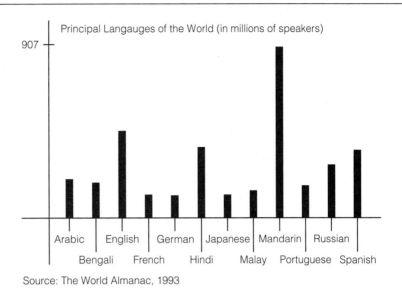

Source: The World Almanac, 1993

Figure 10.22 Bar chart for practice problems.

EXERCISES 10.3

1. Suppose data for a few more years are added to the data of Example 2. What changes will have to be made in the program?

In Exercises 2 through 9, write a program to display the given information in a bar chart.

2. United States Minimum Wage

1951	.75
1961	1.00
1971	1.25
1981	3.35
1991	4.25

3. Number of Computers in U.S. Public Schools, K–12 (in millions)

1985	.8
1987	1.4
1989	1.7
1991	2.2
1993	4.1

Source: Statistical Abstract of the United States, 1995

4. Largest Law Firms in Washington, D.C. (in number of lawyers)

Arnold & Porter	370
Covington & Burling	294
Hogan & Hartson	264
Shaw, Pittman, Potts, and Trowbridge	237
Arent, Fox, Kitner, Plotkin & Kahn	230

Source: Book of Lists 8th Annual 1992–1993 Reference Guide to the Washington Area's Leading Industries

5. Average Tuition and Required Fees at Four-Year Universities

	1970	1975	1980	1985	1990
Public	427	599	840	1388	2006
Private	1809	2614	3811	6826	10400

Source: Statistical Abstract of the United States, 1992

6. Educational Attainment of Persons 25 Years Old and Older (in %)

	1970	1980	1990
High School Graduate	52.3	66.5	77.6
College Graduate	10.7	16.2	21.3

Source: Statistical Abstract of the United States, 1992

7. New Automobile Retail Sales (in millions)

	1975	1980	1985	1990
Domestic	7.1	6.6	8.0	6.9
Imports	1.6	2.4	2.4	2.4

Source: Statistical Abstract of the United States, 1992

8. Principal Languages of the World (in millions of speakers)

Arabic	208	Japanese	126
Bengali	189	Malay	148
English	456	Mandarin	907
French	123	Portuguese	177
German	119	Russian	293
Hindi	383	Spanish	362

Source: The World Almanac, 1993

9. 1990 Federal Funding for Research and Development to Universities and Colleges (in millions of $)

Johns Hopkins Univ.	471	UC, Los Angeles	177
Stanford Univ.	248	Univ. of Michigan	177
MIT	218	UC, San Francisco	167
Univ. of Washington	217	UC, San Diego	165

Source: National Science Foundation

The program that follows draws a circle in the center of the picture box. In Exercises 10 through 12, rewrite the picOutput.Scale statement in order to achieve the stated result.

```
Private Sub cmdDraw_Click ()
  picOutput.Cls
  picOutput.Scale (-5, 5)-(5, -5)
  picOutput.Circle (0, 0), 2
End Sub
```

10. Draw the circle in the left half of the picture box.

11. Draw the circle in the right half of the picture box.

12. Draw the circle in the upper left corner of the picture box.

13. Clustered bar charts are sometimes drawn with overlapping rectangles. See Figure 10.23. What changes would have to be made to do this in the program of Example 2?

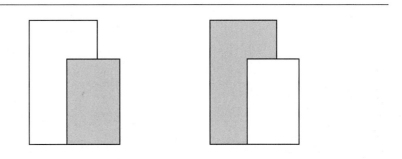

Figure 10.23 Clustered Bar Chart

SOLUTIONS TO PRACTICE PROBLEMS 10.3

1. (a) The number of characters in the labels is so large the labels must be placed in two rows.

 (b) Every other label had to be lowered.

 (c) Short vertical lines extend from the bars to the legends.

2. (a) A slight change in the picOutput.Scale statement will produce extra room at the bottom of the screen. The negative number that specifies the lower range of the y axis should be increased in magnitude.

 (b) The For...Next loop that places the label should be replaced by two loops that increment by 2 and place the labels on two rows.

 (c) The For...Next loops in step (b) should each draw vertical lines at the same spots where tick marks usually appear. The lines should extend from the x axis to the appropriate label. The length of these lines can be determined by experimentation.

10.4 PIE CHARTS

Drawing pie charts requires the Circle method and the FillStyle property. The Circle method draws not only circles, but also sectors (formed by an arc and two radius lines). The FillStyle property determines what pattern, if any, is used to fill a sector. The FillColor property can be used, if desired, to lend color to the fill patterns.

Figure 10.24 shows a circle with several radius lines drawn. The radius line extending to the right from the center of the circle is called the **horizontal radius line**. Every other radius line is assigned a number between 0 and 1 according to the percentage of the circle that must be swept out in the counterclockwise direction in order to reach that radius line. For instance, beginning at the horizontal radius line and rotating 1/4 of the way around the circle counterclockwise, we reach the radius line labeled .25.

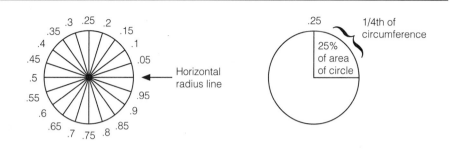

Figure 10.24 Numbers assigned to radius lines.

EXAMPLE 1   In Figure 10.25, what percentage of the area of the circle lies in the shaded sector?

Figure 10.25 Circle for Example 1.

SOLUTION   The percentage of the circle contained between the radius lines labeled .15 and .35 is 35% − 15%, or 20%.

The statement

```
picBox.Circle (x, y), r
```

draws the circle with center (x, y) and radius r. More precisely, the length of the horizontal radius line will be r units in the scale for the x axis determined by the Picture1.Scale statement. If $0 < a < b < 1$ and c is the circumference of the unit circle $(2*\pi)$, then the statement

```
picBox.Circle (x, y), r, , a * c, b * c
```

draws an arc from the end of radius line a to the end of radius line b. See Figure 10.26(a). The statement

```
picBox.Circle (x, y), r, , -a * c, -b * c
```

draws the sector corresponding to that arc. See Figure 10.26(b).

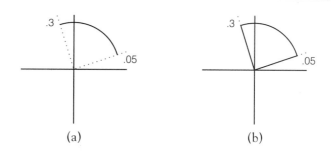

Figure 10.26 (a) Arc of a circle and (b) sector of a circle.

A special case occurs when *a* is 0. The expression –*a* * *c* will be zero rather than a negative number. As a result, Visual Basic does not draw the horizontal radius line associated with *a* = 0. In order to create a sector that has the horizontal radius line as one of its edges, use a small number such as .0000001 for *a*.

EXAMPLE 2   Write a program to draw a sector whose sides are a horizontal radius line and the radius line that is 40 percent of the way around the circle.

SOLUTION   The following program draws the sector with its center at the center of the picture box. The radius was arbitrarily chosen to be 2 and the picOutput.Scale statement was chosen so that the circle would be fairly large. The output displayed in the picture box is shown in Figure 10.27.

```
Private Sub cmdDraw_Click()
  Dim c As Single
  picOutput.Cls
  picOutput.Scale (-3, 3)-(3, -3)    'Specify coordinate system
  Let c = 2 * 3.14159
  Let a = .0000001
  Let b = .4
  Rem Draw sector with radius lines corresponding to 0 and .4
  picOutput.Circle (0, 0), 2, , -a * c, -b * c
End Sub
```

Figure 10.27 Display from Example 2.

A sector can be "painted" using any of the patterns shown in Figure 10.28. Which pattern is used to fill a sector is determined by the value of the FillStyle property. The default value of this property is 1 for transparent. Thus, by default, the interior of a sector is not painted.

Fill Style #	Fill Pattern	Fill Style #	Fill Pattern
0		4	
1		5	
2		6	
3		7	

Figure 10.28 Fill patterns.

EXAMPLE 3 Write a program to draw the sector consisting of the bottom half of a circle and fill it with vertical lines.

SOLUTION Vertical lines correspond to a FillStyle of 3. See Figure 10.29 for the output of the following program.

```
Private Sub cmdDraw_Click()
  Dim c As Single
  Rem Draw bottom half of circle filled with vertical lines
  Let c = 2 * 3.14159
  picSector.Cls
  picSector.Scale (-3, 3)-(3, -3)         'Specify coordinate system
  Let picSector.FillStyle = 3             'Vertical lines
  picSector.Circle (0, 0), 2, , -.5 * c, -1 * c
End Sub
```

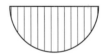

Figure 10.29 Display from Example 3.

The color used to fill the interior of a sector is determined by the value of the FillColor property. If the FillStyle of a picture box is any value except 1, then the statement

```
Let picBox.FillColor = QBColor(c)
```

will cause new circles and sectors drawn in the picture box to be filled with a pattern in color c of Table 10.1 in Section 10.1

EXAMPLE 4 Write a program to subdivide a circle into four quadrants and fill in the second quadrant, that is, the quadrant extending from radius line .25 to radius line .5, with magenta crosshatched lines.

SOLUTION Magenta corresponds to a FillColor of 5. Crosshatched lines correspond to a FillStyle of 6. See Figure 10.30 for the output of the following program.

```
Private Sub cmdDraw_Click()
  Dim c As Single
  Rem Draw quarters of circle and paint upper-left quadrant
  Let c = 2 * 3.14159
  picBox.Cls
  picBox.Scale (-3, 3)-(3, -3)          'Specify coordinate system
  picBox.Circle (0, 0), 2, , -.0000001 * c, -.25 * c
  Let picBox.FillStyle = 6              'Crosshatched
  Let picBox.FillColor = QBColor(5)     'Magenta
  picBox.Circle (0, 0), 2, , -.25 * c, -.5 * c
  Let picBox.FillStyle = 1             'Transparent
  picBox.Circle (0, 0), 2, , -.5 * c, -.75 * c
  picBox.Circle (0, 0), 2, , -.75 * c, -1 * c
End Sub
```

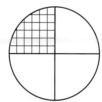

Figure 10.30 Display from Example 4.

The FillStyle and FillColor properties can be used when creating rectangles. The statements

```
Let picBox.FillStyle = s
Let picBox.FillColor = QBColor(c)
picBox.Line (x1, y1)-(x2, y2), , B
```

draw a rectangle filled with the pattern specified by s in the color specified by c. This capability is often used when creating the legend to accompany a graph.

The procedure for drawing a pie chart is as follows:

1. Read the categories and the quantities into arrays, such as *category*() and *quantity*().

2. Determine the radius lines. The number associated with the ith radius line is *cumPercent*(i). This number is a total of *quantity*(i) and the preceding percentages.

3. Draw and fill each sector with a pattern. The first sector extends from the horizontal radius line to radius line 1, the second sector from radius line 1 to radius line 2, and so on.

4. Draw rectangular legends to associate each sector with its category.

EXAMPLE 5   Table 10.3 gives the distribution of the 1991 revenue of Microsoft Corporation. Construct a pie chart that displays the sources of revenue.

	Revenue (in $millions)	Percent of Total Revenue
Operating systems & languages	648	36
Applications software	918	51
Other	234	13

Table 10.3 Sources of revenue: Microsoft Corp., 1991.

SOLUTION   Figure 10.31 shows the output displayed by the following program.

```
Private Sub cmdDraw_Click()
  Dim numItems As Integer, radius As Single
  Rem Draw pie chart of Microsoft Corporation's 1991 revenues
  Let numItems = 3
  ReDim category(1 To numItems) As String
  ReDim quantity(1 To numItems) As Single
  Call ReadData(category(), quantity(), numItems)
  Call DrawData(quantity(), numItems, radius)
  Call ShowLegend(category(), numItems, radius)
  Call ShowTitle(radius)
End Sub


Private Sub DrawData(quantity() As Single, numItems As Integer, _
                  radius As Single)
  Dim circumf As Single, leftEdge As Single, rightEdge As Single
  Dim topEdge As Single, bottomEdge As Single, i As Integer
  Dim startAngle As Single, stopAngle As Single
  Rem Draw and fill each sector of pie chart
  Rem All scaling & text positioning done as a percentage of radius
  Let radius = 1   'actual value used is not important
  Rem Make picture 4 radii wide to provide plenty of space for
  Rem circle and legends. Place origin 1.25 radii from left edge;
  Rem space of 1.75 radii will remain on right for legends.
  Let leftEdge = -1.25 * radius
  Let rightEdge = 2.75 * radius
  Rem Force vertical scale to match horizontal scale;
  Rem center origin vertically
  Let topEdge = 2 * radius * (picRevenue.Height / picRevenue.Width)
  Let bottomEdge = -topEdge
  picRevenue.Cls
  picRevenue.Scale (leftEdge, topEdge)-(rightEdge, bottomEdge)
  Let circumf = 2 * 3.14159
  ReDim cumPercent(0 To numItems) As Single
```

```
      Let cumPercent(0) = .0000001 'a "zero" that can be made negative
      For i = 1 To numItems
        Let cumPercent(i) = cumPercent(i - 1) + quantity(i)
        Let startAngle = cumPercent(i - 1) * circumf
        Let stopAngle = cumPercent(i) * circumf
        Let picRevenue.FillStyle = (8 - i) 'use fill patterns 7, 6, and 5
        picRevenue.Circle (0, 0), radius, , -startAngle, -stopAngle
      Next i
    End Sub


    Private Sub Locate (x As Single, y As Single)
      Let picRevenue.CurrentX = x
      Let picRevenue.CurrentY = y
    End Sub


    Private Sub ReadData(category() As String,quantity() As Single, _
                    numItems As Integer)
      Dim i As Integer
      Rem Load categories and percentages of revenue
      Rem Assume the data have been placed in the file REVENUE.TXT
      Rem (First line in file is "Oper. Systems and Lang.",.36)
      Open "REVENUE.TXT" For Input As #1
      For i = 1 To numItems
        Input #1, category(i), quantity(i)
      Next i
      Close #1
    End Sub


    Private Sub ShowLegend(category() As String, numItems As Integer, _
                    radius As Single)
      Dim lblHght As Single, legendSize As Single
      Dim i As Integer, vertPos As Single
      Rem Place legend centered to right of pie chart
      Rem Make separation between items equal to one line of text
      Rem "Text lines" needed for legends is thus (2*numItems-1)
      Let lblHght = picRevenue.TextHeight(" ")
      Let legendSize = lblHght * (2 * numItems - 1)
      For i = 1 To numItems
        Let picRevenue.FillStyle = (8 - i)
        Let vertPos = (legendSize / 2) - (3 - i) * (2 * lblHght)
        picRevenue.Line (1.1 * radius, vertPos)-(1.4 * radius, _
                    vertPos + lblHght),.,B
        Call Locate(1.5 * radius, vertPos)
        picRevenue.Print category(i)
      Next i
    End Sub

    Private Sub ShowTitle(radius As Single)
      Dim lbl As String, lblWid As Single
      Rem Display title right below circle
      Let lbl = "Sources of Revenue: Microsoft, 1991"
      Let lblWid = picRevenue.TextWidth(lbl)
      Call Locate(-lblWid / 2, -radius)
      picRevenue.Print lbl
    End Sub
```

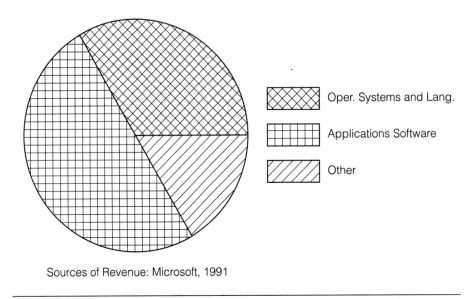

Sources of Revenue: Microsoft, 1991

Figure 10.31 Display from Example 5.

PRACTICE PROBLEMS 10.4

1. Label each of the radius lines in Figure 10.32 with a number from 0 to 1.

Figure 10.32 Circle for Practice Problem 1.

2. Write a program to draw the circle and radius lines in Problem 1 and to fill in the sector consisting of 30 percent of the area of the circle.

EXERCISES 10.4

1. Label each of the radius lines in Figure 10.33(a) with a number from 0 to 1.

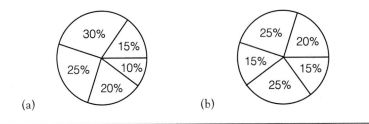

Figure 10.33 Circles for Exercises 1 and 2.

2. Label each of the radius lines in Figure 10.33(b) with a number from 0 to 1.

3. Write a program to draw the circle and radius lines of Figure 10.33(a) and to fill in the sector consisting of 10 percent of the circle.

4. Write a program to draw the circle and radius lines of Figure 10.33(b) and to fill in the sector consisting of 25 percent of the circle.

In Exercises 5 and 6, draw a pie chart to display the given data.

5. United States Recreational Beverage Consumption (1995)

Soft Drinks	52.9%
Beer	14.7%
Bottled Water	11.1%
Other	21.3%

Source: International Bottle Water Association

6. Average Number of Miles from College to Home for College Freshmen

5 or less	10%	51 to 100	15%
6 to 10	8%	101 to 500	28%
11 to 50	30%	more than 500	9%

Source: Higher Education Research Institute

7. Construct a general pie-chart program that prompts the user for the title, the number of sectors (2 through 8), and legends. Try the program with the following data.

Share of Bagel Market, 1996

Supermarkets	54%
Bagel stores	20%
Bakeries	20%
Other	6%

Source: Bakery Production and Marketing magazine, Food Marketing Institute

8. Modify the program in Exercise 7 to accept raw data and convert them to percentages. Try the program with the following data.

Fiscal Year 1997 Operating Budget for Montgomery County, Maryland (in millions of dollars)

Board of Education	915	Health and Human Services	102
Public Works and Transportation	235	Montgomery College	97
Public Safety	207	Other	62
Debt Service	146		

Source: Montgomery County Government Department of Finance

9. Write a program that produces the drawing in Figure 10.34.

Figure 10.34 Drawing for Exercise 9.

10. Write a program that draws a Smiley face. See Figure 10.35.

Figure 10.35 Drawing for Exercise 10.

SOLUTIONS TO PRACTICE PROBLEMS 10.4

1. Each number was obtained by summing the percentages for each of the sectors from the horizontal radius line to the radius line under consideration.

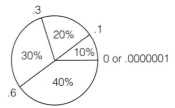

2. The 30 percent sector is the third sector, extending from radius line .3 to radius line .6.

```
Private Sub cmdDraw_Click()
  Dim perc(1 To 4) As Single
  Let perc(0) = .0000001
  Let perc(1) = .1
  Let perc(2) = .3
  Let perc(3) = .6
  Let perc(4) = 1
  picOutput.Cls
  picOutput.Scale (-3, 3)-(3, -3)   'Specify coordinate system
  Let c = 2 * 3.14159
  For i = 1 To 4
    If i = 3 Then
        picOutput.FillStyle = 0    'Solid fill
      Else
        picOutput.FillStyle = 1    'Transparent fill
    End If
    picOutput.Circle (0, 0), 2,, -perc(i - 1) * c, -perc(i) * c   'Draw sector
  Next i
End Sub
```

Chapter 10
Summary

1. Data can be vividly displayed in *line, bar, clustered bar,* and *pie charts.* Screen dumps of these charts produce printed copy.

2. The programmer can select his or her own coordinate system with the Scale method.

3. The Line method draws lines, rectangles, and solid rectangles. Styled lines can be drawn by assigning appropriate values to the DrawStyle property.

4. The Circle method statement is used to draw circles, radius lines, and sectors. Each radius line is specified by a number between 0 and 1. The number $2 * \pi$ (or 6.283185) is used by the Circle method when drawing radii and sectors.

5. The PSet method turns on a single point and is useful in graphing functions.

6. The FillStyle property allows circles, sectors, and rectangles to be filled with one of eight patterns, and the QBColor( ) function allows them to appear in assorted colors.

Chapter 10
Programming Projects

1. Look in magazines and newspapers for four sets of data, one suited to each type of chart discussed in this chapter. Write programs to display the data in chart form.

2. Figure 10.36 is called a *horizontal bar chart.* Write a program to produce this chart.

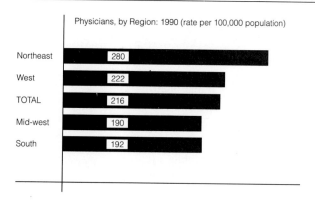

Figure 10.36 Horizontal bar chart.

3. Figure 10.37 is called a segmented bar chart. Write a program to construct this chart.

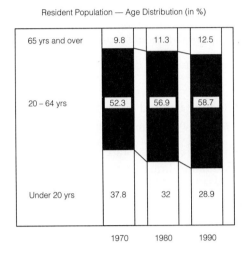

Figure 10.37 Segmented bar chart.

4. Figure 10.38 is called a *range chart*. Using the data in Table 10.4, write a program to produce this chart.

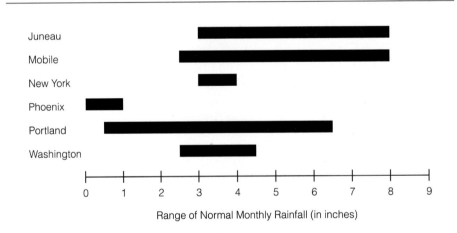

Figure 10.38 Range chart.

	Lowest NMR	Highest NMR
Mobile	2.6	7.7
Portland	.5	6.4
Phoenix	.1	1.0
Washington	2.6	4.4
Juneau	2.9	7.7
New York	3.1	4.2

Table 10.4 Range of normal monthly rainfall for selected cities (in inches).

11

Additional Controls and Objects

11.1 **List Boxes and Combo Boxes / 496**
• The List Box Control • The Combo Box Control
• Drive, Directory, and File List Box Controls

11.2 **Nine Elementary Controls / 508**
• The Frame Control • The Check Box Control
• The Option Button Control • The Horizontal
and Vertical Scroll Bar Controls • The Timer
Control • The Shape Control • The Line Control
• The Image Control

11.3 **Five Additional Objects / 523**
• The Microsoft FlexGrid Control • The Menu Control
• The Clipboard Object • Multiple Forms • The Common
Dialog Control

Summary / 541

Programming Projects / 542

11.1 LIST BOXES AND COMBO BOXES

The dialog box in Figure 11.1 contains one **list box** and three **combo boxes**. The Folders list box displays a list of folders (also known as directories). You click on a folder to highlight it and double-click on a folder to open it. A combo box combines the features of a text box and a list box. In the "File name" combo box, you click on a file to have it duplicated in the associated text box and double-click on a file to open it. (You also can type directly into the associated text box.) With the other two combo boxes (known as dropdown combo boxes), only the text box part is showing. The associated list drops down when you click on the arrow to the right of the text box part.

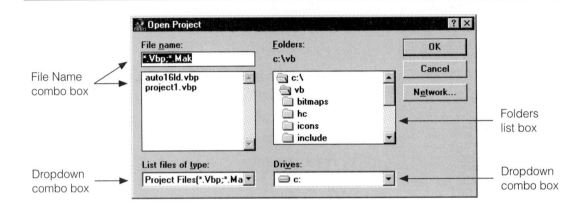

Figure 11.1 Open Project dialog box.

The List Box Control

The fifth row of the standard toolbox (in most editions of Visual Basic) contains the combo box icon on the left and the list box icon on the right. The list boxes discussed in this text will display a single column of strings, referred to as **items**. The items to appear initially can either be specified at design time with the List property or set with code in the Form_Load event procedure. Then code is used to access, add, or delete items from the list. We will first carry out all tasks with code, and then show how the initial items can be specified at design time.

The Sorted property is perhaps the most interesting list box property. When it is set to True, the items will automatically be displayed in alphabetical (that is, ANSI) order. The default value of the Sorted property is False.

If *str* is a string, then the statement

```
List1.AddItem str
```

adds *str* to the list. The item is added at the proper sorted position if the Sorted property is True, and otherwise is added to the end of the list. At any time, the value of

```
List1.ListCount
```

is the number of items in the list box.

Each item in the List1 list box is identified by an index number ranging from 0 through List1.ListCount − 1. The value of

    List1.NewIndex

is the index number of the item most recently added to List1 by the AddItem method. During run time you can highlight an item from a list by clicking on it with the mouse or by moving to it with the up- and down-arrow keys. (The second method triggers the Click event each time an arrow key causes the highlight to move.) The value of

    List1.ListIndex

is the index number of the item currently highlighted in List1.

The string array List1.List( ) holds the list of items stored in the list box. In particular, the value of

    List1.List(*n*)

is the item of List1 having index *n*. For instance, the statement Print List1.List(0) displays the first item of the list box List1. The value of

    List1.List(List1.ListIndex)

is the item (string) currently highlighted in list box List1. Alternatively, the value of

    List1.Text

is the currently highlighted item. Unlike the Text property of a text box, you may not assign a value to List1.Text.

The statement

    List1.RemoveItem *n*

deletes the item of index *n* from List1, the statement

    List1.RemoveItem List1.ListIndex

deletes the item currently highlighted in List1, and the statement

    List1.Clear

deletes every item of List1.

EXAMPLE 1 An oxymoron is a pairing of contradictory or incongruous words. The following program displays a sorted list of oxymorons. When you click an item (or highlight it with the up- and down-arrow keys), it is displayed in a picture box. A command button allows you to add an additional item with an Input box. You can delete an item by double-clicking on it with the mouse. (**Note:** When you double-click the mouse, two events are processed—the Click event and the double-click event.) After running the program, click on different items, add an item or two (such as "same difference" or "liquid gas"), and delete an item.

Object	Property	Setting
frmOxyMor	Caption	OXYMORONS
lstOxys	Sorted	True
cmdAdd	Caption	Add an Item
lblDelete	Caption	[To delete an item, double-click on it.]
picSelected		

```
Private Sub cmdAdd_Click()
  Dim item As String
  Let item = InputBox("Item to Add:")
  lstOxys.AddItem item
End Sub

Private Sub Form_Load()
  lstOxys.AddItem "jumbo shrimp"
  lstOxys.AddItem "definite maybe"
  lstOxys.AddItem "old news"
  lstOxys.AddItem "good grief"
End Sub

Private Sub lstOxys_Click()
  picSelected.Cls
  picSelected.Print "The selected item is"
  picSelected.Print Chr(34) & lstOxys.Text & Chr(34) & "."
End Sub

Private Sub LstOxys_DblClick()
  lstOxys.RemoveItem lstOxys.ListIndex
End Sub
```

[Run and then click on the second item of the list box.]

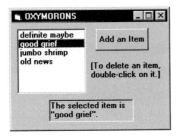

The following steps show how to fill a list box at design time. (This method is used in Example 3.)

1. Select the List property of the list box.

2. Click on the down arrow of the settings box. (A small box will be displayed.)

3. Type in the first item and press Ctrl+Enter. (The cursor will move to the next line.)

4. Repeat Step 3 for each of the other items.

5. When you are finished entering items, press the enter key.

When the Sorted property of a list box is True, the index associated with an item will change when a "lesser" item is added to or removed from the list. In many applications it is important to have a fixed number associated with each item in a list box. Visual Basic makes this possible using the ItemData property. The statement

```
List1.ItemData(n) = m
```

associates the number *m* with the item of index *n*, and the statement

```
List1.ItemData(List1.NewIndex) = m
```

associates the number *m* with the item most recently added to the list box. Thus, the List1 list box can be thought of as consisting of two arrays, List1.List( ) and List1.ItemData( ). The contents of List1.List( ) are displayed in the list box, allowing the user to make a selection while the hidden contents of List1.ItemData( ) can be used by the programmer to index records or, as illustrated in Example 2, to set up parallel arrays that hold other data associated with each item displayed in the list box.

EXAMPLE 2   The following program uses NewIndex and ItemData to provide data about inventions. When an item is highlighted, its ItemData value is used to locate the appropriate entries in the inventor( ) and date( ) arrays. Assume the file INVENTOR. TXT contains the following three lines:

"Ball-point pen", "Lazlo and George Biro", 1938
"Frozen food", "Robert Birdseye", 1929
"Bifocal lenses", "Ben Franklin", 1784

Object	Property	Setting
frmInvent	Caption	Inventions
lstInvents	Sorted	True
lblInventor	Caption	Inventor
lblWho	Caption	(none)
lblYear	Caption	Year
lblWhen	Caption	(none)

```
Rem In the (Declarations) section of (General)
Dim inventor(0 To 10) As String
Dim yr(0 To 10) As Integer

Private Sub Form_Load()
  Dim what As String, who As String, when As Integer, index As Integer
  Open "INVENTOR.TXT" For Input As #1
  Let index = 0
  Do While (index < UBound(inventor)) And (Not EOF(1))
    Input #1, what, who, when
    Let index = index + 1
    lstInvents.AddItem what
```

```
      Let lstInvents.ItemData(lstInvents.NewIndex) = index
      Let inventor(index) = who
      Let yr(index) = when
  Loop
End Sub

Private Sub lstInvents_Click()
  Let lblWho.Caption = inventor(lstInvents.ItemData(lstInvents.ListIndex))
  Let lblWhen.Caption = Str(yr(lstInvents.ItemData(lstInvents.ListIndex)))
End Sub
```

[Run and then highlight the second entry in the list.]

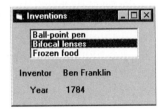

The Combo Box Control

A combo box is best thought of as a text box with a help list attached. With an ordinary text box, the user must type information into the box. With a combo box, the user has the option of either typing in information or just selecting the appropriate piece of information from a list. The two most useful types of combo box are denoted as style 0 and style 1 combo boxes. See Figure 11.2.

Style 0 combo box   Style 1 combo box

Figure 11.2 Styles of combo boxes.

With a style 1 combo box, the list is always visible. With a style 0 combo box, the list drops down when the user clicks on the arrow, and then disappears after a selection is made. In either case, when an item from the list is highlighted, the item automatically appears in the text box at the top and its value is assigned to the Text property of the combo box.

Combo boxes have essentially the same properties, events, and methods as list boxes. In particular, all the statements discussed before for list boxes also hold for combo boxes. The Style property of a combo box is usually specified at design time.

EXAMPLE 3 The following program uses a style 1 combo box to obtain a person's title for the first line of the address of a letter. (**Note:** At design time, first set the combo box's Style property to 1, and then lengthen the combo box.)

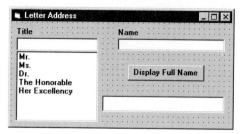

Object	Property	Setting
frmTitle	Caption	Letter Address
lblTitle	Caption	Title
cboTitle	List	Mr.
		Ms.
		Dr.
		The Honorable
		Her Excellency
	Style	1 – Simple Combo
	Text	(blank)
lblName	Caption	Name
txtName	Text	(blank)
cmdDisplay	Caption	Display Full Name
txtDisplay	Text	(blank)

```
Private Sub cmdDisplay_Click()
  Let txtDisplay.Text = cboTitle.Text & " " & txtName.Text
End Sub
```

[Run, select an item from the combo box, type a name into the Name text box, and click the command button.]

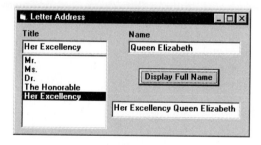

The same program with a style 0 combo box produces the output shown.

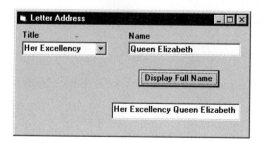

Drive ▣, Directory ▢, and File ▤ List Box Controls

Boxes similar to those inside the Open Project dialog box of Figure 11.1 are available to any Visual Basic program via icons from the Toolbox. Visual Basic does much of the work of providing the appropriate lists for the three boxes. Windows determines the contents of the drive box. The programmer determines the contents of directory list boxes and file list boxes with Path properties.

Most of the properties, methods, and events of list boxes are also valid for the three file-related list boxes. For instance, in the file list box File1, File1.List-Count is the number of files and File1.List(n) is the name of the nth file, where counting begins with 0. The selected items for the three controls are identified by the Drive, Path, and FileName properties, respectively. For instance, in the drive list box Drive1, the selected drive is given by the string Drive1.Drive.

Suppose a form contains a drive list box named Drive1, a directory list box named Dir1, and a file list box named File1. (These names are the default names supplied by Visual Basic.) When the user selects a new drive from the Drive1 list box, the directories in Dir1 should reflect this change. The proper event procedure to effect the change is

```
Private Sub Drive1_Change()
  Dir1.Path = Drive1.Drive
End Sub
```

This event is triggered by clicking on the drive name or using the arrow keys to highlight the drive name and then pressing Enter. When the user selects a new directory in Dir1, the files in File1 can be changed with the event procedure

```
Private Sub Dir1_Change()
  File1.Path = Dir1.Path
End Sub
```

This event procedure is triggered by double-clicking on a directory name. If the preceding two event procedures are in place, a change of the drive will trigger a change of the directory, which in turn will trigger a change in the list of files. The standard prefix for the names of the drive, directory, and file list box controls are drv, dir, and fil, respectively.

EXAMPLE 4   The following program can be used to display the full name of any file on any drive.

Object	Property	Setting
frmFiles	Caption	Select a File
drvList		
dirList		
filList		
cmdDisplay	Caption	Display Complete Name of File
picFileSpec		

```
Private Sub cmdDisplay_Click()
  picFileSpec.Cls
  picFileSpec.Print dirList.Path;
```

```
    If Right(dirList.Path, 1) <> "\" Then
        picFileSpec.Print "\";
    End If
    picFileSpec.Print filList.FileName
End Sub

Private Sub dirList_Change()
  Let filList.Path = dirList.Path
End Sub

Private Sub drvList_Change()
  Let dirList.Path = drvList.Drive
End Sub
```

[Run, select a drive, double-click on a directory, select a file, and then click the command button.]

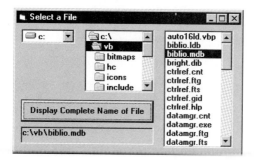

Comments

1. If a list or combo box is too short to display all the items that have been added to it, Visual Basic automatically places a vertical scroll bar on the right side of the list box. The user can then scroll to see the remaining items of the list.

2. When the Style property of a combo box is set to 2, the combo box becomes a dropdown list box. The Drive list box is an example of a dropdown list box.

3. Dropdown combo boxes (Style 0) are used in Windows applications as a text box with a "history list" (list of past entries) from which you can either type a new entry or select an old entry.

4. The standard Windows convention for opening a file is to double-click on a name in a file list box. The program must contain code for a DblClick event procedure to carry out this task.

5. File list boxes can be made to display selective lists based on wildcard characters by setting the Pattern property. For instance, setting File1.Pattern equal to "*.TXT" dictates that only files with the extension TXT will be displayed.

PRACTICE PROBLEMS 11.1

1. Write code to record the contents of a list box into a file.

2. Give a statement that will display the last item in the combo box cboBox.

EXERCISES 11.1

For Exercises 1 through 12, suppose that the list box lstBox is as shown and determine the effect of the code. (Assume the Sorted property is set to True.)

```
Bach
Beethoven
Chopin
Mozart
Tchaikovsky
```

1. `picOutput.Print lstBox.Text`

2. `picOutput.Print lstBox.List(2)`

3. `picOutput.Print lstBox.List(lstBox.ListCount - 1)`

4. `lstBox.AddItem "Haydn"`

5. `lstBox.AddItem "Brahms"`
   `picOutput.Print lstBox.List(lstBox.NewIndex)`

6. `lstBox.RemoveItem 0`

7. `lstBox.RemoveItem lstBox.ListIndex`

8. `lstBox.RemoveItem lstBox.ListCount - 1`

9. `lstBox.Clear`

10. ```
    Open "COMPOSER.TXT" For Output As #1
    For n = 0 To lstBox.ListCount - 1
      Write #1, lstBox.List(n)
    Next n
    Close #1
    ```

11. ```
    For n = 0 To lstBox.ListCount - 1
      If Len(lstBox.List(n)) = 6 Then
          lstBox.RemoveItem n
      End If
    Next n
    ```

12. ```
    For n = 0 To lstBox.ListCount - 1
      Let Composer(n) = lstBox.List(n)   'Composer() is a string array
    Next n
    lstBox.Sorted = False
    lstBox.Clear
    For n = lstBox.ListCount - 1 To 0 Step -1
      lstBox.AddItem Composer(n)
    Next n
    ```
    ```

In Exercises 13 through 24, assume that the combo box cboBox appears as shown and that the Sorted property is set to True. Give a statement or statements that will carry out the stated task.

13. Display the string "Dante".

14. Display the string "Goethe".

15. Display the first item of the list. (The statement should do the job even if additional items were added to the list.)

16. Delete the string "Shakespeare".

17. Delete the string "Goethe".

18. Delete the last item of the list. (The statement should do the job even if additional items were added to the list.)

19. Insert the string "Cervantes". Where will it be inserted?

20. Display every other item of the list in a picture box.

21. Delete every item beginning with the letter "M". (The code should do the job even if additional items were added to the list.)

22. Determine if "Cervantes" is in the list. (The statement should do the job even if additional items were added to the list.)

23. Display the item most recently added to the list.

24. Store the items in the file AUTHOR.TXT.

In Exercises 25 through 30, suppose the form contains a list box containing positive numbers, a command button, and a picture box. Write a click event procedure for the command button that displays the requested information in the picture box.

25. The average of the numbers in the list.

26. The largest number in the list.

27. Every other number in the list.

28. All numbers greater than the average.

29. The *spread* of the list, that is, the difference between the largest and smallest numbers in the list.

30. The median of the numbers in the list.

31. Assume the data in Table 11.1 are contained in the sequential file STATEINF. TXT. Write a program that shows the states in a sorted list box and displays a state's nickname and motto when the state is double-clicked.

State	Nickname	Motto
Wisconsin	Badger State	Forward
Rhode Island	Ocean State	Hope
Texas	Lone Star State	Friendship
Utah	Beehive State	Industry

Table 11.1 State nicknames and mottos.

32. Table 11.2 contains the five U.S. presidents rated highest by history professors. Create a form with a list box and two command buttons captioned "Order by Year Inaugurated" and "Order by Age at Inaugural." Write a program that shows the Presidents in the list box. When one of the command buttons is clicked, the list box should display the presidents in the requested order.

President	Year Inaugurated	Age at Inaugural
Abraham Lincoln	1861	52
Franklin Roosevelt	1933	51
George Washington	1789	57
Thomas Jefferson	1801	58
Theodore Roosevelt	1901	42

Table 11.2 Highest rated U.S. presidents.

33. Table 11.3 contains wind-chill factors for several temperatures (in degrees Fahrenheit) and wind speeds (in miles per hour). Write a program containing the temperatures in one list box and the wind speeds in another. When the user selects an item from each list box and clicks on a command button, the program should display the corresponding wind-chill factor.

		Speed		
	5	10	15	20
0	–5	–22	–31	–39
Temperature 5	0	–15	–25	–31
10	7	–9	–18	–24
15	12	–3	–11	–17

Table 11.3 Wind-chill factors.

34. Suppose a form contains a list box (with Sorted = False), a label, and two command buttons captioned "Add an Item" and "Delete an Item". When the Add an Item button is clicked, the program should request an item with an input box and then insert the item above the currently highlighted item. When the Delete an Item button is clicked, the program should remove the highlighted item from the list. At all times, the label should display the number of items in the list.

35. Consider the Length Converter in Figure 11.3. Write a program to place the items in the list and carry out the conversion. (See the first programming project in Chapter 7 for a table of equivalent lengths.)

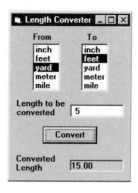

Figure 11.3 Form for Exercise 35.

36. Write a program to ask a person which Monopoly®space he or she has landed on and then display the result in a picture box. The response should be obtained with a combo box listing the squares most commonly landed on—Illinois Avenue, Go, B&O Railroad, and Free Parking. (One possible outcome to be displayed in the picture box is "You have landed on Park Place.")

37. Write a program to question a person about his or her IBM-compatible computer and then display a descriptive sentence in a picture box. The form should contain combo boxes for brand, amount of memory, and size of screen. The lists should contain the most common responses for each category. The most common PCs are Compaq, Dell, Packard Bell, IBM, and Gateway 2000. The most common amounts of memory are 16MB, 24MB, 32MB and 64MB. The most common screen sizes are 14 inch, 15 inch, and 17 inch. (One possible outcome to be displayed in the picture box is "You have a Gateway 2000 computer with 32MB of memory and a 17 inch monitor.")

38. Modify the program in Example 4 so that the names of all the files with extension .frm in the files list box are printed on the printer.

39. Write a program to display a picture (contained in a .bmp file in the Windows directory) in a picture box. A file should be selected with drive, directory, and file list boxes and the picture displayed with a statement of the form Let picBox.Picture = LoadPicture(*full name of file*).

SOLUTIONS TO PRACTICE PROBLEMS 11.1

```
1. Private Sub SaveListBox()
     Dim i As Integer
     Open "LISTDATA.TXT" For Output As #1
     For i = 0 to lstBox.ListCount - 1
       Write #1, lstBox.List(i)
     Next i
     Close #1
   End Sub
```

```
2. picBox.Print cboBox.List(cboBox.ListCount - 1)
```

11.2 NINE ELEMENTARY CONTROLS

In this section, we discuss the nine controls indicated on the Toolbox in Figure 11.4.

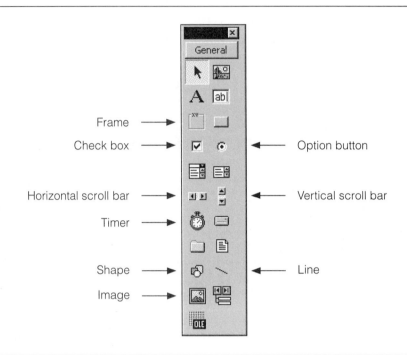

Figure 11.4 Nine elementary controls.

The Frame Control

Frames are passive objects used to group related sets of controls for visual effect. You rarely write event procedures for frames. The preceding frame has a group of three text boxes attached to it. When you drag the frame, the attached controls follow as a unit. If you hide the frame, the attached controls will be hidden as well.

A control must be attached to a frame in a special way. You cannot just double-click to create the control and then drag it into a frame. To attach a control to a frame, first create the frame. Next, single-click on the control icon to activate it, then move the mouse pointer inside the frame to the point where you want to place the upper-left corner of the control. Finally, drag the mouse to the right and down, and then release the mouse button when you are satisfied with the size of the control. This is referred to as the **single-click-draw technique**.

A group of controls also can be attached to a picture box. The advantages of using frames are that they have a title sunk into their borders that can be set with the Caption property and that they cannot receive the focus. As shown later in this section, the frame control is particularly important when working with groups of option button controls. The standard prefix for the name of a frame is fra.

The Check Box Control ☑

A check box, which consists of a small square and a caption, presents the user with a yes/no choice. The form in Example 1 uses four check box controls. The Value property of a check box is 0 when the square is empty and is 1 when the square is checked. At run time, the user clicks on the square to toggle between the unchecked and checked states. So doing also triggers the Click event.

EXAMPLE 1   The following program allows an employee to compute the monthly cost of various benefit packages.

Object	Property	Setting
frmBenefits	Caption	Benefits Menu
chkDrugs	Caption	Prescription Drug Plan ($12.51)
	Value	0 – Unchecked
chkDental	Caption	Dental Plan ($9.68)
	Value	0 – Unchecked
chkVision	Caption	Vision Plan ($1.50)
	Value	0 – Unchecked
chkMedical	Caption	Medical Plan ($25.25)
	Value	0 – Unchecked
lblTotal	Caption	Total monthly payment:
lblAmount	Caption	$0.00

```
Private Sub chkDrugs_Click()
  Call Tally
End Sub

Private Sub chkDental_Click()
  Call Tally
End Sub

Private Sub chkVision_Click()
  Call Tally
End Sub

Private Sub chkMedical_Click()
  Call Tally
End Sub

Private Sub Tally()
  Dim sum As Single
  If chkDrugs.Value = 1 Then
      Let sum = sum + 12.51
  End If
  If chkDental.Value = 1 Then
      Let sum = sum + 9.68
  End If
```

```
    If chkVision.Value = 1 Then
        Let sum = sum + 1.5
    End If
    If chkMedical.Value = 1 Then
        Let sum = sum + 25.25
    End If
    Let lblAmount.Caption = Format(sum, "Currency")
End Sub
```

[Run and then click on the desired options.]

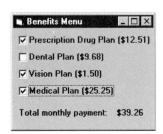

When a check box has the focus, the spacebar can be used to check (or uncheck) the box and invoke the click event. In addition, the state of a check box can be toggled from the keyboard without first setting the focus to the check box if you create an access key for the check box by including an ampersand in the Caption property. (Access keys appear underlined at run time). For instance, if the Caption property for the Dental Plan in Example 1 is set as "&Dental Plan", then the user can check (or uncheck) the box by pressing Alt+D.

Notice that the program code for the solution to Example 1 involved four identical click event procedures. This is a good indication that a control array of check boxes will simplify the program, as shown in Example 2.

EXAMPLE 2   The following program reworks Example 1 using a control array of check boxes, with an access key for each check box. The program has been made more general and easy to update by placing the name and cost of each benefit plan in the data file BENEFITS.TXT. Each line of the file consists of the name of the plan followed by the cost of the plan, as illustrated by the first line of the file:

"&Prescription Drug Plan", 12.51

Object	Property	Setting
frmBenefits	Caption	Benefits Menu
chkPlan( )	Index	0 through 3
lblTotal	Caption	Total monthly payment:
lblAmount	Caption	$0.00

```
Dim price(0 To 3) As Single 'In (Declarations) section of (General)
Dim sum As Single

Private Sub Form_Load()
    Dim i As Integer, plan As String, cost As Single
    Open "BENEFITS.TXT" For Input As #1
```

```
  For i = 0 To 3
    Input #1, plan, cost
    Let price(i) = cost
    Let chkPlan(i).Caption = plan & " (" & Format(cost, "Currency") & ")"
  Next i
  Close 1
  Let sum = 0
End Sub

Private Sub chkPlan_Click(Index As Integer)
  If chkPlan(Index).Value = 1 Then
      Let sum = sum + price(Index)
    Else
      Let sum = sum - price(Index)
  End If
  Let lblAmount.Caption = Format(sum, "Currency")
End Sub
```

The Value property of a check box also can be set to "2-Grayed". When a grayed square is clicked, it becomes unchecked. When clicked again, it becomes checked.

The Option Button Control

Option buttons are used to give the user a single choice from several options. Normally, a group of several option buttons is attached to a frame or picture box with the single-click-draw technique. Each button consists of a small circle accompanied by text that is set with the Caption property. When a circle or its accompanying text is clicked, a solid dot appears in the circle and the button is said to be "on." At most one option button in a group can be on at the same time. Therefore, if one button is on and another button in the group is clicked, the first button will turn off. By convention, the names of option buttons have the prefix opt.

The Value property of an option button tells if the button is on or off. The condition

```
    optButton.Value
```

is True when optButton is on and False when optButton is off. The statement

```
    Let optButton.Value = True
```

turns on optButton and turns off all other buttons in its group. The statement

```
    Let optButton.Value = False
```

turns off optButton and has no effect on the other buttons in its group.

The Click event for an option button is triggered only when an off button is turned on. It is not triggered when an on button is clicked.

EXAMPLE 3   The following program tells you if an option button is on.

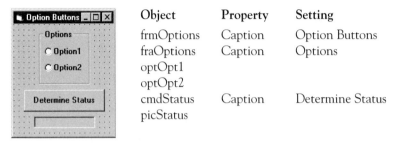

Object	Property	Setting
frmOptions	Caption	Option Buttons
fraOptions	Caption	Options
optOpt1		
optOpt2		
cmdStatus	Caption	Determine Status
picStatus		

```
Private Sub cmdStatus_Click()
  picStatus.Cls
  If optOpt1.Value = True Then
      picStatus.Print "Option1 is on."
    ElseIf optOpt2.Value = True Then
      picStatus.Print "Option2 is on."
  End If
End Sub


Private Sub Form_Load()
   Let optOpt1.Value = False    'Turn off optOpt1
   Let optOpt2.Value = False    'Turn off optOpt2
End Sub
```

[Run, click on one of the option buttons, and then click the command button.]

The text alongside an option button is specified with the Caption property. As with a command button and a check box, an ampersand can be used to create an access key for an option button.

EXAMPLE 4   The following program allows the user to select text size in a text box. The three option buttons have been attached to the frame with the single-click-draw technique.

Object	Property	Setting
frmSize	Caption	Change Size
fraFontSize	Caption	Font Size
opt12pt	Caption	&12
opt18pt	Caption	1&8
opt24pt	Caption	&24
txtInfo	Text	Hello

```
Private Sub opt12pt_Click()
  Let txtInfo.Font.Size = 12
End Sub

Private Sub opt18pt_Click()
  Let txtInfo.Font.Size = 18
End Sub

Private Sub opt24pt_Click()
  Let txtInfo.Font.Size = 24
End Sub
```

[Run and click on the last option button (or press Alt+2).]

A single form can have several groups of option buttons. However, each group must be attached to its own frame or picture box.

The Horizontal and Vertical Scroll Bar Controls

Figure 11.5 shows the two types of scroll bars. When the user clicks on one of the arrow buttons, the thumb moves a small amount toward that arrow. When the user clicks between the thumb and one of the arrow buttons, the thumb moves a large amount toward that arrow. The user can also move the thumb by dragging it. The main properties of a scroll bar control are Min, Max, Value, SmallChange, and LargeChange, which are set to whole numbers. At any time, hsbBar.Value is a number between hsbBar.Min and hsbBar.Max determined by the position of the thumb. If the thumb is halfway between the two arrows, then hsbBar.Value is a number halfway between hsbBar.Min and hsbBar.Max. If the thumb is near the left arrow button, then hsbBar.Value is an appropriately proportioned value near hsbBar.Min, etc. When an arrow button is clicked, hsbBar.Value changes by hsbBar.SmallChange and the thumb moves accordingly. When the bar between the thumb and one of the arrows is clicked, hsbBar.Value changes by hsbBar.LargeChange and the thumb moves accordingly. When the thumb is dragged, hsbBar.Value changes accordingly. The default values of Min, Max, SmallChange, and LargeChange are 0, 32767, 1, and 1, respectively. However, these values are usually reset at design time. **Note:** The setting for the Min property can be a number greater than the setting for the Max property. The Min property determines the values for the left and top arrows. The Max property determines the values for the right and bottom arrows.

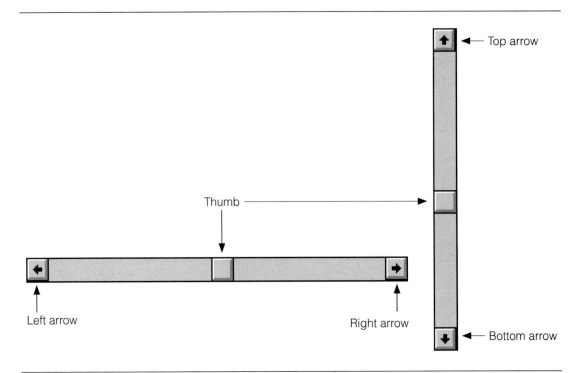

Figure 11.5 Horizontal and vertical scroll bars.

The Change event is triggered whenever an arrow or bar is clicked, or after the thumb has been dragged. The Scroll event is triggered whenever the thumb is being dragged.

EXAMPLE 5 The following program uses scroll bars to move a smiling face around the form. The face is a large Wingdings character J inside a label. The values lblFace.Left and lblFace.Top are the distances in twips of the label from the left side and top of the form. (When printing, 1440 twips equal one inch; on the screen, 1440 twips are more or less an inch.)

Object	Property	Setting
frmFace	Caption	Smiling Face
hsbXPos	Min	0
	Max	3000
	SmallChange	100
	LargeChange	500
	Value	0
vsbYPos	Min	500
	Max	3000
	SmallChange	100
	LargeChange	500
	Value	500
lblFace	Caption	J
	Font	Wingdings
	Font Size	24
	Left	0
	Top	500

```
Private Sub hsbXPos_Change()
  Let lblFace.Left = hsbXPos.Value
End Sub

Private Sub vsbYPos_Change()
  Let lblFace.Top = vsbYPos.Value
End Sub
```

[Run and move the thumbs on the scroll bars.]

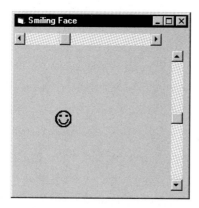

In Example 5, when you drag the thumb, the face does not move until the dragging is completed. This can be corrected by adding the following two event procedures.

```
Private Sub hsbXPos_Scroll()
  Let lblFace.Left = hsbXPos.Value
End Sub

Private Sub vsbYPos_Scroll()
  Let lblFace.Top = vsbYPos.Value
End Sub
```

The Timer Control

The timer control, which is invisible during run time, triggers an event after a specified amount of time. The length of time, measured in milliseconds, is set with the Interval property to be any number from 0 to 65,535 (about 1 minute and 5 seconds). The event triggered each time Timer1.Interval milliseconds elapses is called Timer1_Timer ( ). In order to begin timing, a timer must first be turned on by setting its Enabled property to True. A timer is turned off either by setting its Enabled property to False or by setting its Interval property to 0. The standard prefix for the name of a timer control is tmr.

EXAMPLE 6   The following program creates a stopwatch that updates the time every tenth of a second.

Object	Property	Setting
frmWatch	Caption	Stopwatch
cmdStart	Caption	Start
lblSeconds	Caption	Seconds
lblTime	Caption	(blank)
cmdStop	Caption	Stop
tmrWatch	Interval	100
	Enabled	False

```
Private Sub cmdStart_Click()
  Let lblTime.Caption = " 0"       'Reset watch
  Let tmrWatch.Enabled = True
End Sub

Private Sub cmdStop_Click()
  Let tmrWatch.Enabled = False
End Sub

Private Sub tmrWatch_Timer()
  Let lblTime.Caption = Str(Val(lblTime.Caption) + .1)
End Sub
```

[Run, click on the Start button, wait 10.8 seconds, and click on the Stop button.]

The Shape Control

The shape control assumes one of six possible predefined shapes depending on the value of its Shape property. Figure 11.6 shows the six shapes and the values of their corresponding Shape properties. Shapes are usually placed on a form at design time for decoration or to highlight certain parts of the form. By convention, names of shape controls have the prefix shp.

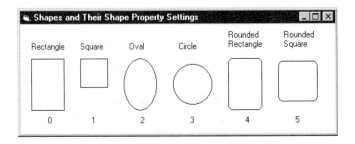

Figure 11.6 The six possible shapes for a shape control.

The most useful properties of shapes are BackStyle (transparent vs. opaque; see Figure 11.7), BorderWidth (thickness of border), BorderStyle (solid, dashed, dotted, etc.), BackColor (background color), FillStyle (fill-in pattern: horizontal lines, upward diagonal lines, etc., as in Figure 10.28), FillColor (color used by FillStyle), and Visible.

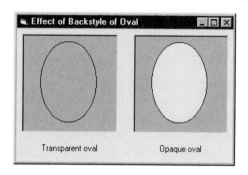

Figure 11.7 Effect of the value of the BackStyle property.

Figure 11.8 shows several effects that can be achieved with shapes. In the first effect, a command is set off by placing it on top of a rounded rectangle shape whose BackStyle is opaque, BackColor is blue, FillStyle is downward diagonal, and FillColor is yellow. In the second effect, the TRFFC20.ICO icon (displayed in an appropriately sized, borderless picture box) is "framed" by placing it on top of an oval shape whose BackStyle is opaque and BackColor is the same as the background color of the icon. In the last effect, two command buttons are tied together by surrounding them with a circle shape whose FillStyle is transparent, BorderWidth is 8, and BorderColor is green, and by placing behind the command buttons an oval shape whose FillStyle is transparent, BorderWidth is 3, and BorderColor is blue.

Figure 11.8 Several effects achieved with shape controls.

The Line Control

The Line control, which produces lines of various thickness, styles, and colors, is primarily used to enhance the visual appearance of forms. The most useful properties of lines are BorderColor (color of the line), BorderWidth (thickness of the line), BorderStyle (solid, dashed, dotted, etc.), and Visible. Figure 11.9 shows several effects that can be achieved with lines. By convention, names of line controls have the prefix lin.

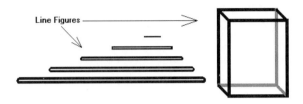

Figure 11.9 Several effects achieved with line controls.

The Image Control

The image control is designed to hold pictures stored in graphics files such as .BMP files created with Windows' Paintbrush or .ICO files of icons that come with Visual Basic. Pictures are placed in image controls with the Picture property. If you double-click on the Picture property during design time, a file-selection dialog box appears and assists you in selecting an appropriate file. However, prior to setting the Picture property, you should set the Stretch property. If the Stretch property is set to False (the default value), the image control will be resized to fit the picture. If the Stretch property is set to True, the picture will be resized to fit the image control. Therefore, with Stretch property True, pictures can be reduced (by placing them into a small image control) or enlarged (by placing them into an image control bigger than the picture). Figure 11.10 shows a picture created with Paintbrush and reduced to several different sizes. By convention, names of image controls have the prefix img.

A picture can be assigned to an image control at run time. However a statement such as

```
Let imgBox.Picture = "filespec"
```

will not do the job. Instead, we must use the LoadPicture function in a statement such as

```
Let imgBox.Picture = LoadPicture("filespec")
```

Image controls enhance the visual appeal of programs. Also, because image controls respond to the Click event and can receive the focus, they can serve as pictorial command buttons.

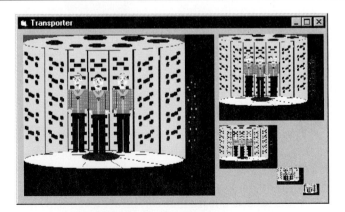

Figure 11.10 A picture created with Paintbrush and reduced several times.

Comment

1. When placing Line and Shape controls on a form, greater precision can be achieved by first turning off the "Align Controls to Grid" option in the Environment section of the Options submenu of the Tools menu.

2. Although frames cannot receive the focus, they can have an access key that sends the focus to the first control inside the frame that can receive the focus.

PRACTICE PROBLEMS 11.2

1. Suppose you create a frame and then drag a preexisting text box into the frame. How will this text box differ from a text box that was attached to the frame by the single-click-draw method?

2. What is the difference between a group of check boxes attached to a frame and a group of option buttons attached to a frame?

EXERCISES 11.2

In Exercises 1 through 18, determine the effect of setting the property to the value shown.

1. `Frame1.Caption = "Income"`
2. `Check1.Value = 1`
3. `Check1.Value = 0`
4. `Check1.Caption = "&Vanilla"`
5. `Option1.Value = False`
6. `Option1.Caption = "Punt"`
7. `Let HScroll2.Value = HScroll2.Max`
8. `Let HScroll2.Value = (HScroll2.Max + HScroll2.Min) / 2`
9. `Let VScroll2.SmallChange = VScroll2.LargeChange`
10. `Timer1.Interval = 5000`
11. `Timer1.Interval = 0`
12. `Timer1.Enabled = False`
13. `Shape1.Shape = 2`
14. `Let Shape2.BackColor = Shape1.BackColor`
15. `Shape1.FillStyle = 6`
16. `Let Line1.Visible = False`
17. `Let Line1.BorderWidth = 2 * Line1.BorderWidth`
18. `Image1.Stretch = True`

In Exercises 19 through 28, write one or more lines of code to carry out the task.

19. A frame has two option buttons attached to it. Move all three objects 100 twips to the right.

20. Clear the small rectangular box of Check1.

21. Turn off Option2.

22. Move the thumb of VScroll2 as high as possible.

23. Move the thumb of HScroll2 one-third of the way between the left arrow and the right arrow.

24. Specify that Timer1 trigger an event every half second.

25. Specify that Timer1 trigger an event every 2 minutes and 10 seconds. **Hint:** Use a global variable called Flag.

26. Make Shape1 a circle.

27. Fill Shape1 with vertical lines.

28. Make Image1 vanish.

In Exercises 29 and 30, determine the state of the two option buttons after the command button is clicked.

29.
```
Private Sub Command1_Click()
    Option1.Value = True
    Option2.Value = True
End Sub
```

30.
```
Private Sub Command1_Click()
    Option1.Value = False
    Option2.Value = False
End Sub
```

31. Which of the controls presented in this section can receive the focus? Design a form containing all of the controls and repeatedly press the Tab key to confirm your answer.

32. Create a form with two frames, each having two option buttons attached to it. Run the program and confirm that the two pairs of option buttons operate independently of each other.

33. Suppose a frame has two option buttons attached to it. If the statement Let Frame1.Visible = False is executed, will the option buttons also vanish? Test your answer.

34. Why are option buttons also called "radio buttons"?

A form contains a command button, a small picture box, and a frame with three check boxes (Check1, Check2, and Check3) attached to it. In Exercises 35 and 36, write a click event for the command button that displays the stated information in the picture box when the command button is clicked.

35. The number of boxes checked.

36. The captions of the checked boxes.

37. A computer dealer offers two basic computers, the Deluxe ($1500) and the Super ($1700). In addition, the customer can order any of the following additional options: multimedia kit ($300), internal modem ($100), 4MB of added memory ($150). Write a program that computes the cost of the computer system selected.

38. Item 33a of Form 1040 for the U.S. Individual Income Tax Return reads as follows:

33a Check if: ☐ **You** were 65 or older, ☐ Blind; ☐ **Spouse** was 65 or older, ☐ Blind ☐
Add the number of boxes checked above and enter the total here   → 33a ☐

Write a program that looks at the checked boxes and displays the value for the large square.

39. Write a program for the Font Style form in Figure 11.11. The style of the words in the text box should be determined by the settings in the two frames.

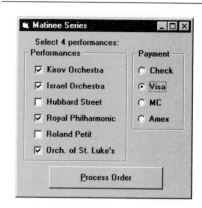

Figure 11.11 Form for Exercise 39.

Figure 11.12 Form for Exercise 40.

40. Subscribers to the Matinee Series for the 1994–1995 season at the Kennedy Center for the Performing Arts must select four performances out of the six shown in the Matinee Series form in Figure 11.12, and must indicate the method of payment. Write the click event procedure for the command button. The procedure should first determine whether exactly four performances have been checked. If not, the user should be so informed with a message box. Then the method of payment should be examined. If no method has been indicated, the user must be reminded to select one. Depending on the method of payment, the user should be told with a message box to either mail in the check with the order form or to give the credit card number with an input box request. At the end of the process, the caption on the command box should change to "Thank You".

41. Create a form with a line, an oval, and a horizontal scroll box. Write a program that uses the scroll bar to alter the thickness of the line and the oval from 1 through 12. At any time, the number for the thickness should be displayed in a label.

42. *Simulation of Times Square Ball.* Create a form with a vertical scroll bar and a timer control. When the program is run, the thumb should be at the top of the scroll bar. Each second the thumb should descend one-tenth of the way down. When the thumb reaches the bottom after 10 seconds, a message box displaying HAPPY NEW YEAR should appear.

43. Write a program to synchronize the two thermometers shown in the Temperatures form in Figure 11.13. When the thumb of either thermometer is moved, the other thermometer moves to the corresponding temperature and each temperature is displayed above the thermometer.

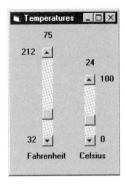

Figure 11.13 Form for Exercise 43.   **Figure 11.14** Form for Exercise 44.

44. Write a program to create a decorative digital clock. The clock in the Digital Clock form in Figure 11.14 is inserted in an image control containing any .BMP picture. The values for hour, minute, and second can be obtained as Hour(Now), Minute(Now), and Second(Now) and can be formatted with the format string "00".

45. The Pictures directory of the CD accompanying this text contains files named MOON1.BMP, MOON2.BMP, . . . , MOON8.BMP, which show eight phases of the moon. Create a form consisting of an image control, a timer control, and a file list box. Set the Path property of the file list box to the directory containing the moon icons (such as "D:\PICTURES"), set the Pattern property to MOON?.BMP, and set the Visible property to False. Every 2 seconds assign another file from the file list box to the Picture property of the Image control to see the moon cycle through its phases every 16 seconds. One phase is shown in Figure 11.15.

Figure 11.15 Form for Exercise 45.

SOLUTIONS TO PRACTICE PROBLEMS 11.2

1. The text box attached by the single-click-draw method will move with the frame, whereas the other text box will not.

2. With option buttons, at most one button can be on at any given time, whereas several check boxes can be checked simultaneously.

11.3 FIVE ADDITIONAL OBJECTS

In this section we discuss three controls and two objects that are not controls. The three controls are the Microsoft FlexGrid control (a custom control), the menu control (not accessed through the toolbox), and the common dialog box control (a custom control). The two objects are the clipboard and the form. The discussion of the form deals with the use of multiple forms. The Microsoft FlexGrid control is not available with the Control Creation Edition of Visual Basic.

The Microsoft FlexGrid Control

The FlexGrid control does not initially appear in your Toolbox. To add the control, click on Components in the Project menu, click the Controls tab, and click on the check box to the left of "Microsoft FlexGrid Control 5.0." Then press the OK button. By convention, names of Microsoft FlexGrids have the prefix *msg*.

A grid is a rectangular array used to display tables or to create spreadsheet-like applications. The grid in Figure 11.16 has 6 rows and 7 columns. The number of rows and columns can be specified at design time with the Rows and Cols properties or at run time with statements such as Let msgFlex.Rows = 6 and Let msgFlex.Cols = 7. Rows and columns are numbered beginning with 0. For instance, the rows in Figure 11.16 are numbered (from top to bottom) as 0, 1, 2, 3, 4, and 5.

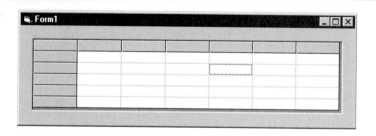

Figure 11.16 A simple FlexGrid control.

The width, measured in twips (there are about 1440 twips to an inch), of each column can be specified only at run time with the ColWidth property. A typical statement is Let Grid1.ColWidth(3) = 1200, which sets the width of column 3 to 1200 twips. (The default column width is 555 twips.) Similarly, the RowHeight property specifies the height of each row. The width and height of the entire grid can be specified at design time by dragging the mouse or by setting the Width and Height properties.

The grayed row and column in Figure 11.16 are referred to as **fixed**. Fixed rows and columns must be at the top and left sides of the grid. The number of fixed rows and columns is specified by the FixedRows and FixedCols properties. The grid in Figure 11.16 has the default settings FixedRows = 1 and FixedCols = 1.

If the width of the grid is too small to show all the columns, a horizontal scroll bar will automatically appear across the bottom of the grid. Then, during run time, the nonfixed columns can be scrolled to reveal the hidden columns. Similarly, a vertical scroll bar appears when the height of the grid is too small to show all the rows. Scroll bars can be suppressed by setting the ScrollBars property of the grid to 0 – flexScrollBarNone. (The default value of the ScrollBars property is 3 – flexScrollBarBoth.)

The individual small rectangles are called **cells.** Each cell is identified by its row and column numbers. At any time, one cell is singled out as the **active cell.** Initially, the cell in row 1, column 1 is the active cell. The pair of statements Let msgFlex.Row = m, Let msgFlex.Col = n set the active cell to the cell in the mth row and nth column. The active cell in a nonfixed row or column is identified by a dotted border. (In Figure 11.16, the cell in row 2, column 4 is the active cell.) Whenever the user clicks on a cell in a nonfixed row or column, that cell becomes the active cell. The horizontal and vertical lines forming the cells can be turned off by setting the GridLines property to 0 – flexGridNone.

When the user clicks on a grayed cell in the top row, the cell below the clicked-on cell becomes active, and the rest of the column is colored blue. We say that the column has been **selected.** Similarly, when the user clicks on a grayed cell in the left column, its row is selected. Also, a rectangular block of cells can be selected by dragging the cursor across them. When a cell is selected, its CellSelected property is True and otherwise is False.

Unfortunately, you can't just place text into a cell by clicking on the cell and typing, as you would with a text box. The statement Let msgFlex.Text = str places text into the active cell and the statement Let str = msgFlex.Text reads the contents of the active cell. The text inside all the nonfixed cells of column n can be displayed left-aligned, right-aligned, or centered with a statement of the form Let msgFlex.ColAlignment(n) = r, where r is 0 for left-alignment, 1 for right-alignment, and 2 for centered. The fixed cells of column n can be justified with a statement of the form Let msgFlex.FixedAlignment(n) = r (**Note:** Due to a bug, the ColAlignment and FixedAlignment properties of the FlexGrid control do not work properly in the first release of Visual Basic 5.0. This bug should be corrected in subsequent releases of VB 5.0. In Example 1, we use the Format function to right-justify numbers instead of relying on ColAlignment.)

EXAMPLE 1   The following program uses a grid to display an improved version of the table of student expenses from Example 5 of Section 3.5. The five expense categories and numeric data for the table are stored in the sequential file STCOSTS.TXT. Each record of the file consists of a string followed by four numbers.

Object	Property	Setting
frmCosts	Caption	Average Expenses of Commuter Students (1993–94)
msgCosts	BorderStyle	0 – flexBorderNone
	Cols	5
	FixedCols	0
	FixedRows	0
	Font	Courier New
	GridLines	0 – flexGridNone
	Rows	9
	ScrollBars	0 – flexScrollBarNone

```
Private Sub Form_Load()
    Dim rowNum As Integer, colNum As Integer
    Dim strData As String, numData As Single
    Rem  Column headings
    Let msgCosts.Row = 0
    Let msgCosts.Col = 1
```

```
      Let msgCosts.Text = Format("Pb 2-yr", "@@@@@@@@@")
      Let msgCosts.Col = 2
      Let msgCosts.Text = Format("Pr 2-yr", "@@@@@@@@@")
      Let msgCosts.Col = 3
      Let msgCosts.Text = Format("Pb 4-yr", "@@@@@@@@@")
      Let msgCosts.Col = 4
      Let msgCosts.Text = Format("Pr 4-yr", "@@@@@@@@@")
      Rem  Read data from data file and obtain column totals
      Dim total(1 To 4) As Single
      Open "STCOSTS.TXT" For Input As #1
      For rowNum = 2 To 6    'row 0 holds headings, row 1 is blank
        For colNum = 0 To 4
          Let msgCosts.Row = rowNum
          Let msgCosts.Col = colNum
          If colNum = 0 Then
              Input #1, strData
              Let msgCosts.Text = strData
            Else
              Input #1, numData
              Let msgCosts.Text = Format(numData, "Currency")
              Let total(colNum) = total(colNum) + numData
          End If
        Next colNum
      Next rowNum
      Rem  Display totals
      Let msgCosts.Row = 8
      Let msgCosts.Col = 0
      Let msgCosts.Text = "Total"
      For colNum = 1 To 4
        Let msgCosts.Col = colNum
        Let msgCosts.Row = 7
        Let msgCosts.Text = "————————"
        Let msgCosts.Row = 8
        Let msgCosts.Text = Format(Format(numData, "Currency"), "@@@@@@@@@")
      Next colNum
      Rem  Set column widths to accommodate data; right-justify dollar amounts
      Let msgCosts.ColWidth(0) = 2000        'Space for category names
      For colNum = 1 To 4
        Let msgCosts.ColWidth(colNum) = 1200    'Space for dollar amounts
      Next colNum
      Rem  Set overall grid size to minimum needed for the data
      Let msgCosts.Width = 2000 + 4 * 1200
      Let msgCosts.Height = 9 * msgCosts.RowHeight(0)
End Sub
```

[Run]

Average Expenses of Commuter Students (1993-94)				
	Pb 2-yr	Pr 2-yr	Pb 4-yr	Pr 4-yr
Tuition & Fees	$1,229.00	$6,175.00	$2,527.00	$11,025.00
Books & Supplies	$533.00	$566.00	$552.00	$556.00
Board	$1,643.00	$1,589.00	$1,601.00	$1,722.00
Transportation	$923.00	$890.00	$870.00	$824.00
Other Expenses	$1,044.00	$970.00	$1,259.00	$1,073.00
	----------	----------	----------	----------
Total	$5,372.00	$10,190.00	$6,809.00	$15,200.00

EXAMPLE 2 The following program creates a simplified spreadsheet. The user places a number into the active cell by typing the number into an input box. The program keeps a running total of the sum of the numbers.

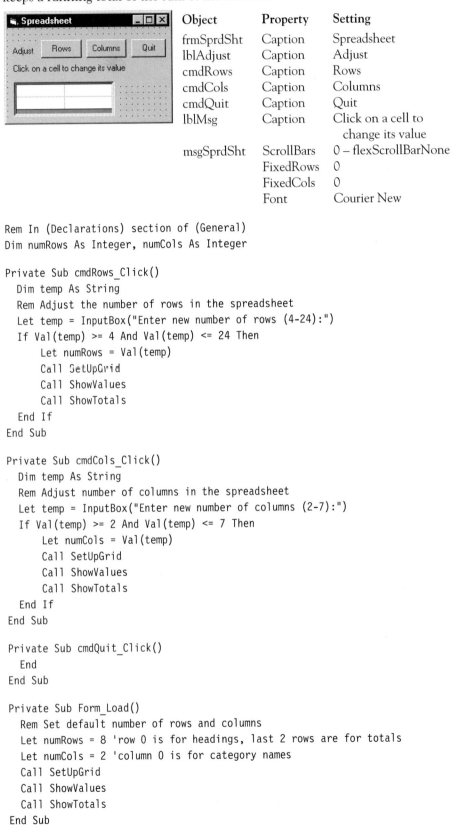

Object	Property	Setting
frmSprdSht	Caption	Spreadsheet
lblAdjust	Caption	Adjust
cmdRows	Caption	Rows
cmdCols	Caption	Columns
cmdQuit	Caption	Quit
lblMsg	Caption	Click on a cell to change its value
msgSprdSht	ScrollBars	0 – flexScrollBarNone
	FixedRows	0
	FixedCols	0
	Font	Courier New

```
Rem In (Declarations) section of (General)
Dim numRows As Integer, numCols As Integer

Private Sub cmdRows_Click()
  Dim temp As String
  Rem Adjust the number of rows in the spreadsheet
  Let temp = InputBox("Enter new number of rows (4-24):")
  If Val(temp) >= 4 And Val(temp) <= 24 Then
      Let numRows = Val(temp)
      Call SetUpGrid
      Call ShowValues
      Call ShowTotals
  End If
End Sub

Private Sub cmdCols_Click()
  Dim temp As String
  Rem Adjust number of columns in the spreadsheet
  Let temp = InputBox("Enter new number of columns (2-7):")
  If Val(temp) >= 2 And Val(temp) <= 7 Then
      Let numCols = Val(temp)
      Call SetUpGrid
      Call ShowValues
      Call ShowTotals
  End If
End Sub

Private Sub cmdQuit_Click()
  End
End Sub

Private Sub Form_Load()
  Rem Set default number of rows and columns
  Let numRows = 8 'row 0 is for headings, last 2 rows are for totals
  Let numCols = 2 'column 0 is for category names
  Call SetUpGrid
  Call ShowValues
  Call ShowTotals
End Sub
```

```
Private Sub msgSprdSht_Click()
  Dim temp As String, message As String
  Rem Obtain new value for cell if it is not in the "total" rows
  If messageSprdSht.Row < numRows - 2 Then
      Let message = "Enter new value for the row "
      Let message = message & Format(msgSprdSht.Row + 1, "#") & " column "
      Let message = message & Format(msgSprdSht.Col + 1, "#") & " cell:"
      Let temp = InputBox(message,,msgSprdSht.Text) 'Propose old value as default
      If msgSprdSht.Col = 0 Then
          Let msgSprdSht.Text = temp
        ElseIf msgSprdsht.Row = 0 Then
          Let msgSprdSht.Text = Format(temp, "@@@@@@@@@@")
        Else
          Let msgSprdsht.Text = Format(Format(Val(temp), "0.00"), "@@@@@@@@@@")
          Call ShowTotals
      End If
  End If
End Sub

Private Sub SetUpGrid()
  Dim colNum As Integer
  Rem Set up grid
  Let msgSprdSht.Col = 0
  Let msgSprdSht.Row = msgSprdSht.Rows - 1
  Let msgSprdSht.Text = "" 'erase "Total" in case increasing rows
  Let msgSprdSht.Rows = numRows
  Let msgSprdSht.Cols = numCols
  Rem Set column widths; right-justify columns with numeric data
  Let msgSprdSht.ColWidth(0) = 2000    'space for category names
  Let msgSprdSht.ColAlignment(0) = 0  'show data left-justified
  For colNum = 1 To numCols - 1
    Let msgSprdSht.ColWidth(colNum) = 1200  'space for dollar amounts
    Let msgSprdSht.ColAlignment(colNum) = 1 'show data right-justified
  Next colNum
  Rem Set overall grid size to minimum needed for the data
  Let msgSprdSht.Width = 2000 + (numCols - 1) * 1200 + 15 * (numCols + 1) + 8
  Let msgSprdSht.Height = numRows*msgSprdSht.RowHeight(0)+15*(numRows + 1)+8
  Rem Adjust form to accommodate grid and other controls
  Let frmSprdSht.Width = msgSprdSht.Left + msgSprdSht.Width + 200
  Let frmSprdSht.Height = msgSprdSht.Top + msgSprdSht.Height + 500
  Let frmSprdSht.Top = 0
  Let frmSprdSht.Left = 0
End Sub

Private Sub ShowTotals()
  Dim colNum As Integer, rowNum As Integer, total As Single
  Rem Compute and display total of each numeric column
  Let msgSprdSht.Row = numRows - 1
  Let msgSprdSht.Col = 0
  Let msgSprdSht.Text = "Total"
  For colNum = 1 To numCols - 1
    Let total = 0
    For rowNum = 1 To numRows - 3
      Let msgSprdSht.Row = rowNum
      Let msgSprdSht.Col = colNum
      Let total = total + Val(msgSprdSht.Text)
    Next rowNum
```

```
      Let msgSprdSht.Row = numRows - 2
      Let msgSprdSht.Text = Format("————", "@@@@@@@@@@")
      Let msgSprdSht.Row = numRows - 1
      Let msgSprdSht.Text = Format(Format(total, "Currency"), "@@@@@@@@@@")
    Next colNum
End Sub

Private Sub ShowValues()
  Dim rowNum As Integer, colNum As Integer
  Rem Refresh values displayed in cells
  For rowNum = 1 To numRows - 1
    For colNum = 1 To numCols - 1
      Let msgSprdSht.Row = rowNum
      Let msgSprdSht.Col = colNum
      Let msgSprdSht.Text = Format(Format(Val(msgSprdSht.Text), "0.00"), _
                            "@@@@@@@@@@")
    Next colNum
  Next rowNum
End Sub
```

[A possible run of the program is shown.]

So far we have used the Text property of grids to place strings into cells. Grids also have a Picture property. A picture (such as a .BMP file created with Paintbrush or an .ICO file from Visual Basic's icon directory) is placed into the active cell with a statement of the form

```
Let msgFlex.Picture = LoadPicture("filespec")
```

If both text and a picture are assigned to a cell, then the picture appears in the upper left portion of the cell, and the text appears to the right of the picture.

The Menu Control

Visual Basic forms can have menu bars similar to the menu bar in the Visual Basic environment. Figure 11.17 shows a typical menu, with the submenu for the Font menu item dropped down. Here, the menu bar contains two menu items (Font and Size), referred to as **top-level** menu items. When the Font menu item is clicked, a dropdown list of two second-level menu items (Courier and TimesRm) appears. Although not visible here, the dropdown list under Size contains the two second-level menu items "12" and "24". Each menu item is treated as a distinct control that responds to only one event—the click event. The click event is triggered not only by the click of the mouse button, but also for top-level items by pressing Alt+*accessKey* and for second-level items by just pressing the access key. The click event for the Courier menu item in Figure 11.17 can be activated directly by pressing the shortcut key F1.

Figure 11.17 A simple menu.

Menus are created with the Menu Editor window available from the Tools menu on the Visual Basic main menu bar. Figure 11.18 shows the Menu Design window used to create the menu in Figure 11.17. Each menu item has a Caption property (what the user sees) and a Name property (used to refer to the item in the program.) For instance, the last menu item in Figure 11.18 has Caption property "24" and Name property "mnu24". The following steps are used to create the Font-Size menu:

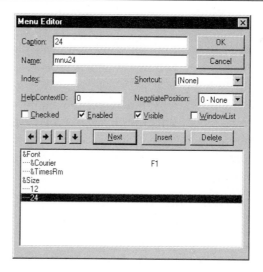

Figure 11.18 The Menu Editor window used to create the menu in Figure 11.17.

1. Type &Font into the Caption box and type mnuFont into the Name box.

2. Click on the Next button.

3. Click on the Right Arrow button. (This creates the ellipses and indents the next menu item, which will be a second-level item.)

4. Type &Courier into the Caption box and type mnuCourier into the Name box.

5. Click on the arrow to the right of the Shortcut box and select F1 from the dropdown list.

6. Click on the Next button.

7. Type &TimesRm into the Caption box and type mnuTimesRm into the Name box.

8. Click on the Next button

9. Click on the Left Arrow button. (This causes the next item to appear flush left to indicate that it is a top-level menu item.)

10. Type &Size into the Caption box and type mnuSize into the Name box.

11. Click on the Next button and then click on the Right Arrow button.

12. Type 12 into the Caption box and type mnu12 into the Name box.

13. Click on the Next button.

14. Type 24 into the Caption box and type mnu24 into the Name box. Your Menu Editor window should now appear as in Figure 11.18.

15. Click the OK button to close the Menu Editor window.

Three of the check boxes on the Menu Editor window are especially useful. When the Checked box is checked, a checkmark appears in front of the menu item. This checkmark can be altered in code with statements such as Let mnuItem.Checked = False and Let mnuItem.Checked = True. When the Enable box is unchecked, the menu item appears gray and does not respond to the click event. The enabled state can be altered in code with statements such as Let mnuItem.Enabled = False and Let mnuItem.Enabled = True. When the Visible property is unchecked, the menu item is invisible.

EXAMPLE 3 The following program creates the application in Figure 11.17, in which the menu is used to alter the appearance of the contents of a text box. The form has caption "Alter Font & Size" and the properties of the menu items are as created before.

```
Private Sub mnu12_Click()
  Let txtInfo.Font.Size = 12
End Sub

Private Sub mnu24_Click()
  Let txtInfo.Font.Size = 24
End Sub

Private Sub mnuCourier_Click()
  Let txtInfo.Font.Name = "Courier"
End Sub

Private Sub mnuTimesRm_Click()
  Let txtInfo.Font.Name = "Times New Roman"
End Sub
```

The Clipboard Object

The clipboard object is used to copy or move text from one location to another. It is maintained by Windows and therefore even can be used to transfer information from one Windows application to another. It is actually a portion of memory that holds text and has no properties or events.

If *str* is a string, then the statement

```
Clipboard.SetText str
```

replaces any text currently in the clipboard with *str*. The statement

```
Let str = Clipboard.GetText()
```

assigns the text in the clipboard to the string variable *str*.

The statement

```
Clipboard.Clear
```

deletes the contents of the clipboard.

A portion of the text in a text box or combo box can be **selected** by dragging the mouse across it or by moving the cursor across it while holding down the Shift key. After you select text, you can place it into the clipboard by pressing Ctrl+Ins. Also, if the cursor is in a text box and you press Shift+Ins, the contents of the clipboard will be inserted at the cursor position. These tasks also can be carried out in code. The SelText property of a text box holds the selected string from the text box and a statement such as

```
Clipboard.SetText txtBox.SelText
```

copies this selected string into the clipboard. The statement

```
Let txtBox.SelText = Clipboard.GetText()
```

replaces the selected portion of txtBox with the contents of the clipboard. If nothing has been selected, the statement inserts the contents of the clipboard into txtBox at the cursor position.

Multiple Forms

A Visual Basic program can contain more than one form. Additional forms are created from the Project menu with Add Form (Alt/P/F). The name of each form appears in the project window, and any form can be made the active form by double-clicking on its name in the project window. (**Hint:** After creating a new form, move it down slightly so that you can see at least the title bars of the other forms. Then you can activate any form by just clicking on its title bar.) The second form has default name Form2, the third form has default name Form3, and so on. Forms are hidden or activated with statements such as

```
Form1.Hide
```

or

```
Form2.Show
```

When a program is run, the first form created is the only one visible. After that, the Hide and Show methods can be used to determine what forms appear. Two or more forms can be visible at the same time.

Often, additional forms, such as message and dialog boxes, are displayed to present a special message or request specific information. When a message or dialog box appears, the user cannot shift the focus to another form without first hiding the message or dialog box by clicking an OK or Cancel command button. If a form is displayed with a statement of the type

```
formName.Show 1
```

then the form will exhibit this same behavior. The user will not be allowed to shift the focus to any other form until *formName* is hidden. Such a form is said to be **modal**. It is customary to set the BorderStyle property of modal forms to "3-Fixed Double".

Each form has its own controls and code. However, code from one form can refer to a control in another form. If so, the control must be prefixed with the name of the other form, followed by a period. For instance, the statement

```
Let Form2.txtBox.Text = "Hello"
```

in Form1 causes text to be displayed in a text box on Form2. (**Note:** Two forms can have a text box named txtBox. Code using the name txtBox refers to the text box in its own form unless prefixed with the name of another form.)

EXAMPLE 4   The following program uses a second form as a dialog box to total the different sources of income. Initially, only frmIncome is visible. The user types in his or her name and then either can type in the income or click on the command button for assistance in totaling the different sources of income. Clicking on the command button from frmIncome causes frmSources to appear and be active. The user fills in the three text boxes and then clicks on the command button to have the amounts totaled and displayed in the income text box of the first form.

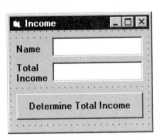

Object	Property	Setting
frmIncome	Caption	Income
lblName	Caption	Name
txtName	Text	(blank)
lblTotal	Caption	Total Income
lblSum	Caption	(blank)
cmdShowTot	Caption	Determine Total Income

Object	Property	Setting
frmSources	Caption	Sources of Income
	BorderStyle	3 – Fixed Double
lblWages	Caption	Wages
txtWages	Text	(blank)
lblInterest	Caption	Interest Income
txtInterest	Text	(blank)
lblDividend	Caption	Dividend Income
txtDividend	Text	(blank)
cmdCompute	Caption	Compute Total Income

```
Private Sub cmdShowTot_Click()
  frmSources.Show 1
End Sub

Private Sub cmdCompute_Click()
  Dim sum As Single
  Let sum = Val(txtWages.Text) + Val(txtInterest.Text) + Val(txtDividend.Text)
  Let frmIncome.lblSum.Caption = Format(Str(sum), "Currency")
  frmSources.Hide
End Sub
```

[Run, enter name, click the command button, and fill in the sources of income.]

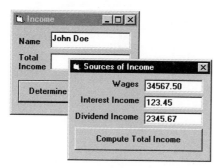

All variables declared and procedures created in a form are local to that form; that is, they are not available to any other form. Such variables and procedures are said to be of **form level**. However, you can declare global variables and procedures that are available to all forms. To do so, select Module from the Insert menu. A code window will appear with Module1 in the title bar. Procedures created in this window will be available to all forms. To declare a variable that is available to all forms, declare it in the Module1 window, but use the word Public instead of Dim. For instance, if the statement

```
Public person As String
```

appears in the Module1 code window, the variable *person* can be accessed anywhere in the program.

The Common Dialog Control

The common dialog control does not initially appear in your Toolbox. To add the control, select Components from the Project menu, click the Controls tab, and click on the check box to the left of "Microsoft Common Dialog Control 5.0." Then press the OK button. By convention, names of common dialog boxes have the prefix dlg.

The common dialog control can produce each of the useful dialog boxes in Figures 11.19 through 11.23, thereby saving the programmer the trouble of designing custom dialog boxes for these purposes. The common dialog control has no events, only methods and properties. Actually, like the Timer control, the common dialog box control is invisible. However, when you execute a statement of the form

```
CommonDialog1.Show_____
```

where the blank line is filled with Open, Save, Color, Font, or Printer, the specified dialog box is produced. Table 11.4 gives the purposes of the various dialog boxes.

Type of Dialog box	Purpose of Dialog Box
Open	Determine what disk file to open
Save As	Determine where and with what name to save a disk file
Color	Select one color from about 1.6 million colors
Font	Select a font for the screen or printer
Print	Help control the printer

Table 11.4 The different types of dialog boxes.

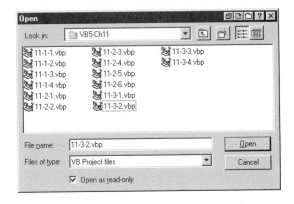

Figure 11.19 An Open common dialog box.

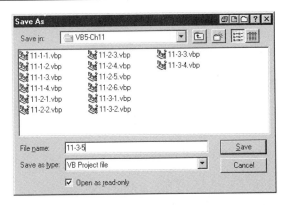

Figure 11.20 A Save As common dialog box.

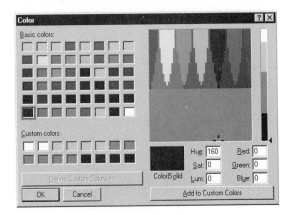

Figure 11.21 A Color common dialog box.

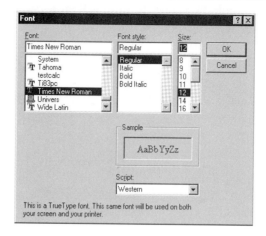

Figure 11.22 A Font common dialog box.

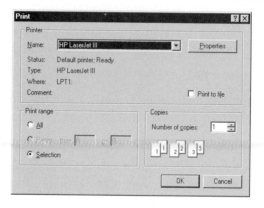

Figure 11.23 A Print common dialog box.

The Flags property influences certain features of the dialog box and should be set prior to setting the Action property. A complete discussion of the Flags property would be too great a digression. For our purposes, we will be well served by always setting the Flags property to 3 with the statement

```
Let dlgBox.Flags = 3
```

After selections are made from a common dialog box and the OK button is clicked, the values of the selections are stored in properties such as FileName, Color, FontName, FontItalic, FontSize and Copies. For instance, the following event procedure specifies the font for the contents of a text box.

```
Private Sub cmdButton_Click()
  Let dlgFont.Flags = 3
  dlgFont.ShowFont              'invoke Font common dialog box
  Rem  Select Font, Font Style, and Size and then click on OK
  Let txtBox.Font.Name = dlgFont.FontName
  Let txtBox.Font.Bold= dlgFont.FontBold
  Let txtBox.Font.Italic = dlgFont.FontItalic
  Let txtBox.Font.Size = dlgFont.FontSize
End Sub
```

Table 11.5 gives the principal properties whose setting are garnered from the common dialog boxes.

Type of Common Dialog Box	Principal Properties
Open	FileName
Save As	FileName
Color	Color
Font	FontName, FontSize, FontBold, FontItalic
Print	Copies, FromPage, ToPage

Table 11.5 Principal properties of the common dialog boxes.

With Open and Save As common dialog boxes, a property is needed to specify what types of files should be displayed. A statement of the form

```
Let dlgFile.Filter ="dscrpt1|filter1|dscrpt2|filter2|dscrpt3|filter3"
```

provides verbal descriptions for the Type box and strings using wildcard characters (filters) to identify the files. A specific statement might be

```
Let dlgFile.Filter = "Text Files|*.TXT|MAK Files|*.MAK|All Files|*.*"
```

After the filter property is set, the FilterIndex property can be used to set the default filter. For instance, if the preceding statement is followed with

```
Let dlgFile.FilterIndex = 1
```

the default will be the first pair of filter items. That is, when the dialog box pops up, the Type box will display Text Files, and the File Name box will show only files with the extension TXT.

Comments

1. In the properties window of a flexGrid control, one setting of the Gridlines property is "0 – flexGridNone." In code, this setting can be invoked with either

```
Let MSFlexGrid1.GridLines = 0
```

or

```
Let MSFlexGrid1.GridLines = flexGridNone
```

2. For detailed information about the different settings of the Flags property for the Common Dialog control, click on "Microsoft Visual Basic Help Topics" in the Help menu, click on the Index tab, type Flags, and press the Enter key. Then double-click on one of the topics Flags Property (Color Dialog), Flags Property (Font Dialog), Flags Property (Open, Save As Dialogs), or Flags Property (Print Dialog).

PRACTICE PROBLEMS 11.3

1. What is the difference between the Row property and the Rows property of a grid?

2. What is the effect of the statement Let txtBox.SelText = ""?

EXERCISES 11.3

In Exercises 1 through 32, describe the effect of executing the statement.

1. `Let msgFlex.Columns = 5`

2. `Let msgFlex.Rows = 3`

3. `Let msgFlex.RowHeight(3) = 400`

4. `Let msgFlex.ColWidth(2) = 2000`

5. `Let msgFlex.FixedCols = 1`

6. `Let msgFlex.FixedRows = 2`

7. `Let msgFlex.Row = 3`

8. `Let msgFlex.Col = 4`

9. `Let msgFlex.Text = "Income"`

10. `Let amount = Val(msgFlex.Text)`

11. `Let msgFlex.ColAlignment(3) = 2`

12. `Let msgFlex.ColAlignment(2) = 1`

13. `Let msgFlex.GridLines = 0`

14. `Let msgFlex.GridLines = 3`

15. `Let msgFlex.ScrollBars = 0`

16. `Let mnuCopy.Enabled = False`

17. `Let mnuCut.Enabled = True`

18. `Let mnuPaste.Checked = True`

19. `Let mnuSave.Checked = False`

20. `Let phrase = Clipboard.GetText()`

21. `Clipboard.Clear`

22. `Clipboard.SetText "Hello"`

23. `Clipboard.SetText txtBox.SelText`

24. `Let txtBox.SelText = Clipboard.GetText()`

25. `frmTwo.Show`

26. `frmTwo.Show 1`

27. `frmOne.Hide`

28. `Global amount As Single`

29. `dlgBox.ShowColor`

30. `dlgBox.ShowFont`

31. `Let dlgBox.Filter = "All Files|*.*|Notepad Files|*.TXT|"`

32. `Let dlgBox.FilterItem = 2`

In Exercises 33 through 64, write one or more lines of code to carry out the task.

33. Set the number of rows in msgFlex to 7.

34. Set the number of columns in msgFlex to 5.

35. Set the width of the first column of msgFlex to 3000 twips.

36. Set the height of the first row of msgFlex to 300 twips.

37. Fix the top two rows of msgFlex.

38. Fix the leftmost column of msgFlex.

39. Specify that the active cell of msgFlex be in the third column (that is, column number 2).

40. Specify that the active cell of msgFlex be in the fourth row (that is, row number 3).

41. Display the contents of the active cell of msgFlex in picBox.

42. Place the number 76 into the active cell of msgFlex.

43. Right-align the contents of the nonfixed cells in the second column of msgFlex.

44. Center the contents of the nonfixed cells in the third row of msgFlex.

45. Show grid lines in msgFlex.

46. Delete grid lines from msgFlex.

47. Disable the menu item mnuExit and make it appear gray.

48. Ungray the menu item mnuExit.

49. Place a check mark to the left of the menu item mnuNormal.

50. Remove a check mark from the left of the menu item mnuBold.

51. Assign the contents of the clipboard to the variable *street*.

52. Clear out the contents of the clipboard.

53. Place the word "Happy" into the clipboard.

54. Copy the selected text in txtBox into the clipboard.

55. Insert the contents of the clipboard at the cursor position in txtBox.

56. Replace the selected portion of txtBox by the contents of the clipboard.

57. Delete the selected portion of txtBox.

58. Display frmTwo as a nonmodal form.

59. Display frmTwo as a modal form.

60. Declare the variable *wholeNumber* as an Integer variable recognized by every form.

61. Remove frmTwo from the screen.

62. Specify that a Save As dialog box be displayed in a common dialog box.

63. Specify that an Open dialog box be displayed in a common dialog box.

64. Specify that the types of files listed in a Save As or Open dialog box's Type list box be of the types "*.mak" or "*.frm".

In Exercises 65 and 66, determine what happens to msgFlex when the command button is clicked.

65.
```
Private Sub cmdButton_Click()
    msgFlex.Row = 4
    msgFlex.Col = 5
    msgFlex.Text = Str(32)
End Sub
```

66.
```
Private Sub cmdButton_Click()
    Dim i As Integer, j As Integer
    For i = 0 To 5
      msgFlex.Row = i
      For j = 0 To 5
        msgFlex.Col = j
        msgFlex.Text = Str(i) & "," & Str(j)
      Next j
    Next i
End Sub
```

67. Write a program to create the powers of two table shown in Figure 11.24.

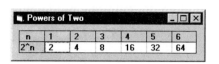

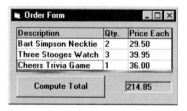

Figure 11.24 Table for Exercise 67.　　**Figure 11.25** Table for Exercise 68.

68. Write a program to create the multiplication table shown in Figure 11.25.

69. Write a program to produce a spreadsheet that serves as an order form. The grid should have three columns headed "Description," "Qty.," and "Price Each". The user should be able to fill in an entry by clicking on it and then responding to an input box. When the command button is clicked, the total cost of the order should appear in a picture box. A sample run is shown in Figure 11.26.

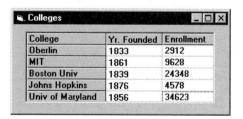

Figure 11.26 Sample run of Exercise 69.

70. The Colleges form in Figure 11.27 contains information about five colleges where the author of this book either attended or taught. Write a program to place the data into a grid as shown. When the heading of a column is clicked, the program should sort the entire grid by that column. For instance, if "Yr. Founded" is clicked, the colleges should reappear in order of their age.

College	Yr. Founded	Enrollment
Oberlin	1833	2912
MIT	1861	9628
Boston Univ	1839	24348
Johns Hopkins	1876	4578
Univ of Maryland	1856	34623

Figure 11.27 Form with data in grid for Exercise 70.

71. Redo Exercise 70 with a menu and include a search capability. The top-level items should be Sort (with second-level items College, Year, Enrollment) and Search (with second-level items College and Year). The sort should be the same as in Exercise 70. The search options should allow the user to enter a college or a year into an input box and should display the relevant information about the row containing the college or year. If the college or year cannot be found, the user should be so informed.

72. Modify the spreadsheet program in Example 2 to add an additional column on the right to hold the sums of the rows. Also, a thin column should be added before the final sums column to set it off.

73. Modify the spreadsheet program in Example 2 to sum only the changed column when the msgSprdSht_Click event is called.

74. Write a program with a single text box and a menu with the single top-level item Edit and the four second-level items Copy, Paste, Cut, and Exit. Copy should place a copy of the selected portion of txtBox into the clipboard, Paste should duplicate the contents of the clipboard at the cursor position, Cut should delete a selected portion of the text box and place it in the clipboard, and Exit should terminate the program.

75. Write a program containing the two forms shown in Figure 11.28. Initially, the Number to Dial form appears. When the Show Push Buttons command button is clicked, the Push Button form appears. The user enters a number by clicking on successive push buttons and then clicks on Enter to have the number transferred to the label at the bottom of the first form.

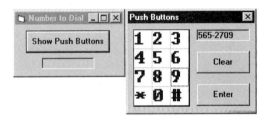

Figure 11.28 Sample run of Exercise 75.

76. Consider the Select Style form shown in Figure 11.29. Write a program to select the color and the font for the text box. When the user clicks on a command button, the corresponding custom dialog box should appear to expedite the choice.

Figure 11.29 Form for Exercise 76.

SOLUTIONS TO PRACTICE PROBLEMS 11.3

1. The Rows property determines how many rows a grid contains, and the Row property specifies which row in the grid contains the active cell.

2. If part of the contents of txtBox has been selected, the selected text will be deleted. Otherwise, nothing happens.

Chapter 11
Summary

1. *List boxes* provide easy access to lists of strings. The lists can be automatically sorted (Sorted property = True), altered (AddItem, RemoveItem, and Clear methods), the currently highlighted item identified (Text property), and the number of items determined (ListCount property). The array List() holds the items stored in the list. Each item is identified by an index number (0, 1, 2, . . .). The most recently inserted item can be determined with the NewIndex property.

2. *Combo boxes* are enhanced text boxes. They not only allow the user to enter information by typing it into a text box (read with the Text property), but allow the user to select the information from a list of items.

3. *Drive, directory,* and *file list boxes* are specialized list boxes managed largely by Windows. The selected items are identified by the Drive, Path, and Filename properties, respectively. A directory list box always displays the subdirectories of the directory identified by its Path property, and a files list box displays the files in the directory identified by its Path property.

4. Selections are made with *check boxes* (allow several) and *option buttons* (allow at most one). The state of the control (*checked vs. unchecked* or *on vs. off*) is stored in the Value property. Clicking on a check box toggles its state. Clicking on an option button gives it the *on* state and turns *off* the other option buttons in its group.

5. *Frames* are used to group controls, especially option buttons, as a unit.

6. *Horizontal* and *vertical scroll bars* permit the user to select from among a range of numbers by clicking or dragging the mouse. The range is specified by the Min and Max properties, and new settings trigger the Click and Change events.

7. The *timer control* triggers an event after a specified amount of time.

8. The *shape* and *line controls* enhance the visual look of a form with rectangles, ovals, circles, and lines of different size, thickness, and color.

9. The *image control*, which displays pictures or icons, can either expand to accommodate the size of the drawing or have the drawing alter its size to fit the image control.

10. A Microsoft FlexGrid control is a rectangular array of cells, each identified by a row and column number. The numbers of rows and columns are specified by the Rows and Cols properties. If the size of the grid is larger than provided by the control, scroll bars can be used to look at different parts of the grid. The FixedRows and FixedCols properties fix a certain number of the top rows and leftmost columns so that they will not scroll. The Row and Col properties are used to designate one cell as *active*. The Text property is used to read or place text into the active cell.

11. *Menus*, similar to the menus of Visual Basic itself, can be created with the Menu Design window.

12. The *clipboard* is filled with the SetText method or by pressing Ctrl+Ins, and is copied with the GetText function or with Shift+Ins.

13. *Additional forms* serve as new windows or dialog boxes. They are revealed with the Show method and concealed with the Hide method.

14. *Common dialog boxes* provide an effortless way of specifying files, colors, and fonts, and of communicating with the printer.

Chapter 11
Programming Projects

1. *Membership List.* Write a menu-driven program to manage a membership list. (See the following Membership List form.) Assume that the names and phone numbers of all members are stored in the sequential file MEMBERS.TXT. The names should be read into the list box when the form is loaded and the phone numbers should be read into an array. When a name is highlighted, both the name and phone number of the person should appear in the text boxes at the bottom of the screen. To delete a person, highlight his or her name and click on the Delete menu item. To change either the phone number or the spelling of the person's name, make the corrections in the text boxes and click on the menu item Modify. To add a new member, type his or her name and phone number into the text boxes and click on the menu item Add. When Exit is clicked, the new membership list should be written to a file and the program should terminate.

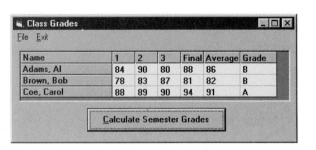

2. *Grade Book.* Write a comprehensive program that a professor could use to record student grades for several classes and save the records in sequential files. (See the preceding Class Grades form.) Each class has three hourly exams and a final exam. The file for a single class should consist of the number of students in the class, call it *n*, and a record of five fields (name, grade1, grade2, grade3, final) for each student, with the records ordered alphabetically by the student's name. (A typical name might appear as "Doe, John".) Initially, the four grade fields should contain zeros. The program should contain a top-level menu item, File, with second-level subitems for Open, Save, Add Student, Remove Student. When a file is opened (via a file list

directory or common dialog box), the data for the students should be loaded into a grid of $n + 1$ rows and 7 columns. (The last two columns should remain blank.) The professor should be able to enter (or alter) exam data by clicking on the cell and responding to an input box. When a student is added, the grid should be enlarged by one row and the student inserted in proper alphabetical position. When a student is deleted, the grid should be reduced by one row. When the Calculate Semester Grades button is clicked, the last two columns should be filled in by the program. (Assume that the final exam counts as two hour exams.) If a grade is changed after the last two columns have been filled in, the corresponding average and grade should be recomputed.

3. *Tic-Tac-Toe*. Write a program that "officiates" a game of tic-tac-toe. That is, the program should allow two players to alternate entering X's and O's into a tic-tac-toe board until either someone wins or a draw is reached. If one of the players wins, the program should announce the winner immediately; in case of a draw, the program should display "Cat's game". The players should enter their plays by clicking on the desired cell in the tic-tac-toe grid, and the program should check that each play is valid. **Optional Enhancement:** Allow the players to enter a number n. The program should officiate a best-of-n tournament, keeping track of the number of games won by each player until one of them wins more than half of the games. Ignore draws.

4. *Hangman*. Write a program to play Hangman. (See the following Hangman form.) A list of 20 words should be placed in a sequential file and one selected at random with Rnd. The program should do the following:

(a) Draw a gallows on the screen with three line controls.
(b) Create a grid having 1 row and 26 columns, and fill the grid with the 26 letters of the alphabet.
(c) Create a second grid of one row and the number of columns equal to the length of the word selected.
(d) Each time the user clicks on one of the letters of the alphabet, that letter should be removed. If the letter is in the selected word, its location(s) should be revealed in the second grid. If the letter is not in the word, another piece of the man should be drawn with a shape control.

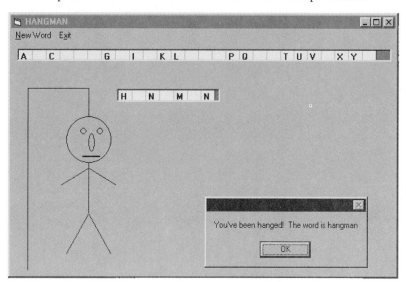

5. *Inventory Control.* Write an inventory program for a book store and save the information in a sequential file. Each record should consist of five fields—title, author, category, wholesale price, and number in stock. (The two categories are fiction and nonfiction.) At any time, the program should display the titles of the books in stock in a list box, for which the user should have the option of displaying either all titles or just those in one of the two categories. When a book is selected from the list, its title, author, category, wholesale price, and number in stock should be displayed in a picture box. The user should be able to add a new book, delete a book, or change the inventory level of a book in stock. At any time, the user should be able to calculate the total value of all books, or the total value of the books in either category.

6. *Voting Machine.* The members of the local Gilligan's Island fan club bring a computer to their annual meeting to use in the election of a new president. Write a program to handle the election. The program should add each candidate to a list box as he or she is nominated. After the nomination process is complete, club members should be able to approach the computer one at a time and double-click on the candidate of their choice. When a "Tally Votes" command button is clicked, a second list box, showing the number of votes received by each candidate, should appear alongside the first list box. Also, the name(s) of the candidate(s) with the highest number of votes should be displayed in a picture box.

7. *Airplane Seating Chart.* An airplane has 30 rows (numbered 1 through 30), with 6 seats (labeled A, B, C, D, E, and F) in each row. Write a program to display a 7-by-31 grid with a cell for each seat. As each passenger selects a seat and a meal (regular, low-calorie, or vegetarian), the ticket agent clicks on the cell corresponding to the seat. A dialog box requests the type of meal and then one of the letters R, L, or V is placed in the cell clicked. At any time, the agent can request the number of seats filled, the number of window seats vacant, and the numbers of each type of meal ordered.

12

Database Management

12.1 **An Introduction To Databases** / **546**
• The Data Control • A Data Control
Walkthrough • Using Code with a Data Control
• The Validation Event

12.2 **Relational Databases and SQL** / **557**
• Primary and Foreign Keys • SQL
• Four SQL Requests • Find Methods

12.3 **Data-bound Grid Control; Creating and
Designing Databases** / **569**
• The Data-Bound Grid Control • Creating a
Database with Visual Data Manager • Creating
a Database in Code with the Professional or
Enterprise Edition • Principles of Database Design

Summary / **584**

Programming Projects / **585**

12.1 AN INTRODUCTION TO DATABASES

The material in this chapter is not accessible with the Control Creation Edition of Visual Basic 5.0 as the CCE lacks the data control. The data control is supplied with all other editions of Visual Basic 5.0 and with all editions of Visual Basic 4.0.

The management of databases is the number one use of computers today. Airlines use databases to handle nearly 1.5 billion passenger reservations per year. The 6500 hospitals in the United States use databases to document the care of over 30 million patients per year. Banks in the United States use databases to monitor the use of 350 million credit cards. Although databases vary considerably in size and complexity, most of them adhere to the fundamental principals of design discussed in this chapter. That is, they are composed of a collection of interrelated tables.

A **table** is a rectangular array of data. Table 12.1 provides information about large cities. Each column of the table, called a **field**, contains the same type of information. (The third column gives the 1995 population in millions and the fourth column gives the projected 2015 population in millions.) The names of the fields are *city, country, pop1995,* and *pop2015*. Each row, called a **record**, contains the same type of information as every other row. Also, the pieces of information in each row are related; they all apply to a specific city. Table 12.2, Countries, has three fields and nine records.

city	country	pop1995	pop2015
Beijing	China	12.4	19.4
Bombay	India	15.1	27.4
Calcutta	India	11.7	17.6
Los Angeles	USA	12.4	14.3
Mexico City	Mexico	15.6	18.8
New York	USA	16.3	17.6
Sao Paulo	Brazil	16.4	20.8
Shanghai	China	15.1	23.4
Tianjin	China	10.7	17.0
Tokyo	Japan	26.8	28.7

Table 12.1 Cities.

country	pop1995	currency
Brazil	155.8	real
China	1185.2	yuan
India	846.3	rupee
Indonesia	195.3	rupiah
Japan	125.0	yen
Mexico	85.6	peso
Nigeria	95.4	naira
Russia	148.2	ruble
USA	263.4	dollar

Table 12.2 Countries

Source: An Urbanized World—Global Report on Human Settlements 1996, a report presented at Habitat II, a UN conference on the world's cities held in Istanbul in June 1996.

A **database** (or **relational database**) is a collection of one or more (usually related) tables that has been created with **database management software**. The best known dedicated database management products are Access, Btrieve, dBase, FoxPro, and Paradox. Every version of Visual Basic 5.0 except the CCE can manage, revise, and analyze a database that has been created with one of these products. However, only the Professional and Enterprise Editions of Visual Basic can create a database programmatically, that is, with code. Section 12.3 shows how to create a database with Visual Data Manager, a miniversion of Access that is supplied with the Learning, Professional, and Enterprise editions of Visual Basic. Section 12.3 also gives a code template for creating a database programmatically.

The databases used in this chapter can be found in the collection of files accompanying this text. The database files have the extension .MDB. For instance, the file MEGACTY1.MDB is a database file containing the two tables presented before. (**Note:** MDB files should be copied from the CD onto a hard drive and accessed from the hard drive.)

The Data Control

Visual Basic communicates with databases through the data control. Data controls can read, modify, delete, and add records to databases. The following walkthrough uses a data control to connect Visual Basic to the database MEGACTY1.MDB.

A Data Control Walkthrough

1. Press Alt/**F**ile/**N**ew Project and double-click on Standard EXE.
2. Double-click on the data control icon. Set its Name to datCities and its caption to Cities.
3. Stretch it horizontally to see the caption Cities.
4. Select the DatabaseName property and set it to the path for the file MEGACTY1.MDB.

   An Open File dialog box will help you locate the file.
5. Select the RecordSource property and click on the down-arrow button at the right of the settings window.

   The names of the two tables in the database, Cities and Countries, are displayed.
6. Select Cities.
7. Place a text box, txtCity, on the form.

   Text boxes are said to be **data-aware** because they can be bound to a data control and access its data.
8. Select txtCity DataSource property.
9. Click on the down arrow to the right of the settings box and select datCities.
10. Select the DataField property and click on the down arrow at the right of the settings box.

    You will see the names of the different fields in the table.
11. Select the field *city*.

    The text box now is said to be **bound** to the data control.

12. Place another text box, txtPop1995, on the form.

13. Select txtPop1995's DataSource property.

14. Click on the down arrow to the right of the settings box and select datCities.

15. Select the DataField property, click on the down arrow at the right of the settings box, and select *pop1995*.

16. Run the program.

    The form will appear as in Figure 12.1. The arrows on the data control, called **navigation arrows**, look and act like VCR buttons. The arrows have been identified by the tasks they perform.

17. Click on the various navigation arrows on the data control to see the different cities and their populations in the Cities table displayed in the text boxes.

18. Change the name of a city or change its population and then move to another record.

    If you look back through the records, you will see that the data have been permanently changed.

Figure 12.1 A Data control with two text boxes bound to it.

Using Code with a Data Control

Only one record can be accessed at a time; this record is called the **current record**. In this walkthrough, the text boxes bound to the data control showed the contents of the *city* and *pop1995* fields of the current record. The user clicked on the navigation arrows of the data control to select a new current record.

The current record also can be changed with code. The methods MoveNext, MovePrevious, MoveLast, and MoveFirst select a new current record as suggested by their names. For instance, the statement

```
Data1.Recordset.MoveLast
```

specifies the last record of the table to be the current record. (The word Recordset is inserted in most data-control statements that manipulate records for reasons that needn't concern us now.)

The entry of the field *fieldName* of the current record is

```
Data1.Recordset.Fields("fieldName").Value
```

For instance, with the status as in Figure 12.1, the statement

```
Let strVar = datCities.Recordset.Fields("city").Value
```

assigns "Beijing" to the variable *strVar* and the statements

```
datCities.Recordset.Edit
Let datCities.Recordset.Fields("city").Value = "Peking"
datCities.Recordset.Update
```

change the *city* field of the current record to "Peking". (The first statement makes a copy of the current record for editing. The second statement alters the copy, and the third statement sends the new copy of the record to the database.)

The number of previously accessed records in the table is given by the RecordCount property. The EOF (End Of File) and BOF (Beginning Of File) run-time properties indicate whether the end or beginning of the file has been reached. For instance, the following two sets of statements each place the cities into a list box.

```
datCities.Recordset.MoveLast
datCities.Recordset.MoveFirst
For i = 1 to datCities.Recordset.RecordCount
  lstBox.AddItem datCities.Recordset.Fields("city").Value
  datCities.Recordset.MoveNext
Next i

datCities.Recordset.MoveFirst
Do While Not datCities.Recordset.EOF
  lstBox.AddItem datCities.Recordset.Fields("city").Value
  datCities.Recordset.MoveNext
Loop
```

The current record can be marked for removal with the statement

```
Data1.Recordset.Delete
```

The record will be removed when a data control navigation arrow is clicked or a Move method is executed. A new record can be added to the end of the table with the statement

```
Data1.Recordset.AddNew
```

followed by

```
Let Data1.Recordset.Fields("fieldName").Value = entryForField
```

statements for each field and a

```
Data1.Recordset.Update
```

statement. Alternately, the AddNew method can be followed by the user typing the information into text boxes bound to the data control and then moving to another record. (**Note:** When you add a record and then click on the Move-Previous arrow, you will not see the next-to-last record, but rather will see the record preceding the record that was current when AddNew was executed.)

The Validation Event

Visual Basic has a device called **validation** that lets you restrict the values a user can enter into a table. For instance, if the Cities table is only to contain cities with a population of more than 1 million, you can use validation to prevent any record with a number less than 1 in the *pop1995* field from being entered.

Validation also allows you to catch (and prevent) errors that might cause a program to crash.

Data controls have an event procedure called Validate that is activated whenever the current record is about to be changed. For instance, it is called when a navigation arrow is clicked or a Move, Update, Delete, or AddNew method is executed. The general form of the Validate event procedure is

```
Private Sub Data1_Validate(Action As Integer, Save As Integer)
   statement(s)
End Sub
```

The value of Action identifies the specific operation that triggered the event and the value of Save specifies whether data bound to the control has changed. You can change the value of the Action argument to perform a different action. Some values of the Action argument are shown in Table 12.3.

Value	Description
1	MoveFirst method
2	MovePrevious method
3	MoveNext method
4	MoveLast method
5	AddNew method
6	Update operation (not UpdateRecord)
7	Delete method
10	Close method

Table 12.3 Some values of the Action argument.

If you assign 0 to the Action argument, the operation will be canceled when the Validate event procedure exited.

The value of Save is –1 (True) if the data in any control attached to the data control have changed and is 0 (False) otherwise. If you set the value of Save to 0 in the Validate event procedure, any changes will not be saved.

Consider the form created in the walkthrough. Suppose the contents of txtPop1995, the 1995 population text box, is changed to .8 and then a navigator arrow is clicked in an attempt to move to another record. The following code prevents the move.

```
Private Sub datCities_Validate(Action As Integer, Save As Integer)
   Dim strMsg As String
   If val(txtPop1995) < 1 then
       Let strMsg = "We only allow cities having a population " & _
                   "at least one million."
       MsgBox strMsg, , "City too small!"
       Let Action = 0
   End If
End Sub
```

If the statement

```
Let Action = 0
```

is changed to

```
Let Save = 0
```

the move will take place, but the previous record will retain its original values. That is, the number .8 will not appear in the table.

EXAMPLE 1 The following program is a general database manager for the Cities table in the MEGACTY1.MDB database. It allows the user to edit the Cities table as needed and to locate information based on the city name. (In the Validate event procedure, the inner If block keeps the message box from appearing when the first or last record is deleted.)

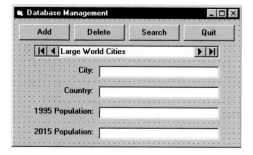

Object	Property	Setting
frmDBMan	Caption	Database Management
cmdAdd	Caption	Add
cmdDelete	Caption	Delete
cmdSearch	Caption	Search
cmdQuit	Caption	Quit
datCities	Caption	Large World Cities
	DatabaseName	MEGACTY1.MDB
	RecordSource	Cities
lblCity	Caption	City:
txtCity	Text	(blank)
	DataSource	datCities
	DataField	City
lblCountry	Caption	Country:
txtCountry	Text	(blank)
	DataSource	datCities
	DataField	Country
lblPop1995	Caption	1995 Population:
txtPop1995	Text	(blank)
	DataSource	datCities
	DataField	pop1995
lblPop2015	Caption	2015 Population:
txtPop2015	Text	(blank)
	DataSource	datCities
	DataField	pop2015

```
Private Sub cmdAdd_Click()
  Rem Add a new record
  datCities.Recordset.AddNew
  txtCity.SetFocus    'Data must be entered and a new record moved to
End Sub

Private Sub cmdDelete_Click ()
  Rem Delete the currently displayed record
  datCities.Recordset.Delete
  Rem Move so that user sees deleted record disappear
  datCities.Recordset.MoveNext
  If datCities.Recordset.EOF Then
      datCities.Recordset.MovePrevious
  End If
End Sub
```

```
Private Sub cmdSearch_Click()
  Dim strSearchFor As String, intFound As Integer
  Rem Search for the city specified by the user
  Let strSearchFor = UCase(InputBox("Name of city to find:"))
  If Len(strSearchFor) > 0 Then
      datCities.Recordset.MoveFirst
      Let intFound = 0
      Do While intFound = 0 And Not datCities.Recordset.EOF
        If UCase(datCities.Recordset.Fields("City").Value) = strSearchFor Then
            Let intFound = 1
          Else
            datCities.Recordset.MoveNext
        End If
      Loop
      If intFound = 0 Then
          MsgBox "Unable to locate requested city.",,"Not Found"
          datCities.Recordset.MoveLast   'move so that EOF is no longer true
      End If
    Else
      MsgBox "Must enter a city.", ,""
  End If
End Sub

Private Sub cmdQuit_Click ()
    End
End Sub

Private Sub datCities_Validate(Action As Integer, Save As Integer)
  Rem Prevent a user from adding a city of population under 1 million
  Dim strMsg As String
  If Val(txtPop1995) < 1 Then
    If Not datCities.Recordset.EOF And Not datCities.Recordset.BOF Then
        Let strMsg = "We only allow cities having a population of " & _
                "at least one million."
        MsgBox strMsg, , "City too small!"
        Let Action = 0
    End If
  End If
End Sub
```

[Run, click the Search button, and enter New York.]

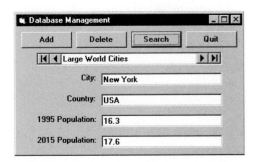

Comments

1. You will most likely alter the file MEGACTY1.MDB while experimenting with the data control or running the program in Example 1. Therefore, we have provided a second copy of the file called MEGACTY1.BAK. You can use it and the copy feature of Windows Explorer or My Computer to obtain a fresh copy of MEGACTY1.MDB.

2. The following controls can be bound to a data control: text box, check box, image, label, picture box, list box, combo box, data bound list box, data bound combo box, and data bound grid.

3. A form can contain more than one data control.

4. Some entries in a table can be empty. For instance, in the Cities table, if the 2015 projected value is not known for a particular city, it can be omitted.

5. Do not use a method such as Move, Delete, or AddNew inside the Validate event procedure. Otherwise, an infinite loop will occur.

6. Field names can be up to 64 characters in length and can consist of letters, numbers, and spaces. If spaces are used in a name, then the name must be enclosed in brackets when used in Visual Basic.

7. Both tables in the database MEGACTY1.MDB have fields called *country*. If there is ever any question about which is being referred to, we can distinguish them by using the two (full) names cities.country and countries.country.

8. In the MEGACTY1.MDB database, the values in the field *city* are all of data type String and the values in the field *pop1995* are all of data type Single. We say that field *city* has type String (also known as Text) and the field *pop1995* has type Single. Two other common data types are Date/Time and Boolean (also known as Yes/No).

9. When a field is first created, a type must be specified. When that type is String (or Text), a maximum length must also be specified. In the MEGACTY1.MDB database, the fields *city* and *country* have maximum length 20 and the field *currency* has maximum length 10.

10. The database MEGACTY1.MDB was created with Visual Data Manager, which has the same format as Access. When the database to be used has been created with other software, such as FoxPro 2.5 or dBase IV, then the walkthrough requires an additional step. Namely, between Steps 3 and 4, the Connect property of the data control has to be set to the name of the software product. (This step was not necessary in our case because Access is the default software.) **Note:** Access database file names end with .MDB, which is an abbreviation for Microsoft Data Base. Btrieve, FoxPro, dBase, and Paradox database file names end with .DAT, .DBF, .DBF, and .DB, respectively.

PRACTICE PROBLEMS 12.1

The Access database BIBLIO.MDB is supplied with Visual Basic 5.0 and is usually stored in the same directory as Visual Basic. How might you determine each of the following quantities?

1. The number of tables in this database

2. The names of the fields in the table Titles

3. The number of records in the table Titles

EXERCISES 12.1

Exercises 1 through 14 refer to the database MEGACTY1.MDB.

1. Write a program to place in a list box the names of the countries in the Countries table in the order they appear in the table.

2. Write a program to place in a list box the names of the countries in the Countries table in the reverse order that they appear in the table.

3. Write a program to place in a list box the names of the cities in the Cities table whose populations are projected to exceed 20 million in the year 2015.

4. Write a program to place in a list box the names of the cities in the Cities table whose 1995 populations are between 12 and 16 million.

5. Write a program to place in a list box the names of the countries in the Countries table, where each name is followed by a hyphen and the name of its currency.

6. Write a program to find and display the city in the Cities table that will experience the greatest percentage growth from 1995 to 2015. [**Note:** The percentage growth is 100 * (pop2015 – pop1995) / pop1995.]

7. Write a program to place the countries from the Countries table in a list box in descending order of their 1995 populations. (**Hint:** Place the countries and their 1995 populations in a pair of parallel arrays and sort the pair of arrays in descending order based on the populations.)

8. Write a program to place the cities from the Cities table in a list box in descending order of their percentage population growth from 1995 to 2015.

9. Write a program to display the name and currency of each city in the table Cities.

10. Write a program to display the names and 1995 populations of the countries in the table Country. The countries should be displayed in descending order of their populations.

11. Write a program to back up the contents of the Cities table in one sequential file and the Countries table in another sequential file. Run the program and compare the sizes of these two sequential files with the size of the file MEGACTY1.MDB.

12. Suppose the sequential file ADDCTRY.TXT contains several records for countries not in MEGACTY1.MDB, where each record consists of the name of a country, its 1995 population (in millions), and the name of its currency. Write a program to add the contents of this file into the Countries table.

13. Suppose the sequential file UPDATE.TXT contains several records, where each record consists of the name of a country, its 1995 population (in millions), and the name of its currency. Write a program to use the information in UPDATE.TXT to update the Countries table. If a record in UPDATE.TXT contains the same country as a record in the Countries table, then the population in 1995 and the name of the currency in the Countries table should be replaced with the corresponding values from UPDATE.TXT. If a record in UPDATE.TXT contains a country that does not appear in the Countries table, a new record should be added to the table.

14. Write a program that allows the user to specify a city and then displays the percentage of its country's population that lives in that city.

Exercises 15 through 18 refer to the BIBLIO.MDB database supplied with Visual Basic.

15. How many tables are in the database?

16. Give the names of the fields in the table Publishers.

17. How many records are in the table Publishers?

18. Write a program that requests the name of a publisher (such as Prentice Hall or Microsoft Press) and gives the publisher's address.

19. The database ST_ABBR.MDB contains one table, States, having two fields, *abbreviation* and *state*. Each record consists of a two-letter abbreviation and the name of a state. Some records are (AZ, Arizona) and (MD, Maryland). Write a program that allows the user to enter a two-letter abbreviation and obtain the name of the state. Of course, if the two-letter abbreviation does not correspond to any state, the user should be so informed.

In Exercises 20 through 25, match the Validate event procedures with the effect in A through F.

    A. When the MoveNext navigator arrow is pressed, data control moves to the previous record.

    B. When you move to a new record, all changes to the previous record are ignored.

    C. When the MoveLast navigator arrow is pressed, the data control moves to the first record.

    D. Navigator arrows won't work. Can't edit.

    E. Every time you move to a new record, the current record is saved, whether or not any changes were made to it.

    F. Whenever the MovePrevious arrow is clicked, an empty record is created.

20.
```
Private Sub Data1_Validate (Action As Integer, Save As Integer)
    If Action = 3 Then
        Let Action = 2
    End If
End Sub
```

21.
```
Private Sub Data1_Validate (Action As Integer, Save As Integer)
    If (Save = –1) And (Action >=1 ) And (Action <= 4) Then
        Let Save = 0
    End If
End Sub
```

22.
```
Private Sub Data1_Validate (Action As Integer, Save As Integer)
    If Action = 4 Then
        Let Action = 1
    End If
End Sub
```

23.
```
Private Sub Data1_Validate (Action As Integer, Save As Integer)
    Let Action = 0
End Sub
```

24.
```
Private Sub Data1_Validate(Action As Integer, Save As Integer)
    If (Action >= 1) And (Action <= 4) Then
        Let Save = –1
    End If
End Sub
```

25.
```
Private Sub Data1_Validate(Action As Integer, Save As Integer)
    If Action = 2 Then
        Let Action = 5
    End If
End Sub
```

26. Write a program similar to Example 1 that uses the Countries table, but does not allow the name of country to be changed.

27. Write a program similar to Example 1 that uses the Countries table, but does not allow a new country to be added unless a value is given for its currency field.

28. A data control can also be connected to an Excel spreadsheet. (Set the Connect property of the data control to Excel 3.0 or Excel 4.0 or Excel 5.0 or Excel 8.0, . . . , and set the DataBaseName property to the name of the spreadsheet.) The Excel 5.0 spreadsheet CHKBOOK.XLS is one of the files on the CD accompanying this text. This spreadsheet has four columns labeled *date*, *checkNum*, *description*, and *amount*. Write a program that displays the rows of the speadsheet in text boxes. The program should allow you to search, delete, and add checks to the spreadsheet. (**Note:** Set the RecordSource property to Checks$. The column names serve as field names and should be specified in the DataField property of the text boxes.)

SOLUTIONS TO PRACTICE PROBLEMS 12.1

Place a data control, call it datBooks, on a form and set its DatabaseName property to the file BIBLIO.MDB.

1. Select the RecordSource property and click on the down-arrow button at the right of its settings box. Count the number of entries in the dropdown list of tables that appears.

2. Set the RecordSource property of datBooks to the table Titles. Place a text box, call it txtBook, on the form and bind it to the data control by setting its DataSource property to datBooks. Select the DataField property of txtBook and click on the down-arrow button at the right of its settings box. Count the number of entries in the dropdown list of fields that appears.

3. Place a picture box and a command button on the screen. Place the statements

```
datBooks.Recordset.MoveLast
picBox.Print datBooks.Recordset.RecordCount
```

in the cmdDisplay_Click event procedure. Run the program and then click on the command button.

12.2 RELATIONAL DATABASES AND SQL

Primary and Foreign Keys

A well-designed table should have a field (or set of fields) that can be used to uniquely identify each record. Such a field (or set of fields) is called a **primary key**. For instance, in the Countries table of Section 12.1, the *country* field is a primary key. In the Cities table, because we are only considering very large cities (of over 1 million population), the *city* field is a primary key. Databases of student enrollments in a college usually use a field of social security numbers as the primary key. Names would not be a good choice because there could be easily two students having the same name.

When a database is created, a field can be specified as a primary key. If so, Visual Basic will insist that every record have an entry in the primary key field and that the same entry does not appear in any other record. If the user tries to enter a record with no data in the primary key, the error message "Index or primary key can't contain a null record." will be generated. If the user tries to enter a record with the same primary key data as another record, the error message "Duplicate value in index, primary key, or relationship. Changes were unsuccessful." will be displayed.

When a database contains two or more tables, the tables are usually related. For instance, the two tables Cities and Countries are related by their *country* field. Let's refer to these two fields as Cities.country and Countries.country. Notice that every entry in Cities.country appears uniquely in Countries.country and Countries.country is a primary key . We say that Cities.country is a **foreign key** of Countries.country. Foreign keys can be specified when a table is first created. If so, Visual Basic will insist on the **Rule of Referential Integrity**, namely, that each value in the foreign key must also appear in the primary key of the other table.

The CD accompanying this book contains a database named MEGACTY2. MDB. It has the same information as MEGACTY1.MDB except that Cities.city and Countries.country have been specified as primary keys for their respective tables, and Cities.country has been specified as a foreign key of Countries.country. If the user tries to add a city to the Cities table whose country does not appear in the Countries table, then the error message "Can't add or change record. Referential integrity rules require a related record in table 'Countries'." will be displayed. The message will also be generated if the user tries to delete a country from the Countries.country field that appears in the Cities.country field. Due to the interdependence of the two tables in MEGACTY2.MDB, this database is called a **relational database**.

A foreign key allows Visual Basic to link (or **join**) together two tables from a relational database in a meaningful way. For instance, when the two tables Cities and Countries from MEGACTY2.MDB are joined based on the foreign key Cities.country, the result is Table 12.4. The record for each city is expanded to show its country's population and its currency. This joined table is very handy if, say, we wanted to click on navigation arrows and display a city's name and currency. We only have to create the original two tables; Visual Basic creates the joined table as needed. The request for a joined table is made in a language called SQL.

city	Cities. country	Cities. pop1995	pop2015	Countries. country	Country. pop1995	currency
Tokyo	Japan	26.8	28.7	Japan	125.0	yen
Sao Paulo	Brazil	16.4	20.8	Brazil	155.8	real
New York	USA	16.3	17.6	USA	263.4	dollar
Mexico City	Mexico	15.6	18.8	Mexico	85.6	peso
Bombay	India	15.1	27.4	India	846.3	rupee
Shanghai	China	15.1	23.4	China	1185.2	yuan
Los Angeles	USA	12.4	14.3	USA	263.4	dollar
Beijing	China	12.4	19.4	China	1185.2	yuan
Calcutta	India	11.7	17.6	India	846.3	rupee
Tianjin	China	10.7	17.0	China	1185.2	yuan

Table 12.4 A join of two tables.

SQL

Structured Query Language (SQL) was developed in the early 1970s at IBM for use with relational databases. The language was standardized in 1986 by ANSI (American National Standards Institute). Visual Basic uses a version of SQL that is compliant with ANSI-89 SQL. There are some minor variations that are of no concern in this book.

SQL is a very powerful language. One use of SQL is to request specialized information from an existing database and/or to have the information presented in a specified order.

Four SQL Requests

We will focus on four basic types of requests that can be made with SQL.

Request I: Show the records in a specified order.

Some examples of orders with MEGACTY2.MDB are

(a) Alphabetical order based on the name of the city.
(b) Alphabetical order based on the name of the country, and within each country group, the name of the city.
(c) In descending order based on the projected 2015 population.

Request II: Show just the records that meet certain criteria.

Some examples of criteria with MEGACTY2.MDB are

(a) Cities that are in China.
(b) Cities whose 2015 population is projected to be at least 20 million.
(c) Cities whose name begins with the letter S.

Request III: Join the tables together, connected by a foreign key, and present the records as in Requests I and II.

Some examples with MEGACTY2.MDB are

(a) Show the cities in descending order of the populations of their countries.
(b) Show the cities whose currency has "u" as its second letter.

Request IV: Make available just *some* of the fields of either the basic tables or the joined table. (For now, this type of request just conserves space and effort by Visual Basic. However, it will be very useful in Section 12.3 when used with a data-bound grid.)

Some examples with MEGACTY2.MDB are

(a) Make available just the city and country fields of the table Cities.
(b) Make available just the city and currency fields of the joined table.

Normally, we set the RecordSource property of a data control to an entire table. Also, the records of the table are normally presented in the order they are physically stored in the table. We make the requests discussed before by specifying the RecordSource property as one of the following kinds of settings.

Request I: SELECT * FROM *Table1* ORDER BY *field1* ASC
          or SELECT * FROM *Table1* ORDER BY *field1* DESC

Request II: SELECT * FROM *Table1* WHERE *criteria*

Request III: SELECT * FROM *Table1* INNER JOIN *Table2* ON *foreign field* =
          primary field WHERE *criteria*

Request IV: SELECT *field1*, *field2*, . . . *fieldN*, FROM *Table1* WHERE *criteria*

The words ASC and DESC specify ASCending and DESCending orders, respectively. A *criteria* clause is a string containing a condition of the type used with If blocks. In addition to the standard operators <, >, and =, *criteria* strings frequently contain the operator Like. Essentially, Like uses the wildcard characters ? and * to compare a string to a pattern. A question mark stands for a single character in the same position as the question mark. For instance, the pattern "B?d" is matched by "Bid", "Bud", and "Bad". An asterisk stands for any number of characters in the same position as the asterisk. For instance, the pattern "C*r" is matched by "Computer", "Chair", and "Car". See Comments 3 through 5 for further information about Like.

In the sentence

```
SELECT fields FROM clause
```

fields is either * (to indicate all fields) or a sequence of the fields to be available (separated by commas), and *clause* is either a single table or a join of two tables. A join of two tables is indicated by a *clause* of the form

```
table1 INNER JOIN table2 ON foreign key of table1=primary key of table2
```

Appending

```
WHERE criteria
```

to the end of the sentence restricts the records to those satisfying *criteria*. Appending

```
ORDER BY field(s) ASC (or DESC)
```

presents the records ordered by the specified *field* or *fields*.

In general, the SQL statements we consider will look like

```
SELECT www FROM xxx WHERE yyy ORDER BY zzz
```

where SELECT *www* FROM *xxx* is always present and accompanied by one or both of WHERE *yyy* and ORDER BY *zzz*. In addition, the *xxx* portion might contain an INNER JOIN phrase.

The settings for the examples mentioned earlier are as follows:

I (a) Show the records from Cities in alphabetical order based on the name of the city.

```
SELECT * FROM Cities ORDER BY city ASC
```

I (b) Show the records from Cities in alphabetical order based first on the name of the country and, within each country group, the name of the city.

```
SELECT * FROM Cities ORDER BY country, city ASC
```

I (c) Show the records from Cities in descending order based on the projected 2015 population.

```
SELECT * FROM Cities ORDER BY pop2015 DESC
```

II (a) Show the records for the Cities in China.

```
SELECT * FROM Cities WHERE country = 'China'
```

II (b) Show the records from Cities whose 2015 population is projected to be at least 20 million.

```
SELECT * FROM Cities WHERE pop2015 >= 20
```

II (c) Show the records from Cities whose name begins with the letter S.

```
SELECT * FROM Cities WHERE city Like 'S*'
```

III(a) Show the records from the joined table in descending order of the populations of their countries.

```
SELECT * FROM Cities INNER JOIN Countries ON Cities.country =
Countries.country ORDER BY Countries.pop1995 DESC
```

III(b) Show the records from the joined table whose currency has "u" as its second letter.

```
SELECT * FROM Cities INNER JOIN Countries ON Cities.country =
Countries.country WHERE currency Like '?u*'
```

IV(a) Make available just the city and country fields of the table Cities.

```
SELECT city, country FROM Cities
```

IV(b) Make available just the city and currency fields of the joined table.

```
SELECT city, currency FROM Cities INNER JOIN Countries ON
Cities.country = Countries.country
```

Note: In several of the statements, the single quote, rather than the normal double quote was used to surround strings. This is standard practice with SQL statements.

We can think of an SQL statement as creating in essence a new "virtual" table from existing tables. For instance, we might regard the statement

```
SELECT city, pop2015 FROM Cities WHERE pop2015>=20
```

as creating the "virtual" table

city	pop2015
Tokyo	28.7
Sao Paulo	20.8
Bombay	27.4
Shanghai	23.4

This table is a subtable of the original table Cities, that is, it consists of what is left after certain columns and rows are deleted.

As another example, the statement

```
SELECT Cities.city, Cities.Country, Country.currency FROM Cities INNER JOIN
Countries ON Cities.country = Countries.country WHERE Countries.country>'K'
```

creates in essence the "virtual" table

Cities.city	Cities.country	currency
New York	USA	dollar
Mexico City	Mexico	peso
Los Angeles	USA	dollar

which is a subtable of a join of the two tables Cities and Countries.

These "virtual" tables don't really exist physically. However, for all practical purposes, Visual Basic acts as if they did. In Visual Basic terminology, a "virtual" table is called a **recordset** and SQL statements are said to create a recordset. In standard relational database books, a "virtual" table is called a **view**.

SQL also can be used in code with a statement of the form

```
Data1.RecordSource = " SELECT ... FROM ..."
```

to alter the order and kinds of records presented from a database. However, such a statement must be followed by the statement

```
Data1.Refresh
```

to reset the information processed by the data control.

EXAMPLE 1   The following program allows the user to alter the order and kinds of information displayed from a database. When the first command button is pressed, the cities are presented in ascending order based on their 1995 populations. When the second command button is pressed, the cities are presented in alphabetical order along with their currencies.

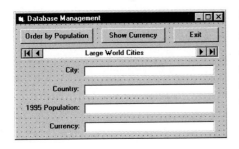

Object	Property	Setting
frmDBMan	Caption	Database Management
cmdOrderByPop	Caption	Order by Population
cmdShowCurrency	Caption	Show Currency
cmdQuit	Caption	Exit
datCities	Caption	Large World Cities
	DatabaseName	MEGACTY2.MDB
	RecordSource	Cities
lblCity	Caption	City:
txtCity	DataSource	datCities
	DataField	city
lblCountry	Caption	Country:
txtCountry	DataSource	datCities
	DataField	country
lblPopulation	Caption	1995 Population:
txtPopulation	DataSource	datCities
	DataField	pop1995
lblCurrency	Caption	Currency:
txtCurrency	DataSource	datCities

```
Private Sub cmdOrderByPop_Click()
    Dim strSQL As String
    Let txtCurrency.DataField = ""
    Let txtCurrency.Text = ""
    Let strSQL = "SELECT * FROM Cities ORDER BY pop1995 ASC"
    Let datCities.RecordSource = strSQL
    datCities.Refresh
End Sub

Private Sub cmdQuit_Click()
    End
End Sub
```

```
Private Sub cmdShowCurrency_Click()
    Dim strSQL As String
    Let strSQL = "SELECT city, Cities.country, Cities.pop1995, currency " & _
                 "FROM Cities INNER JOIN Countries " & _
                 "ON Cities.country=Countries.country " & _
                 "ORDER BY city ASC"
    Let datCities.RecordSource = strSQL
    datCities.Refresh
    Let txtCity.DataField = "city"
    Let txtCountry.DataField = "country"
    Let txtPopulation.DataField = "pop1995"
    Let txtCurrency.DataField = "currency"
End Sub
```

[Run and click on Order by Population.]

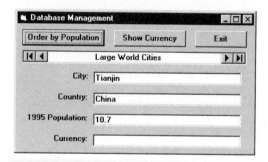

[Click on Show Currency and click on the Next navigator arrow six times.]

The program in Example 1 of Section 12.1 searched a table for a specific record by looping through all the records. Whereas this technique is fine for small tables, it is not efficient for searches of large tables. Visual Basic provides a better way with Find methods.

Find Methods

Suppose a table has been attached to the data control Data1, and an SQL statement has been used to create and order a recordset. Then a statement of the form

```
Data1.RecordSet.FindFirst criteria
```

starts at the beginning of the recordset, searches for the first record in the recordset that satisfies the criteria, and makes that record the current record.

(Here, *criteria* is a string just like a *criteria* phrase that follows WHERE in an SQL statement.) The related methods FindLast, FindNext, and FindPrevious function as their names suggest. (FindLast starts at the end of the recordset. FindNext and FindPrevious start at the current record.) For instance, suppose an SQL statement ordered the cities alphabetically by name. The following statements and their outcomes show the effects of the various Find methods.(In each case, assume that the current record is Mexico City.)

Statement	New Current Record
datCities.Recordset.FindFirst "pop2015 < 20"	Beijing
datCities.Recordset.FindLast "pop2015 < 20"	Tianjin
datCities.Recordset.FindNext "pop2015 < 20"	New York
datCities.Recordset.FindPrevious "pop2015 < 20"	Los Angeles

Visual Basic has two properties, NoMatch and Bookmark, that help when a Find method fails to locate a suitable record.

If BkMk is a string variable, a statement of the form

```
Let BkMk = Data1.Recordset.Bookmark
```

assigns the location of the current record to the variable BkMk. When desired, the statement

```
Let Data1.Recordset.Bookmark = BkMk
```

will return to the original location in the table.

If a Find method does not locate a record matching the criteria, the first or last record (depending on where the search is heading) in the recordset becomes the current record and the NoMatch property is set to True. Therefore, the following lines of code can be used to keep the current record current whenever the Find method is unsuccessful.

```
Let BkMk = Data1.Recordset.Bookmark
Data1.Recordset.FindNext criteria
If Data1.Recordset.NoMatch = True Then
    Data1.Recordset.Bookmark = BkMk
End If
```

EXAMPLE 2   The following program displays the large cities in a country specified by the user. Due to the SQL statement in the setting for datCities.RecordSource, the cities will be presented alphabetically. Notice the handling of the string variable *criteria*. Had the Find statement been

```
datCities.Recordset.FindFirst "country = nom"
```

the error message "Can't bind name 'nom'." would have been generated.

Object	Property	Setting
frmDBMan	Caption	EXAMPLE 12-2-2
lstCities		
cmdFind	Caption	Find Cities
lblCountry	Caption	Country
txtCountry	Caption	(blank)
datCities	Caption	Large World Cities
	DatabaseName	MEGACTY2.MDB
	RecordSource	SELECT * FROM Cities ORDER BY city ASC

```
Private Sub cmdFind_Click()
  Dim nom As String, criteria As String
  lstCities.Clear
  If txtCountry.Text <> "" Then
      Let nom = txtCountry.Text
      Let criteria = "country = " & "'" & nom & "'"
      datCities.Recordset.FindFirst criteria
      Do While datCities.Recordset.NoMatch = False
        lstCities.AddItem datCities.Recordset.Fields("city").Value
        datCities.Recordset.FindNext criteria
      Loop
      If lstCities.ListCount = 0 Then lstCities.AddItem "None"
    Else
      MsgBox "You must enter a country.", , ""
      txtCountry.SetFocus
    End If
End Sub
```

[Run, type China into the text box, and press the command button.]

Comments

1. Each record of the Countries table is related to one or more records of the Cities table, but each record of the Cities table is related to only one record of the Countries table. Therefore, we say that there is a **one-to-many relationship** from the Countries table to the Cities table.

2. SQL statements are insensitive to case. For instance, the following choices for *criteria* have the same effect: City='China', city='china', CITY='china', CiTy='CHINA'.

3. When the Like operator is used, the "pattern" must appear on the right of the operator. For instance, the SQL statement

```
SELECT * FROM Cities WHERE city Like 'S*'
```

cannot be replaced by

```
SELECT * FROM Cities WHERE 'S*' Like city
```

4. The operator Like permits a refinement of the wildcard character "?". Whereas "?" is a placeholder for any letter, an expression such as "[*letter1-letter2*]" is a placeholder for any letter from *letter1* to *letter2*. For instance, the pattern "[A-F]ad" is matched by Bad and Dad, but not Sad.

5. The Like operator can be used in If blocks in much the same way as the operators >, =, and <. In this situation, the operator is case-sensitive. For instance, the condition ("bad" Like "[A-F]ad") is False. However, when Like is used in SQL statements, it is case-insensitive. That is, ("bad" Like "[A-F]ad") is True.

6. Sometimes a pair of fields is specified as a primary key. For instance, in a table of college courses, a single course might have several sections—a course might be identified as CMSC 102, Section 3. In this case, the pair of fields *course, section* would serve as a primary key for the table.

7. The requirement that no record may have a null primary key is called the **Rule of Entity Integrity**.

8. If there is no field with unique entries, database designers usually add a "counter field" containing the numbers 1, 2, 3, and so on. This field then can serve as a primary key.

PRACTICE PROBLEMS 12.2

Consider the procedure cmdSearch_Click( ) of Example 1 in Section 12.1.

1. Rewrite the procedure using an SQL statement to display the requested record.

2. Rewrite the procedure using a Find method to display the requested record.

EXERCISES 12.2

Exercises 1 and 4 refer to the database MEGACTY2.MDB, where the primary keys of Cities and Countries are *city* and *country*, respectively, and *Cities.country* is a foreign key to *Countries.country*. Determine whether the stated action could ever cause a problem. Explain.

1. Add a new record to the Cities table.

2. Delete a record from the Countries table.

3. Delete a record from the Cities table.

4. Add a new record to the Countries table.

In Exercises 5 through 10, use the database BIBLIO.MDB that is provided with Visual Basic. By experimentation, determine the primary keys for each of the tables in Exercises 5 through 8.

5. Authors

6. Publishers

7. Titles

8. Title Author

Determine the foreign keys for the pairs of tables in Exercises 9 and 10.

9. Authors, Titles

10. Publishers, Titles

The following tables are "virtual" tables derived from the MEGACTY2.MDB database. In Exercises 11 through 14, identify the "virtual" table associated with the SQL statement.

(A)

country	pop1995	currency
Russia	148.2	ruble
Indonesia	195.3	rupiah
India	846.3	rupee
Brazil	155.8	real

(B)

country	pop1995	currency
China	1185.2	yuan

(C)

country	pop1995	currency
China	1185.2	yuan
India	846.3	rupee

(D)

country	pop1995	currency
China	1185.2	yuan
Brazil	155.8	real

11. `SELECT * FROM Countries WHERE pop1995>1000 ORDER BY pop1995 ASC`

12. `SELECT * FROM Countries WHERE country<'E' ORDER BY pop1995 DESC`

13. `SELECT * FROM Countries WHERE currency Like 'r*' ORDER BY country DESC`

14. `SELECT * FROM Countries WHERE pop1995>700 ORDER BY country ASC`

The following tables are "virtual" tables derived from the MEGACTY2.MDB database. In Exercises 15 through 18, identify the "virtual" table associated with the SQL statement.

(A)

city	currency
Sao Paulo	real
Shanghai	yuan

(B)

city	currency
Tokyo	yen
Bombay	rupee
Shanghai	yuan

(C)

city	currency
Bombay	rupee
Calcutta	rupee

(D)

city	currency
Tokyo	yen

15. `SELECT city, currency FROM Cities INNER JOIN Countries ON Cities.country = Countries.country WHERE city='Tokyo'`

16. `SELECT city, currency FROM Cities INNER JOIN Countries ON Cities.country=`
    `Countries.country WHERE pop2015>22 ORDER BY pop2015 DESC`

17. `SELECT city, currency FROM Cities INNER JOIN Countries ON Cities.country =`
    `Countries.country WHERE Cities.country='India' ORDER BY Cities.pop1995 DESC`

18. `SELECT city, currency FROM Cities INNER JOIN Countries ON Cities.country =`
    `Countries.country WHERE city Like 'S*' ORDER BY Countries.pop1995 ASC`

Exercises 19 through 22 refer to the database MEGACTY2.MDB. Identify the city in the current record after the following lines of code are executed.

19. `Let datCities.RecordSource = "SELECT * FROM Cities"`
    `datCities.Refresh`
    `datCities.Recordset.FindFirst "pop2015 < 20"`

20. `Let datCities.RecordSource = "SELECT * FROM Cities ORDER BY city ASC"`
    `datCities.Refresh`
    `datCities.Recordset.FindLast "pop2015 < 20"`

21. `Let datCities.RecordSource = "SELECT * FROM Cities ORDER BY pop2015 ASC"`
    `datCities.Refresh`
    `datCities.Recordset.FindFirst "pop2015 < 20"`

22. `Let datCities.RecordSource = "SELECT * FROM Cities WHERE country = 'India'"`
    `datCities.Refresh`
    `datCities.Recordset.FindLast "pop2015 < 20"`

Write a set of statements as in Exercises 19 through 22 to accomplish the following task.

23. Find the city in China that will have the largest population in 2015.

24. Find the city that has the smallest population in 1995.

25. Consider the database MEGACTY2.MDB. Write a program with a single list box and four command buttons captioned "Alphabetical Order", "Order by 1995 Population", "Order by 2015 Population", and "Alphabetical Order by Country and City". Each time one of the command buttons is pressed, the cities from the Cities table should be displayed in the list box as described by the command button.

26. Consider the database BIBLIO.MDB. Write a program that requests a year as input and then displays in a list box the titles and authors of all books published in that year. The program should use the Find method to locate the books.

Exercises 27 and 28 refer to the database PHONEBK.MDB, which holds all the information for the residence listings of a telephone book for a city. Assume the database consists of one table, Names, with the six fields: lastName, firstName, middleInitial, streetNumber, street, and phoneNumber.

27. Write a program that will print out the phone book in the standard form shown in Figure 12.2(a).

28. Write a program that will print out a "criss-cross" directory that gives phone numbers with the entries organized by street as in Figure 12.2(b).

AAKER Larry 3 Main St	874-2345		APPLE ST 3 Carl Aaron	405-2345	
AARON Alex 23 Park Ave	924-3456		5 John Smith	862-1934	
Bob R 17 Elm St	347-3456		7 Ted T Jones	405-1843	
Carl 3 Apple St	405-2345		ARROW RD 1 Ben Rob	865-2345	
(a)			(b)		

Figure 12.2 (a) Standard phone directory and (b)criss-cross directory.

SOLUTIONS TO PRACTICE PROBLEMS 12.2

1.
```
Private Sub cmdSearch_Click ()
    Dim strSearchFor As String, strSQL As String
    Rem Search for the city specified by the user
    Let strSearchFor = InputBox("Name of city to find:")
    If Len(strSearchFor) > 0 Then
        Let strSQL = "SELECT * FROM Cities " & _
                    "WHERE city=" & "'" & strSearchFor & "'"
        datCities.RecordSource = strSQL
        datCities.Refresh
        If txtCity.Text = "" Then
            MsgBox "Unable to locate requested city.",,"Not Found"
            datCities.RecordSource = "SELECT * FROM Cities"
            datCities.Refresh
        End If
    Else
        Msgbox "Must enter a city.",,""
    End If
End Sub
```

2.
```
Private Sub cmdSearch_Click ()
    Dim strSearchFor As String
    Rem Search for the city specified by the user
    Let strSearchFor = InputBox("Name of city to find:")
    If Len(strSearchFor) > 0 Then
        datCities.Recordset.FindFirst "city= " & "'" & strSearchFor & "'"
        If datCities.Recordset.NoMatch = True Then
            MsgBox "Unable to locate requested city.",,"Not Found"
        End If
    Else
        Msgbox "Must enter a city.",,""
    End If
End Sub
```

12.3 DATA-BOUND GRID CONTROL; CREATING AND DESIGNING DATABASES

You use the **data-bound grid** control to view and edit entire tables with minimal code. When you attach the control to a table, it automatically displays the table's records (including the field names) in a grid resembling a spreadsheet. After a discussion of this powerful control, you will learn how to create your own databases. Of course, the best way to view your new creations is with the data-bound grid control.

There are three ways you can create a database:

1. Use Visual Data Manager, a program supplied with the Learning, Standard, Professional, and Enterprise editions of Visual Basic.

2. Use code with the Professional or Enterprise editions of Visual Basic. (Although, the Learning Edition of Visual Basic can edit an existing database, it lacks the statements needed to create a database from scratch.)

3. Use database management software, such as Access, Btrieve, dDase, FoxPro, or Paradox.

In this section, we provide a detailed explanation of how to use Visual Data Manager. We include a code template that you can easily modify to create a database with the Professional or Enterprise editions of Visual Basic.

The Data-Bound Grid Control

Before you can use the data-bound grid control, you may need to add the control to the toolbar using the Components dialog box that is invoked from the Project menu. (Place an x in the check box next to "Microsoft Data Bound Grid Control".) Also, you may have to check the "Microsoft DAO Object Library" using the References dialog box that is invoked from the Project menu.

When you attach the grid control to a table via a data control, it automatically displays the table's records (including the field names) in a spreadsheet-like array with an arrow pointing to the current record. This gives you a great deal of ready-made functionality that allows you to browse and edit entire tables. The rows and columns display the records and fields. The intersection of a row and column is called a **cell**. You can specify the current cell in code or can change it at run time using the mouse or the arrow keys. You can read and edit the contents of each cell either directly or with code.

Two properties of the data-bound grid, AllowAddNew and AllowDelete, let you decide whether the user can add new records and delete existing records directly. The default values for both properties are False. When the AllowAdd New property is set to True, the last row displayed in the DBGrid control is left blank to permit users to enter new records. When the AllowDelete property is set to True, the user can remove a record by clicking on the (gray) rectangle to the left of the record and then pressing the Delete key. Of course, with any property setting, records can always be added or deleted programmatically.

You can prevent the user from making changes directly to an individual cell by setting the AllowUpdate property of the DBGrid to False. The default value is True.

You can use an SQL statement to specify the fields displayed in a data-bound grid. For instance, if the data-bound grid control has datCities as its DataSource and the DatabaseName setting for datCities is MEGACTY2.MDB, then the statement

```
Let datCities.RecordSource = "SELECT city, country FROM Cities"
```

causes the grid to display only the first two columns of the Cities table. The same effect can be achieved at design time by setting the RecordSource property of datCities to

```
SELECT city, country FROM Cities
```

EXAMPLE 1   The following program displays the contents of the Cities table of the MEGACTY2.MDB database. When you click on the command button, the grid displays the cities, their countries, and currency.

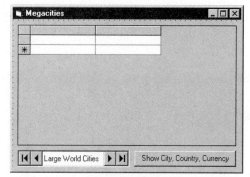

Object	Property	Setting
frm12_3_1	Caption	Megacities
datCities	Caption	Large World Cities
	Database	MEGACTY2.MDB
	RecordSource	Cities
dbgrdCities	DataSource	datCities
cmdShow	Caption	Show City, Country, Currency

```
Private Sub cmdShow_Click()
    Rem Join the two tables and display cities, countries, and currency
    Let datCities.RecordSource = "SELECT city, Cities.country, currency FROM " & _
        "Cities INNER JOIN Countries ON Countries.country = Cities.country"
    datCities.Refresh
End Sub
```

[Run]

[Click on the command button.]

The arrow in the left column points to the current record. When you click on a cell of the grid, its row becomes the current record. If you change the contents of any cell, the table will be updated as soon as the current record changes. (Of course, if a change violates either the rule of referential or entity integrity an error message will be generated and the program will end.)

Creating a Database with Visual Data Manager

You invoke Visual Data Manager (VisData) from Visual Basic by pressing Alt/Add-Ins/Visual Data Manager. The first two entries of the File menu of VisData are Open Database, used to view and alter an existing database, and New, used to create a new database. See Figure 12.3.

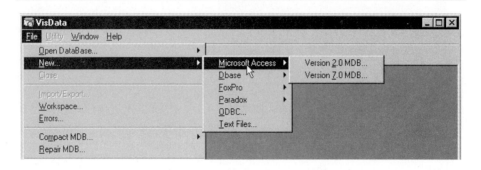

Figure 12.3 Visual Data Manager's File menu

Let's focus on creating a new database. After you select New, you are presented with a drop-down menu used to choose the type of database as shown in Figure 12.3. Choose Microsoft Access and then specify a version. (Version 7.0 is the latest version of Access, the one that comes with the Professional Edition of Office 97.) Then a standard file-naming dialog box titled "Select Microsoft Access Database to Create" appears. See Figure 12.4.

Figure 12.4 Dialog box used to name the database

After you name the database, say as MEGACITY.MDB, and click Save, the Database window and SQL Statement box appear. We will work solely with the Database window.

Figure 12.5 Database window. (Appears after the database is named. Initially the window will contain only the Properties line. Additional lines will appear as tables are created.)

Suppose you want to create a database with two tables. Starting from the Database window, the basic steps are as follows:

1. Create the database and the two tables.

   (a) Click on the right mouse button within the Database window. Click on New Table and use the Table Structure window (Figure 12.6) to name the first table and to specify the fields and their data types. Then return to the Database window by clicking Build the Table.
   (b) Repeat Step 1 for the second table.

2. (Optional) Specify a primary key for a table.

   (a) Highlight the table name in the Database window.
   (b) Press the right mouse button and choose Design to invoke the Table Structure window (Figure 12.6).
   (c) Press the Add Index button to invoke the Add Index window (Figure 12.7) and follow the steps listed after the figure.

3. Place records into a table.

   (**Note:** The VisData toolbar contains three sets of icons. This discussion assumes that the left icon of each of the first two sets has been selected. These are the "Table type Recordset" and "Use Data Control on New Form" icons.)

   (a) Double-click on the table in the Database window to invoke the Table window (Figure 12.8).
   (b) Follow the directions listed after Figure 12.8.

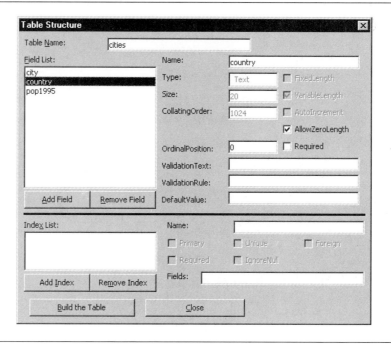

Figure 12.6 Table Structure window. (Invoked from the Database window with the right mouse button by choosing New or Design .)

How to use the Table Structure window

1. Type the name of the table in the Table Name text box.

2. Click on the Add Field button. (An Add Field window will be displayed.)

3. Type the name of a field in the Name text box.

4. Click on the down arrow of the Type combo box and select a type from the dropdown list. (We use primarily the type "Text" for strings, and "Single" or "Integer" for numbers.)

5. If the data type is "Text," type the length of the largest possible string needed in the Size box. (For instance, length 20 should suffice for names of cities. The length must be no longer than 255 characters.)

6. Press OK to add the field to the table.

7. Repeat Steps 3 through 6 until you have added all the fields to the table. When you are through, click on the Close button to return to the Database window.

8. To delete a field, highlight the field by clicking on it in the list box and then press the Remove Field button.

9. When all fields have been specified, press the "Build the Table" button to save the table and return to the Database window. (If we later decide to add a new field or delete an existing field, we can return to the Table Structure window by highlighting the table in the Database window, clicking the right mouse button, and choosing Design.)

(**Note:** The "Build the Table" button appears only for new tables, otherwise, use the Close button return to the Database window.)

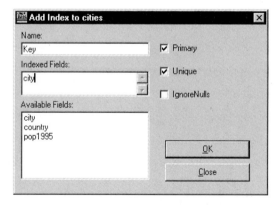

Figure 12.7 Add Index window (Invoked from the Table Structure window by pressing Add Index.)

How to use the Add Index window to specify a primary key

1. Type in a name for an index, such as Principal, click on the field which is to be the primary field, and place check marks in the Primary and Unique check boxes.

2. Click OK and then click Close.

Note: To specify an ordinary index, follow all steps except turning on the Primary check box.

3. Press "Build the Table" or Close to return to the Database window.

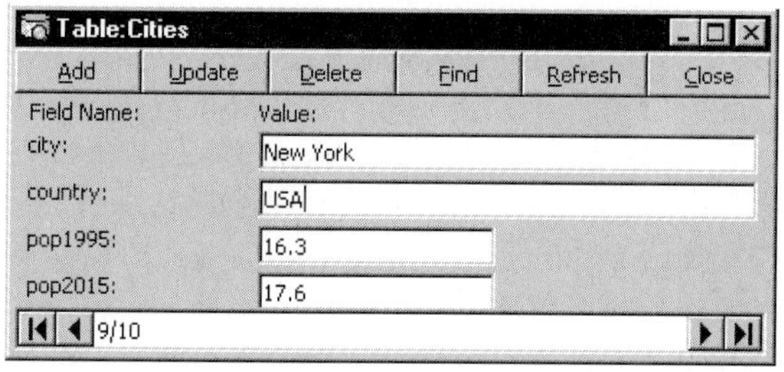

Figure 12.8 Table window (Invoked from the Database window by double-clicking on the table name. Or, choose the table, click on the right mouse button, and click on Open.)

How to use the Table window

1. If the table has no records, the Value text boxes will be blank. To add a record, type data into the fields and press the Update button.

2. To add a new record to the end of a table that already contains records, click the Add button, type data into the fields, and press the Update button. If you make a mistake entering the data, click on the Cancel button.

3. To view an existing record, use the navigator buttons (identical to those of the data control) or the Find button to move to a record of a specified value. Parameters window of Figure 12.9.

4. To remove the current record from the table, click the Delete button. The record is immediately deleted and cannot be recovered.

5. To edit an existing record, make changes in the data and click on the Update button.

6. Press the Close button to return to the Database window.

At any time, the main section of the Database window contains a list of the tables you have specified. Initially the main section is blank except for Properties. (This is a list of properties pertaining to the database.) If you click the right mouse button while highlighting a table, a menu will appear with the following options:

Menu Item	Use
Open	Open the table to allow records to be added
Design	Specify the design (number and types of fields)
Rename	Rename the given table.
Delete	Remove the given table from the database.
Copy Structure	Copies the structure of the given database with or without the data currently contained in the database.
Refresh List	Redisplay the list in the Database window.
New Table	Open the Table Structure window.
New Query	Open the Query Builder window.

Creating a Database in Code with the Professional or Enterprise Edition

The following lines of code create a database named "DBNAME.MDB" with two tables, TABLE1 and TABLE2. TABLE1 has the fields FIELD1A (type Text with maximum length 50) and FIELD1B (numeric of type Single). TABLE2 has analogous fields called FIELD2A and FIELD2B, and also FIELD2C of type Integer. FIELD1A is a primary key of TABLE1 and FIELD2A is a foreign key in TABLE2 referring to FIELD1A of TABLE1. FIELD2C is a primary key of TABLE2. The record ("alpha", 1997) is placed in TABLE1 and the record ("alpha", 2000, 1) is placed in TABLE2. This code, which is contained in the file CREATEDB.TXT accompanying this textbook, is intended as a template that you can modify to create a database programmatically.

```
Dim MyDB As Database, MyWs As Workspace
Dim T1, T2 As TableDef
Dim T1Flds(1 To 2), T2Flds(1 To 3) As Field
Dim TempFld As Field
Dim T1Idx, T2Idx As Index
Dim Rel As Relation
Dim MyRec As Recordset
Rem Create Database
Set MyWs = DBEngine.Workspaces(0)
Set MyDB = MyWs.CreateDatabase("C:\DBNAME.MDB", dbLangGeneral)
Rem Create first Table, TABLE1
Set T1 = MyDB.CreateTableDef("TABLE1")
Rem Specify fields for TABLE1
Rem Note the use of the optional parameter 50 for field size
Rem If 50 is omitted, the size will default to 20
Set T1Flds(1) = T1.CreateField("FIELD1A", dbText, 50)
Set T1Flds(2) = T1.CreateField("FIELD1B", dbSingle)
Rem Add the New fields to the field list in the Table
T1.Fields.Append T1Flds(1)
T1.Fields.Append T1Flds(2)
Rem Specify a primary field for TABLE1
Set T1Idx = T1.CreateIndex("FIELD1A")
T1Idx.Primary = True
T1Idx.Unique = True
T1Idx.Required = True
Set T1Flds(1) = T1Idx.CreateField("FIELD1A")
Rem Add this field to the field list of the Index
T1Idx.Fields.Append T1Flds(1)
Rem Add this Index to the index list of the Table
T1.Indexes.Append T1Idx
Rem Add the Table to the Database
MyDB.TableDefs.Append T1
Rem Create TABLE2
Set T2 = MyDB.CreateTableDef("TABLE2")
Rem Specify fields for TABLE2
Set T2Flds(1) = T2.CreateField("FIELD2A", dbText, 50)
Set T2Flds(2) = T2.CreateField("FIELD2B", dbSingle)
Set T2Flds(3) = T2.CreateField("FIELD2C", dbInteger)
Rem Add the new fields to the field list of the Table
T2.Fields.Append T2Flds(1)
```

```
T2.Fields.Append T2Flds(2)
T2.Fields.Append T2Flds(3)
Rem Set the primary field for TABLE2
Set T2Idx = T2.CreateIndex("FIELD2C")
T2Idx.Primary = True
T2Idx.Unique = True
T2Idx.Required = True
Set T2Flds(3) = T2Idx.CreateField("FIELD2C")
Rem Add this field to the field list of the Index
T2Idx.Fields.Append T2Flds(3)
Rem Add this index to the index list of TABLE2
T2.Indexes.Append T2Idx
Rem Add TABLE2 to the Database
MyDB.TableDefs.Append T2
Rem Set up the relation between the tables
Set Rel = MyDB.CreateRelation("foreign", "TABLE1", "TABLE2")
Rel.Attributes = 0
Rem Mark the primary field in TABLE1
Set T2Flds(1) = Rel.CreateField("FIELD1A")
Rem Mark the foreign key field in TABLE2
T2Flds(1).ForeignName = "FIELD2A"
Rem Add the field to the field list of the relation
Rel.Fields.Append T2Flds(1)
Rem Add the relation to the database
MyDB.Relations.Append Rel
Rem Add a record to each table
Rem Open a recordset referring to TABLE1
Set MyRec = T1.OpenRecordset
Rem Create a record
MyRec.AddNew
MyRec("FIELD1A") = "alpha"
MyRec("FIELD1B") = 1997
Rem Update the recordset
MyRec.Update
Rem Close the recordset referring to TABLE1
MyRec.Close
Rem Open a recordset referring to TABLE2
Set MyRec = T2.OpenRecordset
Rem Create a record
MyRec.AddNew
MyRec("FIELD2A") = "alpha"
MyRec("FIELD2B") = 2000
MyRec("FIELD2C") = 1
Rem Update the recordset
MyRec.Update
Rem Close the recordset
MyRec.Close
Rem Close the database
MyDB.Close
```

Principles of Database Design

In order to design a database, you must decide how many tables to use, what fields to include in each table, what fields to make primary or foreign keys, and what validation criteria to specify. The programming paradigm "Plan first, code later" also applies to databases. Before you design a database, you first must understand how the database will be used. For instance, you must know in what way and how often the user will update the data, and what types of reports the user will want to be generated from the database. Failure to plan ahead can be very costly.

You have no doubt read about the "year 2000 crisis." Databases designed in the 1960s and 1970s saved space by using just two digits to refer to each year. As a result, they cannot distinguish between the year 2000 and the year 1900. Correcting this oversight is predicted to cost government and industry billions of dollars.

Good relational database design is more an art than a science. However, there are certain fundamental guidelines that the designer should keep in mind.

Include the necessary data.

After you have a clear picture of the types of reports the user must generate, you will know what fields and relationships to include. On the other hand, some data that seem relevant do not have to be kept.

Be aware that data should often be stored in their smallest parts.

For instance, city, state, and zip code are usually best stored in three fields. So doing will allow you to sort a mailing by zip code or target a mailing to the residents of a specific city.

Avoid redundancy.

The process of avoiding redundancy by splitting a table into two or more related tables is called **data normalization**. For instance, the excessive duplication in Table 12.5(a) can be avoided by replacing the table with the two related tables, Tables 12.5(b) and 12.3(c).

course	section	name	time	credits	prerequisite
CS102	1001	Intro to Databases	MWF 8–9	3	CS101
CS102	1002	Intro to Databases	MWF 1–2	3	CS101
CS102	1003	Intro to Databases	MWF 2–3	3	CS101
CS102	1004	Intro to Databases	MWF 3–4	3	CS101
CS105	1001	Visual Basic	MWF 1–2	4	CS200

Table 12.5(a) A table with redundant data.

course	section	time
CS102	1001	MWF 8–9
CS102	1002	MWF 1–2
CS102	1003	MWF 2–3
CS102	1004	MWF 3–4
CS105	1001	MWF 1–2

Table 12.5(b)

course	name	credits	prerequisite
CS102	Intro to Databases	3	CS101
CS105	Visual Basic	4	CS200

Table 12.5(c)

Avoid tables with intentionally blank entries.

Tables with entries that are intentionally left blank waste space and are inefficient to use. Table 12.6, which serves as a directory of faculty and students, has an excessive number of blank entries. The table should be split into two tables, each dealing with just one of the groups.

name	ssn	classific- ation	date hired	dept	office number	gpa	credits earned
Sarah Brown	816-34-9012	student				3.7	78
Pat Riley	409-22-1234	faculty	9/1/90	biology	Y-3014		
Joe Russo	690-32-1108	faculty	9/1/88	math	T-2008		
Juan Lopez	509-43-4110	student				3.2	42

Table 12.6 A table with an excessive number of blank entries

Strive for table clarity.

Each table should have a basic topic and all the data in the table should be connected to that topic.

Don't let a table get unnecessarily large.

A bookstore might keep a permanent record of each purchase for the purpose of targeting mailings. A better solution is to add a couple of extra fields to the customer table that identity the types of books of interest to the customer.

Avoid calculated fields.

A calculated field is one whose value can be determined from other fields. For instance, if a table has fields for both the population and area of a state, then there is no need to include a field for the population density.

Comments

1. The data-bound grid control was new to Visual Basic 4.0 and was a welcome addition. Two other appreciated new data-bound controls were the data-bound list and combo controls. When these controls are attached to a field, the items in the field automatically appear in the list. (There is no need to insert them with the AddItem method.) In addition, both DBList and DBCombo support an automated search mode that can quickly locate items in the list without additional code. To attach a DBList or DBCombo control to a field of a table, the following properties must be set: DataSource, DataField, RowSource, BoundColumn, and ListField.

2. You can add additional fields to a database table, but you cannot rename, modify, or delete fields without deleting the entire table and rebuilding each field. For this reason, design your tables carefully.

3. The total length of a record in a table is limited to 2000 bytes.

4. Field names can be up to 64 characters long and can include any combination of letters, numbers, spaces, and special characters except a period (.), an exclamation mark (!), and brackets ([ ]). You cannot use leading spaces or control characters (ANSI values 0 through 32).

5. Be careful if you create a database with empty tables. If you pull it into a program and try to move through it with the navigator arrows, an error will be generated. You must add at least one record before starting to navigate.

6. Databases created with Visual Data Manager or with code have essentially the structure of Access databases. One difference is that tables created with Access must have a primary key, whereas primary keys are optional for tables created with Visual Data Manager or code.

PRACTICE PROBLEMS 12.3

1. Suppose a second command button, cmdDisplay, is added to Example 1. Write code so that all fields of the Countries table will be displayed when the button is pressed.

2. What would be some benefits of storing peoples names in two fields instead of one?

EXERCISES 12.3

For each grid in Exercises 1 through 10, give an SQL statement that can be used to create the grid from the MEGACTY2.MDB database. (*Note:* There is more than one correct answer to each exercise.)

1.

country	pop1995	currency
Indonesia	195.3	rupiah
India	846.3	rupee

2.

country
Mexico
Brazil

3.

country	currency
Japan	yen
Russia	ruble
Brazil	real
Indonesia	rupiah

4.

country	pop1995	currency
India	846.3	rupee
Indonesia	195.3	rupiah
Brazil	155.8	real
Russia	148.2	ruble

5.

city	country	pop1995	pop2015
Shanghai	China	15.1	23.4
Beijing	China	12.4	19.4
Tianjin	China	10.7	17

6.

	city	country	pop1995	pop2015
	Sao Paulo	Brazil	16.4	20.8
▶	Shanghai	China	15.1	23.4
	Bombay	India	15.1	27.4
	Tokyo	Japan	26.8	28.7

7.

	city	country	pop1995	pop2015
	Shanghai	China	15.1	23.4
▶	Bombay	India	15.1	27.4
	Mexico City	Mexico	15.6	18.8

8.

	city	country	pop1995	pop2015
▶	Sao Paulo	Brazil	16.4	20.8
	Mexico City	Mexico	15.6	18.8

9.

	city	pop2015	currency
▶	Bombay	27.4	rupee
	Calcutta	17.6	rupee

10.

	city	Cities.pop1995	Countries.pop1995
▶	Tokyo	26.8	125
	Sao Paulo	16.4	155.8
	New York	16.3	263.4

In Exercises 11 through 14, experiment with a database to determine the effect of setting the given property of a DBGrid control to the given value.

11. Property: RowDividerStyle, Setting: 3-Raised

12. Property: ColumnHeaders, Setting: False

13. Property: HeadLines, Setting: 2

14. Property: RowDividerStyle, Setting: 1-Black line

15. Create the following table of U.S. presidents for a database. Make the number field the primary key. Write a codeless program to display the table in a data-bound grid.

number	name	ageAtInauguration
1	George Washington	57
2	John Adams	61
3	Thomas Jefferson	58

16. Create the following table of leading restaurant chains for a database. Make the rank1996 field the primary field. Write a codeless program to display the table in a data-bound grid.

rank1996	name	segment
1	McDonald's	quick service burgers
2	Burger King	quick service burgers
3	Pizza Hut	full service pizza
4	KFC	quick service chicken
5	Taco Bell	quick service Mexican

17. Create a database having the following two tables. The left table contains famous lines from films that were spoken by the leading male actor. The field *film* in the second table should be a primary key. Use this database in a codeless program that displays a grid of two columns, where the first column contains a famous line and the second column contains the name of the actor who spoke the line.

famousLine	film	film	maleLead
Rosebud.	Citizen Kane	Citizen Kane	Orson Wells
We'll always have Paris.	Casablanca	Casablanca	Humphrey Bogart
You're going to need a bigger boat.	Jaws	Jaws	Roy Scheider
The name is Bond. James Bond.	Goldfinger	Goldfinger	Sean Connery
I stick my neck out for nobody.	Casablanca		

18. Create a database having the following two tables. The left table contains famous novels along with their authors. The right table contains a list of important authors along with their country and year of birth. The field *author* in the right table should be a primary key. Use this database in a codeless program that displays a grid of three columns, where the first column contains a famous novel, the second column contains the country in which it was written, and the third column contains the author's year of birth.

novel	author	author	country	yrOfBirth
War and Peace	Tolstoy	Tolstoy	Russia	1828
My Antonia	Cather	Cather	USA	1873
Anna Karenina	Tolstoy	Hugo	France	1802
Les Miserables	Hugo	Cervantes	Spain	1547
O Pioneers!	Cather			

19. The first Summer Olympic Games were held in Athens, Greece, in 1896. The database OLYMPICS.MDB has a single table called Summer, part of which is displayed in Table 12.7. The *year* field has been designated as the primary key. Unfortunately, the designer of the table Summer used a string of length 2 for the year and we are therefore unable to enter the data for the 1996 summer olympics. Create a new database with an integer field to display the year in Summer, and write a program to transfer the information from the old table into the new table. Then add the record "1996, Atlanta, USA". (**Note:** The Summer Olympic Games were canceled in 1916, 1940, and 1944 due to war.)

year	site	mostMedals
96	Athens	Greece
00	Paris	France
04	St. Louis	USA
.		
.		
.		
88	Seoul	USSR
92	Barcelona	Unified Team

Table 12.7 Summer Olympics.

20. The database BIBLIO.MDB is provided with Visual Basic and is usually found in the directory c:\Program Files\DevStudio\VB\VB5. Use either Visual Data Manager or any other database management program to determine the names of the tables, the primary keys, and the foreign keys in the database.

21. Specify all tables, fields, primary keys, foreign keys, validation rules, and validation text for a database to hold the student registrations for all the courses at a college. The registrar will use the database to print out a course schedule for each student and a class list for each course. Each course schedule should contain the student's name, address, social security number, and the list of courses currently registered for (with course name, section number, time, room, instructor, and number of credits). Each class list should contain the course name, section number, instructor, and list of students (with social security number, name, major, and rank).

22. Specify all tables, fields, primary keys, foreign keys, and validation rules and text for a database to be used by a bank to keep track of all checking account transactions for a month. At the end of the month, the bank will use the database to send out statements for each account. Each statement will contain a name, address, account number, opening balance, closing balance, and a detailed listing of all checks written and deposits made.

23. Reduce redundancy in the following table.

name	address	city	state	zip
R. Myers	3 Maple St.	Seattle	WA	98109
T. Murphy	25 Main St.	Seattle	WA	98109
L. Scott	14 Park Ave.	New York	NY	10199
B. Jones	106 5th St.	Seattle	WA	98109
W. Smith	29 7th Ave	New York	NY	10199
V. Miller	4 Flower Ave	Chicago	IL	60607

24. Reduce redundancy in the following table of members of the U.S. House of Representatives.

name	state	party	statePop	numColleges
J. Dingell	MI	D	9.6	106
W. Gilcrest	MD	R	5.1	57
J. Conyers	MI	D	9.6	106
C. Morella	MD	R	5.1	57
J. Kennedy	MA	D	6.1	117
A. Wynn	MD	D	5.1	57

25. Why use a field for a person's birth date rather than a field for his or her age?

In Exercises 26 and 27, use either Visual Data Manager or code to make the following changes in the Countries table of MEGACTY2.MDB.

26. Add the record "Canada, 29.5, dollar".

27. Add a new field, *postalRate*, and fill in the entries with the costs of mailing a letter. Some postal rates (in cents) are: Brazil, 23; Canada, 33; China, 35; India, 3; Japan, 74; Mexico, 24; USA, 32.

1.
```
Private Sub cmdDisplay_Click()
    Rem Display the contents of the table Countries
    datCities.RecordSource = "SELECT * FROM Countries"
    datCities.Refresh
End Sub
```

2. You can order the records by the last name. Also, you can use the record in a mailing and refer to each person in the salutation by their first name; as in "Dear Mabel."

Chapter 12
Summary

1. A *table* is a group of data items arranged in a rectangular array, each containing the same categories of information. Each data item (row) is called a *record*. Each category (column) is called a *field*. Two tables with a common field are said to be *related*. A *database* is a collection of one or more, usually related, tables.

2. The *data control* is used to access a database. When a text box is bound to a data control through its DataSource and DataField properties, the user can read and edit a field of the database. At any time, one record is specified as the *current record*. The user can change the current record with the data control's *navigator arrows* or with *Move* statements. The properties *Record-Count*, *BOF*, and *EOF* count records and indicate whether the ends of a recordset have been reached. The *Value* property of Fields("*fieldName*") reads the contents of a field of the current record. The *Validate event*, which can be used to control edits, is triggered whenever the current record is about to be changed.

3. A *primary key* is a field or set of fields that uniquely identifies each row of a table. The *rule of entity integrity* states that no record can have a null entry in a primary key. A *foreign key* is a field or set of fields in one table that refers to a primary key in another table. The *rule of referential integrity* states that each value in the foreign key must also appear in the primary key.

4. Structured Query Language (SQL) is used to create a "virtual" table consisting of a subtable of a table or of a join of two tables and imposes an order on the records. The subtable is specified with the reserved words SELECT, FROM, WHERE, ORDER BY, and INNER JOIN . . . ON. The WHERE clause of an SQL statement commonly uses the Like operator in addition to the standard operators. SQL statements are either employed at design time or run time as the setting of the RecordSource property. During run time, the Refresh method for the data control should be executed after the Record-Source property is set.

5. The *data-bound grid control* can show an entire "virtual" table in a spreadsheet-like display. Records can be easily viewed and edited. Records also can be added and deleted if the AllowAddNew and AllowDelete properties are set to True.

6. *Visual Data Manager*, a database management program supplied with most versions of Visual Basic, can be used to create a database and specify primary keys, and validation criteria. A database can be created by code with the Professional or Enterprise editions of Visual Basic.

7. Although good database design is an art, there are several fundamental principles that usually should be followed.

Chapter 12
Programming Projects

1. The database MICROLND.MDB (on the accompanying CD) is maintained by the Microland Computer Warehouse, a mail order computer supply company. Tables 12.8 through 12.10 show parts of three tables in the database. The table Customers identifies each customer by an ID number and gives, in addition to the name and address, the total amount of purchases during the current year. The table Inventory identifies each product in stock by an ID number and gives, in addition to its description and price (per unit), the quantity currently in stock. The table Orders gives the orders received today. Suppose it is now the end of the day. Write a program that uses the three tables to do the following.

(a) Update the *quantity* field of the Inventory table.
(b) Display in a list box the items that are out of stock and therefore must be reordered.
(c) Update the *amtOfSales* field of the Customers table.
(d) Print bills to all customers who ordered during the day. (You can assume that each customer only calls once during a particular day and therefore that all items ordered by a single customer are grouped together. The bill should indicate if an item is currently out of stock. You can just display the bills one at a time in a picture window instead of actually printing them.)

custID	name	street	city	amtPurchases
1	Michael Smith	2 Park St.	Dallas, TX 75201	234.50
2	Brittany Jones	5 Second Ave	Tampa, FL 33602	121.90
3	Warren Pease	7 Maple St	Boston, MA 02101	387.20

Table 12.8 First three records of the Customers table.

itemID	description	price	quantity
PL208	Visual Basic – Standard	89.50	12
SW109	MS Office Upgrade	195.95	2
HW913	PaperPort ix	300.25	8

Table 12.9 First three records of the Inventory table.

custID	itemID	quantity
3	SW109	1
1	PL208	3
1	HW913	2
2	PL208	1

Table 12.10 First four records of the Orders table.

2. Most college libraries have a computerized online catalog that allows you to look up books by author or title. Use the database BIBLIO.MDB to design such a catalog. You should create a new database with the necessary tables and fields and copy all needed information from BIBLIO.MDB into the new database. (One field should hold the number of copies that the library owns and another field should hold the number of copies currently on the shelf. Use the Rnd function to fill the first field with numbers from 1 to 3.) The user should be able to do the following.

(a) View the books by author in either alphabetical or chronological order and then obtain relevant information (publisher, ISBN, copyright year, number of copies available and owned) on a specific book.
(b) Determine if a book with a specified title is owned by the library.
(c) Search for all books containing a certain word in its title.
(d) Check out a book that is on the shelf.
(e) Reserve a book that is currently not on the shelf. (A number can be assigned to each reservation to determine priority.)

The librarian should be able to generate a listing of all books for which there is a waiting list.

13

Object-Oriented Programming

13.1 Classes and Objects / 588

13.2 Collections and Events / 604
  • Collections • Keys • Events

13.3 Class Relationships / 614

13.4 Building ActiveX Controls / 623

Summary / 633

Programming Projects / 634

13.1 CLASSES AND OBJECTS

noun A word used to denote or name a person, place, thing, quality, or act.

verb That part of speech that expresses existence, action, or occurrence.

adjective Any of a class of words used to modify a noun or other substantive by limiting, qualifying, or specifying.

The American Heritage Dictionary of the English Language

"A good rule of thumb for object-oriented programming is that classes are the nouns in your analysis of the problem. The methods in your object correspond to verbs that the noun does. The properties are the adjectives that describe the noun."

Gary Cornell & David Jezak[1]

Practical experience in the financial, scientific, engineering, and software design industries has revealed some difficulties with traditional program design methodologies. As programs grow in size and become more complex, and as the number of programmers working on the same project increases, the number of dependencies and interrelationships throughout the code increases exponentially. A small change made by one programmer in one place may have many effects, both intended and unintended, in many other places. The effects of this change may ripple throughout the entire program, requiring the rewriting of a great deal of code along the way.

A partial solution to this problem is "data hiding" where, within a unit, as much implementation detail as possible is hidden. Data hiding is an important principle underlying object-oriented programming. An object is an encapsulation of data and procedures that act on the data. The only thing of concern to a programmer using an object is the tasks that the object can perform and the parameters used by these tasks. The details of the data structures and procedures are hidden within the object.

Two types of objects will be of concern to us, **control objects** and **code objects**. Examples of control objects are text boxes, picture boxes, command buttons and all the other controls that can be created from the Visual Basic toolbox. Code objects are specific instances of user-defined types that are defined similarly to record types in a separate module. Both types of objects have properties and respond to methods. The main differences are that control objects are predefined and have physical manifestations, whereas code objects must be created by the programmer and exist solely in a portion of memory. In this section, when we use the word "object" without a qualifier, we mean "code object."

Whenever you double-click on the TextBox icon in the toolbar, a new text box is created. Although each text box is a separate entity, they all have the same properties and methods. Each text box is said to be an instance of the class TextBox. In some sense, the TextBox icon in the toolbox is a template for creating text boxes. (When you look at the properties window for a text box, the dropdown list box at the top of the window says something like "Text1 TextBox". "Text1" is the name of the control object and "TextBox" is the name

---

1   ActiveX Visual Basic 5 Control Creation Edition, Prentice-Hall, 1997.

of its class.) You can't set properties or invoke methods of the TextBox icon, only of the specific text boxes that it creates. The analogy is often made between the TextBox icon and a cookie cutter. The cookie cutter is used to create cookies that you can eat, but you can't eat the cookie cutter.

Object-oriented programs are populated with objects that hold data, have properties, respond to methods, and raise events. (The generation of events will be discussed in the next section.) Six examples are as follows.

1. In a professor's program to assign and display semester grades, a student object might hold a single student's name, social security number, midterm grade, and final exam grade. A SemGrade method might calculate the student's semester grade. Events might be raised when improper data is passed to the object.

2. In a payroll program, an employee object might hold an employee's name, hourly wage, and hours worked. A CalculatePay method would tell the object to calculate the wages for the current pay period.

3. In a checking account program, a check register object might record and total the checks written during a certain month, a deposit slip object might record and total the deposits made during a certain month, and an account object might keep a running total of the balance in the account. The account object would raise an event to alert the bank when the balance gets too low.

4. In a bookstore inventory program, a textbook object might hold the name, author, quantity in stock, and wholesale price of an individual textbook. A RetailPrice method might instruct the book object to calculate the selling price of the textbook. An event could be triggered when the book goes out of stock.

5. In a game program, an airplane object might hold the location of an airplane. At any time, the program could tell the object to display the airplane at its current location or to drop a bomb. An event can be triggered each time a bomb moves so that the program can determine if anything was hit.

6. In a card game, a card object might hold the denomination and suit of a specific card. An IdentifyCard method might return a string such as "Ace of Spades." A deck of cards object might consist of an array of card objects. A ShuffleDeck method might thoroughly shuffle the deck and a Shuffling event might indicate the progress of the shuffle.

The most important object-oriented term is **class**. A class is a template from which objects are created. The class specifies the properties and methods that will be common to all objects that are instances of that class. Classes are formulated in class modules. An object, which is an instance of a class, can be created in a program with a pair of statements of the form

```
Private objectName As className    'In General Declarations section
Set objectName = New className     'In procedure
```

In the program, properties of the object is accessed with statements of the form shown in the following table.

Task	Statement
Assign a value to a property	Let *objectName.propertyName* = *value*
Display the value of a property	picBox.Print *objectName.propertyName*
Carry out a method	*objectName.methodName(arg1, ...)*
Raise an event	RaiseEvent *eventName*

The following walkthrough creates a student class and a program that uses that class. The data stored by an object of this class are name, social security number, and grades on two exams (midterm and final).

1. Start a new program.

2. From the Project menu on the toolbar, click on Add Class Module.

3. Double-click on Class Module in the Add Class Module dialog box. (The window that appears looks like an ordinary code window.)

4. If the Property window is not visible, press F4 to display it. (Notice that the class has the default name Class1 and has just one property, Name.)

5. Change the setting of the Name property to CStudent. (We will follow the common convention of beginning each class name with the uppercase letter C.)

6. Type the following lines into the code module.

```
Private m_name As String
Private m_ssn As String
Private m_midterm As Single
Private m_final As Single
```

(These lines of code declare four variables that will be used to hold data. The word Private guarantees that the variables cannot be accessed directly from outside the object. In object-oriented programming terminology, these variables are called **member variables** (or **instance variables**). We will follow the common convention of beginning the name of each member variable with the prefix "m_".)

7. From the Tools menu on the toolbar, click on Add Procedure. (As before, an Add Procedure dialog box will appear.)

8. Type "Name" into the Name text box, click on Property in the Type frame, and click on OK. The following lines will appear in the class module window.

```
Public Property Get Name() As Variant

End Property

Public Property Let Name(ByVal vNewValue As Variant)

End Property
```

9. Change the words Variant to String, the word vNewValue to vName, and type code into the two property procedures as shown below.

```
Public Property Get Name() As String
   Name = m_name
End Property
```

```
Public Property Let Name(ByVal vName As String)
  m_name = vName
End Property
```

The first procedure will be called by our program to retrieve the value of the variable *m_name* and the second procedure will be called to assign a value to the variable *m_name*.

10. In the same manner as in Steps 7–9, create the following pair of property procedures that will be used to retrieve and assign values to the variable *m_ssn*.

```
Public Property Get SocSecNum() As String
  SocSecNum = m_ssn
End Property

Public Property Let SocSecNum(ByVal vNum As String)
  m_ssn = vNum
End Property
```

11. Property procedures can be typed directly into the class module without the use of Add Procedure. Also, property procedures needn't come in pairs. For instance, if we wanted the value of a member variable to be "write only," we would use a Property Let procedure and have no Property Get procedure. Type the following two property procedures into the class module. The inclusion of the word Public is optional.

```
Property Let midGrade(ByVal vGrade As Single)
  m_midterm = vGrade
End Property

Property Let finGrade(ByVal vGrade As Single)
  m_final = vGrade
End Property
```

12. Create the following ordinary Public function with the name SemGrade.

```
Public Function SemGrade() As String
  Dim grade As Single
  Let grade = (m_midterm + m_final) / 2
  Let grade = Int(grade + 0.5)    'Round the grade
  Select Case grade
    Case Is >= 90
      SemGrade = "A"
    Case Is >= 80
      SemGrade = "B"
    Case Is >= 70
      SemGrade = "C"
    Case Is >= 60
      SemGrade = "D"
    Case Else
      SemGrade = "F"
  End Select
End Function
```

(This function will be used by our program to invoke a method requesting an object to calculate a student's semester grade.)

13. From the File menu, click on Save CStudent.cls As and save the class module with the name 13-1-1S.cls. (We chose this name since the class will be used in Example 1. Another good choice of name would have been Student.cls. The extension cls is normally given to files holding class modules.)

14. Press Alt/View/Object to activate the form. We can now write a program that creates an object, call it *pupil*, that is an instance of the class and uses the object to calculate a student's semester grade. The object variable is declared (in the general declarations section of the code module) with the statement

```
Private pupil As CStudent
```

and then an instance of the class is created inside a procedure with the statement

```
Set pupil = New CStudent
```

The object *pupil* will be local to the procedure. That is, it will cease to exist after the procedure has ended. The Property Let procedures are used to assign values to the member variables, and the Property Get procedures are used to retrieve values. The function SemGrade becomes a method for obtaining the student's grade.

Some examples are

```
pupil.Name = "Adams, Al"       'Assign a value to m_name
picBox.Print pupil.Name        'Display the student's name
picBox.Print pupil.SemGrade    'Display the student's semester grade
```

The first statement calls the Property Let Name procedure, the second statement calls the Property Get Name procedure, and the third statement calls the method procedure SemGrade.

EXAMPLE 1   The following program uses the class CStudent to calculate and display a student's semester grade.

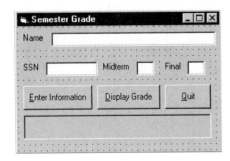

Object	Property	Setting
frm13_1_1	Caption	Semester Grade
lblName	Caption	Name
txtName	Text	(blank)
lblSSN	Caption	SSN
txtSSN	Text	(blank)
lblMidterm	Caption	Midterm
txtMidterm	Text	(blank)
lblFinal	Caption	Final
txtFinal	Text	(blank)
cmdEnter	Caption	&Enter Information
cmdDisplay	Caption	&Display Grade
cmdQuit	Caption	&Quit
picGrade		

```
Rem Student Class (CStudent)
Private m_name As String
Private m_ssn As String
```

```
    Private m_midterm As Single
    Private m_final As Single

    Property Get Name() As String
      Name = m_name
    End Property

    Property Let Name(ByVal vName As String)
      m_name = vName
    End Property

    Property Get SocSecNum() As String
      SocSecNum = m_ssn
    End Property

    Property Let SocSecNum(ByVal vNum As String)
      m_ssn = vNum
    End Property

    Property Let midGrade(ByVal vGrade As Single)
      m_midterm = vGrade
    End Property

    Property Let finGrade(ByVal vGrade As Single)
      m_final = vGrade
    End Property

    Public Function SemGrade() As String
      Dim grade As Single
      Let grade = (m_midterm + m_final) / 2
      Let grade = Int(grade + 0.5)     'Round the grade
      Select Case grade
        Case Is >= 90
          SemGrade = "A"
        Case Is >= 80
          SemGrade = "B"
        Case Is >= 70
          SemGrade = "C"
        Case Is >= 60
          SemGrade = "D"
        Case Else
          SemGrade = "F"
      End Select
    End Function


Rem  Form Code
Private pupil As CStudent           'pupil is an object of class CStudent

Private Sub cmdEnter_Click()
  Set pupil = New CStudent
  Rem Read the values stored in the text boxes
  Let pupil.Name = txtName
  Let pupil.SocSecNum = txtSSN
  Let pupil.midGrade = Val(txtMidterm)
  Let pupil.finGrade = Val(txtFinal)
```

```
      Rem Clear Text Boxes
      Let txtName.Text = ""
      Let txtSSN.Text = ""
      Let txtMidterm.Text = ""
      Let txtFinal.Text = ""
      picGrade.Cls
      picGrade.Print "Student recorded."
End Sub

Private Sub cmdDisplay_Click()
    picGrade.Cls
    picGrade.Print pupil.Name; Tab(28); pupil.SocSecNum(); _
                            Tab(48); pupil.SemGrade
End Sub

Private Sub cmdQuit_Click()
    End
End Sub
```

[Run, enter the data for a student (such as "Adams, Al", "123-45-6789", "82", "87"), press the Enter Information button to send the data to the object, and press the Display Grade button to display the student's name, social security number, and semester grade.]

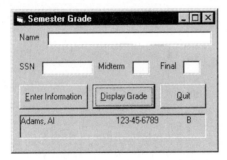

In summary, the following seven steps are used to create a class.

1. Identify a *thing* in your program that is to become an object.

2. Determine the properties and methods you would like the object to have.

3. A class will serve as a template for the object. Add a class module from the Project menu.

4. Set the name property of the class. (A common convention is to begin the name with the letter C.)

5. For each of the properties in Step 2, declare a private member variable with a statement of the form

   ```
   Private m_variableName As dataType
   ```

6. For each of the member variables in Step 5, create one or two public property procedures to retrieve and assign values of the variable. The general forms of the procedures are

```
Public Property Get ProcedureName() As DataType
    ProcedureName = m_variableName
    (Possibly additional code.)
End Property

Public Property Let Procedurename(ByVal vNewValue As DataType)
    Let m_variableName = vNewValue
    (Possibly additional code.)
End Property
```

Note: Since the member variables were declared as Private, they cannot be accessed directly from outside an object. They can only be accessed through Property procedures which allow values to be checked and perhaps modified. Also, a Property procedure is able to take other steps necessitated by a change in a member variable.

7. For each method in Step 2, create a subprogram or function procedure to carry out the task.

EXAMPLE 2 Modify the program in Example 1 to calculate semester grades for students who have registered on a "Pass/Fail" basis. Use a class module to calculate the semester grade.

SOLUTION We will create a new class, named CPFStudent, with the same member variables and property procedures as the class CStudent. The only change needed in the class module occurs in the SemGrade method. The new code for this method is

```
Public Function SemGrade() As String
    Dim grade As Single
    Let grade = (m_midterm + m_final) / 2
    Let grade = Int(grade + 0.5)    'Round the grade
    If grade >= 60 Then
        SemGrade = "Pass"
      Else
        SemGrade = "Fail"
    End If
End Function
```

The only change needed in the Form code is to replace the two occurrences of CStudent with CPFStudent. When the program is run with the same input as in Example 1, the output will be

```
Adams, Al        123-45-6789     Pass
```

The Initialize Event Procedure

The Object drop-down combo box in a class module window displays two items General and Class. When you click on Class, the following template appears.

```
Private Sub Class_Initialize()

End Sub
```

This event procedure is automatically invoked when an object is created from the class. Any code you type into the procedure is then executed. This procedure is used to set default values for member variables and to create other objects associated with this object.

Since methods are created with ordinary functions or subprograms, arguments can be passed to them when they are called. The graphical program in Example 3 makes use of arguments. The program involves "twips," which are a unit of screen measurement. (One inch is about 1440 twips.) The settings for the Top, Left, Height, and Width properties of a control are given in twips. For instance, the statements

```
Let Image1.Width =  1440      '1 inch
Let Image1.Height = 2160      '1.5 inch
Let Image1.Top = 2880         '2 inches
Let Image1.Left =  7200       '5 inches
```

set the size of the image control as 1" by 1.5", and place the control 2 inches from the left side of the form and 5 inches from the top of the form. (See Figure 7.6 in Section 7.3.) Programs using the Height property of the form should have the BorderStyle property of the form set to "0-None" since otherwise the height of the border is included in the height of the form.

EXAMPLE 3   Write a program containing a Circle object. The object should keep track of the center and radius of the circle. (The center is specified by two numbers, called the coordinates, giving the distance from the left side and top of the form. Distances and the radius should be measured in twips.) A Show method should display the circle on the form and a Move method should add 500 twips to each coordinate of the center of the circle. Initially, the circle should have its center at (500, 500) and radius 500. The form should have a command button captioned "Move and Show Circle" that invokes both methods.

SOLUTION

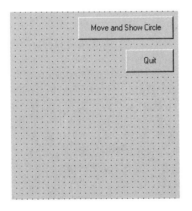

Control	Property	Setting
frmCircles	BorderStyle	0-None
cmdMove	Caption	Move and Show Circle
cmdQuit	Caption	Quit

```
Rem  Class module for CCircle
Private m_x As Integer  'Dist from center of circle to left side of form
Private m_y As Integer  'Distance from center of circle to top of form
Private m_r As Single   'Radius of circle
```

```
Private Sub Class_Initialize()
  Rem  Set the initial center of the circle to the upper
  Rem  left corner of the form and set its radius to 500.
  Let m_x = 0
  Let m_y = 0
  Let m_r = 500
End Sub


Public Property Get Xcoord() As Integer
  Xcoord = m_x
End Property


Public Property Let Xcoord(ByVal vNewValue As Integer)
  m_x = vNewValue
End Property


Public Property Get Ycoord() As Integer
  Ycoord = m_y
End Property


Public Property Let Ycoord(ByVal vNewValue As Integer)
  m_y = vNewValue
End Property


Public Sub Show()
  Rem  Display the circle.
  Rem  See discussion of Circle method in Section 10.4.
  frmCircles.Circle (m_x, m_y), m_r
End Sub


Public Sub Move(Dist)
  Rem  Move the center of the circle Dist twips to the right
  Rem  and Dist twips down.
  Let m_x = m_x + Dist
  Let m_y = m_y + Dist
  Call Show
End Sub


Rem  Form code
Private round As CCircle
Dim x As Integer, y As Integer, r As Single

Private Sub Form_Load()
  Set round = New CCircle
End Sub


Private Sub cmdMove_Click()
  round.Move (500)
End Sub


Private Sub cmdQuit_Click()
  End
End Sub
```

[Run and press the command button five times.]

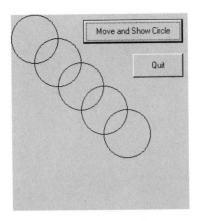

Comments

1. The statement

   ```
   Set objectVar = Nothing
   ```

   dissociates the object variable from the actual object and frees up the memory used by the variable.

2. An object variable declared inside a procedure ceases to exist when the procedure is exited. (We say that the object falls out of scope.) The effect is the same as when the variable is set to Nothing.

3. The counterpart to the Initialize event is the Terminate event procedure which has the template

   ```
   Private Sub Class_Terminate()

   End Sub
   ```

   and is automatically invoked when all references to the object are Set to Nothing or when the object falls out of scope. This procedure is often used to set any objects you may have created inside the class module to Nothing.

4. Methods can be either functions or subprograms. A method that returns a value must be a function; otherwise it can be a subprogram.

5. A program with a class module has at least three components: a form, form code, and class module code. Although the View menu gives you access to the form (Alt/V/B) and the form code (Alt/V/C), only the Project Explorer gives access to all three. To view the code for a class module, double-click on the name of the class in the Project Explorer.

6. A class module is saved in a file whose filename has the extension .cls. Therefore, classes have both a name (C*something*) and a filename (*something*.cls).

7. To insert an existing (saved) class module into a program, click on Add Class Module in the Project menu, click on the Existing tab, and enter the filespec for the class module.

8. To delete a class from a program, right click on the class name in the Project Explorer and click on Remove *className*.

9. An object also can be declared with a statement of the form

```
Private pupil As Object
```

However, objects so declared require more time and effort for Visual Basic to access.

10. The set of properties, methods, and events for a class is called the class **interface**. The classes CStudent and CPFStudent have the same interface, even though they carry out the task of computing a grade differently. The programmer need only be aware of the SemGrade method and needn't be concerned about its implementation. The feature that two classes can have behaviors that are named the same and have essentially the same purpose but different implementations is called **polymorphism**.

11. Sometimes you will have difficulty deciding whether an interface item should be a property or a method. As a rule of thumb, properties should access data and methods should perform operations.

12. The ByVal (which stands for "by value") keyword is automatically inserted before parameters in Property Let statements invoked from the Tools menu. However, this keyword is optional. The default way of passing an argument to a parameter is ByRef (which stands for "by reference"). Usually, passing by value is more efficient than passing by reference.

13. The default parameter name in a Property Let procedure is vNewValue. Although we usually substitute a meaningful name, we retain the convention of beginning the name with the prefix v.

14. We could have preceded our member variables with the keyword Public and allowed direct access to the variables. However, this is considered poor programming practice. By using Property Let procedures to update the data, we can enforce constraints and carry out validation.

15. In a class module, a property is implemented by two procedures, one to set and the other to retrieve the property value. These procedures that access properties are sometimes referred to as **accessor** methods.

PRACTICE PROBLEMS 13.1

1. Which of the following analogies is out of place?

  (a) class : object
  (b) sewing pattern : garment
  (c) blueprint : house
  (d) programmer : program
  (e) cookie cutter : cookie

2. What is the main difference between an object and a record?

EXERCISES 13.1

Exercises 1 through 12 refer to the class CStudent. When applicable, assume that *pupil* is an instance of the class.

1. What will be the effect if the Property Let midGrade procedure is changed to the following?

```
Property Let midGrade(ByVal vGrade As Single)
  Select Case vGrade
    Case Is < 0
       m_midterm = 0
    Case Is > 100
      m_midterm = 100
    Case Else
       m_midterm = vGrade
  End Select
End Property
```

2. What will be the effect if the `Property Let midGrade` procedure is changed to the following?

```
Property Let midGrade(ByVal vGrade As Single)
  m_midterm = vGrade + 10
End Property
```

3. Modify the class module for CStudent so that the following statement will display the student's midterm grade.

```
picBox.Print pupil.midGrade
```

4. Modify the class module for CStudent so that the student's semester average can be displayed with a statement of the form

```
picBox.Print pupil.Average
```

5. Find the error in the following form code.

```
Private scholar As CStudent

Private Sub cmdGo_Click()
  Dim nom as String
  scholar.Name = "Peace, Warren"
  Let nom = scholar.Name
End Sub
```

6. Find the error in the following form code.

```
Private scholar As CStudent

Private Sub cmdGo_Click()
  Dim nom as String
  Set scholar = CStudent
  scholar.Name = "Peace, Warren"
  Let nom = scholar.Name
End Sub
```

7. Find the error in the following form code.

```
Private scholar As CStudent

Private Sub cmdGo_Click()
  Dim nom as String
  Set scholar = New CStudent
  m_Name = "Peace, Warren"
  Let nom = scholar.Name
End Sub
```

8. Find the error in the following form code.

```
Private scholar As CStudent

Private Sub cmdGo_Click()
  Set scholar = New CStudent
  scholar.Name = "Peace, Warren"
  Let nom = m_Name
End Sub
```

9. Find the error in the following form code.

```
Private scholar As CStudent

Private Sub cmdGo_Click()
  Dim grade As String
  Set scholar = New CStudent
  scholar.semGrade = "A"
  Let grade = scholar.semGrade
End Sub
```

10. Write code for the class module that sets the two grades to 10 whenever an instance of the class is created.

11. What is the effect of adding the following code to the class module.

```
Private Sub Class_Initialize()
  m_ssn = "999-99-9999"
End Sub
```

12. What is the output of the following form code?

```
Private pupil As CStudent

Private scholar As CStudent

Private Sub cmdGo_Click()
  Set scholar = New CStudent
  Set pupil = New CStudent
  Let scholar.midterm = 89
  Let pupil.midterm = scholar.midterm
  picBox.Print pupil.midterm
End Sub
```

Exercises 13 through 16 refer to the class CCircle.

13. Consider the program in Example 3. What would be the effect of removing the four Property procedures from the class module?

14. Modify the program in Example 3 so that the four Property procedures are used.

15. Modify Example 3 so that the circle originally has its center at the lowerright corner of the form and moves diagonally upward each time cmdMove is pressed.

16. Modify the form code of Example 3 so that each time cmdMove is pressed, the distance moved (in twips) is a randomly selected number from 0 to 999.

17. Write the class module for a class called CSquare. The class should have three properties, Length, Perimeter, and Area, with their obvious meanings. When a value is assigned to one of the properties, the values of the other two should be recalculated automatically. When the following form code is executed, the numbers 5 and 20 should be displayed in the picture box.

```
Private poly As CSquare

Private Sub cmdGo_Click()
   Set poly = New CSquare
   Let poly.Area = 25
   picBox.Print poly.Length; poly.Perimeter
End Sub
```

18. Modify the class CSquare in the previous exercise so that all squares will have lengths between 1 and 10. For instance, the statement Let poly.Area = .5 should result in a square of length 1, and the statement Let poly.Area = 200 should result in a square of length 10.

19. Write the class module for a class called CPairOfDice. The function Rnd should be used to obtain the value for each die. (**Note:** The value of Int(6 * Rnd) + 1 will be a randomly chosen whole number between 1 and 6.) When the following form code is executed, three numbers (such as 3, 4, and 7) should be displayed in the picture box.

```
Private cubes As CPairOfDice

Private Sub cmdGo_Click()
   Set cubes = New CPairOfDice
   cubes.Roll
   picBox.Print cubes.Die1; cubes.Die2; cubes.SumOfFaces
End Sub
```

20. Write a program to toss a pair of dice 1000 times and display the number of times that the sum of the two faces is 7. The program should use an instance of the class CPairOfDice discussed in the previous exercise.

21. Write the class module for a class called CStopWatch. The class should have the methods Start, Halt, and TimeElapsed. The time elapsed should be given in seconds. (**Note:** The function Timer gives the number of seconds that have elapsed since midnight.) When the following form code is executed, a number (such as 4.8) should be displayed in the picture box.

```
Private timekeeper As CStopWatch

Private Sub cmdGo_Click()
  Rem  Time the execution of a loop
  Dim i As Integer, j As Integer, value As Single
  Set timekeeper = New CStopWatch
  timekeeper.Start
  For i = 1 to 2000
    For j = 1 to 2000
      Let value = Sqr(j)
    Next j
  Next i
  timekeeper.Halt
  picBox.Print Format(timekeeper.TimeElapsed, "#.#")
End Sub
```

22. Write the class module for a class called CCollege. The class should have properties Name, NumStudents, and NumFaculty. The method SFRatio should compute the student-faculty ratio. When the following form code is executed, the number 18.7 should be displayed in the picture box.

```
Private school As CCollege

Private Sub cmdGo_Click()
  Set school = New CCollege
  Let school.Name = "University of Maryland, College Park"
  Let school.NumStudents = 30648
  Let school.NumFaculty =1638
  Print Format(school.SFRatio, "#.#")
End Sub
```

23. Write a program that calculates an employee's pay for a week based on the hourly wage and the number of hours worked. All computations should be performed by an instance of the class CWages.

24. Write a program that a college bookstore can use to keep track of and determine the retail prices of textbooks. All computations should be performed by an instance of the class CTextbooks. The class should have properties Title, Author, Cost (wholesale cost), Quantity (number of copies in stock), and the method Price, that is, the retail price. Assuming that the bookstore marks up book by 25%, the Price should be 1.25 times the Cost.

25. Write a program that calculates an employee's FICA tax, with all computations performed by an instance of a class CFICA. The FICA tax has two components: the Social Security benefits tax, which in 1997 is 6.2 percent of the first $65,400 of earnings for the year, and the Medicare tax, which is 1.45 percent of earnings.

26. Write a program that adds two fractions and displays their sum in reduced form. The program should use a CFraction class that stores the numerator and denominator of a fraction and has a Reduce method that divides each the numerator and denominator by their greatest common divisor. Exercise 39 of Section 6.1 contains an algorithm for calculating the greatest common divisor of two numbers.

SOLUTIONS TO PRACTICE PROBLEMS 13.1

1. (d) A programmer is not a template for creating a program.

2. Whereas both hold data, only an object has methods. Also, as we will see in the next section, objects can have events.

13.2 COLLECTIONS AND EVENTS

"An object without an event is like a telephone without a ringer."

Anonymous

A collection is an entity, similar to an array, that is especially well-suited to working with sets of objects. This section discusses collections of objects and user-defined events for classes.

Collections

A collection of objects is an ordered set of objects where the objects are identified by the numbers 1, 2, 3, ... A collection is declared with a statement of the form

```
Dim collectionName As New Collection
```

and initially contains no objects. (We say that the variable *collectionName* has type Collection.) The statement

```
collectionName.Add objectName
```

adds the named object to the collection and automatically assigns it the next available number. The numbers for the different objects will reflect the order they were added to the collection. The statement

```
collectionName.Remove n
```

deletes the nth object from the collection and automatically reduces the object numbers from $n+1$ on by 1 so that there will be no gap in the numbers. At any time, the value of

```
collectionName.Count
```

is the number of objects in the collection. The value of

```
collectionName.Item(n).propertyName
```

is the value of the named property in the nth object of the collection. The statement

```
collectionName.Item(n).methodName
```

runs the named method of the nth object of the collection.

EXAMPLE 1 In the following program, the user enters four pieces of data about a student into text boxes and selects a type of registration. When the AddStudent button is pressed, the data is used to create and initialize an appropriate object (either from class CStudent or class CPFStudent) and the object is added to a collection. When the Calculate Grades button is pressed, the name, social security number, and semester grade for each student in the collection is displayed in the picture box.

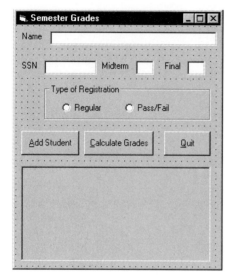

Object	Property	Setting
frm13_2_1	Caption	Semester Grades
lblName	Caption	Name
txtName	Text	(blank)
lblSSN	Caption	SSN
txtSSN	Text	(blank)
fraType	Caption	Type of Registration
lblMidterm	Caption	Midterm
txtMidterm	Text	(blank)
lblFinal	Caption	Final
txtFinal	Text	(blank)
optReg	Caption	Regular
optPF	Caption	Pass/Fail
cmdAdd	Caption	&Add Student
cmdSemGrade	Caption	&Calculate Grades
cmdQuit	Caption	&Quit
picGrades		

```
Rem Student Class (CStudent)
Private m_name As String
Private m_ssn As String
Private m_midterm As Single
Private m_final As Single

Property Get Name() As String
  Name = m_name
End Property

Property Let Name(ByVal vName As String)
  m_name = vName
End Property

Property Get SocSecNum() As String
  SocSecNum = m_ssn
End Property

Property Let SocSecNum(ByVal vNum As String)
  m_ssn = vNum
End Property

Property Let midGrade(ByVal vGrade As Single)
  m_midterm = vGrade
End Property

Property Let finGrade(ByVal vGrade As Single)
  m_final = vGrade
End Property
```

```
Public Function SemGrade() As String
  Dim grade As Single
  Let grade = (m_midterm + m_final) / 2
  Let grade = Int(grade + 0.5)    'Round the grade
  Select Case grade
    Case Is >= 90
      SemGrade = "A"
    Case Is >= 80
      SemGrade = "B"
    Case Is >= 70
      SemGrade = "C"
    Case Is >= 60
      SemGrade = "D"
    Case Else
      SemGrade = "F"
  End Select
End Function

Rem  Pass/Fail Student Class (CPFStudent)
Private m_name As String
Private m_ssn As String
Private m_midterm As Single
Private m_final As Single

Property Get Name() As String
  Name = m_name
End Property

Property Let Name(ByVal vName As String)
  m_name = vName
End Property

Property Get SocSecNum() As String
  SocSecNum = m_ssn
End Property

Property Let SocSecNum(ByVal vNum As String)
  m_ssn = vNum
End Property

Property Let midGrade(ByVal vGrade As Single)
  m_midterm = vGrade
End Property

Property Let finGrade(ByVal vGrade As Single)
  m_final = vGrade
End Property

Public Function SemGrade() As String
  Dim grade As Single
  Let grade = (m_midterm + m_final) / 2
  Let grade = Int(grade + 0.5)    'Round the grade
```

```
    If grade >= 60 Then
        SemGrade = "Pass"
      Else
        SemGrade = "Fail"
    End If
End Function


Rem  Form code
Private pupil As Object
Dim section As New Collection

Private Sub cmdAdd_Click()
  If optReg.Value Then
      Set pupil = New CSTudent
    Else
      Set pupil = New CPFStudent
  End If
  Rem Read the Values stored in the Text boxes
  Let pupil.Name = txtName
  Let pupil.SocSecNum = txtSSN
  Let pupil.midGrade = Val(txtMidterm)
  Let pupil.finGrade = Val(txtFinal)
  section.Add pupil
  Rem Clear Text Boxes
  Let txtName.Text = ""
  Let txtSSN.Text = ""
  Let txtMidterm.Text = ""
  Let txtFinal.Text = ""
  picGrades.Print "Student added."
End Sub


Private Sub cmdSemGrade_Click()
  Dim i As Integer, grade As String
  picGrades.Cls
  For i = 1 To section.Count
    picGrades.Print section.Item(i).Name; _
                    Tab(28); section.Item(i).SocSecNum(); _
                    Tab(48); section.Item(i).SemGrade
  Next i
End Sub


Private Sub cmdQuit_Click()
  End
End Sub


Private Sub Form_Load()
  Rem  Initially, regular student should be selected
  Let optReg = True
End Sub
```

[Run, type in data for Al Adams, press the Add Student button, repeat the process for Brittany Brown and Carol Cole, press the Calculate Grades button, and then enter data for Daniel Doyle.]

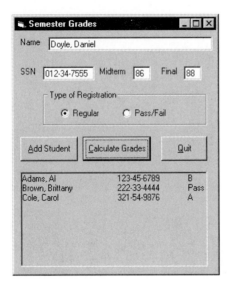

Keys

The items in a collection are automatically paired with the numbers from 1 on. Visual Basic provides an alternative device for accessing a specific item. At the time an item is added to a collection, we can associate a key for the item via a statement of the form

```
collectionName.Add objectName, keyString
```

After that, the object can be referred to as *collectionName.Item(keyString)*.
A property of the object can be accessed with

```
collectionName.Item(keyString).property
```

For instance, consider the situation of Example 1. If we are using social security number as a key, and the object *pupil* contains the data for Brittany Brown, then the statement

```
section.Add pupil, "222-33-4444"
```

would assign the string "222-33-4444" as a key for her data. Then her name property can be accessed with

```
section.Item("222-33-4444").Name
```

EXAMPLE 2   Extend the program of Example 1 so that the grade for an individual student can be displayed by giving a social security number.

SOLUTION   There are no changes in the two classes. In the Sub cmdAdd_Click procedure of the form code, change the line

```
section.Add pupil
```

to

```
section.Add pupil, txtSSN.Text
```

Place an additional command button (cmdDisplay) with the caption "Display Single Grade" on the form and add the following event procedure for this button.

```
Private Sub cmdDisplay_Click()
  Dim ssn As String
  Let ssn = InputBox("Enter the student's social security number.")
  picGrades.Cls
  picGrades.Print section.Item(ssn).Name; _
                Tab(28); section.Item(ssn).SocSecNum(); _
                Tab(48); section.Item(ssn).SemGrade
End Sub
```

When this command button is pressed, the input box in Figure 13.1 appears. To obtain the output in Figure 13.2, run the program, enter the same data as in the execution of Example 1, press the "Display Single Grade" button, type 222-33-4444 into the input box, and press Enter.

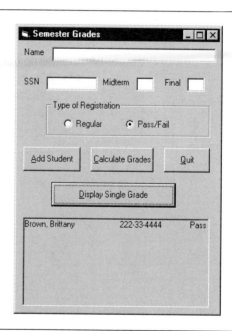

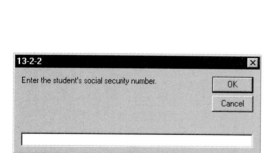

Figure 13.1 Input box

Figure 13.2 Output of program

Events

In the previous section we drew a parallel between objects and controls and showed how to define properties and methods for classes. In addition to the two predefined events for classes, Initialize and Terminate, other events can be defined by the programmer to communicate changes of properties, errors, and the progress of lengthy operations. Such events are called **user-defined events**. The statement for triggering an event is located in the class module and the event is dealt with in the form code. Suppose the event is named UserDefinedEvent and has the arguments *arg1*, *arg2*, and so on. In the class module, the statement

```
Public Event UserDefinedEvent(arg1, arg2, ...)
```

should be placed in the (Declarations) section of (General), and the statement

```
RaiseEvent UserDefinedEvent(arg1, arg2, ...)
```

should be placed at the locations in the class module code at which the event should be triggered. In the form code, an instance of the class, call it object1, must be declared with a statement of the type

```
Private WithEvents object1 As CClassName
```

in order to be able to respond to the event. That is, the word WithEvents must be inserted into the standard declaration statement. The header of an event procedure for *object1* will be

```
Private Sub object1_UserDefinedEvent(par1, par2, ...)
```

EXAMPLE 3   Consider the circle class defined in Example 3 of Section 13.1. Add a user-defined event that is triggered whenever the center of a circle changes. The event should have parameters to pass the center and radius of the circle. The form code should use the event to determine if part (or all) of the drawn circle will fall outside the form. If so, the event procedure should display the message "Circle Off Screen" in a label and cause all future circles to be drawn in red.

SOLUTION   Let's call the event PositionChanged.

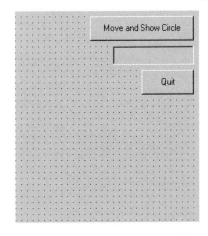

Control	Property	Setting
frmCircles	BorderStyle	0-None
cmdMove	Caption	Move and Show Circle
lblCaution	BorderStyle	1-Fixed Single
	Caption	(blank)
cmdQuit	Caption	Quit

```
Rem  Class module for CCircle
Private m_x As Integer  'Dist from center of circle to left side of form
Private m_y As Integer  'Distance from center of circle to top of form
Private m_r As Single   'Radius of circle
Public Event PositionChanged(x As Integer, y as Integer, r As Single)
Rem  Event is triggered by a change in the center of the circle

Private Sub Class_Initialize()
  Rem  Set the initial center of the circle to the upper
  Rem  left corner of the form and set its radius to 500.
  Let m_x = 0
  Let m_y = 0
  Let m_r = 500
End Sub
```

```
Public Property Get Xcoord() As Integer
  Let Xcoord = m_x
End Property

Public Property Let Xcoord(ByVal vNewValue As Integer)
  Let m_x = vNewValue
End Property

Public Property Get Ycoord() As Integer
  Let Ycoord = m_y
End Property

Public Property Let Ycoord(ByVal vNewValue As Integer)
  Let m_y = vNewValue
End Property

Public Sub Show()
  Rem  Display the circle.
  Rem  See discussion of Circle method in Section 10.4.
  frmCircles.Circle (m_x, m_y), m_r
End Sub

Public Sub Move(Dist)
  Rem  Move the center of the circle Dist twips to the right
  Rem  and Dist twips down.
  Let m_x = m_x + Dist
  Let m_y = m_y + Dist
  RaiseEvent PositionChanged(m_x, m_y, m_r)
  Call Show
End Sub

Rem  Form code
Private WithEvents round As CCircle

Private Sub Form_Load()
  Set round = New CCircle
End Sub

Private Sub cmdMove_Click()
  round.Move (500)
End Sub

Private Sub round_PositionChanged(x As Integer, y As Integer, _
                                  r As Integer)
  Rem  This event is triggered when the center of the circle changes.
  Rem  The code determines if part of the circle is off the screen.
  If (x + r > frmCircles.Width) Or (y + r > frmCircles.Height) Then
      Let lblCaution.Caption = "Circle Off Screen"
      Let frmCircles.ForeColor = QBColor(12) 'Make future circles red
  End If
End Sub

Private Sub cmdQuit_Click()
  End
End Sub
```

[Run and press the "Move and Show Circle" button seven times. **Note:** The last circle will be colored red.]

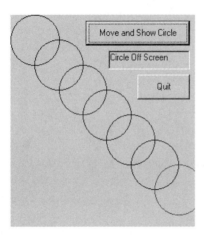

Comments

1. Perhaps a better name for "user-defined events." would be "programmer-defined events."

2. A statement of the form

   ```
   collectionName.Add objectName, keyString
   ```

   can also be written as

   ```
   collectionName.Add Item:=objectName, Key:=keyString
   ```

3. The WithEvents keyword cannot be inserted into a delaraction statement of the form

   ```
   Private objectName As Object
   ```

   It can only be used when a specific class follows the word "As."

4. Collections require more memory than arrays and slow down execution time. If either a collection or an array would suffice, choose an array. This will often be the case when the number of items is fixed. For instance, a deck of cards should be represented as an array of card objects rather than a collection of card objects.

PRACTICE PROBLEMS 13.2

Consider the program in Example 1, but assume that there are no Pass/Fail students. Therefore, in the form code, the statement Private pupil As Object should be replaced by Private pupil As CStudent and the cmdAdd method should be altered accordingly.

1. Alter the Property Let SocSecNum procedure to raise the event ImproperSSN when the social security number does not have 11 characters. The event should pass the length of the social security number and the student's name to the form code.

2. What statement must be placed in the general declarations section of the class module?

3. Write an event procedure for the event ImproperSocSecNum.

4. What statement in the general declaration section of the form code must be altered?

EXERCISES 13.2

1. In Example 1, modify the event procedure cmdSemGrade_Click so that only the students who received a grade of A or Pass are displayed.

The CD accompanying this textbook contains the file STATES.TXT which provides data on the 50 states. Each record contains five pieces of information about a single state: name, abbreviation, date it entered the union, area (in square miles), and projected population in the year 2000. The records are ordered by the date of entry into the union. The first three records are

"Delaware", "DE", "Dec. 7, 1787", 2489, 759000
"Pennsylvania", "PA", "Dec. 12, 1787", 46058, 12296000
"New Jersey", "NJ", "Dec. 18, 1787", 8722, 8135000

2. Create a class CState with five properties to hold the information about a single state, and a method that calculates the density (people per square mile) of the state.

3. Write a program that requests a state's abbreviation in a message box and displays the name of the state and the date the state entered the union. The program should use a collection of CState objects.

4. Write a program that requests a state's name in a message box and displays the states abbreviation, density, and date of entrance into the union.

5. Write a program that displays the names of the states and their densities in a list box ordered by density. The program should use a collection of CState objects.

6. Write a program that reads the data from the file into a collection of CState objects and raises an event whenever the population of a state exceeds ten million. States with large population should have their names and populations displayed in a picture box by the corresponding event procedure.

7. Consider the program described in the opening paragraph of the Practice Problems. Add an event that is raised when the grade entered for a student is negative or greater than 100. Show all changes that must be made and write an event procedure for the event.

8. Consider the class CPairOfDice discussed in Exercise 20 of Section 13.1. Add the event SnakeEyes that is raised whenever two ones appear during a roll of the dice. Write a program that uses the event.

9. Consider the class CStopWatch discussed in Exercise 21 of Section 13.1. Add the event MidnightPassed which is triggered if midnight occurs between the invocations of the Start and Stop methods. Write a program that uses the event.

10. Consider the CFraction class in Exercise 25 of Section 13.1. Add the event ZeroDenominator which is triggered whenever a denominator is set to 0. Write a program that uses the event.

SOLUTIONS TO PRACTICE PROBLEMS 13.2

```
1. Property Let SocSecNum(ByVal vNum As String)
     If Len(vNum) = 11 Then
         m_ssn = vNum
       Else
         RaiseEvent ImproperSSN(Len(vNum),m_name)
     End If
   End Property
```

2. Public Event ImproperSSN(length As Integer, studentName As String)

```
3. Private Sub pupil_ImproperSSN(length As Integer, studentName As string)
     MsgBox "The social security number entered for " & _
            studentName & " consisted of" & Str(length) & _
            " characters. Reenter the data for " & studentName & "."
   End Sub
```

4. The statement

    Private pupil As CStudent

   must be changed to

    Private WithEvents pupil As CStudent

13.3 CLASS RELATIONSHIPS

The three relationships between classes are "use," "containment," and "inheritance." One class **uses** another class if it manipulates objects of that class. We say that class A **contains** class B when a member variable of class A has class B as its type. **Inheritance** is a process by which one class (the child class), inherits the properties, methods, and events of another class (the parent class). Visual Basic does not support the strict academic definition of inheritance. In this section, we present programs that illustrate "use" (Example 1) and "containment" (Example 2).

In this section we will be setting variables to existing objects. In that case, the proper statement is

    Set objVar = existingObject

EXAMPLE 1 Write a program to create and control two airplane objects (referred to as a *bomber* and a *plane*) and a bomb object. The airplane object should keep track of its location (that is, the number of twips from the left side and the top side of the form.), be capable of moving in a direction (Right, Up, or Down) specified by the user from a combo box, and should be able to drop a bomb when so commanded. The last task will be carried out by the bomb object. In the event that a bomb dropped from the bomber hits the plane, the plane should disappear. The airplanes and the bomb will have physical representations as pictures inside image controls. By their locations we mean the upperleft corners of their respective image controls. The picture files AIRPLANE.BMP and BOMB.BMP can be found in the Pictures directory of the CD accompanying this textbook.

SOLUTION

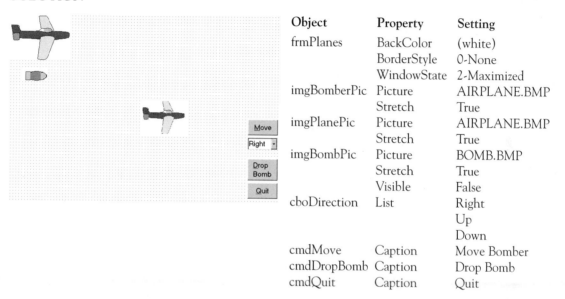

Object	Property	Setting
frmPlanes	BackColor	(white)
	BorderStyle	0-None
	WindowState	2-Maximized
imgBomberPic	Picture	AIRPLANE.BMP
	Stretch	True
imgPlanePic	Picture	AIRPLANE.BMP
	Stretch	True
imgBombPic	Picture	BOMB.BMP
	Stretch	True
	Visible	False
cboDirection	List	Right
		Up
		Down
cmdMove	Caption	Move Bomber
cmdDropBomb	Caption	Drop Bomb
cmdQuit	Caption	Quit

```
Rem Class module for CPlane
Private m_imgPlane As Image 'image control associated with plane

Property Let imagePlane(newPlane As Image)
  Set m_imgPlane = newPlane
End Property

Public Function Present() As Integer
  Rem  Determine if the plane is visible
  Rem  Will be needed by the bomb object.
  If m_imgPlane.Visible Then
      Present = 1
    Else
      Present = 0
  End If
End Function

Public Function X() As Integer
  X = m_imgPlane.Left
End Function

Public Function Y() As Integer
  Y = m_imgPlane.Top
End Function
```

```
Public Function W() As Integer
 W = m_imgPlane.Width
End Function


Public Function H() As Integer
  H = m_imgPlane.Height
End Function


Public Sub Fly(ByVal dir As String, ByVal Height As Integer, ByVal Width As Integer)
  Let m_imgPlane.Visible = True
  Rem  Meanings of variables
  Rem  dir      Direction of airplane (Right, Up, or Down)
  Rem  Height  Height of form
  Rem  Width   Width of form
  If dir = "Up" Then
      Rem Prevent airplane from rising off the screen.
      If (m_imgPlane.Top - 500) >= 0 Then
         Let m_imgPlane.Top = m_imgPlane.Top - 500
       End If
    ElseIf dir = "Down" Then
      Rem Prevent airplane from falling off the screen.
      If (m_imgPlane.Top + m_imgPlane.Height + 500) <= Height Then
          Let m_imgPlane.Top = m_imgPlane.Top + 500
      End If
    ElseIf dir = "Right" Then
      Rem Prevent airplane from moving off the screen.
      If (m_imgPlane.Left + m_imgPlane.Width + 500) <= Width Then
          Let m_imgPlane.Left = m_imgPlane.Left + 500
      End If
  End If
End Sub


Public Sub Destroy()
  m_imgPlane.Visible = False
End Sub


Private Sub Class_Terminate()
  Set m_imgPlane = Nothing
End Sub


Rem Class module for CBomb
Private imgBomb As Image
Public Event BombPositionChanged(X As Integer, Y As Integer, _
                                 W As Integer, H As Integer)
Property Let imageBomb(bomb As Image)
  Set imgBomb = bomb
End Property


Public Sub GoDown(plane As CPlane, ByVal FormHeight As Integer)
  Dim j As Integer
  Let imgBomb.Left = plane.X + 0.5 * plane.W
  Let imgBomb.Top = plane.Y + plane.H
  Let imgBomb.Visible = True
  Do While imgBomb.Top < FormHeight
    Let imgBomb.Top = imgBomb.Top + 5
```

```vb
      RaiseEvent BombPositionChanged(imgBomb.Left, imgBomb.Top, _
                                     imgBomb.Width, imgBomb.Height)
      Rem Pause
      For j = 1 To 2000
      Next j
   Loop
   Let imgBomb.Visible = False
End Sub


Public Sub Destroy()
   Let imgBomb.Visible = False
End Sub


Private Sub Class_Terminate()
   Set imgBomb = Nothing
End Sub


Rem  Form code
Private bomber As CPlane
Private plane As CPlane
Private WithEvents bomb As CBomb

Private Sub Form_Load()
   Set bomber = New CPlane
   Set plane = New CPlane
   Set bomb = New CBomb
   Let bomber.imagePlane = imgBomberPic
   Let plane.imagePlane = imgPlanePic
   Let bomb.imageBomb = imgBombPic
End Sub


Private Sub bomb_BombPositionChanged(X As Integer, Y As Integer, H As Integer, W As Integer)
   Rem  Check to see if Plane is hit, i.e. the bomb is inside plane or vice versa.
   If plane.Present() = 1 Then
      If (plane.X <= X) And (plane.X + plane.W >= X) And _
         (plane.Y <= Y) And (plane.Y + plane.H >= Y) Or _
         (X <= plane.X) And (X + W >= plane.X) And _
         (Y <= plane.Y) And (Y + H >= plane.Y) Then
         plane.Destroy
         bomb.Destroy
      End If
   End If
End Sub


Private Sub cmdMove_Click()
   bomber.Fly cboDirection.Text, frmPlanes.Height, frmPlanes.Width
End Sub


Private Sub cmdDropBomb_Click()
   bomb.GoDown bomber, frmPlanes.Height
End Sub


Private Sub cmdQuit_Click()
   End
End Sub
```

[Run, press the Move button twice, and then press the Drop Bomb button.]

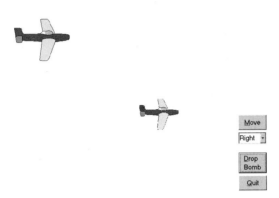

EXAMPLE 2   Write a program to deal a five-card poker hand. The program should have a deck-of-cards object containing an array of 52 card objects.

SOLUTION   Our card object will have two properties, Denomination and Suit, and one method, IdentifyCard. The IdentifyCard method returns a string such as "Ace of Spades."

In the DeckOfCards object, the Initialize event procedure assigns denominations and suits to the 52 cards. The method ReadCard(n) returns the string identifying the nth card of the deck. The method ShuffleDeck uses Rnd to mix-up the cards while making 200 passes through the deck. The event `Shuffling(n As Integer, nMax As Integer)` is triggered during each shuffling pass through the deck and its parameters communicate the number of the pass and the total number of passes, so that the program that uses it can keep track of the progress.

Object	Property	Setting
frmPokerHand	Caption	Poker Hand
picHand		
cmdShuffle	Caption	&Shuffle
cmdDeal	Caption	&Deal
cmdQuit	Caption	&Quit

```
Rem Class module for CCard
Private m_Denomination As String
Private m_Suit As String

Public Property Let Denomination(ByVal vDenom As String)
  m_Denomination = vDenom
End Property

Public Property Let Suit(ByVal vSuit As String)
  m_Suit = vSuit
End Property

Public Property Get Denomination() As String
  Denomination = m_Denomination
End Property
```

```
Public Property Get Suit() As String
  Suit = m_Suit
End Property

Public Function IdentifyCard() As String
  Dim Denom As String
  Select Case Val(m_Denomination)
    Case 1
      Let Denom = "Ace"
    Case Is <= 10
      Let Denom = m_Denomination
    Case 11
      Let Denom = "Jack"
    Case 12
      Let Denom = "Queen"
    Case 13
      Let Denom = "King"
  End Select
  IdentifyCard = Denom & " of " & m_Suit
End Function

Rem  Class module for CDeckOfCards
Private m_deck(1 To 52) As CCard
Public Event Shuffling(n As Integer, nMax As Integer)

Private Sub Class_Initialize()
  Dim i As Integer
  For i = 1 To 52
    Set m_deck(i) = New CCard
    Rem  Make the first thirteen cards hearts, the
    Rem  next thirteen cards diamonds, and so on.
    Select Case i
      Case Is <= 13
        Let m_deck(i).Suit = "Hearts"
      Case Is <= 26
        Let m_deck(i).Suit = "Diamonds"
      Case Is <= 39
        Let m_deck(i).Suit = "Clubs"
      Case Else
        Let m_deck(i).Suit = "Spades"
    End Select
    Rem  Assign numbers from 1 through 13 to the
    Rem  cards of each suit.
    If (i Mod 13 = 0) Then
      Let m_deck(i).Denomination = Str(13)
    Else
      Let m_deck(i).Denomination = Str(i Mod 13)
    End If
  Next i
End Sub

Public Function ReadCard(cardNum As Integer) As String
  ReadCard = m_deck(cardNum).IdentifyCard
End Function
```

```
Private Sub Swap(ByVal i As Integer, ByVal j As Integer)
  Rem Swap the ith and jth card in the deck
  Dim TempCard As New CCard
  Let TempCard.Denomination = m_deck(i).Denomination
  Let TempCard.Suit = m_deck(i).Suit
  Let m_deck(i).Denomination = m_deck(j).Denomination
  Let m_deck(i).Suit = m_deck(j).Suit
  Let m_deck(j).Denomination = TempCard.Denomination
  Let m_deck(j).Suit = TempCard.Suit
End Sub

Public Sub ShuffleDeck()
  Rem  Do 200 passes through the deck. On each pass
  Rem  swap each card with a randomly selected card.
  Dim index As Integer, i As Integer, k As Integer
  Randomize   'Initialize random number generator
  For i = 1 To 200
    For k = 1 To 52
      Let index = Int((52 * Rnd) + 1)
      Call Swap(k, index)
    Next k
    RaiseEvent Shuffling(i, 200)
  Next i
End Sub

Rem   Form Code
Public WithEvents cards As CDeckOfCards

Private Sub Form_Load()
  Set cards = New CDeckOfCards
End Sub

Private Sub cmdShuffle_Click()
  Call cards.ShuffleDeck
End Sub

Private Sub cmdDeal_Click()
Dim str As String
Dim i As Integer
  picHand.Cls
  For i = 1 To 5
    Let str = cards.ReadCard(i)
    picHand.Print str
  Next i
End Sub

Private Sub cards_shuffling(n As Integer, nMax As Integer)
  Rem  n is the number of the specific pass through the deck (1, 2, 3..)
  Rem  nMax is the total number of passes when the deck is shuffled
  picHand.Cls
  picHand.Print "Shuffling Pass:"; n; "out of"; nMax
End Sub

Private Sub cmdQuit_Click()
  End
End Sub
```

[Run, click on the Shuffle button, and click on the Deal button after the shuffling is complete.]

Comment

1. Example 1 illustrates "use" since the GoDown object of the bomb object receives a plane object. In general, class A uses Class B if an object of class B is sent a message by a property or method of class A, or a method or property of class A returns, receives, or creates objects of class B.

EXERCISES 13.3

1. Write a program for the fraction calculator shown in Figure 13.3. After the numerators and denominators of the two fractions to the left of the equals sign are placed in the four text boxes, one of four operations buttons should be pressed. The result appears to the right of the equals sign. The program should use a Calculator class which contains three members of the type CFraction discussed in Exercise 26 of Section 13.1.

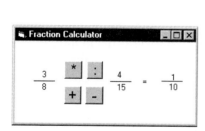

Figure 13.3 Exercise 1

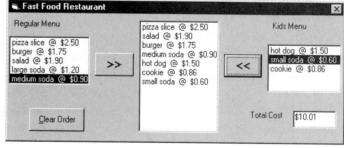

Figure 13.4 Exercise 2

2. Write a program that takes orders at a fast food restaurant. See Figure 13.4. The restaurant has two menus, a regular menu and a kids menu. An item is ordered by highlighting it in one of the list boxes and then pushing the >> or << button to place it in the order list box in the center of the form. As each item is ordered, a running total is displayed in the label at the lower right part of the form. The program should use a Menu class which contains a Food class. (The contents of each of the three list boxes should be treated as Menu objects.) A Food object should hold the name and price of a single food item. A Menu object should have a MenuChanged event that can be used by the form code to update the cost of the order.

3. Write a program for a simple game in which each of two players rolls a pair of dice. The person with the highest tally wins. See Figure 13.5. The program should use a Game class (CHighRoller) having two member variables of the type CPairOfDice discussed in Exercise 19 of Section 13.1.

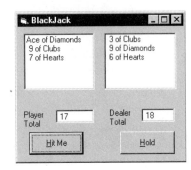

Figure 13.5 Exercise 3   **Figure 13.6** Exercise 4

4. Write a program for the game blackjack. See Figure 13.6. The program should use a Blackjack class (CBlackjack) which contains a member variable of the type CDeckOfCards presented in Example 2 of this section.

5. Write a program to produce an employee's weekly paycheck receipt. The receipt should contain the employees name, amount earned for the week, total amount earned for the year, FICA tax deduction, withholding tax deduction, and take-home amount. The program should use an Employee class (CEmployee) and a Tax class (CTax). The Tax class must have properties for the amount earned for the week, the prior total amount earned for the year, the number of withholding exemptions, and marital status. It should have methods for computing FICA and withholding taxes. The Employee class should store the employees name, number of withholding allowances, marital status, hours worked this week, hourly salary, and previous amount earned for the year. The Employee class should use the Tax class to calculate the taxes to be deducted. The formula for calculating the FICA tax is given in Exercise 25 of Section 13.1. To compute the withholding tax, multiply the number of withholding allowances by $50.96, subtract the product from the amount earned, and use Table 13.1 or Table 13.2.

Adjusted Weekly Income	Income Tax Withheld
$0 to $51	$0
Over $51 to $503	15% of amount over $51
Over $503 to 1067	$67.80 + 28% of amount over $503
Over $1067 to $2426	$225.72 + 31% of amount over $1067
Over $2426 to $5241	$647.01 + 36% of amount over $2426
Over $5241	$1660.41 + 39.6% of amount over $5241

Table 13.1 1997 federal income tax withheld for a single person paid weekly.

Adjusted Weekly Income	Income Tax Withheld
$0 to $124	$0
Over $124 to $874	15% of amount over $124
Over $874 to $1786	$112.50 + 28% of amount over $874
Over $1786 to $3000	$367.86 + 31% of amount over $1786
Over $3000 to $5297	$744.20 + 36% of amount over $3000
Over $5297	$1570.04 + 39.6% of amount over $5297

Table 13.2 1997 federal income tax withheld for a married person paid weekly.

13.4 BUILDING ACTIVEX CONTROLS

"Visual Basic 5.0's ability to create ActiveX controls may prove a good way to create flashy Web pages. It *will* become the most powerful tool for component-based applications development yet created. Of that I am certain."

Dan Appleman[2]

Note: *ActiveX controls can be created with all versions of Visual Basic 5.0 except the Learning Edition.*

ActiveX is the name given to the fundamental technology for a type of 32-bit controls that can be used in Windows applications. Since this technology is supported by the Internet, ActiveX controls play a major part in programming for web pages. However, ActiveX controls are an important part of *all* Visual Basic programming.

There are three types of ActiveX controls.

1. *Sub-classed controls* are created by modifying existing controls.

2. *Aggregate controls* are created by combining existing controls and writing code to link them together.

3. *User-drawn controls* are created from scratch without displaying any standard controls.

In this section we present a detail example of building an aggregate control. However, the constituent controls will be modified in the same way as sub-classed controls.

We will create a customized control that serves as a deposit slip for a checking account. See Figure 13.7. With this control, amounts for dollars and cents are typed into control arrays of text boxes which permit only whole numbers to be entered. Amounts entered into these text boxes are immediately summed and the totals displayed in boxes (labels) at the bottoms of the columns. An additional array of five text boxes identifies the checks. The text boxes and labels are contained inside a picture box.

---

2   Developing ActiveX Components with Visual Basic 5.0, Ziff-Davis Press, 1997.

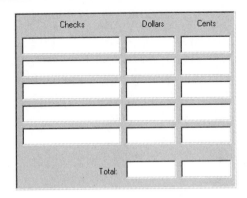

Figure 13.7 User-defined DepositSlip control

Unlike an ordinary printed deposit slip, our electronic deposit slip will allow us to vary the number of entries for checks. The DepositSlip control will have a property, NumChecks, that gives the number of entries for checks on the deposit slip. (When the DepositSlip control is used in a program, NumChecks will appear in the Properties window for the deposit slip.) It has default value 5 and can be set at design time or run time to any number from 0 through 5. The deposit slip will have two methods Total and Clear. The method Total, calculates the total value of the checks as a single-precision number. The method Clear removes all information that has been added to the deposit slip. Also, the DepositSlip control will have an event that will be triggered whenever a change is made to the data in the text boxes. After we build this control, we can put it in the Visual Basic toolbar. From there it can be placed onto a form and used like any other control.

The following steps are used to build an ActiveX control.

1. Press Alt/File/New to invoke the New Project dialog box.

2. Double-click on the ActiveX Control icon. [The form that appears is similar to the form used to create programs. The main difference is that the form's title bar says "Project1-UserControl1 (UserControl)" instead of "Project1-Form1(Form)."]

3. Place controls on the form and write code to link them together. [The code will look like the code in a class module. It will create methods with subprograms or functions and will incorporate the RaiseEvents statement.]

4. Press Alt/File/Make Project1.ocx. . . to compile this new user-defined control as an ocx file. [A Make Project dialog box will appear to assist you in the location and name for the file.]

This newly created file will automatically be registered by Windows and will be available when designing Visual Basic programs. It will be among the list of custom controls that appears when you press Alt/Project/Components.

A Word of Caution: When an ActiveX control is compiled as an ocx file and registered by Windows, it is not easily removed from the Windows registry. Therefore, if you are using a computer that is not your own (such as a computer in a computer lab), you should probably not compile ActiveX controls. In

Example 3, we show how to use an ActiveX control without compiling it to an ocx file.

The code referred to in Step 3 above will look familiar to you, except for a pair of events, called ReadProperties and WriteProperties that are used to communicate the state of the user-defined properties among various parts of the program. Visual Basic uses a device called a Property Bag to hold the state of the properties. The general form of this pair of events is

```
Private Sub UserControl_ReadProperties(PropBag As PropertyBag)
  On Error Resume Next
  Let memberVariable = PropBag.ReadProperty(propertyName, defaultValue)
  Let propertyName = memberVariable
End Sub


Private Sub UserControl_WriteProperties(PropBag As PropertyBag)
  On Error Resume Next
  Call PropBag.WriteProperty(propertyName, memberVariable, defaultValue)
End Sub
```

where *memberVariable* is the Private member variable used to hold the value of the property. The default values are optional, but recommended.

To create a custom control, one puts its constituent controls on the form. We've already discussed this part. Then one decides on what properties and methods the new control will have, and which events it will raise.

For each new property, one writes two procedures: Property Let and Property Get, and also adds one line of code into ReadProperties and WriteProperties events of the control, as seen in Example 1. This is needed so that the newly created property could appear in the Property window of the control, and so that the property value set at design time could persist until run time. The exception of this rule occurs when the property one defines is an object in itself. Then one uses Property Set instead of Property Let procedure. In Example 1, NumChecks is the single (integer-valued) property of the DepositSlip control.

Each method of the control is, in fact, a public procedure (or function) declared in the control's module. In Example 1, the function Total is a method of the DepositSlip control.

If you want your control to raise events (almost any useful control does), you should first declare them using the Public Event syntax (see Example 1), and then raise them at appropriate times using the RaiseEvent statement. The DepositSlip control from Example 1 declares the event Changed. This event is raised whenever the control contents are changed and the total is updated, so that the program that uses our control could make the necessary updates on such occasions.

EXAMPLE 1   Build the DepositSlip control discussed above.

SOLUTION   Double-click on ActiveX Control from the New Project window to invoke the ActiveX designer. The screen resembles the familiar form designer screen that is invoked with Standard EXE. The only differences are in the title bar (it contains the words "UserControl" instead of "Form.") and the rectangular gridded region (it lacks a title bar and is referred to as a *User Control form*).

Design the form below. Begin by placing a picture box on the User Control form. (The other controls will be placed inside the picture box.) Place the words "Checks," "Dollars," and "Cents" in labels, and place an array of five text boxes below each label. Place three labels in the bottom part of the picture box as shown.

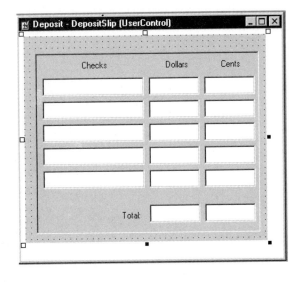

Object	Property	Setting
picBox		
lblChecks	Caption	Checks
lblDollars	Caption	Dollars
lblCents	Caption	Cents
txtChecks()	Index	0 to 4
	Text	(blank)
txtDollars()	Index	0 to 4
	Text	(blank)
txtCents()	Index	0 to 14
	Text	(blank)
lblTotal	Caption	Total:
lblTotDollars	Caption	(blank)
	BorderStyle	1-Fixed Single
lblTotCents	Caption	(blank)
	BorderStyle	1-Fixed Single

```
Rem  Code for the User Control DepositSlip
Rem  The event Changed will be triggered
Rem  whenever the total amount deposited changes.
Private m_numChecks As Integer  'Number of checks listed on deposit slip
Public Event Changed()

Private Sub txtCents_Change(index As Integer)
  Rem  Whenever an amount in the cents column is changed, update
  Rem  the numbers in the two labels holding the total amount.
  Call Update
End Sub

Private Sub txtDollars_Change(index As Integer)
  Rem  Whenever an amount in the dollars column is changed, update
  Rem  the numbers in the two labels holding the total amount.
  Call Update
End Sub

Private Sub txtCents_KeyPress(index As Integer, KeyAscii As Integer)
  Rem  Only allow the digits 0 through 9 and the backspace key
  Rem  to be typed into the cents column. The ANSI values of 0, 9, and
  Rem  the backspace key are 48, 57, and 8.
  If ((KeyAscii < 48) Or (KeyAscii > 57)) And (KeyAscii <> 8) Then
      Let KeyAscii = 0
  End If
End Sub
```

```
Private Sub txtDollars_KeyPress(index As Integer, KeyAscii As Integer)
    Rem  Only allow the digits 0 through 9 and the backspace key
    Rem  to be typed into the dollars column. The ANSI values of 0, 9, and
    Rem  the backspace key are 48, 57, and 8.
    If ((KeyAscii < 48) Or (KeyAscii > 57)) And (KeyAscii <> 8) Then
        Let KeyAscii = 0
    End If
End Sub


Private Sub Update()
    Rem  This routine executes whenever the user types into one of the
    Rem  text boxes. It adds up the amounts of money and places the
    Rem  total amount in the labels at the bottom of the picture box.
    Dim index As Integer, sum As Single, cents As String
    Rem  sum will hold the total amount deposited in cents.
    Let sum = 0
    For index = 0 To m_numChecks - 1
      If txtDollars(index).Text <> "" Then
          Let sum = sum + 100 * Val(txtDollars(index).Text)
      End If
      If txtCents(index).Text <> "" Then
          Let sum = sum + Val(txtCents(index).Text)
      End If
    Next index
    Rem  The number of cents are the rightmost two digits of the sum.
    Let cents = Right(Str(sum), 2)
    Let lblTotalCents.Caption = Format(cents, "00")
    Rem  The number of dollars is the whole number
    Rem  part when the sum is divided by 100.
    Let lblTotalDollars.Caption = Str(Int(sum / 100))
    RaiseEvent Changed
End Sub


Public Function Total() As String
    Dim amount As Single
    Let amount = Val(lblTotalDollars.Caption) + _
                Val(lblTotalCents.Caption) / 100
    Total = amount
End Function


Public Property Get NumChecks() As Integer
    NumChecks = m_numChecks
End Property


Public Property Let NumChecks(ByVal vNumChecks As Integer)
    Dim i As Integer
    If vNumChecks > 5 Then
        Let vNumChecks = 5
    End If
    Let m_numChecks = vNumChecks
```

```
      Rem  Make m_numChecks controls visible.
      For i = 0 To m_numChecks - 1
        Let txtCents(i).Visible = True
        Let txtDollars(i).Visible = True
        Let txtChecks(i).Visible = True
      Next i
      Rem Hide the remaining controls.
      For i = m_numChecks To 4
        Let txtCents(i).Visible = False
        Let txtDollars(i).Visible = False
        Let txtChecks(i).Visible = False
      Next i
      Call Clear
    End Property

    Private Sub UserControl_ReadProperties(PropBag As PropertyBag)
      Rem  Invoked at run time.
      Rem  Allows design time property value for NumChecks to persist.
      On Error Resume Next
      Let m_numChecks = PropBag.ReadProperty("NumChecks", 5)
      Let NumChecks = m_numChecks
    End Sub

    Private Sub UserControl_WriteProperties(PropBag As PropertyBag)
      Rem  Invoked at design time.
      Rem  Allows design time property value for NumChecks to persist.
      On Error Resume Next
      Call PropBag.WriteProperty("NumChecks", m_numChecks)
    End Sub

    Public Sub Clear()
      Dim index As Integer
      For index = 0 To 4
        Let txtChecks(index).Text = ""
        Let txtDollars(index).Text = ""
        Let txtCents(index).Text = ""
      Next index
      Call Update
    End Sub
```

You cannot run the code above by itself. The code is used only to define the properties, methods, and events for the user-defined control. If you decide to compile the control and have it registered (most likely permanently in the Windows registry), press Alt/File/Make Project1.ocx and give it the file name DEPOSIT.OCX. The program in the Example 2 uses the compiled control to update the balance in a checking account. Example 3 carries out the same task without compiling the control.

Note: When you save the code in Example 1, you are prompted for two filenames: a filename with extension vbp for the project, and a filename with extension ctl for the user-defined control. On the CD accompanying this textbook, the files have been given the names 13-4-1.vbp and 13-4-1.ctl.

EXAMPLE 2   Assuming that the DepositSlip control of Example 1 has been compiled to an ocx file, write a program that calculates the new balance in a checking account after a deposit is made. The previous balance and the number of checks should be requested from the user in text boxes. The new balance should be automatically adjusted as each amount is entered into a deposit slip.

SOLUTION   Press Alt/File/New Project to begin a new program. Press Alt/Project/Components (or Ctrl+T) to display the list of control that have been registered in the Windows registry. Find the name Deposit in the Components list, click on the box next to the name, and then click on OK. A new icon, 🔳, will appear in the toolbox. If you hold the mouse cursor over this icon, the identifying word DepositSlip appears. You can place this control on the form as you would any other built-in control. Also, you can set its properties in a property window. We will use the prefix "dsl" for DepositSlip controls. The following form contains a DepositSlip control along with several other familiar controls.

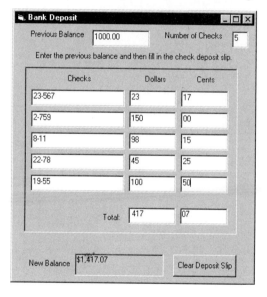

Object	Property	Setting
frm13_4_2	Caption	Bank Deposit
lblOldBal	Caption	Previous Balance
txtOldBal	Text	(blank)
lblNumChecks	Caption	Number of Checks
txtNumChecks	Text	5
lblInstructions	Caption	Enter the previous balance and then fill in the check deposit slip.
dslChecks	NumChecks	5
lblNewBal	Caption	New Balance
lblComputedBal	BorderStyle	1-Fixed Single
	Caption	(blank)
cmdClear	Caption	Clear Deposit Slip

```
Private Sub cmdClear_Click()
  dslChecks.Clear
End Sub

Private Sub dslChecks_Changed()
  Dim newBal As Single
  Let newBal = Val(txtOldBal.Text) + Val(dslChecks.Total)
  Let lblComputedBal.Caption = Format(newBal, "Currency")
End Sub

Private Sub Form_Load()
  Let txtNumChecks.Text = dslChecks.NumChecks
End Sub

Private Sub txtNumChecks_Change()
  Let dslChecks.NumChecks = Val(txtNumChecks)
End Sub
```

[Run the program, enter a previous balance into the first text box, and fill in the check deposit slip. The new balance will be automatically adjusted each time you type a digit into a dollars or cents column. In the sample output below, we have used the American Bankers Association routing numbers to identify each check.]

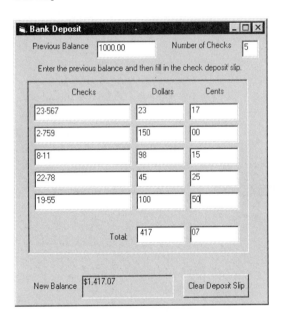

EXAMPLE 3   Redo the program in Example 2 without first compiling the DepositSlip control.

SOLUTION

1. Create the Deposit slip as in Example 1, but do not press Alt/File/Make Project1.ocx to compile it. Alternately, open the project 13-4-1.vbp found on the CD accompanying this textbook.

2. Notice that a grayed DepositSlip icon appears on the toolbar. (Hold the mouse cursor over the control to display the tooltip and confirm that the control is indeed a DepositSlip control.)

3. Close the designer by clicking on the X button at the right side of the Visual Basic toolbar. (Do not click on the X button in the Visual Basic title bar in upper-right corner of the screen.)

4. Notice that the DepositSlip icon is no longer grayed. (The icon was previously grayed since the ActiveX designer was active and had control of the control.)

5. Press Alt/File/Add Project., and then double-click on Standard EXE. (An ordinary form appears.)

6. Proceed as in Example 2 to design the form, enter the code, and run the program.

7. The combination of the ActiveX designer and the form is referred to as a **project group**. When you save the combination by pressing Alt/File/Save Project Group, you are prompted for three filenames with extensions frm, vbp, and vbg.

8. To open a saved project group, open the file with the extension vbg. For instance, to open the project group for this example from the accompanying CD, open 13-4-3.vbg.

Comments

1. ActiveX controls are referred to as "user-defined controls." Perhaps a better name would be "programmer-defined controls."

2. If you decide to compile your controls to ocx files before using them, you might end up with many entries in your list of components. One way to keep the list small is to reuse the control name and filename of an existing ActiveX control and overwrite it.

EXERCISES 13.4

1. Build an ActiveX control, call it PassWord, consisting of a text box suitable for entering passwords. Any characters typed into the text box should appear as asterisks. An event should be triggered each time the contents of the text box changes. Double-clicking on the textbox should toggle the revealing and disguising of the password. (**Hint:** Setting the PasswordChar property of the text box to "*" disguises the password; setting it to "" reveals the password.) Test the control in a form consisting only of a PassWord control. After the user types a word into the PassWord control and double-clicks on the control, the actual password should be displayed.

2. (a) Build an ActiveX control, call it SingleCap, consisting of a small text box that accepts exactly one uppercase letter. An event should be triggered each time the contents of the text box changes.
   (b) Use the SingleCap control in a program that requests a person's first initial and last initial and then displays his of her pair of initials.

3. (a) Build an ActiveX control, call it Phone that resembles the face of a telephone. See Figure 13.8. The numbered buttons should be a control array of command buttons. A phone number should be generated and stored in the corresponding property by pushing a sequence of numbered buttons, and the Flush command button should cancel all numbers dialed. An event should be triggered each time a command button is pressed.
   (b) Write a program consisting of a Phone control and a label. As the user clicks on the push buttons, the numbers dialed should appear in the label.

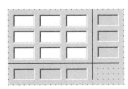

Figure 13.8 Phone control

Figure 13.9 MagicSquare control

4. (a) Exercise 24 of Section 7.5 discusses magic squares. Build an ActiveX control, call it MagicSquare, that is used to find a 3-by-3 magic square by trial and error. See Figure 13.9. A method should indicate whether or not the array is a magic square. As numbers are typed into the white text boxes, the sums of the rows and columns should automatically be displayed in the gray labels and the property of being a magic square should be reevaluated and the corresponding event raised.

   (b) Place a MagicSquare control on a form, run the program, and try to find a 3-by-3 magic square. The background color of the form should turn green [Form.BackColor = QBColor(2)] when the numbers form a magic square and should be red [Form.BackColor = QBColor(4)] otherwise.

5. (a) Build an ActiveX control, call it PaymentForm, that permits a salesperson to indicate the type of payment. See Figure 13.10. The frame (and its contents, four option buttons and a text box) should be visible only when the Credit Card option button is selected. A method should indicate the mode of payment and if a credit card is being used, the method should reveal the card used and the number in the text box.

   (b) Write a program consisting of a PaymentForm control, a command button, and a label. When the command button is pressed, the label should indicate the details of the type of payment. Two possible outcomes are "Paid by personal check" and "Paid by VISA card #1111 2222 3333 4444."

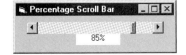

Figure 13.10 PaymentForm control

Figure 13.11 PercentageScrollBar control

6. (a) Build an ActiveX control, call it PercentageScrollBar that is made with a horizontal scroll bar and a label. See Figure 13.11. As the thumb moves, the label should record the percentage of the length of the bar that the thumb has been moved.

(b) Write a program consisting solely of a PercentageScrollBar. Move the thumb and observe the change in the label.

7. (a) Build an ActiveX control, call it FastFoodOrder, that can be used to record an order at a fast food restaurant. See Figure 13.12. The control should consist of three labels, three text boxes (to record the numbers of each item ordered), and two command buttons. Three properties should give the prices of burgers, fries, and shakes. A method should determine the cost of the order. An event should be triggered when either of the buttons are clicked. When the Cancel button is pressed, the three text boxes should be cleared before raising this event.

(b) Write a program consisting of a FastFoodOrder control, five labels, and one text box. When the four text boxes are filled and the Ok button is pressed, the values for the cost and change labels should be calculated and displayed. The prices of the items on the menu can be specified by the Form_Load procedure if desired.

(a) FastFoodOrder control

(b) Exercise 7 during run time

Figure 13.12

Chapter 13
Summary

1. An *object* is an entity that stores data, has methods that manipulate the data, and can trigger events. A *class* describes a group of similar objects. A *method* specifies the way in which an object's data are manipulated. An *event* is a change in the state of an object.

2. Classes are defined in a separate module called a *class module*. Data is stored in member variables and accessed by procedures called methods.

3. Property Let and Property Get procedures are used to set and retrieve values of member variables. These procedures can also be used enforce constraints and carry out validation.

4. The Initialize and Terminate event procedures are automatically invoked when an object is created and falls out of scope, respectively.

5. An object variable is declared in the declarations section of a program with a statement of the form `Private objectName As className` and created with a statement of the form `Set objectName = New className`.

6. A *collection* is a convenient devise for grouping together diverse objects. Objects are added to collections with the Add method and removed with the Remove method. The number of objects in a collection is determined with the Count property and object is returned by the Item method using either a number or a key.

7. Events are declared in the general declarations section of class module with a statement of the form `Public Event UserDefinedEvent(arg1, arg2, ...)` and triggered with a RaiseEvent statement. In the form code, the declaration statement for an object, must include the keyword WithEvents in order for the events coming from the object to be processed.

8. Objects interact through *use* and *containment*.

9. The programmer can build custom-designed ActiveX controls that can be placed on a form and have the same features as the controls on the toolbar.

Chapter 13
Programming Projects

1. *Son of Deep Blue.* Write a program that plays a game of tic-tac-toe in which a person competes with the computer. The game should be played in a control array of nine labels. See Figure 13.13. After the user moves by placing an X in a label, the program should determine the location for the O. The program should use a tic-tac-toe object that raises events when a player moves and when the game is over. The outcome of the game should be announced in a message box.

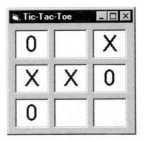

Figure 13.13 Tic-Tac-Toe

2. *Bank Account.* Write a program to maintain a person's Savings and Checking accounts. The program should keep track of and display the balances in both accounts, and maintain a list of transactions (deposits, withdrawals, fund transfers, and check clearings) separately for each account. The two lists of transactions should be stored in sequential files so that they will persist between program sessions.

Consider the form in Figure 13.14. The two drop-down combo boxes should each contain the items Checking and Savings. Each of the four frames corresponds to a type of transaction. (When Savings is selected in the Account combo box, the Check frame should disappear.) The user makes a transaction by typing data into the text boxes of a frame and pressing the command button. The items appearing in the transactions list box should correspond to the type of account that has been selected. The caption of the second label in the Tranfers frame should toggle between "to Checking" and "to Savings" depending on the item selected in the "Transfer from" combo box. If a transaction cannot be carried out, a message (such as "Insufficient funds") should be displayed.

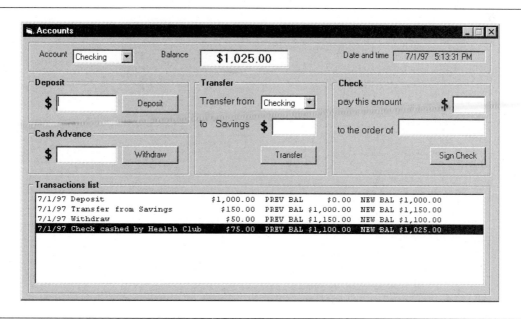

Figure 13.14 Bank accounts

The program should use two classes, CTransaction and CAccount. The class CTransaction should have properties for transaction type, amount, paid to, previous balance, new balance, and transaction date. It should have a method that puts the data into a string that can be added to the Transaction list box, and methods that place data into and retrieve data from a sequential file.

The class CAccount, which will have both a checking account and a savings account as instances, should contain a collection of CTransaction objects. In addition, it should have properties for name (Checking or Savings) and balance. It should have methods to carry out a transaction (if possible), display the list of transactions, and to load and retrieve the set of transactions into or from a sequential file. The events InsufficientFunds and Transaction-Committed should be triggered at appropriate times. [**Hint:** In order to make CAccount object to display a list of transactions, a list box should be passed to a method as an argument. The method might begin with `Public Sub EnumerateTransactions(LB As ListBox)`.]

14

Communicating with Other Applications

14.1 OLE / 638
- OLE Automation • The OLE Container Control
- An Embedding Walkthrough Using Excel
- A Linking Walkthrough Using Word

14.2 Accessing the Internet With Visual Basic / 648
- What Is the Internet? • A Web Browser Walkthrough

14.3 Web Page Programming With VBScript / 654
- HTML • Placing ActiveX controls in HTML documents • Activating a Web Page with VBScript

Summary / 663

14.1 OLE

OLE, which stands for Object Linking and Embedding, is the evolving technology that allows programmers to use Visual Basic to glue together applications like spreadsheets and word processors. The three types of OLE are known as automation, linking, and embedding. With automation, you control an application from outside. With linking and embedding, you bring an application into your program. In this section, OLE is illustrated with Microsoft Excel and Word. However, the programs and walkthroughs can be modified for other spreadsheet and word processing software packages.

OLE Automation

The objects in the Visual Basic toolbox have both properties and methods, and Visual Basic controls them by manipulating their properties and methods. In general, anything with properties and methods that can be controlled by manipulating its properties and methods is called an **object**. In particular, an Excel spreadsheet or a Word document can be specified as an **OLE Automation object**.

We have worked extensively with the data types String, Integer, and Single. There are eight other data types, including one called **Object**. A variable that has been declared as an Object variable can be assigned to refer to an OLE Automation object. The CreateObject function is used to create an OLE Automation object and the Set statement is used to assign the object to an object variable. For instance, the pair of statements

```
Dim objExcel As Objcct
Set objExcel = CreateObject("Excel.sheet")
```

creates an Excel spreadsheet object and assigns it to the Object variable objExcel. Application. The pair of statements

```
Dim objWord As Object
Set objWord = CreateObject("Word.Basic")
```

creates a Word document object and assigns it to the Object variable objWord. After the object is no longer needed, a statement of the form

```
Set objVar = Nothing
```

should be executed to discontinue association of objVar with the specific object and release all the resources associated with the previously referenced object.

An object is controlled by manipulating its properties and methods. For instance, the statement

```
objExcel.Application.Cells(4, 3).Value = "49"
```

places the number 49 into the cell in the fourth row and third column (that is, C4) of the spreadsheet. Some other Excel statements are

```
objExcel.Application.Visible = True              'Display spreadsheet
objExcel.Application.Cells(4, 3).Font.Bold = True     'Make cell bold
objExcel.Application.Cells(7, 3).Formula = "=SUM(C1:C5)"    'Specify that
                'cell C7 hold the sum of the numbers in cells C1 through C5
objExcel.Application.Save filespec                'Save spreadsheet
objExcel.Application.Quit                         'Exit Excel
```

With the Word object, the statement

```
objWord.Insert = "We'll always have Paris."
```

inserts the sentence into the document at the current insertion point. Some other Word statements are

```
objWord.FileNewDefault       'Creates a new document based on
                             'the Normal template
objWord.WordLeft             'Move the insertion point left one word
                             '(Counts period as a word.)
objWord.Bold                 'Change font to bold
objWord.FileSaveAs filespec  'Save document with specified name
objWord.FilePrint            'Print the current document
objWord.FileClose            'Close the current document
```

OLE Automation involves the following four steps:

1. Declare an Object variable with a Dim statement.

2. Create an OLE Automation object with a CreateObject function and assign it to the variable with a Set statement.

3. Transfer commands and/or data to the OLE Automation object to carry out the desired task.

4. Close the object and assign the value Nothing to the Object variable.

EXAMPLE 1 The following program, which requires that Microsoft Excel be present in your computer, creates a spreadsheet for college expenses and uses the spreadsheet to add up the values for the different categories. The user should place numbers into the text boxes and then press the first command button to tabulate total college expenses. This process can be repeated as many times as desired. The final spreadsheet can be saved by pressing the Save button.

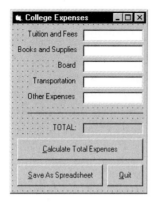

Object	Property	Setting
frm14_1_1	Caption	College Expenses
lblTuitNFees	Caption	Tuition and Fees
txtTuitNFees	Text	(blank)
lblBooksNSuppl	Caption	Books and Supplies
txtBooksNSuppl	Text	(blank)
lblBoard	Caption	Board
txtBoard	Text	(blank)
lblTransportation	Caption	Transportation
txtTransportation	Text	(blank)
lblOther	Caption	Other Expenses
txtOther	Text	(blank)
Line1		
lblTotal	Caption	TOTAL:
lblHoldTotal	Caption	(blank)
cmdCalculate	Caption	&Calculate Total Expenses
cmdSave	Caption	&Save As Spreadsheet
cmdQuit	Caption	&Quit

```
Dim objExcel As Object        'In (Declarations) section of  (General)

Private Sub cmdCalculate_Click()
  Set objExcel = CreateObject("Excel.Sheet")
  Rem Make Excel visible
  objExcel.Application.Visible = True
  Rem Fill in Row Labels
  objExcel.Application.Cells(1, 1).Value = "Tuition & Fees"
  objExcel.Application.Cells(2, 1).Value = "Books & Supplies"
  objExcel.Application.Cells(3, 1).Value = "Board"
  objExcel.Application.Cells(4, 1).Value = "Transportation"
  objExcel.Application.Cells(5, 1).Value = "Other Expenses"
  objExcel.Application.Cells(7, 1).Value = "Total"
  objExcel.Application.Cells(7, 1).Font.Bold = True
  objExcel.Application.Cells(6, 3).Value = "————-"
  Rem Fill in Rows Values
  objExcel.Application.Cells(1, 3).Value = txtTuitNFees.Text
  objExcel.Application.Cells(2, 3).Value = txtBooksNSuppl.Text
  objExcel.Application.Cells(3, 3).Value = txtBoard.Text
  objExcel.Application.Cells(4, 3).Value = txtTransportation.Text
  objExcel.Application.Cells(5, 3).Value = txtOther.Text
  Rem Set up a cell to total the expenses
  objExcel.Application.Cells(7, 3).Formula = "=SUM(C1:C5)"
  objExcel.Application.Cells(7, 3).Font.Bold = True
  Rem Set total as the contents of this cell
  lblHoldTotal = objExcel.Application.Cells(7, 3).Value
  Rem Make Excel invisible
  objExcel.Application.Visible = False
End Sub

Private Sub cmdQuit_Click()
  Rem Close Excel
  objExcel.Application.Quit
```

```
      Rem Release the object variable
      Set objExcel = Nothing
      End
   End Sub

   Private Sub cmdSave_Click()
      Rem Save the new spreadsheet to a File
      objExcel.Application.Save "EXPENSES.XLS"
   End Sub
```

[Run, place numbers into the text boxes, and click on the Calculate Total Expenses button.]

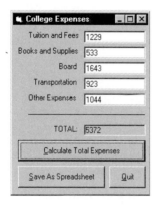

EXAMPLE 2   The following program creates a Word document, prints the contents of the document, and saves the document to a file.

Object	Property	Setting
frm14_1_2	Caption	EXAMPLE 2
cmdCreate	Caption	&Create Word Document

```
   Private Sub cmdCreate_Click()
      Dim objWord As Object
      Set objWord = CreateObject("Word.Basic")
      objWord.FileNewDefault
      objWord.Insert "I can resist everything."
      objWord.Wordleft
      objWord.Bold
      objWord.Insert " except temptation"
      objWord.FilePrint    'Make sure your printer is on
      objWord.FileSaveAs "QUOTE.DOC"
      objWord.FileClose
      Set objWord = Nothing
   End Sub
```

[Run and click the command button. The printer will produce the following output.]

    I can resist everything **except temptation.**

The OLE Container Control

An OLE Container control provides a bridge to Windows applications, such as spreadsheets and word processors. For instance, it can hold an Excel spreadsheet or a Word document. The application can be either linked or embedded through the OLE Container control. With **linking**, a link is established to the data associated with the application and only a snapshot of the data is displayed. Other applications can access the object's data and modify them. For example, if you link a text file to a Visual Basic application, the text file can be modified by any application linked to it. The modified version appears in all documents linked to this text. With **embedding**, all the application's data are actually contained in the OLE Container control and no other application has access to the data.

When you place an OLE Container control on a form, the dialog box in Figure 14.1 appears. You can select an application from the list and then press the OK button (or double-click on the application) to insert it into the control. Alternately, you can click on the "Create from File" option button to produce the dialog box in Figure 14.2. From this second dialog box, you specify a file (such as a Word .DOC file or an Excel .XLS file) by typing it into the text box or clicking the Browse command button and selecting it from a standard file selection dialog box. After the file has been selected, you have the option of checking the Link check box before clicking on the OK button to insert the contents of the file into the OLE Container control.

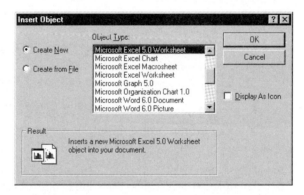

Figure 14.1 An Insert Object dialog box.

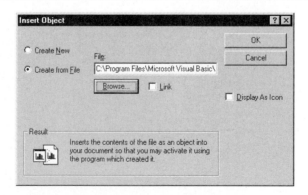

Figure 14.2 Dialog box for inserting contents of a file into an OLE Container control.

An Embedding Walkthrough Using Excel

1. Press Alt/**F**ile/**N**ew Project.

2. Click the OLE icon in the Toolbox and use the single-click-draw technique to create a large rectangle on the form.

3. The Insert Object dialog box appears. Double-click on "Microsoft Excel Worksheet" in the Object Type list.

   Excel will be invoked and you will be able to create a spreadsheet. (Most likely, the Excel menu bar will replace the Visual Basic menu bar. In some cases, the Excel menu bar will appear on the form just below the title bar.)

4. Enter data into cells as shown in the first three rows of the spreadsheet in Figure 14.3

5. Drag to select cells A1 through F3.

6. If you are using Excel 97, click Insert, click Chart, and then proceed to Step 8. If you are using Excel 7.0, click Insert, then Chart, and then On This Sheet.

7. (A new mouse pointer consisting of a thin plus sign and a small bar chart appears.) Move the mouse pointer to cell A5, drag to the bottom-right corner of the OLE Container control, and then release the left mouse button.

   A Chart Wizard dialog box appears.

8. Click on the Finish button.

   Your spreadsheet should be similar to the one in Figure 14.3.

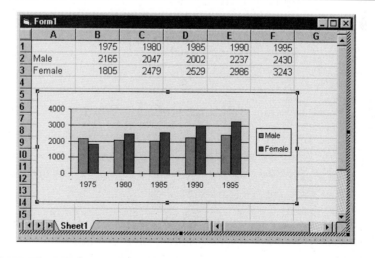

Figure 14.3 An Excel spreadsheet.

9. Click on the form to exit Excel.

   The values you created in Excel are now displayed in the OLE rectangle without any Excel embellishments. If needed, you can resize the OLE rectangle to show any hidden material.

10. Run the program.

11. Double-click on the OLE rectangle to reinvoke Excel.

12. Change the value in one of the cells and then click on any other cell.

    Notice that the change is reflected in the bar chart.

13. Click the End icon to end the program.

    Notice that the changes to the data and graph have been lost. They are permanently gone.

14. Add a command button to the form and caption it Save Sheet.

15. Double-click on the command button to open the Command1_Click event procedure code window.

16. Enter the following program lines into this code window:

```
Dim objExcel As Object
Set objExcel = OLE1.Object
objExcel.Application.Save "MySheet.xls"
Set objExcel = Nothing
```

    The first two lines of this code make the contents of OLE1 into an OLE Automation object.

17. Run the program, double-click on the OLE rectangle to invoke Excel, change the contents of one of the cells, and click on another cell.

18. Click on the Save Sheet command button.

19. Click the End icon to end the program.

    Again the changes to the data and graph have been lost. However, the saved file now can be used to recover the changes if you so desire. To do so, go to the SourceDoc property of OLE1, click on the ellipsis, type MYSHEET.XLS into the text box, click on the OK button, and click on Yes in the "Delete Current Embedded Object?" message box.

A Linking Walkthrough Using Word

1. Before starting Visual Basic, invoke Word, type in a few sentences, and save the document. In this walkthrough we assume that the document you have created now resides on drive A and is named MYWORK.DOC.

2. Invoke Visual Basic.

3. Click the OLE icon in the Toolbox and use the single-click-draw technique to create a large rectangle on the form.

4. Click on the "Create from File" option button, type A:\MYWORK.DOC into the text box, click the Link check box, and click on the OK button.

    The document saved in MYWORK. DOC is displayed in the OLE rectangle.

5. Run the program and double-click the OLE rectangle. The complete Word program is invoked and the document in MYWORK.DOC is displayed.

6. Make some changes to the document, and then press Alt/File/Save and Alt/File/Exit to save your changes and exit Word. The modified document is displayed in the OLE rectangle on the Visual Basic form.

7. End the program and display the form if it is hidden.

   Notice that the document in the OLE rectangle is the original document, not the modified version. Visual Basic maintains an image of this original document in the program to display at run time if it is unable to display the latest version of the data (document).

8. Run the program.

   The document is still the original version.

9. Double-click on the OLE rectangle to invoke Word.

   Notice that the document displayed is the modified version.

10. Exit back to Visual Basic and then end the Visual Basic program.

11. Double-click on the form and add the code

    ```
    Let Ole1.Action = 6  'Update OLE image
    ```

    to the Form_Load event procedure.

12. Run the program.

    Notice that Visual Basic has updated the document to the last version saved while in Word even though you have not yet accessed Word by double-clicking.

Comments

1. OLE requires a powerful computer to operate at a reasonable speed. It works best with a Pentium chip and at least 16 MB of RAM.

2. An embedded application in the container OLE1 can be made into an OLE Automation object by a pair of statements of the form

   ```
   Dim objVar As Object
   Set objVar = OLE1.Object
   ```

3. After an Excel spreadsheet has been opened as an object, data can be assigned to and read from a single cell with statements such as

   ```
   objExcel.Application.Cells(4, 2).Value = "49"
   Let num = objExcel.Application.Cells(1, 3).Value
   ```

   These statements can be replaced by the following statements that use the standard spreadsheet notation for cells.

   ```
   objExcel.Application.Range("B4").Value = "49"
   Let num = objExcel.Application.Range("C1").Value
   ```

4. A linked or embedded application can be activated by double-clicking on the OLE container. They can also be activated with the code

   ```
   Let OLE1.Action = 7
   ```

   and deactivated with the code

   ```
   Let OLE1.Action = 9
   ```

5. The OLE Automation function GetObject, which is similar to CreateObject, can be used to access existing Excel spreadsheets. For instance, if a worksheet resides in the root directory on a diskette in drive A and has the name EXPENSES.XLS, then the spreadsheet can be accessed with the pair of statements

```
Dim objExcel As Object
Set objExcel = GetObject("A:\EXPENSES.XLS")
```

6. Some other Word statements for use in OLE Automation are

```
objWord.FileOpen filespec        'Open the specified document
objWord.FontSize n               'Assigns the value n to the font size
objWord.StartOfLine              'Move the insertion point to the
                                 'beginning of the current line
objWord.EndOfLine                'Move the insertion point to the
                                 'end of the current line
objWord.StartOfDocument          'Move the insertion point to the
                                 'beginning of the document
objWord.EndOfDocument            'Move the insertion point to the
                                 'end of the document
objWord.FileSave                 'Save the current document
objWord.FileClose                'Close the current document
```

7. The following key combinations can be used to carry out tasks with an embedded Excel application:

Ctrl+;	Insert the date in the current cell
Alt+=	Sum continuous column of numbers containing the current cell
Ctrl+Z	Undo the last operation
Shift+F3	Invoke the Function Wizard
F7	Check spelling

8. The standard prefix for the name of an OLE container control is ole.

9. OLE replaces an earlier technology known as Dynamic Data Exchange (DDE) that was used to integrate applications into Visual Basic programs. DDE is slower and more difficult to use than OLE.

PRACTICE PROBLEM 14.1

1. Redo the "Linking Walkthrough Using Word", but do not click the Link check box in Step 4. What differences do you notice as you continue the walkthrough?

EXERCISES 14.1

Exercises 1 through 3 apply to a form containing a command button, a text box, and an OLE container (oleExcel) with an embedded Excel worksheet. Run the program, double-click oleExcel, enter numbers into some of the cells, and then click on cmdDisplay. What will appear in txtOutput? (*Note:* The first two lines of each event procedure make the contents of objExcel into an OLE Automation object.) If you are using Excel 97, insert "worksheets("Sheet1"). " before "Cells."

1.
```
Private Sub cmdDisplay_Click()
    Dim objExcel As Object
    Set objExcel = oleExcel.Object
    Dim n As Integer
    Dim sumVar As Integer
    Let sumVar = 0
    For n = 1 To 3
      Let sumVar = sumVar + objExcel.Cells(n, 1).Value
    Next n
    txtOutput.Text = sumVar
    Set objExcel = Nothing
End Sub
```

2.
```
Private Sub cmdDisplay_Click()
    Dim objExcel As Object
    Set objExcel = oleExcel.Object
    Dim strVar As String
    If objExcel.Application.Cells(1, 1) > objExcel.Cells(2, 1) Then
        Let strVar = "A1 is greater than A2."
      Else
        Let strVar = "A2 is less than or equal to A1."
    End If
    txtOutput.Text = strVar
    Set objExcel = Nothing
End Sub
```

3.
```
Private Sub cmdDisplay_Click()
    Dim objExcel As Object
    Set objExcel = oleExcel.Object
    Let objExcel.Application.Cells(25, 25).Formula = "=MAX(A1:A3)"
    Let txtOutput.Text = objExcel.Cells(25, 25).Value
    Set objExcel = Nothing
End Sub
```

4. Suppose the sequential file NUMBERS.TXT contains a sequence of numbers. Write an OLE Automation program that reads the numbers from the file and uses a spreadsheet to calculate their average. (**Note:** A function such as AVERAGE(C1:C5) averages the numbers in the specified block of cells.)

5. Write a program similar to Example 1 that allows you to input grades for three exams and then uses a spreadsheet to determine the average grade. (**Note:** A function such as AVERAGE(C1:C5) averages the numbers in the specified block of cells.)

6. Write an OLE Automation program to open the document created in Example 2 and insert "A Quotation by Oscar Wilde." at the beginning of the document. (**Note:** The statement objWord.Insert Chr(13) inserts a carriage return and line feed.)

7. Write an OLE Automation program to open the document created in Example 2, and add another paragraph to the end of the document. One possibility is "I always pass on good advice. It is the only thing to do with it. It is never of any use to oneself."

8. Write a program with a text box, two command buttons, and a word processor embedded in an OLE Container control. The program should use the word processor to correct the spelling of a sentence typed into the text box. When the first command button is clicked, the contents of the text box should be placed into the clipboard and the word processor activated. The user can place the sentence into the document with Ctrl+V, press F7 to invoke the spell checker, select the corrected sentence as a block, and press Ctrl+C to put the corrected sentence into the clipboard. When the second command button is pressed, the word processor should be deactivated and the contents of the clipboard should replace the contents of the text box.

9. Write a program with a form containing a command button, a text box, and an OLE container (oleExcel) with an embedded spreadsheet as in Figure 14.3. After you run the program, double-click oleExcel, enter the three grades, and then click on cmdDisplay, the semester grade should be displayed in the text box. The semester grade is obtained by throwing out the lowest grade and averaging the other two grades.

SOLUTIONS TO PRACTICE PROBLEMS 14.1

1. In Step 5, when the OLE rectangle is double-clicked, the complete version of Word is not invoked. Instead, the Standard and Formatting toolbars are overlaid in the middle of the screen. In Step 6, the document cannot be saved because the menu bar is not present, and neither clicking on the Save icon nor pressing Ctrl+S works.

2. With Word, some toolbars appeared on the screen. With Excel there were no toolbars.

14.2 ACCESSING THE INTERNET WITH VISUAL BASIC

What Is the Internet?

The Internet began in the late 1960s as a plan to link computers at scientific laboratories across the country so that researchers could share computer resources. This plan was funded by the Defense Department's Advanced Research Projects Agency (ARPA) and initially was known as ARPANET. Over time, many research institutions and universities connected to this network. Eventually, the National Science Foundation took over ARPANET and ultimately it became what we now know as the Internet. The past few years has seen an amazing amount of growth in this global network. It more than doubles in size every 6 months.

The Internet often is confused with one of its most popular components, the **World Wide Web** (WWW) or "the Web." The Internet is much more than the Web. It also consists of electronic mail (e-mail), file transfer (FTP), Usenet News, and remote login capabilities. E-mail allows people to send messages to one another over the Internet. FTP allows people to transfer files from one machine to another. This is often the preferred method of retrieving shareware or freeware programs over the Internet. Usenet is a large collection of electronic discussion groups called newsgroups. There are newsgroups dedicated to every topic imaginable. People can post messages that all members of the group can read and answer.

The World Wide Web is made up of documents called pages, which contain pictures and text. The pages are accessed through programs called **browsers**. The best known Web browsers are Netscape, Mosaic, Lynx, and Internet Explorer. Web pages usually include links to other pages. These links are often set apart from the regular text by using boldface, underlining, or color. When you click on a link, you call up the page referred to by that link. This technology for connecting documents is called **hypertext**.

To access an initial Web page, you must specify an address called a Uniform Resource Locator (**URL**). You can do this by typing in a URL (or Locator) text box found toward the top of your browser or by typing in the dialog box that appears when selecting the Open command from the File menu or clicking the Open button in the toolbar.

A Web Browser Walkthrough

1. Connect to the Internet either through your commercial service provider or by using your school's network computers.

2. Start up a Web browser such as Netscape, Mosaic, Lynx, or Internet Explorer.

3. In the Location or URL text box toward the top of the browser, type in http://www.whitehouse.gov

4. Press Enter.

   After a little wait, you will see the White House Web page loaded into your browser.

5. Click on one of the highlighted or underlined phrases (links) in the document.

   The page associated with this link will load. For instance, if you click on "The President & Vice President:" you will see pictures of them and their wives along with information on how to send e-mail to them.

6. Click on some other links to see what pages are brought up.

7. When you are through exploring the White House page, try other URL addresses such as:

Microsoft's Visual Basic Page	http://www.microsoft.com/vbasic
Carl and Gary's Visual Basic Page	http://www.apexsc.com/vb
Prentice-Hall's Home Page	http://www.prenhall.com

The remainder of this section is devoted to using Visual Basic to create our own Web browser. The requirements for this task are as follows:

1. Windows 95 or Windows NT 3.51 (or later).

2. A modem—the faster, the better.

3. A Windows 95 TCP/IP stack, usually referred to as a Winsock. (If you are using an Internet connection through your school, it almost certainly meets this requirement. If you are using a dialup connection from home, the Microsoft hookup to the network that comes with Windows 95 will work.)

4. Microsoft Internet Explorer 3.0 (or higher) must be installed.

To Add the Web Browrser Control to Your Visual Basic Toolbox

1. Invoke Visual Basic.

2. Press Ctrl+T to invoke the Components dialog box.

3. Click the check box next to Microsoft Internet Controls.

4. Click the OK button.

The Web Browser icon should now appear in your toolbox.

EXAMPLE 1   The following program creates a simplified Web browser. (Before running the program, be sure you are connected to the Internet as discussed above.) The primary task of the program, accessing the Web, is accomplished with the single statement

```
WebBrowser1.Navigate(txtURL.Text)
```

The On Error Resume Next statement specifies that when a run-time error occurs, control goes to the statement immediately following the statement where the error occurred where execution continues. This statement is needed because the LocationURL of the Web Browser control can easily return an error and crash the program. (For instance, this would happen if the intended web site was down.)

After you run the program as specified in what follows, click on one of the links. **Note:** The home page of Internet Explorer will also be the home page of the Web Browser control.

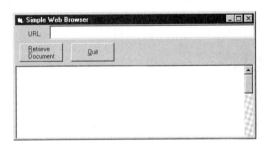

Object	Property	Setting
frm14_2_1	Caption	Simple Web Browser
txtURL	Text	(blank)
cmdRetrieve	Caption	&Retrieve Document
	Default	True
cmdQuit	Caption	&Quit
lblURL	Caption	URL:
WebBrowser1		

```
Private Sub Form_Load()
    WebBrowser1.GoHome              'Calls up Internet Explorer's home page
End Sub

Private Sub cmdRetrieve_Click()
  Rem Calls up the URL typed in the text box
  WebBrowser1.Navigate(txtURL.Text)
End Sub

Private Sub Form_Resize()
  Rem Resizes the WebBrowser control with the Form,
  Rem as long as the form is not minimized.
  Rem occurs when the Form is first displayed
```

```
    If frm14_2_1.WindowState <> 1 Then
        WebBrowser1.Width = frm14_2_1.ScaleWidth
        WebBrowser1.Height = frm14_2_1.ScaleHeight - 740 'Subtract toolbar height
    End If
End Sub

Private Sub WebBrowser1_NavigateComplete (ByVal URL As String) Complete
    Rem Is activated when the HTML control finishes retrieving the
    Rem requested Web page.
    Rem Updates the text box to display the URL of the current page.
    txtURL.Text = WebBrowser1.LocationURL
End Sub

Private Sub cmdQuit_Click()
    End
End Sub
```

[Run. The Internet Explorer's home page will be displayed. Type http://www.whitehouse.gov into the text box, and click on the "Retrieve Document" command button.]

EXAMPLE 2   The following enhancement of Example 1 adds a label that shows the status of the Web Browser control, a command button that returns you back to the most recently accessed page, and a command button that displays the Prentice-Hall web site. (The picture of the Prentice-Hall trademark is contained in the Pictures directory of the accompanying CD.)

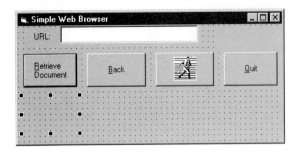

Object	Property	Setting
frm14_2_2	Caption	Simple Web Browser
lblURL	Caption	URL:
txtURL	Text	(blank)
lblStatus	Caption	(blank)
cmdRetrieve	Caption	&Retrieve Document
cmdBack	Caption	&Back
cmdPH	Caption	(none)
	Style	Graphical
	Picture	PHICON.BMP
cmdQuit	Caption	&Quit
WebBrowser1		

Add the following code to the program in Example 1.

```
Private Sub WebBrowser1_StatusTextChange(ByVal Text As String)
  Rem Event is called whenever the address of the page being
  Rem displayed changes. The address is assigned to the string Text.
  Let lblStatus.Caption = Text
End Sub

Private Sub cmdBack_Click()
  WebBrowser1.GoBack    'Return to the previous web site or page
End Sub

Private Sub cmdPH_Click()
  WebBrowser1.Navigate ("http://www.prenhall.com")
End Sub
```

[Run. After the Internet Explore home page appears, click on the command button with the picture of the Prentice-Hall trademark.]

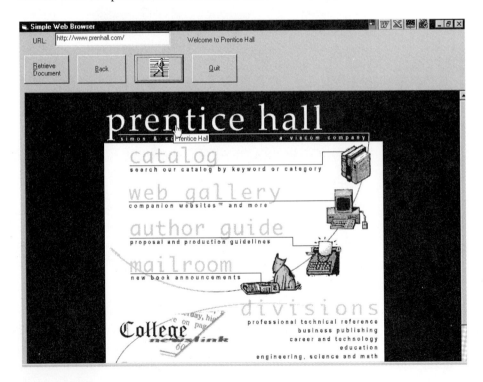

Comments

1. The abbreviation HTTP stands for HyperText Transmission Protocol.

2. If you do not have a copy of Internet Explorer 3 (or later), you can download it from http:\\www.microsoft.com.

3. Some additional properties of the Web Browser control are

LocationURL	Gives the URL of the current page.
LocationName	Gives the title of the current page.
Busy	Has the value True if the control is downloading a file or navigating to a new location.

4. Some additional methods of the Web Browser control are

GoForward	Undoes the most recent GoBack method.
GoSearch	Goes to the user's web searching page.
Stop	Cancels the current operation of the control.

5. Some additional events of the Web Browser control are

BeforeNavigate	Triggered right before the control moves to a new location.
ProgressChange	Triggered periodically as the downloading continues.
DownloadComplete	Triggered when the download is complete, halter, or failed.

6. If a file on your disk is an HTML document, you can view it as a web page with the statement `WebBrowser1.Navigate "filespec"`.

7. Three good books about the Internet are

C. L. Clark, *A Student's Guide to the Internet*, Prentice Hall, Inc. 1996.

B. P. Kehoe, *Zen and the Art of the Internet*, Prentice Hall, Inc. 1996.

K. Hafner and M. Lyon, *Where Wizards Stay Up Late: The Origins of the Internet*, Simon & Schuster, 1996.

PRACTICE PROBLEM 14.2

1. Can a Web browser really be written with just one line of code?

EXERCISES 14.2

1. What is the difference between the Internet and the World Wide Web?

2. Suppose the sequential file CENSORED.TXT contains a list of URLs that you do not want accessed. Modify Example 1 so that the user will not be able to visit these Web pages.

3. Modify the program in Example 2 to contain a Forward button.

4. Modify the program in Example 2 to inform the user when the downloading of the requested web page is complete.

5. Implement a history list for the Web browser of Example 2. This list should be displayed in a list box and should contain the URL addresses of the last ten web addresses visited. The user should be able to revisit one of these 10 sites by double-clicking on the appropriate address.

6. Add a What's Cool list of interesting URL addresses to the Web browser from Example 2. One such list is stored in the file COOL.TXT on the CD accompanying this book. When the program is loaded, the contents of the file should be placed into a list box. The user should be able to visit one of the interesting sites by double-clicking on its address in the list box.

7. Add a BookMarks feature to the Web browser in Example 2. Bookmarks are a customized list of addresses that you frequently use. Create a sequential file called BKMS.TXT containing a few addresses. When you load the program, the contents of BKMS.TXT should be displayed in a list box. The user should be able to visit one of these sites by double-clicking on its address in the list box. Also, the user should be able to create a new bookmark by adding the address in the text box to both the list box and the sequential file.

8. Enhance the program in Exercise 7 to allow the user to delete a bookmark.

9. Type the following text into Windows Notepad and save it with the name WELCOME.HTM. Then write a program to view this file as a Web page.

```
<BODY>
<I> Welcome </I> to <B>Visual Basic 5.0 </B>
</BODY>
```

10. Experiment with the program in Exercise 9 to determine the values of the LocationURL and LocationName properties of the Web Browser control when the control is looking at an HTML file on a disk.

SOLUTION TO PRACTICE PROBLEM 14.2

1. Yes. If the program in Example 1 is simplified to consist solely of the procedure cmdRetrieve_Click(), it will still browse the Web.

14.3 WEB PAGE PROGRAMMING WITH VBSCRIPT

Note: This section requires that the Internet Explorer Web browser be installed on your computer.

Web browsers display Web pages created as text files, called HTML[1] documents. The text files can be written with Notepad or any other word processor. VBScript is a subset of the Visual Basic programming language that is used to make Web pages interactive. In this section, we learn how to create Web pages with HTML, add controls to Web pages, and write VBScript code that manipulates the controls.

HTML

Here is a typical line in an HTML document.

    <B>This sentence will be printed in bold.</B>

---

1 HTML stands for HyperText Markup Language

The items <B> and </B> are called **tags**. Here the letter B stands for Bold and the pair of tags tells the browser to display everything between the two tags in boldface. The first tag is called the **begin tag** and the second tag is called the **end tag**. Most tags come in pairs in which the second tag differs from the first only in the addition of a slash (/). The combination of pair of tags and the data characters enclosed by them is called an **element**. In general, a tag defines a format to apply or an action to take. A pair of tags tells the browser what to do with the text between the tags. Some pairs of tags and their effect on the text between them are as follows.

<I>, </I>	Display the text in italics
<U>, </U>	Display the text underlined.
<Hn>, </Hn>	Display the text in a size n header ($1 \leq n \leq 6$)
<BIG>, </BIG>	Display the text one font size larger.
<SMALL>, </SMALL>	Display the text one font size smaller.
<CENTER>, </CENTER>	Center the text.
<TITLE>, </TITLE>	Place the text in the Web page title bar.

An example of a tag that does not come in pairs is <P>, which tells the browser to start a new paragraph and inserting a blank line. A similar tag is <BR> which inserts a carriage return and a line feed to start a new line. The lines

```
Line One
Line Two
```

in an HTML document will be displayed as

```
Line One Line Two
```

in the Web page, since browsers ignore the blank space at the ends of lines. On the other hand,

```
Line One <BR> Line Two
```

will be displayed as

```
Line One
Line Two
```

and

```
Line One <P> Line Two
```

will be displayed as

```
Line One

Line Two
```

Sometimes the begin tag of a pair of tags contains additional information needed to carry out the task. The pair of tags <A HREF=*address*> and </A> create a hyperlink to the Web page with the specified address and the text between the tags underlined. For instance, the element

<A HREF="http://www.prenhall.com"> This is a link to Prentice-Hall.</A>

in an HTML document will be displayed by the browser as

This is a link to Prentice-Hall.

When you click anywhere on this line, the browser will move to the Prentice-Hall Web site.

HTML documents consist of two parts, called the head and the body, that are delineated by the pairs of tags <HEAD>, </HEAD> and <BODY>, </BODY>. In addition, the entire HTML document is usually enclosed in the pair of tags <HTML>, </HTML>. The HTML document in Figure 14.4 produces the Web page shown in Figure 14.5.

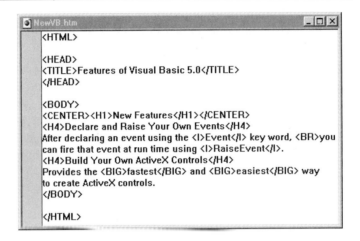

Figure 14.4 HTML document

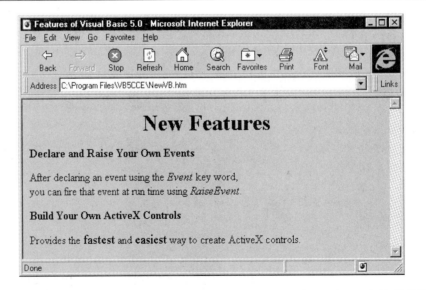

Figure 14.5 Web page

Placing ActiveX controls in HTML documents

With Internet Explorer, ActiveX controls, such as text boxes, command buttons, and user-built controls, can be placed on Web pages. For instance, the element

```
<OBJECT ID="cmdPush" WIDTH=115 HEIGHT=49
 CLASSID="CLSID:D7053240-CE69-11CD-A777-00DD01143C57">
  <PARAM NAME="Caption" VALUE="Push Me">
  <PARAM NAME="Size" VALUE="3037;1291">
  <PARAM NAME="FontCharSet" VALUE="0">
  <PARAM NAME="FontPitchAndFamily" VALUE="2">
  <PARAM NAME="ParagraphAlign" VALUE="3">
  <PARAM NAME="FontWeight" VALUE="0">
</OBJECT>
```

tells Internet Explorer to place a command button (named cmdPush) on the Web page. The string beginning with CLSID is the control's identification number in the Windows registry. The PARAM tags set properties of the control. For instance, the first PARAM tag sets the caption of the command button to "Push Me."

Creating the OBJECT element is so cumbersome that Microsoft has developed a tool, called the ActiveX Control Pad, that makes placing a control on a Web page nearly as easy as placing a control on a Visual Basic form. The ActiveX Control Pad is sometimes included with Internet Explorer. Also, the ActiveX Control Pad can be downloaded separately from the Microsoft Web site. (See Comment 8.)

The ActiveX Control Pad is actually a word processor that looks and acts much like Notepad. The following walkthrough uses the ActiveX Control Pad to create a Web page containing a text box and a command button.

1. Click the Start button on the Windows taskbar, point to Programs, point to Microsoft ActiveX Control Pad, and then click on Microsoft ActiveX Control Pad in the final pop-up list. The window that appears (see Figure 14.6) contains a template for an HTML document.

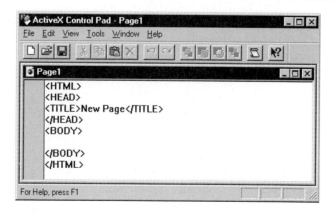

Figure 14.6 ActiveX Control Pad

2. In the Title element, replace "New Page" with "My First Web Page".

3. Just below the begin Body tag, type the following lines.

```
<BIG>"Hello"</BIG>
<P>Type your first name into the box.
```

4. Press Alt/Edit/Insert ActiveX Control. (An Insert ActiveX dialog box appears containing a list of all available controls.)

5. Scroll down the list and double-click on Microsoft Forms 2.0 TextBox. (Two windows appear. One window, titled Edit ActiveX Control, contains a text box and is similar to a Visual Basic form. The other window is an abbreviated text box Properties window)

6. Scroll down the Properties window and click on ID. (The default setting TextBox1 appears next to ID and in the settings text box at the top of the Properties window. The ID property is the same as Visual Basic's Name property.)

7. Replace the words in the settings text box with txtFirstName and click on the Apply button.

8. Go to the Edit ActiveX Control window and make the text box a little larger.

9. Close the windows by clicking on their X buttons. (An OBJECT element for the text box has been added to the ActiveX Control Pad.)

10. Repeat Steps 4 through 9 to add a command button OBJECT element. (Select Microsoft Forms 2.0 Command button, give it the ID cmdShow, and the caption "Show Greeting.")

11. Press Alt/Save As, select a location and name (with extension htm) for the file, and click on the Save button.

12. Invoke Internet Explorer. (There is no need to actually connect to the internet via a phone line.)

13. Type the filespec for your saved HTML page into the address box and press Enter. (The window in Figure 14.7 will appear.)

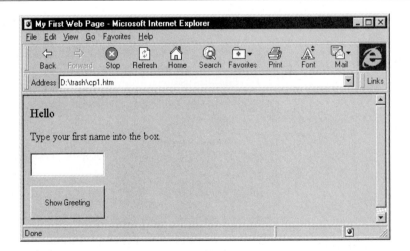

Figure 14.7

14. Feel free to type into the text box and click on the command button. Nothing will happen since no code has yet been written for them.

Activating a Web Page with VBScript

The VBScript programming language is an offshoot of Visual Basic. It has most of the familiar features, such as If blocks, Do loops, Select Case blocks, procedures, and arrays. However, VBScript has some differences from Visual Basic. For instance, all variables are of type Variant and are declared with a statement of the form Dim *variableName*. Whereas in Visual Basic the keyword Let is optional in assignment statements, in VBScript the keyword Let must be omitted. Also, the words Private and Public cannot be used in the heading lines of procedures. See Comment 7. Some additional differences between Visual Basic and VBScript are listed in Comments 5 and 6.

Code is written into a SCRIPT element with begin tag

```
<SCRIPT LANGUAGE="VBSCRIPT">
```

and end tag </SCRIPT>. Let's continue the walkthrough above by adding some code to the HTML document created in the walkthrough. (If you have already closed the HTML document, you can bring it back into the ActiveX Control Pad with Alt/File/Open.)

15. Type the following code into the body element of the document, say just below the OBJECT elements, and then Save the document.

```
<SCRIPT LANGUAGE="VBSCRIPT">
Sub cmdShow_Click()
 Dim nom
 nom = txtFirstName.text
 MsgBox "Greetings " & nom
End Sub
</SCRIPT>
```

16. Return to Internet Explorer and look at the revised Web page. (If you have not changed the Address since the walkthrough, just click on the Refresh icon to load the revised HTML page. Otherwise type in its filespec and press the Enter key.)

17. Type your name, say David, into the text box and click on the command button. A message box will pop up with the message "Greetings David".

Comments

1. You can obtain extensive information about HTML and VBScript from the Help menu in the ActiveX Control Pad. (If the documentation for VBScript is not present on your computer, you can either download the documentation or read it online at http://microsoft.com/vbscript.)

2. HTML tags are not case sensitive. For instance, <b> has the same effect as <B>.

3. A TITLE element must placed inside the HEAD portion of an HTML document.

4. VBScript programs can contain code that is not in any procedure. If so, this code is executed by Internet Explorer as soon as the Web page is displayed. It is analogous to Visual Basic code found in the Form_Load event procedure.

5. Some features of Visual Basic that are not available in VBScript are the Format function, Timer function, On Error Goto statement, arrays declared with lower bound $\neq 0$, line labels, collections, and picture box controls.

6. If i is the index of a For...Next loop, in Visual Basic the final statement should be Next i. In VBScript, the i must be dropped from the final statement.

7. The keywords Private and Public can be used in Sub statements with Internet Explorer 4.0 and VBScript 2.0. However, they cannot be used with earlier versions.

8. To download the ActiveX Control Pad, enter the address

```
http://www.microsoft.com/workshop/author/cpad
```

into your browser and follow the directions.

9. You can place your own custom-built ActiveX controls into an HTML document provided the control has been compiled into an ocx file. However, in order to use these controls you will have to ease Internet Explorer's safety level. To invoke the lowest level of security, select Options from Internet Explorer's View menu, click on the Security tab, click on the Safety Level button, and select None. **Note:** Before you actually connect to the internet, reset the safety level to High.

10. Visual Basic allows you to place controls exactly where you want on a form. The ActiveX Control Pad has a device, called an HTML Layout, that lets you achieve the same result. An HTML Layout is actually an ActiveX control that acts as a container for other controls. It has a grid like a form that allow for precision alignment. The steps for creating an HTML Layout are as follows.

   (a) From the ActiveX Control Pad, click on New HTML Layout in the File menu. (A form-like window and a square toolbar containing about a dozen icons will appear.)
   (b) Place a control on the Layout with the click and drag method. To set the properties of a control in the Layout, double-click on the control to produce a Properties window.
   (c) After all the controls have been drawn and their properties set, save the Layout (in an ALX file).
   (d) To insert the Layout into an HTML document, position the cursor at the insertion point, and click on Insert HTML Layout in the Edit menu to open a file-selection dialog box. Select the location and name of the file, and then press the Open button. (An OBJECT element will be created for the Layout.)
   (e) Whenever you want to alter the Layout, place the cursor anywhere inside the OBJECT element and select Edit HTML Layout from the Edit menu.

PRACTICE PROBLEMS 14.3

What is the effect of each of the following portions of an HTML document.

1. <I>The <B>future</B> isn't what it used to be.</I>

```
2. <SCRIPT LANGUAGE="VBSCRIPT">
   Dim word
   word = "untie!"
   Call Join(word)
   Sub Join(word)
     MsgBox "Bad spellers of the world, " & word
   End Sub
   </SCRIPT>
```

EXERCISES 14.3

In Exercises 1 through 4, determine what will be displayed on the Web page by the portion of the HTML document shown.

1. <I>Keep cool,</I> <B>but don't freeze.</B>
Found on a jar of mayonnaise.

2. So little time<P>and so little to do.

3. Would you like to visit the <A HREF="http://www.prenhall.com" >Prentice-Hall</A> Web site?

4. Talk is cheap because <BIG>supply </BIG>exceeds demand.

In Exercises 5 through 8, find the errors.

5.
```
<SCRIPT LANGUAGE="VBSCRIPT">
Sub cmdShow Click()
  Dim nom
  nom = txtFirstName.text
  MsgBox "<B>Greetings </B>" & nom
End Sub
</SCRIPT>
```

6.
```
<SCRIPT LANGUAGE="VBSCRIPT">
Sub cmdShow_Click()
  MsgBox "Hello"
End Sub

<OBJECT ID="cmdPush" WIDTH=115 HEIGHT=49
CLASSID="CLSID:D7053240-CE69-11CD-A777-00DD01143C57">
  <PARAM NAME="Caption" VALUE="Push Me">
  <PARAM NAME="Size" VALUE="3037;1291">
  <PARAM NAME="FontCharSet" VALUE="0">
</OBJECT>

</SCRIPT>
```

7.
```
<SCRIPT>
Sub cmdShow_Click()
  MsgBox "Keep cool"
End Sub
</SCRIPT>
```

8. Start slow <i> and taper off.<i>

9. Create a Web page that displays the date and time in labels as soon as the Web page appears. Use the functions Date and Time.

10. Create a Web page that displays a message containing "Welcome to my Web page." as soon as the Web page appears.

11. Create a Web page containing a text box, a command button, and a label. Instruct the user to enter a word into the text box and push the command button to see the word written backwards.

12. Create a Web page with a text box, a command button, and a list box. Each time the user presses the button, the contents of the text box should be placed in the list in alphabetical order.

13. Table 14.1 gives the number of colleges in each of the New England states. Write a Web page containing a label and a list box that displays the six states. When the user clicks on one of the states, the number of colleges in the state should be displayed in the label. The Web page should contain instructions for the user.

State	Colleges	State	Colleges
Connecticut	42	New Hampshire	30
Maine	31	Rhode Island	14
Massachusetts	117	Vermont	22

Table 14.1 Colleges in New England

14. Create a Web page with a text box, a command button, and a label. The user should be instructed to type the name of one of the New England states into the text box and then press the command button. When the command button is pressed, the number of colleges in the state should be displayed. (Use the data in Table 14.1)

15. Create a Web page having the same design and results as the program in Example 1 of Section 7.5. (**Note:** replace the picture box with a label.) Use an HTML Layout. Also, add text that instructs the user on how to use the Web page.

16. Create a Web page having the same design and program as Example 3 of Section 11.1. Use an HTML Layout.

17. (This exercise assumes that you have compiled the CheckDeposit ActiveX control discussed in Section 13.4.) Create a Web page that can be used to record checks to be deposited into a checking account and automatically readjust the balance in the account.

SOLUTIONS TO PRACTICE PROBLEMS 14.3

1. *The **future** isn't what it used to be.*

2. As soon as the Web page appears, a message box containing the statement "Bad spellers of the world, untie!" will appear.

Chapter 14
Summary

1. OLE, a technology developed by Microsoft, gives Visual Basic access to other applications.

2. OLE Automation allows you to control other applications with Visual Basic code. The other application is declared as an object with the Set statement and CreateObject function.

3. Other applications can be embedded in or linked to a form with the OLE Container control.

4. The WebBrowser control can be used to create a browser for the World Wide Web.

5. The document-formatting language used by Web browsers is called *HTML*. *Tags* are used to mark up text with display instructions. The combination of a pair of tags and the text enclosed is called an *element*.

6. The ActiveX Control Pad is used to place text, controls, and programs into HTML documents

7. *VBScript* is a subset of Visual Basic that is used to make Web pages interactive.

Appendix A

ANSI Values

ANSI Value	Character	ANSI Value	Character	ANSI Value	Character
000	(null)	040	(	080	P
001	□	041	)	081	Q
002	□	042	*	082	R
003	□	043	+	083	S
004	□	044	,	084	T
005	□	045	−	085	U
006	□	046	.	086	V
007	□	047	/	087	W
008	□	048	0	088	X
009	(tab)	049	1	089	Y
010	(line feed)	050	2	090	Z
011	□	051	3	091	[
012	□	052	4	092	\
013	(carriage return)	053	5	093	]
014	□	054	6	094	^
015	□	055	7	095	_
016	□	056	8	096	`
017	□	057	9	097	a
018	□	058	:	098	b
019	□	059	;	099	c
020	□	060	<	100	d
021	□	061	=	101	e
022	□	062	>	102	f
023	□	063	?	103	g
024	□	064	@	104	h
025	□	065	A	105	i
026	□	066	B	106	j
027	□	067	C	107	k
028	□	068	D	108	l
029	□	069	E	109	m
030	□	070	F	110	n
031	□	071	G	111	o
032		072	H	112	p
033	!	073	I	113	q
034	"	074	J	114	r
035	#	075	K	115	s
036	$	076	L	116	t
037	%	077	M	117	u
038	&	078	N	118	v
039	'	079	O	119	w

ANSI Value	Character	ANSI Value	Character	ANSI Value	Character
120	x	166	¦	212	Ô
121	y	167	§	213	Õ
122	z	168	¨	214	Ö
123	{	169	©	215	×
124	|	170	ª	216	Ø
125	}	171	«	217	Ù
126	~	172	¬	218	Ú
127	□	173	-	219	Û
128	□	174	®	220	Ü
129	□	175	¯	221	Ý
130	‚	176	°	222	þ
131	ƒ	177	±	223	ß
132	„	178	²	224	à
133	…	179	³	225	á
134	†	180	´	226	â
135	‡	181	µ	227	ã
136	ˆ	182	¶	228	ä
137	‰	183	·	229	å
138	Š	184	¸	230	æ
139	‹	185	¹	231	ç
140	Œ	186	º	232	è
141	□	187	»	233	é
142	□	188	¼	234	ê
143	□	189	½	235	ë
144	□	190	¾	236	ì
145	'	191	¿	237	í
146	'	192	À	238	î
147	"	193	Á	239	ï
148	"	194	Â	240	õ
149	•	195	Ã	241	ñ
150	–	196	Ä	242	ò
151	—	197	Å	243	ó
152	~	198	Æ	244	ô
153	™	199	Ç	245	õ
154	š	200	È	246	ö
155	›	201	É	247	÷
156	œ	202	Ê	248	ø
157	□	203	Ë	249	ù
158	□	204	Ì	250	ú
159	Ÿ	205	Í	251	û
160		206	Î	252	ü
161	¡	207	Ï	253	ý
162	¢	208	Ð	254	þ
163	£	209	Ñ	255	ÿ
164	¤	210	Ò		
165	¥	211	Ó		

Appendix B

How To

HOW TO: Install, Invoke, and Exit Visual Basic

A. Install the Control Creation Edition of Visual Basic

1. Place the CD accompanying this book into your CD drive.
2. From the Windows Desktop, double-click on My Computer.
3. (A window showing the different disk drives will appear.) Double-click on the icon containing a picture of a CD (along with a drive) and labeled "Cce" (followed by a drive letter).
4. (A new window appears.) Double-click on the icon labeled Vb5ccein.exe in the new window.
5. (The following message appears. "Would you like to install Visual Basic 5.0 Control Creation Edition? You will be prompted for an install directory. This application requires Microsoft Windows 95 or greater, or else Microsoft Windows NT 4.0 or greater.") Click on the Yes button.
6. (A license agreement appears.) Click on the Yes button to signify that you accept the terms of the agreement.
7. (You will be shown a list of the folders and files on your hard drive, and you will be asked "Where you would like to copy the Visual Basic 5.0 CCE files?") We recommend that you use the default location C:\Program Files\VB5CCE.
8. (The following statement will appear. "The folder C:\Program Files\VB5CCE does not exist. Do you want to create it?") Click on the Yes button.
9. (After little wait, the following message will appear. "VB5.0 Control Creation installation complete.") Click on the OK button.
10. Return to My Computer and double-click on the file Ccehelp.exe in the Help folder of the CD to install the Visual Basic help files.
11. (Optional) The DOCS folder on the CD contains six programs which install extensive (32 MB) documentation about Visual Basic. Most of the material is not relevant to the topics covered in this textbook. To install some of the documentation, return to My Computer and double-click on one of the files.
12. Close the My Computer window and any other related windows that are open by clicking on the X buttons in their upper-right corners.
13. We recommend that you create a shortcut icon to invoke Visual Basic. This can be accomplished with the following steps.
    a. From the Windows desktop, position the mouse pointer over a blank spot and press the right mouse button.
    b. (A pop-up menu will appear.) Point to New and then click on Shortcut in the second pop-up menu that appears.
    c. (A dialog box will appear.) Type in the location and name "C:\Program Files\VB5CCE\VB5CCE.EXE."

    d. Click on the Next button.

    e. (A dialog box requesting a name will appear.) Type in your choice of name, such as VB5CCE.

    f. Click on the Finish button.

B. Install the Learning, Professional, or Enterprise Editions of Visual Basic.

1. Place the CD containing the software into your CD drive.
2. From the Windows Desktop, double-click on My Computer.
3. (A window showing the different disk drives will appear.) Double-click on the icon containing a picture of a CD and having a label beginning "VB50."
4. Double-click on the Setup folder.
5. Double-click on Setup.
6. Follow the directions given by the setup process.

C. Invoke Visual Basic after installation.

1. Click the Start button.
2. Point to Programs.
3. Point to Microsoft Visual Basic 5.0.
4. Point to Visual Basic 5.0.
5. Click on Visual Basic Control Creation Edition or similar name.

D. Exit Visual Basic.

1. Press the Esc key
2. Press Alt/F/X.
3. If an unsaved program is present, Visual Basic will prompt you about saving it.

Note: In many situations, Step 1 is not needed.

HOW TO: Manage Programs

A. Run a program from Visual Basic.

1. Click on the Start icon (right arrowhead).

    or

1. Press F5.

    or

1. Press Alt/R and make a selection from the Run menu.

B. Save the current program on a disk.

1. Press Alt/F/V [or click the Save Project icon (shows a diskette) on the Toolbar].
2. Fill in the requested information. Do not give an extension as part of the project name or the file name. Two files will be created —one with extension .VBP and the other with extension .FRM. The .VBP file holds a list of files related to the project. The .FRM file actually holds the program.

Note: After a program has been saved once, updated versions can be saved with the same filenames by pressing Alt/F/V. Alt/F/E is used to save the program with new filenames.

C. Begin a new program.

　　1. Press Alt/F/N.
　　2. If an unsaved program is present, Visual Basic will prompt you about saving it.

D. Open a program stored on a disk.

　　1. Press Alt/F/O [or click the Open Project icon (shows an open folder) on the Toolbar].
　　2. Click on one of the two tabs, Existing or Recent.
　　3. If you selected Existing, choose a folder for the "Look in:" box, type a filename into the "File name:" box, and press the Enter key. Alternatively, double-click on one of the filenames displayed in the large box in the middle of the dialog box.
　　4. If you selected Recent, double-click on one or the files in the list.

Note 1: (In Steps 3 and 4, if an unsaved program is present, Visual Basic will prompt you about saving it.)

Note 2: The form for the project may not appear, but can be accessed through the Project Explorer window.

E. Use the Project Explorer.

Note: Just below the Project Explorer title bar are three icons (View Code, View Object, and Toggle Folders), and below them is the List window. At any time, one item in the List window is selected.

　　1. Click on View Code to see the code associated with the selected item.
　　2. Click on View Object to see the Object (usually the form) associated with the selected item.

F. Display the form associated with a program.

　　1. Press Alt/V/B.

　　or

　　1. Press Shift+F7.

　　or

　　1. Press Alt/V/P to activate the Project Explorer window.
　　2. Click on the View Object button.

HOW TO: Use the Editor

A. Mark a section of text as a block.

　　1. Move the cursor to the beginning or end of the block.
　　2. Hold down a Shift key and use the direction keys to highlight a block of text.
　　3. Release the Shift key.

　　or

　　1. Move the mouse to the beginning or end of the block.
　　2. Hold down the left mouse button and move the mouse to the other end of the block.
　　3. Release the left mouse button.

Note 1: To unblock text, press a direction key or click outside the block.

Note 2: To select a word, double-click on it. To select a line, move the mouse pointer just far enough into the left margin so that the pointer changes, and then single-click there.

B. Delete a line of a program.

1. Move the cursor to the line.
2. Press Ctrl+Y.

   or

1. Mark the line as a block. (See item A of this section.)
2. Press Alt/E/T or press Ctrl+X.

Note: In the preceding maneuvers, the line is placed in the clipboard and can be retrieved by pressing Ctrl+V. To delete the line without placing it in the clipboard, mark it as a block and press Del.

C. Move a line within the Code window.

1. Move the cursor to the line and press Ctrl+Y.
2. Move the cursor to the target location.
3. Press Ctrl+V.

D. Use the clipboard to move or duplicate statements.

1. Mark the statements as a block.
2. Press Ctrl+X to delete the block and place it into the clipboard. Or, press Ctrl+C to place a copy of the block into the clipboard.
3. Move the cursor to the location where you desire to place the block.
4. Press Ctrl+V to place a copy of the text from the clipboard at the cursor.

E. Search for specific text in the program.

1. Press Alt/E/F or Ctrl+F.
2. Type sought-after text into the rectangle.
3. Select desired options if different from the defaults.
4. Press the Enter key.
5. To repeat the search, press Find Next or press Cancel and then F3.

F. Search and change.

1. Press Alt/E/E or Ctrl+H.
2. Type sought-after text into first rectangle.
3. Press Tab.
4. Type replacement text into second rectangle.
5. Select desired options if different from the defaults.
6. Press the Enter key.
7. Press Replace to make the change or press Replace All to make all such changes.

G. Cancel a change.

1. Press Alt/E/U to undo the last change made to a line.

HOW TO: Get Help

A. Obtain information about a Visual Basic topic.

    1. Press Alt/H/M.
    2. Click on the Index tab and follow the instructions.
    3. To display a topic, double-click on it.
    4. If a second lists pops up, double-click on it.

B. View the syntax and purpose of a Visual Basic keyword.

    1. Type the word into a Code window.
    2. Place the cursor on, or just following, the keyword.
    3. Press F1.

C. Display an ANSI table.

    1. Press Alt/H/M and click on the Index tab.
    2. Type ANSI and press the Enter key.
    3. To move between the displays for ANSI characters 0-127 and 128-255, click on "See Also," and then click on the Display button.

D. Obtain a list of Visual Basic's reserved words.

    1. Press Alt/H/M.
    2. Type "keywords," press the down-arrow key, and double-click on a category of keywords from the list below the blue bar.

E. Obtain a list of shortcut keys.

    1. Press Alt/H/M and click on the Contents tab.
    2. Double-click on the Additional Information book.
    3. Double-click on the Keyboard Guide book.
    4. Double-click on one of the collections of shortcut keys.

F. Obtain information about a control.

    1. Click on the control at design time.
    2. Press F1.

G. Exit Help.

    1. Press Esc.

HOW TO: Manipulate a Dialog Box

A. Use a dialog box.

A dialog box contains three types of items: rectangles (text boxes), option lists, and command buttons. An option list is a sequence of option buttons of the form ○ *option* or ☐ *option*.

    1. Move from item to item with the Tab key. (The movement is from left to right and top to bottom. Use Shift+Tab to reverse the direction.)
    2. Inside a rectangle, either type in the requested information or use the direction keys to make a selection.
    3. In an option list, an option button of the form ○ *option* can be activated with the direction keys. A dot inside the circle indicates that the option has been activated.

4. In an option list, an option button of the form ☐ *option* can be activated or deactivated by pressing the space bar. An X or ✓ inside the square indicates that the option has been activated.
5. A highlighted command button is invoked by pressing the Enter key.

B. Cancel a dialog box

1. Press the Esc key.

or

1. Press the Tab key until the command button captioned "Cancel" is highlighted and then press the Enter key.

HOW TO: Manage Menus

A. Open a pull-down menu.

1. Click on the menu name.

or

1. Press Alt.
2. Press the first letter of the name of the menu. Alternatively, use the Right Arrow key to move the highlighted cursor bar to the menu name, and then press the Down Arrow key.

B. Make a selection from a pull-down menu.

1. Open the pull-down menu.
2. Click on the desired item.

or

1. Open the pull-down menu. One letter in each item that is eligible to be used will be underlined.
2. Press the underlined letter. Alternatively, use the Down Arrow key to move the cursor bar to the desired item and then press the Enter key.

C. Obtain information about the selections in a pull-down menu.

1. Press Alt/H/M and click on the Contents tab.
2. Double-click on the Interface Reference book
3. Double-click on the Menu book
4. Double-click on the name of the menu of interest.
5. Double-click on the selection of interest.

D. Look at all the menus in the menu bar.

1. Press Alt/F.
2. Press the Right Arrow key each time you want to see a new menu.

E. Close a pull-down menu.

1. Press the Esc key or click anywhere outside the menu.

HOW TO: Utilize the Windows Environment

A. Place a section of code in the Windows clipboard.

1. Mark the section of code as a block as described in the How to Use the Editor section.
2. Press Ctrl+C.

B. Access Windows' Notepad.

> 1. Click the Start button.
> 2. Point to Programs.
> 3. Point to Accessories.
> 4. Click Notepad.

C. Display all characters in a font.

> 1. Click the Start button.
> 2. Point to Programs.
> 3. Point to Accessories.
> 4. Click Character Map.
> 5. Click on the underlined down arrow at the right end of the Font box.
> 6. Highlight the desired font and press the Enter key or click on the desired font.

D. Display an ANSI or ASCII code for a character with a code above 128.

> 1. Proceed as described in item C above to display the font containing the character of interest.
> 2. Click on the character of interest. Displayed at the right end of the bottom line of the font table is Alt+0xxx, where xxx is the code for the character.

HOW TO: Design a Form

A. Display the ToolBox.

> 1. Press Alt/V/X.

B. Place a new control on the form.

> *Option I:* (new control with default size and position)
>
> 1. Double-click on the control's icon in the ToolBox. The new control appears at the center of the form.
> 2. Size and position the control as described in item H, which follows.
>
> *Option II:* (a single new control sized and positioned as it is created)
>
> 1. Click on the control's icon in the ToolBox.
> 2. Move the mouse to the approximate position on the form desired for the upper-left corner of the control.
> 3. Press and hold the left mouse button.
> 4. Move the mouse to the position on the form desired for the lower-right corner of the control. A dashed box will indicate the overall shape of the new control.
> 5. Release the left mouse button.
> 6. The control can be resized and repositioned as described in what follows.
>
> *Option III:* (create multiple instances of the same control)
>
> 1. Click on the control's icon in the ToolBox while holding down the Ctrl key.
> 2. Repeatedly use steps 2 through 5 of Option II to create instances of the control.

3. When finished creating instances of this control, click on the arrow icon in the ToolBox.

C. Create a related group of controls.

1. To hold the related group of controls, place a PictureBox or Frame control on the form.
2. Use Option II or III in item B of this section to place controls on the PictureBox or Frame.

D. Set the focus to a particular control.

1. Click on the control.

   or

1. Press the Tab key until the control receives the focus.

E. Delete a control.

1. Set the focus to the control to be deleted.
2. Press the Del key.

F. Delete a related group of controls.

1. Set the focus to the PictureBox or Frame holding the related group of controls.
2. Press the Del key.

G. Move a control, related group of controls, or form to a new location.

1. Move the mouse onto the control, the PictureBox or Frame containing the related group of controls, or the title of the from.
2. Drag the object to the new location.

H. Change the size of a control.

1. Set the focus to the desired control.
2. Move the mouse to one of the eight sizing handles located around the edge of the control. The mouse pointer will change to a double arrow which points in the direction that resizing can occur.
3. Drag to the desired size.

I. Change the size of a Project Container window.

1. Move the mouse to the edge or corner of the window that is to be stretched or shrunk. The mouse pointer will change to a double arrow which points in the direction that resizing can occur.
2. Drag to the desired size.

J. Use the color palette to set foreground and background colors.

1. Set the focus to the desired control or the form.
2. Press Alt/V/L to activate the Color Palette.
3. If the Color Palette obscures the object you are working with, you may wish to use the mouse to grab the Color Palette by its title bar and move it so that at least some of the object shows.
4. To set the foreground color, click on the square within a square at the far left in the Color Palette and click on the desired color from the palette.

5. To set the background color, click on the region within the outer square but outside the inner square and click on the desired color from the palette.

   or

1. Set the focus to the desired control or the form.
2. Press Alt/V/W to activate the Properties window.
3. To set the foreground color, click on the down arrow to the right of the ForeColor settings box, click on the Palette tab, and click on the desired color.
4. To set the background color, click on the down arrow to the right of the BackColor settings box, click on the Palette tab, and click on the desired color.

HOW TO: Work with the Properties of an Object

A. Activate the Properties window.

1. Press Alt/V/W.

   or

1. Press F4.

   or

1. Click on an object on the form with the right mouse button.
2. In the shortcut menu, click on Properties.

B. Highlight a property in the Properties window.

1. Activate the Properties window and press the Enter key.
2. Use the Up or Down Arrow keys to move the highlight bar to the desired property.

   or

1. Activate the Properties window.
2. Click on the up or down arrow located at the ends of the vertical scroll bar at the right side of the Properties window until the desired property is visible.
3. Click on the desired property.

C. Select or specify a setting for a property.

1. Highlight the property whose setting is to be changed.
2. Click on the settings box or press Tab to place the cursor in the settings box.
   a. If a black down arrow appears at the right end of the settings box, click on the down arrow to display a list of all allowed settings, and then click on the desired setting.
   b. If an ellipsis (three periods: . . .) appears at the right end of the settings box, press F4 or click on the ellipsis to display a dialog box. Answer the questions in the dialog box and click on OK.
   c. If the cursor moves to the settings box, type in the new setting for the property.

D. Change a property setting of an object.

    1. Set the focus to the desired object.
    2. Activate the Properties window .
    3. Highlight the property whose setting is to be changed.
    4. Select or specify the new setting for the property.

E. Let a label change size to accommodate its caption.

    1. Set the label's AutoSize property to True. (The label will shrink to the smallest size needed to hold the current caption. If the caption is changed, the label will automatically grow or shrink horizontally to accommodate the new caption. If the WordWrap property is set to True as well, the label will grow and shrink vertically, keeping the same width.)

F. Let a label caption use more than one line.

    1. Set the label's WordWrap property to True. [If the label is not wide enough to accommodate the entire caption on one line, part of the caption will wrap to additional lines. If the label height is too small, then part or all of these wrapped lines will not be visible (unless the AutoSize property is set to True).]

G. Let a text box display more than one line.

    1. Set the text box's MultiLine property to True. (If the text box is not wide enough to accommodate the text entered by the user, the text will scroll down to new lines. If the text box is not tall enough, lines will scroll up out of view, but can be redisplayed by moving the cursor up.)

H. Assign a hot key to a label or command button.

    1. When assigning a value to the Caption property, precede the desired hot key character with an ampersand (&).

I. Allow a particular command button to be activated by a press of the Enter key.

    1. Set the command button's Default property to True.

Note: Setting the Default property True for one command button automatically sets the property to False for all the other command buttons on the form.

J. Adjust the order in which the Tab key moves the focus.

    1. Set the focus to the first object in the tabbing sequence.
    2. Change the setting of the TabIndex property for this object to 0.
    3. Set the focus to the next object in the tabbing sequence.
    4. Change the setting of the TabIndex property for this object to 1.
    5. Repeat Steps 3 and 4 (adding 1 to the Tab Index property) until all objects on the form have been assigned a new TabIndex setting.

Note: In Steps 2 and 4, if an object is moved to another position in the sequence, then the TabIndex property for the other objects will be renumbered accordingly.

K. Allow the pressing of Esc to activate a particular command button.

    1. Set the command button's Cancel property to True. (Setting the Cancel property to True for one command button automatically sets it False for all other command buttons.)

L. Keep the contents of a picture box from being erased.

    1. Set the picture box's AutoRedraw property to True. (The default is False. Unless the property is set to True, the contents will be erased when the picture box is obscured by another window.)

HOW TO: Manage Procedures

A. Access the Code Window.

    1. Press the Esc key followed by F7. (It is not always necessary to press the Esc key.)

    or

    1. Press Alt/V/C.

    or

    1. Press Alt/V/P to activate the Project Explorer window.
    2. Click on the "View Code" button.

B. Look at an existing procedure.

    1. Access the Code Window.
    2. Press Ctrl+Down Arrow or Ctrl+Up Arrow to see all the procedures.

    or

    1. Access the Code Window.
    2. Click on the Down Arrow at the right of the Object box and then select an object. [For general procedures select (General) as the Object.]
    3. Click on the Down Arrow at the right of the Procedure box and then select a procedure.

C. Create a procedure.

    1. Access the Code Window.
    2. Move to a blank line that is not inside a procedure.
    3. Type Private Sub (for a subprogram) or Private Function (for a function) followed by the name of the procedure and any parameters.
    4. Press the Enter key. (The Code Window will now display the new procedure heading and an End Sub or End Function statement.)
    5. Type the procedure into the Code Window.

    or

    1. Access the Code Window.
    2. Press Alt/T/P. (A dialog box will appear.)
    3. Type the name of the procedure into the Name rectangle.
    4. Select the type of procedure.
    5. Select the Scope by clicking on Public or Private. (In this book, we primarily use Private.)

6. Press the Enter key. (The Code window will now display the new procedure heading and an End Sub or End Function statement.)
7. Type the procedure into the Code Window.

D. Alter a procedure.

1. View the procedure in the Code Window as described in item B of this section.
2. Make changes as needed.

E. Remove a procedure.

1. Bring the procedure into the Code Window as described in item B of this section.
2. Mark the entire procedure as a block. That is,
    a. Press Ctrl+PgUp to move the cursor to the beginning of the procedure.
    b. Hold down the Shift key and press Ctrl+PgDown to move the cursor to the start of the next procedure.
    c. Press the Up Arrow key until just after the end of the procedure to be deleted.
3. Press the Del key.

F. Insert an existing procedure into a program.

1. Open the program containing the procedure.
2. View the procedure in the Code Window as described in item B of this section
3. Mark the entire procedure as a block, as described in item E of this section.
4. Press Ctrl+C to place the procedure into the clipboard.
5. Open the program in which the procedure is to be inserted and access the Code Window.
6. Move the cursor to a blank line.
7. Press Ctrl+V to place the contents of the clipboard into the program.

HOW TO: Manage Windows

A. Zoom the active window to fill the entire screen.

1. Click on the maximize button (page icon; second icon from the right) on the title bar of the window.
2. To return the window to its original size, click on the restore (double-page) button that has replaced the maximize button.

B. Move a window.

1. Move the mouse to the title bar of the window.
2. Drag the window to the desired location.

C. Change the size of a window.

1. Move the mouse to the edge of the window which is to be adjusted or to the corner joining the two edges to be adjusted.
2. When the mouse becomes a double arrow, drag the edge or corner until the window has the desired size.

D. Close a window.

   1. Click on the X button on the far right corner of the title bar.

HOW TO: Use the Printer

A. Obtain a printout of a program.

   1. Press Alt/F/P.
   2. Press the Enter key.

Note: To print just the text selected as a block or the active (current) window, use the direction keys to select the desired option.

B. Obtain a printout of the form during run time.

   1. Place the statement PrintForm in the Form_Click( ) or other appropriate procedure of the program which will be executed at the point when the desired output will be on the form.

HOW TO: Use the Debugger

A. Stop a program at a specified line.

   1. Place the cursor on the desired line.
   2. Press F9 or Alt/D/T to highlight the line in red. (This highlighted line is called a *breakpoint*. When the program is run it will stop at the breakpoint before executing the statement.)

Note: To remove this breakpoint, repeat steps 1 and 2.

B. Remove all breakpoints.

   1. Press Alt/D/C or Ctrl+Shift+F9.

C. Run a program one statement at a time.

   1. Press F8. The first executable statement will be highlighted. (An event must first occur for which an event procedure has been written.)
   2. Press F8 each time you want to execute the currently highlighted statement.

Note: You will probably need to press Alt+Tab to switch back and forth between the form and the VB environment. Also, to guarantee that output is retained while stepping through the program, the AutoRedraw property of the form and any picture boxes may need to be set to True.

D. Run the program one statement at a time, but execute each procedure call without stepping through the statements in the procedure one at a time.

   1. Press Shift+F8. The first executable statement will be highlighted.
   2. Press Shift+F8 each time you want to execute the currently highlighted statement.

E. Continue execution of a program that has been suspended.

   1. Press F5.

Note: Each time an attempt is made to change a suspended program in a way that would prevent the program from continuing, Visual Basic displays a dialog box warning that the program will have to be restarted from the beginning and gives the option to cancel the attempted change.

F. Have further stepping begin at the line containing the cursor (no variables are cleared).

   1. Press Alt/D/R or Ctrl+F8.

G. Set the next statement to be run in the current procedure.

   1. Place the cursor anywhere in the desired statement.
   2. Press Alt/D/N or Ctrl+F9.

H. Determine the value of an expression during run time.

   1. Press Alt/D/A (Add Watch)
   2. Type the expression into the Expression text box, adjust other entries in dialog box (if necessary), and click on OK.

Note: The value of the expression will appear in the Watches window during break mode.

Appendix C

Visual Basic Statements, Functions, Methods, Properties, Events, Data Types, and Operators

This appendix applies to the following objects: form, printer, text box, command button, label, and picture box. The last four are also called *controls*. Terms in brackets follow some of the discussions. These terms refer to supporting topics presented at the end of this appendix.

Abs The function Abs strips the minus signs from negative numbers while leaving other numbers unchanged. If x is any number, then the value of Abs(x) is the absolute value of x.

Action The type of a common dialog box can be determined by the setting of the Action property (1-Open, 2-Save As, 3-Color, 4-Font, 5-Print). This use is obsolete. Instead, use the methods ShowOpen, ShowSave, ShowColor, ShowFont, and ShowPrinter. For an OLE control, the setting of the Action property during run time determines the action to take.

Add A statement of the form *collectionName*.Add *objectName* adds the named object to a collection. A statement of the form *collectionName*.Add *objectName keyString* adds the named object to a collection with the key keyString.

AddItem The AddItem method adds an additional item to a list box or combo box and adds an additional row to a grid. A statement of the form List1.AddItem *str* inserts the string either at the end of the list (if Sorted = False) or in its proper alphabetical position (if Sorted = True). The statement List1.AddItem *str, n* inserts the item at the position with index n. The use of an index is not recommended when Sorted = True. The statement MSFlexGrid1.AddItem "", n inserts a new row into the grid at position n.

AddNew The AddNew method is used with a data control to set the stage for the addition of a new record to the end of a file. It clears any controls bound to the data control. The actual addition takes place after Value and Update statements are executed.

Alignment The Alignment property of a text box or label affects how the text assigned to the Text property is displayed. If the Alignment property is set to 0 (the default), text is displayed left-justified; if set to 1, text is right-justified; and if set to 2, text is centered.

681

And (Logical Operator) The logical expression *condition1* And *condition2* is true only if both *condition1* and *condition2* are true. For example, (3<7) And ("abc">"a") is true because 3<7 is true as is "abc">"a", and ("apple">"ape") And ("earth">"moon") is false because "earth">"moon" is false.

And (Bitwise Operator) The expression *byte1* And *byte2* is evaluated by expressing each byte as an 8-tuple binary number and then Anding together corresponding digits, where 1 And 1 equals 1, 1 And 0, 0 And 1, and 0 And 0 all equal 0. For example, the expression 37 And 157 translated to binary 8-tuples becomes 00100101 And 10011101. Anding together corresponding digits gives the binary 8-tuple 00000101 or decimal 5. Thus, 37 And 157 is 5.

Array If *arglist* is a comma-delimited list of values, then the value of the function Array(*arglist*) is a variant containing an array of these values. See Dim for discussion of arrays.

Asc Characters are stored as numbers from 0 to 255. If *str* is a string of characters, then Asc(*str*) is the number corresponding to the first character of *str*. For any *n* from 0 to 255, Asc(Chr(*n*)) is *n*.

Atn The trigonometric function Atn, or *arctangent*, is the inverse of the tangent function. For any number *x*, Atn(*x*) is an angle in radians between –pi/2 and pi/2 whose tangent is *x*. [radians]

AutoRedraw The AutoRedraw property determines what happens to graphics and Printed material on a form or picture box after another object (for example, another picture box) or program temporarily obscures part of the form or picture box. If AutoRedraw is True, then Visual Basic will restore the graphics and Printed material from a copy that it has saved in memory. If AutoRedraw is False, then Visual Basic does not keep track of graphics and Printed material that have been obscured, but does invoke the Paint event of the form or picture box when the obstruction is removed. Thus, only graphics and Printed material generated by the Paint event will be restored when AutoRedraw is False.

AutoSize If the AutoSize property of a label or picture box is True, Visual Basic automatically sets the width and height of the label so that the entire caption can be accommodated. If the AutoSize property is False, the size of the label is not adjusted by Visual Basic, and captions are clipped if they do not fit.

BackColor The BackColor property determines the background color of an object. For a Command Button, the background color is the color of the dotted rounded rectangle that surrounds the caption when the command button has the focus. If the BackColor of a form or picture box is changed while a program is running, all graphics and Printed text directly on the form or picture box are erased. [color]

BackStyle The BackStyle property of a label or shape is opaque (1) by default. The rectangular, square, circular, or oval region associated with the control is filled with the control's background color and possibly caption. If the BackStyle is set to transparent (0), whatever is behind the control remains visible; the background color of the control essentially becomes "see through."

Beep The statement Beep produces a sound of frequency 800 Hz that lasts a fraction of a second.

BOF When the BOF property of a data control is True, the current record position in the file is before the first record.

Boolean A variable of type Boolean requires 2 bytes of memory and holds either the value True or False. If boolVar is a Boolean variable, then the statement Print boolVar displays –1 when the value is True and displays 0 when the value is False.

BorderColor The BorderColor property determines the color of a line or shape control. [color]

BorderStyle The BorderStyle property determines the border style for a form [0-none, 1-fixed single, 2-sizeable (default), 3-fixed double], line or shape [0-transparent, 1-solid, 2-dash, 3-dot, 4-dash-dot, 5-dash-dot-dot, 6-inside solid], grid image, label, picture box, and text box [0-none, 1-fixed single (default)]. You cannot change the borders of forms and text boxes during run time.

BorderWidth The BorderWidth property (with settings from 1 through 8192) determines the thickness of a line or shape control.

Byte A variable of type Byte uses a single byte of memory and holds a value from 0 to 255.

Call A statement of the form Call *SubprogramName(argList)* is used to execute the named subprogram, passing to it the variables and values in the list of arguments. Arrays appearing in the list of arguments should be specified by the array name followed by empty parentheses. The value of a variable argument may be altered by the subprogram unless the variable is surrounded by parentheses. After the statements in the subprogram have been executed, program execution continues with the statement following Call. **Note:** The keyword Call may be omitted. In this case, the parentheses are omitted and the statement is written *SubprogramName argList*.

Cancel The Cancel property provides a means of responding when the user presses the Esc key. At most one command button on a form may have its Cancel property set to True. If the Esc key is pressed while the program is running, Visual Basic will execute the click event procedure of the command button whose Cancel property is True.

Caption The Caption property holds the text that is to appear as the caption for a form, command button, data control, or label. If an ampersand (&) is placed in the caption of a command button or label, the ampersand will not be displayed, but the character following the ampersand will become a hot key. Hot keys provide a quick way to access a command button or the control (usually a text box) following (in tab index order) a label. Hot keys are activated by holding down the Alt key and pressing the hot key character.

CBool The function CBool converts byte, currency, double-integer, integer, long integer, and single-precision numbers to the Boolean values True or False. Nonzero values are converted to True and zero is converted to False. If x is any number, then the value of CBool(x) is the Boolean value determined by x.

CByte The function CByte converts integer, long integer, single-precision, double-precision, and currency numbers to byte numbers. If x is any number, then the value of CByte(x) is the byte number determined by x.

CCur The function CCur converts byte integer, long integer, single-precision, and double-precision numbers to currency numbers. If x is any number, then the value of CCur(x) is the currency number determined by x.

CDate The function CDate converts byte, currency, double-integer, integer, long integer, and single-precision numbers to dates. If x is any number, then the value of CDate(x) is the date determined by x.

CDbl The function CDbl converts byte, integer, long integer, single-precision, and currency numbers to double-precision numbers. If x is any number, then the value of CDbl(x) is the double-precision number determined by x.

Change The Change event occurs when the contents of a combo box, directory list box, drive list box, label, picture box, scroll bar, or text box are altered in a specific way. The alterations are: (a) change of text (combo box or text box), (b) user selects a new directory or drive (directory and drive list boxes), (c) thumb moves (scroll bar), (d) change of Caption property (label), and (e) change of Picture property (picture box).

ChDir The statement ChDir *path* changes the current directory on the specified disk drive to the subdirectory specified by *path*. For example, ChDir "C:\" specifies the root directory of the C drive as the current directory. Omitting a drive letter in *path* causes the default drive to be used. [directories]

ChDrive The statement ChDrive *drive* changes the default drive to the drive specified by *drive*. For example, ChDrive "A" specifies the A drive as the new default drive.

Chr If n is a number from 0 to 255, then a statement of the form *objectName*.Print Chr(n) displays the nth character of the current font.

CInt The function CInt converts byte, long integer, single-precision, double-precision, and currency numbers to integer numbers. If x is any number from -32768 to 32767, the value of CInt(x) is the (possibly rounded) integer constant that x determines.

Circle The graphics method *objectName*.Circle (x, y), r, c, $r1$, $r2$, a draws on *objectName* a portion, or all, of an ellipse. The center of the ellipse is the point (x, y) and the longer radius is r. The color of the ellipse is determined by c. If $r1$ and $r2$ are present, then the computer draws only the portion of the ellipse that extends from the radius line at an angle of Abs($r1$) radians with the horizontal radius line to the radius line at an angle of Abs($r2$) radians with the horizontal radius line in a counterclockwise direction. If either $r1$ or $r2$ is negative, the computer also draws its radius line. The ratio of the length of the vertical diameter to the length of the horizontal diameter will be a. After the Circle method is executed, the value of *objectName*.CurrentX becomes x and the value of *objectName*.CurrentY becomes y. [color] [coordinate systems] [radians]

Clear The method ClipBoard.Clear clears the clipboard, setting its contents to the null string. The statements List1.Clear and Combo1.Clear remove all items from the control's list.

Click The Click event applies to check boxes, combo boxes, command buttons, directory list boxes, file list boxes, forms, frames, grids, images, labels, list boxes, menu items, OLE controls, option buttons, picture boxes, and text boxes. A Click event occurs whenever the left mouse button is pressed and released while the mouse cursor is over the control or over a blank area on the form. In the case of a command button, the Click event is also called if the spacebar or Enter key is pressed while the command button has the focus, or if the button's access key is used.

CLng The function CLng converts byte, integer, single-precision, double-precision, and currency numbers to long integer numbers. If x is any number from –2,147,483,648 to 2,147,483,647, the value of CLng(x) is the (possibly rounded) long integer constant that x determines.

Close The statement Close #n closes the file that has been opened with reference number n. By itself, Close closes all open files. The Close method for a data control closes the database.

Cls The method *formName*.Cls clears the form *formName* of all text and graphics that have been placed directly on the form with methods like *formName*.Print, *formName*.Circle, and so on. The method *pictureBox*.Cls clears the named picture box. The Cls method resets the CurrentX and CurrentY properties of the cleared object to the coordinates of the upper-left corner [usually (0, 0)].

Col and Row The Col and Row properties specify the active cell of a grid. The statements Let MSFlexGrid1.Col = m and Let MSFlexGrid1.Row = n specify the cell in column m and row n to be the active cell. The statement MSFlexGrid1.Text = str places the string into the active cell.

ColAlignment The statement MSFlexGrid1.ColAlignment(m) = n, where n = 0 (left-align (default)), 1 (right-align), or 2 (centered), aligns the text in the nonfixed cells of the mth column of the grid.

Color The value of the Color property of a Color common dialog box identifies the selected color.

Cols and Rows The Cols and Rows properties of a grid specify the numbers of rows and columns.

ColWidth The statement Let MSFlexGrid1.Colwidth(m) = n specifies that column m of the grid be n twips wide. (There are about 1440 twips in an inch.)

Const The statement Const *constantName* = *expression* causes Visual Basic to replace every occurrence of *constantName* with the value of the expression. This replacement takes place before any lines of the program are executed. Unlike Let, Const does not set up a location in the program's memory for a variable. A *constantName* may appear in only one Const statement and may not appear on the left side of a Let statement. We call *constantName* a "symbolic constant" or "named constant."

Control The Control data type may be used in the parameter lists of Sub and Function definitions to allow the passing of control names to the procedure.

ControlBox The ControlBox property determines whether or not a form has a Control-menu button displayed in the upper left corner. If the ControlBox property is set to True (the default), the Control-menu button is displayed. Among the operations available from the ControlBox menu is the ability to close the form and thereby end the program. If the ControlBox property of a form is set to False, the Control-menu button is not displayed. Because, in this case, the user cannot end the program using the Control-menu button or by pressing Alt+F4, it is important to provide a command button for this purpose.

Connect The Connect property of a data control identifies the format (such as Access, FoxPro, Dbase) of the database determined by the DatabaseName property.

Cos The value of the trigonometric function Cos(x) is the cosine of an angle of x radians. [radians]

Count The value of *collectionName*.Count is the number of objects in the collection.

CreateObject If *appName* is the name of an application and *objectType* is the type or class of the object to create, then the value of the function Create-Object(*appName. objectType*) is an OLE Automation object. For instance, Create-Object("Excel.sheet") creates an Excel worksheet and CreateObject("Word.Basic") creates a Word document.

CSng The function CSng converts byte, integer, long integer, and double-precision numbers to single-precision numbers. If x is any number, the value of CSng(x) is the single-precision number that x determines.

CStr The function CStr converts byte, integer, long integer, single-precision, double-precision, currency, and variant numbers to strings. If x is any number, the value of CStr(x) is the string determined by x. Unlike the Str function, CStr does not place a space in front of positive numbers. [variant]

CurDir The value of the function CurDir(*drive*) is a string specifying the current directory on the drive specified by *drive*. The value of CurDir("") or CurDir is a string specifying the current directory on the default drive. [directories]

Currency The currency data type is extremely useful for calculations involving money. A variable of type Currency requires 8 bytes of memory and can hold any number from –922,337,203,685,477.5808 to 922,337,203,685,477.5807 with at most four decimal places. Currency values and variables may be indicated by the type tag @: 21436587.01@, Balance@.

CurrentX, CurrentY The properties CurrentX and CurrentY give the horizontal and vertical coordinates of the point on a form, picture box, or the printer at which the next Print or graphics method will begin. Initially, CurrentX and CurrentY are the coordinates of the upper-left corner of the form or picture box. [coordinate systems]

CVar The function CVar converts strings and byte, integer, long integer, single-precision, double-precision, and currency numbers to variants. If x is any string or number, the value of CVar(x) is the variant determined by x. [variant]

CVDate The function CVDate converts a numeric or string expression to an equivalent serial date. If x is any expression representing a valid date, the value of CVDate(x) is the serial date determined by x. Valid numeric values are –657434 (January 1, 100 AD.) to 2958465 (December 31, 9999). Valid string expressions either look like one of these valid numeric values (for example, "19497" corresponding to May 18, 1953) or look like a date (for example, "10 Feb 1955", "August 13, 1958", etc.) [date]

DatabaseName The value of the DatabaseName property of a data control is the filespec of the file containing the database.

DataField After the DataSource property of a data-aware control has been set to bind the control to a data control, the DataField property is set to a field of the table accessed by the data control.

DataSource To bind a data-aware control to a data control at design time, set the value of the DataSource property of the data-aware control to the name of the data control.

Date The value of the function Date is the current date returned as a string of the form mm-dd-yyyy. If *dateStr* is a string of this form, the statement Date = *dateStr* resets the date as specified by *dateStr*.

Date A variable of type Date requires 8 bytes of memory and holds numbers representing dates from January 1, 100 to December 31, 9999. Literal date values can be assigned to date variables with statements such as Let *dateVar* = #5/12/1996#, Let *dateVar* = #5 Jan, 1997#, and Let *dateVar* = #February 10, 2004#. However, values of *dateVar* are displayed in the form month/day/year (for example, 5/12/1996).

DateSerial The value of the function DateSerial(*year, month, day*) is the serial date corresponding to the given year, month, and day. Values from 0 to 9999 are acceptable for *year*, with 0 to 99 interpreted as 1900 to 1999. Values of 1 to 12 for *month*, and 1 to 31 for *day* are normal, but any integer value is acceptable. Often, numeric expressions are used for *month* or *day* that evaluate to numbers outside these ranges. For example, DateSerial(1993, 2, 10 + 90) is the date 90 days after Feb. 10, 1993. [date]

DateValue The value of the function DateValue(*str*) is the serial date corresponding to the date given in *str*. DateValue recognizes the following date formats: "2-10-1955", "2/10/1955", "February 10, 1955", "Feb 10, 1955", "10-Feb-1955", and "10 February 1955". For the years 1900 through 1999, the initial "19" is optional. [date]

Day The function Day extracts the day of the month from a serial date. If *d* is any valid serial date, the value of Day(*d*) is an integer from 1 to 31 giving the day of the month recorded as part of the date and time stored in *d*. [date]

DblClick The DblClick event applies to combo boxes, file list boxes, forms, frames, grids, images, labels, list boxes, OLE controls, option buttons, picture boxes, and text boxes. A DblClick event occurs whenever the left mouse button is pressed and released twice, in quick succession, while the mouse cursor is over the control or over a blank area on the form. Double-clicking on an object will first cause that object's Click event to occur, followed by its DblClick event. **Note:** When you double-click on an item in a drive list box, the item is automatically assigned to the Path property. When you double-click on an item in a file list box, the item is automatically assigned to the FileName property.

Default When the Default property of a command button is set to True and the focus is on an object that is not another command button, pressing the enter key has the same effect as clicking on the button. At most, one command button on a form can have True as the value of its Default property.

DefInt, DefLng, DefSng, DefDbl, DefStr, DefCur, DefVar, DefByte, DefBool, DefDate, DefObj A variable can be assigned a type by either a type-declaration tag or an As clause. A statement of the form DefInt *letter* specifies that any "untyped" variable whose name begins with the specified letter will have integer type. A statement of the form DefInt *letter1-letter2* specifies that all "untyped" variables whose names begin with a letter in the range *letter1* through *letter2* will have integer type. The statements DefLng, DefSng, DefDbl, DefStr, DefCur,

DefVar, DefByte, DefBool, DefDate, and DefObj specify the corresponding types for long integer, single-precision, double-precision, string, currency, variant, byte, boolean, date, and object variables, respectively. Def*Type* statements are placed in the (Declarations) section of (General). [variant]

Delete The Delete method for a data control deletes the current record.

Dim The statement Dim *arrayName*(m To n) As *variableType* declares an array with subscripts ranging from m to n, inclusive, where m and n are in the normal integer range of –32768 to 32767. The *variableType* must be Integer, Long, Single, Double, Currency, String, String*n, Variant, Boolean, Byte, Date, or a user-defined type. A statement of the form Dim *arrayName*(m To n, p To q) As *variableType* declares a doubly subscripted, or two-dimensional, array. Three- and higher-dimensional arrays are declared similarly. If m and p are zero, the preceding Dim statements may be changed to Dim *arrayName*(n) As *variableType* and Dim *arrayName*(n, q) As *variableType*. The statement Dim *arrayName*( ) As *variable-Type* defines an array whose size is initially unknown but must be established by a ReDim statement before the array can be accessed. The statement Dim *variable-Name* As *variableType* specifies the type of data that will be stored in *variable-Name*. Variables and arrays Dimmed in the (Declarations) section of (General) are available to all procedures. In procedures, Dim is used to declare variables, but ReDim is often used to dimension arrays. [dynamic vs. static] [variant]

Dir If *fileTemplate* specifies a file (or a collection of files by including ? or *), then the value of the function Dir(*fileTemplate*) is the filespec of the first file matching the pattern specified by *fileTemplate*. If this value is not the null string, the value of the function Dir is the next file that matches the previously specified pattern. For example, the value of Dir("*.VBP") will be a string specifying the first file in the current directory of the default drive whose name has the .VBP extension. [directories] [filespec]

Do/Loop A statement of the form Do, Do While *cond*, or Do Until *cond* is used to mark the beginning of a block of statements that will be repeated. A statement of the form Loop, Loop While *cond*, or Loop Until *cond* is used to mark the end of the block. Each time a statement containing While or Until followed by a condition is encountered, the truth value of the condition determines whether the block should be repeated or whether the program should jump to the statement immediately following the block. A Do loop may also be exited at any point with an Exit Do statement.

DoEvents Executing the statement DoEvents permits Visual Basic to act on any events may have occurred while the current event procedure has been executing.

Double A variable of type Double requires 8 bytes of memory and can hold 0, the numbers from 4.94065×10^{-324} to $1.797693134862316 \times 10^{308}$ with at most 17 significant digits and the negatives of these numbers. Double values and variables may be indicated by the type tag #: 2.718281828459045#, Pi#.

DrawMode The property DrawMode determines whether graphics are drawn in black, white, foreground color, or some interaction of these colors with the current contents of the form or picture box. The following table lists the allowed values for the DrawMode property and the rules for what RGB color number will be assigned at a given point when the RGB color number for the color currently displayed at that point is *display* and the RGB color number for the draw color is *draw*. [color]

DrawMode	Color Produced	
1	&H00000000& (Black)	
2	Not draw And Not display	(inverse of #15)
3	display And Not draw	(inverse of #14)
4	Not draw	(inverse of #13)
5	draw And Not display	(inverse of #12)
6	Not display	(inverse of #11)
7	draw Xor display	
8	Not draw Or Not display	(inverse of #9)
9	draw And display	
10	Not (draw Xor display)	(inverse of #7)
11	display	(transparent)
12	display Or Not draw	
13	draw (draw color)	
14	draw Or Not display	
15	draw Or display	
16	&H00FFFFFF& (White)	

DrawStyle When DrawWidth is 1 for a form or picture box (the default), the property DrawStyle determines whether graphics are drawn using a solid line or some combinations of dots and dashes. Use a DrawStyle of 0 (the default) for solid lines, 1 for dashed lines, 2 for dotted lines, 3 for dash-dot lines, or 4 for dash-dot-dot lines. A DrawStyle of 5 produces "invisible" graphics.

When thick lines are drawn as a result of setting DrawWidth to values greater than 1, graphics are always drawn using solid lines. In this case, DrawStyle can be used to either center the thick line over where line with a DrawWidth of 1 would be drawn or, when drawing closed figures like ellipses and rectangles, to place the thick line just inside where the line with a DrawWidth of 1 would be drawn. To draw thick graphics inside the normal closed figure, use a DrawStyle of 6. DrawStyles 1 through 4 will center thick graphics over the normal location.

DrawWidth The property DrawWidth determines the width in pixels of the lines that are drawn by graphics methods. The default is 1 pixel. Values from 1 to 32,767 are permitted.

Drive The Drive property of a drive list box gives the contents of the currently selected item.

Enabled The property Enabled determines whether or not a form or control responds to events. If the Enabled property of a form or control is set to True (the default), and if an event occurs for which an event procedure has been written, the event procedure will be executed. When the Enabled property of a form or control is set to False, all events relating to that control are ignored; no event procedures are executed.

End The statement End terminates the execution of the program and closes all files. Also, the statements End Def, End Function, End If, End Select, End Sub, and End Type are used to denote the conclusion of multiline function definitions, function blocks, If blocks, Select Case blocks, subprograms, and user-defined, record-type declarations.

EndDoc The method Printer.EndDoc is used to indicate that the document currently being printed is complete and should be released to the printer.

Environ Visual Basic has an environment table consisting of equations of the form "*name=value*" that is inherited from DOS when Windows is invoked. If *name* is the left side of an equation in Visual Basic's environment table, then the value of the function Environ("*name*") will be the string consisting of the right side of the equation. The value of Environ(*n*) is the *n*th equation in Visual Basic's environment table.

EOF Suppose a file has been opened for sequential input with reference number *n*. The value of the function EOF(*n*) will be True (–1) if the end of the file has been reached and False (0) otherwise. [**Note:** The logical condition Not EOF(*n*) is true until the end of the file is reached.] When used with a communications file, EOF(*n*) will be true if the communications buffer is empty and false if the buffer contains data.

Err After an error occurs during the execution of a program, the value of Err.Number will be a number identifying the type of error. Err.Number is used in conjunction with the On Error statement. If *n* is a whole number from 0 to 32,767, then the statement Err.Raise *n* generates the run-time error associated with the number *n*.

Eqv The logical expression *condition1* Eqv *condition2* is true if *condition1* and *condition2* are both true or both false. For example, (1>2) Eqv ("xyz"<"a") is true because both 1>2 and "xyz"<"a" are false, whereas ("apple">"ape") Eqv ("earth"> "moon") is false because "apple">"ape" is true but "earth">"moon" is false.

Erase For static arrays, the statement Erase *arrayName* resets each array element to its default value. For dynamic arrays, the statement Erase *arrayName* deletes the array from memory. **Note:** After a dynamic array has been Erased, it may be ReDimensioned. However, the number of dimensions must be the same as before. [dynamic vs. static]

Error The statement Error *n* simulates the occurrence of the run-time error identified by the number *n*, where *n* may range from 1 to 32,767. It is a useful debugging tool.

Error The value of the function Error is the error message corresponding to the run-time error that has most recently occurred. The value of the function Error(*errNum*) is the error message corresponding to the run-time error designated by *errNum*.

Event A statement of the form Public Event *UserDefinedEvent*(arg1, arg2, . . .), appearing in the general declarations section of a code module, declares a user-defined event and passes the arguments to the event procedure. After this declaration is made, the RaiseEvent statement can be used to fire the event.

Exit The Exit statement may be used in any of five forms: Exit For, Exit Sub, Exit Function, Exit Property, Exit Def, and Exit Do. The Exit statement causes program execution to jump out of the specified structure prematurely: Exit For jumps out of a For/Next loop to the statement following Next, Exit Sub jumps out of a subprogram to the statement following the Call statement, and so on.

Exp The value of the function Exp(*x*) is e^x, where *e* (about 2.71828) is the base of the natural logarithm function.

False A predefined constant whose value is 0. False is used when setting the value of properties that are either True or False. For example, Picture1.FontItalic = False.

Fields The Fields property of a recordset is used to read or set the Value property of the Recordset. For instance, a statement of the form Print Data1.Record-Set.Fields(*fieldName*).Value displays the value in the specified field of the current record of the database table associated with the data control. The preceding Print statement can be abbreviated to Print Data1.RecordSet(*fieldName*).

FileAttr After a file has been opened with reference number *n*, the value of the function FileAttr (*n*, 1) is 1, 2, 4, 8, or 32 depending on whether the file was opened for Input, Output, Append, Random, or Binary, respectively. The value of the function FileAttr (*n*, 2) is the file's DOS file handle, a number that uniquely identifies the file and is used in assembly language programming.

FileCopy The statement FileCopy *source*, *destination* creates the file specified by *destination* by making a copy of the file specified by *source*. Both *source* and *destination* may specify drive and path information. If the file specified by *destination* already exists, it will be overwritten without a warning being issued.

FileDateTime The value of the function FileDateTime(*filename*) is a string giving the date and time that the file specified by the *filename* was created or last modified.

FileLen The value of the function FileLen(*filename*) is the length in characters (bytes) of the file specified by *filename*.

FileName The FileName property of a file list box is the contents of the currently selected item.

FillColor When the FillStyle property of a form or picture box is set to a value other than the default of 1, the property FillColor determines what color is used to paint the interior of ellipses and rectangles drawn with the Circle and Line graphics methods. The FillColor property may be assigned any valid RGB color number. The default value for FillColor is black (0). [color]

FillStyle The property FillStyle determines what pattern is used to paint the interior of ellipses and rectangles drawn on forms or picture boxes with the Circle and Line methods. The default value for FillStyle is transparent (1), which means that interiors are not painted. Other values available for FillStyle are solid (0), horizontal lines (2), vertical lines (3), diagonals running upward to the right (4), diagonals running downward to the right (5), vertical and horizontal lines [crosshatched] (6), and diagonal crosshatched (7). **Note:** Using BF in a Line method has the same effect as setting the FillStyle to 0 and the FillColor to the color of the bordering line.

FindFirst, FindLast, FindNext, FindPrevious A statement of the form Data1.RecordSet.Find*What criteria* selects a new current record in the table of the database associated with the data control in the expected way, based on the specifications of the string *criteria*.

Fix The value of the function Fix(*x*) is the whole number obtained by discarding the decimal part of the number *x*.

FixedAlignment The statement MSFlexGrid1.FixedAlignment(*m*) = *n*, where *n* = 0 (left-align (default)), 1 (right-align), or 2 (centered), aligns the text in the fixed cells of the *m*th column of the grid.

FixedCols and FixedRows The FixedCols and FixedRows properties of a grid specify the number of fixed rows and fixed columns of a grid. Fixed rows and columns are used for headings and never disappear due to scrolling.

Flags The Flags property of a common dialog box sets a variety of options.

FontBold The property FontBold determines whether the characters Printed on a form, picture box, or printer, or assigned to a text box, command button, or label appear in bold or normal type. If the FontBold property is set to True (the default), then for a form, picture box, or printer, subsequent Printed characters appear bold. For a text box, command button, or label, the text or caption is immediately changed to bold. If the FontBold property is set to False, subsequent characters are Printed in normal type and characters assigned to the text or caption property change immediately to normal type.

FontCount The value of the property Screen.FontCount is the number of fonts available for use on the screen. Similarly, the value of the property Printer.FontCount is the number of fonts available on the printer. The FontCount property is set according to your Windows environment and generally used to determine the limit on the index for the Fonts property.

FontItalic The property FontItalic determines whether or not the characters Printed on a form, picture box, or printer, or assigned to a text box, command button, or label appear in italic or upright type. If the FontItalic property is set to True, then for a form, picture box, or printer, subsequent characters appear in italic. For a text box, command button, or label, the text or caption is immediately changed to italic. If the FontItalic property is set to False (the default), subsequent characters are Printed in upright type and characters assigned to the text or caption property change immediately to upright type.

FontName The property FontName determines what type face is used when characters are Printed on a form, picture box, or printer, or assigned to a text box, command button, or label. If the FontName property of a form, picture box, or printer is set to a font obtained from the Fonts property, all subsequently Printed characters will appear in the new type face. When the FontName property of a text box, command button, or label is set to a new font, characters assigned to the text or caption property change immediately to the new type face.

Fonts The value of the property Screen.Fonts(*fontNum*) is the name of a screen font available in the current Windows environment. The index *fontNum* can range from 0 to Screen.FontCount–1. Similarly, the value of the property Printer.Fonts(*fontNum*) is the name of an available printer font. The values in the Fonts property are set by your Windows environment and are generally used to determine which fonts are available for setting the FontName property.

FontSize The property FontSize determines the size, in points, of characters Printed on forms, picture boxes, and the printer or displayed in text boxes and on command buttons and labels. Available font sizes depend on your Windows environment, but will always be between 1 and 2048. Default font sizes are usually between 8 and 12 point. **Note:** One point equals 1/72nd of an inch.

FontStrikeThru The property FontStrikeThru determines whether or not the characters Printed on a form, picture box, or printer, or assigned to a text box, command button, or label appear in a strikethru or standard font. If the FontStrikeThru property is set to True, then for a form, picture box, or printer, subsequent Printed characters appear with a horizontal line through the middle of each character. For a text box, command button, or label, the text or caption is immediately changed so that a horizontal line goes through the middle of each character. If the FontStrikeThru property is set to False (the default), subsequent characters are Printed in standard type and characters assigned to text or caption property change immediately to standard type.

FontTransparent   The property FontTransparent determines the degree to which characters Printed to forms and picture boxes obscure existing text and graphics. If the FontTransparent property is set to True (the default), the existing text and graphics are obscured only by the dots (pixels) needed to actually form the new character. If the FontTransparent property is set to False, then all text and graphics are obscured within the character box (small rectangle surrounding a character) associated with the new character. Those dots (pixels) not needed to form the character are changed to the background color.

FontUnderline   The property FontUnderline determines whether or not the characters printed on a form, picture box, or printer, or assigned to a text box, command button, or label appear with an underline. If the FontUnderline property is set to True, then for a form, picture box, or printer, subsequent characters Printed appear underlined. For a text box, command button, or label, the text or caption is immediately changed to underlined. If the FontUnderline property is set to False (the default), subsequent characters are Printed without underlines characters assigned to the text or caption property change immediately to nonunderlined.

For Each/Next   A multistatement block beginning with For Each *var* In *array-Name* and ending with Next *var*, where *arrayName* is an array of type variant and *var* is a variant variable, executes the statements inside the block for each element of the array.

For/Next   The statement For *index* = *a* To *b* Step *s* sets the value of the variable *index* to *a* and repeatedly executes the statements between itself and the statement Next *index*. Each time the Next statement is reached, *s* is added to the value of *index*. This process continues until the value of *index* passes *b*. Although the numbers *a*, *b*, and *s* may have any numeric type, the lower the precision of the type, the faster the loop executes. The statement For *index* = *a* To *b* is equivalent to the statement For *index* = *a* To *b* Step 1. The index following the word Next is optional.

ForeColor   The property ForeColor determines the color used to display text, captions, graphics, and Printed characters. If the ForeColor property of a form or picture box is changed, subsequent characters will appear in the new color. For a text box, command button, or label, text or caption is immediately changed to the new color. [color]

Format   The value of the function Format(*expression*, *str*) is a string representing *expression* (a number, date, time, or string) formatted according to the rules given by *str*. Format is useful when assigning values to the Text property and when Printing to a form, picture box, or the printer.

   Numeric output can be formatted with commas, leading and trailing zeros, preceding or trailing signs (+ or –), and exponential notation. This is accomplished either by using for *str* the name of one of several predefined numeric formats or by combining in *str* one or more of the following special numeric formatting characters: #, 0, decimal point (period), comma, %, E–, and E+. The expression to be formatted can evaluate to one of the numeric types or a string representing a number.

Predefined numeric formats include "General Number," which displays a number as is; "Currency," which displays a number with a leading dollar sign, commas every three digits to the left of the decimal, displays two decimal places, and encloses negative numbers in parentheses; "Fixed," which displays two digits to the right and at least one digit to the left of the decimal point; "Standard," which displays a number with commas and two decimal places but does not use parentheses for negative numbers; "Percent," which multiplies the value by 100 and displays a percent sign after two decimal places; and "Scientific," which displays numbers in standard scientific notation. For example, Format(–5432.352, "Currency") gives the string "($5,432.35)".

The symbol # designates a place for a digit. If the number being formatted does not need all the places provided by the #'s given in *str*, the extra #'s are ignored. The symbol 0, like #, designates a place for a digit. However, if the number being formatted does not need all the places provided by the 0's given in *str*, the character 0 is displayed in the extra places. If the number being converted has more whole part digits than there is space reserved by #'s and 0's, additional space is used as if the format string had more #'s at its beginning. For example, Format(56, "####") yields "56", Format(56, "#") yields "56", Format(0, "#") yields "", Format(56, "0000") yields "0056", Format(56, "0") yields "56", and Format(0, "0") yields "0".

The decimal point symbol (.) marks the location of the decimal place. It separates the format rules into two sections, one applying to the whole part of the number and the other to the decimal part. When included in the format string, a decimal point will always appear in the resulting string. For example, Format(56.246, "#.##") yields "56.25", Format(.246, "#.##") yields ".25", Format(.246, "0.##") yields "0.25", and Format(56.2, "0.00") yields "52.20".

The comma symbol (,) placed to the left of the decimal point between #'s and/or 0's causes commas to be displayed to the left of every third digit to the left of the decimal point, as appropriate. If commas are placed to the immediate left of the decimal point (or to the right of all #'s and 0's when the decimal point symbol is not used), then before the number is formatted, it is divided by 1000 for each comma, but commas will not appear in the result. In order to divide by 1000's and display commas in the result, use format strings like "#,#,.00", which displays the number with commas in units of thousands, and "#,#,,.00", which displays the number with commas in units of millions. For example, Format(1234000, "#,#") yields "1,234,000", Format(1234000, "#,") yields "1234", Format(1234000, "#,.") yields "1234.", Format(1234000, "#,,.0") yields "1.2", and Format(1234000, "#,0,.0") yields "1,234.0".

The percent symbol (%) placed to the right of all #'s, 0's, and any decimal point causes the number to be converted to a percentage (multiplied by 100) before formatting and the symbol % to be displayed. For example, Format(.05624, "#.##%") yields "5.62%", and Format(1.23, "#%") yields "123%".

The symbols E+ and E– placed to the right of all #'s, 0's, and any decimal point cause the number to be displayed in scientific notation. Places for the digits in the exponent must be reserved to the right of E+ or E– with #'s or 0's. When E+ is used and the exponent is positive, a plus sign appears in front of the exponent in the result. When E– is used and the exponent is positive, no sign or space precedes the exponent. When scientific notation is used, each position reserved by #'s to the left of the decimal point is used whenever possible. For example, Format(1234.56, "#.##E+##") yields "1.23E+3", Format(1234.56, "##.##E-##") yields "12.34E2", Format(1234, "###.00E+##") yields "123.40E+1", and Format(123, "###E+00") yields "123E+00".

Date and time output can be formatted using numbers or names for months, putting the day, month, and year in any order desired, using 12-hour or 24-hour notation, and so on. This is accomplished either by letting *str* be the name of one of several predefined date/time formats or by combining in *str* one or more special date/time formatting characters. The expression to be formatted can evaluate to a number that falls within the range of valid serial dates or to a string representing a date/time.

Predefined date/time formats include "General Date," which displays a date in mm/dd/yyyy format and, if appropriate, a time in hh:mm:ss PM format; "Long Date," which displays the day of week, the full name of month, the day, and a four-digit year; "Medium Date," which displays the day, abbreviated month name, and two-digit year; "Short Date," which displays "mm/dd/yy"; "Long Time," which displays the time in hh:mm:ss PM format; "Medium Time," which displays time in hh:mm PM format; and "Short Time," which display time in 24-hour format as hh:mm. For example, let dt = DateSerial(55,2,10) + TimeSerial(21,45,30). Then Format(dt, "General Date") yields "2/10/55 9:45:30 PM", Format(dt, "Medium Date") yields "10-Feb-55", and Format(dt, "Short Time") yields "21:45".

Format symbols for the day, month, and year include d (day as number but no leading zero), dd (day as number with leading zero), ddd (day as three-letter name), dddd (day as full name), m (month as number but no leading zero), mm (month as number with leading zero), mmm (month as three-letter name), mmmm (month as full name), yy (year as two-digit number), and yyyy (year as four-digit number). Separators such as slash, dash, and period may be used as desired to connect day, month, and year symbols into a final format. For example, Format("August 13, 1958", "dddd, d.mmm.yy") yields "Wednesday, 13.Aug.58" and Format("July 4, 1776", "ddd: mmmm dd, yyyy") yields "Thu: July 04, 1776". Additional format symbols for dates include w (day-of-week as number 1–7), ww (week-of-year as number 1–53), q (quarter-of-year as number 1–4), y (day-of-year as number 1–366), ddddd (same as short date), and dddddd (same as long date).

Format symbols for the second, minute, and hour include s (seconds with no leading zero), ss (seconds as two-digit number), n (minutes with no leading zero), nn (minutes as two-digit number), h (hours with no leading zero), hh (hours as two-digit number), AM/PM (use 12-hour clock and uppercase), am/pm (use 12-hour clock and lowercase), A/P (use 12-hour clock and single uppercase letter), a/p (use 12-hour clock and single lowercase letter), and ttttt (same as general date). Separators such as colons and periods may be used as desired to connect hour, minute, and second symbols into a final format. For example, Format("14:04:01", "h:nn AM/PM") yields "2:04 PM", Format("14:04:01", "h.n.s") yields "14.4.1", and Format(0.75, "h:nna/p") yields "6:00p".

String output can be formatted as all uppercase, all lowercase, left-justified or right-justified. Symbols used to format strings are @ (define a field for at least as many characters as there are @ symbols; if less characters than @ symbols, fill remainder of field with spaces; if more characters than @ symbols, display the extra characters—don't clip), & (reserve space for entire output string), < (convert all characters to lowercase before displaying), > (convert all characters to uppercase before displaying), ! (left justify within field defined by @ symbols;

default is to right justify). For example, Format("Red", "@") yields "Red", Format("Red", "@@@@@@") yields " Red" (3 leading spaces), Format("Red", "!>@@@@@@") yields "RED " (3 trailing spaces), and Format("Red", "<&") yields "red".

FreeFile When files are opened, they are assigned a reference number from 1 to 255. At any time, the value of the function FreeFile is the next available reference number.

FromPage, ToPage The FromPage and ToPage properties of a Print common dialog box identify the values selected for the From and To text boxes.

Function A function is a multistatement block usually beginning with a statement of the form Private Function *FunctionName(parList)* As *returnType*, followed on subsequent lines by one or more statements for carrying out the task of the function, and ending with the statement End Function. The parameter list, *parList*, is a list of variables through which values will be passed to the function when the function is called. Parameter types may be numeric, (variable-length) string, variant, object, user-defined record type, or array. The types of the parameters may be specified with type-declaration tags, Def*Type* statements, or As clauses. Array names appearing in the parameter list should be followed by an empty pair of parentheses. Functions are named with the same conventions as variables. The value of a variable argument used in calling a function may be altered by the function unless the variable is surrounded by parentheses. The value returned can be of any type (declared in *returnType*). Variables appearing in a function are local to the function unless they have been declared in the (Declarations) section of (General) and are not redeclared in Dim or Static statements within the function. A statement of the form Function *FunctionName(parList)* Static specifies that all variables local to the function be treated as static by default, that is, they are invisible outside of the function but retain their values between function calls. Functions may invoke themselves (called *recursion*) or other procedures. However, no procedure may be defined inside a function.

Get User-defined record types provide an efficient means of working with random-access files. After a user-defined record type is defined and a variable of that type, call it *recVar*, is declared, the file is opened with a length equal to Len (*recVar*). The *r*th record of the random-access file is retrieved and assigned to *recVar* with the statement Get #n, r, recVar.

The Get statement is also used to retrieve data from a binary file and assign it to any type of variable. Suppose *var* is a variable that holds a value consisting of *b* bytes. (For instance, if *var* is an integer variable, then *b* is 2. If *var* is an ordinary string variable, then *b* will equal the length of the string currently assigned to it.) The statement Get #n, p, var assigns to the variable *var*, the *b* consecutive bytes beginning with the byte in position *p* of the binary file having reference number *n*. (**Note:** The positions are numbered 1, 2, 3, ...) If *p* is omitted, then the current file position is used as the beginning position. [binary file]

GetAttr The value of the function GetAttr(*filename*) is a number indicating the file attributes associated with the file specified by *filename*. Let *attrib* be a variable holding the value returned by GetAttr. Then the file specified by *filename* is a read-only file if *attrib* And 1 = 1, is a hidden file if *attrib* And 2 = 2, is a system file if *attrib* And 4 = 4, is a volume label if *attrib* And 8 = 8, is a directory name if *attrib* And 16 = 16, or has been modified since the last backup if *attrib* And 32 = 32. See SetAttr.

GetObject If *filespec* specifies a file for an application that supports OLE Automation, then the value of the function GetObject(*filespec*) is an OLE Automation object.

GetText The value of the method ClipBoard.GetText is a string containing a copy of the data currently stored in the clipboard.

Global The Global statement is used to create variables, including arrays, that are available to all procedures in all forms and BAS modules associated with a project. The Global statement must be placed in the (Declarations) section of a BAS module, and has the same structure as a Dim statement. For example, the statement Global classList(1 to 30) As String, numStudents As Integer creates an array and a variable for use in all procedures of the project.

GoSub A statement of the form GoSub *lineLabel* causes a jump to the first statement following the specified line label. When the statement Return is reached, the program jumps back to the statement following the GoSub statement. The GoSub statement and its target must be in the same procedure. [line label] [subroutine]

GotFocus A GotFocus event occurs when an object receives the focus, either through a user action or through code, via the SetFocus method.

GoTo The statement GoTo *lineLabel* causes an unconditional jump to the first statement after the specified line label. The GoTo statement and its target must be in the same procedure. [line label]

GridLines Grid lines are the light gray lines in a grid that separate columns and rows. The GridLines property determines whether the grid lines are visible (GridLines = True) or not (GridLines = False.)

Height The property Height determines the vertical size of an object. Height is measured in units of twips. For the Printer object, Height may be read (ph = Printer.Height is OK) but not assigned (Printer.Height = 100 causes an error).

Hex If *n* is a whole number from 0 to 2,147,483,647, then the value of the function Hex(*n*) is the string consisting of the hexadecimal representation of *n*.

Hide The Hide method removes a form from the screen.

Hour The function Hour extracts the hours from a serial date. If *d* is any valid serial date, then the value of Hour(*d*) is a whole number from 0 to 23 indicating the hours recorded as part of the date and time store in *d*. [date]

If (block) A block of statements beginning with a statement of the form If *condition* Then and ending with the statement End If indicates that the group of statements between If and End If are to be executed only when *condition* is true. If the group of statements is separated into two parts by an Else statement, then the first part will be executed when *condition* is true and the second part when *condition* is false. Statements of the form ElseIf *condition* may also appear and define groups of statements to be executed when alternate conditions are true.

If (single line) A statement of the form If *condition* Then *action* causes the program to take the specified action if *condition* is true. Otherwise, execution continues at the next line. A statement of the form If *condition* Then *action1* Else *action2* causes the program to take *action1* if *condition* is true and *action2* if *condition* is false.

If TypeOf To test for the type of a control when the control name is passed to a procedure, use If TypeOf *controlName* Is *controlType* Then *action1* Else *action2* in either the single line or block form of the If statement. ElseIf TypeOf is also permitted. For *controlType*, use one of the control names that appear in the Form Design ToolBox (CommandButton, Label, TextBox, etc.) for example, If TypeOf objectPassed Is Label Then. . . .

Imp The logical expression *condition1* Imp *condition2* is true except when *condition1* is true and *condition2* is false. For example, (3<7) Imp ("abc">"a") is true because both 3<7 and "abc">"a" are true, and ("apple">"ape") Imp ("earth"> "moon") is false because "apple">"ape" is true but "earth">"moon" is false. Imp is an abbreviation for "logically implies."

Index When a control is part of a Control array, it is identified by the number specified by its Index Property.

Input The statement *str* = Input(*n*, *m*) assigns the next *n* characters from the file with reference number *m* (opened in Input or Binary mode) to *str*.

Input# The statement Input #*n*, *var* reads the next item of data from a sequential file that has been opened for Input with reference number *n* and assigns the item to the variable *var*. The statement Input #*n*, *var1*, *var2*, . . . reads a sequence of values and assigns them to the variables.

InputBox The value of the function InputBox(*prompt*) is the string entered by the user in response to the prompt given by *prompt*. The InputBox function automatically displays the prompt, a text box for user input, an OK button, and a Cancel button in a dialog box in the center of the screen. If the user selects Cancel, the value of the function is the null string (""). For greater control, use the function InputBox(*prompt*, *title*, *defaultStr*, *xpos*, *ypos*), which titles the dialog box with *title*, displays *defaultStr* as the default value in the text box, and positions the upper-left corner of the dialog box at coordinates (*xpos*, *ypos*) on the screen. [coordinate systems]

InStr The value of the function InStr(*str1*, *str2*) is the position of the string *str2* in the string *str1*. The value of InStr(*n*, *str1*, *str2*) is the first position at or after the *n*th character of *str1* that the string *str2* occurs. If *str2* does not appear as a substring of *str1*, the value is 0.

Int The value of the function Int(*x*) is the greatest whole number that is less than or equal to *x*.

Integer A variable of type Integer requires 2 bytes of memory and can hold the whole numbers from −32,768 to 32,767. Integer values and variables may be indicated by the type tag %: 345%, Count%.

Interval The Interval property of a Timer control is set to the number of milliseconds (1 to 65535) required to trigger a Timer event.

IsDate The value of the function IsDate(*str*) is True (−1) if the string *str* represents a date between January 1, 100 and December 31, 9999. Otherwise, the value is False (0). [date]

IsEmpty The value of the function IsEmpty(*v*) is True (−1) if *v* is a variable of unspecified type (that is, is a variant) that has not yet been assigned a value. In all other cases the value of IsEmpty is False (0). [variant]

IsNull The value of the function IsNull(*v*) is True (−1) if *v* is a variant variable that has been assigned the special value Null. In all other cases the value of IsNull is False (0). [variant]

IsNumeric The value of the function IsNumeric(v) is True (-1) if v is a number, numeric variable, or a variant variable that has been assigned a number or a string that could be obtained by Formatting a number. In all other cases the value of IsNumeric is False (0). [variant]

Item The value of *collectionName*.Item(n) is the nth object in the named collection. The value of *collectionName*.Item(*keyString*) is the nth object in the named collection, where *keyString* is the key given to the object when it was added to the collection. If the value of n or *keyString* doesn't match an existing object of the collection, an error occurs.

ItemData When you create a list or combo box, Visual Basic automatically creates a long integer array referred to as ItemData. The statement Let List1.ItemData(m) = n assigns the value n to the mth subscripted variable of the array. It is commonly used with the NewIndex property to associate a number with each item in a list, and thereby create a minidatabase. The ItemData property is especially useful for lists in which Sorted = True.

KeyPress The KeyPress event applies to command buttons, text boxes, and picture boxes. A KeyPress event occurs whenever the user presses a key while one of the preceding controls has the focus. A code identifying which key was pressed will be passed to the event procedure in the KeyAscii parameter. This information can then be used to determine what action should be taken when a given key is pressed.

Kill The statement Kill "*filespec*" erases the specified disk file. [filespec]

LargeChange When a scroll bar is clicked between the thumb and one of the arrow buttons, the Value property of the scroll bar changes by the value of the LargeChange property and the thumb moves accordingly.

LBound For a one-dimensional array *arrayName*, the value of the function LBound(*arrayName*) is the smallest subscript value that may be used. For any array *arrayName*, the value of the function LBound(*arrayName*, n) is the smallest subscript value that may be used for the nth subscript of the array. For example, after the statement Dim example(1 To 31, 1 To 12, 1990 To 1999) is executed, the value of LBound(example, 3) is the smallest value allowed for the third subscript of example( ), which is 1990.

LCase The value of the string function LCase(*str*) is a string identical to *str* except that all uppercase letters are changed to lowercase.

Left The property Left determines the position of the left edge of a form or control. The units of measure are twips for forms. The units of measure for a control are determined by the ScaleMode property of the container (form, picture box, etc.) upon which the control has been placed, with the position of the control measured from the edge of its container using the coordinate system established by the various Scale. . . properties for the container. By default, the unit of measure for a container is twips, with a value of 0 for the Left property placing the control against the left edge of the container.

Left The value of the function Left(*str*, n) is the string consisting of the leftmost n characters of *str*. If n is greater than the number of characters in *str*, the value of the function is *str*.

Len The value of Len(*str*) is the number of characters in the string *str*. If *var* is not a variable-length string variable, the value of Len(*var*) is the number of bytes needed to hold the value of the variable in memory. That is, Len(*var*) is 1, 2, 2, 4, 4, 8, or 8 for byte, Boolean, integer, long integer, single-precision, double-precision, and currency variables. Len(*var*), when *var* is a variable with a user-defined record type, is the number of bytes of memory needed to store the value of the variable. If *var* is a variant variable, Len(*var*) is the number of bytes needed to store var as a string. [variant]

Let   The statement Let *var* = *expr* assigns the value of the expression to the variable. If *var* is a fixed-length string variable with length n and Len(*expr*) is greater than n, then just the first n characters of *expr* are assigned to *var*. If Len(*expr*) < n, then *expr* is padded on the right with spaces and assigned to *var*. If *var* has a user-defined type, then *expr* must be of the same type. The statement *var* = *expr* is equivalent to Let *var* = *expr*.

Line   The graphics method *objectName*.Line (*x1*, *y1*)–(*x2*, *y2*) draws a line connecting the two points. The graphics method *objectName*.Line –(*x2*, *y2*) draws a line from the point (*objectName*.CurrentX, *objectName*.CurrentY) to the specified point. The object *objectName* can be a form, picture box, or the Printer. The line is in color c if *objectName*.Line (*x1*, *y1*)–(*x2*, *y2*), c is executed. The statement *objectName*.Line (*x1*, *y1*)–(*x2*, *y2*), ,B draws a rectangle with the two points as opposite vertices. (If B is replaced by BF, a solid rectangle is drawn.) After a Line method is executed, the value of *objectName*.CurrentX becomes *x2* and the value of *objectName*.CurrentY becomes *y2*. [color] [coordinate systems]

Line Input#   After a file has been opened as a sequential file for Input with reference number n, the statement Line Input #n, *str* assigns to the string variable *str* the string of characters from the current location in the file up to the next pair of carriage return/line feed characters.

List   The List property of a combo box, directory list box, drive list box, file list box, or list box is used to access items in the list. When one of these controls is created, Visual Basic automatically creates the string array List to hold the list of items stored in the control. The value of List1.List(n) is the item of List1 having index n. The value of List1.List (List1.ListIndex) is the item (string) currently highlighted in list box List1.

ListCount   For a list or combo box, the value of List1.ListCount or Combo1.ListCount is the number of items currently in the list. For a directory list box, drive list box, or file list box, the value of *control*.ListCount is the number of subdirectories in the current directory, the number of drives on the computer, or the number of files in the current directory that match the Pattern property, respectively.

ListIndex   The ListIndex property gives the index of the currently selected item is a combo box, directory list box, drive list box, file list box, or list box.

Load   The Load event applies only to forms and occurs only once, immediately when a program starts. This is the appropriate place to put code that should be executed every time a program is run, regardless of the user's actions.

Load   If *controlName* is the name of a control in a control array whose Index property was assigned a value during form design and *num* is a whole number that has not yet been used as an index for the *controlName*() array, then the statement Load *controlName*(*num*) copies properties of *controlName*(0) and creates the element *controlName*(*num*) of the *controlName*() array.

LoadPicture The statement *objectName*.Picture = LoadPicture(*pictureFile*), where *objectName* is a form or picture box, places the picture defined in the file specified by *pictureFile* on *objectName*

Loc This function gives the current location in a sequential, random-access, or binary file. For a sequential file with reference number n, Loc(n) is the number of blocks of 128 characters read from or written to the file since it was opened. For a random-access file, Loc(n) is the current record (either the last record read or written, or the record identified in a Seek statement). For a binary file, Loc(n) is the number of bytes from the beginning of the file to the last byte read or written. For communications, the value of Loc(n) is the number of bytes waiting in the communications buffer with reference number n. [binary file]

Lock The Lock command is intended for use in programs that operate on a network. The DOS command Share enables file sharing and should be executed from DOS prior to using the Lock statement. After a file has been opened with reference number n, the statement Lock #n denies access to the file by any other process. For a random-access file, the statement Lock #n, $r1$ To $r2$ denies access to records $r1$ through $r2$ by any other process. For a binary file, this statement denies access to bytes $r1$ through $r2$. The statement Lock #n, $r1$ locks only record (or byte) $r1$. For a sequential file, all forms of the Lock statement have the same effect as Lock #n. The Unlock statement is used to remove locks from files. All locks should be removed before a file is closed or the program is terminated. [binary file]

LOF After a file has been opened with reference number n, the number of characters in the file (that is, the length of the file) is given by LOF(n). For communications, the value of LOF(n) equals the number of bytes waiting in the communications buffer with reference number n.

Log If x is a positive number, the value of Log(x) is the natural logarithm (base e) of x.

Long A variable of type Long requires 4 bytes of memory and can hold the whole numbers from $-2,147,483,648$ to $2,147,483,647$. Long values and variables may be indicated by the type tag &: 12345678&, Population&.

LostFocus A LostFocus event occurs when an object loses the focus, either through a user action or through code, via the SetFocus method.

LSet If *str* is a string variable, then the statement LSet *str1* = *str2* replaces the value of *str1* with a string of the same length consisting of *str2* truncated or padded on the right with spaces. LSet also can be used to assign a record of one user-defined type to a record of a different user-defined type.

LTrim The value of the function LTrim(*str*) is the string obtained by removing all the spaces from the beginning of the string *str*. The string *str* may be either of fixed or variable length.

Max and Min The Max and Min properties of scroll bars give the values of horizontal (vertical) scroll bars when the thumb is at the right (bottom) and left (top) arrows, respectively.

MaxButton The MaxButton property determines whether or not a form has a maximize button in the upper-right corner. If the value of the MaxButton property is set to True (the default), a maximize button is displayed when the program is run. The user then has the option to click on the maximize button to cause the form to enlarge and fill the entire screen. If the value of the MaxButton property is set to False, the maximize button is not displayed when the program is run, and the user is thus unable to "maximize" the form.

MaxLength The property MaxLength determines the maximum number of characters that a text box will accept. If the MaxLength property for a text box is set to 0 (the default), an unlimited number of characters may be entered in the text box.

Mid The value of the function Mid(*str*, *m*, *n*) is the substring of *str* beginning with the *m*th character of *str* and containing up to *n* characters. If the parameter *n* is omitted, Mid(*str*, *m*) is all the characters of *str* from the *m*th character on. The statement Mid(*str*, *m*, *n*) = *str2* replaces the characters of *str*, beginning with the *m*th character, by the first *n* characters of the string *str2*.

MinButton The MinButton property determines whether or not a form has a minimize button in the upper-right corner. If the value of the MinButton property is set to True (the default), a minimize button is displayed when the program is run. The user then has the option to click on the minimize button to cause the form to be replaced by a small icon at the bottom of the screen. If the value of the MinButton property is set to False, the minimize button is not displayed when the program is run, and the user is thus unable to "minimize" the form.

Minute The function Minute extracts the minutes from a serial date. If *d* is any valid serial date, the value of Minute(*d*) is a whole number from 0 to 59 giving the minutes recorded as part of the date and time stored in *d*. [date]

MkDir The statement MkDir *path**dirName* creates a subdirectory named *dirName* in the directory specified by *path*. [directories]

Mod The value of the expression *num1* Mod *num2* is the whole number remainder when *num1* is divided by *num2*. If either *num1* or *num2* is not a whole number, it is rounded to a whole number before the Mod operation is performed. If one or both of *num1* and *num2* are negative, the result of the Mod operation will have the same sign as *num1*. For example, 25 Mod 7 is 4, 18.7 Mod 3.2 is 1, –35 Mod –4 is –3, and 27 Mod –6 is 3.

Month The function Month extracts the month from a serial date. If *d* is any valid serial date, the value of Month(*d*) is a whole number from 1 to 12 giving the month recorded as part of the date and time stored in *d*. [date]

MousePointer The property MousePointer determines what shape the mouse pointer takes when the mouse is over a particular form or control. Valid values for the MousePointer property are whole numbers from 0 to 12. A value of 0 (the default) indicates that the mouse pointer should take on the normal shape for the control it is over. (The normal shape over text boxes is an I-beam, and for a form, picture box, label, or command button it is an arrow.) Use a MousePointer value of 1 for an arrow, 2 for cross-hairs, 3 for an I-beam, 4 for a small square within a square, 5 for a four-pointed arrow, 6 for a double arrow pointing up to the right and down to the left, 7 for a double arrow pointing up and down, 8 for a double arrow pointing up to the left and down to the right, 9 for a double arrow pointing left and right, 10 for an up arrow, 11 for an hourglass, and 12 for a "do not" symbol (circle with diagonal line).

Move The method *objectName*.Move *xpos*, *ypos* moves the named form or control so that its upper left corner has coordinates (*xpos*, *ypos*). For forms, positioning is relative to the upper left corner of the screen. For controls, positioning is relative to the upper left corner of the form, frame, or picture box to which the control is attached. The method *objectName*.Move *xpos*, *ypos*, *width*, *height* also resizes the named form or control to be *width* units wide and *height* units high. The Move method may be used whether or not a form or control is visible. If you wish to specify just a new width for an object, you CANNOT use *objectName*.Move , , *width*. Instead, use *objectName*.Move *objectName*.Left, *objectName*.Top, *width*. Similar considerations apply for changing just *ypos*, *height*, *width* and *height*, and so on.

MoveFirst, MoveLast, MoveNext, MovePrevious The data control methods MoveNext, MovePrevious, MoveLast, and MoveFirst select new current records in the expected way.

MsgBox (Statement and Function) The statement MsgBox *prompt* displays *prompt* in a dialog box with an OK button. The more general statement MsgBox *prompt*, *buttons*, *title* displays *prompt* in a dialog box titled with *title* and containing from one to three buttons as determined by the value of *buttons*. The value of *buttons* also determines which button is the default (has the focus) and which, if any, of four icons is displayed. The value to use for *buttons* can be computed as follows:

$$buttons = \text{set number} + \text{default number} + \text{icon number}$$

where set number, default number, and icon number are determined from the following tables:

Buttons Set	Set Number
OK	0
OK, Cancel	1
Abort, Retry, Ignore	2
Yes, No, Cancel	3
Yes, No	4
Retry, Cancel	5

Focus Default	Default Number
First Button	0
Second Button	256
Third Button	512

Icon	Icon Number
Stop sign	16
Question mark	32
Exclamation mark	48
Information	64

The value of the function MsgBox(*prompt*, *buttons*, *title*) indicates which of the displayed buttons the user pushed; in all other aspects the MsgBox statement and function act in the same manner. The values returned for each of the possible buttons pressed are 1 for OK, 2 for Cancel (or Esc), 3 for Abort, 4 for Retry, 5 for Ignore, 6 for Yes, and 7 for No.

MultiLine The property MultiLine determines whether or not a text box can accept and display multiple lines. If the MultiLine property of a text box is set to True, then text entered in the text box will wrap to a new line when the right side of the text box is reached. Pressing the Enter key will also start a new line. If the MultiLine property of a text box is set to False (the default), input is restricted to a single line that scrolls if more input is entered than can be displayed within the width of the text box.

Name (Property) The property Name is used at design time to give a meaningful name to a form or control. This new name will then be used by Visual Basic in naming all event procedures for the form or control.

Name (Statement) The statement Name "*filespec1*" As "*filespec2*" is used to change the name and/or the directory of *filespec1* to the name and/or directory specified by *filespec2*. The two filespecs must refer to the same drive. [filespec]

New The keyword New is used with Set, to create an instance of a class. A typical statement is Set *objectVariable* As New *className*.

NewIndex The NewIndex property of a combo box or list box gives the index number of the item most recently added to the list.

NewPage The method Printer.NewPage indicates that the current page of output is complete and should be sent to the printer. A form feed (Chr(12)) will also be sent to the printer to cause the paper to advance to the top of a new page.

Not (Bitwise Operator) The expression Not *byte1* is evaluated by expressing the byte as an 8-tuple binary number and then Notting each individual digit, where Not 1 is equal to 0, while Not 0 is equal to 1. For example, the expression Not 37 translated to binary 8-tuples becomes Not 00100101. Notting each digit gives the binary 8-tuple 11011010 or decimal 218; thus Not 37 is 218.

Not (Logical Operator) The logical expression Not *condition1* is true if *condition1* is false and false if *condition1* is true. For example, Not (3<7) is false because 3<7 is true, and Not ("earth">"moon") is true because "earth">"moon" is false.

Nothing The keyword Nothing is used with Set to discontinue the association of an object variable with a specific object. A typical statement is Set *objectVariable* = Nothing. Assigning Nothing to an object variable releases all the system and memory resources associated with the previously referenced object when no other variable refers to it.

Now The value of the function Now( ) is the serial date for the current date and time as recorded on the computer's internal clock. [date]

Oct If *n* is a whole number between 0 and 2,147,483,647, Oct(*n*) is the octal (that is, base 8) representation of *n*.

On Error The statement On Error GoTo *lineLabel* sets up error-trapping. An error then causes a jump to the error-handling routine beginning with the first statement following the specified line label. The On Error statement and its target must be in the same procedure. [line label]

On...GoSub and On...GoTo The statement On *expression* GoSub *lineLabel1*, *lineLabel2*, ... causes a GoSub to *lineLabel1*, *lineLabel2*, ... depending on whether the value of the expression is 1, 2, ... Similarly, the GoTo variation causes an unconditional jump to the appropriate line label. The GoSub or GoTo statement and its target must be in the same procedure. [line label]

Open The statement Open "*filespec*" For *mode* As #*n* allows access to the file *filespec* in one of the following modes: Input (information can be read sequentially from the file), Output (a new file is created and information can be written sequentially to it), Append (information can be added sequentially to the end of a file), or Binary (information can be read or written in an arbitrary fashion). The statement Open "*filespec*" For Random As #*n* Len = *g* allows random-access to the file *filespec* in which each record has length *g*. Throughout the program, the file is referred to by the reference number *n* (from 1 through 255). Another variation of the Open statement is Open "LPT1" For Output As #*n*, which allows access to the printer as if it were a sequential file.

In a network environment, two enhancements to the Open statement are available. (The DOS command Share enables file sharing and should be executed from DOS prior to the use of the enhanced variations of the Open statement.) Visual Basic accesses data files in two ways: it reads from them or writes to them. When several processes may utilize a file at the same time, accurate file handling requires that certain types of access be denied to anyone but the person who has opened the file. The statement Open "*filespec*" For *mode* Lock Read As #*n* or Open "*filespec*" For Random Lock Read As #*n* Len = *g* opens the specified file and forbids any other process from reading the file as long as the file is open. Lock Write forbids any other process from writing to the file as long as the file is open. Lock Read Write forbids any other process from reading or writing to the file as long as the file is open. Lock Shared grants full access to any other process, except when a file is currently opened and locked by a process for a certain access mode, then another process attempting to open the file for the same mode will receive the message "Permission denied" and be denied access. [filespec] [binary file]

Option Base After the statement Option Base *m* is executed, where *m* is 0 or 1, a statement of the form Dim *arrayName*(*n*) defines an array with subscripts ranging from *m* to *n*. Visual Basic's extended Dim statement, which permits both lower and upper subscript bounds to be specified for each array, achieves a wider range of results, making its use preferable to Option Base.

Option Compare The statement Option Compare Text, placed in the (Declarations) section of (General), causes string comparisons to be case-insensitive. Thus, if Option Compare Text is in effect, the comparison "make" = "MaKe" will be true. The statement Option Compare Binary placed in the (Declarations) section produces the default comparison rules, which are case-sensitive and use the character order given in the ANSI/ASCII character tables.

Option Explicit If the statement Option Explicit appears in the (Declarations) section of (General), each variable must be declared before it is used. A variable is declared by appearing in a Const, Dim, Global, ReDim, or Static statement, or by appearing as a parameter in a Sub or Function definition.

Or (Bitwise Operator) The expression *byte1* Or *byte2* is evaluated by expressing each byte as an 8-tuple binary number and then Oring together corresponding digits, where 1 Or 1, 1 Or 0, and 0 Or 1 are all equal to 1, while 0 And 0 is equal to 0. For example, the expression 37 Or 157 translated to binary 8-tuples becomes 00100101 Or 10011101. Oring together corresponding digits gives the binary 8-tuple 10111101 or decimal 189. Thus, 37 Or 157 is 189.

Or (Logical Operator) The logical expression *condition1* Or *condition2* is true except when both *condition1* and *condition2* are false. For example, ("apple">"ape") Or ("earth">"moon") is true because "apple">"ape" is true, and (1>2) Or ("moon"< "earth") is false because both (1>2) and ("moon"<"earth") are false.

Path   The Path property for a directory list box is the contents of the currently selected item, and for a files list box is the path identifying the directory whose files are displayed.

PathChange   For a files list box, the PathChange event is triggered by a change in the value of the Path property.

Pattern   The Pattern property of a files list box uses wildcard characters to determine which file names are displayed. A typical statement is Let File1.Pattern = "*.TXT."

PatternChange   For a files list box, the PatternChange event is triggered by a change in the value of the Pattern property.

Picture   The property Picture allows a form or picture box to be assigned a picture or icon for display. If *iconOrPicture* is a file defining an icon or bitmapped picture, then *objectName*.Picture = LoadPicture(*iconOrPicture*) places the icon or picture on the form or picture box identified by *objectName*.

Point   The value of the method *objectName*.Point(x, y) is the RGB number of the color of the point with coordinates (x, y) on the form or picture box identified by *objectName*. Thus, if the point with coordinates (x, y) has been painted using color RGB(r, g, b), then the value of Point(x, y) will be $r+256*g+65536*b$. If the coordinates (x, y) identify a point that is not on *objectName*, the value of Point(x, y) will be –1. [color] [coordinate systems]

Print   The print method is used to display data on the screen or printer. The statement *objectName*.Print *expression* displays the value of the expression at the current position of the cursor in the named object (form, picture box, or Printer) and moves the cursor to the beginning of the next line. (Numbers are displayed with a trailing space and positive numbers with a leading space.) If the statement is followed by a semicolon or comma, the cursor will not move to the next line after the display, but will move to the next position or print zone, respectively. Several expressions may be placed in the same Print method if separated by semicolons (to display them adjacent to one another) or by commas (to display them in successive zones).

Print#   After a file has been opened as a sequential file for output or append with reference number *n*, the statement Print #*n*, *expression* places the value of the expression into the file in the same way the Print method displays it in a picture box.

Printer   The Printer object provides access to the printer. Methods available are Print to send text to the printer, NewPage to execute a form feed to begin a new page, EndDoc to terminate the printing process, and the graphics methods. Many properties available for forms and picture boxes, such as fonts and scaling, are also available for the printer.

PrintForm   The method *formName*.PrintForm prints on the printer an image of the named form and all its contents.

Property Get/End Property   A Property Get procedure is a multistatement block in a class module beginning with a statement of the form Public Property Get *name*(*parList*), followed on subsequent lines by one or more statements for carrying out the task of the procedure, and ending with the statement End Property. The parameter list *parList* is a list of variables through which values will be passed to the procedure when the property value of an associated object is retrieved. The name and data type of each parameter in a Property Get procedure must be the same as the corresponding parameter in a Property Let procedure (if one exists).

Property Let/End Property   A Property Let procedure is a multistatement block in a class module beginning with a statement of the form Public Property Let *name(parList)*, followed on subsequent lines by one or more statements for carrying out the task of the procedure, and ending with the statement End Property. The parameter list *parList* is a list of variables through which values will be passed to the procedure when an assignment is made to the property of an associated object. The name and data type of each parameter in a Property Let procedure must be the same as the corresponding parameter in a Property Get procedure (if one exists).

PSet   The graphics method *objectName*.PSet(*x*, *y*) displays the point with coordinates (*x*, *y*) in the foreground color. The method *objectName*.PSet(*x*, *y*), *c* causes the point (*x*, *y*) to be displayed in the RGB color specified by *c*. The size of the point is determined by the value of the DrawWidth property. The actual color(s) displayed depend on the values of the DrawMode and DrawStyle properties. After a PSet method is executed, the value of *objectName*.CurrentX becomes *x* and the value of *objectName*.CurrentY becomes *y*. [color] [coordinate systems]

Put   The Put statement is used to place data into a random-access file. Suppose *recVar* is a variable of a user-defined record type and that a file has been opened with a statement of the form Open *fileName* For Random As #*n* Len = Len(*recVar*). The statement Put #*n*, *r*, *recVar* places the value of *recVar* in the *r*th record of the file.

The Put statement is also used to place data into a file opened as a binary file. Suppose *var* is a variable that holds a value consisting of *b* bytes. (For instance, if *var* is an integer variable, then *b* is 2. If *var* is an ordinary string variable, then *b* will equal the length of the string currently assigned to it.) The statement Put #*n*, *p*, *var* writes the successive bytes of *var* into the *b* consecutive locations beginning with position *p* in the binary file with reference number *n*. (**Note:** The positions are numbered 1, 2, 3, ...) If *p* is omitted, the current file position is used as the beginning position. [binary file]

QBColor   The function QBColor provides easy access to 16 standard colors. If *colorAttrib* is a whole number from 0 to 15, the value of the functions QBColor (*colorAttrib*) is the RGB color number associated with *colorAttrib*. The following table names the colors produced by each of the possible values of *colorAttrib*.

0 Black	4 Red	8 Gray	12 Light Red
1 Blue	5 Magenta	9 Light Blue	13 Light Magenta
2 Green	6 Brown	10 Light Green	14 Yellow
3 Cyan	7 White	11 Light Cyan	15 Intense White

RaiseEvent   After an event has been declared in the general declarations section of a class module, the statement RaiseEvent *EventName(arg1, arg2, . . .)* generates the event.

Randomize   The statement Randomize automatically uses the computer's clock to seed the random-number generator. If a program includes a Randomize statement in the Form_Load event procedure, the list of numbers generated by Rnd will vary each time the program is executed. Randomize *n* seeds the generator with a number determined by *n*. If a program does not seed the random-number generator or seeds it with a set number, the list of numbers generated by Rnd will be the same each time the program is executed.

RecordCount The value of Data1.Recordset.RecordCount is the number of records in the database table associated with the data control.

RecordSource The value of the RecordSource property of a data control is the table of the database determined by the DatabaseName property. The value can also be an SQL statement used to specify a virtual table.

ReDim The statement ReDim *arrayName*(...) erases the array from memory and recreates it. The information inside the parentheses has the same form and produces the same results as that in a Dim statement. After the ReDimensioning, all elements have their default values. Although the ranges of the subscripts may be changed, the number of dimensions must be the same as in the original Dimensioning of the array. ReDim may be used only within procedures; it may not be used in the (Declarations) section of (General). To establish an array that is available to all procedures and also can be resized, Dim it with empty parentheses in the (Declarations) section of (General) and then ReDim it as needed within appropriate procedures.

Refresh The method *objectName*.Refresh causes the named form or control to be refreshed, that is, redrawn reflecting any changes made to its properties. Generally, refreshing occurs automatically, but if not, it may be forced with the Refresh method.

Rem The statement Rem allows documentation to be placed in a program. A line of the form Rem *comment* is ignored during execution. The Rem statement may be abbreviated as an apostrophe.

Remove A statement of the form *collectionName*.Remove *n* deletes the *n*th object from the collection and automatically reduces the object numbers from *n* on by 1 so that there is no gap in the numbers. A statement of the form *collectionName*.Remove *keyString* deletes the object identified by the key *key-String*. If the value of *n* or *keyString* doesn't match an existing object of the collection, an error occurs.

RemoveItem The RemoveItem method deletes items from list and combo boxes and deletes rows from grids. The statement List1.RemoveItem *n* (where *n* is 0, 1, . . .) deletes the item with index *n*. For instance, List1.RemoveItem 0 deletes the top item and List1.RemoveItem ListCount − 1 deletes the bottom item in the list. The statement MSFlexGrid1.RemoveItem *n* deletes row *n* from the grid.

Reset The statement Reset closes all open files. Using Reset is equivalent to using Close with no file reference numbers.

Resume When the statement Resume is encountered at the end of an error-handling routine, the program branches back to the statement in which the error was encountered. The variations Resume *lineLabel* and Resume Next cause the program to branch to the first statement following the indicated line label or to the statement following the statement in which the error occurred, respectively. (The combination of On Error and Resume Next is similar to the combination GoSub and Return.) [line label]

Return When the statement Return is encountered at the end of a subroutine, the program branches back to the statement following the one containing the most recently executed GoSub. The variation Return *lineLabel* causes the program to branch back to the first statement following the indicated line label. [line label] [subroutine]

RGB The value of the function RGB(*red, green, blue*) is the color number corresponding to a mixture of *red* red, *green* green, and *blue* blue. This color number is assigned to color properties or used in graphics methods to produce text or graphics in a particular color. Each of the three color components may have a value from 0 to 255. The color produced using RGB(0, 0, 0) is black, RGB(255, 255, 255) is white, RGB(255, 0, 0) is bright red, RGB(10, 0, 0) is a dark red, and so on. (The value of the function RGB(*r, g, b*) is the long integer $r+256*g+65536*b$.) [color]

Right The value of the function Right(*str, n*) is the string consisting of the rightmost *n* characters of *str*. If *n* is greater than the number of characters of *str*, then the value of the function is *str*.

RmDir If *path* specifies a directory containing no files or subdirectories, then the statement RmDir *path* removes the directory. [directories]

Rnd The value of the function Rnd is a randomly selected number from 0 to 1, not including 1. The value of Int(*n**Rnd)+1 is a random whole number from 1 to *n*.

RowHeight The statement Let MSFlexGrid1.RowHeight(*m*) = *n* specifies that row *m* of the grid be *n* twips high. (There are about 1440 twips in an inch.)

RSet If *str1* is a string variable, the statement RSet *str1* = *str2* replaces the value of *str1* with a string of the same length consisting of *str2* truncated or padded on the left with spaces.

RTrim The value of the function RTrim(*str*) is the string obtained by removing all the spaces from the end of the string *str*. The string *str* may be either fixed-length or variable-length.

Scale The method *objectName*.Scale (*x1, y1*)–(*x2, y2*) defines a coordinate system for the form or picture box identified by *objectName*. This coordinate system has horizontal values ranging from *x1* at the left edge of *objectName* to *x2* at the right edge and vertical values ranging from *y1* at the top edge of *objectName* to *y2* at the bottom edge. Subsequent graphics methods and control positioning place figures and controls in accordance with this new coordinate system. As a result of using the Scale method, the ScaleMode property of *objectName* is set to 0, the ScaleLeft property to *x1*, the ScaleTop property to *y1*, the ScaleHeight property to *y2–y1*, and the ScaleWidth property to *x2–x1*. The method *objectName*.Scale without arguments resets the coordinate system of *objectName* to the default coordinate system where the unit of measure is twips and the upper-left corner of *objectName* has coordinates (0, 0).

ScaleHeight The property ScaleHeight determines the vertical scale on a form or picture box. After the statement *objectName*.ScaleHeight = *hght* is executed, the vertical coordinates range from *objectName*.ScaleTop at the top edge of *objectName* to *objectName*.ScaleTop + *hght* at the bottom edge. The default value of the ScaleHeight property is the height of *objectName* when measured in the units specified by *objectName*'s ScaleMode property.

ScaleLeft The property ScaleLeft determines the horizontal coordinate of the left edge of a form or picture box. After the statement *objectName*.ScaleLeft = *left* is executed, the horizontal coordinates will range from *left* at the left edge of *objectName* to *left* + *objectName*.ScaleWidth at the right edge. The default value of the ScaleLeft property is 0.

ScaleMode The property ScaleMode determines the horizontal and vertical unit of measure for the coordinate system on a form or picture box. If the ScaleMode property of a form or picture box is set to 1 (the default), the unit of measure becomes twips. Other possible values for ScaleMode are 2 for points (72 points = 1 inch), 3 for pixels, 4 for characters (1 horizontal unit = 120 twips; 1 vertical unit = 240 twips), 5 for inches, 6 for millimeters, and 7 for centimeters. A value of 0 for the ScaleMode property indicates that units of measure are to be determined from the current settings of the ScaleHeight and ScaleWidth properties. Visual Basic automatically sets the ScaleMode property of an object to 0 when any of the object's Scale... properties are assigned values.

ScaleTop The property ScaleTop determines the vertical coordinate of the top edge of a form or picture box. After the statement *objectName*.ScaleTop = *top* is executed, the vertical coordinates range from *top* at the top edge of *objectName* to *top* + *objectName*.ScaleHeight at the bottom edge. The default value for the ScaleTop property is 0.

ScaleWidth The property ScaleWidth determines the horizontal scale on a form or picture box. After the statement *objectName*.ScaleWidth = *wdth* is executed, the horizontal coordinates range from *objectName*.ScaleLeft at the left edge of *objectName* to *objectName*.ScaleLeft + *wdth* at the right edge. The default value of the ScaleWidth property is the width of *objectName* when measured in the units specified by *objectName*'s ScaleMode property.

ScrollBars The ScrollBars property of a grid or text box specifies whether the control has horizontal (setting = 1), vertical (setting = 2), both (setting = 3), or no (setting = 0) scroll bars. In order for a text box to have scroll bars, the MultiLine property must be set to True.

Second The function Second extracts the seconds from a serial date. If *d* is any valid serial date, the value of Second(*d*) is a whole number from 0 to 59 giving the seconds recorded as part of the date and time stored in *d*. [date]

Seek The statement Seek #*n*, *p* sets the current file position in the binary or random-access file referenced by *n* to the *p*th byte or record of the file, respectively. After the statement is executed, the next Get or Put statement will read or write bytes, respectively, beginning with the *p*th byte or record. The value of the function Seek(*n*) is the current file position either in bytes or by record number. After a Put or Get statement is executed, the value of Seek(*n*) is the number of the next byte or record. [binary file]

Select Case The Select Case statement provides a compact method of selecting for execution one of several blocks of statements based on the value of an expression. The Select Case block begins with a line of the form Select Case *expression* and ends with the statement End Select. In between are statements of the form Case *valueList* and perhaps the statement Case Else. The items in the *valueList* may be individual values or ranges of values such as "*a* To *b*" or "Is < *a*". Each of these Case statements is followed by a block of one or more statements. The block of statements following the first Case *valueList* statement for which *valueList* includes the value of *expression* is the only block of statements executed. If none of the value lists includes the value of expression and a Case Else statement is present, then the block of statements following the Case Else statement is executed.

SendKeys The statement SendKeys *str* places in the keyboard buffer the characters and keystrokes specified by *str*. The effect is exactly the same as if the user had typed the series of characters/keystrokes at the keyboard. The statement SendKeys str, True places keystrokes in the keyboard buffer and waits until these keystrokes are processed (used) before allowing program execution to continue with the next statement in the procedure containing the SendKeys statement. Keystrokes can be specified that do not have a displayable character or that result from using the Shift, Ctrl, or Alt keys. See the Visual Basic reference manual or Help for further details.

Set Essentially, Set is "Let for objects." Whereas the Let statement is used to assign ordinary values to variables or properties, the Set statement is used to assign objects to variables or properties.

The statement Set *controlVar* = *objectExpression* associates the name *controlVar* with the object identified by *objectExpression*. For example, if the statements Dim Scenery As PictureBox and Set Scenery = Picture1 are executed, then Scenery becomes another name for Picture1, and references like Scenery.Print *message* are equivalent to Picture1.Print *message*. Also, the Set statement assigns an object to an object variable. When you want to release the memory used for the object, execute Set *objVar* = Nothing.

SetAttr The statement SetAttr *fileName*, *attribute* sets the file attribute of the file specified by *fileName*. A file's attribute can be 0 for "Normal" or a combination of 1, 2, or 4 for "Read-only", "Hidden", and "System." In addition, a file can be marked as "changed since last backup" by adding 32 to its attribute. Thus, for example, if a file's attribute is set to 35 (1 + 2 + 32), the file is classified as a Read-only Hidden file that has been changed since the last backup.

SetFocus The method *objectName*.SetFocus moves the focus to the named form or control. Only the object with the focus can receive user input from the keyboard or the mouse. If *objectName* is a form, the form's default control, if any, receives the focus. Disabled and invisible objects cannot receive the focus. If an attempt is made to set focus to a control that cannot receive the focus, the next control in tab order receives the focus.

SetText The method ClipBoard.SetText *info* replaces the contents of the clipboard with the string *info*.

Sgn The value of the function Sgn(x) is 1, 0, or –1, depending on whether x is positive, zero, or negative, respectively.

Shell If *command* is a DOS command, the function Shell(*command*) causes *command* to be executed. If the DOS command requires user input, execution of the Visual Basic program will be suspended until the user input is supplied. Using the function Shell with no arguments suspends program execution and invokes a copy of DOS. Entering the command Exit resumes execution of the Visual Basic program. The value returned by the Shell function is a number used by Windows to identify the new task being performed.

Show The Show method makes an invisible form visible. The statement Form1.Show 1 also makes a form modal. No user input to any other form will be accepted until the modal form is hidden.

Sin For any number x, the value of the trigonometric function $Sin(x)$ is the sine of the angle of x radians. [radians]

Single A variable of type Single requires 4 bytes of memory and can hold 0, the numbers from 1.40129×10^{-45} to 3.40283×10^{38} with at most seven significant digits, and the negatives of these numbers. Single values and variables may be indicated by the type tag !: 32.156!, Meters!.

SmallChange When a scroll bar arrow button is clicked, the Value property of the scroll bar changes by the value of the SmallChange property and the thumb moves accordingly.

Sorted When the Sorted property of a list or combo box is set to True, the items are automatically presented in alphabetical order.

Space If n is an integer from 0 to 32767, the value of the function $Space(n)$ is the string consisting of n spaces.

Spc The function Spc is used in Print and Print# statements to generate spaces. For instance, the statement Print *str1*; Spc(n); *str2* skips n spaces between the displays of the two strings.

Sqr For any nonnegative number x, the value of the square root function $Sqr(x)$ is the non-negative number whose square is x.

Static A statement of the form Static *var1*, *var2*, ... can be used at the beginning of the definition of a procedure to specify that the variables *var1*, *var2*, ... are static local variables in the procedure. Memory for static variables is permanently set aside by Visual Basic, allowing static variables to retain their values between successive calls of the procedure. The type of each variable is either determined by a Def*Type* statement, a type-declaration tag, or an As clause. Static variables have no connection to variables of the same name outside the procedure, and so may be named without regard to "outside" variables. Arrays created in a procedure by ReDim are lost when the procedure is exited. Arrays that are local to a procedure yet retained from one invocation of the procedure to the next can be created by dimensioning the array in the procedure with a Static statement rather than a ReDim statement. Dimensions for static arrays must be numeric constants. A local static array whose size is to be determined at run time is declared by listing its name followed by empty parentheses in a Static statement, and then dimensioning the array in a subsequent ReDim statement.

Stop The statement Stop suspends the execution of a program. Execution can be resumed beginning with the first statement after the Stop statement by pressing F5.

Str The Str function converts numbers to strings. The value of the function $Str(n)$ is the string consisting of the number n in the form normally displayed by a print statement.

StrComp The value of the function StrComp(*str1*, *str2*, *compMode*) is –1, 0, 1, or Null depending on whether *str1* < *str2*, *str1* = *str2*, *str1* > *str2*, or either of *str1* and *str2* is Null. The comparison will be case-sensitive if *compMode* is 0 and case-insensitive if *compMode* is 1.

StrConv   The value of StrConv(*str*, 3) is the value of *str* with the first letter of every word converted to uppercase. The value of StrConv(*str*, 1) is the same as UCase(*str*) and the value of StrConv(*str*, 2) is the same as LCase(*str*).

Stretch   When the Stretch property of an image control is set to False (the default value), the image control will be resized to fit the picture If the Stretch property is set to True, the picture will be resized to fit the image control

String   A variable of type String can hold a string of up to 32,767 characters. String values are enclosed in quotes: "January 1, 2001". String variables can be indicated by the type tag $: FirstName$. A variable of type String*n* holds a string of *n* characters, where *n* is a whole number from 1 to 32,767. Variables of this type have no type tag and must be declared in a Dim, Global, or Static statement. Until assigned a value, these variables contain a string of *n* Chr(0)'s.

String   If *n* is a whole number from 0 to 32767, the value of String(*n*, *str*) is the string consisting of the first character of *str* repeated *n* times. If *m* is a whole number from 0 to 255, the value of the function String(*n*, *m*) is the string consisting of the character with ANSI value *m* repeated *n* times.

Style   The Style property of a combo box determine whether the list is always visible (Style = 1) or whether the list drops down when the user clicks on the arrow and then disappears after a selection is made (Style = 0).

Sub/End Sub   A subprogram is a multistatement block beginning with a statement of the form Sub *SubprogramName*(*parList*), followed on subsequent lines by one or more statements for carrying out the task of the subprogram, and ending with the statement End Sub. The parameter list *parList* is a list of variables through which values will be passed to the subprogram whenever the function is called. (See the discussion of Call.) Parameters may be numeric or (variable-length) string variables as well as arrays.

Tab   The function Tab(*n*) is used in Print and Print# statements to move the cursor to position *n* and place spaces in all skipped-over positions. If *n* is less than the cursor position, the cursor is moved to the *n*th position of the next line.

TabIndex   The property TabIndex determines the order in which the tab key moves the focus about the objects on a form. Visual Basic automatically assigns successive tab indexes as new controls are created at design time. Visual Basic also automatically prevents two controls on the same form from having the same tab index by renumbering controls with higher tab indexes when the designer or program directly assigns a new tab index to a control.

Tan   For any number *x* (except for $x = \pi/2$, $-\pi/2$, $3 * \pi/2$, $-3 * \pi/2$, and so on), the value of the trigonometric function Tan(*x*) is the tangent of the angle of *x* radians. [radians]

Text   For a text box, the Text property holds the information assigned to a text box. A statement of the form Let *textBoxName*.Text = *str* changes the contents of *textBoxName* to the string specified by *str*. A statement of the form *str* = *textBoxName*.Text assigns the contents of *textBoxName* to *str*. For a list or combo box, *control*.Text is the contents of the currently highlighted item or the item in the text box, respectively. For a grid, MSFlexGrid1.Text is the contents of the active cell.

TextHeight This method applies to forms, picture boxes, and printer objects. The value of the method *objectName*.TextHeight(*strVar*) is the amount of vertical space required to display the contents of *strVar* using the font currently assigned for *objectName*. These contents may include multiple lines of text resulting from the use of carriage return/line feed pairs (Chr(13) + Chr(10)) in *strVar*. The units of height are those specified by the ScaleMode and ScaleHeight properties of *objectName*. (The default is twips.)

TextWidth This method applies to forms, picture boxes, and printer objects. The value of the method *objectName*.TextWidth(*strVar*) is the amount of horizontal space required to display the contents of *strVar* using the font currently assigned for *objectName*. When carriage return/line feed pairs (Chr(13) + Chr(10)) create multiple lines in *strVar*, this will be the space required for the longest line.

Time The value of the function Time is the current time expressed as a string of the form hh:mm:ss. (The hours range from 0 to 23, as in military time.) If *timeStr* is such a string, the statement Time = *timeStr* sets the computer's internal clock to the corresponding time.

Timer The value of the function Timer is the number of seconds from midnight to the time currently stored in the computer's internal clock.

Timer The Timer event is triggered by the passage of the amount of time specified by the Interval property of a timer control whose Enabled property is set to True.

TimeSerial The value of the function TimeSerial(*hour*, *minute*, *second*) is the serial date corresponding to the given hour, minute, and second. Values from 0 (midnight) to 23 (11 p.m.) for *hour*, and 0 to 59 for both *minute* and *second* are normal, but any Integer value may be used. Often, numeric expressions are used for *hour*, *minute*, or *second* that evaluate to numbers outside these ranges. For example, TimeSerial(15–5, 20–30, 0) is the serial time 5 hours and 30 minutes before 3:20 p.m.

TimeValue The value of the function TimeValue(*str*) is the serial date corresponding to the time given in *str*. TimeValue recognizes both the 24-hour and 12-hour time formats: "13:45:24" or "1:45:24PM".

Top The property Top determines the position of the top edge of a form or control. The units of measure are twips for forms. The units of measure for a control are determined by the ScaleMode property of the container (form, picture box, etc.) on which the control has been placed, with the position of the control measure from the edge of its container using the coordinate system established by the various Scale... properties for the container. By default, the unit of measure for a container is twips, with a value of 0 for the Top property placing the control against the top edge of the container.

Trim The value of the function Trim(*str*) is the string obtained by removing all the spaces from the beginning and end of the string *str*. The string *str* may be either fixed-length or variable-length.

True A predefined constant whose value is –1. True is used when setting the value of properties that are either True or False. For example, Picture1.FontItalic = True.

Type/End Type A multistatement block beginning the Type *typeName* and ending with End Type creates a user-defined record type. Each statement inside the block has the form *elt* As *type*, where *elt* is a variable and *type* is either Integer, Boolean, Byte, Date, Long, Single, Double, Currency, Variant, String*n (that is, fixed-length string), or another user-defined record type. After a statement of the form Dim *var* As *typeName* appears, the element corresponding to the statement *elt* As *type* is referred to as *var.elt*. Type declaration blocks must be placed in the (Declarations) section of a BAS module. [variant]

TypeName If var is variable, then the value of the function TypeName(var) is a string identifying the type of the variable. The possible values of the function are Byte, Integer, Long, Single, Double, Currency, Date, String, Boolean, Error, Empty (uninitialized), Null (no valid data), Object (an object that supports OLE Automation), Unknown (an OLE Automation object whose type is unknown), and Nothing (an object variable that doesn't refer to an object).

UBound For a one-dimensional array *arrayName*, the value of the function UBound(*arrayName*) is the largest subscript value that may be used. For any array *arrayName*, the value of the function UBound(*arrayName*, n) is the largest subscript value that may be used for the nth subscript of the array. For example, after the statement Dim example(1 To 31, 1 To 12, 1990 To 1999) is executed, the value of UBound(example, 3) is the largest value allowed for the third subscript of example( ), which is 1999.

UCase The value of the string function UCase(*str*) is a string identical to *str* except that all lowercase letters are changed to uppercase.

Unlock The Unlock command is intended for use in programs that operate on a network. The DOS command Share enables file sharing and should be executed from DOS prior to using the Lock and Unlock statements. After a Lock statement has been used to deny access to all or part of a file (see the discussion of Lock for details), a corresponding Unlock statement can be used to restore access. Suppose a data file has been opened as reference number n. The locks established by the statements Lock #n; Lock #n, *r1*; and Lock #n, *r1* To *r2* are undone by the statements Unlock #n; Unlock #n, *r1*; and Unlock #n, *r1* To *r2*, respectively. There must be an exact correspondence between the locking and the unlocking statements used in a program, that is, each set of paired statements must refer to the same range of record numbers or bytes.

Update The Update method of a data control is used to save changes made to the database.

Val The Val function is used to convert strings to numbers. If the leading characters of the string *str* corresponds to a number, then Val(*str*) will be the number represented by these characters. For any number n, Val(Str(n)) is n.

Validate The Validate event procedure is activated whenever the current record of a database table is about to be changed. The heading of the procedure has the form Private Sub Data1_Validate(Action As Integer, Save As Integer), where the value of Action identifies the specific operation that triggered the event and the value of Save specifies whether data bound to the control has changed. You can change the value of the Action argument to convert one operation into another.

Value The Value property of a scroll bar is a number between the values of the Min and Max properties of the scroll bar that is related to the position of the thumb. The Value property of an option button is True when the button is on and False when the button is off. The Value property of a check box is 0 (unchecked), 1 (checked), or 2 (grayed). The Value property of Fields("*field-Name*") reads the contents of a field of the current record.

Variant A variable of type variant can be assigned numbers, strings, and several other types of data. Variant variables are written without type-declaration tags. [variant]

VarType The value of the function VarType(var) is a number indicating the type of value stored in var. This function is primarily used to check the type of data stored in a variant variable. Some values returned by VarType are 0 for "Empty," 1 for "Null," 2 for Integer, 3 for Long Integer, 4 for Single Precision, 5 for Double Precision, 6 for Currency, 7 for Date, 8 for String, 9 for OLE Automation object, 10 for Error, 11 for Boolean, 13 for Non-OLE Automation object, and 17 for Byte. For nonvariant arrays, the number assigned is 8192 plus the number assigned to the type of the array. [variant]

Visible The property Visible determines whether or not a form or control is displayed. If the Visible property of an object is True, the object will be displayed (if not covered by other objects) and respond to events if its Enabled property is True. If the Visible property of an object is set to False, the object will not be displayed and cannot respond to events.

WeekDay The value of the function WeekDay(*d*) is a number giving the day of the week for the date store in *d*. These values will range from 1 for Sunday to 7 for Saturday.

While/Wend A While ... Wend loop is a sequence of statements beginning with a statement of the form While *condition* and ending with the statement Wend. After the While statement is executed, the computer repeatedly executes the entire sequence of statements inside the loop as long as the condition is true.

Width (Property) The property Width determines the horizontal size of an object. Width is measured in units of twips. For the Printer object, Width may be read (pw = Printer.Width is OK) but not assigned (Printer.Width = 100 causes an error).

Width (Statement) If *s* is an integer less than 255 and *n* is the reference number of a file opened in sequential mode, the statement Width #n, *s* causes Visual Basic to permit at most *s* characters to be printed on a single line in the file. Visual Basic will send a carriage return/line feed pair to the file after *s* characters have been printed on a line, even if the Print# or Write# statement would not otherwise start a new line at that point. The statement Width #n, 0 specifies infinite width, that is, a carriage return/line feed pair will be sent to the printer only when requested by Print# or Write#.

With/End With A multistatement block begun by With *recName* or With *objName* and ended by End With is used to assign values to the fields of the named record variable or to properties of the named object. The statements inside the block have the form .*fieldName* = *fieldValue* or .*propertyName* = *propertyValue*. When you use this block, you only have to refer to the record variable or object once instead of referring to it with each assignment.

WithEvents   If a class has events attached to it, and form code intends to make use of these events, then the keyword WithEvents should be inserted into the statement declaring an instance of the class. A typical declaration statement is Private WithEvents *objectVariable* As *className*.

WordWrap   The WordWrap property of a label with AutoSize property set to True determines whether or not long captions will wrap. (When a label's AutoSize property is False, word wrap always occurs, but the additional lines will not be visible if the label is not tall enough.) Assume a label's AutoSize property is True. If its WordWrap property is set to True, long captions will wrap to multiple lines; if its WordWrap property is False (the default), the caption will always occupy a single line. If a label has its WordWrap and AutoSize property set to True, the label's horizontal length is determined by its Width property, with long captions being accommodated by having the label expand vertically so that word wrap can spread the caption over several lines. If a label's WordWrap property is set to False while its AutoSize property is True, the label will be one line high and will expand or shrink horizontally to exactly accommodate its caption.

Write#   After a sequential file is opened for output or append with reference number n, the statement Write #n, *exp1*, *exp2*, . . . records the values of the expressions one after the other into the file. Strings appear surrounded by quotation marks, numbers do not have leading or trailing spaces, all commas in the expressions are recorded, and the characters for carriage return and line feed are placed following the data.

Xor   (Logical Operator) The logical expression *condition1* Xor *condition2* is true if *condition1* is true or *condition2* is true, but not if both are true. For example, (3<7) Xor ("abc">"a") is false because both 3<7 and "abc">"a" are true, and ("apple">"ape") Xor ("earth">"moon") is true because "apple">"ape" is true and "earth">"moon" is false.

Xor   (Bitwise Operator) The expression *byte1* Xor *byte2* is evaluated by expressing each byte as an 8-tuple binary number and then Xoring together corresponding digits, where 1 Xor 0 and 0 Xor 1 both equal 1, while 1 Xor 1 and 0 Xor 0 both equal 0. For example, the expression 37 Xor 157 translated to binary 8-tuples becomes 00100101 Xor 10011101. Xoring together corresponding digits gives the binary 8-tuple 10111000 or decimal 184. Thus, 37 Xor 157 is 184.

Year   The function Year extracts the year from a serial date. If *d* is any valid serial date, then the value of Year(*d*) is a whole number from 100 to 9999 giving the year recorded as part of the date and time stored in *d*. [date]

Supporting Topics

[**binary file**]:   A file that has been opened with a statement of the form Open "*filespec*" For Binary As #n is regarded simply as a sequence of characters occupying positions 1, 2, 3, ... At any time, a specific location in the file is designated as the "current position." The Seek statement can be used to set the current position. Collections of consecutive characters are written to and read from the file beginning at the current position with Put and Get statements, respectively. After a Put or Get statement is executed, the position following the last position accessed becomes the new current position.

[color]: Numbers written in base 16 are referred to as hexadecimal numbers. They are written with the digits 0, 1, 2, 3, 4, 5, 6, 7, 8, 9, A (=10), B (=11), C (=12), D (=13), E (=14), and F (=15). A hexadecimal number such as *rst* corresponds to the decimal integer $t + 16 * s + 16^2 * r$. Each color in Visual Basic is identified by a long integer (usually expressed as a hexadecimal number of the form &H...&) and referred to as an RGB color number. This number specifies the amounts of red, green, and blue combined to produce the color. The amount of any color is a relative quantity, with 0 representing none of the color and 255 representing the maximum available. Thus, black corresponds to 0 units each of red, green, and blue, and white corresponds to 255 units each of red, green, and blue. The RGB color number corresponding to *r* units of red, *g* units of green, and *b* units of blue is $r + 256 * g + 65536 * b$, which is the value returned by the function RGB(r, g, b). Hexadecimal notation provides a fairly easy means of specifying RGB color numbers. If the amount of red desired is expressed as a two-digit hexadecimal number, *rr*, the amount of green in hexadecimal as *gg*, and the amount of blue in hexadecimal as *bb*, then the RGB color number for this color is &H00*bbggrr*&. For example, the RGB color number for a bright green would come from 255 (FF in hexadecimal) units of green, so the RGB color number in hexadecimal is &H0000FF00&.

[coordinate systems]: The default coordinate system for a form, picture box, or the printer defines the upper-left corner as the point (0, 0). In this coordinate system, the point (x, y) lies *x* units to the right of and *y* units below the upper-left corner. The unit of measure in the default coordinate system is a twip. A twip is defined as 1/1440 of an inch (though varying screen sizes may result in 1440 twips not appearing as exactly an inch on the screen). Custom coordinate systems can be created using the Scale method and ScaleMode property.

[date]: Functions dealing with dates and times use the type 7 variant data type. Dates and times are stored as serial dates, double-precision numbers, with the whole part recording the date and the decimal part recording the time. Valid whole parts range from –657434 to 2958465, which correspond to all days from January 1, 100 to December, 31, 9999. A whole part of 0 corresponds to December 30, 1899. All decimal parts are valid, with .0 corresponding to midnight, .25 corresponding to 6 a.m., .5 corresponding to noon, and so on. In general, the decimal equivalent of *sec*/86400 corresponds to *sec* seconds past midnight. If a given date corresponds to a negative whole part, then times on that day are obtained by adding a negative decimal part to the negative whole part. For example, October, 24, 1898, corresponds to a whole part of –432. A time of 6 p.m. corresponds to .75, so a time of 6 p.m. on 10/24/1898 corresponds to –432 +–.75 = –432.75.

[directories]: Think of a disk as a master folder holding other folders, each of which might hold yet other folders. Each folder, other than the master folder, has a name. Each folder is identified by a *path*: a string beginning with a drive letter, a colon, and a backslash character, ending with the name of the folder to be identified, and listing the names of the intermediate folders (in order) separated by backslashes. For instance the path "C:\DAVID\GAMES" identifies the folder GAMES, which is contained in the folder DAVID, which in turn is contained in the master folder of drive C.

Each folder is called a *directory* and the master folder is called the *root directory*. When a folder is opened, the revealed folders are referred to as its *subdirectories*. Think of a file as a piece of paper inside one of the folders. Thus, each directory contains files and subdirectories.

[dynamic vs. static arrays]: Visual Basic uses two methods of storing arrays: dynamic and static. The memory locations for a static array are set aside the instant the program is executed and this portion of memory may not be freed for any other purpose. The memory locations for a dynamic array are assigned when a particular procedure requests that an array be created (a ReDim statement is encountered) and *can* be freed for other purposes. Although dynamic arrays are more flexible, static arrays can be accessed faster. Arrays Dimensioned in the (Declarations) section of (General) use static allocation, except for arrays declared using empty parentheses. Arrays created by using the ReDim statement in procedures use dynamic allocation.

[filespec]: The filespec of a file on disk is a string consisting of the letter of the drive, a colon, and the name of the file. If directories are being used, the file name is preceded by the identifying path.

[line label]: Program lines that are the destinations of statements such as GoTo and GoSub are identified by placing a line label at the beginning of the program line or alone on the line proceeding the program line. Line labels may be placed only at the beginning of a line, are named using the same rules as variable, and are followed by a colon. Line numbers may be used in place of line labels, but program readability is greatly improved by using descriptive line labels.

[radians]: The radian system of measurement measures angles in terms of a distance around the circumference of the circle of radius 1. If the vertex of an angle between 0 and 360 degrees is placed at the center of the circle, the length of the arc of the circle contained between the two sides of the angle is the radian measure of the angle. An angle of d degrees has a radian measure of (pi/180) $* d$ radians.

[subroutine]: A subroutine is a sequence of statements beginning with a line label and ending with a Return statement. A subroutine is meant to be branched to by a GoSub statement and is usually placed after an Exit Sub or Exit Function statement at the bottom of a procedure so that it cannot be entered inadvertently.

[variant]: Variant is a generic variable type. Any variable that is used without a type declaration tag ($, %, &, !, #, @) or without being declared as a specific type using an As clause or a DefType statement is treated as a variant variable. A variable of type Variant can hold any type of data. When values are assigned to a variant variable, Visual Basic keeps track of the "type" of data that has been stored. Visual Basic recognizes many types of data: type 0 for "Empty" (nothing yet has been stored in the variable; the default), type 1 for "Null" (the special value Null has been assigned to the variable), type 2 for Integer, type 3 for Long integer, type 4 for Single precision, type 5 for Double precision, type 6 for Currency, type 7 for Date/time, type 8 for String, type 10 for Error, type 11 for

Boolean, and type 17 for Byte. A single variant variable may be assigned different data types at different points in a program, although this is usually not a good programming technique. The data assigned to a variant array need not all be of the same type. As a result, a variant array can be used in much the same way as a user-defined type to store related data.

Appendix D

Visual Basic Debugging Tools

Errors in programs are called *bugs* and the process of finding and correcting them is called *debugging*. Since Visual Basic does not discover errors due to faulty logic, they present the most difficulties in debugging. One method of discovering a logical error is by **desk-checking**, that is, tracing the values of variables on paper by writing down their expected value after "mentally executing" each line in the program. Desk checking is rudimentary and highly impractical except for small programs.

Another method of debugging involves placing Print methods at strategic points in the program and displaying the values of selected variables or expressions until the error is detected. After correcting the error, the Print methods are removed. For many programming environments, desk checking and Print methods are the only debugging methods available to the programmer.

The Visual Basic debugger offers an alternative to desk checking and Print methods. It allows you to pause during the execution of your program in order to view and alter values of variables. These values can be accessed through the Immediate, Watch, and Locals windows, known collectively as the three Debug windows.

The Three Program Modes

At any time, a program is in one of three modes design mode, run mode, or break mode. The current mode is displayed in the Visual Basic title bar.

Title bar during design time.

Title bar during run time.

Title bar during break mode.

At design time you place controls on a form, set their initial properties, and write code. Run time is initiated by pressing the Start button. Break mode is invoked automatically when a run-time error occurs. While a program is running, you can manually invoke Break mode by pressing Ctrl+Break, clicking on Break in the Run menu, or clicking on the Break icon ▣ (located between the Start and Stop icons). While the program is in break mode, you can use the Immediate window to examine and change values of variables and object settings. When you enter break mode, the Start button on the toolbar changes to a Continue button. You can click on it to proceed with the execution of the program.

The Immediate Window

You can set the focus to the Immediate window by clicking on it (if visible), by pressing Ctrl+G, or by choosing "Immediate Window" from the View menu. Although the Immediate window can be used during design time, it is primarily used in break mode. When you type a statement into the Immediate window and press the Enter key, the statement is executed at once. A statement of the form

```
Print expression
```

displays the value of the expression on the next line of the Immediate window. In Figure 1, three statements have been executed. (When the program was interrupted, the variable *numVar* had the value 10.) In addition to displaying values of expressions, the Immediate window also is commonly used to change the value of a variable with a Let statement before continuing to run the program. **Note:** Any statement in the Immediate window can be executed again by placing the cursor anywhere on the statement and pressing the Enter key.

Figure D.1 Three Print statements executed in the Immediate window.

The Watch Window

You can designate an expression as a watch expression or a break expression. Break expressions are of two varieties: those that cause a break when they become true and those that cause a break when they change value. At any time, the Watch window shows the current values of all watch and break expressions. In the Watch window of Figure 2, the type of each expression is specified by an icon as shown in Table 1.

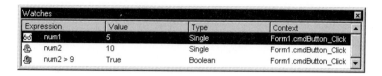

Figure D.2 The Watch window.

Icon	Type of expression
6ờ	Watch expression
	Break when expression is true
	Break when expression has changed

Table D.1 Watch type icons

The easiest way to add an expression to the Watch window is to right-click on a variable in the code window and then click on "Add Watch" to call up an Add Watch dialog box. You can then alter the expression in the Expression text box the and select one of the three Watch types. To delete an expression from the Watch window, right-click on the expression and then click on "Delete Watch." To alter an expression in the Watch window, right-click on the expression and click on "Edit Watch."

The Locals Window

The Locals window, invoked by clicking on "Locals Window" in the View menu, is a feature new to Visual Basic in version 5.0. This window automatically displays the names, values, and types of all variables in the current procedure. See Figure 3. You can alter the values of variables at any time. In addition, you can examine and change properties of controls through the Locals window.

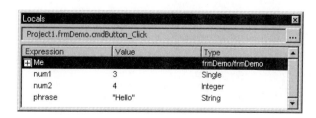

Figure D.3 The Locals window.

Stepping Through a Program

The program can be executed one statement at a time, with each press of an appropriate function key executing a statement. This process is called **stepping** (or **stepping into**). After each step, values of variables, expressions, and conditions can be displayed from the debug windows, and the values of variables can be changed.

When a procedure is called, the lines of the procedure can be executed one at a time, referred to as "stepping through the procedure," or the entire procedure can be executed at once, referred to as "stepping over a procedure." A step over a procedure is called a **procedure step**. In addition, you can execute the remainder of the current procedure at once, referred to as "stepping out of the procedure."

Stepping begins with the first line of the first event procedure invoked by the user. Program execution normally proceeds in order through the statements in the event procedure. However, at any time the programmer can specify the next statement to be executed.

As another debugging tool, Visual Basic allows the programmer to specify certain lines as **breakpoints**. Then, when the program is run, execution will stop at the first breakpoint reached. The programmer can then either step through the program or continue execution to the next breakpoint.

The tasks discussed above are summarized below, along with a means to carry out each task. The tasks invoked with function keys can also be produced from the menu bar.

Step Into:	Press F8
Step Over:	Press Shift+F8
Step Out:	Press Ctrl+Shift+F8
Set a breakpoint:	Move cursor to line, press F9
Remove a breakpoint:	Move cursor to line containing breakpoint, press F9
Clear all breakpoints:	Press Ctrl+Shift+F9
Set next statement:	Press Ctrl+F9
Continue execution to next breakpoint or the end of the program:	Press F5
Run to cursor:	Press Ctrl+F8

Six Walkthroughs

The following walkthroughs use the debugging tools with the programming structures covered in Chapters 3, 4, 5, and 6.

Stepping Through an Elementary Program: Chapter 3

The following walkthrough demonstrates several capabilities of the debugger.

1. Create a form with a command button (cmdButton) and a picture box (picBox). Set the AutoRedraw property of the picture box to True. (During the debugging process, the entire form will be covered. The True setting for AutoRedraw prevents the contents of the picture box from being erased.)

2. Double-click on the command button and enter the following event procedure:

```
Private Sub cmdButton_Click()
    Dim num As Single
    picBox.Cls
    Let num = Val(InputBox("Enter a number:"))
    Let num = num + 1
    Let num = num + 2
    picBox.Print num
End Sub
```

3. Press F8, click the command button, and press F8 again. A yellow arrow points to the picBox.Cls statement and the statement is highlighted in yellow. This indicates that the picBox.Cls statement is the next statement to be executed. (Pressing F8 is referred to as stepping. You can also step to the next statement of a program with the Step Into option from the Debug menu.)

4. Press F8. The picBox.Cls statement is executed and the statement involving InputBox is designated as the next statement to be executed.

5. Press F8 to execute the statement containing InputBox. Respond to the request by typing 5 and clicking the OK button.

6. Press F8 again to execute the statement Let num = num + 1.

7. Let the mouse sit over any occurrence of the word "num" for a second or so. The current value of the variable will be displayed in a small box. See Figure 4.

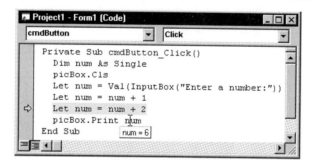

Figure D.4 Obtaining the value of a variable.

8. Click on the End icon to end the program.

9. Move the cursor to the line

```
Let num = num + 2
```

and then press F9. A red dot appears to the left of the line and the line is displayed in white text on a red background. This indicates that the line is a breakpoint. (Pressing F9 is referred to as toggling a breakpoint. You also can toggle a breakpoint with the Toggle Breakpoint option from the Debug menu.)

10. Press F5 and click on the command button. Respond to the request by entering 5. The program executes the first three lines and stops at the breakpoint. The breakpoint line is not executed.

11. Open the Immediate window by pressing Ctrl+G. If necessary, clear the contents of the window. Type the statement

```
Print "num ="; num
```

into the Immediate window and then press Enter to execute the statement. The appearance of "num = 6" on the next line of the Immediate window confirms that the breakpoint line was not executed.

12. Press F7 to return to the Code window.

13. Move the cursor to the line Let num = num + 1 and then press Ctrl+F9 to specify that line as the next line to be executed. (You can also use the Set Next Statement option from the Debug menu.)

14. Press F8 to execute the selected line.

15. Press Ctrl+G to return to the Immediate window. Move the cursor to the line containing the print statement and press Enter to confirm that the value of *num* is now 7, and then return to the Code window.

16. Move the cursor to the breakpoint line and press F9 to deselect the line as a breakpoint.

17. Press F5 to execute the remaining lines of the program. Observe that the value displayed in the picture box is 9.

General Comment: As you step through a program, the form will become hidden from view. However, the form will be represented by a button on the Windows 95 taskbar at the bottom of the screen. The button will contain the name of the form. You can see the form at any time by clicking on its button.

Stepping Through a Program Containing an Ordinary Procedure: Chapter 4

The following walkthrough uses the single-stepping feature of the debugger to trace the flow through a program and a subprogram.

1. Create a form with a command button (cmdButton) and a picture box (picBox). Set the AutoRedraw property of the picture box to True. Then enter the following two procedures:

```
Private Sub cmdButton_Click()
  Dim p As Single, b As Single
  picBox.Cls
  Let p = 1000     'Principal
  Call GetBalance(p, b)
  picBox.Print "The balance is"; b
End Sub
```

```
Private Sub GetBalance(prin As Single, bal As Single)
   Rem Calculate the balance at 5% interest rate
   Dim interest As Single
   Let interest = .05 * prin
   Let bal = prin + interest
End Sub
```

2. Press F8, click the command button, and press F8 again. The picBox.Cls statement is highlighted to indicate that it is the next statement to be executed.

3. Press F8 two more times. The Call statement is highlighted.

4. Press F8 once and observe that the heading of the subprogram GetBalance is now highlighted in yellow.

5. Press F8 three times to execute the Let statements and to highlight the End Sub statement. (Notice that the Dim and Rem statements were skipped.)

6. Press F8 and notice that the yellow highlight has moved back to the cmdButton_Click event procedure and is on the statement immediately following the Call statement.

7. Click on the End icon to end the program.

8. Repeat Steps 2 and 3, and then press Shift+F8 to step over the procedure GetBalance. The procedure has been executed in its entirety.

9. Click on the End icon to end the program.

Communication Between Arguments and Parameters

The following walkthrough uses the Locals window to monitor the values of arguments and parameters during the execution of a program.

1. If you have not already done so, type the preceding program into the Code window.

2. Press F8 and click on the command button.

3. Select "Locals Window" from the View window. Notice that the variables from the cmdButton_Click event procedure appear in the Locals window.

4. Press F8 three more times to highlight the Call statement. Notice that the value of the variable p has changed.

5. Press F8 to call the subprogram. Notice that the variables displayed in the Locals window are now those of the procedure GetBalance.

6. Press F8 three times to execute the procedure.

7. Press F8 to return to cmdButton_Click event procedure. Notice that the value of the variable b has inherited the value of the variable bal.

8. Click on the End icon to end the program.

Stepping Through Programs Containing Selection Structures: Chapter 5

If Blocks

The following walkthrough demonstrates how an If statement evaluates a condition to determine whether to take an action.

1. Create a form with a command button (cmdButton) and a picture box (picBox). Set the AutoRedraw property of the picture box to True. Then open the Code window and enter the following procedure:

```
Private Sub cmdButton_Click()
   Dim wage As Single
   picBox.Cls
   Let wage = Val(InputBox("wage:"))
   If wage < 5.15 Then
       picBox.Print "Below minimum wage."
     Else
       picBox.Print "Wage Ok."
   End If
End Sub
```

2. Press F8, click the command button, and press F8 twice. The picBox.Cls statement will be highlighted and executed, and then the statement containing InputBox will be highlighted.

3. Press F8 once to execute the statement containing InputBox. Type a wage of 3.25 and press the Enter key. The If statement is highlighted, but has not been executed.

4. Press F8 once and notice that the highlight for the current statement has jumped to the statement picBox.Print "Below minimum wage." Since the condition "wage < 5.15" is true, the action associated with Then was selected.

5. Press F8 to execute the picBox.Print statement. Notice that Else is skipped and End If is highlighted.

6. Press F8 again. We are through with the If block and the statement following the If block, End Sub, is highlighted.

7. Click on the End icon to end the program.

8. If desired, try stepping through the program again with 5.75 entered as the wage. Since the condition "wage < 5.15" will be false, the Else action will be executed instead of the Then action.

Select Case Blocks

The following walkthrough illustrates how a Select Case block uses the selector to choose from among several actions.

1. Create a form with a command button (cmdButton) and a picture box (picBox). Set the AutoRedraw property of the picture box to True. Then open the Code window and enter the following procedure:

```
Private Sub cmdButton_Click()
  Dim age As Single, price As Single
  picBox.Cls
  Let age = Val(InputBox("age:"))
  Select Case age
    Case Is < 12
      Let price = 0
    Case Is < 18
      Let price = 3.5
    Case Is >= 65
      Let price = 4
    Case Else
      Let price = 5.5
  End Select
  picBox.Print "Your ticket price is ";Format(price,"Currency")
End Sub
```

2. Press F8, click on the command button, and press F8 twice. The picBox.Cls statement will be highlighted and executed, and then the statement containing InputBox will be highlighted.

3. Press F8 once to execute the statement containing InputBox. Type an age of 8 and press the Enter key. The Select Case statement is highlighted, but has not been executed.

4. Press F8 twice and observe that the action associated with Case Is < 12 is highlighted.

5. Press F8 once to execute the Let statement. Notice that End Select is highlighted. This demonstrates that when more than one Case clause is true, only the first is acted upon.

6. Click on the End icon to end the program.

7. If desired, step through the program again, entering a different age and predicting which Case clause will be acted upon. (Some possible ages to try are 12, 14, 18, 33, and 67.)

Stepping Through a Program Containing a Do Loop: Chapter 6

Do Loops

The following walkthrough demonstrates use of the Immediate window to monitor the value of a condition in a Do loop that searches for a name.

1. Access Windows' Notepad, enter the following line of data, and save the file on the A drive with the name DATA.TXT

```
Bert, Ernie, Grover, Oscar
```

2. Return to Visual Basic. Create a form with a command button (cmdButton) and a picture box (picBox). Set the AutoRedraw property of the picture box to True. Then double-click on the command button and enter the following procedure:

```
Private Sub cmdButton_Click()
  Rem Look for a specific name
  Dim searchName As String, nom As String
  picBox.Cls
  Let searchName = InputBox("Name:")   'Name to search for in list
  Open "A:DATA.TXT" For Input As #1
  Let nom = ""
  Do While (nom <> searchName) And Not EOF(1)
    Input #1, nom
  Loop
  If nom = searchName Then
      picBox.Print nom
    Else
      picBox.Print "Name not found"
  End If
  Close #1
End Sub
```

3. Press F8 and click on the command button. The heading of the event procedure is highlighted in yellow.

4. Double-click on the variable *searchName*, click the right mouse button, click on "Add Watch," and click on OK. The variable *searchName* has been added to the Watch window.

5. Repeat Step 4 for the variable *nom*.

6. Drag the mouse across the words

   `(nom <> searchName) And Not EOF(1)`

   to highlight them. Then click the right mouse button, click on "Add Watch," and click on OK. Widen the Watch window as much as possible in order to see the entire expression.

7. Press F8 three more times to execute the picBox.Cls statement and the statement containing InputBox. Enter the name "Ernie" at the prompt.

8. Press F8 repeatedly until the entire event procedure has been executed. Pause after each keypress and notice how the values of the expressions in the Watch window change.

9. Click on the End icon to end the program.

Answers

To Selected Odd-Numbered Exercises

CHAPTER 1

Exercises 1.2

1. The program is busy carrying out a task; please wait.
3. Double-clicking means clicking the left mouse button twice in quick succession.
7. Starting with an uppercase W, Windows refers to Microsoft's Windows program. Starting with a lowercase w, windows refers to the rectangular regions of the screen in which different programs are displayed.
9. Double-click on the Notepad icon.
11. A toggle is a key like the Ins, NumLock, and CapsLock keys that changes keyboard operations back and forth between two different typing modes.
13. PgDn

15. Backspace
17. NumLock
19. CapsLock
21. End
23. Shift
25. Alt/F/P
27. Ctrl+Home
29. Alt
31. Alt
33. Alt/F/A
35. End/Enter

Exercises 1.3

1. A filename cannot contain a question mark
3. Forward slashes (/) are not allowed in filespecs. Use a backslash (\) to separate folders in a filespec.
5. 4
7. 4 (Answers may vary)
9. Files are sorted by size.

11. Files are sorted by the date they were last modified.
13. Create a new directory called TEMP on your hard drive and then copy the file from the first diskette to TEMP. Place the second diskette in the diskette drive and then copy the file from TEMP to the second diskette. Delete the file and TEMP from the hard drive.

CHAPTER 3

Exercises 3.1

1. Command buttons appear to be pushed down and then let up when they are clicked.

3. After a command button is clicked, its border becomes boldfaced and a rounded rectangle of small dots surrounds the caption.

(In Exercises 7 through 27, begin by pressing Alt/F/N to create a new form.)

7. Click on the Properties window or Press F4 to activate the Properties window.
   Press Shift+Ctrl+C to highlight the Caption property.
   Type in "CHECKING ACCOUNT".
9. Double-click the text box icon in the toolbox.
   Activate the Properties window and highlight the BackColor property.

Click on the "..." icon to the right of the Settings box.
Click on the Palette tab.
Click on the desired yellow in the palette.
Press Shift+Ctrl+T followed by three down arrows to highlight the Text property.
Click on the settings box and delete "Text1".
Click on the form to see the empty, yellow text box.

11. Double-click on the text box icon in the toolbox.

    Activate the Properties window and highlight the Text property.

    Type the requested sentence.

    Highlight the MultiLine property.

    Double-click on the highlighted MultiLine property to change its value to True.

    Highlight the Alignment property.

    Double-click twice on the highlighted Alignment property to change its value to 2-Center.

    Click on the form.

    Use the mouse to resize the text box so that the sentence occupies three lines.

13. Double-click on the text box icon in the toolbox.

    Activate the Properties window and highlight the Text property.

    Type "VISUAL BASIC".

    Highlight the Font property.

    Click on the ellipsis to the right of the Settings box.

    Click on "Courier" in the Font box and click OK.

    Click on the form to see the resulting text box.

15. Double-click on the command button icon in the toolbox.

    Activate the Properties window and highlight the Caption property.

    Type "PUSH".

    Highlight the Font property and click on the ellipsis.

    Click on Italic in the Font Style box.

    Click on 24 in the Size box.

    Click OK.

    Click on the form to see the resulting command button.

    Resize the command button to properly accommodate its caption.

17. Double-click on the command button icon in the toolbox.

    Activate the Properties window and highlight the Caption property.

    Type "PUS&H".

    Click on the form to see the resulting command button.

19. Double-click on the label icon in the toolbox.

    Activate the Properties window and highlight the Caption property.

    Type "ALIAS".

    Click on the form to see the resulting label.

21. Double-click on the label icon in the toolbox.

    Activate the Properties window and highlight the Alignment property.

    Double-click twice on the highlighted Alignment property to change its value to "2-Center".

    Highlight the Caption property.

    Type "ALIAS".

    Double-click on the BorderStyle property to change its value to "1–Fixed Single".

    Highlight the Font property and click on the ellipsis.

    Click on Italic in the Font Style box and click OK.

    Click on the form to see the resulting label.

23. Double-click on the label icon in the toolbox.

    Activate the Properties window and highlight the Font property.

    Click on the ellipsis to the right of the Settings box.

    Click on Wingdings in the Font box.

    Click on the largest size available (72) in the Size box.

    Click OK.

    As one means of determining which keystroke in the Wingdings font corresponds to a diskette, follow steps a–g.

    (a) Click the Start button.
    (b) Point to Programs and then point to Accessories.
    (c) Click the Character Map.
    (d) Click on the down arrow in the font box and click on Wingdings.
    (e) Click on the diskette character (fourth from the right end of the first row).
    (f) Note at the bottom of the font map window that the keystroke for the diskette character is a less than sign.
    (g) Close the Character Map and Accessories windows and return to Visual Basic.

    Highlight the Caption property.

    Change the caption setting to a less than sign by pressing <.

    Click on the label and enlarge it.

25. Double-click on the picture box icon in the toolbox.

    Activate the Properties window and highlight the BackColor property.

    Click on the ". . ." icon to the right of the Settings box.

    Click on the Palette tab.

    Click on the desired yellow in the palette.

    Click on the form to see the yellow picture box.

27. Double-click on the picture box icon in the toolbox.

    Increase the size of the picture box so that it can easily hold two standard size command buttons.

    Click (do NOT double-click) on the command button icon in the toolbox.

    Move the mouse to the desired location in the picture box of the upper-left corner of the first command button.

    Press and hold the left mouse button and drag the mouse down and to the right until the rectangle attains the size desired for the first command button

    Release the left mouse button.

    Repeat the preceding four steps (starting with clicking on the command button icon in the toolbox) to place the second command button on the picture box.

29. Create a new project. Change the form's caption to "Dynamic Duo". Place two command buttons on the form. Enter as the caption of the first "&Batman" and of the second "&Robin". Increase the font size for both command buttons to 13.5.

31. Create a new project. Change the form's caption to "Fill in the Blank". Place a label, a text box, and another label on the form at appropriate locations. Change the caption of the first label to "Toto, I don't think we're in" and of the second label to "A Quote from the Wizard of Oz". Delete "Text1" from the text property of the text box. Resize and position the labels as needed.

33. Create a new project. Change its caption to "An Uncle's Advice". Place a picture box on the form and increase its size to provide plenty of space. Place on the picture box five labels and three command buttons. Change the captions of each label to the appropriate text. Change the BorderStyle property of the last label to "1–Fixed Single". Change the captions of the command buttons to "1", "2", and "3". Resize and position the labels and command buttons as is appropriate. Finally, the size of the picture box can be adjusted down as appropriate.

Exercises 3.2

1. The word Hello.

3. The word Hello in italic letters.

5. The text box vanishes; nothing is visible.

7. The word Hello in green letters.

9. The word Hello in big, fixed-width letters.

11. The name of the control has been given but not the property being assigned. Let frmHi ="Hello" needs to be changed to Let frmHi.Caption = "Hello".

13. Text boxes do not have a Caption property. Information to be displayed in a text box must be assigned to the Text property.

15. Only 0 and 1 are valid values for the BorderStyle property of a label.

17. `Let lblTwo.Caption = "E.T. phone home."`

19. `Let txtBox.ForeColor = &HFF&`
    `Let txtBox.Text = "The stuff that dreams are made of."`

21. `Let txtBox.Text = ""`

23. `Let lblTwo.Visible = False`

25. `Let picBox.BackColor = &HFF0000&`

27. `Let txtBox.Font.Bold = True`
    `Let txtBox.Font.Italic = True`
    `Let txtBox.Text = "Hello"`

29. `cmdButton.SetFocus`

31. `Let lblTwo.BorderStyle = 1`
    `Let lblTwo.Alignment = 2`

37.
```
Private Sub cmdLeft_Click()
   Let lblShow.Alignment = 0
   Let lblShow.Caption = "Left Justify"
End Sub

Private Sub cmdCenter_Click()
   Let lblShow.Alignment = 2
   Let lblShow.Caption = "Center"
End Sub

Private Sub cmdRight_Click()
   Let lblShow.Alignment = 1
   Let lblShow.Caption = "Right Justify"
End Sub
```

35. Create a new project. Change the form's caption to "Picture Box Icon." Place a picture box and a label on the form. Change the label's caption property to the sentence shown. Change the label's Background property to white, and its Font Size property to 18. Access the picture box's picture property and select the picture file picbox.bmp from the Pictures folder on the CD accompanying this textbook.

39.
```
Private Sub cmdRed_Click()
   Let txtShow.BackColor = &HFF&
End Sub

Private Sub cmdBlue_Click()
   Let txtShow.BackColor = &HFF0000&
End Sub

Private Sub cmdWhite_Click()
   Let txtShow.ForeColor = &HFFFFFF&
End Sub

Private Sub cmdYellow_Click()
   Let txtShow.ForeColor = &HFFFF&
End Sub
```

41.
```
Private Sub txtLife.GotFocus()
   Let txtQuote.Text = "I like life, it's something to do."
End Sub

Private Sub txtFuture.GotFocus()
   Let txtQuote.Text = "The future isn't what it used to be."
End Sub

Private Sub txtTruth.GotFocus()
   Let txtQuote.Text = "Tell the truth and run."
End Sub
```

43.

Object	Property	Setting
cmdLarge	Caption	Large
cmdSmall	Caption	Small
cmdBold	Caption	Bold
cmdItalics	Caption	Italic
txtShow	Text	(blank)

```
Private Sub cmdLarge_Click()
   Let txtShow.Font.Size = 18
End Sub

Private Sub cmdSmall_Click()
   Let txtShow.Font.Size = 8.25
End Sub

Private Sub cmdBold_Click()
   Let txtShow.Font.Bold = True
   Let txtShow.Font.Italic = False
End Sub

Private Sub cmdItalics_Click()
   Let txtShow.Font.Italic = True
   Let txtShow.Font.Bold = False
End Sub
```

45.

Object	Property	Setting
frmEx45	Caption	Face
lblFace	Font.Name	Wingdings
	Caption	K
	Font.Size	24
cmdVanish	Caption	Vanish
cmdReappear	Caption	Reappear

```
Private Sub cmdVanish_Click()
  Let lblFace.Visible = False
End Sub


Private Sub cmdReappear_Click()
  Let lblFace.Visible = True
End Sub
```

47.

Object	Property	Setting
cmdPush1	Caption	Push Me
cmdPush2	Caption	Push Me
cmdPush3	Caption	Push Me
cmdPush4	Caption	Push Me

```
Private Sub cmdPush1_Click()
  Let cmdPush1.Visible = False
  Let cmdPush2.Visible = True
  Let cmdPush3.Visible = True
  Let cmdPush4.Visible = True
End Sub

Private Sub cmdPush2_Click()
  Let cmdPush1.Visible = True
  Let cmdPush2.Visible = False
  Let cmdPush3.Visible = True
  Let cmdPush4.Visible = True
End Sub

Private Sub cmdPush3_Click()
  Let cmdPush1.Visible = True
  Let cmdPush2.Visible = True
  Let cmdPush3.Visible = False
  Let cmdPush4.Visible = True
End Sub

Private Sub cmdPush4_Click()
  Let cmdPush1.Visible = True
  Let cmdPush2.Visible = True
  Let cmdPush3.Visible = True
  Let cmdPush4.Visible = False
End Sub
```

Exercises 3.3

1. 12

3. .03125

5. 8

7. 3E+09

9. 4E–08

11. Valid

13. Valid

15. Not valid

17. 10

19. 16

21. 9

23.
```
Private Sub cmdCompute_Click()
   picOutput.Cls
   picOutput.Print 7 * 8 + 5
End Sub
```

25.
```
Private Sub cmdCompute_Click()
   picOutput.Cls
   picOutput.Print .055 * 20
End Sub
```

27.
```
Private Sub cmdCompute_Click()
   picOutput.Cls
   picOutput.Print 17 * (3 + 162)
End Sub
```

29.

x	y
2	0
2	6
11	6
11	6
11	6
11	7

31. 6

33. 1 2 3 4
11

35. 1
64

37. 27   12

39. The third line should read Let c = a + b

41. The first line should not contain a comma. The second line should not contain a dollar sign.

43.
```
Private Sub cmdCompute_Click()
   picOutput.Cls
   picOutput.Print 1; 2; 1 + 2
End Sub
```

45.
```
Private Sub cmdCompute_Click()
   picOutput.Cls
   Let revenue = 98456
   Let costs = 45000
   Let profit = revenue - costs
   picOutput.Print profit
End Sub
```

47.
```
Private Sub cmdCompute_Click()
    picOutput.Cls
    Let price = 19.95
    Let discountPercent = 30
    Let markDown = (discountPercent / 100) * price
    Let price = price - markDown
    picOutput.Print price
End Sub
```

49.
```
Private Sub cmdCompute_Click()
    picOutput.Cls
    Let balance = 100
    Let balance = balance + balance * .05
    Let balance = balance + balance * .05
    Let balance = balance + balance * .05
    picOutput.Print balance
End Sub
```

51.
```
Private Sub cmdCompute_Click()
    picOutput.Cls
    Let balance = 100
    Let balance = balance * (1.05 ^ 10)
    picOutput.Print balance
End Sub
```

53.
```
Private Sub cmdCompute_Click()
    picOutput.Cls
    Let acres = 30
    Let yieldPerAcre = 18
    Let corn = yieldPerAcre * acres
    picOutput.Print corn
End Sub
```

55.
```
Private Sub cmdCompute_Click()
    picOutput.Cls
    Let distance = 233
    Let elapsedTime = 7 - 2
    Let averageSpeed = distance / elapsedTime
    picOutput.Print averageSpeed
End Sub
```

57.
```
Private Sub cmdCompute_Click()
    picOutput.Cls
    Let waterPerPersonPerDay = 1600
    Let people = 260000000
    Let days = 365
    Let waterUsed = waterPerPersonPerDay * people * days
    picOutput.Print waterUsed
End Sub
```

Exercises 3.4

1. Hello
1234

3. 12 12 TWELVE

5. A ROSE IS A ROSE IS A ROSE

7. 1234 Main Street

9. "We're all in this alone." Lily Tomlin

11. 17 2
-20 16

13. The number of digits in 3567 is 4

15. The variable phone should be declared as type String, not Single.

17. The sentence in the second line should be enclosed by quotation marks.

19. End is a keyword and cannot be used as a variable name.

21.
```
Private Sub cmdButton_KeyPress(KeyAscii As Integer)
    cmdButton_Click
End Sub
```

23.
```
Private Sub cmdDisplay_Click()
    Dim firstName As String, middleName As String
    Dim lastName As String, yearOfBirth As Single
    picOutput.Cls
    Let firstName = "Thomas"
    Let middleName = "Alva"
    Let lastName = "Edison"
    Let yearOfBirth = 1847
    picOutput.Print firstName; " "; middleName; " "; lastName; ","; yearOfBirth
End Sub
```

25.
```
Private Sub cmdDisplay_Click()
    Dim publisher As String
    picOutput.Cls
    Let publisher = "Prentice Hall, Inc."
    picOutput.Print Chr(169) & " " & publisher
End Sub
```

27.
```
Private Sub cmdCompute_Click()
    picSum.Print Val(txtNum1.Text) + Val(txtNum2.Text)
End Sub
```

29.
```
Private Sub cmdCompute_Click()
    Let lblNumMiles.Caption = Str(Val(txtNumSec.Text) / 5)
End Sub
```

31.
```
Private Sub cmdCompute_Click()
    Dim cycling As Single, running As Single, swimming As Single, pounds As Single
    picWtLoss.Cls
    Let cycling = Val(txtCycle.Text)
    Let running = Val(txtRun.Text)
    Let swimming = Val(txtSwim.Text)
    Let pounds = (200 * cycling + 475 * running + 275 * swimming) / 3500
    picWtLoss.Print pounds; "pounds were lost."
End Sub
```

33.

Object	Property	Setting
frmEx33	Caption	Net Income
lblRevenue	Caption	Revenue
txtRevenue	Text	(blank)
lblExpenses	Caption	Expenses
txtExpenses	Text	(blank)
cmdCompute	Caption	Display Net Income
picOutput		

```
Private Sub cmdCompute_Click()
   Dim income As Single
   Rem Compute Net Income based on revenue and expenses
   picOutput.Cls
   Let income = Val(txtRevenue.Text) - Val(txtExpenses.Text)
   picOutput.Print "The company's net income is"; income
End Sub
```

35.

Object	Property	Setting
frmEx35	Caption	Price to Earnings Ratio
lblPrice	Caption	Price
txtPrice	Text	(blank)
lblEarnings	Caption	Earnings
txtEarnings	Text	(blank)
cmdCompute	Caption	Display PER
picOutput		

```
Private Sub cmdCompute_Click()
   Dim per As Single
   Rem Compute Price to Earnings Ratio
   picOutput.Cls
   Let per = Val(txtPrice.Text) / Val(txtEarnings.Text)
   picOutput.Print "The price to earnings ratio is"; per
End Sub
```

37.

Object	Property	Setting
frmEx37	Caption	Grass Seed
lblOunces	Caption	Ounces of seed recommended for 2000 square feet of lawn
txtOunces	Text	(blank)
lblLawnWidth	Caption	Width of lawn in feet
txtLawnWidth	Text	(blank)
lblLawnLength	Caption	Length of lawn in feet
txtLawnLength	Text	(blank)
cmdCompute	Caption	Display Seed Needed
picOutput		

```
Private Sub cmdCompute_Click()
   Dim lbSeedPerFt As Single,area As Single, grassSeed As Single
   Rem Compute amount of grass seed needed for a given lawn.
   picOutput.Cls
   Let lbSeedPerFt = (Val(txtOunces.Text) / 16) / 2000
   Let area = Val(txtLawnWidth.Text) * Val(txtLawnLength.Text)
   Let grassSeed = lbSeedPerFt * area
   picOutput.Print grassSeed; "pounds of grass seed are needed."
End Sub
```

39.

Object	Property	Setting
cmdIncrement	Caption	Increment
lblCounter	Caption	0

```
Private Sub cmdIncrement_Click()
   Let lblCounter.Caption = Str(Val(lblCounter.Caption) + 1)
End Sub
```

41.

Object	Property	Setting
frmEx41	Caption	Tipping
lblAmount	Caption	Amount of bill:
txtAmount	Text	(blank)
lblPercentTip	Caption	Percentage Tip
txtPercentTip	Text	(blank)
cmdComputeTip	Caption	Compute Tip
picOutput		

```
Private Sub cmdComputeTip_Click()
   picOutput.Cls
   picOutput.Print "The tip is"; Val(txtAmount.Text) * Val(txtPercentTip.Text) / 100
End Sub
```

Exercises 3.5

1. 16

3. baseball

5. Age: 20

7. setup

9. The White House has 132 rooms.

11.
```
1 OneTwo 2
2
1
```

13. Harvard University is 360 years old.

15. You might win 180 dollars.

17. Hello John Jones

19. 1 one   won

21. one   two

23. 1234567890
              5

25. 1234567890
          one
                      two

27. 1234567890
              one two

29. The Input#1 statement will assign "John Smith" to str1, leaving nothing left to assign to str2. An "Input past end of file" error will occur.

31. Each line in the file consists of three items, but the Input#1 statements are reading just two. As a result, the second Input#1 statement will assign the numeric data 110 to the string variable *building* and 0 to ht. This is not what was intended.

33. The response is to be used as a number, so the input from the user should not contain commas. With the given user response, the value in the variable statePop will be 8.

35. It should be "Font.Name". Also, the name of the font to the right of the equal sign must be surrounded by quotes.

37. The caption information to the right of the equal sign must be surrounded by quotes.

39. When assigning properties of the form, the correct object name is Form1, not Form. Also, Spc(5) can only be used with a Print method and semicolons are not valid.

41.

category	amount	total
(undefined)	(undefined)	(undefined)
""	(undefined)	(undefined)
""	0	(undefined)
""	0	0
""	0	0
"phone"	35.25	0
"phone"	35.25	35.25
"postage"	14.75	35.25
"postage"	14.75	50
"postage"	14.75	50
"postage	14.75	50
(undefined)	(undefined)	(undefinded)

43.
```
Private Sub cmdDisplay_Click()
    Dim course As String, percent1982 As Single, percent1987 As Single
    Rem Compute course enrollment percentage change
    picOutput.Cls
    Open "DATA.TXT" For Input As #1
    Input #1, course, percent1982, percent1987
    picOutput.Print "The percentage change for "; course; " was"; percent1987 - percent1982
    Input #1, course, percent1982, percent1987
    picOutput.Print "The percentage change for "; course; " was"; percent1987 - percent1982
    Close #1
End Sub
```

45.
```
Private Sub cmdDisplay_Click()
    Dim begOfYearPrice As Single, endOfYearPrice As Single, percentIncrease As Single
    Rem Report percent increase for a basket of goods
    picOutput.Cls
    Let begOfYearPrice = 200
    Let endOfYearPrice = Val(InputBox("Enter price at the end of the year:"))
    Let percentIncrease = 100 * (endOfYearPrice - begOfYearPrice) / begOfYearPrice
    picOutput.Print "The percent increase for the year is"; percentIncrease
End Sub
```

47. MsgBox "The future isn't what it used to be.", , ""

49.
```
Private Sub cmdSummarize_Click()
    Dim account As String, beginningBalance As Single
    Dim deposits As Single, withdrawals As Single
    Dim endOfMonth As Single, total As Single
    Rem Report checking account activity
    picReport.Cls
    Open "DATA.TXT" For Input As #1
    Rem 1st account
    Input #1, account, beginningBalance, deposits, withdrawals
    Let endOfMonth = beginningBalance + deposits - withdrawals
    Let total = endOfMonth
    picReport.Print "Monthly balance for account "; account; " is $"; endOfMonth
    Rem 2nd account
    Input #1, account, beginningBalance, deposits, withdrawals
    Let endOfMonth = beginningBalance + deposits - withdrawals
```

```
      Let total = total + endOfMonth
      picReport.Print "Monthly balance for account "; account; " is $"; endOfMonth
      Rem 3rd account
      Input #1, account, beginningBalance, deposits, withdrawals
      Let endOfMonth = beginningBalance + deposits - withdrawals
      Let total = total + endOfMonth
      picReport.Print "Monthly balance for account "; account; " is $"; endOfMonth
      picReport.Print "Total for all accounts ="; total
      Close #1
    End Sub
```

51.
```
    Private Sub cmdComputeAvg_Click()
      Dim socNmb As String, exam1 As Single, exam2 As Single, exam3 As Single
      Dim final As Single, average As Single, total As Single
      Rem Compute semester averages
      picOutput.Cls
      Open "DATA.TXT" For Input As #1
      Rem 1st student
      Input #1, socNmb, exam1, exam2, exam3, final
      Let average = (exam1 + exam2 + exam3 + final * 2) / 5
      Let total = average
      picOutput.Print "Semester average for "; socNmb; " is"; average
      Rem 2nd student
      Input #1, socNmb, exam1, exam2, exam3, final
      Let average = (exam1 + exam2 + exam3 + final * 2) / 5
      Let total = total + average
      picOutput.Print "Semester average for "; socNmb; " is"; average
      Rem 3rd student
      Input #1, socNmb, exam1, exam2, exam3, final
      Let average = (exam1 + exam2 + exam3 + final * 2) / 5
      Let total = total + average
      picOutput.Print "Semester average for "; socNmb; " is"; average
      picOutput.Print "Class average is"; total / 3
      Close #1
    End Sub
```

53.
```
    Private Sub cmdCompute_Click()
      Dim athlete As String, sport As String
      Dim winnings As Single, income As Single
      Rem Display a table of sports salaries
      picOutput.Cls
      picOutput.Print , , "Salary or"
      picOutput.Print "Athlete", "Sport", "Winnings", "Endorsements", "Total"
      Open "DATA.TXT" For Input As #1
      Input #1, athlete, sport, winnings, endorsements
      picOutput.Print athlete, sport, winnings, endorsements, winnings + endorsements
      Input #1, athlete, sport, winnings, endorsements
      picOutput.Print athlete, sport, winnings, endorsements, winnings + endorsements
      Input #1, athlete, sport, winnings, endorsements
      picOutput.Print athlete, sport, winnings, endorsements, winnings + endorsements
      Input #1, athlete, sport, winnings, endorsements
      picOutput.Print athlete, sport, winnings, endorsements, winnings + endorsements
      Close #1
    End Sub
```

55.
```
    Private Sub txtPhoneNum_GotFocus()
      MsgBox "Be sure to include the area code!", , ""
    End Sub
```

57.
```
    Private Sub cmdCompute_Click()
      Dim price As Single, quantity As Single, revenue As Single
      picOutput.Cls
      Open "DATA.TXT" For Input As #1
      Input #1, price
      Input #1, quantity
      Let revenue = price * quantity
      picOutput.Print "The revenue is"; revenue
      Close #1
    End Sub
```

Exercises 3.6

1. MCD'S
3. 10
5. 6
7. AB
9. e
11. 4
13. 0
15. now
17. 2
19. 3
21. -3
23. 0
25. Lul
27. ullaby
29. LULLABY
31. 0
33. by
35. 8lab
37. Today is Thu
39. o
41. I guess your answer is yes
43. 1937 YANKEES
45. 320,000.00
47. 32.00
49. 0.03
51. ($23.00)

53. $0.75
55. $10.50
57. 0
59. -2345
61. -1
63. 6.25%
65. 100.00%
67. 2.50%
69. 2.00E-04
71. 1.00E+02
73. -1.41E+00
75. Saturday, January 01, 2000
77. 02-Jan-00
79. Manhattan $24.00
81. Name   Salary
    Bill $123,000.00
83. "Currency"
85. "@@@@@"
87. "Scientific"
89. "Standard"
91. 1234567890
            abcd
93. 1234567890
        1234.559
95. 1234567890
        $25.00

97. The two arguments of Left should be interchanged.
99. Cannot take the square root of a negative number.
101. The second argument of Format must be a string; Standard should be "Standard".
103. The function name Format is missing in front of the parenthesis.
105. Yes
107. Integers from 10 through 19
109. Integers from 1 through 52
111. The 26 lowercase letters a through z
113. `2 * Rnd + 2`
115. `Int(2 * Rnd)`
117. `Chr(Int(7 * Rnd) + 65)`
119.
```
Rem Display an area code from a phone number entered in the form xxx-xxx-xxxx
picOutput.Print Left(txtPhone.Text, 3)
```
121.
```
Private Sub cmdDisplay_Click()
    Dim grad As Integer
    Rem Display number of graduation tickets
    picOutput.Cls
    Let grad = Val(InputBox("Enter number of graduates:"))
    picOutput.Print Int(2000 / grad); "tickets will be distributed to each student"
End Sub
```
123.
```
Private Sub cmdDisplay_Click()
    Dim q As Single, h As Single, c As Single
    Rem Compute optimal inventory size
    Let q = Val(InputBox("Enter quantity:"))
    Let h = Val(InputBox("Enter ordering cost:"))
    Let c = Val(InputBox("Enter storage cost:"))
    picOutput.Print "The optimum inventory size is"; Int(Sqr(2 * q * h / c))
End Sub
```

125.
```
Private Sub cmdRound_Click()
    Dim number As Single, decPlaces As Integer
    Rem Round a number
    Let number = Val(InputBox("Number to round:"))
    Let decPlaces = Val(InputBox("Decimal places to which number should be rounded:"))
    Let number = Int(number * 10 ^ decPlaces + .5) / 10 ^ decPlaces
    picOutput.Cls
    picOutput.Print "The rounded number is"; number
End Sub
```

127.
```
Private Sub cmdComputeChange_Click()
    Dim cents As Integer, quarters As Integer
    Rem Quarters in change
    Let cents = Val(InputBox("Number of cents (between 1 and 99):"))
    Let quarters = Int(cents / 25)
    picResult.Cls
    picResult.Print "The change will contain"; quarters; "quarters."
End Sub
```

129.
```
Private Sub cmdConvertHours_Click()
    Dim nautHour As Integer
    Rem Convert hours
    Let nautHour = Val(InputBox("Nautical hour (0 to 23):"))
    picResult.Cls
    picResult.Print "The standard hour is"; nautHour Mod 12
End Sub
```

131.
```
Private Sub cmdFindDigits_Click()
    Dim num As String, ptPos As Integer
    Rem Determine number of digits before and after the decimal point
    Let num = InputBox("Enter a number containing a decimal point:")
    Let ptPos = Instr(num, ".")
    picOutput.Cls
    picOutput.Print "There are"; ptPos - 1; "digits before the decimal point"
    picOutput.Print "and"; Len(num) - ptPos; "digits after the decimal point."
End Sub
```

133.

Object	Property	Setting
frmCompoundInterest	Caption	Compound Interest
lblPrincipal	Caption	Principal
txtPrincipal	Text	(blank)
lblInterestRate	Caption	Interest Rate
		Alignment 2 – Center
txtInterestRate	Text	(blank)
cmdCompute	Caption	Compute Balance
lblBalance	Caption	Balance after 10 years
		Alignment 2 – Center
lblOutput	Caption	(blank)

```
Private Sub cmdCompute_Click()
    Dim principal As Single, intRate As Single, balance As Single
    Rem Show growth of money in a savings account
    Let principal = Val(txtPrincipal.Text)
    Let txtPrincipal.Text = Format(principal, "Currency")
    Let intRate = Val(txtInterestRate.Text)
    Let txtInterestRate.Text = Format(intRate, "Percent")
    Let balance = principal * (1 + intRate) ^ 10
    Let lblOutput.Caption = Format(balance, "Currency")
End Sub

Private Sub txtPrincipal_GotFocus()
    Let txtPrincipal.Text = ""
End Sub

Private Sub txtInterestRate_GotFocus()
    Let txtInterestRate.Text = ""
End Sub
```

135.
```
Private Sub cmdPrintStateData_Click()
    Dim state As String, capital As String, population As Single, Area As Single
    Dim nicePop As String, niceArea As String, niceDens As String
    Rem State data
    Open "3-6-E135.TXT" For Input As #1
    Printer.Font.Name = "Courier"
    Printer.Font.Bold = True
    Printer.Print "State"; Tab(12); "Capital"; Tab(24); "Population";
    Printer.Print Tab(38); "Area"; Tab(48); "Density"
    Printer.Font.Bold = False
    Input #1, state, capital, population, area
    Let nicePop = Format(population, "#,#")
    Let niceArea = Format(area, "#,#")
    Let niceDens = Format(population / area, "Standard")
    Printer.Print state; Tab(12); capital; Tab(24); Format(nicePop, "@@@@@@@@@");
    Printer.Print Tab(38);Format(niceArea,"@@@@@@@");Tab(48);Format(niceDens,"@@@@@@")
    Input #1, state, capital, population, area
    Let nicePop = Format(population, "#,#")
    Let niceArea = Format(area, "#,#")
    Let niceDens = Format(population / area, "Standard")
    Printer.Print state; Tab(12); capital; Tab(24); Format(nicePop, "@@@@@@@@@");
    Printer.Print Tab(38);Format(niceArea,"@@@@@@@");Tab(48);Format(niceDens,"@@@@@@")
    Input #1, state, capital, population, area
    Let nicePop = Format(population, "#,#")
    Let niceArea = Format(area, "#,#")
    Let niceDens = Format(population / area, "Standard")
    Printer.Print state; Tab(12); capital; Tab(24); Format(nicePop, "@@@@@@@@@");
    Printer.Print Tab(38);Format(niceArea,"@@@@@@@");Tab(48);Format(niceDens,"@@@@@@")
    Printer.EndDoc
    Close #1
End Sub
```

137.
```
Private Sub cmdPrintRndDate_Click()
    Dim m As Integer, y As Integer
    Rem Select a random month and year during the 1990s
    Randomize
    Let m = Int(12 * Rnd) + 1
    Let y = Int(10 * Rnd) + 1990
    picOutput.Cls
    picOutput.Print m; "/"; y
End Sub
```

139.
```
Private Sub txtNyahNyah_KeyPress(KeyAscii As Integer)
    Rem Replace the users keystroke with a random letter from A to Z
    Let KeyAscii = Int(26 * Rnd) + 65
End Sub
```

CHAPTER 4

Exercises 4.1

1. It isn't easy being green.
                Kermit the frog

3. Why do clocks run clockwise?
Because they were invented in the northern
hemisphere where sundials move clockwise.

5. Divorced, beheaded, died;
Divorced, beheaded, survived.

7. Keep cool, but don't freeze.
Source: A jar of mayonnaise.

9. 88 keys on a piano

11. It was the best of times.
It was the worst of times.

13. Your name has 7 letters.
The first letter is G

15. abcde

17. 144 items in a gross

19. 30% of M&M's Plain Chocolate Candies are brown.

21. 1440 minutes in a day

23. t is the 6 th letter of the word.

25. According to a poll in the May 31, 1988
        issue of PC Magazine, 75% of the people polled
        write programs for their companies.
        The four most popular languages used are as follows.
        22 percent of the respondents use BASIC
        16 percent of the respondents use Assembler
        15 percent of the respondents use C
        13 percent of the respondents use Pascal

27. President Bush is a graduate of Yale University
President Clinton is a graduate of Georgetown University

29. The first 6 letters are Visual

31. The negative of worldly is unworldly

33. 24 blackbirds baked in a pie.

35. There is a parameter in the subprogram, but no argument in
the statement calling the subprogram.

37. Since *Print* is a keyword, it cannot be used as the name of a
subprogram.

39.
```
Private Sub cmdDisplay_Click()
    Dim num As Integer
    Rem Display a lucky number
    picOutput.Cls
    Let num = 7
    Call Lucky(num)
End Sub

Private Sub Lucky(num As Integer)
    Rem Display message
    picOutput.Print num; "is a lucky number."
End Sub
```

41.
```
Private Sub cmdDisplay_Click()
    Dim tree As String, ht As Single
    Rem Information about trees
    picOutput.Cls
    Open "TREES.TXT" For Input As #1
    Input #1, tree, ht
    Call Tallest(tree, ht)
    Input #1, tree, ht
    Call Tallest(tree, ht)
    Close #1
End Sub

Private Sub Tallest(tree As String, ht As Single)
    Rem Display information about tree
    picOutput.Print "The tallest "; tree; " in the U.S. is"; ht; "feet."
End Sub
```

43.
```
Private Sub cmdCompute_Click()
    Dim num As Single
    Rem Given a number, display its triple
    picResult.Cls
    Let num = Val(InputBox("Enter a number:"))
    Call Triple(num)
End Sub

Private Sub Triple(num As Single)
    Rem Multiply the value of the number by 3
    picResult.Print "The number's triple is"; 3 * num
End Sub
```

45.
```
Private Sub cmdDisplay_Click()
    Dim word As String, col As Integer
    Rem Enter a word and column number to display
    picOutput.Cls
    Let word = InputBox("Enter a word:")
    Let col = Val(InputBox("Enter a column number between 1 and 10:"))
    Call PlaceNShow(word, col)
End Sub

Private Sub PlaceNShow(word As String, col As Integer)
    Rem Display the word at the given column number
    picOutput.Print Tab(col); word
End Sub
```

47.
```
Private Sub cmdDisplay_Click()
   Rem Intended college majors
   picOutput.Cls
   Call DisplaySource
   Call Majors(18, "business")
   Call Majors(2, "computer science")
End Sub


Private Sub DisplaySource()
   Rem Display the source of the information
   picOutput.Print "According to a 1991 survey of college freshmen"
   picOutput.Print "taken by the Higher Educational Research Institute:"
   picOutput.Print
End Sub


Private Sub Majors(students As Single, field As String)
   Rem Display the information about major
   picOutput.Print students; "percent said they intend to major in "; field
End Sub
```

49.
```
Private Sub cmdDisplay_Click()
   Dim num As Single
   Rem Favorite number
   picOutput.Cls
   Let num = Val(txtBox.Text)
   Call Sum (num)
   Call Product(num)
End Sub


Private Sub Product(num As Single)
   picOutput.Print "The product of your favorite number with itself is"; num * num
End Sub


Private Sub Sum(num As Single)
   picOutput.Print "The sum of your favorite number with itself is"; num + num
End Sub
```

51.
```
Private Sub cmdDisplay_Click()
   Dim animal As String, sound As String
   Rem Old McDonald Had a Farm
   picOldMcDonald.Cls
   Open "FARM.TXT" For Input As #1
   Input #1, animal, sound
   Call ShowVerse(animal, sound)
   picOldMcDonald.Print
   Input #1, animal, sound
   Call ShowVerse(animal, sound)
   picOldMcDonald.Print
   Input #1, animal, sound
   Call ShowVerse(animal, sound)
   picOldMcDonald.Print
   Input #1, animal, sound
   Call ShowVerse(animal, sound)
   Close #1
End Sub


Private Sub ShowVerse(animal As String, sound As String)
   Rem Display a verse from Old McDonald Had a Farm
   picOldMcDonald.Print "Old McDonald had a farm. Eyi eyi oh."
   picOldMcDonald.Print "And on his farm he had a "; animal; ".  Eyi eyi oh."
   picOldMcDonald.Print "With a "; sound; " "; sound; " here, ";
   picOldMcDonald.Print "and a "; sound; " "; sound; " there."
   picOldMcDonald.Print "Here a "; sound; ", there a "; sound;
   picOldMcDonald.Print ", everywhere a "; sound; " "; sound; "."
   picOldMcDonald.Print "Old McDonald had a farm. Eyi eyi oh."
End Sub
```

53.
```
Private Sub cmdDisplay_Click()
    Rem Display a table for occupation growth
    picOutput.Cls
    Open "4-1-E53.TXT" For Input As #1
    picOutput.Print "Occupation"; Tab(40); 1982; Tab(48); 1991; Tab(56);"Change"
    picOutput.Print
    Call ComputeChange
    Call ComputeChange
    Call ComputeChange
    Close #1
End Sub

Private Sub ComputeChange()
    Dim occupation As String, num82 As Single, num91 As Single, perChange As Single
    Rem Read data and compute percent change, display all data
    Input #1, occupation, num82, num91
    Let perChange = 100 * (num91 - num82) / num82
    picOutput.Print occupation; Tab(40); num82; Tab(48); num91; Tab(58); Format(perChange, "0"); "%"
End Sub
```

Exercises 4.2

1. 9

3. Can Can

5. 25

7. Less is more

9. Gabriel was born in the year 1980

11. Buckeyes

13. 0

15. 1 1

17. discovered Florida

19. The variable c should be a parameter in the subprogram. That is, the Sub statement should be Private Sub Sum (x As Single, y As Single, c As Single).

21.
```
Private Sub cmdCompute_Click()
    Dim price As Single, tax As Single, cost As Single
    Rem Calculate sales tax
    picOutput.Cls
    Call InputPrice(price)
    Call Compute(price, tax, cost)
    Call ShowData(price, tax, cost)
End Sub

Private Sub Compute(price As Single, tax As Single,
        cost As Single)
    Rem Calculate the cost
    Let tax = .05 * price
    Let cost = price + tax
End Sub

Private Sub InputPrice(price As Single)
    Rem Get the price of the item
    Let price = Val(InputBox("Enter the price of the item:"))
End Sub

Private Sub ShowData(price As Single, tax As Single,
        cost As Single)
    Rem Display bill
    picOutput.Print "Price: "; price
    picOutput.Print "Tax: "; tax
    picOutput.Print "————"
    picOutput.Print "Cost: "; cost
End Sub
```

23.
```
Private Sub cmdDisplay_Click()
    Dim length As Single, wdth As Single, area As Single
    Rem Compute area of rectangle
    picOutput.Cls
    Call InputSize(length, wdth)
    Call ComputeArea(length, wdth, area)
    Call ShowArea(area)
End Sub

Private Sub ComputeArea(length As Single, wdth As Single, area As Single)
    Rem Calculate the area
    Let area = length * wdth
End Sub
```

```
   Private Sub InputSize(length As Single, wdth As Single)
     Rem Get the dimensions of the rectangle
     Let length = Val(txtLength.Text)
     Let wdth = Val(txtWidth.Text)
   End Sub


   Private Sub ShowArea(area As Single)
     Rem Display the area of the rectangle
     picOutput.Print "The area of the rectangle is"; area
   End Sub
```

25. `Dim nom As String   'place in the (Declarations) section of (General)`

27.
```
   Private Sub cmdDisplay_Click()
     Dim first As String, last As String, fInit As String, lInit As String
     Rem Display initials
     picOutput.Cls
     Call InputNames (first, last)
     Call ExtractInitials(first, last, fInit, lInit)
     Call DisplayInitials(fInit, lInit)
   End Sub


   Private Sub DisplayInitials(fInit As String, lInit As String)
     Rem Display the initials
     picOutput.Print "The initials are "; fInit; "."; lInit; "."
   End Sub


   Private Sub ExtractInitials(first As String, last As String, fInit As String, lInit As String)
     Rem Determine the initials of the first and last names
     Let fInit = Left(first,1)
     Let lInit = Left(last,1)
   End Sub


   Private Sub InputNames(first As String, last As String)
     Rem Get the person's first and last name
     Let first = InputBox("Enter your first name:")
     Let last = InputBox("Enter your last name:")
   End Sub
```

29.
```
   Private Sub cmdCompute_Click()
     Dim cost As Single, price As Single, markup As Single
     Rem Calculate percentage markup
     picMarkup.Cls
     Call InputAmounts(cost, price)
     Call ComputeMarkup(cost, price, markup)
     Call DisplayMarkup(markup)
   End Sub


   Private Sub ComputeMarkup(cost As Single, price As Single, markup As Single)
     Let markup = 100 * ((price - cost) / cost)
   End Sub


   Private Sub DisplayMarkup(markup As Single)
     picMarkup.Print "The markup is "; Format(markup, "0"); " percent."
   End Sub


   Private Sub InputAmounts(cost As Single, price As Single)
     Let cost = Val(InputBox("Enter the cost:"))
     Let price = Val(InputBox("Enter the selling price:"))
   End Sub
```

31.
```
   Private Sub cmdCompute_Click()
     Dim nom As String, atBats As Integer, hits As Integer, ave As Single
     Rem Calculate batting average
     picAverage.Cls
     Open "4-2-E31.TXT" For Input As #1
     Call ReadStats(nom, atBats, hits)
     Call ComputeAverage(atBats, hits, ave)
     Call DisplayInfo(nom, ave)
     Close #1
   End Sub
```

```
Private Sub ComputeAverage(atBats As Integer, hits As Integer, ave As Single)
  Let ave = hits / atBats
End Sub


Private Sub DisplayInfo(nom As String, ave As Single)
  picAverage.Print "Name", "Batting Average"
  picAverage.Print nom,
  picAverage.Print Format(ave,".000")
End Sub


Private Sub ReadStats(nom As String, atBats As Integer, hits As Integer)
  Input #1, nom, atBats, hits
End Sub
```

33.
```
Private Sub cmdDisplay_Click()
  Rem Display Hat Rack mall comparison table
  picTable.Cls
  picTable.Print Tab(15); "Rent per"
  picTable.Print Tab(15); "Square"; Tab(25); "Total"; Tab(35); "Monthly"
  picTable.Print "Mall Name"; Tab(15); "Foot"; Tab(25); "Feet"; Tab(35); "Rent"
  picTable.Print
  Open "MALLS.TXT" For Input As #1
  Call DisplayInfo
  Call DisplayInfo
  Call DisplayInfo
  Close #1
End Sub


Private Sub ComputeRent(rent As Single, feet As Single, total As Single)
  Rem Compute monthly rent given rent/foot and number of feet
  Let total = rent * feet
End Sub


Private Sub DisplayInfo()
  Dim mall As String, rentPerFoot As Single, squareFeet As Single, rent As Single
  Rem Display the information for a single mall
  Input #1, mall, rentPerFoot, squareFeet
  Call ComputeRent(rentPerFoot, squareFeet, rent)
  picTable.Print mall; Tab(15); rentPerFoot; Tab(25); squareFeet; Tab(35); rent
End Sub
```

35.
```
Dim total As Single   'In (Declarations) section of (General)


Private Sub cmdProcessItem_Click()
  Dim item As String, price As Single
  Rem Process item; display part of sales receipt
  Call InputData(item, price)
  Let total = total + price
  Call ShowData(item, price)
  Let txtItem.Text = ""
  Let txtPrice.Text = ""
  txtItem.SetFocus
End Sub


Private Sub cmdDisplay_Click()
  Dim tax As Single
  Rem Display sum, tax, and total
  Let tax = total * .05
  Let tax = Int(100 * tax + .5) / 100
  picReceipt.Print Tab(15); "——-"
  Call ShowData("Sum", total)
  Call ShowData("Tax", tax)
  Call ShowData("Total", total + tax)
End Sub


Private Sub InputData(item As String, price As Single)
  Rem Input item name and price
  Let item = txtItem.Text
  Let price = Val(txtPrice.Text)
End Sub
```

```
Private Sub ShowData(strItem As String, numItem As Single)
  Rem Display data on specified line
  picReceipt.Print strItem; Tab(15); Format(numItem,"Standard")
End Sub
```

Exercises 4.3

1. 203

3. The population will double in 24 years.

5. Volume of cylinder having base area 3.14159
and height 2 is 6.28318
Volume of cylinder having base area 28.27431
and height 4 is 113.0972

7. train

9. moral has the negative amoral
political has the negative apolitical

11. The first line of the function definition should end with
As String not *As Single*.

13.
```
Private Sub cmdCompute_Click()
    Dim radius As Single, height As Single
    Rem Tin Needed for a Tin Can
    picOutput.Cls
    Call InputDims(radius, height)
    Call ShowAmount(radius, height)
End Sub

Private Function CanArea(radius As Single, height As Single) As Single
  Rem Calculate surface area of a cylindrical can
  CanArea = 6.28 * (radius * radius + radius * height)
End Function

Private Sub InputDims(radius As Single, height As Single)
  Let radius = Val(InputBox("Enter radius of can:"))
  Let height = Val(InputBox("Enter height of can:"))
End Sub

Private Sub ShowAmount(radius As Single, height As Single)
  picOutput.Print "A can of radius", radius, "and height"; height
  picOutput.Print "requires"; CanArea(radius, height); "square units to make."
End Sub
```

15.
```
Private Sub cmdRound_Click()
    Dim m As Single, n As Integer
    Rem Round a positive number m to n decimal places
    picResult.Cls
    Call InputData(m, n)
    Call RoundIt(m, n)
End Sub

Private Sub InputData(m As Single, n As Integer)
  Let m = Val(InputBox("Enter a number to round:"))
  Let n = Val(InputBox("Round it to how many decimal places?"))
End Sub

Private Function Rounded(m As Single, n As Integer) As Single
  Rem Round a number to a given number of decimal places
  Rounded = Int(m * 10 ^ n  + .5) / (10 ^ n)
End Function

Private Sub RoundIt(m As Single, n As Integer)
  picResult.Print m; "rounded to"; n; "places is"; Rounded(m, n)
End Sub
```

17.
```
Private Sub cmdCompute_Click()
    Dim popcorn As Single, butter As Single, bucket As Single, price As Single
    Rem Popcorn Profits
    picProfit.Cls
    Call InputAmounts(popcorn, butter, bucket, price)
    Call ShowProfit(popcorn, butter, bucket, price)
End Sub
```

```
    Private Sub InputAmounts(popcorn As Single,butter As Single,bucket As Single,price As Single)
      Let popcorn = Val(InputBox("What is the cost of the popcorn kernels?"))
      Let butter = Val(InputBox("What is the cost of the butter?"))
      Let bucket = Val(InputBox("What is the cost of the bucket?"))
      Let price = Val(InputBox("What is the sale price?"))
    End Sub

    Private Function Profit(popcorn As Single,butter As Single,bucket As Single,price As Single) As Single
      Rem Calculate the profit on a bucket of popcorn
      Profit = price - (popcorn + butter + bucket)
    End Function

    Private Sub ShowProfit(popcorn As Single,butter As Single,bucket As Single,price As Single)
      picProfit.Print "The profit is";
      picProfit.Print Profit(popcorn, butter, bucket, price)
    End Sub
```

19.
```
    Private Sub cmdCompute_Click()
        Dim weight As Single
        Rem Original Cost of Airmail
        picCost.Cls
        Call InputWeight(weight)
        Call ShowCost(weight)
    End Sub

    Private Function Ceil(x As Single) As Single
      Ceil = -Int(-x)
    End Function

    Private Function Cost(weight As Single) As Single
      Rem Calculate the cost of an airmail letter
      Cost = .05 + .10 * Ceil(weight - 1)
    End Function

    Private Sub InputWeight(weight As Single)
      Let weight = Val(txtOunces.Text)
    End Sub

    Private Sub ShowCost(weight As Single)
      picCost.Print "The cost of mailing the letter is $"; Cost(weight)
    End Sub
```

21.
```
    Private Sub cmdGreetSenator_Click()
        Dim nom As String
        Rem Display a greeting for a senator
        picGreeting.Cls
        Let nom = InputBox("Enter the senator's name:")
        picGreeting.Print
        picGreeting.Print "The Honorable "; nom
        picGreeting.Print "United States Senate"
        picGreeting.Print "Washington, DC 20001"
        picGreeting.Print
        picGreeting.Print "Dear Senator "; LastName(nom); ","
    End Sub

    Private Function LastName(nom As String) As String
      Rem Determine the last name of a two-part name
      Let spaceNmb = Instr(nom, " ")
      LastName = Mid(nom, spaceNmb + 1, Len(nom) - spaceNmb)
    End Function
```

CHAPTER 5

Exercises 5.1

1. True
3. True
5. True
7. True
9. False
11. False
13. True
15. True
17. False
19. False

21. False
23. True
25. Equivalent
27. Not Equivalent
29. Equivalent
31. Not Equivalent
33. Equivalent
35. a <= b
37. (a >= b) Or (c = d)
39. (a = "") Or (a >= b) Or (Len(a) >= 5)

Exercises 5.2

1. Less than ten
3. Tomorrow is another day.
5. 10
7. Cost of call: $11.26
9. The number of vowels is 2
11. positive
13. Incorrect conditional. Should be If (1 < num) And (num < 3) Then

15. no Then
17. Comparing numeric and string data
19. Incorrect conditional. Should be If (j = 4) Or (k = 4) Then
21. Let a = 5
23.
```
If j = 7 Then
    Let b = 1
  Else
    Let b = 2
End If
```

25.
```
Let message = "Is Alaska bigger than Texas and California combined?"
Let answer = InputBox(message)
If UCase(Left(answer, 1)) = "Y" Then
    picOutput.Print "Correct"
  Else
    picOutput.Print "Wrong"
End If
```

27.
```
Private Sub cmdComputeTip_Click()
    Dim cost As Single, tip As Single
    Rem Give waiter a tip
    picTip.Cls
    Let cost = Val(InputBox("Enter cost of meal:"))
    Let tip = cost * .15
    If tip < 1 Then
        Let tip = 1
    End If
    picTip.Print "Leave "; Format(tip, "Currency"); " for the tip."
End Sub
```

29.
```
Private Sub cmdOrderDisks_Click()
    Dim num As Single, cost As Single
    Rem Order diskettes
    picCost.Cls
    Let num = Val(InputBox("Number of diskettes:"))
    If num < 25 Then
        Let cost = num
      Else
        Let cost = .7 * num
    End If
    picCost.Print "The cost is "; Format(cost, "Currency")
End Sub
```

31.
```
Private Sub txtNum_KeyPress(KeyAscii As Integer)
    If KeyAscii > 31 And KeyAscii < Asc("0") Or KeyAscii > Asc("9") Then
        Rem Ignore all regular keystrokes except the digits 0 through 9
        Let KeyAscii = 0
    End If
End Sub
```

33.
```
Private Sub cmdComputeBalance_Click()
    Dim balance As Single, amount As Single
    Rem Savings account withdrawal
    picBalance.Cls
    Let balance = Val(InputBox("Current balance:"))
    Let amount = Val(InputBox("Amount of withdrawal:"))
    If (balance >= amount) Then
        Let balance = balance - amount
        picBalance.Print "New balance is "; Format(balance, "Currency")
        If balance < 150 Then
            picBalance.Print "Balance below $150"
        End If
      Else
        picBalance.Print "Withdrawal denied."
    End If
End Sub
```

35.
```
Private Sub cmdRunLottery_Click()
    Dim d1 As Integer, d2 As Integer, d3 As Integer, lucky As String
    Rem Lottery
    picLuckySeven.Cls
    Randomize
    Let d1 = Int(10 * Rnd)
    Let d2 = Int(10 * Rnd)
    Let d3 = Int(10 * Rnd)
    Let lucky = "Lucky seven"
    If d1 = 7 Then
        If (d2 = 7) Or (d3 = 7) Then
            picLuckySeven.Print lucky
        End If
      Else
        If (d2 = 7) And (d3 = 7) Then
            picLuckySeven.Print lucky
        End If
    End If
End Sub
```

37.
```
Private Sub cmdConvert_Click()
    Dim word As String, first As String
    Rem Convert to Pig Latin
    picPigLatin.Cls
    Let word = InputBox("Enter a word (use all lowercase):")
    Let first = Left(word, 1)
    If Instr("aeiou", first) <> 0 Then
        Let word = word & "way"
      Else
        Let word = Mid(word, 2, Len(word) - 1) & first & "ay"
    End If
    picPigLatin.Print "The word in pig latin is "; word
End Sub
```

39.
```
Dim status As Integer   'In (Declarations) section of (General)

Private Sub cmdBogart_Click()
  If status = 0 Then
      picCasablanca.Print "I came to Casablanca for the waters."
      Let status = 1
    ElseIf status = 2 Then
      picCasablanca.Print "I was misinformed."
      Let status = 0
  End If
End Sub

Sub cmdRaines_Click ()
  If status = 1 Then
      picCasablanca.Print "But we're in the middle of the desert."
      Let status = 2
  End If
End Sub
```

41.

Object	Property	Setting
frmPresidentQuiz	Caption	Yankee Doodle President
lblQuestion	Caption	Which U.S. President was born on July 4?
txtAnswer	Text	(blank)
cmdCheckAnswer	Caption	Check Answer
lblCount	Caption	0
lblGuesses	Caption	guesses so far.

```
Private Sub cmdCheckAnswer_Click()
  Dim msg As String
  Rem lblCount keeps track of the number of guesses; increase number of guesses by 1
  Let lblCount.Caption = Format(Val(lblCount.Caption) + 1 ,"#")
  If Instr(UCase(txtAnswer.Text), "COOLIDGE") > 0 Then
      MsgBox "Calvin Coolidge was born on July 4, 1872.", , "Correct"
    ElseIf Val(lblCount.Caption) = 3 Then
      Let msg = "He once said, 'If you don't say anything,"
      Let msg = msg & " you won't be called upon to repeat it.'"
      MsgBox msg, , "Hint"
    ElseIf Val(lblCount.Caption) = 7 Then
      MsgBox "His nickname was 'Silent Cal.'", , "Hint"
    ElseIf Val(lblCount.Caption) = 10 Then
      MsgBox "Calvin Coolidge was born on July 4, 1872.", , "You've run out of guesses"
      End
  End If
End Sub
```

43.
```
Private Sub cmdCalcNJTax_Click()
  Dim income As Single, tax As Single
  Rem Calculate New Jersey state income tax
  picNJTax.Cls
  Let income = Val(InputBox("Taxable income:"))
  If income <= 20000 Then
      Let tax = .02 * income
    Else
      If income <= 50000 Then
          Let tax = 400 + .025 * (income - 20000)
        Else
          Let tax = 1150 + .035 * (income - 50000)
      End If
  End If
  picNJTax.Print "Tax is "; Format(tax, "Currency")
End Sub
```

Exercises 5.3

1.
```
The price is $3.75
The price is $3.75
```

3.
```
Mesozoic Era
Paleozoic Era
?
```

5.
```
Nope.
He worked with the developer, von Neumann, on the ENIAC.
Correct
```

7.
```
The less things change, the more they remain the same.
Less is more.
Time keeps everything from happening at once.
```

9. Should have a Case clause.

11. Works. However, you should not compare numeric
(0 To 9) and string data (string variable *a*).

13. Error in second Case.

15. Case a < 5 should be Case Is < 5

17. Valid

19. Invalid

21. Valid

23.
```
Select Case a
  Case 1
    picOutput.Print "one"
  Case Is > 5
    picOutput.Print "two"
End Select
```

25.
```
Select Case a
  Case 2
    picOutput.Print "yes"
  Case Is < 5
    picOutput.Print "no"
End Select
```

27.
```
Private Sub cmdCompute_Click()
    Dim percent As Single
    Rem Determine degree of cloudiness
    picCloudCover.Cls
    Let percent = Val(InputBox("Percentage of cloud cover:"))
    Select Case percent
      Case 0 To 30
        picCloudCover.Print "Clear"
      Case 31 To 70
        picCloudCover.Print "Partly cloudy"
      Case 71 To 99
        picCloudCover.Print "Cloudy"
      Case 100
        picCloudCover.Print "Overcast"
      Case Else
        picCloudCover.Print "Percentage must be between 0 And 100."
    End Select
End Sub
```

29.
```
Private Sub cmdFindNumDays_Click()
    Dim monthName As String, days As Integer
    Rem Give number of days in month
    picNumDays.Cls
    Call InputMonth(monthName)
    Call GetDays(monthName, days)
    Call ShowDays(days, monthName)
End Sub

Private Sub GetDays(monthName As String, days As Integer)
  Dim answer As String
  Rem Compute number of days in the month
  Select Case UCase(monthName)
    Case "FEBRUARY"
      Let answer = InputBox("Is it a leap year?")
      If UCase(Left(answer, 1)) = "Y" Then
          Let days = 29
        Else
          Let days = 28
      End If
    Case "APRIL", "JUNE", "SEPTEMBER", "NOVEMBER"
      Let days = 30
    Case "JANUARY","MARCH","MAY","JULY","AUGUST","OCTOBER","DECEMBER"
      Let days = 31
  End Select
End Sub

Private Sub InputMonth(monthName As String)
  Rem Input a month of the year
  Let monthName = InputBox("Enter a month (do not abbreviate):")
End Sub

Private Sub ShowDays(days As Integer, monthName As String)
  Rem Report number of days in month
  picNumDays.Print monthName; " has"; days; "days."
End Sub
```

31.
```
Private Sub cmdProcessScore_Click()
    Dim score As Integer
    Rem Give letter grade for number score
    picLetterGrade.Cls
    Call InputScore(score)
    Call ShowGrade(score)
End Sub


Private Function Grade(score As Integer) As String
    Rem Return letter grade for score
    Select Case score
        Case 90 To 100
            Grade = "A"
        Case 80 To 89
            Grade = "B"
        Case 70 To 79
            Grade = "C"
        Case 60 To 69
            Grade = "D"
        Case 0 To 59
            Grade = "F"
        Case Else
            Grade = "Invalid"
    End Select
End Function


Private Sub InputScore(score As Integer)
    Rem Input a number score
    Let score = Val(InputBox("What is the score?"))
End Sub


Private Sub ShowGrade(score As Integer)
    Rem Show letter grade for score
    picLetterGrade.Print "The letter grade is "; Grade(score)
End Sub
```

33.
```
Private Sub cmdCompute_Click()
    Dim amount As Single
    Rem Determine cash award
    picReward.Cls
    Let amount = Val(InputBox("How much was recovered?"))
    Select Case amount
        Case Is <= 75000
            Let amount = .1 * amount
        Case Is <= 100000
            Let amount = 7500 + .05 * (amount - 75000)
        Case Is > 100000
            Let amount = 8750 + .01 * (amount - 100000)
            If amount > 50000 Then
                Let amount = 50000
            End If
    End Select
    picReward.Print "The amount given as reward is "; _
                    Format(amount, "Currency")
End Sub
```

35.

Object	Property	Setting
frmEx5_3_35	Caption	Presidential Trivia
lblQuestion	Caption	Last name of one of the four most recent Presidents
	Alignment	1 – Right Justify
txtName	Text	(blank)
cmdGetFacts	Caption	OK
picTrivia		

```
Private Sub cmdGetFacts_Click()
    Dim pres As String, state As String, trivia As String
    Let pres = txtName.Text
    Select Case UCase(pres)
        Case "CARTER"
            Let state = "Georgia"
            Let trivia = "The only soft drink served in the Carter "
            Let trivia = trivia & "White House was Coca-Cola."
        Case "REAGAN"
            Let state = "California"
            Let trivia = "His secret service code name was Rawhide."
        Case "BUSH"
            Let state = "Texas"
            Let trivia = "He was the third left-handed president."
        Case "CLINTON"
            Let state = "Arkansas"
            Let trivia = "In college he did a good imitation of Elvis Presley."
        Case Else
            Let state = ""
            Let trivia = ""
    End Select
```

```
        If state <> "" Then
            picTrivia.Cls
            picTrivia.Print "President " & pres & "'s ";
            picTrivia.Print "home state was " & state & "."
            picTrivia.Print trivia
        End If
        Let txtName.Text = ""
        txtName.SetFocus
    End Sub
```

37.
```
    Private Sub cmdHumor_Click()
        Let lblSentence.Caption = HumorMsg(Val(txtNumber.Text))
    End Sub


    Private Sub cmdInsult_Click()
        Let lblSentence.Caption = InsultMsg(Val(txtNumber.Text))
    End Sub


    Private Function HumorMsg(num As Integer) As String
      Dim temp As String
      Select Case num
        Case 1
          HumorMsg = "I can resist everything except temptation"
        Case 2
          HumorMsg = "I just heard from Bill Bailey. He's not coming home."
        Case 3
          Let temp = "I have enough money to last the rest of my life,"
          HumorMsg = temp & " unless I buy something."
        Case Else
          HumorMsg = ""
          txtNumber.Text = ""
      End Select
    End Function


    Private Function InsultMsg(num As Integer) As String
      Select Case num
        Case 1
          InsultMsg = "How much would you charge to haunt a house?"
        Case 2
          InsultMsg = "I bet you have no more friends than an alarm clock."
        Case 3
          InsultMsg = "When your IQ rises to 30, sell."
        Case Else
          InsultMsg = ""
          txtNumber.Text = ""
      End Select
    End Function
```

CHAPTER 6

Exercises 6.1

1. `17`

3. You are a super programmer!

5. `2`

7. Program never stops

9. Do and Loop interchanged.

11. `While num >= 7`

13. `Until response <> "Y"`

15. `Until nom = ""`

17. `Until (a <= 1) Or (a >= 3)`

19. `While n = 0`

21.
```
Private Sub cmdDisplay_Click()
    Dim nom As String, num As Integer
    Rem Request and display three names
    picOutput.Cls
    Let num = 0
    Do While num < 3
      Let nom = InputBox("Enter a name:")
      picOutput.Print nom
      Let num = num + 1
    Loop
End Sub
```

23.
```
Private Sub cmdDisplayConvTable_Click()
    Dim celsius As Single
    Rem Convert Celsius to Fahrenheit
    picTempTable.Cls
    picTempTable.Print "Celsius"; Tab(10); "Fahrenheit"
    Let celsius = -40
    Do While celsius <= 40
      Call ShowFahrenheit(celsius)
      Let celsius = celsius + 5
    Loop
End Sub

Private Function Fahrenheit(celsius As Single) As Single
  Rem Convert Celsius to Fahrenheit
  Fahrenheit = (9 / 5) * celsius + 32
End Function

Private Sub ShowFahrenheit(celsius As Single)
  Rem Give Fahrenheit equivalent
  picTempTable.Print celsius; Tab(10); Fahrenheit(celsius)
End Sub
```

25.
```
Private Sub cmdComputeOdds_Click()
    Dim counter As Integer, sevens As Integer, dieOne As Integer, dieTwo As Integer
    Randomize
    Let counter = 0
    Let sevens = 0
    Do While sevens < 10
      Let dieOne = Int(6 * Rnd) + 1
      Let dieTwo = Int(6 * Rnd) + 1
      Let counter = counter + 1
      If dieOne + dieTwo = 7 Then
        Let sevens = sevens + 1
      End If
    Loop
    picOdds.Cls
    picOdds.Print "The approximate odds of two die totaling seven is 1 in ";
    picOdds.Print Format(counter / sevens, "Standard")
End Sub
```

27.
```
Private Sub cmdDisplay_Click()
    Dim x As Integer, y As Integer, temp As Integer
    Rem First terms in the Fibonacci sequence
    Let x = 1
    Let y = 1
    picFibonacci.Cls
    picFibonacci.Print "Terms in the Fibonacci sequence between 1 and 100 are:"
    picFibonacci.Print x;
    Do While y <= 100
      picFibonacci.Print y;
      Let temp = x + y
      Let x = y
      Let y = temp
    Loop
End Sub
```

29.
```
Private Sub cmdDisplay_Click()
    Dim minuteHandPos As Single, hourHandPos As Single, difference As Single
    Rem When after 6:30 do clock hands exactly overlap?
    Let minuteHandPos = 0
    Let hourHandPos = 30
    Do While hourHandPos - minuteHandPos >= .0001
      Let difference = hourHandPos - minuteHandPos
      Let minuteHandPos = minuteHandPos + difference
      Let hourHandPos = hourHandPos + difference / 12
    Loop
    picOutput.Print "The hands overlap at"; minuteHandPos; "minutes after six."
End Sub
```

31.
```
Private Sub cmdBounceBall_Click()
    Dim height As Single, bounceFactor As Single, bounces As Integer, distance As Single
    Rem Bounce a ball and find total distance traveled
    picTotalDistance.Cls
    Call InputData(height, bounceFactor)
    Call BounceBall(height, bounceFactor, bounces, distance)
    Call ShowData(bounces, distance)
End Sub

Private Sub BounceBall(hght As Single, bFactor As Single, bounces As Integer, dist As Single)
    Let bounces = 1            ' first bounce
    Let dist = hght
    Do While hght * bFactor >= 10
        Let bounces = bounces + 1
        Let hght = hght * bFactor
        Let dist = dist + 2 * hght        ' up then down again
    Loop
End Sub

Private Sub InputData(height As Single, bounceFactor As Single)
    Dim prompt As String
    Rem Input height and coefficient of restitution
    Let prompt = "What is the coefficient of restitution of the ball (0 to 1)? " _
            & "Examples are .7 for a tennis ball, .75 for a basketball, " _
            & ".9 for a super ball, and .3 for a softball."
    Let bounceFactor = Val(InputBox(prompt))
    Let height = Val(InputBox("From how many meters will the ball be dropped?"))
    Let height = height * 100        ' convert to centimeters
End Sub

Private Sub ShowData(bounces As Integer, distance As Single)
    picTotalDistance.Print "The ball bounced"; bounces; "times and traveled about ";
    picTotalDistance.Print Format(distance / 100,"Standard"); " meters."
End Sub
```

33.
```
Private Sub cmdEstimate_Click()
    Dim amt As Single, yrs As Integer
    Rem Years to deplete savings account
    picResult.Cls
    Let amt = Val(InputBox("Enter initial amount in account:"))
    Let yrs = 0
    If amt * 1.05 - 1000 >= amt Then
        picResult.Print "Account will never be depleted."
      Else
        Do
            Let amt = amt * 1.05 - 1000
            Let yrs = yrs + 1
        Loop Until amt <= 0
        picResult.Print "It takes"; yrs; "years to deplete the account."
    End If
End Sub
```

35.
```
Private Sub cmdDetermineAge_Click()
    Dim age As Integer
    Rem Solution to age problem
    picResult.Cls
    Let age = 1
    Do While 1980 + age <> age * age
        Let age = age + 1
    Loop
    picResult.Print "The solution is"; age; "years old."
End Sub
```

37.
```
Private Sub cmdCapSentence_Click()
    Rem Capitalize entire sentence
    picOutput.Cls
    picOutput.Print Ucase(txtSentence.Text)
End Sub
```

```
    Private Sub cmdCapInitial_Click()
      Dim info As String, word As String
      Rem Capitalize first letter of each word
      picOutput.Cls
      Let info = LTrim(txtSentence.Text) 'discard any leading spaces
      Do While info <> ""
        Let word = NextWord(info)
        picOutput.Print UCase(Left(word, 1)) & Mid(word, 2) & " ";
      Loop
    End Sub

    Private Function NextWord(info As String) As String
      Dim spacePos As Integer
      Rem Take word from beginning of info; space assumed to be the word separator
      Let spacePos = Instr(info, " ")
      If spacePos = 0 Then
          Let NextWord = info
          Let info = ""
        Else
          Let NextWord = Left(info, spacePos - 1)
          Let info = LTrim(Mid(info, spacePos))
      End If
    End Function
```

39.
```
    Private Sub cmdFindGCD_Click()
      Dim m As Single, n As Single, t As Single, q As Single
      Rem Greatest common divisor
      picGCD.Cls
      Call InputIntegers(m, n)
      Do While n <> 0
        Let t = n
        Let n = m Mod n
        Let m = t
      Loop
      picGCD.Print "The greatest common divisor is"; m
    End Sub

    Private Sub InputIntegers(m As Single, n As Single)
      Rem Input two integers
      Let m = Val(InputBox("Enter first integer:"))
      Let n = Val(InputBox("Enter second integer:"))
    End Sub
```

Exercises 6.2

1. 13

3. pie
    cake
    melon

5. A
    Apple
    Apricot
    Avocado

    B
    Banana
    Blueberry

    G
    Grape

    L
    Lemon
    Lime

7. A group of ducks is called a brace

9. counters

11. Loop statement missing. Also, loop cannot be entered because the value of num is 0.

13. Last president in file will not be printed.

15.
```
Private Sub cmdDisplay_Click()
    Dim largest As Single, num as Single
    Rem Find largest of a collection of numbers
    picOutput.Cls
    Let largest = 0
    Open "DATA.TXT" For Input As #1
    Do While Not EOF(1)
      Input #1, num
      If num > largest Then
          Let largest = num
      End If
    Loop
    picOutput.Print "The largest number is"; largest
End Sub
```

17.
```
Private Sub cmdDisplay_Click()
    Dim total As Single, numGrades As Integer, grade As Single
    Dim average As Single, aaCount As Integer
    Rem Display percentage of grades that are above average
    picOutput.Cls
    Open "GRADES.TXT" For Input As #1
    Let total = 0
    Let numGrades = 0
    Do While Not EOF(1)
      Input #1, grade
      Let total = total + grade
      Let numGrades = numGrades + 1
    Loop
    Close #1
    If numGrades > 0 Then
        Let average = total / numGrades
        Let aaCount - 0
        Open "GRADES.TXT" For Input As #1
        Do While Not EOF(1)
          Input #1, grade
          If grade > average Then
              Let aaCount = aaCount + 1
          End If
        Loop
        Close #1
        picOutput.Print Format(aaCount / numGrades, "Percent"); "of grades are above the average of";
        picOutput.Print Format(average, "Standard")
    End If
End Sub
```

19.
```
Private Sub cmdShowPresident_Click()
    Dim n As Integer, num As Integer, nom As String
    Rem Display the name of the nth president
    Let n = Val(txtPresNum.Text)
    If (1 <= n) And (n <= 42) Then
        picPresident.Cls
        Open "USPRES.TXT" For Input As #1
        Let num = 0
        Do
          Input #1, nom
          Let num = num + 1
        Loop Until num = n
        picPresident.Print nom; " was President number"; n
        Close #1
    End If
End Sub
```

21.
```
Private Sub cmdTestAlgorithm_Click()
    Dim n As Single, numSteps As Single
    Rem Half problem
    picResult.Cls
    Let n = Val(txtInitialNum.Text)
    Let numSteps = 0
    Do While n <> 1
      Let numSteps = numSteps + 1
      If (n / 2) = Int(n / 2) Then
          Let n = n / 2
          picResult.Print n;
      Else
          Let n = 3 * n + 1
          picResult.Print n;
      End If
    Loop
    picResult.Print
    picResult.Print "It took"; numSteps; "steps to reach 1."
End Sub
```

23.
```
Private Sub cmdProcessSonnet_Click()
    Dim totalWords As Integer, lineCount As Integer, sonnetLine As String
    Dim wordCount As Integer, word As String
    Rem Analyze a Shakespeare sonnet
    picAnalysis.Cls
    Let totalWords = 0
    Let lineCount = 0
    Open "SONNET.TXT" For Input As #1
    Do While Not EOF(1)
      Input #1, sonnetLine
      Let lineCount = lineCount + 1
      Let wordCount = 0
      Do While sonnetLine<>""
        Let word = nextWord(sonnetLine)
        Let wordCount = wordCount + 1
      Loop
      Let totalWords = totalWords + wordCount
    Loop
    picAnalysis.Print "The sonnet contains an average of"; totalWords / lineCount
    picAnalysis.Print "words per line and a total of "; totalWords; "words."
    Close #1
End Sub


Private Function NextWord(info As String) As String
  Dim spacePos As Integer
  Rem Take word from beginning of info; space assumed to be the word separator
  Rem This function modifies the parameter
  Let spacePos = Instr(info, " ")
  If spacePos = 0 Then
      NextWord = info
      Let info = ""
    Else
      NextWord = Left(info, spacePos - 1)
      info = LTrim(Mid(info, spacePos))
    End If
End Function
```

25.
```
Private Sub cmdRemoveParens_Click()
    Dim sentence As String, parensFlag As Integer, position As Integer, letter As String
    Rem Remove parentheses and their contents from a sentence
    picOutput.Cls
    Let sentence = txtSentence.Text
    Let parensFlag = 0
    Let position = 1
    Do Until position > Len(sentence)
      Let letter = Mid(sentence, position, 1)
      Select Case letter
        Case "("
          Let parensFlag = 1
        Case ")"
          Let parensFlag = 0
        Case Else
          If parensFlag = 0 Then
              picOutput.Print letter;
          End If
      End Select
      Let position = position + 1
    Loop
End Sub
```

27.
```
Private Sub cmdDisplay_Click()
    Dim money As Single, liquid As String, price As Single
    Rem Display liquids available given an amount of money
    picOutput.Cls
    Let money = Val(txtAmount.Text)
    picOutput.Print "You can purchase one gallon of any of the following liquids."
    Open "DATA.TXT" For Input As #1
    Do While Not EOF(1)
      Input #1, liquid, price
      If price <= money Then
          picOutput.Print liquid
      End If
    Loop
    Close #1
End Sub
```

Exercises 6.3

1. Pass # 1
Pass # 2
Pass # 3
Pass # 4

3. 2 4 6 8 Who do we appreciate?

5. 5 6 7 8 9 10 11 12 13

7. Steve Cram   3:46.31
Steve Scott   3:51.6
Mary Slaney   4:20.5

9. 1   4   7   10
2   5   8   11
3   6   9   12

11. *******Hooray*******

13. Loop is never executed because 1 is less than 25.5 and the step is negative.

15. A For statement can only have one Next statement.

17.
```
For num = 1 To 10 Step 2
    picOutput.Print num
Next num
```

19.
```
Private Sub cmdDisplay_Click()
    Dim i As Integer
    Rem Display a row of 10 stars
    picOutput.Cls
    For i = 1 To 10
      picOutput.Print "*";
    Next i
End Sub
```

21.
```
Private Sub cmdDisplay_Click()
    Dim i As Integer, j As Integer
    Rem Display 10 x 10 array of stars
    picOutput.Cls
    For i = 1 To 10
      For j = 1 To 10
        picOutput.Print "*";
      Next j
      picOutput.Print
    Next i
End Sub
```

23.
```
Private Sub cmdComputeSum_Click()
    Dim sum As Single, denominator As Integer
    Rem Compute the sum 1 + 1/2 + 1/3 + 1/4 + ... + 1/100
    picOutput.Cls
    Let sum = 0
    For denominator = 1 To 100
      Let sum = sum + 1 / denominator
    Next denominator
    picOutput.Print "The sum is"; sum
End Sub
```

25.
```
Private Sub cmdAnalyzeOptions_Click()
    Dim result1 As Single, result2 As Single
    Rem Compare salaries
    picResults.Cls
    Call Option1(result1)
    Call Option2(result2)
    If result1 > result2 Then
        picResults.Print "Option 1";
      Else
        picResults.Print "Option 2";
    End If
    picResults.Print " pays better"
End Sub

Private Sub Option1(result1 As Single)
    Dim i As Integer
    Rem Compute total salary for 10 days
    Rem with a flat salary of $100/day
    Let result1 = 0
    For i = 1 To 10
      Let result1 = result1 + 100
    Next i
    picResults.Print "Option 1 = "; Format(result1, "Currency")
End Sub

Private Sub Option2(result2 As Single)
    Dim i As Integer, daySalary As Single
    Rem Compute the total salary for 10 days
    Rem starting at $1 and doubling each day
    Let result2 = 0
    Let daySalary = 1
    For i = 1 To 10
      Let result2 = result2 + daySalary
      Let daySalary = daySalary * 2
    Next i
    picResults.Print "Option 2 = "; Format(result2, "Currency")
End Sub
```

27.
```
Private Sub cmdCompIdealWeights_Click()
    Dim lower As Integer, upper As Integer
    Rem Ideal weights for men and women
    picWeightTable.Cls
    Call InputBounds(lower, upper)
    Call ShowWeights(lower, upper)
End Sub


Private Function IdealMan(height As Integer) As Single
  Rem Compute the ideal weight of a man given the height
  IdealMan = 4 * height - 128
End Function


Private Function IdealWoman(height As Integer) As Single
  Rem Compute the ideal weight of a woman given the height
  IdealWoman = 3.5 * height - 108
End Function


Private Sub InputBounds(lower As Integer, upper As Integer)
  Rem Input the lower and upper bounds on height
  Let lower = Val(InputBox("Enter lower bound on height in inches:"))
  Let upper = Val(InputBox("Enter upper bound on height in inches:"))
End Sub


Private Sub ShowWeights(lower As Integer, upper As Integer)
  Dim height As Integer
  Rem Display table of weights
  picWeightTable.Print
  picWeightTable.Print "Height", "Wt - Women", "Wt - Men"
  picWeightTable.Print
  For height = lower To upper
    picWeightTable.Print height, IdealWoman(height), IdealMan(height)
  Next height
End Sub
```

29.
```
Private Sub cmdCountSibilants_Click()
    Rem Number of sibilants in sentence
    picResults.Cls
    picResults.Print "There are"; Sibilants(txtSentence.Text); "sibilants."
End Sub


Private Function Sibilants(sentence As String) As Single
  Dim numSibs As Integer, i As Integer, letter As String
  Rem Count number of sibilants
  Let numSibs = 0
  For i = 1 To Len(sentence)
    Let letter = UCase(Mid(sentence, i, 1))
    If (letter = "S") Or (letter = "Z") Then
        Let numSibs = numSibs + 1
    End If
  Next i
  Sibilants = numSibs
End Function
```

31.
```
Private Sub cmdCalcBalance_Click()
    Dim amt As Single, yearNum As Integer
    Rem Bank interest for 10 years
    picBalance.Cls
    Let amt = 800
    For yearNum = 1 To 10
      Let amt = amt * 1.04 + 100
    Next yearNum
    picBalance.Print "The final amount is "; Format(amt, "Currency")
End Sub
```

33.
```
Private Sub cmdDecay_Click()
    Dim grams As Single, yearNum As Integer
    Rem Radioactive decay
    picOutput.Cls
    Let grams = 10
    For yearNum = 1 To 5
      Let grams = .88 * grams
    Next yearNum
    picOutput.Print "Of 10 grams of cobalt 60,"
    picOutput.Print Format(grams, "Standard"); " grams remain after 5 years."
End Sub
```

35.
```
Private Sub cmdDraw_Click()
    Dim stars As Integer, i As Integer
    Rem Draw a hollow box
    picOutput.Cls
    picOutput.Font.Name = "Courier"
    Let stars = Val(txtNum)
    Call DrawSide(stars)
    For i = 1 To stars - 2
      Call DrawRow(stars)
    Next i
    Call DrawSide(stars)
End Sub


Private Sub DrawRow(stars As Integer)
    Dim i As Integer
    Rem Draw a row (put spaces between the two stars)
    picOutput.Print "*";
    For i = 1 To stars - 2
      picOutput.Print " ";
    Next i
    picOutput.Print "*"
End Sub


Private Sub DrawSide(stars As Integer)
    Dim i As Integer
    Rem Draw a solid side of stars
    For i = 1 To stars
      picOutput.Print "*";
    Next i
    picOutput.Print
End Sub
```

37.
```
Private Sub cmdDisplay_Click()
    Dim m As Integer, n As Integer, row As Integer, col As Integer
    Rem Create a multiplication table
    picTable.Cls
    picTable.Font.Name = "Courier"
    Let m = Val(InputBox("Enter number of rows:"))
    Let n = Val(InputBox("Enter number of columns:"))
    For row = 1 To m
      For col = 1 To n
        picTable.Print RightJustify6(row * col);
      Next col
      picTable.Print
    Next row
End Sub


Private Function RightJustify6(what As Integer) As String
    Dim s As String
    Let s = Format(what, "#")
    RightJustify6 = Format(s, "@@@@@@")
End Function
```

39.
```
Private Sub cmdCompute_Click()
    Dim testValue As Single, amount As Single, i As Integer
    Rem Gambling casino problem
    picLoser.Cls
    Let testValue = 4
    Do
      Let testValue = testValue + 1     'Start test with $5
      Let amount = testValue
      For i = 1 To 3        'One iteration for each casino
        Let amount = amount - 1     'Entrance fee
        Let amount = amount / 2     'Funds lost
        Let amount = amount - 1     'Exit fee
      Next i
    Loop Until amount = 0
    picLoser.Print "Starting amount = "; Format(testValue, "Currency")
End Sub
```

41.
```
Private Sub cmdSelectWord_Click()
    Dim which As Integer, i As Integer, word As String
    Rem Select random word from file of 20 words
    Randomize
    picOutput.Cls
    Let which = Int(20 * Rnd) + 1
    Open "DATA.TXT" For Input As #1
    For i = 1 To which
      Input #1, word
    Next i
    picOutput.Print "The selected word is "; word
    Close #1
End Sub
```

43.
```
Private Sub cmdPickWinner_Click()
    Dim entries As Integer, nom As String
    Dim which As Integer, i As Integer, word As String
    Rem Select random name from file with unknown number of names
    Randomize
    picWinner.Cls
    Let entries = 0
    Open "DATA.TXT" For Input As #1
    Do While Not EOF(1)
      Input #1, nom
      Let entries = entries + 1
    Loop
    Close #1
    Let which = Int(entries * Rnd) + 1
    Open "DATA.TXT" For Input As #1
    For i = 1 To which
      Input #1, nom
    Next i
    picWinner.Print "The winner is "; nom
    Close #1
End Sub
```

CHAPTER 7

Exercises 7.1

1. 3 7 0

3. Stuhldreher
Crowley

5. 6 2 9 11 3 4

7. The Dim statement in the (Declarations) section of (General) dimensions companies() with subscripts from 1 to 100 and makes companies available to all procedures. Therefore, the ReDim statement in the Form_Load event procedure produces the error message "Array already dimensioned."

9. Array subscript out of range (when k > 4).

11. Improper syntax in first Dim statement.

13.

river(1)	river(2)	river(3)	river(4)	river(5)
Thames	Ohio	Amazon	Volga	Nile

river(1)	river(2)	river(3)	river(4)	river(5)
Ohio	Amazon	Volga	Nile	Thames

15. (a) 2
(b) 7
(c) 10
(d) 9

17. Replace lines 18 through 24 with
```
Rem Display all names and difference from average
picTopStudents.Cls
For student = 1 To 8
  picTopStudents.Print nom(student), score(student) - average
Next student
```

19.
```
Dim bestPicture(1975 To 1995) As String
```

21.
```
Dim marx(1 To 4) As String 'In (Declarations) section
                              'of (General)
Private Sub Form_Load()
    Let marx(1) = "Chico"
    Let marx(2) = "Harpo"
    Let marx(3) = "Groucho"
    Let marx(4) = "Zeppo"
End Sub
```

23.
```
Dim i As Integer
Rem Reverse array a() and store in b()
For i = 1 To 4
  Let b(i) = a(5 - i)
Next i
```

```
      Integer, k As Integer
      play the elements of the array a()
    = 1 To 26 Step 5
   or k = 0 To 4
      picArray.Print Tab(10 * k + 1); a(i + k);
   Next k
   picArray.Print
 Next i
```

27.
```
Dim i As Integer, differFlag As Integer
Rem Compare arrays a() and b() for same values
Let differFlag = 0
For i = 1 To 10
  If a(i) <> b(i) Then
      Let differFlag = 1
  End If
Next i
If differFlag = 1 Then
    picOutput.Print "The arrays are not identical."
  Else
    picOutput.Print "The arrays have identical values."
End If
```

29.
```
Dim i As Integer
Rem Curve grades by adding 7
For i = 1 To 12
  Let grades(i) = grades(i) + 7
Next i
```

31.
```
Private Sub cmdDisplay_Click()
   Dim range As Integer, dataElement As Integer, score As Integer, interval As Integer
   Rem Create and display the frequency of scores
   picTable.Cls
   Dim frequency(1 To 5) As Integer
   Rem Set array elements to 0
   For range = 1 To 5
     Let frequency(range) = 0
   Next range
   Rem Read scores, count scores in each of five intervals
   Open "DATA.TXT" For Input As #1
   For dataElement = 1 To 30
     Input #1, score
     Let range = Int(score / 10) + 1    'Number in the range of 1-5
     Let frequency(range) = frequency(range) + 1
   Next dataElement
   Close #1
   Rem Display frequency in each interval
   picTable.Print "Interval"; Tab(12); "Frequency"
   picTable.Print
   For interval = 1 To 5
     picTable.Print 10 * (interval - 1); "to"; 10 * interval;
     picTable.Print Tab(14); frequency(interval)
   Next interval
End Sub
```

33.
```
Private Sub cmdDisplay_Click()
   Dim i As Integer, total As Single
   Rem Display names, percentage of total units for top ten pizza chains
   picOutput.Cls
   Dim nom(1 To 10) As String, units(1 To 10) As Single
   Rem Read from data file and record names and number of units
   Rem Compute total units
   Open "DATA.TXT" For Input As #1
   Let total = 0                    'Total units
   For i = 1 To 10
     Input #1, nom(i), units(i)
     Let total = total + units(i)
   Next i
   Close #1
   Rem Display names and percentage of total units
   picOutput.Print "Name"; Tab(30); "Percentage of units"
   For i = 1 To 10
     picOutput.Print  nom(i); Tab(30); Format(units(i) / total, "Percent")
   Next i
End Sub
```

35.
```
Dim monthNames(1 To 12) As Single   'In (Declarations) section of (General)

Private Sub Form_Load()
  Let monthNames(1) = "January"
  Let monthNames(2) = "February"
  Let monthNames(3) = "March"
  Let monthNames(4) = "April"
  Let monthNames(5) = "May"
  Let monthNames(6) = "June"
  Let monthNames(7) = "July"
  Let monthNames(8) = "August"
  Let monthNames(9) = "September"
  Let monthNames(10) = "October"
  Let monthNames(11) = "November"
  Let monthNames(12) = "December"
End Sub

Private Sub cmdDisplay_Click()
  Dim monthNum As Integer
  Rem Display month name
  picOutput.Cls
  Let monthNum = Val(InputBox("Enter month number:"))
  picOutput.Print "Month name is "; monthNames(monthNum)
End Sub
```

37.
```
Private Sub cmdDisplay_Click()
  Dim i As Integer, roll As Integer
  Rem Report results of 1000 rolls of a die
  Randomize
  picOutput.Cls
  Dim results(1 To 6) As Integer
  For i = 1 To 1000
    Let roll = Int(6 * Rnd) + 1
    Let results(roll) = results(roll) + 1
  Next i
  For i = 1 to 6
    picOutput.Print i; "came up"; results(i); "times"
  Next i
End Sub
```

Exercises 7.2

1. No.

3. Michigan

5. less than
greater than
equals
less than

7. The total rainfall for the first quarter is 10

9. Change picOutput.Print city to picOutput.Print city (1). You can't display an entire array with one statement.

11. n is incremented by 1 even if the user enters 0 to stop and see the product. Move the incrementing inside the If block just before the statement Let num(n) = number.

13.
```
Private Sub CopyArray(a() As Integer, b() As Integer)
  Dim i As Integer
  Rem Place a's values in b
  For i = 1 to UBound(a)
    Let b(i) = a(i)
  Next i
End Sub
```

15.
```
Private Sub Ascending()
  Dim order As Integer, i As Integer
  Rem Determine if array is ascending
  Let order = 1
  For i = 1 To Ubound(scores) - 1
    If scores(i) > scores(i + 1) Then
      Let order = 0
    End If
  Next i
  If order = 1 Then
    picOutput.Print "Array is ascending."
  Else
    picOutput.Print "Array is not ascending."
  End If
End Sub
```

17.
```
Private Sub WhatOrder()
    Dim ascend As Integer, descend As Integer, i As Integer
    Rem Determine if order is ascending, descending, both, or neither
    Let ascend = 1
    Let descend = 1
    For i = 1 To Ubound(scores) - 1
      If scores(i) > scores(i + 1) Then
          Let ascend = 0
        ElseIf scores(i) < scores(i + 1) Then
          Let descend = 0
      End If
    Next i
    If (ascend = 1) And (descend = 1) Then
        picOutput.Print "Array is both"
      ElseIf (ascend = 0) And (descend = 0) Then
        picOutput.Print "Array is neither ascending nor descending."
      ElseIf (ascend = 1) Then
        picOutput.Print "Array is ascending."
      Else
        picOutput.Print "Array is descending."
    End If
End Sub
```

19.
```
Private Sub MergeOrderedWithDups()
    Dim indexA As Integer, indexB As Integer, indexC As Integer
    Dim doneA As Integer, doneB As Integer
    Rem Merge ascending arrays, with duplications
    ReDim c(1 To 40) As Single
    Let indexA = 1
    Let indexB = 1
    Let doneA = 0
    Let doneB - 0
    For indexC = 1 To 40
      If ((a(indexA) <= b(indexB)) And doneA = 0) Or doneB = 1 Then
          Let c(indexC) = a(indexA)
          If indexA < 20 Then
              Let indexA = indexA + 1
            Else
              Let doneA = 1
          End If
        Else
          Let c(indexC) = b(indexB)
          If indexB < 20 Then
              Let indexB = indexB + 1
            Else
              Let doneB = 1
          End If
      End If
    Next indexC
End Sub
```

21.
```
Dim state(1 To 50) As String    'In (Declarations) section of (General)
Dim numStates As Integer
Rem Maintain a list of states

Private Sub cmdInsState_Click()
  Dim nom As String, i As Integer, j As Integer
  Rem Enter a new state in the correct position
  If numStates = UBound(state) Then
      MsgBox "Fifty states have already been entered.", , ""
    Else
      Let nom = txtState.Text
      Let state(numStates + 1) = nom
      Let i = 1
      Do While state(i) < nom
        Let i = i + 1
      Loop
```

```
        If (nom = state(i)) And (i <= numStates) Then
            MsgBox "State already exists"
          Else   'shuffle array, insert state
            For j = numStates To i Step -1
              Let state(j + 1) = state(j)
            Next j
            Let state(i) = nom
            Let numStates = numStates + 1
        End If
    End If
End Sub

Private Sub cmdDelState_Click()
  Dim nom As String, i As Integer, k As Integer
  Rem Delete a state from the list
  Let nom = txtState.Text
  Let i = 1
  Do While (i < numStates) And (nom > state(i))
    Let i = i + 1
  Loop
  If (numStates = 0) Or (nom <> state(i)) Then
      MsgBox "State does not exist"
    Else   ' Shuffle rest of array down by 1
      Let numStates = numStates - 1
      For k = i To numStates
        Let state(k) = state(k + 1)
      Next k
  End If
End Sub

Private Sub cmdDisplay_Click()
  Dim i As Integer
  Rem Display the states in the list
  picStates.Cls
  For i = 1 To numStates
    picStates.Print state(i)
  Next i
End Sub

Private Sub cmdQuit_Click()
  End
End Sub
```

23.
```
Dim grades(1 To 100) As Integer   'In (Declarations) section of (General)
Dim numScores As Integer
Rem Report the number of students scoring above the class average

Private Sub cmdRecordScore_Click()
  If numScores = 100 Then
      MsgBox "100 scores have been entered. Cannot process more data.", , ""
    Else
      Let numScores = numScores + 1
      Let grades(numScores) = Val(txtScore.Text)
  End If
End Sub

Private Sub cmdCalcAverage_Click()
  Dim average As Single, aboveAverage As Integer
  picOutput.Cls
  Let average = Avg(grades(), numScores)
  Let aboveAverage = AboveAvg(grades(), numScores, average)
  picOutput.Print aboveAverage; "students scored above the average"
End Sub

Private Function Avg(scores() As Integer, num As Integer) As Single
  Rem Compute the average and number of students above it
  Dim sum As Integer, i As Integer
  Let sum = 0
  For i = 1 To num
    Let sum = sum + scores(i)
  Next i
```

```
      If num <> 0 Then
          Avg = sum / num
      Else
          Avg = 0
      End If
  End Function


      Private Function AboveAvg(scores() As Integer, num As Integer, classAvg As Single) As Integer
        Dim i As Integer, tot As Integer
        Rem Count number of scores above average
        For i = 1 To num
          If scores(i) > classAvg Then
              Let tot = tot + 1
          End If
        Next i
        AboveAvg = tot
      End Function
```

25.
```
      Private Sub cmdSelectPeople_Click()
        Rem Choose 50 people from a data file containing 100 names
        Dim person(1 To 100) As Integer
        Call ClearArray(person())
        Call SelectPeople(person())
        Call ShowPeople(person())
      End Sub


      Private Sub ClearArray(person() As Integer)
        Dim i As Integer
        Rem Clear all array elements (no one selected yet)
        For i = 1 To 100
          Let person(i) = 0
        Next i
      End Sub


      Private Sub SelectPeople(person() As Integer)
        Dim i As Integer, num As Integer
        Rem Select 50 people (person i selected when person(i)=1)
        Randomize
        For i = 1 To 50
          Do
            Let num = Int(Rnd * 100) + 1
          Loop Until person(num) = 0
          Let person(num) = 1
        Next i
      End Sub


      Private Sub ShowPeople(person() As Integer)
        Dim i As Integer, nom As String
        Rem Display selected people
        picOutput.Cls
        Open "DATA.TXT" For Input As #1
        For i = 1 To 100
          Input #1, nom
          If person(i) = 1 Then
              picOutput.Print nom
          End If
        Next i
        Close #1
      End Sub
```

Exercises 7.3

5. The width of text box txtBox is cut in half.

7. The text box will move left or right so that the upper-left corner of text box txtBox is of equal distance from the top and the left edge of the form.

9. The text box txtBox will extend all the way across the form. If the left edge of the text box is not at the left edge of the form, then part of the text box will extend beyond the right edge of the form but will not be visible.

11.
```
Private Sub cmdButton_Click(Index As Integer)
    Let cmdButton(Index).Visible = False
End Sub
```

13.
```
Private Sub cmdButton_Click(Index As Integer)
    Dim otherIndex As Integer
    Let otherIndex = (Index + 1) Mod 2
    Let cmdButton(Index).Font.Italic = True
    Let cmdButton(otherIndex).Font.Italic = False
End Sub
```

15.
```
Private Sub cmdButton_Click(Index As Integer)
    Dim othrIdx As Integer
    Let othrIdx = (Index + 1) Mod 2
    Let cmdButton(Index).Left = cmdButton(othrIdx).Left + cmdButton(othrIdx).Width + 100
End Sub
```

17.
```
Private Sub cmdButton_Click(Index As Integer)
    Let cmdButton(Index).Width = 2 * cmdButton(Index).Width
End Sub
```

19.
```
Load txtBox(1)
Let txtBox(1).Top = txtBox(0).Top + txtBox(0).Height + 100
Let txtBox(1).Visible = True
```

21. The first line of the event procedure should not have (1) in it, but instead should have (Index As Integer) after Click.

23. The index of the For loop should start at 1, not 0, or If i > 0 Then . . . End If should be put around the Load statement and the Let statement that sets the Top property. With a value of zero for *i*, an attempt will be made to load lblID(0), which has already been created at design time, and to set the Top property of lblID(0) based on the Top and Height properties of lblID(−1), which cannot be done.

25. Home expenses for winter were $4271.66

27. Summer bills exceeded winter by $67.09

29. The form displays a vertical column of four text boxes, separated from each other by one-half the height of a text box and labeled on the left with "Row #". The column is headed by "Col 1".

31. The form displays a horizontal row of four touching text boxes labeled above by "Col #". The row is labeled on the left by "Row 1".

33.
```
Private Sub txtWinter_LostFocus(Index As Integer)
    Rem recompute totals
    Call Retotal
End Sub

Private Sub txtSpring_LostFocus(Index As Integer)
    Rem recompute totals
    Call Retotal
End Sub

Private Sub txtSummer_LostFocus(Index As Integer)
    Rem recompute totals
    Call Retotal
End Sub

Private Sub txtFall_LostFocus(Index As Integer)
    Rem recompute totals
    Call Retotal
End Sub

Private Sub Retotal()
    Dim total(1 To 4) As Single
    Dim i As Integer, cTotal As Single
    Rem recompute totals
    For i = 1 To 4
        Let total(1) = total(1) + Val(txtWinter(i).Text)
        Let total(2) = total(2) + Val(txtSpring(i).Text)
        Let total(3) = total(3) + Val(txtSummer(i).Text)
        Let total(4) = total(4) + Val(txtFall(i).Text)
    Next i
    For i = 1 to 4
        Let lblQuarterTot(i).Caption = Str(total(i))
    Next i
    For i = 1 to 4
        Let cTotal = 0
        Let cTotal = Val(txtWinter(i).Text) + Val(txtSpring(i).Text)
        Let cTotal = cTotal + Val(txtSummer(i).Text) + Val(txtFall(i).Text)
        Let lblCategTot(i).Caption = Str(cTotal)
    Next i
End Sub
```

35.
```
Private Sub picTrafficLight_LostFocus(Index As Integer)
   Let picTrafficLight(Index).BackColor = &HFFFFFF
   Select Case Index
     Case 0
       Let picTrafficLight(1).BackColor = &HFFFF&
     Case 1
       Let picTrafficLight(2).BackColor = &HFF&
     Case 2
       Let picTrafficLight(0).BackColor = &HFF00&
   End Select
End Sub
```

37.
```
Dim correctNum As Single  'In (Declarations) section of (General)

Private Sub cmdAnswer_Click(Index As Integer)
  If Index = correctNum Then
     Call CorrectAnswer
  Else
     Call IncorrectAnswer
  End If
End Sub


Private Sub CorrectAnswer()
  Dim response As String
  Let response = InputBox("Correct. Would you like another question? (Y/N)")
  Let response = Ucase(Left(response,1))
  If response = "N" Then
     Close #1
     End
  Else
     If Not EOF(1) Then
        Call GetQuestion
     Else
       MsgBox "There are no more questions.", , ""
       Close #1
       End
     End If
  End If
End Sub


Private Sub Form_Load()
  Open "7-3-E37.TXT" For Input As #1
  Call GetQuestion
End Sub


Private Sub GetQuestion()
  Dim i As Integer, info As String
  For i = 0 to 4
    Input #1, info        'obtain question and 4 possible answers
    Let lblSentence(i).Caption = info
  Next i
  Input #1, correctNum   'number of the correct answer
End Sub


Private Sub IncorrectAnswer()         Private Sub cmdQuit_Click()
  MsgBox "Incorrect, Try Again", , ""   Close #1
End Sub                                 End
                                      End Sub
```

Exercises 7.4

1. 200 100

3. 11 7 Numbers interchanged.

5. Items not properly swapped.

7. Sequential

9. 4 swaps

11. $(n-1) + (n-2) + \ldots + 1$ or $n(n-1)/2$

13. 4 swaps

15. 8 comparisons

17. Go through the list once and count the number of times that each of the four integers occurs and then list the determined number of 1's, followed by the determined number of 2's, etc.

19. 16; 8 1/2; 5

21.
```
Private Sub TripleSwap(x As Single, y As Single, z As Single)
    Dim temp As Single
    Rem Interchange the values of x, y, and z
    Let temp = x
    Let x = y
    Let y = z
    Let z = temp
End Sub
```

23.
```
Private Sub cmdDisplay_Click()
    Rem Display exhibits and number of visitors in alphabetical order
    Dim exhibit(1 To 10) As String, visitors(1 To 10) As Integer
    Call ReadData(exhibit(), visitors())
    Call SortData(exhibit(), visitors())
    Call ShowData(exhibit(), visitors())
End Sub

Private Sub ReadData(exhibit() As String, visitors() As Integer)
    Dim i As Integer
    Rem Read exhibit names, visitors
    Open "DATA.TXT" For Input As #1
    For i = 1 To 10
      Input #1, exhibit(i), visitors(i)
    Next i
    Close #1
End Sub

Private Sub ShowData(exhibit() As String, visitors() As Integer)
    Dim i As Integer, temp As String
    Rem Display exhibit names and visitors
    picTopExhibits.Cls
    picTopExhibits.Print "Exhibit"; Tab(30); "Attendance (in thousands)"
    picTopExhibits.Print
    For i = 1 To 10
      Let temp = Format(visitors(i),"#")
      picTopExhibits.Print exhibit(i); Tab(36); Format(temp,"@@@@")
    Next i
End Sub

Private Sub SortData(exhibit() As String, visitors() As Integer)
    Dim elements As Integer, gap As Integer, doneFlag As Integer, index As Integer
    Dim strTemp As String, numTemp As Integer
    Rem Shell sort data by exhibit names
    Let elements = 10
    Let gap = Int(elements / 2)
    Do While gap >= 1
      Do
        Let doneFlag = 1
        For index = 1 To elements - gap
          If exhibit(index) > exhibit(index + gap) Then
              Let strTemp = exhibit(index)
              Let exhibit(index) = exhibit(index + gap)
              Let exhibit(index + gap) = strTemp
              Let numTemp = visitors(index)
              Let visitors(index) = visitors(index + gap)
              Let visitors(index + gap) = numTemp
              Let doneFlag = 0
          End If
        Next index
      Loop Until doneFlag = 1
      Let gap = Int(gap / 2)
    Loop
End Sub
```

25.
```
Private Sub cmdDisplay_Click()
  Rem Input list of words, insert additional element
  picWords.Cls
  Dim wordList(1 To 11) As String
  Call InputWords(wordList())
  Call InsertWord(wordList())
  Call ShowWords(wordList())
End Sub

Private Sub InputWords(wordList() As String)
  Dim i As Integer
  Rem Input first 10 words
  picWords.Print "Input ten words, in alphabetical order"
  For i = 1 To 10
    Let wordList(i) = InputBox("Enter word number " & Format(i, "#") & ":")
  Next i
End Sub

Private Sub InsertWord(wordList() As String)
  Dim word As String, i As Integer
  Rem Insert eleventh word in alphabetical order
  picWords.Print
  Let word = InputBox("Word to add:")
  Let wordList(11) = word
  Let i = 1
  Do While word > wordList(i)
    Let i = i + 1
  Loop
  Rem word belongs in slot i; move elements i through 10 up one slot
  For k = 10 To i Step -1
    Let wordList(k + 1) = wordList(k)
  Next k
  Let wordList(i) = word
End Sub

Private Sub ShowWords(wordList() As String)
  Dim i As Integer
  Rem Show list of 11 words
  picWords.Cls
  For i = 1 To 11
    picWords.Print wordList(i); " ";
  Next i
End Sub
```

27.
```
Private Sub cmdDisplay_Click()
  Rem Sort array of 200 numbers
  Dim nums(1 To 200) As Integer
  Dim dist(0 To 63) As Integer
  Call FillArray(nums())
  Call GetOccurrences(nums(), dist())
  Call ShowDistribution(dist())
End Sub

Private Sub FillArray(nums() As Integer)
  Dim i As Integer
  Rem Generate numbers from 0 to 63 and place in array
  Let nums(1) = 5
  For i = 2 To 200
    Let nums(i) = (9 * nums(i - 1) + 7) Mod 64
  Next i
End Sub

Private Sub GetOccurrences(nums() As Integer, dist() As Integer)
  Dim i As Integer
  Rem Record occurrences for each number
  For i = 1 To 200
    Let dist(nums(i)) = dist(nums(i)) + 1
  Next i
End Sub
```

```
  Private Sub ShowDistribution(dist() As Integer)
     Dim colWid As Integer, col As Integer, colNum As Integer, i As Integer
     Rem Display distribution array
     picDistribution.Cls
     Let colWid = 12                'Width allotted for a column
     For colNum = 0 To 3            'Display headings at top of four column
       Let col = colWid * colNum + 1
       picDistribution.Print Tab(col); " # Occur";
     Next colNum
     picDistribution.Print
     For i = 1 To 63                'Display numbers & count of occurrences
       Let colNum = (i - 1) Mod 4
       Let col = colWid * colNum + 1
       picDistribution.Print Tab(col); i; Tab(col + 4); dist(i);
       If col = 3 Then
           picDistribution.Print
       End If
     Next i
  End Sub
```

29.
```
    Dim codes() As String  'In (Declarations) section of (General)

    Private Sub Form_Load()
      Dim i As Integer
      ReDim codes(Asc("A") To Asc("Z")) As String
      Open "7-4-E29.TXT" For Input As #1
      For i = Asc("A") To Asc("Z")
        Input #1, codes(i)
      Next i
      Close #1
    End Sub


    Private Sub cmdConvertToMorse_Click()
      Dim word As String
      Rem Encode word in Morse Code
      Let word = UCase(txtWord.Text)
      Call ShowCode(word)
    End Sub


    Private Sub ShowCode(word As String)
      Dim index As Integer, letter As String
      Rem Show code for each index in word
      picMorse.Cls
      For index = 1 To Len(word)
        Let letter = Mid(word, index, 1)
        picMorse.Print codes(Asc(letter)), letter
      Next index
    End Sub
```

31.
```
    Private Sub cmdCalcAvg_Click()
       Dim nom As String
       Rem Compute average of five highest test scores
       Dim score(1 To 7) As Integer
       Call InputData(nom, score())
       Call SortData(score())
       Call ShowData(nom, score())
    End Sub

    Private Sub InputData(nom As String, score() As Integer)
      Dim i As Integer
      Rem Input student's name and seven test scores
      Let nom = InputBox("Student's name:")
      For i = 1 To 7
        Let score(i) = Val(InputBox("Test score " & Format(i, "#") & ":"))
      Next i
    End Sub
```

```
Private Sub ShowData(nom As String, score() As Integer)
  Dim sum As Integer, passNum As Integer
  picAvg.Cls
  Let sum = 0
  For passNum = 1 To 5
    Let sum = sum + score(passNum)
  Next passNum
  picAvg.Print nom, sum / 5
End Sub


Private Sub SortData(score() As Integer)
  Dim passNum As Integer, index As Integer, temp As Integer
  Rem Bubble sort scores in descending order
  For passNum = 1 To 6
    For index = 1 To 7 - passNum
      If score(index) < score(index + 1) Then
          Let temp = score(index)
          Let score(index) = score(index + 1)
          Let score(index + 1) = temp
      End If
    Next index
  Next passNum
End Sub
```

33.
```
Private Sub cmdCalcMedian_Click()
    Dim n As Integer
    Rem Input array of measurements and determine their median
    Call InputNumberOfMeasurements(n)
    ReDim nums(1 To n) As Single
    Call InputNums(nums())
    Call DisplayMedian(nums())
End Sub


Private Sub DisplayMedian(nums() As Single)
  Rem Display the median of the n measurements
  picMedian.Cls
  picMedian.Print "The median is"; Median(nums())
End Sub


Private Sub InputNumberOfMeasurements(n As Integer)
  Rem Input number of measurements
  Let n = Val(InputBox("Number of measurements:"))
End Sub


Private Sub InputNums(nums() As Single)
  Dim i As Integer
  Rem Input list of measurements
  For i = 1 To UBound(nums)
    Let nums(i) = Val(InputBox("Enter measurement #" & Format(i, "#") & ":"))
  Next i
End Sub


Private Function Median(nums() As Single) As Single
  Dim n As Integer
  Call SortNums(nums())
  Let n = UBound(nums)
  If Int(n / 2) = n / 2 Then      'n is even
      Let m = n / 2
      Median = (nums(m) + nums(m + 1)) / 2
    Else                          'n is odd
      Median = nums((n + 1) / 2)
  End If
End Function


Private Sub SortNums(nums() As Single)
  Dim n As Integer, i As Integer, j As Integer, temp As Single
  Rem Bubble sort list of numbers
  Let n = UBound(nums)
```

```
      For i = 1 To n - 1
        For j = 1 To n - i
          If nums(j) > nums(j + 1) Then
              Let temp = nums(j)
              Let nums(j) = nums(j + 1)
              Let nums(j + 1) = temp
          End If
        Next j
      Next i
    End Sub
```

Exercises 7.5

1. 12

3. Dorothy

5. 4 1 6
    5 8 2

7. 1 3 5

9. The dimension statement should read Dim a(1 To 4, 1 To 3) As Integer (currently, the error is Subscript Out of Range.)

11.
```
Private Sub FillArray(a() As Single)
    Dim row As Integer, col As Integer
    Rem Fill an array
    For row = 1 To 10
      For col = 1 To 10
        Let a(row, col) = col
      Next col
    Next row
End Sub
```

13.
```
Private Sub Exchange(a() As Single)
    Dim col As Integer, temp As Single
    Rem Interchange values of 2nd and 3rd row
    For col = 1 To 10
      Let temp = a(2, col)
      Let a(2, col) = a(3, col)
      Let a(3, col) = temp
    Next col
End Sub
```

15.
```
Private Sub cmdDisplay_Click()
    Rem Program to calculate inventory
    Dim inv(1 To 2, 1 To 3) As Single, sales(1 To 2, 1 To 3) As Single
    Call ReadArrays(inv(), sales())
    Call ShowInventory(inv(), sales())
End Sub

Private Sub ReadArrays(inv() As Single, sales() As Single)
    Dim store As Integer, item As Integer
    Rem Read beginning inventory and sales for day
    Rem Beginning inventory is assumed to reside in BEGINV.TXT
    Rem Sales for day is assumed to reside in SALES.TXT
    Open "BEGINV.TXT" For Input As #1
    Open "SALES.TXT" For Input As #2
    For store = 1 To 2
      For item = 1 To 3
        Input #1, inv(store, item)
        Input #2, sales(store, item)
      Next item
    Next store
    Close #1
    Close #2
End Sub

Private Sub ShowInventory(inv() As Single, sales() As Single)
    Dim total As Single, store As Integer, item As Integer
    Rem Calculate and show inventory at end of the day
    picInventory.Cls
    Let total = 0
    For store = 1 To 2
      For item = 1 To 3
        Let inv(store, item) = inv(store, item) - sales(store, item)
        picInventory.Print inv(store, item),
        Let total = total + inv(store, item)
      Next item
      picInventory.Print
    Next store
    picInventory.Print "Total inventory is now"; total
End Sub
```

17.
```
Private Sub cmdCompute_Click()
    Rem Compute course enrollments by campus, no. of students by course
    picEnroll.Cls
    Dim enrollment(1 To 3, 1 To 10) As Single
    Call ReadData(enrollment())
    Call ShowCampusTotals(enrollment())
    Call ShowCourseTotals(enrollment())
End Sub

Private Sub ReadData(enrollment() As Single)
  Dim campus As Integer, course As Integer
  Rem Read enrollment data
  Rem Course enrollment data are assumed to reside in ENROLL.TXT
  Open "7-5-E17.TXT" For Input As #1
  For campus = 1 To 3
    For course = 1 To 10
      Input #1, enrollment(campus, course)
    Next course
  Next campus
  Close #1
End Sub

Private Sub ShowCampusTotals(enrollment() As Single)
  Dim campus As Integer, total As Single, course As Integer
  Rem Compute and show total enrollments for each campus
  For campus = 1 To 3
    Let total = 0
    For course = 1 To 10
      Let total = total + enrollment(campus, course)
    Next course
    picEnroll.Print "The total course enrollments on campus"; campus; "is"; total
  Next campus
End Sub

Private Sub ShowCourseTotals(enrollment() As Single)
  Dim course As Integer, total As Single, campus As Integer
  Rem Compute total enrollment for each course
  For course = 1 To 10
    Let total = 0
    For campus = 1 To 3
      Let total = total + enrollment(campus, course)
    Next campus
    picEnroll.Print "The total enrollment in course"; course; "is"; total
  Next course
End Sub
```

19.
```
Private Sub cmdCalcGolfStats_Click()
    Rem Compute golf statistics
    picStats.Cls
    Dim nom(1 To 3) As String, score(1 To 3, 1 To 4) As Integer
    Call ReadData(nom(), score())
    Call ComputeTotalScore(nom(), score())
    Call ComputeAveScore(nom(), score())
End Sub

Private Sub ComputeAveScore(nom() As String, score() As Integer)
  Dim round As Integer, total As Integer, player As Integer
  Rem Compute average score for each round
  For round = 1 To 4
    Let total = 0
    For player = 1 To 3
      Let total = total + score(player, round)
    Next player
    picStats.Print "The average for round"; round; "was"; total / 3
  Next round
End Sub
```

```
Private Sub ComputeTotalScore(nom() As String, score() As Integer)
  Dim player As Integer, total As Integer, round As Integer
  Rem Compute total score for each player
  For player = 1 To 3
    Let total = 0
    For round = 1 To 4
      Let total = total + score(player, round)
    Next round
    picStats.Print "The total score for "; nom(player); " was"; total
  Next player
  picStats.Print
End Sub


Private Sub ReadData(nom() As String, score() As Integer)
  Dim player As Integer, round As Integer
  Rem Results of 1997 Masters assumed to reside in GOLF.TXT
  Rem Read names and scores
  Open "7-5-E19.TXT" For Input As #1
  For player = 1 To 3
    Input #1, nom(player)
    For round = 1 To 4
      Input #1, score(player, round)
    Next round
  Next player
  Close #1
End Sub
```

21.
```
Rem In the (Declarations) section of (General)
Dim prog(1 To 3) As String, univ(1 To 3, 1 To 5) As String


Private Sub cmdDisplayRankings_Click()
  Dim university As String
  Rem Access information from University Rankings Table
  Let university = Trim(txtUnivName.Text)
  Call ShowRankings(university)
End Sub


Private Sub Form_Load()
  Dim dept As Integer, ranking As Integer
  Rem Read university rankings in three departments
  Open "7-5-E21.TXT" For Input As #1
  For dept = 1 To 3
    Input #1, prog(dept)
    For ranking = 1 To 5
      Input #1, univ(dept, ranking)
    Next ranking
  Next dept
  Close #1
End Sub


Private Sub ShowRankings(university As String)
  Dim foundFlag As Integer, dept As Integer, ranking As Integer
  Rem Show rankings of university
  picRankings.Cls
  picRankings.Print university; " departments ranked in the top 5:"
  Let foundFlag = 0
  For dept = 1 To 3
    For ranking = 1 To 5
      If univ(dept, ranking) = university Then
          picRankings.Print prog(dept), ranking
          Let foundFlag = 1
      End If
    Next ranking
  Next dept
```

```
      If foundFlag = 0 Then
          picRankings.Print "Sorry! No information listed."
      End If
      txtUnivName.Text = ""
      txtUnivName.SetFocus
    End Sub
```

23.

Object	Property	Setting
lblStudent	Caption	Name of Student #1:
txtStudent	Text	(blank)
lblExam	Caption	Exam Scores:
txtExam	Index	1 to 5
	Text	(blank)
cmdRecordData	Caption	Record Student Data
picGrades		

```
Rem In (Declarations) section of (General)
Dim nom(1 To 15) As String, score(1 To 15, 1 To 5) As Integer
Dim student As Integer

Private Sub cmdRecordData_Click()
  Dim exam As Integer
  Rem Record name and five exam scores for another student
  Rem Exam scores are entered in a control array of five text boxes
  Rem When last student is entered, process data and prevent further data entry
  Let student = student + 1
  Let nom(student) = txtStudent.Text
  For exam = 1 To 5
    Let score(student, exam) = Val(txtExam(exam).Text)
  Next exam
  If student = UBound(nom) Then
      Call ProcessData
      Let cmdRecordData.Visible = False
    Else
      Let txtStudent.Text = ""
      For exam = 1 To 5
        Let txtExam(exam).Text = ""
      Next exam
      Let lblStudent.Caption = "Name of student #" & Format(student, "0") & ":"
      txtStudent.SetFocus
  End If
End Sub

Private Sub ProcessData()
  Rem Analyze exam scores
  picGrades.Cls
  Call ShowAverages(nom(), score())
  Call SortScores(score())
  Call ShowMedians(score())
End Sub

Private Sub ShowAverages(nom() As String, score() As Integer)
  Dim index As Integer, sum As Integer, exam As Integer
  Rem Compute and show semester score averages
  picGrades.Print "Name"; Tab(15); "Semester average"
  For index = 1 To UBound(nom)
    Let sum = 0
    For exam = 1 To 5
      Let sum = sum + score(index, exam)
    Next exam
    picGrades.Print nom(index); Tab(20); Format(sum / 5, "#")
  Next index
End Sub
```

```
   Private Sub ShowMedians(score() As Integer)
     Dim entries As Integer, exam As Integer, middle As Integer
     Rem Show medians for each exam
     Let entries = UBound(nom)
     For exam = 1 To 5
       picGrades.Print "The median on exam"; exam; "was";
       If Int(entries / 2) = entries / 2 Then    'If even number of entries
           Let middle = entries / 2           'First index of the two "middle" entries
           picGrades.Print (score(middle, exam) + score(middle + 1, exam)) / 2
         Else
           Let middle = (entries + 1) / 2
           picGrades.Print score(middle, exam)
       End If
     Next exam
   End Sub


   Private Sub SortScores(score() As Integer)
     Dim entries As Integer, exam As Integer, passNum As Integer
     Dim index As Integer, temp As Integer
     Rem Bubble sort scores
     Let entries = UBound(nom)
     For exam = 1 To 5
       For passNum = 1 To entries - 1
         For index = 1 To entries - passNum
           If score(index, exam) > score(index + 1, exam) Then
               Let temp = score(index, exam)
               Let score(index, exam) = score(index + 1, exam)
               Let score(index + 1, exam) = temp
           End If
         Next index
       Next passNum
     Next exam
   End Sub
```

25.
```
   Private Sub cmdCalcTotSales_Click()
     Rem Compute total sales for each store and for entire company
     Dim sales(1 To 3, 1 To 5) As Integer, cost(1 To 5) As Single
     Call ReadData(sales(), cost())
     Call ShowRevenues(sales(), cost())
   End Sub


   Private Sub ReadData(sales() As Integer, cost() As Single)
     Dim store As Integer, item As Integer
     Rem Read sales and cost
     Open "7-5-E25B.TXT" For Input As #1
     For store = 1 To 3
       For item = 1 To 5
         Input #1, sales(store, item)
       Next item
     Next store
     Close #1
     Open "7-5-E25A.TXT" For Input As #1
     For item = 1 To 5
       Input #1, cost(item)
     Next item
     Close #1
   End Sub


   Private Sub ShowRevenues(sales() As Integer, cost() As Single)
     Dim totalRevenue As Single, store As Integer, storeRevenue As Single
     Dim item As Integer, totalStr As String
     Rem Compute and show revenues
     picTotalSales.Font.Name = "Courier"
     picTotalSales.Cls
     picTotalSales.Print "Store";Tab(12);"Total"
     Let totalRevenue = 0
```

```
For store = 1 To 3
  Let storeRevenue = 0
  For item = 1 To 5
    Let storeRevenue = storeRevenue + sales(store, item) * cost(item)
  Next item
  Let totalRevenue = totalRevenue + storeRevenue
  Let totalStr = Format(storeRevenue, "Currency")
  picTotalSales.Print " "; store; Tab(7); Format(totalStr, "@@@@@@@@@@")
Next store
picTotalSales.Print "Total revenue for the company was "; Format(totalRevenue, "Currency")
End Sub
```

CHAPTER 8

Exercises 8.1

1. `Hello`

3. `Hello`
`Aloha`
`Bon Jour`

5. Copies Hello and Bon Jour into the file "WELCOME".

7. No quotes surrounding file name.

9. Using EOF(1) as the terminating value in a For loop.

11. In the Open statement, remove the quotation marks surrounding nom. Otherwise, the new file will have the name NOM instead of the intended name NEW.GREET.TXT

13.
```
Private Sub cmdCreateFile_Click()
    Rem Create file of names and prices of items bought by cowboys
    Open "COWBOY.TXT" For Output As #1
    Write #1, "Colt Peacemaker", 12.20
    Write #1, "Holster", 2
    Write #1, "Levi Strauss Jeans", 1.35
    Write #1, "Saddle", 40
    Write #1, "Stetson", 10
    Close #1
End Sub
```

15.
```
Private Sub cmdAddItem_Click()
    Rem Add Winchester rifle to end of file COWBOY
    Open "COWBOY.TXT" For Append As #1
    Write #1, "Winchester rifle", 20.5
    Close #1
End Sub
```

17.
```
Private Sub cmdAddItem_Click()
    Dim newItem As String, newPrice As Single
    Rem Insert an item into COWBOY file in proper sequence
    Call InputItemData(newItem, newPrice)
    Call AddItemData(newItem, newPrice)
End Sub

Private Sub AddItemData(newItem As String, newPrice As Single)
    Dim insertedFlag As Integer, item As String, price As Single
    Rem Create second COWBOY file with new inserted item
    Open "COWBOY.TXT" For Input As #1
    Open "COWBOY2.TXT" For Output As #2
    Let insertedFlag = 0      'Tells if item has been inserted
    Do While Not EOF(1)
        Input #1, item, price
        If (insertedFlag = 0) And (item >= newItem) Then
            Write #2, newItem, newPrice
            Let insertedFlag = 1
        End If
        Write #2, item, price
    Loop
    If insertedFlag = 0 Then
        Write #2, newItem, newPrice
    End If
    Close #1
    Close #2
End Sub

Private Sub InputItemData(newItem As String, newPrice As Single)
    Rem Input new item name and price
    Let newItem = InputBox("New item to be inserted:")
    Let newPrice = Val(InputBox("Price of the new item:"))
End Sub
```

19.
```
Private Sub cmdRemoveItem_Click()
    Dim item As String, price As Single
    Rem Produce COWBOY4.TXT with Holster removed
    Open "COWBOY.TXT" For Input As #1
    Open "COWBOY4.TXT" For Output As #2
    Do While Not EOF(1)
        Input #1, item, price
        If item <> "Holster" Then
            Write #2, item, price
        End If
    Loop
    Close #1
    Close #2
End Sub
```

23.
```
Private Sub cmdProcess_Click()
    Dim searchTitle As String,filename As String,title As String
    Rem Access publisher's inventory files
    picInventory.Cls
    Call InputData(searchTitle, filename)
    Open filename For Input As #1
    Let title = ""
    Do While (title <> searchTitle) And (Not EOF(1))
        Input #1, title, copies
    Loop
    If (title = searchTitle) And (searchTitle <> "") Then
        picInventory.Print "No. of copies in inventory:"; copies
    Else
        picInventory.Print "Book is not listed."
    End If
    Close #1
End Sub


Private Sub InputData(searchTitle As String, filename As
String)
    Rem Input book name and determine file name
    Let searchTitle = txtTitle.Text
    Let bookType = txtType.Text
    If UCase(bookType) = "H" Then
        Let filename = "HARDBACK.INV"
    Else
        Let filename = "PAPERBCK.INV"
    End If
End Sub
```

21.
```
Private Sub cmdFind_Click()
    Dim search As String, nom As String, yob As Integer
    Rem Search for a name in YOB.TXT
    picOutput.Cls
    Let search = txtName.Text
    Open "YOB.TXT" For Input As #1
    Let nom = ""
    Do While (search > nom) And (Not EOF(1))
        Input #1, nom, yob
    Loop
    If (nom = search) And (search <> "") Then
        picOutput.Print nom; "'s age is"; 1995 - yob
    Else
        picOutput.Print search; " is not in YOB.TXT"
    End If
    Close #1
End Sub
```

25.
```
Private Sub cmdDelOpenFile_Click()
    On Error GoTo ErrorHandler
    Dim item As String, price As Single
    picOutput.Cls
    Open "COWBOY.TXT" For Input As #1
    Input #1, item, price
    picOutput.Print item, price
    Kill "COWBOY.TXT"
    Input #1, item, price
    picOutput.Print item, price
    Close #1
    Exit Sub
ErrorHandler:
    Rem 55 = file already open
    If Err = 55 Then
        picOutput.Print "ERROR"; Err; ":Can't kill file"
    End If
    Rem  Skip line that tries to kill the open file
    Resume Next
End Sub
```

Exercises 8.2

1.
```
Private Sub cmdCreateFile_Click()
    Rem Add initial batting average record to AVERAGE.TXT
    Write #1, txtPlayer.Text, 0, 0        'Initialize counters
    Let txtPlayer.Text = ""
    txtPlayer.SetFocus
End Sub


Private Sub cmdQuit_Click()
    Close #1
End Sub


Private Sub Form_Load()
    Open "AVERAGE.TXT" For Output As #1
End Sub
```

3.
```
Private Sub cmdUpdateFile_Click()
    Rem Add a player to the end of the file AVERAGE.TXT
    Open "AVERAGE.TXT" For Append As #1
    Write #1, txtPlayer.Text, 0, 0
    Close #1
End Sub
```

5.
```
Private Sub cmdProcess_Click()
    Dim nom As String, subscriber As String
    Rem NY Times subscribers on the block
    Open "BLOCK.TXT" For Input As #1
    Open "TIMES.TXT" For Input As #2
    Open "NAMES.TXT" For Output As #3
    Let subscriber = ""
    Do While Not EOF(1)
        Input #1, nom
        Do While (subscriber < nom) And (Not EOF(2))
            Input #2, subscriber
        Loop
        If subscriber = nom Then
            Write #3, subscriber
        End If
    Loop
    Close #1
    Close #2
    Close #3
End Sub
```

7.
```
Private Sub cmdCountRepeats_Click()
    Dim max As Single, lastNum As Single, numRepeats As Single, number As Single
    Rem Count maximum number of repeated integers
    picOutput.Cls
    Open "NUMBERS.TXT" For Input As #1
    Let max = 0
    Let lastNum = 0
    Let numRepeats = 0
    Do While Not EOF(1)
      Input #1, number
      If number <> lastNum Then
          If numRepeats > max Then
              Let max = numRepeats
          End If
          Let lastNum = number
          Let numRepeats = 1
        Else
          Let numRepeats = numRepeats + 1
      End If
    Loop
    picOutput.Print "The maximum number of repeats is"; max
    Close #1
End Sub
```

9.
```
Private Sub cmdProcessTicketSales_Click()
    Dim cntrlVar As Integer, gradeTotal As Integer, total As Integer
    Dim grade As Integer, nom As String, nmbTix As Integer
    Rem Display student raffle ticket totals
    picOutput.Cls
    Open "RAFFLE.TXT" For Input As #1
    Let cntrlVar = 0
    Let gradeTotal = 0
    Let total = 0
    Do While Not EOF(1)
      Input #1, grade, nom, nmbTix
      If cntrlVar = 0 Then          'Reset cntrlVar after first grade is read
          Let cntrlVar = grade
      End If
      If (grade <> cntrlVar) Then    'Display gradeTotal if new grade found
          picOutput.Print "Grade"; cntrlVar; "sold"; gradeTotal; "tickets"
          Let total = total + gradeTotal
          Let gradeTotal = 0
          Let cntrlVar = grade
      End If
      Let gradeTotal = gradeTotal + nmbTix
      If EOF(1) Then               'At end-of-file, print last grade's total
          picOutput.Print "Grade"; cntrlVar; "sold"; gradeTotal; "tickets"
          Let total = total + gradeTotal
      End If
    Loop
    picOutput.Print
    picOutput.Print "Total = "; total
    Close #1
End Sub
```

11.
```
Private Sub cmdUpdate_Click()
    Dim mstName As String, mstNmb As String, nom As String, newNmb As String
    Rem Update phone number master file
    Open "MASTER.TXT" For Input As #1
    Open "MOVED.TXT" For Input As #2
    Open "TEMP.TXT" For Output As #3
    Do While Not EOF(2)
      Input #2, nom, newNmb
      Do
        Input #1, mstName, mstNmb
        If mstName = nom Then
            Write #3, mstName, newNmb
          Else
            Write #3, mstName, mstNmb
        End If
      Loop Until mstName = nom
    Loop
    Do While Not EOF(1)
      Input #1, mstName, mstNmb
      Write #3, mstName, mstNmb
    Loop
    Close #1
    Close #2
    Close #3
    Open "MASTER.TXT" For Output As #1
    Open "TEMP.TXT" For Input As #2
    Do While Not EOF(2)
      Input #2, mstName, mstNmb
      Write #1, mstName, mstNmb
    Loop
    Close #1
    Close #2
    Kill "TEMP.TXT"
End Sub
```

13. Split the file into two or more files that can be stored in arrays, sort these files using arrays, and then merge the sorted files.

CHAPTER 9

Exercises 9.1

1. `Pacific   Mississipp`

3. heights are same
170
eye colors are same

5. The variables used in the Let statements are invalid. They should be astrology.nom and astrology.sign.

7. `Let employee.name = "Bob"` is invalid and there is no `End Type` statement.

9. Number is an invalid data type.

11.
```
Public Type planet
    planetName As String * 20
    distanceFromSun As Single
End Type
```

13.
```
Public Type car
    make As String * 20
    model As String * 20
    yr As Single
    mileage As Single
End Type
```

15.
```
Private Sub cmdDisplay_Click ()
    Rem Input three words and display them in first three zones
    picOutput.Cls
    picOutput.Font.Name = "Courier"
    Dim word1 As String * 14
    Dim word2 As String * 14
    Dim word3 As String * 14
    Let word1 = txtWord1.Text
    Let word2 = txtWord2.Text
    Let word3 = txtWord3.Text
    picOutput.Print word1; word2; wprd3
End Sub
```

Exercises 9.2

1. VA

3. TX
    WI
    VA
    3

5.
Virginia Tech	VA	1872
Harvard	MA	1636

7. Milwaukee Area Tech. Col.   WI   1912

9. Cannot take length of a variable type. Should be Len(actor).

11. Cannot print record variable.

13.
```
Public Type typeNums
    num1 As Single
    num2 As Single
    num3 As Single
End Type

Dim numbers As typeNums
Open "NUMBERS.TXT" For Random As #1 Len = Len(numbers)
```

15.
```
Rem In BAS Module
Public Type typePerson
    nom As String * 15
    yob As Integer
End Type

Rem in Form Module
Private Sub cmdConvertFile_Click()
    Dim recNum As Single, nom As String, yob As Integer
    Rem Make random file YOB2.TXT from sequential file YOB.TXT
    Dim person As typePerson
    Open "YOB.TXT" For Input As #1
    Open "YOB2.TXT" For Random As #2 Len = Len(person)
    Let recNum = 1
    Do While Not EOF(1)
        Input #1, nom, yob
        Let person.nom = nom
        Let person.yob = yob
        Put #2, recNum, person
        Let recNum = recNum + 1
    Loop
    Close #1
    Close #2
End Sub
```

CHAPTER 10

Exercises 10.1

1. picBox.Scale (-1, 30)-(7, -5)

3.
```
picBox.Line (-1, 0)-(4, 0)      'x-axis
picBox.Line (0, -8)-(0, 40)     'y-axis
```

5.
```
Private Sub cmdDraw_Click()
    Rem Draw axes and line
    picOutput.Scale (-2, 240)-(12, -40)
    picOutput.Line (-2, 0)-(12, 0)        'Draw x-axis
    picOutput.Line (0, -40)-(0, 240)      'Draw y-axis
    picOutput.Line (3, 200)-(10, 150)     'Draw line
    picOutput.Circle (3, 200), .05
    picOutput.Circle (10, 150), .05
End Sub
```

7.
```
Private Sub cmdDraw_Click()
    Rem Draw axes and line
    picOutput.Scale (-.2 * 4, 1.2 * .5)-(1.2 * 4, -.2 * .5)
    picOutput.Line (-.2 * 4, 0)-(1.2 * 4, 0)     'Draw x-axis
    picOutput.Line (0, -.2 * .5)-(0, 1.2 * .5)   'Draw y-axis
    picOutput.Line (2, .5)-(4, .3)               'Draw line
    picOutput.Circle (2, .5), .03
    picOutput.Circle (4, .3), .03
End Sub
```

9.
```
Private Sub cmdDraw_Click()
    Rem Draw a circle in the center of the screen
    picOutput.Scale (-10, 10)-(10, -10)
    picOutput.Circle (0, 0), 4
End Sub
```

11.
```
Private Sub cmdDraw_Click()
    Rem Draw a tick mark at 70 on the y-axis
    picOutput.Scale (-10, 100)-(100, -10)
    picOutput.Line (0, -10)-(0, 100)        'y-axis
    picOutput.Line (-1, 70)-(1, 70)
End Sub
```

13.
```
Private Sub cmdDraw_Click()
    Rem Draw points in the 4 corners of the picture box
    picOutput.Scale (0, 10)-(10, 0)
    picOutput.Circle (0, 0), 1
    picOutput.Circle (0, 10), 1
    picOutput.Circle (10, 0), 1
    picOutput.Circle (10, 10), 1
End Sub
```

15.
```
Private Sub cmdDraw_Click()
    Rem Draw a rectangle
    picOutput.Scale (0, 10)-(10, 0)
    picOutput.Line (1, 1)-(1, 6)
    picOutput.Line (1, 6)-(6, 6)
    picOutput.Line (6, 6)-(6, 1)
    picOutput.Line (6, 1)-(1, 1)
End Sub
```

17.
```
Private Sub cmdDraw_Click()
    Dim r As Single
    Rem Draw five concentric circles
    picOutput.Scale (0, 10)-(10, 0)
    For r = .5 To 2.5 Step .5
        picOutput.Circle (5, 5), r
    Next r
End Sub
```

19.
```
Private Sub cmdDraw_Click()
    Rem Draw a circle and tangent line
    picOutput.Scale (0, 10)-(10, 0)
    picOutput.Circle (5, 5), 1
    picOutput.Line (6, 0)-(6, 10)
End Sub
```

21. The circle will be smaller.

23. The circle will be the same size as in Exercise 21.

25.
```
Private Sub cmdDraw_Click()
    Dim maxX As Single, maxY As Single
    Rem Graph the Square Function
    Let maxX = 10
    Let maxY = maxX * maxX
    picOutput.Scale (-.2 * maxX, 1.2 * maxY)-(1.2 * maxX, -.2 * maxY)
    picOutput.Line (-.2 * maxX, 0)-(1.2 * maxX, 0)   'Draw x-axis
    picOutput.Line (0, -.2 * maxY)-(0, 1.2 * maxY)   'Draw y-axis
    For x = 0 To maxX Step .01
        picOutput.PSet (x, x * x)
    Next x
End Sub
```

27.
```
Private Sub cmdDraw_Click()
    Dim maxNum As Integer, interval As Single
    Dim i As Integer, xPos As Single, ticLabel As String
    Rem Draw a number line
    Let maxNum = Val(InputBox("Enter maximum number to be displayed:"))
    picOutput.Cls
    picOutput.Scale (-10, 10)-(110, -10)
    picOutput.Line (0, 0)-(100, 0)          'Draw x-axis
    Let interval = 100 / (maxNum + 1)
    For i = 1 To maxNum
      Let xPos = interval * i
      picOutput.Line (xPos, -.5)-(xPos, .5)
      Let ticLabel = Format(i, "0")
      Let picOutput.CurrentX = interval * i - picOutput.TextWidth(ticLabel) / 2
      Let picOutput.CurrentY = -1
      picOutput.Print ticLabel;
    Next i
End Sub
```

29.
```
Private Sub cmdDraw_Click()
    Dim x As Integer, y As Integer
    Rem Draw a sheet of graph paper
    picOutput.Scale (0, 50)-(100, 0)
    For x = 0 To 100 Step 5
      picOutput.Line (x, 0)-(x, 50)
    Next x
    For y = 0 To 50 Step 5
      picOutput.Line (0, y)-(100, y)
    Next y
End Sub
```

Exercises 10.2

1. `picOutput.Scale (-1, 1600)-(6, -250)`

Exercises 10.3

1. The variable numYears will have to be increased and the new data added to the data file.

11. `picOutput.Scale (-7.5, 5)-(2.5, -5)`

13. Only procedure DrawData needs to be changed
```
Private Sub DrawData(male() As Single, female() As Single, numYears As Integer)
    Dim i As Integer
    Rem Draw rectangles
    For i = 1 To numYears
      picEnroll.Line (i - .4, male(i))-(i, 0), , BF
      picEnroll.Line (i - .2, female(i))-(i + .2, 0), , B
    Next i
End Sub
```

Exercises 10.4

1. Counterclockwise the numbers are 0, .15, .45, .70, .and .90.

3. Assume that the data .15, .30, .25, .20, and .10 have been placed in the file DATA.TXT.

```
Private Sub cmdDraw_Click()
    Dim circumf As Single, i As Integer, startAngle As Single, stopAngle As Single, radius As Single
    Dim percent(1 To 5) As Single, cumPercent(0 To 5) As Single
    Rem Draw circle and radius lines and fill one sector
    picOutput.Scale (-10, 10)-(10, -10)
    Let radius = 5
    Let circumf = 2 * 3.14159
    Let cumPercent(0) = .0000001 'a "zero" that can be made negative
    Open "DATA.TXT" For Input As #1
    For i = 1 To 5
      Input #1, percent(i)
      Let cumPercent(i) = cumPercent(i - 1) + percent(i)
      Let startAngle = cumPercent(i - 1) * circumf
      Let stopAngle = cumPercent(i) * circumf
      If percent(i) = .1 Then
          Let picOutput.FillStyle = 0 'solid fill
        Else
          Let picOutput.FillStyle = 1 'transparent fill
      End If
      picOutput.Circle (0, 0), radius, , -startAngle, -stopAngle
    Next i
    Close #1
End Sub
```

9.
```
Private Sub cmdDraw_Click()
    Dim circumf As Single
    Rem Draw Pacman
    picOutput.Scale (-4, 4)-(4, -4)
    Let circumf = 2 ^ 3.14159
    picOutput.Circle (0, 0), 2, , -(1 / 8) * circumf, -(7 / 8) * circumf
End Sub
```

CHAPTER 11

Exercises 11.1

1. The currently selected item in lstBox is displayed in picOutput.

3. The last item in lstBox is displayed in picOutput.

5. Brahms is added to the list (after Beethoven) and is displayed in picOutput.

7. The currently selected item in lstBox is deleted.

9. All items are removed from lstBox.

11. Chopin is removed from the list. (Mozart is not removed because the deletion of Chopin changes the index of Mozart from 3 to 2 while the value of *n* in the next pass through the For...Next loop is 3.)

13. `picOutput.Print cboBox.List(0)`

15. `picOutput.Print cboBox.List(0)`

25.
```
Private Sub cmdDisplay_Click()
    Dim i As Integer, total As Single
    Let total = 0
    For i = 0 to lstNumbers.ListCount - 1
      Let total = total + Val(lstNumbers.List(i))
    Next i
    picOutput.Print "The average of the numbers is"; total / lstNumbers.ListCount
End Sub
```

17. `cboBox.RemoveItem 1`

19. `cboBox.AddItem "Cervantes"   'Will appear first in the list`

21.
```
Private Sub DeleteMs()
    Dim i As Integer
    Rem Delete all items beginning with M
    Let i = 0
    Do While i <= cboBox.ListCount - 1
      If Left(cboBox.List(i), 1) = "M" Then
          cboBox.RemoveItem i
        Else
          Let i = i + 1
      End If
    Loop
End Sub
```

23. `picOutput.Print cboBox.List(cboBox.NewIndex)`

27.
```
Private Sub cmdDisplay_Click()
    Dim i As Integer
    For i = 0 to lstNumbers.ListCount - 1 Step 2
      picOutput.Print lstNumbers.List(i)
    Next i
End Sub
```

29.
```
Private Sub cmdDisplay_Click()
    Dim i As Integer, largest As Single, smallest As Single
    Let largest = Val(lstNumbers.List(0))
    Let smallest = largest
    For i = 1 to lstNumbers.ListCount - 1
      If Val(lstNumbers.List(i)) < smallest Then
          Let smallest = Val(lstNumbers.List(i))
        ElseIf Val(lstNumbers.List(i)) > largest Then
          Let largest = Val(lstNumbers.List(i))
      End If
    Next i
    picOutput.Print "The spread of the numbers is"; largest - smallest
End Sub
```

31.

Object	Property	Setting
frmStates	Caption	State Facts
lstStates	Sorted	True
picStates		

```
Dim nickName(4) As String, motto(4) As String    'In (Declarations) section of (General)


Private Sub Form_Load()
  Dim i As Integer, state As String
  Open "STATEINF.TXT" For Input As #1
  For i = 1 To 4
    Input #1, state, nickName(i), motto(i)
    lstStates.AddItem state
    Let lstStates.ItemData(lstStates.NewIndex) = i
  Next i
  Close 1
End Sub


Private Sub lstStates_DblClick()
  picStates.Cls
  picStates.Print "Nickname: "; nickName(lstStates.ItemData(lstStates.ListIndex))
  picStates.Print "Motto: "; motto(lstStates.ItemData(lstStates.ListIndex))
End Sub
```

35.

Object	Property	Setting
frmLengths	Caption	Length Converter
lblFrom	Caption	From
lblTo	Caption	To
lstFrom		
lstTo		
lblLength	Caption	Length to be converted
txtLength	Text	(blank)
cmdConvert	Caption	Convert
lblConverted	Caption	Converted Length
lblNewLen	Caption	(blank)

```
Private Sub Form_Load()
  lstFrom.AddItem "inch"
  lstFrom.AddItem "feet"
  lstFrom.AddItem "yard"
  lstFrom.AddItem "meter"
  lstFrom.AddItem "mile"
  lstTo.AddItem "inch"
  lstTo.AddItem "feet"
  lstTo.AddItem "yard"
  lstTo.AddItem "meter"
  lstTo.AddItem "mile"
End Sub
```

```
Private Sub cmdConvert_Click()
  Dim fromFact As Single, toFact As Single, newDist As Single
  Rem fromFact is # of inches in "from" unit
  Select Case lstFrom.ListIndex
    Case 0
      Let fromFact = 1
    Case 1
      Let fromFact = 12
    Case 2
      Let fromFact = 36
    Case 3
      Let fromFact = 100 / 2.54 '100 centimeters / 2.54 cm per inch
    Case 4
      Let fromFact = 63360      '5280 feet per mile * 12 inches per foot
  End Select
  Rem toFact is # of inches in "to" units
  Select Case lstTo.ListIndex
    Case 0
      Let toFact = 1
    Case 1
      Let toFact = 12
    Case 2
      Let toFact = 36
    Case 3
      Let toFact = 100 / 2.54 '100 centimeters / 2.54 cm per inch
    Case 4
      Let toFact = 63360        '5280 feet per mile * 12 inches per foot
  End Select
  Let newDist = Val(txtLength.Text) * fromFact / toFact
  If newDist >= 1 Then
      Let lblNewLen.Caption = Format(newDist, "Standard")
    Else
      Let lblNewLen.Caption = Format(newDist, "0.000000")
  End If
End Sub
```

Exercises 11.2

1. The word "Income" becomes the caption embedded in the top of Frame1.

3. The Check1 check box becomes unchecked.

5. The Option1 option button becomes unselected.

7. The scroll bar thumb will move to its rightmost position.

9. Clicking on the arrow on either end of the scroll bar will move the thumb the same ("large") distance as clicking on the bar between the thumb and an arrow.

11. The Timer1 control is disabled (that is, stopped).

13. The Shape1 control becomes an oval.

15. The Shape1 control becomes filled with a crosshatch pattern.

17. The thickness of the Line1 control doubles.

19. `Let Frame1.Left = Frame1.Left + 100`

21. `Let Option2.Value = False`

23. `Let HScroll2.Value = HScroll2.Min + (HScroll2.Max - HScroll2.Min) / 3`

25.
```
Dim flag As Integer 'In (Declarations) section of (General)
Private Sub Form_Load()
  Let flag = 0
  Let Timer1.Interval = 65000  'One minute and five seconds
  Let Timer1.Enabled = True
End Sub

Private Sub Timer1_Timer()
  If flag = 0 Then
      Let flag = 1
    Else
      Let flag = 0
      Call Event  'Event is procedure that is invoked every 2 minutes and 10 seconds
  End If
End Sub
```

CHAPTER 12

Exercises 12.1

1.

Object	Property	Setting
datCountries	DatabaseName	MEGACTY1.MDB
	RecordSource	Countries
lstCountries		
cmdList	Caption	List Countries

```
Private Sub cmdList_Click()
  datCountries.Recordset.MoveFirst
  Do While Not datCountries.Recordset.EOF
    lstCountries.AddItem _
    datCountries.Recordset.Fields("country").Value
    datCountries.Recordset.MoveNext
  Loop
End Sub
```

3.

Object	Property	Setting
datCities	DatabaseName	MEGACTY1.MDB
	RecordSource	Cities
lstCities		
cmdList	Caption	List Megacities

```
Private Sub cmdList_Click()
  datCities.Recordset.MoveFirst
  Do While Not datCities.Recordset.EOF
    If datCities.Recordset.Fields("pop2015").Value > 20 Then
      lstCities.AddItem _
              datCities.Recordset.Fields("city").Value
    End If
    datCities!Recordset.MoveNext
  Loop
End Sub
```

15. 5   **17.** 67   **21.** B   **23.** D   **25.** F

27.

Object	Property	Setting
frmDBMan	Caption	Database Management
lblCountry	Caption	Country:
	DataSource	datCountries
txtCountry	DataField	country
	DataSource	datCountries
lblCurrency	Caption	Currency:
txtCurrency	DataField	currency
	DataSource	datCountries
lblPop1995	Caption	1995 Population:
txtPop1995	DataField	pop1995
	DataSource	datCountries
datCountries	Caption	Populous Countries
	DatabaseName	MEGACTY1.MDB
	RecordSource	Countries
cmdAdd	Caption	Add
cmdSearch	Caption	Search
cmdDelete	Caption	Delete
cmdQuit	Caption	Quit

```
Private Sub cmdAdd_Click()
  Rem Add a new record
  datCountries.Recordset.AddNew
  Rem Data must be entered before moving or no record is added
  txtCountry.SetFocus
End Sub

Private Sub cmdDelete_Click()
  Rem Delete the currently displayed record
  datCountries.Recordset.Delete
  Rem Move so that user sees deleted record disappear
  datCountries.Recordset.MoveNext
  If datCountries.Recordset.EOF Then
      datCountries.Recordset.MovePrevious
  End If
End Sub

Private Sub cmdSearch_Click()
  Dim strSearchFor As String, intFound As Integer
  Rem Search for the country specified by the user
  Let strSearchFor = UCase(InputBox("Name of country to find:"))
  If Len(strSearchFor) > 0 Then
      datCountries.Recordset.MoveFirst
      Let intFound = 0
```

```
        Do While intFound = 0 And Not datCountries.Recordset.EOF
          If UCase(datCountries.Recordset.Fields("country").Value) = _
                  strSearchFor Then
              Let intFound = 1
          Else
              datCountries.Recordset.MoveNext
          End If
        Loop
        If intFound = 0 Then
            MsgBox "Unable to locate requested country."
            Rem  Move so that EOF is no longer true
            datCountries.Recordset.MoveLast
        End If
      Else
        MsgBox "Must enter a country.", , "Not Found"
    End If
  End If
End Sub

Private Sub datCountries_Validate(Action As Integer, Save As Integer)
  Rem Does not allow record to be added without currency
  Dim strMsg As String
  If Not datCountries.Recordset.EOF And Not datCountries.Recordset.BOF Then
    If (txtCurrency.Text = "") Then
        MsgBox "A currency is required."
        Let Action = 0
    End If
  End If
End Sub

Private Sub cmdQuit_Click()
  End
End Sub
```

Exercises 12.2

1. Could cause a problem if the country was not one of the countries in the Countries table.

3. No problem.

5. Au_ID

7. ISBN

9. None

11. B

13. A

15. D

17. C

19. Beijing

21. Los Angeles

23.
```
datCities.RecordSource = "SELECT * FROM Cities ORDER BY pop2015 ASC"
datCities.Refresh
datCities.Recordset.FindLast "country = 'China'"
```

25.

Object	Property	Setting
frmDBMan	Caption	Database Management
cmdAlphabetical	Caption	&Alphabetical Order
cmd1995Pop	Caption	Order by &1995 Population
cmd2015Pop	Caption	Order by &2015 Population
cmdAlphCoCity	Caption	Alphabetical Order by Country and City
lstCities	DataField	city
	DataSource	datCities
datCities	Caption	Large World Cities
	DatabaseName	MEGACTY2.MDB
	RecordSource	Cities
cmdQuit	Caption	Exit

```
Private Sub cmd1995Pop_Click()
  Dim strSQL As String
  strSQL = "SELECT * FROM Cities ORDER BY pop1995 ASC"
  datCities.RecordSource = strSQL
  datCities.Refresh
  Call FillList
End Sub
```

```
Private Sub cmd2015Pop_Click()
  Dim strSQL As String
  strSQL = "SELECT * FROM Cities ORDER BY pop2015 ASC"
  datCities.RecordSource = strSQL
  datCities.Refresh
  Call FillList
End Sub

Private Sub cmdAlphabetical_Click()
  Dim strSQL As String
  strSQL = "SELECT * FROM Cities ORDER BY City ASC"
  datCities.RecordSource = strSQL
  datCities.Refresh
  Call FillList
End Sub

Private Sub cmdAlphCoCity_Click()
  Dim strSQL As String
  Rem Order alphabetically by country and city
  strSQL = "SELECT * FROM Cities ORDER BY country, city ASC"
  datCities.RecordSource = strSQL
  datCities.Refresh
  Call FillList
End Sub
```

```
Private Sub FillList()
  Rem Fill list box with city names
  lstCities.Clear
  datCities.Recordset.MoveFirst
  Do While Not datCities.Recordset.EOF
    lstCities.AddItem datCities.Recordset.Fields("city")
    datCities.Recordset.MoveNext
  Loop
End Sub

Private Sub cmdQuit_Click()
  End
End Sub
```

Exercises 12.3

1. `SELECT * FROM Countries WHERE country Like 'I*' ORDER BY pop1995 ASC`

3. `SELECT country, currency FROM Countries WHERE pop1995>100 AND pop1995<200 ORDER BY pop1995 ASC`

5. `SELECT * FROM Cities WHERE country='China' ORDER BY pop2015 DESC`

7. `SELECT * FROM Cities WHERE pop1995>15 AND pop1995<16 ORDER BY pop1995 ASC, pop2015 ASC`

9. `SELECT city,Cities.pop2015,currency FROM Cities INNER JOIN Countries ON Countries.country=Cities.country WHERE Countries.country='India' ORDER BY pop2015 DESC`

15. Suppose the table is named Presidents.

Object	Property	Setting
frmPresidents	Caption	Presidents
datPresidents	Caption	U.S. Presidents
	DatabaseName	PRES.MBD
	RecordSource	Presidents
dbgrdPresidents	DataSource	datPresidents

17. Suppose the two tables are named Lines and Actors.

Object	Property	Setting
frmFilms	Caption	Famous Movie Lines
datLines	Caption	Famous Lines
	DatabaseName	LINES.MDB
	RecordSource	SELECT famousLine, maleLead FROM Lines INNER JOIN Actors ON Lines.film=Actors.film
dbgrdFilms	DataSource	datLines

19. OLYMPNEW.MDB is an empty database created in Visual Data Manager with the same structure as OLYMPICS.MDB, except for the year field which is now of type Integer.

Object	Property	Setting
frmOlympics	Caption	Summer Olympics
datNew	Caption	New database
	DatabaseName	OLYMPNEW.MDB
	RecordSource	Summer
cmdCopy	Caption	&Copy and Update the Database
cmdExit	Caption	Done
	Enabled	False
datOld	Caption	Old database
	DatabaseName	OLYMPICS.MDB
	RecordSource	Summer
dbgrdOld	DataSource	datOld
dbgrdNew	DataSource	datNew

```
Private Sub cmdCopy_Click()
  Dim yrStr As String    ' gets the 2-character year from old DB
  Dim yrInt As Integer  ' holds the integer year for new DB
  Dim century As Integer
  Dim site As String, mostMedals As String
  Rem  Modify old Olympics database, with 2 chars for year,
  Rem  and copy into new DB with year stored as integer
  Rem
  Rem Get first record; should be 1896 Olympics
  datOld.Recordset.MoveFirst
  Call GetOldData(yrStr, site, mostMedals)
  Let yrInt = Val(yrStr) + 1800
  Call PutNewData(yrInt, site, mostMedals)
  datOld.Recordset.MoveNext
  Rem Read old database, fill new database
  Let century = 1900
  Do While Not datOld.Recordset.EOF
    Call GetOldData(yrStr, site, mostMedals)
    Let yrInt = Val(yrStr) + century
    Call PutNewData(yrInt, site, mostMedals)
    datOld.Recordset.MoveNext
  Loop
  Rem Insert 1996 Olympics (in Atlanta)
  Let yrInt = 1996
  Let site = "Atlanta"
  Let mostMedals = "USA"
  Call PutNewData(yrInt, site, mostMedals)
  Let cmdExit.Enabled = True
  Let cmdCopy.Enabled = False
End Sub

Private Sub GetOldData(yr As String, site As String, mostMedals As String)
  Rem Get data from current record of old database
  Let yr = datOld.Recordset.Fields("year").Value
  Let site = datOld.Recordset.Fields("site").Value
  Let mostMedals = datOld.Recordset.Fields("mostMedals").Value
End Sub

Private Sub PutNewData(yr As Integer, site As String, mostMedals As String)
  Rem Add record at end of new database
  datNew.Recordset.AddNew
  Let datNew.Recordset.Fields("year").Value = yr
  Let datNew.Recordset.Fields("site").Value = site
  Let datNew.Recordset.Fields("mostMedals").Value = mostMedals
  datNew.Recordset.Update
End Sub

Private Sub cmdExit_Click()
  End
End Sub
```

CHAPTER 13

Exercises 13.1

1. Any negative grade will be recorded as 0 and any grade greater than 100 will be recorded as 100.

3.
```
Property Get midGrade() As Single
  midGrade = m_midterm
End Property
```

5. The object variable *scholar* was not created with a Set scholar = New CStudent statement before it was used.

7. The member variable *m_Name*, which is Private, was assigned a value from outside the class code.

9. The method semGrade returns a value, but cannot set a value.

11. The member variable *m_ssn* will have the value "999-99-9999" whenever an instance of the class is created.

13. None.

15. Add the following lines to the Form_Load event procedure, and change 500 to –500 in the cmdMove_Click event procedure.

```
Let round.Xcoord = frmCircles.Width
Let round.Ycoord = frmCircles.Height
```

Count, 604, 686
Control, 44
    aggregate, 623
    arrays, 335–339
    bound, 547
    Check box, 509–512
    Combo box, 496, 500–501, 503
    Command button, 45, 51–52
    Common dialog box, 533
    Data, 547ff
    Directory list box, 502–503
    Drive list box, 502–503
    File list box, 502–503
    FlexGrid, 523–528
    Frame, 508–509
    Horizontal scroll bar, 513–515
    Image, 518
    Label, 45, 52
    Line, 517–518
    List box, 496–499, 503
    Menu, 528–530
    Option button, 511–513
    Picture box, 45, 52–53, 71
    Shape, 516–517
    Text box, 46–51, 88–89
    Timer, 515–516
    variable, 274, 295, 415
    Vertical scroll bar, 513–515
Control array, 335–341
    creating at run time, 339
    creating at design time, 336
    event procedure, 338
    nonzero initial index, 341
Control break processing, 414ff
Control-menu button, 13
Coordinate systems, 456, 718
Cooper, Alan, 29
Copies property, 536
Copying text, 531, 670
Counter, 260, 262
    variable, 295, 322
CreateObject function, 638, 686
Criteria clause, 559
Ctrl key, 10, 15
Ctrl+Del key combination, 10
Ctrl+Down Arrow key combination, 150
Ctrl+End key combination, 13
Ctrl+Home key combination, 13
Currency format string, 123, 694
Current record, 548
CurrentX property, 461, 686
CurrentY property, 461, 686
Cursor, 8
Curving grades, 392

D

Data control, 547ff
Data aware, 547
Data file, 17
Database, 547
    creating with code, 578–580
    creating with Visual Data Manager, 572ff
    design principles, 577ff
DataBaseName property, 547, 686
Data-bound grid control, 570–572
DataField property, 547, 686
Data Source property, 547, 687
Day of week, 245
DblClick event, 503, 687
Debugging, 26, 33, 679–680, 721ff
Declaring variables, 87, 92
Decision, 191
    structures, 38, 198ff
(Declarations), 167, 303
Default value, 91
Del key, 10, 15
Delete method, 549, 688
Deleting a breakpoint, 679
Depreciation, 299
Descending order, 320
Design
    modular, 151, 189ff
    top-down, 150, 169, 189–190
Desk-checking, 42, 721
Desktop, 7
Dialog box
    Input, 102
    Load Picture, 53
    Message box, 106
    moving around in, 20
    Save As, 12
    Save File As, 50
    Save Project As, 50
Dijkstra, Edsger W., 27
Dim statement, 87, 88, 303, 312, 368,
        439, 688
Dimension of an array, 303
Dir function, 400, 688
Directory, 17, 718–719
    list box control, 502–503
Direct-access file, 449
Diskette, 2, 16
    drive, 2
Displaying a procedure, 144, 150
Divide and conquer method, 37
Dividend, 120
Division, 71
Divisor, 120

Do loop, 248ff, 295, 688
   nested, 260
   pass, 248
Documentation, 34, 107–108
Dollar sign, 88, 123
Double-click, 5
Double-subscripted variable, 368
Double variable, 88, 688
Dragging, 6
DrawStyle property, 471, 689
Drive property, 502, 689
Drive list box control, 502–503
Driver, 193
Dynamic array, 719

E

Eckert, J. Presper, 26
Edit method, 549
Editing commands, 669–670
Editor
   smart, 77, 149, 227
   text, 9
   using, 669–670
Efficiency of sorts, 354
Element,
   of an array, 303
   of an HTML page, 655
Else, 203, 220
ElseIf, 206
Embedding (OLE), 642, 643–644
Empty string, 91
End
   Function, 177
   icon, 49
   key, 10, 15, 49
   statement, 65, 689
   tag, 655
End Select, 221
End Sub, 59, 142
End Type, 440
EndDoc method, 107, 690
Ending Windows, 12
Enter key, 9, 15
EOF function, 260, 549, 690
Error
   Array not defined, 312
   detecting, 65
   File not found, 400
   For without Next, 280
   handling routine, 403
   Input past end of file, 107
   Invalid procedure call or
      argument, 127
   Next without For, 280

Subscript out of range, 312
   syntax, 78
   trapping, 403
Esc key, 11, 15
Event procedure, 59
Events, 58ff, 609, 690
Excel, 638, 639–640, 643–644, 646
Exiting Visual Basic, 668
Exponent, 72, 73, 79
Exponentiation, 71
Expression, 136
   numeric, 74
   string, 86

F

F1 key, 671
F4 key, 46, 675
F5 key, 49, 724
F7 key, 679, 724
F8 key, 678, 724
F9 key, 679, 724
Faggin, Federico, 28
FICA tax, 207, 235
Field,
   of a database table, 546, 553
   of a record, 404, 438
   length, 438
Fields property, 548, 691
File, 17
   adding items to, 399
   binary, 717
   closing, 400
   creating with Windows' Notepad, 7ff
   data, 17
   direct-access, 449
   length, 449
   list box control, 502–503
   merging, 412
   name, 12, 17, 19, 398
   opening for append, 399, 400
   opening for input, 99
   opening for output, 398
   processing data from, 261
   random-access, 404, 446ff, 454
   reading from, 99ff
   reference number of, 99, 398
   relative, 449
   saving, 12, 20, 50
   specifying, 20
   sequential, 398
   sorting, 411
   writing to, 398
File not found error, 400
FileName property, 536, 691

Filespec, 17, 719
Fill pattern, 486
FillColor property, 486, 517, 691
FillStyle property, 485–486, 517, 691
Filter, 536
FilterIndex property, 536
Find methods, 563–564, 691
Fixed-length string, 436, 442, 453
Fixed columns, 523, 692
Fixed rows, 523, 692
FixedAlignment property, 524, 691
Flag, 260, 263, 295
Flags property, 535, 692
Flagged bubble sort, 361
FlexGrid control, 523–528
Flowchart, 35, 192
Flowline, 35
Focus, 50, 53
Folder, 17
    copy a, 19
    create a, 18
    delete a, 19
    move a, 19
    remove a , 19
    rename a, 19
Font,
    Bold property, 59, 536, 692
    common dialog box, 534
    dialog box, 48–49
    Italic property, 536, 692
    Name property, 536, 692
    Size property, 49, 59, 536, 692
For, 274
For without Next error, 280
ForeColor property, 48, 693
Foreign key, 557
Form(s), 45
    design, 673–674
    multiple, 531–533
    level procedure, 533
    level variable, 533
Form level variable, 167, 303, 309, 369, 533
Format a diskette, 20
Format function, 122–125, 693–696
Format string, 123
Form_Load event, 168, 305
For. . .Next loop, 274ff, 295, 660, 693
    body, 274
    control variable, 274, 293
    initial value, 274
    nested, 278
    terminating value, 274
Frame control, 508–509
Frequency table, 311
FromPage property, 536, 696

Function, 118ff, 176ff, 696
    Asc, 90, 682
    BOF, 549, 566, 682
    Chr, 90, 684
    Ceil, 182
    EOF, 260, 549, 690
    InStr, 121, 127, 698
    Int, 118, 698
    key, 9
    LBound, 329, 699
    LCase, 127, 699
    Left, 121, 127, 699
    Len, 121, 446, 699
    Loc, 450, 701
    managing, 677–678
    Mid, 121, 127, 702
    numeric, 118
    Randomize, 126, 707
    Right, 121, 127, 709
    Rnd, 125–126, 127, 709
    RTrim, 437, 709
    Spc, 103, 712
    Sqr, 118, 712
    Str, 88–89, 92–93, 712
    string, 121
    string-valued, 127
    Tab function, 105, 109, 713
    Timer, 361, 714
    Trim, 121, 714
    UBound, 329, 715
    UCase, 121, 127, 361, 715
    user-defined, 176, 194
    Val, 88, 92, 715
Fylstra, Dan, 28

G

Game of Life, 394
Gap in a Shell sort, 353
Gates, Bill, 33
(General), 144
General procedures, 142
Get statement, 448, 450, 696
GetObject function, 646, 697
GetText property, 533, 697
Global variable, 533, 697
GotFocus event, 62, 64, 338, 697
GoTo, 42, 196, 697
Graphics coordinate systems, 456, 718
Graphical User Interface, 22
GridLines property, 524, 697

H

Hangman, 543

Hard copy, obtaining, 679
Hardware, 4
Height property, 339–341, 697
Help, 404, 671
Hide method, 531, 697
Hierarchy chart, 35, 37
Hoff, Ted, 28
Hollerith, Herman, 25
Home key, 10, 15, 49
Hopper, Grace M., 26
Horizontal
    bar chart, 493
    radius line, 483
    scroll bar control, 513–515
Hourglass, 5
HTML, 654–656
    layout, 660
Hypertext, 649, 656
Hypertext Markup Language,
    654–656

I

I-Beam, 5
Icon, 6
If, 203, 697
    block, confusing, 209
    ElseIf, 206
Image control, 518
Income tax, 236, 244
Index property, 336, 698
Inheritance, 614
Inequality, 198, 227
Infinite loop, 252
Initial value, 274
Initialize event, 595
Inner Join operation, 559
Input, 3, 32, 88, 99, 102
Input# statement, 99, 100, 108, 109, 698
Input box, 102
Input past end of file error message, 109
InputBox function, 102, 698
Inputting from a file, 99
Ins key, 10, 15
Insert mode, 10
Insert Object dialog box, 642
Installing Visual Basic, 667
Instance variable, 590
Instr function, 121–122, 127, 698
Int function, 118, 698
Integer
    division, 127
    variable, 88, 698
Internet, 648–649, 653
Interval property, 515, 698

Invalid procedure call or argument error, 127
Invoking Visual Basic, 668
Is, 221, 227
Item
    of a collection, 604, 699
    of a list box, 496
ItemData property, 499, 699
Iteration, 191, 248ff

J

Jacopini, Guiseppe, 27
Jobs, Stephen, 28

K

Kapor, Mitchell D., 29
Kemeny, John G., 27
Key
    access, 11, 529
    Alt, 11, 15
    Alt+F4, 49
    Backspace, 9, 15
    Caps Lock, 10, 15
    for a collection, 608
    Ctrl, 10, 15
    Ctrl+Del, 10
    Ctrl+End, 13
    Ctrl+Home, 13
    Ctrl+Y, 668
    Cursor Down, 15
    Del, 10, 15
    End, 10, 15
    Enter, 7, 15
    Esc, 11, 15
    F1, 671
    F4, 46, 675
    F5, 49, 668, 625, 724
    F8, 679, 724
    F9, 679, 724
    foreign, 557
    function, 9
    Home, 10, 15
    Ins, 10, 15
    Num Lock, 9, 15
    PgDn, 13, 15
    PgUp, 13 15
    primary, 557, 574
    sequence, 13
    Shift, 10, 15
    Shift+F8, 680, 724
    Tab, 11, 15
    toggle, 9
Key field of an array, 361
KeyAscii variable, 90–91

Keyboard, 2, 10
Keypad, numeric, 9
KeyPress event, 90, 91
Keyword, 65, 77
Kill statement, 400, 699
Knuth, Donald E., 28
Kurtz, Thomas E., 27

L

Label (diskette), 16
Label, line, 404, 697, 719
Label control, 45, 52ff
Large change, 513, 588
Layout, 660
LBound function, 329, 699
LCase function, 127, 699
Leading space, 76
Least squares approximation, 297–298
Left arrow, 512
Left property, 339–340, 699
Left function, 121, 127, 699
Len function, 121, 446, 699
Length
    field, 438
    file, 449
    string, 121
Let statement 59, 74,75, 85, 442, 700
Level of precedence
    arithmetic operators, 77
    logical operators, 199
Library, 168
Like operator, 559, 566
Line method, 458, 480, 493, 700
Line
    chart, 468ff
    clipping, 463
    continuation character, 106
    control, 517–518
    feed, 76
    horizontal radius, 483
    method, 458, 700
    style, 471, 493
Linking, 642, 644–645
List box control, 496–500, 503
List Properties/Methods, 61
List property, 497, 700
ListCount property, 496, 700
ListIndex property, 497, 700
Load Picture dialog box, 53
LoadPicture function, 518, 701
Loading a program, 667
Loc function, 450, 701
Local variable, 165, 194, 306, 369
LOF function, 449, 701

Logical operator, 199, 243
    level of precedence, 200
Long
    division, 120
    variable type, 88, 701
Long Date format string, 123, 695
Lookup, table, 359
Loop, 248
    Do, 248, 295, 688
    For. . .Next, 274, 295, 693
    infinite, 252
    nested, 260, 265, 278
    structure, 40
Looping, 191
LostFocus event, 62, 701

M

Machine language, 3
Managing
    functions, 677–678
    menus, 672
    procedures, 677–678
    programs, 668–669
    subprograms, 677–678
    windows, 678–679
Mathematical notation, 71
Mauchley, John, 26
Max property, 513, 701
Maximize button, 13
Mazer, Stan, 28
Mean of data, 391
Medium Date format string, 123, 695
Member variable, 590, 594
Memory, 2, 74, 163
Menu bar, 8, 9
Menus, managing, 672
Menu control, 528–530
Menu Editor window, 529
Merge algorithm, 324
Merging files, 412
Message box, 106
Methods, 71, 595, 599
Microprocessor, 2
Mid function, 121, 127, 702
Mills, Harlan B., 27
Min property, 513, 701
Minimize button, 13
Mod, 127, 702
Mode
    insert, 10
    overwrite, 10
Modular design, 150, 189
Module, 37, 189
Modulo, 127

Monitor, 2
Mouse, 5
    clicking, 5
    cursor, 5
    double-clicking, 5, 53
    dragging, 6
    pointing, 5
    using a, 5–6
Move methods, 548, 703
Moving text, 670
MsgBox, 106, 703
MultiLine property, 49, 55, 703–704
Multiple forms, 531–533
Multiplication, 71
My Computer, 7, 17–19

N

Name property, 54, 704
Name statement, 400, 704
Navigate, 650
Navigation arrows, 548
Nested loop, 260, 265, 278
Nesting, 209
New, 589, 604, 704
New program, starting, 50, 669
NewIndex property, 497, 704
NewPage method, 107, 704
Next, 274ff
Next without For error, 280
NoMatch property, 564
Not logical operator, 199, 704
Notation
    mathematical, 71
    scientific, 72–73
    Visual Basic, 71
Notepad, 7–12, 109
Nothing keyword, 598, 638, 704
Noyce, Robert, 28
Null string, 91
Num Lock key, 9, 15
Numeric
    constant, 71
    function, 118
    keypad, 9
    variable, 73–74

O

Object data type, 638
Objects, 44ff, 588ff
    grouping, 55
    setting properties of, 46–47, 59, 66
Object-oriented programming, 588ff

OCX files, 628, 630, 660
OLE, 638–646
    automation, 638
    automation object, 638
    container control, 642
    embedding, 642, 643–644
    Insert Object dialog box, 642
    linking, 642, 644–645
On Error, 404, 644–645, 704
Open common dialog box, 534
Open statement, 398, 446, 704–705
Opening a file for
    append, 399, 400
    input, 99
    output, 398
    random, 446, 450
Operator
    \, 127
    And, 199, 682
    integer division, 127
    Like, 559
    logical, 200, 243
    Mod, 127, 702
    Not, 199, 704
    Or, 199, 704
    relational, 198, 243
Option button control, 511–513
Option Explicit, 92, 705
Or logical operator, 199, 705
Order
    ascending, 320
    descending, 321
Ordered array, 320
    search of, 321, 322
Output, 3, 32, 98–99, 104, 106–107
Oval shape, 516
Overwrite mode, 10

P

Palindrome, 334
Parallel arrays, 312
Parameter, 145, 147, 177
    Info, 150
Parenthesis, 77
Pascal, 252
Pass, 349
Passing, 144
    arrays, 325
by reference, 164
    by value, 183
    records, 441
    values, 165
    variables, 163, 177

Path, 17
Path property, 503, 707
Pattern property, 503, 707
Payroll case study, 235ff
Percent format string, 123, 694
Personal computer, 2
PgDn key, 13, 15
PgUp key, 13, 15
Picture box control, 45, 52–53, 71
Picture property, 53, 518, 706
Pie chart, 483ff
Point, with mouse, 5
Pointing device, 5
Poker, 393, 618
Positioning text, 461
Primary key, 557
Print common dialog box, 534
Print method, 71, 75–76, 104, 706
Print zone, 104, 106, 109
Printer, 2
Printer object, 106
PrintForm method, 107, 706
Printing a Notepad file, 13
Printing a program, 679
Printing the screen, 107
Private, 59, 595, 660
Problem solving, 4
Procedure, 143, 183, 194
  creating, 143
  displaying 144, 150, 677
  event, 59
  form level, 533
  general, 142
  global, 533
  list box, 60
  managing, 677–678
  step, 679, 724
Processing, 3, 32
  control break, 414–416
  data from a file, 261
Program, 3
  clearing from memory, 50
  development cycle, 33
  documentation, 107
  opening, 51, 669
  printing, 679
  running, 49, 668
  saving, 50, 668
  starting new, 50
  terminating, 49
Programmer, 4
Programming
  stub, 193
  style, 150, 209, 252

Polymorphism, 599
PRG file, 630
Project, 50
  group, 630
Project Explorer window, 45
Properties window, 45, 54
  how to access, 675–676
Property, 599
Property Get, 590, 591, 595, 706
Property Let, 590, 591, 595, 599, 707
Property Set, 625
PSet method, 459, 707
Pseudocode, 35, 37, 42
Public, 439, 533, 599, 660
Put statement, 447, 450, 707

Q

QBColor function, 464, 707
Quadratic formula, 244
Quick Info, 103
Question mark, 559
Quotation mark, 91
Quotient, 120

R

Radian measure, 719
Radioactive decay, 285
RaiseEvent, 610, 707
Random number, 125
Randomize function, 126, 707
Random-access file, 404, 446ff, 449, 450, 454
Range, 390
  array, 303, 310
  chart, 494
  determining for an array, 329
  specifying in Case, 221
  Subscript out of range error, 312
Reading from a file, 99ff
Record, 404, 437, 453
  current, 548
  passing, 440
  type, 441
  variable, 439
RecordSet, 562
RecordSource property, 547, 708
Rectangle shape, 516
ReDim statement, 308, 312, 708
Reference number of a file, 99, 398
Referential integrity, 557
Relational database, 547, 557
Relational operator, 198, 243
Relative file, 449

Rem statement, 107, 708
Remainder, 120
Remove. 604, 708
RemoveItem method, 497, 708
Removing a breakpoint, 679, 729
Reserved word, 65
Restricted keyword, 77
Reusable, 193
Right function, 121, 127, 709
Right arrow, 514
Right-justification, 123–124
Rnd function, 125–126, 127, 709
Root folder (directory), 17
Rounded rectangle shape, 516
Rounded square shape, 516
Roundoff error, 280
Row property, 524, 685
RowHeight property, 523, 709
Rows property, 523, 709
RTrim function, 437, 709
Rule,
    of entity integrity, 566
    of referential integrity, 557
Running a program, 49, 668

S

Save As common dialog box, 534
Save File As dialog box, 50
Saving a program, 50, 668
Scale method, 458, 463, 709
Scientific format string, 123, 694
Scientific notation, 72–73
Screen dump, 107
SCRIPT tag, 659
Scroll
    arrow, 8
    bars, 8
    box, 8
    event, 514
Scroll bar controls, 513–515
ScrollBars property, 523–524, 710
Search
    binary, 356, 357
    of ordered array, 321, 322
    sequential, 328, 356
Search and replace, editor command, 670
Second-level menu item, 528
Sector of a circle, 484–485
Segmented bar chart, 494
Select Case block, 219, 221, 222, 226–227,
    243, 710
Selected, 531
    object, 46
Select statement (SQL), 559ff

Selector, 219, 221, 243
Semicolon, 76, 77
Sequence, 191
    structure, 38
Sequential
    file, 398, 404
    file sorting, 411
    search, 328, 356, 391
Set, 592, 598, 638. 711
SetFocus method, 65, 711
SetText property, 531, 711
Setting a breakpoint, 679, 724
Settings box, 47
Shape control, 516–517
Shell, Donald, 27
Shell sort, 27, 348, 353
Shift key, 10, 15
Shockley, William, 27
Show method, 531, 712
ShowColor method, 533
ShowFont method, 533
ShowPrinter method, 533
ShowSave method, 533
Simple variable, 302
Simulation, 126
Single variable, 87, 88, 712
Single-click-draw technique, 508
Single-subscripted variable, 367
Sizing handles, 46
SmallChange property, 513, 712
Smart editor, 77, 227
Social security tax, 207, 235
Software, 4
Sort
    array, 348
    bubble, 349
    efficiency, 354
    a file, 411
    flagged bubble sort, 361
    gap in Shell sort, 353
    Shell, 27, 348, 353
Sorted property, 496, 712
Sorting, 349, 353
Space
    leading, 76
    trailing, 76
Spaghetti code, 191
Spc function, 103, 712
Specifying a coordinate system, 456
Spreadsheet case study, 381ff
Sqr function, 118, 712
Square shape, 516
Standard deviation, 391
Standard format string, 123, 694
Start button, 6–7

Static, 712
Static array, 719
Step, 276
Stepping to debug, 679–680, 724–725
Stepwise refinement, 189
Str function, 88–89, 92–93, 712
Stretch property, 5186, 713
String, 84–85, 87
    constant, 84
    empty, 91
    expression, 86
    in a file, 108
    fixed-length, 436, 453
    format, 123
    function, 121
    null, 91
    string-valued function, 127
    substring, 122
    variable, 85
String-valued function, 127
Structure
    decision, 38, 191
    loop, 40, 191
    sequence, 38, 191
Structured programming, 28, 191
Structured query language, 558ff
Stub programming, 193
Style
    of a combo box, 500, 713
    of a line, 471, 493
Sub, 59, 142, 713
Subdirectory, 17, 719
Subfolder, 17
Subprogram, 59, 142, 194
    creating, 143–144, 677
    inserting into a program, 677
    managing, 677–678
    removing, 150, 678
Subroutine, 719
Subscript, 303
Subscript out of range error, 312
Subscripted variable, 303
Substring, 122
Subtraction, 71
Supply and demand, 285
Sydnes, William L., 29
Syntax error, 78
System unit, 2

T

Tab function, 105, 109, 713
Tab key, 11, 15, 53
Table
    ANSI (or ASCII), 89–90, 665–666

Data window, 576
    of a database, 546
    frequency, 311
    lookup, 359
    Structure window, 573–574
    window, 575
Tag, 655
Terminate, 598
Terminating value, 274
Text
    copying, 670
    editor, 8
    mark as a block, 669–670
    moving, 670
    positioning, 461
    property, 47, 497, 713
Text box control, 45–51, 88–89
Then, 203
Thumb, 514
Tic-tac-toe, 543, 634
Title
    bar, 8
    tag, 655, 659
Timer control, 515–516
Timer event, 515, 712
Timer function, 361, 714
To
    in Case, 221
    in For, 274
Toggle key, 9
Toolbar, 45
Toolbox, 45
Top arrow, 514
Top level menu item, 528
Top property, 341–342, 714
Top-down
    chart, 37
    design, 149, 169, 189
ToPage property, 536, 696
Trailing space, 76
Trim function, 121, 127, 714
Truth value, 201
Turing, Alan, 25
Twip, 339
Two-dimensional array, 367
Type, 438, 715
Type declaration tag, 88
Type mismatch error, 91

U

UBound function, 329, 715
UCase function, 121, 127, 361, 715
Ulam, Stanislaw, 26
Unconditional branch, 42

Underscore, 106
Until, 250, 252
Update method, 549, 715
URL, 649
Use, 614, 621
User, 4
User-defined
    control, 630
    event, 609–610
    function, 176, 194
Using the editor, 669–670

V

Val function, 88, 92, 715
Validation event, 549–561
Value
    ANSI (ASCII), 89–90, 665–666
    default, 91
    initial, 274
    list, 219
    passing, 163
    property, 509, 511, 513, 548, 592, 716
    step, 276
    terminating, 274
    truth, 201
Variable, 73–74, 137, 302
    array, 302
    control, 274, 295, 415
    counter, 295, 323
    declaring, 87, 92
    double, 88, 688
    double-subscripted, 368
    form level, 167, 533
    global, 533
    instance, 590
    integer, 88, 698
    local, 165, 194
    member, 590, 594
    numeric, 73–74
    passing, 163, 177
    record, 439
    simple, 302
    single, 87, 712
    single-subscripted, 367
    string, 85, 713
    subscripted, 303

Variant data type, 719–720
VBScript, 659, 660
Vertical scroll bar control, 513–515
View, 562
Virtual table, 561
Visible property, 54, 340, 517, 716
Visual Basic, 4
    Control Creation Edition, 25
    controls, 44ff
    creating a program, 58
    events, 58ff
    exiting, 668
    HOW TOs, 667–680
    installing, 44, 667–668
    introduction to, 22–25
    invoking, 44, 668
    notation, 71
    objects, 44ff
    printing programs, 679
    properties, 45ff
    statements, etc., 681ff
    versions, 25
Visual Data Manager, 572ff
Von Neumann, John, 26

W

Web page, 649, 654
Where clause (SQL), 559
While, 248, 252, 716
Width property, 339–340, 716
Wildcard characters, 536, 559
Wilkes, Maurice V., 26
Windows
    ending, 13
    how to utilize environment, 673
    introduction to, 4–14
    managing, 678–679
    starting, 6
WithEvents, 610, 612, 717
Word Basic, 638, 646
Word palindrome, 334
Work area, 8
World Wide Web, 648
Wozniak, Stephen, 28
Write# statement, 398, 717
Writing to a file, 398–400

ACCOMPANYING CD

The CD in this book contains the files needed to install the Control Creation Edition of Visual Basic 5.0. To install the software, follow the steps in the first part of Appendix B.

In addition, the CD contains all the programs from the examples and case studies of this textbook, many of the TXT files needed for the exercises, and several BMP (picture) files. The programs (and TXT files) are contained in the folder PROGRAMS, in sub-folders called CH3, CH4, CH5, and so on. The picture files are contained in the folder PICTURES. We recommend that you copy the entire contents of the folder PROGRAMS onto a diskette.

Each program has a name of the form *chapter-section-number*.VBP. For instance, the program in Chapter 3, Section 2, Example 4 has the name 3-2-4.VBP. Many of the programs make use of TXT files that are also in the subfolder. Before you run one of these programs, you may have to alter the filespec of a TXT file that is used by the program so that it contains a path to the location of the file. If you do not specify a path, Visual Basic most likely will look for the file in the Visual Basic folder, usually "C:\Program Files\VB5CCE" for the Control Creation Edition and "C:\Program Files\DevStudio\Vb" for the other versions of Visual Basic. Some people just copy all the TXT files from the CD into the Visual Basic folder.

MICROSOFT SOFTWARE LICENSE

READ THIS FIRST. Your use of the Microsoft software (the "SOFTWARE") is governed by the legal agreement below.

BY OPENING THE SEALED CD PACKAGE YOU ARE AGREEING TO BE BOUND BY THE TERMS AND CONDITIONS SET BELOW. IF YOU DO NOT AGREE WITH SUCH TERMS AND CONDITIONS, YOU SHOULD RETURN THE UNOPENED CD PACKAGE TOGETHER WITH THE BOOK TO THE PLACE YOU OBTAINED THEM FOR A REFUND.

1. GRANT OF LICENSE. Microsoft grants to you the right to use the enclosed SOFTWARE. You may make additional copies for demonstration purposes.

2. COPYRIGHT. The SOFTWARE is owned by Microsoft or its suppliers and is protected by United States copyright laws and international treaty provisions.

3. OTHER RESTRICTIONS. You may not rent, sell, or lease the SOFTWARE. You may not reverse engineer, decompile or disassemble the SOFTWARE.

DISCLAIMER OF WARRANTY AND LIMITED WARRANTY

THE SOFTWARE AND ACCOMPANYING WRITTEN MATERIALS (INCLUDING INSTRUCTIONS FOR USE) ARE PROVIDED "AS IS" WITHOUT WARRANTY OF ANY KIND. FURTHER, MICROSOFT DOES NOT WARRANT, GUARANTEE, OR MAKE ANY REPRESENTATIONS REGARDING THE USE, OR THE RESULTS OF THE USE, OF THE SOFTWARE OR WRITTEN MATERIALS IN TERMS OF CORRECTNESS, ACCURACY, RELIABILITY, CURRENTNESS, OR OTHERWISE. THE ENTIRE RISK AS TO THE RESULTS AND PERFORMANCE OF THE SOFTWARE IS ASSUMED BY YOU. IF THE SOFTWARE OR WRITTEN MATERIALS ARE DEFECTIVE YOU, AND NOT MICROSOFT OR ITS DEALERS, DISTRIBUTORS, AGENTS, OR EMPLOYEES, ASSUME THE ENTIRE COST OF ALL NECESSARY SERVICING, REPAIR, OR CORRECTION.

The CD in this book was reproduced by Prentice Hall, Inc. under a special arrangement with Microsoft Corporation. For this reason, Prentice Hall, Inc., is responsible for the product warranty and for support. If your CD is defective, please return it to Prentice Hall, Inc., which will arrange for its replacement. In no event shall Microsoft's liability and your exclusive remedy as to defective software, written materials, and disks be other than either (a) return of the purchase price or (b) replacement of the disk, which is returned to Microsoft with a copy of the receipt. If failure of the disk has resulted from accident, abuse, or misapplication, Microsoft shall have no responsibility to replace the disk or refund the purchase price. Any replacement disk will be warranted for thirty (30) days.

NO OTHER WARRANTIES. MICROSOFT DISCLAIMS ALL OTHER WARRANTIES, EITHER EXPRESS OR IMPLIED, INCLUDING BUT NOT LIMITED TO IMPLIED WARRANTIES OF MERCHANTABILITY AND FITNESS FOR A PARTICULAR PURPOSE, WITH RESPECT TO THE SOFTWARE AND ANY AC-COMPANYING HARDWARE. THIS LIMITED WARRANTY GIVES YOU SPECIFIC LEGAL RIGHTS. YOU MAY HAVE OTHERS, WHICH VARY FROM STATE TO STATE.

NO LIABILITY FOR CONSEQUENTIAL DAMAGES. IN NO EVENT SHALL MICROSOFT OR ITS SUPPLIERS BE LIABLE FOR ANY DAMAGES WHATSOEVER (INCLUDING WITHOUT LIMITATION DAMAGES FOR LOSS OF BUSINESS PROFITS, BUSINESS INTERRUPTION, LOSS OF BUSINESS INFOR-MATION, OR OTHER PECUNIARY LOSS) ARISING OUT OF THE USE OR INABILITY TO USE THIS MICROSOFT PRODUCT EVEN IF MICROSOFT HAS BEEN ADVISED OF THE POSSIBILITY OF SUCH DAMAGES. BECAUSE SOME STATES DO NOT ALLOW THE EXCLUSION OR LIMITATION OF LIABIL-ITY FOR CONSEQUENTIAL OR INCIDENTAL DAMAGES, THE ABOVE LIMITATION MAY NOT APPLY TO YOU.

U.S. GOVERNMENT RESTRICTED RIGHTS

The SOFTWARE and documentation are provided with RESTRICTED RIGHTS. Use, duplication, or disclosure by he Government is subject to restrictions as set forth in subparagraph (c)(1)(ii) of the Rights in Technical Data and mputer software clause at DFARS 252.227-7013 or subparagraphs (c)(1) and (2) of the Commercial Computer are—Restricted Rights at 48 CFR 52.227-19, as applicable. Manufacturer is Microsoft Corporation/One t Way/Redmond, WA 98052-6399.

red this product in the United States, this Agreement is governed by the laws of the State of Washington.